Introduction to Investments, 2e

Haim Levy
Hebrew University of Jerusalem

Assisted by
Deborah Gunthorpe
University of Tennessee

South-Western College Publishing
an International Thomson Publishing company I(T)P®

Cincinnati • Albany • Boston • Detroit • Johannesburg • London • Madrid • Melbourne • Mexico City
New York • Pacific Grove • San Francisco • Scottsdale • Singapore • Tokyo • Toronto

Publisher/Team Director:	Jack W. Calhoun
Acquisitions Editor:	Michael B. Mercier
Developmental Editor:	Thomas S. Sigel
Production Editor:	Sharon L. Smith
Internal Design:	Craig LaGesse Ramsdell
Cover Design:	Ann Small, A Small Design Studio, Cincinnati and Craig LaGesse Ramsdell
Cover Photography:	J. A. Kraulis/Masterfile
Cover Photo Digital Retouching:	Alan Brown, Photonics Graphics, Cincinnati
Production House:	Pre-Press Company, Inc.
Marketing Manager:	Lisa L. Lysne

Library of Congress Cataloging-in-Publication Data
Levy, Haim.
    Introduction to investments / Haim Levy.—2nd ed.
      p.   cm.
    Includes bibliographical references and index.
    ISBN 0-538-87737-5 (hardcover)
    1. Investments.   2. Corporations—Finance.   I. Title.
HG4521.L628   1998
658.15'54—dc21   98-29096
                                        CIP

1 2 3 4 5 6 7 8 D1 4 3 2 1 0 9 8

Printed in the United States of America

I(T)P®
International Thomson Publishing
South-Western College Publishing is an ITP Company.
The ITP trademark is used under license.

This book is devoted to investment analysis in the capital market. The three main issues discussed are security selectivity (security valuation models); portfolio diversification (the portfolio composition of the selected securities); and changes in portfolio composition over time, known as dynamic asset allocation (with emphasis on three classes of assets: stocks, bonds, and cash).

If the market is efficient, the fundamental and technical analyses commonly employed in security selectivity are worthless. Similarly, the use of industry and macroeconomic analyses to predict the market (that is, the stock market's peak and trough), which is needed for dynamic asset allocation, is a waste of time. Therefore, what is left in efficient markets is the risk reduction that is due to portfolio diversification. However, if the market is inefficient or even partially inefficient, then security analyses, as well as industry and macroeconomic analyses, may be financially beneficial. Is the market efficient? Let us start with an anecdote regarding this issue.

A university professor who wrote his doctoral dissertation on the topic of market efficiency was walking past the New York Stock Exchange at 11 Wall Street with his 10-year-old son when the boy suddenly exclaimed, "Dad, there's a $100 bill on the sidewalk!" "That's impossible," replied the professor. "The market is efficient, and in an efficient market, $100 bills cannot be found on the sidewalk!"

This anecdote serves to illustrate the main implication of the belief in market efficiency: If the market is indeed perfectly efficient, there will be no bargains in the market; there will be no $100 bills lying around just waiting to be found. In an efficient market, all risky assets will be correctly priced, and all available information on a given stock will be duly reflected in its current market price. Under such circumstances, valuation models of stocks, bonds, and options will not be helpful in security selection. In other words, such models cannot be applied to obtain abnormal profits. Similarly, a dynamic asset allocation incurs transaction costs, with no benefit.

The story of the $100 bill also illustrates the absurdity of the concept of market efficiency pushed to the extreme. There is a $100 bill on the sidewalk, and you are the first one to find it. You cannot believe your eyes! True, it is impossible for the $100 bill to remain on the sidewalk for very long. However, it is equally true that if it happens to be lying there, you might be the first one to see it and pick it up. Is there a moral to this story? Even if the market is not perfectly efficient, sophisticated investors who succeed in reaping a profit from undervalued assets will push the stock prices up to an equilibrium price, as predicted by the efficient market hypotheses. For the ordinary investor, the market is usually very efficient. For you, the student taking this course—the sophisticated investor of the future—the market is probably inefficient, so you may succeed in reaping a profit.

Indeed, some well-known professional investors do not believe in efficient markets and claim they are reaping a profit because the markets are inefficient. This view is summarized in an article published in *Fortune* in which Sequoia Fund's William Ruane, Berkshire Hathaway's Charles Munger and Warren Buffett, and money manager Walter Schloss all say that they do not believe in efficient markets. Says Buffett, "I'd be a bum on the street with a tin cup if the market were efficient."[1]

In light of such statements regarding market efficiency, this book has been organized and written around the new developments and challenges facing the capital market. Indeed, recent years have witnessed a fourfold revolution in the field of finance and investment in the capital market. First, the argument as to whether the market is efficient or inefficient has resurfaced. This issue is crucial, because it carries implications regarding the value of some of the topics taught in investment courses, as well as the justification for many of the jobs on Wall Street (which, basically, does not believe in market efficiency). The author accepts that there is disagreement on this issue and, in writing this book, has maintained an open mind and tolerance toward the views expressed by both the proponents and antagonists of market efficiency.

Second, the capital market has been bombarded with new investment strategies. Derivatives have hit the headlines, and financial engineering is popular. The role of options as a speculative investment tool, as well as a hedging risk investment tool, has expanded rapidly in the last few years. The number of contracts traded on the options exchanges grew from 106.5 million contracts in 1992 to 273.0 million contracts in 1997, with positive growth in each year. At the same time, many institutions and firms have recently lost in the derivatives markets. The biggest loss (over a

---

1. Terence P. Pare, "Yes, You Can Beat the Market," *Fortune,* April 3, 1995, p. 47.

billion dollars) was by Barings Bank, then England's oldest bank. (After its collapse, Barings Bank was purchased by Holland's ING Group.) The last part of the book focuses on the role that derivative securities, such as options, play in portfolio management. This discussion will help readers gain a better understanding of these popular, but often misunderstood and sometimes mismanaged, financial instruments.

Third, the market has become truly global. Because of fast-flowing communication systems, transactions between all parts of the planet can be executed with a computer keystroke. This fast communication system and market globalization are noticed in particular when short-term panic occurs in the market, as in the October 1987 crisis and the October 1997 crash. The 1997 crash started in Asia, and the effects reverberated throughout most stock markets around the world. In those two events, almost all major stock markets worldwide fell sharply. The long-run correlation between stock market movements of some countries is also very high, which limits the potential gain from international diversification. This is true for many European countries, and the positive correlation may even increase in the near future, when most Western European nations will use one currency, the Euro. However, for some countries there is no correlation, or even a negative correlation, between stock prices in the long run, and not all markets rise or fall in tandem. Thus, in the long run, the correlation between some markets is not very high, and investors can gain from international diversification.

In particular, in recent years the two largest economies in the world, the United States and Japan, moved sharply in different directions (that is, there was a negative correlation). To demonstrate, in the early 1990s the Dow was at the 3,000 level. In July 1998 it reached approximately the 9,200 level. That is, more than a 200% rate of return in a short period of time. In contrast, investing in Japan during this period was devastating to Japanese investors, let alone to U.S. investors. In 1989, the Nikkei index was close to 40,000 points. By July 1998, it had fallen to 16,188. This represents about a 60% drop in the index. For Americans who invested in the Nikkei, the rates of return were affected both by the Nikkei index fall and the changes in foreign exchange rates. A depreciation of the yen added to the losses. For example, from 1995 to 1998, the Nikkei index did not change much. However, in 1995, one yen was worth 1.2 American cents, whereas in July 1998, it was worth about 0.70 cents. Thus, even with no change in the Nikkei index, the investor who invested $1.20 in 1995 in Japan (100 yen) could withdraw only 0.70 cents in 1998. Hence, there was a loss of 42% on the foreign exchange even with no change in the Nikkei index, and the loss was intensified with any additional drop in the Nikkei.

Short-run panics do not necessarily reflect a weakness of the economy, but long-run movements in stock prices do reflect the weaknesses and strengths of the economy. For example, the sharp drop in the Nikkei index and the deterioration of the yen relative to the dollar reflect the recent slow growth in the Japanese economy. Between 1987 and 1991, Japan had an annual growth in gross domestic product (GDP) of 4% to 6%. This growth rate sharply dropped in recent years (with the exception of 1996), reaching a mere 0.9% growth rate in 1997. The sluggish economy induces financial distress and a flow of bad debt, which in turn affect the bankruptcy rates in Japan. For the year ending March 1998, the bankruptcy rates of firms increased by 17% relative to the previous year. In contrast, there were periods when the yen became stronger relative to the dollar; investing in Japan then was profitable to U.S. investors, whereas those investing in the United States incurred losses. Thus, in portfolio investment, investors must distinguish between short-term shifts in the stock market (and, in particular, short-term panic, which generally is followed by a market correction and which tends to cover all markets in the world) and long-term trends (which are not necessarily in the same direction but rather reflect the fundamental characteristics of the various economies).

The fluctuations in the stock market and in foreign exchange rates affect the internationally diversified portfolio's risk and return. This text discusses ways to benefit from international diversification via control of foreign exchange risk. Finally, executives face growing pressure, both public and internal, to ensure ethical practices in the financial marketplace.

All these rapid changes can make the field of investments more difficult for students to understand and for professors to teach. At the same time, however, the changes also make the field more challenging and interesting.

A WORD OF CAUTION

The second edition of this book was completed in the middle of 1998, when the Dow Jones broke the 9,000 level. Stocks, strong for about 3 years, have been good to investors, offering a relatively high rate of return. This trend has been accompanied by a wave of mergers, including the biggest merger in U.S. history (an $83 billion deal) between Citicorp and Travelers Group, as well as the acquisition of Chrysler by Daimler-Benz for more than $40 billion. Moreover, the longest bull market started in October 1990 and continued to April 1998. This bull market lasted 2,734 days, over which the Dow gained 282%.

Some analysts predict that the Dow will continue its rally, meeting the Nikkei index somewhere around 15,000 points. However, some are skeptical and predict that the Dow will fall sharply. For example, Alan Greenspan, the chairman of the Federal Reserve Board, said in April 1998 that stock prices are based on forecasts. He stated that the U.S. economy had entered a new era of continuous steep gains in productivity, and noted that as a central banker, he has always had great skepticism about new eras and changing structures of how the world functions.[2] Greenspan may be right this time in his prediction, but in a December 5, 1996, speech, he rattled his audience when he asked whether the market might be exhibiting "irrational exuburance." In 1998 we know that he was wrong in 1996, because at that time the Dow Jones stood at 6,400 points, and during sixteen months it escalated to 9,100—a 42% gain during that period.

This story indicates only that it is very hard to predict when the market will reach its peak or trough. In the presence of the market upswing euphoria in recent years, we tend to forget the periods with negative returns. A sharp drop of more than 20% in stock prices in one day, as occurred in the crash of October 1987, does not occur often. However, apart from the crashes and the years with a negative rate

2. *USA Today,* April 3, 1998.

of return, there are very long periods with a negative or only a small positive return, in contrast to recent years. For example, from 1973 to 1977, the average annual rate of return on stocks was 0.2%; in the period from 1926 to 1941 it was 1.2%. From November 14, 1972 to January 8, 1987, the Dow climbed from 1,000 to 2,000 points; that is, it doubled in about 14 years with only about a 5% annual rate of return. This annual rate of return is much smaller when inflation, personal tax, and capital gains tax on individuals are deducted.

Moreover, when the market is up sharply in the last rally, we are tempted to believe that any investment in the stock market is profitable. This is not the case. For example, in the 5-year period ending March 31, 1998, which is a bull period, we find mutual funds with total returns of hundreds of percentage points (for example, Fidelity Sel Electronic at 347% and Seligman Communication at 304%) and mutual funds that lost almost all their value (for example, Steadman Tech & Growth at −81% and Frontier Equity Fund at −66%).

Thus, even in a bull market, investors need to remember the risk of changing trends in the whole market, as well as the risk of some stocks falling sharply. Therefore, this book focuses on return and risk, with the goal of minimizing risk for a given expected rate of return.

INTENDED AUDIENCE

This book is geared to both undergraduate and graduate students. The subject matter can be covered in a two-semester course, but the text can also be used for a one-semester course by selecting the chapters considered most important. Generally, this course is taken after principles of finance have been studied. However, the concepts needed for this book (such as discounting) are discussed here, in order to achieve a self-contained text. With regard to mathematics, no more than high school–level algebra is assumed.

The student who studies principles of finance before taking an investments course will probably wonder why some of the material, such as risk and return analysis, appears in both courses. Many issues are common to both areas. Both the corporate manager and the portfolio manager face the problems of asset evaluation and risk reduction by diversification. However, there is one distinction: portfolio managers diversify the portfolio across the many stocks available in the market, whereas corporate managers focus their activities on a relatively small number of projects contained in the firm's portfolio of projects. The selection of a portfolio from a large number of assets requires specialized tools, and these tools are introduced and discussed in this book.

ORGANIZATION OF THE BOOK

The anecdote of the $100 bill lying on the Wall Street sidewalk serves as a guideline in structuring this book. Part 1 is devoted to the market environment and to a description of the various securities and how they are traded. Part 2 covers modern portfolio theory, with an emphasis on the gain from diversification. Part 3 expands the available opportunities by adding the riskless asset and also focuses on international diversification. Part 4 introduces the concept of efficient markets and the technical analyses that rely on the belief that the market is inefficient. Part 5 describes bonds and stock valuation models, and Part 6 is devoted to options and financial engineering.

Investment analysis (in Part 2 of the text) begins with modern portfolio theory for two reasons:

1. Portfolio theory furnishes the basic tools needed for fundamental analysis, and especially for assessing risk. A solid understanding of the concepts related to risk is needed in order to analyze issues such as why long-term bonds are generally riskier than short-term bonds and how to construct a portfolio of bonds or stocks.
2. If the efficient market hypothesis is pushed to the extreme, and it is assumed that it is not possible to distinguish between good and bad investments (neither in the short run nor in the long run), we have to conclude that the models for valuating stocks, bonds, and options are not helpful. The only investment tools that are helpful are those provided by modern portfolio theory.

After a discussion of modern portfolio theory, one chapter is devoted to the theory and empirical evidence of market efficiency. Because the value of fundamental and technical analyses is limited in a highly efficient market, it is important to have a good understanding of the concept of market efficiency first.

After an analysis of the arguments for and against market efficiency, models for the valuation of bonds, stocks, and futures are introduced. If investors believe that some models are capable of "beating the market" or inducing "abnormal" profits, they can use these models to distinguish between good and bad investments. However, they can do so only if the market is indeed inefficient or at least not perfectly efficient.

Although the common view among academics in the past was that investors could not beat the market, recently some academics have expressed the opposite view, which enhances the importance of studying these valuation models. In fact, a study by Josef Lakonishok of the University of Illinois, Andrei Schleifer of Harvard University, and Robert W. Vishny of the University of Chicago showed that stock-picking strategies using simple measures outperform both a strategy emphasizing growth stocks and the market as a whole.[3]

This new and improved edition features improvements in clarity and readability. In addition, the following changes have been introduced:

- Part 2 of the first edition has been divided into two parts, and the order of the chapters has been changed. In the second edition, the chapter that includes the risk–return relationship known as the capital asset pricing model, or CAPM

---

3. Josef Lakonishok, Andrei Schleifer, and Robert W. Vishny, "Contrarian Investment, Extrapolation, and Risk," *Journal of Finance* 49, no. 5 (December 1994). This study was also cited in *Fortune,* April 3, 1995.

(Chapter 9), immediately follows the chapter that describes the gain from diversification. The chapter on international diversification (Chapter 11) now wraps up Part 3. This change gives the reader a smooth transition from portfolio choices without the riskless asset to portfolio choices with the riskless asset and then a discussion of the CAPM.

- The chapter order in Part 6 has been changed. The new order provides a more logical discussion of forward and future simple transactions and then leads into the more complicated topics of options and option valuation. The book concludes with a chapter on financial engineering.

- Stock valuation models in most textbooks rely heavily on discounted futures dividends. However, these models are not applicable to firms such as Microsoft, which never paid dividends. Therefore, Chapter 18 discusses the free cash flow model (FCFM) method for stock valuation and compares it with the other common valuation methods. The method appears in an appendix, thus allowing the instructor to skip this material if so desired.

- The economic value-added (EVA) model for stock valuation is also discussed in an appendix to Chapter 18.

- A discussion of value at risk (VaR), which banks have recently adopted, and of the use of derivatives to affect the VaR has been added to Chapter 25.

- The effect of recent merger waves on stock prices is discussed in end-of-chapter problem-solving sections.

- Current events such as the 1997 currency crisis in Asia are covered either in the text or in the form of end-of-chapter problems and minicases. In addition to the risk of investing in securities, currency and political risk are also addressed.

- New innovations in the stock market (such as the trade in diamonds and spiders, as well as "terminated" mutual funds) appear in the book, either in end-of-chapter problem sections or discussions in the text.

- Where possible, data have been updated through the spring of 1998. In many cases, data are from Internet sources; thus, the reader can go directly to the sources to find the very latest information.

- Many of the articles in Investments in the News have been updated. The text includes new boxes and minicases. At the same time, the unique articles and boxes with special features from the first edition have been retained.

- Articles that appeared in the financial media in 1997 and 1998 are used to create new end-of-chapter problems, further enhancing the connection between theory and practice, which is the main thrust of the book.

- Chapter 3, which contains a discussion of the mechanics of trading securities, now has additional numerical examples.

- In Chapter 4 there is a discussion of the possible conflict of interest between the broker who manages the investor's portfolio and the investor. Issues of portfolio turnover and taxes are discussed, and the importance of business ethics is emphasized.

- Chapter 5 ("Calculating Rates of Return") has been simplified. An appendix that discusses the dollar-weighted average rate of return has been added.

- Chapter 12 ("Efficient Markets: Theory and Evidence") has been rewritten to reflect the most recent developments. The average monthly rates of return on various investment classes for various periods are discussed, with emphasis on the January 1998 effect of small stocks.

- A discussion of the discount (and premium) of closed-end mutual funds has been added, as well as a discussion of recent public pressure to open up closed-end funds.

SPECIAL FEATURES

This text and its special features were carefully developed by the author and evaluated by a dedicated panel of reviewers. The goal throughout has been to spark the interest of students and enhance their motivation to learn about the field of investments. Included are articles and discussions from sources such as the *Wall Street Journal, Barron's Business Week,* and *Fortune,* as well as the financial statements of corporations, in order to introduce students to real-life scenarios that will give them the opportunity to apply and develop investment techniques. Each chapter opens with one or more newspaper articles highlighting the main topic discussed in the chapter. Each chapter closes with a full-page minicase dealing with a practical issue taken from the financial media related to the material studied in the chapter.

ETHICAL ISSUES

There is growing concern in the financial community regarding ethical issues and regulation in the area of finance. This text devotes a whole chapter (Chapter 4) to this topic. This extensive coverage is a unique feature of this book.

FINANCIAL ENGINEERING

A separate chapter (Chapter 25) is devoted to financial engineering and how its innovative investment strategies can be employed in practice. This coverage is also unique to this investments text. In view of the ever-growing importance of financial engineering and the many innovations in this area, much can be learned from this chapter.

FOCUS ON PRACTICE

The book emphasizes the practicalities of investing. To enable the student to relate theory to everyday applications, each chapter offers the following features:

- **Investments in the News** offers articles from the *Wall Street Journal* and other sources that are used to launch the discussion of each chapter.
- **Connecting Theory to Practice and Making the Connection** present students with current investment news from the *Wall Street Journal, Fortune,* and other sources. The goal of these features is to show students how to analyze arti-

cles on current issues appearing in the financial media, using concepts learned in the chapter.

- **Cases from the *Wall Street Journal, Fortune,* and Other Sources** close each chapter and allow students to apply the concepts introduced in the chapter to real-world events.
- **Practice Boxes** show how the issues raised in each chapter are treated in the financial media and serve to connect the theory to practice.
- **Review and Practice Problems** at the end of each chapter apply the concepts discussed in that chapter. Many problems are taken from the financial media and use actual cases to show the relevance of the material studied.
- **Special CFA examination questions** are practice problems that prepare students for the series of Chartered Financial Analyst (CFA) examinations administered by the Association for Investment Management and Research (AIMR). For more information regarding the CFA Candidate Program, address inquiries to the following:

Association for Investment Management and Research
Department of Candidate Programs
5 Boar's Head Lane
P.O. Box 3668
Charlottesville, VA 22903-0668

ANCILLARY MATERIALS

Study Guide Prepared by Timothy Dye of Texas A&M University, a completely new Study Guide features learning objectives; key concept reinforcement; and self-evaluation questions and problems, including true-and-false, multiple choice, and short essay questions. In addition, sample CFA questions, used by permission from the AIMR, help students master the concepts that are necessary to pass the Level 1 examination.

Instructor's Manual Enhanced and updated by Richard Gendreau of Bemidji State University, the Instructor's Manual recaps learning objectives for each chapter. In addition, Professor Gendreau offers lecture hints and ideas and makes recommendations on where to use Power Point slides during the lecture. This manual also provides suggestions to the instructor on enlivening and enriching classroom teaching. Extra enrichment problems with answers are also included. A new feature includes Internet references that lead professors and students to pertinent investment-related Web sites. As an added bonus, Professor Gendreau weaves throughout the manual an interactive investments simulation that links professors and students to the Thomson Investors Network.

Solutions Manual Answers to questions and problems in the end-of-chapter Review, Practice, and Applying Theory to Practice sections have been provided by Haim Levy.

Microsoft PowerPoint Slides Also created by Richard Gendreau, Power-Point slides accompany the suggested lecture outline in the Instructor's Manual. The slides are designed to allow the instructor to modify and adapt each slide to meet individual classroom needs. Slides are available on disk or can be downloaded from the Levy Web site (http://www.levy.swcollege.com).

Software Spreadsheet software is provided free to adopters of the text in order to give students the opportunity to implement techniques presented in the text. The spreadsheets contain both generic models for solving a class of problems and solutions to many specific text examples and end-of-chapter problems. An additional set of tutorial software tools, written by John O'Brien and Sanjay Srivastava of Carnegie Mellon University, is available to adopters of the text at special bundled discounts. Modules available for bundling include the following:

- *Modern Portfolio Theory and CAPM Tutor.*
- *Option Valuation and Option Tutor.*
- *Bond Valuation and Bond Tutor.*

Test Bank The new and improved Test Bank, written and updated by Joseph Vu of DePaul University, includes multiple choice, true-and-false, and essay questions.

Thomson World Class Learning™ Testing Tools All the questions in the printed Test Bank are included in electronic form in this easy-to-use test creation software, which is compatible with Microsoft Windows. World Class Test enables users to add or edit questions, instructions, and answers; select questions by previewing the questions on the screen; let the system select questions randomly; select questions by question number; view summaries of the test or the test bank chapters; set up the page layout for tests; and print tests in a variety of formats.

Thomson Investors Network Thomson Investors Network, a powerful Web site, provides instructors, students, and individual investors with a wealth of information and tools, including portfolio tracking software, live stock quotations, and company and industry reports. Instructors can use Thomson Investors Network to create handouts with real-world company and industry data, or they can use it live in the classroom as a pedagogical aid. Suggestions on how to integrate this resource into a course are presented in the Instructor's Manual. A preview of this invaluable tool is available by visiting http://www.thomsoninvest.net. Contact your ITP sales representative for more information about this feature.

ACKNOWLEDGMENTS

This project could never have been completed without the help of many colleagues and friends. I would like to thank the many reviewers who provided valuable feedback for both the first and second editions:

Michael J. Alderson
St. Louis University

Hames J. Angel
Georgetown University

Yakov Amihud
New York University

Sung C. Bae
Bowling Green State University

Kegian Bi
University of San Francisco

Avi Bick
Simon Fraser University

Gilbert Bickum
Eastern Kentucky University

Richard H. Borgman
University of Maine

Denis O. Boudreaux
University of Southern Louisiana

Stephen Caples
McNeese State University

John Clark
University of Alabama

John Clinebell
University of Northern Colorado

Charles J. Corrado
University of Missouri-Columbia

Arthur T. Cox
University of Northern Iowa

Richard F. DeMong
University of Virginia

Giorgio De Santis
University of Southern California

Elroy Dimson
London School of Business

John W. Ellis
Colorado State University

Thomas H. Eyssell
University of Missouri at St. Louis

Daniel Falkowski
Canisius College

James Feller
Middle Tennessee State University

J. Howard Finch
University of Tennessee at Chattanooga

Adam K. Gehr, Jr.
DePaul University

Deborah W. Gregory
University of Otago

Deborah L. Gunthorpe
University of Tennessee

Frank M. Hatheway
Pennsylvania State University

David Heskel
Bloomsburg College

Stan Jacobs
Central Washington University

Vahan Janjigian
Boston College

Hazel J. Johnson
University of Louisville

Edward M. Kaitz
Marymount University

Andrew Karolyi
Ohio State University

Mike Keenan
New York University

Yoram Kroll
Hebrew University

Ladd Kochman
Kennesaw State College

Thomas Krueger
University of Wisconsin LaCrosse

Yoram Landskroner
Hebrew University

Graham K. Lemke
Pennsylvania State University

Azriel Levy
Hebrew University

K. C. Lim
City Polytechnic, Hong Kong

K. C. Ma
Investment Research Company

Steven V. Mann
University of South Carolina

Ralph D. May
Southwestern Oklahoma State University

William M. Mayfield
Northwestern Oklahoma State University

Micharel L. McBain
Marquette University

Robert McConkie
Sam Houston State University

Robert McElreath
Clemson University

Bruce McManis
Nicholls State University

Edward Miller
University of New Orleans

Lalatendu Misra
University of Texas at San Antonio

Santhosh B. Mohan
Ohio Northern University

Eli Ofek
New York University

Joseph P. Ogden
State University of New York at Buffalo

Rajeev N. Parikh
St. Bonaventure University

Rose Prasad
Michigan State University

Hugh M. Pratt
University of Manitoba

Jerry Prock
University of Texas

Shafiqur Rahman
Portland State University

Venkateshward K. Reddy
University of Colorado, Colorado Springs

William Reichenstein
Baylor University

Stan Reyburn
*Commercial Investment Counselor,
Professional Realty Associates*

Meir Schneller
Virginia Polytechnic Institute

Latha Shanker
Concordia University

Neil Sicherman
University of South Carolina

Raymond W. So
Louisiana State University

Meir Statman
Santa Clara University

Stacey L. Suydam
Montana State University, Billings

Antoinette Tessmer
University of Illinois

David E. Upton
Virginia Commonwealth University

Gopala K. Vasudevan
Suffolk University

Joseph D. Vu
DePaul University

William Wells
Merrimack University

Darin While
Union University

James A. Yoder
University of South Alabama

I would also like to thank Hyla Berkowitz and Maya Landau for their editorial help, as well as Yael Ben-David, Daniel Berkowitz, Natali Eisof, Allon Cohen, Eitan Goldman, and Doron Lavee for their assistance in preparing the manuscript. Special thanks also go to Mary Berry for her excellent and thorough copyediting, Susan Orttung for obtaining copyright permissions, Carla Atkinson for attentively consolidating all editorial changes onto a master copy for the compositor, and Jenna Schulman at Pre-Press Company for overseeing production of the book.

I want to extend special thanks to Deborah Gunthorpe and Boaz Leibovitch for their significant contribution in updating and revising this edition. They spent countless hours researching and also reviewing and responding to queries in the copyediting stage.

Finally, I would like to thank the hardworking team at South-Western College Publishing, which includes Michael Mercier, acquisitions editor, and Sharon Smith, production editor. In particular, I thank Thomas Sigel, developmental editor, for coordinating and driving this entire project.

A NOTE TO THE STUDENT

What are the potential benefits of studying investments?

Why study investments? There are several reasons why it is worthwhile to study finance and, in particular, investments. First, in this day and age, you can hardly go through life totally oblivious to terms such as *swaps, options, bonds, stocks,* and *yields.* The media will not let you. To understand the financial news, you need some understanding of such terms.

Second, no matter what job you eventually get, you hope to be able to save some of your income. Should you buy mutual funds, or should you personally diversify across various stocks? Should you play it safe and buy certificates of deposit, or should you take on risk and invest in emerging markets? The material in this book will help you make decisions regarding your own savings.

Third, studying finance is very challenging. It is a practical field in which highly sophisticated models are applied. For example, the beta risk index is used and published by Value Line and Standard & Poors in ranking stocks. The Black-Scholes option pricing model is employed regularly by practitioners and traders in the financial markets. Thus, the topics covered in this book are not only intellectually challenging but also important in day-to-day decision making.

Indeed, the theoretical underpinnings of this field finally received recognition by the Nobel Committee in 1990, when it awarded the Nobel Prize in economics to financial economists Harry Markowitz, Merton Miller, and William Sharpe. A large part of this book relies on the work of Markowitz and Sharpe, which laid the foundation for portfolio decision-making models and equilibrium risk-return relationships. (Miller's main contribution is in the area of corporate finance.) In 1997, Robert Merton and Myron Scholes won the Nobel Prize in economics for their contribution to research in derivatives with an emphasis on options valuation models.

Perhaps the most important reason for studying this subject is the hope that the yield will be truly profitable. Indeed, the rewards of a career in this area can be awesome. Moreover, a job on Wall Street spells prestige. To acquire such a job—and the competition is stiff—you will usually need an MBA degree. The following table will give you an idea of what to expect in pursuing a career in investments:

"Still Making Out on Wall Street"[4]

Total Compensation: Salary and Bonus Position	Junior Professional (3–5 years' experience), in Thousands	Senior Professional (10+ years' experience), in Thousands
Stock research analyst	$150–$250	$350–$500
Bond trader	$300–$500	$650–$850
Corporate finance generalist	$250–$400	$700–$1,000
Institutional bond salesperson	$200–$300	$600–$800

Who said no one wants to be a statistic! But what's the catch? To receive these high salaries, you need 3 to 5 years or more than 10 years of experience. The catch-22 here is this: How can you get a job when you have no experience, and how can you get experience without a job? The aim of this book is to provide you with enough knowledge for your first job, even with no experience. Indeed, it is hoped that mastery of the material presented in this book will be a good substitute for the experience needed to acquire your first position and to be successful in your job. Who knows, within no time, you may be part of the salary statistics appearing in the table!

Haim Levy
Jerusalem, Israel

---

4. Based on an article by Ford S. Worthy, *Fortune*, April 6, 1992, p. 71.

Dr. Haim Levy is the Miles Robinson Professor of Finance at Hebrew University of Jerusalem. He has also taught at the Universities of California (Berkeley), Pennsylvania, Illinois, and Florida. In addition to his teaching responsibilities, he is an active consultant to firms and governments worldwide.

Dr. Levy is the most published and most frequently cited researcher in modern finance. In addition to almost 200 journal articles, he has published numerous books, including *Principles of Corporate Finance* (South-Western College Publishing, 1998). He has also found time to serve on the editorial boards of the *Journal of Finance*, *Journal of Banking and Finance*, *Journal of Portfolio Management*, and the *Financial Analysts Journal*.

BRIEF CONTENTS

PART 1
The Investment Environment

1 Introduction 1
2 Bonds, Stocks, and Other
Financial Securities 29
3 Security Markets 71
4 Regulation and Ethics 119

PART 2
Return and Risk

5 Calculating Rates of Return 145
6 Foundation of Risk Analysis 191
7 Portfolio Mean and Variance 215
8 The Gain from Portfolio Diversification 249

PART 3
Equilibrium Prices:
Expanding the Portfolio Universe

9 Return and Risk: The Linear Relationships
and CAPM 288
10 Index Models and the Arbitrage
Pricing Theory 337
11 International Investment 369

PART 4
Efficient Markets and
Portfolio Performance

12 Efficient Markets: Theory and Evidence 407
13 Technical Analysis 450
14 Investment Companies and Mutual Funds 482
15 Performance Measurement 521

PART 5
Security Analysis

16 Interest Rates and Bond Valuation 555
17 Bonds—Analysis and Management 612
18 Common Stocks—Valuation 656
19 Common Stock Selection 704
20 Market and Industry Analysis 734
21 Financial Statement Analysis 765

PART 6
Options, Futures, and
Financial Engineering

22 Options—Basics and Strategies 805
23 Valuing Stock Options 840
24 Futures 884
25 Financial Engineering 930

Appendix A Information Markets 963

**Appendix B Code of Ethics and Standards of
Professional Conduct 968**

Glossary 973

Name Index 985

Subject Index 989

CONTENTS

PART 1   THE INVESTMENT ENVIRONMENT

1 Introduction   1

Investments in the News
Greenspan Gives No Hint of Rate Boost   1
Tokyo Stocks Retreat Broadly to Profit-Taking—European and Latin American Bourses Rebound   2
AIG's Net Jumps 14% to $826 Million, Buoyed by Strength at Home and Abroad   2

1.1 FACTORS AFFECTING ASSETS PRICE   4

1.2 THE DIFFERENCE BETWEEN CORPORATE FINANCE AND INVESTMENTS   6

1.3 THE DIFFERENCE BETWEEN PHYSICAL AND FINANCIAL ASSETS   7
Connecting Theory to Practice 1.1: What Are Your Odds?   8   1.3.1 Divisibility   8   1.3.2 Marketability   10   1.3.3 The Holding Period   10   1.3.4 Information Availability   10

1.4 THE BENEFITS OF STUDYING INVESTMENTS   11

1.5 THE INVESTMENT PROCESS   12
1.5.1 Investor Characteristics   12   1.5.2 Investment Vehicles: The Trade-off between Risk and Return   14   1.5.3 Strategy Development   14   *Connecting Theory to Practice 1.2: Diversification: Your Guide to Investing*   15   1.5.4 Strategy Implementation   17   1.5.5 Strategy Monitoring   17

1.6 WHERE DO WE GO FROM HERE? A BRIEF OVERVIEW OF THE BOOK   17

Summary   18   Chapter at a Glance   19   Key Terms   20   Review   20   Practice   20   CFA Problems   22

Your Turn: Applying Theory to Practice: Turmoil in Dow Jones Industrials Leaves Investors Seeking Security   22

Selected References **23**   Supplemental References **24**

APPENDIX 1A REVIEW OF TIME VALUE CONCEPTS **24**

Practice **28**

2 Bonds, Stocks, and Other Financial Securities   **29**

Investments in the News
  Bonds Rise as Stocks Post Meager Gains **29**

2.1 BONDS **30**
2.1.1 Basic Characteristics of Bonds **31**   2.1.2 Types of Bonds **32**

2.2 STOCKS **41**
2.2.1 Basic Characteristics of Common Stock **41**   2.2.2 Classifications of Common Stocks **42**   2.2.3 Preferred Stocks **43**   2.2.4 Reading the Stock Pages **44**

2.3 DERIVATIVE SECURITIES **46**
2.3.1 Stock Options **46**   2.3.3 Convertible Bonds **46**   2.3.3 Futures **47**
2.3.4 Swaps **47**

2.4 RISKS OF BONDS AND STOCKS **48**
Connecting Theory to Practice 2.1: In a Surprise, South Korea Ends Its Attempts to Defend Its Currency **53**

2.5 INTERNATIONAL SECURITIES **54**

2.6 MUTUAL FUNDS **56**

Summary **60**   Chapter at a Glance **61**   Key Terms **61**   Review **62**   Practice **62**
CFA Problems **64**

Your Turn: Applying Theory to Practice: A Bank Plays with Yield **65**

Selected References **66**   Supplemental References **66**

APPENDIX 2A TAXES **66**

3 Security Markets   **71**

Investments in the News
  Investing in the Future **71**

3.1 THE ROLE OF SECURITY MARKETS **73**

3.2 THE PRIMARY SECURITY MARKET **75**
3.2.1 Investment Bankers and Underwriting **76**   3.2.2 IPOs versus Private Placement **80**   3.2.3 Underpricing IPOs and Price Discovery **81**

3.3 THE SECONDARY SECURITY MARKET **83**
Connecting Theory to Practice 3.1: The Big Board's Bicentennial: 200 Years Later, Small Investors Find Clout at America's Premier Exchange **85**

3.4 TRADING MECHANICS 87
3.4.1 Securities Trading Systems 87   *Connecting Theory to Practice 3.2: Regulated Exchanges around the Globe* 89   3.4.2 Goals of Trading Systems 89   3.4.3 Participants in Securities Markets 90   3.4.4 Establishing Market Prices 92   3.4.5 Automated Trading 92   *Connecting Theory to Practice 3.3: Blind Bids Become Popular in Big Trades* 93   3.4.6 Types of Orders 95   3.4.7 Placing an Order 96   3.4.8 Margin Trading 97   3.4.9 Short Selling 101   3.4.10 Brokers 101   3.4.11 Financial Planners 103

3.5 WORLD SECURITY MARKETS 104
3.5.1 World Bond Markets 105   3.5.2 World Stock Markets 107   3.5.3 World Derivative Markets 108

Summary 110   Chapter at a Glance 111   Key Terms 112   Review 113   Practice 113

Your Turn: Applying Theory to Practice: Bitter Lesson: When That "Hot" IPO Is Really a Lemon 115

Selected References 117   Supplemental References 118

4 Regulation and Ethics 119

Investments in the News
    Following a Broker's Advice Can Reap Nice Gains—Until You Get the Tax Bill 119

4.1 HISTORY OF SECURITIES REGULATION 120

4.2 SECURITIES LAW AND FINANCIAL INNOVATION 126
Connecting Theory to Practice 4.1: "Derivatives" Draw Warnings from Regulators 127

4.3 CORPORATE GOVERNANCE 128

4.4 ETHICS AND FRAUD 128
Connecting Theory to Practice 4.2: The New Crisis in Business Ethics 129   4.4.1 Unethical versus Fraudulent Behavior 131   *Connecting Theory to Practice 4.3: Legal Ethics Shouldn't Be an Oxymoron* 132   4.4.2 Independent Judgment 135   4.4.3 Insider Trading 135   *Connecting Theory to Practice 4.4: Front-Running Putnam Suit Spotlights Personal Trades, Fund Track* 136   4.4.4 Commission Brokers and Churning 137   4.4.5 Commission Brokers and IPOs 137   4.4.6 Financial Planners and Product Sales Commissions 137   4.4.7 CEO's Compensation and Performance 138   4.4.8 Improving the Conduct of Investment Managers 138

Summary 138   Chapter at a Glance 139   Key Terms 139   Review 140   Practice 140   CFA Problems 143

Your Turn: Applying Theory to Practice: IG Metall Chief Faces Pressure to Step Down 143

Selected References 144   Supplemental References 144

PART 2   RETURN AND RISK

5 Calculating Rates of Return   145

Investments in the News
   The Best Mutual Funds—U.S. Stock Funds   145

5.1 USING RATES OF RETURN   146

5.2 RATE-OF-RETURN CALCULATIONS   148
5.2.1   Simple Rates of Return   148   5.2.2 Bond Returns on an Accrual Basis   154

5.3 AFTER-TAX RATES OF RETURN   156

5.4 INFLATION-ADJUSTED RATES OF RETURN   158

5.5 FOREIGN EXCHANGE AND RATES OF RETURN   160
Connecting Theory to Practice 5.1: Germany's Rate Decision May Determine Whether Dollar's Slide Will Continue   160

5.6 AVERAGE RATE OF RETURN   162

5.7 ADJUSTED RATE OF RETURN   165

5.8 INDEXES   167
5.8.1 Types of Indexes   168   5.8.2 Bond Indexes   174   5.8.3 Stock Indexes   176

5.9 TRACKING RATES OF RETURN OVER TIME   177

Summary   181   Chapter at a Glance   181   Key Terms   183   Review   183
Practice   183

Your Turn: Applying Theory to Practice: Rates of Return—The Various Definitions   188

Selected References   189   Supplemental References   189

APPENDIX 5A DOLLAR-WEIGHTED
AVERAGE RATE OF RETURN   189

6 The Foundation of Risk Analysis   191

Investments in the News
   Why Risk Matters   191

6.1 THE CASE OF CERTAINTY   192

6.2 THE NATURE OF RISK   194

6.3 ALTERNATIVE INVESTMENT CRITERIA   196
6.3.1 Maximum Return Criterion   196   6.3.2 Maximum Expected Return
Criterion   197

6.4 RISK AVERSION 199
6.4.1 Definition of Risk Averters 199   6.4.2 Risk Premium 200

6.5 CALCULATING VARIANCE 201

6.6 THE MEAN-VARIANCE CRITERION 202

6.7 OTHER ATTITUDES TOWARD RISK 205

Summary 207   Chapter at a Glance 207   Key Terms 208   Review 208
Practice 209

Your Turn: Applying Theory to Practice: Mean and Variance of Bonds and Stocks 213

Supplemental References 214

7 Portfolio Mean and Variance 215

Investments in the News
  Mutual Funds, Navigating the Future 215
  Diversification Made Simple: Fidelity Asset Manager™ 215

7.1 THE PORTFOLIO 216

7.2 AN ASSET'S RISK WHEN HELD
WITH OTHER ASSETS IN A PORTFOLIO 216

7.3 THE EXPECTED RATE OF RETURN ON A PORTFOLIO 220

7.4 COVARIANCES 222

7.5 CORRELATION COEFFICIENT 227

7.6 THE PORTFOLIO VARIANCE 231
7.6.1 The Direct Method 232   7.6.2 The Indirect Method 233

7.7 ANOTHER LOOK AT MUTUAL FUNDS 237

7.8 THE VARIANCE OF A PORTFOLIO
COMPOSED OF n ASSETS 238

Summary 238   Chapter at a Glance 239   Key Terms 240   Practice 240

*Your Turn: Applying Theory to Practice: Portfolio Mean and Variance: Bonds and
Stocks* 243

APPENDIX 7A THE VARIANCE OF A
PORTFOLIO COMPOSED OF n ASSETS 244

8 The Gain from Portfolio Diversification 249

Investments in the News
  More of a Mix 249

8.1 THE EFFECT OF CORRELATION
ON A PORTFOLIO'S RISK REDUCTION 251
8.1.1 The Investment Weights That Guarantee a Perfect Return on the Portfolio—
When the Correlation Is $p = -1$ 255 *Connecting Theory to Practice 8.1: How to Build
a Stock Portfolio Even If You Aren't a Moneybags—Continued* 260 8.1.2 The Effect of
the Number of Assets in a Portfolio on Risk Reduction 261 8.1.3 A Little Diversification Goes a Long Way 264

8.2 EFFICIENT AND INEFFICIENT INVESTMENT STRATEGIES 266
8.2.1 Efficient and Inefficient Frontiers in the Two-Asset Case 267 8.2.2 Two Assets with Different Correlations 269 8.2.3 Efficient and Inefficient Frontiers with
Many Assets 270

8.3 THE GAIN FROM DIVERSIFICATION
IN UNRELATED FIRMS IN PRACTICE 272
Summary 274   Chapter at a Glance 275   Key Terms 275   Review 275
Practice 276

Your Turn: Applying Theory to Practice: Portfolio Poll—The Ideal Portfolio? 281

Supplemental Reference 283

APPENDIX 8A CALCULATING THE EFFICIENT FRONTIER 283

**PART 3   EQUILIBRIUM PRICES:
EXPANDING THE PORTFOLIO UNIVERSE**

9 Risk and Return: The Linear Relationships and the Capital Asset Pricing Model 288

*Investments in the News
The Ultimate Index Funds* 288

9.1 INDIFFERENCE CURVES 290

9.2 EFFICIENT INVESTMENT OPPORTUNITIES WITH RISK-FREE
BORROWING AND LENDING AND A SINGLE RISKY ASSET 292

9.3 THE CAPITAL MARKET LINE (CML) 297

9.4 THE SEPARATION PROPERTY 299

9.5 THE SECURITY MARKET LINE (SML)
AND THE CAPITAL ASSET PRICING MODEL (CAPM) 301
9.5.1 Beta as a Measure of Risk 301 9.5.2 The Meaning of Beta—Characteristic
Lines 303 *Connecting Theory to Practice 9.1: How Savvy Fund Investors Tally the Risk*
307 9.5.3 U.S. Market Portfolio and the World Market Portfolio 309 9.5.4 The
Security Market Line (SML) 310 9.5.5 The Risk Premium 315

9.6 SYSTEMATIC AND UNSYSTEMATIC RISK 317

9.7 A PROOF OF THE CAPM   319
Connecting Theory to Practice: Stock Picks That Are Stopping the Presses 322

9.8 USING THE CAPM FOR STOCK SELECTION 323

9.9 USING ALPHA AND BETA IN PRACTICE 325

9.10 SHORTCOMINGS OF THE CAPM 325

Summary 328   Chapter at a Glance 329   Key Terms 330   Review 330
Practice 331   CFA Problems 334

*Your Turn: Applying Theory to Practice 9.1: Super Diversifiers: Adding Commodities to
Your Portfolio without All the Stomach-Churning* 335

Selected References 336   Supplemental References 336

10 Index Models and the Arbitrage Pricing Theory 337

*Investments in the News
   Practicing What They Teach* 337

10.1 THE SINGLE INDEX MODEL 338
10.1.1 Common-Factor and Firm-Specific Rates of Returns 338   10.1.2 Why the
SIM Drastically Reduces the Amount of Computations 342   10.1.3 Systematic
and Unsystematic Risk and Portfolio Size 343   10.1.4 Risk and Expected Return
with the SIM 344

10.2 THE ARBITRAGE PRICING THEORY 345
10.2.1 Examples of Arbitrage 346   *Connecting Theory to Practice 10.1: Program
Trading* 349   10.2.2 The APT: Assumptions and Risk-Return Relationship 350
*Connecting Theory to Practice 10.2: Surprise, Surprise! Unexpected Announcements Affect
Stock Prices* 352   10.2.3 The Linear APT Relationship 354

10.3 THE APT AND THE CAPM 360

10.4 MULTIFACTOR APT MODEL 361

Summary 363   Chapter at a Glance 363   Key Terms 364   Review 364
Practice 365

*Your Turn: Applying Theory to Practice: Calculating Asset Covariance by the Single Index
Model (SIM)* 367

Selected Reference 368   Supplemental References 368

11 International Investment 369

*Investments in the News
   International Investing Raises Questions on Allocation, Diversification, Hedging* 369

11.1 RISKS AND RETURNS IN INTERNATIONAL INVESTMENTS 371
Connecting Theory to Practice 11.1: Equity Market Globalization: A View from 11 Wall Street 372   11.1.1 Diversifying Internationally 374   11.1.2 Currency Risk 380 11.1.3 International Diversification: Various Points of View 385

11.2 INTERNATIONAL PARITY RELATIONSHIPS 389
11.2.1 Purchasing Power Parity 389   11.2.2 International Fisher Relationship 392 11.2.3 Foreign Exchange Expectations 393   11.2.4 Interest Rate Parity 394

Summary 398   Chapter at a Glance 399   Key Terms 399   Review 399 Practice 400

Your Turn: Applying Theory to Practice: International Diversification in the Bond Market 404

Selected References 405   Supplemental References 405

PART 4   EFFICIENT MARKETS AND PORTFOLIO PERFORMANCE

12 Efficient Markets: Theory and Evidence   407

Investments in the News
  Luck or Logic? Debate Rages On over "Efficient-Market" Theory 407

12.1 EFFICIENT MARKET DEFINED 409

12.2 WHAT CONSTITUTES THE APPROPRIATE INFORMATION SET? 410
12.2.1 Weak Form of the EMT 411   12.2.2 Semistrong Form of the EMT 412 12.2.3 Strong Form of the EMT 414   *Connecting Theory to Practice 12.1: Court Allows Broader Meaning of Insider Trading* 415

12.3 INVESTMENT STRATEGY IN AN EFFICIENT MARKET 417
12.3.1 Resource Allocation and the EMT 417   12.3.2 Portfolio Selection and the EMT 417   12.3.3 Passive versus Active Portfolio Management 419 *Connecting Theory to Practice 12.2: Reaching All Your Goals—Why Choosing the Right Mix Is Job #1* 420

12.4 INVESTMENT STRATEGY IN AN INEFFICIENT MARKET 421

12.5 EMPIRICAL EVIDENCE RELATED TO THE EMT 421
12.5.1 Evidence Related to the Weak Form of the EMT 422   12.5.2 Evidence Related to the Semistrong Form of the EMT 427   *Connecting Theory to Practice 12.3: Zacks Quarterly Earnings Update* 430   12.5.3 Evidence Related to the Strong Form of the EMT 431   *Connecting Theory to Practice 12.4: "Cheat Sheets" on IPOs Raise Fairness Issue* 432

12.6 MARKET ANOMALIES 433
Connecting Theory to Practice 12.5: Warm to the January Effect but New Year Comes Earlier for Small-Caps 438

Summary **439**   Chapter at a Glance **440**   Key Terms **440**   Review **440**   Practice **441**   CFA Problems **446**

Your Turn: Applying Theory to Practice: The Investor's Plan of Attack **446**

Selected References **448**   Supplemental References **448**

13 Technical Analysis **450**

Investments in the News
   Technicians Turn Bearish on U.S. Stocks **450**

13.1 IN DEFENSE OF TECHNICAL ANALYSIS **451**

13.2 CHARTING **453**
13.2.1 Bar Charts **453**   13.2.2 Point-and-Figure Charts **457**   13.2.3 Candlestick Charts **459**

13.3 THEORETICAL BASIS OF TECHNICAL ANALYSIS **463**
13.3.1 Dow Theory **463**   *Connecting Theory to Practice 13.1: Adherents of the Dow Theory on Stock Trends Disagree over When the Bull Market Will End* **464**   13.3.2 Moving Averages **465**   13.3.3 Relative Strength **467**

13.4 TECHNICAL INDICATORS **468**
13.4.1 Breadth Indicators **469**   *Connecting Theory to Practice 13.2: Heavy Volume and Lagging Blue Chips May Point to Coming Decline in Stocks* **471**   13.4.2 Sentiment Indicators **472**

Summary **473**   Chapter at a Glance **473**   Key Terms **474**   Review **474**   Practice **475**

Your Turn: Applying Theory to Practice: Voodoo or Science? **479**

Selected References **481**   Supplemental References **481**

14 Investment Companies and Mutual Funds **482**

Investments in the News
   The Terminator **482**
   Fund Survey: Enough Already **482**

14.1 TYPES OF FUNDS **483**
14.1.1 Closed-End Funds (Investment Trusts) **485**   *Connecting Theory to Practice 14.1: Should You Be a Bull in China's Shop?* **491**   *Connecting Theory to Practice 14.2: At Closed-End Funds, a Big Push to Open Up Conversions Can Mean Windfalls for Shareholders* **494**   14.1.2 Open-End Funds (Mutual Funds) **495**

14.2 BENEFITS AND COSTS OF INVESTING IN MUTUAL FUNDS **503**
14.2.1 Benefits of Investing in Mutual Funds **503**   14.2.2 Costs of Investing in Mutual Funds **506**   *Connecting Theory to Practice 14.3: Magellan, the Flagship of*

Fidelity, Will Close to Most New Investors **509**   *Connecting Theory to Practice 14.4: Without Portfolio: The Case for Picking Your Own Stocks* **510**

Summary **511**   Chapter at a Glance **512**   Key Terms **513**   Review **513** Practice **513**

Your Turn: Applying Theory to Practice: The Discount Indicator **518**

Selected References **519**   Supplemental References **519**

15 Performance Measurement   521

Investments in the News
  U.S. Equity Funds **521**

15.1 HOW TO MEASURE RISK **523**

15.2 PERFORMANCE INDEXES **525**
15.2.1 Sharpe's Performance Index (PI_s) **525**   15.2.2 Treynor's Performance Index (PI_T) **528**   15.2.3 Jensen's Performance Index (PI_J) **531**   15.2.4 Performance Indexes with APT (PI_A) **533**   15.2.5 Summary of Performance Indexes **533** *Connecting Theory to Practice 15.1: A Happy Few Manage to Beat the S&P* **534**

15.3 EMPIRICAL EVIDENCE OF THE PERFORMANCE OF MUTUAL FUNDS **536**

15.4 TIMING THE MARKET **537**

15.5 A WORD OF CAUTION ABOUT PERFORMANCE INDEXES IN PRACTICE **539** *Connecting Theory to Practice 15.2: What Money Managers Really Sell* **539**

15.6 PERFORMANCE ATTRIBUTION **541**

15.7 INDEXING AND INTERNATIONAL DIVERSIFICATION **543** *Connecting Theory to Practice 15.3: At Last. A Simple Strategy for International Investing. Use the Power of Indexing* **544**

Summary **545**   Chapter at a Glance **546**   Key Terms **546**   Review **547** Practice **547**

Your Turn: Applying Theory to Practice: Measuring the Performance of Small Stocks and Corporate Bonds **552**

Selected References **553**   Supplemental References **553**

PART 5   SECURITY ANALYSIS

16 Interest Rates and Bond Valuation   555

Investments in the News
  Bond Pros: Where to Ride Out a Jittery Market **555**
  Zeroing In **555**

16.1 INTEREST RATE CHANGES 556

16.2 THE YIELD CURVE 558

16.3 EXPLAINING THE SHAPE OF THE YIELD CURVE 562
Connecting Theory to Practice 16.1a: Curve on Yields Poses Dilemma for Bond Buyer 562
*Connecting Theory to Practice 16.1b: Bond Prices Continue Their Decline as Treasury
Prepares Sale of $38 Billion in New Securities* 564   16.3.1 Spot Rates, Forward Rates,
Forward Contracts, and Holding Period Rates 565   16.3.2 The Expectations
Hypothesis 568   16.3.3 The Liquidity Preference Hypothesis 569   16.3.4 The
Market Segmentations Hypothesis 570

16.4 OTHER MEASURES OF BOND YIELDS 571

16.5 PRICING BONDS IN PRACTICE 573

16.6 SPREADS OVER TREASURIES 576
16.6.1 Bond Ratings 577   *Connecting Theory to Practice 16.2a: Value of Bond Ratings
Questioned by a Growing Number of Studies* 579   *Connecting Theory to Practice 16.2b:
Moody's Bond-Rating Changes* 581   16.6.2 Bond Ratings and Spreads over Treasuries
582   16.6.3 Junk Bonds 586   16.6.4 Inflation-Indexed Bonds 587   16.6.5 International Bond Markets 588

16.7 THE IMPACT OF EMBEDDED OPTIONS 590
16.7.1 The Call Feature 590   16.7.2 The Conversion Feature 592

Summary 593   Chapter at a Glance 594   Key Terms 594   Review 595
Practice 595   CFA Problems 599

*Your Turn: Applying Theory to Practice: Enhancing Portfolio Return with Convertible
Bonds* 599

Selected References 601   Supplemental References 602

APPENDIX 16A SIMPLE EQUATIONS FOR BOND PRICING 603
Appendix Practice 605

APPENDIX 16B INCORPORATING ACCRUED
INTEREST AND PARTIAL PERIODS 605
Appendix Practice 609

APPENDIX 16C METHODS OF COMPOUNDING
INTEREST RATES 609
Appendix Practice 611

17 Bonds—Analysis and Management 612

*Investments in the News
    Bond's Duration Is Handy Guide on Rates* 612

17.1 BOND PRICING PRINCIPLES 613

17.1.1 Principle 1: Bond Prices Change with the Passage of Time **613**   17.1.2 Principle 2: Bond Prices Are Inversely Related to the Yield to Maturity **614** 17.1.3 Principle 3: The Longer the Maturity, the More Sensitive the Bond's Price to Changes in the Yield to Maturity **615**   17.1.4 Principle 4: The Sensitivity of the Price of a Bond to Changes in the Yield to Maturity Increases at a Decreasing Rate with the Length to Maturity **618**   *Connecting Theory to Practice 17.1: TVA Is Mulling Sale of 50-Year Bonds* **619**   17.1.5 Principle 5: There Is a Linear Relationship between a Bond's Coupon Rate and Its Price **620**

17.2 DURATION AND CONVEXITY **624**
17.2.1 Duration Principles **632**   17.2.2 Convexity **637**

17.3 IMMUNIZATION **639**
17.3.1 Income Immunization **639**   17.3.2 Price Immunization **641**

17.4 PASSIVE VERSUS ACTIVE BOND MANAGEMENT STRATEGIES **642** *Connecting Theory to Practice 17.2: Building a Bond Ladder Is Safe Way to Increase Yield* **642**   17.4.1 Contingent Immunization **643**   17.4.2 Popular Active Bond Management Strategies **643**   *Connecting Theory to Practice 17.3: Vanguard's Investment Grade Bond Fund* **644**

Summary **645**   Chapter at a Glance **646**   Key Terms **646**   Review **647** Practice **647**   CFA Problems **650**

Your Turn: Applying Theory to Practice: Will You Ride Down the Yield Curve or Take the "Haircut" on Yield? **650**

Selected References **653**   Supplemental References **654**

APPENDIX 17A COMPUTATIONAL EQUATION FOR DURATION **654**

18 Common Stocks—Valuation   656

Investments in the News
  Rating Your Broker's Stock Picks **656**

18.1 USES OF STOCK VALUATION MODELS **657**
18.1.1 Assessing Investment Opportunities **658**   18.1.2 Valuing a Common Stock Issue **658**   18.1.3 Estimating the Appropriate Discount Rate **658**   18.1.4 Understanding the Financial Media **659**

18.2 THE DISCOUNTED CASH FLOW PRINCIPLE **659**

18.3 THE CONSTANT DIVIDEND GROWTH MODEL **664**

18.4 SOURCES OF GROWTH **665**
18.4.1 Source 1: Reinvestment of Earnings **666**   18.4.2 Source 2: Opportunities for Extraordinary Profits **666**   18.4.3 Normal-Growth Firms **667**   18.4.4 Super-growth Firms **670**   18.4.5 Supergrowth Firms for a Limited Time Period **671**

18.5 CONSTANT DIVIDEND GROWTH MODEL VALUATION WHEN ALL THE EARNINGS ARE PAID AS CASH DIVIDENDS **674**

18.6 FINDING THE COST OF EQUITY CAPITAL WITH THECONSTANT DIVIDEND GROWTH MODEL **675**

18.7 PICKING STOCKS USING THE P/E RATIO **676**
Connecting Theory to Practice 18.1: Stocks Are in a Stratosphere, by Some Measures— Valuation Meter Indicates Prices off the Charts **678**

Summary **682** Chapter at a Glance **683** Key Terms **684** Review **684** Practice **685** CFA Problems **690**

Your Turn: Applying Theory to Practice: Sara Lee—Valuation, Growth Rate, and Cost of Equity **691**

Selected References **692** Supplemental References **692**

APPENDIX 18A FREE CASH FLOW MODEL (FCFM) FOR NORMAL-GROWTH FIRMS **693**
Connecting Theory to Practice 18.2: Man from the Pru Banks on New Image **694**
Connecting Theory to Practice 18.3: Seeking Shelter **699**

APPENDIX 18B PICKING STOCKS WITH EVA **701**

19 Common Stock Selection **704**

Investments in the News
  Finding the Common Denominator of Winning Stocks **704**

19.1 THE ANATOMY OF A STOCK MARKET WINNER **705**

19.2 HOW ANALYSTS VIEW THE STOCK VALUATION PROCESS **706**

19.3 MANAGING A STOCK PORTFOLIO **707**
19.3.1 Sources of Risk for Common Stock **710** 19.3.2 Market Signals of a Crash: An Analyst's View **712** *Connecting Theory to Practice 19.1: Vertigo* **712** 19.3.3 Duration of Common Stock **714**

19.4 ESTIMATING DIVIDEND DISCOUNT MODEL INPUTS **716**
19.4.1 Estimating the Dividend Growth Rate (g) **716** 19.4.2 Estimating the Investors' Required Rate of Return (k) **719**

19.5 IMPLEMENTING DIVIDEND DISCOUNT MODELS **720**
19.5.1 DDM Assumptions **721** 19.5.2 Proper Inputs **722** 19.5.3 Interpreting the Results of a DDM Calculation **722**

Summary **723** Chapter at a Glance **724** Key Terms **725** Review **725** Practice **725**

Your Turn: Applying Theory to Practice: Ace Stock Picker Names Some Tactics That Work in This Year's Market **730**

Selected References **731**   Supplemental References **732**

**APPENDIX 19A ESTIMATING THE
GROWTH RATE OF DIVIDENDS** **732**

20 Market and Industry Analysis   734

Investments in the News
   The Dollar's Decline Has an Upside **734**

20.1 MACROECONOMIC EVALUATION   **736**
20.1.1 Understanding Gross Domestic Product **736**   20.1.2 The Business Cycle and Economic Indicators **740**   20.1.3 Fiscal and Monetary Policy **741**

20.2 THE ECONOMY AND THE FINANCIAL MARKETS   **744**
20.2.1 Bond Market **745**   20.2.2 Stock Market **746**

20.3 VALUING THE OVERALL STOCK MARKET   **746**
20.3.1 Book Value **746**   20.3.2 Dividends **748**   *Connecting Theory to Practice 20.1: Low Dividend Yield May No Longer Be the Red Flag for Stocks It Once Was* **749**   20.3.3 Earnings **750**   *Connecting Theory to Practice 20.2: Are Stocks Overvalued? Not a Chance* **751**

20.4 INDUSTRY ANALYSIS   **751**
20.4.1 The Industrial Life Cycle **753**   20.4.2 Demand and Supply Analysis **753** *Connecting Theory to Practice 20.3: Biotechs on the Blink* **754**   20.4.3 Industry Profitability **756**   20.4.4 International Competition and Markets **756**

Summary **756**   Chapter at a Glance **757**   Key Terms **757**   Review **758** Practice **758**   CFA Problems **761**

Your Turn: Applying Theory to Practice: The Big Picture—What Macroeconomic and Political Factors Should Be Considered in Selecting the Type of Investment? **761**

Selected References **763**   Supplemental References **763**

21 Financial Statement Analysis   765

Investments in the News
   "We Were Great!"—Except for . . . **765**
   Yes, You Can Beat the Market **765**

21.1 FINANCIAL STATEMENTS   **766**
21.1.1 Financial Accounting Concepts **767**   *Connecting Theory to Practice 21.1: As IBM's Woes Grew, Its Accounting Tactics Got Less Conservative* **768**   21.1.2 Balance Sheet **770**   21.1.3 Income Statement **778**   21.1.4 Statement of Cash Flows **780**

21.2 EARNINGS PER SHARE (EPS)   **783**

21.3 RATIO ANALYSIS   **784**

Connecting Theory to Practice 21.2: How Chartered Financial Analysts View Financial Ratios **786**

Summary **794**   Chapter at a Glance **794**   Key Terms **795**   Review **795**   Practice **796**

Your Turn: Applying Theory to Practice: What If Ben Graham Had Had a PC? **799**

Selected References **803**   Supplemental References **803**

PART 6   OPTIONS, FUTURES, AND FINANCIAL ENGINEERING

22 Forward and Futures Contracts 805

Investments in the News
  Commodities and Financial Futures **805**
  Chicago's Two Futures Exchanges Agree to Consolidate Their Clearinghouses **805**
  Using Derivatives by Dow **805**

22.1 FORWARD CONTRACTS **807**

22.2 FUTURES CONTRACTS **809**
22.2.1 Characteristics of Futures Contracts **809**   22.2.2 Reading Financial Data on Futures **812**

22.3 BUYING AND SELLING FUTURES CONTRACTS **816**
22.3.1 Trading a Futures Contract **816**   22.3.2 The Clearinghouse **818**   22.3.3 Margin Requirements **818**   *Connecting Theory to Practice 22.1: CFTC Weighs Block Trades of Contracts* **821**

22.4 INVESTMENT STRATEGIES WITH FUTURES CONTRACTS **822**
22.4.1 Hedging **824**   22.4.2 Speculating **825**   22.4.3 Arbitrage **826**   22.4.4 Portfolio Diversification **826**   *Connecting Theory to Practice 22.2: Institutions Buy Futures to Cut Risks* **826**

22.5 PRICING FUTURES CONTRACTS **827**
22.5.1 The Basis **827**   22.5.2 Pricing Stock Index Futures **828**   22.5.3 Pricing Currency Futures **830**   22.5.4 Pricing Commodity Futures **833**

Summary **834**   Chapter at a Glance **834**   Key Terms **835**   Review **835**   Practice **835**   CFA Problems **836**

Your Turn: Applying Theory to Practice: Futures Prices **837**

Selected References **838**   Supplemental References **838**

23 Options—Basic Concepts and Strategies 840

Investments in the News
  The $1 Billion Lesson of Nicholas Leeson **840**
  What Are Derivatives, and How Could You Lose $382 Million with Them? **840**

23.1 THE DEVELOPMENT OF MODERN OPTION TRADING   841

23.2 BUYING AND SELLING OPTIONS   843
23.2.1 The Option Buyer 843   23.2.2 The Option Seller 844   23.2.3 The Option
Contract 844   23.2.4 Investing in Options versus Investing in Stock 848   23.2.5
The Underlying Asset and the Option 849   *Connecting Theory to Practice 23.1: New
Tools for the Options Crowd* 850

23.3 OVERVIEW OF OPTION MARKETS   851

23.4 OPTION VALUES AT EXPIRATION   852
23.4.1 Option Prices: Intrinsic and Time Value Components 852   23.4.2 Payoff
Diagrams 854

23.5 INVESTMENT STRATEGIES USING OPTIONS   862
23.5.1 Protective Put Buying 863   23.5.2 Covered Call Writing 865   23.5.3 Bull
Spread 866

Summary 868   Chapter at a Glance 868   Key Terms 870   Review 870
Practice 870   CFA Problems 872

Your Turn: Applying Theory to Practice: Option-Stock Hedges: A Strategy for Caterpillar 872

Selected References 873   Supplemental References 874

APPENDIX 23A TAXES   874

APPENDIX 23B MARGIN REQUIREMENTS   875
Appendix Practice 879

APPENDIX 23C OTHER OPTION STRATEGIES   879
Appendix Practice 883

24 Valuing Options   884

*Investments in the News
   Trick or Treat? Risk Management Tools May Be the Risk* 884

24.1 OPTION BOUNDARIES   886
24.1.1 Call Option Boundaries 887   24.1.2 Put Option Options 890   24.1.3 Put-
Call Parity 893

24.2 BLACK-SCHOLES OPTION PRICING MODEL (BSOPM)   895
24.2.1 Call Options 895   24.2.2 Put Options 897   24.2.3 Estimating Inputs to the
BSOPM 897   24.2.4 Sensitivity Analysis of the BSOPM 899   24.2.5 Empirical
Evidence Regarding the BSOPM 899   *Connecting Theory to Practice 24.1: The Holes
in Black-Scholes* 902

24.3 APPLICATIONS OF THE BSOPM   903

24.3.1 Valuing Portfolio Insurance Using the BSOPM 904   24.3.2 Convertible Securities 905   24.3.3 Valuing Warrants 906   24.3.4 Options on Futures Contracts 906

Summary 909   Chapter at a Glance 910   Key Terms 911   Review 911 Practice 911

Your Turn: Applying Theory to Practice: Option Valuation: Does It Work in Practice? **914**

Selected References and Supplemental References 915

APPENDIX 24A BINOMIAL OPTION PRICING MODEL 915
Appendix Practice 922

APPENDIX 24B AN EXAMPLE USING THE
BLACK-SCHOLES OPTION PRICING MODEL 922

APPENDIX 24C CONTINUOUSLY COMPOUNDED
INTEREST RATES 926

APPENDIX 24D CALCULATING CONTINUOUSLY
COMPOUNDED STANDARD DEVIATIONS 927

25 Financial Engineering 930

Investments in the News
    Derivatives Are a Sensible Way to Manage Risk 930

25.1 WHAT IS FINANCIAL ENGINEERING? 931
25.1.1 Financial Engineering at Magma Copper Company 932   25.1.2 Indexed Bonds 934   25.1.3 Symmetric and Asymmetric Hedging Strategies 935   *Connecting Theory to Practice 25.1: States Hitting Options Pits to Hedge Risk* 935

25.2 WHY PURSUE FINANCIAL ENGINEERING STRATEGIES? 939
25.2.1 Unique Situations 939   25.2.2 When Markets Are Perceived to Be Inefficient 940   25.2.3 When Markets Are Perceived to Be Efficient 941

25.3 SWAPS 946
25.3.1 Interest Rate Swaps 946   *Connecting Theory to Practice 25.2: Let's Swap* 947
25.3.2 Currency Swaps 949   25.3.3 Commodity Swaps 950   *Connecting Theory to Practice 25.3: Big-Stakes Hedge Starts Branching Out* 950

25.4 RECENT FINANCIAL ENGINEERING INNOVATIONS 951

25.5 THE VALUE AT RISK (VaR) 952

Summary 954   Chapter at a Glance 955   Key Terms 955   Review 956 Practice 956

Your Turn: Applying Theory to Practice: Salomon Debt Links Returns to Stock of Computer Firm 959

Selected References 960   Supplemental References 961

APPENDIX A: INFORMATION MARKETS 963

APPENDIX B: CODE OF ETHICS AND STANDARDS
OF PROFESSIONAL CONDUCT 968

GLOSSARY 973

NAME INDEX 985

SUBJECT INDEX 989

CHAPTER 1

INTRODUCTION

LEARNING OBJECTIVES

After studying this chapter you should be able to:

1. Compare and contrast corporate finance and investments.

2. Differentiate between investments in real assets and investments in financial assets (securities).

3. State some good reasons for the study of investments.

4. Summarize the overall investment process.

INVESTMENTS IN THE NEWS

GREENSPAN GIVES NO HINT OF RATE BOOST

Economy Is 'Exceptional.'

Prices Are Nearly Stable;

Stocks and Bonds Soar

WASHINGTON—Federal Reserve Chairman Alan Greenspan testified for three hours on Capitol Hill yesterday and gave no hint that an interest-rate increase is imminent, sending stocks and bonds soaring. . . .

Financial markets cheered the absence of any threats about inflation or higher rates. The Dow Jones Industrial Average rose 154.93 to close at a high of 8061.65. Rising bond prices pushed yields on 30-year bonds to the lowest level since early December.

The Fed chief said it is difficult to tell if the "exceptional economic situation" reflects only temporary factors—such as the strong dollar and the lull in health-care cost increases—or the more significant long-term uptrend in productivity trends that he has been talking about for years.

Mr. Greenspan long has argued that computer technology may pay a significant productivity dividend, and lately he has suggested that it finally may be showing up. "Important pieces of information . . . could be read as indicating basic improvements in the longer-term efficiency of our economy," he said, raising the possibility that the world is undergoing "a once- or twice-in-a-century phenomenon that will carry productivity trends nationally and globally to a new higher track."

Source: *Wall Street Journal*, "Greenspan Gives No Hint of Rate Boost," July 23, 1997, p. A2. Reprinted by permission of *The Wall Street Journal*, © 1997 Dow Jones & Co., Inc. All Rights Reserved Worldwide.

TOKYO STOCKS RETREAT BROADLY TO PROFIT-TAKING; EUROPEAN AND LATIN AMERICAN BOURSES REBOUND

Tokyo stocks declined broadly Tuesday on profit-taking. Many European markets rebounded, aided by a stronger U.S. dollar and Wall Street's opening gains, and Latin American Bourses staged explosive recoveries, following hints that the U.S. wouldn't tinker with monetary policy for now, igniting New York equities.

The Dow Jones World Stock Index was at 173.18, up 2.31, reflecting gains in the Americas, Europe/ Africa and Asia/Pacific markets. . . .

In Tokyo the Nikkei 225-index fell 92.30 points to 20157.02.

But trading was thin, as many investors stayed out of the market ahead of U.S. Federal Reserve Chairman Alan Greenspan's semiannual testimony to a congressional banking committee, later in the day.

In London, the Financial Times-Stock Exchange 100-share index gained 41 points to 486.7

In Frankfurt, the DAX 30-stock index jumped 122.02 points, or 3%, to a record 4230.42.

The U.S. dollar's rise to a six-year high against the mark was the driving force behind equities' gains in heavy volume. . . .

In Mexico City, shares advanced 1.4% in a positive reaction to the Greenspan comments in Washington and to Wall Street's record high.

Source: "Tokyo Stocks Retreat Broadly to Profit-Taking; European and Latin American Bourses Rebound," *Wall Street Journal*, July 23, 1997. Reprinted by permission of *The Wall Street Journal*, © 1997 Dow Jones & Co., Inc. All Rights Reserved Worldwide.

In July 1998 the Nikkei index was about 15,000, reflecting the slowing growth of the Japanese economy.

AIG'S NET JUMPS 14% TO $826.5 MILLION, BUOYED BY STRENGTH AT HOME AND ABROAD

NEW YORK—American International Group Inc. reported a 14% increase in second-quarter net income, as it continued to perform well in a competitive domestic market and posted strong gains abroad. . . .

In New York Stock Exchange composite trading, AIG's shares rose $3.625, or 2.4%, to close at $156.50. "AIG is a very good company reporting very good results," said Alan Zimmermann, an analyst with Morgan Stanley. "Their worldwide diversification gives them a broad spread of risk, which leads to excellent underwriting results."

Source: "AIG's Net Jumps 14% to $826.5 Million, Buoyed by Strength at Home and Abroad," *Wall Street Journal*, July 25, 1997, p. A4. Reprinted by permission of *The Wall Street Journal*, © 1997 Dow Jones & Co., Inc. All Rights Reserved Worldwide.

An investor is an individual who is willing to forgo consumption today to achieve the goal of a higher level of consumption in the future. In this book we look at the opportunities available to investors and the techniques that investors can use to select proper investment vehicles to achieve their goal. We also focus on the information available to investors, because prudent investment decisions require the best use of this information. As described in the articles in this chapter's Investments in the News, stocks and bonds are typical financial securities used for investment purposes. The situations described, however, show that investors need more than familiarity with these vehicles. Investors also must follow the types of events that can cause the values of investment vehicles to change.

An analysis of the opening articles can illustrate how external factors in the economy, changes in a given industry, or events within a firm might affect stock and bond prices. Such an analysis can also clarify the interrelationships among interest rates, foreign exchange rates, and index changes in the stock markets in various countries.

The first article illustrates the effect of macroeconomic factors such as inflation, unemployment, and interest rates. Macroeconomic factors influence the entire stock and bond market in the United States and abroad. Thus, market analysis seeks to address questions like the following: How does the Federal Reserve Bank's interest rate policy affect stock and bond prices? Why did stock and bond prices surge in response to this news? What is the interrelationship between the overall economy and the securities markets? How do macroeconomic factors affect the trend in prices of stocks and bonds? What macroeconomic factors would be expected to affect the stock market? What news is considered to be positive, and what news is considered to be negative?

Federal Reserve Bank chairman Alan Greenspan indicates in the article that the computer industry is a key factor in the increased productivity in the United States and in the world. This statement implies that not all industries have the same potential growth. Therefore, industry analyses play an important role in investment selection. The question for the investor is whether it is reasonable to expect a particular industry to continue to grow. The investor should ask, How do I determine if one industry is in better shape than another industry? Why does the stock index of some industries go up while, at the same time, others go down?

The second quotation emphasizes the globalization of the capital market. In Tokyo, the Nikkei index fell, and the market was thin because investors were waiting for Greenspan's testimony. In most other countries, the stock indexes soared, and the strong dollar was mentioned as being an important factor driving the markets up. This quotation shows that the various markets are interrelated. It also illustrates how the stock market in other countries soared when the interest rate was not increased in the face of a strong economy in the United States. (A strong economy implies a strong dollar; that is, each dollar is worth more, say, German marks.) The explanation is that exporters in these countries make more money when the dollar is strong, because each dollar of an export then brings home more revenue in terms of the local currency. Therefore, the exporters make a higher profit, and the market surges. Clearly, knowledge of international investment, currency, and exchange rates are of crucial importance to investors.

The third quotation provides information regarding a specific company. A 14% increase in AIG's second-quarter earnings induced a 2.4% increase in the firm's stock price. (Once again, worldwide diversification is mentioned as a vehicle adopted by AIG to reduce risk.) How does new information regarding individual firms affect their securities? What type of information affects the stock price of an individual firm? Analysis of this type of information will help us explain why one stock goes up when the industry goes down. Thus, as part of our study of investments, we consider macroeconomic analyses and industry analyses, as well as security analyses.

1.1 FACTORS AFFECTING ASSETS PRICE

Most of this textbook is devoted to exploring the issues mentioned in the analysis of the three quotations in Investments in the News. We examine models for determining the value of various financial assets (for example, bonds and stocks) and show how changes in expected earnings or in the interest rate affect the current price of these assets. The book discusses industry and macroeconomic analyses. In particular, it shows how a change in interest rates may affect the value of individual stocks, as well as an individual's portfolio composition. Throughout the book there is an emphasis on market globalization, the gain from international diversification, and the effect of the currency exchange rate on return in overseas investments.

Generally, academics and practitioners agree on the effects on stock and bond prices of changes in the most important factors. For example, almost all agree that when the Federal Reserve cuts interest rates more than expected, or when it announces no increase in the interest rate when such an increase is expected, the overall stock market will go up. If the Federal Reserve cuts interest rates less than expected, the overall stock market will go down. Such an overall rise in the stock market or in an individual security is called a **rally.** Note that the factor must change by *more than expected* to influence prices. The current price reflects investors' best estimates of future changes in the factors. Thus, when the Federal Reserve cuts interest rates by more than expected, the present value of future cash flows such as dividends increases, and so do stock prices. (Appendix 1A reviews the present value concept.)

Investors routinely observe that when a firm announces greater-than-expected quarterly earnings and dividends, the stock price of the firm goes up. The only questionable issue is the *extent* to which such news will or should affect prices. Indeed, the valuation models presented in the chapters that follow attempt to evaluate both stock and bond prices and the effect of various levels of interest rates and dividends on these prices.

Because there is general agreement on the effect of the main factors on security prices, it would seem that the investor's task should be very simple. If investors know, for example, that tomorrow the Federal Reserve will cut interest rates, investors should invest in stocks today and enjoy the stock market rally tomorrow. Unfortunately, however, investing is not that simple. What if the Federal Reserve does not cut the interest rate, or the cut is less than what investors expected? In either case, the market will be disappointed, and prices will fall as a result. In general, investors do not completely agree on future forecasts. For example, some investors predict a cut in interest rates while some do not; hence, each investor pursues a different investment strategy. What is safe to assume is that no one has perfect foresight. Rather, investors can only estimate the probability of future events.

Even if one knows with certainty that some event will occur, no one knows for certain how the stock market will react to the event. Even though the stock market typically rallies when interest rates fall, there is no guarantee that a rally will occur in response to such an interest rate change. For example, from July 1991 through April 1992, the Japanese interest rate was cut from 6% to 3.75%, yet the Japanese stock market fell approximately 20%. Thus, even if investors know for sure that interest rates will be cut in the future, they should not put all their money in the stock market. There is always a risk that the stock market will not react favorably to an interest rate cut.

Suppose an investor believes that for General Motors (GM), there is a 50% chance that cash dividends and earnings will increase and a 50% chance that they will decrease. For AT&T, the same investor predicts a 75% chance of an increase in earnings and dividends and a 25% chance of a decrease. If investors were certain about the future events, they would buy only one stock—the one with the highest increase in value. However, the future of both stocks is subject to uncertainty. The GM stock could go up and AT&T could go down, despite the odds. To minimize the chance of a loss, the investor may decide to diversify and buy a quantity of both GM and AT&T stocks. Experts recommend that investors diversify by holding several different assets. Analysts further tell investors to study the many investment opportunities outside the United States. These markets may provide an opportunity for substantial risk reduction (see AIG's policy in the third article of Investments in the News).

In reality, information on future earnings, dividends, interest rates, inflation, and productivity is not known with certainty. Thus, the best policy is to invest in a group of securities known as a *portfolio,* a strategy that reduces the overall risk exposure. Indeed, a large part of this book is devoted to portfolio analysis and how to construct portfolios when perfect knowledge regarding future prices is not available.

Some of the information in this book will be familiar to readers from work in other classes—particularly corporate finance. This introductory chapter begins by comparing corporate finance and investments. It then compares investments in physical and financial assets. Investors have different goals than financial managers, and understanding the investor's aspirations and goals is a good place to start. The chapter explains reasons for studying investments and examines careers in the field. The chapter also looks at the types of investments available and the way investors can organize their investment strategies.

1.2 THE DIFFERENCE BETWEEN CORPORATE FINANCE AND INVESTMENTS

Virtually all students who take an investments course are required to have had at least one corporate finance (or principles of finance) course. In a corporate finance course, students are exposed to investment-related concepts, such as yield to maturity, portfolio variance, and the dividend valuation model. Students often wonder why they need to study investments again. What is the difference between physical project analysis studied in corporate finance classes and security analysis? After all, both involve an initial investment and the hope of getting the largest possible return in the future.

There are many similarities between project analysis and investment analysis. For example, both rely on estimating future cash flows and discounting these future cash flows to the present. However, there are also many differences between these two types of analysis. Therefore, specific tools are needed in financial asset investment analysis that are not needed in project analysis.

Corporate finance typically covers issues such as project analysis, capital structure, capital budgeting, and working capital management. Project analysis is concerned with determining whether a project should be undertaken; for example, whether a new warehouse should be built. Capital structure addresses the question of what type of long-term financing is best. Capital budgeting addresses the question of what long-term investments to undertake. Working capital management addresses how to manage a firm's day-to-day cash flow. Corporate finance is also concerned with how to allocate profits. Profits are divided among the government (through taxes), shareholders (through dividends), and the firm itself (through retained earnings).

Firms raise money by issuing stocks and bonds. These securities are subsequently traded in the financial market, where they are bought and sold by investors. Thus, both investors and the firm have an interest in the workings of financial markets. Corporate finance involves the interaction between firms and financial markets, whereas the field of investments addresses the interaction between investors and financial markets. Investors bring to the financial market a set of objectives (for example, to earn, on average, a 12% return) and constraints (for example, to strive to preserve original capital in down markets).

Investment is the use of financial capital in an effort to create more financial capital in the future. That is, an investor forgoes consumption today in an attempt to achieve an even higher level of consumption in the future. Investment in the **money market** (securities with maturities of less than 1 year) can be distinguished from investment in the **capital market** (securities with maturities greater than 1 year). Generally, investment in the money market is less risky than investment in the capital market because of the relatively short maturities of these securities. One exception is the case of derivative securities, such as put and call options. Exhibit 1-1 provides examples of the securities in each of the three market categories.

Investment also refers to a vehicle used to make more money. Some investments are **speculative,** meaning they involve a high degree of risk. However, many in-

EXHIBIT 1-1
Examples of
Financial
Securities
by Market
Classification

Money market securities

Treasury bills

Commercial paper

Negotiable certificates of deposit

Eurodollars

Banker's acceptances

Repurchase agreements

Capital market securities

Fixed-income securities: Debt instruments issued by the U.S. Treasury, federal agencies (e.g., Fannie Mae), municipalities, and corporations

Equity securities: Common stock and preferred stock

Derivative market securities

Options

Futures contracts

vestors in speculative vehicles undertake strategies to **hedge** against the risk of a major loss. Hedging is a technique used to limit loss potential. Risk reduction can also be achieved by holding a portfolio of assets. A **portfolio** is a group of securities that are held together in an effort to achieve some future consumption (or rate of return) and risk desire.

The primary focus of this book is on the relationship between financial markets and investors. Hence, issues related to corporate finance will be addressed only to the extent that they influence prices and perceptions of riskiness in financial markets. The basic formulas employed in both areas—corporate finance and investments—are covered. In fact, some of the same techniques used to evaluate assets in project analysis are used in financial assets analysis. Therefore, Appendix 1A reviews the basic formulas—present value, internal rate of return, and so forth—that you studied in your corporate finance course. This review will serve as a bridge between the two courses and will help later, because stock and bond valuation formulas are based on present value and internal rate of return methods.

1.3 THE DIFFERENCE BETWEEN PHYSICAL AND FINANCIAL ASSETS

An **asset** is something that is owned by a business, institution, partnership, or individual and that has monetary value. There are two categories of assets: **financial assets,** which are intangible, such as corporate stocks and bonds, and **physical assets** (also called **real assets** or **tangible assets**), which are tangible, such as precious metals or real estate. Although financial assets are typically represented by tangible certificates of ownership, the financial asset itself is intangible. Financial assets are also called **securities.** A key distinction between financial and real (physical) assets is that real assets are income-generating assets used to produce goods or services. Financial assets, in contrast, represent claims against the income generated by real assets.

Investment in real assets differs from investment in financial assets in several ways. Investing in the capital market typically involves a commitment of money to various financial assets, such as bonds and stocks, as opposed to real assets, such as machines. The use of the term *investment* in this book is confined strictly to investments in financial assets. Connecting Theory to Practice 1.1 describes the historical performance of financial and some physical assets. Notice that the chance to earn a positive rate of return depends on the length of time investors are willing to invest their money.

CONNECTING THEORY TO PRACTICE 1.1

WHAT ARE YOUR ODDS?

Wall Street's bread-and-butter investments continue to be stocks. Indeed, as shown in the first table on page 9, in 1996 the Dow Jones Industrial Average, which is made up of blue chip stocks, earned a healthy 29% return. In contrast, in 1996 precious metals such as gold experienced a loss of 5.1%, and at this writing were still declining in value.

Before you rush to invest in stocks, however, review the second table, which demonstrates that spectacular returns on common stocks are not without risk. If your focus is short term—a position not advocated by financial theory or this textbook—there is also a 26% chance that you will lose your investment. This essence of risk and return will pervade the discussions throughout this textbook.

MAKING THE CONNECTION

The second table on page 9 shows that the longer the holding period, the smaller the chance of having an extreme result (that is, a loss of more than 20% rate of return). The first table reveals that in the years 1994 to 1996, precious metals, art, and rare coins were relatively poor investments whose returns fell short of the return on stocks. However, in some years (not reported in the tables), precious metals and collectibles outperformed both stocks and bonds.

1.3.1 Divisibility

One unique characteristic of investments in financial assets (as opposed to investments in real assets) is that financial assets are easily divisible. For example, you can buy a small fraction of General Electric (GE) through common stock. (You do not have to buy the entire company.) Thus, you can buy or sell a portion of a corporation with

Total Return on Investments

Type of Investment	1996	1995	1994
Stocks			
Dow Jones Industrial Average	29.1%	36.8%	5.9%
Standard & Poor's 500	23.0	37.6	1.3
Wilshire 5000	21.2	36.4	−0.1
Bonds			
Treasury bonds	−0.8	30.7	−7.6
Corporate bonds	1.6	26.9	−5.8
Municipal bonds	4.1	17.4	−5.2
Bank instruments			
Certificates of deposit	5.0	5.4	4.0
Money market accounts	2.7	2.9	2.4
Precious metals			
Gold	−5.1	1.0	−2.0
Silver	−9.6	5.9	−4.0
Collectibles			
Art	−1.3	9.4	−17.2
Rare coins	4.1	0.4	−2.9

Source: *Wall Street Journal,* January 2, 1997, p. R12. Reprinted by permission of *The Wall Street Journal,* © 1997 Dow Jones & Co., Inc. All Rights Reserved Worldwide.

What Are Your Odds?

Here are your chances of making or losing money in the leading United States stocks[a] over various holding periods. Shorter holding periods carry much more risk.

If You Hold	Your Chance of Losing Money	Your Chance of Making 0–10% per Year	Your Chance of Making 0–20% per Year	Your Chance of Making 20% or More per Year
1 year	26%	18%	20%	37%
3 years	14	28	39	19
5 years	10	31	49	10
10 years	4	42	53	1
20 years	0	37	63	0

[a]Standard & Poor's 500-stock average, annualized monthly returns since 1926, with all dividends reinvested.

Source: "What Are Your Odds?" *Newsweek,* November 10, 1997, p. 38, © 1997, Newsweek, Inc. All rights reserved. Reprinted by permission; as cited in Ibbotson Associates. Used with permission. ©1998 Ibbotson Associates, Inc. All rights reserved. [Certain portions of this work were derived from copyrighted works of Roger G. Ibbotson and Rex Sinquefield.]

common stock. It is much harder, however, to buy or sell a portion of a manufacturing plant or other physical asset. An asset is said to be **divisible** if you can buy and sell small portions of it. Financial assets are divisible, whereas most physical assets are not.

1.3.2 Marketability

Financial assets (or securities) can be classified by how easily they can be bought and sold. **Marketable securities,** such as 100 shares of AT&T stock, can easily be bought and sold by a phone call to a broker or via the Internet and are therefore very liquid. **Nonmarketable securities,** such as stamps or Chinese ceramics, cannot be readily sold. Marketability does not necessarily reflect market value, but simply the ease and speed with which an asset can be traded without having to incur a substantial price concession. Clearly, if you wanted to sell a house in one day, you would have to offer a substantial discount to attract someone to buy it immediately.

Marketability is a characteristic of financial assets that is not shared by real assets. Marketability, or **liquidity,** reflects the feasibility of converting an asset into cash quickly and without significantly affecting its price. Stocks with a large number of shares outstanding that are actively traded are very liquid. These securities are preferred by investors who trade large quantities of securities, because their trading activity will have no (or minimal) impact on the security's price. Many financial assets are very easy to buy and sell. However, most real assets are not very liquid and hence are described as *illiquid*. An investor who owns textile machines and who wants to sell them, for example, will generally have difficulty doing so.

1.3.3 The Holding Period

When investors acquire a real asset, they normally plan to hold it for a relatively long period. Buying new steel-producing machines, for example, requires large installation costs. Therefore, no one would plan to hold these machines for a month or even just a year. However, the transaction costs of buying securities are relatively low, and investing for a month or a year may be reasonable. Thus, the planned holding period of securities can be much shorter than the corresponding holding period of most real assets.

1.3.4 Information Availability

Information about financial assets is abundant. Although in principle, all investors can obtain information on real assets, it is typically hard to acquire and may be costly. For example, suppose you inquire about buying an oil-drilling machine. Where would you get information on the value of the machine? What are the transportation and installation costs of the machine? Probably only a few people in the oil industry have the information to determine these costs. The situation is different with stocks and bonds. Anyone can open the *Wall Street Journal* or call a broker to find out how much a share of AT&T stock costs. Similarly, a person who wants to buy shares of AT&T stock can obtain information (at almost no cost) on earnings, dividends, and so forth. Today, almost every large firm has an Internet site, and an investor can obtain all needed information free of charge with just the push of a button. Because this information is publicly available, the impact of many published factors on the value of the financial asset can be analyzed. This type of analysis cannot be easily done with real assets, at least not by all investors.

Four factors—divisibility, marketability (also called liquidity), holding period, and information availability—make investments in financial assets different from investments in real assets. Thus, we need different tools to analyze these types of investments. In particular, because of the divisibility property of financial assets, this book will focus on how to build portfolios of securities.

1.4 THE BENEFITS OF STUDYING INVESTMENTS

People study investments for at least two main reasons. First, a thorough knowledge of the investment process can greatly enhance a person's welfare. Second, this knowledge can lead to a rewarding career. By understanding how to make wise investments and manage finances prudently, people can greatly reduce the amount of income required to support a better lifestyle.

Many people spend most of their lives trying to generate additional income rather than focusing on properly managing the income that they currently generate. For example, consider a group of physicians who focus on running an office practice and providing for their patients, but neglect their day-to-day cash flow management. As a result, the group has over $30,000 in a checking account that does not earn interest. By taking a little time, they could immediately generate an additional $800 per year. That is, they could open a money market account from which they could write checks (usually in excess of some minimum amount, say, $250). Suppose the money market account is earning about 4% per year. Hence, by moving $20,000 to the money market account (leaving $10,000 for daily cash flow), the physicians could earn $800 ($20,000 × 0.04) a year. Just as the physician's office could make $800 a year, so all individuals can save money by wisely managing their personal finances. The proper management of personal finances can result in a significantly higher future income. From the efficient management of day-to-day cash flow to retirement planning, a thorough knowledge of investments will provide lifelong benefits. Thus, even nonprofessional investors can benefit from understanding investments.

As the financial markets become increasingly complex, job opportunities for professional investors increase. Even though job opportunities declined after the October 1987 stock market crash, the overall trend has been expansion. Increasingly, firms are looking for people with specialized skills. In 1998, the stock indexes in the United States hit an all-time high, with the Dow Jones index passing the 9,000-point mark. This bull market increases the demand for finance majors with specialized skills. For example, several major brokerage firms have hired aerospace engineers to program the computers that are designed to take advantage of mispriced assets across international markets. Also, the needs of the complex interest rate swap market have prompted a few active participants in these markets to advertise in card players' magazines. (Apparently, the ability to bluff is highly valued.) Exhibit 1-2 provides a sampling of job opportunities in the investments field.

1.5 THE INVESTMENT PROCESS

The study of investments is never completed. The investment process is dynamic and ongoing. Thus, the job of the investment analyst is never finished. However, there are always five basic components in the investment process: investor characteristics, investment vehicles, strategy development, strategy implementation, and strategy monitoring. Exhibit 1-3 shows the relationship of the components in the investment process.

1.5.1 Investor Characteristics

The first element in the investment process is the investor. The investor may be an individual or an institutional investor, such as a manager of an employee retirement account or bank trust department. The investor should first establish the **investment policy,** a written document detailing the objectives and constraints (characteristics) of the investor.

EXHIBIT 1-2   **Job Opportunities in Investments**

Title	Typical Firms	Description
Broker, registered representative, account executive	Brokerage firms, financial institutions	Provide sales and financial planning services
Analyst	Brokerage firms, financial institutions	Conduct research and security analysis
Financial planner	Private firms, certified public accountant (CPA) firms	Advise individual investors
Portfolio manager	Mutual fund groups, pension funds, money managers	Perform asset allocation and security selection
Asset/liability manager	Insurance companies, financial institutions	Perform research, actuarial work, and asset allocation
Auditor	All firms	Monitor and devise internal controls
Regulator	Government agencies, exchanges	Oversee and police market activity
Surveillance	Exchanges	Oversee and monitor trading behavior

EXHIBIT 1-3
The Investment Process

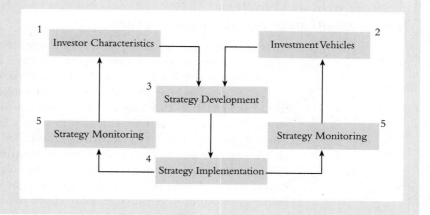

The investment policy should have specific objectives regarding the return requirement and risk tolerance. For example, the investment policy may state that the portfolio's target average return should exceed 8% and the portfolio should avoid exposure to more than 10% in losses. Typically, identifying the tolerance for risk is the most important objective, because every investor would like to earn the greatest return possible.

The investment policy should also state any constraints that will affect the day-to-day management of the funds. Constraints include any liquidity needs, projected time horizons, tax considerations, and legal and regulatory considerations, as well as unique needs, circumstances, and preferences. For example, the policy may call for 5% of the portfolio to remain liquid. The projected time horizon may be short, long, or indefinite. The policy will usually state the tax status of the account. If the account is an endowment, it is tax exempt, and the investment manager need not be concerned about the tax ramifications of different trading strategies.

Here are some typical questions the individual investor must address before reaching an investment decision: What is the investor's current financial situation? What are the available investable resources? What is the investable income over the foreseeable future? What cash flows are needed at different dates in the future? How much risk can be tolerated by the investor? What type of investments would cause the investor to lose sleep? What is the tax status of the investment funds?

These types of questions must be addressed at the beginning of the investment management process. For example, parents who want to invest for the college education of their newborn child have different answers, and therefore different investment policies, than an investor who is planning to get married and who wants to buy a house in one year. It is important to understand that although precise information is not necessary, good estimates are essential. A thorough assessment of investor characteristics is covered in Part 2 of this book.

1.5.2 Investment Vehicles:
The Trade-off between Risk and Return

After an assessment has been made of the investor's characteristics, the available investment opportunities can be explored. Financial assets are broadly classified as money market, capital market, and derivative market securities.

Let us look at three categories of investment vehicles: bonds, stocks, and derivative securities. Bonds are financial assets that represent a creditor relationship with an entity. They are debt instruments of a firm. Stocks represent an ownership position in a corporation. Derivative securities (also called *contingent claims*), such as options and futures, are tied to the performance of another security (hence, the term *derivative*). Of the three categories, bonds are generally the least risky and also offer the lowest return. Stocks offer a higher return on average; however, they are generally riskier than bonds. Derivative securities have the highest potential risk level, as well as the highest potential return. Exhibit 1-4 describes these three major classes of investment opportunities and gives some general information about them. Of course, the information in Exhibit 1-4 is general and therefore not true for every security.

1.5.3 Strategy Development

The next element in the investment process is to optimize the competing constraints of the various investment vehicles and the investor's characteristics. Investors generally seek an investment strategy that provides the highest possible expected return within the constraints of the desired cash flow, risk level, and other important variables (such as liquidity).

The precise strategy developed depends on the investor's perception of how good capital markets are at processing information. If the capital markets process information quickly and accurately, we say that the markets are efficient. An **efficient market** is one in which stock prices reflect all relevant information about the stock.

If an investor believes that the market is efficient, the investment focus will be on designing well-diversified portfolios. (The investor sees no benefit in trying to uncover mispriced securities.) However, the investor who does not believe that the markets are efficient may wish to acquire all of the latest information and attempt to buy underpriced securities and sell overpriced securities.

EXHIBIT 1-4 **Summary of Investment Vehicles**	**Vehicle**	**Potential Risks**	**Potential Return**	**Marketability**	**Dividend and Interest Cash Flows**
	Bonds[a]	Low	Low	Low/moderate	High
	Stocks	Moderate/high	Moderate/high	Usually good	Low
	Derivative securities	Very high	Potentially high	Low	None

[a]Short- or moderate-term bonds. Long-term bonds are somewhere between short-term bonds and stocks in their characteristics.

Parts 2 and 3 of this book address the development of strategies when the investor believes that the market is efficient. Part 4 addresses the development of strategies when the investor does not believe that the market is efficient. Most investors are somewhere in between these two extreme views. They typically believe the market is somewhat efficient, so they diversify and try to design optimal portfolios, as discussed in Parts 2 and 3. However, investors are ever watchful for securities that may be temporarily mispriced due to some unforeseen event.

When developing a strategy, some investors like to avoid as much risk as possible. For example, investors who need money to pay tuition next year would put all their money in very safe securities, such as short-term bonds. Some investors who are not willing to miss a possible high return are willing to expose themselves to the risk and put all or most of their money in stocks or derivative securities. However, it is not necessary to go to the extreme and put all available money in one security. The investor can buy a little bit of each category of asset. By doing so, the investor may benefit from a relatively high return but not be exposed to a very high risk. This concept is known as *asset allocation*.

Asset allocation is the proportioning of an investment portfolio among various asset categories, such as cash, bonds, stocks, and real estate. Asset allocation plays a key role in investment management. Securities within each asset class—for example, stocks—tend to move together over time. This co-movement is called **correlation.** Thus, asset allocation is essential, because assets in different classes do not tend to move together. This lack of co-movement helps reduce portfolio risk.

After the asset allocation decision has been made, the investor can turn to the task of individual security selection. **Security selection** is the decision-making process used to determine the specific securities within each asset class that are most suitable for a client's needs.

Connecting Theory to Practice 1.2 illustrates the asset allocation strategies recommended by GIT Investment Services, Inc. Note that different diversification strategies among cash (actually, money market securities), bonds (fixed income), stocks (equity), and international equity depend on the risk an investor is willing to accept (which, in turn, depends on the investor's age). Individual investors choose the policy that fits their needs and risk tolerance. How to select an optimal allocation strategy and how to evaluate the resulting risk exposure is the heart of this book and is covered in Parts 2 and 3.

CONNECTING THEORY TO PRACTICE 1.2

DIVERSIFICATION: YOUR GUIDE TO INVESTING

Your investment portfolio should reflect your investment goals and objectives. These goals are unique for every individual, based on factors such as an investor's age, financial condition, and risk tolerance, as well as whether money invested represents tax-deferred retirement assets. The following are hypothetical diversified portfolios for informational purposes only. The portfolios are based on a program of long-term investing.

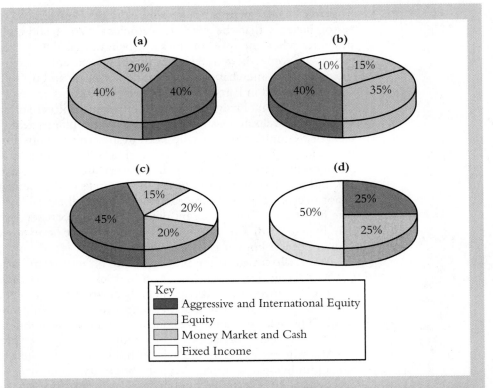

(a)

20%

40%   40%

(b)

10% 15%

40%   35%

(c)

15%

20%

45%

20%

(d)

25%

50%

25%

Key
■ Aggressive and International Equity
☐ Equity
▨ Money Market and Cash
☐ Fixed Income

Young investors (Graph a) have the luxury of time to take more risks. They can choose funds that invest in rapidly expanding companies in the United States or overseas.

Investors entering their 40s (Graph b) should reduce their money market holdings as they begin investing for retirement or a child's education. Add fixed-income funds for greater portfolio diversification.

Investors in their prime earning years (Graph c) should continue to build their retirement portfolios. As they approach retirement, fixed-income securities (bonds) become a greater percentage of the overall portfolio.

The key concerns of retired investors (Graph d) are preserving the purchasing power of their assets while generating regular income.

Source: © 1995, 1996, 1997, GIT Investment Services, Inc., as cited in http://www.gitfunds.com/divasset.htm.

MAKING THE CONNECTION

The investor's ability to tolerate risk influences how money is allocated to different asset classes. Young investors have the luxury of tolerating more risk and thus can focus on equity (stocks). Older individuals focus on a more conservative portfolio, with 50% invested in lower-risk fixed-income securities (bonds).

1.5.4 Strategy Implementation

After a strategy has been developed, the asset allocation decisions are implemented and the specific securities selected. Successful implementation of the asset allocation decision is difficult in practice, because it involves changing securities in the portfolio frequently. One problem is transaction costs: changing the asset allocation decision is costly because it requires liquidating many securities.[1] These costs directly reduce the benefits expected from the allocation strategy.

A second problem is changing economic and market factors. Economies and markets are in constant flux, which changes the optimal allocation strategy. These changes result in assets either being allocated in a suboptimal fashion or incurring transaction costs. For example, in the late 1980s, interest rates were high, and inflation was expected to fall. This situation induced some investors to allocate a large portion of their assets to bonds. Bonds were paying high interest, and inflation was not a major problem. Also, as interest rates fell in the early 1990s, bond prices rose. This condition further increased the allocation to bonds. In contrast, when interest rates are relatively low and there is an expectation that firms will earn a lot of money, as occurred in the prosperity of the late 1990s, investors want to invest mainly in stocks. These constantly changing circumstances result in the need of investors to constantly change their asset allocations.

A third problem is changing investor objectives and constraints. Over time, the needs of an individual or fund change, requiring reallocation of assets. For example, an investor's aversion to risk may change if she inherits a large sum of money.

An investor must also decide the best course of day-to-day strategy implementation—that is, the most cost-effective way to acquire the desired financial assets. For example, should the investor buy a stock from a stock exchange or from some other source?

1.5.5 Strategy Monitoring

Once the investment process has begun, it is important to periodically reevaluate the approach. This monitoring is necessary because financial markets change, tax laws change, and other events alter stated goals. For example, in 1997, a reduction in the capital gains tax from 28% to 20% took place. How should this reduction affect an investor's asset allocation strategy? Perhaps a much better security than was previously available is created. Investors must regularly examine and question their strategy to make sure it is the best. Primarily, they need to monitor goals and objectives and review the available financial assets.

1.6 WHERE DO WE GO FROM HERE?
A BRIEF OVERVIEW OF THE BOOK

This book has six parts. The remainder of Part 1 provides an overview of the investment environment. Chapter 2 introduces the basic securities used in the investment

---

1. A recent solution to avoiding these costs is to use futures and options contracts on broad-based indexes. (See Chapters 22, 23, and 24.)

process: stocks, bonds, and derivative securities. Chapter 3 surveys the security markets, focusing on the practical issues investors encounter when they actually implement an investment strategy. Chapter 4 addresses the regulatory environment and ethical issues. Laws constrain the actions of investors in an effort to make trading fair for all investors. Ethics are principles that are generally agreed on by investors in an effort to gain the trust of potential investors.

Part 2 focuses on the basic components of risk and return. Chapter 5 surveys the methods used for calculating rates of return, focusing on the professionally accepted standards. Chapter 6 reviews the foundations of risk assessment. The chapter examines different attitudes toward risk and its influence on returns. Chapters 7 and 8 introduce the relationships between returns of different securities and discuss how to capitalize on these relationships.

Part 3 discusses equilibrium prices and includes Chapters 9, 10, and 11. Chapters 9 and 10 survey the modern pricing models. Chapter 11 extends diversification concepts to include international securities.

Part 4 presents efficient markets and portfolio performance. Chapter 12 addresses the notion of efficient markets and reviews the related empirical evidence for and against this hypothesis. Chapter 13 presents the fundamental ideas related to technical analysis. Chapter 14 focuses on using mutual funds and investment companies to fulfill investment objectives. Finally, Chapter 15 discusses measurement tools for assessing how well securities are performing.

With this background in portfolio management, Part 5 turns to security analysis. Portfolio management is covered first because it is applicable to all investors. Chapters 16 and 17 are devoted to bonds, and Chapters 18 and 19 are devoted to stocks. Chapter 20 introduces overall market analysis, the question of whether to invest in bonds or stocks, as well as industry analysis. Finally, Chapter 21 surveys the basic issues related to evaluating financial statements.

Part 6 covers derivative securities, with Chapter 22 devoted to futures, and Chapters 23 and 24 devoted to options. The book concludes with Chapter 25, on financial engineering, a new and growing area of finance. Financial engineering is the process by which firms find creative solutions to complex financial problems, often by creating custom-design derivative securities.

SUMMARY

Compare and contrast corporate finance and investments. Corporate finance typically covers project analysis, capital structure, capital budgeting, and working capital management. Corporate finance addresses the relationship between the financial markets and firms, whereas the field of investments addresses the relationship between investors and the financial markets. The investments field typically covers issues related to security analysis. It also covers issues unique to investments in securities, such as portfolio diversification and hedging.

Differentiate between investments in real assets and investments in financial assets (securities).   The differences include the divisibility of investment in securities (you can buy a small fraction of a firm); marketability (you can sell a $100,000 investment in stock with one phone call to a broker); the investment holding period (which can be shorter for financial assets); and the more abundant information available on financial assets as compared with real assets.

State some good reasons for the study of investments. The benefits of understanding investments include helping you become a better manager of your own personal wealth and learning about the possibilities of a dynamic and exciting career.

Summarize the overall investment process.   The investment process consists of five components: investor characteristics, investment vehicles, strategy development, strategy implementation, and strategy monitoring.

CHAPTER AT A GLANCE

1. *Various factors influence security prices:*
   a. Macroeconomic factors (for example, interest rates).
   b. Industry factors (for example, the role of computers in the growth of the economy).
   c. Security factors (for example, the earnings of AIG).

2. *The level of certainty regarding information about securities affects the strategy:*
   a. If the information is certain, the investment decision is relatively clear-cut. Investors will put all their resources in the investment with the highest return.
   b. If the information is not certain, the investment decision is less clear-cut. Investors tend not to put all their resources in one investment but rather to diversify among many assets.

3. *Investing in financial assets (securities) differs from investing in real assets because financial assets have the following characteristics:*
   a. They are divisible.
   b. They are more marketable.
   c. They have a flexible holding period.
   d. They have a vast amount of available information.

4. *Studying investments is rewarding because it will improve your ability to do the following:*
   a. Manage your own money.
   b. Pursue a challenging career.

5. *The investment process can be categorized as follows:*
   a. Investor's preferences for risk, liquidity, and income.
   b. The trade-off of various investment vehicles regarding risk and return.
   c. The process of developing a strategy.
   d. The process of implementing the strategy.
   e. Monitoring the performance of the strategy.

1.1 In general, how can macroeconomic information be used to make an investment decision? Give an example.

KEY TERMS

Asset 7	Investment 6	Rally 4
Asset allocation 15	Investment policy 12	Real asset 7
Capital market 6	Liquidity 10	Security 8
Correlation 15	Marketable security 10	Security selection 15
Divisible 10	Money market 6	Speculative 6
Efficient market 14	Nonmarketable security 10	Tangible asset 7
Financial asset 7	Physical asset 7	
Hedge 7	Portfolio 7	

REVIEW

1.1 In general, how can macroeconomic information be used to make an investment decision? Give an example.

1.2 Explain the primary differences between corporate finance and investments.

1.3 What does it mean to make an investment?

1.4 What are financial assets?

1.5 Explain the difference between financial assets and real assets.

1.6 How does divisibility help us differentiate between physical assets and securities?

1.7 What is marketability? Why are stocks said to be marketable?

1.8 What are the primary reasons we study investments, other than the fact that it is a required course?

1.9 In your own words, how would you characterize the investment process?

1.10 Explain the relationship between expected return and risk. How do the investor's characteristics influence the securities that are acquired?

1.11 Differentiate among bonds, stocks, and derivative securities. What are the main characteristics of each of these types of securities?

1.12 What is *asset allocation,* and what are the major asset classes? How is asset allocation distinguished from security selection?

1.13 A widow who has no current income has $100,000 to invest. Referring to the pie charts in Connecting Theory to Practice 1.2, how would you recommend that she invest the $100,000?

PRACTICE

1.1 Two stocks are sold today for $100 each. You know for sure that at the end of the year, one stock will be sold for $110 and the other, for $115. Would you diversify between the two? Why or why not?

1.2 Suppose you have a car, a house, an acre of land in the Bahamas, and a very nice shirt from the Chicago Bulls 1998 NBA championship. Rank these assets by their liquidity, and explain your answer.

1.3 How would you change your answer to Question 1.2 if you were told that for some reason, the uncertainty about the future price of cars had increased but there was no change in the degree of uncertainty regarding the prices of the other assets?

1.4 Selling a house involves advertising costs, realtor commissions, and lawyer fees to write contracts. Is a house a liquid asset? Why or why not?

1.5 Suppose that selling a stock involved 1% to 2% transaction costs and selling a bond involved 0.5 to 1% transaction costs. Also, assume that stocks are more volatile than bonds. Which are more liquid? What is the relationship between volatility of price and liquidity?

1.6 You are considering either purchasing 100 textile machines and building a fabric factory or purchasing shares of a textile stock traded on the New York Stock Exchange. Which of these two investments may have a more flexible investment holding period? Which is more liquid? Explain your answer.

1.7 Assume that the expected return on land is 15%; on rare coins, 12%; and on stocks, 19%. How do you think these assets should be ranked according to their risk?

1.8 Suppose you have $5,000 extra cash to invest in one of the following assets: real estate in South Florida, rare coins and stamps, or shares of stock in Microsoft Corporation. Rank these assets from the least to the most liquid. Which of the assets are financial assets and which are real assets?

1.9 Assume your mother, who is 67 years old and a retired high school teacher, has come to you for investment advice. She tells you that she is frustrated with the 3.5% she is earning on her savings and knows there must be a better way for her to invest her savings. What advice would you give her? What factors should you consider in offering her investment advice?

1.10 Suppose that you have $1 million today. This year you consume $100,000 and invest $900,000 at

a −1% real investment rate. Are you necessarily an irrational investor?

1.11 A partnership of lawyers has cash inflows and cash outflows. As a consultant, you determine that during the year, the partnership checking account held $500,000 more than they needed for their operation. Suppose that money market accounts yield 5% per year, and the business checking account yields no interest. Suggest an improvement in the money management of the partnership. How much would you save the partnership per year?

1.12 Suppose that you have $1 million in cash, and 1 year from now you have a debt payout of $950,000. If you do not pay this $950,000, you will incur great damage, (for example, bankruptcy). You can invest your money in stocks whose rate of return is either −10% or 30% with equal probability, or in bonds whose return is either −1% or 15% with equal probability. What are your investment options? What will your cash flows be? Can you invest some proportion of your money in stocks without risking your future payment needs? Determine this proportion. What will the return be if you lose 1% in bonds but earn 30% in stocks under this strategy?

1.13 The following graph describes the prices of four assets over time:

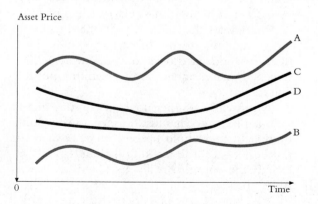

How many asset classes exist? Which assets belong to the same asset class?

CFA PROBLEMS

1.1 a. List the objectives and constraints that must be considered in developing an investment policy statement.

b. Explain why the asset allocation decision is the primary determinant of total portfolio performance over time.

c. Describe three reasons why the successful implementation of asset allocation decisions is even more difficult in practice than in theory.

For Internet questions visit the Levy Investment Web site at http://levy-invst.swcollege.com.

YOUR TURN: APPLYING THEORY TO PRACTICE

TURMOIL IN DOW JONES INDUSTRIALS LEAVES INVESTORS SEEKING SECURITY

New York—The turmoil lately in the Dow Jones Industrial Average reminds investors: Wall Street is a two-way street.

While stocks have managed to recoup 24 of the 104 points they surrendered late last week, many market professionals are still nervous. Last week's sudden drop "showed how tender the market is," says Morgan Stanley strategist Byron Wien.

If the market were to turn south for a while, which stocks would hold up best? There are no guarantees, but money managers say cheap stocks that pay a dividend and don't have too much debt often weather downturns pretty well.

As a sign of the times, Harry Klein of Market Base notes that these days it's hard to locate secure-looking stocks. In fact, he finds fewer than two dozen stocks out of nearly 2,000 screened that clear the hurdles defining possible safe havens.

Meanwhile, Katherine Hensel, strategist at Lehman Brothers, has just finished a major study of which stocks hold up best in weak markets. Cyclical stocks, the market's darlings lately, "are exactly the ones that really get killed" in downturns, she says.

Ms. Hensel says investors who expect a decline should beware of hotel, semiconductor, homebuilding, and air-freight stocks. But they should consider beefing up holdings of oil, food, and utility stocks.

To reach these conclusions, the Lehman study reviewed nine market "corrections" since 1962, or every downturn of 5% or more that didn't precede a recession. For her part, Ms. Hensel expects a "classic correction" of 10% to 15% in the next few months, now that the Federal Reserve has begun to raise interest rates.

The study found three main characteristics that predict how fragile a stock will be in a downturn. The first is volatility, measured by what market professionals call "beta."

A stock with a beta of one is precisely as volatile as the overall market. A stock with a beta of 1.5 tends to move half again as far as the market: If the market rises 10%, such a stock can be expected to soar 15%—and vice versa. When stocks are falling, investors do better with low-beta stocks.

Second, the study found that "hot stocks," or those that had the best gains in the prior year, typically fell more than most in down markets. Third, stocks with above-average dividend yields usually withstood market slumps better.

What stocks meet those criteria today? In the oil group, Ms. Hensel points to Imperial Oil,

Pennzoil, and Atlantic Richfield. "The news is not going to get a lot worse" for oils, now that the price of oil has sunk to around $14 a barrel, she says.

In this case, we accept Hensel's claim that beta measures stock volatility (or risk). (We discuss this risk index in detail in Chapter 9.)

1. Suppose the price of a stock is $100, and its beta is equal to 1.5. Calculate the market price of the stock if the following price changes occur in the overall market—for example, the Dow Jones Industrial Average or the Standard & Poor's index: +10%, −5%, 0%, +20%, and −10%.

2. Assume the following betas:

Firm	Beta
Imperial Oil	1.5
Pennzoil	2
Atlantic Richfield	0.8

Calculate the percentage price change in these stocks if the overall market goes up by 10% and if it goes down by 10%.

3. Suppose there is a 50% probability of the market's going up by 20% and a 50% probability of the market's going down by 10%. Thus, the expected (or average) rate of return on the market is as follows:

$$\frac{1}{2} \times 20\% + \frac{1}{2} (-10\%)$$
$$= 10\% - 5\%$$
$$= 5\%$$

Calculate the expected rate of return on the stocks in Question 2 on the assumption that beta measures risk. For simplicity, assume that if beta is equal to zero, the corresponding rate of return is zero. Draw the line (with beta on the horizontal axis and expected return on the vertical axis) showing the relationship between risk and expected return for these three stocks. Show where the market is located on this line.

SELECTED REFERENCES

Ayling, David E. *The Internationalisation of Stockmarkets.* Brookfield, Vt.: Gower Publishing, 1986.

This book provides a basic overview of the issues related to stockmarkets' becoming increasingly interrelated.

Caires, Bryan de, and David Simmonds, eds. *The GT Guide to World Equity Markets 1989.* London: Euromoney Publications, 1989.

This book provides a brief synopsis of all the major world stock exchanges.

Careers in Finance. 2d ed. Tampa, Fla.: Financial Management Association, 1990.

This book "provides information on what professionals in finance do, what types of decisions they make, . . . what types of interrelationships they must deal with, and what skills and abilities they must have in order to be successful" (from the Preface). This book is usually available through local student Financial Management Association (FMA) groups.

Downes, John, and Jordan Elliot Goodman. *Dictionary of Finance and Investment Terms.* 2d ed. New York: Barron's Educational Series, 1987.

This is a good dictionary of investment terms.

Eatwell, John, Murray Milgate, and Peter Newman, eds. *New Palgrave Dictionary of Money and Finance.* New York: W.W. Norton, 1989.

This is a detailed dictionary of financial concepts. The terms are defined and discussed by leading academics in finance.

Huang, Roger D., and Hans R. Stoll. *Major World Equity Markets: Current Structure and Prospects for Change.* Monograph Series in Finance and Economics, Monograph 1991-3. New York: New York University Salomon Center, 1991.

This monograph looks in depth at the equity markets in London, Toronto, Paris, Tokyo, and Germany. Specifically, it examines the market microstructures.

SUPPLEMENTAL REFERENCES

Erb, Claude B., Campbell R. Harvey, and Tadas E. Viskanta. "Expected Return and Volatility in 135 Countries." *Journal of Portfolio Management,* Spring 1996, pp. 46–58.

Maginn, John L., and Donald L. Tuttle, eds. *Managing Investment Portfolios: A Dynamic Process.*

2d ed. New York: Warren, Gorham & Lamont, 1990.

Malkiel, Burton. *A Random Walk Down Wall Street.* 5th ed. New York: W.W. Norton, 1991.

Appendix 1A   Review of Time Value Concepts

This appendix reviews a selection of corporate finance topics that are directly related to investments. Understanding the time value of money is crucial to making prudent investments. When you make investments, you reallocate cash flows over time. Specifically, you pay out money now with the expectation of receiving more in the future. Here, we review the concepts of future value, present value, uneven cash flows, net present value, and internal rate of return.

FUTURE VALUE

Future value represents the value of a set of expected cash flows at a specific point in the future if compounded at a given interest rate. For a single cash flow today (CF_0) with an interest rate (i) for a period of a certain length (n), we have the future value (FV_n) as follows:

$$FV_n = CF_0(1 + i)^n \qquad (1A.1)$$

For example, a \$100 investment today ($CF_0 = \$100$) at 10% ($i = 0.10$) for 5 years ($n = 5$) will be worth

$$FV_5 = \$100(1 + 0.10)^5 = \$100(1.6105) \cong \$161.05$$

in 5 years.

The future value of a \$1 annuity (which is \$1 cash flow each period starting next period and denoted $FVIFA_{i,n}$, or future value interest factor for an annuity) can be found using the following equation:

$$FVIFA_{i,n} = \frac{[(1 + i)^n - 1]}{i} \tag{1A.2}$$

This type of annuity is known as an *ordinary annuity*, because the first cash flow occurs one period from today, and we are determining the value when the final cash flow occurs. Another type of annuity occurs when the cash flows start today. The value one period is after the last payment occurs. This type of annuity is known as an *annuity due*. All references in this appendix are to ordinary annuities. The future value of an annuity (FVA) with a given payment stream (denoted PMT) is therefore

$$FVA_n = PMT(FVIFA_{i,n})$$
$$= PMT\frac{[(1 + i)^n - 1]}{i} \tag{1A.3}$$

For example, a \$100 annuity (PMT = \$100) at 10% for 5 years will be worth \$610.50 at the end of 5 years:

$$FVA_5 = \$100\frac{[(1 + 0.1)^5 - 1]}{0.1} \cong \$100\frac{(1.6105 - 1)}{0.1}$$
$$= \$100(6.105) = \$610.50$$

PRESENT VALUE

Present value represents the value today of future cash flows discounted at a specified interest rate. For a single cash flow n periods from now (CF_n) with a specified interest rate (i), the present value is represented as follows:

$$PV = \frac{CF_n}{(1 + i)^n} \tag{1A.4}$$

Note that because CF_n is the future value, we can write $CF_n = FV_n$. If we let $CF_n = \$161.05$, $i = 0.10$, and $n = 5$, we have the following:

$$PV = \frac{\$161.05}{(1 + 0.10)^5} \cong \$100$$

The present value interest factor of a $1 annuity (denoted $PVIFA_{i,n}$) can be found using the following equation:

$$PVIFA_{i,n} = \frac{\left\{1 - \left[\frac{1}{(1+i)^n}\right]\right\}}{i} \qquad (1A.5)$$

For a given periodical payment amount (PMT), we have the present value of an annuity as

$$PVA_n = PMT(PVIFA_{i,n}) = PMT\frac{\left\{1 - \left[\frac{1}{(1+i)^n}\right]\right\}}{i} \qquad (1A.6)$$

For example, a $100 annuity discounted at 10% for 5 years is worth $379.10 today:

$$PVA_5 = \$100 \frac{\left[1 - \frac{1}{(1+0.1)^5}\right]}{0.1}$$

$$\cong \$100 \frac{0.37908}{0.1} = \$379.08$$

UNEVEN CASH FLOWS

In many cases, the series of cash flows are not the same amount each period (that is, the cash flows do not represent an annuity). Dividends, for example, are not necessarily the same each period. In this case, each cash flow must be discounted separately. Specifically, the present value of a set of future cash flows is as follows:[2]

$$PV = \sum_{t=1}^{n} \frac{CF_t}{(1+i)^t} \qquad (1A.7)$$

where CF_t represents the cash flow occurring at time t (for example CF is the cash flow at the 1 period). For example, a 3-year bond that pays $100 coupon at the end of each year, returns the original investment of $1,000 at the end of 3 years, and is discounted at 8% is worth the following:

2. Recall that

$$\sum_{i=1}^{n} x_i = x_1 + x_2 + \cdots + x_n$$

For example, if $x_1 = 11$, $x_2 = 19$, and $x_3 = 5$, we have

$$\sum_{i=1}^{3} x_i = x_1 + x_2 + x_3 = 11 + 19 + 5 = 35$$

$$PV = \frac{\$100}{(1 + 0.08)^1} + \frac{\$100}{(1 + 0.08)^2} + \frac{\$100 + \$1,000}{(1 + 0.08)^3}$$

$$\cong \$92.59 + \$85.73 + \$873.22 = \$1,051.54$$

NET PRESENT VALUE

Net present value (NPV) is simply the present value of future cash flows minus any initial investment or cash outlay. Specifically, if the investment is represented as a negative cash flow, then NPV is as follows:

$$NPV = \sum_{t=0}^{n} \frac{CF_t}{(1 + i)^t} \qquad (1A.8)$$

where for $t = 0$ (rather than $t = 1$), we have the cash outflow CF_0, which is negative. For example, suppose we purchased the bond just described for $1,020. The NPV would be as follows:

$$NPV = \frac{-\$1,020}{(1 + 0.08)^0} + \frac{\$100}{(1 + 0.08)^1} + \frac{\$100}{(1 + 0.08)^2} + \frac{\$100 + \$1,000}{(1 + 0.08)^3}$$

Because $(1 + 0.08)^0 = 1$, we have

$$NPV \cong \$31.54$$

INTERNAL RATE OF RETURN

The internal rate of return (IRR) calculation finds the interest rate (i), which will result in a zero NPV. Specifically, let IRR denote the interest rate that solves the following:

$$\sum_{t=0}^{n} \frac{CF_t}{(1 + IRR)^t} = 0 \qquad (1A.9)$$

Unfortunately, solving for IRR is complicated and requires a calculator or trial-and-error techniques. For example, the IRR that solves the previous bond illustration was found, using a financial calculator, to be 9.207%. Thus, we observe the following:

$$\frac{-\$1,020}{(1 + 0.09207)^0} + \frac{\$100}{(1 + 0.09207)^1} + \frac{\$100}{(1 + 0.09207)^2} + \frac{\$100 + \$1,000}{(1 + 0.09207)^3}$$

$$\cong -\$1,020 + \$91.57 + \$83.85 + \$844.58$$

$$= 0$$

The IRR on future cash flows of a bond is called *yield to maturity*.

PRACTICE

1.1 Suppose there is a security that offers $100 at the end of each year for the next 10 years. This type of security is known as an *annuity*. If the appropriate interest rate is 10%, how much is this security worth?

1.2 Given the results in Question 1.1, what is the future value of this investment in 10 years?

1.3 Suppose you purchase Commonwealth Edison common stock (a public utility) for $30 per share. You are expecting to receive a $3 dividend at the end of each year for the next 3 years, at which time you anticipate being able to sell the stock for $40. If the interest rate is 11%, what is the present value of your investment? What is the net present value?

1.4 Find the internal rate of return for the investment described in Question 1.3.

1.5 The future value 2 years from now ($n = 2$) of a single cash flow today of $CF_0 = \$100$ is $110.25. What is the interest rate employed to find the future value?

1.6 Suppose you have a new patent and would like to sell it to a manufacturing firm. The firm offers you a lump sum of $1,000 or an annuity of $200 for 7 years in return for the patent. What option do you prefer, given that the discount rate is 10%?

1.7 Suppose a bond traded in the market for $900 pays $50 in interest at the end of the year for each of the next 10 years. At the end of the tenth year the bond is redeemed and you get $1,000. If you buy the bond today for $900, what is the internal rate of return (IRR) on your investment?

1.8 A bond is sold for $100 and pays $10 at the end of each year for the next n years. At the end of the nth year, it pays back $100.

a. Assuming $n = 10$, what is the *IRR* of this bond?

b. Is the IRR affected by the assumed number of years, n? What is the IRR if $n = 5$?

CHAPTER 2

BONDS, STOCKS, AND OTHER FINANCIAL SECURITIES

LEARNING OBJECTIVES

After studying this chapter you should be able to:

1. Describe basic characteristics and types of bonds and stocks.

2. Compare different types of derivative securities.

3. Explain the risks involved in bond and stock investment.

4. Describe investment opportunities in international securities and mutual funds.

INVESTMENTS IN THE NEWS

BONDS RISE AS STOCKS POST MEAGER GAINS

Thursday's Markets

Bond investors celebrated the release of more data offering reassurance that the economy isn't overheating, but wary money managers still aren't convinced that it's time to jump back into the stock market.

Major stock indexes ended another day of above-average volatility with relatively small gains. While the Dow Jones Industrial Average traded in a 132-point range throughout the day, it ended only 13.71 points higher at 7942.03, failing to break back above 8000. The Standard & Poor's 500-stock average gained 2.75 points to 924.77, while the NASDAQ Composite Index rose 3.29 to 1586.69.

The meager gains puzzled many analysts, especially given the bond market's rally in the wake of the report that consumer prices rose only 0.2%, exactly as many economists had forecast. The on-target reading eliminates, in many analysts' opinions, any chance that Federal Reserve policymakers will raise interest rates at their meeting next Tuesday.

"It's practically the perfect scenario for the bonds for now," says Stuart Hoffman, chief economist at PNC Bank Corp. of Pittsburgh. But stock investors, he says, continue to fret that signs of resurgent demand from consumers will translate into inflationary pressures and thus higher interest rates later in the year.

Marshall Acuff, market strategist at Smith Barney, admitted to being puzzled by the stock market's ho-hum response to a rally that took the price of the bellwether bond nearly a whole point higher.

"It's surprising not to see follow-through in interest rate-sensitive stocks," he says.

Source: Suzanne McGee, "Bonds Rise as Stocks Post Meager Gains," *The Wall Street Journal*, 15 August 1997, p. C1. Reprinted by permission of *The Wall Street Journal*, © Dow Jones & Co., Inc. All Rights Reserved Worldwide.

Bond prices are affected by the economy. In this chapter's Investments in the News, the release of data showing that the consumer price index rose only 0.2 led to low expectations for an increase in the interest rate and, hence, a gain in the bond market. The stock market had been expected to respond positively to this news, but it surprised analysts by not doing so. However, by mid-1998 the Dow Jones surged above the 9,000-point level.

What are the characteristics of bonds and stocks? What are the cash flows to the bondholder and to the stockholder? Why does the inflation rate directly affect bond prices, whereas it does not directly affect stock prices?

This chapter describes the basic characteristics of bonds and stocks, describes the cash flows attached to each of these two important securities, discusses inflation, and shows why low inflation is expected to have a positive effect on bond prices. The chapter also illustrates how to read the financial quotes as they appear in the financial media. This chapter discusses options briefly; and separate chapters in Parts 4 and 5 discuss the valuation and management of options and futures, as well as provide more detailed analyses of each.

During the 71 years from 1926 to 1996 (inclusive), U.S. common stocks have provided average annual arithmetic returns of approximately 12.7%, whereas U.S. corporate bonds have provided average annual returns of only 6.0%.[1] The reason for the difference in average returns stems from the basic structure of these securities and the risk accompanying them. For example, the standard deviation of annualized returns for common stock, which is a measure of variability or risk, was 20.3%, whereas for corporate bonds it was 8.7%. A description of bonds and stocks will illustrate why this difference in return has occurred.

2.1 BONDS

A **bond** is a financial contract. The bond issuer, such as a corporation, will pay the bond's buyer periodic interest. Then, at the end of the specified term, the issuer pays the principal. In return, the bondholder pays the firm a given sum of money today. Bonds are traded in the bond market and have a market price that may change over time. A bond is a security that is basically an IOU from the issuer. It carries no corporate ownership privileges. For example, a 10-year AT&T bond gives you the right to receive periodic coupon (interest) payments and the principal (or face value) at maturity. As a bondholder, you have no voice in the affairs of the corporation. Most bonds are fixed-income securities, because the stated payments are contractual and constant over time. However, some bonds pay variable income and are referred to as floating-rate bonds. With a floating-rate or fixed-rate bond, the issuer is obligated to pay the bondholder specified amounts of money at specified dates. As long as the maturity of the bond is not too long, the risks are generally low, with

---

1. From data from Ibbotson Associates, *Stocks, Bonds, Bills, and Inflation* (Homewood, Ill.: Dow Jones-Irwin, 1997). The data are taken from the available computer diskette.

correspondingly low returns. Bonds are usually less liquid than stocks and generate relatively high periodic cash flows.

Bonds are interest-bearing obligations of governments or corporations.[2] With every passing day, investors are offered new types of bonds with different characteristics. Among the newest types of bonds are century bonds, which mature in 100 years. Dresser Industries issued $200 million worth of century bonds in 1996, which will mature in 2096.[3] This section examines common characteristics of bonds and the most popular types of bonds traded today.

2.1.1 Basic Characteristics of Bonds

Bonds have three major identifying characteristics. First, they are typically securities issued by a corporation or governmental unit. Second, they usually pay fixed periodic interest installments, called **coupon payments.** Also available are variable coupon payment bonds, or bonds whose coupon payment changes as market interest rates change. Third, bonds pay a lump sum at maturity that is called the **par value, face value,** or **principal.**

Bonds are typically classified into two groups based on their length of time to maturity. **Money market securities** are short-term (less than 1 year) obligations and usually require a minimum of $25,000 to purchase. In contrast, **capital market securities** are long-term securities (more than 1 year) such as Treasury bonds (usually having initial maturities in excess of 10 years). The term *capital market securities* also applies to stock.

Exhibit 2-1a shows the cash flow characteristics of a bond in general. Exhibit 2-1b shows an example of cash flows from a particular bond. The downward-pointing arrows in Exhibit 2-1 depict the cash payments from the investor, and the upward-pointing arrows depict cash receipts to the investor. Hence, by investing the current market price of the bond today ($Price), there is a promised stream of cash receipts in the future, called coupon payments ($C), and principal payment (or par value, $Par). The bond price today is the present value of its future coupons and par value. Note that if inflation decreases, the discount rate will decrease and the present value of the future cash flows ($C and $Par) will increase, thus increasing the price of the bond. (See this chapter's Investments in the News and Appendix 1A.)

The advantages of bonds to an investor are that they are good sources of current income, and their investment is relatively safe from large losses (unless, of course, the bonds have a large risk of default by the issuing company). Another advantage is that bondholders receive their payments before shareholders can be compensated. A major disadvantage of bonds is that the potential profit is limited. Also, bond prices are sensitive to interest rate changes. The larger the change in the interest rate, the larger the potential losses or gains.

---

2. It is common to make a distinction between bonds and fixed-income securities. Fixed-income securities include all interest-bearing securities, whereas bonds refer only to securities that are long term.

3. *The Wall Street Journal,* 6 August 1996, p. B4.

EXHIBIT 2-1
Cash Flow Charac-
teristics of Bonds

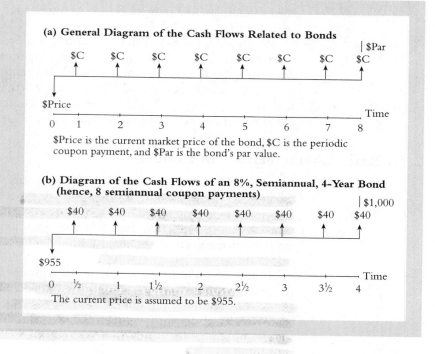

(a) General Diagram of the Cash Flows Related to Bonds

$Price is the current market price of the bond, $C is the periodic coupon payment, and $Par is the bond's par value.

(b) Diagram of the Cash Flows of an 8%, Semiannual, 4-Year Bond (hence, 8 semiannual coupon payments)

The current price is assumed to be $955.

2.1.2 Types of Bonds

Several types of bonds are available to investors, including short term and long term, high risk and low risk, and taxable and nontaxable. Exhibit 2-2 lists the different types of bonds, classified by whether they are money market securities or capital market securities. The following section provides a brief description of various types of bonds.

EXHIBIT 2-2
Types of
Bonds

Money Market Securities	Capital Market Securities
Treasury bills	U.S. Treasury notes
Commercial paper	U.S. Treasury bonds
Bankers' acceptances	Federal agency bonds
Negotiable certificates of deposit	Municipal bonds
Repurchase agreements	Corporate bonds
Federal funds	Mortgages and mortgage-backed securities
Eurodollars	

MONEY MARKET SECURITIES

The money market includes a wide range of securities, including Treasury bills, commercial paper, bankers' acceptances, negotiable certificates of deposit, repurchase agreements, federal funds, and Eurodollars.

U.S. Treasury bills (also called T-bills) are securities representing financial obligations of the U.S. government. They have the unique feature of being issued at a discount from their stated value at maturity. In other words, a sum of money is paid today for a greater fixed dollar amount in the future at maturity; usually the payment at maturity is $100,000 (no coupon payments are made). For example, Treasury bills may sell for $98,000 when issued and have a maturity value of $100,000 in six months. Thus, the return to the investor is $2,000. During this six-month period, the investor earns interest, although the interest is not paid in cash but is merely accrued.

Treasury bills have maturities of less than 1 year. T-bills are issued on an auction basis. The U.S. Treasury accepts competitive bids and allocates bills to those offering the highest prices. Noncompetitive bids are also accepted. A noncompetitive bid is an offer to purchase the bills at a price that equals the average of the competitive bids. By the end of 1996, the Treasury bill market exceeded $775 billion.[4] The market for T-bills is one of the most active in the world.

Exhibit 2-3 shows recent quotes for U.S. Treasury bills. The first column gives the coupon rate, followed by the maturity date. Next, the bid and asked discount rates are given, followed by the change from the previous day. The **discount rate** is a method of quoting interest rates for T-bills.[5] The **bid rate** is the discount rate at which you, the investor, can sell a T-bill. The **asked rate** is the discount rate at which you can buy it from a dealer. The higher the discount rate, the lower the price. The bid discount rates exceed asked discount rates, because dealers are willing to sell only at prices higher than they are willing to buy. The final column gives the internal rate of return of the asked discount rate of the T-bill. It is calculated using a different approach than the discount rate, and it measures the yields so they are comparable to yields on Treasury and corporate bonds.[6]

Another type of money market security is **commercial paper,** which is a vehicle of short-term borrowing by large corporations. Large, well-established corporations have found that borrowing directly from investors via commercial paper is cheaper than relying solely on bank loans. Commercial paper is unsecured notes of corporations, usually issued at a discount. *Unsecured* means that these loans are not backed by specific assets. That is, the only thing backing the loans is the "full faith and credit" of the firm. Commercial paper is issued either directly from the firm to the investor or through an intermediary.

Issuers of commercial paper are typically corporations that have a high credit rating. However, other firms can use the commercial paper market if they "enhance" the credit quality of the commercial paper. Firms can enhance their credit

---

4. *Economic Report of the President* (Washington, D.C.: U.S. Government Printing Office, 1997), p. 398.
5. The actual mathematical calculation is discussed in detail in Chapter 16.
6. The approach is known as the *bond equivalent method* and is explained in Chapter 16.

EXHIBIT 2-3 Illustration of U.S. Treasury Bill Quotes

TREASURY BONDS, NOTES & BILLS

Tuesday, November 18, 1997

Representative and Indicative Over-the-Counter quotations based on $1 million or more.

Treasury bond, note and bill quotes are as of mid-afternoon. Colons in bond and note bid-and-asked quotes represent 32nds; 101:01 means 101 1/32. Net changes in 32nds. Treasury bill quotes in hundredths, quoted in terms of a rate discount. Days to maturity calculated from settlement date. All yields are based on a one-day settlement and calculated on the offer quote. Current 13-week and 26-week bills are boldfaced.

GOVT. BONDS & NOTES

Rate	Maturity Mo/Yr	Bid	Asked	Chg.	Ask Yld.
5 3/8	Nov 97n	99:30	100:00	....	5.24
6	Nov 97n	99:31	100:01	....	4.82
5 1/4	Dec 97n	99:29	99:31	....	5.42
6	Dec 97n	100:00	100:02	....	5.33
7 7/8	Jan 98n	100:11	100:13	....	5.09
5	Jan 98n	99:26	99:28	....	5.55
5 5/8	Jan 98n	99:30	100:00	....	5.53
7 1/4	Feb 98n	100:11	100:13	....	5.43
8 1/8	Feb 98n	100:18	100:20	....	5.36
5 1/8	Feb 98n	99:26	99:28	....	5.52
5 1/8	Mar 98n	99:26	99:28	....	5.44
6 1/8	Mar 98n	100:06	100:08	....	5.38
7 7/8	Apr 98n	100:29	100:31	....	5.38
5 1/8	Apr 98n	99:25	99:27	– 1	5.47
5 7/8	Apr 98n	100:04	100:06	....	5.43
6 1/8	May 98n	100:08	100:10	....	5.47
9	May 98n	101:21	101:23	....	5.39
5 3/8	May 98n	99:27	99:29	....	5.55
6	May 98n	100:06	100:08	....	5.51

Rate	Maturity Mo./Yr.	Bid	Asked	Chg.	Ask Yld.
13 3/4	Aug 04	143:03	143:09	+ 1	5.68
7 7/8	Nov 04n	111:05	111:09	....	5.88
11 5/8	Nov 04	132:09	132:15	....	5.89
7 1/2	Feb 05n	109:09	109:11	....	5.89
6 1/2	May 05n	103:18	103:20	....	5.89
8 1/4	May 00-05	105:14	105:16	+ 1	5.84
12	May 05	136:08	136:14	....	5.91
6 1/2	Aug 05n	103:19	103:21	+ 1	5.90
10 3/4	Aug 05	129:16	129:22	....	5.91
5 7/8	Nov 05n	99:24	99:26	+ 1	5.90
5 5/8	Feb 06n	98:02	98:04	....	5.91
9 3/8	Feb 06	122:12	122:18	+ 1	5.88
6 7/8	May 06n	106:10	106:12	+ 1	5.91
7	Jul 06n	107:07	107:09	+ 1	5.91
6 1/2	Oct 06n	103:30	104:00	+ 1	5.91
3 3/8	Jan 07i	98:24	98:25	....	3.53
6 1/4	Feb 07n	102:12	102:14	+ 1	5.90
7 5/8	Feb 02-07	106:05	106:07	....	5.94
6 5/8	May 07n	105:09	105:10	+ 1	5.89
6 1/8	Aug 07n	102:02	102:03	+ 1	5.84

Source: *The Wall Street Journal*, 19 November 1997, p. C20. Reprinted by permission of *The Wall Street Journal*, © Dow Jones & Co., Inc. All Rights Reserved Worldwide.

U.S. Notes and Bonds

Rate	Mo/Yr	Bid	Asked	Fri. Chg.	Ask Yld.
5	Jan 98n	99:29	99:31	— 1	5.91
5 5/8	Jan 98n	99:30	100:00	....	5.48
7 1/4	Feb 98n	100:02	100:04	....	5.31
8 1/8	Feb 98n	100:04	100:06	— 1	5.28
5 1/8	Feb 98n	99:28	99:30	— 1	5.60
5 1/8	Mar 98n	99:28	99:30	— 2	5.37
6 1/8	Mar 98n	100:03	100:05	— 1	5.21
7 7/8	Apr 98n	100:17	100:19	— 2	5.19
5 1/8	Apr 98n	99:28	99:30	— 1	5.29
5 7/8	Apr 98n	100:02	100:04	— 2	5.35
6 1/8	May 98n	100:06	100:08	— 1	5.27
9	May 98n	101:03	101:05	— 2	5.21
5 3/8	May 98n	99:29	99:31	— 2	5.42
6	May 98n	100:05	100:07	— 1	5.34
5 1/8	Jun 98n	99:28	99:30	— 1	5.25
6 1/4	Jun 98n	100:11	100:13	— 2	5.30
8 1/4	Jul 98n	101:11	101:13	— 2	5.28
5 1/4	Jul 98n	99:28	99:30	— 2	5.37
6 1/4	Jul 98n	100:13	100:15	— 2	5.34
5 7/8	Aug 98n	100:06	100:08	— 2	5.42
9 1/4	Aug 98n	102:03	102:05	— 3	5.35
4 3/4	Aug 98n	99:17	99:19	— 3	5.43
6 1/8	Aug 98n	100:12	100:14	— 2	5.37
4 3/4	Sep 98n	99:16	99:18	— 2	5.39
6	Sep 98n	100:11	100:13	— 3	5.38
7 1/8	Oct 98n	101:06	101:08	— 2	5.35
4 3/4	Oct 98n	99:13	99:15	— 2	5.45
5 7/8	Oct 98n	100:08	100:10	— 3	5.45
5 1/2	Nov 98n	100:00	100:02	— 3	5.41
8 7/8	Nov 98n	102:22	102:24	— 3	5.38
5 1/8	Nov 98n	99:23	99:25	— 3	5.38
5 5/8	Nov 98n	100:04	100:06	— 3	5.39
5 1/8	Dec 98n	99:23	99:25	— 3	5.36
5 3/4	Dec 98n	100:09	100:11	— 3	5.37
6 3/8	Jan 99n	100:29	100:31	— 3	5.35
5	Jan 99n	99:18	99:20	— 3	5.38
5 7/8	Jan 99n	100:14	100:16	— 3	5.37
5	Feb 99n	99:17	99:19	— 3	5.39
8 7/8	Feb 99n	103:18	103:20	— 3	5.34
5 1/2	Feb 99n	100:02	100:04	— 3	5.38
5 7/8	Feb 99n	100:15	100:17	— 3	5.37
5 7/8	Mar 99n	100:17	100:19	— 3	5.35
6 1/4	Mar 99n	100:30	101:00	— 4	5.36
7	Apr 99n	101:28	101:30	— 3	5.35
6 3/8	Apr 99n	101:10	101:12	— 3	5.24
6 1/2	Apr 99n	101:11	101:13	— 3	5.34
6 3/8	May 99n	101:06	101:08	— 4	5.37
9 1/8	May 99n	104:22	104:24	— 3	5.33
6 1/4	May 99n	101:07	101:09	— 3	5.26
6 3/4	May 99n	101:24	101:26	— 3	5.34
6	Jun 99n	100:27	100:29	— 3	5.34
6 3/4	Jun 99n	101:28	101:30	— 3	5.34
6 3/8	Jul 99n	101:13	101:15	— 3	5.33
5 7/8	Jul 99n	100:22	100:24	— 3	5.36
6 7/8	Jul 99n	102:05	102:07	— 3	5.34
6	Aug 99n	100:29	100:31	— 3	5.35
8	Aug 99n	103:28	103:30	— 4	5.35
5 7/8	Aug 99n	100:23	100:25	— 4	5.36
6 7/8	Aug 99n	102:09	102:11	— 3	5.33
5 3/4	Sep 99n	100:19	100:21	— 3	5.33

Source: *Barron's* (January 19, 1998): p. MW58. Reprinted by permission of *Barron's*, © 1998 Dow Jones & Co., Inc. All Rights Reserved Worldwide.

by purchasing a guarantee from another, more well-established firm or by pledging collateral of quality assets with the issue.

Commercial paper is riskier than Treasury bills, because there is a greater risk of default by a corporation. (There is virtually zero probability of default by the federal government.) Also, commercial paper is not easily bought and sold after it is issued, because most investors in commercial paper hold it until maturity. The majority of investors in this market are institutions like money market mutual funds and pension funds. By the end of 1996, the commercial paper market in the United States exceeded $475 billion.[7]

Bankers' acceptances are short-term obligations that are based on a customer's request to pay a supplier at a future date. Bankers' acceptances arise from the financial needs of corporations engaged in international commerce. The supplier desires immediate payment, and the customer desires to pay once the goods are delivered and inspected. A bankers' acceptance allows both the supplier's and the customer's desires to be achieved, but not without cost.

To demonstrate how a firm and its customer use bankers' acceptances, suppose a U.S. firm ships a 3-ton engine to a Swiss firm, and delivery takes two months. The U.S. firm would like payment from the sale today, and the Swiss firm wants to wait until the engine is delivered. Neither the U.S. firm's bank nor the Swiss firm's bank wants to provide the capital for this loan. The Swiss firm's bank could pay the U.S. firm a discounted amount now. The Swiss bank could then sell this short-term loan contract to an outside party, recouping its initial outlay. This short-term loan contract will typically have a higher interest rate than similar money market securities, making it attractive to investors. Because of its complexity, the market for bankers' acceptances does not have active trading of its securities. Its market, which is much smaller than that for commercial paper, was only about $12 billion in October 1996.[8]

Negotiable certificates of deposit (CDs) developed from investors' demand for liquidity in their CD investments. Most CDs cannot be traded, and they incur penalties for early withdrawal. To accommodate large money market investors, financial institutions allowed their large-denomination CD deposits to be traded as negotiable CDs. Negotiable CDs can be as small as $100,000, but tend to trade in increments of $5 million. The largest investors in this market are money market mutual funds and investment companies. By the end of 1996, the large-denomination CD market was approximately $500 billion.[9]

The **repurchase agreement** (repos) market affords additional liquidity to the money market. Firms are able to raise additional capital by selling securities held in inventory to another institution with an agreement to buy them back at a specified higher price at a specified time. In effect, a repurchase agreement is a short-term loan. The securities are usually government securities. Because of concerns about default risk, the length of maturity of a repurchase agreement is usually very short. Typically, repos are used for overnight borrowing needs.

As an example of how repos work, suppose that for cash management purposes, Ford Motor Corporation holds $4 million in three-month U.S. Treasury bills yielding 5%. Now Ford has an immediate need for $4 million so it can purchase a specialized piece of equipment being offered at a bankruptcy liquidation. Ford's cash manager also knows that in a week, Ford will receive a $4 million payment for auto sales in Canada. What can Ford do?

7. *Economic Report of the President,* p. 379
8. *Ibid.*
9. *Ibid.*

One solution would be to take a bank loan at, say, 11%. Ford could also sell the T-bills and buy them back in one week. Ford would incur two transaction costs when the bills had to be repurchased. In addition, there would be price risk in this transaction: the price of the T-bills could rise in a week. Alternatively, Ford could enter into a repurchase agreement using its T-bills. Ford could sell the T-bills to an outside firm with a guarantee to buy them back in two weeks at a specified price. From the difference between the sale price and the purchase price, an implied interest rate, known as the *repo rate,* can be computed. Obviously, Ford should employ the transaction that is the cheapest after all transaction costs are considered.

The firm that holds short-term financial assets and, in particular, bank deposits, can invest in the repo market. The firm can make more money than it can earn in deposit accounts, and with a lower risk. How is this possible? Security dealers who need to borrow money are not allowed to enter the deposit market. Therefore, they are willing to pay a firm that lends them money in a repo agreement a very high interest rate. In addition, a firm that lends money to dealers holds the securities as collateral, whereas the deposits in the bank are uninsured. Thus, a higher return and a lower risk on the firm's money is obtained compared with a bank deposit. For example, by investing in repos, Dupont/Canoco reports an annual income increase of $2 million.

There are many variations in the design of repurchase agreements. A **term repo** has a longer holding period. A **reverse repo** is the opposite of a repo. In this transaction, a corporation buys the securities with an agreement to sell them at a specified price and time. The repo market was about $190 billion at the end of 1996.[10]

The **federal funds** market helps banks place reserves on deposit at the Federal Reserve Bank. Banks that do not have sufficient funds on reserve can borrow from other banks that have excess reserves. Most of this borrowing is for one day, although some agreements are for as long as six months.

Finally, **Eurodollars** are U.S. dollar deposits held outside of the United States. These deposits are not subject to the same regulations as bank deposits held within the United States. Hence, the interest rate offered on Eurodollar deposits is typically different from the rate offered in the United States. The interest rate quoted for these deposits between major banks is referred to as the LIBOR, or London Interbank Offer Rate. It is the rate that one bank asks from another bank for borrowing. London is the main trading center for Eurodollars. The LIBID, or London Interbank Bid Rate, is the rate at which major banks will offer Eurodollars as deposits to other banks. The interest on loans is sometimes linked to the LIBOR. Quotes such as "LIBOR + 1%" or "LIBOR + 2%" are very common, where the riskier the borrower, the higher the increase in the interest rate above the LIBOR.

CAPITAL MARKET SECURITIES

Like T-bills, **U.S. Treasury notes and U.S. Treasury bonds** are government securities used to finance the government debt. In contrast to T-bills, which have maturities of less than 1 year, U.S. Treasury notes and bonds have maturities greater

---

10. *Ibid.*

than 1 year at the time they are issued. They pay stated coupon amounts semiannually and are exempt from state and local taxes. When first issued, notes have maturities of 2 to 10 years, and bonds have maturities of more than 10 years. The minimum denomination is $1,000. Treasury notes and bonds are quoted on a price basis and as a percent of par (in 32nds).

Exhibit 2-4 illustrates Treasury bond and Treasury note quotes. The bid price of the August 05 bond is quoted as 127:20, which means $127\frac{20}{32}$ of par value. (Recall that par value is the lump sum paid at maturity.) If par is $1,000 (which is standard),

EXHIBIT 2-4
Illustration of U.S. Treasury Bond and Note Quotes

TREASURY BONDS, NOTES & BILLS

Tuesday, October 21, 1997

Representative and Indicative Over-the-Counter quotations based on $1 million or more.

Treasury bond, note and bill quotes are as of mid-afternoon. Colons in bond and note bid-and-asked quotes represent 32nds; 101:01 means 101 1/32. Net changes in 32nds. Treasury bill quotes in hundredths, quoted in terms of a rate discount. Days to maturity calculated from settlement date. All yields are based on a one-day settlement and calculated on the offer quote. Current 13-week and 26-week bills are boldfaced. For bonds callable prior to maturity, yields are computed to the earliest call date for issues quoted above par and to the maturity date for issues quoted below par. n-Treasury note. i-Inflation-indexed. wi-When issued. iw-Inflation-indexed when issued; daily change is expressed in basis points.

Source: Dow Jones/Cantor Fitzgerald.

U.S. Treasury strips as of 3 p.m. Eastern time, also based on transactions of $1 million or more. Colons in bid-and-asked quotes represent 32nds; 99:01 means 99 1/32. Net changes in 32nds. Yields calculated on the asked quotation. ci-stripped coupon interest. bp-Treasury bond, stripped principal. np-Treasury note, stripped principal. For bonds callable prior to maturity, yields are computed to the earliest call date for issues quoted above par and to the maturity date for issues below par.

Source: Bear, Stearns & Co. via Street Software Technology Inc.

GOVT. BONDS & NOTES

Rate	Maturity Mo/Yr	Bid	Asked	Chg.	Ask Yld.
$5\frac{5}{8}$	Oct 97n	99:31	100:01	....	4.23
$5\frac{3}{4}$	Oct 97n	99:31	100:01	....	4.35
$7\frac{3}{8}$	Nov 97n	100:02	100:04	− 1	5.28
$8\frac{7}{8}$	Nov 97n	100:05	100:07	− 1	5.30
$5\frac{3}{8}$	Nov 97n	99:31	100:01	− 1	4.97
6	Nov 97n	100:01	100:03	− 1	5.00
$5\frac{1}{4}$	Dec 97n	99:30	100:00	− 2	5.17
6	Dec 97n	100:03	100:05	− 1	5.08
$7\frac{7}{8}$	Jan 98n	100:17	100:19	− 2	5.16
5	Jan 98n	99:26	99:28	− 2	5.40
$5\frac{5}{8}$	Jan 98n	100:00	100:02	− 2	5.33
$7\frac{1}{4}$	Feb 98n	100:15	100:17	− 2	5.46
$8\frac{1}{8}$	Feb 98n	100:24	100:26	− 2	5.42
$5\frac{1}{8}$	Feb 98n	99:27	99:29	− 2	5.35
$5\frac{1}{8}$	Mar 98n	99:26	99:28	− 2	5.40
$6\frac{1}{8}$	Mar 98n	100:08	100:10	− 2	5.38
$7\frac{7}{8}$	Apr 98n	101:02	101:04	− 2	5.47
$5\frac{1}{8}$	Apr 98n	99:24	99:26	− 1	5.49
$5\frac{7}{8}$	Apr 98n	100:04	100:06	− 2	5.50
$6\frac{1}{8}$	May 98n	100:09	100:11	− 1	5.49
9	May 98n	101:27	101:29	− 2	5.52
$5\frac{3}{8}$	May 98n	99:26	99:28	− 1	5.58
6	May 98n	100:06	100:08	− 1	5.56
$5\frac{1}{8}$	Jun 98n	99:21	99:23	− 1	5.53
$6\frac{1}{4}$	Jun 98n	100:13	100:15	− 1	5.53
$8\frac{1}{4}$	Jul 98n	101:26	101:28	− 1	5.58
$5\frac{1}{4}$	Jul 98n	99:21	99:23	− 1	5.61
$6\frac{1}{4}$	Jul 98n	100:13	100:15	− 1	5.61
$5\frac{7}{8}$	Aug 98n	100:02	100:04	− 1	5.70
$9\frac{1}{4}$	Aug 98n	102:23	102:25	− 1	5.69
$4\frac{3}{4}$	Aug 98n	99:05	99:07	− 1	5.69
$6\frac{1}{2}$	Apr 99n	100:28	100:30	− 1	5.85
$6\frac{3}{8}$	May 99n	100:22	100:24	− 1	5.86
$9\frac{1}{8}$	May 99n	104:24	104:26	− 1	5.86
$6\frac{1}{4}$	May 99n	100:21	100:23	− 1	5.77
$6\frac{3}{4}$	May 99n	101:08	101:10	− 1	5.88
6	Jun 99n	100:04	100:06	− 1	5.88
$6\frac{3}{4}$	Jun 99n	101:11	101:13	− 1	5.86
$6\frac{3}{8}$	Jul 99n	100:24	100:26	− 1	5.87
$5\frac{7}{8}$	Jul 99n	99:28	99:30	− 1	5.91
$6\frac{7}{8}$	Jul 99n	101:18	101:20	− 1	5.89
6	Aug 99n	100:03	100:05	− 1	5.90
8	Aug 99n	103:16	103:18	− 1	5.89
$5\frac{7}{8}$	Aug 99n	99:29	99:30	− 1	5.91
$6\frac{7}{8}$	Aug 99n	101:20	101:22	− 1	5.90
$5\frac{3}{4}$	Sep 99n	99:23	99:24	− 1	5.89
$7\frac{1}{8}$	Sep 99n	102:06	102:08	....	5.88
6	Oct 99n	100:07	100:09	− 1	5.85
$7\frac{1}{2}$	Oct 99n	102:29	102:31	− 2	5.92
$5\frac{7}{8}$	Nov 99n	99:27	99:29	− 1	5.92
$7\frac{7}{8}$	Nov 99n	103:22	103:24	− 1	5.92
$7\frac{3}{4}$	Nov 99n	103:16	103:18	− 1	5.92
$7\frac{3}{4}$	Dec 99n	103:20	103:22	− 1	5.92
$6\frac{3}{8}$	Jan 00n	100:30	101:00	....	5.88
$7\frac{3}{4}$	Jan 00n	103:23	103:25	− 1	5.94
$5\frac{7}{8}$	Feb 00n	99:25	99:27	− 1	5.94
$8\frac{1}{2}$	Feb 00n	105:12	105:14	− 1	5.94
$7\frac{1}{8}$	Feb 00n	102:16	102:18	....	5.94
$6\frac{7}{8}$	Mar 00n	102:00	102:02	− 1	5.95
$5\frac{1}{2}$	Apr 00n	98:30	99:00	....	5.94
$6\frac{3}{4}$	Apr 00n	101:25	101:27	....	5.95
$6\frac{3}{8}$	May 00n	100:29	100:30	− 2	5.97
$8\frac{7}{8}$	May 00n	106:28	106:30	....	5.92
$13\frac{3}{8}$	Aug 01	124:15	124:21	− 1	6.04
$6\frac{1}{2}$	Aug 01n	101:13	101:15	....	6.06
$6\frac{3}{8}$	Sep 01n	101:00	101:02	....	6.07
$6\frac{1}{4}$	Oct 01n	100:18	100:20	....	6.07
$7\frac{1}{2}$	Nov 01n	104:31	105:01	− 1	6.08
$15\frac{3}{4}$	Nov 01	134:11	134:17	+ 1	6.04
$5\frac{7}{8}$	Nov 01n	99:06	99:08	....	6.08
$6\frac{1}{8}$	Dec 01n	100:03	100:05	....	6.08
$6\frac{1}{4}$	Jan 02n	100:17	100:19	....	6.09
$14\frac{1}{4}$	Feb 02	130:15	130:21	....	6.07
$6\frac{1}{4}$	Feb 02n	100:17	100:19	....	6.09
$6\frac{5}{8}$	Mar 02n	101:31	102:01	....	6.09
$6\frac{5}{8}$	Apr 02n	102:08	102:10	+ 1	6.03
$7\frac{1}{2}$	May 02n	105:18	105:20	+ 1	6.07
$6\frac{1}{2}$	May 02n	101:24	101:26	+ 1	6.04
$6\frac{1}{4}$	Jun 02n	100:17	100:19	....	6.10
$3\frac{5}{8}$	Jul 02i	99:30	99:31	+ 1	3.63
6	Jul 02n	99:19	99:21	....	6.08
$6\frac{3}{8}$	Aug 02n	101:05	101:07	+ 1	6.08
$6\frac{1}{4}$	Aug 02n	100:18	100:19	....	6.10
$5\frac{7}{8}$	Sep 02n	99:06	99:07	+ 1	6.06
$11\frac{5}{8}$	Nov 02	123:21	123:27	+ 1	6.08
$6\frac{1}{4}$	Feb 03n	100:20	100:22	+ 2	6.09
$10\frac{3}{4}$	Feb 03	120:20	120:26	....	6.10
$10\frac{3}{4}$	May 03	121:13	121:19	+ 1	6.11
$5\frac{3}{4}$	Aug 03n	98:05	98:07	+ 1	6.12
$11\frac{1}{8}$	Aug 03	123:31	124:05	− 1	6.12
$11\frac{7}{8}$	Nov 03	128:17	128:23	+ 1	6.13
$5\frac{7}{8}$	Feb 04n	98:22	98:24	....	6.11
$7\frac{1}{4}$	May 04n	105:27	105:29	+ 1	6.14
$12\frac{3}{8}$	May 04	132:31	133:05	....	6.16
$7\frac{1}{4}$	Aug 04n	105:30	106:00	+ 1	6.16
$13\frac{3}{4}$	Aug 04	141:15	141:21	+ 1	6.17
$7\frac{7}{8}$	Nov 04n	109:18	109:20	+ 2	6.17
$11\frac{5}{8}$	Nov 04	130:20	130:26	+ 1	6.18
$7\frac{1}{2}$	Feb 05n	107:18	107:20	+ 1	6.19
$6\frac{1}{2}$	May 05n	101:25	101:27	+ 1	6.19
$8\frac{1}{4}$	May 00-05	104:29	104:31	+ 1	6.12
12	May 05	134:13	134:19	....	6.20
$6\frac{1}{2}$	Aug 05n	101:25	101:27	....	6.20
$10\frac{3}{4}$	Aug 05	127:20	127:26	+ 1	6.20
$5\frac{7}{8}$	Nov 05n	97:28	97:30	+ 1	6.20
$5\frac{5}{8}$	Feb 06n	96:06	96:08	+ 1	6.21
$9\frac{3}{8}$	Feb 06	120:13	120:19	....	6.17
$6\frac{7}{8}$	May 06n	104:09	104:11	+ 1	6.21
7	Jul 06n	105:05	105:07	+ 2	6.21
$6\frac{1}{2}$	Oct 06n	101:28	101:30	+ 1	6.21
$3\frac{3}{8}$	Jan 07i	98:06	98:07	− 1	3.60
$6\frac{1}{4}$	Feb 07n	100:08	100:10	+ 1	6.20
$7\frac{5}{8}$	Feb 02-07	105:05	105:07	+ 1	6.22
$6\frac{5}{8}$	May 07n	103:01	103:02	+ 3	6.20
$6\frac{1}{8}$	Aug 07n	99:28	99:29	+ 2	6.14
$7\frac{7}{8}$	Nov 02-07	107:22	107:24	+ 1	6.07
$8\frac{3}{8}$	Aug 03-08	110:27	110:31	+ 1	6.10
$8\frac{3}{4}$	Nov 03-08	112:09	112:13	+ 1	6.26

Source: *The Wall Street Journal*, 22 October 1997, p. C15. Reprinted by permission of *The Wall Street Journal*,

then this quote results in a price of $1,276.25. Because $^{20}/_{32} = 0.625$, the price is 127.625% of par. Because the par value is $1,000, we get $(127.625/100) \cdot \$1,000 = \$1,276.25$ today and get only $1,000 in the future. We do not lose money, because we also receive coupon payments every semiannual period up to the maturity date. The notation 02–07 for the February $7\frac{5}{8}$'s bond means that the bond is first callable in 2002, and it matures in February 2007. **A callable bond** can be bought back by the issuing entity at a stated price in the future. The Change (Chg.) column is in 32nds. Hence, the $7\frac{5}{8}$, Feb 02–07 rose $\frac{1}{32}$ from the previous day.

Government agencies, such as the Federal National Mortgage Association (FNMA—pronounced "Fannie Mae"), issue **federal agency bonds.** They are usually in $100,000 denominations. Exhibit 2-5 illustrates some federal agency bond quotes. The 6.82% FNMA issue pays a coupon rate of 6.82% and has a stated maturity of April 2002 (4-02). The bid price is 102.5% (or 102 and $^{16}/_{32}$nds) of par, and the asked price is 102.625% (or 102 and $^{20}/_{32}$nds) of par. At these prices, the internal rate of return is 6.15%.

Agency securities differ from Treasury securities. Agency securities are issued by federal government-sponsored corporations, such as the Federal Home Loan Banks, and not directly from the U.S. government. Agency securities are perceived to be slightly more risky than Treasuries from a default risk viewpoint. The U.S. government may not be as likely to come to the rescue of an agency as it would be for securities issued by the U.S. Treasury.

State and local governments issue **municipal bonds** to finance highways, water systems, schools, and other capital projects. There are two basic types of municipal

---

EXHIBIT 2-5
Illustration of Federal Agency Bond Quotes

GOVERNMENT AGENCY & SIMILAR ISSUES

Tuesday, October 21, 1997

Over-the-Counter mid-afternoon quotations based on large transactions, usually $1 million or more. Colons in bid-and-asked quotes represent 32nds; 101:01 means 101 1/32.

All yields are calculated to maturity, and based on the asked quote. * – Callable issue, maturity date shown. For issues callable prior to maturity, yields are computed to the earliest call date for issues quoted above par, or 100, and to the maturity date for issues below par.

Source: Bear, Stearns & Co. via Street Software Technology Inc.

FNMA Issues

Rate	Mat.	Bid	Asked	Yld.
6.05	11-97	100:01	100:02	4.60
9.55	11-97	100:06	100:08	3.75
9.55	12-97	100:18	100:19	4.80
6.05	1-98	100:04	100:05	5.24
5.38	1-98*	99:28	99:29	5.72
8.65	2-98	100:16	100:18	6.55
5.01	2-98	99:28	99:30	5.16
5.51	2-98	100:01	100:03	5.18
8.20	3-98	100:30	101:00	5.46
5.30	3-98*	99:28	99:30	5.39
5.71	3-98	100:04	100:04	5.36
5.25	3-98	99:25	99:27	5.61
5.79	3-98	100:04	100:06	5.35
5.92	4-98	100:03	100:05	5.54

Rate	Mat.	Bid	Asked	Yld.
6.15	12-01*	98:18	98:22	6.51
6.38	1-02	100:17	100:21	6.19
6.41	2-02	100:20	100:24	6.21
7.50	2-02	104:18	104:22	6.24
6.23	3-02	100:00	100:04	6.19
6.49	3-02	101:09	101:13	6.12
7.12	4-02*	100:26	100:30	6.46
7.55	4-02	105:06	105:10	6.18
6.82	4-02	102:16	102:20	6.15
6.70	5-02	101:21	101:25	6.24
6.59	5-02	101:12	101:16	6.20
6.23	7-02	99:26	99:30	6.24
6.95	9-02*	100:02	100:08	0.00
6.54	9-02*	100:08	100:12	6.39
6.78	9-02*	99:27	99:31	6.79

Federal Home Loan Bank

Rate	Mat.	Bid	Asked	Yld.
5.45	11-97	100:00	100:01	4.45
5.63	12-97*	100:01	100:02	5.17
5.65	1-98*	100:02	100:03	5.18
5.75	1-98*	100:02	100:03	5.22
5.78	1-98	100:03	100:04	5.23
5.87	1-98	100:04	100:05	5.27
5.99	2-98	100:04	100:06	5.28
5.80	2-98*	100:02	100:04	3.19
4.98	2-98	99:24	99:26	5.50
6.08	4-98	100:07	100:09	5.47
5.26	4-98*	99:26	99:28	5.51
5.95	5-98	100:04	100:06	5.61
5.91	6-98	100:03	100:05	5.64
5.86	7-98*	100:00	100:02	5.76
6.04	8-98*	99:31	100:01	5.99
5.90	9-98*	99:29	99:31	5.23
5.89	10-98*	100:00	100:02	5.46
6.10	10-98	100:05	100:07	5.86
9.25	11-98	103:16	103:18	5.83
6.32	12-98*	100:01	100:03	5.36
9.30	1-99	104:00	104:03	5.87
5.43	2-99	99:08	99:11	5.94
6.44	4-99	100:22	100:25	5.88
8.60	6-99	104:00	104:03	5.99
6.11	6-99	100:08	100:11	5.88
8.45	7-99	104:14	104:17	5.70
6.26	8-99	99:11	99:14	6.59

Rate	Mat.	Bid	Asked	Yld.
6.38	5-01	101:08	101:12	5.94
6.75	1-02	101:18	101:22	6.28
12.38	10-02	123:24	123:30	6.64
5.25	9-03	96:06	96:12	5.99
6.38	7-05	100:20	100:26	6.24
6.63	8-06	102:06	102:14	6.26
8.25	9-16	114:12	114:20	6.85
8.63	10-16	118:08	118:16	6.86
9.25	7-17	125:14	125:22	6.86
7.63	1-23	110:30	111:06	6.70
8.88	3-26	123:27	124:03	6.92

Financing Corporation

Rate	Mat.	Bid	Asked	Yld.
10.70	10-17	137:07	137:15	7.15
9.80	11-17	132:27	133:03	6.76
9.40	2-18	123:28	124:04	7.13
9.80	4-18	132:13	132:21	6.82
10.00	5-18	134:04	134:12	6.86
10.35	8-18	137:22	137:30	6.89
9.65	11-18	131:01	131:09	6.83
9.90	12-18	133:09	133:17	6.87
9.60	12-18	130:00	130:08	6.87
9.65	3-19	130:27	131:03	6.86
9.70	4-19	131:06	131:14	6.88
9.00	6-19	122:22	122:30	6.94
8.60	9-19	118:18	118:26	6.92

bonds: general obligation bonds and revenue bonds. **General obligation bonds** are backed by the full faith and power of the municipality. **Revenue bonds** are backed by the income generated from a specific project, such as a toll bridge. The income from these bonds is exempt from federal, state, and local taxes if the investor lives in that locality, but the income is subject to state and local taxes if the investor does not live in the locality issuing the bonds. Because investors are interested in after-tax returns, we would not anticipate the yields to be as high as the fully taxable counterparts. Everything else being equal, investors would prefer a tax-free bond. Exhibit 2-6 illustrates some recent quotes for municipal bonds. The Tampa Sports Authority bonds have a stated coupon of 5.25% and mature on January 1, 2027. The current price is 96% of par and has a yield (or internal rate of return) based on the bid price of 5.53%.

Corporate bonds are issued to finance investment in new plant equipment (real assets). These bonds usually have a par or face value of $1,000. Corporate bonds vary in their riskiness and their returns to investors. Some highly rated bonds are very safe but pay low interest. **Junk bonds,** in contrast, are very risky and thus pay much higher interest. For such bonds, there is a higher risk that the firm will go bankrupt and the investor will lose the entire investment—hence, the name junk bonds.

Some bonds do not pay any interest and are called **zero-coupon bonds.** The Time Warner zr13 bond in Exhibit 2-7 is a zero-coupon bond. Bonds that make coupon payments during the life of the bond are **coupon-bearing bonds.** For example, "Viacm 7s03B" denotes Viacom's 7% semiannual coupon-bearing bonds that mature in the year 2003. This means that Viacom pays coupons at a rate of 3.5% of the stated maturity value each semiannual period. Other bonds, such as the USX bonds listed in Exhibit 2-7, are convertible into common stock. Convertible bonds are discussed in more detail below.

EXHIBIT 2-6
Illustration of Municipal Bond Quotes

TAX-EXEMPT BONDS

Representative prices for several active tax-exempt revenue and refunding bonds, based on institutional trades. Changes rounded to the nearest one-eighth. Yield is to maturity. n-New. Source: The Bond Buyer.

ISSUE	COUPON	MAT	PRICE	CHG	BID YLD	ISSUE	COUPON	MAT	PRICE	CHG	BID YLD
Atlanta Ga Wtr&Swr 97	5.250	01-01-27	96	— ⅛	5.52	No Centrl Tx Hlth Fac	5.375	02-15-26	96⅜	— ⅛	5.63
Ca Gen Obligate Bds	5.000	10-01-23	93½	...	5.47	No Tx Tollway Auth	5.000	01-01-20	93⅝	...	5.49
Ca Gen Obligate Bds	5.125	10-01-27	94½	...	5.50	NYC Muni Fin Auth	5.000	06-15-21	93¾	— ⅛	5.47
Cal Hlth Fac Ser 97	5.250	08-01-27	95⅝	...	5.55	NYC Muni Wtr Auth	5.125	06-15-30	94	...	5.52
Charlotte-M Hsp N C	5.125	01-15-22	94⅜	— ⅛	5.54	NYC Trans Fin Auth	5.125	08-15-21	95⅛	...	5.49
Chgo Ill Wtr Rev Ser1	5.250	11-01-27	95⅛	— ⅛	5.59	NYC Trans Fin Auth	5.000	08-15-27	92⅞	+ ¼	5.48
Dade Fla Aviat rev Bds	5.125	10-01-27	94¼	...	5.51	PR Elec Pwr Auth	5.375	07-01-27	98⅛	...	5.51
Denver Colo Arpt 97E	5.250	11-15-23	95¾	...	5.55	PR Pub Bldg Auth	5.000	07-01-27	94⅛	— ⅛	5.40
Fairfax Co Wtr Auth Va	5.000	04-01-29	92⅜	...	5.51	PR Pub Imprvmt Bds	5.375	07-01-25	96⅜	...	5.61
Houston Tx Wtr & Swr	5.000	12-01-25	92⅜	— ¼	5.51	Pt St Lucie Fla Util	5.125	09-01-27	94½	...	5.50
Houston Tx Wtr & Swr	5.400	12-01-23	97¾	— ⅛	5.56	Pub Hwy Auth Colo	5.000	09-01-26	92½	...	5.51
Jacksonville Hlth Fla	5.125	08-15-27	93⅞	— ⅛	5.55	Salt River Proj Agri	5.000	01-01-20	94½	+ ⅛	5.42
Jefferson Co Hlth 97	5.125	10-01-27	93¼	— ⅜	5.59	San Joaquin Hills Ca	5.375	01-15-29	97⅜	...	5.55
Mass Bay Transp Auth	5.000	03-01-24	92⅜	— ⅛	5.54	San Joaquin Hills Ca	5.250	01-15-30	95¾	...	5.53
Mass Hlth & Ed Fac	5.375	07-01-24	96⅝	— ⅛	5.62	Santa Clara Fin Auth	5.000	11-15-22	93½	...	5.47
Mass Spcl Oblig Ser A	5.000	06-01-17	94¾	...	5.43	Tampa Sports Auth	5.250	01-01-27	96	— ⅛	5.53
Mass Tpk Auth Ser A	5.000	01-01-27	92⅜	...	5.51	Tarrant Co Hlth Fac Tx	5.000	02-15-26	91⅞	— ⅛	5.57
Mass Tpk Auth Ser A	5.000	01-01-37	91⅜	— ⅛	5.54	Tarrant Co Hlth Fac Tx	5.250	02-15-22	95⅜	...	5.60
Nashvll&Davidson Cnty	5.125	05-15-25	94¾	...	5.50	Tx Wtr Revolving Fd	5.000	07-15-19	94	— ⅛	5.47
No Centrl Tx Hlth Fac	5.125	02-15-22	93¾	— ⅛	5.59	Wisc Hlth & Ed Fac	5.250	08-15-27	94⅜	— ⅛	5.63

EXHIBIT 2-7
Illustration of Corporate Bond Quotes

NEW YORK EXCHANGE BONDS

Quotations as of 4 p.m. Eastern Time
Tuesday, October 21, 1997

Volume $954,000

SALES SINCE JANUARY 1
(000 omitted)

1997	1996	1995
$4,235,658	$4,564,978	$5,948,888

	Domestic		All Issues	
	Tue.	Mon.	Tue.	Mon.
Issues traded	270	237	276	242
Advances	104	79	105	81
Declines	104	102	109	104
Unchanged	62	56	62	57
New highs	10	7	10	7
New lows	3	3	3	3

Dow Jones Bond Averages

–1996–		–1997–			---1997---			--1996--	
High	Low	High	Low		Close	Chg.	%Yld	Close	Chg.
106.09	100.99	104.70	101.09	20 Bonds	104.12	+0.08	7.01	103.00	+ 0.20
102.43	97.46	102.38	97.64	10 Utilities	101.75	+0.15	7.02	99.78	+ 0.18
109.94	104.06	107.23	104.54	10 Industrials	106.49	+0.01	7.00	106.22	+ 0.23

CORPORATION BONDS
Volume, $14,262,000

Bonds	Cur Yld.	Vol.	Close	Net Chg.
AMR 8.10s98	8.0	25	101	– ⅛
ATT 4⅜99	4.5	25	97¼	– ¼
ATT 6s00	6.0	10	99¼	...
ATT 5⅛01	5.3	11	96⅛	...
ATT 7⅛02	7.0	120	102½	– ¼
ATT 6¾04	6.6	65	101⅝	+ ⅛
ATT 8.2s05	8.0	5	102⅜	– ⅝
ATT 7½06	7.1	15	105⅝	– ⅛
ATT 7¾07	7.3	5	106⅜	– 2⅛
ATT 8⅛22	7.8	89	104¼	+ ¼
ATT 8⅛24	7.8	15	104	+ ⅞
Aames 10½02	10.1	20	104	+ ¼
AcmeM 12½02	11.5	5	108½	– ½
AlskAr 6⅞14	cv	2	107	...
Allwst 7¼14	cv	75	101¼	+ ¼
Alza 5s06	cv	36	99¾	+ ¼
AForP 5s30	7.1	20	70	– ⅛
AExC 6⅛00	6.1	10	100¼	+ ⅞
Amresco 10s03	9.7	10	103½	+ ½
Anhr 8⅝16	8.4	5	103	– ½
AnnTaylr 8¾00	8.7	48	100¾	...
Argosy 12s01	cv	11	90	...
Argosy 13¼04	12.8	142	103⅝	– ⅛
IllBel 7⅝06	7.5	25	101⅝	...
IllPwr 8s23	7.9	15	101	– 1
IntgHlt 6s03	cv	2	103¼	– 1¾
IBM 6⅜97	6.4	25	99 29/32	...
IBM 6⅜00	6.3	60	100½	+ ⅛
IBM 7¼02	7.0	100	103¼	+ ⅛
IBM 8⅜19	7.3	40	114¼	+ ⅝
IPap dc5⅛12	6.4	10	80⅛	– ⅛
JCPL 7⅛04	7.0	4	101½	+ 1⅛
JumboSp 4½00	cv	10	69½	...
KentE 4½04	cv	149	100¼	– ¼
Kolmrg 8¾09	cv	5	103	– 1
Koppers 8½04	8.0	305	105¾	+ 3⅜
Loews 3⅛07	cv	35	114	+ 7
LgIsLt 7.3s99	7.2	5	101	+ ¼
LgIsLt 7.05s03	7.0	35	100½	– ½
LgIsLt 8⅝04	8.4	43	102⅜	+ ⅛
LgIsLt 8½06	8.3	20	102¼	+ ¼
LgIsLt 8.9s19	8.4	60	105⅜	– ¼
LgIsLt 9¾21	9.5	58	102⅛	– ⅛
LgIsLt 9s22	8.2	25	110¼	– ¼
LgIsLt 9⅝24	9.5	30	101⅝	– ⅜
Lucent 7¼06	7.0	15	104¼	– ⅛
MacNS 7⅞04	cv	12	103¼	+ ¼
StoneCn 11⅞98	11.4	20	104⅜	...
StoneCn 11s99	10.6	109	104	+ ⅛
StoneC 9⅞01	9.6	474	102¾	+ ⅜
StoneC 10¾02A	10.6	448	101⅞	– ¼
StoneC 10¾02O	10.0	40	107¼	+ ⅛
StoneC 11½04	10.6	52	108¾	+ ¼
StoneCn 6¾07	cv	11	83	+ ½
TVA 7.45s01	7.3	25	102	– 1½
TVA 6⅞02	6.8	10	100⅞	...
TVA 6⅞02	6.8	20	101⅝	+ ⅜
TVA 6⅛03	6.2	45	98¾	...
TVA 7⅝22	7.5	201	102¼	+ ¼
TVA 7¾22	7.6	42	102½	...
TVA 8.05s24	8.0	255	101	– 1¼
TVA 8⅝29	8.0	58	108	+ ¼
TVA 8¼34	8.1	6	102¼	– ⅜
TVA 6⅞43	7.2	25	95¾	– ¾
TerR 4s19r	5.7	25	70	...
Texco 9s97	9.0	10	99 31/32	+ 1/32
Texco 9s99D	8.6	20	104⅝	...
Texco 8½03	7.8	40	108⅞	– 1
TmeWar 7.98s04	7.6	5	105⅝	+ ⅜
TmeWar 7¾05	7.5	70	103⅞	– ¾
TmeWar 8.18s07	7.6	96	107	– ⅝
TmeWE 7¼08	7.1	20	101⅞	+ 1
TmeWar 9⅛13	7.9	132	115⅝	...
TmeWar zr13	...	5	48¾	+ ¼
TmeWar 9.15s23	7.8	2	117⅛	...
TollCp 9½03	9.1	20	104⅛	...
TollCp 4¾04	cv	1	115½	+ 3½
TucEP 8⅛01	8.0	12	101	...
USX 5¾01	cv	100	97½	+ 1
Unisys 8¼00	cv	173	142¼	– ¾
US Filt 4½01	cv	10	120	+ 3
Viacm 7s03A	7.4	127	94⅞	+ ⅜
Viacm 7s03B	7.4	30	95⅛	+ ⅝
WMX dc2s05	cv	3	88½	– ½
Wainoco 7¾14	cv	19	98	...
WasteM zr01	...	8	107	– 2
Webb 9¾03	9.5	585	102⅛	+ ⅝
Webb 9s06	8.9	88	100⅝	+ ⅛
Webb 9¾08	9.5	935	102¼	+ ⅜
Weirton 11½98	11.4	60	101¼	...
Weirton 10⅞99	10.4	73	104⅜	...
Weirton 10¾05	10.1	15	106¼	...
WstbrgC 11s02	10.9	50	101	+ ¼
WhlPit 9⅜03	9.0	51	103¾	...
WldColor 07	cv	40	97	...
Wrldcp 7s04	cv	5	65	+ 4½
XrxCr 10s99	9.4	10	106⅞	...
Zenith 6¼11	cv	50	77¼	– ¼

Source: *The Wall Street Journal*, 22 October 1997. Reprinted by permission of *The Wall Street Journal*, © 1997 Dow Jones & Co., Inc. All Rights Reserved Worldwide.

The first column of Exhibit 2-7 gives the corporation's name, the stated annual coupon rate, and the maturity date. The current yield column is the stated annual coupon amount divided by the current price. For example, the Viacom 7% bonds have a current yield of about 7.4%, or (7/95.125). The volume column is the number of bonds traded for that day. Thus, 30 Viacom 7% bonds were traded on October 21, 1997. The last two columns give the closing price (95.125) as a percentage of par and the change from the previous day (up ⅝).

Mortgages are bonds in which the borrower (the mortgagor) provides the lender (the mortgagee) collateral, which is usually real estate.[11] You are probably most familiar with mortgages on homes. Default risk related to mortgages can be

11. Other mortgage bonds are collateralized by corporate assets, such as property and equipment.

insured either privately or through government insurance agencies such as the Federal Housing Authority (FHA) or the Veterans Administration (VA). Mortgages are typically pooled (packaged together in portfolios) and sold. These pools of securities are called **mortgage-backed securities.** The originator of the mortgage will sell the mortgage through another firm (called a **conduit**), such as the Federal National Mortgage Association (FNMA). Mortgage-backed securities may or may not be backed by a federal agency. The most difficult aspect of managing a mortgage portfolio is assessing the risk that the mortgages will be prepaid. Mortgage holders prepay when interest rates are down.

2.2 STOCKS

This section covers the basic characteristics of common and preferred stock. It compares and contrasts the different types of stock issues and concludes with a description of published stock quotations.

2.2.1 Basic Characteristics of Common Stock

A **common stock** represents part ownership in a firm. A stock certificate is evidence of this ownership share. Common stocks are also referred to as *common shares* or *equity*. Typically, each common stock owned entitles an investor to one vote in corporate stockholders meetings. Stockholders vote on such issues as who will be in senior management positions, who will be the outside auditor, and what to do with merger offers. Historically, common stocks on the whole have provided a higher return than bonds, but they also have higher risk. For example, in the stock market crash of October 19, 1987, the overall value of the market declined more than 20% in one day. The crash of 1987 was more severe than the plunge of the market on October 28, 1997, when the Dow Jones Industrial Average fell 554.26 points, a one-day loss of 7.2%.

With common stocks, the ownership of the firm is residual; that is, common stockholders receive what is left over after all other claims on the firm have been satisfied. Because they are residual claims, common stocks have no stated maturity. In other words, unlike corporate bonds, common stocks do not have a date on which the corporation must buy them back. If you own common stock and wish to sell it, you must find a willing buyer.

Also, **cash dividends** are paid to stockholders only after other liabilities have been paid. Cash dividends are cash payments made to stockholders from the firm that issued the stock. The stockholder receives these residual benefits in the form of dividends, capital gains, or both. Typically, the firm does not pay all its earnings in cash dividends. Usually the firm will retain some of its earnings to reinvest in other projects in an effort to enhance the firm's value. For example, a pharmaceutical company will take some of its earnings and invest them in research and development in an effort to discover new and better drugs, thereby earning future profits.

Corporations try to maintain a constant dividend payment, because this situation tends to enhance share prices (or at least it is perceived by some to enhance share prices). An investor earns **capital gains** (the difference between the asset's purchase price and selling price, when this difference is positive) when he or she sells stocks at a price higher than the purchase price. If the stock is sold at a price below the purchase price, a **capital loss** is incurred. The tax consequences of capital gains are discussed in Appendix 2A.

To understand the risk and rewards of investing in a common stock, most analysts begin with the firm's financial statements. (Chapter 21 describes the various financial statements.) **Fundamental analysis** is the process of examining financial statements, along with other relevant information, to determine the underlying value of a firm. The purpose of fundamental analysis is to find the intrinsic worth of the firm. The intrinsic worth is the "true" value of the firm, not its current market value. Practitioners of fundamental analysis compare this true value to the current price of the stock to make investment decisions.

Several dates are important when investing in dividend-paying common stock. Dividends are typically paid quarterly, although there are many other payment methods. The **declaration date** is the day when the board of directors actually announces that stockholders on the date of record will receive a dividend. The **date of record** is the day on which the stockholder must actually own the shares to be able to receive the dividend. The date of record is usually several weeks after the declaration date. The **ex-dividend date** is the first day on which, if the stock is purchased, stockholders are no longer entitled to receive the dividend. Stocks on the New York Stock Exchange (NYSE) go ex-dividend four trading days before the date of record. This allows for the official records to be adjusted. Finally, the **payment date** is the day that the company actually mails the dividend checks to its stockholders. The payment date is about three weeks after the ex-dividend date.

2.2.2 Classifications of Common Stocks

Stocks are usually classified using the following categories: (1) growth, (2) income, (3) blue chip, (4) speculative, (5) cyclical, and (6) defensive. A stock may be classified in more than one category. For example, WalMart stock is rated as both growth and blue chip. Some stocks may fall into only one or two categories, and other stocks may defy classification because of their unique features.

Growth stocks are usually common stocks of smaller firms having sales and earnings growth in excess of the industry average. The company pays very low or no dividends and reinvests its earnings for expansion. For example, Microsoft Corporation had recorded sales and earnings growth rates in excess of 20% per year from 1988 through 1997. To date, Microsoft has not paid any cash dividends.

Income stocks are common stocks of older, more mature firms that pay high dividends and are not growing rapidly. Stocks of utility companies are examples of income stocks. Income stocks are usually in low-risk industries, and their price increases little, if at all. For example, Duke Power Company has paid dividends consistently for at least the last 20 years without ever decreasing the amount paid. In the last 10 years, Duke has consistently increased its dividend at a rate of about 5% per year.[12] Hence, Duke Power Company has been a solid source of income and a very stable firm.

Blue chip stocks are common stocks of large, financially sound corporations with a good history of dividend payments and consistent earnings growth. These stocks tend to have very little risk of default. For example, Procter and Gamble recorded sales of over $3,046 million in 1996. The company has increased its dividend every year for at least the past 20 years, through 1996. Blue chip stocks typically have more capital gains potential than do income stocks.

Speculative stocks are the opposite of blue chip stocks. These are stocks with a higher than average possibility of gain or loss, due to the fact that they are very risky and have considerable short-term volatility. For example, Texas Instruments recorded a 94% decrease in net income for the fiscal year ending in 1996. However, for the fiscal year 1995, Texas Instruments experienced an increase in net income of over 57%. Hence, investing in Texas Instruments during this time period was very risky. For the 52-week period ending October 13, 1997, Texas Instrument stock experienced a 52-week low of $30.50 and a high of $71.25. Also note that this 52-week period does not include the large decline experienced on October 28, 1997, when the Dow Jones Industrial Average fell over 550 points in one day.

Cyclical stocks are common stocks that tend to move with the business cycle. When the economy is doing well, these stocks do well. When the country is in recession, these stocks do poorly. Ford Motor Company is a cyclical stock, as are other automobile makers. Automobile sales are typically a leading indicator of economic activity. Hence, as the economy slips into a recession, so do the earnings of automobile companies. Ford recorded large income gains during the expansion years in the late 1980s, but the company experienced sizable losses in the recession of the early 1990s.

Defensive stocks are the opposite of cyclical stocks, in a sense. Defensive stocks tend to do relatively well in recessionary periods but do not do very well when the economy is booming. These stocks are more difficult to find than cyclical stocks. Stocks of automobile-parts makers may be defensive. When the economy is in a recession, consumers are much more likely to attempt to maintain their motor vehicles rather than purchase new ones. Hence, sales by auto-parts makers tend to increase in recessions and decrease in expansions.

2.2.3 Preferred Stocks

Preferred stocks typically pay a stated dividend and have preference over the payments to common stockholders. Thus, preferred stock is a "hybrid security" that has some properties of bonds and some properties of stocks. Investors are attracted to this type of investment, but they sometimes overlook the risk. It is true that preferred stock may provide a relatively high yield, but this high yield is not guaranteed.

---

12. This means that if Duke paid a $1 dividend last year, then on average, it will pay $1.05 this year.

Also, if the firm goes bankrupt, the preferred stockholder stands in the credit line behind bondholders. A company's failure to pay preferred stock dividends, however, does not result in bankruptcy. Sometimes the firm can even call back the preferred stock, thus avoiding the high dividend. Finally, owners of preferred stock do not enjoy the same benefits as owners of common stock when the firm is doing well. That is, the common stock price could increase sharply, offering stockholders high capital gains. However, the preferred stock price gains are limited, much like the earning potential of bonds.

Cumulative preferred stocks are preferred stocks whose dividends accumulate if they are not paid. That is, before common shareholders can receive a dividend, the preferred shareholders receive all prior dividends that are due. **Participating preferred stocks** are preferred stocks whose dividends are tied to the success of the firm according to some stated formula in the earnings of the firm.

Dividends on preferred shares are not tax deductible. However, in 1995, the Internal Revenue Service (IRS) approved a new type of preferred shares whose dividends are tax deductible. Thus, the firm can enjoy a cheaper source of obtaining funds to finance operations.[13]

2.2.4 Reading the Stock Pages

Exhibit 2-8 shows a stock page from the financial pages of a newspaper. The first two columns give the 52-week high and low stock prices, followed in the third column by the company's abbreviated name. For example, AT&T had a 52-week high of 47¾ (a new 52-week high, as shown by the ▲ symbol) and a 52-week low of 30¾. The *s* by Aames Financial means the firm has recently had a stock split. A **stock split** occurs when a company issues more new shares in return for existing shares. For example, a 2-for-1 split means that a company issues two new shares for every one share currently outstanding. Stock splits are a method that firms use to control the per-share cost of its stock. After a 2-for-1 split, a firm's stock will trade at about half of its previous value.

Note in the "Explanatory Notes" in Exhibit 2-8 that *pr* stands for *preference shares,* and *pf* stands for *preferred shares.* **Preference shares** are preferred stock with a higher claim to any dividend payments than other preferred stock issues. That is, in hard times these shares' dividends are paid before any other dividends are paid.

The fourth column gives the company's unique ticker symbol. The fifth column gives the dollar dividend paid per share over the past 52 weeks, and the sixth column gives the dividend yield. The dividend yield is found by dividing the annual (52-week) dollar dividend (denoted by D) by the closing price per share (denoted by P) (Column 11) and is stated in percentages. Specifically,

$$\text{Dividend Yield} = (D/P)100$$

which for AT&T (see Exhibit 2-8) is

$$\text{Dividend Yield} = (\$1.32/49.75)100 \cong 2.7\%$$

---

13. See Andrew Bary, "What a Deal: New Breed of Preferred Issues Helps Everybody but the Tax Man," *Barron's,* 27 February 1995.

EXHIBIT 2-8 **Illustration of Stock Price Quotes**

NEW YORK STOCK EXCHANGE COMPOSITE TRANSACTIONS

Quotations as of 5 p.m. Eastern Time
Tuesday, October 21, 1997

52 Weeks Hi	Lo	Stock	Sym	Div	Yld %	PE	Vol 100s	Hi	Lo	Close	Net Chg
		-A-A-A-									
38 7/16	24 1/4	AAR	AIR	.48	1.3	24	523	36	35 1/16	35 13/16	+ 13/16
29 3/16	15 1/2	ABM Indus	ABM	.40	1.4	25	226	28 3/8	28	28 3/8	+ 1/2
n 24 7/16	18 3/8	ABN AMRO ADR	AAN	.25p	...	...	629	20 1/4	19 15/16	20 3/16	+ 3/16
11	10	ACM Gvt Fd	ACG	.90a	8.3	...	911	10 13/16	10 11/16	10 13/16	+ 1/16
8 1/4	7	ACM OppFd	AOF	.63	7.9	...	106	7 15/16	7 7/8	7 15/16	+ 1/16
10 1/4	8 7/8	ACM SecFd	GSF	.90	9.0	...	1547	10 1/16	10	10	− 1/16
7	6 1/4	ACM SpctmFd	SI	.57	8.8	...	1488	6 1/2	6 7/16	6 1/2	+ 1/16
15	11 1/2	ACM MgmdInc	ADF	1.35	9.1	...	252	14 7/8	14 3/4	14 13/16	− 1/16
10 1/2	9 1/4	ACM MgdIncFd	AMF	.90	8.9	...	363	10 1/8	10 1/16	10 1/16	− 1/16
14 1/4	12 1/4	ACM MuniSec	AMU	.90	6.4	...	84	14 1/16	14	14	− 1/16
27 7/16	16 3/4	♣ ACX Tch A	ACX		...	dd	101	26 1/2	26 7/16	26 7/16	+ 1/8
s 49 5/8	**20 3/16**	**♣ AES Cp**	**AES**		**...**	**50**	**5277**	**47 5/16**	**41 3/4**	**47 3/16**	**+ 3 9/16**
57 7/8	36 1/8	♣ AFLAC	AFL	.46	.9	12	1700	53 15/16	52 1/4	53 11/16	+ 1 7/16
36 5/16	23 7/8	AGCO Cp	AG	.04	.1	12	4110	31 1/4	30 11/16	30 7/8	− 1/4
22	18 1/4	AGL Res	ATG	1.08	5.7	13	525	18 7/8	18 1/2	18 7/8	+ 3/8
20 1/4	11 1/2	AgSvcAm	ASV		...	20	37	19 5/16	19 1/8	19 3/16	− 1/16
n 25 3/4	25	AICI CapTr pf		.35p	...	...	99	25 5/16	25 1/4	25 5/16	...
19 5/8	13 1/4	AJL PepsTr	AJP	1.44	8.7	...	132	16 5/8	16 5/16	16 5/8	+ 1/4
24 3/4	20 5/8	♣ AMLI Resdntl	AML	1.72	7.3	19	1281	23 3/4	23 3/8	23 11/16	+ 1/16
56 11/16	32 7/8	♣ AMP	AMP	1.04	2.0	43	1461	51 3/4	51 1/8	51 5/8	+ 5/8
▲ 122 1/4	78 1/4	AMR	AMR		...	10	5735	123 1/2	120 3/4	123 7/16	+ 3 1/16
51 1/4	40 7/8	♣ ARCO Chm	RCM	2.80	5.5	45	202	51 1/4	51	51 1/16	− 1/16
41	28 5/16	ASA	ASA	1.20	4.0	...	885	30 1/16	29 13/16	29 15/16	+ 1/16
▲ 47 3/4	30 3/4	AT&T	T	1.32	2.7	16	138958	50 1/16	47 7/8	49 3/4	+ 2 1/4
35 1/4	28 1/4	AXA-UAP ADR	AXA	.65p	...	...	223	34 1/2	34 1/8	34 3/8	− 1/16
s 34 5/16	**10 1/2**	**AamesFnl**	**AAM**	**.13**	**.9**	**9**	**12800**	**15 3/4**	**14 3/16**	**14 1/2**	**− 1 3/16**
n 26 5/16	24 1/2	AbbeyNtl		2.19	8.3	...	12	26 5/16	26 1/4	26 5/16	+ 1/16
68 15/16	49 3/8	AbbotLab	ABT	1.08	1.7	24	13500	63 7/8	63 5/16	63 11/16	+ 1/8
28	12 1/2	Abercrombie A	ANF		...	...	571	24	23 1/4	23 1/4	− 1/2
21	12 5/8	Abitibi g	ABY	.40	...	...	2591	16 1/2	16 3/16	16 1/4	− 3/16
28 5/8	17 3/4	♣ AcceptIns	AIF		...	13	65	27 7/16	27 1/8	27 7/16	+ 5/16
32	15 3/4	AccuStaff	ASI		...	49	6890	29 5/8	28 1/8	29	+ 3/8
101 1/16	51 1/2	ACE Ltd	ACL	.88	.9	14	245	98 15/16	96	98 7/8	+ 2 7/8
10 3/8	6 1/8	AcmeElec	ACE		...	cc	202	7 11/16	7 1/4	7 9/16	+ 5/16
21 5/8	13	AcmeMetals	AMI		...	dd	171	14 7/16	14	14 1/4	− 1/16
24 5/8	**14**	**ACNielsen**	**ART**		**...**	**45**	**1174**	**24 1/2**	**22 5/8**	**24 1/2**	**+ 1 11/16**
29 3/4	18 1/8	Acuson	ACN		...	79	941	26 7/8	26 3/8	26 3/4	+ 1/8
25 1/2	19 1/4	♣ AdamsExp	ADX	1.72e	6.8	...	750	25 5/16	24 7/8	25 1/4	+ 5/16
n 26 1/2	13 3/4	Administaff	ASF		...	...	74	23 7/8	23 1/2	23 7/8	+ 1/2
48 1/2	17	♣ AdvMicro	AMD		...	dd	24170	29 3/4	28 1/4	29 7/16	+ 1 3/8
27 1/2	9	Advest	ADV	.09e	.4	19	123	25 11/16	25 3/16	25 5/8	+ 7/16
21 1/4	11	Advo	AD		...	dd	1544	21 1/8	20 3/8	20 11/16	− 1/16
12 15/16	5 7/8	♣ Advocat	AVC		...	11	20	10 15/16	10 13/16	10 13/16	− 1/16
87 1/8	51 1/8	♣ AEGON NV	AEG	1.52e	1.9	22	172	81 15/16	81 7/16	81 13/16	+ 1/8
12 1/2	3 1/8	♣ Aeroflex	ARX		...	35	1732	12 1/4	11 3/4	12	− 1/2
57 1/2	30 3/4	AeroVick	ANV	.80	1.4	17	2078	56	54	55 5/8	+ 1 3/4
n 73 5/8	**48**	**AES Tr pfA**		**2.69**	**3.7**	**...**	**1158**	**72**	**67 7/16**	**72**	**+ 4 9/16**
27 1/2	26 5/8	AetnaMIPS pfA		2.37	8.8	...	94	27 1/16	27	27	...
118 1/8	60 1/8	Aetna	AET	.80	1.0	23	8999	77 7/16	75 7/8	77 3/8	+ 1 13/16
104	65 3/8	Aetna pfC		4.76	6.2	...	557	76 7/8	75 13/16	76 3/4	+ 15/16
s 32	19 1/2	AffilCptrSvc	AFA		...	24	76	25 3/8	25	25 3/16	+ 1/16
15 1/4	8	♣ AgnicoEgl	AEM	.10	1.1	...	470	9 3/16	8 15/16	9 1/8	+ 3/16
22 3/8	18 3/4	AgreeRlty	ADC	1.84f	8.5	15	110	21 3/4	21 1/4	21 5/8	− 1/16

EXPLANATORY NOTES

The following explanations apply to New York and American exchange listed issues and the Nasdaq Stock Market. NYSE and Amex prices are composite quotations that include trades on the Chicago, Pacific, Philadelphia, Boston and Cincinnati exchanges and reported by the National Association of Securities Dealers.

Boldfaced quotations highlight those issues whose price changed by 5% or more if their previous closing price was $2 or higher.

Underlined quotations are those stocks with large changes in volume, per exchange, compared with the issue's average trading volume. The calculation includes common stocks of $5 a share or more with an average volume over 65 trading days of at least 5,000 shares. The underlined quotations are for the 40 largest volume percentage leaders on the NYSE and the Nasdaq National Market. It includes the 20 largest volume percentage gainers on the Amex.

The 52-week high and low columns show the highest and lowest price of the issue during the preceding 52 weeks plus the current week, but not the latest trading day. These ranges are adjusted to reflect stock payouts of 1% or more, and cash dividends or other distributions of 10% or more.

Dividend/Distribution rates, unless noted, are annual disbursements based on the last monthly, quarterly, semiannual, or annual declaration. Special or extra dividends or distributions, including return of capital, special situations or payments not designated as regular are identified by footnotes.

Yield is defined as the dividends or other distributions paid by a company on its securities, expressed as a percentage of price.

The P/E ratio is determined by dividing the closing market price by the company's primary per-share earnings for the most recent four quarters. Charges and other adjustments usually are excluded when they qualify as extraordinary items under generally accepted accounting rules.

Sales figures are the unofficial daily total of shares traded, quoted in hundreds (two zeros omitted; f-four zeros omitted.)

Exchange ticker symbols are shown for all New York and American exchange common stocks, and Dow Jones News/Retrieval symbols are listed for Class A and Class B shares listed on both markets. Nasdaq symbols are listed for all Nasdaq NMS issues. A more detailed explanation of Nasdaq ticker symbols appears with the NMS listings.

FOOTNOTES: **▲**-New 52-week high. **▼**-New 52-week low. **a**-Extra dividend or extras in addition to the regular dividend. **b**-Indicates annual rate of the cash dividend and that a stock dividend was paid. **c**-Liquidating dividend. **cc**-P/E ratio is 100 or more. **dd**-Loss in the most recent four quarters. **e**-Indicates a dividend was declared in the preceding 12 months, but that there isn't a regular dividend rate. Amount shown may have been adjusted to reflect stock split, spinoff or other distribution. **ec**-Emerging Company Marketplace issue. **FD**-First day of trading. **f**-Annual rate, increased on latest declaration. **g**-Indicates the dividend and earnings are expressed in Canadian money. The stock trades in U.S. dollars. No yield or P/E ratio is shown. **gg**-Special sales condition; no regular way trading. **h**-Temporary exemption from Nasdaq requirements. **i**-Indicates amount declared or paid after a stock dividend or split. **j**-Indicates dividend was paid this year, and that at the last dividend meeting a dividend was omitted or deferred. **k**-Indicates dividend declared this year on cumulative issues with dividends in arrears. **m**-Annual rate, reduced on latest declaration. **n**-Newly issued in the past 52 weeks. The high-low range begins with the start of trading and doesn't cover the entire period. **p**-Initial dividend; no yield calculated. **pf**-Preferred. **pp**-Holder owes installment(s) of purchase price. **pr**-Preference. **r**-Indicates a cash dividend declared in the preceding 12 months, plus a stock dividend. **rt**-Rights. **s**-Stock split or stock dividend, or cash or cash equivalent distribution, amounting to 10% or more in the past 52 weeks. The high-low price is adjusted from the old stock. Dividend calculations begin with the date the split was paid or the stock dividend occurred. **stk**-Paid in stock in the last 12 months. Company doesn't pay cash dividend. **un**-Units. **v**-Trading halted on primary market. **vj**-In bankruptcy or receivership or being reorganized under the Bankruptcy Code, or securities assumed by such companies. **wd**-When distributed. **wi**-When issued. **wt**-Warrants. **ww**-With warrants. **x**-Ex-dividend, ex-distribution, ex-rights or without warrants. **z**-Sales in full, not in 100s.

Source: *The Wall Street Journal*, 22 October 1997, p. C3. Reprinted by permission of *The Wall Street Journal*, © 1997 Dow Jones & Co., Inc. All Rights Reserved Worldwide.

The seventh column gives the price/earnings (P/E) ratio, which is the closing price divided by the past four quarters' earnings per share. The P/E ratio is a widely used statistic in evaluating common stocks. A firm that is expected to experience significant growth in the future will have a higher P/E ratio. That is, the current price will reflect this perceived growth and be much higher than its current earnings. The current P/E ratio is 16 for AT&T; in other words, the stock price is 16 times larger than the annual earnings per share. With the P/E ratio and the closing price, we can infer an earnings per share (EPS). That is,

$$P/E = P/EPS, \text{ and therefore } EPS = P/(P/E)$$

For example, we find AT&T's EPS to be

$$EPS = \$49.75/16 \cong \$3.11$$

Thus, AT&T's EPS over the past year is approximately $3.11. This is an approximation, because the reported P/E is rounded. When the earnings are negative or very close to zero, the P/E ratio is meaningless and hence not reported.

Column 8 gives the volume of shares trading, in 100s. Common stocks are typically traded in groups of 100, which are referred to as **round lots.** In Exhibit 2-8 we see that 138,958 round lots were traded for AT&T. Thus, 13,895,800 shares of AT&T stock were traded on this day.

Columns 9 and 10 give the previous day's high and low prices, respectively. Column 11 gives the closing price, which is the price of the last trade. The final column gives the change from the previous trading day.

2.3 DERIVATIVE SECURITIES

A derivative security is one whose value depends directly on, or is derived from, the value of another asset. Four types of derivative securities are stock options, convertible bonds, futures, and swaps.

2.3.1 Stock Options

A **call option** on common stock gives the holder of the option (the buyer) the right to buy a specified stock at a specified price on or before a specified date. A **put option** gives the holder the right to sell a specified stock at a specified price on or before a specified date. Investors buy call options in hopes that the stock price will rise so they may buy the stock at a discount. Investors buy put options hoping that the stock price will fall so they may sell the stock at a premium.

The advantage of call options is that when stock prices rise, these options provide a much higher return than the comparable return from stock ownership. However, there is a risk that the call option will expire worthless if stock prices fall. Options are useful tools in managing the risks of a portfolio. For example, options can be used to insure the downside risk of a stock portfolio. (We examine this issue in Chapter 23.)

2.3.2 Convertible Bonds

Convertible bonds provide a unique investment opportunity. A **convertible bond** is a corporate bond with an option to convert the bond into stock. The bondholder receives coupon payments that generally have a higher yield than the dividend yield of the underlying stock. Because the bond is convertible, it provides the opportunity to participate in any rise in stock price. In essence, a convertible bond is an ordinary bond with a call option attached.

Suppose Cray Research 6⅛, 2011 convertible bonds were trading at 85¾. That is, the bonds offer a 6⅛% coupon and will mature in 2011. The price of 85¾ refers to percentage of par. The par value of the bonds is $1,000; hence, the quoted price of the bond is $857.50 (or 0.8575 · $1,000).

To understand the price of the Cray Research bond, we need more information. We need the **conversion ratio,** the number of common shares a bondholder will receive if the bond is tendered for conversion. For Cray Research convertible bonds, the conversion ratio is 12.82. That is, each bond with $1,000 par is convertible into 12.82 shares of stock. The **conversion price** is the par value of a bond divided by the conversion ratio, which for Cray is about $78 (that is, $1,000/12.82). Cray Research stock is currently trading at $42 per share. The **conversion value** is the current value of a bond if it is converted. If we converted the Cray bonds, our equity would be worth $538.44 (that is, $42 · 12.82), which is far less than the bonds' current trading price of $857.50. The **conversion premium** is the value of the option to convert, which is the difference between the current market value of the bonds and the comparable market price of a nonconvertible bond. In this case, the option to convert at $78 when the stock is presently trading at $42 is not worth very much.

2.3.3 Futures

A futures contract is a security that *obligates* one to buy or sell a specified amount of an asset at a stated price on a particular date. For example, the buyer of a 5,000-bushel corn futures contract that matures in three months agrees to buy 5,000 bushels of a specified grade of corn at a specific location at a specific price (the futures price).

Futures contracts exist on most major commodities; metals; energy products; interest rates; currencies; and various indexes, mainly stock indexes. Futures are used to hedge financial price risk and to speculate on the direction of future prices. For example, a multinational corporation that has a large accounts receivable in Japanese yen may sell yen futures contracts to hedge against a weakening yen relative to the dollar. A speculator who believes the dollar will weaken against the yen may buy yen futures in hopes of profiting. Thus, futures provide the ability to transfer financial price risk from the hedger to the speculator.

2.3.4 Swaps

A newer type of financial security is the swap. Swaps can be thought of as a portfolio of futures contracts involving multiple delivery dates. A **swap** is an agreement to exchange specific assets at future points in time. For example, a currency swap is an agreement to exchange currencies—say, U.S. dollars for French francs—at specific dates and for specific amounts in the future.

The first major swap occurred between IBM and the World Bank in 1981. IBM held fixed-rate debt in German marks (DM) and Swiss francs (SF). Because of recent changes in the foreign exchange rates, IBM wanted to convert its DM and SF liabilities to U.S. dollar liabilities. In August 1981, the World Bank issued fixed-rate bonds in $2 denominations with the exact maturities of the IBM debt. The World Bank and IBM then agreed to "swap" the interest payments. The interest payments were calculated based on the par value of the bonds. This par value is referred to as the **notional principal.** The net result of these transactions was that the World Bank would, in effect, make IBM's debt payments in DM and SF, and IBM would make the World Bank's debt payments in U.S. dollars. Thus, IBM eliminated its currency risk.[14] Why did the World Bank take this currency risk? Probably, it had assets in Germany and Switzerland that generated DM and SF cash flow. These assets could then be used to pay the World Bank's debts with no concern about changes in exchange rates. Thus, both sides of this transaction benefited.

2.4 RISKS OF BONDS AND STOCKS

Exhibit 2-9 compares the risk and average (or expected) return characteristics of the financial securities introduced in this chapter. If held in isolation, options and futures are the most risky, but they also provide the highest potential return. Short-term government bonds are the safest, but they also offer the smallest return. In between these two extremes are securities offering different levels of risk and return. Although stocks are typically riskier than bonds, they also offer a higher return on average. Long-term bonds have a higher risk and generally also a higher return than short-term bonds. Finally, corporate bonds must offer a higher return on average to induce investors to take on default risk.

Investing in bonds and stocks has nine major sources of risk. (The order of coverage here does not suggest priority of risks, as risks vary among different securities.) The risk sources follow:

1. *Default risk*. One risk that affects bond investors is that of default. The municipality or corporation may fail to pay either the coupon payment or face value at maturity. Bond investors in the Seabrook Nuclear Power Plant suffered from default risk when the plant's owner, the New Hampshire Power Company, failed to pay the coupon payments. In 1995, TWA failed to pay the interest on its bonds. Firms may default if they have too much debt (relative to the cash flows they generate). In this event, both stockholders and bondholders may lose. Of course, federal government bonds do not have default risk, because the Treasury Department can print money. Corporate and municipal bonds, however, are exposed to default risk.

2. *Interest rate risk*. A second source of risk to bond investors is that of a change in interest rates. Would you want to buy a bond offering an annual 8% coupon rate when the market is paying 10% on newly issued bonds? Recall that bonds typi-

14. See Alan Tucker, *Financial Futures, Options, and Swaps* (New York: West Publishing, 1991), p. 481.

EXHIBIT 2-9   **Risk and Return on Various Assets**

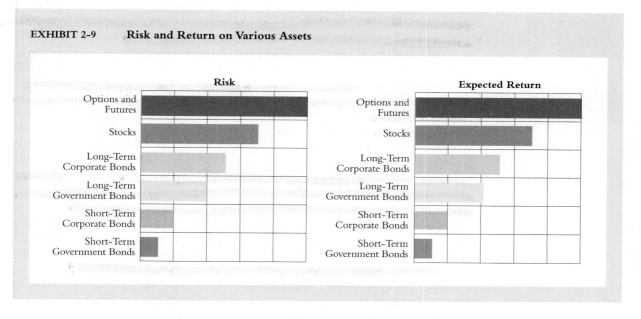

cally have a fixed coupon. If you have an 8% coupon bond, it is an agreement to pay you 8% of par value every year. Now suppose interest rates increase to 10%, and you are locked into a bad agreement; then you lose money. To be more specific, investors will sell the 8% bond, causing its price to fall. The falling price will result in rising yields. For example, if an 8% coupon bond is selling for 90% of the price of the new 10% bond, for the same investment you can buy more of the old bond and earn more interest. The selling will continue until both the old and new bonds yield 10%. These higher yields imply that you can reinvest the coupon payment at a higher yield. However, if the yield goes down, the coupon reinvestment rate will be smaller. This change in the reinvestment rate is called the **reinvestment rate risk.** In contrast, the change in the bond price because of an increase in the interest rate described above is called the **price risk.** In this case, the low coupon rate causes you to lose money. The rise in interest rates could be caused by factors outside a firm's control: a rise in the Federal Reserve discount rate, a change in monetary policy, or a change in the inflation rate.

Of course, changes in interest rates may also be a source of gain. If you hold a bond with a fixed coupon of 8% and the interest rate goes down in the market to 6%, you are locked into a good agreement. Everyone will buy the 8% bond, and its market price will go up (which gives you a capital gain as a bondholder) until both the old and new bonds yield the same return of 6%.

Although changes in the interest rate may result in a gain for bondholders, interest rate changes are usually referred to as *interest rate risk,* because the uncertainty caused by these changes in general is undesirable to investors. In other words, if investors could buy one of two bonds, where the first bond's price did not change and the second bond's price would have a $50 gain or a $50 loss with equal probability, most investors would choose the first bond.

Stockholders also can lose or win when interest rates change. For example, in the first half of 1994, overall interest rates rose, which helped push overall stock prices lower. Higher interest rates make bonds relatively more attractive, causing some investors to sell stocks and buy bonds. This stock selling results in lower stock prices.

3. *Inflation rate risk.* Interest rate changes may be caused by many factors that are very hard to predict. One of these factors is a change in the inflation rate, which is referred to as the *inflation rate risk* or *purchasing power risk*. These terms refer to the risk of losing the purchasing power of future cash receipts. That is, the value of the dollars received in the future is less than expected, and therefore, the investor is unable to purchase as many goods and services as anticipated.

For example, suppose a 1-year bond is offering a 5% yield, but inflation is 6%. At the end of the year, investors would be able to buy *less* with the bond's proceeds than they could with the initial investment at the beginning of the year. Inflation is a threat to the future benefits provided from investing.

Recently, new bonds called inflation-indexed Treasury securities have been issued. The interest and principal of the bonds are linked to the cost of living index, which shields these bonds from inflation rate risk.

PRACTICE BOX

Problem

A government bond sold at $1,000. It pays an annual interest of 5% a year at the end of each year, and it matures in exactly 2 years. The par value is $1,000, and the bond has a yield of 5%. What is the capital gain if interest rates go down to 3%? What is the capital loss if interest rates go up to 7%? How would your results change if the bonds had 10 years to maturity? Which bond is riskier, the 2-year bond or the 10-year bond?

Solution

Using present value tables, a calculator, or software, we calculate the present value of the bonds' cash flows. The results are:

Interest Rates	Market Price of 2-Year Bond	Market Price of 10-Year Bond
3%	$1,038	$1,171
5	1,000	1,000
7	964	860

Thus, the 2-year bond provides a $38 capital gain when rates fall to 3%, whereas the 10-year bond provides a $171 capital gain. However, the losses are similar in magnitude ($36 and $140, respectively), making the 10-year bond riskier.

4. *Risk of call.* Another potential risk to bondholders is the risk of call. Many bonds contain a call provision that allows the issuing firm to repurchase its bonds at a stated price after a stated date. The purchase price is usually the face value plus 1 year of coupon payments. This call provision can adversely affect the value of the bonds if interest rates decline dramatically.

For example, an 8% coupon bond with a face value of $1,000 that matures in 15 years may have a call provision after 8 years. According to the call provision, the firm could repurchase the bonds any time after the 8th year if it is willing to pay the face value ($1,000) plus 1 year of interest ($80), or $1,080.

If interest rates fall to 5%, the bond gains from having an 8% coupon. However, there is a risk that the bond will be taken away from the investor, who then will not fully benefit from the drastic change in the interest rate. The firm could call the bonds and issue new ones at 5%, saving 3% per year. Also, the investor faces an investment decision of what to do with the proceeds from the bond at the time the firm chooses to buy the bond back. Bonds are typically called after interest rates have fallen substantially. Thus, bond investors will be reinvesting the proceeds at a time when rates are low.

A callable bond, like all other bonds, also suffers losses when interest rates go up (because the price falls). Also, a callable bond's price will not go up in the same way as a noncallable bond's price. Thus, why would anyone want to buy such bonds, which seem to be an inferior investment? The reason is simple. The firm issuing the bonds must issue them at a higher interest rate than the rate for noncallable bonds for a rational investor to buy the callable bonds. Thus, in the event that the interest rate does not go down and the bonds are not called, the bondholder enjoys a relatively high interest rate.

5. *Liquidity risk.* Another risk of investing in certain bonds and stocks is that they may not be liquid. That is, if the bonds or stocks have to be sold unexpectedly, it could be very costly to the investor. There may be no one who wishes to buy the securities at that time. To get a buyer quickly, the investor may have to sell the security at an unreasonably low price relative to its true value and thus incur a substantial price concession. Investors typically do not have a liquidity risk problem with government bonds and actively traded bonds of larger corporations, such as those issued by AT&T and GM. However, investors must anticipate a liquidity risk with the bonds or stocks of small firms, because they are not actively traded. To compensate for the lack of liquidity, small firms must offer investors a higher yield on bonds or a higher expected return on the stock. No one would buy them otherwise.

6. *Political and regulatory risk.* Bonds and stocks are also exposed to political risk. This risk refers to unforeseen changes in the tax or legal environment that have an impact on stock and bond prices. For example, suppose Congress decided to double the income tax rate and cut the capital gains tax rate in half. What impact would this have on coupon-bearing bonds? In such a case, the tax liabilities of the coupon payments would double, and investors would have an incentive to buy stocks rather than bonds because the change in capital gains tax would favor

stocks. Therefore, coupon-bearing bonds would decline in value as a result of the new tax laws. As Connecting Theory to Practice 2.1 illustrates, a government policy that falls in the category of political risk is a significant consideration in investment decisions.

7. *Business risk.* Stocks and corporate bond prices are influenced greatly by the prosperity of the particular company, as well as by the economy in general. Stock and bond prices are directly influenced by how well a company is performing. Furthermore, because the firm is often involved with risky research and development projects, stocks are influenced by company performance much more than bonds. Company performance is usually directly linked to the performance of the overall economy.

8. *Market risk.* Much of the research conducted on securities markets has documented that the prices of all securities in a particular market tend to move together. For example, the U.S. Treasury bond market exhibits a high level of co-movement of its bond prices. This principle is also true for corporate bonds and stocks. Even a good stock tends to perform poorly when the overall market is going down. Hence, it is important to know what influences overall market movements.

9. *Exchange rate risk.* As an American investor, why would you buy U.S. bonds yielding only 4.12% when you could earn 10.15% in the United Kingdom? The answer is simple: When you invest in the United Kingdom, you have to convert your U.S. dollars to British pounds. However, when you want your money back—say, at the end of the year—you must sell the U.K. bonds for British pounds and then convert the proceeds to U.S. dollars. Of course, there is a risk that for each pound you receive, you may get fewer dollars because of changes in the exchange rate. In dollars, you may end up with a yield much lower than 10.15%; indeed, the yield may be even less than the 4.12% that you can get on the U.S. bonds. Thus, the high yield of 10.15% may be an illusion. Bonds are bought and sold in local currencies, not in U.S. dollars. This exchange rate adds one more layer of risk for the international investor.

The risks of investing in government and corporate bonds, as well as in common stocks, are summarized in Exhibit 2-10. Corporate bonds of similar maturities to government bonds have a higher yield because of default risk. Stocks do not induce default risk, because not paying dividends does not cause the firm to be declared in default. However, stockholders are exposed to risk of default by the firm from other factors (for example, a big financial loss or lawsuit).

Interest rates influence both the bond market and the stock market. Typically, if the interest rates fall, both the bond market and the stock market rally. Inflation risk has exactly the same influence as interest rate risk. Stocks are not callable, whereas most corporate bonds are. The call feature introduces an opportunity loss if interest rates fall. Liquidity risk is present in all securities; however, the government market is the most liquid. Political and regulatory risk, market risk, and foreign exchange risk are present in both the bond and the stock markets. However, business risk applies only to corporate securities, not to securities issued by governments.

EXHIBIT 2-10 Risk Exposure for Bonds and Stocks	Risks	Government Bonds	Corporate Bonds	Common Stocks
	Default	No	Yes	Yes
	Overall level of interest rates in the economy	Yes	Yes	Yes
	Inflation rate	Yes	Yes	Yes
	Call	Some Issues	Most issues	No
	Liquidity	Little	Yes	Yes
	Political and regulatory	Yes	Yes	Yes
	Business	No	Yes	Yes
	Market	Yes	Yes	Yes
	Foreign exchange rate	Yes	Yes	Yes

Yes: Investors in bonds or stocks of this category are exposed to this risk.

No: Investors in bonds or stocks of this category are not exposed to this risk.

Little: Investors in bonds of this category are exposed to some, but not much, of this risk.

CONNECTING THEORY TO PRACTICE 2.1

IN A SURPRISE, SOUTH KOREA ENDS ITS ATTEMPTS TO DEFEND ITS CURRENCY

WASHINGTON, Nov. 17—South Korea suspended efforts to defend its currency with its own, fast-depleting financial reserves today as American, Asian and European officials scrambled to determine if the world's 11th largest economy—and one of America's largest trading partners—will become the latest Asian nation needing an economic bailout.

. . . South Korea is estimated to have $67 billion to $77 billion in short-term debt owned by financial institutions and investors worldwide, and there is good reason to question whether it has the resources to pay that back.

Source: *The New York Times,* 18 November 1997, p. C1, Copyright © 1997 by The New York Times Company. Reprinted by Permission.

MAKING THE CONNECTION

The actions of the South Korean government to suspend efforts to support its currency serve as a reminder of the risks associated with investing in stocks

(continued)

and bonds. Although short-term bonds are typically considered one of the least risky investments in financial securities, in this case investors are reminded of the additional risks involved. Whereas default risk, inflation risk, and liquidity risk are routinely associated with debt, this example highlights two additional forms of risk: political and regulatory.

2.5 INTERNATIONAL SECURITIES

International securities include stocks and bonds issued in foreign countries by foreign firms, as well as securities issued by some domestic firms that pay interest or dividends in a different currency. For example, McDonald's Corporation issued bonds that pay interest in New Zealand dollars. International securities are increasing in importance for several reasons. First, as technologies are improving, the costs of trading international securities are declining. These costs include the cost of actually trading, taxes, and other market impediments. Second, markets are dominated more and more by institutional investors. Institutional investors—such as banks, pension funds, insurance companies, endowments, and mutual funds—trade large quantities of securities. These larger firms have the economies of scale to invest the energy needed to explore foreign markets. Third, technological advances in communications have been astounding. Fiber-optic telecommunication lines now link several trading firms directly to each other, as well as to multiple securities exchanges. These lines allow information to be communicated at a rate nearing the speed of light.

The major benefits of investing in international securities include the possibility of higher returns and diversification. For example, many international bonds offer a higher yield than similar U.S. bonds. However, the investor must also consider how the bond's price will change over time, as well as how changes in the foreign exchange rate will influence the return on international bonds.

Exhibit 2-11 provides a sampling of international stock quotes. Notice that they are traded in their local currencies. Therefore, although the stock may rise, the gain could be eliminated with an adverse move in the foreign exchange rate.

People can invest in international securities in three ways. First, investors can buy foreign bonds or stocks directly in their own markets. Second, many domestic exchanges trade **American Depository Receipts** (ADRs),[15] which are receipts for foreign shares held in a U.S. bank. ADR holders are entitled to the dividends and capital gains of the foreign shares. ADRs trade just like shares of common stock. For example, ADRs trade on the NYSE for Honda Motor Company, a Japanese-based automobile manufacturer. Honda Motor's ADRs trade on the NYSE with ticker

---

15. American Depository Receipts are also sometimes referred to as American Depository Shares, or ADSs.

EXHIBIT 2-11   A Sampling of International Stock Quotes

Fujitsu	1580	+	20
Furukawa Elec	726		....
Green Cross	410	+	12
Haseko	109	−	3
Hirose Elec	8670	−	30
Hitachi Cable	944	−	30
Hitachi Credit	2380	+	80
Hitachi Ltd	1190	+	10
Hitachi Maxell	2950	−	90
Hitachi Metals	635	−	16
Honda Motor	3630	+	30
Hosiden Elec	1320		....
Hoya	5550	−	50
IHI	377	+	12
Ind Bank Japan	1720	+	30
Intec	1340	+	10
Isetan	1230	−	20
Isuzu	355	−	3
Ito-yokado	x6810	−	104
Itochu Corp	520	+	9
Iwatsu Elec	291	−	4
JAL	475	+	6
Japan Aviat El	922	+	20
Japan Energy	220	+	5
Japan Radio	1230		....
JEOL	770	+	9
JUSCO	3180	+	40
Kajima	666	+	12
Kandenko	850	+	5
Kansai Elec	2240	+	20
Kao Corp	1800	−	10
Kawasaki Hi	489	+	16
Kawasaki Steel	299	+	1
KDD	7900	+	230
Kinden	1640	+	40
Kirin	999	−	1
Kobe Steel	170		....
Kokusai Elec	2270	+	70
Kokuyo	2840	−	50
Komatsu Ltd	853	+	18
Konica	701	+	3

Nihon Unisys Ltd	945	+	5
Nikko Securities	590	+	5
Nikon Corp	2230	+	30
Nintendo	10500	+	100
Nippon Chemi-con	578	+	3
Nippon Columbia	369	−	2
Nippon El Glass	2140		....
Nippon Express	813	+	5
Nippon Hodo	848	+	30
Nippon Meat	1480	−	30
Nippon Oil	559	+	10
Nippon Paper	669	+	3
Nippon Sanso	415	+	6
Nippon Shinpan	301	+	4
Nippon Steel	305	−	4
Nissan Motor	777	+	18
Nissin Food	2820	−	20
Nitsuko	640	+	15
NKK	188	−	4
Nomura Securitie	1650	+	20
NSK	651	+	32
NTN	580	+	15
NTT	1150000	+	30000
Obayashi Corp	764	−	17
Odakyu Railway	613	−	7
Oki Elec Ind	446	+	7
OKK	270	+	6
Okuma Corp	755	+	5
Olympus Optical	879	+	9
Omron	2340	−	10
Ono Pharm	4050	−	60
Onward	1920	−	10
Orient Corp	385		....
Pioneer Electron	2660	+	30
Renown	210		....
Ricoh Co	1750	−	10
Royal Co	2110		....
Ryobi	361	+	5
Sakura Bank	740	−	5
Sankyo Co	3850	−	30
Sanrio	937	+	12

Tokyo Style	1420	−	20
Tokyu Corp	634	−	4
Tonen Corp	1140	+	30
Toppan Print	1800	−	40
Toray	814	+	5
Toshiba	730	+	9
Toto	1300	+	40
Toyo Seikan	2080	−	10
Toyobo	232	+	2
Toyoda Mach	1230	+	20
Toyota Motor	3220	+	100
Tsugami	259	+	6
Uny	2320	+	40
Ushio	1370	+	30
Wacoal	1370	−	10
Yamaha	2010	+	10
Yamaichi Sec	237	+	2
Yamanouchi Phm	2910	−	10
Yamatake-Hnywl	2190	−	10
Yamato Tran	1460		....
Yamazaki Baking	1700	+	10
Yasuda Fire	711	−	11
Yokogawa Elec	820	+	15

LONDON
(in pound/pence)

	Close	Net Chg.
Abbey National	8.225	− 0.070
Allied-Domecq	4.625	− 0.040
Arjo Wiggins	1.815	− 0.005
Assoc Brit Fds	5.055	+ 0.020
BAA PLC	5.600	− 0.035
Barclays	14.040	− 0.010
Bass	8.125	....
BAT Indus	5.335	+ 0.195
BG	2.615	− 0.020
Blue Circle	4.165	+ 0.080
BOC Group	11.080	+ 0.005
Body Shop	1.520	+ 0.005

Source: *The Wall Street Journal*, August 26, 1997. Reprinted by permission of *The Wall Street Journal*, © 1997 Dow Jones & Co., Inc. All Rights Reserved Worldwide.

symbol HMC, and Honda Motor also trades on the Tokyo Stock Exchange (TSE) in yen. Each ADR allows the holder the rights to two common shares.[16] When HMC was trading at $61⅞ on the NYSE, Honda Motor was trading at 3,630 yen on the TSE. The price difference can be explained in the following fashion. On this particular day, the dollar exchange rate for yen was 0.00846 dollar per yen. Because one ADR equals two common shares, the dollar value of two Honda common shares is about $61.42, or $2 \cdot 3{,}630$ yen $\cdot \$0.00846$. Although stock in Honda Motor can be bought in two ways, either on the TSE or on the NYSE, the price is about the same.[17] Finally, some mutual funds specialize in international markets. It is now possible to buy a portfolio of international securities with one phone call. International investing is discussed in more detail in Chapter 11.

2.6 MUTUAL FUNDS

Many investors choose to invest their money in **mutual funds,** which receive money from investors with the common objective of pooling the funds and then investing them in securities. There are many different types of mutual funds, as well as a range of ways to classify them. For example, there are **open-end funds,** which can issue additional shares upon demand and eliminate shares when they are redeemed. Conversely, **closed-end funds** cannot increase or decrease the number of shares easily.[18] Shares of open-end funds are purchased and sold exclusively with the fund. Closed-end funds sell their shares on stock exchanges. Some open-end funds are no load (NL), and some are load. The load is a sales charge paid by an investor who buys a share in a load mutual fund. A fund that does not charge this fee is called a no-load fund.

Exhibit 2-12 provides a sampling of data for mutual funds. (Exhibit 2-13 illustrates how to read such data.) The most important figure in the exhibit is the NAV, which is similar to the price quotation for other assets, such as stocks. "NAV" stands for **net asset value,** which is the current market value of the assets per share (based on the market value of the underlying securities in the mutual fund). Investors will receive the net asset value if they sell an open-end mutual fund share. From time to time, detailed data on mutual funds are published, including data on performance in the last 5 years.

Exhibit 2-14 provides selected data on closed-end funds. In closed-end funds, market supply and demand drives the trading prices. Closed-end funds trade at a premium above, or at a discount below, net asset value, depending on a range of factors

---

16. Information from *The Value Line Investment Survey,* 21 November 1997.

17. Also, there are enough traders watching the relationship between these securities. In their desire to make any possible profit from price differences, these traders, who are known as *arbitrageurs,* insure that the pricing difference will not be too great. By trading large blocks between markets, arbitrageurs influence prices, drawing them closer together.

18. A closed-end fund, with shareholder approval, can undertake a new issue or change the nature of the fund (for example, change it to an open-end fund).

EXHIBIT 2-12
A Sampling of Mutual Fund Data

MUTUAL FUND QUOTATIONS

LIPPER INDEXES

Tuesday, August 19, 1997

Equity Indexes	Prelim. Close	Prev.	Percentage chg. since Wk ago	Dec. 31
Capital Appreciation ...	1812.89	+ 1.46	+ 0.48	+ 16.46
Growth Fund	6000.67	+ 1.53	+ 0.50	+ 22.65
Small Cap Fund	608.98	+ 1.33	+ 0.50	+ 11.46
Growth & Income	5791.65	+ 1.22	− 0.05	+ 21.78
Equity Income Fd	3063.19	+ 0.94	− 0.34	+ 19.93
Science and Tech Fd ...	576.06	+ 2.37	+ 2.59	+ 24.04
International Fund	642.41	+ 0.28	− 1.79	+ 13.67
Gold Fund.................	113.18	− 0.52	− 1.05	− 22.13
Balanced Fund...........	3534.82	+ 0.79	+ 0.19	+ 15.35
Emerging Markets......	106.69	− 0.36	− 3.56	+ 15.44
Bond Indexes				
Corp A-Rated Debt......	717.28	+ 0.01	+ 0.87	+ 5.10
US Government	271.05	− 0.01	+ 0.85	+ 4.64
GNMA	295.13	− 0.02	+ 0.58	+ 5.21
High Current Yield......	733.56	+ 0.07	+ 0.21	+ 8.47
Intmdt Inv Grade.......	197.99	− 0.00	+ 0.76	+ 4.94
Short Inv Grade	183.62	− 0.01	+ 0.32	+ 4.00
General Municipal	520.92	+ 0.08	+ 0.41	+ 5.03
High Yield Municipal ..	252.47	+ 0.09	+ 0.36	+ 5.26
Short Municipal	113.39	+ 0.01	+ 0.10	+ 2.70
Global Income	195.30	− 0.09	+ 0.55	+ 1.16
International Income...	121.54	− 0.21	+ 0.52	− 1.78

Indexes are based on the largest funds within the same investment objective and do not include multiple share classes of similar funds. The Yardsticks table, appearing with Friday's listings, includes all funds with the same objective.
Source: Lipper Analytical Services, Inc. The Lipper Funds Inc. are not affiliated with Lipper Analytical Services.

Ranges for investment companies, with daily price data supplied by the National Association of Securities Dealers and performance and cost calculations by Lipper Analytical Services Inc. The NASD requires a mutual fund to have at least 1,000 shareholders or net assets of $25 million before being listed. Detailed explanatory notes appear elsewhere on this page.

Name	NAV	Net Chg	YTD %ret
AAL Mutual A:			
Bond p	9.86	...	+ 4.9
CGrowth p	25.01	+ 0.40	+ 22.9
HiYBdA	10.30	+ 0.02	NS
Intl p	12.11	+ 0.04	+ 10.5
MidCap p	15.36	+ 0.19	+ 13.1
MuniBd p	11.37	+ 0.02	+ 5.5
SmCap p	12.64	+ 0.19	+ 12.9
Utility p	12.24	+ 0.08	+ 8.8
AAL Mutual B:			
CGrowth p	24.93	+ 0.40	NS
Intl p	12.04	+ 0.03	NS
MidCap	15.30	+ 0.19	NS
SmCap p	12.58	+ 0.18	NS
AARP Invst:			
BalS&B	20.86	+ 0.14	+ 16.0
BdInc	15.15	...	NS
CaGr	56.01	+ 0.95	+ 33.1
DivGr	16.87	+ 0.12	NS
DivInc	15.83	+ 0.04	NS
GiniM	15.11	...	+ 4.6
GlblGr	18.74	+ 0.18	+ 15.0
GthInc	55.64	+ 0.62	+ 24.0
HQ Bd	16.06	...	+ 4.1
IntlSkt	16.68	+ 0.07	NS
SmCoStk	18.38	− 0.11	NS
TxFBd	18.28	+ 0.01	+ 4.7
USStkl	17.63	+ 0.26	NS

EXHIBIT 2-13   Interpreting Mutual Fund Data

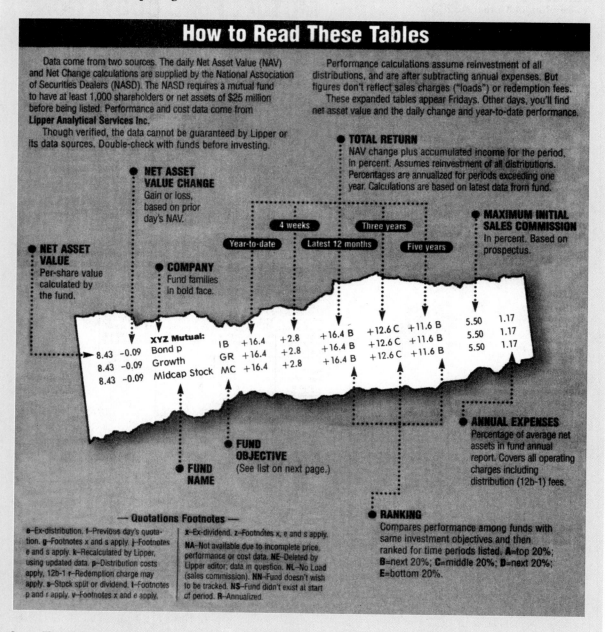

How to Read These Tables

Data come from two sources. The daily Net Asset Value (NAV) and Net Change calculations are supplied by the National Association of Securities Dealers (NASD). The NASD requires a mutual fund to have at least 1,000 shareholders or net assets of $25 million before being listed. Performance and cost data come from **Lipper Analytical Services Inc.**

Though verified, the data cannot be guaranteed by Lipper or its data sources. Double-check with funds before investing.

Performance calculations assume reinvestment of all distributions, and are after subtracting annual expenses. But figures don't reflect sales charges ("loads") or redemption fees.

These expanded tables appear Fridays. Other days, you'll find net asset value and the daily change and year-to-date performance.

● **NET ASSET VALUE CHANGE**
Gain or loss, based on prior day's NAV.

● **TOTAL RETURN**
NAV change plus accumulated income for the period, in percent. Assumes reinvestment of all distributions. Percentages are annualized for periods exceeding one year. Calculations are based on latest data from fund.

● **MAXIMUM INITIAL SALES COMMISSION**
In percent. Based on prospectus.

● **NET ASSET VALUE**
Per-share value calculated by the fund.

● **COMPANY**
Fund families in bold face.

| | | | 4 weeks | | | Three years | | | | |
| | | Year-to-date | | Latest 12 months | | | Five years | | | |

XYZ Mutual:										
8.43	–0.09	Bond p	IB	+16.4	+2.8	+16.4 B	+12.6 C	+11.6 B	5.50	1.17
8.43	–0.09	Growth	GR	+16.4	+2.8	+16.4 B	+12.6 C	+11.6 B	5.50	1.17
8.43	–0.09	Midcap Stock	MC	+16.4	+2.8	+16.4 B	+12.6 C	+11.6 B	5.50	1.17

● **FUND NAME**

● **FUND OBJECTIVE**
(See list on next page.)

● **ANNUAL EXPENSES**
Percentage of average net assets in fund annual report. Covers all operating charges including distribution (12b-1) fees.

● **RANKING**
Compares performance among funds with same investment objectives and then ranked for time periods listed. **A**=top 20%; **B**=next 20%; **C**=middle 20%; **D**=next 20%; **E**=bottom 20%.

— **Quotations Footnotes** —

e–Ex-distribution. **f**–Previous day's quotation. **g**–Footnotes x and s apply. **j**–Footnotes e and s apply. **k**–Recalculated by Lipper, using updated data. **p**–Distribution costs apply, 12b-1 **r**–Redemption charge may apply. **s**–Stock split or dividend. **t**–Footnotes p and r apply. **v**–Footnotes x and e apply.

x–Ex-dividend. **z**–Footnotes x, e and s apply. **NA**–Not available due to incomplete price, performance or cost data. **NE**–Deleted by Lipper editor; data in question. **NL**–No Load (sales commission). **NN**–Fund doesn't wish to be tracked. **NS**–Fund didn't exist at start of period. **R**–Annualized.

Source: *The Wall Street Journal*, 24 October 1997, p.C20. Reprinted by permission of *The Wall Street Journal*, © 1997 Dow Jones & Co., Inc. All Rights Reserved Worldwide.

(including how well the fund is run, the expenses charged, and the particular focus of the fund). Mutual funds are discussed in more detail in Chapter 14.

The graphs in Exhibit 2-14 show that in the third quarter of 1997, the closed-end fund index rose while the Dow Jones Industrial Index fell. As a result, the prices of the shares of closed-end funds rose more sharply than the prices of the assets held; hence, the discount rose from −12% to −8%. However, there are some funds that are traded at a premium; for example, MFS Special Val traded at a 26.8% premium.

EXHIBIT 2-14 Closed-End Mutual Funds

CLOSED-END FUNDS

Closed-end funds sell a limited number of shares and invest in securities. Unlike open-end funds, closed-ends generally do not buy their shares back from investors who wish to sell. Instead, shares trade on a stock exchange. The following list, provided by Lipper Analytical Services, shows the ticker symbol and exchange where each fund trades (A: American; C: Chicago; N: NYSE; O: Nasdaq; T: Toronto; z: does not trade on an exchange). The data also include the fund's most recent net asset value (NAV), as well as its closing share price on its respective exchange on the last day NAV was calculated, and the percentage difference between the market price and NAV (the premium or discount), unless indicated by a footnote otherwise. For equity funds, the final column provides 52-week returns based on market prices plus dividends; for bond funds, the past 12 months' income distributions as a percentage of the current market price. Footnotes: a: the Net Asset Value and the market price are ex dividend. b: the NAV is fully diluted. c: NAV, market price and premium or discount are as of Thursday's close. d: NAV market price and premium or discount are as of Wednesday's close. e: NAV assumes rights offering is fully subscribed. v: NAV is converted at the commercial Rand rate. y: NAV and market price are in Canadian dollars. N/A: Information is not available or is not applicable. ♣Free annual or semi-annual reports are available by phoning 1-800-965-2929 or faxing 1-800-747-9384.

Fund Name (Symbol)	Stock Exch	NAV	Market Price	Prem /Disc	52 week Market Return
Friday, October 03, 1997					
General Equity Funds					
Adams Express (ADX)	♣N	30.01	25 1/8	− 16.3	32.4
Alliance All-Mkt (AMO)	N	34.75	32 5/16	− 7.0	78.6
Avalon Capital (MIST)	O	14.48	13 1/4	− 8.5	20.5
Baker Fentress (BKF)	♣N	25.15	21 5/16	− 15.3	22.4
Bergstrom Cap (BEM)	A	161.31	143 3/4	− 10.9	29.4
Blue Chip Value (BLU)	♣N	10.90	11	+ 0.9	37.8
Central Secs (CET)	A	31.67	33 3/8	+ 5.4	46.7
Corp Renaissance (CREN)-c	O	8.08	5 13/16	− 28.1	− 26.2
Engex (EGX)	A	14.14	10 1/4	− 27.5	− 13.7
Equus II (EQS)	♣A	33.02	25 3/4	− 22.0	65.2
Gabelli Equity (GAB)	N	11.67	11	− 5.7	28.0
General American (GAM)	♣N	31.78	27 13/16	− 12.5	33.1
Librty AllStr Eq (USA)	♣N	14.24	14 1/2	+ 1.8	43.2
Librty AllStr Gr (ASG)	♣N	13.54	13 1/16	− 3.5	51.9
MFS Special Val (MFV)	N	15.82	20 1/16	+ 26.8	26.2
Morgan FunShares (MFUN)-c	O	12.37	10	− 19.2	19.4
Morgan Gr Sm Cap (MGC)	♣N	14.97	14	− 6.5	44.1
NAIC Growth (GRF)-c	C	N/A	N/A	N/A	N/A
Royce Value (RVT)	♣N	18.38	16 15/16	− 7.8	43.1
Royce,5.75 '04Cv-w	N	142.04	128 1/8	− 9.8	31.9
Salomon SBF (SBF)	N	20.99	18 1/2	− 11.9	32.9
Source Capital (SOR)	N	53.49	49 7/8	− 6.8	32.0
Tri-Continental (TY)	♣N	36.32	29 7/8	− 17.7	31.9
Zweig (ZF)	♣N	13 24	13 7/16	+ 1 5	29.6

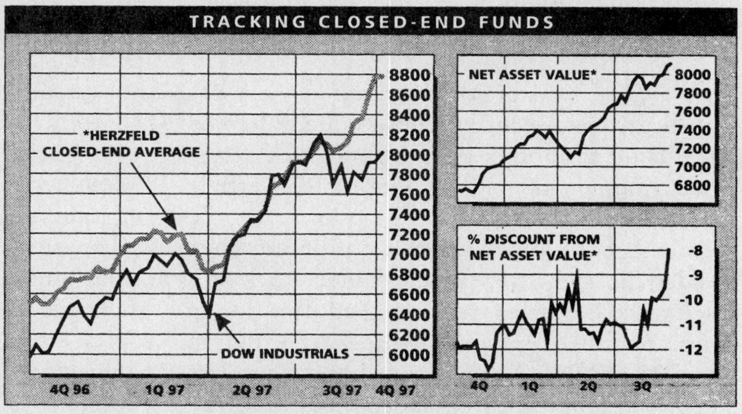

The Herzfeld Closed-End Average measures 16 equally-weighted closed-end funds based in the U.S. that invest principally in American equities. The net asset value is a weighted average of the funds' NAVs. *The net asset value and % discount charts lag the market by one week. Source: Thomas J. Herzfeld Advisors Inc., Miami. 305-271-1900

Source: *Barron's* (October 6, 1997): p. MW76. Reprinted by permission of *Barron's*, © 1997 Dow Jones & Co., Inc. All Rights Reserved Worldwide.

New investment vehicles have recently begun to compete with mutual funds. On January 1998, the American Stock Exchange began trading unit trusts called *Diamonds*. Each of these unit trusts represents a stake in the 30 stocks that make up the Dow Jones Index. In effect, Diamonds turn the Dow into publicly trading stock, thus enabling investors to buy and sell the index at any time during the trading day. Each Diamond is sold for the equivalent of 1% of the value of the index. Thus, if the index is traded for, say, 8,000, the Diamond price is determined as $80. Diamonds complement the Amex's popular *Spiders,* which are unit trusts based on the stocks included in the Standard & Poor's 500 Index. Diamonds and Spiders provide a solid alternative to mutual funds.

SUMMARY

Describe basic characteristics and types of bonds and stocks.   Bonds are instruments that are useful primarily when investors have specific income requirements, whereas stocks are purchased primarily for growth potential. Money market securities are short-term obligations, including Treasury bills, commercial paper, bankers' acceptances, negotiable certificates of deposit, repurchase agreements, federal funds, and Eurodollars. Capital market securities are long-term obligations, including Treasury notes and bonds, federal agency bonds, municipal bonds, corporate bonds, mortgages and mortgage-backed securities, and stocks.

Compare different types of derivative securities.   A derivative security is a security whose value is derived from the value of another asset. Examples of derivative securities include stock options, convertible bonds, futures, and swaps. A call option gives the holder the right to buy, whereas a put option gives the holder the right to sell, a specified stock at a specified price on or before a specified date (for an American option). (Options are discussed further in Chapters 23 and 24.) A convertible bond is just like a regular bond, but with an added feature: if you own a convertible bond, you can convert the bond into a specified number of stocks. A futures contract is a security that obligates the investor to buy or sell a specified amount of an asset at a stated price on a particular date (see also Chapter 22). A swap is similar to a futures contract, except that it is an agreement to exchange specific assets at future points in time. Swaps are discussed further in Chapter 25.

Explain the risks involved in bond and stock investment. There are nine categories of risks related to bonds and stocks: default risk, interest rate risk, inflation rate risk, risk of call, liquidity risk, political and regulatory risk, business risk, market risk, and exchange rate risk. U.S. government bonds do not have default risk or business risk. Common stocks are not callable. Understanding the risks related to investments is an important first step in successful money management.

Describe investment opportunities in international securities and mutual funds.   International securities increase the investor's opportunities. International securities can be purchased directly from an international stock exchange, indirectly through an American Depository Receipt, or indirectly through a mutual fund. Mutual funds receive money from investors with common objectives, pool the funds together, and then invest them in securities. Shares of open-end funds are purchased and sold exclusively with the fund, whereas shares of closed-end funds are traded on stock exchanges.

CHAPTER AT A GLANCE

MAIN TYPES OF SECURITIES | ENTITLE INVESTORS TO THE FOLLOWING

Equity ⟶ Common Stocks — Variable dividends depending on profits
Preferred Stocks — Fixed dividends

Debt ⟶ Government Bonds — Fixed interest, default-free
Corporate Bonds — Fixed interest, default possible
Convertible Bonds — Fixed interest with chance to participate in earnings of firm, default possible

		BUYER'S VIEWPOINT	SELLER'S VIEWPOINT
Derivative Assets	Call Option	Profits if stock goes up	Profits if stock goes down
	Put Option	Profits if stock goes down	Profits if stock goes up
	Futures	Profits if asset goes up	Profits if asset goes down

KEY TERMS

American Depository Receipt (ADR)   54
Asked rate   33
Bankers' acceptance   35
Bid rate   33
Blue chip stock   43
Bond   30
Call option   46
Callable bond   38
Capital gains   42
Capital loss   42
Capital market security   31
Cash dividend   41
Closed-end fund   56
Commercial paper   33
Common stock   41
Conduit   41
Conversion premium   47
Conversion price   47
Conversion ratio   47
Conversion value   47
Convertible bond   46
Corporate bond   39
Coupon-bearing bond   39
Coupon payment   31

Cumulative preferred stock   44
Cyclical stock   43
Date of record   42
Declaration date   42
Defensive stock   43
Diamonds   60
Discount rate   33
Eurodollar   36
Ex-dividend date   42
Face value   31
Federal agency bond   38
Federal funds   36
Fundamental analysis   42
General obligation bond   39
Growth stock   42
Income stock   42
Junk bond   39
Money market security   31
Mortgage   40
Mortgage-backed security   41
Municipal bond   38
Mutual fund   56
Negotiable certificate of deposit   35
Net asset value   56

Notional principal   48
Open-end fund   56
Par value   31
Participating preferred stock   44
Payment date   42
Preference share   44
Price risk   49
Principal   31
Put option   46
Reinvestment rate risk   49
Repurchase agreement   35
Revenue bond   39
Reverse repo   36
Round lot   46
Speculative stock   43
Spiders   60
Stock split   44
Swap   47
Term repo   36
U.S. Treasury bill   33
U.S. Treasury bond   36
U.S. Treasury note   36
Zero-coupon bond   39

REVIEW

2.1 What are the advantages and disadvantages of investing in bonds?

2.2 What are the major identifying characteristics of bonds?

2.3 Explain what is meant by the following statement: "The ownership of the firm is residual in nature."

2.4 Explain the dates that are important in relation to the dividends paid on common stocks.

2.5 What is the P/E ratio, and how is it calculated?

2.6 What is a derivative security?

2.7 Give an example of how futures are used to hedge financial price risk and to speculate on the direction of future prices.

2.8 Why are international securities increasing in importance?

PRACTICE

2.1 Joe-Bob from L.A. decided to invest $950 (price) in a 12% semiannual, 3-year bond. What is the yield to maturity (internal rate of return, or IRR) if the par value is $1,000?

2.2 A bond is sold for $700 and matures in 5 years. It pays $20 at the end of each year. The par value is $1,000. Calculate the yield to maturity (IRR) on the bond using a calculator or software.

2.3 A junk bond is trading for $800 and matures exactly 1 year from now at $1,000. There is no interest paid between now and maturity.
a. Calculate the yield to maturity on the bond.
b. How do you explain your results, knowing that the interest rate on government bonds is only 5% a year?

2.4 The bid and asked yields on zero-coupon bonds with a $1,000 par value are 6.2% and 6%, respectively. The maturity is 5 years. What are the implied bid and asked prices of these two bonds? (Assume annual interest compounding.)

2.5 You have two different bonds, both of which were just issued for 10-year maturities: (1) a zero-coupon bond with a par value of $1,000 and (2) a bond that pays $50 interest at the end of each year with a par value of $1,000. Both of these bonds have the same 10% annual yield to maturity.
a. Calculate the market price of these two bonds, and explain your results.

b. Suppose that immediately after the issue of the bonds, the interest rate goes up to 12%. Which bond will suffer larger losses? Why?

2.6 The P/E ratio of a stock is 10. The price is $100 per share. What is the implied earnings per share?

2.7 The net asset value of a mutual fund is $12. The share price is $13.
a. Is it an open-end fund or a closed-end fund?
b. Calculate the premium or discount.

2.8 The dividend yield on IBM stock is 2%. The yield to maturity on IBM bonds is 8%. Does this mean that you will be better off buying the bonds than buying the stock?

2.9 A municipal bond and a corporate bond offer you the same yield of 8%. Both have the same risk of default.
a. Which bond would you prefer if you were a tax-exempt investor?
b. Which bond would you prefer if you pay 31% tax on interest received? Explain.

2.10 Suppose you buy a stock for $100. You receive $4 as a cash dividend at the end of the year. The stock price at the end of the year is $95.
a. What is the rate of return on your investment?
b. What is the dividend yield as measured at the beginning of the year? At the end of the year?

c. What is your total dollar return on this investment?

2.11 Suppose you buy a stock on January 1 for $100 and consider selling it on December 20. The stock price is $150. Your income tax rate is 31%. Is it worthwhile for you to wait a few days before selling? How many days should you wait, assuming the stock price will remain at $150? What will be your gain from waiting?

2.12 You have the following data regarding two firms (all numbers are in millions):

Year	Firm A Earnings	Firm A Dividends	Firm B Earnings	Firm B Dividends
1	$1	$0	$100	$50
2	1.2	0	101	50
3	1.5	0	98	50
4	1.7	0	100	55

Which firm would be classified as a growth firm, and which would not? Calculate the annual growth rate of earnings and dividends of each of these two firms.

2.13 The prices of the stock of Alamo Rent-A-Car and the S&P 500 index are as follows:

Year	1	2	3	4
Alamo	$100	$114	$110	$112
S&P	300	280	240	260

Is Alamo's stock a defensive stock? Why?

2.14 Suppose a bond is sold for $1,000 and pays an annual interest rate of 10% on the par value, which is also $1,000. The bond was issued 20 years ago and will mature in one week. You own some of these bonds. The yield on these bonds suddenly goes way up, to 15%. Calculate your loss. Explain your results.

2.15 Suppose government bonds yield 6%, and junk bonds for the same maturity yield 24%. Now suppose you are told that the average yield on these two bonds is the same. Calculate the implied proba-

bility of default on the junk bonds. Assume that in case of default, you lose the whole investment.

2.16 Suppose you buy a bond that matures in 1 year, pays no interest, and has a par value of $1,000. You buy the bond for $950. The inflation rate was 10% for this year. What did you earn on this bond? Explain.

2.17 You hold a bond that matures in 20 years. The yield to maturity is 10%, and the coupon rate is 10%. The market, as well as the face value of the bond, is $1,000. Suppose the yield to maturity drops to 5% after you buy the bond. Determine your immediate gain under the following conditions:
a. If the bond is not callable.
b. If the bond is callable at $1,100 and the firm does call the bond whenever the price is above $1,100.

2.18 Suppose that as an American investor, you buy 1-year, zero-coupon German government bonds that yield 12% in German marks. You hold this investment for 1 year and find that the rate of return in U.S. dollars is only 8%. Calculate the change in the exchange rate between the U.S. dollar and the German mark.

2.19 Suppose you hold a convertible bond whose par value is $1,000, and the market value is $1,500. You are allowed to convert the bond for 50 shares of stock. The stock price is $35 per share. You need cash very badly now. Would you convert the bonds or sell the bonds in the market? Show your cash flow for each option.

2.20 Suppose a bond has a par value of $1,000 and a market value of $1,100. It is convertible into 40 shares of stock, and the current stock price is $26.
a. What is the conversion ratio?
b. What is the conversion price?
c. What is the conversion value?

2.21 Suppose you buy a mutual fund for $10,000 and have to pay a 4% load. The mutual fund made 10% on its investment for each of the following 2 years. Calculate your rate of return if you hold the fund for 1 year and, alternatively, if you hold the fund for 2 years. Do your results explain why buyers of mutual funds generally have a long investment horizon?

2.22 An ADR of Honda Motor is traded on the NYSE for $22. The exchange rate is 100 yen per dollar. Suppose that Honda Motor is trading in Japan for 2,500 yen. How can you use this information to make a profit? Explain.

2.23 Suppose you are considering purchasing one of the following two bonds. Ignoring taxes and transactions costs, and assuming that the risk of each bond is identical, which bond should you select, and why?

	Bond A	Bond B
Face value	$1,000	$1,000
Coupon rate	10%	12%
Time to maturity	5 years	5 years
Interest paid	Semiannually	Semiannually
Current price	$1,000	$929.76

2.24 Assume that Bond B in Question 2.23 was selling for $1,000 versus $929.76. How would your answer to the question change?

2.25 Suppose that there are two closed-end mutual funds, A and B. Both trade at $8, where the net asset value per share is $10. Fund A is a terminated fund. (A terminated fund is a fund with a termination date, the date at which the assets are liquidated and distributed to the shareholders. See also Chapter 14.) Its termination date is in 1 year from now. Fund B is not a terminated fund.
a. Calculate the premium or discount corresponding to these two funds.
b. Suppose that the net asset value of both funds will increase to $12 one year from now. Calculate the rate of return to the investor in Fund A for this year. Can you calculate the rate of return corresponding to Fund B under these circumstances?

CFA PROBLEMS

2.1 Robert Devlin and Neil Parish are portfolio managers at the Broward Investment Group. At their regular Monday strategy meeting, the topic of adding international bonds to one of their portfolios came up. The portfolio, an ERISA-qualified pension account for a U.S. client, was currently 90% invested in U.S. Treasury bonds and 10% invested in 10-year Canadian government bonds.[19]

Devlin suggested buying a position in 10-year German government bonds, whereas Parish argued for a position in 10-year Australian government bonds.
a. Briefly discuss the three major issues that Devlin and Parish should address in their analysis of the return prospects for German and Australian bonds relative to those of U.S. bonds.

Having made no changes to the original portfolio, Devlin and Parish hold a subsequent strategy meeting and decide to add positions in the government bonds of Japan, the United Kingdom, France, Germany, and Australia.
b. Identify and discuss two reasons for adding a broader mix of international bonds to the pension portfolio.

2.2 Fundamental to investing is controlling investment risk while maximizing total investment return. Identify four primary sources of risk faced by investors, and explain the possible impact on investment returns.

For Internet questions visit the Levy Investment Web site at http://levy-invst.swcollege.com.

---

19.   ERISA denotes the Employees' Retirement Income Securities Act of 1974, which regulates the management of retirement accounts.

YOUR TURN: APPLYING THEORY TO PRACTICE
THE COMPOUNDED RATE OF RETURN ON PREFERRED CONVERTIBLE BONDS: A BANK PLAY WITH YIELD

Despite the runup by bank stocks, Michael Zuk, a Kansas City, Mo.–based regional banking analyst for Fahnestock & Co., thinks several of the bank convertible preferred issues are still attractively priced for both yield and capital appreciation.

One of Zuk's favorites is the $1.75 convertible preferred of Wichita-based, $5.5 billion (assets) Fourth Financial Corp. The company operates Bank IV Kansas, the largest bank in the state, and is expanding into Oklahoma and Missouri. For the first quarter of 1993, Fourth Financial's return on equity was 18.9%, return on assets was 1.7%, and the ratio of equity to assets was 8.9%. Zuk estimates that Fourth Financial will earn at least $2.5 a share this year, versus $2.17 in 1992.

Fourth Financial's 22.4 million common shares, which trade over-the-counter, have risen 79% since early 1991, to a recent 28¼. It sold 4 million shares of convertible preferred to the public in February 1992 at $25 apiece. Each is convertible into 0.862 shares of common. The preferred can be called in March 1997 at $25.

The recent O-T-C price of the preferred stock was 29, for a 21% conversion premium. Yield: 6%. Zuk's target price for the common, come 1997, is 40. This would put a value of 34½ on the preferred at that time. So the preferred offers the prospect of nearly 20% capital appreciation over the period. This works out to a compounded total annual return through March 1997 of 10.1%.

Source: "Streetwalker," Thomas Jaffee, ed. *Forbes,* 5 July 1993, p. 144. Reprinted by Permission of *Forbes* Magazine © Forbes Inc., 1993.

Note: The preferred-convertible stocks pay $1.75 dividend a year. The preferred stocks can be converted into common stocks, exactly like convertible bonds. If not converted by March 1997, the firm can call back the preferred stock at $25 apiece. Note that the article was written on July 5, 1993, and the return was calculated up to March 1997. To simplify the calculation, assume that exactly 4 years are left before the possible call of the preferred stocks.

Questions
1. Suppose the price of the common stock falls below $25, the firm calls the stocks in March 1997, and you did not convert the preferred stock into common stock. Calculate the internal rate of return (IRR) on the preferred stock. Assume that the $1.75 dividends are paid at the end of each year.

2. Explain how, in your view, the value of $34½ on the preferred stocks is obtained. How is the 20% capital appreciation calculated?

3. Calculate the IRR of the investment if conversion takes place at $40 a share. Explain the relationship of the IRR and the 10.1% compounded annual rate of return on the preferred stocks mentioned in the article.

4. What is the IRR on the investment if you buy common stocks rather than preferred stocks? Assume that a $2.5 dividend per share is paid annually at the end of each year and that the shares reach the target price of $40. Compare your answer to the IRR obtained in Question 3. In light of your results, why don't all investors buy the stocks with the higher IRR?

5. The bank also has a bond that matures in 1997 and pays 8% interest per year. What are the pros and cons of investing in the bond versus investing in the preferred stock? Explain.

SELECTED REFERENCES

Fabozzi, Frank J., and D. Fabozzi. *Bond Market Analysis and Strategies.* Englewood Cliffs, N.J.: Prentice-Hall, 1989.

Fabozzi, Frank J., and Irving M. Pollack, eds. *Handbook of Fixed Income Securities.* Homewood, Ill.: Dow Jones–Irwin, 1987.

Kelly, Jonathan M., Luis F. Martin, and John H. Carlson, "The Relationship Between Bonds and Stocks in Emerging Markets." *Journal of Portfolio Management,* Spring 1998, pp. 110–122.

Kihn, John, "To Load or Not to Load? A Study of the Marketing and Distribution Changes of Mutual Funds." *Financial Analysts Journal,* May/June 1996, pp. 28–37.

Lederman, Jess, and Keith Park, eds. *Global Bond Markets.* Chicago: Probus, 1991.

Lederman, Jess, and Keith Park, eds. *Global Equity Markets.* Chicago: Probus, 1991.

Stigum, Marcia. *The Money Market.* 3d ed. Homewood, Ill.: Dow Jones–Irwin, 1989.

SUPPLEMENTAL REFERENCES

Baumol, William, Steven Goldfeld, Lilli Gordon, and Michael Koehn. *The Economics of Mutual Funds Markets.* Boston: Kluwer, 1989.

Cook, Timothy Q., and Timothy D. Rowe, eds. *Instruments of the Money Market.* Richmond, Va.: Federal Reserve Bank of Richmond, 1986.

Mutual Fund Fact Book. Washington, D.C.: The Investment Company Institute. Various issues.

Solnik, Bruno. *International Investments.* 2d ed. Reading, Mass.: Addison-Wesley, 1991.

Appendix 2A: Taxes

In July 1997 a new tax law was almost completed after long discussion in Congress. The main item in the new law is a reduction in capital gains tax from 28% to 20%. If an asset is held for less than 18 months, the ordinary income tax rates apply. If an asset is held for 5 years before it is sold, the capital gains tax is reduced, according to the new law, to only 18%.

Taxes are an important consideration in the investment process, because they affect an investor's net income. Investments differ in how they determine an investor's tax bill. For example, selling a stock that has greatly appreciated in price and buying a different stock will result in an investor's having to pay tax on the stock that has appreciated. No taxes would have to be paid yet, if the investor did not sell the stock.

Unfortunately, taxes are very complicated. Tax rules change often and typically the tax rates are determined more by political negotiation than by economic forces. This appendix briefly reviews some of the major tax consequences of investing in bonds and stocks.

Although there are many different taxes, the most significant tax is the federal income tax. State and local income taxes take a smaller percentage of an investor's return.

The tax rate applied to investment profits depends on whether the profits are classified as ordinary income (or loss) or capital gain (or loss). Most profits related to interest or cash dividend payments are considered ordinary income. If you own 1,000 shares of CWE, Inc., which paid $3 per share in cash dividends, then you have $3,000, or $3 · 1,000, in ordinary income. Most profits or losses related to price changes are considered capital gains or losses. If you purchased 100 shares of ABM at $30 and subsequently sold it at $35, you have a capital gain of $500 [($35 − $30) · 100], or $5 per share (ignoring commissions).

Capital gains and losses are further divided into short-term and long-term gains and losses. If a security is held for less than or equal to 18 months (according to the new 1997 law), the proceeds are classified as a short-term capital gain or loss. If a security is held for more than 18 months, it is classified as a long-term capital gain or loss. Before the new 1997 law was employed, net long-term gains were taxed at a maximum rate of 28%. If your ordinary income tax rate was lower than 28%, net long-term capital gains were taxed at the ordinary income tax rate. Short-term capital gains are taxed at the ordinary income tax rate. With the new 1997 tax law, the 28% rate was reduced to 20% (or 18% if the investment is held for 5 years or more).

Commissions paid to brokers for making security transactions are deducted only after a security is sold. Commissions paid to buy a stock, for example, are considered as increasing the purchase price of the security. If 200 shares purchased at $30 resulted in a $60 commission, then the price, including commission (known as the *basis*), is

$$\text{Basis} = \frac{(\$30 \cdot 200) + \$60}{200} = \$30.30 \text{ per share}$$

If an investor sells 100 shares for $33 (with a $30 commission) after four weeks, the investor's short-term capital gain is

$$(\$33 \cdot 100) - \$30 - (\$30.30 \cdot 100) = \$240$$

Exhibit 2A-1 lists the marginal tax rates—the amount of tax imposed on an additional dollar of income—for the four different categories of taxpayers, as well as the corporate tax rates. The tax rates are progressive, because they increase with a taxpayer's income. Hence, tax planning increases in importance as income increases. Exhibit 2A-2 lists the maximum capital gains for various holding periods. The investor can use these various rates to help decide what the holding period should be.

BONDS

In general, bond coupon payments are considered ordinary income for tax purposes. When a bond is sold before maturity, the bond price changes are treated as capital gains and losses. However, not all bonds are taxable. The most important consideration is whether the bond's coupon payments are subject to federal income

EXHIBIT 2A-1
Individual and Corporate
Tax Rates

Part a: Tax Rates for Individual Investors in 1997

Single—Schedule X

If line 5 is:		The tax is:	of the amount over—
Over—	But not over—		
$0	$24,650	....................15%	$0
24,650	59,750	$3,697.50 + 28%	24,650
59,750	124,650	13,525.50 + 31%	59,750
124,650	271,050	33,644.50 + 36%	124,650
271,050	....	86,348.50 + 39.6%	271,050

Married filing jointly or Qualifying widow(er)—Schedule Y-1

If line 5 is:		The tax is:	of the amount over—
Over—	But not over—		
$0	$41,200	....................15%	$0
41,200	99,600	$6,180.00 + 28%	41,200
99,600	151,750	22,532.00 + 31%	99,600
151,750	271,050	38,698.50 + 36%	151,750
271,050	....	81,646.50 + 39.6%	271,050

Head of household—Schedule Z

If line 5 is:		The tax is:	of the amount over—
Over—	But not over—		
$0	$33,050	....................15%	$0
33,050	85,350	$4,957.50 + 28%	33,050
85,350	138,200	19,601.50 + 31%	85,350
138,200	271,050	35,985.00 + 36%	138,200
271,050	....	83,811.00 + 39.6%	271,050

Married filing separately—Schedule Y-2

If line 5 is:		The tax is:	of the amount over—
Over—	But not over—		
$0	$20,600	....................15%	$0
20,600	49,800	$3,090.00 + 28%	20,600
49,800	75,875	11,266.00 + 31%	49,800
75,875	135,525	19,349.25 + 36%	75,875
135,525	....	40,823.25 + 39.6%	135,525

EXHIBIT 2A-1
(continued)

Part b: U.S. Corporate Tax Rate Schedule for 1997

Tax Rate	Taxable Income
15%	$0–$50,000
25%	$50,001–$75,000
34%	$75,001–$100,000
39%[a]	$100,001–$335,000
34%	$335,001–$10,000,000
35%	$10,000,001–$15,000,000
38%[b]	$15,000,001–$18,333,333
35%	Over $18,333,333

[a]Includes additional 5% recapture tax under 1986 law.

[b]Includes additional 3% recapture tax under 1993 law.

Source: Internal Revenue Service

EXHIBIT 2A-2
Capital Gains Tax Summary

Holding Period of Asset or Stock	Maximum Capital Gains Tax as of 1997	Maximum Capital Gains Tax Prior to 1997
If held between 0 and 12 months:	39.6%	39.6%
If held between 12 and 18 months:	28	28
If held between 18 and 60 months:	20	28
If held more than 60 months but acquired after 2000:	18	28

Note: The 20% rate applies to assets sold between 5/6/97 and 7/29/97 and held between 12 and 18 months. Investors should confirm the applicable tax rates relevant to their situation with the Internal Revenue Service Tax Code.

taxes. Municipal bonds are exempt from federal income tax. Because of this exemption, municipal bonds typically trade at higher prices (lower yields) than comparable corporate bonds. (See Chapter 17.) Investors in the highest tax bracket may find municipal bonds attractive on an after-tax basis.

Numerous other minor issues should be examined. For example, municipal bonds are typically also exempt from state or local income taxes in the locality where they are issued. Municipal bonds issued by, say, the state of Alabama are exempt from Alabama income tax. Also, investment in some bonds issued at a deep discount (for example, zero-coupon bonds) requires that income tax be paid on the interest accrued each year, even though the interest is not paid until the bond matures. The worst of both worlds can occur with such bonds. An investor might buy a 20-year zero-coupon bond, pay taxes each year on the implied interest (even though the investor receives no interest), and then have the bond default in the last year.

STOCKS

The cash dividends received from stocks are considered ordinary income. However, stock splits are not considered ordinary income. When a stock splits (say, two shares for each one share owned), the cost basis is adjusted.

For example, if you purchase 100 shares of Microsoft for $90 per share and pay a $50 brokerage commission, your cost basis is

$$\text{Basis} = (\$90 \cdot 100) + \$50 = \$9,050$$

or $90.50 ($9,050/100) per share. If Microsoft splits 2-for-1, you receive two new shares for every one old share. The new basis per share is $45.25 ($9,050/200), and you own 200 shares. If 100 shares are sold after nine months at $50 per share (with a commission of $30), you will have a short-term capital gain of

$$\text{Capital Gain} = (100 \cdot \$50) - \$30 - (100 \cdot \$45.25)$$

$$= \$5,000 - \$30 - \$4,525$$

$$= \$445$$

Like dividends on common stocks, preferred stock dividends are not tax deductible for the company (whereas interest payments are tax deductible).[20] However, 70% of the dividend on preferred stocks is tax exempt to most corporate owners. Thus, companies that purchase preferred shares do not have to pay taxes on 70% of the preferred dividends, although individuals must pay the full income tax rate. Therefore, corporations have an incentive to hold preferred stock, and preferred stock is most suitable for corporate clients.

This appendix has described only the major tax consequences of investment in bonds and stocks. For more information, see Ray Sommerfeld's *Essentials of Taxation* (Reading, Mass.: Addison-Wesley, 1989).

---

20. A financial innovation called the monthly income preferred security, or MIPS, was introduced on the market in the mid 1990s. The firm issuing the MIPS can deduct the preferred dividends for tax purposes (see *Barron's*, February 27, 1995).

CHAPTER 3

SECURITY MARKETS

LEARNING OBJECTIVES

After studying this chapter you should be able to:

1. Describe the function of security markets.

2. Contrast the primary and secondary markets.

3. Summarize the operation of the secondary market.

4. Describe the basic structure of security markets.

5. Survey world security markets.

INVESTMENTS IN THE NEWS

INVESTING IN THE FUTURE

In 1990, the New York Stock Exchange initiated after-hour trading with the idea of building a round-the-clock operation by the year 2000. Recently, it fully automated trading, leaving the traditional manual methods—and paper-strewn floor—far behind. Now, technology, specifically the Internet, is further changing the way we invest in financial securities. Indeed, computers have influenced every aspect of our home and work lives—from new "smart homes" (like the one Bill Gates of Microsoft Corporation built), which have sensors that turn on lights, music, and digital artwork, to the way we buy and sell stocks. Several investment firms, such as Fidelity Investments®, and Charles Schwab & Co. Inc., as well as small brokerage companies, such as E-Trade Group, Inc., and Ameritrade, currently provide online stock trading. Some of the advantages of the Internet cited by investors are the ability to access information directly at any time and from several locations rather than waiting to contact a broker during regular business hours, the immediacy of that information (which is delivered in real time), and the low cost of transactions. As the chart shows, Internet investing, at a mere 2.96 million in 1997, is projected to reach 14.38 million accounts by the year 2002. What will help propel this growth? Well, in addition to the use of PCs, the industry is working on additional technology, such as WebTV and "Smart phones," to win over skeptics.

Source: Condensed from "Investing in the Future," *Fidelity Focus: The Magazine for Fidelity's Investors,* Winter 1997, pp. 8–13. Reprinted with permission.

Internet Investing Takes Off

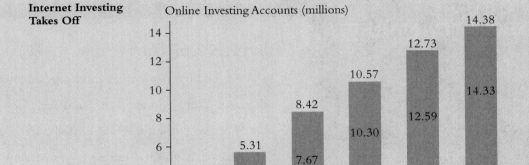

Online Investing Accounts (millions)

Dial-up or Online Service
Internet

Source: Forrester Research, Inc. Reprinted with permission.

This chapter is a study of security markets—the markets where investors buy and sell the financial assets described in Chapter 2. This task is not as simple as it might seem, because security markets have changed dramatically as technology has improved and Internet investing is increasing. In a sense, learning about security markets is like aiming at a moving target.

As this chapter's Investments in the News illustrates, Internet investing is taking off. In many ways the Internet is ideal technology for investment tasks. It's *dynamic:* an investor can get stock quotes that are ahead of those on the "crawler" ticker at the bottom of the television screen and daily NAVs before they are printed in the next morning's paper. The Internet is *inexpensive:* brokerages often offer lower trade commissions online, because it's cheaper for them to accept trades that way. It's *automated:* normal office hours do not apply, which is crucial in an era when everyone leads hectic lives. It's *searchable:* you can find a wealth of free, sophisticated information that was once available only to wealthy individuals, investment analysts, and larger corporations.

Regardless of the changes in security markets, these markets are designed to allow firms to raise funds for growth and capital investment. They are the arenas in which investors—both individual investors and institutional investors—execute their buying and selling decisions. It is this function of security markets that we study in this chapter.

Our investigation of markets begins with Section 3.1, a discussion of the reasons markets exist and the benefits they offer to society. Sections 3.2 and 3.3 explain the institutional structure of security markets. They describe the primary market, where securities are first sold, and the secondary market, where securities are subsequently traded. Another way to think about security markets is in a theoretical sense—that is, how they should be constructed to facilitate trading. Section 3.4 takes this approach as it describes and compares different methods of trading. Yet another way of studying security markets is to observe how they actually function. In Section 3.5, world security markets are discussed. Finally, security markets can be viewed in terms of historical development. By studying how markets developed in the past, we can learn how markets will evolve in the future. The legal history of security markets is described in Chapter 4.

3.1 THE ROLE OF SECURITY MARKETS

A **market** is the means by which products and services are bought and sold, directly or through an agent. A market need not be a physical location. Indeed, it can be a computer network or a telecommunications system, as described in Investments in the News. In a security market, you do not have to possess the security you wish to sell; you can sell a security that you do not own but that you can borrow.

A security market that functions effectively provides society with two benefits. First, it allocates scarce resources—in this case, investors' funds—to those firms that will make the best economic use of them. That is, a well-functioning security market helps suppliers of funds find those who demand funds and will make the best use of them. For example, consider two firms that both need several hundred million dollars for investment. Firm A can make 20% on this investment, whereas Firm B can make only 15% (assume the risk is similar). Suppose there is a limited supply of funds. If the market is efficient and all information is available to potential investors, these investors will be more inclined to buy Stock A than Stock B. Therefore, more money will be allocated to the more profitable firm. Second, a well-functioning security market will reduce the cost of moving in and out of securities, which in turn enlarges the set of investors willing to supply funds; hence, firms will have more funds to invest in production.

A well-functioning security market also benefits buyers and sellers in three ways: by making information available, by establishing prices, and by increasing the liquidity of the assets being bought or sold.

INFORMATION AVAILABILITY

Buyers and sellers must be able to communicate with each other and have access to timely and accurate information in a well-functioning security market. Notice that neither criterion requires the buyer and seller (or their representatives) to meet at a physical location.

PRICE SETTING

In a well-functioning security market, prices should reflect all the available information. That is, the market price should not misrepresent known information. Price setting has its costs, and for a market to function well, these costs should be minimal. We call these costs of price setting **execution costs,** and they include *transaction costs, market impact effects*, and *inaccurate price discovery.*

Transaction costs include the costs related to communication systems, the costs related to the party who is willing to buy or sell the securities, and any other fees or expenses. When transaction costs are low, more investors are willing to participate in the market.

Market impact effects are price changes that result from buying or selling pressure. For example, a stock may be quoted at $100, but if it has to fall to $90 for an investor to be able to sell 10,000 shares, this market impact effect represents a major cost to the investor.

Inaccurate price discovery refers to securities trading at prices that do not reflect true value. Clearly, buying a stock that is 10% overpriced will be costly. In a well-functioning security market, prices adjust quickly to new information, and securities are correctly priced. If there is a lag between the time when information is available and a price change, price discovery will be inaccurate during this period.

LIQUIDITY

The liquidity of a security market is the ease with which securities can be purchased or sold without a dramatic impact on their prices. When markets are liquid, transactions are completed quickly. For example, the market for U.S. Treasury bills is more liquid than the market for real estate, because $10 million in U.S. Treasury bills can be traded in seconds at their fair market price, whereas trading real estate may take months. The market for stocks and bonds of big companies is more liquid than the market for securities of smaller firms. When markets are liquid, market participants execute trades at existing prices. This certainty of quoted prices is called **price continuity.** If prices are fairly certain and only small changes occur when a trade takes place, we say we have price continuity.

We can measure the liquidity of different security markets by looking at the depth, breadth, and resiliency of transactions that occur in each market. If a sufficient number of orders exist at prices above and below the price at which shares are currently trading, the transaction has **depth.**[1] Otherwise the market is **shallow.** If a large volume of orders exists at prices above and below the current price, the transaction has **breadth.** Otherwise, it is called a *thin market.* If new orders come into the market rapidly when prices change due to an imbalance of orders, the transaction has **resiliency.**[2]

Exhibit 3–1 illustrates this concept when the current price is assumed to be $99⅛. The exhibit shows hypothetical stock orders at various bid prices as they ap-

---

1. These orders are known as *limit orders* and are covered in Section 3.4.
2. For more information, see Robert A. Schwartz, *Equity Markets: Structure, Trading, and Performance* (New York: Harper & Row, 1988).

pear in the Market Maker limit order book. (The concepts of bid price and limit order will be explained later in the chapter.) Column A demonstrates a thin and shallow market; Column B, a thin and deep market; Column C, a broad and shallow market; and Column D, a broad and deep market. If the market for a given stock is broad and deep, as well as resilient, it is considered to be a relatively liquid market. A transaction can be made in such a market quickly, with no significant price change.

3.2   THE PRIMARY SECURITY MARKET

Securities are traded on two basic markets: the primary market and the secondary market. The **primary market** is the mechanism through which a firm can raise additional capital by selling stocks, bonds, and other securities. All securities are first traded in the primary market, and the proceeds from the sale of securities go to the issuing firm. The issuers of new securities include both corporate and government entities. The **secondary market** is where previously issued securities trade among investors. Note that the issuing firm does not receive any funds when its securities are traded in the secondary market. However, the secondary market provides liquidity for the newly issued securities in the primary market. Investors are much more willing to buy securities in the primary market when they know there will be a market in which to trade them in the future. The existence of a well-functioning secondary market thus makes buying securities in the primary market more appealing.

Historically, new issues have been a profitable investment over the short run. To attract willing investors, new issues have been underpriced; that is, they have been sold at a small discount from their fair market value. Thus, the appeal of buying securities in the primary market over the secondary market is the potential for making above-average returns.

EXHIBIT 3-1 Hypothetical Stock Orders	Alternative Hypothetical Orders			
Bid Price	A	B	C	D
$100	400	400	1,000	1,000
99⅛	500	500	1,000	1,000
99¾	0	600	0	1,200
99⅝	0	650	0	1,400
99½	0	700	0	1,500
99⅛	0	700	0	1,600
99	0	700	0	1,700
Market condition:	Thin and shallow	Thin and deep	Broad and shallow	Broad and deep

Securities traded in the primary market for the very first time are referred to as **initial public offerings (IPOs).** A company can have only one IPO. If a company has sold stock previously, a new stock offering is called a **primary offering** or a **seasoned new issue.** After the initial trading, the securities move to the secondary market. To issue securities in the primary market, a firm must provide a **prospectus,** a legal document containing the business plan and other information that will help investors make prudent investment decisions.

3.2.1 Investment Bankers and Underwriting

Security issues in the primary market are usually handled by **investment bankers,** who assist firms needing funds by locating individuals and firms wanting to invest funds. Investment bankers act as **underwriters** of a new issue—intermediaries between the buyers and sellers of a new issue, who may also guarantee that the new issue is successful.

Underwriters perform different services to firms. Of course, the more services they provide, the larger the underwriting fee. Underwriters may do the following:

1. *Give advice.* Underwriters provide advice as to the type and terms of security to offer and the timing of the issue.
2. *Provide a firm commitment.* In this arrangement the underwriter buys the issue at a predetermined price from the issuing corporation with the expectation of reselling shares of the issue at a higher price.
3. *Make a best effort.* In this arrangement the underwriter markets the new issue as best it can and takes no price risk. The underwriter does not take ownership of the securities.
4. *Issue a standby commitment.* In this arrangement the underwriter buys the remainder of an issue that could not be sold above a specified price. The price that the underwriter must pay is substantially less than the market price; hence, the standby commitment is less risky than the firm commitment (see below).

The largest underwriters are listed in Exhibit 3-2. In terms of equity capital, Morgan Stanley/Dean Witter are the largest; however, Goldman Sachs earned the highest profit in 1996.

Underwriters generate revenues from the firm commitment arrangement, through the difference between the firm commitment price (P_{FC}) and the price received when issued (P_I). The difference between these two prices is referred to as the **gross spread (GS)** or the **underwriter's discount.** Thus,

Gross Spread = Price Received by the Issue − Firm Commitment Price

or

$$GS = P_I - P_{FC} \tag{3.1}$$

To illustrate how an investment banker profits from a firm commitment, consider the following example. In 1993, Morgan Stanley helped issue 100,000,

| EXHIBIT 3-2 | In Billions | | |
How They Stack Up: Profits at Some of Wall Street's Biggest Securities Firms	Firm	1996 Profit	Equity Capital
	Goldman	$2.60[a]	$ 5.40
	Morgan Stanley, Dean Witter	1.96[b]	12.20
	Merrill Lynch	1.62	7.30
	Salomon	0.62	5.90
	Bear Stearns	0.58[c]	3.28
	Lehman	0.42	4.10
	PaineWebber	0.36	1.84

[a]Goldman profits are stated before taxes and payments to partners

[b]Morgan Stanley, Dean Witter's profits have been restated to reflect this year's merger

[c]Annualized net income for the 12 months ended Dec. 31, 1996

Source: *Wall Street Journal*, August 5, 1997, p. C1. Reprinted by permission of *The Wall Street Journal*, © 1997 Dow Jones & Co., Inc. All Rights Reserved Worldwide.

$1,000 par Gulf Stages Inc., 20-year bonds. The firm commitment price was 98.5% of par (P_{FC} = 985), and the issuing price turned out to be 100.50% of par (P_I = $1,005.00$). The gross spread per bond was GS = $1,005 - $985 = $20, or $2,000,000, for the issue (or $20 · 100,000).

The gross spread, given as a percentage of the total proceeds to the firm, varies with the type of issue and its size. For IPOs of bonds it is about 14% for small issues (less than $1 million), and it drops to about 1% for large issues ($50 million or more). For preferred stocks, the range (for the corresponding issue size) is 1.5% to 17%. The range is 3.5% to 22% for common stocks. If the issue has already traded in the market, the gross spread is much smaller: for stocks, about 15% for an issue of less than $1 million and about 4% for large issues of more than $50 million. For stock right issues, the fees are much smaller: about 8% for small issues and 4% for large issues. (A stock right issue is an issue of a common stock to existing shareholders, who hold rights at a discount from the price at which this stock will later be offered to the public.) The reason the spread is smaller for right issues is that rights are offered to the public at a price much lower than the current market price; hence, the underwriter's risk is relatively small. If the stocks are sold as best efforts, the underwriter does not take any risk, and the fee is about one-third (or much less, for large issues) of the gross fee. Usually, even a relatively small fee covers the administrative costs of handling the issue and makes a profit for the investment bank.

The main risk faced by underwriters with firm commitments is the possibility of enormous losses between the time the underwriter makes a firm commitment and the time the underwriter sells the securities to the public. If the underwriter is wrong in the anticipated issue price, it could prove costly.

The risks of an IPO are demonstrated by the experience of Orbital Science Corporation, a space technologies firm. Orbital Science Corporation specializes in launching satellites into orbit from underneath the wing of a large plane. The firm and underwriter originally scheduled an IPO of stock to occur a month before the first rocket launch. Then an article appeared in the *Wall Street Journal* describing how this first launch could make or break the company. Obviously, there was a risk that the launch would fail and the stock's value would diminish. To reduce the price risk, Orbital Science and the underwriter delayed the issue until the outcome of the launch was known. On April 5, 1990, at 12:10 Pacific Daylight Time, Orbital Science successfully launched its first rocket. On April 24, 1990, Orbital Science sold about 2.4 million shares of stock at $14 per share during its initial public offering.[3] Clearly, an unsuccessful launch would have greatly influenced the issuing price.

Suppose an IPO of stock was believed to be worth $300 million, and the PaineWebber Group (PW) took it as an underwriter with a firm commitment. Suppose PW was unable to sell it to the public at its anticipated price because of some crisis, and the stock value fell 73%. PaineWebber's loss would be enormous, at $219 million (73% · $300). Now suppose PW, with $1.84 billion in total consolidated capital (see Exhibit 3-2), decided to underwrite this $300 million common stock issue with an anticipated gross spread of 3%. Thus, PW anticipates revenues from the deal of $9 million ($300 million · 3%). Comparing the size of the issue ($300 million) with PW's equity ($1.84 billion) shows that PW is exposing a substantial portion of its capital in one issue.

To reduce this risk exposure, underwriters form **syndicates** (purchase groups), groups of investment bankers that agree to participate in the risk related to the sale of an IPO. Participation includes accepting part of the risk, as well as part of the potential revenues. The syndicate also forms a selling group that includes the investment bankers in the syndicate, as well as others whose sole focus is distribution of the shares in the IPO. The selling group typically does not take any risk. Exhibit 3-3 shows an announcement of an IPO. The syndicate (purchase group) is NationsBanc Montgomery Securities, Inc. (the lead investment banker); BancAmerica Robertson Stephens; and Wessels, Arnold & Henderson, L.L.C. The remaining firms listed make up the selling group. Such an announcement is called a *tombstone*.

The investment banking industry also underwrites issues that are not IPOs, namely, stocks of firms that have outstanding shares. In this case, the market price is known. Generally, when additional shares are issued, the price of identical shares outstanding is temporarily depressed, and the underwriter must take this into account. The firm is trying to sell a large number of shares at one time, and there may not be willing buyers. Price pressure from the new supply of shares can result in a significant stock price reduction. For example, on April 27, 1992, General Motors announced its plans to issue $2.9 billion in new stock. The stock price sank $2.7 per share, to $39.625 (a decline of more than 6%).

---

3. Based on several articles appearing in *Wall Street Journal,* February 13, March 23, March 26, April 6, and April 25, 1990.

EXHIBIT 3-3
Announcement of an IPO

This advertisement is neither an offer to sell nor a solicitation of an offer to buy these securities.
The offer is made only by the Prospectus.

NEW ISSUE
November 4, 1997

3,335,000 Shares

CONCORD
The Total View

Common Stock
Price $14 Per Share

Copies of the Prospectus may be obtained in any State only from such of
the undersigned as may lawfully offer these securities in such State.

NATIONSBANC MONTGOMERY SECURITIES, INC.

BANCAMERICA ROBERTSON STEPHENS

WESSELS, ARNOLD & HENDERSON, L.L.C.

BEAR, STEARNS & CO. INC.	BT ALEX. BROWN	COWEN & COMPANY
CREDIT SUISSE FIRST BOSTON		HAMBRECHT & QUIST
MORGAN STANLEY DEAN WITTER	PRUDENTIAL SECURITIES INCORPORATED	
ADAMS, HARKNESS & HILL, INC.		INCORPORATED CRUTTENDEN ROTH
FIRST ALBANY CORPORATION	HAMPSHIRE SECURITIES CORPORATION	
SOUNDVIEW FINANCIAL GROUP, INC.		INCORPORATED TUCKER ANTHONY
VOLPE BROWN WHELAN & COMPANY	H.C. WAINWRIGHT & CO., INC.	

Source: *Wall Street Journal*, November 4, 1997, p. C2.

In response to this type of problem, in 1982 the Securities and Exchange Commission (SEC) allowed for *"shelf registration"* under Rule 415 for certain types of securities. This rule allows large firms to register security issues and sell the issues in pieces during the 2 years following the initial registration (possibly on short notice). Thus, firms can reduce the losses due to price pressure by issuing the shares when the market is strong.

PRACTICE BOX

Problem	Suppose Kidder Peabody was the underwriter of a 3 million common stock issue under a firm commitment. The IPO was issued at $10 per share, and the firm commitment was for $9.875 per share. What was Kidder Peabody's gross spread? What is the gross spread as a percentage of the firm's proceeds?
Solution	The gross spread is the difference between the issue price and firm commitment price, or $10 − $9.875 = $0.125 per share, or ($0.125 · 3 million) = $375,000. The firm's proceeds are $9.875 · 3 million = $29.625 million. Hence, the percentage gross spread is $375,000/$29,625,000 = 0.01266, or 1.266%.

3.2.2 IPOs versus Private Placement

An alternative way to raise capital in the primary market is through a private placement. A **private placement** is an offering of a security directly to one investor or group of investors. For example, on January 21, 1998, the Macerich Company (MAC) raised $100 million from a private placement with Security Capital Group Incorporated (SCZ). A private placement bypasses the public marketplace and is therefore generally less costly than IPOs.

Initial public offerings in the United States require prior review by the SEC, as well as compliance with a large number of costly regulations.[4] Section 4(2) of the Securities Act of 1933 exempts "nonpublic" or private offerings. Regulation D adopted by the SEC in 1982 gave specific guidelines for what is exempt under Section 4(2) of the 1933 act. These guidelines require no general advertising for private issues. However, the sale must be to "sophisticated" investors who can evaluate the risk and return and who have substantial economic resources.[5]

Why do firms sometimes select private placements rather than public issues? In the United States, private placements do not require a prospectus. However, a **private placement memorandum,** which provides information regarding the new issue, is required. A private placement memorandum is less exhaustive than a prospectus. Prior to April 1990, private placements could not be resold for 2 years. This restriction greatly hampered the private placement market by effectively eliminating any liquidity. In April 1990, however, the SEC adopted Rule 144A, which allows

---

4. Chapter 4 discusses in detail the major regulations related to investments.
5. For more details, see Frank J. Fabozzi and Franco Modigliani, *Capital Markets Institutions and Instruments* (Englewood Cliffs, N.J.: Prentice-Hall, 1992).

"large" institutions to trade private placements with other "large" institutions without having to wait 2 years or register the placement with the SEC.

Exhibit 3-4 is an advertisement by the Teachers Insurance and Annuity Association (TIAA) soliciting more private placements. Firms may solicit private placements, but issuers cannot advertise them. As the advertisement indicates, TIAA is a money management firm that manages a multibillion-dollar portfolio for college professors' retirement. The ad shows that TIAA would like to lend money; it has made many private placements and would like to make other private placements.

3.2.3 Underpricing IPOs and Price Discovery

Most IPOs have no preexisting market price. Thus, the underwriter has to evaluate and estimate the "fair" price for the stock. Pricing IPOs is very complicated and requires tools that are covered in the remainder of this book. Setting aside the issue of

EXHIBIT 3-4
TIAA's Advertisement for Private Placements

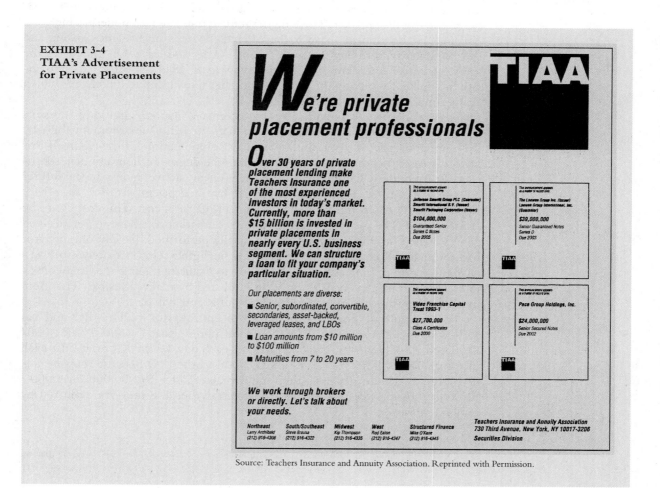

Source: Teachers Insurance and Annuity Association. Reprinted with Permission.

determining the appropriate value of a security, let us examine why underwriters tend to underprice IPOs relative to their "fair" value.

Underwriters face a dilemma in pricing IPOs. If they overprice the issue, then the investors who buy the IPOs will lose both money and trust in the investment bankers. If they underprice the issue, then the issuing firm will lose both capital and trust in the investment bankers. On average, underwriters historically have underpriced IPOs.[6] The ethical issues related to pricing IPOs are discussed in Chapter 4 (see Section 4.4).

Several explanations are often given for IPO underpricing:

1. *Information asymmetry.* Differences in the information available to the firm, investment banker, and potential investors is known as **information asymmetry.** For example, the firm and the investment banker may have better information than investors. If this is the case, the investors who are less informed will have greater uncertainty about the issue and therefore will not buy it unless they are offered a lower price. Higher potential returns must be offered to attract investors to participate in the IPO market. These higher returns translate into underpricing.

2. *Scalping.* Higher returns have to be offered, because investment bankers and their affiliates tend to buy the really "good" issues and leave the "scraps" to the investing public. This skimming of quality issues is called **scalping.** To compensate the public for buying the "scraps," a higher return should be offered, which again implies underpricing.

3. *Liquidity.* One benefit provided by the secondary market is liquidity. Investors will not buy IPOs that subsequently are hard to sell. One argument for why IPOs are underpriced is that underpricing is compensation for the relatively low liquidity. Also, there is uncertainty regarding the degree of liquidity that a security subsequently will command. Will there be any active trading in the future? This lack of liquidity is paid for by the firm by underpricing its IPO.

4. *Appraisal costs.* Assessing the fair value of an IPO has a cost. This cost has to be compensated. The prospectus must be studied, market data have to be collected and evaluated, and industry analysis is usually performed. If only one investor had to incur this cost, perhaps it would be negligible. Unfortunately, stock exchanges require a wide ownership of shares to facilitate trading and limit corporate control. Thus, every IPO must be evaluated by many investors. The more investors there are, the higher the total appraisal cost will be.

   For example, if one investor buys the entire $100 million IPO and has $1,000 appraisal costs, the IPO should be underpriced by 0.001% ($1,000/$100,000,000). However, if 1,000 investors each buy $100,000 of the IPO, each investor's cost will be 1% ($1,000/$100,000), so the IPO likewise must be underpriced by 1%. In this case, the total appraisal cost is $1,000,000, or 1,000 · $1,000. Thus, private placements are less costly because they are evaluated by only one investor.

6. See Clifford W. Smith, "Investment Banking and the Capital Acquisition Process," *Journal of Financial Economics* 15 (January–February 1986): 3–29.

3.3 THE SECONDARY SECURITY MARKET

In the secondary market, previously issued securities are traded between investors. The proceeds of selling a security go to the current owner of the security, not to the original issuing company. The secondary market provides liquidity to individuals who acquire securities in the primary market. The secondary market consists of major stock exchanges and over-the-counter markets. Major stock exchanges are the New York Stock Exchange (NYSE), the American Stock Exchange (AMEX), and the Tokyo Stock Exchange (TSE). Over-the-counter markets are the National Association of Securities Dealers' Automated Quotations system (NASDAQ), interbank markets, and major commodity and derivative exchanges. The Chicago Board of Trade (CBOT) and the Chicago Mercantile Exchange (CME) are exchanges where commodity and derivative securities such as stock options are traded.

The New York Stock Exchange is the oldest (established in 1792) and the largest stock exchange in the United States. It is also called the Big Board or simply The Exchange. The NYSE is a corporation governed by a board of directors composed of twenty individuals representing the public and the exchange membership. The board is elected by the members of the exchange. The total number of voting members is fixed at 1,366 "seats," which are owned by individuals, usually officers of security firms. When members die or retire, the seats are usually auctioned off to bidders approved for membership by the NYSE. The price of the seats varies from as low as $35,000 in 1977 to more than $1 million in 1987. In November 1997, the *Wall Street Journal* reported that a seat on the NYSE sold for $1,575,000; the bid price was $1.3 million with the offer price of $2 million.[7] In comparison, a seat on the AMEX sold for $400,000 on November 6, 1997—considerably lower than a seat on the NYSE.[8] The higher the potential income of the member because of the ownership of a seat, the higher the price of the seat.

More than 1,600 corporations are listed on the NYSE. The stocks, bonds, options, rights, and warrants of these corporations are traded in about four hundred *trading posts* located on the *floor*. Every one of these corporations is assigned to one of these posts.

A large range of trading activity is conducted in the secondary market. Transactions in this market are categorized as follows.

First market transactions are trades of securities that are actually made on the floor of the exchange on which the security is listed. For example, AT&T is a stock that is traded on the NYSE. When AT&T is traded on the NYSE, it is said to be traded in the first market.

Second market transactions are over-the-counter (OTC) trades that are made on the over-the-counter market. The **over-the-counter market** is a telephone- and computer-linked network for trading securities. Securities listed on the OTC

---

7. See "Big Board Seat Is Sold," *Wall Street Journal,* November 17, 1997, p. A12.
8. See "AMEX STATS" at http://www.AMEX.com. Note that this price was down $20,000 from a prior seat sale on October 27, 1997, for $420,000.

market are not listed on an exchange. For example, Microsoft stock is traded over the counter and is listed on the NASDAQ system, not on an exchange. (The OTC market will be discussed in more detail later in the chapter.)

Third market transactions are trades in *exchange-listed* issues that take place off the exchange floor with the aid of brokers. An example would be an AT&T trade that is conducted through an OTC market. (Recall that AT&T is listed on the NYSE.)

Fourth market transactions are trades in exchange-listed issues that are arranged by the buyers and sellers, off the exchange floor, without the aid of brokers. An example would be trading AT&T with your uncle.[9]

Upstairs market transactions are trades that are arranged from a network of trading desks that negotiate large block transactions.

Securities can be listed on more than one exchange. This is known as **dual listing.** Dual listing enhances the level of competition and is thought to lower the cost of trading.[10] Dual listing in international markets, as well as on the East and West Coasts in the United States, expands the hours when trading can occur. There are various regulations restricting dual listings. For example, securities listed on the NYSE cannot also be listed on the AMEX.

The NYSE is the most important U.S. exchange, and it celebrated its 200th birthday in 1992. As Connecting Theory to Practice 3.1 explains, the composition of trading on the NYSE has changed over the past 30 years. Specifically, ownership of shares by households and nonprofit organizations has fallen from 91.3% in 1950 to 47.7% in the third quarter of 1996.[11] The remaining shares are owned primarily by institutional investors, including mutual funds. As will be discussed later, the NYSE has responded to this changing composition and is catering more to institutional investors (although not neglecting the needs of individual investors).

The brokers mentioned in Connecting Theory to Practice 3.1 who were left out in the cold did not give up. They continued trading stocks of smaller companies that the NYSE members had no interest in trading. It is interesting to note that at the turn of the century, 85% of the business "on the curb" (outside the NYSE) was executing orders transmitted to it by the NYSE.[12] The curb market moved indoors in 1921 to 86 Trinity Place, the present-day location of the AMEX. Today, the AMEX also trades many new, innovative derivative securities.[13]

In order for stocks to trade on exchanges, minimum requirements have to be met. Exhibit 3-5 presents the minimum listing requirements for the NYSE, AMEX, and NASDAQ.

---

9. The back of a stock certificate, like a title to an automobile, contains the appropriate forms for transferring ownership. The stock certificate is then mailed to the corporate registrar, who will issue a new certificate.

10. Some argue that dual listing actually increases the cost of trading, because multiple dealers all have to cover the same fixed expenses with lower volume.

11. See "Mutual Funds: Navigating the Future," *Fortune,* November 24, 1997, p. S4.

12. See Stuart Bruchey, *Modernization of the American Stock Exchange 1971–1989* (New York: Garland Publishing, 1991), p. 16.

13. These innovations include warrants on foreign stock indexes (Nikkei, CAC 40 [Index of Common Stocks on the Paris Bourse], and the *Financial Times* [United Kingdom]), commodity trust units, and foreign currency warrants.

CONNECTING THEORY TO PRACTICE 3.1

THE BIG BOARD'S BICENTENNIAL: 200 YEARS LATER, SMALL INVESTORS FIND CLOUT AT AMERICA'S PREMIER EXCHANGE

New York—In the spring of 1837, brokers at the New York Stock & Exchange Board noticed a small hole in the brick wall of their building.

They discovered it had been bored by a broker who wasn't a member and was speculating in stocks on a street curb outside the exchange. The broker, like countless investors before and since, wanted desperately to know what was going on inside. The exchange, just as determined to keep out the broker and his ilk, filled the hole and continued trading behind closed doors.

Even as the Big Board defends itself against increased competition from regional, over-the-counter and foreign markets, it is celebrating the first time that insiders formalized their control of New York's fledgling stock market. In May 1792, stocks were auctioned alongside bonds and lottery tickets whenever wealthy investors needed some cash. A few auctioneers attempted to dominate stock trading, prompting 24 brokers to band together in defense of their businesses.

They signed the Buttonwood Agreement, named after a buttonwood tree on Wall Street under which securities traders met. The pact obligated them to "give preference" to one another in stock trading and collect a minimum fixed commission on stock sales. Buttonwood's effect became clear when winter came. The 24 brokers moved their business to a cozy back room of Wall Street's Tontine Coffee House, leaving other auctioneers and brokers shivering in the cold.

Charles Merrill, meanwhile, pioneered selling stock to "retail," or individual investors—the brokerage business's term for the ultimate outsiders. . . . In 1965, individual households controlled a whopping 84.1% of the U.S. stock market.

But the 1970s and 1980s were marked by the rise of a new group of Wall Street insiders—big pension funds, insurance companies, money managers and foreign investors who were diversifying beyond bonds by pouring cash into U.S. stocks. Institutional stock ownership soared from 20% of the market in 1970 to 46.5% last year, or $2.03 trillion of stocks. Meanwhile, individual households' share of the stock market has shrunk to a record-low 53.5% (though more Americans own stocks than do the citizens of any other country).

(continued)

MAKING THE CONNECTION

From its very inception, the NYSE has focused on maintaining an effective market for stock trading. The Buttonwood Agreement resulted in the communication of better information between buyers and sellers. With this concentration of information, traders are better able to set prices, resulting in a fair and orderly market. Finally, because the majority of stock trading occurs at one place, traders are able to provide better liquidity. Hence, for over 200 years the NYSE has provided a well-functioning securities market by focusing on three key elements: information availability, price setting, and liquidity.

The NYSE and the AMEX are national exchanges; they trade securities that command a national, and sometimes international, investor following. There are other stock exchanges in the United States besides the NYSE and the AMEX that cater to securities that have only regional interest. The trading volume on these exchanges is much lower. Regional stock exchanges include the Midwest Stock Exchange, the Pacific Stock Exchange, the Boston Stock Exchange, and the Philadelphia Stock Exchange.

An alternative to trading on a stock exchange is the OTC market. The OTC market is traditionally for securities of smaller companies. However, there are exceptions, such as Intel and Microsoft, which are large firms whose stocks trade on the OTC market. The decision of where to list a security is primarily made by the company issuing stock to the public.

Stock trades on the OTC market in several ways. First, the OTC trades are generally less active issues that are usually traded in regional brokerage offices. For example, a small Alabama firm's stock may trade only within the Southeast. This firm could opt for a regional stock exchange. Second, the OTC market trades less active issues that have trading activity nationally. For these issues, quotations are reported daily on "pink sheets" that are mailed nationally to brokers by the National Quotations Bureau. Third, the OTC market trades issues that are listed on the NASDAQ. The NASDAQ lists over 5,540 domestic and foreign companies. In 1996, share volume was 138.1 billion shares, with a dollar volume of $3.3 trillion, surpassing the other

EXHIBIT 3-5 Listing Requirements for the NYSE, AMEX, and NASDAQ	Characteristic	NYSE	AMEX	NASDAQ
	Minimum shares publicly held	1.1 million	0.3 million	0.3 million
	Minimum number of shareholders	2,000	800	300
	Minimum pretax income last year	$2.5 million	$0.75 million	—
	Minimum market capitalization	$18 million	$3 million	$1 million

Source: *NYSE Fact Book*, 1996; Web site at http://www.directipo.com, January 24, 1998.

markets.[14] Finally, the OTC market's most actively traded issues are listed on the NASDAQ's more sophisticated system called the National Market System (NMS).

An interesting event occurring at the precise time this book was being revised is the possible merger between NASDAQ and AMEX. If approved by the membership of both exchanges, as well as the SEC, the make-up of the financial markets will change. Among the benefits cited are better quality trades and lower costs. In April 1998 the merger was approved by both NASDAQ and AMEX boards of directors.

The secondary market must be sensitive to investor needs. Providing a secondary market is a competitive business, with the market share's going to those exchanges that best serve the investors at the lowest cost. An exchange is constantly trying to attract firms that will allow it to trade their shares. Exchanges have distinguished themselves in many different ways. For example, the NYSE and the AMEX cater to larger firms, whereas the OTC market primarily caters to smaller firms. The NYSE and other exchanges are moving quickly toward twenty-four-hour trading to increase trading activity and respond to investor demand. Some markets already offer investors the opportunity to trade twenty-four hours a day. The idea that twenty-four-hour trading will increase trading activity has been validated in many circumstances. For example, U.S. dollar index futures contracts experienced a 35% increase in trading during the first month of twenty-four-hour trading.[15]

3.4 TRADING MECHANICS

The actual mechanisms in a financial market to facilitate trading are known as the **market microstructure,** or the institutional setup of a securities market. This section identifies some typical setups and discusses some underlying principles of market design. It reviews some of the goals of trading systems, various participants in securities markets, and the establishment of market prices. Also included is an overview of automated trading systems and various issues important to investors when they are trying to execute a trade.

3.4.1. Securities Trading Systems

The trading of securities is conducted by members of the exchange or by an official of the exchange. However, trades are not conducted in the same manner in all stock exchanges around the world (or even in the United States). The three main trading systems are the call market, continuous market, and mixed market.

In the **call market,** trading and prices are determined at a specified time during the day by a designated person collecting all of the buy and sell orders and then determining the equilibrium price (that is, the price where supply and demand are equal). For example, suppose that by 2:00 PM the total accumulated buy orders by all investors in Sabra stock is as follows:

14. See the NASDAQ Web site at http://www.NASDAQ.com.
15. Based on a letter dated March 31, 1992, by Peter Burton, director of Financial Instruments Exchange (FINEX), a division of the New York Cotton Exchange.

Buy 60 shares at $13 per share or less.
Buy 70 shares at $12 per share or less.
Buy 80 shares at $11 per share or less.
Buy 100 shares at $10 per share or less.

Note that the higher price is associated with a smaller number of shares demanded. Similarly, the following might be the aggregate supply of orders:

Sell 10 shares at $11 per share or more.
Sell 40 shares at $12 per share or more
Sell 70 shares at $13 per share or more.
Sell 150 shares at $14 per share or more.

Note that the higher the price, the more shares that are made available to sell. From the aggregate supply and demand information, we see that the equilibrium price is $13 per share and 60 shares traded. Those investors wanting to sell securities at a higher price than $13 will be unable to find a buyer, and those wishing to buy securities at a price less than $13 will be unable to find a seller. Also note that in our example a total of 70 shares were offered for sale at a price of $13; however, only 60 investors were willing to purchase the stock at this price, leaving 10 sell orders not executed. In practice, demand is always equal to supply at a given price. The designated person must then change the price—say, to $12½—in order to create new demand and supply functions until equilibrium is reached. When trade in one security is finished, trade in the second security takes place, and so on until all securities are traded. All unfulfilled orders can be resubmitted the following day or the next time the security is traded. Call market trading usually occurs once a day, but in some countries it can occur two to three times a day.

Call market trading is common in Hong Kong, Israel (with some stocks), Austria, and Norway. In most large exchanges (for example, in the United States, Canada, and the United Kingdom), where the volume of trading and the number of listed securities is large, the **continuous market** system of trading is employed. As the name indicates, trades in each security occur at any time the stock exchange is open. If there are a seller and a buyer of IBM shares at an agreed price, for example, at 10:00 AM, the transaction is conducted in a matter of minutes. Five minutes later, another transaction in the same stock may be executed at a different price. For example, on some of the business television news networks in the United States, you can view the NYSE and NASDAQ transactions occurring throughout the day by watching the information scrolling across the television screen. This information includes, for example, the ticker symbol of the stock, volume traded, last price, and change in price from the previous price.

In some countries (for example, Switzerland and France), a **mixed market** exists. In this system, a group of stocks is traded continuously for, say, a half hour, and then another group of stocks is traded continuously for a half hour, and so forth throughout the day.

Connecting Theory to Practice 3.2 summarizes the impact of automation on the regulated exchanges around the world. Several of the exchanges have adopted automated systems modeled after the NASDAQ (developed in 1971). Others (for example, German exchanges) combine a number of different trading structures.

Automation has played an important part in changing the regulated exchanges around the world. A summary of some of the largest exchanges follows:

Exchange Site	Exchange Characteristics
United States	Largest single marketplace is the NYSE, which is principally a floor-based system; OTC market introduced an automated system in 1971 (NASDAQ), which is an interdealer quotation system; real-time trade reporting was established in 1982; National Market System (NMS) legislation was enacted in 1975.
Japan	Among the eight stock exchanges, 80% of the trading volume occurs on the Tokyo Stock Exchange (TSE), which is principally a floor-based system; equities may trade through the JASDAQ, which was modeled after NASDAQ; bulk of bond trading occurs on the OTC market.
Europe	Quote-driven dealer market; screen-based trading system (modeled after NASDAQ) allows dealers to disseminate price quotes; in September 1995, Tradepoint, a new trading system, went into effect in the United Kingdom, London Stock Exchange (LSE), and permits investors and broker-dealers to trade directly and anonymously with one another.
Paris	Continuous order-driven screen-based trading system replaced the periodic call auctions with open outcry in 1986; a new exchange was established in Paris in 1996 for young, innovative, high-risk companies to trade; similar markets have opened in Germany, Belgium, and the Netherlands.
Germany	Combines three different trading structures: (1) floor trading (still used in eight regional exchanges, Frankfurt being the most important); (2) electronic trading system; and (3) off-exchange telephone market; an interesting feature is that many companies are listed on several exchanges, and prices often vary across exchanges.

Source: *Financial Market Trends,* no. 65, November 1996, p. 21.

3.4.2 Goals of Trading Systems

Markets facilitate trading, and investors will trade on the market that provides the best service at the most competitive price. When a new market is being developed, several questions need to be addressed by the market designers:[16]

1. *Should all information be made public?* For example, how can information known only to insiders, such as corporate executives, be used? Exchanges do not permit insider trading, because it is illegal.

---

16. Based on Joel Hasbrouck, "Security Markets, Information and Liquidity," *Financial Practice and Education* 1(Fall–Winter 1991): 7–16.

2. *If all information is not made public, then should at least the trading record be public infor-*
    mation? For example, should you be able to know who is doing the trading? On
    the NYSE, investors may trade without revealing who they are. Thus, the
    NYSE has decided that it is in the best interest of investors to be able to trade in
    secret. Although corporate executives must report their trading activities to the
    appropriate regulatory agencies, they do not have to reveal their trading activi-
    ties until *after* the trade has been executed.

3. *Are traders able to buy and sell without greatly influencing market prices?* For example,
    the NYSE has an appointed person whose job description requires that "on
    those occasional instances when there is a temporary shortage of either buyers
    or sellers, [he or she] will buy or sell for their own accounts, against the trend of
    the market."[17]

4. *Are prices allowed to gyrate wildly, or are there constraints on how much prices can move?*
    Are there daily price limits? The NYSE has adopted a circuit breaker system in
    response to the stock market crash of 1987. By Rule 80B, when the Dow Jones
    Industrial Average (DJIA) falls by 350 points from the previous day's close, trad-
    ing is stopped for ½ hour. If the DJIA continues to fall to 550 points below the
    previous day's close, trading is stopped for 1 hour.[18] The idea is that these trading
    halts will give potential buyers an opportunity to assess the market and be will-
    ing to place orders to buy.

5. *Will the market attract a large number of traders who will provide the necessary liquidity?*

6. *Will this market require an individual to specialize in providing liquidity for a particular*
    security? For example, the NYSE has such a person, whereas the OTC market
    does not.

Several of these issues are conflicting. For example, how can there be an infor-
mationally efficient market (Question 1) and, at the same time, a market that dis-
allows large price swings (Question 4)? This is impossible, because information can
arrive in a dramatic fashion. Consider the possible effect on a market of the news of
an earthquake, major accident, or political event.

3.4.3 Participants in Securities Markets

All participants in security markets are referred to generically as *traders*. The most
important traders are the **market makers,** or the individuals determining the bid
and asked price quotes. The **bid price** is the price at which the public can sell securities and the market maker must buy securities. The **asked price** is the price at
which the public can buy securities and the market maker must sell securities.
Clearly, for the market maker to make a living, the bid price must be less than the
asked price. That is, the market maker must be buying at the bid price for less than
what he or she is selling at the asked price.

The members of the exchange are involved in transactions in the listed securities. They have various functions and, hence, various sources of income. The main

---

17. *NYSE Fact Book for the Year 1996* (New York: New York Stock Exchange, Inc. 1996), pp. 22–23.
18. *Ibid.*, p. 21.

players on the floor of most exchanges, such as the NYSE, include commission brokers, dealers, floor brokers, registered competitive traders, and specialists. Some exchange members buy or sell for their own account. Some function as **brokers** (also now called *registered representatives*). Generally, brokers are persons who act as intermediaries between a buyer and a seller, a service for which they charge a commission. Brokers must register with the exchange where the stocks are traded (hence, the name *registered representative*).

COMMISSION BROKERS

Commission brokers buy and sell securities for clients of brokerage houses. They are connected to the brokerage houses (for example, Merrill Lynch) by either telephones or computer terminals, and they receive requests to buy or sell securities, execute the trade, and then send back a confirmation message to the brokerage firm. For this service, they charge a commission fee. Of course, commission brokers also trade for their own accounts and thus also act as dealers (discussed next).

DEALERS

Dealers maintain their own inventory of securities and buy and sell securities from this inventory; thus, dealers are market makers. In this capacity, they do not serve as an intermediary but rather take the risk of holding the securities in their own account. Because most brokerage firms operate both as commission brokers and as dealers, the term *broker-dealer* is often used. Dealers earn their incomes from selling securities they own at a higher price than they paid for them.

FLOOR BROKERS

Floor brokers are individuals on the floor of the NYSE who handle the overflow orders from other exchange members. They are sometimes referred to as freelance brokers. For example, floor brokers, for a fee, will work with commission brokers who get too busy to handle all their clients' orders on time. Floor brokers help insure that orders are handled in a timely fashion.

REGISTERED COMPETITIVE TRADERS

Registered competitive traders own seats on the exchange and buy and sell for their own accounts. Like dealers, they earn their incomes solely by profiting from their buy and sell decisions.

SPECIALISTS

The **specialist** is a unique feature of the NYSE. Specialists are members of the NYSE who are charged with the responsibility of maintaining a fair and orderly market for one or more securities. They are called **registered equity market makers** on the AMEX. Specialists buy and sell (or even short sell) securities for their own accounts to counteract any temporary imbalance in supply and demand for the stock. In this way, they work to prevent large fluctuations in the price of the stock in which they trade. Specialists are prohibited from buying or selling securities for their own accounts if there are any outstanding orders that have not been executed for the same security at the same price in the *specialist's book*. The specialist's book is essentially a log of limit orders (discussed later in this section) that have been received by the specialist; the log records orders in each price category in the sequence in which they are received by the specialist.

The specialist has an important role in making the market a continuous market. To illustrate, suppose that the highest limit order to buy IBM stock is $100, whereas the lowest limit order to sell is $102. As market buy and sell orders come to the floor, the market price of IBM stock fluctuates from $100 to $102. The specialist is expected, and has agreed, to reduce this relatively large fluctuation by stepping in and buying and selling IBM stock for his or her own account at bid and ask prices between these two prices such that the range would be only between ¼ and ½. In this way, the specialist provides continuity.

Specialists earn income in two ways. First, as brokers, they receive commission fees for executing orders. Second, as dealers, they receive income by selling securities held in their own inventory at prices greater than the original purchase price.

3.4.4 Establishing Market Prices

The difference between the asked price and the bid price—what determines the market maker's income—is known as the **bid-asked spread.** For example, Microsoft stock may be quoted at 83 bid and 83⅛ asked. Thus, the bid-asked spread is ⅛ of a dollar, or $0.125 per share.

The bid-asked spread set by the market maker is determined by several factors:

1. Fixed operating costs (such as leasing an office and computer terminals) and anticipated volume of activity.
2. Nonfinancing variable cost per transaction (labor and supplies).
3. Cost of financing the inventory of securities.
4. Risk of price depreciation if inventory is held and risk of price appreciation if sales have exceeded inventory.[19]
5. Likelihood of trading with those who have superior information (insiders). Because the first three factors are relatively stable, many investors monitor the size of the bid-asked spread for clues regarding how the market maker views the volatility of a stock. Larger bid-asked spreads signal larger uncertainty.

3.4.5 Automated Trading

All traders will probably rely more heavily on technology in the years ahead. As technological advances continue at top speed, the potential for computerized trading has become a reality (see this chapter's Investments in the News). The changes have sparked an intense debate on the efficiency of floor traders versus traders who

---

19. See the discussion of short selling later in this section. The market maker is short if the sales have exceeded the inventory.

use computerized machines. To determine what is most efficient, we need to determine the primary tasks that exchanges seek to accomplish.

The primary task of an exchange is determining the current price that will support the quantity of trading desired. That is, whatever trading framework is adopted, one must be able to identify efficiently the current price and the quantity with which trading can occur at that price.

One innovation used to carry out this task using automated trading is a strategy known as **program trading,** which is the simultaneous purchase or sale of at least fifteen different stocks with a total value of $1 million or more. The computer program constantly monitors the stock, futures, and option markets. It gives a buy or sell signal when opportunities for arbitrage profits (sure profits with no risk) occur, or when market conditions warrant portfolio accumulation or liquidation. Program trading was blamed for the large decline in the stock market that occurred on Black Monday (October 19, 1987), because when the market was down, the computer program triggered a sale order that enhanced the price fall. Nevertheless, program trading has increased in volume, reaching about 16% of the total volume on the New York Stock Exchange in 1997. Connecting Theory to Practice 3.3 illustrates the blind bid, which has become popular in program trading. In blind bidding, massive baskets of various stocks are bid on without the traders' actually knowing what stocks they will get. The blind bid reduces the risk of the many fund managers and increases the role of the broker in sharing the risk.

Program trading does not necessarily have to be transacted via computer. The idea of trading "baskets" of securities has been around for a long time; however, it wasn't until the advent of computerized trading that it became very efficient. The volume of program trading is enormous. For example, program trading on the NYSE averaged 16.8% of the average daily trading volume for November 10–14, 1997.[20]

The GLOBEX trading system, which was developed by a joint venture between the Chicago Mercantile Exchange and Reuters (a British information distribution company), promises to be the security exchange of the future. GLOBEX is a global OTC market where many different types of securities trade. Reuters has more than 200,000 terminals in more than 120 countries. Hence, GLOBEX has a phenomenal degree of direct access to trading.

CONNECTING THEORY TO PRACTICE 3.3

BLIND BIDS BECOME POPULAR IN BIG TRADES

How's this for risky?

Wall Street program traders are routinely committing up to $1 billion of their firm's capital to buy huge baskets of various stocks from big fund managers on a few hours' notice.

(continued)

---

20. See "NYSE Program Trading Averages 16.8 Percent of Volume," at http://www.f2.yahoo.com/finance/971120/NYSE_program_trading_1.html.

But here's the kicker: The traders don't even know what stocks they're getting.

These so-called blind bids to either buy or sell massive portfolios have surged in popularity as many fund managers, under pressure to keep pace with market indexes, seek ways to maximize their profit on trades. Because funds trade such big chunks of stocks, they can run the risk of pushing up prices when they buy and sending them lower when they sell. The blind-bid transactions allow managers to get a uniform price for their stocks, eliminating at least some market risk.

Blind-bid transactions have helped propel program trading to 16% of total volume on the New York Stock Exchange this year, up from 10% in 1989. Programs recently accounted for more than 25% of one week's volume, a record for a week that didn't include expirations of stock options. And they've relegated old-fashioned index arbitrage program trading—designed to capture fleeting price discrepancies between stocks and stock-index futures—to just a quarter of total program trading.

"We see customer transactions in the billions, not millions," says David Baker.

Mr. Baker estimates the cost to a fund manager of a typical blind-bid program has fallen 50% to between three cents and nine cents a share in the last 18 months. Where five years ago brokers took on risk in less than 5% of program trades—acting only as agent in the remainder—now broker capital is on line in at least half of all program trades, he estimates. Most blind-bid trades are at least $100 million to buy or sell and $1 billion trades come along every six to eight weeks. . . .

In a blind bid, a broker typically guarantees a fund manager that the fund will receive that day's closing price for each stock in a basket. That eliminates a serious and growing cost to fund managers: the lost profit of seeing stocks rise while they're trying to buy them or fall while they're trying to sell them.

"You've eliminated the most important part of your risk, which is market risk during implementation," says Kevin Alger, global head of equity trading at J. P. Morgan Investment Management, a big user of program trades to manage its stock portfolios. "You've cut back on market impact. The trade is done, the decisions are in the portfolio, and you're fully invested in the market."

Such concerns have risen as stock prices have become more volatile in the last six to 12 months, says Ravi Singh, head of global portfolio trading at Lehman Brothers. "The clients see a big benefit to getting [a trade] done entirely in one day, and the only way is to have a broker bid on the basket and promise the close."

Here's how a recent blind bid worked. At about 2 PM, Lehman's program desk received a 10-page fax from a money manager wanting to sell several hundred stocks valued at about $500 million from an index portfolio at the same time it wanted to buy less than a hundred stocks for an active portfolio. The money manager didn't name the stocks, but he did describe how closely the two baskets tracked the S&P 500, how liquid the stocks were, which industry groups they belonged to, and the market capitalization of each company's stock. Lehman traders analyzed the fax for about 20 minutes before submitting a blind bid of less than 10 cents a share as a commission.

Shortly after the 4 PM close of the stock market, Lehman learned it had won the trade, and the manager relayed the names of the stocks. Lehman traders set to work analyzing the stocks, to see how much of the trade it could match from internal inventory, whether it could use the stocks to generate or complement other trading business, and how much of the position it would like to get rid of immediately. Meantime, the actual transactions were completed in London and thus never appeared on the "tape" of regular U.S. stock exchange transactions. Over the next week, Lehman program and block traders executed the trades necessary to eliminate most of the unwanted risk taken on with the position.

The risk, of course, is that the stocks the broker has bought from the money manager will drop in price before the broker can resell them. But in a diversified portfolio, the risk of any particular stock falling is offset by that of another rising. In fact, the more bids the program trader wins, the more the risks offset each other. Those unusual economies of scale are largely why the price of risk programs has fallen so rapidly.

MAKING THE CONNECTION

Blind program trading has become very popular and accounts for a large portion of the trades on the NYSE. The broker guarantees a closing price and, hence, takes some of the risk. The fund management does not know in advance what stocks it will buy or sell but does know the stock's category, industry, risk profile, and so on. Because of the very large volume of trades, the broker reserves a large amount of dollar commissions, and the fund manager is guaranteed that the high volume of buy-sell orders will not affect the securities prices.

3.4.6 Types of Orders

Investors can use different types of orders to buy and sell securities. The most common is a **market order,** which is an order to buy or sell a specified quantity of a specified security *at the best price currently available.* In contrast, a **limit order** is an order to buy or sell a specified quantity of a specified security *at a specified price or better.* The trade will occur only when the specified price is available.

For example, suppose the current bid and asked prices for Microsoft stock are $89\frac{7}{8}$ bid and $90\frac{1}{8}$ asked. A market order to buy Microsoft stock would be executed with the market maker at $90\frac{1}{8}$. A market order to sell Microsoft stock would be executed at $89⅞. Rather than issue a market order, the investor could issue a limit order to buy, say, 100 shares (one round lot) of Microsoft common stock at $89. This order would not be executed until the asked price dropped to $89 or lower. If the price did fall—say, to $89—then the market maker would sell 100 shares of Microsoft at $89 to the investor. In the same fashion, a limit order to sell Microsoft stock could be placed at $91. This sell order would not be executed until the bid price rose to $91 or higher.

All orders are **day orders** unless otherwise specified. That is, all limit orders expire at the end of the trading day if not executed. Market orders are day orders by definition, because they occur very quickly. An alternative to a day order is the **good-till-canceled (GTC) order**, a limit order that remains in effect until it is executed or canceled.

Other specialized orders include the not-held order and the stop order. A **not-held (NH) order,** given to a floor broker, allows the broker to try and obtain a better price, but the broker is not held responsible if he or she is unsuccessful. For example, on a NH order to sell, the broker is not liable if the price falls sharply and the broker does not successfully sell an order at the higher price. A **stop order** is an order to sell if the price falls below a specified price or to buy if the price rises above a specified price. Stop orders are used to limit losses or protect accumulated gains. If you purchased Microsoft when it was trading at $50, and it rose to $200, you could limit your risk of losing this gain with a stop order to sell if the price falls below $190. Exhibit 3-6 lists other unusual types of orders that currently exist.

Finally, although most orders are for **round lots** (increments of 100 shares), trading can be in **odd lots,** which is any number of shares not in increments of 100. For example, a 50-share trade would be an odd-lot trade. Odd-lot trades, however, incur substantially higher fees; thus, it is more economical to trade round lots. In 1996, 104.6 *billion* shares in round lots traded on the NYSE, whereas only 381,932 *million* odd-lot shares were purchased.[21]

3.4.7 Placing an Order

Investors can place buy or sell orders in one of three ways. The standard method is a phone call to a broker, who executes the trades. Investors can also trade from their personal computers. Trading through a personal computer is typically done with a modem and dial-in capabilities with a broker. Trades can also be initiated with a call on a touch-tone phone to a broker's computer.

Although there are different ways to initiate a trade, the path the trade takes after the order is given is typically the same (Exhibit 3-7). The client contacts the broker with an order (1). The broker keys the order into the firm's computer (2). The computer is programmed to locate the exchange with the best available price to make the trade (3). Depending on the type of order, the trade will be executed either electronically (4) or by the firm's trader responsible for the order (5). Once the trade is executed, the relevant information is sent back to the firm via a computer network (6) and given to the broker (7), who passes it on to the client (8).

---

21. *NYSE Fact Book for the Year 1996* (New York: New York Stock Exchange, Inc., May 1997), p. 11.

EXHIBIT 3-6 Specialized Orders for Securities	Type of Order	Definition
	All-or-none order	Partial execution of an order is prohibited. For example, assume you have a seller wishing to sell 1,000 shares of IBM stock at $80 per share, and the buy limit order is for 2,000 shares at $80. Because the order would be only partially filled, it would not be executed.
	Minimum-fill order	Execution of the order will take place at a prespecified minimum volume of trading.
	Market opening/closing order	Order is executed only at the opening or closing of the market.
	Last-sale-price order	Order must be executed at a price equal to or better than the last sale price.
	Mid-market order	Execution of this order must be at the middle of the most recent bid-offer spread only.
	Basket trade	Purchase (or sale) of a given security may be executed only in conjunction with the sale (or purchase) of another security.
	Index-related trade	The execution price is related to the value of a specified market index (could be considered a type of limit order).
	Spot/future trade	Execution of a cash position is only permitted if a prespecified and simultaneous execution occurs in a futures market.

Source: *Financial Market Trends,* no. 65, November 1996, pp. 16–17.

All orders are settled on the *settlement date,* which is three days after the order is executed. At this time, the brokerage firm remits the proceeds from the sale of securities to the client, or the client must remit the funds to the brokerage firm for the purchase of securities.

Each exchange has a clearinghouse (or is affiliated with a clearinghouse) that keeps track of all the intricate details of trading. The trading information is also communicated to the clearinghouse (9).

3.4.8 Margin Trading

Investors may engage in **margin trading.** That is, they may borrow a portion of the funds needed to buy stock from their brokers. By borrowing, the investor can take a larger position than otherwise would be possible; hence, the investor is able to "lever" the investment. One advantage of margin trading is that if the stock price appreciates, the investor's return is enhanced. If the stock price declines, however, the investor's losses are magnified.

The interest rate charged by the broker on the borrowed funds is known as the **call loan rate** or the **broker loan rate.** The maximum amount that can be borrowed is established by the Federal Reserve Board's Regulation T and is currently

EXHIBIT 3-7
The Path of a Stock Trade

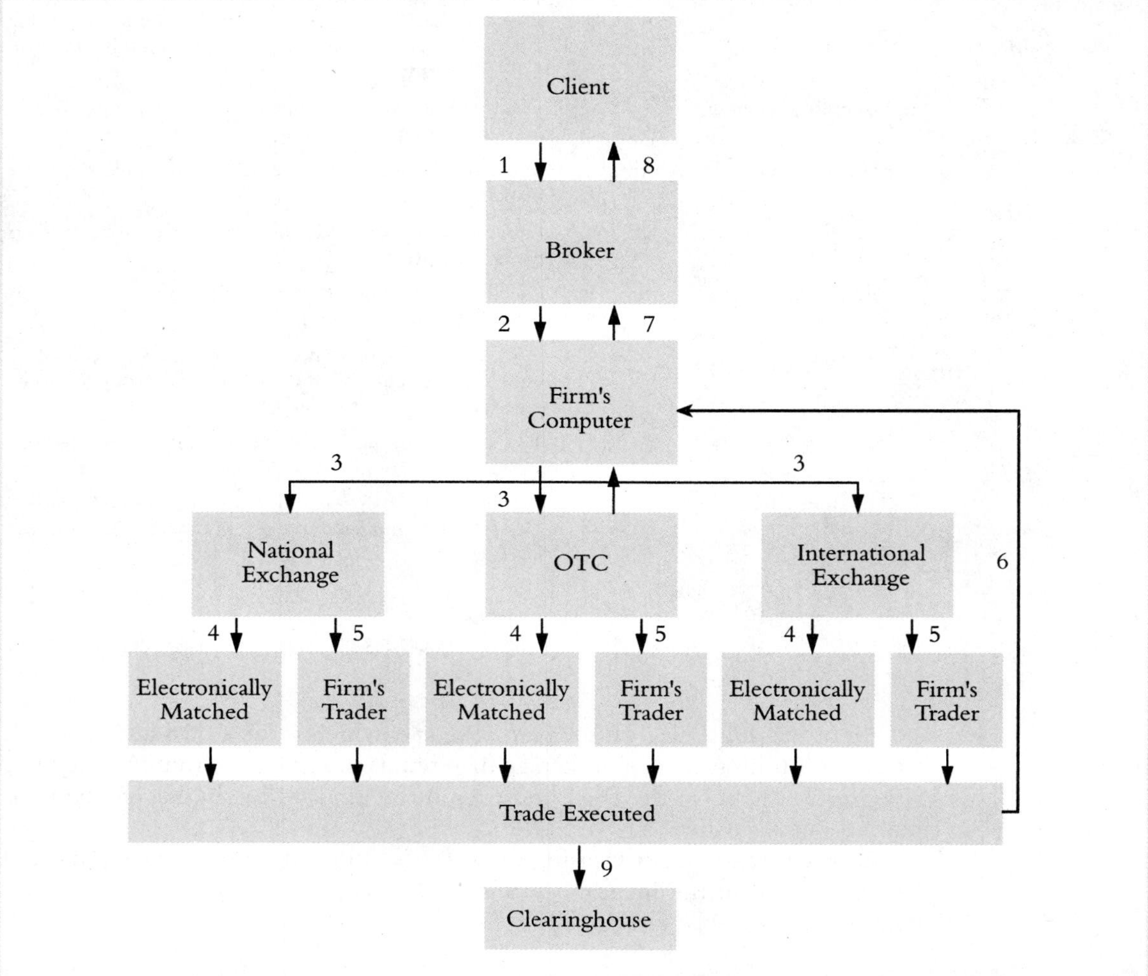

50% of the purchase price.[22] However, brokers may require investors to put up more than 50% of the purchase price.

As stock prices fall, the percentage of borrowed money in relation to security value will rise. If this percentage rises above the allowable limit, the investor must

22. The margin requirement has been 50% since January 3, 1974. The margin requirement has been as high as 100% (in 1946) and as low as 40% (in the late 1930s and early 1940s). (See *NYSE Fact Book for the Year 1996*, p. 79.)

supply more funds to reduce the amount borrowed. When a broker calls for more money, it is a **margin call.** One factor to consider before buying on margin is at what price level a margin call will go out.

The **initial margin** *(IM)* is the percentage of the dollar amount originally required by the lender to be put up by the borrower:

$$IM = \frac{\text{Total Amount Put Up by Investor}}{\text{Total Value of the Shares}}$$

which can be expressed in symbols as

$$IM = \frac{(N \cdot P) - B}{N \cdot P} \tag{3.2}$$

where N is the number of shares, P is the purchase price of the security, and B is the amount borrowed. For example, if you purchased 200 shares ($N = 200$) of AT&T at $60 per share ($P = \$60$), then the total cost is $12,000. An initial margin of 50% would require that you borrow no more than 50% of $12,000, namely, $6,000:

$$IM = \frac{(200 \cdot \$60) - \$6,000}{200 \cdot \$60} = 0.5, \text{ or } 50\%$$

The percentage of the total current market value that an investor originally put up is known as the **actual margin.** As prices fall, the actual margin will also fall. For example, if the AT&T stock price falls to $55 ($P = \$55$), then the investor's actual margin (AM) is

$$AM = \frac{(N \cdot P) - B}{N \cdot P} = \frac{(200 \cdot \$55) - \$6,000}{200 \cdot \$55} = 0.45, \text{ or } 45\%$$

To minimize the risk of default by the investor, the broker has a minimum margin requirement, known as the **maintenance margin,** which is the percentage of the dollar amount of the securities market value that must always be set aside as margin. The maintenance margin is always less than the initial margin. The maintenance margin (MM) can be written as

$$MM = \frac{(N \cdot P') - B}{N \cdot P'} \tag{3.3}$$

where P' is the price at which a margin call will be issued. Solving for P', we find

$$P' = \frac{B}{N(1 - MM)} \tag{3.4}$$

Suppose you purchased 100 shares ($N = 100$) of Microsoft common stock for $90 ($P = 90$) by borrowing $4,500 ($B = 4,500$) and providing $4,500 of your own funds (because of the initial margin of 50%). Now suppose the maintenance margin is 40% ($MM = 0.4$). The price below which you will receive a margin call is

$$P' = \frac{4,500}{100(1 - 0.4)} = \frac{4,500}{60} = \$75$$

Hence, you will not receive a margin call as long as the price remains above $75. If the price suddenly falls to $60, how much will you have to add in cash to hold this position? You will have to add the amount of cash that will bring the maintenance margin back to 40%, or from Equation 3.3,

$$MM = \frac{(N \cdot P') - B + \text{Cash}}{N \cdot P'}$$

or

$$\text{Cash} = (MM \cdot N \cdot P') - (N \cdot P') + B$$

If the price falls to $60, you will have

$$\text{Cash} = (0.4 \cdot 100 \cdot \$60) - (100 \cdot \$60) + \$4,500 = \$900$$

Indeed, the amount borrowed decreases to $4,500 - 900 = $3,600, and the maintenance margin (MM) is

$$\frac{(100 \cdot 60) - \$3,600}{(100 \cdot 60)} = \frac{6,000 - 3,600}{6,000} = \frac{2,400}{6,000} = 0.40, \text{ or } 40\%$$

as required.

Most investors buy securities in the expectation that they will appreciate in value. Margin trading is one method to enhance the return when a security's price rises.

PRACTICE BOX

Problem

Suppose you purchased 1,000 shares of GE common stock for $65 by borrowing $30,000. Thus, the initial margin is $35,000 [($65 · 1,000) − $30,000], or 53.85% ($35,000/$65,000). Now suppose the maintenance margin is 25%. What is the price below which you would receive a margin call?

Solution

Given the information above, $N = 1,000$, $B = \$30,000$, and $MM = 0.25$. Therefore, from Equation 3.4, you have

$$P' = \frac{\$30,000}{1,000(1 - 0.25)} = \$40$$

If the stock price fell below $40, you would receive a margin call.

3.4.9 Short Selling

How can you profit when stock prices are falling? Is selling your own stocks the best that you can do? **Short selling** is a method that allows you to profit when a stock's price falls by selling securities that you borrow. Actually, your broker borrows these securities from the inventory of other clients. If the price falls, the short seller can buy the securities back at a lower price. By selling high and buying low, the short seller can make a profit. Thus, the short seller is hoping prices will fall.

To demonstrate how a short sale works, assume you borrow from your broker 100 shares of GM stock, and you sell them for $40. Assume further that the price falls to $38. Now you buy the stock back and return it to the broker. From this transaction, you make a profit of $2 per share. However, if the price goes up to $42, you have to pay $42 to buy it, and you lose $2 per share.

The short seller must pay any dividends due to the original owner of the shorted securities. Also, the proceeds from the short sale are held by the broker as collateral for the borrowed securities. The short seller must provide additional money to insure against default. If 100 shares of GM are sold short at $40, and GM's stock price rises to $50, then the brokerage firm will lose $1,000, or $100(\$50 - \$40)$, if the short seller defaults. The current minimum initial margin requirement for short selling set by the Federal Reserve is 50%.[23]

Stocks can be sold short only if prior to the short sale they have traded on an **uptick** or **zero–plus tick.** Trading on an uptick refers to a security's last trade price exceeding the previous trade price (for example, $101\frac{1}{8}$, then $101\frac{1}{4}$). Trading on a zero–plus tick refers to a security's last trade price being the same as the previous trade price, but the previous trade price exceeding the one before it (for example, $101\frac{1}{8}$, then $101\frac{1}{4}$, then $101\frac{1}{4}$).

Short selling is a high-risk position, because the securities may continue to rise. For example, if an investor had sold short 100 shares of Microsoft when it was trading at $50 per share in the late 1980s, the investor would be required to cover this short position by buying Microsoft. Microsoft common stock is currently trading for about $250 (adjusting for splits). In this case, the investor is facing a $200 loss per share. The investor could wait, but then the price might go even higher.

When investors buy stock (a long position), the most they can lose is the investment itself (when or if the stock price falls to zero). However, when investors sell short (a short position), their loss has no bounds because there is no upper limit to the stock price. The higher the price, the larger the loss.

3.4.10 Brokers

There are two basic types of brokers: full-service brokers and discount-service brokers. Full-service brokers earn commissions based on the volume of trading they transact. At a full-service brokerage firm, an investor is assigned to a broker, and that broker notifies the investor about prospects on various securities. The broker also shares advice from the firm's research group as to the anticipated direction of security

---

23. See *Federal Reserve Bulletin,* December 1992 (Washington, D.C.: Board of Governors of the Federal Reserve System), p. A26.

prices. Full-service brokers typically have analyses of most major corporations. The commission can be as high as 2% of the value of the transaction.

Discount-service brokers are paid a set salary. Investors do not receive any investment advice from discount-service brokers. However, the cost of trading is from 50% to 70% less than the prices charged by full-service brokers.

COMMISSION SCHEDULE

The typical discount brokerage's equities transaction costs are listed in Exhibit 3-8.[24] For example, purchasing 400 shares of $20 stock would cost $83.00, or $35 + (0.006 · 20 · 400). Most firms have both maximum and minimum fees. Trading odd lots is more expensive.

There are big differences in commission rates among firms, as the advertisement in Exhibit 3-9 reveals. For a 200-share transaction with a price of $25 per share, Schwab charges $89, which implies that the commission as a percentage of the transaction is $89/(200 shares · $25) = $89/$5,000 = 0.0178, or 1.78%. NDB charges just a little more than a fourth of the commission.

BROKERAGE SERVICES

Discount-service and full-service brokerage firms offer several services. These services vary widely, so investors should compare brokerage firms before choosing one. Most firms offer an 800 (toll-free) telephone number to buy and sell securities. They also provide a toll-free number to receive current stock quotes and provide execution capabilities on all U.S. security markets. Some brokerage firms also handle international trades and provide real-time quotes via the Internet. Several houses offer money market rates for idle cash between investments, as well as checking services. Most firms provide complete safekeeping and record-keeping services (usually monthly). Finally, most brokerage houses offer insurance up to $500,000 through the Securities Investor Protection Corporation (SIPC). The SIPC insurance covers the risk that the brokerage firm might become insolvent. It does not, however, cover losses from a fall in security prices.[25]

EXHIBIT 3-8 Equities (Stocks and Warrants) Transaction Costs	Dollar Amount of Transaction	Commission Rate
	Under $2,500	$25 + 0.010 of dollar amount
	$2,500–$9,999.99	$35 + 0.006 of dollar amount
	$10,000–$29,999.99	$55 + 0.003 of dollar amount
	$30,000 and over	$85 + 0.002 of dollar amount
	Source: Brown & Company.	

24. This commission schedule is from Brown & Company. Full-service brokerage fees are usually much more complicated. Typically, they will be at least 100% more than the fee schedule given here.

25. To gain a greater understanding of the services provided by different brokerage firms, call a few local brokerage houses (see "Stock Brokers" in the telephone book) and request information.

EXHIBIT 3-9
Example of Commission Rates for Stock Trades

Flat Fee Trading® Makes The Difference

	200 sh. @$25	300 sh. @$20	500 sh. @$18	1000 sh. @$14
Schwab	89.00	95.60	106.60	123.60
Fidelity	88.50	95.10	106.10	123.10
Quick & Reilly	60.50	65.00	81.50	94.00
NDB	**24.95/ 27.95***	**24.95/ 27.95***	**24.95/ 27.95***	**24.95/ 27.95***

BROKER-ASSISTED RATES BASED ON SURVEY DONE 8/28/97.

*DOMESTIC STOCK, MARKET ORDER VS. LIMIT ORDER. LISTED ORDERS IN EXCESS OF 5,000 SHARES WILL INCUR A 1 PERCENT PER SHARE CHARGE ON THE ENTIRE ORDER. OTHER PRODUCTS AND SERVICES ARE AVAILABLE AT OTHER PRICES AND FEES.

National Discount
BROKERS

1-800-4-1-PRICE
www.ndb.com

help@ndb.com • 1-800-888-3999 • Member NASD, SIPC, MSRB and Discount Brokers Association.
A National Discount Brokers Group Company • Listed on the NYSE (Symbol: NDB)

NDB Listed NYSE

Source: *Barron's*, October 6, 1997, p. 64.

3.4.11 Financial Planners

Rather than dealing directly with brokers, individual investors sometimes use financial planners. Financial planners evaluate an investor's situation and formulate a strategic investment plan. The academic field of financial planning is still in its infancy. Although financial planning has gone on for centuries, the label *financial planner* is new. Just about anyone can be a financial planner in the United States simply by paying $150 and registering with the SEC. (Some states require registration with state officials as well.)

Most financial planners generate their revenues from commissions. Hence, investors must exercise care when soliciting their advice. It is now possible to call state securities departments to find out if a particular financial planner has ever been in trouble. The North American Administrators Association and the National Association of Securities Dealers (NASD) have developed a computer database of financial planners that covers all fifty states. The system, known as the Central Registration Depository, lists a financial planner's education, employment, any bankruptcy filings, any legal injunctions against his or her business, and any criminal convictions.[26]

Financial planners may have various professional degrees and certifications:

- *Doctor of jurisprudence* (JD). Usually these individuals are lawyers working in the investments area, specializing in tax law.
- *Certified public accountant* (CPA). CPAs working in the investments area usually specialize in tax accounting.
- *Chartered financial analyst* (CFA). This degree is granted by the Institute of Chartered Financial Analysts and requires a minimum of 3 years' experience as a financial analyst. The CFA degree requires successful completion of three 6-hour examinations covering all phases of investment activities. In addition, members of the institute must adhere to very strict ethical standards.
- *Certified financial planner* (CFP). The CFP degree requires passing six 3-hour exams administered by the College of Financial Planning in Denver, Colorado.
- *Chartered financial consultant* (Ch.FC). This degree is similar to the CFP but is conducted by the American College in Bryn Mawr, Pennsylvania.
- *Registered investment advisor*. This degree requires a $150 registration fee at the federal level and, possibly, registration with the state.
- *Registered representative* (Reg. Rep.). This degree is required to make securities transactions. These financial planners must pass the Association of Security Dealers Series 7 exam, which requires only knowledge of securities laws.

3.5 WORLD SECURITY MARKETS

So far the chapter's description of security markets has covered only the workings of U.S. markets. With today's technology, however, investors can routinely search the entire globe for the securities that best meet their needs. Most major brokerage firms have offices on every continent and can effectively conduct international securities transactions. Trading firms, especially those trading derivative securities, routinely "pass the book." Passing the book occurs when a New York brokerage firm communicates to its office on the West Coast of the United States what kind of securities are currently held and the nature of the risks involved. The West Coast firm passes the book to Singapore or Tokyo. The process continues until the London desk passes the book back to New York. Indeed, the sun never sets on many active trading firms.

The history of world security markets is long and varied. Babylonian merchants financed their activities from the savings of the rich around 2000 B.C. By 400 B.C. the Greeks had their equivalent of a modern joint-stock company and markets for handling currencies and interest-bearing securities.[27] With the exception of the

---

26. Based on an article by Ellen E. Schultz, *Wall Street Journal,* September 13, 1990, p. C1.

27. See D. E. Ayling, *The Internationalisation of Stockmarkets* (Brookfield, Vt.: Gower Publishing, 1986), p. 44, and Web site at http://www.ibbotson.com/research/wealth.htm, Laurence B. Siegel, "The $40 Trillion Market: Global Stock and Bond Capitalization and Returns."

Middle Ages and major wars, the move toward more sophisticated security markets has never stopped. Today's world security markets include bond, stock, and derivative markets.

3.5.1 World Bond Markets

The world bond market has increased more than fifteenfold in the past 30 years—from $700 billion in 1966 to over $21 trillion as of year-end 1994.[28] As Exhibit 3-10 illustrates, the majority of this debt is from governments. Notice that government borrowing makes up approximately 62% of the total bond market.

There have been numerous advances in the international money market. For example, Germany moved into the commercial paper (CP) market in 1991, when "certain amendments to section 795 of the German Civil Code made it possible to issue short-dated domestic securities."[29] The market for deutscheMark CP has developed rapidly and is being widely used by German firms, as well as German subsidiaries of foreign firms.

U.S. Treasury securities constitute one of the largest and most liquid capital markets in the world. Other major governments, however, also have substantial treasury issues. Exhibit 3-11 summarizes the major government bond markets and their sizes. The U.S. government bond market is larger than the total value of the major non–U.S. markets; it makes up 48.5% of the market. The Japanese market follows, with 26.3%, and then the German market, with 10.9%. Thus, the government bond market is highly concentrated in just a few countries.

EXHIBIT 3-10
World Distribution of Bonds, Year-End 1994

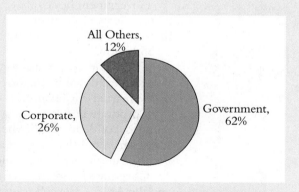

Source: Web site at http://www.ibbotson.com/research/wealth.htm, Laurence B. Siegel, "The $40 Trillion Market: Global Stock and Bond Capitalization and Returns." Used with permission. © 1998 Ibbotson Associates, Inc. All rights reserved. [Certain portions of this work were derived from copyrighted works of Roger G. Ibbotson and Rex Sinquefield.]

28. For perspective, $1 million in tightly bound $1,000 bills makes a stack approximately 4 inches tall. Thus, $20 trillion in tightly bound $1,000 bills makes a stack approximately 1,290 miles high!
29. See Peter Lee, "Deutschmark CP Gets into Gear," *Euromoney*, August 1991, p. 51.

EXHIBIT 3-11
Major National
Government
Bond Markets as
of Year-End 1994

Nation	Market Value (billions $, U.S.)	Percentage (numbers are rounded)
United States	5,489	48.5
Japan	2,977	26.3
Germany	1,236	10.9
France	513	4.5
Canada	335	3.0
United Kingdom	331	2.9
Netherlands	253	2.2
Australia	82	0.7
Denmark	72	0.6
Switzerland	37	0.3
Total	11,325	100

Source: Web site at http://www.ibbotson.com/research/wealth.htm, Laurence B. Siegel, "The $40 Trillion Market: Global Stock and Bond Capitalization and Returns."

Government bonds are traded on the major exchanges and the over-the-counter market, as well as in interbank markets. For example, as of December 31, 1996, there were 640 government issues listed on the NYSE with a total par value of $2.55 billion.[30]

The world corporate bond market stands over $5.4 trillion. Exhibit 3-12 provides a breakdown by major country. Again, the United States dominates, with 41% of the market. Five countries capture all but 14% of the market.

Corporate bonds are an attractive means to raise capital, because the interest expense is tax deductible (whereas dividend payments are not—see Appendix 2A). However, recall that corporate bonds also increase the likelihood that the firm will go bankrupt in hard economic times.

Corporate bonds are traded on most major stock exchanges, such as the NYSE and the AMEX, as well as on the over-the-counter market. The international arena, has a special type of bond, called a **crossborder bond.** Crossborder bonds are bonds issued in a different country than the issuer. For example, a bond that a U.S. firm issues that is denominated in Swiss francs, paying interest and principal in Swiss francs, would be classified as a crossborder bond. The crossborder bond has been one of the fastest-growing segments of the bond market.

30. See *NYSE Fact Book for the Year 1996,* p. 84.

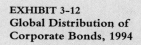

EXHIBIT 3-12
Global Distribution of
Corporate Bonds, 1994

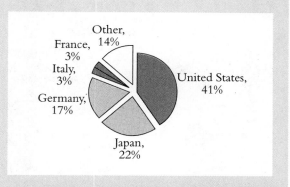

3.5.2 World Stock Markets

The market value of world equities now exceeds $17.8 trillion. Exhibit 3-13 shows a pie chart of equity markets by major countries. Once again, the United States is the largest market, but here it is very closely followed by Japan.

Exhibit 3-14 presents a brief description of the major world stock exchanges, including the year they were established. The oldest exchange is the Frankfurt Stock Exchange in Germany, which was established in 1402. From the investor's viewpoint, the process of trading on different exchanges is about the same—the investor

EXHIBIT 3-13
Global Stock Market
Capitalization, Year-End 1994

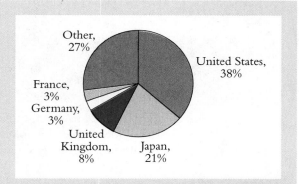

EXHIBIT 3-14 **Major World** **Stock Exchanges**	**Exchange**	**Country**	**Year** **Established**
	Melbourne SE	Australia	1865
	Brussels SE	Belgium	1801
	Sao Paulo SE	Brazil	1850[a]
	Montreal SE	Canada	1874
	Toronto SE	Canada	1852
	Vancouver SE	Canada	1907
	Copenhagen SE	Denmark	1690[a]
	Paris SE	France	N/A
	Frankfurt SE	Germany	1402
	Hong Kong SE	Hong Kong	1891
	Tel Aviv SE	Israel	1953
	Milan SE	Italy	1808
	Tokyo SE	Japan	1878
	Amsterdam SE	Netherlands	1611[a]
	SE of Singapore	Singapore	1973
	Madrid SE	Spain	1831
	Zurich SE	Switzerland	1877
	Taiwan SE	Taiwan	1961
	Intern. SE	United Kingdom	1600[a]
	New York SE	United States	1792

[a]Approximately.

N/A = Not available.

SE = Stock Exchange.

Source: Bryan de Caires and David Simmonds, *The GT Guide to World Equity Markets 1989* (London, England: Euromoney Publications, 1989). Reprinted with permission.

calls a broker. However, each exchange has its own unique way of handling transactions. For example, the Tokyo Stock Exchange is a call market, whereas the NYSE is a continuous market (see Connecting Theory to Practice 3.2).

3.5.3 World Derivative Markets

Options and futures are traded in world derivative markets. Some believe that futures trading dates as far back as 2000 B.C. in India. There is also evidence of futures and options market trading at least as far back as the 1500s in the tulip bulb industry in the Netherlands. Rice futures began trading in Osaka, Japan, in the 1730s.[31] At least eighty-seven exchanges worldwide now trade options or futures.

The market for swaps is entirely over the counter. By June 1995, this market had exploded, with $13.923 trillion in notional principal outstanding, of which $10.816 trillion is for interest rate swaps.[32] (Notional principal forms the basis from which the interest payments are calculated.) Swaps are now available in currencies and energy products as well. (Swaps are discussed in more detail in Chapter 25.)

Exhibit 3-15 summarizes the types of contracts traded on a selection of exchanges. Notice that most exchanges specialize in one or two types of contracts. For example, the Chicago Board Options Exchange (CBOE) focuses on interest-rate-based and stock-index-based options contracts.

EXHIBIT 3-15 World Derivative Exchanges	Exchange	Futures	Options
	American Stock Exchange		SI
	Australian Options Market		SI, PM
	Chicago Board Options Exchange		IR, SI
	Chicago Board of Trade	IR, SI, PM, SA	IR, PM, SA
	Chicago Mercantile Exchange (CME)	SA	
	Chicago Rice and Cotton Exchange	SA	
	CME—Index and Options Market	SI	IR, SI, FX, SA
	CME—International Monetary Market	IR,FX	
	Coffee, Sugar & Cocoa Exchange	SI	SI
	Commodity Exchange Inc.	IR, PM, BM	
	Copenhagen Stock Exchange	IR, SI	IR, SI
	European Options Exchange NV		IR, SI, FX, PM
	Financial Instrument Exchange	IR, FX	IR, FX
	The Futures & Options Exchange—London	SA	SA
	Hong Kong Futures Exchange Ltd.	SI, PM, SA	
	Kansas City Board of Trade	SI, SA	SA
	London Grain Futures Market	SA	SA
	London International Financial Futures Exchange	IR, SI, FX	IR, FX
	London Metal Exchange	PM	PM
	London Traded Options Market		SI
	Marche a Terme International de France (MATIF)	IR, SI, SA	IR, SA

(continued)

31. See Malcolm J. Robertson, *Directory of World Futures and Options* (Englewood Cliffs, N.J.: Prentice-Hall, 1990), p. 0/13.
32. Based on International Swap Dealers Association Survey, 1994.

EXHIBIT 3-15 (continued)	Exchange	Futures	Options
	Marche des Options Negociables de la Bourse de Paris (MONEP)		SI
	Mid-American Commodity Exchange	IR, FX, PM, SA	PM, SA
	Minneapolis Grain Exchange	SA	SA
	The Montreal Exchange	IR	IR, PM
	Nagoya Grain & Sugar Exchange	SA	
	Nagoya Stock Exchange		SI
	New York Cotton Exchange	SA	SA
	New York Futures Exchange	IR, SI	SI
	New York Stock Exchange		SI
	Osaka Securities Exchange	SI	SI
	Osaka Sugar Exchange	SA	
	Osaka Textile Exchange	SA	
	Pacific Stock Exchange		SI
	Philadelphia Board of Trade	SI, FX	
	Philadelphia Stock Exchange		SI, FX
	Rotterdam Energy Futures Exchange	OG	
	Singapore International Monetary Exchange	IR, SI, FX, PM	IR, FX
	Swiss Options and Financial Futures Exchange		SI
	Sydney Futures Exchange Ltd.	IR, SI, FX, SA	IR, SI, FX
	Tokyo International Financial Futures Exchange	IR, FX	
	Toronto Futures Exchange	IR, SI	IR, PM

BM = base metals.

FX = foreign exchange or currencies.

IR = interest rates.

OG = energy, oil, and gas.

PM = precious metals.

SA = softs (such as cotton) and agriculture.

SI = stock indexes.

Source: Malcolm J. Robertson, *Directory of World Futures and Options* (Englewood Cliffs, N.J.: Prentice-Hall, 1990), p. App/1.

SUMMARY

Describe the function of security markets. A security market that functions effectively provides accurate information, accurate prices, and liquidity. Buyers and sellers have access to timely and accurate infor- mation. Market prices reflect all known informa- tion. When markets are liquid, transactions are completed quickly.

Contrast the primary and secondary markets. The primary market is the mechanism through which a firm can raise additional capital by selling stocks, bonds, and other securities. The secondary market is where previously issued securities trade among investors. An alternative to raising capital by an initial public offering is with a private placement. The secondary market includes national exchanges such as the New York Stock Exchange (NYSE) and the American Stock Exchange (AMEX), regional exchanges such as the Pacific Stock Exchange and the Boston Stock Exchange, and the over-the-counter (OTC) market.

Describe the basic structure of security markets. Security exchanges seek to have a trading mechanism that satisfies competing constraints. For example,

determining what information must be made public and what information is to remain private is a difficult task. Market makers are individuals who set the bid and asked price quotes. The bid price is the price at which investors can sell securities, and the asked price is the price at which investors can buy securities.

Survey world security markets. The world security markets include bond, stock, and derivative markets. The $21 trillion bond market is dominated by the United States. The $17.8 trillion stock market is led in size by the United States, followed closely by Japan. The world security markets also include more than eighty-seven security exchanges that trade derivative securities, such as options and futures.

CHAPTER AT A GLANCE

1. *Primary determinants of a good security market:*
   a. Information availability.
   b. Price setting with full information.
   c. Liquidity.

2. *In the primary market, underwriters act in the following capacities:*
   a. Advisors.
   b. Providers of a firm commitment to buy the issue.
   c. Providers of a best-efforts agreement to sell the issue.
   d. Issuers of a standby commitment to buy the right offering issue at a lower price if unable to sell the entire issue.

3. *An alternative to an IPO is a private placement, which is less costly but less liquid.*

4. *Explanations for IPO underpricing include the following:*
   a. Information asymmetry.
   b. Scalping of good issues by underwriters.
   c. Compensation for providing liquidity.
   d. Appraisal costs incurred by many buyers.

5. *Secondary market trading is conducted in the following ways:*
   a. On the exchanges.
   b. On the OTC market.
   c. Directly between buyers and sellers.

6. *Within the secondary market, there are five categories of markets:*
   a. Exchange-traded securities on the exchange.
   b. Over-the-counter (OTC)–traded securities traded on the OTC market.

   c. Exchange-listed securities traded on the OTC market.
   d. Exchange-listed securities traded directly between buyer and seller.
   e. Large block trades (known as the *upstairs market*).

7. *Markets are designed in three major formats:*
   a. Call—trading occurs only at specified points in time with a market-clearing price.
   b. Continuous—trading can occur when the market is open (most popular in United States).
   c. Mixed—trading is continuous, but a given time interval is allocated to each group of stocks.

8. *Orders to buy or sell securities can be either of the following:*
   a. Market orders—the best available price.
   b. Limit orders—only at a specified price, or better.

9. *Margin trading is trading in part with borrowed funds. It makes use of the following concepts:*

Initial Margin

Maintenance Margin

$$IM = \frac{(N \cdot P) - B}{N \cdot P}$$

$$MM = \frac{(N \cdot P') - B + \text{Cash}}{N \cdot P'}$$

Margin Call Price

$$P' = \frac{B}{N(1 - MM)}$$

10. *World security markets include the following:*
   a. Bond markets.
   b. Stock markets.
   c. Derivative markets.

KEY TERMS

Actual margin 99	First market 83	Market microstructure 87
Asked price 90	Floor broker 91	Market order 95
Bid price 90	Fourth market 84	Mixed market 88
Bid-asked spread 92	Good-till-canceled (GTC)	Not-held (NH) order 96
Breadth 74	order 96	Odd lot 96
Broker 91	Gross spread 76	Over-the-counter market 83
Broker loan rate 97	Information asymmetry 82	Price continuity 74
Call loan rate 97	Initial margin 99	Primary market 75
Call market 87	Initial public offering (IPO) 76	Primary offering 76
Commission broker 91	Investment banker 76	Private placement 80
Continuous market 88	Limit order 95	Private placement memorandum
Crossborder bond 106	Maintenance margin 99	80
Day order 96	Margin call 99	Program trading 93
Depth 74	Margin trading 97	Prospectus 76
Dual listing 84	Market 73	Registered competitive trader
Execution cost 74	Market maker 90	91

Registered equity market maker 91	Second market 83	Third market 84
Resiliency 74	Secondary market 75	Underwriter 76
Round lot 96	Short selling 101	Underwriter's discount 76
Scalping 82	Specialist 91	Upstairs market 84
Seasoned new issue 76	Stop order 96	Uptick 101
	Syndicate 78	Zero-plus tick 101

REVIEW

3.1 What are the main explanations given for IPOs being underpriced?

3.2 How are the U.S. secondary market transactions categorized?

3.3 Describe the three major categories of secondary markets.

3.4 Describe the market maker on the NYSE.

3.5 What factors affect the bid-asked spread?

3.6 What is margin trading, and why is it considered risky?

PRACTICE

3.1 Suppose you purchase 500 shares of Wal–Mart common stock at $75 per share by borrowing funds, and your initial margin is 65%. The maintenance margin is 55%.
a. How much of your own money will you have to provide?
b. What is the price at which you would begin to receive a margin call?

3.2 Using the commission schedules provided in this chapter, how much would you pay in commission to a discount-service brokerage firm if you bought 700 shares of Ford Motor Company's common stock at $25 per share?

3.3 Suppose IBM stock is trading for $70 a share. You borrow from your broker 100 shares and sell them. Calculate your dollar profit if IBM's stock price drops to $60 a share. Also calculate your dollar loss if IBM's stock price rises to $80 a share. Are your profits limited? Are your losses limited? Explain.

3.4 Suppose you are an underwriter who has a firm commitment to sell a million shares at $100 a share. You have an agreement to give the issuing firm $95

per share. Suppose there is a chance of ½ that all shares will be sold at $100 and a chance of ½ that the issue will not go well and the market price will end up being only $92 per share. What is, on average, the underwriter spread?

3.5 Suppose you invested $400,000 with your broker, and the broker went bankrupt. Are you insured? Suppose now that the value of your assets went down to $200,000 because of bankruptcies of firms that issued the shares you hold. Are you insured now?

3.6 A specialist of Xerox Corporation has an asked price of $20⅛ and a bid price of $20⅙. A specialist of a firm smaller than Xerox has an asked price of $20⅛ and a bid price of $19½. How can you explain these differences in the bid and asked prices?

3.7 The bid price of Stock A is $1, and the asked price is $1⅛. The bid and asked prices of Stock B are $100 and $100⅛, respectively. Which stock do you think is more volatile?

3.8 Suppose you buy a stock for $2,500, and the rate of return after six months is 5%. What is the rate of return after transaction costs? What would be the rate of return if you invested $10,000? (Use the commission figures in the text.) Assume that you add to the investment the transaction costs, and you have not sold the stock yet (hence, there is no transaction cost at the end of the six months).

3.9 Suppose an underwriter has a firm commitment on two issues, each issue at $10 per share and for 1 million shares. Suppose the price falls to $9 in both issues. Would the underwriter be better off by having one issue of 2 million shares and having the price of the issue fall from $10 to $9?

3.10 In light of your answer to Question 3.9, why do underwriters form syndicates?

3.11 Suppose Ford invests in the repo market. They sell Treasury bills for $1,000,000 and have agreed to buy them back in one month for $1,005,000. What is the implied repo rate?

3.12 The stock price is $P = \$100$, and you bought 1,000 shares of this particular stock. The initial margin you use is 20%. How much did you borrow? (Use Equation 3.2.)

3.13 The price (P'), below which you will be called for the maintenance margin can be expressed without the amount borrowed (B). (See Equation 3.4.) Develop and explain this formula.

3.14 If the initial margin is 50%, the maintenance margin is 40%, the stock price is $100, and you buy 100 shares, what is the price below which you will receive a maintenance margin call? (Use Equation 3.4, as well as the formula derived in Question 3.13.)

3.15 Suppose you know the loan balance per share, but you do not know the number of shares involved in a margin transaction. The current price is P. Can you write a formula for the price P' for a maintenance margin call?

3.16 You sell short 100 shares of IBM at $95 a share. The broker holds the cash receipt and gives you ½% interest per month. After one month you buy back the 100 shares. Determine your total profit or loss under the following conditions:
a. The stock price falls to $90 a share.
b. The stock price rises to $100 a share.

3.17 The price of Exxon common stock is $33. You bought it when it was $20. You want to secure at least 100% on your initial investment. What kind of sell order can you give? At what price?

3.18 Ford Motor Company holds $1,000,000 three-month Treasury bills yielding 5%. The manager urgently needs $1,000,000 for only one week. Ford can either borrow at 12% per year (or 0.218% per week) or use the repo market, selling the Treasury bills and agreeing to buy them back in a week for $1,002,500. Which borrowing strategy would you recommend? How would you change your answer if Ford can buy back the bills at $1,002,000?

3.19 Suppose you have $10,000. The stock price of Intel is $100 per share. You decide to buy 1,000 shares of Intel and simultaneously short sell 1,000 shares.
a. What will be your net dollar return if the price of Intel one month later is $110? What if the price is $90? Assume there are no dividends and no transaction costs.
b. How would you change your answer if there is a 1% transaction cost on buy and sell orders?

3.20 Suppose you have no money, but you would like to short sell 100 shares of Intel and use the proceeds to buy 100 shares of Intel. Your investment horizon is six months. The stock price is $100 per share.
a. What is your dollar return in six months?
b. How would you change your answer if you have to deposit the proceeds with your broker, who pays you 2% for six months, and you can borrow from the bank at 3% for six months?

3.21 Suppose you buy a round lot (100 shares) of IBM stock at $103 per share. You want to sell the stock if the price rises to $110 per share but also want to protect yourself in case the price drops to $97 per share. What could you do?

3.22 Assume you have decided to purchase 200 shares (2 round lots) of Walt Disney common stock on margin. The stock currently sells for $160 per share. The initial margin requirement of your broker is 60% (that is, 10% greater than required under Regulation T). How much money must you send your broker?

3.23 Suppose you short sell 100 shares of IBM, and with the proceeds you buy 100 shares of IBM. The share price is $90. You intend to hold this financial position in IBM for one month. Assume that no dividends are paid during this month.
a. In the absence of transaction costs, what is the cash flow today and one month hence?

b. Suppose the stock of IBM will be traded one month hence for $110. You sell the stocks held and buy them back to cover the short sale. Describe the cash flow on your position six months hence.
c. Suppose now that closing the position this way involves $10 transaction costs. Is there a better way to close the position?
d. In light of the above answers, is it rational to hold such an investment composed of short selling 100 stocks and buying 100 shares of IBM?

For Internet questions visit the Levy Investment Web site at http://levy-invst.swcollege.com.

YOUR TURN: APPLYING THEORY TO PRACTICE
BITTER LESSON: WHEN THAT "HOT" IPO IS REALLY A LEMON

Minneapolis money manager Ray Hirsch was on the verge of buying stock in American Dental Laser Inc. last spring—until he called a few local dentists.

What Mr. Hirsch learned saved him a lot of money. Despite the excitement on Wall Street about American Dental's hand-held laser for gum surgery, he discovered that dentists were put off by the device's $50,000 price tag. American Dental went public at $13 a share last June. But Mr. Hirsch, who runs the $226 million IDS Discovery mutual fund, steered clear of the stock even though underwriters assured him it would be a hot offering.

Since then, American Dental's stock has slumped 73% to $3.50 a share as of yesterday. A major reason for the drop: disappointing sales of its lasers. That sales decline has left American Dental with net losses in the past two quarters and made the company one of the worst performing initial public stock offerings of late.

Even though the stock market is booming, buying IPOs remains a high-risk, high-reward game. Plenty of IPOs have doubled in price over the past year. But an analysis by Securities Data Co. shows that since January 1991, 53 IPOs have skidded at least 20% from their initial offering price.

It may be too late for investors who bought duds such as American Dental, Maverick Tube Corp., or Tocor II Inc.—all of which now trade at less than half their offering price (see next table). But with a bit of work, investment pros say, it is possible to spot the IPO lemons ahead of time—and thereby avoid buying them.

In some cases, such as American Dental, investors who check with customers and suppliers of a company's products can uncover warning signs. In other cases, potential trouble spots can be found in a company's prospectus, which is the official offering document in a stock offering.

Chip Morris, manager of T. Rowe Prices' $200 million Science and Technology fund, says he is nervous when a company's revenue and earnings show a zigzag pattern in the years immediately before the company goes public. He is much more comfortable when he sees "a steady progression of earnings and revenue."

(continued)

10 IPO Lemons

	Date of IPO	Current Price	Drop from IPO Price
American Dental	Jun –91	$3.50	73%
Maverick Tube	Mar –91	4.63	66
OESI Power	May –91	4.75	66
Tocor II	Jan –92	14.00	65
Salton/Maxim	Oct –91	4.75	60
IDEC Pharm.	Sept –91	6.75	55
DNX	Dec –91	6.00	54
Cephalon	Apr –91	8.50	53
Univax Biologics	Feb –92	6.00	50
Physicians Computer	Nov –91	4.88	46

Source: Securities Data Co.

Mr. Morris also prefers companies that have "lots of small contracts, rather than relying on one or two big customers." That way, the loss of any single contract, or delays on any big project, can't hurt a company's prospects too much.

Source: "Bitter Lesson: When That 'Hot' IPO Is Really a Lemon," *Wall Street Journal*, April 21, 1994, p. C1. Reprinted by permission of *The Wall Street Journal*, © 1994 Dow Jones & Co., Inc. All Rights Reserved Worldwide.

Questions

1. If American Dental's prospectus showed 10 years of steady sales of the $50,000 device, would the risk of the IPO be smaller? Explain.

2. You consider investing in a portfolio of ten IPOs or, alternatively, in a portfolio of ten stocks in the same industry already traded on the NYSE. On which portfolio will the expected rate of return be higher? Why?

3. Suppose that according to the prospectus, the earnings per share (EPS) of IPO A and IPO B for the last 4 years were as follows:

Year	1	2	3	4
IPO A	1	0.5	1	0.5
IPO B	0.75	0.75	0.75	0.75

Which IPO is less risky? Why?

4. What "potential trouble spots" can be revealed by examining a company's prospectus? Give a few examples.

5. Chip Morris prefers IPOs with (a) "a steady progression of earnings and revenue" and (b) "lots of small contracts, rather than . . . one or two big customers." Why would such IPOs be preferred?

6. An investment banker underwrites a stock issue of General Motors (whose stocks are already listed on the NYSE) and a new IPO. The earnings per share of both firms are $5. For General Motors, the underwriter suggested a firm commitment of $60 and a selling price of $64. For the IPO, the selling price to the public is also $64, and the firm commitment is $55. Calculate the gross spread of these issues, and explain the underwriter's pricing policy. (Note: Gross spread = price to the public per share − receipts per share to the firm.)

7. Suppose you short sell 100 shares of American Dental at $13 and buy them back at $3.50. You have to pay the broker a $100 transaction fee. The proceeds from the short sale are deposited with the broker, and you receive $50 interest for the period that you deposit the money. During this period, American Dental distributes a $7-per-share dividend. Show your cash flows and the dollar profit on this transaction. What would the profit (loss) be if, when you buy back the stock of American Dental, it is traded for $23 a share? Explain the risk involved with short sales. (Note: Short selling means you borrow the stock from the broker; sell it; and after a given time, buy it back and return it to the broker.)

SELECTED REFERENCES

Benos, A., and M. Crouhy. "Changes in the Structure and Dynamics of European Markets." *Financial Analyst Journal* (May–June 1995): 37–50.

This article provides a description of changes in European securities markets and the prevailing tracking systems in the various exchanges in Europe.

Eatwell, John, Murray Milgate, and Peter Newman, eds. New Palgrave Dictionary of Money and Finance. New York: W.W. Norton, 1989.

This is a detailed dictionary of financial concepts. The terms are defined and discussed by leading academics in finance.

Fabozzi, Frank J., and Franco Modigliani. *Capital Markets Institutions and Instruments.* Englewood Cliffs, N.J.: Prentice-Hall, 1992.

This text provides a detailed analysis of world capital markets, with special emphasis on the United States.

Fridson, Martin S., and Gao Yan. "Primary versus Secondary Pricing of High-Yield Bonds." *Financial Analyst Journal* (May–June 1996): 20–27.

This article analyzes the underpricing of newly floated securities vis-à-vis secondary market price levels.

Griffin, Mark W. "A Global Perspective on Pension Fund Asset Allocation." *Financial Analyst Journal* (March–April 1998): 60–68.

This article provides a detailed comparison of pension fund asset allocation around the globe with an emphasis on equities versus bonds.

Hasbrouck, Joel. "Security Markets, Information and Liquidity." *Financial Practice and Education* 1, no. 2 (Fall–Winter 1991): 7–16.

This article is a good summary of market microstructure.

Lederman, Jess, and Keith K. H. Park, eds. *The Global Bond Markets State-of-the-Art Research, Analysis and Investment Strategies.* Chicago: Probus Publishing, 1991.

This book surveys the major world bond markets and addresses some of the more sophisticated global bond investment strategies.

Livingston, Miles. *Money and Capital Markets: Financial Instruments and Their Uses.* Englewood Cliffs, N.J.: Prentice-Hall, 1990.

This text provides many useful technical details of capital markets, with an emphasis on pricing.

Mann, Steven V., and Robert W. Seijas. "Bid-Ask Spreads, NYSE Specialists and NASD Dealers." *Journal of Portfolio Management,* Fall 1991, pp. 54–58.

This article describes the salient differences between the NYSE specialist system and the NASD dealer system of making a market. The authors view these different systems as "cousins" and not "twins."

Robertson, Malcolm J. *Directory of World Futures and Options.* Englewood Cliffs, N.J.: Prentice-Hall, 1990.

This is an exhaustive directory of futures and options markets worldwide.

Scarlata, Jodi G. "Institutional Developments in the Globalization of Securities and Futures Markets." *Federal Reserve Bank of St. Louis,* January–February 1992, pp. 17–30.

This article provides a good survey of recent developments in globalization. Particularly helpful is the summary of computerized trading systems.

Schwartz, Robert A. *Equity Markets: Structure, Trading, and Performance.* New York: Harper & Row, 1988.

This book provides the institutional detail of U.S. security markets and focuses on market microstructure issues and regulations.

Tucker, Alan L. *Financial Futures, Options, and Swaps.* St. Paul, Minn.: West Publishing, 1991.

This is a detailed introduction to futures, options, and swaps.

SUPPLEMENTAL REFERENCES

AMEX Fact Book. Annual. New York: American Stock Exchange.

Bae, Sung C., and Haim Levy. "The Valuation of Firm Commitment Underwriting Contracts for Seasoned New Equity Issues: Theory and Evidence." *Financial Management,* Summer 1990, pp. 48–59.

Glosten, Lawrence R. "Insider Trading, Liquidity, and the Role of the Monopolist Specialist." *Journal of Business,* April 1989, pp. 211–235.

NASD Fact Book. Annual. Washington, D.C.: National Association of Securities Dealers.

NYSE Fact Book. Annual. New York: New York Stock Exchange.

Smith, Clifford W. "Investment Banking and the Capital Acquisition Process." *Journal of Financial Economics* 15(January–February 1986): 3–29.

Tokyo Stock Exchange Fact Book. Annual. Tokyo: Tokyo Stock Exchange.

CHAPTER 4

REGULATION AND ETHICS

LEARNING OBJECTIVES

After studying this chapter you should be able to:

1. Describe key regulations designed to control the securities industry.

2. Explain why financial innovation can create problems with investors and regulators.

3. Contrast the goals of corporate managers and corporate owners.

4. Describe situations in which investment professionals may act unethically.

INVESTMENTS IN THE NEWS

FOLLOWING A BROKER'S ADVICE CAN REAP NICE GAINS—UNTIL YOU GET THE TAX BILL

How do you like your brokerage house stock picks lately? Pretty well, probably—unless you match them against the leading market indexes, and unless you worry about your tax bill.

The Standard & Poor's 500-Stock Index was up 34.7% in the 12 months through June. According to a continuing study by *The Wall Street Journal* and Zacks Investment Research Inc. of Chicago, only three out of 16 major brokerage houses did that well.

Still, the stocks on the recommended list at the typical brokerage house were up more than 29%, which is enough to keep most customers happy. Until they look at their tax bill, anyway.

For tax reasons, many individual investors have long preferred to hold their stocks for at least a year and a day to qualify for long-term capital-gains treatment. As such, their gains have been taxed at a top federal rate of 28%, compared with effective rates as high as 39.6% for profits on stocks held for a year or less. Under the new tax law, profits on stocks held more than 18 months will qualify for an even better deal: a top tax rate of 20%.

Yet brokerage houses often act as if most customers were short-term traders. Rick Chrabaszewski of Zacks recently analyzed the turnover rates on brokerage-house recommended lists in the past three years and in the first half of 1997. He found that most brokerage houses are fickle, changing their minds frequently about which stocks are their favorites.

Among 16 houses in the study, nine had turnover rates of 100% or more in 1996. Eleven houses are on track to exceed 100% turnover in 1997.

Such frequent additions and deletions from the recommended list could lead to adverse tax consequences for people who follow the firms' advice. And it may be emblematic of a general tendency to overtrade—always a temptation for brokers and brokerage houses, which earn a good chunk of their revenue from trading commissions.

Source: John R. Dorfman, "Following a Broker's Advice Can Reap Nice Gains—Until You Get the Tax Bill," *Wall Street Journal*, August 15, 1997. Reprinted by permission of *The Wall Street Journal* © 1997 Dow Jones & Co., Inc. All Rights Reserved Worldwide.

As this chapter's Investments in the News shows, the broker who advises a client on a buy-sell transaction may not operate in the client's best after-tax interest. The broker who gets a commission for each transaction would like to have a large turnover in the client's portfolio. However, the turnover affects the client's tax bill. A holding period of less than 1 year implies a possible 39.6% marginal tax on all profits, including capital gains. Holding the financial asset for a longer period may result in only a 28% tax on capital gains. Laws passed in 1997 will reduce some capital gains from 28% to 20%.

Does a broker's conduct like that just described represent unethical activity? It is hard to tell. If the broker believes that selling and buying securities indeed improve the portfolio's performance, then the broker's recommendations are ethical. However, if the broker controls the client's account, and the motive for the large turnover is to increase commission fees, the behavior is unethical and may even be illegal (against government regulations). However, proving that "excessive" turnover took place is tricky (see Section 4.4).

What are the differences between regulations and ethics? **Regulations** are rules established by governments for the purpose of identifying unacceptable behavior. **Ethics** are the principles on which the correctness of specific actions is determined.[1] A behavior that is unacceptable based on ethical standards may be found acceptable by existing regulations. Indeed, it is hard to legislate ethical behavior.

This chapter outlines the history of securities regulation in the United States and discusses current regulation and financial innovation. Next, it describes problems that arise when the goals of managers differ from the goals of a company's owners. Finally, it reviews some of the major ethical problems confronting market participants.

4.1 HISTORY OF SECURITIES REGULATION

Prior to the twentieth century, family-owned firms were very secretive about their financial affairs and profits. The firms did not want others to know how well they were doing. During the early 1900s there was a fundamental shift in corporate design. The family members who ran the firms (known as "enterprise capitalists") were turning the day-to-day affairs of corporate life over to professional managers, who increasingly relied on financial institutions for their necessary capital.

Corporate reporting gradually increased because of changes in the marketplace and the need to provide information to investors.[2] Corporate managers recognized the need to report to their shareholders, who, as part owners of the firm, had a right to corporate information. Powerful investor groups began to voice criticism of the way firms were conducting themselves. Financial institutions needed to assess the riskiness of corporations before making loans to them. These factors led to the standardization of accounting practices.

---

1. From Gerald F. Cavanagh, *American Business Values,* 3d ed. (Englewood Cliffs, N.J.: Prentice-Hall, 1990), p. 2.
2. For more details, see David Hawkins, *Corporate Financial Reporting and Analysis,* 2d ed. (Homewood, Ill.: Dow Jones–Irwin, 1986).

At the turn of the century, there were no standard accounting practices or disclosure requirements. In 1902, United States Steel Corporation published an annual report, but few other corporations followed suit. Common accounting practices began to emerge, making it easier to require firms to report their financial affairs in a consistent manner. Although there were some attempts at regulation by legislators and lobbying groups, the relatively good economy in the early part of the twentieth century caused the regulatory attempts to be ignored.

The fall of the Dow Jones Industrial Average from a high of 358 on October 11, 1929, to a low of 41 on July 8, 1932, provided the appropriate environment for those who desired to regulate the securities industry. During the decade following the stock market crash of 1929, the U.S. Congress passed five major securities acts designed to protect investors.

The **Securities Act of 1933** requires disclosure of information about an initial public offering (IPO) and registration with the Federal Trade Commission (FTC). The financial information disclosed has to be certified by an independent accountant. The 1933 act also addresses fraudulent activities and regulates the primary market; it requires a registration statement and a prospectus. Because of the nature of this legislation, it is sometimes referred to as the *truth-in-issuance act*.

The Glass-Steagall Banking Act of 1933 created the Federal Deposit Insurance Corporation (FDIC) and required the separation of commercial and investment banking. Currently, the FDIC insures each bank deposit up to $100,000. If a bank fails, then the government (through the FDIC) pays depositors for any deposits up to $100,000. The separation of commercial and investment banking activities was motivated by the investment bankers' practice of using their commercial banking resources to manipulate stock prices.

The **Securities Exchange Act of 1934** regulates the secondary market. It also created the Securities and Exchange Commission (SEC) and gave it the power to regulate commission rates established by the exchanges, to prohibit manipulative trading practices, and to monitor traders' practices. The 1934 act provides for the registration of exchanges, which are to be self-regulatory organizations. The exchanges are owned and operated by their members. The 1934 act gave exchanges the authority to discipline their membership and gave the Federal Reserve Board the authority to establish margin requirements. The 1934 act also forbids trading based on inside information.

The Public Utility Holding Company Act of 1935 (the PUHCA) forces public utility holding companies to register with the SEC. This law requires utilities to file financial statements and other documents. The registration process puts more information about a company into the public domain. This legislation gave the SEC broad powers related to the management of public utilities.

The Maloney Act of 1938 amended the 1934 act to bring the over-the-counter market under SEC jurisdiction and encourages the development of associations like the NYSE. The Maloney Act resulted in the development of the National Association of Securities Dealers (NASD), which was registered with the SEC in 1939.

Other legislation in the early development of the U.S. securities market included the Trust Indenture Act of 1939, which requires that bond issues have both a disinterested trustee and provisions to protect the rights of the bondholders. For example, the board of directors cannot pay a large cash dividend to common stockholders and then immediately default on the bond payment. Also, bondholders are required to receive from the firm a semiannual report documenting the firm's adherence to terms of the bond indenture.

In 1940, two acts were passed. The Investment Company Act provides for the basic regulation of investment companies. The Investment Advisors Act requires the registration and regulation of investment advisors.

The Williams Act of 1968 provided legislation on attempts to take over a publicly held firm. An attempt to buy large portions of a publicly held firm is known as making a **tender offer.** The Williams Act was enacted in response to a series of unannounced takeovers, during which stockholders had to make decisions under duress. This act requires parties attempting to buy a company to file an information document with the SEC, as well as with the company under consideration. This document must contain information on the terms of the offer, the source of financing, the competence of the bidder, and a company plan after the takeover.

The U.S. government acquired an interest in the management of brokerage firms when it passed the Securities Investor Protection Act of 1970. In the event of default by a brokerage firm, this act provides insurance to customers' accounts of up to $500,000 each by the Securities Investor Protection Corporation (SIPC).

The Employee Retirement Income Security Act of 1974 (ERISA) regulates the management of pension funds and retirement accounts. Managers of these types of accounts have a **fiduciary** relationship. A fiduciary is a person who acts in the best interest of his or her clients on issues related to their relationship. In other words, money managers must act in the best interest of their clients. A money manager is a fiduciary under ERISA when at least one of the following criteria is true: (1) the money manager exercises any authority related to portfolio management decisions, (2) the money manager is paid a fee for investment advice, and/or (3) the money manager has any control over the administration of a portfolio.[3]

Based on ERISA, an investment manager must be loyal. This requires that any expenses charged to an ERISA account must be reasonable, and the fund must be managed with the client's best interests in mind. Specifically, an investment manager must act prudently. That is, the manager should always act with care and work diligently when conducting business for clients. One recently added requirement is that a manager must diversify a customer's account to minimize losses. (See Part 2 of this book for a complete discussion of the benefits of diversification.)

The Securities Acts Amendments of 1975 provided major changes to the Securities Exchange Act of 1934. Specifically, these amendments eliminated fixed commissions charged by brokers in order to make the exchanges more competitive and called for the establishment of a national market system.

The Foreign Corrupt Practices Act of 1977 places restrictions on the behavior of domestic firms operating in international markets. Specifically, firms are not allowed to bribe foreign officials, even if bribery is legal in that country. In 1983, firms were given the ability to sell new securities over a period of time rather than

---

3. See Section 404(a)(1) of ERISA of 1974.

all at once. As Chapter 3 described, this ability helps firms that have to sell securities at depressed prices; it is called *shelf registration*.

In 1984 and 1988, two acts were passed that gave the SEC greater enforcement powers. The 1984 Insider Trading Sanctions Act made it illegal to trade a security while in possession of material nonpublic information. Although the act is vague as to what kind of information is material and when information is nonpublic, it has been used to restrict insider trading. The 1988 Insider Trading and Securities Fraud Enforcement Act increased the fines and punishment for insider trading and other fraudulent activities.

In 1990 several new regulations were enacted, ranging from expanding the SEC's enforcement powers to facilitating the resale of a private placement. In 1995, under the Securities Exchange Act of 1934, two new rules were enacted that became effective in January 1997. The **"Display Rule"** (Rule 11Ac1-4) requires that limit orders placed by customers and priced better than a specialist's or market maker's quote must be displayed. Similarly, the "Quote Rule" (Rule 11Ac1-1) requires market makers to publish quotations for any listed security when a quote represents more than 1% of the aggregate trading volume for that security. The intent of these two rules is to enhance competition and pricing efficiency by openly disclosing the trading activity on each security. The major U.S. legislation related to investment management is summarized in Exhibit 4-1.

EXHIBIT 4-1   **Summary of U.S. Securities Laws**

Year	Legislation	Purpose
1933	Securities Act	Requires IPO disclosure, registration with Federal Trade Commission (FTC), and certification; addresses fraud
1933	Glass-Steagall Banking Act	Created Federal Deposit Insurance Corporation (FDIC), separates commercial banking from investment banking
1934	Securities Exchange Act	Regulates secondary market, established Securities and Exchange Commission (SEC), provides for exchange self-rule, gives Fed authority to establish margin, forbids insider trading
1935	Public Utility Holding Company Act	Requires utilities to register with SEC
1938	Maloney Act	Places OTC market under SEC supervision, results in development of National Association of Securities Dealers (NASD)
1939	Trust Indenture Act	Requires a bond trustee and protective provisions in bond indentures
1940	Investment Company Act	Regulates investment companies
1940	Investment Advisors Act	Requires registration of investment advisors and regulates activities

(continued)

EXHIBIT 4-1   *(continued)*

Year	Legislation	Purpose
1968	Williams Act	Regulates tender offers
1970	Securities Investor Protection Act	Provides governmental insurance through the Securities Investor Protection Corporation (SIPC) for defaults by brokers
1974	Employee Retirement Income Security Act	Regulates the management of pension funds
1975	Securities Acts Amendments	Eliminates fixed commissions, requires the development of a national market system
1977	Foreign Corrupt Practices Act	Makes it illegal to bribe foreign officials, regulates internal controls of multinational corporations
1983	Shelf Registration	Allows for the sale of securities over a period of time rather than a specific day
1984	Insider Trading Sanctions Act	Makes it illegal to trade while in possession of "material nonpublic" information
1988	Insider Trading and Securities Fraud Enforcement Act	Increases potential liabilities for insider trading or other fraudulent activities
1990	Shareholder Communications Improvement Act	Requires banks and brokers holding shares for beneficial owners of securities in nominee name to forward to the beneficial owners the proxy and information statements of investment companies
1990	Securities Law Enforcement Remedies Act	Provides the SEC with significant additional enforcement powers; civil penalties can now go up to $500,000; officers or directors whose conduct demonstrates "substantial unfitness" can be barred
1990	Market Reform Act	A response to the October 1987 and October 1989 market breaks; permits the SEC, during "periods of extraordinary volatility," to "prohibit or constrain" trading practices such as program trading
1990	Rule 144A	Designed to facilitate the resale of privately placed securities without SEC registration: the SEC wanted to develop "a more liquid and efficient institutional resale market for unregistered securities"
1995	Rule 11Ac1-4	"Display Rule" requires that limit orders placed by customers and priced better than a specialist's or market maker's quote must be displayed
1995	Rule 11Ac1-1	"Quote Rule" requires market makers to publish quotations for any listed security when a quote represents more than 1% of the aggregate trading volume for that security

Source: C. Steven Bradford, "Rule 144A and Integration," *Securities Regulation Law Journal* 20 (1992): 37; Web site at http://www.sec.gov/rules/final/34-38110.txt.

Although security legislation is designed to protect investors from fraud, many of the actual fraud convictions are based on broader laws. The guilty pleas of Michael Milken (head of the high-yield bond department at the failed Drexel Burnham Lambert, Inc.) on April 24, 1990, are good examples (see Exhibit 4-2). Conspiracy, mail fraud, and assisting the filing of a false tax return are not violations of security laws, but they were used successfully in the prosecution of Michael Milken. These convictions resulted in Milken's receiving a 10-year prison sentence. Milken actually served only 2 years in prison, because he cooperated with government officials. He also was required to perform 2,400 hours of community work over a 3-year period.[4]

EXHIBIT 4-2   **Criminal Convictions of Michael Milken**

Charge	Background	Maximum Sentence
Conspiracy	Involved unlawful securities transactions between Milken and Ivan Boesky and David B. Solomon . . . that were intended to enrich the coconspirators and to enhance Drexel's ability to complete transactions.	5 years
Aiding and abetting the filing of a false SEC document	Failed to disclose Drexel's interest in the Boesky Organization's holdings in Fischbach Corp.	5 years
Securities fraud	Enlisted the Boesky Organization to artificially support the price of MCA common stock while Golden Nugget, a Drexel client, was disposing of its MCA holdings.	5 years
Aiding and abetting net-capital violations	Provided unlawful assistance to the Boesky Organization by "parking" Boesky's holdings in Helmerich & Payne at Drexel, which allowed the Boesky Organization to free up additional cash and overstate the amount of net capital it reported to the SEC.	5 years
Mail fraud	Defrauded investors in the Finsbury Fund, an investment fund for foreign investors managed by David Solomon.	5 years
Assisting the filing of a false tax return	Entered into prearranged trades with Solomon that were designed to reduce Solomon's federal income tax liability.	3 years

Source: Laurie P. Cohen, "Milken Pleads Guilty to Six Felony Counts and Issues an Apology," *Wall Street Journal,* April 25, 1990, p. A6. Reprinted by permission of *The Wall Street Journal,* © 1990 Dow Jones & Co., Inc. All Rights Reserved Worldwide.

4. See Jonathan M. Moses, "Milken to Work in Antidrug Program," *Wall Street Journal,* June 4, 1993, p. B8.

4.2 SECURITIES LAW AND FINANCIAL INNOVATION

There is a natural tension between accounting and regulatory bodies on the one hand and financial innovation on the other. The innovators (called *financial engineers*) want the freedom to design, sell, and trade whatever complex security they desire. However, regulators want to make sure potential investors in these securities fully understand the securities, acquire full information, and are not cheated by the more sophisticated traders.

Regulators are concerned about the rights of the different security holders. With simple common stock and traditional bonds, these rights are clear. When more innovative securities are offered, however, it is sometimes unclear whose interest is at stake.[5]

The financial innovation by Americus Trust of prime shares and score shares is a classic example. The idea is very straightforward: Some people buy common stocks for dividends, whereas others buy common stocks for capital appreciation. Why not split the stock into two parts—dividends and appreciation—and let the two parts trade separately? After lengthy legal and tax battles, Americus Trust was granted permission to set up a trust, and the American Stock Exchange allowed trading of the resulting securities.

The dividend part was known as *prime shares*, and the appreciation part was known as *score shares*. The prime shareholders maintained all voting rights and received all dividends. The score shareholders received no dividends and had no voting rights, but they profited if the underlying share price appreciated.

In principle, these securities allow an investor to purchase either prime shares for dividends or score shares for capital appreciation. Corporate executives at major U.S. firms, however, expressed concern over these securities and their impact on securities law. Specifically, the executives argued that the voting prime shareholders would be "dividend hungry pests." The issuance of prime shares and score shares in principle made operating under existing securities law difficult for corporate executives.

It is clear that this financial innovation complicates the fiduciary duty of managers. To whom should upper management cater—prime shareholders seeking dividends or score shareholders seeking increases in firm value? In practice, this is not a major problem, because these trusts account for a very small percentage of shares outstanding. It is clear, however, that such financial innovations are causing difficulties for lawyers and accountants.[6]

The relationship between financial innovation and corporate law is captured in the following quotation by law professor Henry T. C. Hu: "Financial innovation—especially relating to equity securities—has not only rendered this fundamental principle of corporate law (a corporation is to be primarily run for the benefit of its shareholders) maddeningly ambiguous, but has dramatically heightened the costs of the legal indeterminacy."[7] Connecting Theory to Practice 4.1 further illustrates the tension between financial innovation and securities law.

---

5. See Henry T. C. Hu, "New Financial Products: The Modern Process of Financial Innovation and the Puzzle of Shareholder Welfare," *Financial Management Collection* 7, no. 1 (Winter 1992): 1–13, for a detailed discussion of these issues.

6. In 1984, prime and score shares were in effect eliminated because of unfavorable tax rulings pushed by senior corporate executives.

7. Hu, "New Financial Products," p. 2.

CONNECTING THEORY TO PRACTICE 4.1
"DERIVATIVES" DRAW WARNINGS FROM REGULATORS

NEW YORK—After two years of behind-the-scenes warnings, financial regulators are going public with their fears of a future crisis in the booming global "derivatives" market.

This shadowy multitrillion-dollar market—of swaps, options, futures and custom made financial instruments—has revolutionized how corporations and financial institutions manage risks. With derivatives sold by banks and securities firms, big institutions can hedge against sudden moves in interest rates, currencies or the cost of raw materials. Much of this complex trading, involving a global web of interconnected financial obligations, doesn't show up on the balance sheets of banks and brokers.

But international financial regulators are increasingly worried that this booming market is growing too fast, has too little regulation and is being used by some traders as a speculative arena. With so many institutions obligated to one another, regulators fear that a big loss by a single financial firm could cause dangerous waves in world financial markets.

The regulators' warning bell was sounded in January in a speech by E. Gerald Corrigan, the powerful president of the Federal Reserve Bank of New York.

"The growth and complexity of off-balance sheet activities and the nature of the credit, price and settlement risk they entail should give us all cause for concern," Mr. Corrigan said in a speech to the New York State Bankers Association.

"High tech banking and finance has its place, but it's not all that it's cracked up to be. . . . I hope this sounds like a warning, because it is."

In the current climate, concludes John J. Kriz, a vice president at Moody's Investors Service Inc., "More regulations on the derivatives market seems to be a foregone conclusion. It's now a question of when, not if."

Source: Steven Lipin and William Power, "'Derivatives' Draw Warnings from Regulators," *Wall Street Journal,* March 25, 1992, p. C1. Reprinted by permission of *The Wall Street Journal,* © 1992 Dow Jones & Co., Inc. All Rights Reserved Worldwide.

MAKING THE CONNECTION

It is apparent from this excerpt that regulators are concerned about the explosive growth in the derivatives market. Because many derivative securities are tailor-made, they do not fit neatly into regulatory definitions. In fact, legal uncertainty is a major risk faced by investors in this market. Regulators such as E. Gerald Corrigan are trying to expand the regulatory authority of various government agencies to be able to control the actions of market participants.

(continued)

In 1994, the U.S. House of Representatives introduced a bill titled the Derivatives Safety and Soundness Act (H.R. 4503), which was designed to expand regulatory control of derivatives. By its very nature, financial innovation remains a step ahead of financial regulation.

4.3 CORPORATE GOVERNANCE

As the interests of the different investors become increasingly difficult to assess, examination of the issue of how corporations are controlled is essential. Suppose investors and corporate managers obey all laws and security regulations. Who guarantees that the corporate managers will always act in the best interest of stockholders? Specifically, who regulates the corporate managers' actions even within the wide range of existing laws and SEC regulations? Managers of corporations must be kept honest. One mechanism for maintaining honesty is the shareholders' right to elect board members.

Corporate governance is the method or system of controlling the corporation. Corporate control usually rests with a board of directors. This group of individuals is usually elected by the common shareholders and given specific powers as allowed in the corporate charter and bylaws. The most important power of the board of directors is the appointment of senior managers, who carry out the day-to-day affairs of the corporation and delegate authority to employees. The board also determines the chief executive officer's compensation.

Corporate governance is important because it is the framework through which shareholders can be assured of legal compliance, and it establishes the appropriate ethical conduct of the corporation. Through judicious use of corporate governance, shareholders can implement strict ethical standards throughout the corporation.

With the increasing concentration of shares held by large institutional investors, the role of active corporate governance on the part of shareholders will certainly increase. When shares of a company are widely held by individual investors, it is difficult for any one shareholder to exercise much control. However, when a few large institutional investors get together, they can easily exercise control of a corporation. One major concern is what happens if institutional money managers fail to keep as their priority the interests of their clients. For example, if institutional money managers use their authority to vote themselves on the board of directors so they can personally benefit, they are no longer acting in their clients' best interest.

4.4 ETHICS AND FRAUD

In 1992, the Research Foundation of the Institute of Chartered Financial Analysts interviewed four hundred investment analysts and published a survey regarding ethics in the investment profession. Here are a few observations:

- Almost one-quarter of the respondents had observed unethical behavior by a colleague during the previous twelve months.
- The three most frequent violations (in descending order) were failing to use diligence and thoroughness in making recommendations, writing reports with predetermined conclusions, and communicating inside information.
- Most frequently, analysts observing unethical behavior within their firms made the activity known to a supervisor. More than one-third, however, did nothing.
- More than one-fifth of the respondents had at some time in their careers been asked to do something unethical.
- A large majority believe that senior managements seek high ethical standards for their firms.
- Respondents believe that the home environment is the most important source of education and training for ethical behavior, but that senior management leadership and company training programs should be more important than they currently are.
- The threat of government sanctions and moral/religious beliefs are significantly more important deterrents to unethical behavior than are self-regulatory sanctions or published codes of ethics.[8]

The survey results suggest that unethical behavior is widespread in the investment community. For example, analyst recommendations are not necessarily based on diligent, independent analysis. Thus, there is a crisis in the investment community with regard to ethical conduct, as Connecting Theory to Practice 4.2 illustrates.

CONNECTING THEORY TO PRACTICE 4.2

THE NEW CRISIS IN BUSINESS ETHICS

To meet goals in these tough times, more managers are cutting ethical corners. The trend hurts both the culprits and their companies, even if they don't get caught.

As this economic slowdown lingers like some stubborn low-grade infection, managers are putting the heat on subordinates. Many of the old rules no longer seem to apply. Says Gary Edwards, president of the Ethics Resource Center, a consulting firm in Washington: "The message out there is, reaching objectives is what matters, and how you get there isn't that important."

The result has been an eruption of questionable and sometimes plainly criminal behavior throughout corporate America. We are not dealing here so much with the personal greed that propelled Wall Street operators of the '80s

(continued)

8. E. Theodore Viet and Michael R. Murphy, *Ethics in the Investment Profession: A Survey* (Charlottesville, Va.: The Research Foundation of Chartered Financial Analysts, 1992), pp. 4, 28.

into federal prisons. Today's miscreants are more often motivated by the most basic of instincts—fear of losing their jobs or the necessity to eke out some benefit for their companies. If that means fudging a few sales figures, abusing a competitor, or shortchanging the occasional customer, so be it.

People lower down on the corporate food chain are telling the boss what they think he wants to hear, and outright lying has become commonplace at many companies. Michael Josephson, a prominent Los Angeles ethicist who consults for some of America's largest public corporations, says his polls reveal that between 20% and 30% of middle managers have written deceptive internal reports. . . .

The Justice Department has become far keener on catching and punishing white-collar criminals since the S&L crisis and the BCCI scandal.[a] Last November tough new sentencing guidelines for corporate crimes went into effect. Warns Josephson: "We are going to see a phenomenal number of business scandals during the 1990s. We are swimming in enough lies to keep the lawyers busy for the next ten years." . . .

In tough times it's all the more important to remember that ethics pay off in the end, and on the bottom line. Ten years ago James Burke, chief executive of Johnson & Johnson, put together a list of major companies that paid a lot of attention to ethical standards. The market value of the group, which included J&J, Coca-Cola, Gerber, IBM, Deere, Kodak, 3M, Xerox, J. C. Penney, and Pitney Bowes, grew at 11.3% annually from 1950 to 1990. The growth rate for Dow Jones industrials as a whole was 6.2% a year over the same period.

The case is probably easier to make in the negative: Doing the wrong thing can be costly. Under the new federal sentencing guidelines, corporations face mandatory fines that reach into the hundreds of millions for a broad range of crimes—antitrust violations, breaking securities and contract law, fraud, bribery, kickbacks, money laundering, you name it. And that's if just one employee gets caught.

Even if you don't land in court, you might find yourself on the front page or the evening news, which could be worse. In the past few years, most media have given much more coverage to business. Newspapers and magazines all over the U.S. now employ investigative reporters with MBAs and business experience to dig into the affairs of companies. The old advice is still the best: Don't do anything on the job you wouldn't want your mother to read about with her morning coffee. . . .

Source: Kenneth Labich, "The New Crisis in Business Ethics," *Fortune,* April 20, 1992, pp. 167–176. Reprinted from the April 20, 1992, issue of *Fortune* by special permission. Copyright 1992, Time Inc.

a. The S&L crisis refers to the massive defaults of savings and loan institutions in the United States during the late 1980s and early 1990s. These defaults occurred for a variety of reasons, one of which was the fraudulent practices of managers. The BCCI scandal refers to the billions of dollars alleged to have been fraudulently taken from BCCI Holdings, an international financial institution.

MAKING THE CONNECTION

It is easier for corporate managers to behave ethically when business is going well. It is when business is slow that corporate managers face greater temptations. Based on the evidence of James Burke, chief executive of Johnson & Johnson, it pays to manage a corporation based on high ethical standards. Not only is it the right thing to do, but also it appears that ethical management results in businesses being more profitable.

4.4.1 Unethical versus Fraudulent Behavior

In today's business climate, the words *unethical* and *fraudulent* are used almost in the same breath. However, there is a clear distinction between the two. *Fraud* involves breaking the law or the existing regulations. *Ethics* is more difficult to define.

Ethics generally influence behavior more than written laws do. Ethics are typically applied at three levels within a corporation. The first level is in defining the corporate mission. Why is the corporation in existence? What are its objectives? A company's ethical responsibilities are usually clear from its corporate objectives. For example, Pfizer's "Statement of Corporate Philosophy" states that one of the firm's objectives is to "contribute to the economic strength of society and function as a good corporate citizen on a local, state, and national basis in all countries in which we do business."[9]

The second level of applying ethics applies to constituency relations. This level relates to the corporation's responsibilities to employees, communities, customers, suppliers, shareholders, governments, and the general public. For example, whose interests take priority? Is it the customers, who desire reasonably priced, safe products, or is it the shareholders, who desire a high rate of return on their investment?

The third level at which ethics influence a corporation is in establishing corporate policies and practices. A clearly defined statement of ethics provides the foundation on which to build corporate policy. How are employees to carry out day-to-day activities? Are employees to maintain a high standard of conduct, even if it reduces a firm's profits?[10] Many professions have codes of ethics to establish what activities and behaviors are considered acceptable. The Association for Investment Management and Research (AIMR) has adopted the following code of ethics to be adhered to by over thirty thousand members (and over twenty-five thousand candidates):[11]

A financial analyst should conduct himself with integrity and dignity and act in an ethical manner in his dealings with the public, clients, customers, employees, and fellow analysts.

A financial analyst should conduct himself and should encourage others to practice financial analysis in a professional and ethical manner that will reflect credit on himself and his profession.

---

9. Pfizer, Inc.'s "Statement of Corporate Philosophy," p. 3, n.d.
10. See Ronald E. Berenbeim, *Corporate Ethics* (New York: The Conference Board, 1987), p. 1.
11. See Web site at http://www.AIMR.org/aimr/cfa/cfaprofile.

A financial analyst should act with competence and should strive to maintain and improve his competence and that of others in the profession.

A financial analyst should use proper care and exercise independent professional judgment.[12]

Connecting Theory to Practice 4.3 shows how Arthur Levitt, the chairman of the SEC, is trying to end some unethical issues concerning the municipal bond market.

CONNECTING THEORY TO PRACTICE 4.3

LEGAL ETHICS SHOULDN'T BE AN OXYMORON

The American Bar Association, now meeting in San Francisco, has an opportunity to exercise moral leadership on an issue that is crucial to the integrity of the $1.3 trillion municipal bond market. It's an issue that's been a top priority of mine since I became chairman of the Securities and Exchange Commission four years ago. At that time, the need for reform in the municipal market was obvious. Corruption and conflicts of interest that would have stirred the envy of Boss Tweed had tarnished the reputation of the municipal market, overshadowing the many honest and diligent people who work there.

At the center of our effort to clean up the market has been a drive to eliminate "pay-to-play," the practice of making political contributions to candidates for local office in exchange for favorable consideration in the award of contracts relating to municipal bonds. These contracts can be for legal, underwriting, or advisory services.

There's little doubt that pay-to-play damages the integrity of the municipal bond market. It creates the impression that contracts are awarded on the basis of political influence, not professional competence. Pay-to-play also breeds contempt for the political process. Four years ago I resolved to try to bring an end to the practice before it could become ingrained in the minds of a new generation of leaders in the industry. But the SEC's regulatory touch on the municipal market is light; Congress designed it that way. Ultimately, more than any SEC rule or enforcement action, it is the daily actions of market participants that demonstrate the integrity of this market and earn the public's trust.

In 1993 key municipal bond dealers upheld that trust by voluntarily agreeing to ban political donations by firms seeking underwriting business. This cultural shift has since been reinforced with a formal rule by the Municipal Securities Rulemaking Board. But lawyers have been slow to follow the bankers' lead. No meaningful nationwide measure has yet been put in place by our country's lawyers to bring an end to pay-to-play.

---

12. Adapted with permission from *Standards of Practice Handbook*, 5th ed. Copyright 1990, Association for Investment Management and Research, Charlottesville, Va. All rights reserved.

Lawyers in the Empire State have been a courageous exception. A report by the Association of the Bar of the City of New York demonstrates the need for action, and the City Bar has proposed a measure to curb pay-to-play statewide. Since ending pay-to-play in one state is not enough, the City Bar has also called upon the ABA to pass a resolution to encourage all state bar associations to adopt policies to end this pernicious practice.

The City Bar proposal simply calls on bond lawyers to cut the tie between campaign contributions and selection as bond counsel. This is eminently reasonable, yet several prominent lawyers have launched harsh attacks on it, arguing that it would violate their First Amendment rights. But the courts have upheld the constitutionality of similiar measures for dealers. Besides, the bar is known for its creativity; it should be able to devise untainted mechanisms for expressing political support.

Others have tried to divert the debate, claiming the problem should be addressed through comprehensive campaign finance reform. But for the SEC, ending pay-to-play is a matter of *market* reform. Still others have blamed the politicians who ask for money. But true character lies in accepting responsibility, not shirking it.

Finally, some have said, "We must first marshal the evidence to be sure that 'pay-to-play' exists." The regional and national press—as well as the legal trade press—have extensively reported the problem and issued calls for action. No one knows this market better than the bond dealers, who have already acted to end the practice and now call upon lawyers to join them. It may be that for those who resist reform, the evidence will never be strong enough.

There are other benefits to ending pay-to-play. Public opinion of lawyers is at a dismal low. A recent ABA survey found that less than 25% of respondents thought lawyers were generally "honest and ethical." The issue of pay-to-play presents an opportunity (though certainly not the only one) to address the public's growing cynicism about lawyers. Instead of commissioning survey after survey and fretting about the results, here is a chance for the bar actually to *do* something honest and ethical.

Pay-to-play presents just about as clear an ethical choice as the legal community is ever going to get. Attempts to rationalize, temporize or dodge the issue reflect precisely the kind of behavior that has given lawyers a bad name. A strong stand against a shady pracitce would help restore public confidence in the profession.

Tomorrow I will call on the ABA's House of Delegates to curb pay-to-play. For the sake of our markets, and for the credibility of the legal profession, I hope the delegates will act to end this odious practice.

(continued)

MAKING THE CONNECTION

Making contributions to politicians who run for local offices is unethical when the firms that donate the money expect to get contracts relating to municipal bonds. The politicians may treat the donors favorably when bonds are issued. Arthur Levitt, the chairman of the SEC, is making an effort to curb this unethical practice.

The following example illustrates how difficult it can be to distinguish between unethical conduct and fraudulent conduct. A recent lawsuit was brought by a shareholder of Image Films Entertainment, Inc., against the co-chief executives Ron Howard and Brian Grazer. Howard and Grazer apparently planned either to leave the company or to make a tender offer to buy the outstanding shares. The shareholder claimed that Howard and Grazer were very talented and should not be allowed to leave this firm because the "prospects, revenue, profit, and reputation depend on the creative talents and reputation of these two principals." Alternatively, if Howard and Grazer chose to buy the firm, they would be taking unfair advantage of shareholders.[13]

Aside from whether the shareholders have a legal case, it is unclear whether the principals were acting unethically. Shareholders apparently bought the shares believing that these two principals would manage the firm. Thus, they may have felt betrayed and afraid that they would lose money if the principals left the firm. An ethical issue exists, however, only if the principals had led the shareholders to believe that they would manage the firm for a long time. Managers are free to leave a firm and move to another company, or even to retire. However, managers should represent themselves honestly and truthfully.

Many unethical actions are regulated. For example, insider trading was considered unfair and hence is restricted by law. Therefore, anyone who participates in insider trading is simply breaking the law and can be put behind bars. In contrast, many actions in investments are considered unethical but are not unlawful. Regulators cannot impose laws and regulations on every possible unethical action that investors can take. Furthermore, in a discussion of ethics and regulations, sometimes the issues are mixed.

As an example of an issue that involves ethics but not law, say a CEO nominates people who are dependent on her to the board of directors, which determines her compensation. This action is clearly unethical. It is not unlawful, however. In the future we may see a law regulating the nomination of the board of directors, and if such a law is passed, this CEO's action will move from the unethical category to the unlawful category.

Unlawful acts are considered by most people to be unethical. That is, most ethical frameworks hold as essential the responsibility to obey the law. For example, the AIMR's *Standards of Professional Conduct* require that "the financial analyst shall not

13. "Shareholder of Image Sues Its Two Principals," *Wall Street Journal,* May 11, 1992, p. B4A.

knowingly participate in, or assist, any acts in violation of any applicable law, rule, or regulation of any government, governmental agency, or regulatory organization governing his professional, financial, or business activities."[14] As the illustration involving the CEO and the board of directors demonstrates, however, not all unethical acts are unlawful.

Ethical issues in investing include independent judgment, insider trading, churning, selling IPOs, commission-based selling, and CEO compensation.

4.4.2 Independent Judgment

Exercising independent judgment is a cornerstone of the AIMR's *Code of Ethics*. It is critical that financial analysts issue their own assessment of the value of individual securities. If analysts' judgments are influenced by outside pressures, then the value of their recommendations is highly suspect.

The financial analyst is not to succumb to outside pressure; rather, the analyst should "exercise diligence and thoroughness in making an investment recommendation to others."[15] Analysts should do their own homework and clearly present their own opinions about a given security. They should not rely exclusively on other analysts' opinions but rather have a credible basis for their own recommendations.

4.4.3 Insider Trading

Many investors rely on the independent judgments of investment advisors, as well as their own ability to acquire information. Investors are allowed to use any information that is acquired lawfully. However, they are not allowed to base investment decisions on information that is not publicly available. For example, a person cannot buy stock in a company based on inappropriately acquired information of a pending takeover. However, if the pending takeover was announced, say, in the *Wall Street Journal,* a public source, then the investor can buy shares legally.

In 1984, the Ninety-eighth Congress of the United States passed the Insider Trading Sanctions Act of 1984 "[t]o amend the Securities Exchange Act of 1934 to increase the sanctions against trading in securities while in possession of material nonpublic information."[16] Specifically, the 1984 act states that the SEC can bring court action against anyone who has purchased or who sells "a security while in possession of material nonpublic information. The amount of such penalty shall be determined by the court in light of the facts and circumstances, but shall not exceed three times the profit gained or loss avoided as a result of such unlawful purchase or sale, and shall be payable into the Treasury of the United States."[17]

The Insider Trading and Securities Fraud Enforcement Act of 1988 dramatically increases maximum jail terms and fines for inside trades, provides for cash bounties

---

14. Association for Investment Management and Research, *Code of Ethics and Standards of Professional Conduct,* Standard II (B), May 2, 1992.

15. *Ibid.,* Standard III (A) 1, May 2, 1992.

16. Public Law 98-376, 98th Cong., August 10, 1984 (98 Stat. 1264), H.R. 559.

17. *Ibid.*

to informers, allows for lawsuits by those claiming to have been harmed, and attempts to induce firms to institute better internal controls. This act was passed in response to insider trading litigation and was intended to dampen the amount of insider trading done.[18] Connecting Theory to Practice 4.4 demonstrates some of the issues concerning personal trading by a big fund manager.

Exactly defining "material nonpublic information," however, may be difficult. For example, is there a difference between rumor and substantive facts? Outside of blatant criminal activity, such as bribing corporate executives, trading on material nonpublic information is sometimes an ethical decision.

CONNECTING THEORY TO PRACTICE 4.4

FRONT-RUNNING PUTNAM SUIT SPOTLIGHTS PERSONAL TRADES, FUND TRACK

A legal skirmish between Putnam Investments and a former staff attorney for the big, Boston-based mutual-fund company has opened a window onto the murky world of personal trading by fund managers. . . .

The suit also charges, however, that during the late 1980s, some senior fund managers at Putnam asked colleagues to hold off on trades for clients so that the managers could complete trades in the same stocks for themselves. These allegations raise issues of "front running," an illegal practice. When front running, a money manager seeks to profit personally as the firm's massive buying power eventually pushes up the price of a stock he bought previously.

Source: Robert McGough, "Putnam Suit Spotlights Personal Trades, Fund Track," *Wall Street Journal,* August 14, 1997. Reprinted by permission of *The Wall Street Journal,* © 1997 Dow Jones & Co., Inc. All Rights Reserved Worldwide.

MAKING THE CONNECTION

Suppose that a manager of a mutual fund intends to have a large buy order of a given stock, which might affect the stock price. If the manager delays the transaction because he wishes to buy stock for himself and thus then enjoy the stock price's appreciation when the big buy order is translated, it is called *front running* and is illegal. The article from the *Wall Street Journal* demonstrates such activity and the legal suit that followed.

---

18. The impact of this regulation is an open question. Nasser Arshadi and Thomas H. Eyssell ("Regulatory Deterrence and Registered Insider Trading: The Case of Tender Offers," *Financial Management,* Summer 1991, pp. 30–39) found that the more stringent regulations reduced both the amount and profitability of insider trading before tender offers. However, H. Nejat Seyhun ("The Effectiveness of Insider-Trading Sanctions," *Journal of Law and Economics,* April 1992, pp. 149–182) claims there is no evidence that the more stringent legislation had any effect on the profitability or volume of overall insider trading.

4.4.4 Commission Brokers and Churning

Full-service brokers face some difficult ethical decisions. The broker is paid by commission. The fees earned are determined by the amount of trading the broker convinces the clients to undertake. However, the buy and hold strategy may be the best for many clients. What should a broker recommend to clients? Should the broker recommend that the client buy one security and hold on to it for 25 years or buy twenty-five securities and hold each for only 1 year, which would generate 25 times the commission? Which would the client prefer?

A broker's buying and selling excessive amounts for a client is called **churning.** Specifically, "churning exists when a stockbroker has control over an account and causes it to be traded excessively for the primary purpose of generating commissions."[19] However, defining the term *excessively* is tricky. From the investor's viewpoint, if the broker is making money for the investor, then a large amount of trading is fine. If the broker is trading a lot and losing money, then from the investor's viewpoint the broker is churning.

Churning is illegal under SEC rules (specifically, Rule 10b-[5]), as well as under the rules of all major exchanges. In most cases it is difficult to prove whether churning has occurred or whether the broker was pursuing some sort of investment management strategy. The courts have used three tests to determine whether excessive trading existed:

1. Annualized turnover ratio (how frequently securities are traded).
2. Ratio of commissions to invested equity.
3. The proportion of commissions derived by the broker from the account in question compared with all other accounts handled by that broker.[20]

In spite of these criteria, the issue of churning is left mainly in the ethical arena.

4.4.5 Commission Brokers and IPOs

Another ethical problem that commission brokers face is that their firms are also major underwriters of new securities. Thus, these brokers have to sell a set number of these securities, whether the client needs them or not. These brokers are working for two competing parties. The firm issuing the securities wants the highest price for the securities. The client wants the lowest price. The broker must exercise considerable fortitude to make sure the clients are well served.

4.4.6 Financial Planners and Product Sales Commissions

In most cases, financial planners who manage and advise investors are compensated from commissions generated by the sale of financial products such as mutual funds. Thus, when dealing with financial planners, an investor is basically dealing with a salesperson. If you were a salesperson, which products would you sell? Many salespeople would sell the products having the largest commission. However, these

---

19. See Richard A. Booth, "Damages in Churning Cases," *Securities Regulation Law Journal* 20, no. 3 (Fall 1992): 3.
20. *Ibid.*, p. 5.

are not necessarily the best products for the client. Thus, the product choice is unethical.

4.4.7 CEO's Compensation and Performance

The CEO's compensation generally is indexed to the firm's performance. However, recently the compensation of many CEOs has increased even though their firms were losing money. The financial media is full of criticism of this phenomenon. Clearly, excessive compensation of executives will result in shareholders' losing return on their investments. The corporate governance of the firm is supposed to prevent executive interest from replacing that of shareholders' interest.

How can the excessive compensation packages of CEOs be explained? The CEO is the most powerful person in the firm, and the CEO directly or indirectly nominates the board of directors and the compensation committee. Consider the hypothetical case in which the compensation committee of Firm A includes the CEO of Firm B, and the compensation committee of Firm B includes the CEO of Firm A. The risk of mutual bias in setting compensation then exists. Compensation might be based on personal favors exchanged rather than on actual performance. If so, did the CEOs break the law? They probably did not, but they certainly conducted themselves in an unethical manner. Executives should act in a fiduciary capacity on behalf of shareholders, not merely in their own best interest.

4.4.8 Improving the Conduct of Investment Managers

Many ethical issues like those described so far could be solved by establishing incentive structures that foster a highly ethical securities market that is satisfactory to potential investors. Specifically, fiduciaries should align their own reward systems so they correspond with their clients' desires. For example, financial planners should create a reward system that would reward them for designing optimal after-tax strategies for their clients.

It would not be difficult for financial analysts to produce reports that were based on independent judgment if they were rewarded for doing so. Also, brokers would most likely act in the best interest of their clients if their compensation were tied to how well the client were served rather than to how many times the broker could persuade the client to trade. Similarly, if the CEO's compensation were linked to earnings or the stock price, the CEO would try to maximize the stock price and thus satisfy stockholders.

SUMMARY

Describe key regulations designed to control the securities industry.   Since the depression in the early 1930s, many laws have been enacted that were designed to make financial markets fair and orderly. For example, the Securities Act of 1933 requires disclosure of information about an initial public offering and has general antifraud provisions. The Glass–Steagall Banking Act of 1933 created the Federal Deposit Insurance Corporation and required the separation of commercial and investment banking. The Securities Exchange Act of 1934 provides regulation for the secondary market and created the Securities and Exchange Commission. The 1990 Market Reform Act permits the SEC to "prohibit or constrain" program trading during periods when the market is showing "extraordinary" movements. The 1995 rules provide regulation related to limit orders and quotations that are published by the market makers.

Explain why financial innovation can create problems with investors and regulators.   There is a natural tension between accounting and regulatory bodies on the one hand and financial innovation on the other. Prime and score shares are good examples of this tension. This financial innovation split common stock into two new shares: a prime share that yields dividends and a score share that yields capital appreciation. Unfortunately, this financial innovation also changed the language of securities laws because senior management did not know whether to cater to prime shareholders seeking dividends or score shareholders seeking capital appreciation.

Contrast the goals of corporate managers and corporate owners.   Corporate governance is the method or system of controlling a corporation. How a corporation is controlled is important, because it is the framework through which shareholders can be assured of legal compliance, and it establishes the appropriate ethical conduct of the corporation.

Describe situations in which investment professionals may act unethically.   Ethics are the principles on which the correctness of specific actions is determined. Several common ethical issues arise in investments, including independent judgment, insider trading, churning, selling IPOs, commission-based selling, and CEO compensation.

CHAPTER AT A GLANCE

1. The day-to-day affairs of corporate management are influenced by the following:
   Securities regulations.
   Corporate governance.
   Ethics.

2. The major U.S. securities regulations were created in the wake of the 1929 depression (see Exhibit 4-1).

3. Corporate governance is typically exercised as follows: Shareholders elect a board of directors, who hire upper management, who delegate authority to employees.

4. Ethics involves integrity, dignity, competence, proper care, and independent professional judgment. Ethical problems in investments include the following:
   a. Independent judgment.
   b. Insider trading.
   c. Commission brokers and churning.
   d. Commission brokers and IPOs.
   e. Financial planners and product sales commissions.
   f. CEO compensation and performance.

KEY TERMS

Churning   137
Corporate governance   128
Display Rule   123
Ethics   120

Fiduciary   122
Quote Rule   123
Regulation   120
Securities Act of 1933   121

Securities Exchange Act of 1934   121
Tender offer   122

REVIEW

4.1 In the early 1900s, as firms shifted from family-owned firms to publicly held firms, corporate reporting gradually increased. What factors contributed to this increase?

4.2 What was the major impetus for the initial securities regulations?

4.3 What are the differences between the Securities Act of 1933 and the Securities Exchange Act of 1934?

4.4 Which act resulted in the development of the NASD?

4.5 What is the relationship between financial innovation and securities law?

PRACTICE

4.1 The banks in your town offer you 10% interest if you invest $200,000 or more. If you invest $100,000, you receive only 9.5%. You wish to invest $200,000. You consider putting $100,000 in each of two banks or $200,000 in one bank. Calculate the dollar profit under each strategy. What are the pros and cons of each choice?

4.2 Keith Loeb's wife was a close relative of Ira Waldbaum. One evening, Keith's wife told him that Ira planned to tender a controlling block of Waldbaum, Inc., stock to the Great Atlantic and Pacific Tea Company for $50 per share. The next day Keith phoned his broker, Robert Chestman, and told him about the deal. Suppose Robert immediately purchased 3,000 shares of Waldbaum stock for his own account at $24 per share. Next, Robert purchased 7,000 shares for his clients' discretionary accounts at $26 per share. Finally, Robert purchased 1,000 shares for Keith at $27 per share. That evening the tender offer was made public, and the next morning the share price was $50.

a. How much money did the respective parties make if we assume they sold their positions at $50 per share?

b. What criminal activities were conducted, and by whom?

c. Were there any ethical violations?

d. If you were Keith Loeb, what would particularly bother you about Robert Chestman's activities?

(Note: Keith Loeb agreed to cooperate with the government, paid a $25,000 fine, and agreed to disgorge a $25,000 profit on the Waldbaum stock. Robert Chestman was found guilty of various crimes, including violating Rule 14e-3. This rule prohibits trading on the basis of material nonpublic information concerning a pending tender offer that the investor knows or has reason to know has been acquired "directly or indirectly" from an insider of the issuer, or someone working on the investor's behalf.)[21]

4.3 Suppose you give your broker $10,000 to invest, and the broker makes a 22% gross return (before commissions). Your friend gives another broker $10,000, and this broker makes a 20% gross return. If commissions cost $200 per transaction, and your broker made three transactions and your friend's broker made only one transaction, who is now better off?

4.4 Suppose you were playing a very good game of golf (even par) one day with Bill, your golfing partner. On the thirteenth fairway, Bill mentions in passing that his firm is going to be bought out at $50 per share in the next few weeks, and it's affecting his golf game. (He is losing.) The next morning you discover that Bill's firm is trading at $30 per share.

a. If you purchase 1,000 shares of stock in Bill's firm at $30 and sell it one month later at $50, what

---

21.   This question is based, in part, on information contained in Brian M. McNamara and Robert A. Barron, "Quarterly Survey of SEC Rulemaking and Major Appellate Decisions," *Securities Regulation Law Journal* 20 (1992): 103–106. There is no claim that these are the actual facts of this case.

is your dollar profit? What was your monthly rate of return?

b. Is it ethical to purchase this stock?

c. Would you be committing a crime if you buy this stock?

4.5 Your broker manages your portfolio. She recommends that you change 50% of your portfolio almost every two months. The broker charges a 2% transaction cost on each buy or sell transaction. Thus, a round turn—purchase and sale of a security within a short time—transaction cost is 4%. How much do you pay in transaction costs, on average, as a percentage of your portfolio on an annual basis? What are the possible motives for such turnover?

Suppose the broker earns 14% annually on your portfolio before transaction costs. You could put your money in Treasury bills earning 5% annually with no transaction costs. Which strategy is better?

4.6 You are sitting on the board of directors of a firm that plans to repurchase its stock at $12 per share. The current price is $10 per share. You told your son to buy 10,000 shares before this information became public.

a. What is the profit if the price indeed jumps later to $12 per share?

b. Would your son's purchase be illegal?

4.7 As an underwriter, you have in your hand 1 million shares. You have a firm commitment to pay the firm $10 per share. The initial public offering was unsuccessful, and the price was only $8 per share.

a. What is your loss in such a case?

b. Suppose you convince the clients whose portfolios you manage to buy the stock for $10 per share. Is this unethical?

4.8 Assume the following: A lawsuit filed against General Motors alleges that the company falsified test results regarding the safety of its pickup trucks, and the firm's stock price falls 15%. Kodak is accused in a lawsuit filed by Konica, one of its competitors, of infringing on a 35-millimeter film-processing patent held by Konica, and the stock price of Kodak falls 5%. Interpret these results, assuming that there are no other events (either company, industry, or economic factors) that would have an impact on either stock price.

4.9 The earnings per share (EPS) of Evon Perfumes and the CEO's compensation are as follows:

	Year			
	1	2	3	4
EPS	5	4.5	4	1
CEO's Compensation (in million $)	1	1.1	1.5	2

The wages and bonuses of two out of the three members of the compensation committee are determined by the CEO. Analyze these data. Do the data indicate illegal action? Unethical action?

4.10 A pharmaceutical firm had initial encouraging results on tests of a new drug. The results were discussed at the board of directors meeting, but the public did not yet learn of the new discovery. A day after the board meeting, the firm's stock was traded for $10. A month later, when the information on the drug was made public, the stock was traded for $25. A board member's relative bought 100,000 shares at $10 a day after the meeting. The average stock price of firms in the industry rose 10% during this month.

a. Was the purchase of stock the day after the meeting illegal? Unethical?

b. What was the gain on the relative's transaction?

4.11 A broker has control of Dan Smith's account. Dan Smith finds the following changes in the number of shares of IBM in his account:

Date	Number of Shares
Jan. 1, 1999	5,000
Feb. 1, 1999	3,000
March 1, 1999	5,000
April 1, 1999	2,000

The broker's fee is 2% of the volume of transaction. Suppose that the stock of IBM was traded for $100 in the whole period between January 1, 1999, and April 1, 1999, and there were no new events or information released on IBM.

a. Calculate the broker's fee.

b. Can churning be suspected? What other information do you need to answer this question.

4.12 The table at the top of column 2 presents insider trading reporting for nonbank companies.

a. How is an insider defined in the table? When, according to the table, does the insider have to report the transaction to the SEC?

b. Suppose that the three insider traders of Whole Foods Market who sold 42% of their ownership in the firm made the transaction on December 28. Suggest how to examine whether the insider trading was illegal.

c. Suppose that on December 26, Whole Foods Market made a public announcement of information, and a few days earlier there was a large volume of sales of this stock by people who play golf with these three insiders. Is this illegal trading?

4.13 In 1997, the value of announced mergers was $781 billion:

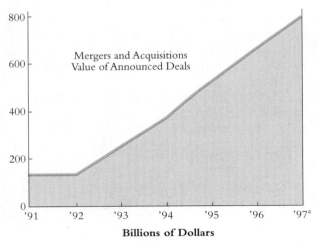

a. Through November 6.

Source: Data from Securities Data Company.

a. Suppose that the mergers were made public on a given date, and one month earlier the stock price went up, on average, by 30%. Are these results necessarily due to illegal insider trading? Suggest how to examine this hypothesis.

RECENT FILINGS

PURCHASES

Company	Symbol (Exch.)	% Chg. in Holdings	# of Insiders	# of Shares	$ Value (millions)
Data General DGN (N)		200	1	4,000	$0.079
Lilly Ind LI (N)		91	1	2,000	0.039*
Rational Software RATL (O)		80	1	100,000	0.933
Coventry CVTY (O)		57	1	10,000	0.158
Paging Network PAGE (O)		43	1	7,000	0.086*
Equity Inns ENN (N)		27	1	45,935	0.693
Pilgrim Amer Cap PACC (O)		26	1	2,000	0.042
Simpson Ind SMPS (O)		25	1	2,000	0.023
Utah Medical Prods UM (N)		16	2	7,000	0.050
Coach USA CUI (N)		2	2	7,000	0.200

SALES

Company	Symbol (Exch.)	% Chg. in Holdings	# of Insiders	# of Shares	$ Value (millions)
Encore Wire WIRE (O)		−55	2	70,000	$2.134
Airgas ARG (N)		−54	2	11,641	0.167
Tandy TAN (N)		−46	2	11,338	0.499
Whole Foods Market WFMI (O)		−42	3	504,825	20.602
CoreStaff CSTF (O)		−39	2	45,000	1.262
Advanced Fibre AFCI (O)		−15	2	365,000	11.748
Quickturn Des Sys QKTN (O)		−15	2	10,400	0.137
On Assignment ASGN (O)		−12	2	10,500	0.254
Wal-Mart WMT (N)		−10	2	49,384	1.959
McDonald MDD (N)		−7	2	16,200	0.382

An insider is any officer, director, or owner of 10% or more of a class of a company's securities. An insider must report any trade to the SEC by the 10th of the month following the transaction. The tables highlight companies that filed with the SEC in the seven-day period ended December 23, 1997. The tables do not include pension-plan or employee stock-option activity, trades by beneficial owners of 10% or more, trades under $2 per share, or trades under 100 shares. The "Purchases" column includes only open-market and private purchases; the "Sales" column includes only open-market and private sales, and excludes trades preceded by option exercise in the twelve months prior to the reported event. N = New York Stock Exchange. O = stock is included in NASDAQ National Market or NASDAQ Small Cap listings, or is traded over the counter and quoted only in "pink sheets" listings.

Source: CDA/Investnet, Fort Lauderdale, Fla. Adapted from *Barron's*, December 29, 1997, p. 49.

b. Suppose you discover that insiders who invested $10 billion in all these mergers pushed the price of the target firm, on average, from $100 to $110. Thus, the investors bought on average the stocks at $110. When this merger was announced the stock price, on average, jumped to $130. Given the above $10 billion volume invested in this merger, what is the total dollar amount of the insider traders' profit?

CFA PROBLEMS

4.1 Ann Carter, CFA, recently became a portfolio manager at Riverside Bank. She has both ERISA–qualified retirement plans and personal trust accounts. She knows she will be acting in a fiduciary capacity for both kinds of accounts and that her duties and responsibilities for both kinds of accounts will be similar.

Explain what a fiduciary is, and describe an investment manager's specific duties as a fiduciary under ERISA.

For Internet questions visit the Levy Investment Web site at http://levy-invst.swcollege.com.

YOUR TURN: APPLYING THEORY TO PRACTICE
IG METALL CHIEF FACES PRESSURE TO STEP DOWN

FRANKFURT—Franz Steinkuehler, the chairman of Germany's big IG Metall union, came under increasing pressure to step down a day after he confirmed that his personal stock dealings have come under the scrutiny of an insider-trading probe.

Mr. Steinkuehler, who sits on the supervisory board of Daimler–Benz AG, on Monday, confirmed press reports that he purchased 2,100 shares of Mercedes AG Holding (MAH) for just under one million marks ($619,700) in the two weeks ahead of Daimler-Benz's April 2 announcement of a stock swap that triggered a surge in MAH shares. He also confirmed that he bought the last 1,000 MAH shares only a day before the announcement, putting them in his son's account.

But the union boss said he hadn't had access to any insider information or any prior knowledge of the impending announcement when making the purchases.

Insider trading still isn't a prosecutable offense in Germany, although legislation is in the pipeline.

But public opinion appeared to be stacked against the union leader on Tuesday. Commentators focused not so much on whether he had insider information, but whether he should have been trading Mercedes stock at all because of his seat on Daimler-Benz's board.

The mass-circulation Bild newspaper trumpeted that while Mercedes was laying off workers, their union leader was speculating in its stock. The Handelsblatt financial daily asked how Mr. Steinkuehler can persuade workers to go on strike for a 50-mark pay raise "when he can pick up the telephone and earn more than a hundred thousand marks."

Source: "IG Metall Chief Faces Pressure to Step Down," *Wall Street Journal*, May 19, 1993, p. 2. Reprinted by permission of *The Wall Street Journal*, © 1993 Dow Jones & Co., Inc. All Rights Reserved Worldwide.

Questions

1. The stock price of Mercedes went up in two weeks (from the date of the first purchase by Steinkuehler to the announcement date of the swap), from 476 to 540 German Marks per share. What is the profit in German Marks? What is the rate of return on the investment for two weeks? What is the rate of return on an annual basis? What is the total profit on Steinkuehler's investment in German Marks? Assume that all 2,100 shares were bought at the beginning of the two weeks preceding the announcement.

2. Did Steinkuehler break the law in Germany? What is the corresponding law in the United States?

3. Do the Mercedes employees have a legal case against Steinkuehler? What about an ethical case? Discuss.

SELECTED REFERENCES

Association for Investment Management and Research. *Standards of Practice Handbook*. 5th ed. Charlottesville, Va.: AIMR, 1990.
  This is the standard reference for chartered financial analysts regarding ethics and standards of conduct.

Baker, H. Kent, ed. *Good Ethics: The Essential Element of a Firm's Success*. Charlottesville, Va.: Association for Investment Management and Research, 1994.
  This is a series of articles on the importance of good ethics for a firm's success.

Berenbeim, Ronald E. *Corporate Ethics*. New York: The Conference Board, 1987.
  This monograph examines the results of a survey of three hundred executives regarding twenty-five highly visible and complex ethical issues.

Hawkins, David. *Corporate Financial Reporting and Analysis*. 2d ed. Homewood, Ill.: Dow Jones–Irwin, 1986.
  This book is an excellent source of information related to the history of corporate reporting practices.

Hu, Henry T. C. "New Financial Products, The Modern Process of Financial Innovation and the Puzzle of Shareholder Welfare." *Financial Management Collection* 7, no. 1 (Winter 1992): 1–13.
  This article originally appeared in the Texas Law Review *(69, no. 6 (May 1991): 1273–1317) and provides a good summary of how financial innovation is influencing securities law.*

Securities Regulation Law Journal
  This quarterly publication reviews recent court cases related to securities law. Each edition contains a section titled "Quarterly Survey of SEC Rulemaking and Major Appellate Decisions." There are also good articles that discuss and debate the ramifications of new laws and regulations.

Viet, E. Theodore, and Michael R. Murphy. *Ethics in the Investment Profession: A Survey*. Charlottesville, Va.: The Research Foundation of the Institute of Chartered Financial Analysts, 1992.
  This forty-page monograph reports the results of a survey of four hundred investment analysts on ethical issues.

Williams, Gerald J. *Ethics in Modern Management*. New York: Quorum Books, 1992.
  This book provides a nice summary of some of the more popular ethical (moral) theories, such as cultural moral relativism, utilitarianism, and natural law.

More data on ethics is available in the following journals: *Ethics; Journal of Business Ethics; Professional Ethics.*

The following Web sites offer updated (1998) data about ethics:

http://www.condor.depaul.edu/ethics
http://www.babson.edu/
http://www.ethics.ubc.ca/

SUPPLEMENTAL REFERENCES

Casey, John L. *Ethics in the Financial Marketplace*. New York: Scudder, Stevens & Clark, 1990.

Cavanagh, Gerald F. *American Business Values*. 3d ed. Englewood Cliffs, N.J.: Prentice-Hall, 1990.

Hammer, Richard M., Gilbert Simonetti, Jr., and Charles T. Crawford, eds. *Investment Regulation around the World*. Somerset, N.J.: Ronald Press, 1983.

Lowenstein, Louis. *What's Wrong with Wall Street*. Reading, Mass.: Addison-Wesley, 1988.

Meulbroek, Lisa K. "An Empirical Analysis of Illegal Insider Trading." *Journal of Finance* 47 (1992): 1661–1699.

Schwartz, Robert A. *Equity Markets Structure, Trading, and Performance*. New York: Harper & Row, 1988.

Shefrin, Hersh, and Meir Statman. *Ethics, Fairness, Efficiency and Financial Markets*. Charlottesville, Va.: The Research Foundation of the Institute of Chartered Financial Analysts, 1992.

Tewles, Richard J., and Edward S. Bradley. *The Stock Market*. 5th ed. New York: Wiley, 1987.

CHAPTER 5

CALCULATING RATES OF RETURN

LEARNING OBJECTIVES

After studying this chapter you should be able to:

1. Understand the different methods for computing rates of return.

2. Analyze the impact of taxes and inflation on rate-of-return calculations.

3. Describe how returns can increase or decrease when exchange rates change.

4. Contrast the different types of stock indexes.

5. Compare the historical risk-return trade-off for stocks and bonds.

INVESTMENTS IN THE NEWS

THE BEST MUTUAL FUNDS—U.S. STOCK FUNDS

It's been a great market for investors, but a frustrating one for

mutual fund managers. Only 49 of the funds listed beat the

S&P's 19.8% average annual five-year return, and that's before

subtracting sales loads and taxes. Even the very best fund on our

list, PBHG Growth, had a tricky time of it. The fund boasts a

terrific five-year adjusted return of 24.8%, but that masks a

horrible stretch over the past year, when PBHG was down 4%

compared with the overall market's 20% gain. . . .

Source: Maria Atanasov, "The Best Mutual Funds," *Fortune*, December 29, 1997, pp. 122–136. Reprinted from the December 29, 1997, issue of *Fortune* by special permission © 1997 Time, Inc.

Investors are willing to defer current consumption for future consumption because they expect to earn a return by investing. This chapter looks at returns from investments in financial securities and the measure used to determine how much an investment has earned—specifically, the **rate of return,** which is most simply calculated by dividing the dollar profit by the amount originally invested. Rates of return are most often expressed in percentages, as in this chapter's Investments in the News. Investors must understand how rates of return are calculated and reported to make inferences from them. This chapter describes various methods for calculating rates of return.

Rates of return are reported in the financial media, as illustrated in Investments in the News, to rank the performance of various financial assets. Mutual funds are evaluated based on their previous 1-year and 5-year performances. The rates of return for mutual funds are compared with these of the S&P 500, because that index represents the average performance of the stock market during that period. Such data on historical rates of return are used to evaluate money managers and to help investors make decisions about future investments.

Rates of return measure the profitability of an investment in various assets. As Chapters 6 through 11 will show, rates of return, and in particular their dispersion, are also used to measure risk. Indeed, the rest of the article in Investments in the News, which appeared in *Fortune,* reported (not shown here) that the average annual rate of return on the corporate bond funds it analyzed was only 5.3%, compared with the 19.8% average annual 5-year rate of return on the S&P 500. If stocks have unusual returns relative to bonds, why do investors invest in bonds? Chapters 6 through 11 are devoted to examining why one would invest in bonds. First, however, a knowledge of how to calculate rates of return is necessary.

5.1 USING RATES OF RETURN

One important use of rates of return is in a comparison of the profitability of different investments. It is standard practice for investment managers to present the profitability of financial assets in percentage figures rather than in dollar amounts. Profitability in percentages enables investors to compare the rates of return on various assets of different levels of investment. For example, you can determine which of two investments is more profitable by comparing the rate of return on AT&T with that of Microsoft. Suppose you could earn $200 on AT&T stock and $100 on Microsoft stock. Is the investment in AT&T better than Microsoft? If you had to invest $1,000 in AT&T but only $200 in Microsoft, the investment in Microsoft would surely be better. Comparing the profit in percentage form gives you the information you need. AT&T's rate of return is $200/$1,000 = 0.20, or 20%. Microsoft's rate of return is $100/$200 = 0.50, or 50%.

Recall that unlike an investment in physical assets (such as machinery), you can increase (or decrease) the size of an investment in the stock market. That is, financial assets are divisible, whereas most physical assets are not. You could invest $1,000 (instead of $200) in Microsoft and receive $500 (= $100 · 5). Thus, for a higher investment in Microsoft, you would receive a higher dollar return. Because the investment scale can be changed, for comparing profitability on financial assets, the absolute dollar profit is meaningless. The percentage figures are more appropriate.

In addition to comparing investments in different assets, investors and investment analysts have the following three other uses for rates of return:

1. *Measuring historical performance.* Suppose you have two mutual funds managed by two professional managers, Abraham and Alita. The managers of the two funds are free to invest in all available assets. You want to compensate managers who do a good job and fire those who do a bad job. An important measure of a manager's performance is the historical rate of return, or the **realized rates of return** on the funds. Realized rates of return are rates of return that have already been earned, as opposed to rates of return *expected* for the future. Realized rates of return are also called **ex-post rates of return.** In contrast, ex-ante rates of return are rates of return that are expected to occur in the future.

    Rates of return may not be entirely sufficient to rank these two managers, because you also need to know how much risk each manager has taken. Nevertheless, if Abraham has earned an average of +1% over the past 10 years and Alita has earned an average of +10% over the past 10 years, and the annual risk-free rate was 3%, then you can rank the managers solely on rates of return. Because Alita outperformed Abraham by such a substantial margin and Abraham earned less than the risk-free interest rate, Abraham should be fired, or at least not highly rewarded.

2. *Determining future investment.* Investors may use historical rates of return to estimate future returns and risk of various securities—estimates that are needed to make portfolio investment decisions (see Chapter 8). Most stock prices fluctuate over time. However, over long periods of time, some types of stock are expected to yield a higher average rate of return than others. For example, because of the higher risks, an investor expects to get a higher return on Microsoft (a software development company with erratic earnings) than on Pacific Gas Corporation (a regulated public utility with stable earnings).

    When you plan your investment holdings, you can look at the historical average rates of return of Microsoft and Pacific Gas Corporation, and those averages can serve as the best estimate of what will happen in the future. For example, suppose the average rate of return on Microsoft over the past 10 years was 20%, and you plan to invest for 1 year. In the absence of more information regarding the future of Microsoft, you expect that your investment in Microsoft, on average, will earn 20% next year. This is your best estimate of the future. However, the realized return next year may be dramatically different from this figure.

    Also, generally speaking, future fluctuations in rates of return can be estimated by looking at historical rates of return. The fluctuations of Microsoft's rate of return are higher than the fluctuations of Pacific Gas Corporation's rate of return. You wish to measure and use these fluctuations in constructing your investment holdings (your portfolio; see Chapter 8).

3. *Estimating cost of capital.* Finally, rates of return can be used to estimate a firm's cost of equity, as studied in corporate finance. Recall that financial managers use the cost of equity (or cost of capital) in capital budgeting decisions. One method for

estimating the appropriate discount rate to use in net-present-value calculations utilizes historical rates of return on equity.

5.2 RATE-OF-RETURN CALCULATIONS

Rates of return can be calculated in more than one way. Some methods yield different results than others, and money managers, who are rated on their performance, have an incentive to use those methods that make them look best. With this problem in mind, in 1992 the Committee for Performance Presentation Standards (CPPS) of the Association of Investment Management and Research (AIMR) established strict guidelines for its members to follow in presenting historical performance measures. The AIMR is the largest association of financial analysts in the world, with over thirty thousand members in 1997. The AIMR standards are probably the ones you will have to adhere to if you become involved in the money management industry. This section reviews the techniques used in complying with the AIMR standards.[1]

5.2.1 Simple Rates of Return

Investors hold a security for a given period. The rate of return measured for this period is called the *holding period return* (HPR). There are several ways to measure security returns. This discussion begins with the simple rate of return.

The simple rate of return measures by how much the value of a given investment increases or decreases over a given period of time. The **simple rate of return** (R) is given by

$$R = \frac{EMV - BMV + I}{BMV} \tag{5.1}$$

where *EMV* is the ending market value, *BMV* is the beginning market value, and *I* is income received from the investment. This is the most common and simplest way of estimating the rate of return. Equation 5.1 gives rates of return in decimal form. To get percentages, simply multiply by 100.

To demonstrate the simple-rate-of-return calculation, assume you purchased 200 shares of stock at the beginning of the year for $100 per share. At the end of the year, you receive an $8 cash dividend per share. The stock is trading at the end of the year at $110 per share. The rate of return in this case is

$$R = \frac{(200 \cdot \$110) - (200 \cdot \$100) + (200 \cdot \$8)}{(200 \cdot \$100)}$$

$$= \frac{200}{200}\left(\frac{\$110 - \$100 + \$8}{\$100}\right) = \frac{\$18}{\$100} = 0.18, \text{ or } 18\%$$

Note that the rate of return does not depend on whether you buy 200, 100, or even 1 share of stock, because the number of shares (200, in this example) is common to every term in the equation and hence cancels. (This is not always the case, as will be illustrated later.)

Determining a stock's or a portfolio's performance using the simple-rate-of-return calculation is useful when the period selected has no income except at the end. The simple rate of return has some limitations, however. It does not accurately account for the timing of cash dividends that are paid more frequently than once a year. Clearly, an investor would rather have the dividends at the beginning of the year than at the end. Also, when investing in bonds, one must account for accrued interest. That is, the buyer in the secondary market must pay to the seller any interest accrued up to the selling date.

It is easier to see the timing problem if we rewrite Equation 5.1 as follows:

$$R = \frac{EMV - BMV}{BMV} + \frac{I}{BMV} \qquad (5.1')$$

or

Rate of Return = Capital Gain or Loss + Cash Flow Yield

There are two components to the simple rate of return: (1) capital gains or losses and (2) the cash flow yield. The first term on the right of the equals sign is the capital gain or loss as a percentage of the initial investment in the security. The second term is the cash flow yield, such as the dividend yield on a stock. The capital gain or loss component is realized at the end of the period. It is assumed in this equation that the income is also received at the end of the period. Clearly, if a dividend has been paid in the middle of the period, it could have been invested to earn even more by the end of the period. Thus, the simple-rate-of-return method ignores the timing of income payments.

Note that Equation 5.1 can also be written as

$$R = \frac{EMV + I}{BMV} - \frac{BMV}{BMV} = \frac{EMV + I}{BMV} - 1$$

and hence,

$$1 + R = \frac{EMV + I}{BMV}$$

which, in the earlier example, would be

$$1 + R = \frac{(200 \cdot \$110) + (200 \cdot \$8)}{(200 \cdot \$100)} = \$1.18$$

which tells us that the value of $1 at the end of the period is $1.18. That is, $1 invested one period earlier would be worth $1.18 at the end of the period.

5.2.2 Adjusted Rate of Return

The simple rate of return is not accurate, because it does not take into account the timing of dividends. To illustrate, consider two stocks, each with a $100 price at the beginning of the year and a $110 price at the end of the year. The cash dividend is $10 for each stock. However, on one stock, the $10 is paid in January, whereas on the other stock it is paid in December. The simple rate of return shows a 20% rate of return on both stocks, regardless of the timing of the cash dividends. However, investors are not indifferent to the timing of cash dividends. The earlier the dividends are obtained, the better off are the investors.

The **adjusted rate of return** is used to calculate rates of return by taking into account the timing of cash dividends. Because the adjusted rate of return takes into account the timing of the cash flows, it is called the **time-weighted rate of return.** This correct rate of return is used in the rest of the chapter, so it will be called *the rate of return* to distinguish it from the *simple rate of return*. The rate of return assumes that all interim cash flows are reinvested in the security under consideration. For example, if an investor wants to measure the rate of return for 1998 on Xerox stock, and $10 dividends are paid in January, then the $10 is used to purchase more Xerox stock immediately after the dividends are received. The AIMR explains the philosophy of this adjustment as follows.

If cash flows occur during the period, they must theoretically be used, in effect, "to buy additional units" of the portfolio at the market price on the day that they are received. Thus, the most accurate approach is to calculate the market value of the portfolio on the date of each flow, calculate an interim rate of return for the subperiod [according to Equation 5.1], and then link the subperiod returns to get the return for the month or quarter.[2]

PRACTICE BOX	
Problem	Suppose you began the year owning 1,000 shares of Borland International, Inc. (BI), common stock, which was trading for $25 per share. In May, BI declared a 3-for-1 stock split. That is, each owner of 1 BI share received three new shares instead of the 1 share held. BI paid no cash dividends. At the end of the year, BI common stock was trading for $10 per share. What is the dollar return and rate of return from investing in BI?
Solution	From Equation 5.1, $I = \$0$, $BMV = 1{,}000 \cdot \$25 = \$25{,}000$, and $EMV = 3{,}000 \cdot \$10 = \$30{,}000$ (because of 3-for-1 splits). Therefore, the dollar return is $5,000 (or $30,000 − $25,000), and the rate of return is $$R = \frac{\$30{,}000 - \$25{,}000 + \$0}{\$25{,}000} = 0.20, \text{ or } 20\%$$

Thus we need to properly incorporate the timing of the cash flows to the investor or to adjust for the fact that dividends are generally not paid at the end of the

2. AIMR, p.28.

year. There are two approaches to computing the time-weighted rate of return (which we call the *rate of return* in order to distinguish it from the simple rate of return). The **linking method** calculates the simple rate of return to each subperiod when the cash dividend date determines the end of each subperiod, and then calculates the rate of return from these simple rates of return. The **index method** focuses on the notion that cash flows are used to purchase additional units of the portfolio. Both approaches yield the same adjusted rate-of-return values. The index method is useful in understanding time-weighted computations, whereas the linking method is simpler to calculate in practice. The following numerical example illustrates these two approaches to computing rates of return.

Assume you are investing in shares of ABC, Inc. Exhibit 5–1a shows the necessary data for your calculations. Notice that ABC, Inc., paid quarterly cash dividends, and its stock price fluctuated considerably during this year.[3] Specifically, notice that the price fell early in the year, rose during the latter part of the year, and fell again to its original level by year's end.

By the linking method, the simple rate of return (r_t) is calculated for each subperiod (t). Then the rate of return (R) for the entire period is obtained by the following formula:

EXHIBIT 5-1
Calculating a Time-Weighted Rate of Return for ABC, Inc.

(a) Table of Input Information

Date	Dollar Dividend per Share	Market Price When Dividend Is Received
January 1		$100
February 15	$2	80
May 15	2	95
August 15	2	105
November 15	2	120
December 31		100

(b) Calculating a Time-Weighted Rate of Return by the Linking Method

Date	Interim Period	Interim Rate of Return	Time-Weighted Rate of Return
January 1			
February 15	1	−0.18	−0.18
May 15	2	0.2125	−0.0057
August 15	3	0.1263	0.1198
November 15	4	0.1619	0.3011
December 31	5	−0.1667	0.0842

3. Dividends are typically declared about a month after the end of a fiscal quarter and paid two weeks later. Hence, most firms pay dividends in February, May, August, and November.

$$R = [(1 + r_1)(1 + r_2) \ldots (1 + r_m)] - 1$$

where m is the number of subperiods.

Exhibit 5-1b illustrates the linking method of computing returns. The simple rate of return over Period 1 (January 1 through February 15) is -0.18 [($80 - $100 + $2)/$100], and over Period 2 (February 15 through May 15) it is 0.2125 [($95 - $80 + $2)/$80]. Thus, the time-weighted rate of return over the period January 1 through May 15 is given by -0.0057 ([1 + (-0.18)][1 + 0.2125] $- 1$). Continuing this procedure, the time-weighted rate of return for the whole year is found to be 0.0842, or 8.42% (see the last entry in the last column of Exhibit 5-1b).

Note that an 8% return is obtained [($100 - $100 + $2 \cdot 4)/$100] if the timing of dividends is ignored and the simple rate of return given by Equation 5.1 is used. How can the 42-basis-point difference in the rates of return (8.42% $-$ 8.00%) be explained?[4] This question can be answered by working through the index method for the same investment (see Exhibit 5-2).

With the index method, we see that the 42-basis-point difference results from the additional shares received by reinvesting the dividends. For example, on February 15 each shareholder received $2 per share in dividends, which could have been invested in the stock at a cost of $80 per share. Thus, Exhibit 5-2 shows that on February 15, the owner of 100 shares of ABC, Inc., would receive $200 (or $2 \cdot 100), with which the shareholder could purchase 2.5 additional shares ($200/$80). Therefore, on May 15 this shareholder would receive $2 dividends on the original 100 shares, as well as $2 dividends on the additional 2.5 shares. Exhibit 5-2 illustrates how this reinvestment process would work throughout the entire year.

The additional shares purchased in Period t (AS_t) are calculated by the following formula:

$$AS_t = \frac{N_{t-1}D_t}{P_t} \tag{5.2}$$

where N_{t-1} is the number of shares owned at the end of Period $t - 1$ (for example, the number of shares owned on the ex-dividend date), D_t is the cash dividend paid

EXHIBIT 5-2 Calculating a Time-Weighted Rate of Return for ABC, Inc., by the Index Method	Date	Dollar Dividend per Share	Market Price When Dividend Is Received	Additional Shares Purchased	Number of Shares Owned
	January 1		$100		100
	February 15	$2	80	2.5	102.5
	May 15	2	95	2.1579	104.6579
	August 15	2	105	1.9935	106.6514
	November 15	2	120	1.7775	108.4289
	December 31		100		108.4289

4. Recall that a basis point is 1% of 1%.

in Period t, and P_t is the price per share in Period t after the dividends are paid. For example, 2.1579 additional shares are purchased on May 15, where

$$AS_t = (102.5 \text{ shares} \cdot \$2)/\$95$$

The number of shares owned is simply the number from the previous period plus any additional shares purchased during the period. Specifically,

$$N_t = N_{t-1} + AS_t$$

Notice in Exhibit 5-2 that when share prices are low, the dividends' receipts will buy more shares than when share prices are high. Because share prices are low early in the year, this investor is able to buy more shares early and hence receive more dividends during the rest of the year. By year's end, the investor has approximately 108.43 shares worth $100 per share. The rate of return over this year can be found by dividing the value of the investment at the end by the amount invested at the beginning and subtracting 1. That is,

$$R = \frac{P_n N_n}{P_0 N_0} - 1 = \frac{100 \cdot 108.4289}{100 \cdot 100} - 1 = 0.084289, \text{ or } 8.4289\% \qquad (5.3)$$

where P_n is the stock price at the end of the year, N_n is the number of shares owned at the end of the year, P_0 is the stock price at the beginning of the year, and N_0 is the number of shares owned at the beginning of the year. Equation 5.3 is similar to the equation for the simple rate of return given in Equation 5.1. Equation 5.3 assumes income to be zero, but the ending market value contains the dividends, as well as earnings on dividends, that were reinvested during the year.

The result of using the index method given in Equation 5.3 is exactly the same as the time-weighted rate of return found by the linking method (ignoring rounding errors). Therefore, by using the index method we can see that the time-weighted rate-of-return method appropriately handles interim cash flows such as dividend payments on common stocks.

To sum up this example, the 8% rate of return using the simple-rate-of-return method given by Equation 5.1 assumes that when the dividends are received they are either idle or consumed, whereas the time-weighted rate of return assumes reinvestment of the cash dividends. The time-weighted rate of return is the superior calculation for two reasons:

1. The time-weighted rate-of-return method appropriately addresses the timing of cash flows. Investors prefer to receive money now rather than later, a fact that is ignored by the simple method. For example, suppose that Firms A and B have the same data as those given in Exhibit 5-1, with only one difference: Firm A pays an $8 cash dividend at the beginning of the period, whereas Firm B pays an $8 cash dividend at the end of the period. Are investors indifferent regarding the dividend payment date, as Equation 5.1 implies? They are not, because of the time value of money. However, the simple-rate-of-return calculation can mislead investors into believing that the rate of return for both firms is the same.

2. The time-weighted rate-of-return method appropriately accounts for the investment of interim cash flows. Investors want to know how well different securities have performed over time. Thus, interim cash flows must be assumed to be invested in the security itself. For example, suppose you want to compare the historical rates of return on two firms, A and B. You invest $100 in Firm A and $100 in Firm B. Firm A pays you $50 in dividends after one day. Firm B does not pay dividends at all. Using the simple method to calculate rates of return does not make sense, because your investment in Firm A is reduced by $50 after one day. Thus, by the simple method, you actually compare the return on an investment of $100 in Firm B to $50 in Firm A. Therefore, the reinvestment assumption is incorporated in order to have an accurate measure of the performance of a particular security independent of its dividend policy.

Notice that the different calculation methods do not attempt to identify the best strategy for the investor but rather to measure the correct rate of return. For example, sometimes reinvesting the dividends is bad (for example, when the stock price falls). However, only the time-weighted rate-of-return method gives the true, objective, historical rate of return on a given asset.

PRACTICE BOX

Problem

Suppose you purchased 100 shares of GE on January 1 at $50 per share. GE pays $2.30 annual dividend per share on March 15, when the stock is trading at $55. GE declares a 3-for-2 stock split effective May 30, when the stock is trading at $60. (A 3-for-2 stock split implies 3 new shares for 2 old shares.) If GE closed on December 31 at $35 per share, what was your rate of return using the index method?

Solution

Using the index method, construct the following table:

Date	Dividend and Split	Market Price	AS_t[a]	$N_t = N_t + AS_t$
January 1		$50		100
March 15	$2.3	$55	4.182[b]	104.182
May 30	3-for-2	$60	52.091[c]	156.273
December 31		$35		156.273

a. See Equation 5.2.

b. Based on Equation 5.2, $(100 \cdot \$2.3)/\$55 = 4.182$.

c. For a 3-for-2 stock split, the number of shares owned after the split is $(3/2)(104.182) = 156.273$. Therefore, the added number of shares is $156.273 - 104.182 = 52.091$.

The rate of return from Equation 5.3 is

$$R = \frac{156.273 \cdot \$35}{100 \cdot \$50} - 1 \cong 0.0939, \ or \ 9.39\%.$$

5.2.3 Bond Returns on an Accrual Basis

Calculating the rate of return on bonds raises one more issue regarding the timing of cash flows. Whereas the cash dividends on stocks are paid on a periodic (most often quarterly) basis, bond coupon interest accrues *daily*. Thus, the equation for calculating bond returns must incorporate that accrued interest. The bond prices quoted by the financial media and market makers do not include accrued interest in most cases. However, the actual price paid for the bonds includes accrued interest. Therefore, when calculating the interim return of bonds, the investor must incorporate accrued interest. The CPPS of the AIMR describes the underlying philosophy of rate-of-return calculations for bonds:

The Standards clearly state that an accrual basis, rather than a cash basis, should be used for calculating interest income. The guiding premise, again, should be to include that income to which the portfolio was truly entitled if the security were sold at the end of the performance interval. Stock dividends do not become payable unless the stock is owned on the ex-dividend date. Dividends should therefore be accrued as income as of their ex-date. Interest on most fixed-income securities becomes payable pro rate as long as the security is held. Interest should therefore be accrued according to whatever method is appropriate for the specific issue.[5]

Rates of return for bonds calculated on a *cash* basis ignore the accrued interest (which the buyer has to pay), so they are not accurate. To account for accrued interest, simply add the values for accrued interest at the beginning and end of the period to the respective beginning and ending prices in Equation 5.1. Formally, the simple rate of return (R_t) can be expressed as

$$R_t = \frac{[(P_t + AI_t) - (P_{t-1} + AI_{t-1}) + C_t]}{(P_{t-1} + AI_{t-1})} \tag{5.4}$$

where the data on which a coupon C_t is paid is determined to the end of the subperiod corresponding to the simple-rate-of-return calculation and P_t is the price of the bond at the end of Period t, P_{t-1} is the price of the bond at the end of Period $t - 1$, AI_t is the accrued interest as of the end of Period t (investors get it if they sell the bonds), AI_{t-1} is the accrued interest as of the end of Period $t - 1$ (investors have to pay it when they buy the bonds), and C_t is the coupon paid at the end of Subperiod t. As is discussed later, if the coupon is paid at the end of the period, the accrued interest will be zero.

Let us illustrate how to calculate rates of return for bonds on an accrual basis. Consider a coupon bond that pays 8% on a semiannual basis. Assume that $40 in interest is paid on November 15 and January 15. Exhibit 5-3a illustrates how to calculate the time-weighted rate of return with the linking method. The exhibit lists the coupon payments, market prices, and accrued interest for each date. Recall from Equation 5.1 that the simple rate of return requires calculating the beginning and ending market values. The accrual basis incorporates accrued interest in these

5. Adapted with permission from *Report of the Performance Presentation Standards Implementation Committee*, December 1991, pp. 31–32. Copyright 1991, Association for Investment Management and Research, Charlottesville, Va. All rights reserved.

values. For example, consider the simple return during the period January 1 to May 15, where the beginning market value is $1,000 ($990 + $10, where $10 is accrued interest). The calculation of accrued interest will be handled in detail in Chapter 16. Until then, accrued interest can be estimated as the fraction of the period since the last payment times the payment amount. In this case, it is (1½ months/6 months) · $40 = $10. The 1½ months is November 15 to January 1. The ending market value is $1,030. The income paid in this period is the coupon payment of $40. Thus, the simple rate of return for the first interim period is

$$R_1 = \frac{[\$1,030 - (\$990 + \$10) + \$40]}{\$990 + \$10} = \frac{\$70}{\$1,000} = 0.07, \text{ or } 7\%$$

Note that the accrued interest at the end of Period i will be zero if there is a coupon payment. That is, all interest that has been accrued was paid via the coupon payment. From Exhibit 5-3 we find that the rate of return over this year was 9.03%.

EXHIBIT 5-3
Calculating the Rate of Return for an 8% Semi-annual Coupon-Bearing Bond

(a) Computing the Rate of Return by the Linking Method

Date (t)	Interim Period	Coupon	Market Price	Accrued Interest	Accrued Rate of Return	Rate of Return to t
Jan. 1			$ 990	$10[a]		
May 15	1	$40	$1,030	$ 0	0.08	0.07
Nov. 15	2	$40	$1,020	$ 0	0.0291	0.1011[b]
Dec. 31	3		$1,000	$10[a]	−0.0098	0.0903[c]

a. (1,000)(0.08)(1.5/12) = $10. (Interest is paid on May 15 and November 15.)

b. (1 + 0.07) · (1 + 0.0291) − 1 = 0.1011.

c. (1 + 0.1011) · (1 − 0.0098) − 1 = 0.0903.

(b) Computing Time-Weighted Rate of Return by the Index Method

Date (t)	Interim Period	Coupon	Market Price	Accrued Interest	Additional Bonds Purchased	Number of Bonds Owned
Jan. 1			$ 990	$10[a]		100
May 15	1	$40	$1,030	$ 0	3.8835[b]	103.8835
Nov. 15	2	$40	$1,020	$ 0	4.0738[c]	107.9573
Dec. 31	3		$1,000	$10		107.9573

a. (1,000)(0.08)(1.5/12) = $10. (Interest is paid on May 15 and November 15.)

b. ($40 · 100 bonds)/$1,030 = 3.8835 bonds.

c. ($40 · 103.8835 bonds)/$1,020 = 4.0738 bonds.

Exhibit 5-3b illustrates how to calculate the rate of return with the index method. Assuming the investor buys 100 bonds, the rate of return, using the index method, is

$$R = \frac{(\$1,000 + \$10)(107.9573)}{(\$990 + \$10)(100)} - 1 \cong 0.09037$$

or approximately 9.037%. Once again the results of the index method are approximately equal to the time-weighted rate of return, and the slight difference is due to rounding.

5.3 AFTER-TAX RATES OF RETURN

Taxes generally change the return an investor receives. Although many pension funds and other portfolios are tax exempt, the security holdings of many investors are taxable. The procedure for calculating after-tax returns is conceptually similar to the simple-rate-of-return calculations in Section 5.2. The only difference is the reduction of income (dividends or coupon payments) resulting from taxes. To include the impact of taxes on the simple-rate-of-return calculation, adjust the simple-rate-of-return calculation when it is not the last interim period:

$$R_t = \frac{EMV_t - BMV_t + I_t(1 - T)}{BMV_t} \tag{5.5}$$

where R_t is the interim after-tax rate of return, EMV_t is the market value at the end of Interim Period t, BMV_t is the market value at the beginning of Interim Period t, I_t is the income (cash dividends or coupon payments) paid at the end of Interim Period t, and T is the income tax rate.

Capital gains taxes are incorporated only at year-end, when it is assumed that the security is sold.[6] Assume you buy the stock and then sell it after holding it for one period. Thus, the after-tax, simple rate of return for the *last* interim period (R_n) ending at year-end is

$$R_n = \frac{EMV_n - BMV_n - N_0(P_n - P_0)T_g + I_n(1 - T)}{BMV_n} \tag{5.6}$$

where EMV_n is the market value of the security at the end of Period n, BMV_n is the market value of the security at the beginning of Period n, N_0 is the number of shares owned at the beginning of the year, P_n is the price of the stock at the end of Period n, P_0 is the price of the stock at the beginning of the nth period, T_g is the capital gains rate, I_n is the income (cash dividends or coupon payments) paid at the end of interim Period n, and T is the income tax rate.[7] Assuming no splits or stock dividends, the term $-N_0(P_n - P_0)T_g$ accounts for the loss due to payment of capital

---

6. If the time horizon of the portfolio is long term, one could assume that capital gains taxes were incurred.

7. The tax system in most countries distinguishes between income and capital gains; they usually are taxed at different rates.

gains taxes (or gains due to tax reduction with capital losses). This is actually only an approximation because of the reinvestment-of-dividends assumption.

Assuming a 25% tax rate on dividends, Exhibit 5-4 uses the information from Exhibit 5-1 on ABC, Inc., stock and illustrates the after-tax computations for five periods. It is assumed that shares are bought on January 1 and sold on December 31. The simple rate of return for the first period is -0.1850 {[$80 $-$ $100 + $2 (1 $-$ 0.25)]/$100 = $-18.50/100$}. This is lower than the interim rate of return of -0.18 calculated with no taxes in Exhibit 5-1b. Notice that taxes reduced the time-weighted rate of return. The rate of return was 8.42% before taxes (see Exhibit 5-1b), and taxes reduced the return to 6.27% (see Exhibit 5.4). Also notice that, in this example, there are no capital gains, because the beginning price is equal to the ending price.[8]

An alternative method used to adjust for taxes is to employ the following equation:

$$R_{AT} = R_{BT}(1 - T) \qquad (5.7)$$

where R_{AT} is the after-tax return, R_{BT} is the time-weighted rate of return before taxes, and T is the income tax rate. This approach is an approximation that assumes that all income tax is paid at the end of the performance interval and that the income tax rate is the same as the capital gains tax rate. In our example,

$$R_{AT} = 0.0842(1 - 0.25) = 0.0632$$

which results in an estimation error of five basis points $(0.0632 - 0.0627)$. The difference is more significant when the underlying price makes a significant move from its original value and capital gains taxes are incurred.

5.4 INFLATION-ADJUSTED RATES OF RETURN

Thus far we have calculated rates of return in nominal dollars, ignoring the effect of inflation.[9] Inflation causes investors to lose purchasing power when they sell their

EXHIBIT 5-4 Calculating a Time-Weighted Rate of Return for ABC, Inc., on an After-Tax Basis Assuming a 25% Income and Capital Gains Tax	Date (t)	Interim Period	Dollar Dividend	Market Price	Simple Rate of Return	Rate of Return to t
	Jan. 1			$100	N/A	N/A
	Feb. 15	1	$2	$ 80	-0.1850	-0.1850
	May 15	2	$2	$ 95	0.2063	-0.0169
	Aug. 15	3	$2	$105	0.1211	0.1022
	Nov. 15	4	$2	$120	0.1571	0.2753
	Dec. 31	5		$100	-0.1667	0.0627

8. Technically, one should also consider the capital gains and losses on reinvested dividends. However, this would greatly increase the computational difficulties without significantly altering the results.

9. *Inflation* is the increase over time in the cost of goods and services. *Deflation* refers to the decrease over time in the cost of goods and services.

assets in the future and wish to buy goods with the proceeds. Investors would probably rather have no inflation than positive inflation.

The consumer price index (denoted CPI in the U.S. financial press) measures the inflation rate. The CPI is the percentage change in the price of a specified basket of consumer goods. The index was normalized to 100 in 1982. That is, the value of the basket of goods in 1982 was divided by itself and multiplied by 100. The value of the basket of goods for each year is divided by the basket's value in 1982 and multiplied by 100. For example, in May 1997, the CPI was 160.1, and in May 1998 the CPI was 162.8. Hence, the inflation rate (h) for the year May 1997–May 1998 was

$$h = \frac{CPI_1 - CPI_0}{CPI_0} \tag{5.8}$$

Using this formula we have

$$h = \frac{162.8 - 160.1}{160.1} \cong 0.0169$$

1.69%, where CPI_1 denotes the CPI at the end of the period and CPI_0 denotes the CPI at the beginning of the period.

Inflation reduces the purchasing power of an investment. That is, a person may invest $1,000 with the expectation of getting $1,100 back in a year and of using this sum to purchase goods and services. If the overall cost of these goods and services rises more than 10% over the year, however, this investment will not be sufficient. To demonstrate, suppose upon graduation, Brian wants to buy a suit and briefcase. He has saved $1,000 for both items, but because of inflation, the cost increases to $1,150. Brian's savings during this same period increase only from $1,000 to $1,100. Although he has made a 10% nominal rate of return [($1,100 − $1,000)/$1,000] on his investment, the inflation rate has been 15% [($1,150 − $1,000)/$1,000], which means that in real terms, Brian lost money. To include inflation in our calculations, we must determine the real rate of return.

The **real rate of return** is the nominal rate of return adjusted for inflation. The real rate of return (R_{real}) is calculated as

$$R_{real} = \frac{1 + R_{nom}}{1 + h} - 1 \tag{5.9}$$

where R_{nom} is the nominal rate of return and h is the inflation rate.[10] Thus, in Brian's case, the real rate of return is

$$R_{real} = \frac{1 + 0.1}{1 + 0.15} - 1 \cong -0.0435, \text{ or } -4.35\%$$

Note two properties of real rates of return:

10. Equation 5.9 can be approximated by $R_{real} = R_{nom} - h$, where R_{real} is the real rate of return, R_{nom} is the nominal rate of return and h is the inflation rate. This is known as the *Fisher relationship*, which was originally proposed by I. Fisher, *The Theory of Interest* (New York: Macmillan, 1930).

1. If there is no inflation ($h = 0$), then the real rate of return is equal to the nominal rate of return.

2. If the nominal rate of return is equal to the inflation rate ($R_{nom} = h$), then in real terms, the rate of return is zero. In Brian's case, suppose the prices of goods go up only from \$1,000 to \$1,100. In this case, Brian gets a zero real rate of return.

5.5 FOREIGN EXCHANGE AND RATES OF RETURN

Today, many investors invest abroad either directly or indirectly (through mutual funds). Exchange rates can alter the rate of return realized on an international investment. Although a falling dollar may be good for U.S. investors in a foreign country, it is bad for foreign investors in the United States. This section illustrates how foreign exchange influences rates of return. Connecting Theory to Practice 5.1 describes the impact of foreign exchange changes on international investments.

CONNECTING THEORY TO PRACTICE 5.1

GERMANY'S RATE DECISION MAY DETERMINE WHETHER DOLLAR'S SLIDE WILL CONTINUE

NEW YORK—How low can the dollar go?

Yesterday, the U.S. currency momentarily fell to a 1992 low against the mark. With the dollar—after dropping for the better part of four months—now flirting just above its post–World War II low, traders and investors are wondering how much longer the slide will continue.

The slumping dollar has widespread consequences for U.S. and foreign businesses and investors. A weak dollar should help make U.S. industry more competitive by lowering the prices of U.S. exports, while increasing the prices that American consumers must pay for goods manufactured abroad.

A falling dollar is also good news for those U.S. investors who already own foreign stocks and bonds. That's because foreign securities become more valuable when converted into dollars. But foreign investors who own U.S. stocks and bonds aren't as lucky. Indeed, the falling dollar has already reduced the value of their U.S. investments. Thus, if the dollar continues to fall, foreigners could shy away from U.S. markets.

Source: Michael R. Sesit, "Germany's Rate Decision May Determine Whether Dollar's Slide Will Continue," *Wall Street Journal*, July 16, 1992, p. C1. Reprinted by permission of *The Wall Street Journal*, © 1992 Dow Jones & Co., Inc. All Rights Reserved Worldwide.

MAKING THE CONNECTION

This excerpt illustrates that there are both rewards and dangers in foreign investing. In this instance, U.S. investors in Germany are profiting as the dollar slumps, whereas German investors in the United States are losing.

A weak dollar means U.S. products that are sold overseas will generate greater profits in U.S. dollars. Alternatively, foreign products in the United States will be more expensive. It is worth mentioning that on July 15, 1992, the exchange rate was DM 1.487 per dollar. On April 3, 1995, the exchange rate dropped to DM 1.375 per dollar. On June 29, 1998, the tables turned; the dollar became stronger, up to DM 1.818 per dollar. Similarly, by July 1998 the yen deteriorated relative to the dollar (up to 140 yen per dollar), inducing a big loss to American investors who held yen. Obviously, the exchange rates cannot be ignored in measuring the rate of return on foreign investments.

Exhibit 5-5 traces the path of a $100 investment by a U.S. investor in a German stock. Step 1 is to convert the U.S. dollars ($) to deutsche Marks (DM). Suppose the foreign exchange rate today is fx_0 ($/DM) = 0.6. That is, one deutsche Mark will buy $0.60 (or 60 cents). Alternatively, 1 U.S. dollar will buy 1.67 deutsche Marks. That is, fx_0 (DM/$) = $1/fx_0$ ($/DM) = 1/0.6 = 1.67. Therefore, the $100 investment is worth DM 166.67.

Step 2 is to invest in the German stock. In this example, the rate of return on the stock is 15% in Germany during the year. The U.S. investor ends up with DM 191.67, or DM 166.67 · (1 + 0.15). Finally, Step 3 is to convert the DM 191.67 back to U.S. dollars at the new exchange rate, which has fallen to $0.5/DM. The investor is left with $95.8. That is, the U.S. dollar became more valuable relative to Marks. At the beginning of the year, $1 would buy DM 1.67 ($1/$0.6 per DM). At the end of the year, $1 would buy DM 2 ($1/$0.5 per DM). Thus, we say that the dollar rallied. Alternatively, the Mark would buy $0.6 at the beginning of the year and only $0.5 at the end. Hence, we say the Mark depreciated.

In this case, the actual return to the U.S. investor was a loss of 4.2%, or ($95.8/$100) − 1. Although the investor earned 15% in the *local* currency of German Marks, the exchange rate decline from 0.6 to 0.5 wiped out all of the rate of return and produced a 4.2% loss as well. Thus, foreign investments contain two components: the return in local currency and the return on foreign exchange.

EXHIBIT 5-5
The Return to a U.S.
Investor in a German Stock

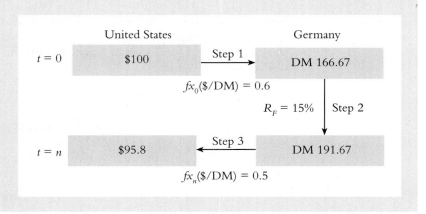

Formally, the rate of return adjusted for foreign exchange risk (R_D) is as follows:

$$R_D = \frac{fx_n(DC/FC)}{fx_0(DC/FC)}(1 + R_L) - 1 \qquad (5.10)$$

where $fx_n(DC/FC)$ is the foreign exchange rate at time n in domestic currency (DC) per foreign currency (FC), $fx_0(DC/FC)$ is the rate at time 0, and R_L is the rate of return in the foreign investment in local currency.

Note that the rate of return on foreign exchange alone (R_{fx}) can be calculated as

$$R_{fx} = \frac{fx_n(DC/FC)}{fx_0(DC/FC)} - 1 \qquad (5.11)$$

For example, in the case of German Marks,

$$R_{fx} = \frac{\$0.5/DM}{\$0.6/DM} - 1 \cong -0.167$$

or -16.7%. Thus, this investor lost 16.7% simply from changes in exchange rates. Substituting Equation 5.11 into Equation 5.10, we have an alternative method to compute returns in domestic currency:

$$R_D = (1 + R_{fx})(1 + R_L) - 1$$

In our illustration with the German investment, we have

$$R_D = (1 - 0.167)(1 + 0.15) - 1 \cong 0.042$$

Exhibit 5-6 illustrates the risk related to foreign exchange. The graph clearly shows that the returns to a U.S. investor in French stocks are much different than the returns to a French investor.

PRACTICE BOX

Problem

Suppose you invested in the Japanese stock market last year. At the beginning of the year, the foreign exchange rate was $0.008/yen, and by the end of the year it had risen to $0.01/yen. If your Japanese portfolio was down 15% that year, what was your rate of return?

Solution

From Equation 5.10, we have

$$R_D = \frac{\$0.01/yen}{\$0.008/yen}(1 - 0.15) - 1 = 0.0625$$

or 6.25%. Thus, although the market was down by 15%, you would still have earned 6.25% by investing in Japanese stocks.

EXHIBIT 5-6   **Monthly Rates of Retrun on French Stocks, in French Francs and U.S. Dollars (57 months, 3/93 to 12/97)**

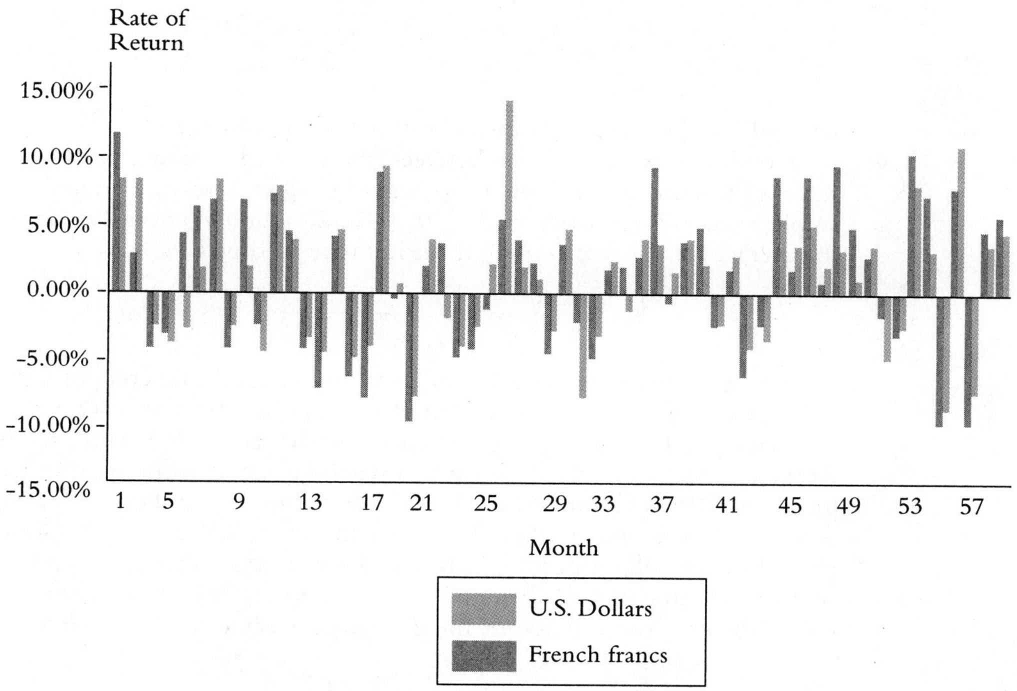

Source: Derived from Morgan Stanley Capital International (MSCI) France Index at Web site http://www.ms.com/MSCIDATA.

5.6 AVERAGE RATE OF RETURN

To measure the return on a portfolio of assets in a given year or to measure the return on a specific security (or a portfolio) across years, some averages must be calculated. There are two main methods for calculating averages of financial assets. These methods use the **arithmetic average** and the **geometric average.** Because the two methods yield different results, it is important to study them and be able to understand the interpretation of these two averages. Section 5.7 analyzes various indexes that also measure the average change in a basket of assets.

This section discusses the historical averages, called ex-post averages, to distinguish them from expected values or means, which relate to future values (ex-ante values). The **arithmetic method** of determining the average rate of return adds the realized rate of return over different periods[11] identified by subscript t (R_t) and divides by the number of observations (m). That is,

$$\overline{R}_A = \frac{\sum_{t=1}^{m} R_t}{m} \tag{5.12}$$

where $\overline{R}_A$ is the average (or mean) arithmetic rate of return.

Recall that we distinguish between the forward-looking, or ex-ante, expected returns [denoted as $E(R)$] and historical, or ex-post, returns (denoted as $\overline{R}$). For example, if AT&T stock returned −10%, 0%, 25%, and 9% over the past 4 years, then the average rate of return using the arithmetic method is

$$\overline{R}_A = \frac{-0.10 + 0.0 + 0.25 + 0.09}{4} = 0.06, \text{ or } 6\%$$

The **geometric method** is an averaging method that compounds rates of return. That is, if $1 is invested in Period 1, then it will be worth $(1 + R_1)$ at the end of Period 1. The geometric method assumes that $(1 + R_1)$ is invested in Period 2. At the end of Period 2, the investment will be worth the amount invested at the beginning of Period 2 times the value of a dollar invested in Period 2. That is, the investment at the end of Period 2 is worth $(1 + R_1)(1 + R_2)$. Continuing this procedure over all ex-post periods would give us the value at the end of m periods of a $1 investment at the beginning of the period. This total return is averaged by taking the mth root. Therefore, the geometric average can be expressed as[12]

$$\overline{R}_G = \left[\prod_{t=1}^{m} (1 + R_t) \right]^{1/m} - 1 \tag{5.13}$$

where $\overline{R}_G$ is the average (or mean) geometric rate of return. Using the example of AT&T stock, we have

$$\overline{R}_G = [(1 - 0.1)(1 + 0)(1 + 0.25)(1 + 0.09)]^{1/4} - 1 \cong 0.0523,$$

or 5.23%. Notice that the geometric average of 5.23% is different from the arithmetic average of 6%.

Let us look at a more dramatic case to illustrate the different results obtained from these two methods. Suppose a mutual fund paid no dividends and began with a market value of $100 per share. At the end of the first year, the fund was worth $50 per share, and at the end of the second year, the fund was once again worth $100 per

---

11. At this point, the length of the period (t) does not matter. It can be a year, a quarter, or even a day.

12. The symbol $\prod$ means "Take the product of." For example, $y = \prod^{3} x_i$ means $y = x_1 \cdot x_2 \cdot x_3$. Thus, if $x_1 = 1$, $x_2 = 2$, $x_3 = 3$, then $y = 1 \cdot 2 \cdot 3 = 6$.

share. The rate of return in the first year was [($50 − $100)/$100] = −0.50, or a loss of 50%. The rate of return in the second year was [($100 − $50)/$50] = 1.0, or an increase of 100%. The arithmetic average is (−0.5 + 1.0)/2 = 0.25, or 25%. The geometric average, however, is $[(1 − 0.5)(1 + 1)]^{1/2} − 1 = 0\%$.

Suppose you invest for 2 years in the fund. Which averaging method is correct—the 0% geometric average rate of return or the 25% arithmetic average rate of return?

In this case, you originally invested $100 and after 2 years ended up with $100. Clearly, from an investor's viewpoint, there was no profit, or a 0% rate of return. The geometric average, therefore, is the correct calculation, because it shows a zero rate of return that reflects the change in the value to the investor. Indeed, the geometric average can be interpreted as being the actual growth of the assets, and the arithmetic average is meaningless in this case.

In two situations, however, the arithmetic average is accurate and should be used:

1. The arithmetic method is correct when estimating the average performance across different securities for one period of time. For example, you would use the arithmetic average when calculating the average return for securities within a specific industry. If you wanted to assess the performance of the automobile industry over last year, you would take the arithmetic average of rates of return of automobile stocks. That is, you would not be measuring growth over time but rather performance during one period of time.

2. The arithmetic average is an unbiased estimate of future expected rates of return.[13] Suppose we want to invest in Microsoft for just 1 year. By taking the arithmetic average of the last 10 years, we get the best estimate of next year's rate of return. To see this, recall the mutual fund example. Looking at past performance, we know that in one year the rate of return was −50%, and in the second year it was +100%. Suppose further that these are the only two possible outcomes for the future. Because we do not know which outcome will occur next year, our best estimate is that on average, we will make 25%, a case where the arithmetic average is relevant. Note that we are *not* addressing the long-run performance of the fund but only what we expect to earn over the next year. For portfolio investment decisions discussed in Chapters 7 and 8, we use the arithmetic average as an estimate of the expected rate of return on the portfolio.

The arithmetic average will exceed the geometric average as long as rates of returns are not constant. Hence, the arithmetic average is sometimes said to be upwardly biased. The difference between these two averages is greater when the volatility of returns is larger. If there is zero volatility, then the arithmetic average is equal to the geometric average.

---

13. This assumes, of course, that the probability distribution is stable. That is, the distribution from which historical observations were made is the same as the distribution from which future observations will be made. The mathematical proof of this assertion can be found in most basic statistics books.

PRACTICE BOX

Problem

Calculate the arithmetic and geometric annual average rates of return for the Abbott and Costello mutual funds. Explain the differences between the two results.

Year	Abbott Fund	Costello Fund
1	10%	8%
2	5	12
3	−15	11
4	40	9

Solution

Writing the rates of return in decimal figures, the arithmetic averages are

$$\overline{R}_{A,\,Abbott} = \frac{0.1 + 0.05 - 0.15 + 0.4}{4} = 0.10$$

$$\overline{R}_{A,\,Costello} = \frac{0.08 + 0.12 + 0.11 + 0.09}{4} = 0.10$$

The geometric averages are

$$\overline{R}_{G,\,Abbott} = [(1 + 0.1)(1 + 0.05)(1 - 0.15)(1 + 0.4)]^{1/4} - 1 \cong 0.083$$

$$\overline{R}_{G,\,Costello} = [(1 + 0.08)(1 + 0.12)(1 + 0.11)(1 + 0.09)]^{1/4} - 1 \cong 0.0999$$

The difference between the geometric and arithmetic averages is larger for the Abbott Fund because it has greater volatility (−15% to 40%). The more volatile the returns, the greater the difference between the geometric average and the arithmetic average.

5.7 INDEXES

Indexes are widely used to measure historical rates of return across several securities. Almost all evening newscasts and newspapers report the changes in the Dow Jones index. What is the Dow Jones index? What do these changes mean, and why is the index important?

A securities index measures the performance of a certain basket of securities in the same way the CPI measures consumer prices. For example, the Dow Jones Industrial Average (DJIA) is a stock index that consists of thirty blue chip stocks. Exhibit 5-7 lists the thirty stocks that made up the DJIA as of July 6, 1998, as well as the original twelve stocks that were included in the index. It is interesting to note that of the original stocks, only General Electric is still in the index. However, GE has been removed and reinstated twice since the inception of the index. Many other indexes are used in the securities markets, and new ones are being introduced constantly.

EXHIBIT 5-7
The Dow Jones Industrial Average Then and Now

Thirty Stocks Included in the DJIA as of July 6, 1998

AT&T Corporation	Hewlett-Packard Company
Allied Signal Inc.	International Business Machines
Aluminum Company of America	International Paper Company
American Express Company	Johnson & Johnson
Boeing Company	McDonald's Corporation
Caterpillar Inc.	Merck & Company
Chevron Corporation	Minnesota Mining & Manufacturing
Coca-Cola Company	J. P. Morgan & Company
Walt Disney Company	Philip Morris Companies
DuPont Company	Procter & Gamble Company
Eastman Kodak Company	Sears, Roebuck & Company
Exxon Corporation	Travelers Group Inc.
General Electric Company	Union Carbide Corporation
General Motors Corporation	United Technologies Corporation
Goodyear Tire & Rubber Company	Wal-Mart Stores Inc.

Twelve Stocks Originally Included in the DJIA

American Cotton Oil	LaClede Gas
American Sugar	National Lead
American Tobacco	North American
Chicago Gas	Tennessee Coal & Iron
Distilling & Cattle Feeding	U.S. Leather Preferred
General Electric	U.S. Rubber

Source: Web site at http://stocks.miningco.com/library/weekly/aa013797.html.

Indexes are important for several reasons. First, stock indexes measure the general performance of an economy. It is unusual to have a stock market that is sharply rising if the economy is sharply falling.[14] Second, indexes are useful as a benchmark for gauging the performance of money managers. For example, bond fund managers could be evaluated against a bond index to determine how well they are doing. Also, stock mutual fund managers are typically evaluated against some index (such as the S&P 500, as in this chapter's Investments in the News). Third, indexes serve as a guide for passively managed mutual funds. That is, an investor who wanted to match the performance of the DJIA could invest in a mutual fund that mimics the DJIA. Nowadays, an investor can buy Spiders, which mimic the Standard and Poors 500 index, and Diamonds, which mimic the Dow Jones index. (For more

14. There are exceptions, such as the U.S. bull market in the early 1990s.

details see Chapter 25). Fourth, indexes are used by investment analysts to assess the overall direction of the market. Fifth, indexes are used to estimate statistical parameters such as beta, a measure of risk typically introduced in an introductory finance course and further developed in Chapter 10 of this book. Finally, indexes are used as underlying securities in various derivative securities (see Part 5 of this book).

The various indexes differ in three major aspects: (1) in which securities are included in the index and how many, (2) in how the index is adjusted over time for changes in securities (such as a takeover), and (3) in which method is used to calculate the index. The following sections focus on these three factors as they examine some of the more popular indexes.

5.7.1 Types of Stock Indexes

Indexes are designed to monitor the performance of some sector of the financial markets. For example, the Gold/Silver Stock Index tracks mining stocks, whereas the Wilshire Small Cap Index tracks small-company stocks. The number of securities within an index varies widely. For example, the Gold/Silver Stock Index has seven stocks, whereas the Wilshire 5000 Index has five thousand stocks.

Indexes can generally be categorized as price-weighted, value-weighted, or equally weighted indexes. The difference depends on how much significance, or weight, is given to each security. The price-weighted index weights its component securities according to their market price, whereas the value-weighted index weights its component securities by their equity market value. The equally weighted indexes weight each security equally. For example, the Dow Jones Industrial Average is based on the stock price of each security, whereas the S&P 500 is based on the market value of each firm's equity.

PRICE-WEIGHTED INDEX

The value of a price-weighted index is found by adding the prices of each security and dividing by a divisor. Namely, the index (I_t) at date t is given by

$$I_t = \frac{1}{divisor} \sum_{i=1}^{n} P_{i_t} \qquad (5.14)$$

where n is the number of assets in the index, and P_{i_t} is the price of asset i in period t.

The **divisor** is a number that is adjusted periodically for stock dividends, stock splits, and other changes. For example, when a stock splits 2-for-1, the stock price typically falls by about 50%, but the economic value of the stock holding has not changed. Changing the divisor affords a means to adjust an index for these artificial changes so that the index continues to reflect the actual value of the securities.

Exhibit 5-8 provides a simple illustration of how a price-weighted index is calculated for three securities. The divisor is set equal to 3 here, for simplicity. Exhibit 5-8 shows five periods for each security price, index value, and percentage change. Notice that from Period 1 to Period 2, all three securities rise by 10%. As expected, this results in a 10% increase in the index. However, in the next three periods, only

EXHIBIT 5-8		Period (t)				
Calculating a Price-Weighted Index	**Security** **Price**	**1**	**2**	**3**	**4**	**5**
	1 P_1	$150	$165	$181.50	$181.50	$181.50
	% change		10%	10%	0%	0%
	2 P_2	$100	$110	$110	$121	$121
	% change		10%	0%	10%	0%
	3 P_3	$50	$55	$55	$55	$60.50
	% change		10%	0%	0%	10%
	Index (I_t)[a]	100	110	115.50	119.17	121
	% change		10%	5%[b]	3.18%	1.54%

a. $I_t = \sum_{i=1}^{n} Q_i P_{i_t}$ where $Q_i = 1/\text{divisor} = 1/3$.

b. Let us illustrate one of the calculations. The 5% rate of return in Period 3 is obtained in the following way. The index is $I_3 = 1/3(\$181.50) + 1/3(\$110) + 1/3(\$55) = 115.50$, and the index percentage change is $(115.50/110) - 1 = 0.05$, or a 5% increase.

one security rises by 10%, and the rest remain the same. Notice that a 10% increase in the highest-priced security has a greater influence on the index than a 10% increase in the lowest-priced security. When only Security 1 rises by 10%, to $181.50, the index rises by 5%. However, when only Security 3 rises by 10%, to $60.50, the index rises only by 1.54%. This pattern is generally true for price-weighted indexes. High-priced securities influence the index more than lower-priced securities. We know that a firm's stock price is a function of the number of shares outstanding and is easily changed by stock splits. Therefore, there is no intuitive justification for higher-priced stocks' having more influence.

The popular Dow Jones Industrial Average is a price-weighted average of thirty U.S. industrial stocks. Hence, this index can be expressed as

$$I_{DJIA,t} = \frac{1}{divisor} \sum_{i=1}^{30} P_{i_t}$$

To avoid adverse effects of artificial changes such as stock splits on this price-weighted index, a procedure has been developed to adjust the divisor to get the index back to its original level before an artificial change. The divisor of the DJIA was initially set at 30 in 1928. With time, stock dividends, and stock splits, however, the divisor continued to decrease, and it is now only a small fraction. Daily newspapers and television programs report the closing value of the DJIA, and each week *Barron's* reports the value of the divisor.

A price-weighted index has to be adjusted when a security in the index has a stock split. Recall that when a stock splits, its price falls, which would result in an artificial decline in a price-weighted index if no adjustments were made. For example, on May 15, 1992, Disney stock split 4-for-1. The stock price before the split was $152\frac{7}{8}$. As soon as the stock was split, one share was worth only $38.21875 ($152.875/4). On the day of the split, the DJIA was reported at 3353.09. Had the DJIA not been adjusted for the Disney Stock split, it would have fallen to 3143.27, a 6.26% decline [(3143.27 − 3353.09)/3353.09]. Before Disney had the stock split, the divisor was 0.54643593, and the sum of the other twenty-nine stocks totaled 1679.375. Thus, the DJIA, if unadjusted for the stock split of Disney, would have been

$$I_{DJIA,unadjusted} = \frac{1}{0.54643593}(1679.375 + 38.21875) = 3143.27$$

In the case of Disney, the adjusted divisor is 0.51225107, and thus

$$I_{DJIA,adjusted} = \frac{1}{0.51225107}(1679.375 + 38.21875) = 3353.03$$

which is equal to the original level of the DJIA except for slight rounding errors. Although the adjustment in the divisor makes sure that the index is unaffected by stock dividends and stock splits, the influence of Disney stock on the DJIA also becomes much smaller after the split, because the stock's price is lower (see Exhibit 5-8).

One advantage of price-weighted indexes is that it is relatively easy to mimic the rate of return of the index by simply buying the same number of shares of each stock in the index. Many mutual funds, for example, are in essence "index funds" that strive only to mimic a particular index, such as the DJIA. However, the bias of price-weighted indexes toward high-priced stocks lacks any economic justification, because a stock's price is easily manipulated with stock splits. For example, why should Disney's stock become less influential within the index after its split?[15] The value-weighted indexes were developed to address this shortcoming of price-weighted indexes.

VALUE-WEIGHTED INDEX

A value-weighted index is based on the total market value of each security or a firm's equity value rather than merely on the price of each share. If we let N_{i_t} represent the number of shares of stock *outstanding* of Firm i at time t, then the firm's equity value, or its **market capitalization,** is $N_{i_t} \cdot P_{i_t}$. Shares of stock are called outstanding if they are not held by the company that issued them. The value-weighted index is given by

$$I_t = \left(\frac{100}{\sum_{i=1}^{n} N_{i_1} P_{i_1}}\right) \sum_{i=1}^{n} N_{i_t} P_{i_t} \tag{5.15}$$

15. In particular, after the 4-for-1 split, a portfolio seeking to mimic the DJIA would have to sell three-fourths of its Disney stocks, because price-weighted indexes assume that the same number of shares are held. The proceeds must be reinvested equally in all the stocks within the index.

where 100 represents the beginning value of the index. Note that the term within the parentheses is constant across time. Also, when $t = 1$, the two summation equations are identical, and the value of the index is 100.

For the securities given in Exhibit 5-8, assume that $N_1 = 300$, $N_2 = 150$, and $N_3 = 100$. Therefore, each stock has different market capitalizations: \$45,000 ($300 \cdot$ \$150) for Security 1, \$15,000 ($150 \cdot$ \$100) for Security 2, and \$5,000 ($100 \cdot$ \$50) for Security 3. For simplicity, further assume that the number of shares outstanding remains the same during these five periods. From the prices of the three securities in Exhibit 5-8 and the values of N_i, the denominator of Equation 5.15 is

$$\sum_{i=1}^{3} N_{i_1} P_{i_1} = (300 \cdot \$150) + (150 \cdot \$100) + (100 \cdot \$50) = \$65,000$$

Substituting this result in Equation 5.15 yields

$$I_t = \frac{100}{65,000} \sum_{i=1}^{3} N_{i_t} P_{i_t} \tag{5.16}$$

Exhibit 5-9 carries out the calculations for these five periods. Notice that for value-weighted indexes, a 10% change in all securities has the same influence on the percentage change in the index. However, when all prices are not changed by the same percentage, the value-weighted index depends directly on each security's relative market capitalization. The greater the market capitalization of a security, the larger its influence (see the percentage change of the index in Columns 3, 4, and 5 of Exhibit 5-9).

The main advantage of the value-weighted index is that it is not affected by stock splits and stock dividends. For example, if the firm with Security 1 in Exhibit 5-9 declared a 2-for-1 split in Period 4, then $N1_4 = 300 \cdot 2$, but also $P1_4 = 181.50/2$, and the total market capitalization remains \$54,450. From Equation 5.16 we see that the index is not affected by this change, because the 2 in $N1_4$ cancels with the 2 in the denominator of $P1_4$ [or $(300 \cdot 2)(181.5/2) = (300 \cdot 181.5)$].

EQUALLY WEIGHTED INDEX

An equally weighted index is calculated by giving each security the same weight, regardless of its price or market capitalization. If we think of the index as a portfolio, we imagine that investors purchase an equal *dollar* amount of each security.

Two methods are used to construct an equally weighted index: the arithmetic method and the multiplicative method. (The multiplicative method is also known as the *geometric method*.) Both methods employ the rate of return corresponding to some interim period on the securities in the index. The interim period is typically one day. The value of an index by the arithmetic method is found using the following formula:

$$I_t = I_{t-1}\left(1 + \frac{1}{n}\sum_{i=1}^{n} R_{i_t}\right) \tag{5.17}$$

EXHIBIT 5-9	**Period (t)**				
Calculating a Value-Weighted Index	**1**	**2**	**3**	**4**	**5**
P_1	$150	$165	$181.50	$181.50	$181.50
$N_1 P_1$	$45,000	$49,500	$54,450	$54,450	$54,450
% change		10%	10%	0%	0%
P_2	$100	$110	$110	$121	$121
$N_2 P_2$	$15,000	$16,500	$16,500	$18,150	$18,150
% change		10%	0%	10%	0%
P_3	$50	$55	$55	$55	$60.5
$N_3 P_3$	$5,000	$5,500	$5,500	$5,500	$6,050
% change		10%	0%	0%	10%
Index (I_t)[a]	100	110	117.6[b]	120.2	121
% change		10%	6.9%	2.2%	0.67%

a. $Q_{i_t} = 100 \left(\dfrac{N_{i_t}}{\sum\limits_{i=1}^{n} N_{i_t} P_{i_t}} \right)$ and $I_t = \sum\limits_{i=1}^{n} Q_{i_t} P_{i_t}$, where $N_1 = 300$, $N_2 = 150$, and $N_3 = 100$.

b. For example, the index value (based on the information in Equation 5.16) is

$$I_3 = (100/65,000) \cdot [(300 \cdot \$181.50) + (150 \cdot \$110) + (100 \cdot \$55)]$$
$$= 0.001538(54,450 + 16,500 + 5,500) = 117.6$$

and the percentage change in the index is

$$\% \text{ Change} = (117.6/110) - 1 = 0.069, \text{ or } 6.9\%$$

The term $\dfrac{1}{n}\sum R$ is an arithmetic average of the rates of return of all the securities in the index. Exhibit 5-10 provides the index calculations for this method. From $t = 1$ to $t = 2$, the rates of return on all three securities are 10%. Thus, the index value at $t = 2$ is

$$I_2 = 100[1 + (1/3)(0.1 + 0.1 + 0.1)] = 100(1.1) = 110$$

From $t = 2$ to $t = 3$, only Security 1 changes, and the new index level is

$$I_3 = 110\,[1 + (1/3)(0.1 + 0.0 + 0.0)] = 110(1.033) = 113.63$$

Thus, we see that the percentage change in the index is 3.3% (see the last row in Exhibit 5-10), regardless of the stock's price level or market capitalization.

The arithmetic method is used in the equally weighted index series provided by the Center for Research in Securities Prices (CRSP) and is available in two versions. One version includes dividends in the return corresponding to each interim period calculation, and one version does not. The index is also calculated with either daily prices or monthly prices. The CRSP also provides a value-weighted series.[16]

---

16. The CRSP is an organization that supplies security data and is widely used by academic investment researchers.

EXHIBIT 5-10 Calculating an Equally Weighted Index with the Arithmetic Method	Period (t)					
Security	Price	1	2	3	4	5
1	P_1	$150	$165	$181.50	$181.50	$181.50
	% change		10%	10%	0%	0%
2	P_2	$100	$110	$110	$121	$121
	% change		10%	0%	10%	0%
3	P_3	$50	$55	$55	$55	$60.5
	% change		10%	0%	0%	10%
	Index (I_t)[a]	100	110	113.63	117.38	121.25
	% change		10%	3.3%	3.3%	3.3%

a. $I_t = I_{t-1}\left(1 + \dfrac{1}{n}\sum_{i=1}^{n} R_{i_t}\right)$

The multiplicative method differs from the arithmetic method solely on how returns are averaged across securities. Specifically, the value of an index by the multiplicative method is found with the following formula:

$$I_t = I_{t-1}\left(\prod_{i=1}^{n}(1 + R_{i_t})\right)^{1/n} \tag{5.18}$$

Exhibit 5–11 shows the index calculations for the multiplicative method. A comparison of Exhibits 5–10 and 5–11 reveals that the arithmetic method of averaging results in higher values than the multiplicative method.

Value Line, a securities analysis firm that offers opinions on the investment potential of various securities, provides an index constructed using the multiplicative method. The Kansas City Board of Trade provides derivative securities based on this index.

5.7.2 Bond Indexes

Bond indexes are designed to track different segments of the bond market. Bond indexes that incorporate total returns (coupon and price changes) were developed in the 1970s. Prior indexes ignored coupon payments, which make up a large portion of a bond's return.

Bond indexes have several problems that stock indexes do not have. First, because bonds have a finite maturity, the set of bonds within an index is always changing. A change in a bond's maturity affects the risk of the basket of bonds. Also, because of the call features within bonds, the overall set of bonds is constantly changing. When interest rates fall sharply, most firms call their bonds and reissue new bonds with lower coupon rates. For example, after 8 years, a 10-year bond in the index will be a

EXHIBIT 5-11
Calculating an
Equally Weighted
Index with the
Multiplicative
Method

Security	Price	Period (t)				
		1	2	3	4	5
1	P_1	$150	$165	$181.50	$181.50	$181.50
	% change		10%	10%	0%	0%
2	P_2	$100	$110	$110	$121	$121
	% change		10%	0%	10%	0%
3	P_3	$50	$55	$55	$55	$60.5
	% change		10%	0%	0%	10%
	Index (I_t)[a]	100	110	113.55[b]	171.2	121
	% change		10%	3.2%	3.2%	3.2%

a. $I_t = I_{t-1}\left(\prod_{i=1}^{n}(1 + R_i)\right)^{1/n}$

b. For example, the index value is

$$I_3 = 110[1 + 0.1)(1 + 0.0)(1 + 0.0)]^{1/3}$$
$$= 110(1.1)^{1/3} = 110 \cdot 1.03228 \cong 113.55$$

and the percentage change in the index is

$$\% \text{ Change} = (113.55/110) - 1 \cong 0.032, \text{ or } 3.2\%$$

2-year bond, and 2-year bonds have different risk characteristics than 10-year bonds. Second, many bonds are not actively traded, which leads to pricing problems. How do you compute the value of a bond index at the end of the day when a particular bond within the index did not trade? Do you use the price from the last time the bond traded, which could be days earlier, when market conditions were much different? Do you estimate the current market price by some other method? Thus, an investor should be cautious when using bond indexes that contain inactive bonds.

Exhibit 5-12 lists the characteristics of four major bond indexes. Notice that the approaches vary. The Ryan Index uses equal weighting, whereas the others use value weighting. Lehman Brothers ignores the reinvestment of intramonth cash flows, and Salomon Brothers assumes the monies are invested at the one-month Treasury bill rate. Over the long run, the movements of these indexes are very similar; however, in the short run they may not move in tandem. Notice that three of the four indexes are broad based. Thus, we know that they will contain prices that are not based on literal trades and that the component bonds will be changing constantly. For example, in 1996, several firms issued long-maturity bonds; International Business Machines issued 100-year bonds, and Time-Warner issued 40-year bonds. If this trend continues, then these indexes will represent, on average, longer-maturity bonds. Thus, the maturity structure of the index itself will be changing over time.[17]

17. For more details, see Frank K. Reilly, G. Wenchi Kao, and David J. Wright, "Alternative Bond Market Indexes," *Financial Analysts Journal*, May–June 1992, pp. 44–58.

EXHIBIT 5-12 Characteristics of Four Bond Indexes	Characteristic	Lehman Brothers	Merrill Lynch	Ryan	Salomon Brothers
	Number of issues within the index	Over 6,500	Over 5,000	7 Treasury issues	Over 5,000
	Maturity	Greater than 1 year	Greater than 1 year	Greater than 2 years	Greater than 1 year
	Weighting	Value	Value	Equal	Value
	Reinvestment of intramonth cash flows	No	Yes, in specific bond	Yes, in specific bond	Yes, at one-month T-bill rate

Source: Adapted with permission from Frank K. Reilly et al., "Alternative Bond Market Indexes," *Financial Analysts Journal,* May–June 1992, p. 47. Copyright 1992, Association for Investment Management and Research, Charlottesville, Va. All Rights Reserved.

5.7.3 Major Stock Indexes Around the World

Indexes for stocks are easier to develop and maintain than bond indexes. Exhibit 5-13 presents a partial listing of stock indexes. Notice that most indexes are value weighted; price weighting is the next most popular method. Recall that a value-weighted index has the advantage of automatically adjusting for stock splits and is weighted based on market capitalization.

Most major exchanges have indexes that track how the stocks on their particular exchange are performing. For example, the NYSE Composite Index is a value-weighted index of all the stocks on the New York Stock Exchange. Similarly, the TOPIX Index covers 1,100 stocks on the Tokyo Stock Exchange. One widely watched index is the S&P 500, which is value weighted. Many professional money managers are evaluated based on how well they perform relative to the S&P 500. Many vendors of indexes now maintain a whole range of indexes. For example, Dow Jones now has indexes that cover the entire globe, as well as indexes covering each major industry. Similarly, Wilshire maintains a whole set of different indexes.

5.8 TRACKING RATES OF RETURN OVER TIME

An analysis of the historical rates of return of financial securities reveals that common stocks have been far more volatile than corporate bonds or Treasury bills. This increased volatility has been accompanied by higher average rates of return. The pattern is clear: the higher the volatility (or standard deviation), the higher, on average, the return. This is the classic risk–return trade-off (see Exhibit 5-14).

The mean columns in Exhibit 5-14 give the average rate of return for each security type. The standard deviation column provides a measure of risk. Small-company stocks historically have offered the highest average returns (arithmetic mean of 17.7%), but they also have had the highest standard deviation (34.1%). U.S.

EXHIBIT 5-13   **A Partial Listing of Stock Indexes**

Stock Index Name	Weighting Method	Purpose of Index
AMEX Composite Index	Value	American Stock Exchange
Australian Options Market	Value	Australian Stock Exchange
CAC 40 Stock Index	Value	Marché à Terme International de France (MATIF), French stocks
Center for Research in Security Prices (CRSP)	Arithmetic and value	NYSE/AMEX and OTC, with and without dividends
Computer Technology Stock Index	Value	Computer technology stocks
Dow Jones Indices	Price and value	U.S. blue chip stocks and broad-based, global indexes
European Options Exchange Dutch Stock Index	Price	Stocks of the Netherlands
Financial Times–Stock Exchange 100 Stock Index	Value	100 large United Kingdom stocks
Finnish Options Stock Index (FOX)	Value	Finnish stocks
Gold/Silver Stock Index	Value	Index of 7 large mining stocks
Institutional Stock Index	Value	Index of 75 stocks largely held by institutions
International (ADR) Market Stock Index	Value	Index of 50 foreign stocks traded on the NYSE as American Depository Receipts
Major Market Stock Index	Price	Index of 20 blue chip stocks, mimics the DJIA
Nagoya Option 25 Stock Index	Price	25 large Japanese stocks
National OTC Stock Indices	Value	U.S. OTC stocks
Nikkei 225 Stock Average	Value	Japanese stocks
NYSE Composite Stock Index	Value	All NYSE stocks
Oil Stock Index	Price	U.S. index of oil stocks
Russell Indices	Value	Russell 3000—3,000 largest U.S. stocks; Russell 1000—1,000 of the highest of the 3,000 stocks in Russell 3000, ranked by size; Russell 2000—consists of the other 2000 stocks.
S&P Indices	Value	Large U.S. stocks
Swiss Market Index (SMI)	Value	25 large Swiss stocks
Tokyo Stock Price (TOPIX) Index	Value	1,100 stocks on the Tokyo Stock Exchange
Toronto 35 Stock Index	Value	35 large Canadian stocks
Value Line	Geometric	Over 1,650 smaller U.S. stocks
Wilshire Indices	Value	Small U.S. stocks

Source: Malcolm J. Robertson, *Directory of World Futures and Options* (Englewood Cliffs, N.J.: Prentice-Hall, 1990).

EXHIBIT 5-14 Annual Total Returns from 1926 to 1996	Series	Geometric Mean[a]	Arithmetic Mean[a]	Standard Deviation[b]
	Large-company stocks	10.7%	12.7%	20.3%
	Small-company stocks	12.6	17.7	34.1
	Long-term corporate bonds	5.6	6.0	8.7
	Long-term government bonds	5.1	5.4	9.2
	Intermediate-term government bonds	5.2	5.4	5.8
	U.S. Treasury bills	3.7	3.8	3.3
	Inflation	3.1	3.2	4.5

a. The arithmetic and geometric means are calculated by the formulas in Equations 5.12 and 5.13, respectively.

b. The standard deviation (SD) is calculated by the formula

$$SD = \left[\sum_{t=1}^{m} (R_t - \overline{R})^2 / (m - 1) \right]^{1/2}$$

where R_t is the rate of return in year t, $\overline{R}$ is the arithmetic average, and m is the number of years.

Source: Derived from data in Ibbotson Associates, "Stocks, Bonds, Bulls, and Inflation" (Chicago: Ibbotson Associates) 1997 Yearbook. Used with permission, © 1997 Ibbotson Associates, Inc. All rights reserved. [Certain portions of this work were derived from copyrighted works of Roger G. Ibbotson and Rex Sinquefield.]

Treasury bills, on the other extreme, offer the lowest average return (3.8%), but they also have had the lowest standard deviation (3.3%). The relationship between risk and return is almost perfect. The exception is intermediate-term government bonds, which have the same average return as long-term government bonds but a lower standard deviation.

Exhibit 5-15 presents international stock returns over the period January 1993 through January 1998 in both local currency and U.S. dollars. Clearly, actual performance is affected by the exchange rate. For example, in the United Kingdom, the monthly return in local currency was only 1.09% per month, whereas in U.S. dollars it was 1.27% (a whopping 0.16% increase per month because of currency fluctuations). In Italy, for example, the pattern was reversed, with local currency returns at 1.60% and U.S. dollar returns at only 1.35%.

Exhibit 5-16 provides the rates of return for the first two weeks of January 1998 (actually, until January 16, 1998), on the indexes of various countries where rates of return are given in U.S. dollars. Thus, if the local currency loses value against the dollar, a negative rate of return is recorded, even if the stock index in local currency does not change. In January 1998 there were sharp changes in the various stock market indexes, with a deterioration of the value of the local currencies versus the U.S. dollar. Also some sharp corrections were registered in January. More than 10% daily rates of return were common. As Exhibit 5-16 shows, the rate of return on the Indonesian stock market in U.S. dollar was −44.11% in 16 days. In South Korea, the rate of return was 34.55% during the same period. The big fluctuations were in the Latin America and the Pacific region, where some of the economies were near collapse.

| EXHIBIT 5-15 | | In U.S. $ | | In Local Currency | |
International Stock Returns and Standard Deviations, 1993–1998, in U.S. Dollars and in Local Currency	Country	Mean	SD	Mean	SD
Based on Monthly Index, 1/22/93 to 1/22/98 (59 months) Selected Data for 1993–1998	Europe	1.37	0.11	1.44	0.14
	France	0.99	0.20	1.19	0.27
	Germany	1.38	0.18	1.60	0.25
	USA	1.45	3.13	1.45	3.13
	The World Index	1.125	0.098	1.127	0.10
	Italy	1.35	0.54	1.60	0.47
	Hong Kong	1.152	0.759	1.154	0.755
	Japan	0.14	0.43	0.16	0.32
	Korea	−1.52	0.84	−0.44	0.52
	United Kingdom	1.27	0.124	1.09	0.115

Source: Based on the Morgan Stanley Capital International indexes at Web site http://www.ms.com/mscidata, January 22, 1998.

EXHIBIT 5-16   Dow Jones Global Indexes

Region/ Country	DJ Global Indexes, Local Curr. Latest Fri.	Wkly % Chg.		DJ Global Indexes, U.S. $ Latest Fri.	Wkly % Chg.		DJ Global Indexes, U.S. $ on 12/31/97	Point Chg. From 12/31/97		% Chg. From 12/31/97 (U.S. $)	
Americas				222.43	+	3.35	227.09	−	3.66	−	1.61
Brazil	1162004.61	+	2.44	400.49	+	1.89	443.41	−	42.92	−	9.68
Canada	183.09	+	1.95	147.21	+	1.43	153.74	−	6.52	−	4.24
Chile	190.74	−	3.03	156.77	−	2.39	183.14	−	26.37	−	14.40
Mexico	338.68	+	2.03	126.85	+	1.78	142.90	−	16.05	−	11.23
U.S.	911.82	+	3.52	911.82	+	3.52	922.34	−	10.52	−	1.14
Venezuela	625.94	−	2.68	76.07	−	3.16	89.64	−	13.56	−	15.13
Latin America				193.22	+	1.02	217.42	−	24.19	−	11.13
Europe/Africa				185.90	+	0.89	187.02	−	1.13	−	0.60
Austria	124.39	−	2.71	103.48	−	3.04	107.17	−	3.69	−	3.44
Belgium	215.98	+	1.43	179.02	+	0.79	177.85	+	1.17	+	0.66
Denmark	221.32	+	1.66	187.60	+	1.04	184.13	+	3.47	+	1.88
Finland	426.91	+	2.29	319.84	+	1.83	313.08	+	6.77	+	2.16
France	181.74	+	1.84	153.31	+	1.18	157.12	−	3.80	−	2.42
Germany	229.43	−	1.20	189.53	−	1.82	196.17	−	6.64	−	3.39

(continued)

EXHIBIT 5-16   *(continued)*

Region/ Country	DJ Global Indexes, Local Curr. Latest Fri.	Wkly % Chg.	DJ Global Indexes, U.S. $ Latest Fri.	Wkly % Chg.	DJ Global Indexes, U.S. $ on 12/31/97	Point Chg. From 12/31/97	% Chg. From 12/31/97 (U.S. $)
Greece 6.70	232.60	−	5.08	141.27 −	5.22	151.41 −	10.15 −
Ireland	287.87	+ 2.04	251.56	+ 3.24	243.14	+ 8.43	+ 3.47
Italy	240.10	+ 2.90	164.40	+ 2.20	155.68	+ 8.72	+ 5.60
Netherlands	319.31	+ 2.09	263.81	+ 1.43	266.29	− 2.48	− 0.93
Norway	199.10	+ 0.44	157.60	− 0.47	170.44	− 12.85	− 7.54
Portugal	330.69	+ 1.78	238.43	+ 1.21	227.56	+ 10.88	+ 4.78
South Africa	173.83	− 1.84	95.78	− 2.48	103.68	− 7.89	− 7.61
Spain	305.32	+ 3.46	190.85	+ 2.90	182.74	+ 8.11	+ 4.44
Sweden	339.08	+ 0.17	233.92	− 0.33	238.60	− 4.68	− 1.96
Switzerland	351.65	+ 0.13	318.30	− 1.29	326.87	− 8.56	− 2.62
United Kingdom	202.36	+ 1.31	176.84	+ 2.50	175.25	+ 1.59	+ 0.91
Pacific Region			77.27	+ 6.28	77.93	− 0.66	− 0.85
Australia	155.87	+ 0.40	136.39	+ 3.67	133.78	+ 2.61	+ 1.95
Hong Kong	182.05	− 1.20	182.70	− 1.22	224.25	− 41.55	− 18.53
Indonesia	160.07	+ 30.18	38.42	+ 26.26	68.73	− 30.32	− 44.11
Japan	75.22	+ 4.68	72.57	+ 6.86	70.38	+ 2.19	+ 3.11
Malaysia	102.33	+ 7.62	66.61	+ 18.97	80.28	− 13.67	− 17.03
New Zealand	147.71	− 2.67	160.87	+ 0.58	167.54	− 6.67	− 3.98
Philippines	178.14	+ 6.94	111.95	+ 14.47	129.23	− 17.27	− 13.37
Singapore	115.01	+ 7.41	107.70	+ 10.30	123.15	− 15.45	− 12.54
South Korea	81.30	+ 18.46	38.09	+ 32.52	28.31	+ 9.78	+ 34.55
Taiwan	183.95	+ 0.86	140.51	+ 1.78	153.17	− 12.66	− 8.27
Thailand	63.91	+ 13.90	29.27	+ 17.66	30.24	− 0.97	− 3.21
Europe/Africa (ex. South Africa)			190.89	+ 0.99	191.64	− 0.74	− 0.39
Europe/Africa (ex. U.K. & S. Africa)			204.09	+ 0.24	206.21	− 2.12	− 1.03
Nordic Region			217.47	+ 0.23	220.30	− 2.83	− 1.29
Pacific Region (ex. Japan)			120.44	+ 4.62	135.01	− 14.57	− 10.79
World (ex. U.S.)			123.99	+ 2.62	125.56	− 1.57	− 1.25
DOW JONES WORLD STOCK INDEX			164.63	+ 3.07	166.63	− 1.99	− 1.20

Indexes based on 6/30/82 = 100 for U.S., 12/31/91 = 100 for World.

SUMMARY

Understand the different methods for computing rates of return. Rates of return can be calculated using different methods. The simple rate of return is the dollar profit divided by the investment. It ignores the time value of money. The method that uses the adjusted rate of return, or the time-weighted rate of return (which we call *rate of return* to distinguish it from the simple rate of return), has the endorsement of the Association of Investment Management and Research (AIMR). Rates of return are found by first calculating simple rates of return and then linking these returns together.

The idea of time-weighted rates of return is that any interim cash flow is reinvested in the asset under consideration. An alternative way to calculate time-weighted rates of return is known as the *index method*. It yields the same results as the time-weighted rate-of-return method, and in addition provides the intuition behind that method. The appropriate method to handle the rates of return of bonds is the accrual method, which basically assumes that the bonds were actually purchased at the beginning of the performance period and sold at the end.

Analyze the impact of taxes and inflation on rate-of-return calculations. Taxes and inflation influence the rate-of-return calculation and reduce the overall rate of return. In the case of taxes, there is a reduction of income (tax payment), which reduces the after-tax rate of return. In the inflation case, there is a reduction in the investor's purchasing power, which reduces the real rate of return to the investor.

Describe how returns can increase or decrease when exchange rates change. A weaker dollar is beneficial for U.S. investors who have invested internationally. Their international investment can be converted into more U.S. dollars when the investment is liquidated. A stronger dollar has the reverse effect. When liquidated, international investments will be converted into fewer U.S. dollars.

The average rate of return can be calculated in two ways—the arithmetic average and the geometric average, which yield different results.

Contrast the different types of stock indexes. The price-weighted index is found by adding the prices of each security and dividing by a divisor. The value-weighted index is based on the total market value of each security or a firm's equity value rather than merely on the price of each share. Equally weighted indexes are calculated by giving each security the same weight, regardless of its price or market capitalization.

Compare the historical risk-return trade-off for stocks and bonds. Historically, common stocks have been more volatile than bonds. Also, common stocks have offered a higher average return than bonds. There appears to be a positive relationship between volatility and return.

CHAPTER AT A GLANCE

1. The simple rate of return is given by

$$R = \frac{EMV - BMV + I}{BMV}$$

2. There are two methods to calculate time-weighted or adjusted rates of return, called *rates of return:*
   a. The linking method "links" the interim rates of returns by

   $$R = [(1 + r_1)(1 + r_2) \ldots (1 + r_n)] - 1$$

where RtV is the simple rate of return for Period t ($t = 1, 2, \ldots n$).

   b. The index method creates an index of the value of a portfolio, assuming all interim cash flows are reinvested in the security.

3. Rates of return must be adjusted for the following:
   a. Taxes.
   b. Inflation.
   c. Foreign exchange.
   d. Timing of dividends.

4. There are several indexes:
   a. The price-weighted index must be adjusted when a security in the index has a stock split. It is computed as follows:

   $$I_t = \frac{1}{divisor} \sum_{i=1}^{n} P_{i_t}$$

   where n is the number of assets in the index.

   b. The value-weighted index is computed as follows:

   $$I_t = \left(\frac{100}{\sum_{i=1}^{n} N_{i_1} P_{i_1}} \right) \sum_{i=1}^{n} N_{i_t} P_{i_t}$$

   where N_{i_t} is the number of shares outstanding of Firm i in Period t, and n is the number of securities making up the index. The term in parentheses remains constant.

   c. The equally weighted index is computed by the arithmetic method as follows:

   $$I_t = I_{t-1} \left(1 + \frac{1}{n} \sum_{i=1}^{n} R_{i_t} \right)$$

   d. The equally weighted index is computed by the geometric (multiplicative) method as follows:

   $$I_t = I_{t-1} \left(\prod_{i=1}^{n} (1 + R_{i_t}) \right)^{1/n}$$

5. The arithmetic method of averaging follows:

   $$\overline{R}_A = \frac{\sum_{t=1}^{m} R_t}{m}$$

where m is the number of periods (years).

6. The geometric method of averaging follows:

$$\overline{R}_G = \left[\prod_{t=1}^{m} (1 + R_t) \right]^{1/m} - 1$$

KEY TERMS

Adjusted rate of return   165
Arithmetic average   162
Arithmetic method   163
Divisor   169
Dollar-weighted average rate of
    return   190
Ex-post rate of return   147

Geometric average   162
Geometric compounding   166
Geometric method   164
Index method   150
Linking method   150
Market capitalization   171
Rate of return   146

Real rate of return   159
Realized rate of return   147
Simple rate of return   148
Time-weighted rate of
    return   165

REVIEW

5.1 Give four ways that investment analysts use rates of return.

5.2 What is the difference between the arithmetic average and the geometric average? Describe when each is used.

5.3 Explain the difference between $\overline{R}$ and $E(R)$.

5.4 The AIMR has adopted the time-weighted rate-of-return method for reporting the historical performance of money managers. What is the basic philosophy behind this method of rate-of-return reporting?

5.5 List three different ways that indexes can be constructed, and describe each one.

PRACTICE

5.1 A stock that was purchased in January for $50 paid a $3 dividend in December, when its price was $55.
a. Calculate the dollar *return* on this investment if 100 shares were purchased.
b. Calculate the *rate of return* on this investment if 100 shares were purchased.

c. How would your answers to Parts a and b change if 200 shares were purchased?
d. How would your answers to Parts a and b change if the stock split 3-for-1 before the end of the year? (Hence, the $55 is the price after the stock split was taken.)

5.2 A zero-coupon bond was purchased in January for $875 per $1,000 par. In December the bond was trading for $950.

a. Calculate the return and rate of return on this bond.

b. If the tax rate were 30%, what was the after-tax rate of return?

c. If deflation of 3% occurred during the year (that is, −3% inflation), what was the real, after-tax rate of return?

5.3 Suppose a United Kingdom bond was purchased by an American investor in January for 500 British pounds when the exchange rate was $2.0/pound. Assume no coupon payments; also, the bond was sold for 475 pounds in December, when the exchange rate was $2.2/pound.

a. What was the rate of return on the bond in British pounds?

b. What was the rate of return to the American investor on the exchange rate only?

c. What was the rate of return in U.S. dollars?

5.4 Use the data in Question 5.3, and assume that the inflation rate was 5% in the United States and 10% in the United Kingdom.

a. What was the real rate of return in British pounds?

b. What was the real rate of return in U.S. dollars?

5.5 The following table gives the NYSE composite index over a recent 15-year period:

End of Year	NYSE Composite
1981	71.11
1982	81.03
1983	95.18
1984	96.38
1985	121.58
1986	138.58
1987	138.23
1988	156.26
1989	195.04
1990	180.49

End of Year	NYSE Composite
1991	229.44
1992	240.21
1993	259.08
1994	250.94
1995	329.51
1996	392.30

a. Ignoring dividends, calculate the simple annual rates of return.

b. Calculate the arithmetic average of the annual rates of return.

c. Calculate the geometric average of the annual rates of return.

d. Compare your answers to Parts b and c. How do you account for the difference between these averages?

5.6 The following table gives the Consumer Price Index (CPI) over a recent 10-year period:

End of Year	CPI
1986	109.6
1987	113.6
1988	118.3
1989	124.0
1990	130.7
1991	136.2
1992	140.3
1993	144.5
1994	148.2
1995	152.4
1996	156.9

a. Compute the inflation rates for each year over this 10-year period.

b. Compute the geometric-average inflation rate over this 10-year period.

c. Calculate the real rate of return on the NYSE Composite (using the data in Question 5.5) for each year.

5.7 Suppose we have the following information on Xerox, Inc.:

Dividends Paid ($)	Date
0.75	February 2
0.75	May 4
0.75	July 30
0.75	October 25

Stock Price ($)	Date
61¼	January 4
52⅜	February 2
64⅞	May 4
70½	July 30
75¾	October 25
71	December 30

a. Calculate the simple rate of return for the period January 4 through December 30.
b. Calculate the rate of return for the period January 4 through December 30 using the linking method.
c. Calculate the rate of return for the period January 4 through December 30 using the index method.
d. Explain any differences in rates of return.

5.8 Rework Question 5.7b, assuming that the income tax rate on dividends is 25% and the capital gains tax rate is 15%.

5.9 Using the data in Question 5.7, suppose Xerox, Inc., also had a rights issue of one share for each existing share. In a rights issue, the firm gives its existing shareholders the right to buy additional shares of common stock at a specified price. For each share owned, a shareholder receives one right. Rights trade in the secondary market. In this case, Xerox began trading the rights on October 25 at $1 per right. Rework Question 5.7c, incorporating the effects of this rights offering.

5.10 Suppose you purchased 1,000 shares of Hardin Bread Company on January 1 at $60 per share. Hardin pays $1.50 annual dividend on April 22, when the stock is trading at $42. Hardin declares a 5-for-1 stock split effective August 28, when the stock is trading at $54.
a. If Hardin closed on December 29 at $15 per share, what was your rate of return by the index method?
b. If the inflation rate was 7.8%, what was your real rate of return?

5.11 a. Given the following information on Goodyear, October 15, 1999, 7.35% coupon-bearing bonds, calculate the annual rate of return based on the index method.

Date	Coupon	Price (in % of $1,000 par)	Accrued Interest
January 3		101¾	$15.3
April 15	$36.75	93⅛	
October 15	$36.75	97¾	
December 27		99¾	$15.2

b. How does your answer to Part a compare with the simple-rate-of-return calculation? Explain.

5.12 Suppose you invest in Honda Motor Company on January 4 for 5,064 yen per share when the exchange rate is $0.0079/yen. On April 20, Honda pays a 253.2-yen dividend when the exchange rate is $0.008/yen and the stock price is 5,003 yen. On December 29, the price of Honda is 6,014 yen per share, and the exchange rate is $0.007/yen.
a. Calculate the rate of return in local currency.
b. Calculate the rate of return in U.S. dollars. (Be sure to address how the 253.2-yen dividend is handled.)
c. If U.S. inflation was 3.9%, what was the real rate of return?

5.13 The Gold/Silver Stock Index is a value-weighted index of seven mining stocks. The following gives some information regarding this index:

Number	Company	Shares	Price ($)
Year 1			
1	ASA[a]	1.5 million	41
2	Battle Mtn Gold	10 million	7
3	Echo Bay	8 million	15
4	Hecla[b]	5 million	114
5	Homestakes[a]	9 million	15
6	Newmont	5 million	50
7	Placer Dome	17 million	11
Year 2			
1	ASA[a]	3 million	20
2	Battle Mtn Gold	10 million	8
3	Echo Bay	8 million	23
4	Hecla[b]	15 million	40
5	Homestakes[a]	18 million	21
6	Newmont	5 million	48
7	Placer Dome	17 million	21

a. 2-for-1 split between Years 1 and 2.

b. 3-for-1 split between Years 1 and 2.

a. If Year 1 is the base year with 100 index value, calculate the index value in Year 2.

b. Calculate the rate of return on the Gold/Silver Stock Index.

5.14 The Major Market Stock Index (MMI) is a price-weighted index of twenty stocks designed to move closely with the Dow Jones Industrial Average. The following table gives recent prices for the MMI:

Company	Day 1 Price	Change from Previous Day
American Express	$23\frac{7}{8}$	$+\frac{1}{8}$
AT&T	$43\frac{3}{8}$	. . .
Chevron	69	$-\frac{3}{8}$
Coca-Cola	$40\frac{5}{8}$	. . .
Dow Chemical	$53\frac{5}{8}$	. . .
DuPont	$49\frac{1}{4}$	$-1\frac{1}{2}$
Eastman Kodak	$41\frac{5}{8}$	$+\frac{1}{2}$

Company	Day 1 Price	Change from Previous Day
Exxon	63	$-\frac{3}{8}$
General Electric	$76\frac{7}{8}$	. . .
General Motors	39	. . .
IBM	$92\frac{3}{4}$	$+\frac{1}{4}$
International Paper	$63\frac{3}{8}$	$-\frac{1}{8}$
Johnson & Johnson	$45\frac{3}{4}$	$-\frac{3}{8}$
Merck	$49\frac{1}{8}$	$-\frac{1}{2}$
3-M	$98\frac{1}{4}$	. . .
Mobil	$64\frac{1}{2}$	-1
Philip Morris	$77\frac{3}{4}$	. . .
Procter & Gamble	50	$-\frac{1}{2}$
Sears	$38\frac{1}{2}$	$-\frac{1}{8}$
USX	$28\frac{1}{2}$	. . .

a. If the MMI was calculated to be 348.07 on Day 1, what is the value of the divisor?

b. What is the value of the MMI on Day 0, assuming no change in the divisor?

5.15 Suppose you have the following rates of return:

Year	Stock A	Stock B
1	10%	5%
2	10%	15%

Calculate the arithmetic average and geometric average for each stock. Explain your results.

5.16 Suppose you invested $100 in the S&P 500 index, and the annual rate of return is 10% per year for all years. After how many years will your investment double?

5.17 Suppose you invested $100 in the S&P 500 index, and the annual rate of return is −10%. After how many years will your investment be worth $50?

5.18 Suppose you invested $100 in a given stock for 4 years. In 2 out of 4 years, the rate of return was +20% a year, and in the other 2 years it was −20% a year.

What is the value of your investment after 4 years? Does it make a difference which 2 of the 4 years had a +20% rate of return and which 2 years had a −20% rate of return?

5.19 Suppose that for Stock A you observe returns of $R_{A,t}$, where t = 1, 2, . . . n. Suppose now that for Stock B you have returns of $R_{B,t}$, expressed as

$$1 + R_{B,t} = a(1 + R_{A,t})$$

where $a > 1$. By how much will the geometric mean of Stock B exceed the geometric mean of Stock A? By how much will the arithmetic mean of Stock B exceed the arithmetic mean of Stock A?

5.20 The stock price at the beginning of the year was $100, and at the end of the year it was $50. The firm paid no dividends but split its stock 2-for-1 in February and then again 5-for-1 in July. Calculate the annual rate of return on the stock.

5.21 Suppose you buy an inflation-indexed bond with a par value of $1,000. The bond matures in 1 year. The principal is linked to the inflation rate, and the coupon interest payment is equal to the inflation rate.
a. How much will you get back at the end of the year if there is 10% inflation? What is your real rate of return?
b. If there is zero inflation and you pay 30% tax on interest, what is the after-tax real rate of return? How would you change your answer if there is 10% inflation? Explain why the real rate of return drops even when it is linked to inflation.

5.22 An American invests in German stocks. There is no inflation in the United States, but there is inflation in Germany. Moreover, it is known that even if there is inflation of $h\%$ in Germany, the foreign exchange market loses $h\%$ relative to the U.S. dollar and hence is a loss in foreign exchange to the U.S. investor. Compare the real rate of return to a German who invests in Germany and to an American who invests in Germany.

5.23 Recently the U.S. Treasury issued index-linked bonds. Suppose that you find that the bonds trade for $1,000 (at par value), and the interest is paid at the end of the year and is 3.5%. Both the principal and interest are linked to the cost-of-living index. You expect 3% inflation next year, and the bond will mature at the end of the year.

a. Calculate the nominal rate of return on the bond.
b. Calculate the real rate of return on the bond.
c. Calculate the after-tax real rate of return on the bond when you must pay 39.6% income tax on all cash flows received beyond the bond's purchase price of $1,000.

5.24 Two stocks, A and B, are traded today for $100. Suppose that eighteen months after the stock purchase, Stock A is traded for $120, whereas Stock B is traded for $110. Stock A does not pay dividends, whereas Stock B pays $10 dividends at the end of the eighteen-month investment period.
a. Calculate the pretax rate of return on the two stocks.
b. Calculate the after-tax rate of return on the two stocks, where the capital gains tax rate is 20% and the income tax rate is 39.6%.
c. How would you change your answer if all the figures are as before but relate to 1 year rather than eighteen months after the investment?

5.25 Mr. Loop bought 1,000 shares of IBM at $10 per share at the beginning of the year. At the end of the year, the stock price was $6. In June the firm split its stock at a ratio of 2:1. On October 1, Mr. Loop sold 1,000 shares of IBM at $5. There were no cash dividends and no taxes. The money was used to buy DuPont stock.
a. What is the annual rate of return on IBM stock?
b. Suppose that Mr. Loop sells DuPont stock at the end of the year at a 20% profit. What is the rate of return on DuPont on an annual basis?
c. What is Mr. Loop's total annual rate of return on his investment in the two stocks?

5.26 Suppose you invest in 100 shares of Coca-Cola. The stock price at the beginning of the year is $40. Suppose that the stock price at the end of the year is $20, and no cash dividend was paid. It is a given that on two dates during the year, the firm paid 10% stock dividends and split its stock 2-for-1. For calculating the annual rate of return, is it important to know whether the stock dividend took place before or after the split? Calculate the annual rate of return.

5.27 The stock of Firm A was traded for $100 at the beginning of the year. The firm did not pay dividends and did not split its stock. With a 20% capital gains tax rate, the rate of return on an annual basis was recorded as 25%. Calculate the rate of return on this stock for a tax-free institution (for example, your university).

5.28 If a stock is held for 5 years, by the new tax laws the capital gains tax is 18%. Suppose that the tax rate on interest on income bonds is 39.6%. An investor considers either putting her money in a savings account with an annual interest of 4% or buying stock (which does not pay dividends) with a rate of return of R for the 5 years. What should be the minimum value of R such that the two investments (stocks and savings account) yield the same after-tax rate of return? Assume that all taxes are paid at the end of the fifth year, when the investment is liquidated.

5.29 *Barron's* reports the 1997 top ten winners and the top ten losers on stocks listed on the NYSE as follows:

	Closing Price	Net Change	Percentage Change
Capital Tr.A SBI	$11\frac{1}{4}$	$+8\frac{1}{2}$	+309.1
NS Group	$17\frac{1}{4}$	$+12\frac{3}{4}$	+283.3
Mail-Well	$40\frac{1}{2}$	$+29\frac{9}{16}$	+271.0
Best Buy	$36\frac{7}{8}$	$+26\frac{1}{4}$	+247.1
Dynamics Am	$91\frac{3}{4}$	$+63\frac{1}{2}$	+224.8
Grubb & Ellis	$13\frac{11}{16}$	$+9\frac{3}{16}$	+204.2
MotivePower Indu	$23\frac{1}{4}$	$+15\frac{7}{16}$	+197.6
Suiza Foods	$59\frac{9}{16}$	$+39\frac{5}{16}$	+194.1
Grupo Iusacell L	$21\frac{11}{16}$	$+14\frac{1}{16}$	+184.4
Buckle Inc	$34\frac{1}{4}$	$+21\frac{3}{4}$	+174.0
Westbridge Cap	$\frac{13}{32}$	$-9\frac{11}{32}$	−95.8
Mercury Fin	$\frac{9}{16}$	$-11\frac{11}{16}$	−95.4
L.A. Gear Inc	$\frac{3}{32}$	$-1\frac{29}{32}$	−95.3
Centennial Techn	3	−49	−94.2
Tri Polyta	$\frac{11}{16}$	$-5\frac{9}{16}$	−89.0
Amer Eagle	$\frac{9}{16}$	$-4\frac{3}{16}$	−88.1
Levitz Furniture	$\frac{7}{16}$	$-2\frac{11}{16}$	−86.0
Payless Cash	$\frac{5}{16}$	$-1\frac{11}{16}$	−84.4
Diana Corp	5	$-22\frac{1}{4}$	−81.7
JumboSprts	$1\frac{7}{16}$	$-6\frac{5}{16}$	−81.4

Source: *Barron's*, January 5, 1998, p. 32.

Suppose that you had no knowledge of how to select between the twenty stocks and therefore invested 5% of your wealth in each of the twenty stocks.
a. What would be your average return in 1997 on this investment portfolio? Explain why the average rate of return on such a portfolio generally is expected to be positive.
b. What would be the average rate of return if you had a selectivity ability and invested 10% in each of the winning stocks?
c. What would be your average rate of return if you invested 10% in each of the losing stocks?
d. How are your results in Parts a, b, and c related?

5.30 Suppose you invested $10,000 in a stock for 2 years. The rate of return was −50% in the first year and −50% in the second year. Do you agree that this means you lost all of your money?

5.31 a. Suppose you invest for 2 years. If the personal tax rate on dividends is equal to the capital gains tax, and the firm pays the dividend only at the end of the second year, then you are indifferent as to whether you get paid in income or capital gains. Do you agree?
b. How would you change your answer if the firm pays dividends at the end of each year?

For Internet questions visit the Levy Investment Web site at http://levy-invst.swcollege.com.

YOUR TURN: APPLYING THEORY TO PRACTICE
RATES OF RETURN—THE VARIOUS DEFINITIONS

The following reader's question appeared in the *Boston Globe*:

Different funds and publications use various terms that confuse me—annual total return, average annual return, annual average return, average annual total return, cumulative total return, average annual compounded total return, and load-adjusted total return. Please explain the differences.—E.H., Cape Cod

Source: *Boston Globe,* June 10, 1993.

Questions

1. Discuss the various terms mentioned, and answer the reader's question.

2. Assume the following 3-year data:

	Year		
	1	2	3
Stock price at beginning of year	$100	$ 95	$120
Stock price at end of year	95	120	140
Dividends paid at end of year	5	5	10

Calculate the various measures of return mentioned in the reader's question. In calculating the load-adjusted total return, assume transaction costs of $2 when the stock is bought and $2 when it is sold. Assume that the stock is held for 3 years and that there are no transaction costs on reinvestment of dividends. What is the relationship between the average annual compounded total return appearing in the reader's question and the internal rate of return (IRR) studied in your "Principles of Finance" course (see also Appendix 1A in Chapter 1)?

3. How do the measures of return mentioned in the reader's question relate to arithmetic and geometric mean returns?

4. Suppose you observe the performance of two stocks A and B, over a period of 2 years. Stock A had an *average* arithmetic annual rate of return of 12% and a *cumulative total* return of 20%. Stock B had an *average* arithmetic annual rate of return of 10% and a *cumulative total* return of 21%. Which investment performed better over the 2-year period? Explain.

SELECTED REFERENCES

Association for Investment Management and Research. *Report of the Performance Presentation Standards Implementation Committee.* Charlottesville, Va.: AIMR, December 1991.

This forty-seven-page monograph explains the recently adopted standards for reporting rates of returns by the AIMR, a leading financial analysts' association.

Reilly, Frank K., G. Wenchi Kao, and David J. Wright. "Alternative Bond Market Indexes." *Financial Analysts Journal,* May–June 1992, pp. 44–58.

This article is a detailed analysis of the major alternative bond market indexes.

Siegel, Jeremy J. "The Equity Premium: Stock and Bond Returns since 1802." *Financial Analysts Journal,* January–February 1992, pp. 28–46.

SUPPLEMENTAL REFERENCES

Eiteman, David K., Arthur I. Stonehill, and Michael H. Moffett. *Multinational Business Finance*. 6th ed. Reading, Mass.: Addison-Wesley, 1992, p. 25.

Fisher, I. *The Theory of Interest*. New York: Macmillan, 1930.

Levy, Haim, and Marshall Sarnat. *Portfolio and Investment Selection: Theory and Practice*. Englewood Cliffs, N.J.: Prentice-Hall International, 1984.

Appendix 5 Dollar-Weighted Average Rate of Return

This chapter discussed arithmetic and geometric rates of return (see Section 5.6). Both measure the average rate of return per $1 invested. These two averages are not affected by the dollar amount invested. However, in some cases the dollar amount invested across time changes. The **dollar-weighted average rate of return** takes this factor into account.

To illustrate, consider the following example. Suppose a stock's price at the beginning of the first year is $100, and at the end of the first year it is $110. At the end of the second year, the share price is $132. For simplicity, assume that no dividend is paid and that an investor buys 1 share at the beginning of the first year and buys one more share at the beginning of the second year. Then, at the end of the second year, the 2 shares are sold. The rate of return for the first year is 10%, or ($110/$100) − 1, and for the second year it is 20%, or ($132/$110) − 1. In this case, the arithmetic average (per Equation 5.12) is

$$\overline{R}_A = \frac{10\% + 20\%}{2} = 15\%$$

and the geometric average (per Equation 5.13) is

$$\overline{R}_G = [(1 + 0.1)(1 + 0.2)]^{1/2} - 1 \cong 0.1489, \text{ or } 14.89\%$$

These two averages are not affected by the dollar amount invested in each year. They will be the same if the investor buys, say, 5 shares rather than 1 share at the beginning of the first year.

The dollar-weighted average rate of return is the internal rate of return (IRR; see Appendix 1A) that solves the following equation:

$$-100 - \frac{1 \cdot \$110}{1 + IRR} + \frac{2 \cdot \$132}{(1 + IRR)^2}$$

where $110 is the dollar amount invested in purchasing one more share. Using a hand calculator, we find that IRR = 16.54%.

Note that 1 share was bought for $100 at the beginning of the first year and another share was bought at the beginning of the second year. Then, at the end of the second year, 2 shares are sold for $132 each. Thus, the IRR is the rate of return on the investment, taking into account that $100 is invested at the beginning of the first year and that an additional $110 is invested in the second year. If the investor buys, say, an additional 5 shares rather than 1 share at the end of the first year, the IRR will be given by the IRR that solves the following equation:

$$-100 - \frac{5 \cdot \$110}{(1 + IRR)} + \frac{6 \cdot \$132}{(1 + IRR)^2}$$

Hence, IRR = 18.48%

Thus, the IRR is affected by the amount invested in each period of time—hence, the term *dollar-weighted average rate of return*. In our example, investing more monies in the second year increases the rate of return. This result is not surprising, however, because in this case, the rate of return the first year is 10% and in the second year, 20%. The concept of the dollar-weighted average rate of return is important, because dividends are often reinvested (for example, in mutual funds), and additional shares of stock are purchased.

CHAPTER 6

THE FOUNDATION OF RISK ANALYSIS

LEARNING OBJECTIVES

After studying this chapter you should be able to:

1. Compare the maximum return and maximum expected return criteria as investment selection methods.

2. Explain what a risk averter is.

3. Calculate the risk premium.

4. Apply the mean-variance criterion in asset selection.

INVESTMENTS IN THE NEWS

WHY RISK MATTERS

How important is a fund's risk profile? This important: It can tell you more—and sometimes a lot more—than past performance.

This year, beginning in our annual summer Retirement Guide and continuing in this year-end investment issue, we've introduced into our list of best mutual funds a statistical measure called "standard deviation." Even if you are only a casual follower of mutual funds, chances are you've heard of it, since standard deviation, which in this case gauges a fund's volatility, has become an increasingly popular yardstick of risk. Simply put, standard deviation tells you how much a fund's short-term results vary from its long-term average; the higher the standard deviation, the more the fund's results jump around. If investing is like a roller-coaster ride—and that's as good as any analogy— then standard deviation tells you what to expect in the way of dips and rolls. It tells you how scared you'll be. . . . The fact is, standard deviation can be an important tool for investors—one that can offer some insight not only into how risky a fund is but even into how it might perform in a given market environment in the future. . . .

Source: David Whitford, "Why Risk Matters," *Fortune*, December 29, 1997, pp. 147–152. Reprinted from the December 29, 1997, issue of *Fortune* by special permission. © 1997, Time, Inc.

The goal of investors is to maximize their wealth. There is a chance that this goal will not be achieved, however, because most investments are risky. This chapter's Investments in the News highlights not only the importance of risk but also the practical use of one measure of risk—standard deviation. Although the article focuses on the standard deviation (the square root of variance) of mutual fund performance, this statistical measure is also used to examine the volatility of an individual stock or bond.

This chapter examines volatility; defines a quantitative measure of risk; and explores how the larger the volatility, the worse off investors are because their risk increases. The chapter formally introduces the concepts of risk, risk aversion, risk premium, and variance of returns. For simplicity in introducing these concepts, it is assumed that investors hold a portfolio of only one asset.

The following three chapters further discuss the concepts in the context of a portfolio (a holding of several assets). They also address the meaning of an asset's risk, its measurement, and how the market compensates investors for bearing this risk. In particular, the higher the risk of an asset, the higher its expected return. To gain a clear perspective on how asset prices change when risk prevails, this chapter first examines how current asset prices change in the unrealistic case where future prices are known with certainty.

6.1 THE CASE OF CERTAINTY

We saw in Chapter 5 that different assets can yield different average rates of return. Why don't all financial assets available in the market yield, on average, the same rate of return? We would expect the same rate of return on all assets if the future were known with certainty; otherwise, investors would sell the asset with the lowest rate of return and switch their investment to the asset with the highest rate of return. Because we are now assuming that the future is known with certainty, all investors will hold the asset offering the highest rate of return. However, we will also see that when the future is uncertain, then the higher the volatility, the higher the expected rate of return.

To demonstrate how asset prices change with risk, as well as the effect of volatility on the expected return from an asset, we first look at the behavior of asset prices when future prices are known with certainty. We start with two investments and demonstrate how current prices are established on these two assets when future prices are known with certainty.

Suppose two assets exist, A and B, each with a market price of $100. We know with certainty that Asset A's future price will be $110 and Asset B's future price will be $120, and no dividend or interest is paid on these assets. Is the market in equilibrium? No, it is not. Because Assets A and B have the same current price of $100, and Asset B provides a higher certain future return, an investor currently holding Asset A should sell it and buy Asset B. The investor would be sure of earning $10, or $120 − $110, in the future with no investment. This type of trading strategy, in which profits are made with no risk and no investment, is known as **arbitrage**. (Remember, this is a world of certainty.) This arbitrage trading will cause the price of

Asset A to fall (because there will be a glut of Asset A on the market) and the price of Asset B to rise (because it will be in great demand) until the two assets yield the same certain rate of return.

To find the equilibrium price of the two assets, turn to the definition of *rate of return* given in Chapter 5. Recall that the total return on an investment over Period *i* is

$$R_i = \frac{EMV_i - BMV_i + I_i}{BMV_i}$$

where EMV_i is the ending market value of the investment, BMV_i is the beginning market value of the investment, and I_i is the income earned during Period *i*. In this case, by assumption, $I_i = 0$, because by assumption, there are no intermediate cash payments, such as dividends. Therefore, we have

$$R_i = \frac{EMV_i - BMV_i}{BMV_i}$$

Assuming that $i = 1$, R_i can be rewritten as:

$$R_1 = \frac{P_1 - P_0}{P_0} = \frac{P_1}{P_0} - 1$$

where P_1 represents the price at the end of the period (EMV_i) and P_0 represents the price at the beginning of the period (BMV_i). Because the rates of return for Assets A and B must be identical in equilibrium, we can set the respective rate-of-return equations equal to each other:

$$\frac{P_{A,1}}{P_{A,0}} - 1 = \frac{P_{B,1}}{P_{B,0}} - 1$$

or

$$\frac{P_{A,1}}{P_{A,0}} = \frac{P_{B,1}}{P_{B,0}}$$

or, in our example,

$$\frac{\$110}{P_{A,0}} = \frac{\$120}{P_{B,0}}$$

From this equation we can calculate the equilibrium price of one asset as a function of the price of the other asset. For example, we can calculate the price of Asset B if we know the original purchase price of Asset A. Suppose the equilibrium price for Asset A is $P_{A,0} = \$95$. Then $P_{B,0} \cong \$103.64$, which is calculated from

$$\frac{\$110}{\$95} = \frac{\$120}{P_{B,0}}$$

must be the equilibrium price of Asset B. For this market price, the return on Asset A is

$$(\$110/\$95) - 1 \cong 0.158, \text{ or } 15.8\%$$

and the rate of return on Asset B is

$$(\$120/\$103.64) - 1 \cong 0.158, \text{ or } 15.8\%$$

Once the certain returns on the two assets are identical, the market is said to be in equilibrium for these two specific assets.

Rates of return on various assets actually observed in the markets are in fact different, however, which clearly indicates that future returns are uncertain. Outside the realm of textbooks, uncertainty regarding the future rates of return prevails. Moreover, even average rates of return across years on various assets are not identical. The different average returns reflect the market compensation for the differential uncertainty or risk characterizing various assets.

There is one asset, however, that is very close to being a certain asset. U.S. short-term Treasury bills (T-bills) yield almost a certain return. Ignoring inflation and the chance of a revolution in the United States, the T-bill will pay with certainty the stated yield. Also, because it is a short-term asset, changes in interest rates do not significantly affect the price (see Chapter 16). Therefore, it is common to refer to the yield on T-bills as the *riskless interest rate*. It is true that over time, the yield on T-bills changes. However, when you purchase a given T-bill, the rate of return you earn is fixed if you hold it to maturity. Understanding that the rates of return on most assets are uncertain, we are now prepared to introduce risk into the investment analysis.

PRACTICE BOX	
Problem	Suppose there are two stocks worth $110 and $200, respectively, 1 year from now. The current price of the first stock is $100. What is the equilibrium price of the second stock?
Solution	In equilibrium, the rate of return on both securities must be identical and be equal to 10%, because $110/$100 − 1 = 0.10, or 10%. Therefore, $110/$100 = $200/$P_2$, or $P_2 = (\$200 \cdot \$100)/\$110 \cong \$181.82$. Notice that with this price, the rate of return on this asset is also 10%.

6.2 THE NATURE OF RISK

Suppose you invest for 1 year in a government bond with a zero–coupon rate and $100 face value. The price of the bond is $90. The bond matures exactly 1 year from today. What rate of return will you earn on this bond if you hold it to maturity? Remember, the bond is riskless.[1]

---

1. For simplicity, assume no inflation. Otherwise, the bond is risky in real terms. Also for simplicity, assume no change in the interest rate. If there is inflation, then the rate of return on bonds whose principal and interest are linked to the cost of living index is riskless. Such bonds are issued by the U.S. government and are called inflation-indexed Treasury securities.

A simple calculation reveals that the rate of return is

$$(\$100/\$90) - 1 \cong 0.111, \text{ or } 11.1\%$$

Because the $100 is received with *certainty* when the bond matures 1 year from now, the 11.1% represents a certain rate of return. Also, because the government cannot realistically go bankrupt, there is no default risk on this investment.

Now suppose instead that you purchase a share of IBM common stock for $100. Obviously, unlike the government bond that matures 1 year from now, the value of the stock 1 year from now is uncertain. Suppose no dividends are paid, and the stock price at the end of the year is either $130 with probability ½ or $80 with probability ½. Given that the stock price today is $100, the rate of return will also be uncertain with the following values: either ($130/$100) − 1 = 0.3 or 30% with probability ½ or ($80/$100) − 1 = −0.2 or −20% with probability ½.

In such a case we say that the investment in the stock is risky, which means that a rate of return obtained in the future is not known with certainty. Namely, the distribution of possible rates of return is known, but which of the outcomes will occur is unknown.

These two investment examples indicate that an investor can distinguish between two alternative situations:

1. **Certainty**, the situation in which the future value of the asset (or the rate of return) is known with a probability of 1. (A probability of 1 means that the asset's future value or rate of return is certain.)

2. **Uncertainty** or **risk**, situations in which there is more than one possible future value of the asset (or more than one possible rate of return). In this case, the asset value is a *random variable*. If investors know the probability of each random outcome, they face *risk*. If the probability of each outcome is unknown to investors, they face *uncertainty*. Note that in both uncertainty and risk, more than one future value is possible.

Actual probabilities that are known (as in a coin–flipping experiment) are called **objective probabilities.** In actual decision making by investors and, in particular, in decisions made by people in business, the true probabilities are rarely known. Normally, the investor can collect some rates of return taken from the past few years on the same stock and, based on these data, estimate the probabilities of possible future rates of return. These probability estimates are called **subjective probabilities.** Thus, even if the objective probabilities are unknown, an investor can attach subjective probabilities to each possible future value of an asset. By doing so, the investor faces a situation defined as risk rather than uncertainty. Because an investor can always assign subjective probabilities to the various possible outcomes, the rest of this book uses the words *uncertainty* and *risk* interchangeably to mean that certainty does *not* prevail.

Note that although some assets in the market yield an almost certain rate of return (short-term government T-bills), most assets (stocks, long-term debt, options, investments in real estate, and so forth) yield uncertain rates of return. Therefore, an investor must develop systematic rules to use in choosing among assets characterized by uncertain returns and, in particular, to find the best diversification strategy among such assets. Different assets have different average rates of return, as well as different degrees of risk, so investors need criteria for selecting the best asset. The historical record given in Chapter 5, Exhibit 5-14, shows that on average, assets with higher risk also offer higher returns. How does an investor go about selecting the best asset for a particular investor?

6.3 ALTERNATIVE INVESTMENT CRITERIA

Two alternative investment criteria are the maximum return criterion and the maximum expected return criterion. These two criteria provide a framework for a broader investment selection procedure, called the *mean-variance criterion* (see Section 6.6). The mean–variance criterion, which was developed by Harry Markowitz,[2] for which he won the 1990 Nobel Prize in economics, is the foundation of modern portfolio theory.

6.3.1 Maximum Return Criterion

An investor using the **maximum return criterion (MRC)** selects the asset with the highest rate of return. To examine this selection technique, consider the four securities illustrated in Exhibit 6-1. All four investments require the same initial outlay of $10,000. According to the maximum return criterion, investment in Security A clearly is better than investment in Security B, because 6% is greater than 5%. Deciding between Securities A and C, however, is not so straightforward. If we look at the −10% return from Security C and compare it with Security A's return, then Security A is superior by this rule. However, if we take the +20% return from Security C and compare it with Security A's return, then Security C turns out to be better.

EXHIBIT 6-1   **Possible Rates of Return on Four Securities with a $10,000 Investment**

Security A		Security B		Security C		Security D	
Rate of Return (%)	Probability	Rate of Return (%)	Probability	Rate of Return (%)	Probability	Rate of Return (%)	Probability
6	1	5	1	−10	1/4	−20	1/4
				0	1/4	10	1/2
				20	1/2	40	1/4

2. See Harry Markowitz, "Portfolio Selection," *Journal of Finance* 7, no. 1 (1952): 77–91.

It is impossible to apply the MRC in this case or any case where returns are uncertain. The MRC simply reflects an investor's desire for *more* profit rather than *less* profit. When uncertainty prevails, however, the MRC does not rank the various investments, because one of the possible returns may be smaller and one larger than the return on the certain asset. When returns are uncertain, which is a more typical situation, one method for choosing among assets with multiple possible returns is simply to select the asset with the highest *expected* return.

6.3.2 Maximum Expected Return Criterion

The **maximum expected return criterion (MERC)** compares assets with uncertain returns and gives a clear ranking of the various assets. With MERC, we first calculate the expected value of the returns on each asset and then choose the one with the highest expected return. The expected return is given by

$$E(R) = \sum_{i=1}^{m} P_i R_i \qquad \qquad (6.1)$$

where R_i is the rate of return on an asset in a given state (the ith return), P_i is the probability corresponding to R_i, m is the number of possible returns (or possible values of R), and the E stands for the "expected" return.

The **expected return** is the average of the potential rates of return. The expected return is also known as the *mean return* or *average return* and, when the context is clear, simply as the **mean.** Expected returns have two components: probabilities and rates of return on an asset. The probabilities and rates of return are multiplied and then summed across *states*. States refer to each estimate of probability and return. When using historical data, states are time periods, such as years. When estimating future outcomes, states are based on different projections of events. When each return is equally probable—that is, $P_i = \frac{1}{m}$ for each i—then for Equation 6.1 we have

$$E(R) = \sum_{i=1}^{m} \frac{1}{m} R_i = \frac{1}{m} \sum_{i=1}^{m} R_i$$

(We can move the $\frac{1}{m}$ term outside of the summation, because it is a constant.)

Applying this formula to the examples in Exhibit 6-1, we have

Security	Expected Return, $E(R)$
A	$E(R_A) = 1(6) = 6$
B	$E(R_B) = 1(5) = 5$
C	$E(R_C) = (\frac{1}{4})(-10) + (\frac{1}{4})0 + (\frac{1}{2})20 = 7.5$
D	$E(R_D) = (\frac{1}{4})(-20) + (\frac{1}{2})10 + (\frac{1}{4})40 = 10$

From this ranking we see that Security D is the best, because it yields the largest expected rate of return (10%).

PRACTICE BOX

Problem

Calculate the expected rate of return on Boston Celtics and Boston Edison common stock, given the following historical rates of return. (Assume that each of the following rates of return is equally probable.)

Year	Boston Celtics	Boston Edison
1	7%	8%
2	−5	4
3	12	9
4	6	7

Solution

From Equation 6.1, we have

$$E(R_{Celtics}) = \tfrac{1}{4}(0.07) - \tfrac{1}{4}(0.05) + \tfrac{1}{4}(0.12) + \tfrac{1}{4}(0.06) = 0.05, \text{ or } 5\%$$

and

$$E(R_{Edison}) = \tfrac{1}{4}(0.08) + \tfrac{1}{4}(0.04) + \tfrac{1}{4}(0.09) + \tfrac{1}{4}(0.07) = 0.07, \text{ or } 7\%.$$

Although the MERC provides a clear-cut ranking of alternative investments, its rankings in some situations are questionable. For example, compare Securities C and D. Although Security D provides the highest expected return, it also exposes the investor to the maximum possible loss, −20%. To understand the drawback of the MERC, suppose that Bobby Jones, a student in a business school in Berkeley, California, has an initial wealth of $10,000. To pay for tuition and living expenses next year, he needs a minimum of $9,000. If he invests in Security C and the lowest return occurs, he will still have $9,000 at year-end:

$$\$10,000[1 + (-0.1)] = 10,000(0.9) = \$9,000$$

where −0.10 is the lowest possible rate of return. If Jones invests in Security D and the worst outcome occurs, he will end up with

$$\$10,000[1 + (-0.2)] = \$10,000(0.8) = \$8,000$$

and he will not have the minimum funds he needs for school next year. Jones is an ambitious student; hence, he would see it as a disaster if he had to drop out of school because of a lack of money. Therefore, he will avoid investment in Security D, because it puts his college career at risk.

However, for other investors who need a minimum of, say, only $5,000 next year, Security D may be preferable. (Again, assume a $10,000 starting amount.) In a nutshell, Security D has the advantage of having the largest mean return, but it also has the disadvantage of having the lowest possible rate of return, −20%. Therefore, it is also the most risky. Thus, the choice between Securities A, C, and D is difficult and may vary from one investor to another, depending on the investor's future financial needs or obligations. An investor with a strong distaste for risk may prefer Security C, whereas an investor who is more willing to take risk (in pursuit of higher returns) may prefer Security D. The next section links investor preference with asset risk.

6.4 RISK AVERSION

In the example illustrated in Exhibit 6-1, a tough decision had to be made. In contrast, Exhibit 6-2 presents an easier case where the mean return on the two assets is identical. Both Security A and Security B have the expected dollar return of $120 on a $100 investment. The return on Security A is certain ($120 with a probability of 1.0), whereas the return on Security B is uncertain, because it yields $110 with a probability of ½ and $130 with a probability of ½.

Which investment would you prefer? Empirical evidence and data taken from the stock market reveal that most investors would prefer Security A.

6.4.1 Definition of Risk Averters

The investors who prefer Security A over Security B are called **risk averters.** Risk averters, other things being equal, are investors who dislike volatility or risk. They always prefer a certain investment over an uncertain investment (namely, they prefer Security A over Security B) *as long as* the expected returns on the two investments are identical. Thus, for risk averters to be convinced to buy Security B, they would have to be compensated by a higher expected return. The difference between the expected rate of return on a risky asset and the riskless interest rate is known as the **risk premium.**

To provide an intuitive explanation of why most investors are risk averters, consider Leslie Chin, a junior in the business school at New York University, who gets $120 per week for food from her parents. The $120 is exactly enough for food and one movie a week (no soda or popcorn). If we offer Chin $110 with a probability of

EXHIBIT 6-2 Dispersion of Returns: Returns on Securities A and B with a $100 Investment	Security A		Security B	
	Return ($)	Probability	Return ($)	Probability
	120	1	110	½
			130	½
	Mean return ($)	120	120	
	Variance	0	100[a]	
	Mean return (%)	20	20	

a. Variance $= \sigma^2 = \frac{1}{2}(110 - 120)^2 + \frac{1}{2}(130 - 120)^2 = 100$ (see Equation 6.3 in Section 6.5).

½ and $130 with a probability of ½ rather than the option of getting $120 for sure, she would probably refuse the offer. The reason is that on the one hand, with $110, she would have to cut out the movie. With $130, on the other hand, she could go to two movies a week. However, because the satisfaction she would derive from having a second movie per week is less than the loss of satisfaction induced by giving up one movie per week, Chin would prefer $120 with certainty. Leslie Chin is called a risk averter, because when she is faced with two alternative investments with identical expected returns, she chooses the safest one.

6.4.2 Risk Premium

Let us return to the example in Exhibit 6-2, where investments in Securities A and B have the same expected rate of return, +20%. Suppose all investors in the market are risk averters. Then all will buy Security A and none will buy Security B. Is this possible? Of course not; someone must hold Security B. Assets in the financial markets are at times like the infamous hot potato. If you don't want it, you have to sell it. To induce someone to buy an undesirable asset, you have to lower its price to make it more attractive to the buyer.

Thus, the market mechanism is as follows: The price of Security B will fall (because it has no demand), say, to $95. At this price, some investors may find it an attractive investment. Assume that at this price, the market is in equilibrium; no one wants to sell or buy stocks. The rate of return on Security B with a current purchase price of $95 is

$$(\$110/\$95) - 1 \cong 15.79\% \text{ with a probability of } \tfrac{1}{2}$$

and

$$(\$130/\$95) - 1 \cong 36.84\% \text{ with a probability of } \tfrac{1}{2}$$

The mean rate of return on Security B is therefore

$$\tfrac{1}{2}(15.79\%) + \tfrac{1}{2}(36.84\%) \cong 26.31\%$$

whereas the mean return on Security A remains 20% (or $120 per $100 invested). Suppose the market is in equilibrium. That is, at these prices there is neither excess demand nor excess supply, and all available assets are bought by investors. Because the rate of return on Security A is certain, the difference in the mean return on these two assets when the market is in equilibrium is called the *risk premium*. Namely,

$$26.31\% - 20\% = 6.31\%$$

is the premium on Security B required by the market to compensate investors for the risk involved with this asset.

Thus, we can say that the mean rate of return on risky assets is composed of the following two elements:

Mean Rate of Return on Risky Asset	=	Mean Rate of Return on Riskless Asset	+	Risk Premium	(6.2)

The more risk averse investors are (for example, the prospect of not finishing college, the danger of going bankrupt, and so forth), the lower the equilibrium price of Security B and, hence, the larger the required risk premium.

In Exhibit 6-2, Security B has only two possible outcomes ($110 and $130). It is clear that the larger the deviation of these outcomes from the $120 mean (for example, $100 and $140), the greater the risk. When there are more than two outcomes, however, an investor needs to find a quantitative measure for the risk. One common measure of the risk is the variability (or variance) of the rates of return.

PRACTICE BOX

Problem

Investment A yields a 10% rate of return with certainty. Investment B yields −10% with a probability of ½ and 40% with a probability of ½, and the market is in equilibrium. Calculate the risk premium.

Solution

From Equation 6.2, we know that the risk premium is equal to the mean rate of return on the risky asset less the mean rate of return on the riskless asset. In this case, the mean return on the risky asset is

$$E(R_B) = \tfrac{1}{2}(-10\%) + \tfrac{1}{2}(40\%) = 15\%$$

Thus, the risk premium is 15% − 10% = 5%.

6.5 CALCULATING VARIANCE

The **variance** of returns is a measure of the dispersion around the mean and is used as a measure of risk.[3] The variance of the possible returns for an asset is denoted by σ^2 (σ is the Greek letter sigma) and is calculated as follows:

$$\sigma^2 = \sum_{i=1}^{m} P_i[R_i - E(R)]^2 \tag{6.3}$$

where P_i is the probability of outcome i, m is the number of possible states, R_i is the rate of return on the asset in State i, and $E(R)$ is the expected return on R (see Equation 6.1). Thus, the variance is the sum of the probability times the squared deviations from the mean.

For example, consider an investment that has two states. In State 1 the investment offers 0% with probability of ½, and in State 2 it offers 30% with probability of ½ over next year. The expected return 1 year from now is ½(0%) + ½(30%) = 15%, and the variance is

$$\sigma^2 = \tfrac{1}{2}(0.0 - 0.15)^2 + \tfrac{1}{2}(0.30 - 0.15)^2 = 0.0225$$

---

3. Variance is not the only measure of risk, but it is the most widely used. Other risk measures include semivariance, risk of loss, and beta.

To calculate the variance over a number of years, simply substitute $\frac{1}{m}$ for P_i, where m is the number of years:[4]

$$\sigma^2 = \sum_{i=1}^{m} \frac{1}{m}[R_i - E(R)]^2 \qquad (6.4)$$

For example, the rates of return over the past 3 years for Idaho Power common stock were 37%, −17%, and 17%. The expected return is

$$E(R_{Idaho}) = (0.37 - 0.17 + 0.17)/3 \cong 0.123$$

and the variance is

$$\sigma^2_{Idaho} = \frac{1}{3}(0.37 - 0.123)^2 + \frac{1}{3}(-0.17 - 0.123)^2 + \frac{1}{3}(0.17 - 0.123)^2 \cong 0.1491$$

Note that if the rates of return are expressed in percentage figures, then the unit of variance is *percent squared*. If the rates of return are in dollar figures, then the unit of variance is *dollars squared*. These terms are difficult to interpret. Therefore, it is common to take the square root of the variance, which is called the **standard deviation.** The standard deviation is stated in percentages or dollars and is expressed as

$$\sigma = \left\{ \sum_{i=1}^{m} \frac{1}{m}[R_i - E(R)]^2 \right\}^{1/2} \qquad (6.5)$$

In the preceding example, we found the variance to be 0.1491. Therefore, the standard deviation is

$$\sigma_{Idaho} = (0.1491)^{1/2} \cong 0.3861, \text{ or } 38.61\%$$

6.6 THE MEAN-VARIANCE CRITERION

Now that we know that most investors are risk averse, we can refine our investment selection criteria. To include this risk aversion characteristic in the decision of security selection, we turn to the **mean-variance criterion (MVC).** We see from the variance formula that the greater the uncertainty of future returns, the higher the variance. Therefore, the MVC is used to select those assets with (1) the lowest variance for the same (or higher) expected return or (2) the highest expected return for the same (or lower) variance.

---

4. Sometimes, when we have sample data (data based on a sample of the whole population) rather than population data (data based on the whole population), we denote the mean by $\bar{R} = \sum R_i / m$, and the sample variance is obtained by dividing by $m - 1$ rather than m. Specifically,

$$\sigma^2 = \sum_{i=1}^{m} [R_i - E(R_i)]^2 / (m - 1)$$

By dividing by $m - 1$, we obtain an unbiased formula for the variance. (See any basic statistics book.) The rest of the book assumes population data rather than sample data; thus, we divide by m. However, dividing by m or by $m - 1$ does not affect the analysis discussed in this book.

The MVC is defined as follows: Asset A is preferred over Asset B if *either* of the following two conditions holds:

$$\text{a. } E(R_A) \geq E(R_B) \text{ and } \sigma_A^2 < \sigma_B^2$$

or

$$\text{b. } E(R_A) > E(R_B) \text{ and } \sigma_A^2 \leq \sigma_B^2$$

The MVC assumes that investors like higher mean rates of return and dislike higher variances (that is, higher risk). Going back to Exhibit 6-2, let us calculate the variances of the two assets:

$$\sigma_A^2 = (120 - 120)^2 = 0$$

and

$$\sigma_B^2 = \tfrac{1}{2}(110 - 120)^2 + \tfrac{1}{2}(130 - 120)^2 = \frac{100}{2} + \frac{100}{2} = 100$$

Security A has the same mean (expected) profitability as Security B ($120) and a lower variance than Security B. Hence, using the MVC, an investor would choose Security A. Thus, in the specific case of the example given in Exhibit 6-2, the MVC leads to the assertion that Security A is preferred over Security B, because both have the same mean profitability, and Security B is more risky.

Exhibit 6-3 shows that the variance can be increased with no change in the mean return. Security A yields $130 with certainty, Security B yields $120 and $140 with equal probability, and Security C yields $110 and $150 with equal probability. As we move from A to B to C, $10 is added and subtracted with equal probability, creating a larger dispersion (variance) without changing the mean return. This movement, which increases the variance but does not change the mean return, causes the risk averter to be worse off, according to the MVC.

EXHIBIT 6-3 Volatility and Variance: Returns on Securities A, B, and C with a $100 Investment	Security A		Security B		Security C	
	Return ($)	Probability	Return ($)	Probability	Return ($)	Probability
	130	1	120	½	110	½
			140	½	150	½
	Mean	130	130[a]		130[b]	
	Variance	0	100[c]		400[d]	

a. ½(120) + ½(140) = 130.

b. ½(110) + ½(150) = 130.

c. ½(120 − 130)² + ½(140 − 130)² = 100.

d. ½(110 − 130)² + ½(150 − 130)² = 400.

The reason risk averters would not like this movement is that the joy or satisfaction they get from the increase of $10 is smaller for them than the sorrow or damage caused by a loss of $10 in the case where the lower income is realized. Thus, for risk averters, Security A is preferred to Security B, and Security B is preferred to Security C. Risk averters prefer to avoid the honey (higher return) not because they do not like honey but because they know there is a probability that they could get stung!

Assuming that all or most investors are risk averters, the stock price of Security B must drop, and the stock price of Security C must drop even further relative to Security A. Once all available assets have been purchased and the market is cleared, we will find that, in fact, there is a risk premium on Securities B and C and that the risk premium on Security C is larger than the risk premium on Security B.

For example, if the price of Security A is $100, the price of Security B may drop to $98, and the price of Security C may drop to $95. Suppose that at these prices, the market is in equilibrium; hence, there is neither an excess demand nor an excess supply of securities. In this case, the mean rate of return would be

Security A: $(\$130/\$100) - 1 = 0.3$ or 30%

Security B: $[\frac{1}{2}(\$120/\$98) + \frac{1}{2}(\$140/\$98)] - 1$

$$= [(\frac{1}{2} \cdot 1.22) + (\frac{1}{2} \cdot 1.43)] - 1 \cong 0.325 \text{ or } 32.5\%$$

Security C: $[\frac{1}{2}(\$110/\$95) + \frac{1}{2}(\$150/\$95)] - 1$

$$= [(\frac{1}{2} \cdot 1.16) + (\frac{1}{2} \cdot 1.58)] - 1 \cong 0.37 \text{ or } 37\%$$

Therefore, for these assumed equilibrium prices, the risk premiums on Securities A, B, and C are as follows:

Security A: Certainty, hence zero risk premium.

Security B: Risk Premium = 32.5% − 30% = 2.5%.

Security C: Risk Premium = 37% − 30% = 7%.

As you can see, the larger the variance, the lower the price, and the larger the risk premium.

PRACTICE BOX	
Problem	If you do not insure your car, its value at the end of the year will be either $10,000 with a probability of 98% (no accident) or $0 (total loss in an accident) with a probability of 2%. An insurance firm is willing to give you $10,000 in the case of a total loss, for a fee of $800. Calculate the mean and variance of your wealth with and without the insurance coverage. What is the risk premium in dollars?
Solution	Without the insurance, the expected value (where *ni* denotes "no insurance") is

$$E(Car_{ni}) = (0.98 \cdot \$10,000) + (0.02 \cdot \$0) = \$9,800$$

and the variance is   *(continued)*

$$\sigma_{ni}^2 = 0.98(\$10,000 - \$9,800)^2 + 0.02(\$0 - \$9,800)^2 = \$1,960,000$$

With the insurance, you have to deduct the cost from each potential outcome. The expected value (where wi denotes "with insurance" and $10,000 is the value of the car whether you have a crash or not, thanks to the insurance) is

$$E(Car_{wi}) = 0.98(\$10,000 - \$800) + 0.02(\$10,000 - \$800) = \$9,200$$

and the variance is

$$\sigma_{wi}^2 = 0.98(\$9,200 - \$9,200)^2 + 0.02(\$9,200 - \$9,200)^2 = 0$$

We see that the insurance eliminates the risk (zero variance), but also reduces the expected value.

The risk premium is the difference between the expected value of the car without the insurance and the expected value of the car with the insurance. Thus, the risk premium in dollars is $9,800 − $9,200 = $600.

6.7 OTHER ATTITUDES TOWARD RISK

Investors who are **risk neutral** completely ignore an asset's variance and make investment decisions based on only the asset's expected return. These investors choose an investment by the MERC. In the example given in Exhibit 6-2, the risk–neutral investor will be indifferent between Securities A and B. If all investors were risk neutral, no risk premium would be required, and Securities A and B would have the same market price.

Investors are defined as **risk seekers** if they like risk or variance. These investors will be ready to pay a higher price for an asset whose variance increases. In Exhibit 6-2, risk seekers will prefer Security B over Security A. There is ample evidence that some people are risk seekers, at least during some periods of time and for small dollar amounts. For example, most gambling activities, such as state lotteries, have expected payoffs less than the cost to play, yet some people still buy lottery tickets.

If all investors were either risk neutral or risk seeking, there would be no positive risk premium. One way to assess whether financial markets are dominated by risk seekers or risk averters is to examine historical rates of return. If riskier securities earn, on average, higher returns, then we can infer that on the whole, the market participants are risk averse. A recent study examined returns on all NYSE stocks (a value-weighted index) and compared their average rate of return with the average rate of return on Treasury bills. After adjusting for inflation, NYSE stocks averaged 6.4% per year compared with 0.5% per year for Treasury bills. This result implies a risk premium of 5.9% (6.4% − 0.5%) after adjusting for inflation. For the years 1926–1996, we obtain similar results: 7.4% average (geometric) and real rate of return on stocks and 0.6% on Treasury bills, with a risk premium of 6.8%.[5] Because

5. *Stocks, Bonds, Bills and Inflation 1997, Yearbook* (Chicago: Ibbotson Associates, 1997).

positive risk premiums are found in the market, we can conclude that risk aversion is the dominating preference in the marketplace. Therefore, in the rest of the book, we assume that investors are risk averse.[6]

Historical returns also confirm the relationship between risk and return. For example, Exhibit 6-4 provides the rates of return on IBM and AT&T stock over a 10-year period. The riskless rate over this period was 6.1%. We see that the average rate of return for IBM was higher than for AT&T. However, the variance and standard deviation were also higher for IBM. The risk premium for IBM was 10.65% − 6.1% = 4.55%, and the risk premium for AT&T was 9.2% − 6.1% = 3.1%. Thus, IBM offers a higher risk and a higher return than AT&T.

EXHIBIT 6-4 **Rates of Return on IBM and AT&T Stock over a 10-Year Period**	**Year**	**IBM**	**AT&T**
	1	0.15%	0.08%
	2	0.135	0.09
	3	−0.04	0.05
	4	0.16	0.10
	5	0.08	0.12
	6	−0.10	0.03
	7	0.24	0.15
	8	0.02	0.06
	9	0.30	0.14
	10	0.12	0.10
	Average rate of return[a]	0.1065%	0.092%
	Variance	0.013	0.001
	Standard deviation	0.114	0.032

a. The average rate of return, variance, and standard deviation are calculated using $P_i = \frac{1}{m}$, where $m = 10$.

So far, we have seen that an asset's variability determines its risk premium. Although this is true when each asset is held in isolation, the investor who holds several assets and constructs a portfolio should take the other factors into account as well. The next chapter examines these issues.

6. See Jeremy J. Siegel, "The Equity Premium: Stock and Bond Returns since 1802," *Financial Analysts Journal,* January–February 1992, pp. 28–38.

SUMMARY

This chapter first discussed asset pricing under the assumption of certainty. Under certainty, in equilibrium all assets will yield the same rate of return. However, we live in a world of uncertainty, where different assets have different expected returns.

Compare the maximum return and maximum expected return criteria as investment selection methods. An investor using the maximum return criterion selects the asset with the highest rate of return. This investment selection method does not work in uncertainty. The maximum expected return criterion selects the asset with the highest *expected* rate of return. This investment selection method does not consider an investment's riskiness.

Explain what a risk averter is. A risk averter, other things being equal, dislikes volatility. Such an investor will always prefer a certain investment over an uncertain investment as long as the expected returns on the two investments are identical. To be induced to take risk, risk averters must be offered a risk premium.

Calculate the risk premium. Given the assets, when we hold only one asset, the larger the deviations of the returns from the mean, the more risky the asset and the larger the required risk premium. The quantitative risk measure in this case is the variance of the rates of return or the square root of the variance, which is the standard deviation. The risk premium can be calculated as the (mean rate of return on risky asset) − (mean rate of return on riskless asset).

Apply the mean-variance criterion in asset selection. The mean-variance criterion (MVC) provides a simple method to assess choices between risky assets. Investor risk aversion results in a risk premium. The risk premium is the additional average return required to compensate the investor for the risk exposure. The stock and bond markets are dominated by risk averters. Investors with other risk attitudes include those who are risk neutral (who are indifferent to the quantity of risk) and risk seekers (who pay a higher price for risky assets).

CHAPTER AT A GLANCE

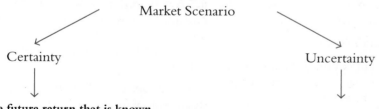

Certainty	Uncertainty
There is only one future return that is known with probability.	**There is more than one possible future return.**
1. The mean return equals the riskless interest rate.	1. The mean return is greater than the riskless interest rate.
2. The variance is zero.	2. The variance is greater than zero.
3. The risk premium is zero.	3. The risk premium is positive (with risk aversion).

Main Equations

With Data Estimating Future Outcomes

Expected return:

$$E(R) = \sum_{i=1}^{m} P_i R_i$$

Variance:

$$\sigma^2 = \sum_{i=1}^{m} P_i [R_i - E(R)]^2$$

Standard deviation:

$$\sigma = \sqrt{\sum_{i=1}^{m} P_i [R_i - E(R)]^2} = \sqrt{\sigma^2}$$

With Historical Data or Equal Probability

Expected return:

$$E(R) = \sum_{i=1}^{m} \frac{1}{m} R_i = \frac{1}{m} \sum_{i=1}^{m} R_i$$

Variance:

$$\sigma^2 = \sum_{i=1}^{m} \frac{1}{m} [R_i - E(R)]^2$$

Standard deviation:

$$\sigma = \sqrt{\sum_{i=1}^{m} \frac{1}{m} [R_i - E(R)]^2} = \sqrt{\sigma^2}$$

KEY TERMS

Arbitrage   192
Certainty   195
Expected return   197
Maximum expected return
   criterion (MERC)   197
Maximum return criterion
   (MRC)   196

Mean   197
Mean-variance criterion
   (MVC)   202
Objective probability   195
Risk   195
Risk averter   199
Risk neutral   205

Risk premium   199
Risk seeker   205
Standard deviation   202
Subjective probability   195
Uncertainty   195
Variance   201

REVIEW

6.1 What is the difference between risk and uncertainty? How are these differences resolved?

6.2 What is an arbitrage transaction?

6.3 Suppose the market is in equilibrium, and there are no mispriced assets. What do different average rates of return in the market reflect?

6.4 When is the MRC the proper investment rule to use?

6.5 What is the relationship between an investor's level of risk aversion and the required risk premium?

6.6 You prefer to get $100 with a probability of ½ and $200 with a probability of ½ over getting $150 with certainty. Are you a risk averter or a risk seeker?

6.7 A firm requires at least a 12% rate of return on a project, the cost of capital is 12%, and the riskless interest rate is 5%. What can we learn about the average stockholder's risk preferences? What is the risk premium?

6.8 Consider the following rates of return for two stock mutual funds:

Year	Fund A (%)	Fund B (%)
1	−10	−15
2	+20	+23
3	+10	+8
4	+12	+15

Examine whether one fund dominates the other by MVC.

PRACTICE

6.1 What is the annual rate of return on a riskless, 2-year zero-coupon bond with a face value of $200 that cost you $170?

6.2 Suppose there are two assets, X and Y, and the current price of Asset X is $100. If it is known with certainty that Asset X will be worth $120 in 1 year and Asset Y will be worth $144, what is the equilibrium price of Asset Y today?

6.3 a. Suppose there are two assets, X and Y, as in Question 6.2. Firm X splits its stock 2-for-1, thus the current price of Firm X is $50. What is the equilibrium price of Asset Y today, if Asset X will be worth $60 in 1 year?
b. Now suppose that Asset Y also splits its stock 2-for-1 and will be worth $72. What is the equilibrium price of Asset Y today? How does your answer compare with that of Question 6.1?

6.4 Suppose a stock that has a current price of $80 has a 50% chance of rising to $120 in 1 year and a 50% chance of falling to $60. What is the expected price of the stock? What is the expected dollar profit? What is the expected rate of return?

6.5 Consider the following data related to Assets A, B, C, and D (given in percentages):

Asset A		Asset B	
Rate of Return (%)	**Probability**	**Rate of Return (%)**	**Probability**
5	1	−10	¼
		10	¾

Asset C		Asset D	
Rate of Return (%)	**Probability**	**Rate of Return (%)**	**Probability**
−20	⅓	−20	¼
15	⅓	10	½
30	⅓	40	¼

Which asset is preferable by the maximum expected return criterion (MERC)? Explain.

6.6 From Question 6.5, which asset is preferable by the mean-variance criterion (MVC)? Discuss.

6.7 During a recent 10-year period, the following rates of return were earned on General Electric (GE) and Duke Power Company (DP). Assume that these are the population distributions and that each year has a probability of $1/m$, where m is the number of years.

Year	GE	DP
1	0.11	0.1
2	0.13	0.12
3	−0.06	0.09
4	0.12	0.17
5	0.03	0.05
6	−0.04	−0.01
7	0.34	0.12
8	0.05	0.06
9	0.26	0.02
10	0.16	0.08

a. Calculate the expected rate of return, variance, and standard deviation of each stock.
b. Assume that the riskless interest rate is 4%. What is the risk premium on these two assets? Explain your results.

6.8 The rate of return on a stock is estimated to be −10% with a probability of ½ and +40% with a probability of ½. These are the estimated returns before tax. Suppose the investor pays a personal tax of 31% on this profit. If the investor loses, he can reduce the tax burden; namely, he gets back money.
a. Calculate the expected value and variance of the before-tax returns. Explain your results.
b. Calculate the expected value and variance of the after-tax returns. Explain your results.

6.9 Next year a security will yield $90 with a probability of ½ and $110 with a probability of ½. An investor is willing to pay $80 for this asset today. The risk-free interest rate is 15%.
a. Is this investor a risk seeker or a risk averter?
b. What is the risk premium?

6.10 Answer Question 6.9 assuming that the investor is ready to pay $95 for this asset.

6.11 Investment A costs $1,000 today, and the return next year is either $900 or $1,300, with an equal probability. Investment B costs $100 today, and the return next year is either $90 or $130, with an equal probability.

a. Calculate the means and variances of future returns (in dollars) on these two assets.

b. Calculate the means and variances of future *rates* of return on these two assets.

c. Suppose Investments A and B are two stocks that exist in the market, and you can buy as much as you wish from these two stocks, but you can buy only one (A or B). Which investment would you prefer?

6.12 Suppose both Stock A and Stock B cost $100. The future returns on these two stocks are as follows:

Stock A		Stock B	
Probability	Return ($)	Probability	Return ($)
½	90	⅓	90
½	150	⅔	150

a. Calculate the expected rates of return and the variances of the rates of return on these two assets.

b. Which investment is better, according to the MVC?

c. Given that the riskless interest rate is 5%, calculate the risk premium on each of these two assets.

6.13 Repeat Question 6.12 when the return on Stockt B is $90 with a probability of ⅔ and $150 with a probability of ⅓. The information on Stock A is unchanged.

6.14 "The variance is always a larger number than the standard deviation." Is this assertion true? Give an example to demonstrate your answer.

6.15 If you buy U.S. Treasury bills with 6 months to maturity, you get for each $100 investment only $103 six months from now.

a. Assuming that this investment is riskless, what is the annual riskless interest rate?

b. Would you say that short-term U.S. Treasury bills are absolutely riskless? (Hint: Consider real returns.)

6.16 a. Calculate the mean real rate of return (for the six-month period) and the variance of the U.S. Treasury bills given in Question 6.15 on the assumption that the future inflation rate would be 1% for the next six months, with certainty.

b. Repeat the calculations when it is known that the inflation rate will be 0% with a probability of ½ and 2% with a probability of ½.

6.17 "Indexing Bonds for Inflation Backed by Fed"[7]

WASHINGTON—*Federal Reserve Chairman Alan Greenspan endorsed the concept of indexing certain government bonds for inflation, saying there is "no question" that such an arrangement would be beneficial to policy makers at the central bank.*

Mr. Greenspan's views came during testimony before the House Government Operations subcommittee on monetary affairs, which began a series of hearings on the indexing idea.

Some economists believe that the Treasury should issue a portion of its long-term bonds as indexed securities, which would have both their principal and interest payments adjusted upward to protect investors from inflation.

Treasury officials didn't comment immediately on the notion, but they've rejected it in the past.

Rep. Doug Barnard (D., Ga.),[8] chairman of the panel, argued that the introduction of indexed bonds would create an attractive investment vehicle and might even save the Treasury money. That's because investors, once insulated from inflation, would accept lower rates of interest on those instruments.

As you can see, it has been suggested that the principal and interest be indexed to inflation. Suppose you have a U.S. bond maturing in 1 year whose price is $100 today and that gives you $105 principal plus interest at the end of the year. The inflation rate is $h = 2\%$ with a probability of ½ and $h = 4\%$ with a probability of ½.

a. Calculate the expected *nominal* rate of return and nominal variance (ignoring inflation).

---

7. Rick Wartzman, *Wall Street Journal,* June 17, 1992, p. A5. Reprinted by permission of *The Wall Street Journal* © 1992 Dow Jones & Co., Inc. All Rights Reserved Worldwide.

8. This means he is a Democrat from Georgia.

b. Calculate the expected value and variance of the real rates of return (after adjusting for inflation). Which are relevant for you, the nominal rates of return or the real rates of return? Explain.

c. Suppose now that the future $105 return is "indexed" to the inflation rate. Specifically, in the future you get $105(1 + h)$, where h is the observed future inflation rate. Calculate the expected rates of return and variance in nominal and real terms. Does indexation reduce your risk? Explain.

6.18 By indexing its bonds, the government reduces the investors' risk, but on average, the government does not want to pay a higher interest rate in real terms.

a. Using the data from Question 6.17, what should be the future payment on an indexed bond (instead of $105) such that on average, the expected real rate of return to the investor is unchanged?

b. Would you be better off with the original bond given in Question 6.17 or the indexed bond you developed in Part a of this question?

6.19 Suppose the government indexed its bonds. The distribution of the inflation is known and is given in Question 6.17, and the future cash flows are determined as in Question 6.18 such that on average, neither the government nor the investors lose money from the indexation.

a. Are the investors who are risk averters better off?

b. Suppose most investors are risk averters, and they are better off because of indexation. Hence, the risk is reduced, and they are ready to pay $101 for the bonds rather than $100. Calculate the mean and variance of the real rates of return with the new $101 price. Does the government gain from such indexation?

6.20 Suppose you consider holding either Asset A or Asset B with the following rates of return:

Asset A		Asset B	
Rate of Return (%)	Probability	Rate of Return (%)	Probability
+30	½	+20	½
0	½	−10	½

Which asset is preferred by MERC? By the MVC?

6.21 a. You buy a triple-B, zero-coupon corporate bond (moderately risky) for $900 that promises to pay $1,000 at the end of the year. There is a $\frac{1}{100}$ probability that the firm will go bankrupt and you will lose all your investment. Is this bond riskless? Calculate the mean rate of return and the variance of the rates of return.

b. Now suppose you purchase a zero-coupon corporate bond with a rating of D− (very risky). Its current market price is $700, and it matures in 1 year (par = $1,000). Investors are risk neutral; that is, they are indifferent to which bond (the triple B or the D− bond) to buy as long as the bonds offer the same expected rate of return. Estimate the probability of bankruptcy of this bond (again, assume that in the case of bankruptcy, the principal and interest are totally lost) implied by the $700 price.

6.22 Suppose you have the following return on a $100 investment in a given stock:

Probability	Return ($)
½	90
¼	120
¼	140

a. Calculate the mean and variance of the dollar return, as well as the mean and variance of the rate of return.

b. Suppose you pay a $5 transaction cost when you sell the stock (at the end of the year). Calculate the mean and variance of the net of the transaction cost for both the return and the rate of return.

c. Repeat Part b, but now suppose you pay 5% of the end-of-period return as transaction costs. Calculate the mean and variance of both return and rate of return.

d. Explain your results Parts a, b, and c.

6.23 Suppose the value of your house is $100,000 if fire does not break out and $10,000 if fire does break out. The probability of a fire is 1%. An insurance company asks for $2,000 to insure your house against fire.

a. Calculate the mean and variance of your wealth with and without an insurance policy.

b. If you decide to buy this insurance policy, are you displaying risk-averse behavior?

6.24 Consider the following investments, which all require a $100 investment:

		Outcomes		
State of the Economy	Probability	Asset A	Asset B	Asset C
Good	⅙	10%	5%	−10%
Normal	⅔	12	5	12
Recession	⅙	−10	5	10

Without calculating the expected returns and variances, what can you discern by studying the three probability distributions? For example, how would you characterize Asset B, and what is the relationship between Asset A and Asset C? What can you say about the return and variance of Asset B? What can you say about the return and variance of Assets A and C?

6.25 Imagine a stock currently selling at $100. One year hence, the stock price will be either $80 or $160, with an equal probability. There are no dividends or stock splits.
a. Calculate the expected value and the standard deviation of rates of return.
b. Assume that the capital gains tax is 20%, with full offset for losses. Calculate the expected rate of return and the standard deviation on an after-tax basis. Does the tax reduce the risk? Explain your results.

6.26 Assume that a stock of one firm is traded for $10 per share, whereas the stock of another firm is traded for $100 per share. Suppose that both stocks have equal probability of falling by 10% or increasing by 30%. Your friend tells you, "The stock whose market value is $100 is much more risky because in dollar terms of the terminal value of the investment, it has a much higher standard deviation." Calculate the standard deviation of the terminal value of each stock, and discuss whether your friend is right or wrong.

6.27 Assume a stock with a market price of $100. The future price 1 year from now is either $80 or $140, with an equal probability. Your broker says that if the stock price falls below $90, she will guarantee you $90. If the price is $130, she will not intervene. It costs you $8 today to buy the insurance. Calculate the expected rate of return and standard deviation with and without the insurance.

6.28 The following exhibit reports the average return and standard deviation of international mutual funds:

Here's What You Get after Loads and Taxes[a]

	Returns		Return	Fees		Risk
	Avg. Annual 5 Yr.	1 Yr.	Avg. Annual 5 Yr.	Sales Load	Annual Expenses	Standard Deviation
International Group Avg.[b] →	13.2%	5.5%	12.1%			
GAM International A	21.0%	21.4%	18.1%	5.00%	1.56%	19.7
Fidelity Diversified International[c]	17.1%	12.4%	16.5%	None	1.27%	13.4
Putnam International Growth A	17.8%	16.6%	16.1%	5.75%	1.74%	15.0
Hotchkis & Wiley International	16.4%	9.0%	15.8%	None	1.00%	13.0
Oakmark International	16.2%	9.1%	15.2%	None	1.32%	16.0
Preferred International	15.7%	8.7%	15.2%	None	1.25%	14.2
Managers Inernational Equity	14.9%	8.7%	14.4%	None	1.53%	12.0
USAA International	15.0%	9.4%	14.2%	None	1.09%	14.0
Vanguard International Growth	14.2%	2.4%	13.7%	None	0.57%	14.9
AIM International Equity A	14.9%	4.5%	13.2%	5.50%	1.57%	15.1
Warburg Pincus Intl. Equity	12.9%	−2.9%	12.4%	None	1.37%	17.2
T. Rowe Price International Stock	12.4%	0.6%	11.6%	None	0.88%	14.3
Scudder International	12.3%	5.9%	11.5%	None	1.15%	13.5

(continued)

| | Returns | | Return | Fees | | Risk |
	Avg. Annual 5 Yr.	1 Yr.	Avg. Annual 5 Yr.	Sales Load	Annual Expenses	Standard Deviation
SIT International Growth	12.0%	1.2%	11.4%	None	1.50%	15.3
Templeton Foreign I	14.1%	10.0%	11.4%	5.75%	1.12%	10.7

a. Performance is through Nov. 14, 1997, and net of annual expenses, brokerage costs, and sales loads; also net of taxes, assuming the new 20% long-term rate for capital gains and income distributions.

b. Average annual return for all funds tracked by Morningstar in each category.

c. Fund will not declare capital gains Dec. 7–31, 1997.

Source: Maura Atanasov, "The Best Mutual Funds," *Fortune,* December 29, 1997, p. 126. Reprinted from the December 29, 1997, issue of FORTUNE by special permission; copyright 1997, Time Inc.

a. Out of the fifteen international mutual funds, which are inferior by the MVC? Explain your results. If you are risk averse and use the MVC to choose your investment, and given that the historical data reflect the future expected data, in which mutual fund would you *not* invest?

b. Putnam International will not be selected by the MVC. To encourage sales of the fund, suppose that the fund's management decreases the annual management fee from 1.74% to 0.50%. Will this induce investors to invest in the fund under the MVC? Explain.

For Internet questions visit the Levy Investment Web site at http://levy-invst.swcollege.com.

YOUR TURN: APPLYING THEORY TO PRACTICE

MEAN AND VARIANCE OF BONDS AND STOCKS

The following table provides the monthly rates of return on the S&P 500 index, small stocks, and corporate and government bonds for the year 1996:

Monthly Rates of Return on Stocks and Bonds for 1996 (%)

Month	S&P 500	Small Stocks	Long-Term Corporate Bonds	Long-Term Government Bonds
1	3.44	0.28	0.14	−0.11
2	0.96	3.69	3.73	−4.83
3	0.96	2.28	1.30	−2.10
4	1.47	8.48	1.60	−1.65
5	2.58	7.49	0.05	−0.54
6	0.41	−5.82	1.72	2.03
7	−4.45	−9.43	0.10	0.18
8	2.12	4.76	−0.70	−1.39
9	5.62	2.91	2.59	2.90
10	2.74	1.75	3.61	4.04
11	7.59	2.88	2.63	3.51
12	−1.96	2.04	−1.86	−2.56

Source: *Stocks, Bonds, Bills, and Inflation 1996, Yearbook* (Chicago: Ibbotson Associates, 1996). Used with permission © 1996 Ibbotson Associates, Inc. All rights reserved. [Certain portions of this work were derived from copyrighted works of Roger G. Ibbotson and Rex Sinquefield.]

Questions

1. Suppose that 1996 was a typical year and can be taken to represent the future monthly rates of return. Calculate the mean, variance, and standard deviation of each of the preceding four assets. Assign a probability of $\frac{1}{12}$ for each month.

2. Which investment would you select, according to the maximum expected return criterion?

3. Suppose you are a risk averter, and therefore, the larger the standard deviation of the return, the greater your required risk premium. Which of the four investments in Question 1 would you prefer? Discuss your results.

4. The table provides data for 1 year only (1996). Discuss your answer to Question 3 in light of the following data, which are based on a period of 71 years (January 1926 to December 1996). Answer the following questions:

Assets	Annual Mean Return (%)	Standard Deviation (%)
S&P 500	12.7	20.3
Small stocks	17.7	34.1
Long-term corporate bonds	6.0	8.7
Long-term government bonds	5.4	9.2

Source: *Stocks, Bonds, Bills and Inflation 1996, Yearbook* (Chicago: Ibbotson Associates, 1996). Used with permission. © 1996 Ibbotson Associates, Inc. All rights reserved. [Certain portions of this work were derived from copyrighted works of Roger G. Ibbotson and Rex Sinquefield.]

a. Which investment is preferred, according to the mean-variance criterion?

b. Suppose there are two investors, A and B. It is given that Investor A is more risk averse than Investor B. Who is more likely to invest in bonds? Explain.

c. What can you learn from 1 year of monthly data regarding investment decision making? Which is more reliable, 1 year of monthly data or 71 years of annual data?

SUPPLEMENTAL REFERENCES

Arrow, K. J. "Alternative Approaches to the Theory of Choice in Risk-Taking Situations." *Econometrica,* October 1951.

Arrow, K. J. "The Role of Securities in the Optimal Allocation of Risk-Bearing." *Review of Economic Studies,* April 1964.

Good, R. Walter. "Yes, Virginia, There Is a Risk Premium, But. . . ." *Financial Analysts Journal,* January/February 1994.

Hirshleifer, J. H. "On the Theory of Optimal Investment Decision." *Journal of Political Economy,* August 1958.

Levy, H., and A. Cohen. "On the Risks of Stocks in the Long Run: Revisited." *The Journal of Portfolio Selection,* Spring 1998.

Markowitz, H. M. *Portfolio Selection.* New York: Wiley, 1959.

Markowitz, H. M. *Mean-Variance Analysis in Portfolio Choice and Capital Markets.* New York: Basil Blackwell, 1987.

Markowitz, Harry. "Portfolio Selection." *Journal of Finance 7,* no. 1 (March 1952): 77–91.

Sharpe, W. F. "Risk Aversion in the Stock Market: Some Empirical Evidence." *Journal of Finance,* June 1976.

CHAPTER 7

PORTFOLIO MEAN AND VARIANCE

LEARNING OBJECTIVES

After studying this chapter you should be able to:

1. Explain the effect of an asset's risk on a portfolio's risk.

2. Discuss the rate of return, expected rate of return, and variance of a portfolio.

3. Explain covariances and correlation coefficients between assets.

4. Explain the role of correlation within a portfolio.

INVESTMENTS IN THE NEWS

MUTUAL FUNDS, NAVIGATING THE FUTURE

Sixty-three million people, representing more than 36 million American households, own mutual funds, according to the Investment Company Institute. That's more than one out of every three households. According to Edward McVey, senior vice president of Franklin Templeton Funds, that number will continue to grow as more people use mutual funds to solve their retirement and other investment needs. [The following table shows the growth in mutual funds between 1978 and 1997.] Steven Norwitz, vice president of T. Rowe Price, agrees. "Mutual funds are a favorite for good reason: they provide professional management and diversification at reasonable cost." Franklin Templeton and T. Rowe Price are two of the nation's largest mutual fund complexes. . . .

Total Number of Mutual Funds

	July 31, 1997	December 31, 1978
Stock funds	2,881	294
Bond/income funds	2,754	150
Money market funds	1,011	61
Total	6,646	505

Source: Adapted from "Mutual Funds, Navigating the Future," *Fortune*, October 13, 1997, pp. 52–56. Reprinted from the October 13, 1997, issue of *Fortune* by special permission; copyright 1997, Time Inc.

YOU CAN LOWER YOUR RISK . . . AND STILL PURSUE GROWTH

Investors should understand that the market's daily ups and downs mean not only high potential rewards but also greater risk. As a result, you may have a gain or loss when you sell your shares. . . . Although the market will experience ups and downs, the Fund is managed to moderate the effects of market fluctuations while remaining poised for long-term growth.

DIVERSIFICATION MADE SIMPLE: FIDELITY ASSET MANAGER™

Now there's an easier way to diversify across a broad range of securities . . . in one simple investment. Fidelity Asset Manager seeks high total return with reduced risk over the long term by allocating its assets among stocks, bonds, and money market instruments. You simply make one investment with no sales charge, and join a diversified portfolio which is carefully watched and gradually adjusted by Fidelity professionals who seek to enhance your return in any market environment.

Source: Fidelity Investments, Inc. Reprinted with permission.

The first article in this chapter's Investments in the News reveals that the number of American households investing in mutual funds, as well as the growth in the number of mutual funds, has increased markedly over the last two decades. (In fact, the total number of mutual funds has grown by 1,216% in the last 20 years.) As of mid-1997, over $4.25 trillion was invested in the more than six thousand available funds, and of this, $2.3 trillion was invested in stock funds.[1]

Why have mutual funds experienced such dramatic growth? One major reason was cited in the article—the ability of investors to conveniently and effectively reduce risk by diversifying their portfolios. The risk and return of a portfolio of assets is the essence of this chapter. Specifically, this chapter measures the mean and risk of a portfolio of assets. It moves from analyzing a single asset, as in Chapter 6, to analyzing a portfolio of assets. Chapter 8 then uses the information given here on the risk and return of a portfolio to show how the diversification of assets minimizes risk in a portfolio.

7.1 THE PORTFOLIO

A portfolio is a combination of assets. However, at times, we use the term *portfolio* to refer to a holding of only one asset. In general, an investor has a portfolio that diversifies wealth in a number of assets, which can be combined in a variety of proportions, or weights. Because the weights are nothing but the proportion of wealth invested in each available asset, the sum of the weights must be equal to 1 (or 100%). Namely,

$$w_1 + w_2 + \ldots + w_n = \sum_{i=1}^{n} w_i = 1 \qquad (7.1)$$

where n is the number of assets included in the portfolio, i is a specific asset, and w_i is the weight (proportion) allocated to the ith asset. The investor does not have to diversify in all available assets. Thus, only the weights of the assets included in the portfolio are summed. If an asset is not in the portfolio, then its proportion is zero, and it is not included in the analysis.

7.2 AN ASSET'S RISK WHEN HELD WITH OTHER ASSETS IN A PORTFOLIO

As Chapter 6 described, the higher the variance (or standard deviation) of the return on an asset, the higher the required risk premium. Hence, the variance of the returns on an asset appears to measure the risk of that asset. Although this is true if an investor holds only one asset, it is not the sole measure of risk if the investor holds more than one risky asset. In a portfolio, the risk of an individual asset is a

1. "Mutual Funds, Navigating the Future," *Fortune,* October 13, 1997, pp. 52–56.

function not only of its own variance but also of its degree of dependency on the other assets in the portfolio.[2]

The degree of dependency measures how the returns on two assets move together. If both go up or down together, we say they have *positive dependency*. If one asset goes up when the other goes down or vice versa, we say that they have *negative dependency*. In general, the more negative the degree of dependency between assets in a portfolio, the lower the risk of the portfolio, and hence, the lower the required risk premium for each specific asset. The precise measure of risk of each asset in a portfolio context is discussed in subsequent chapters. This section demonstrates that a risk-averse investor will require a risk premium that decreases as the degree of dependency between the risky assets in the portfolio decreases.

As it turns out, in the market, an asset may have a high variance but a very low or even zero required risk premium. To illustrate, suppose there are two assets, A and B, whose returns in dollars are given in Exhibit 7-1. Each asset yields +$20 and −$10 with an equal probability of ½. Also, assume that the investment in each asset is $50; hence, a dollar return of $20 implies a 40% rate of return, and a −$10 return implies a −20% rate of return. The mean dollar return is

$$\frac{1}{2}(\$20) + \frac{1}{2}(-\$10) = \$5$$

and the variance is

$$\frac{1}{2}(20 - 5)^2 + \frac{1}{2}(-10 - 5)^2 = 225$$

(The standard deviation is $15.)

Suppose that you invest $100, buying both Assets A and B. Exhibit 7-2 lists the distributions of the returns from these two assets together under different assumptions regarding the dependence between the two assets' distributions. The left column of Exhibit 7-2 assumes positive dependency between the returns on the two assets. Namely, if +$20 is realized on Asset A, this return is also sure to be realized

EXHIBIT 7-1 Return on Assets A and B		Return on Asset A		Return on Asset B	
		Return	Probability	Return	Probability
		+$20	½	+$20	½
		−$10	½	−$10	½
Mean		$5[a]		$5	
Variance		225[b]		225	

a. Mean = ½($20) + ½(−$10) = $5.

b. Variance = ½(20 − 5)² + ½(−10 − 5)² = 225.

2. The degree of dependency between two assets is formally measured by correlation or covariance, which is developed later in the chapter (see Section 7.5).

EXHIBIT 7-2		Positive Dependency		No Dependency		Negative Dependency	
Return on		Return	Probability	Return	Probability	Return	Probability
Portfolio							
Composed		+$40	½	+$40	¼	+$10	1
of Asset A and		−$20	½	+$10	½		
Asset B				−$20	¼		
The Investment							
in the Portfolio	Mean	$10		$10		$10	
Is $100	Variance	900[a]		450[b]		0	

a. Variance = ½(40 − 10)² + ½(−20 − 10)² = 900.

b. Variance = ¼(40 − 10)² + ½(10 − 10)² + ¼(−20 − 10)² = 450.

on Asset B. Hence, from the two assets combined, we get +$40 with a probability of ½. Similarly, if an event occurs with a negative return on Asset A (−$10), the same event also causes a loss on Asset B of −$10. Thus, with a probability of ½, we get −$10 on each asset, or −$20 on the portfolio composed of these two assets.

The right column in Exhibit 7-2 represents the distribution corresponding to negative dependency between the two assets. Namely, if Asset A has a return of +$20, Asset B has a return of −$10, with a total of +$10 on the portfolio of the two assets. Similarly, if the low return is realized on Asset A (−$10), a high cash flow is received on Asset B (+$20), and once again we end up with a +$10 return on the portfolio. Hence, no matter what eventually occurs, the total return obtained on the two assets is +$10, so we get +$10 with a probability of 1, or with certainty; therefore, the variance is equal to zero.

Finally, the middle column of Exhibit 7-2 reports an intermediate case where the returns have no dependency; there is no association, either positive or negative, between the returns on these two assets. Thus, we get +$20 on Asset A with a probability of ½ and +$20 on Asset B with a probability of ½, ending up with $40 with a probability of ½ · ½ = ¼. Similarly, we get −$20 with a probability of ¼. Note, however, that +$10 is obtained with a probability of ½, because it encompasses two events: +$20 on Asset A and −$10 on Asset B, and −$10 on Asset A and +$20 on Asset B. Because each event has a probability of ¼, we end up with $10 with a probability of ½.

The bottom part of Exhibit 7-2 clearly indicates that although the mean return on the combined two assets is $10, no matter what the assumed degree of dependency between the two assets, the variance of the portfolio returns is a function of their dependency; also, the lower the dependency, the lower the variance. In the extreme case of negative dependency, the variance is reduced to zero.

Let us return to the relationship between risk premium and variance, taking the case of a negative dependency. At the end of the investment period of, say, 1 year, an investor receives with certainty a profit of $10. Hence, for an investment of $100 in Stocks A and B, the end-of-period wealth is $110 with certainty. Suppose that at the end of the period, the investor is offered a certain sum of money instead of the two assets that he holds (Assets A and B). What should this sum be in order to make the investor indifferent between the two choices? The answer is clearly $110, or $10 added to the investor's wealth. Because the mean return on the two assets is $10, it implies that the investor requires no risk premium at all. This makes sense; no risk is involved in holding a portfolio of these two assets, because the return on them is $10 with certainty. However, if you offer the investor $111 at the end of the period for the portfolio he holds, you are "bribing" him, and he will sell the portfolio to you.

The important conclusion from this example is that although each of the two assets, when held *separately*, is risky (with a variance of 225 [see Exhibit 7-1]), the two assets are considered to be riskless when included in a portfolio. The negative dependency between the returns on these two assets completely eliminates the uncertainty involved in the returns. Hence, an asset's own variance should be the measure of risk only when the asset is held separately. When the asset is held in a portfolio with other assets, however, the degree of dependency should be incorporated into the measurement of risk, and hence into the risk premium. Thus, in this case, the portfolio's variance is the measure of risk, not the individual asset's variance.

Indeed, the portfolio's variance is equal to zero, which reflects the certainty of the future return. Exhibit 7-2 shows that as negative dependency shifts to no dependency and then to positive dependency, the portfolio variance becomes larger.

In general, the higher the degree of dependency of a particular asset with other risky assets included in a portfolio, the higher will be this asset's contribution to the portfolio's risk, and the higher will be the risk premium required for the asset. Therefore, the required risk premium is a function of not only the asset's variance but also its dependency with other assets.

The discussion so far can be summarized as follows:

1. If an investor holds only one risky asset, the variance is the measure of risk. The higher the variance, the higher will be the required risk premium from the individual assets in the portfolio.
2. If an investor holds more than one risky asset in a portfolio, the risk of each asset is a function of both the asset's own variance and its degree of dependency with the other assets held in the portfolio.
3. The larger the *portfolio's* variance, the higher the required risk premium on the *portfolio.* Therefore, on average, the larger will be the required risk premium on each asset.

Thus, the portfolio's variance, rather than the individual asset's variance, is the key factor in determining the required risk premium. Let us first define the portfolio's expected rate of return and portfolio variance and then turn to how the portfolio's risk can be reduced by diversifying among different assets.

7.3 THE EXPECTED RATE OF RETURN ON A PORTFOLIO

When you invest in many assets, the **portfolio expected return,** denoted by $E(R_p)$, is the weighted average of the expected returns of all the assets held in your portfolio, where the weights are the investment proportions (w_i). Namely,

$$E(R_p) = \sum_{i=1}^{n} w_i E(R_i) \tag{7.2}$$

where n is the number of assets in the portfolio, $E(R_i)$ is the expected rate of return on the ith asset, and w_i is the weight invested in the ith asset. (Note that the weights must sum to 1.0; that is, $\sum w_i = 1.0$.)

For example, if there are only two assets in the portfolio ($n = 2$) with expected rates of return of 5% on the first asset and 20% on the second asset, and if $w_1 = \frac{1}{2}$ and $w_2 = \frac{1}{2}$, we have

$$E(R_p) = \frac{1}{2}(0.05) + \frac{1}{2}(0.2) = 0.125, \text{ or } 12.5\%$$

Of course, when the investment proportions change, the expected rate of return on the portfolio also changes. For example, if $w_1 = \frac{1}{4}$ and $w_2 = \frac{3}{4}$, then

$$E(R_p) = \frac{1}{4}(0.05) + \frac{3}{4}(0.2) = 0.1625, \text{ or } 16.25\%$$

We can confirm that this formula yields the correct expected returns by first calculating the rate of return for each possible scenario and then determining its weighted average based on the probability of each scenario. To illustrate, assume three possible scenarios: the economy may grow, the economy may remain stable, or the economy may go into a recession (see Exhibit 7-3). Note that Asset B provides a higher return in a recession; for example, it may be a firm that produces an inexpensive, low-quality product that is in great demand in a recessionary period. Each scenario has a probability of $\frac{1}{3}$. For example, we have a $\frac{1}{3}$ probability that the economy will grow with a 5% rate of return on Asset A, 10% on Asset B, and 30% on Asset C.

Suppose you construct a portfolio half of which is Asset B and half of which is Asset C (Column 6). If growth occurs, you realize a return of

$$\begin{pmatrix} \text{Weight} \\ \text{in} \\ \text{Asset B} \end{pmatrix} \cdot \begin{pmatrix} \text{Rate of} \\ \text{Return} \\ \text{on B} \\ \text{if Growth} \\ \text{Occurs} \end{pmatrix} + \begin{pmatrix} \text{Weight} \\ \text{in} \\ \text{Asset C} \end{pmatrix} \cdot \begin{pmatrix} \text{Rate of} \\ \text{Return} \\ \text{on C} \\ \text{if Growth} \\ \text{Occurs} \end{pmatrix} = \begin{pmatrix} \text{Rate of} \\ \text{Return on} \\ \text{Portfolio} \\ \text{if Growth} \\ \text{Occurs} \end{pmatrix}$$

$$(\tfrac{1}{2} \cdot 0.1) \qquad + \qquad (\tfrac{1}{2} \cdot 0.3) \qquad = \quad 0.2, \text{ or } 20\%$$

If the economy is stable, you receive

$$\tfrac{1}{2}(0.05) + \tfrac{1}{2}(0.15) = 0.1, \text{ or } 10\%$$

on the portfolio. If the economy is in recession, you receive

EXHIBIT 7-3   **Rates of Return on Three Assets and Two Portfolios**

1	2	3	4	5	6 Portfolio $\frac{1}{2}B + \frac{1}{2}C$	7 Portfolio $\frac{1}{2}A + \frac{1}{4}B + \frac{1}{4}C$
Scenario	Probability	Asset A	Asset B	Asset C		
Growth	$\frac{1}{3}$	0.05	0.10	0.30	0.20[a]	0.125
Stable	$\frac{1}{3}$	0.05	0.05	0.15	0.10	0.075
Recession	$\frac{1}{3}$	0.05	0.15	0.15	0.15	0.10
Portfolio expected rate of return		0.05	0.10	0.20[b]	0.15[c]	0.10

Demonstration of some of the calculations:

a. $\frac{1}{2}(0.10) + \frac{1}{2}(0.30)$.

b. $\frac{1}{3}(0.30) + \frac{1}{3}(0.15) + \frac{1}{3}(0.15)$.

c. $\frac{1}{3}(0.20) + \frac{1}{3}(0.10) + \frac{1}{3}(0.15)$.

$$\tfrac{1}{2}(0.15) + \tfrac{1}{2}(0.15) = 0.15, \text{ or } 15\%$$

Each scenario (growth, stable, or recession) has a probability of $\frac{1}{3}$. The expected rate of return on the portfolio can be calculated just as we would calculate the expected return on an individual asset:

$$E(R_p) = \tfrac{1}{3}(0.20) + \tfrac{1}{3}(0.10) + \tfrac{1}{3}(0.15) = 0.15, \text{ or } 15\%$$

Equation 7.2 calculates the weighted average of the expected rates of return of the three securities in the portfolio, where the invested proportions serve as weights:

$$\begin{pmatrix} \text{Weight} \\ \text{in} \\ \text{Asset B} \end{pmatrix} \cdot \begin{pmatrix} \text{Expected} \\ \text{Rate of} \\ \text{Return on} \\ \text{Asset B} \end{pmatrix} + \begin{pmatrix} \text{Weight} \\ \text{in} \\ \text{Asset C} \end{pmatrix} \cdot \begin{pmatrix} \text{Expected} \\ \text{Rate of} \\ \text{Return on} \\ \text{Asset C} \end{pmatrix} = \begin{pmatrix} \text{Expected} \\ \text{Rate of} \\ \text{Return on} \\ \text{Portfolio} \end{pmatrix}$$

$$(\tfrac{1}{2} \cdot 10\%) \qquad + \qquad (\tfrac{1}{2} \cdot 20\%) \qquad = \qquad 15\%$$

Thus, both methods provide the same results.

Now suppose we construct another portfolio composed of Assets A, B, and C in Exhibit 7-3 with one-half Asset A, one-fourth Asset B, and one-fourth Asset C (see Column 7 in Exhibit 7-3). Using Equation 7.2, we get a portfolio expected return of

$$E(R_p) = \tfrac{1}{2}(0.05) + \tfrac{1}{4}(0.10) + \tfrac{1}{4}(0.20) = 0.1, \text{ or } 10\%,$$

where 0.05, 0.10, and 0.20 are the expected rates of return on Assets A, B, and C, respectively (see Exhibit 7-3). If we first calculate the three possible rates of return on this portfolio and then calculate their mean, we get the same expected rate of return, 10%.

PRACTICE BOX

Problem

Assume the following historical rates of return for General Motors (GM) and British Petroleum (BP). Calculate the expected rate of return on a portfolio that has one-third of your wealth invested in GM and two-thirds of your wealth invested in BP. Use Equation 7.2, and first compute the portfolio rates of return. (Assume that each year is equally probable.)

Year	GM	BP
1	10%	15%
2	−5%	10%
3	8%	0%
4	15%	−1%

Solution

To answer this problem, first note that the probability of each outcome is ¼, because each year is equally probable, and there are 4 years. Thus, construct the following table:

		Rates of Return		
Year	Probability	GM	BP	Portfolio: ⅓ GM and ⅔ BP
1	¼	0.10%	0.15%	0.1333%[a]
2	¼	−0.05	0.10	0.05
3	¼	0.08	0.0	0.0267
4	¼	0.15	−0.01	0.0433
Expected rate of return		0.07[b]	0.06[c]	0.0633[d]

a. ⅓(0.10) + ⅔(0.15).

b. ¼(0.10) + ¼(−0.05) + ¼(0.08) + ¼(0.15).

c. ¼(0.15) + ¼(0.10) + ¼(0.0) + ¼(−0.01).

d. ¼(0.1333) + ¼(0.05) + ¼(0.0267) + ¼(0.0433).

Using Equation 7.2 and the results in the table, you have

$$E(R_p) = ⅓(0.07) + ⅔(0.06) \cong 0.0633$$

which is equal to the expected rate of return obtained in the table.

In summary, the expected rate of return on a portfolio can be calculated in two ways:

1. First calculate all possible returns on the portfolio, and then calculate its expected rate of return.
2. Calculate the portfolio expected rate of return using Equation 7.2.

Both methods produce the same results. Actually, one method serves as a verification of the other. The expected rate of return on a portfolio, then, is simply the sum of the expected returns of the various individual assets multiplied by the weights of each asset in the portfolio. Obviously, the higher the proportion of wealth (w_i) invested in the ith security, the higher its individual effect on the portfolio's expected return (or mean). In the extreme, when all the wealth (100%) is invested in only one security, the portfolio's mean rate of return is simply the mean rate of return on a selected security.

7.4 COVARIANCES

How can the dependency between two assets be measured? An understanding of this dependency enhances an investor's ability to manage risk within a portfolio.

Whereas the variance measures the variability of the rates of return on a given asset or portfolio, the **covariance** measures the "co-movements," or degree of dependency, of the rates of return of two assets. If the rates of return of two assets tend to go up and down together, they have a positive covariance. If one asset's return is relatively high and the other asset's return is relatively low, the covariance is negative.

Exhibit 7-4 gives the rates of return for two stocks over a 4-year period. This exhibit shows a positive co-movement or positive covariance between the two stocks. When one stock is doing relatively well, the other is also doing relatively well, and vice versa.

It is easiest to see positive co-movement in a graph. Exhibit 7-5 shows the rates of return for both stocks plotted in a single graph. Each point represents the pair of returns for both stocks in a given year. For example, in Year 2, Stock A's rate of return was 15% and Stock B's rate of return was 20%. When Stock A's rate of return is down, so is Stock B's rate of return. When Stock A's rate of return is up, so is Stock B's rate of return. Notice that the pattern moves upward as you look from left to right. This upward pattern characterizes a positive covariance.

In some cases the pattern is not so clear. Consider the example in Exhibit 7-6. This example is like the one in Exhibit 7-4, but with one change: when Stock A realizes the highest return, $+25\%$, Stock C realizes a -5% rate of return. Thus, in 3 years the stocks tend to move up and down together, but in the fourth year they move in opposite directions. Is this covariance positive or negative? Look closely at

EXHIBIT 7-4	Year	Stock A	Stock B
Rates of Return for Two Stocks	1	0.05	0.10
Over a 4-Year	2	0.15	0.20
Period	3	−0.05	−0.10
	4	0.25	0.60

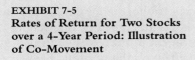

EXHIBIT 7-5
Rates of Return for Two Stocks over a 4–Year Period: Illustration of Co–Movement

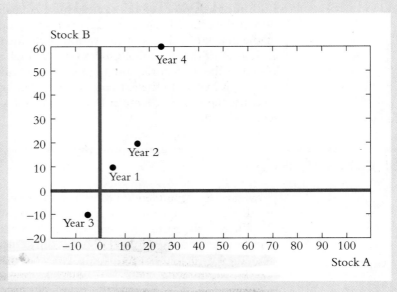

Exhibit 7-7. Obviously, we cannot answer that question through observation alone. We need to define *covariance* more precisely.

The covariance of two assets is given by the following formula:

$$Cov(R_A, R_B) = E\{[R_A - E(R_A)][R_B - E(R_B)]\} \qquad (7.3)$$

where E is the expectation operator. Equation 7.3 can be rewritten as

$$Cov(R_A, R_B) = \sum_{i=1}^{m} P_i[R_{A,i} - E(R_A)][R_{B,i} - E(R_B)] \qquad (7.3')$$

where m is the number of observations and P_i is the probability of getting the returns in each year—namely, the probability of getting the pair of returns $R_{A,i}$ and $R_{B,i}$ on these two assets. $Cov(R_A, R_B)$ denotes the covariance of returns on Assets A

EXHIBIT 7-6	Year	Stock A	Stock C
Rates of Return for Two Stocks Over a 4–Year Period	1	0.05	0.10
	2	0.15	0.20
	3	−0.05	−0.10
	4	0.25	−0.05

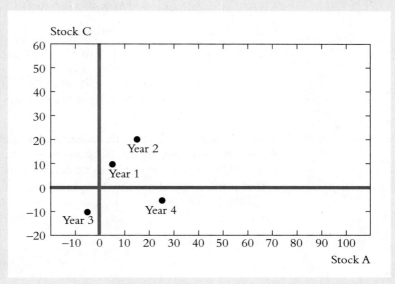

EXHIBIT 7-7
Rates of Return for Two Stocks over a 4-Year Period: Illustration of Little Correlation

and B.[3] As before, $E(R_A)$ and $E(R_B)$ are the expected rates of return on the two stocks.

Equation 7.3 shows that covariance is the expected value of the product of deviations from the mean. If both stock returns are above their mean or both stock returns are below their mean at the same time, then the product will be positive and, hence, the covariance will be positive. However, if one stock return is above its mean when the other stock return is below its mean, then the product will be negative; if this occurs frequently, the covariance will be negative.

In the previous example, assume that each of the 4 years has an equal probability of ¼. Let us calculate the covariance of the three stocks for the two cases given in Exhibits 7-4 and 7-6. From Exhibit 7-4, the expected rates of return are

$$E(R_A) = ¼(0.05) + ¼(0.15) + ¼(-0.05) + ¼(0.25) = 0.10, \text{ or } 10\%$$

$$E(R_B) = ¼(0.10) + ¼(0.20) + ¼(-0.10) + ¼(0.60) = 0.20, \text{ or } 20\%$$

Using Equation 7.3′, we find the covariance between these two assets as follows:

$$\begin{aligned} Cov(R_A, R_B) &= ¼[(0.05 - 0.1)(0.1 - 0.2)] + ¼[(0.15 - 0.1)(0.2 - 0.2)] \\ &\quad + ¼[(-0.05 - 0.1)(-0.1 - 0.2)] + ¼[(0.25 - 0.1)(0.6 - 0.2)] \\ &= 0.00125 + 0 + 0.01125 + 0.015 = 0.0275 \end{aligned}$$

Thus, we see that the covariance is positive, as Exhibit 7-5 suggested.

Turning now to the data in Exhibit 7-6, the expected rate of return for Stock C is

3. For brevity, we usually denote this covariance by σA,B.

$$E(R_C) = \frac{1}{4}(0.10) + \frac{1}{4}(0.20) + \frac{1}{4}(-0.10) + \frac{1}{4}(-0.05) = 0.0375, \text{ or } 3.75\%$$

Using Equation 7.3', the covariance is

$$\begin{aligned}
Cov(R_A, R_C) &= \frac{1}{4}[(0.05 - 0.1)(0.1 - 0.0375)] + \frac{1}{4}[(0.15 - 0.1)(0.2 - 0.0375)] \\
&\quad + \frac{1}{4}[(-0.05 - 0.1)(-0.1 - 0.0375)] \\
&\quad + \frac{1}{4}[(0.25 - 0.1)(-0.05 - 0.0375)] \\
&= -0.00078 + 0.00203 + 0.00516 - 0.00328 \\
&= 0.00313
\end{aligned}$$

The calculation reveals that the covariance is slightly positive. When the direction of the fourth year's rate of return was reversed, the covariance decreased from 0.0275 to 0.00313.[4] In other words, the stock returns of Stock A and Stock B move together more closely than the stock returns of Stock A and Stock C.

With larger sets of data, it is more efficient to use the following covariance equation:

$$Cov(R_A, R_B) = \sum_{i=1}^{m} P_i R_{A,i} R_{B,i} - E(R_A)E(R_B) \tag{7.4}$$

Notice that the first term is just the expected value of $R_{A,i} R_{B,i}$. Exhibit 7-8 illustrates how Equation 7.4 can be used to compute the covariances of Stocks A and B, as well as of Stocks A and C, given in Exhibits 7-4 and 7-6. Exhibit 7-8 can be used to compute the covariance of Stocks A and B:

$$Cov(R_A, R_B) = 0.0475 - (0.1)(0.20) = 0.0275$$

and the covariance of Stocks A and C:

$$Cov(R_A, R_C) = 0.00688 - (0.1)(0.0375) = 0.00313$$

EXHIBIT 7-8 Covariance Calculation Using Equation 7.4	Year	Stock A R_A	Stock B R_B	Stock C R_C	$R_A R_B$	$R_A R_C$
	1	0.05	0.10	0.10	0.005[a]	0.005
	2	0.15	0.20	0.20	0.03	0.03
	3	−0.05	−0.10	−0.10	0.005	0.005
	4	0.25	0.60	−0.05	0.15	−0.0125
	Expected value	0.10	0.20	0.0375	0.0475[b]	0.00688

a. 0.05(0.10).

b. $\frac{1}{4}$(0.005) + $\frac{1}{4}$(0.03) + $\frac{1}{4}$(0.005) + $\frac{1}{4}$(0.15).

4. Note that covariances are not in units such as percentages. If percentages were used rather than decimals, the results would be in percent squared. See Section 7.5, on correlation.

Exhibit 7-9 illustrates three cases. In Case I, the two stocks have a positive co-variance. Notice that when Stock A has negative rates of return, so does Stock B, and when Stock A has positive rates of return, so does Stock B. The pattern, looking from left to right, is clearly upward; hence, the covariance is positive. In Case II, the two stocks have a covariance that is approximately equal to zero. That is, there is no discernible pattern. Finally, in Case III, the two stocks move in different directions and, hence, have a negative covariance. That is, the pattern, looking from left to right, is clearly downward; hence, the covariance is negative.

Finally, the covariance of an asset with itself is simply its own variance. From Equation 7.3′, we have (substituting A for B)

$$Cov(R_A,R_A) = \sum_{i=1}^{m} P_i[R_{A,i} - E(R_A)][R_{A,i} - E(R_A)]$$

Rearranging, we find

$$Cov(R_A,R_A) = \sum_{i=1}^{m} P_i[R_{A,i} - E(R_A)]^2 = \sigma_A^2$$

which can also be written as

$$\sigma_A^2 = \sum_{i=1}^{m} P_i R_{A,i}^2 - E(R_A)^2 \tag{7.5}$$

From Exhibit 7-10 and Equation 7.5, we can calculate the variances as follows:

$$\sigma_A^2 = 0.0225 - 0.1^2 = 0.0125$$

$$\sigma_B^2 = 0.105 - 0.2^2 = 0.065$$

$$\sigma_C^2 = 0.10563 - 0.0375^2 = 0.0142$$

Equation 7.5 is more efficient to use in calculating asset variances than is the more common variance expression given in Equation 6.3 in Chapter 6.

7.5 CORRELATION COEFFICIENT

Positive and negative covariances tell an investor that the stocks in a portfolio either move together or move in opposite directions, but they do not tell the investor much about the strength of this association. The co-movement of two variables depends, in part, on how volatile each one is independently. For example, suppose we find a covariance of 0.003. Is this covariance very large? Is it modestly large? Is it twice as strong as a covariance of 0.0015? If the two variables are not very volatile, then 0.003 may indicate a strong dependency. However, if the two variables are highly volatile, then a covariance of 0.003 may indicate a weak dependency.

By dividing the covariance by the standard deviations of each asset, we can determine the strength of their dependency, or their **correlations**. The number we obtain is called the *correlation coefficient,* or ρ (pronounced "row" or "rho"):

EXHIBIT 7-9
**Illustrations of Positive, Zero,
and Negative Covariance**

Case I: Rates of Return with Positive Covariance

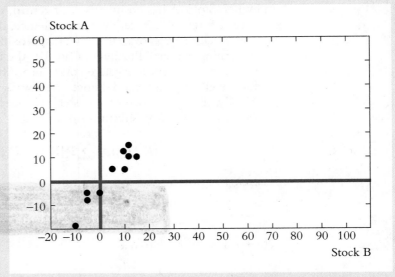

Case II: Rates of Return with Zero Covariance

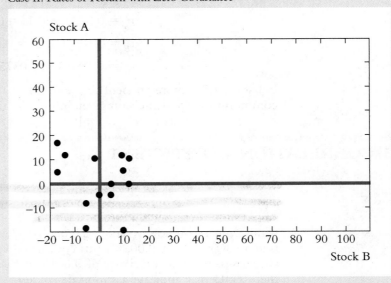

(continued)

EXHIBIT 7-9
(continued)

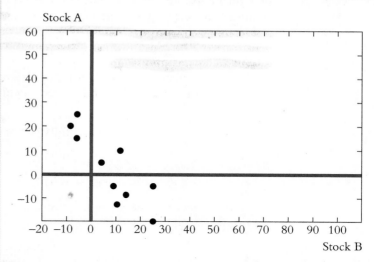

Case III: Rates of Return with Negative Covariance

$$\rho_{A,B} = \frac{Cov(R_A, R_B)}{\sigma_A \sigma_B} \tag{7.6}$$

Both covariance and correlation measure the association between the rates of return on two assets. When the covariance is positive, the correlation also will be positive, and vice versa. The advantage of correlation though, is that it is an absolute number ranging between −1 and +1, and it is not in units, such as dollars or per-

EXHIBIT 7-10
Variance Calculation Using Equation 7.5

Year	Stock A R_A	Stock B R_B	Stock C R_C	R_A^2	R_B^2	R_C^2
1	0.05	0.10	0.10	0.0025	0.01	0.01
2	0.15	0.20	0.20	0.0225	0.04	0.04
3	−0.05	−0.10	−0.10	0.0025	0.01	0.01
4	0.25	0.60	−0.05	0.0625	0.36	0.0025
Expected value	0.10	0.20	0.0375	0.0225[a]	0.105	0.01563

a. ¼(0.0025) + ¼(0.0225) + ¼(0.0025) + ¼(0.0625).

centages. Thus, correlations are directly comparable. For example, if the correlation of rates of return between Stocks A and B is 0.8 and the correlation between rates of return between Stocks C and D is 0.6, we can state with confidence that Stocks A and B have a stronger positive dependency. If there is a perfect positive association between rates of return, then the correlation is $+1$. If there is a perfect negative association, the correlation is -1. If the rates of return are unrelated (that is, uncorrelated), the correlation is zero.

Let us calculate the correlation coefficient for the data given in Exhibits 7-4 and 7-6. From Exhibit 7-10 and related calculations, the standard deviations are as follows:

$$\sigma_A = 0.0125^{1/2} \cong 0.1118$$

$$\sigma_B = 0.065^{1/2} \cong 0.255$$

$$\sigma_C = 0.0142^{1/2} \cong 0.119$$

Thus, the correlation coefficient for Stocks A and B [recall that the covariance was previously found to be $Cov(R_A,R_B) = 0.0275$] is

$$\rho_{A,B} = \frac{0.0275}{0.1118 \cdot 0.255} \cong 0.965$$

and the correlation coefficient for Stocks A and C [recall that the covariance was previously found to be $Cov(R_A,R_C) = 0.00313$] is

$$\rho_{A,C} = \frac{0.00313}{0.1118 \cdot 0.119} \cong 0.235$$

Thus, the correlation coefficient is much lower when Year 4's outcome for Stock C is changed. We can conclude that the rates of return of Stocks A and B have a stronger positive dependency when compared with the rates of return of Stocks A and C. Correlation thus is useful for comparing the benefits of diversifying an investment among several assets.

PRACTICE BOX

Problem

Suppose you are given the following information about Stocks A and B. Calculate the correlation coefficient.

State of the Economy	Probability	Rates of Return	
		R_A	R_B
Growth	½	0.15	0.30
Stable	¼	0.10	0.05
Recession	¼	0.05	0.10

(continued)

Solution

Following the procedures outlined in Exhibits 7-8 and 7-10, based on Equations 7.4 and 7.5, construct the following table:

State of the Economy	Probability	R_A	R_B	$R_A R_B$	R_A^2	R_B^2
Growth	½	0.15	0.30	0.045	0.0225	0.09
Stable	¼	0.10	0.05	0.005	0.01	0.0025
Recession	¼	0.05	0.10	0.005	0.0025	0.01
Expected value		0.1125	0.1875	0.025	0.01438	0.04812

From Equation 7.4, the covariance is

$$Cov(R_A, R_B) = 0.025 - (0.1125)(0.1875) \cong 0.00391$$

$$E\{[R_A - E(R_A)][R_B - E(R_B)]$$
$$= 0.00391$$

$$E(R_A R_B) - [E(R_A) E(R_B)]$$

and from Equation 7.5, the variances are as follows:

$$\sigma_A^2 = 0.01438 - 0.1125^2 \cong 0.00172$$
$$\sigma_B^2 = 0.04812 - 0.1875^2 \cong 0.0130$$

Therefore, the standard deviations are

$$\sigma_A = 0.00172^{1/2} \cong 0.04147$$
$$\sigma_B = 0.013^{1/2} \cong 0.1140$$

Thus, the correlation coefficient is

$$\rho_{A,B} = \frac{0.00391}{0.04147 \cdot 0.1140} \cong 0.827$$

We see that Stocks A and B are highly positively correlated. This is not surprising, because when growth occurs, which is likely (50% chance), both stocks are up, and when a stable economy or a recession occurs, both stocks are below their means. The relationship is not perfect, however, because the magnitudes of each asset's return in a given state vary.

7.6 THE PORTFOLIO VARIANCE

Recall from Chapter 6 that investors seek to maximize their expected return and minimize their risk as measured by variance. However, Chapter 6 assumed that investors held only one asset. This section examines the more realistic case where investors hold many assets (i.e., a portfolio of assets).

The **variance** of a portfolio can be calculated in two ways. With the first method, the rates of return on the portfolio are calculated for each period, and then the variance of a single security equation such as Equation 7.5 is employed on the portfolio returns. This approach is the *direct method*. In the second method, the variance of a portfolio is computed using an equation based on asset variances and covariances. This approach is the *indirect method*, because the portfolio variance is computed indirectly by using the asset variances and covariances. Both methods are useful. The direct method is easy to compute, whereas the indirect method demonstrates the relationship between the portfolio variance and individual asset covariances. It also has the advantage of simplicity if an investor wishes to calculate the variance of various portfolios with various diversification strategies (weights).

7.6.1 The Direct Method

The variance of a portfolio can be calculated directly from its return, as shown in Exhibit 7-11. First, compute the rates of return on the portfolio for each year. For example, in Year 1 for Portfolio 1, the rate of return is

$$R_p = \tfrac{1}{2}(0.05) + \tfrac{1}{2}(0.10) = 0.075 \text{ (Year 1)}$$

Similarly, the rates of return for Years 2 and 3 are found to be

$$R_p = \tfrac{1}{2}(0.10) + \tfrac{1}{2}(0.05) = 0.075 \text{ (Year 2)}$$

$$R_p = \tfrac{1}{2}(0.15) + \tfrac{1}{2}(0.30) = 0.225 \text{ (Year 3)}$$

Now the variance of Portfolio 1 can be calculated using Equation 7.5:

$$\sigma_p^2 = \tfrac{1}{3}(0.075^2) + \tfrac{1}{3}(0.075^2) + \tfrac{1}{3}(0.225^2) - 0.125^2 = 0.005$$

Calculating the portfolio variance by the direct method is straightforward, because the portfolio is treated like any other single asset. Once a series of returns and the corresponding probabilities have been determined, the variance can be easily calculated. (See Portfolios 2 and 3 in Exhibit 7-11.)

EXHIBIT 7-11 Rates of Return on Assets A and B and on Various Portfolios		Individual Asset		Portfolios		
				1	2	3
Year	Probability	A	B	$\tfrac{1}{2}$A + $\tfrac{1}{2}$B	$\tfrac{1}{5}$A + $\tfrac{4}{5}$B	$\tfrac{4}{5}$A + $\tfrac{1}{5}$B
1	$\tfrac{1}{3}$	0.05	0.10	0.075	0.009	0.06
2	$\tfrac{1}{3}$	0.10	0.05	0.075	0.06	0.09
3	$\tfrac{1}{3}$	0.15	0.30	0.225	0.27	0.18
Expected rate of return		0.10	0.15	0.125	0.14	0.11
Variance		0.00167[a]	0.01167	0.005[b]	0.0086	0.0026

Demonstration of some of the calculations:

a. $\tfrac{1}{3}(0.05^2) + \tfrac{1}{3}(0.10^2) + \tfrac{1}{3}(0.15^2) - 0.10^2$.

b. $\tfrac{1}{3}(0.075^2) + \tfrac{1}{3}(0.075^2) + \tfrac{1}{3}(0.225^2) - 0.125^2$ (direct method).

7.6.2 The Indirect Method

The indirect method of calculating the variance of a portfolio shows the relationship between the covariances of the assets and the variance of the portfolio. Using the definition of each asset's variance, as well as the definition of the covariance, we can show that the portfolio's variance (σ_p^2), when the portfolio is composed of two assets, A and B, is

$$\sigma_p^2 = w_A^2 \sigma_A^2 + w_B^2 \sigma_B^2 + 2w_A w_B \sigma_{A,B} \qquad (7.7)$$

↙ covariance

Exhibit 7–12 first shows numerically that Equation 7.7 indeed yields the same variance as the direct calculation given in Exhibit 7–11. Exhibit 7–12 also demonstrates that this formula is indeed the correct formula for the three portfolios under consideration, as given in Exhibit 7–11. When we calculate the variance directly from the portfolio's return, as is done in Exhibit 7–11, or by applying Equation 7.7 (see Exhibit 7–12), we get the same results. For example, Portfolio 1 in Exhibit 7–12 yields the following:

$$\sigma_p^2 = (\tfrac{1}{2})^2(0.00167) + (\tfrac{1}{2})^2(0.01167) + 2(\tfrac{1}{2})(\tfrac{1}{2})0.00333 = 0.005$$

which is exactly the same result found by using the direct method in Exhibit 7–11.

Now that we have shown numerically that Equation 7.7 yields the correct figures for the portfolio's variance, let us prove that with two risky assets, the portfolio's variance as given by Equation 7.7 is correct. First, recall that the portfolio's rate of return (R_p) is given by

$$R_p = w_1 R_1 + w_2 R_2$$

(we replace A and B with 1 and 2, respectively) with an expected value of

$$E(R_p) = w_1 E(R_1) + w_2 E(R_2)$$

Second, the definition of the portfolio variance is given by

$$\sigma_p^2 = E[R_p - E(R_p)]^2$$

Substituting for R_p and $E(R_p)$ yields

$$\sigma_p^2 = E\{w_1 R_1 + w_2 R_2 - [w_1 E(R_1) + w_2 E(R_2)]\}^2$$

EXHIBIT 7-12 The Portfolio Variance of the Three Portfolios in Exhibit 7-11	Portfolio	Allocations (strategy)	$w_A^2 \sigma_A^2$	$w_B^2 \sigma_B^2$	$2w_A w_B \sigma_{A,B}$	$= \sigma_p^2$
	1	$\tfrac{1}{2}A + \tfrac{1}{2}B$	$(\tfrac{1}{2})^2 0.00167$ +	$(\tfrac{1}{2})^2 0.01167$ +	$2(\tfrac{1}{2})(\tfrac{1}{2})0.00333^a$	$= 0.005$
	2	$\tfrac{1}{5}A + \tfrac{4}{5}B$	$(\tfrac{1}{5})^2 0.00167$ +	$(\tfrac{4}{5})^2 0.01167$ +	$2(\tfrac{1}{5})(\tfrac{4}{5})0.00333$	$= 0.0086$
	3	$\tfrac{4}{5}A + \tfrac{1}{5}B$	$(\tfrac{4}{5})^2 0.00167$ +	$(\tfrac{1}{5})^2 0.01167$ +	$2(\tfrac{4}{5})(\tfrac{1}{5})0.00333$	$= 0.0026$

a. $\sigma_{A,B} = (\tfrac{1}{3})(0.05)(0.10) + (\tfrac{1}{3})(0.10)(0.05) + (\tfrac{1}{3})(0.15)(0.30) - (0.10)(0.15) = 0.00333.$

Covariance $\sum P R_A R_B - E(R_A) \times E(R_B)$

which can be rewritten as

$$\sigma_p^2 = E\{w_1[R_1 - E(R_1)] + w_2[R_2 - E(R_2)]\}^2$$

Opening the brackets and employing the rule $(A + B)^2 = A^2 + B^2 + 2AB$, we get

$$\sigma_p^2 = E\{w_1^2[R_1 - E(R_1)]^2 + w_2^2[R_2 - E(R_2)]^2$$
$$+ 2w_1w_2[R_1 - E(R_1)][R_2 - E(R_2)]\}$$

Taking the expectation,[5] and because w_1 and w_2 are constants and not random variables, we get

$$\sigma_p^2 = w_1^2 E[R_1 - E(R_1)]^2 + w_2^2 E[R_2 - E(R_2)]^2$$
$$+ 2w_1w_2 E[R_1 - E(R_1)][R_2 - E(R_2)]$$

which by the definitions of variance and covariance yields

$$\sigma_p^2 = w_1^2\sigma_1^2 + w_2^2\sigma_2^2 + 2w_1w_2\sigma_{1,2} \qquad (7.8)$$

where $\sigma_{1,2}$ denotes the covariance between Assets 1 and 2, and σ_1^2 and σ_2^2 are the variances of Assets 1 and 2, respectively, exactly as claimed in Equation 7.7.

PRACTICE BOX

Problem

Recalculate the variance of the portfolio ½B + ½C given in Exhibit 7–3, where the probability of growth is ½ and the probabilities of a stable economy or a recession are ¼ each. Carry out a direct calculation as in Exhibit 7–11, and then apply Equation 7.7. Do you get the same result?

Solution

The calculation by the direct method results in the following (note the change in the mean):

$$\sigma_p^2 = \tfrac{1}{2}(0.20^2) + \tfrac{1}{4}(0.10^2) + \tfrac{1}{4}(0.15^2) - 0.1625^2 \cong 0.0017$$

where

$$0.20 = \tfrac{1}{2}(0.10) + \tfrac{1}{2}(0.30)$$

$$0.10 = \tfrac{1}{2}(0.05) + \tfrac{1}{2}(0.15)$$

$$0.15 = \tfrac{1}{2}(0.15) + \tfrac{1}{2}(0.15)$$

Using Equation 7.7, we first have to find the variances and covariances with the new probabilities. We find

(continued)

---

5. We use the following rule (where a and b are constants and x and y are random variables):

$$E(ax + by) = E(ax) + E(by) = aE(x) + bE(y)$$

That is, we take the expectation term by term and note that $E(a) = a$ and $E(b) = b$.

$$\sigma_B^2 = \tfrac{1}{2}(0.10^2) + \tfrac{1}{4}(0.05^2) + \tfrac{1}{4}(0.15^2) - 0.10^2 = 0.00125$$

$$\sigma_C^2 = \tfrac{1}{2}(0.30^2) + \tfrac{1}{4}(0.15^2) + \tfrac{1}{4}(0.15^2) - 0.225^2 \cong 0.00563$$

$$Cov(R_B, R_C) = \tfrac{1}{2}[0.10(0.30)] + \tfrac{1}{4}[0.05(0.15)] + \tfrac{1}{4}[0.15(0.15)]$$
$$- (0.10)(0.225) = 0.0$$

Substituting these results into Equation 7.7, we have

$$\sigma_p^2 = (\tfrac{1}{2})^2 0.00125 + (\tfrac{1}{2})^2 0.00563 + 2(\tfrac{1}{2})(\tfrac{1}{2})0$$
$$= 0.0003 + 0.0014 = 0.0017$$

which yields identical results.

Equation 7.8 can also be written by employing the Σ notation. Although the Σ notation is not needed for two assets, it is crucial when there are n assets in the portfolio. We first employ the Σ notation to the two–assets case and then extend this formula to the general case in which the portfolio is composed of n assets.

Equation 7.8 can be rewritten with the Σ notation as follows:

$$\sigma_p^2 = \sum_{i=1}^{2} \sum_{j=1}^{2} w_i w_j \sigma_{i,j} \tag{7.9}$$

where w_i is the proportion invested in asset i, w_j is the proportion invested in asset j, and $\sigma_{i,j}$ is the covariance between assets i and j.

To see that Equations 7.8 and 7.9 are identical, recall that we have to cover all possibilities—namely, $i = 1,2$ and $j = 1,2$. Let us enumerate all these possibilities. When $i = 1$ and $j = 1$, we get the first term, $w_1^2 \sigma_{1,1} = w_1^2 \sigma_1^2$ ($\sigma_{1,1}$ is the covariance of the first asset with itself, which is its variance). When $i = 1$ and $j = 2$, we get $w_1 w_2 \sigma_{1,2}$. When $i = 2$ and $j = 1$, we get $w_2 w_1 \sigma_{2,1}$. Finally, when $i = 2$ and $j = 2$, we get $w_2^2 \sigma_2^2$. Because $\sigma_{1,2} = \sigma_{2,1}$,[6] we have $w_1 w_2 \sigma_{1,2} + w_2 w_1 \sigma_{2,1} = 2 w_1 w_2 \sigma_{1,2}$. Indeed, Equations 7.8 and 7.9 are identical.

Finally, because the correlation between Assets 1 and 2 is defined as

$$\rho_{1,2} = \frac{\sigma_{1,2}}{\sigma_1 \sigma_2}$$

or

$$\sigma_{1,2} = \rho_{1,2} \sigma_1 \sigma_2$$

we can substitute $\rho_{1,2} \sigma_1 \sigma_2$ for $\sigma_{1,2}$ to express the portfolio's variance in terms of its correlation as

---

6. Denoting Asset 1 by x and Asset 2 by y, we get

$$\sigma_{1,2} = \sum p_i [x_i - E(x)][y_i - E(y)]$$

and

$$\sigma_{1,2} = \sum p_i [y_i - E(y)][x_i - E(x)]$$

Of course, the order of the multiplication is irrelevant, namely,

$$[x_i - E(x)][y_i - E(y)] = [y_i - E(y)][x_i - E(x)]$$

Therefore, $\sigma_{1,2} = \sigma_{2,1}$.

$$\sigma_p^2 = w_1^2\sigma_1^2 + w_2^2\sigma_2^2 + 2w_1w_2\rho_{1,2}\sigma_1\sigma_2 \qquad (7.10)$$

Let us summarize these findings schematically:

The Four Terms of the Double Summation Formula of Equation 7.9

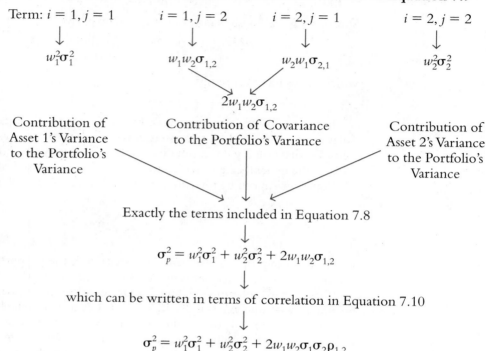

What is the advantage of using Equation 7.10 over the direct calculation of the portfolio's variance? Although the direct calculation has the advantage of being simple, it is silent regarding the various factors affecting the portfolio variance. Equation 7.10, in contrast, sheds light on a major factor affecting the risk reduction—namely, the correlation between the two assets.

PRACTICE BOX	
Problem	Prove that the covariance of Asset x with the riskless interest rate r is equal to zero.
Solution	Because r is riskless, $E(r) = r$. Therefore:

$$\sigma_{x,r} = \sum_{i=1}^{m} P_i[x_i - E(x)][r - E(r)] = \sum_{i=1}^{m} P_i[x_i - E(x)] \cdot 0 = 0$$

which is exactly the definition of variance.

7.7 ANOTHER LOOK AT MUTUAL FUNDS

The diversification benefits of mutual funds stated at the beginning of the chapter are demonstrated nicely by Exhibit 7-3. To demonstrate, suppose a fund or an investor has a goal of getting a mean rate of return of 10% per year. Clearly, Asset B is in line with this target. However, by having a portfolio composed of $\frac{1}{2}A + \frac{1}{4}B + \frac{1}{4}C$, we get a mean return of 10% (see Exhibit 7-3, Column 7), as required, but with a much smaller variance.

Using Exhibit 7-3 and the direct method, the portfolio variance is found to be

$$\sigma_p^2 = \tfrac{1}{3}(0.125 - 0.10)^2 + \tfrac{1}{3}(0.075 - 0.10)^2 + \tfrac{1}{3}(0.10 - 0.10)^2 \cong 0.00042$$

The variance for Asset B is 0.00125; thus, diversifying into Assets A and C greatly reduces the variance.

Exhibit 7-13 demonstrates the returns on Asset B, as well as on the portfolio just discussed. As we can see, the fluctuations on the portfolio are much smaller (7.5%, 10%, and 12.5%) than Asset B's fluctuations (5%, 10%, and 15%). This is exactly what the article in Investments in the News means when it says that one benefit of investing in mutual funds is achieving diversification. By diversifying, the portfolio's risk is reduced—a goal that most investors desire.

We have seen that the portfolio variance is 0.00042. We can also calculate this portfolio variance by the indirect method. With three securities, the variance of the portfolio can be expressed as

$$\sigma_p^2 = \sum_{i=1}^{3}\sum_{j=1}^{3} w_i w_j \sigma_{i,j}$$

EXHIBIT 7-13
Distribution of Returns for Asset B and a Portfolio[a]

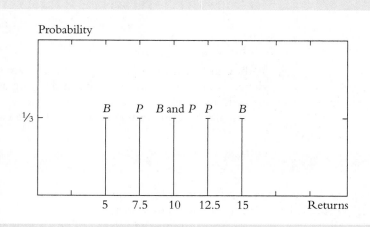

a. B denotes Asset B, and P denotes the portfolio. "B and P" shows that the rate of return is identical for B and P.

Let $1 = A$, $2 = B$, and $3 = C$. Recall that the variance of a constant is zero, and the covariance with a constant is zero. Thus, $\sigma_1^2 = 0$ and $\sigma_{1,2} = \sigma_{1,3} = 0$. Also, the covariance of B with C was found to be zero in the previous Practice Box. Thus,

$$\sigma_p^2 = w_2^2\sigma_2^2 + w_3^2\sigma_3^2 = (\tfrac{1}{4})^2(0.00125) + (\tfrac{1}{4})^2(0.00563) = 0.00043$$

which once again confirms that both approaches to computing the variance of a portfolio yield identical results.

7.8 THE VARIANCE OF A PORTFOLIO COMPOSED OF n ASSETS

Calculating the variance of a portfolio composed of n assets is a simple extension of Equation 7.9, which deals with two assets. The only difference is that we replace 2 with n:

$$\sigma_p^2 = \sum_{i=1}^{n}\sum_{j=1}^{n} w_i w_j \sigma_{i,j} \tag{7.11}$$

Appendix 7A shows how this formula is derived. However, the formula is a natural extension of Equation 7.9 for $n = 2$, which implies that the portfolio variance is nothing but a combination of all the assets' variances as well as all the covariances; and the lower the covariances, the larger the reduction in the portfolio fluctuation achieved by diversification. Therefore, we want to include assets with low covariances in the invested portfolio.

The equation for the variance of a portfolio can also be expressed as follows (see Appendix 7A):

$$\sigma_p^2 = \sum_{i=1}^{n} w_i^2\sigma_i^2 + 2\sum_{i=1}^{n}\sum_{\substack{j=1\\j>i}}^{n} w_i w_j \sigma_{i,j} \tag{7.11'}$$

Although Equation 7.11 is rather complicated, it is clear that the portfolio variance depends on the variances of the underlying assets, the correlations, and the choice of weights.

Finally, in Equations 7.11 and 7.11′, we can substitute $\rho_{i,j}\sigma_i\sigma_j$ for $\sigma_{i,j}$.

SUMMARY

Explain the effect of an asset's risk on a portfolio. When an asset is held with other assets in a portfolio, that asset's risk depends not only on the asset's variance but also on the degree of dependency with other assets. When two assets are perfectly negatively correlated, each asset could be very risky in isolation, but when placed together with the correct weights, a riskless portfolio can be created. The dependency among assets plays an important role in a portfolio's risk and hence in determining the risk premium.

Discuss the expected rate of return and variance of a portfolio. The expected rate of return of a portfolio is the sum of the weights (proportions) invested in an asset times the expected return on that asset, where we sum for all assets. The formula for the variance of a portfolio is much more complicated; the variance of a portfolio is a function of the proportions invested in each asset, the variance of each asset, and the covariances (or correlations) among assets.

Explain covariances and correlation coefficients between assets. Covariances (or correlation coefficients) mea-sure the degree of dependency between two assets. The correlation coefficient, ρ, is a number such that $-1 \le \rho \le 1$, the higher the ρ, the higher the degree of dependency between the assets. Also, covariance (or correlation) plays a major role in determining a portfolio's variance.

Explain the role of correlation within a portfolio. When everything else is held constant, the lower the corre-lation of each pair of assets included in a portfolio, the lower the portfolio's variance will be. Low vari-ance is an attractive feature to risk-averse investors.

CHAPTER AT A GLANCE

1. *The expected rate of return on a portfolio is given by*

$$E(R_p) = \sum_{i=1}^{n} w_i E(R_i)$$

where w_i is the proportion invested in the ith asset and $E(R_i)$ is the expected rate of return on the ith asset.

2. *The covariance between the rates of return of two stocks is given by*

$$Cov(R_1, R_2) = \sum_{i=1}^{m} P_i [R_{1,i} - E(R_1)][R_{2,i} - E(R_2)]$$

where P_i is the probability of State i (typically, $1/m$ for historical data), $R_{1,i}$ is the rate of return on Asset 1 for State i, and $R_{2,i}$ is the rate of return on Asset 2 for State i, where *state* stands for the state of the economy.

3. *The correlation coefficient between the rates of return for two stocks is given by*

$$\rho_{1,2} = \frac{Cov(R_1, R_2)}{\sigma_1 \sigma_2} = \frac{\sigma_{1,2}}{\sigma_1 \sigma_2}$$

where $Cov(R_1, R_2)$ is the covariance between Assets 1 and 2 (also denoted by $\sigma_{1,2}$), σ_1 is the standard devi-ation of Asset 1, and σ_2 is the standard deviation of Asset 2.

4. *The variance of a portfolio of n stocks is given by*

$$\sigma_p^2 = \sum_{i=1}^{n} \sum_{j=1}^{n} w_i w_j \sigma_{i,j}$$

which can also be expressed as

$$\sigma_p^2 = \sum_{i=1}^{n} w_i^2 \sigma_i^2 + 2 \sum_{\substack{i=1 \\ }}^{n} \sum_{\substack{j=1 \\ j>i}}^{n} w_i w_j \sigma_{i,j}$$

Also, $\sigma_{i,j}$ can be substituted for $\rho_{i,j} \sigma_i \sigma_j$ in the formula for the variance of a portfolio given above.

KEY TERMS

Correlation   227
Covariance   222

Portfolio expected return   220
Variance   231

PRACTICE

7.1 Suppose you are given the following information regarding the rates of return on three assets:

State of the Economy	Scenario Probability	Asset		
		A	B	C
1	⅓	5%	10%	30%
2	⅓	5	5	15
3	⅓	5	15	15

Calculate the expected return, variance, and standard deviation for each asset, as well as the covariances and correlation coefficients.

The following are daily price data for the Major Market Index (MMI), American Express (AXP), GE, and Exxon (XON), which will be used for Questions 7.2 through 7.5.

Day	MMI	AXP	GE	XON
1	616.4000	23.0000	74.6250	59.0000
2	617.4600	22.5000	74.0000	58.1250
3	621.3200	22.8750	74.8750	59.8750
4	614.1600	22.6250	75.0000	58.7500
5	625.6200	22.1250	74.0000	57.3750

7.2 Calculate the daily rates of return for the MMI, AXP, GE, and XON.

7.3 Calculate the average rate of return, variance, and standard deviation for the MMI, AXP, and GE.

7.4 Calculate the covariance and correlation coefficient for AXP and GE.

7.5 Suppose you had $100,000 to invest in AXP and GE. Calculate the expected rate of return and standard deviation of a portfolio in which an equal dollar amount is invested in each security.

7.6 Suppose you invested 30% in Asset A, which returned 40%; invested 25% in Asset B, which returned −10%; and invested 45% in Asset C, which returned 15%. What was the rate of return on the portfolio?

7.7 Repeat Question 7.6, except assume that instead of rates of return, the returns given are *expected* rates of return. Thus, calculate the expected rate of return on this portfolio.

7.8 "Correlation does not really reduce the risk of a portfolio, because the underlying securities remain risky." Evaluate this statement, and defend your answer using a portfolio of two securities with identical standard deviations of 30% and in which 50% is invested in each security.

7.9 Prove that the covariance of Asset X with $\frac{1}{2} \cdot X$ is equal to one-half the variance of Asset X.

7.10 Calculate the variance of a portfolio that is equally divided among four uncorrelated assets with standard deviations of 10%, 20%, 30%, and 40%.

7.11 The following are the rates of return on Assets A and B:

Year	R_A	R_B
1	−10%	+10%
2	20	17
3	−2	0
4	4	8
5	12	19

a. What is the rate of return on the portfolio if Year 4 occurs and when $w_A = \frac{1}{5}$ and $w_B = \frac{4}{5}$? How would you change your answer if the investment weights were $w_A = \frac{1}{2}$ and $w_B = \frac{1}{2}$?

b. If each year has a probability of $\frac{1}{3}$, calculate the portfolio mean and variance when $w_A = \frac{1}{2}$ and $w_B = \frac{1}{2}$. First do the calculations by constructing the portfolio rates of return and calculating the mean and variance of these rates of return. Then do the calculations by employing Equation 7.3 in the text. Which method is easier?

7.12 You have two stocks, A and B, with $\sigma_A = 10\%$ and $\sigma_B = 20\%$. The investment proportions in a portfolio are $w_A = w_B = \frac{1}{2}$. It is known that the portfolio standard deviation is $\sigma_p = 5\%$. What is the covariance, or $Cov(R_A, R_B)$?

7.13 You have two stocks with the following rates of return:

Year	R_A	R_B
1	+10%	+10%
2	−5	−5
3	15	15

The probability of each year is $\frac{1}{3}$.
a. Calculate the correlation between Stock A and Stock B.
b. Calculate the variance of a portfolio composed of $w_A = \frac{1}{2}$ and $w_B = \frac{1}{2}$. Calculate the variance of a portfolio composed of $w_A = \frac{1}{3}$ and $w_B = \frac{2}{3}$. Explain your results.

7.14 Suppose you have two stocks, A and B. It is given that $w_A = w_B = \frac{1}{2}$ and that

$$\sigma_A^2 = \sigma_B^2 = \sigma_{A,B} = 10$$

"By employing Equation 7.10 of the text, the portfolio variance must also be equal to 10." Do you agree? If yes, prove it. If no, calculate the portfolio variance.

7.15 It is given that for two assets, A and B,

$$\sigma_A^2 = \sigma_B^2$$

and

$$Cov(R_A, R_B) = \frac{\sigma_A^2}{2}$$

Employ Equation 7.6 to find the portfolio variance (in terms of σ_A^2) when the investment proportions are $w_A = \frac{1}{2}$ and $w_B = \frac{1}{2}$.

7.16 The following is the rate of return on a German stock traded on the Frankfurt stock exchange with the following probabilities:

Probability	Rate of Return
$\frac{1}{2}$	+10%
$\frac{1}{4}$	20
$\frac{1}{4}$	−10

An American investor buys the stock for 1 year. The investor converts \$50 to DM 100 (a 2-for-1 exchange rate) and buys the stock. The same stock is bought also by a German investor.
a. Calculate the expected rate of return and variance on the stock for both a German investor and an American investor, assuming that the exchange rate is constant at DM 2 for \$1.
b. How would you change your answer if it were known with certainty that at the end of the year, the exchange rate would be DM 1.9 per \$1?
c. Recalculate the mean and variance when it is known that at the end of the year, the exchange rate will be DM 1.9 per \$1 with a probability of $\frac{1}{2}$ and DM 2.1 per \$1 with a probability of $\frac{1}{2}$. (Assume that the exchange rates are independent of the stock's rates of return.) Discuss your results.

7.17 You have two securities, A and B, and the investment proportions are $w_A = w_B = \frac{1}{2}$.
a. Is it possible to have a correlation such that the portfolio variance will be larger than both σ_A^2 and σ_B^2?
b. Is it possible that the portfolio variance will be larger than either σ_A^2 or σ_B^2?
c. Is it possible that the portfolio variance will be smaller than both σ_A^2 and σ_B^2?

7.18 Suppose you have three stocks with the following parameters:

$$\sigma_1^2 = 1, \ \sigma_2^2 = 2, \ \sigma_3^2 = 3, \ \sigma_{1,2} = 0,$$
$$\sigma_{1,3} = 1, \text{ and } \sigma_{2,3} = 5$$

You invest $\frac{1}{3}$ in each stock.

a. Calculate the portfolio variance.
b. How would you change your results if all covariances were zero?

c. How would you change your results if $\sigma_{1,2} = 10$ rather than zero?

d. How would you change your results if $\sigma_{2,3} = -2$ rather than $+5$?

e. Explain your answers to Parts b, c, and d.

7.19 You have n assets. The following is known for all assets:

$$\sigma_i^2 = 10 \text{ for } i = 1, 2, \ldots, n$$

$$\sigma_{i,j} = 10 \text{ for all pairs } i \text{ and } j$$

Employ Equation 7.11 to calculate the portfolio variance. Explain your results. First solve the equation for $n = 2$ assets and then for the general case of $n > 2$ assets.

7.20 Suppose you have the following information:

Probability	Stock Price in 1 Year
⅓	$100
⅓	90
⅓	110

The current stock price is $95. You have two ways to pay transaction costs. You must decide which method of payment to use before purchasing the stock: pay a $2 fee at the end of the year (when the stock is sold) regardless of the stock price, or pay 2% of the selling price at the end of the year. Calculate the mean and variance of the gross rate of return, as well as the net rate of return under these two options. Which option would you prefer? Defend your answer.

7.21 Suppose that for two stocks, you have $\sigma_1^2 = 10$, $\sigma_2^2 = 20$, and $\sigma_{1,2} = 5$. For investment proportions $w_1 = \frac{1}{4}$ and $w_2 = \frac{3}{4}$, calculate the portfolio variance.

7.22 "If $\sigma_{i,j} = 0$ for all i and j, no matter whether i equals j or i does not equal j, the portfolio variance must be equal to zero." Evaluate this statement.

7.23 Suppose you have the following information on two stocks:

Probability	Asset A	Asset B
½	−5%	7%
½	20	22

Calculate the portfolio mean and variance for the following two alternative strategies. Also explain the meaning of these two investment strategies.

a. $w_A = \frac{1}{4}$, $w_B = \frac{3}{4}$.

b. $w_A = -\frac{1}{2}$, $w_B = 1\frac{1}{2}$.

7.24 Consider the following two assets:

	Asset A	Asset B
Expected return	10%	10%
Standard deviation	12	12

Assume that you construct a portfolio consisting of only these two assets and hold an equal proportion of your wealth in each of the two assets. You find that the standard deviation of the portfolio is 12%. What is the implied correlation coefficient of returns between Asset A and Asset B? Prove your answer.

7.25 Given the information in Question 7.24, would the implied correlation coefficient between Asset A and Asset B change if you changed the proportion of your wealth that you held in each asset? For example, what if you invested 20% in Asset A and 80% in Asset B, and the standard deviation of the portfolio remained 12%? Explain your results.

7.26 Suppose that there are n securities in a portfolio, the variance of each security is $\sigma_i^2 = 10$, and the covariance of each pair (i,j) is also $\sigma_{i,j} = 10$. Show that no matter what the selected investment proportions $(w_1, w_2, \ldots, w_n)$, the portfolio variance (σ_p^2) will be always equal to 10.

(Hint: Recall that $\sum_{j=1}^{n} w_j = 1$, where w_j is the investment proportion in the jth asset.)

7.27 The following data relate to two stocks, A and B:

	Rate of Return	
Year	Stock A	Stock B
1	10%	5%
2	0	10
3	−12	20
4	40	−5

The investor decides to invest in a portfolio composed of the investment proportions $w_A = \frac{1}{4}$ and $w_B = \frac{3}{4}$.

a. Calculate the portfolio's variance.

b. Calculate the proportion of the three components of the portfolio's variance given by Equation 7.10.

7.28 You consider investing in a stock and in a riskless asset with the following rates of return:

Year	Riskless Interest Rate	Stock (Rate of Return)
1	6%	20%
2	6	−5
3	6	30
4	6	15

a. Calculate the average and standard deviation of the rates of return on each of these two assets.

b. Calculate the correlation of the rates of return on these two assets.

c. What is the expected rate of return and variance of a portfolio composed of 25% of the riskless asset and 75% of the stock?

For Internet questions visit the Levy Investment Web site at http://levy-invst.swcollege.com.

YOUR TURN: APPLYING THEORY TO PRACTICE
PORTFOLIO MEAN AND VARIANCE: BONDS AND STOCKS

The following tables provide the means, standard deviations, and correlations of four types of assets for the last 780 months. All parameters are based on monthly rates of return.

	Mean Return	Standard Deviation
S&P 500	1.01%	5.67%
Small stocks	1.35	8.69
Corporate bonds	0.48	1.97
Government bonds	0.44	2.22

Correlations

	S&P 500	Small Stocks	Corporate Bonds	Government Bonds
S&P 500	1.00%	0.85%	0.22%	0.16%
Small stocks	0.84	1.00	0.18	0.10
Corporate bonds	0.23	0.18	1.00	0.84
Government bonds	0.18	0.10	0.85	1.00

Source: *Stocks, Bonds, Bills, and Inflation 1996 Yearbook* (Chicago: Ibbotson Associates, 1996). Used with permission. © 1996 Ibbotson Associates, Inc. All rights reserved. [Certain portions of this work were derived from copyrighted works of Roger G. Ibbotson and Rex Sinquefield.]

Questions

1. Suppose you decide to invest in two assets and diversify with the following weights: $w_1 = \frac{1}{2}$ and $w_2 = \frac{1}{2}$ (of course, $w_1 + w_2 = 1$). Calculate the *portfolio's* mean and variance for S&P 500 and small stocks, then for corporate bonds and government bonds, and finally for small stocks and government bonds. Which of these strategies is most desirable? Explain.

2. Calculate the portfolio mean and variance for a portfolio composed of weights $w_i = \frac{1}{4}$ ($i = 1, 2, 3, 4$) for each of the above four assets.

3. How would the result in Question 2 change if all correlations reported above were $+1$? Graph your results to Questions 2 and 3 in a mean–standard deviation space. Is the investor better off with high or low correlations? Explain.

REFERENCES

See Chapter 6.

Appendix 7A The Variance of a Portfolio Composed of *n* Assets

The variance of a portfolio (σ_p^2) that is composed of *n* assets is given by Equation 7.11:

$$\sigma_p^2 = \sum_{i=1}^{n}\sum_{j=1}^{n} w_i w_j \sigma_{i,j}$$

This appendix provides a brief sketch of the proof. We write the portfolio rate of return as

$$R_p = \sum_{i=1}^{n} w_i R_i$$

with the mean rate of return

$$E(R_p) = \sum_{i=1}^{n} w_i E(R_i)$$

Then the variance is given by

$$\sigma_p^2 = E[R_p - E(R_p)]^2 = E[\sum w_i R_i - \sum w_i E(R_i)]^2$$
$$= E\{w_1 R_1 + w_2 R_2 + \ldots + w_n R_n$$
$$- [w_1 E(R_1) + w_2 E(R_2) + \ldots + w_n E(R_n)]\}^2$$

Rearranging terms,

$$\sigma_p^2 = E\{w_1[R_1 - E(R_1)] + w_2[R_2 - E(R_2)] + \ldots$$
$$+ w_n[R_n - E(R_n)]\}^2$$

Opening the square bracket, it can be shown that it includes the product of each pair of terms inside the brackets, as well as the product of each term with itself. Thus,

$$\sigma_p^2 = \sum_{i=1}^{n}\sum_{j=1}^{n} w_i w_j E\{[R_i - E(R_i)][R_j - E(R_j)]\}$$

However, because

$$\sigma_i^2 = E[R_i - E(R_i)]^2$$

and

$$\sigma_{i,j} = E\{[R_i - E(R_i)][R_j - E(R_j)]\}$$

we get Equation 7.11 in the text.

How can we count all the terms appearing in the above formula, which consists of all variances, as well as all covariances between all pairs of assets? The formula for the portfolio's variance with $n = 2$ assets can be extended to any number of assets simply by substituting n for 2 in Equation 7.9. To see this, suppose there are n risky assets in the selected portfolio. Then, in principle, the portfolio's variance should be calculated in the same manner given in Equation 7.8 but should be extended to include all individual assets, variances, and covariances of all pairs of Assets i and j.

The procedure is as follows. First, calculate all variances and covariances. Then multiply the ith variance by w_i^2, getting $w_i^2\sigma_i^2$, and multiply covariance $\sigma_{i,j}$ by $w_i w_j$. Finally, sum all these terms to obtain the portfolio's variance.

EXHIBIT 7A-1   **Individual Assets' Variances and Covariances and the Portfolio's Variance**

(a) Variances and Covariances

		Asset j				
		1	2	3	...	n
Asset i	1	$\sigma_1^2(=\sigma_{1,1})$	$\sigma_{1,2}$	$\sigma_{1,3}$	...	$\sigma_{1,n}$
	2	$\sigma_{2,1}$	$\sigma_2^2(=\sigma_{2,2})$	$\sigma_{2,3}$	...	$\sigma_{2,n}$
	3	$\sigma_{3,1}$	$\sigma_{3,2}$	$\sigma_3^2(=\sigma_{3,3})$	...	$\sigma_{3,n}$
	⋮	⋮	⋮	⋮	⋮	⋮
	n	$\sigma_{n,1}$	$\sigma_{n,2}$	$\sigma_{n,3}$	...	$\sigma_n^2(=\sigma_{n,n})$

(b) Variance and Covariance Multiplied by the Corresponding Weights

		Asset j				
		1	2	3	...	n
Asset i	1	$w_1^2\sigma_1^2$	$w_1 w_2 \sigma_{1,2}$	$w_1 w_3 \sigma_{1,3}$	...	$w_1 w_n \sigma_{1,n}$
	2	$w_2 w_1 \sigma_{2,1}$	$w_2^2\sigma_2^2$	$w_2 w_3 \sigma_{2,3}$	...	$w_2 w_n \sigma_{2,n}$
	3	$w_3 w_1 \sigma_{3,1}$	$w_3 w_2 \sigma_{3,2}$	$w_3^2\sigma_3^2$	...	$w_3 w_n \sigma_{3,n}$
	⋮	⋮	⋮	⋮	⋮	⋮
	n	$w_n w_1 \sigma_{n,1}$	$w_n w_2 \sigma_{n,2}$	$w_n w_3 \sigma_{n,3}$	...	$w_n^2\sigma_n^2$

Exhibit 7A–1 demonstrates this procedure. The diagonal in the matrix in the exhibit gives the variances σ_1^2, σ_2^2, ..., σ_n^2. If one wants to keep Exhibit 7A–1 symmetric, σ_1^2 can be rewritten as $\sigma_{1,1}$, σ_2^2 as $\sigma_{2,2}$, and so forth, where $\sigma_{i,i}$ is the covariance of the ith asset with itself, which of course is equal to the variance. The off-diagonal terms in the exhibit give all the covariances; for example, $\sigma_{1,3}$ is the covariance corresponding to Assets 1 and 3, and so forth. Obviously, $\sigma_{1,3} = \sigma_{3,1}$, because the covariance of Assets 1 and 3 is equal to the covariance of Assets 3 and 1. Part b of Exhibit 7A–1 is obtained from Part a simply by multiplying the ith variance σ_i^2 by w_i^2, and by multiplying the covariance $\sigma_{i,j}$ by $w_i w_j$. The portfolio's variance is nothing but the sum of all terms appearing in Part b of Exhibit 7A–1. Thus, the double summation formula in Equation 7.11 is nothing but the sum of all terms in Part b of Exhibit 7A–1.

Let us now write all the terms appearing in Exhibit 7A–1, Part b, in a formula that is the portfolio's variance formula. Looking carefully at all terms appearing in Exhibit 7A–1, Part b, we see that the portfolio's variance of n assets can be written in general as

$$\sigma_p^2 = \sum_{i=1}^{n}\sum_{j=1}^{n} w_i w_j \sigma_{i,j} \tag{7A.1}$$

The following is an explanation of the terms appearing in Equation 7A.1 (recall that $\sigma_{i,i} = \sigma_i^2$). First, we denote the rows in Exhibit 7A–1 by i (where $i = 1, 2, \ldots,$ n) and the columns by j (where $j = 1, 2, \ldots, n$). When $i = j$, we have $w_i^2 \sigma_i^2$. Therefore, for $i = j$ (see the diagonal terms in Exhibit 7A–1, Part b), we get all the variance terms of the individual assets.

Now let us look at the terms when $i \neq j$. For example, when $i = 1$ and $j = 2,$ $3, \ldots, n,$ we sum all the terms in the first row of Exhibit 7A–1, Part b, apart from the variance. In this case, we have

$$w_1 w_2 \sigma_{1,2} + w_1 w_3 \sigma_{1,3} + \ldots + w_1 w_n \sigma_{1,n} = \sum_{j=2}^{n} w_1 w_j \sigma_{1,j} \tag{7A.2}$$

which reflects the covariances of the first asset with all other $n - 1$ assets. Similarly, for $i = 2$, we have all the terms in the second row (apart from $w_2^2 \sigma_2^2$). Thus, as we increase i, we go down to a lower row in the table and sum all the elements in the row. In short, Equation 7A.1 for the portfolio's variance captures all elements in Exhibit 7A–1, Part b.

Sometimes the portfolio's variance is written in another equivalent way. Equation 7A.3 breaks the portfolio's variance into two terms:

$$\sigma_p^2 = \sum_{i=1}^{n} w_i^2 \sigma_i^2 + \sum_{\substack{i=1 \\ }}^{n}\sum_{\substack{j=1 \\ j \neq i}}^{n} w_i w_j \sigma_{i,j} \tag{7A.3}$$

The first term is the sum of all the individual variances appropriately weighted that appear on the diagonal of Part b of Exhibit 7A-1. The second term sums up all the other terms appearing in Exhibit 7A-1, apart from the variances. To guarantee that we will not have double counting of terms that appear in the diagonal of the exhibit, we add to the second term the constraint $j \neq i$; namely, sum all terms except those appearing in the diagonal (recall that $i = j$ means that a term is in the diagonal of the exhibit).

Note that in the second term of Equation 7A.3, each term appears twice. For example, we have $w_1 w_2 \sigma_{1,2}$ and $w_2 w_1 \sigma_{2,1}$, but because $\sigma_{1,2} = \sigma_{2,1}$, these two terms are equal. In general, for every term above the diagonal of Exhibit 7A-1, there is an identical term below the diagonal. Therefore, the variance formula can also be written as

$$\sigma_p^2 = \sum_{i=1}^{n} w_i^2 \sigma_i^2 + 2 \sum_{i=1}^{n} \sum_{\substack{j=1 \\ j>i}}^{n} w_i w_j \sigma_{i,j} \qquad (7A.4)$$

We multiply the second term of the variance by 2, indicating that each term appears twice. However, we must also add the constraint $j > i$ so that we count only terms above the diagonal (and the 2 takes care of the term below the diagonal). For example, if $i = 1$ and $j = 2$, we have the term $w_1 w_2 \sigma_{1,2}$. Because $j > i$, we do not count the term $w_2 w_1 \sigma_{2,1}$ (here $j < i$, because $i = 2$, $j = 1$). However, not counting this term specifically is correct, because we multiply the first term, $w_1 w_2 \sigma_{1,2}$, by 2, which takes care of the "missing" term that is below the diagonal.

Equations 7A.1, 7A.2, 7A.3, and 7A.4 are all ways to sum up all the terms appearing in Part b of Exhibit 7A-1. Hence, they yield the same results. Finally, because $\rho_{i,j} \sigma_i \sigma_j = \sigma_{i,j}$, we can substitute $\rho_{i,j} \sigma_i \sigma_j$ for $\sigma_{i,j}$ in Equations 7A.1, 7A.2, 7A.3, and 7A.4 and express the portfolio's variance in terms of correlations $\rho_{i,j}$ rather than covariances $\sigma_{i,j}$.

EXHIBIT 7A-2   Calculating the Covariance of a Three-Asset Portfolio

(a) Variances and Covariances of Three Assets

		Asset j		
		1	2	3
	1	0.12	0.1	−0.15
Asset i	2	0.10	0.40	0.12
	3	−0.15	0.12	0.16

(continued)

EXHIBIT 7A-2   *(continued)*

((b) The Product of the Investment Weights and the Variances and Covariances

		Asset j			
		1	**2**	**3**	
	1	$(0.1)^2(0.12)$	$0.1(0.3)(0.1)$	$0.1(0.6)(-0.15)$	
Asset i	2	$0.3(0.1)(0.10)$	$(0.3)^2 0.40$	$0.3(0.6)(0.12)$	
	3	$0.6(0.1)(-0.15)$	$0.6(0.3)(0.12)$	$(0.6)^2(0.16)$	
Sum of columns		-0.0048	0.0606	0.0702	Sum of sums 0.126

Exhibit 7A-2 illustrates this calculation with three stocks, $n = 3$. Part a of the exhibit gives the assumed variances and covariances of the various stocks that have been arbitrarily selected for this demonstration. Part b gives these variances multiplied by the portfolio investment weights, where, in this illustration, $w_1 = 0.1$, $w_2 = 0.3$, and $w_3 = 0.6$. The covariances $\sigma_{i,j}$ are multiplied by $w_i w_j$. Then the portfolio's variance is nothing but the sum of all elements in this exhibit, which in this case is $\sigma_p^2 = 0.126$ (see the sum of all numbers at the bottom of Exhibit 7A-2). Obviously, using the basic data of Part a of Exhibit 7A-2, one can calculate other portfolio variances by simply substituting the results in Part b of this exhibit and using other investment weights (w_i).

CHAPTER 8

THE GAIN FROM PORTFOLIO DIVERSIFICATION

LEARNING OBJECTIVES

After studying this chapter you should be able to:

1. Describe the effect of correlation on the risk reduction of a portfolio.

2. Explain how the number of assets in a portfolio affects the portfolio's risk.

3. Locate the efficient and inefficient investment strategies.

INVESTMENTS IN THE NEWS

MORE OF A MIX

Janice Crotty's $34,000 retirement portfolio is modestly diversified. But it has no foreign equity funds, and the stock of one of her former employers—International Data Group—occupies a big slice of the asset pie. Barbara Gilliard, a financial planner, suggested a more diversified approach for the 31-year-old woman.

Current Allocation

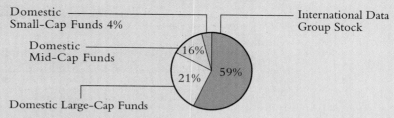

Domestic Small-Cap Funds 4%
Domestic Mid-Cap Funds — 16%
Domestic Large-Cap Funds — 21%
International Data Group Stock — 59%

Suggested Allocation

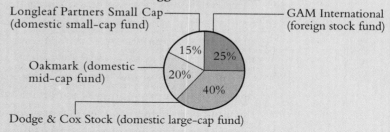

Longleaf Partners Small Cap (domestic small-cap fund) — 15%
Oakmark (domestic mid-cap fund) — 20%
GAM International (foreign stock fund) — 25%
Dodge & Cox Stock (domestic large-cap fund) — 40%

Gilliard generally recommends that Crotty roll the $34,000 in retirement funds into a more diversified portfolio that emphasizes long-term growth. "She's so young and she wouldn't need to touch it until she was 59," Gilliard said.

The $34,000 should be transferred to mutual funds, the planner advises. She would put 40% in the Dodge & Cox Stock fund, which invests in large companies like Coca-Cola and IBM; 25% in GAM International, a foreign fund; 20% in Oakmark, a mid-cap fund, and 15% in Longleaf Partners Small Cap. (Cap is

(continued)

short for capitalization, the total shares value in $'s of the firm. Thus we can refer to mid-, small-, and large-cap to distinguish between firms' share value.) Over the last 3 years, the average annual returns of the four funds have been impressive: 28%, 20%, 25%, and 21%, respectively . . .

"You want to be exposed to a range of markets" to help minimize the risk, Gilliard said in explaining her fund choices. While her recommendations include funds specializing in companies of different sizes—just as Crotty's current fund choices do—Gilliard's funds allow for more ways to diversify the assets. The foreign fund offers one such route, but perhaps the most important is the removal of the high risk of keeping 59% of Crotty's retirement money in the stock of just one company—in this case, IDG.

Source: Adapted with permission from Laurie J. Flynn, "Creating a Parachute for a New Solo Flier," *New York Times*, July 27, 1997, p. 4F. Copyright © 1997 by The New York Times Co. Reprinted by Permission.

HOW TO BUILD A STOCK PORTFOLIO EVEN IF YOU AREN'T A MONEYBAGS

To increase diversification, advisers recommend choosing securities in different industries.

"You don't want more than one company in an industry, and you don't want companies in related industries," says Mr. Lipson [president of Horizon Financial Advisors]. For example, an auto manufacturer and a steel company that supplies auto manufacturers will move together. Further, "you also don't want industries that respond to the economic cycle the same way, such as trucking and basic manufacturing," he says.

While Mr. Lipson believes that investors need at least 15 stocks to be adequately diversified, other advisers are comfortable with a smaller number. "It's not so much the number of names that makes you diversified, but how you spread them out," says George Vanderheiden, who heads the equity growth group for Fidelity Investments.

Investors can add to their diversification by including some international exposure. "To be really well diversified, you need 10% of your portfolio in international stocks," says John Markese, president of the American Association of Individual Investors, an investor-education group based in Chicago.

Kenneth Jessen, 53, an engineer for Hewlett-Packard Co. in Loveland, Colo., follows much of this advice. He holds at least 10 stocks and diversifies into emerging sectors like waste management and foreign stocks. Right now, he says his research has led him to two British companies: Hanson PLC ("20 years of consistent increase in earnings per share") and Glaxo Holdings PLC.

Source: Ellen E. Schultz, "How to Build a Stock Portfolio Even If You Aren't a Moneybags," *The Wall Street Journal*, April 10, 1992, pp. C1, C13. Reprinted by permission of *The Wall Street Journal*, © 1992 Dow Jones & Co., Inc. All Rights Reserved Worldwide.

The first article in this chapter's Investments in the News compares current portfolio allocations with suggested ones. The financial planner emphasizes that holding 59% of one asset is too risky and that adding 25% of international stock helps reduce risk. This reduction is impossible when all assets are invested in one market.

As the second article reports, the experts who manage portfolios believe that selecting stocks—both domestic and foreign—from unrelated industries leads to less risk than simply selecting a large number of stocks. The better an investor is at offsetting the bad performance of one stock by the good performance of another, the more that investor can reduce the risk associated with the portfolio.

As Chapter 7 described, the "relatedness" of stocks can be measured with the correlation coefficient. When the correlation coefficient of stocks in a portfolio is positive and large, the risk reduction is limited. Stocks with negative correlations are preferable, but it is hard to find stocks that are negatively correlated. Therefore, experts recommend finding "unrelated" stocks—that is, stocks with zero correlation.

This chapter focuses on the effects on portfolio risk of the correlation between assets. Specifically, it explains how diversification into different assets can result in lower risk. As assets with lower correlations are selected, the overall portfolio risk is reduced. The chapter also examines how many assets are needed to reduce risk adequately and why investing a high proportion of the portfolio in only one asset may be very risky. After discussing how portfolio risk can be manipulated, the chapter develops the well-known mean-variance rule.

The equilibrium pricing model, which is based on the mean-variance rule, is introduced in Chapter 9. The role of the international market in risk reduction is discussed in detail in Chapter 11.

8.1 THE EFFECT OF CORRELATION ON A PORTFOLIO'S RISK REDUCTION

In reality, both the level of risk and the profitability, or expected return, of a portfolio determine an investor's optimal portfolio. However, for the time being, in order to examine the relationship between correlation and a portfolio's risk, we hold the expected return constant.

Consider a portfolio with just two stocks, A and B, each with the same expected rate of return, $E(R_A) = E(R_B) = 10\%$, but with different variances, σ_A^2 and σ_B^2. Because the expected rate of return of the two assets is 10%, the expected return on the portfolio is also 10%, no matter what proportions of each stock we choose.

PRACTICE BOX	
Problem	Demonstrate that if two securities, Security A and Security B, have the same expected return, then any portfolio composed of these two securities will have that same expected return. *(continued)*

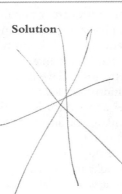

Solution

Recall that the portfolio's expected rate of return in this case is

$$E(R_p) = w_A E(R_A) + w_B E(R_B)$$

However, it is given that $E(R_A) = E(R_B) = Z$, where Z is some given number. Thus, we have

$$E(R_p) = w_A Z + w_B Z = (w_A + w_B)Z$$

We know that the sum of the weights in a portfolio is equal to 1. Hence,

$$E(R_p) = Z$$

and the portfolio's expected return is always equal to the individual security's expected return.

The portfolio's variance, however, will change depending on the proportion of each asset held. This variance is the common measure of the portfolio's risk, just as a stock's variance reflects the stock's level of risk.

We can see how a portfolio's variance is influenced by the weights of the individual assets and their respective variances by looking at the equation for calculating portfolio variance from Chapter 7 (Equation 7.8, where $A = 1$ and $B = 2$):

$$\sigma_p^2 = w_A^2 \sigma_A^2 + (1 - w_A)^2 \sigma_B^2 + 2w_A(1 - w_A)\rho_{A,B}\sigma_A\sigma_B$$

where w_A is the investment proportion (weights) in Asset A and $w_B = 1 - w_A$ is the proportion invested in Asset B. Exhibit 8-1 gives the portfolio's variance, σ_p^2, for various correlations, $\rho_{A,B}$, and for various investment weights, w_A, ($w_B = 1 - w_A$). A denotes ABC Company and B denotes BAT Company. It is assumed in the construction of Exhibit 8-1 that $\sigma_A^2 = 9$ and $\sigma_B^2 = 4$.

Two main conclusions can be drawn from Exhibit 8-1:

1. For a given correlation, the weights selected affect the portfolio's variance.
2. The lower the correlation for a given set of weights, the smaller the portfolio variance and, hence, the larger the gain from diversification between the two assets. For example, for a selected weight of $w_A = \frac{1}{2}$, the portfolio variances for $\rho_{A,B} = -1$, $\rho_{A,B} = -\frac{1}{2}$, $\rho_{A,B} = 0$, $\rho_{A,B} = +\frac{1}{2}$, and $\rho_{A,B} = 1$ are 0.25, 1.75, 3.25, 4.75, and 6.25, respectively. The lower the correlation, the more movement to the left in the direction of the arrow in Exhibit 8-2.

These two conclusions are very important for portfolio management. The manager can minimize a portfolio's risk by carefully selecting assets with low correlation and by balancing the investment weights. The two factors—correlations and weights—are crucial, because they determine the investor's risk exposure.

Exhibit 8-3 quantifies the gain from diversification and shows the impact of correlation on achieving this gain. Assets A and B have equal rates of return; each yields +20% and −10% with equal probability. The mean return on each asset is 5%, and

EXHIBIT 8-1 The Variance[a] of a Portfolio for Various Degrees of Correlation	**Proportion of Wealth Invested in ABC Company (w_A) and BAT Company (w_B)**		**Various Degrees of Correlation ($\rho_{A,B}$)**				
	w_A	w_B	-1	$-\frac{1}{2}$	0	$+\frac{1}{2}$	1
	0	1	4.00	4.00	4.00	4.00	4.00
	0.1	0.9	2.25	2.79	3.33	3.87	4.41
	0.2	0.8	1.00	1.96	2.92	3.88	4.84
	0.3	0.7	0.25	1.51	2.77	4.03	5.29
	0.4	0.6	0.00	1.44	2.88	4.32	5.76
	0.5	0.5	0.25	1.75	3.25	4.75	6.25
	0.6	0.4	1.00	2.44	3.88	5.32	6.76
	0.7	0.3	2.25	3.51	4.77	6.03	7.29
	0.8	0.2	4.00	4.96	5.92	6.83	7.84
	0.9	0.1	6.25	6.79	7.33	7.87	8.41
	1.0	0	9.00	9.00	9.00	9.00	9.00

a. Calculated by the following formula:

$$\sigma_p^2 = w_A^2 \sigma_A^2 + (1 - w_A)^2 \sigma_B^2 + 2w_A(1 - w_A)\sigma_A\sigma_B\rho_{A,B}$$

where

$$\sigma_A = 3 \qquad \sigma_A^2 = 9$$
$$\sigma_B = 2 \qquad \sigma_B^2 = 4$$

and the correlation coefficient (ρ) varies between -1 and $+1$, as given in the exhibit.

EXHIBIT 8-2
Portfolio
Variance for
Different
Correlations
where
$w_A = w_B = \frac{1}{2}$

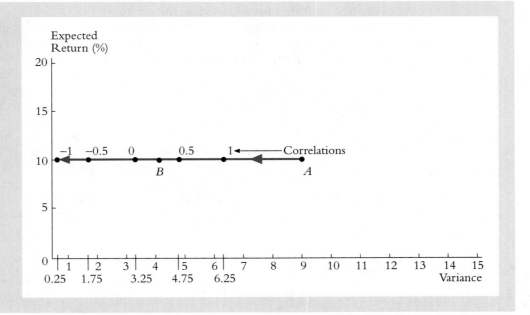

the variance on each is 0.0225 (see Exhibit 8-3a). Exhibit 8-3b gives the returns on a portfolio composed of ½ of Asset A and ½ of Asset B.[1] If there is a perfect positive correlation, $\rho_{A,B}$ = +1, it means that if +20% occurs on Asset A, then +20% also occurs on Asset B; hence, the return on the portfolio will be ½(0.2) + ½(0.2) = 0.20, or 20%. Note that we get ½ of 20% on each asset, because only ½ of the wealth (or a weight of ½) is invested in each asset. Similarly, if −10% occurs on Asset A, the same occurs on Asset B and the portfolio return is −10%. Therefore, for $\rho_{A,B}$ = +1, the portfolio's return and variance are equal to those of either Asset A or Asset B, and no gain from diversification exists.

Now let us turn to the case where the returns on the two assets are independent, which means a correlation of $\rho_{A,B}$ = 0. In this case, the probability of earning +20% on the first asset and +20% on the second asset is similar to the probability of having two heads appear when two coins are tossed; the probability of this occurring is ½(½) = ¼. Similarly, the probability of earning +20% on Asset A and −10% on Asset B is ½(½) = ¼. (Recall that the returns are independent, which implies that $\rho_{A,B}$ = 0.) In this case, the return on the portfolio is

$$½(0.20) + ½(−0.10) = 0.05, \text{ or } 5\%$$

However, an investor may also realize −10% on Asset A and +20% on Asset B with a probability of ¼, yielding once again +5%. Therefore, the total probability of ending with +5% is ¼ + ¼ = ½. Finally, there is a probability of ½ · ½ = ¼ of earning −10% on the two assets, yielding ½(−0.10) + ½(−0.10) = −0.10, or −10%.

The last column of Exhibit 8-3b corresponds to the case of a perfect negative correlation, $\rho_{A,B}$ = −1. If Asset A has a return of +20%, then Asset B's return is −10%. This will result in a portfolio rate of return of ½(+0.20) + ½(−0.10) = 0.05, or 5%. Similarly, if Asset A has a −10% return, then Asset B has a +20% return, and once again a 5% return is earned on the portfolio.

As mentioned above, Exhibit 8-3b shows that if two similar assets are perfectly positively correlated ($\rho_{A,B}$ = +1), no diversification gains are achieved. The investor must live with feast or famine and might as well hold only one asset rather than two. In contrast, when $\rho_{A,B}$ = 0, some stabilization of the portfolio's return is achieved. If the investor loses on one asset, the other asset provides some support, hence lessening the risk. Finally, for the extreme case where $\rho_{A,B}$ = −1 (perfect negative correlation, which is rarely observed in practice), the investor obtains a portfolio with a completely stable rate of return.[2]

Note that the portfolio's mean return is +5%, regardless of the correlation. Thus, in this specific example, an investor can safely assert that it is the degree of correlation that influences the portfolio's level of risk. The lower the correlation, the larger the gain from diversification. The portfolio's variance is reduced from 0.0225 when $\rho_{A,B}$ = +1, to 0.01125 when $\rho_{A,B}$ = 0, and to 0 when $\rho_{A,B}$ = −1.

1. We focus here on events that are firm specific, so these probabilities are related to firm-specific outcomes that may or may not have a relationship with other firms.
2. A zero variance is not always achieved when the correlation coefficient is −1. The achieved variance depends on the investment proportions selected; see the discussion that follows.

EXHIBIT 8–3   The Gain from Diversification

(a) The Return on Two Assets

	Asset A		Asset B	
	Rate of Return	Probability	Rate of Return	Probability
	+0.20	½	+0.20	½
	−0.10	½	−0.10	½
Expected return	0.05		0.05	
Variance	0.0225		0.0225	
Standard deviation	0.15		0.15	

(b) The Rate of Return on a Portfolio Composed of ½A and ½B under Various Correlations

	Correlation = +1		Correlation = 0		Correlation = −1	
	Rate of Return	Probability	Rate of Return	Probability	Rate of Return	Probability
	0.20	½	0.20	¼	0.05	1
	−0.10	½	0.05	½		
			−0.10	¼		
Portfolio mean	0.05		0.05		0.05	
Portfolio variance	0.0225[a]		0.01125[b]		0	
Standard deviation	0.15		0.106		0	

a. $\frac{1}{2}(0.20 - 0.05)^2 + \frac{1}{2}(-0.10 - 0.05)^2 = 0.0225$.

b. $\frac{1}{4}(0.20 - 0.05)^2 + \frac{1}{2}(0.05 - 0.05)^2 + \frac{1}{4}(-0.10 - 0.05)^2 = 0.01125$.

8.1.1 The Investment Weights That Guarantee a Certain Return on the Portfolio—When the Correlation Is $\rho = -1$

Exhibit 8-4 demonstrates a perfect negative correlation of two assets, A and B. Suppose we have stock price data for several years and find that the stock price behavior is described by the two lines in Exhibit 8-4 (which represent the movement of the prices of Stocks A and B). As Figure 8-4 shows, whenever the stock price of A goes up, the stock price of B goes down, and vice versa. Hence, by putting half of the invested wealth in Asset A and half in Asset B, we have a portfolio with perfect stability. This portfolio has a *risk-free return*. The following discussion examines how to determine the weights in each asset that provide a risk-free return when two assets are perfectly negatively correlated.[3]

3. Admittedly, the idea that there would be two securities that were perfectly negatively correlated is very unrealistic. However, this extreme case illustrates concepts that will be used in the more realistic cases later.

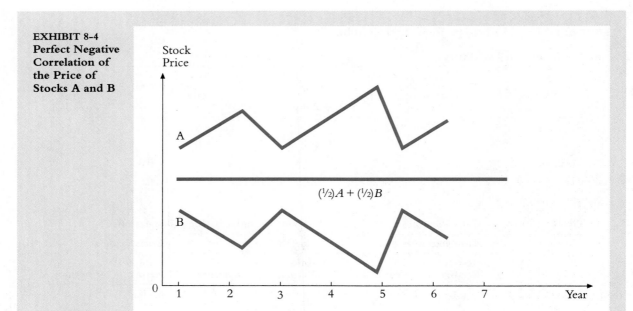

EXHIBIT 8-4
Perfect Negative Correlation of the Price of Stocks A and B

Exhibit 8-4 shows that a portfolio with equal weights guarantees a portfolio with a certain rate of return. This result occurs because in this specific example, Assets A and B are mirror images of each other. If an investor elects not to invest an equal proportion in these two stocks, however, the variance will not equal zero even when $\rho = -1$ (see the Practice Box).

PRACTICE BOX

Problem

How will the portfolio mean and variance change in Exhibit 8-3b when the correlation is -1 and the weight invested in Asset A is $\frac{1}{3}$ and in Asset B is $\frac{2}{3}$?

Solution

In this case, when $+0.20$ is the outcome for A, -0.10 is the outcome for B, and the rate of return is

$$R_p = w_A R_A + w_B R_B = \frac{1}{3}(0.20) + \frac{2}{3}(-0.10) = 0.0$$

and when -0.1 is the outcome for A, $+0.20$ is the outcome for B and the rate of return is

$$R_p = w_A R_A + w_B R_B = \frac{1}{3}(-0.10) + \frac{2}{3}(0.20) \cong 0.10$$

(continued)

Both of these outcomes are equally likely; hence, the expected rate of return is

$$E(R_p) = \tfrac{1}{2}(0.0) + \tfrac{1}{2}(0.10) = 0.05$$

and the variance is

$$\sigma_p^2 = \tfrac{1}{2}(0.0 - 0.05)^2 + \tfrac{1}{2}(0.167 - 0.05)^2 = 0.0025$$

Thus, just because there is a correlation of -1, it does not mean that the portfolio's variance is zero (see the next section).

Let us generalize the case where a portfolio variance equal to zero can be achieved when the correlation coefficient is -1. In general, it is possible to have a correlation coefficient of -1 when two assets do not behave exactly as mirror images of each other. In this case, an investor can still construct a portfolio with an absolutely certain rate of return, but the invested weights that achieve this absolutely certain return are not given by $w_A = w_B = \tfrac{1}{2}$.

Let us solve for the investment weights that achieve an absolutely certain return on the portfolio when $\rho_{A,B} = -1$. In general, the portfolio variance is

$$\sigma_p^2 = w_A^2\sigma_A^2 + w_B^2\sigma_B^2 + 2w_Aw_B\rho_{A,B}\sigma_A\sigma_B$$

If there is a perfect negative correlation, we can substitute -1 for $\rho_{A,B}$ to get

$$\sigma_p^2 = w_A^2\sigma_A^2 + w_B^2\sigma_B^2 - 2w_Aw_B\sigma_A\sigma_B$$

which can be rewritten as follows:[4]

$$\sigma_p^2 = (w_A\sigma_A - w_B\sigma_B)^2$$

Therefore, if $w_A\sigma_A = w_B\sigma_B$, the portfolio variance is $\sigma_p^2 = 0$, which implies no variability of the portfolio's return; in other words, the portfolio yields a certain return. For example, if $\sigma_A = 10\%$, $\sigma_B = 20\%$, then we have to choose weights w_A and w_B such that the following holds:

$$w_A(0.1) = w_B(0.2)$$

or

$$\frac{w_A}{w_B} = \frac{0.2}{0.1} = \frac{2}{1} = 2 \text{ or } w_A = 2w_B$$

Because $w_A + w_B = 1$ by definition, we have (by substituting $2w_B$ for w_A) $2w_B + w_B = 1$, or $3w_B = 1$, and $w_B = \tfrac{1}{3}$. Hence, if we invest $\tfrac{1}{3}$ in Asset B and $\tfrac{2}{3}$ in Asset A, we achieve a portfolio with zero risk. Note, as intuition tells us, that less than 50% is invested in the asset with the relatively large variance. Obviously, if $\sigma_A = \sigma_B$, weights of $w_A = w_B = \tfrac{1}{2}$ will bring the portfolio's variance to zero.

Exhibit 8–5 shows the rates of return on two assets whose correlation is -1. In State 1, the return on Asset A is low (zero), but on Asset B it is high; the opposite

---

4. Denote $w_A\sigma_A = a$ and $w_B\sigma_B = b$, and use the formula $(a - b)^2 = a^2 + b^2 - 2ab$.

| EXHIBIT 8-5 | The Investment Weights That Yield a Certain Return on a Portfolio When Correlation Is -1 | | | |

State of the World	Probability	Rate of Return on Asset A	Rate of Return on Asset B	Rate of Return on Portfolio $\frac{3}{4}A + \frac{1}{4}B$
1	½	0	0.30	0.075
2	½	0.10	0	0.075
Expected rate of return		0.05	0.15	0.075
Variance		0.0025	0.0225	0
Standard deviation		0.05	0.15	0

holds for State 2. Assume that the probability of each state occurring is ½. We can easily calculate the mean, variance, and standard deviation of the return on each asset. Because $\sigma_A = 5$ and $\sigma_B = 15$, the weights that bring the portfolio variance to zero are

$$\frac{w_A}{w_B} = \frac{\sigma_B}{\sigma_A} = \frac{0.15}{0.05} = 3$$

Therefore, $w_A = 3w_B$, and because $w_A + w_B = 1$, we get $3w_B + w_B = 4w_B = 1$. Hence, $w_B = \frac{1}{4}$, and $w_A = \frac{3}{4}$. Indeed, with these weights, we get portfolio returns of 7.5% in each state (see Exhibit 8-5):

$$\text{State 1: } \tfrac{3}{4}(0.0) + \tfrac{1}{4}(0.30) = 0.075, \text{ or } 7.5\%$$

$$\text{State 2: } \tfrac{3}{4}(0.10) + \tfrac{1}{4}(0.0) = 0.075, \text{ or } 7.5\%$$

No matter which state occurs, the investor receives a certain return on the portfolio.

Assets A and B are risky when the mean and variance of Asset B are higher than those of Asset A. By diversifying ¾ in Asset A and ¼ in Asset B, a Portfolio p is achieved with zero variance and an expected value of 7.5%. If we select other weights (for example, $w_A = \frac{1}{2}$ and $w_B = \frac{1}{2}$), we get another portfolio with the following rates of return:

$$\text{State 1: } \tfrac{1}{2}(0.0) + \tfrac{1}{2}(0.30) = 0.15, \text{ or } 15\%$$

$$\text{State 2: } \tfrac{1}{2}(0.10) + \tfrac{1}{2}(0.0) = 0.05, \text{ or } 5\%$$

The portfolio expected return is

$$\tfrac{1}{2}(0.15) + \tfrac{1}{2}(0.05) = 0.10, \text{ or } 10\%$$

and the portfolio variance is

$$\tfrac{1}{2}(0.15 - 0.10)^2 + \tfrac{1}{2}(0.05 - 0.10)^2 = 0.0025$$

and the standard deviation is 0.05, or 5%. This is labeled by point p' in Exhibit 8-6. Any other diversification strategy like point p' leads to a portfolio with a nonzero

**EXHIBIT 8-6
Risk and
Expected
Return for
Various
Combinations
of a Two-Stock
Portfolio with
a Correlation
of −1**

B denotes Asset
B, *A* denotes
Asset A,
p denotes the
zero variance
portfolio, and
p′ denotes a
portfolio of *A*
and *B* with the
same standard
deviation as *A*.

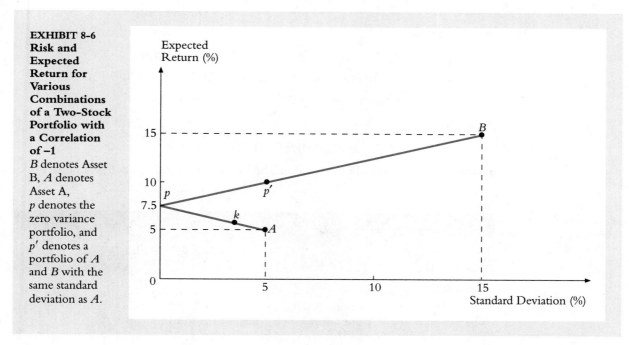

variance. Therefore, we conclude that when the correlation is −1, there is only *one* strategy with particular weights (in the example, ¾ and ¼) that yield a portfolio with a certain return and no risk.[5]

Finally, if the correlation were neither +1 nor −1 but rather $-1 < \rho < +1$, a curve would replace the straight lines in Exhibit 8-6. This case will be discussed later in this chapter.

PRACTICE BOX

Problem

Using the data in Exhibit 8-5, calculate the expected rate of return and variance of a portfolio composed of $w_A = {}^9\!/_{10}$ and $w_B = {}^1\!/_{10}$. Where would this portfolio be located on the graph given in Exhibit 8-6? (Recall that the correlation is −1.)

Solution

The expected rate of return is

$$E(R_p) = {}^9\!/_{10}(0.05) + {}^1\!/_{10}(0.15) = 0.06, \text{ or } 6\%$$

(continued)

---

5. Note that we put the standard deviation, not the variance, on the horizontal axis. If we put the variance on the horizontal axis, we would not get the straight lines. However, we still get the variance of the portfolio as zero for $w_A = {}^3\!/_4$ and $w_B = {}^1\!/_4$.

and the variance is

$$\sigma_p^2 = w_A^2 \sigma_A^2 + (1 - w_A)^2 \sigma_B^2 + 2w_A(1 - w_A)\rho_{A,B}\sigma_A\sigma_B$$

$$= 0.9^2(0.0025) + 0.1^2(0.0225) - 2(0.9)(0.1)(0.05)(0.15)$$

$$= 0.002025 + 0.000225 - 0.00135 = 0.0009$$

Thus, the standard deviation is

$$\sigma_p = (0.0009)^{1/2} = 0.03, \text{ or } 3\%$$

and this portfolio would be located on the lower line of Exhibit 8-6 (see point k).

CONNECTING THEORY TO PRACTICE 8.1

HOW TO BUILD A STOCK PORTFOLIO EVEN IF YOU AREN'T A MONEYBAGS—CONTINUED

You don't need a mountain of cash to buy individual stocks.

Would-be investors are often told that unless they have more than $100,000 to put into stocks, they should stick with mutual funds.

"People espousing this are worried that you won't get enough diversification and that transaction costs on small portfolios are too high," says Arthur Micheletti, chief economist at Bailard, Biehl & Kaiser, a money-management firm in San Mateo, Calif.

But he and other investment advisers and portfolio managers say individuals can build an adequately diversified, high quality portfolio of individual stocks with as little as $25,000.

People who buy even as few as 10 stocks can be adequately diversified, if they buy securities in different industries and use a variety of selection criteria. And they can keep transaction costs low by buying round lots, using discount brokers and keeping trading to a minimum.

How do you build a small portfolio?

First consider the number of stocks needed. Academic research on diversification suggests that individuals need 10 to 20 securities. "So if you assume an average stock price of $20, you could buy 15 stocks in round lots of 100 shares for $30,000," says Elliot Lipson, president of Horizon Financial Advisors.

ONE INVESTMENT ADVISER'S MODEL PORTFOLIO

Elliot Lipson, president of Horizon Financial Advisors, illustrates how a small portfolio of stocks can achieve a lot of diversification, if the stocks come from industries that respond differently to economic and other factors.[a]   *(continued)*

a. Buying 100 shares of each stock would cost about $33,000. For added diversification, Mr. Lipson would put $5,000 into each of two mutual funds: Vanguard Explorer, a small-stock fund, and Harbor International, a fund that buys stocks of companies outside the United States.

Stock	Industry
PepsiCo	Beverage
Bird Corp.	Bldg. Materials
Turner "B"	Broadcasting
Bear Stearns	Brokerage
Everex Systems	Computer
Groundwater Tech.	Environmental
Humana	Hospital
American Bankers Insurance Group	Insurance
Asarca	Metals, misc.
Petroleum & Resources	Oil
United Dominion Realty	Real Estate
GTE	Telephone
Casey's General Stores	Retail Grocery
UST Inc.	Tobacco
Gleason	Tools

Source: Ellen E. Schultz, "How to Build a Stock Portfolio Even If You Aren't a Moneybags," *The Wall Street Journal,* April 10, 1992, p. C1. Reprinted by permission of *The Wall Street Journal,* © 1992 Dow Jones & Co., Inc. All Rights Reserved Worldwide.

MAKING THE CONNECTION

Small investors can diversify adequately by carefully selecting stocks that are not highly correlated, asserts Elliot Lipson, president of Horizon Financial Advisors. He recommends picking stocks from unrelated industries. Lipson is clearly basing his opinion on the benefits of diversification.

Lipson also considers a portfolio of ten to fifteen stocks adequate. However, most professional money managers are widely diversified.

8.1.2 The Effect of the Number of Assets in a Portfolio on Risk Reduction

One decision a portfolio manager must make is how many stocks to buy in order to achieve a high level of return with adequate diversification. Connecting Theory to Practice 8.1 illustrates the problem. It suggests that ten to fifteen stocks are sufficient for investors to achieve the benefits of diversification. In contrast, the Fidelity Magellan mutual fund, as of the third quarter 1997, invested in 489 different stocks.[6] Do investors need to own 489 stocks, or are ten to fifteen sufficient? The answer depends on several factors.

6. Information provided by Fidelity; telephone 800-544-8888. Fidelity's Magellan mutual fund managed $53.8 billion as of February 28, 1997.

From the standpoint of reducing risk, in general, the more assets there are in a portfolio, the better off the investor is. To see this, consider three identical securities, A, B, and C (see Exhibit 8–7). Assume that the rates of return of the three assets are unrelated; namely, their correlation is zero. On the right side of the exhibit are the returns on two portfolios, one composed of only two assets (A and B) and one composed of three assets (A, B, and C). Notice that although the means of the assets, as well as the means of the two portfolios, are identical, the variances of the portfolios are smaller than the variances of the individual securities. Also, the variance of the portfolio with three assets is smaller than the variance of the portfolio with two assets.

Let us look more closely at the probable returns of the two portfolios. First, remember that the rates of return are assumed to be independent (correlation $\rho_{i,j} = 0$). The portfolio composed of Assets A and B ($\frac{1}{2}A + \frac{1}{2}B$) has four possible combinations: a 2% return on both Asset A and Asset B, a 4% return on both Asset A and Asset B, a 2% return on Asset A and a 4% return on Asset B, and a 4% return on Asset A and a 2% return on Asset B. The probabilities of the first two combinations are each $\frac{1}{4}$, with a 2% return on the first combination and a 4% return on the second. The probabilities of the second two combinations are also each $\frac{1}{4}$, but because the combinations are in effect identical (2% and 4% or 4% and 2%), the probability of a 3% return [$\frac{1}{2}(2\%) + \frac{1}{2}(4\%)$] is $\frac{1}{2}$.

In contrast, the portfolio composed of the three assets ($\frac{1}{3}A + \frac{1}{3}B + \frac{1}{3}C$) has eight possible asset combinations, each with a probability of $\frac{1}{8}$. The combinations and their respective returns follow:

EXHIBIT 8–7   **Rates of Return on Three Independent Assets and on Two Portfolios**

Assets						Portfolios			
A		**B**		**C**		$\frac{1}{2}A+\frac{1}{2}B$		$\frac{1}{3}A+\frac{1}{3}B+\frac{1}{3}C$	
Rate of Return	Proba-bility	Rate of Return	Proba-bility	Rate of Return	Proba-bility	Rate of Return	Proba-bility	Rate of Return	Proba-bility
0.02	$\frac{1}{2}$	0.02	$\frac{1}{2}$	0.02	$\frac{1}{2}$	0.02	$\frac{1}{4}$	0.02	$\frac{1}{8}$
0.04	$\frac{1}{2}$	0.04	$\frac{1}{2}$	0.04	$\frac{1}{2}$	0.03	$\frac{1}{2}$	0.0267	$\frac{3}{8}$
						0.04	$\frac{1}{4}$	0.0333	$\frac{3}{8}$
								0.04	$\frac{1}{8}$
$E(R)$ 0.03		0.03		0.03		0.03		0.03	
σ_p^2 0.0001		0.0001		0.0001		0.00005[a]		0.00003[b]	

a. $\sigma_p^2 = \frac{1}{4}(0.02 - 0.03)^2 + \frac{1}{2}(0.03 - 0.03)^2 + \frac{1}{4}(0.04 - 0.03)^2 \cong 0.00005$.

b. $\sigma_p^2 = \frac{1}{8}(0.02 - 0.03)^2 + \frac{3}{8}(0.0267 - 0.03)^2 + \frac{3}{8}(0.0333 - 0.03)^2 + \frac{1}{8}(0.04 - 0.03)^2 \cong 0.00003$.

Portfolio Return

Asset A	Asset B	Asset C	$\frac{1}{3}A + \frac{1}{3}B + \frac{1}{3}C$	Probability
2	2	2	2	$\frac{1}{8}$
2	2	4	$2\frac{2}{3}$	$\frac{1}{8}$
2	4	2	$2\frac{2}{3}$	$\frac{1}{8}$
2	4	4	$3\frac{1}{3}$	$\frac{1}{8}$
4	2	2	$2\frac{2}{3}$	$\frac{1}{8}$
4	2	4	$3\frac{1}{3}$	$\frac{1}{8}$
4	4	2	$3\frac{1}{3}$	$\frac{1}{8}$
4	4	4	4	$\frac{1}{8}$

Because the return of $2\frac{2}{3}$ appears three times with a probability of $\frac{1}{8}$, the probability of getting $2\frac{2}{3}\%$ is $\frac{3}{8}$ ($\frac{1}{8} + \frac{1}{8} + \frac{1}{8}$) as given in Exhibit 8-7. The same is true regarding the return of $3\frac{1}{3}$. As can be seen from Exhibit 8-7, the variance of the return of a portfolio composed of the three assets is $\frac{1}{3}$ of the asset variance, and the variance on a portfolio composed of two assets is $\frac{1}{2}$ of the asset variance. Thus, Exhibit 8-7, demonstrates the common wisdom asserting that the larger the number of assets in a portfolio, the smaller the portfolio's variance.

The calculation of the portfolio variance can be verified by employing Equation 7.11' from Chapter 7 with $\rho_{i,j} = 0$ (which means also that $\sigma_{i,j} = 0$ for $i \neq j$). This calculation gives us, once again, the opportunity to verify the portfolio variance formula. For the two-asset portfolio, we have $\sigma_p^2 = (\frac{1}{2})^2 0.0001 + (\frac{1}{2})^2 0.0001 = 0.00005$. For the three-asset portfolio, we have $\sigma_p^2 = (\frac{1}{3})^2 0.0001 + (\frac{1}{3})^2 0.0001 + (\frac{1}{3})^2 0.0001 \cong 0.00003$, exactly as was obtained with the direct calculation in Exhibit 8-7.

In general, when there are n independent assets, all with the same mean $E(R_j) = E(R_i)$ and the same variance $\sigma_j^2 = \sigma_i^2$,[7] the best strategy is to invest $\frac{1}{n}$ in each of the n available assets. Because all assets have the same mean and variance, there is no reason to prefer one asset over the other. If all assets are independent, all correlations are zero. Hence, the portfolio variance is

$$\sigma_p^2 = w_1^2 \sigma_1^2 + w_2^2 \sigma_2^2 + \ldots + w_n^2 \sigma_n^2$$

With equal weight $w_i = \frac{1}{n}$ invested in each asset, the portfolio's variance can be rewritten as

$$\sigma_p^2 = \left(\frac{1}{n}\right)^2 \sigma_o^2 + \left(\frac{1}{n}\right)^2 \sigma_o^2 + \ldots + \left(\frac{1}{n}\right)^2 \sigma_o^2 = \frac{n}{n^2} \sigma_o^2 = \sigma_o^2/n$$

where $\frac{1}{n}$ is the weight invested in each asset, and σ_o^2 is the variance of each individual asset.

In the example given in Exhibit 8-7, $\sigma_o^2 = 0.0001$ (for each Asset, A, B, and C). Indeed, for a portfolio with two assets ($n = 2$), $\sigma_p^2 = 0.00005$, and for a portfolio composed of three assets ($n = 3$), $\sigma_p^2 = 0.00003$, as the previous formula suggests. When the number of assets becomes very large, the variance approaches zero.

7. $\sigma_i = \sigma_j$ for all assets $i, j, i \neq j$.

Exhibit 8-8 demonstrates the effect of diversification on a portfolio's mean and variance when all individual assets have the same expected return (10%) and variance (1) and they are statistically independent. Assuming the same mean for all securities allows a focus on portfolio variance. Point p_1 represents a portfolio that includes only one asset ($n = 1$). Point p_2 represents a portfolio composed of two assets, and p_3 represents a portfolio composed of three assets. Note that point p_2 is half the variance of point p_1, and point p_3 is one-third the variance of point p_1. Although the portfolio variance continues to approach zero as n becomes larger, most of the portfolio's variance reduction is achieved with a relatively small n. The magnitude of the reduction in the portfolio's variance as a function of the number of assets included in the portfolio is discussed in the next section.

8.1.3 A Little Diversification Goes a Long Way

Unlike the three stocks in Exhibit 8-7, actual stocks rarely have identical variance. However, the principle of achieving gains from diversification still holds even when the variances differ across assets, and even when the assets are not independent. In general, the greater the number of assets in a portfolio, the lower the portfolio's variance. However, as the number of assets increases, the incremental contribution to the reduction in the portfolio's variance becomes smaller and smaller. The greatest gain is achieved by diversifying in a relatively few assets—as is often said, a little diversification goes a long way.

Exhibit 8-9 illustrates a portfolio's variance reduction that is due to an increase in the number of assets in the portfolio (assuming zero correlations). We assume that

**EXHIBIT 8-8
Effect of
Diversification
on a
Portfolio's
Variance
(individual
assets are
identical and
statistically
independent)**

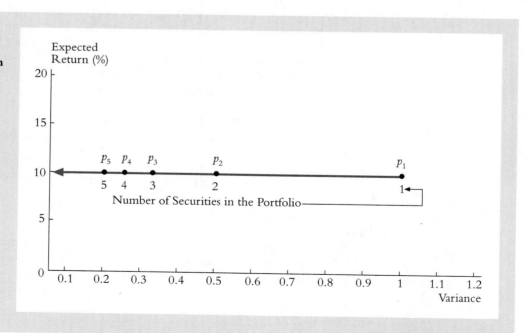

$\sigma_o^2 = 100$ for all assets. For $n = 1$, $\sigma_o^2 = 100$; for $n = 2$, the variance is $\sigma_o^2/2 = 50$, a reduction of 50. The increase in the number of assets from two to three, however, reduces the variance only from $^{100}\!/_2$ to $^{100}\!/_3$, a reduction of $16\frac{2}{3}$. The increase in the number of assets from three to four results in a reduction in the variance of $8\frac{1}{3}$. An increase in the number of assets from four to five further reduces the variance, but only by 5. The effect of increasing the number of assets from one to two is ten times greater than the effect of increasing the number of assets from four to five. With a larger number of assets, the marginal reduction in the variance is minimal. Most of the gain is achieved by diversifying in a relatively small number of assets.

When assets are correlated and the correlation is not as extreme as $+1$ or -1 (instead, a correlation of about 0.3 to 0.5, which is typical for many stocks in the U.S. market), it can be shown that about 90% of the maximum potential benefit of the risk reduction is achieved with a portfolio composed of twelve to eighteen stocks. This is a dramatically small number of stocks, considering that the financial markets in the U.S. trade several thousand stocks. The NYSE alone, for example, lists over 2,900 stocks.[8]

These findings are very important in portfolio management, especially for small investors. Suppose you have $100,000 to invest. Investing in all available stocks would yield the lowest possible portfolio variance. However, to diversify $100,000 in several thousand stocks is impossible, because the transaction costs would be prohibitively high.[9] Thus, financial experts are correct in saying that an investor can reap most of the gain of risk reduction by investing in about ten stocks.

Given this conclusion, why is the Fidelity Magellan fund holding 489 stocks? The following two reasons can be given. First, even though the benefit from including more assets in the portfolio diminishes, it is still positive, and there is some gain.

EXHIBIT 8-9 Portfolio Variance as a Function of the Number of Assets When All Assets Are Independent	Number of Assets in the Portfolio	Portfolio Variance $\sigma_p^2 = \sigma_o^2/n(\sigma_o^2 = 100)$		Marginal Reduction in the Variance
	1		100	—
	2	$^{100}\!/_2 =$	50	50
	3	$^{100}\!/_3 =$	$33\frac{1}{3}$	$16\frac{2}{3}$
	4	$^{100}\!/_4 =$	25	$8\frac{1}{3}$
	5	$^{100}\!/_5 =$	20	5
	10	$^{100}\!/_{10} =$	10	1.11
	20	$^{100}\!/_{20} =$	5	0.263
	50	$^{100}\!/_{50} =$	2	0.041
	100	$^{100}\!/_{100} =$	1	0.010

8. See *New York Stock Exchange Fact Book for the Year 1996,* New York Stock Exchange Inc., New York.

9. This strategy would require owning odd lots, which are much more expensive to trade. Also, transaction costs are inversely related to trade size, even for round lots.

An individual investor who faces large transaction costs cannot study thousands of firms. For Fidelity Magellan, however, the cost of data and information collection per \$1 invested is so small that it is still worthwhile to increase the number of assets in the portfolio and enjoy the little ensuing benefit from risk reduction. Thus, whereas small investors may stop at five or ten stocks, large investors may stop at a much larger number of assets in their portfolios. Second, Fidelity Magellan, with billions of dollars in assets, cannot concentrate in only a few stocks, because the fund's buying and selling would greatly affect those stocks. For example, buying 200,000 shares of a stock that typically has a daily trading volume of only 5,000 shares would exert upward price pressure on the stock. To avoid this, the company must diversify in many stocks.[10]

PRACTICE BOX

Problem

Suppose a mutual fund holds 100 stocks in equal proportions. All stocks are independent, and each stock has a standard deviation of 30%. What is the standard deviation of the mutual fund portfolio?

Solution

Because the stocks are independent and have the same standard deviations (σ_o), we know that

$$\sigma_p^2 = \left(\frac{1}{n}\right)^2 \sigma_o^2 + \left(\frac{1}{n}\right)^2 \sigma_o^2 + \ldots + \left(\frac{1}{n}\right)^2 \sigma_o^2 = \frac{n}{n^2} \sigma_o^2 = \sigma_o^2/n$$

Because $\sigma_o = 0.3$ and $\sigma_o^2 = 0.3^2$, the variance of the portfolio is

$$\sigma_p^2 = \frac{0.3^2}{100} = 0.0009$$

and the standard deviation is the square root of 0.0009, or 0.03 (3%).

8.2 EFFICIENT AND INEFFICIENT INVESTMENT STRATEGIES

So far this discussion of risk reduction has assumed that the expected returns of all available assets are the same. This assumption allowed us to focus on the impact of diversification on the portfolio's variance. The larger the number of assets in the portfolio and the lower their correlations, the smaller the portfolio's risk. In practice, however, it is very rare to have identical expected returns on all individual assets in a portfolio. The analysis changes with assets that have different expected returns and different variances. As will be discussed later, the analysis must include the trade-off between risk and expected return of various portfolios. Recall that by changing the portfolio weights, the portfolio manager may change both the mean and variance of the portfolio. After all

---

10. Mutual funds are required by Regulation M of the Internal Revenue Service not to own more than 5% of any company's stock. Clearly, this requirement influences billion-dollar funds such as Fidelity Magellan. For more information, see Chapter 14.

possible portfolio combinations have been checked and investment weights changed, some portfolios will be more appealing than others. Within the set of all possible investment strategies, the set of strategies with the smallest variance for a given mean is called the **mean-variance frontier** (also known as the **mean-variance set**).

The mean-variance frontier can be divided into an efficient frontier and an inefficient frontier. To introduce these concepts, this section first considers portfolios composed of two assets and then extends the discussion to portfolios composed of n assets.

8.2.1 Efficient and Inefficient Frontiers in the Two-Asset Case

Suppose that you have two portfolios, 1 and 2. If Portfolio 1 has a higher mean and smaller variance than Portfolio 2, we say that Portfolio 1 *dominates* Portfolio 2, and that Portfolio 2 is thus **inefficient.** A portfolio that is not dominated by *any* other portfolio is called an **efficient portfolio.**

These concepts can be demonstrated by the example given in Exhibit 8-10. This exhibit shows the means and variances of two assets, A and B, whose correlation is assumed to be zero. As the exhibit shows, by decreasing the proportion invested in the asset with the lowest expected return (Asset A), the portfolio's expected return increases.

EXHIBIT 8-10	**(a) The Two Assets**		
Efficient- and Inefficient- Frontier Zero- Correlation		**Asset A**	**Asset B**
	Mean return	10%	20%
	Variance	10%	15%

(b) Efficient and Inefficient Strategies

w_A	w_B	Mean[a]	Strategy Variance[b]	Is the Portfolio Efficient?
1	0	10	10	No
0.9	0.1	11	8.25	No
0.8	0.2	12	7	No
0.7	0.3	13	6.25	No
0.6	0.4	14	6 MPV	Yes
0.5	0.5	15	6.25	Yes
0.4	0.6	16	7	Yes
0.3	0.7	17	8.25	Yes
0.2	0.8	18	10	Yes
0.1	0.9	19	12.25	Yes
0	1	20	15	Yes

a. $E(R_p) = w_A(10) + (1 - w_A)20$.

b. Because $\rho_{A,B} = 0$, we have $\sigma_p^2 = w_A^2 10 + (1 - w_A)^2 15$.

This result is obvious, because one invests a higher proportion in the asset with the higher expected return (Asset B). Thus, the effect of a reduction in w_A on the portfolio's mean is unambiguous: the higher the proportion invested in Asset B, the higher the expected return on the portfolio. In the extreme case where $w_A = 0$ and $w_B = 1$, the portfolio's mean return is 20%, because the portfolio is composed of Asset B alone.

The variance column does not show such unambiguous results. The portfolio variance first decreases as w_A decreases (and w_B increases); it reaches its minimum at proportion $w_A = 0.60$, and then it starts to increase. The portfolio corresponding to $w_A = 0.60$ is called the **minimum variance portfolio, or MVP**. The MVP is the portfolio with the smallest variance from the mean-variance frontier. The relationship between the portfolio's variance and the investment proportion is quite general, bending toward the vertical axis (apart from the extreme case of $\rho_{A,B} = +1$).

What is the implication for portfolio management? The most important conclusion is that not all diversification strategies are desirable (that is, some are inefficient). In Exhibit 8-10, all investment strategies with $w_A > 0.60$ are undesirable, because they have both lower expected returns and higher variances. They are all considered inefficient investment strategies because at least one portfolio exists that will provide a higher expected return with the same variance.

Exhibit 8-11 shows the results of Exhibit 8-10 graphically. The curve AB describes the expected returns and standard deviations of portfolios composed of various combinations of Assets A and B, where point B corresponds to 100% investment in Asset B and point A corresponds to 100% investment in Asset A. As the investment proportion in Asset A decreases, the portfolio mean is always increasing. The variance, however, decreases only up to point MVP, and then it starts increasing. It

**EXHIBIT 8-11
Portfolio
Combinations of
Two Securities**
The solid line
represents the
efficient frontier,
the dashed line
represents the
inefficient frontier.
p' and p'' are
portfolios on the
efficient frontiers,
and p is a portfolio
on the inefficient
frontier with the
same variance
as p'.

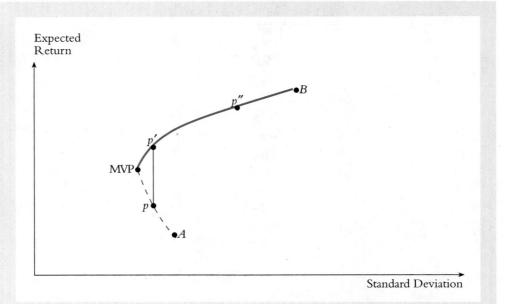

is obvious from this graph that no investor would select portfolios from the segment below point MVP, because for each portfolio on this segment, there is at least one portfolio taken from the segment above point MVP that will offer a higher expected return. For example, consider Portfolio p: Portfolio p' dominates Portfolio p, because it has a higher portfolio mean and the same variance.

Although AB is the mean-variance frontier, only a portion of it is the efficient frontier. The segment below point MVP is called the **inefficient frontier,** which corresponds to inefficient investment strategies. That is, there is a portfolio on the segment above point MVP that yields a higher expected return, hence making portfolios on the segment below point MVP inefficient. The segment above point MVP is called the **efficient frontier,** and it corresponds to efficient investment strategies. Any investment strategy taken from the segment above point MVP may be selected by some investors, because there is no other portfolio that dominates it. For example, compare p' with p''. Portfolio p'' has a higher mean and a higher variance than Portfolio p'; hence, neither p' nor p'' dominates the other. The same holds for all portfolios on the segment above point MVP.

It is common to represent (or draw) the efficient segment of the curve with a solid line and the inefficient segment with a dashed line, reminding the reader that no investor would select portfolios from the dashed segment. For every portfolio on the dashed line, there is another available portfolio with the same standard deviation and a higher mean (represented by the solid line above the dashed line). It is interesting to note that a portfolio composed of 100% of the asset with the highest mean and highest variance (Asset B) is efficient, whereas a portfolio composed of 100% of the asset with the lowest mean and lowest variance is inefficient.

8.2.2 Two Assets with Different Correlations

This section examines how the correlation coefficient influences the mean-variance frontier for the two-asset case. Exhibit 8-12 is the same as Exhibit 8-10 except that it compares four different correlations of Assets A and B: $\rho_{A,B} = -1, -\frac{1}{2}, +\frac{1}{2},$ and $+1$, respectively. The results for $\rho_{A,B} = -\frac{1}{2}$ and $\rho_{A,B} = \frac{1}{2}$ are very similar to the case of $\rho_{A,B} = 0$. The only difference is that the gain from diversification is smaller for $\rho_{A,B} = +\frac{1}{2}$ than for $\rho_{A,B} = 0$, and it is larger when $\rho_{A,B} = -\frac{1}{2}$. For example, in a portfolio with a mean of 12%, when $\rho_{A,B} = -\frac{1}{2}$ the variance is 5.04, and when $\rho_{A,B} = +\frac{1}{2}$ the variance is 8.96, whereas when $\rho_{A,B} = 0$ the variance is 7. In general, the higher the value of $\rho_{A,B}$, the smaller the gain from diversification.

Exhibit 8-13 uses the results of Exhibits 8-10 and 8-12 to demonstrate the effect of the prevailing correlation on the efficient and inefficient segments. For $\rho_{A,B} = +1$, the efficient frontier is a straight line, AB. All investment strategies lying on this line are efficient. For correlation $\rho_{A,B} = -1$, the line from B to point MVP is the set of all efficient investment strategies, and the line from MVP to A is the inefficient set. The two straight lines touch the vertical axis, which implies that for some investment proportions, a perfectly stable portfolio (zero variance) can be achieved. Any correlation between -1 and $+1$ yields the same general results as the correlation $\rho_{A,B} = 0$ case. However, as the correlation declines, the curve bulges to the left, which implies larger risk reduction because of diversification.

EXHIBIT 8-12   **Two-Asset Portfolio Mean and Variance for Various Levels of Correlation**

(a) Basic Inputs—The Assets' Mean and Variance

	Asset A	Asset B
Mean return	10%	20%
Variance	10%	15%

(b) Portfolio Mean[a] and Variance[b] for Various Weights and Asset Correlations

Invested Weights		Correlation $\rho = -1$		Correlation $\rho = -\frac{1}{2}$		Correlation $\rho = +\frac{1}{2}$		Correlation $\rho = +1$	
w_A	$w_B = 1-w_A$	Mean	Variance	Mean	Variance	Mean	Variance	Mean	Variance
1	0	10.0	10	10.0	10	10.0	10	10.0	10
0.9	0.1	11.0	6.05	11.0	7.15	11.0	9.35	11.0	10.45
0.8	0.2	12.0	3.08	12.0	5.04	12.0	8.96	12.0	10.92
0.7	0.3	13.0	1.11	13.0	3.68	13.0	8.82	13.0	11.39
0.6	0.4	14.0	0.12	14.0	3.06	14.0	8.94	14.0	11.88
0.55	0.45	14.5	0.00	14.5	3.03	14.5	9.09	14.5	12.12
0.5	0.5	15.0	0.13	15.0	3.19	15.0	9.31	15.0	12.37
0.4	0.6	16.0	1.12	16.0	4.06	16.0	9.94	16.0	12.88
0.3	0.7	17.0	3.11	17.0	5.68	17.0	10.82	17.0	13.39
0.2	0.8	18.0	6.08	18.0	8.04	18.0	11.96	18.0	13.92
0.1	0.9	19.0	10.05	19.0	11.15	19.0	13.35	19.0	14.45
0	1	20.0	15	20.0	15	20.0	15	20.0	15

a. The mean is calculated as $E(R) = w_A 10 + (1 - w_A)20$.

b. The variance is calculated as

$$\sigma_p^2 = w_A^2 10 + (1 - w_A)^2 15 + 2w_A(1 - w_A)\rho\sqrt{10}\sqrt{15}$$

where ρ is the assumed correlation and $\sqrt{10}$ and $\sqrt{15}$ are the standard deviations of the two assets, respectively.

8.2.3 Efficient and Inefficient Frontiers with Many Assets

So far the gain from diversification has been demonstrated in the case of n risky assets with the same means and variances and zero correlation, or when a nonzero correlation exists but only two assets are available. Actual portfolio choices are much more complicated: there are more than two assets to choose from, assets do not have the same mean or variance, and nonzero correlations prevail. In actual portfolio choices, we first have to find the mean-variance frontier (or mean-variance set) and then identify the efficient set and the inefficient set.[11]

11. With only two assets, every possible portfolio that could be constructed is a member of the mean-variance frontier.

**EXHIBIT 8-13
The Impact of
Correlation
on Efficient
and Inefficient
Frontiers**

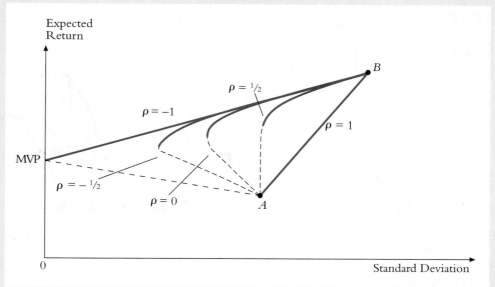

With many assets, an investor may find some investment strategies that are on the mean-variance frontier and some investment strategies that are interior to the frontier—lying to the right of the frontier. Exhibit 8-14 shows five stocks labeled by *A, B, C, D,* and *E*. An investor can benefit by diversifying in any combination of two, three, four, or five of these assets. The graph shows three such diversification strategies, *AB, CD,* and *DE;* all are labeled "2," indicating that two-asset portfolios are created. Of course, there are other two-asset portfolio possibilities (for example, *AE*) that, for simplicity are not shown in the exhibit. Similarly, the curves labeled "3," "4," and "5" stand for three-asset, four-asset, and five-asset portfolios, respectively. There are an infinite number of possible diversification strategies.[12]

Curve 5 in this case, for a given mean rate of return, has the lowest standard deviation when compared with the other curves. Therefore, it is the mean-variance frontier. Note that for any point *p,* there is on curve 5 a point *p'* that yields the same mean return and lower standard deviation. Only part of the *A*-MVP-*E* curve is mean-variance efficient, though. The segment from MVP to *E* of the frontier is mean-variance inefficient, whereas the segment from MVP to *A* is the efficient segment.

Unlike the case with two assets, with many assets other investment strategies are feasible but are not on the mean-variance frontier—for example, point *D;* curves 2, 3, and 4; and so forth. All these strategies are interior to the frontier. Because no investor would choose a portfolio that was interior to the mean-variance frontier, the

12. The more assets considered, the more likely it is that the mean-variance frontier could be improved and shift further to the left.

**EXHIBIT 8-14
The Efficient
and Inefficient
Frontier with
Many Assets**

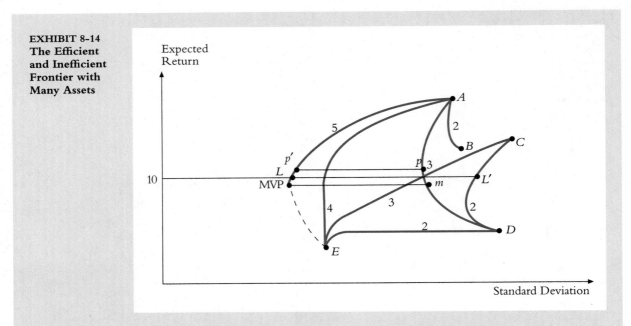

best way to find an optimal portfolio is first to locate the mean-variance frontier and then to identify the efficient and inefficient sets. Appendix 8A explains how to find the frontier with actual data.

8.3 THE GAIN FROM DIVERSIFICATION IN UNRELATED FIRMS IN PRACTICE

So far this chapter has demonstrated that the lower the correlation of the returns on two stocks, the larger the gain from diversification. However, how should we choose these unrelated firms? As a rule of thumb, we should first look for stocks taken from *different* industries, because stocks in the same industry tend to move up and down together (they are highly positively correlated).

Exhibit 8-15 shows the rates of return on two stocks taken from the same industry (Ford and General Motors [GM]—both automobile companies), and Exhibit 8-16 shows the rates of return on two stocks taken from different industries (GM and Upjohn—a pharmaceutical company). As you can see, the correlation between GM and Ford is very high, 0.8, whereas for GM and Upjohn the correlation is negative, −0.3. Thus, one would expect to obtain much greater risk reduction by diversifying in GM and Upjohn. By varying the investment proportions in the stocks, as explained in Section 8.2, we get various portfolios, as shown in Exhibit 8-17.

EXHIBIT 8-15 Summary Statistics for Annual Rates of Return[a] (in %) on Ford and General Motors (GM)	Year	Ford	GM
	1	−11.0	−9.9
	2	132.1	70.7
	3	65.4	24.2
	4	12.9	15.4
	5	34.1	−1.2
	6	51.9	0.2
	7	39.1	−0.6
	8	40.5	45.2
	9	−8.3	8.3
	10	−34.0	−12.7
	Mean	32.3	14.0
	Standard deviation	44.6	25.0
	Correlation	0.8	

a. Note that these are historical rates of return, so the assumed probability of each year is $P_i = 1/m = 1/10$.

EXHIBIT 8-16 Summary Statistics for Annual Rates of Return[a] (in %) on General Motors (GM) and Upjohn	Year	GM	Upjohn
	1	−9.9	−17.5
	2	70.7	−9.5
	3	24.2	33.0
	4	15.4	23.7
	5	−1.2	95.9
	6	0.2	42.3
	7	−0.6	−2.1
	8	45.2	−1.8
	9	8.3	37.8
	10	−12.7	1.3
	Mean	14.0	20.3
	Standard deviation	25.0	32.2
	Correlation	−0.3	

a. Note that these are historical rates of return, so the assumed probability of each year is $P_i = 1/m = 1/10$.

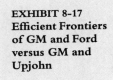

EXHIBIT 8-17
Efficient Frontiers
of GM and Ford
versus GM and
Upjohn

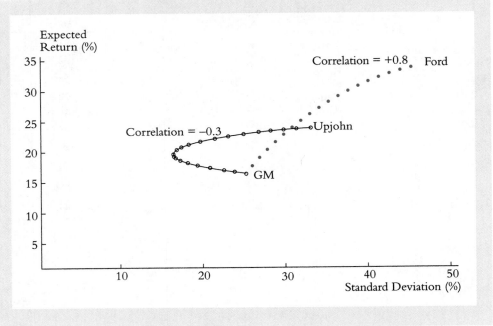

Indeed, the efficient frontier for Ford and GM is almost a straight line, because the correlation between these two stocks is almost perfect (+1). Thus, no meaningful risk reduction can be obtained by diversifying in Ford and GM. However, an investor obtains a substantial risk reduction by diversifying between Upjohn and GM. In this case, the variance of the minimum variance portfolio is much smaller than the variance of each asset separately.

In practice, an investor can begin building a portfolio with stocks from unrelated industries. Historical data analysis can give insight into how different industries and securities are correlated. Clearly, significant risk reduction can be achieved by diversifying across different industries. Chapter 11 examines how international investing can produce further diversification benefits.

SUMMARY

Describe the effect of correlation on the risk-return reduction of a portfolio. Financial planners emphasize the benefits of portfolio diversification. Correlation plays an important role in the risk reduction of a portfolio. Specifically, the lower the correlation, the greater the risk reduction. Expected returns are not influenced by correlation, whereas portfolio variance is.

Explain how the number of assets in a portfolio affects the portfolio's risk. The larger the number of assets in a portfolio, the larger the gain from diversification. However, a little diversification goes a long way. In any case, when managing very large portfolios, even a small amount of risk reduction is very beneficial. Although the debate over how many securities will produce adequate diversification is far from over, it is clear that the level of diversification required depends on how correlated the selected securities are, as well as how large the portfolio is.

Locate the efficient and inefficient investment strategies for a given combination of assets. Efficient and inefficient investment strategies can be examined in a mean-variance context. The mean-variance frontier (or mean-variance set) is the set of portfolios yielding the smallest level of standard deviation (or the least variance) for a given mean rate of return. For each inefficient portfolio, there is one portfolio on the efficient frontier that dominates.

CHAPTER AT A GLANCE

1. The variance of a two-security portfolio is given by the following:

$$\sigma_p^2 = w_A^2 \sigma_A^2 + (1 - w_A)^2 \sigma_B^2 + 2w_A(1 - w_A)\rho_{A,B}\sigma_A\sigma_B$$

2. If the securities have the same variance (σ_o) and are uncorrelated, then the variance of an equally weighted portfolio is given by the following:

$$\sigma_p^2 = \left(\frac{1}{n}\right)^2 \sigma_o^2 + \left(\frac{1}{n}\right)^2 \sigma_o^2 + \ldots + \left(\frac{1}{n}\right)^2 \sigma_o^2 = \frac{n}{n^2}\sigma_o^2 = \sigma_o^2/n$$

KEY TERMS

Inefficient portfolio 267
Efficient portfolio 267
Efficient frontier 269

Inefficient frontier 269
Mean-variance frontier 267
Mean-variance set 267

Minimum variance portfolio
(MVP) 268

REVIEW

8.1 "Diversification across different mutual funds is redundant, because mutual funds are already diversified." Evaluate this statement.

8.2 Consider the two sets of portfolios that can be derived by investing in Assets A and B shown in the following graph.
a. Which line represents the lowest correlation? Why?
b. Is it possible that Line 1 and Line 2 cross? Why or why not? Explain.

8.3 You hear a discussion between an individual investor (with $100,000 to invest) and a money manager (with $10 million to invest). The individual

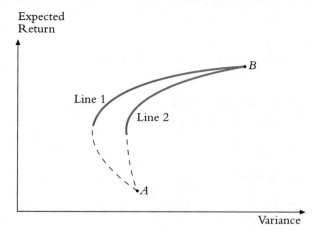

investor claims that investing in five to seven securities is sufficient diversification, whereas the money manager claims that it takes at least one hundred securities to diversify effectively. How do you reconcile these two viewpoints?

8.4 Suppose you are considering investing in one of the following five mutual funds. Rank these mutual funds by the mean-variance rule.

	1	2	3	4	5
Mean	20%	5%	12.5%	15%	6%
Standard deviation	10%	15%	12.5%	10%	3%

8.5 What is the mean-variance frontier, and how is it different from the set of efficient portfolios?

8.6 "You don't want to invest in more than one company in an industry, and you don't want to invest in companies in related industries." Evaluate this statement.

8.7 Suppose you were hired as a consultant for a mutual fund that must invest solely in stocks of an obscure province of western Antarctica. There are one thousand different companies that have traded stocks. It is interesting to note that all one thousand stock prices are strongly correlated with weather conditions. What would you recommend regarding the level of diversification?

8.8 "Investors with less than $100,000 should stick with mutual funds because of diversification benefits." Evaluate this statement.

8.9 "For every portfolio on the efficient frontier, there exists another portfolio on the mean-variance frontier with identical standard deviation, but it is inefficient." Evaluate this statement.

8.10 Suppose we have two securities, A and B. Illustrate graphically the behavior of the efficient frontier as the correlation moves from $+1$ to -1.

PRACTICE

8.1 Calculate the variance of a portfolio that has 15% of its wealth in Stock A with a standard deviation of 10% and the remainder of its wealth in Stock B with a standard deviation of 30%. The correlation coefficient is 0.3.

8.2 Redo Question 8.1, now assuming that the correlation coefficient is 0.2. Explain your results.

8.3 Return to Question 8.1, now assuming that the weight in Asset A is 20%. Explain the difference from your answer to Question 8.1.

8.4 Demonstrate graphically how reducing the correlation decreases the risk related to a portfolio using two perfectly negatively correlated assets with mean of 10%.

8.5 The following shows 11 years of rates of return on Chevron and Mobil, which are energy firms, and on Sears and United States Steel (USX), which are firms in unrelated businesses.

Year	Chevron	Mobil	Sears	USX
1	0.749	0.537	-0.073	0.478
2	-0.061	-0.423	0.164	0.308
3	-0.158	0.149	0.759	-0.229
4	0.165	0.228	0.301	0.435
5	-0.004	0.074	-0.086	-0.076
6	0.275	0.193	0.283	0.080
7	0.267	0.373	0.112	-0.045
8	-0.022	0.088	-0.037	0.453
9	0.220	0.216	0.271	0.049
10	0.464	0.382	-0.007	0.252
11	0.129	-0.020	-0.313	-0.102

Calculate the correlation and portfolio variance with $w_A = w_B = \frac{1}{2}$ for the following firms:
a. Chevron and Mobil.
b. Sears and USX.

8.6 Using the data given in Question 8.5, determine the variance of a portfolio of 25% in each security.

8.7 The following table lists 10 years of rates of return for six major U.S. companies:

Year	AT&T	Coca-Cola	Dow
1	0.311	0.122	−0.110
2	0.118	0.502	0.109
3	0.146	0.099	0.350
4	0.283	0.209	−0.095
5	0.328	0.368	0.472
6	0.087	0.354	0.413
7	0.157	0.071	0.559
8	0.125	0.213	0.028
9	0.523	0.604	0.267
10	−0.334	0.243	−0.310

Year	DuPont	GE	GM
1	−0.025	0.003	−0.070
2	0.059	0.579	0.577
3	0.446	0.271	0.239
4	0.030	0.013	0.157
5	0.383	0.315	0.003
6	0.280	0.221	0.033
7	0.145	0.109	0.083
8	0.076	0.062	0.395
9	0.394	0.430	0.098
10	−0.038	−0.059	−0.108

a. Calculate the average rate of return and standard deviation for each security.
b. Rank the securities in ascending order by the standard deviation. Compute the portfolio standard deviations for $n = 2, 3, 4, 5,$ and 6, where $n = 2$ means the two securities with the lowest standard deviations, $n = 3$ means the three securities with the lowest standard deviations, and so forth. Assume that the portfolios are equally weighted. Discuss your results.

8.8 Assume that four assets are independent and identically distributed, with an equal probability of receiving $2 or $4. Calculate the portfolio variance when you invest in $n = 1, 2, 3,$ and 4 assets (equal weights).

8.9 Suppose all stocks are independent and identically distributed with a mean of 10% and a variance of 10%. You can invest $\frac{1}{n}$ in each stock.
a. Calculate the efficient frontier with $n = 1, 2, \ldots,$ 10 stocks. Will the investor diversify in all n stocks?
b. Show graphically the efficient frontier if you have the following transaction costs: if $n = 1$, you pay $\frac{1}{10}$% (that is, the mean is reduced to 9.9%); if $n = 2$, you pay $\frac{2}{10}$% for each stock; and so forth. Do investors necessarily hold all ten stocks?

8.10 Suppose that you have two independent stocks with rates of return as follows:

Stock A		Stock B	
Probability	R_A	Probability	R_B
½	2%	1	3%
½	4%		

What is the mean and variance of a portfolio composed of $\frac{1}{2}A + \frac{1}{2}B$? What is the covariance of A with B?

8.11 Suppose there are two assets, A and B, where the mean of Asset A is 8%, the mean of Asset B is 20%, the standard deviation of Asset A is 10%, the standard deviation of Asset B is 20%, and the correlation coefficient is +1. Calculate the mean and standard deviation of a portfolio with the following investment proportions:

w_A	w_B
0.0	1.0
0.1	0.9
0.2	0.8
0.3	0.7
0.4	0.6
0.5	0.5
0.6	0.4
0.7	0.3
0.8	0.2
0.9	0.1
1.0	0.0
1.5	−0.5

Express your results graphically, and identify the efficient and inefficient frontiers.

8.12 Repeat Question 8.11, but this time assume that the correlation is −1.

8.13 Suppose you can invest in either Market A or Market B. In Market A there are fifty stocks, all of which have a mean of 10% and a standard deviation of 10%. Also in Market A, all stocks have a correlation coefficient of zero. In Market B there are only two stocks, both with a mean of 10% and a standard deviation of 10%. However, in Market B the correlation coefficient is −0.5. In which Market would you prefer to invest? Explain.

8.14 Suppose there are two stocks, A and B, where the mean and standard deviation of A exceeds B and the correlation coefficient is +1. "If short sales are not allowed, then the efficient frontier is equal to the mean-variance frontier." Do you agree? (Hint: See Appendix 8A.)

8.15 Prove that if you invest 50% of your assets in each of two available stocks and if the correlation coefficient is +½, then the portfolio variance is given by

$$\sigma_p^2 = \frac{\sigma_1^2 + \sigma_2^2 + \sigma_1\sigma_2}{4}$$

8.16 The rates of return on two assets are as follows:

Year	A	B
1	15%	−1%
2	−5%	30%

Assuming that each year has a probability of ½, calculate the investment proportions that make the portfolio variance equal to zero.

8.17 The rates of return on two assets, A and B, are as follows:

Year	A	B
1	15%	30%
2	−5%	−1%

Assuming that each year has a probability of ½, calculate the investment proportions that make the portfolio variance equal to zero.

8.18 Suppose you have n stocks, and all have the same distribution. The rate of return of each of the n stocks has the following possible outcomes. All n stocks are uncorrelated.

Probability	Rate of Return
½	10%
½	20%

Calculate the portfolio variance for the following values of n: 1, 2, 3, 5, 10, 15, 20, 50, and 100. Assume that $\frac{1}{n}$ is invested in each security. Draw a graph showing the relationship between n and the variance of the portfolio. What conclusions can be made?

8.19 The following are the rates of return on two stocks and the inflation rates for the corresponding year:

Year	Rate of Return		Inflation
	Stock A	Stock B	
1	15%	8%	4%
2	7	5	2
3	20	12	8

a. Using nominal rates of return, calculate the correlation coefficient between Stock A and Stock B.
b. Using real rates of return, calculate the correlation coefficient between Stock A and Stock B.
c. Analyze your results.

8.20 Suppose you can invest in two stocks that have a perfect negative correlation (−1). The additional parameters are as follows: The expected rate of return on Stock 1 is 7%, the expected rate of return on Stock 2 is 4%, the standard deviation of Stock 1 is 5%, and the standard deviation of Stock 2 is 10%.

Alternatively, you also can invest in the riskless asset that has an interest rate of 4.5% and a zero variance. Suppose you desire a zero variance. Which alternative is preferable?

8.21 Use the data given in the first article in this chapter's Investments in the News to calculate the mean and variance of the current portfolio and the portfolio suggested by the financial planner under the following assumptions.

a. Assume that the mean rate of return of each of the eight assets appearing in the pie charts is 10%, the standard deviation is 10%, and all pairs have a correlation of $\rho = 0.6$. Does the financial planner portfolio dominate the current portfolio?

b. Assume again that the mean is 10% and all correlations are $\rho = 0.6$ except those invested internationally, whose correlation is zero with all other assets. Does the financial planner portfolio dominate the current portfolio?

Discuss your results in Parts a and b above.

8.22 Consider the following five assets:

Asset	Standard Deviation
A	10%
B	10
C	10
D	10
E	10

Answer the following, assuming that the correlation between all pairs of assets is zero and you invest an equal proportion of your wealth in each asset.

a. What is the variance of the portfolio consisting of Assets A and B only?

b. What is the variance of the portfolio consisting of Assets A, B, and C only?

c. What is the variance of the portfolio consisting of Assets A, B, C, and D only?

d. Explain how the standard deviation of the portfolio changes as you successively add an additional independent asset to your portfolio.

8.23 Using the information provided in Question 8.22, how would your answer to Part b change if you invested 30% of your wealth in Asset A, 60% of your wealth in Asset B, and 10% of your wealth in Asset C? Explain the difference between your answer here and your answer to Question 8.22b.

8.24 The following data report the closing price of five possible investments. Assume that the percent-

age change in the index is the total rate of return to the investor.

Weekly Financial and Stock Indicators
The following table lists the weekly statistics as originally reported in Barron's Market Laboratory for the market week as indicated.

Week Ended	DJI Avg. Close	S&P 500 Index	NYSE Comp. Index	Wilshire 5000 (Bil $)	Gold Futures ($)
1997					
Dec. 26	7679.31	936.46	493.60	8976.00	295.20
19	7756.29	946.78	497.39	9043.11	289.50
12	7838.30	953.39	500.00	9097.85	282.80
5	8149.13	983.79	514.31	9407.88	288.40
Nov. 28	7823.13	955.40	499.10	9142.43	296.90
21	7881.07	963.09	502.85	9220.06	305.90
14	7572.48	928.35	487.17	8932.58	303.70
7	7581.32	927.51	487.29	8962.17	311.20
Oct. 31	7442.08	914.62	481.14	8865.25	312.10
24	7715.41	941.64	495.76	9137.09	307.30
17	7847.03	944.16	496.57	9154.76	324.30
10	8045.21	966.98	506.85	9384.40	328.90
3	8038.58	965.03	505.69	9340.08	334.60
Sept. 26	7922.18	945.22	495.20	9147.19	326.90
19	7917.27	950.51	496.56	9172.69	321.60
12	7742.97	923.91	483.30	8940.11	323.90
5	7822.41	929.05	484.64	8943.92	323.80
Aug. 29	7622.42	899.47	470.48	8679.98	324.50
22	7887.91	923.55	478.93	8815.84	326.20
15	7694.66	900.81	469.10	8631.36	325.70
8	8031.22	933.54	483.79	8881.84	326.10
1	8194.04	947.14	490.98	8977.58	324.70
July 25	8113.44	938.79	486.80	8885.70	326.10
18	7890.46	915.30	475.97	8697.78	328.90
11	7921.82	916.68	478.12	8682.70	322.20
3	7895.81	916.92	477.68	8639.34	324.20
June 27	7687.72	887.30	463.30	8399.76	335.90
20	7796.51	898.70	467.84	8484.51	337.70
13	7782.04	893.27	465.17	8409.93	340.90
6	7435.78	858.01	448.13	8140.16	343.20

(continued)

Week Ended	DJI Avg. Close	S&P 500 Index	NYSE Comp. Index	Wilshire 5000 (Bil $)	Gold Futures ($)
May 30	7331.04	848.28	441.78	8038.50	344.80
23	7345.91	847.03	440.28	8000.32	342.80
16	7194.67	829.75	432.44	7832.41	344.90
9	7169.53	824.78	429.23	7781.11	348.30
2	7071.20	812.97	422.97	7655.70	341.60
Apr. 25	6738.87	765.37	400.38	7216.51	342.40
18	6703.55	766.34	402.64	7269.47	341.50
11	6391.69	737.65	389.47	7059.97	347.00
4	6256.07	757.90	398.02	7213.96	348.80
Mar. 27	6740.59	773.88	407.43	7376.83	350.20
21	6804.79	784.10	412.80	7468.07	353.00
14	6935.46	793.17	417.70	7580.93	352.60
7	7000.89	804.97	423.83	7617.12	349.90
Feb. 28	6877.74	790.82	415.51	7559.42	364.70
21	6931.62	801.77	421.01	7668.96	354.10
14	6988.96	808.48	423.48	7737.86	347.80
7	6855.80	789.56	413.80	7582.92	343.30
Jan. 31	6813.09	786.16	411.98	7575.79	344.90
24	6696.48	770.52	405.51	7467.21	353.40
17	6833.10	776.17	409.31	7501.83	355.70
10	6703.79	759.50	400.76	7362.73	360.20
3	6544.09	748.03	394.06	7243.28	362.00

Source: *Barron's Market Week*, January 5, 1998.

a. Calculate the monthly rate of return for the periods January 3–January 31, February 7–February 28, March 7–March 27 and so on, finally ending with the period December 5–December 26. Thus, you get twelve rates of return corresponding to the twelve months. (Ignore the fact that not all twelve rates of return covered periods of exactly the same length).

b. Using these rates of return, calculate the monthly average rate of return, the standard of rates of return on each asset, and all the pairwise correlations.

c. Draw the five assets in the mean–standard deviation space, and draw the following on the same graph:

1. The efficient frontier of the following two assets: Dow Jones index and S&P 500 index.

2. The two-assets frontier corresponding to the Dow Jones index and Gold Futures (in drawing the graph, use 10 points with investments weighing weights $w = 0, 0.1, 0.2, \ldots, 1$. $(1 - w)$ is determined accordingly when w is the investment weight on one of the assets. Compare the two efficient frontiers, and explain your results.

d. Suppose that you diversify equally among the five assets ($w_i = \frac{1}{5}$; $i = 1, 2, \ldots, 5$). Calculate the mean and standard deviation of this portfolio. Draw it on the same graph given in Part c (also include the five assets on the same graph). Analyze your results. Which of the investments on this graph is efficient, and which is not?

e. Repeat Part d, but this time by investing $\frac{1}{4}$ in each of the four stock indexes and zero in Gold Futures. Discuss your results.

For Internet questions visit the Levy Investment Web site at http://levy-invst.swcollege.com.

YOUR TURN: APPLYING THEORY TO PRACTICE
PORTFOLIO POLL: THE IDEAL PORTFOLIO?

The ideal portfolio?

O Neutral weighting from Morgan Stanley Capital International world equity index and Salomon Brothers world government-bond index

A Merrill Lynch
B Lehman Brothers
C Nikko Securities
D Daiwa Europe
E Crédit Agricole
F Robeco Group Asset Management
G Bank Julius Baer (Zurich)
H UBS International Investment
I Commerz International Capital Management
J Credit Suisse Asset Management

(continued)

- **Holdings by Instrument (%)**

	A	B[a]	C	D	E	F	G	H	I	J
Equities	60	50	65	58	70	50	45	38	50	36
Bonds	30	25	35	37	25	40	43	54	50	58
Cash	10	20	0	5	5	10	12	8	0	6

- **Equity Holdings by Area (%)**

	O	A	B	C	D	E	F	G	H	I	J
Americas											
U.S.	37	37	22	42	30	30	30	30	30	40	33
Others	2	5	7	2	1	5	4	3	0	5	6
Europe											
Britain	10	9	8	10	10	8	10	16	6	8	9
Germany	4	3	6	4	6	8	2	6	8	3	8
France	4	3	12	5	7	18	5	10	12	4	9
Others	11	7	22	0	11	3	8	11	16	18	10
Far East											
Japan	24	28	10	25	23	22	32	12	18	15	17
Others	8	8	13	12	12	6	9	12	10	7	8
	100	100	100	100	100	100	100	100	100	100	100

- **Bond Holdings by Currency (%)**

	O	A	B	C	D	E	F	G	H	I	J
Dollar	39	35	47	50	40	50	15	20	59	65	37
Yen	18	24	12	20	13	15	10	0	10	5	11
Sterling	6	4	5	10	10	10	5	10	3	5	6
DM	10	6	4	8	13	5	10	15	14	5	12
FFr	6	5	8	9	9	0	20	25	6	0	14
Others	21	26	24	3	15	20	40	30	8	20	20
	100	100	100	100	100	100	100	100	100	100	100

5% held in gold.

The table shows the portfolio composition of ten institutional investors. For the purpose of this case, focus here only on the upper part of the table, namely, on the diversification between equities, bonds, gold, and cash. In addition, we have the following estimated parameters:

(continued)

	Equity	Bond	Gold	Cash
Expected return (%)	14	9	8	4
Standard deviation (%)	16	10	3	0

The correlation between equities and bonds is 0.2. The correlation between gold and each of the above assets is zero. Cash yields a certain return of 4%.

Questions

1. What is the correlation between cash and equities?

2. Calculate the portfolio mean and portfolio standard deviation for each of the ten portfolios. Is any one investment strategy better than the others? Discuss.

3. The article that accompanied the above table (which, for the sake of brevity, is not given here) states that "the latest poll of big fund managers finds them starting the new year cautiously. On *average*, they have cut back their holding of both equity (from 54% of their portfolios three months ago to 52% today) and bonds (from 41% to less than 40%). They prefer the liquidity of cash which now accounts for 8% of assets instead of 5%."

Suppose that in view of the uncertainty felt by the fund managers, their estimate of the standard deviation of equity is 18% and of bonds, 12% (rather than the figures given in the table above). Calculate the mean and standard deviation of the funds' *average portfolio* with the old weights and old estimates of the standard deviation, and compare these findings with the new weights (after increasing the proportion of cash) and the new standard deviations. Calculate the mean return and standard deviation of the average portfolio if the weights are not changed. Discuss the fund managers' adjustment to the increased uncertainty.

SUPPLEMENTAL REFERENCE

Summit, Paul–Choudry. "Taking Care of Correlation." *Risk,* February 1998, pp. S2–S9.

Appendix 8A Calculating the Efficient Frontier

Whereas the graphical demonstration of the efficient frontier in the chapter is quite simple, finding the investment proportions corresponding to the frontier and its efficient segment is not an easy task. Typically, it requires computer software.

Finding the efficient frontier requires solving the following problem: Find the portfolio weights $w_1, w_2, \ldots, w_n$ that minimize the portfolio's variance

$$\sigma_p^2 = \sum_{i=1}^{n}\sum_{j=1}^{n} w_i w_a \rho_{i,j} \sigma_i \sigma_j$$

subject to the constraints

a. $\sum_{i=1}^{n} w_i E(R_i) = E(R_p)$ (a given expected return)

b. $\sum_{i=1}^{n} w_i = 1$ (fully invested portfolio)

For example, suppose an investor desires a portfolio that yields a mean return of $E(R_p) = 10\%$. All diversification strategies that lie on the line LL' (see Exhibit 8-14) yield a mean return of 10%. By minimizing the portfolio's variance σ_p^2, we find the investment strategy corresponding to point L, which is a point on the mean-variance frontier. Namely, there is no other portfolio with a mean return of 10% with a lower variance than the variance of Portfolio L. Hence, point L represents a frontier portfolio.

Solving the problem once again for another value of $E(R_p)$—say, 11%—we get another point on the frontier, point p'. By changing $E(R_p)$, we identify the whole mean-variance frontier, as well as the efficient set of investment strategies; in our specific case, it is the segment MVP to A (see Exhibit 8-14).

You might reasonably assume that w_i must be greater than or equal to zero in the equation for portfolio variance. However, in fact, w_i can be negative if short sales are permitted. Short sales occur when an investor sells stocks he does not already own. For example, suppose you borrow from your broker a share of AT&T when the current market price is $100. Then you sell the stock and receive $100 in cash. Suppose that after one month, the stock price drops to $80. Then you buy it back in the market for $80, return the stock to your broker, and net a profit of $20. Of course, if the stock price goes up to $120, you lose $20. (See Chapter 3 for more details on short selling.)

Technically, if $w_i < 0$, it implies short sale of stock i (that is, you hold a negative amount of this asset). To illustrate, suppose there are only two stocks, and an investor selected $w_1 = -0.5$ and $w_2 = 1.5$. This means that for each dollar that the investor has from her own resources, she sells short $0.50 of Asset 1, gets the cash from the sale, and invests $1.50 in Asset 2. Of course, the efficient frontier when short sales are allowed cannot be worse in comparison with the efficient frontier with no short sales, because the investor has more investment strategies from which to choose.

Exhibit 8A-1 demonstrates the n-asset efficient frontier with and without short sales. Obviously, with short sales, the frontier is located to the left of the no-short-sale frontier, because the investor has more investment opportunities when w_i is greater than or less than 0 (she can always select $w_i > 0$ if she prefers this). Thus, the investor cannot do worse than the no-short-sales case.

Exhibit 8A-2 provides historical estimates of the expected returns, standard deviations, and correlation coefficients for five major asset groups. These values are used to determine the efficient frontiers (with and without short sales). Exhibit 8A-3, Part a, shows the computer output of the five groups when short sales are not allowed. Part b of Exhibit 8A-3 uses the same data and demonstrates the portfolio

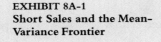

EXHIBIT 8A-1
Short Sales and the Mean-
Variance Frontier

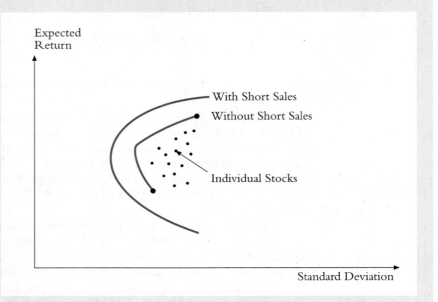

composition when short sales are allowed. Exhibit 8A-4 compares the mean-variance frontier with and without short sales. As this graph shows, the efficient frontier with short sales dominates the one with no short sales.

Exhibit 8A-2 shows that bonds had very low mean returns over the historical period. Investors should still consider these securities for their portfolios, however, because of the diversification benefits. In Exhibit 8A-3a, where there are no short sales, consider a target return of 11.1%. From the weights, we see that we should invest in the two groups of stocks, and more than one-third of the portfolio should be invested in intermediate bonds. However, to achieve a target return of 15.1%, we should invest only in stocks. As the mean increases, fewer assets are included in the portfolio, and the standard deviation is higher.

Exhibit 8A-3b provides similar results, except that short sales are allowed. Notice that in this case, the portfolio standard deviations are lower. For example, with a mean of 7.1%, when short sales are allowed, the portfolio standard deviation is 5.7%; in contrast, when short sales are not allowed, the portfolio standard deviation is 6.7%. Clearly, short selling results in a lower standard deviation. Also notice that rarely is a security not included in the portfolio. Finally, it is important to remember that the efficient frontier is constructed based on estimates of means, standard deviations, and correlations. The actual relationship may be much different in future periods; hence, the portfolio composition may be different.

EXHIBIT 8A-2   **Historical Estimate of Five Major U.S. Asset Groups (based on annual rates of return from 1926 to 1996)**

Asset Group	Mean(%)	SD(%)	Large Company	Small Company	Correlation Long-Term Corp. Bonds	Long-Term Gov. Bonds	Inter.-Term Gov. Bonds
Large–company stock	12.7	20.3	1	0.81	0.25	0.18	0.01
Small–company stock	17.7	34.1		1	0.11	0.03	−0.03
Long-term corporate bonds	6.0	8.7			1	0.94	0.9
Long-Term government bonds	5.4	9.2				1	0.91
Intermediate–term government bonds	5.4	5.8					1

Source: "Stocks, Bonds, Bills, and Inflation," *Annual Yearbook*. Ibbotson Associates, Inc., Chicago, Illinois, 1997.

EXHIBIT 8A-3   **Efficient Frontier—With and Without Short Sales**

(a) Without Short Sales

	Global MVP		Efficient Portfolios								
Mean (%)	5.8		7.1	8.5	9.8	11.1	12.4	13.7	15.1	16.4	17.7
Standard deviation (%)	5.7		6.7	9.1	12.1	15.3	18.7	22.1	25.6	29.6	34.1
Investment Weights (%)											
Large-company stock	1.9	11.2	20.4	29.6	38.9	48.1	56.6	52.8	26.4	0	
Small-company stock	2.3	7.6	12.8	18.1	23.3	28.5	33.7	47.2	73.6	100	
Long-term corporate bonds	0.0	0.0	0.0	0.0	0.0	0.0	9.6	0.0	0.0	0	
Long-term government bonds	0.0	0.0	0.0	0.0	0.0	0.0	0.0	0.0	0.0	0	
Intermediate-term government bonds	95.7	81.3	66.8	52.3	37.8	23.3	0.0	0.0	0.0	0	

(b) With Short Sales

	Global MVP		Efficient Portfolios								
Mean (%)	5.8		7.1	8.4	9.7	11.0	12.3	13.6	14.9	16.2	17.5
Standard deviation (%)	4.5		5.7	8.1	11.1	14.2	17.4	20.7	24.0	27.3	30.6
Investment Weights (%)											
Large-company stock	6.2	13.9	21.7	29.4	37.2	44.9	52.7	60.5	68.2	76.0	
Small-company stock	1.0	5.2	9.5	13.8	18.0	22.3	26.6	30.8	35.1	39.3	
Long-term corporate bonds	−31.2	4.4	40.0	75.6	111.2	146.8	182.4	218.0	253.6	289.2	
Long-term government bonds	−50.5	−78.2	−105.9	−133.6	−161.3	−189.0	−216.7	−244.4	−272.1	−299.8	
Intermediate-term government bonds	174.6	154.7	134.8	114.8	94.9	75.0	55.1	35.1	15.2	−4.7	

EXHIBIT 8A-4   **The Efficient Frontier With and Without Short Sales**

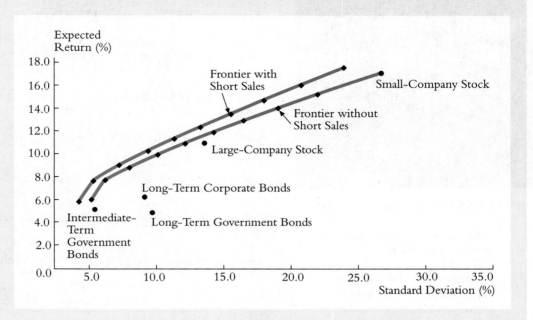

CHAPTER 9

RISK AND RETURN: THE LINEAR RELATIONSHIPS AND THE CAPITAL ASSET PRICING MODEL

LEARNING OBJECTIVES

After studying this chapter you should be able to:

1. Identify the best investment opportunities with risk-free borrowing and lending.

2. Understand the capital market line (CML), which contains only efficient portfolios.

3. Understand the separation property, which asserts that in Stage 1, all investors choose the same risky portfolio, and in Stage 2, investors borrow or lend according to their risk preferences.

4. Understand why beta is the appropriate measure of risk.

5. Understand why the security market line (SML) and the capital asset pricing model (CAPM) describe the equilibrium relationship between risk and expected rate of return.

6. Understand how practitioners who believe in market inefficiency use alpha and beta to select underpriced stocks.

INVESTMENTS IN THE NEWS

THE ULTIMATE INDEX FUNDS

Pick any moment, any market condition, and the Rydex fund group is virtually guaranteed to have an offering at the top of the performance chart. It's also guaranteed to have one at the bottom. How's that? Rydex runs two enhanced index funds, Nova and Ursa, that track the S&P 500 in opposite ways. Rydex Nova is a bull's dream vehicle: with the help of options and futures, manager Tom Michael seeks to deliver 1.5 times the performance of the S&P 500—which puts the fund up sharply in good markets and down sharply in bad ones. At Rydex Ursa, manager Mike Byrum goes the other way, short selling stock-index futures. His objective: a negative 1.0 beta with the S&P 500, meaning that in a 10% market decline, the Ursa fund would be basking in a 10% gain. . . .

Source: Andrea L. Prochniak, "The Ultimate Index Funds," *Fortune,* May 12, 1997. Reprinted from the May 12, 1997, issue of *Fortune* by special permission. © 1997, Time, Inc.

Part 2 of this book showed how investors gain from diversification and also showed that generally, portfolios dominate individual securities; hence, most investors diversify their investment or buy shares of diversified funds. However, Part 2 did not show which portfolio is the optimum one. The problem of portfolio selection is the theme of this chapter's Investments in the News because mutual funds are really nothing more than portfolios. The article introduces a new measure of risk, beta, which helps investors rank portfolios (and individual assets) by their risk. The beta of Rydex Ursa is negative (-1), meaning that its share price fluctuates opposite to the Standard and Poor's (S&P 500) index.

Investors would like to select a portfolio that will minimize the risk for a given expected return. However, how should one construct a portfolio from the large number of individual assets that exist in the market? Does the financial planner need to know the investor's preference in order to make portfolio choices? What is the relationship between sigma (σ), introduced in Chapter 7, and beta (β), introduced in this chapter? What is the expected return on a portfolio (like Rydex) whose beta is negative?

This part of the book expands the investment universe. This chapter adds the risk-free asset, which allows us to derive the equilibrium prices of risky assets and to establish beta as a measure of risk. Chapter 10 expands the risk-return relationship by allowing investors to short sell assets and to keep the proceeds from these short sales. This discussion allows us to develop to one factor a multifactor arbitrage pricing theory (APT). Chapter 11 expands the investment universe by allowing international diversification.

This chapter shows that in the selection of the optimum portfolio of risky assets, there is no need to know the investor's preference. However, the result hinges on the assumption that investors can borrow and lend at a risk-free interest rate, where *risk-free* means that the return on the risk-free asset has zero variance. It is common among practitioners to use the rate of return on short-term Treasury bills as proxy to a risk-free interest rate. The existence of the risk-free assets allows us to derive the equilibrium price of an asset, which is its fair price.

First, this chapter shows what indifference curves look like (indifference curves provide the trade-off between risk and expected return) and demonstrates that the investor's goal is to reach the highest possible indifference curve (utility). Then it shows that when risk-free assets exist, investors can mix any risky asset (individual assets and portfolios) with the risk-free asset and can choose a portfolio (a mix of the risky asset and the risk-free asset) from a set of portfolios where all are located on the straight line called the *opportunity line*. The optimum portfolio choice can be found by the tangency point of the indifference curve to this straight line.

The investor's dilemma is what risky asset (or assets) to mix with the risk-free asset. This chapter shows that the optimum portfolio of risky assets to be mixed with the risk-free asset is the one that provides an opportunity line with the highest slope. This line is called the *capital market line* (CML), and the corresponding portfolio of risky assets is called the *market portfolio*. All investors, regardless of their preference, will choose the market portfolio as their optimum portfolio of risky assets. All portfolios located on the CML are efficient. For efficient portfolios, either the standard deviation (σ) or beta (β) can be used to evaluate risk. For inefficient portfolios (for example, some mutual funds) and for individual securities, sigma is a misleading measure of risk, and beta is the appropriate measure. This chapter also discusses how beta is used in practice for portfolio selection.

As this chapter will show, beta is the correct measure for risk for individual assets and portfolios alike, regardless of whether or not these portfolios are efficient. However, for efficient portfolios, the investor can use either sigma or beta (which will be defined in Section 9.5) to size up risk without affecting the ranking of the portfolios by their risk. Because beta corresponds to individual securities as well as portfolios, this chapter uses the word *asset* where it refers to both individual assets and portfolios. When the discussion refers to individual assets only, it explicitly states this.

9.1 INDIFFERENCE CURVES

As the previous chapters have shown, investors like large expected returns and dislike risk. Risk is represented by standard deviation (later on, we discuss its relationship to beta). Suppose an investor holds an asset that has an expected return of $E(R_A)$ and a standard deviation of σ_A. This asset can be graphed as point A in Exhibit 9-1.[1] Will this investor be better off exchanging Asset A for Asset A_1? We can safely say that the investor would *not* prefer Asset A_1 to Asset A, because Asset A_1 has the same expected return as Asset A but has higher risk ($\sigma_{A_1} > \sigma_A$). Thus, Asset A is preferred to Asset A_1. Now let us compare Asset A to Asset A_2. Will the investor be willing to exchange Asset A for Asset A_2? The answer is yes, because Asset A_2 offers a higher expected return, $E(R_{A_2}) > E(R_A)$, with the same risk as Asset A.

Thus, Asset A is preferable to Asset A_1, and Asset A_2 is preferable to Asset A. If we move along the curve in Exhibit 9-1 from Assets A_1 to A_2, we follow an investor who is moving from an asset that is less preferable to Asset A to an asset that is more preferable to Asset A. As we move along this curve, we pass through a point, A_3, where the investor is indifferent between Asset A and Asset A_3. We can present the same argument that Asset B_2 is preferable to A, whereas Asset B_1 is less desirable than Asset A. Hence, there must be a point, B_3, where the investor is indifferent between Asset A and Asset B_3.

We can repeat this exercise for other points that are closer to or farther away from point A, and we will obtain a curve consisting of all points of indifference, such as B_3, A, and A_3. This curve I is called an **indifference curve,** because the investor who viewed each asset on the curve as equivalent in risk and return would be indifferent to exchanging one asset on the curve for another. Moving along the curve, an investor either takes on more risk for greater expected return or incurs less

---

1. Because the variance is the standard deviation squared, we can say that investors dislike variance. The rest of the chapter uses the terms *standard deviation* and *variance* interchangeably as measures of portfolio risk.

**EXHIBIT 9-1
Indifference Curves**

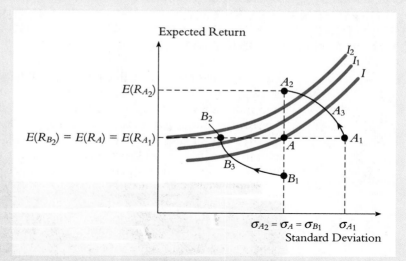

risk for lower expected return. Either way, the investor has the same preference for these various assets, as long as they lie on the same indifference curve.

If we repeat the same exercise but start with a point vertically above point A, we get another indifference curve, I_1, that is higher than I. The higher the indifference curve, the better off investors are, because they can attain a higher expected return for a given level of risk. Thus, indifference curves are measures of investor welfare or **utility**; the higher the indifference curve, the higher the investor's welfare or utility. Exhibit 9-1 demonstrates a set of indifference curves.

The basic characteristics of indifference curves follow:

1. All combinations $[E(R), \sigma_R]$ lying on a given indifference curve provide the investor with the same level of utility.[2]
2. Moving to a higher indifference curve (for example, a shift from I to I_1 or from I_1 to I_2) increases the investor's utility.
3. The indifference curve represents an individual investor's own personal assessment of the trade-off between expected return and risk. In other words, indifference curves are subjective, and their shapes differ from one investor to another.

The rest of this chapter assumes that each investor seeks to reach the highest possible indifference curve, which is tantamount to reaching the highest utility.

---

2. Actually, indifference curves represent *expected utility*, because the investment is risky. Thus, on a given indifference curve, all combinations of mean return, $E(R)$, and risk, σ_R, yield the same expected utility. For simplicity, we use the term *utility* rather than *expected utility*.

9.2 EFFICIENT INVESTMENT OPPORTUNITIES WITH RISK-FREE BORROWING AND LENDING AND A SINGLE RISKY ASSET

The asset yielding the risk-free rate is called the *risk-free asset* or the *riskless asset*. Let us assume that there is a risk-free interest rate at which investors can borrow and lend money. For example, if the risk-free asset yields 5%, an investor who lends at the risk-free rate invests in the asset and earns 5%. An individual who borrows pays a risk-free rate of 5%. We first examine how risk-free borrowing and lending alters the efficient frontier and then make inferences concerning the optimum selected portfolio based on the properties of indifference curves previously discussed.

The properties of the efficient frontier discussed in Chapter 8 (see Section 8.2) are altered by the addition of the possibility of borrowing and lending at the risk-free interest rate. Instead of a curve, we obtain a straight line in the expected return–standard deviation space. This straight line is induced by the fact that the risk-free asset has zero variability and zero covariance with all other risky assets, as well as by the assumption that the lending rate is equal to the borrowing rate. Because the risk-free asset plays a key role in determining the shape of the efficient frontier, we examine more formally the properties of an asset that is risk-free and this asset's effect on the investor's optimum portfolio choice from this efficient frontier.

When we lend money, we say that we invest in the risk-free asset. Because the risk-free interest is $r\%$, we receive $r\%$ on the investment. Similarly, when we borrow money, we pay $r\%$. Because r is obtained (or paid) with certainty (with probability 1), the asset's expected return is also r. Because r is certain, the variance of the return on the risk-free asset is zero.[3]

The *feasible set* is defined as all possible investments (individual assets and portfolios alike) available to the investor. To see how the feasible set changes when the investor can borrow or lend at the risk-free rate, let us start by assuming that the investor has only one risky asset available, denoted by R_A (see Exhibit 9-2a). This risky asset can be an individual asset or a portfolio; to simplify, we call it Portfolio R_A in the rest of this chapter. Thus, the investor holds Portfolio R_A with an expected return of $E(R_A)$ and a standard deviation of σ_A. Now let us add a risk-free asset with a certain rate of return (r) to the portfolio. Because r is certain, its return (and expected return) is r, and its standard deviation is zero (as it has a zero variance). Then the rate of return (R) on a mix composed of Portfolio R_A and the risk-free asset is

$$R = (w_r \cdot r) + (1 - w_r)R_A \qquad (9.1)$$

---

3. The covariance of r with any other random variable (y) is also equal to zero, because

$$Cov(r,y) = \sum_{i=1}^{N} P_i(r - r)[y_i - E(y)] = \sum_{i=1}^{N} P_i \cdot 0 \cdot [y_i - E(y)] = 0$$

where P_i is the probability that y will have the specific value y_i, r is the interest rate as well as its expected value, and N is the number of possible outcomes of y. The risk-free asset (r) has a zero variance (and a zero covariance with other assets) and hence will always be located on the vertical axis in the expected return–standard deviation space (see Exhibit 9-2).

Note that N denotes the number of possible outcomes (or observations) to avoid confusion with the number of securities in a portfolio, which is denoted as n. This book previously used m for the number of observations, but because this chapter uses m to denote the market profits, it uses N for the number of observations.

EXHIBIT 9-2
Investment Opportunities
with a Risk-Free Asset

Part a: Borrowing and Lending Opportunities

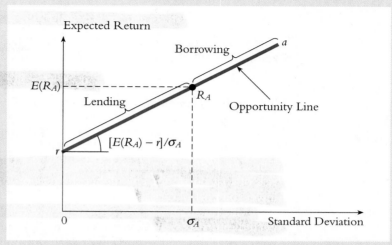

Part b: Influence of Borrowing and Lending on the Investor's Utility

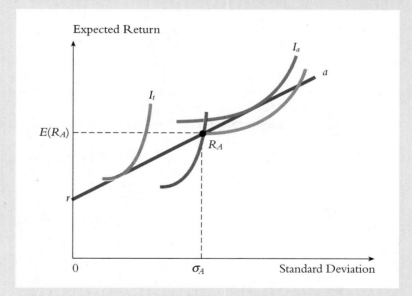

where w_r is the proportion (or investment weight) of the risk-free asset in the portfolio. The expected return $E(R)$ is

$$E(R) = (w_r \cdot r) + (1 - w_r)E(R_A) \qquad (9.2)$$

To calculate the standard deviation of the portfolio, find the variance of R given by (see Chapter 7, Equation 7.11)

$$\sigma_R^2 = w_r^2 \sigma_r^2 + (1 - w_r)^2 \sigma_A^2 + 2w_r(1 - w_r)Cov(r, R_A)$$

The variance of r is zero, and its covariance with any other random variables is also zero; therefore, the portfolio variance is reduced to

$$\sigma_R^2 = (1 - w_r)^2 \sigma_A^2$$

Taking the square root of both sides to obtain the standard deviation, we get

$$\sigma_R = (1 - w_r)\sigma_A \tag{9.3}$$

Thus, by adding a positive amount of a risk-free asset to a portfolio, we lower the risk of that portfolio. The higher the proportion invested in the risk-free asset, the lower the portfolio risk.

Unfortunately, when we lower the overall risk of a portfolio, we lower its expected return as well. Equations 9.2 and 9.3 can be used to show how the portfolio return is related to the portfolio risk. From Equation 9.3 we can solve for the proportion of wealth invested in the risky asset to obtain

$$(1 - w_r) = \frac{\sigma_R}{\sigma_A}$$

Solving for w_r, we obtain

$$w_r = 1 - \frac{\sigma_R}{\sigma_A} \tag{9.3'}$$

Substituting for $(1 - w_r)$ and w_r in Equation 9.2 yields

$$E(R) = \left(1 - \frac{\sigma_R}{\sigma_A}\right)r + \left(\frac{\sigma_R}{\sigma_A}\right)E(R_A)$$

or

$$E(R) = r + \frac{[E(R_A) - r]}{\sigma_A}\sigma_R \tag{9.4}$$

Thus, the portfolio expected return, $E(R)$, is positively related to its standard deviation, σ_R. Moreover, this association is linear, as is evident from Equation 9.4, which yields a straight line. This line is known as the **opportunity line**. The opportunity line describes all available portfolios created by mixing r with R_A (see Exhibit 9-2a). Thus, given Portfolio R_A, only this portfolio is available to investors. Adding the risk-free asset (point r), the investor can mix r and R_A, creating an indefinitely large number of portfolios all lying on the straight line ra, which is the opportunity line. Investors can move along this line by varying the proportion of the risk-free asset according to their preferences.

Exhibit 9-2b shows that the risk-free asset allows investors a range of possible portfolios with different risk and expected return characteristics that allow them to reach higher indifference curves. Without the risk-free asset, only Portfolio R_A is available; with the risk-free asset, all portfolios lying on line ra are attainable. Thus, the feasible set of portfolios is expanded. The more adventurous investors borrow and invest heavily in the risky portfolio, R_A. The more timid investors lend a large proportion of their portfolio at the risk-free rate and invest only a small portion in the risky portfolio. Exhibit 9-2b illustrates these two types of investors, where the indifference curve I_t denotes the timid investor, and I_a denotes the adventurous investor. Note that the indifference curves representing the investors' preferences do not change when the risk-free asset is added. However, as the feasible set changes, the tangency point changes, too (see Exhibit 9-2b). With a risk-free asset, both investors are able to reach a higher indifference curve—the adventurous, through borrowing, and the timid, through lending.

The opportunity line has the following characteristics:

1. The intercept of the opportunity line is r. Thus, if an investor wants a portfolio with zero risk ($\sigma_R = 0$), the return will be r. This result is achieved simply by investing 100% in risk-free assets ($w_r = 1$) so that risk is completely eliminated. Indeed, if we substitute 1 for w_r in Equation 9.1, we obtain a certain return of r.

2. The slope of the opportunity line is $(ER_A - r)/\sigma_A$, where $E(R_A)$ and σ_A are the mean return and standard deviation of the available risky portfolio, R_A. Clearly, the higher the expected portfolio rate of return or the lower the portfolio standard deviation, the steeper the slope. As Chapter 15 will show, the slopes of such lines are useful measures of how well the various portfolios available in the market (or mutual funds) are performing.

3. If we choose a degree of risk (σ_R) to be equal to σ_A ($\sigma_R = \sigma_A$), Equation 9.4 shows that we obtain an expected return of $E(R) = E(R_A)$. This is not surprising because in this case, nothing is invested in the risk-free asset, which can be seen also from Equation 9.2:

$$E(R) = 0(r) + 1[E(R_A)] = E(R_A)$$

In this case, the portfolio has mean $E(R_A)$ and risk σ_A. This is given by point R_A in Exhibit 9-2.

4. If investors lend some part of the investment (that is, $0 < w_r < 1$), some positive proportion of wealth is invested in risk-free bonds (lending), and some proportions are invested in Asset R_A. The mean return on such a portfolio will be less than $E(R_A)$, and the standard deviation will be less than σ_A.

   For example, if $w_r = 0.25$ and $1 - w_r = 0.75$, we get an expected return of $E(R) = 0.25r + 0.75E(R_A)$. As for the risky investment R_A, we assume that $E(R_A) > r$ (because investors are averse to risk), and we obtain $E(R) < E(R_A)$. Similarly, the standard deviation of the portfolio is $\sigma_R = 0.75\sigma_A$ (see Equation 9.3); hence, the portfolio composed of positive proportions of R_A and risk-free bonds (which is the risky asset) must lie on the segment rR_A of the line given in Exhibit 9-2.

Indeed, all portfolios that lie on the segment rR_A are constructed by mixing risk-free bonds with Portfolio R_A, yielding a mean and standard deviation smaller than $E(R_A)$ and σ_A, respectively. By holding some positive investment weight in the risk-free asset, we reduce the mean return but also reduce the risk of the portfolio.

5. If investors borrow (that is, $w_r < 0$, $(1 - w_r) > 1$), they are investing more than their own wealth in R_A; namely, they borrow at the risk-free interest rate and invest their own money plus the borrowed money in the risky portfolio. This is a strategy of leveraging. The segment to the right of point R_A in Exhibit 9-2a represents these **levered portfolios,** which are portfolios that are partially financed by borrowing and have relatively high expected returns and high risk.

To see this, suppose an investor has \$1 to invest. If the investor borrows an additional \$1 at r and invests both dollars in Portfolio R_A, the mean return and risk will increase. The return (R) on the levered portfolio will be $R = 2R_A + (-1)r$. The return on the investment in Asset R_A is $2 \cdot R_A$, because \$2 is invested in R_A, and we subtract $1 \cdot r$, which is interest on the borrowed money. The expected return on such a leveraged investment is $E(R) = 2E(R_A) - (1 \cdot r) = E(R_A) + [E(R_A) - r]$, and the expected return is larger than $E(R_A)$. [Recall that $E(R_A) > r$.] The standard deviation is also larger, because $\sigma_R = 2\sigma_A$.

The most important finding of the previous discussion follows: When a risk-free asset does *not* exist, the investor has only one possible portfolio, given by point R_A. When risk-free borrowing and lending is added, this point is expanded to the straight line given in Exhibit 9-2, Parts a and b. Thus, apart from Investment R_A, many other portfolios are now available to the investor. In this respect, we say that the efficient frontier is expanded when risk-free borrowing or lending is allowed. Investors can always refuse to borrow and lend, a case where they confine themselves to point R_A. However, unless the indifference curve is exactly tangent at point R_A, a higher utility can be achieved by borrowing or lending. Note that with borrowing and lending, both the timid and the adventurous investor reach a higher indifference curve I_a and I_t (see Exhibit 9-ab); hence, the availability of the risk-free asset increases the investor's utility.

PRACTICE BOX

Problem   You have a risky asset, A, with mean of 10% and a standard deviation of 15%. The risk-free interest rate is 5%. Construct the opportunity line. Suppose you select a portfolio with a standard deviation of 20%. How much, if any, do you borrow or lend?

Solution   The opportunity line is given by Equation 9.4 and is

$$E(R) = 0.05 + [(0.10 - 0.05)/0.15]\sigma_R \cong 0.05 + 0.333\sigma_R$$

(continued)

Because $\sigma_R = (1 - w_r)\sigma_A$, to obtain a portfolio with a standard deviation of 20%, the proportion of the investment in the risk-free asset is (see Equation 9.3')

$$w_r = 1 - (\sigma_R/\sigma_A) = 1 - (0.20/0.15) \cong -0.333$$

In other words, you borrow 33.3% of your initial wealth.

9.3 THE CAPITAL MARKET LINE (CML)

In the analysis of Exhibit 9-2, we assumed that there was only one point R_A that could be a portfolio or an individual asset, and the investors mixed R_A with the risk-free asset, obtaining a straight line given by Equation 9.4. Now we analyze investors' choices in more realistic scenarios where there are many risky assets rather than just one. Therefore, investors can mix each of the available assets with the risk-free assets, creating many lines like the one given by Equation 9.4. We show that all investors, regardless of their preferences, will choose the same risky portfolio and mix it with the risk-free asset. The chosen portfolio is the one that maximizes the slopes of the straight lines given by Equation 9.4. As we shall see in this chapter, this choice is important for the following reasons:

1. It reveals the optimum portfolio of risky assets.
2. It allows us to identify the risk measure of each asset when the optimum portfolio is selected.
3. Given the asset's risk measure, this choice allows us to derive an equilibrium price and possibly find "bargains" in the market (in case the market is off equilibrium).

Exhibit 9-3 represents the investor's available choices when one risk-free asset and many risky assets are available. Segment LZ represents the efficient frontier consisting of only risky assets.[4] The dots located to the right of curve ALZ and the two dots labeled A and Z (which are on the line ALZ) represent individual risky assets. Points A and Z correspond to the individual assets with the lowest and highest mean returns, respectively. All other points on the curves represent portfolios. As shown in Exhibit 9-2, the investor can mix any portfolio or asset taken from Exhibit 9-3 with the risk-free asset, creating opportunity lines such as Lines 1 and 2 in Exhibit 9-3. The opportunity line is the set of portfolios that can be constructed using one risky asset, such as Asset c, and the risk-free interest rate. The question is, of course, Which opportunity line puts the investor on the highest indifference curve?

In Exhibit 9-3, line ra has the highest slope. By choosing this line, the investor can reach the highest possible indifference curve (for example, indifference curve I_2 rather than I_1). The portfolios that fall along line ra, which is tangent to the curve LZ, are achieved by mixing Portfolio m with the risk-free asset. Portfolio m, which

---

4. Curve LZ represents the set of all points between L and Z on the mean-variance frontier. The segment AL represents the inefficient part of the frontier.

EXHIBIT 9-3
The Efficient Frontier with
Borrowing and Lending of a
Risk-Free Asset

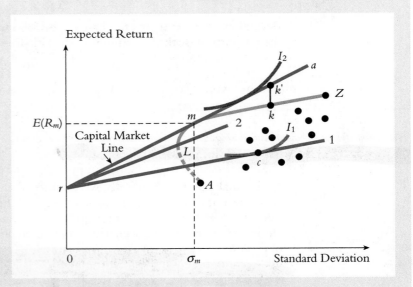

maximizes the slope of the opportunity line, is called the **market portfolio,** or the optimum portfolio of marketable risky assets.[5] We assume that all possible risky assets are considered in constructing curve *LZ*. The market portfolio provides all investors, regardless of their preferences, the highest utility they can achieve when risk-free borrowing and lending is available. Note that *m* (see Exhibit 9-3) is a portfolio and not an individual asset, and by mixing it with the risk-free asset, we end up holding a portfolio of risky assets and the risk-free asset.

We can employ Equation 9.4 for Portfolio m to obtain the formula for line *ra:*

$$E(R) = r + \frac{[(E(R_m) - r)]}{\sigma_m} \sigma_R \qquad (9.5)$$

All portfolios on line *ra* in Exhibit 9-3 are efficient by the mean–variance criterion (MVC), and all other portfolios (and individual assets) are inefficient. The opportunity line that maximizes the slope is called the **capital market line (CML).** The CML is a straight line composed of all possible combinations of the market portfolio (point *m* in Exhibit 9-3), and the risk-free asset (*r*). Note that in the absence of borrowing and lending, the efficient frontier is given by the curve *LZ* (see Exhibit 9-3). By adding the possibility of borrowing and lending, the efficient frontier now becomes the straight line *ra*.

---

5. As will be shown later, in equilibrium, Portfolio m must include all available assets in the market—hence the name *market portfolio.*

Line *ra* clearly dominates the set of risky assets *LZ*, because for any portfolio on curve *LZ*, there is a better portfolio on line *ra* (except for Portfolio m, which lies on both *LZ* and *ra*). For example, Portfolio k′ on line *ra* is superior to Portfolio k on curve *LZ*, because it has the same risk but a higher mean return. Thus, by allowing borrowing and lending at *r*, the efficient frontier is expanded or improved. Also, note that no portfolio taken from line *ra* dominates another portfolio taken from this line. Thus, line *ra* includes all efficient portfolios.

To summarize, the straight line obtained by mixing Portfolio m with borrowing and lending of the risk-free asset is called the CML. Any such mix of *m* and *r* creates a portfolio that includes all the risky assets composing Portfolio m. Because all the portfolios lying on line *ra* are efficient, the linear return-risk relationship given by Equation 9.5 is appropriate *only for efficient portfolios* consisting of various combinations of *r* and *m*.[6]

PRACTICE BOX

Problem

Portfolio A has a mean of 10% and a standard deviation of 8%. Portfolio B has a mean of 15% and a standard deviation of 30%. The risk-free asset has a return of 5%. Which of these two portfolios combined with the risk-free assets provides a higher slope?

Solution

Recall from Exhibit 9-3 that we seek to maximize the slope of the opportunity line. Thus, we seek the portfolio where the slope of this line is the largest. Thus, for two alternative slopes, we obtain

$$\text{Portfolio A: } (0.10 - 0.05)/0.08 = 0.625$$

$$\text{Portfolio B: } (0.15 - 0.05)/0.30 \cong 0.333$$

Although Portfolio B offers a higher mean rate of return, investors will be better off with Portfolio A.

9.4 THE SEPARATION PROPERTY

All investors, regardless of their preferences, will choose to mix Portfolio m with the risk-free asset (*r*). That is, different combinations of Portfolio m and the risk-free asset (*r*) will yield an opportunity line steeper than any other possible lines attained by mixing the risk-free asset with other risky portfolios. Hence, by selecting to invest in Portfolio m, investors can achieve higher expected returns for a given risk level.

---

6. Note that borrowing and lending the risk-free asset is similar to going long (holding a long position) or short (holding a short position) in Treasury bills.

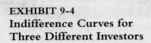
EXHIBIT 9-4
Indifference Curves for
Three Different Investors

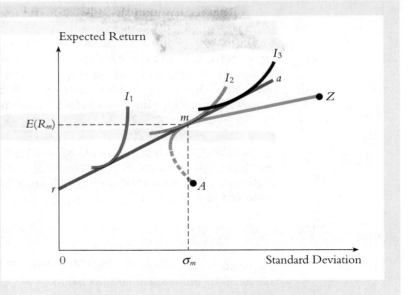

Exhibit 9-4 illustrates the indifference curves of three possible investors. Investor I_1, a lender, puts some proportion of his money in the riskless asset and some in a portfolio of risky assets denoted by m. Investor I_3 borrows money and invests all of her own wealth, plus the amount borrowed, in Portfolio m. Investor I_2 follows the old adage "Neither a borrower nor a lender be." All three investors have one common strategy: they invest in the same Portfolio m of risky assets.

The possibility of borrowing and lending at interest rate r allows a separation of the investment process into two stages:

1. At Stage 1, we find Portfolio m, which is located at the point where the CML and the efficient frontier of risky assets are tangent. This tangency portfolio is the portfolio of risky assets that is desired by all investors.
2. At Stage 2, all investors maximize their utility by borrowing or lending.

Stage 1 is objective and common to all investors; there is no need to know each investor's unique preference (that is, the indifference curves) in order to find Portfolio m. Stage 2 is subjective, and each investor's preference does need to be known; it is determined by indifference curves that vary from one investor to another. This separation of the investment decision into two stages is called the separation property or **separation theorem.** That is, the portfolio selection procedure can be divided into two stages: (1) choose the best portfolio of marketable risky assets, which will be the same portfolio for *all* investors (the market portfolio), and (2) choose the optimal mix of the market portfolio determined in Stage 1 with the risk-free asset to adjust the risk and return preferences of the individual investor.

Because all investors hold the same portfolio of marketable risky assets (m), we can derive a linear relationship between the expected return and risk of each individual asset, as discussed in the next section.

9.5 THE SECURITY MARKET LINE (SML) AND THE CAPITAL ASSET PRICING MODEL (CAPM)

The CML given by Equation 9.5 is a linear relationship between the *efficient* portfolios' standard deviation and their expected return. The CML does not relate to individual assets or even to portfolios that are inefficient (located below line *ra* in Exhibit 9-3). Therefore, the CML does not show us the relationship between the expected rate of return and risk of individual assets (or inefficient portfolios).

How can we determine the relationship between the risk and return of a single asset, such as the stock of Apple Computer or Exxon, that may not be on the efficient frontier? With individual securities, beta (denoted β) is the appropriate measure of risk. Unlike the security's own variance (or standard deviation, σ), beta also captures the covariances with all other assets.

9.5.1 Beta as a Measure of Risk

If only one asset is held in a portfolio, then the standard deviation of this asset is the appropriate risk measure. In a portfolio with many risky assets (as we have seen in Chapters 7 and 8), the covariances among these assets also determine the portfolio's risk. Beta takes all these covariances into account and is thus the appropriate measure of risk. Let's take a closer look at beta.

Beta is the risk measure of an individual asset, such as the common stock of Exxon, IBM, or Ford Motor Company. However, what is beta? Why does it measure the risk of individual assets?

The beta of Asset i, denoted by β_i, is defined as

$$\beta_i = \frac{Cov(R_i, R_m)}{\sigma_m^2} \tag{9.6}$$

where R_i is the rate of return on the *i*th asset, and R_m is the rate of return on the market portfolio (m). Thus, beta measures the co-movement of Asset i and the market.

Because the market portfolio is a combination of risky assets, $R_m = \sum_{j=1}^{n} w_j R_j$, where n is the number of assets included in the market portfolio and w_j is the weight of Asset j in the portfolio. Therefore, beta can also be written as follows:[7]

---

7. We apply the rule

$$Cov(x, ay + bz) = a\, cov(x, y) + b\, cov(x, z)$$

where a and b are some constants and x, y, and z are random variables.

$$\beta_i = Cov\left(R_i, \sum_{j=1}^{n} w_j R_j\right)/\sigma_m^2 = \sum_{j=1}^{n} w_j Cov(R_i, R_j)/\sigma_m^2$$

and the beta of Asset i provides one value that incorporates all the possible covariances of this asset with all other assets ($j = 1, 2, \ldots, n$). Beta can be calculated as follows with historical data when equal probability is assigned to each observation period:[8]

$$\beta_i = \frac{\frac{1}{N}\left(\sum_{t=1}^{N} R_{i,t} R_{m,t}\right) - \overline{R}_i \overline{R}_m}{\frac{1}{N}\left(\sum_{t=1}^{N} R_{m,t}^2\right) - \overline{R}_m^2} \tag{9.6'}$$

where N denotes the number of observations and t denotes historical periods (for example, years, months, and so forth).

Obviously, beta also can be calculated for portfolios (efficient and inefficient alike), and mutual funds. For example, the beta of the market portfolio that is, of course, an efficient portfolio (see point m, Exhibit 9-3), is $+1$ (see later in this chapter).

PRACTICE BOX

Problem

The rate of return for 3 years on the market portfolio (market return) and on Exxon stock is as follows:

Year	Exxon Stock	Market Return
1	0.12	0.10
2	0.20	0.15
3	0.10	0.08

Calculate the beta of Exxon where the probability of each annual outcome is ⅓.

Solution

Let Exxon's rates of return be denoted by R_i and the market's rate of return be denoted by R_m. Construct the following table:

(continued)

---

8. Recall from Equation 7.3 that

$$Cov(R_i, R_m) = E[R_i - \overline{R}_i)(R_m - \overline{R}_m)] = \frac{1}{N}\sum_{t=1}^{N}(R_{i,t} - \overline{R}_i)(R_{m,t} - \overline{R}_m)$$

which can be rewritten as

$$Cov(R_i, R_m) = \frac{1}{N}\sum_{t=1}^{N}(R_{i,t} R_{m,t}) - \overline{R}_i \overline{R}_m$$

Note that throughout the book, we generally denote the number of observations (years) by m. Here we replace it with N to distinguish it from the market portfolio, which is denoted m.

i	R_i	R_m	$R_i \cdot R_m$	R_m^2
1	0.12	0.10	0.012	0.0100
2	0.20	0.15	0.030	0.0225
3	0.10	0.08	0.008	0.0064
Sum	0.42	0.33	0.050	0.0389
Average	0.14	0.11	0.0167	0.0130

Using Equation 9.6'

$$\beta_i = \frac{0.0167 - 0.14 \cdot 0.11}{0.013 - 0.11^2} = \frac{0.0013}{0.0009} \cong 1.44$$

Thus, Exxon's beta is 1.44.

9.5.2 The Meaning of Beta—Characteristic Lines

Why does beta measure risk? Note that β (or β_i, where i stands for Asset i) is nothing but the slope of the regression line given by[9]

$$R_{i_t} = \alpha_i + \beta_i R_{m_t} + e_{i_t} \qquad (9.7)$$

where R_{i_t} is the rate of return on the ith stock in Period t, α_i is the intercept of the line, R_{m_t} is the rate of return on the market portfolio for the same Period t, and e_{i_t} is the deviation from the regression line, called the *error term*. In practice, the error term is not directly observable. However, it can be calculated from Equation 9.7, because R_{i_t} and R_{m_t} are directly observable, and α_i and β_i are estimated.[10] The regression line describing the relationship between R_i and R_m is called the **characteristic**

---

9. In running the following kind of regression,

$$y = \alpha + \beta x + e$$

the slope of the regression line is β, given by

$$\beta = \frac{Cov(x,y)}{\sigma_x^2}$$

Thus, for $y = R_i$ and $x = R_m$, we get

$$\beta_i = \frac{Cov(R_i, R_m)}{\sigma_m^2}$$

Also, a well-known statistical result is

$$\alpha = \bar{y} - \beta \bar{x}$$

and in our specific case we have

$$\alpha_i = \bar{R}_i - \beta_i \bar{R}_m$$

10. Section 9.8 will show that alpha (α) has an economic meaning; it measures the return in excess of the risk-adjusted return as implied by the CAPM and therefore is called the *abnormal return* (see Section 9.8 and Footnote 21).

line.[11] The slope of the regression line is equal to β_i and is thus the risk of the ith asset. The following discussion sheds more light on this risk measure.

If you hold a well-diversified portfolio, you can eliminate a large portion of the risk by diversification; however, the risk of the market portfolio cannot be eliminated. Even if you hold the market portfolio, you cannot avoid the fluctuations of the whole market. For example, on October 19, 1987, the whole stock market went down by more than 20%. Exhibit 9-5 shows the ten biggest one-day declines of the Dow Jones Industrial Average in terms of both the index points and the percentage change. No matter how well diversified your portfolio was on October 19, 1987, or any of the other days shown in Exhibit 9-5, you could not have avoided this loss.

Similarly, no amount of diversification can avoid the risk of economic recession. Thus, macroeconomic factors such as unemployment, the trade balance, budget deficits, interest rates, or events such as war can significantly affect the market rate of return. This risk cannot be diversified away, because it affects the whole market. Beta captures this macroeconomic risk, and therefore it is also called *market risk*.

Beta measures the slope of the line given by Equation 9.7; it measures the sensitivity of the ith stock to market fluctuations. For example, if $\beta_i = 2$, when the market rate of return increases by 1%, this stock's rate of return is expected to go up by 2% on average. However, when the market rate of return goes down by 1%, the stock's rate of return is expected to fall by 2%. Thus, this stock is considered to be an **aggressive stock,** or a stock that is more risky than the market portfolio. This stock fluctuates twice as much as the market portfolio. Similarly, if $\beta_i = \frac{1}{2}$, the stock fluctuates half as much as the market and is considered not to be very risky; it is called a **defensive stock.** A defensive stock "defends" the investor from large losses but also denies the investor large gains. Finally, if $\beta_i = 1$, the stock moves exactly with the market on average. It is called a **neutral stock.**

What is the beta of the market portfolio? Recall from Chapter 7 that the covariance of an asset with itself is nothing but its variance (see Equation 7.5). Thus, the beta of the market portfolio (from Equation 9.6) equals 1, because

$$\beta_m = \frac{Cov(R_m, R_m)}{\sigma_m^2} = \frac{\sigma_m^2}{\sigma_m^2} = 1.0$$

Exhibit 9-6a presents pairs of rates of return on the market portfolio and on the ith stock, along with the regression line that best fits this "cloud" of points that is the corresponding characteristic line. The intercept of the line is α_i, the slope is β_i, and the vertical deviations of the points from the line are the error terms, e_i (see Exhibit 9-6a). The closer the points are to the line, the better the fit.

Exhibit 9-6b describes characteristic lines corresponding to aggressive, defensive, and neutral stocks. Computer firms, such as Apple Computer and Microsoft, are considered to be aggressive stocks. When the market is up by x%, they are usually up by more than x%; when the market is down by x%, they are usually down by

---

11. The characteristic line measures the expected rate of return on the ith asset for a given R_m. Thus, for any R_m, a point on the line is given by $\bar{R}_i = \alpha_i + \beta_i R_m$. If R_m is, say, 10%, and $\beta = 2$ and $\alpha = 5\%$, we have $\bar{R}_i = 5\% + (2 \cdot 10\%) = 25\%$. However, if R_m changed from 10% to 14%, the average rate of return on the stock would be $\bar{R}_i = 5\% + (2 \cdot 14\%) = 33\%$, and the *change* in the expected rate of return would be 8%, as a beta of 2 would predict.

EXHIBIT 9-5
Biggest One-Day Declines in DJIA

Days with Greatest Net Loss in Index Points

Rank	Date	Close	Net Change	% Change
1	10/27/97	7161.15	−554.26	−7.19
2	10/19/87	1738.74	−508.00	−22.61
3	08/15/97	7694.66	−247.37	−3.11
4	06/23/97	7604.26	−192.25	−2.47
5	10/13/89	2569.26	−190.58	−6.91
6	10/23/97	7847.77	−186.88	−2.33
7	03/08/96	5470.45	−171.24	−3.04
8	07/15/96	5349.51	−161.05	−2.92
9	03/13/97	6878.89	−160.48	−2.28
10	11/12/97	7401.32	−157.41	−2.08

Days with Greatest Percentage Loss in Index Points

Rank	Date	Close	Net Change	% Change
1	10/19/87	1738.74	−508.00	−22.61
2	10/28/29	260.64	−38.33	−12.82
3	10/29/29	230.07	−30.57	−11.73
4	11/06/29	232.13	−25.55	−9.92
5	12/18/29	58.27	−5.57	−8.72
6	08/12/32	63.11	−5.79	−8.40
7	03/14/07	76.23	−6.89	−8.29
8	10/26/87	1793.93	−156.83	−8.04
9	07/21/33	88.71	−7.55	−7.84
10	10/18/37	125.73	−10.57	−7.75

more than $x\%$. The stocks of utilities such as Florida Gas or Florida Power and Light, are considered to be defensive. When the market is up by $x\%$, the demand for gas or electricity increases, but by less than $x\%$. When the market is down by $x\%$, the demand for gas and electricity goes down less sharply than the overall demand for other products; hence, the stock of these firms decreases by less than $x\%$.

Thus, beta measures the sensitivity of the ith stock or the portfolio rate of return to changes in the market portfolio rates of return. There are many mutual funds in the market, each of which is composed of numerous risky assets (bonds and stocks). The funds are generally below curve LZ of Exhibit 9-3, because they do not hold all assets available in the market. It is common among practitioners to compare the funds' performance by examining their return and risk, when the risk is measured by beta. Connecting Theory to Practice 9.1 further illustrates how practitioners use beta.

EXHIBIT 9-6
The Characteristic Line

Part a: The Line That Fits Best the "Cloud" of Points

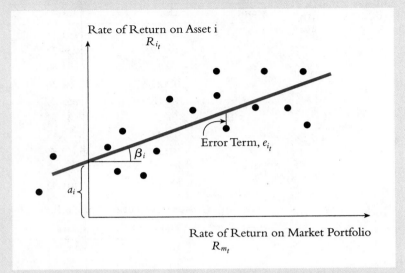

Part b: Examples of the Characteristic Line

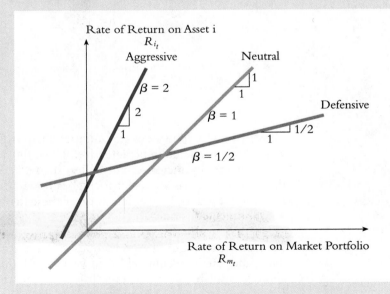

CONNECTING THEORY TO PRACTICE 9.1

HOW SAVVY FUND INVESTORS TALLY THE RISK

Commonly associated with measuring volatility of individual stocks, beta tracks how closely a fund follows the ups and downs of the stock market. It's calculated by looking at the month-to-month fluctuations of a fund's total return over a three-year period, compared with similar movements of the S&P 500-stock index. For purposes of comparison, the S&P 500 is assigned a beta of 1.00. A fund with a beta of less than 1.00 is less volatile than the broader market. A figure higher than 1.00 means a fund is more volatile, and thus its risk—and potential reward—is higher.

"BETA" MEASURES A FUND'S VOLATILITY
AGAINST THE S&P 500

A look at the top performers so far this year illustrates how beta can be used. The Janus Fund generated a total return of 47.2% through Sept. 8, making it the eighth-best performer, according to Chicago-based Morningstar. Better yet, its beta is 0.71, the lowest of the top 10 funds. By contrast, the Twentieth Century Giftrust Investors fund, which generated a slightly higher return of 49.6%, has a beta of 1.36—meaning it is 36% more volatile than the market. So in a market downturn, it's more likely to lose more value. Janus investors receive almost identical returns, while taking less risk.

Expert Opinion: There are drawbacks to beta. For one, it isn't statistically valid in comparing specialized funds, such as gold funds, which can move inversely to the stock market in response to bullion prices. Also, beta, pegged to the S&P, is designed only to measure the U.S. equities market.

Bond funds' betas are calculated using Shearson Lehman Hutton's Government/Corporate Bond Index. But for some, such as junk-bond funds, beta isn't meaningful since there is little relation between their behavior and the broader bond market.

Calculating beta takes an expert. It's best to consult mutual fund directories, available at brokerage houses and libraries. You can also find statistics on volatility in services provided by firms such as Morningstar. Morningstar's *Mutual Fund Values* costs $55 for three monthly sets of detailed information on 1,100 funds. And on computer disk, *Business Week*'s Mutual Funds Scoreboard—compiled by Morningstar—also includes a volatility measure.

Source: "How Savvy Fund Investors Tally the Risk," by John Meehan. Reprinted from the October 2, 1989, issue of *Business Week* by special permission, copyright © 1989 by The McGraw-Hill Companies, Inc.

(continued)

MAKING THE CONNECTION

Mutual funds are ranked by their total return and risk, where risk is measured by beta. The Standard & Poor's 500 stock index is used as a proxy to the market portfolio. A fund with a high total return but also a high beta is not necessarily considered to be a well-managed fund. However, the Janus Fund is considered to be a success: it is the eighth-best performer in total returns, and its beta (risk) is the lowest of the top ten funds. Thus, both total return and beta are employed in examining a fund's success.

Beta is commonly used in many publications as a measure of the risk of an investment (or as an index for safety). Beta is a risk index for portfolios (mutual funds), as well as for individual securities. The larger the beta, the more risky the corresponding asset or portfolio. Exhibit 9-7 illustrates how beta is used as a risk measure of individual stocks and mutual funds.

EXHIBIT 9-7   Uses of Beta

Part a: Callaway Golf

Key Stock Statistics

S&P EPS Est. 1997	2.00	Tang. Bk. Value/Share	5.71
P/E on S&P Est. 1997	16.5	**Beta**	**1.27**
S&P EPS Est. 1998	2.40	Shareholders	6,700
Dividend Rate/Share	0.28	Market cap. (B)	$ 2.4
Shs. outstg. (M)	73.8	Inst. holdings	54%
Avg. daily vol. (M)	0.420		

Part b: Vanguard PrimeCap Fund (VPMCX)

Growth of $10,000 (Ending Value = $70,805)

MPT Statistics

Total Returns	NAV	Load Adj.		3 Yr.	5 Yr.	10 Yr.
Year-To-Date	18.31%	—	Std Dev	12.25	11.80	18.65
1 Month	−1.33%	—	Alpha(%)	1.10	2.18	−1.28
3 Month	7.16%	—	**Beta**	**1.03**	**1.04**	**1.12**
1 Year	18.31%	18.31%	R Sq(%)	65	57	81
3 Year Avg	21.32%	21.32%	Sharpe	1.31	1.16	0.51
5 Year Avg	18.10%	18.10%	Treynor	1.22	1.03	0.67

(continued)

EXHIBIT 9-7   *(continued)*

Total Returns	NAV	Load Adj.
10 Year Avg	15.02%	15.02%
15 Year Avg	—	—
20 Year Avg	—	—
Since Inception	17.58%	17.57%

Part c: Ratings & Reports

Page	Ticker	Company	Recent Price	P/E	Yield %	Beta	Financial Strength
1682	AZO	AutoZone Inc.	29	20.1	Nil	1.10	B++
Industry Sector: Retail (Special Lines)							
2198	BMCS	BMC Software	66	29.9	Nil	1.30	B++
Industry Sector: Computer Software & Svcs							
904	ETH	Ethan Allen Interiors	39	20.0	0.3	1.30	B+
Industry Sector: Furn./Home Furnishings							
681	HBOC	HBO & Co.	48	45.7	0.2	1.30	B++
Industry Sector: Healthcare Information							
1881	HAL	Halliburton Co.	49	24.9	1.0 ·	0.90	B++
Industry Sector: Oilfield Services/Equip.							
317	LDRY	Landry's Seafood	24	20.7	Nil	1.35	B+
Industry Sector: Restaurant							
1064	LLTC	Linear Technology	57	26.5	0.4	1.40	A
Industry Sector: Semiconductor							
2153	KRB	MBNA Corp.	27	20.8	1.2	1.55	B++
Industry Sector: Financial Services							

Source: Part a: Standard & Poor's Stock Reports 1997. Reprinted by permission of Standard & Poor's, a division of The McGraw-Hill Companies. Part b: *Investment Companies Yearbook 1997,* CDA/Wiesenberger, Investment Companies Service, p. 1274. Reprinted by permission. Part c: *The Value Line Investment Survey,* January 9, 1998, p. 6424. Reprinted with permission.

9.5.3 U.S. Market Portfolio and the World Market Portfolio

At this stage, one should ask, What is the composition of the market portfolio (*m*)? Conceptually, it should include all available risky assets.

Should international securities markets be included in Portfolio m? In other words, can we get a steeper CML by diversifying internationally? In principle, the answer is yes, we can gain from international diversification. In the age of electronic communications, the world market has become one large market, and it is easy to invest in the securities of foreign countries. However, most macroeconomic shocks affect all markets. For example, the 1987 crash was not just a U.S. phenomenon but a world phenomenon. Still, as long as correlations between markets are not perfect, the investor can benefit from an international diversification.

International diversification achieves two objectives: (1) it increases the number of assets available, and (2) it decreases, but does not eliminate, the market portfolio risk. It is possible to reduce the market portfolio fluctuations by investing in the world market portfolio, but certainly these fluctuations cannot be completely eliminated. Thus, in principle, when calculating beta, Portfolio m should be taken as the world market, not just the U.S. market. However, for practical reasons, in calculating beta, only the U.S. market is used (or at best, the U.S. market plus some markets in Western Europe and Japan, which have accessible databases on rates of return).

9.5.4 The Security Market Line (SML)

So far, we have seen that beta is the risk of an individual asset. However, how is the expected return on an individual asset related to beta? To answer this question, we first calculate the beta of Apple Computer and investigate its corresponding expected return.

The following table presents the rates of return for a recent 5-year period for both the market portfolio and Apple Computer:

Year	Apple Computer	Market Portfolio
1	−0.13	−0.03
2	0.05	0.02
3	0.15	0.08
4	0.27	0.12
5	0.10	0.07

Following the procedure explained in the previous problem, we obtain the following:

i	R_i	R_m	$R_i \cdot R_m$	R_m^2
1	−0.13	−0.03	0.0039	0.0009
2	0.05	0.02	0.0010	0.0004
3	0.15	0.08	0.012	0.0064
4	0.27	0.12	0.0324	0.0144
5	0.10	0.07	0.0070	0.0049
Sum	0.44	0.26	0.0563	0.027
Average	0.088	0.052	0.01126	0.0054

Thus,

$$\beta_i = \frac{0.01126 - (0.088)(0.052)}{0.0054 - 0.052^2} \cong 2.48$$

Because beta is greater than 1, Apple Computer is classified as an aggressive stock.

What is the expected rate of return required from Apple Computer stock, given that its risk as measured by beta is 2.48? Answering such a question requires the introduction of a new concept, the security market line (SML).

Each asset has its own risk–return profile. If the expected return exactly compensates investors for the risk exposure, we say that the market is in *equilibrium*. There is no incentive to sell or buy stocks, and no investors will wish to change their portfolio compositions. When the market is in equilibrium, all assets are correctly priced, and there are no "bargains" in the market.

The asset pricing model that determines the equilibrium relationship between the expected return and risk of individual assets, as well as portfolios, is called the **capital asset pricing model (CAPM).** The linear relationship between expected return and beta that follows from the CAPM is called the **security market line (SML).** Although we use the terms SML and CAPM interchangeably for the linear risk–return relationship, keep in mind that the CAPM is an equilibrium pricing model, whereas the SML is the end result of this model. We first describe the SML and then discuss and prove the CAPM.

The main results of the CAPM are summarized in the SML linear relationship, which describes the risk–return relationship of individual assets as well as portfolios, whether they are efficient or not. The SML asserts that the following linear risk–return relationship should hold:[12]

$$E(R_i) \quad = \quad r \quad + \quad [E(R_m) - r]\beta_i \qquad (9.8)$$

$$\text{Expected Rate of Return} \quad = \quad \text{Risk–Free Rate} \quad + \quad \text{Risk Premium}$$

where $E(R_i)$ = the expected rate of return on the ith asset, $E(R_m)$ = the expected rate of return of the market portfolio, r = the risk-free interest rate, and β_i = the risk of the ith asset (or its beta). The SML asserts that the expected rate of return on Asset i is equal to the risk-free rate plus a risk premium. This risk premium is equal to the market risk premium $[E(R_m) - r]$ multiplied by the asset's beta.

Exhibit 9-8a demonstrates the SML. Note first that if $\beta_i = 0$, the ith asset is risk-free. Indeed, if we substitute zero for β_i in Equation 9.8, we obtain $E(R_i) = r$. Thus, as expected, the return on a risk-free asset is r. Second, if $\beta_i = 1$, then $E(R_i) = E(R_m)$. In this case, the asset's price fluctuates, on average, in tandem with the market, therefore, the asset has the same risk as the market and hence yields, on average, the same rate of return as the market portfolio, $E(R_m)$. If the stock is a defensive stock ($\beta_i < 1$), the expected return will be smaller than $E(R_m)$. When $\beta_i > 1$, the stock is aggressive—that is, more risky than the market portfolio. Therefore, in equilibrium, the aggressive stock will be characterized by a higher expected return than the market $[E(R_i) > E(R_m)]$.

Thus, in general, the mean return on the ith stock can be broken down into two components: r, the risk-free interest rate, and $[E(R_m) - r]\beta_i$, the risk premium.

---

12. The linear relationship between $E(R_i)$ and β_i holds for any security or portfolio as long as Portfolio m is mean-variance efficient. However, to develop the equilibrium model, we must assume that all investors are risk averse and that they select their portfolios according to the mean-variance rule. In addition, we must assume homogeneous expectations among investors, the absence of transaction costs, and the availability of the risk-free asset. Under these assumptions, all investors hold Portfolio m (the separation property), from which the CAPM follows.

Part a: The Security Market Line (SML)

EXHIBIT 9-8
The Security Line (SML) and
the Capital Market Line (CML)

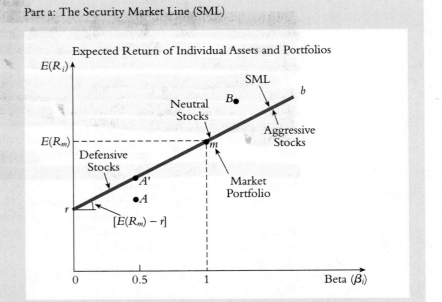

Part b: The Capital Market Line (CML)

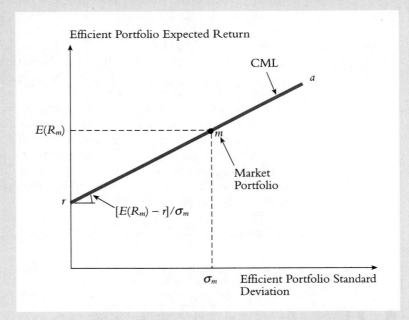

Because $E(R_m) - r$, the slope of line rb in Exhibit 9-8a, is the same for all stocks, we conclude that the higher β_i is, the greater the risk and thus the higher the required risk premium. Therefore, for a high β_i, the corresponding $E(R_i)$ will also be relatively large.

Exhibit 9-8b shows the CML. The CML represents only efficient portfolios; therefore, the risk measure is the portfolio's standard deviation (or variance). Notice that the slope of the CML is $[E(R_m) - r]/\sigma_m$, whereas the slope of the SML is $E(R_m) - r$. Note also that if we invest in an efficient portfolio whose standard deviation is σ_m (the market portfolio), we receive, by employing the CML, an expected return of $E(R_m)$. This is consistent with the SML, because for the market portfolio we have $\beta_m = 1$ and the expected return of $E(R_m)$. Also, because all portfolios and the CML are simply a mix of m and the risk-free asset, by increasing the proportion invested in Portfolio m, one also increases β. Therefore, the risk of *efficient portfolios* can be measured by either σ or β.[13]

PRACTICE BOX

Problem	Suppose the mean rate of return on the market is 10%, and the risk-free interest rate is 5%. Given that beta is 2.48 for Apple Computer, what is the expected rate of return on Apple Computer stock?
Solution	Based on Equation 9.8, the expected rate of return is $E(R_i) = 5\% + (10\% - 5\%)2.48 \cong 17.4\%$.

The SML is a line on which each asset's mean rate of return and beta are plotted. The beta of each asset and a portfolio are calculated by using some market portfolio rates of return. Therefore, the beta and hence the SML depend on the selected market portfolio. If all pairs of expected rate of return and beta lie on one line, the SML, then the market is in equilibrium. However, when historical data are used to estimate the expected rate of return and beta, generally some assets plot above or below the SML, indicating either disequilibrium or a statistically insignificant deviation from the line (because of sampling errors).

To illustrate how the selection of the market portfolios affects beta and the SML, we can take a sample of 5 years' monthly rates of return on the U.S. stock market and on the "world" market for the period January 1993 to January 1998.[14] Of course, the beta of the U.S. market calculated with itself is $+1$. Similarly, the beta of the world market calculated with itself is $+1$. However, using the world market rates of return as the market portfolio to calculate the beta of the U.S. market, we find that beta is equal to 0.74. Using these 5-year data, the average monthly rates of return on the U.S. market and the world market are 1.45% and 1.13%, respectively.

---

13. Consider a Portfolio R, where $R = (w_r \cdot r) + (1 - w_r)R_m$ located on the CML when w_r is the investment proportion in the risk-free asset. Then $\sigma_R = (1 - w_r)\sigma_{Rm}$ and $\beta_R = (1 - w_r)\beta_m = (1 - w_r) \cdot 1$. Thus, as w_r decreases, both σ_R and β_R increase (see also footnote 7).

14. Data from Morgan Stanley Web site at http://www.ms.com/MSCIDATA.

Exhibit 9-9 illustrates the SML, both with the U.S. market as the market portfolio and with the world market as the market portfolio. Line A denotes the SML with the U.S. market as the market portfolio. Point m_1 stands for the U.S. market index as the market portfolio; hence, its beta in this specific example is equal to 1. Its mean rate of return is 1.45%. Point m_3 stands for the world market portfolio; beta for this portfolio is also equal to 1, and the portfolio's mean rate of return is 1.13%. However, when the U.S. market beta is calculated with the world market portfolio, we find that the beta of the U.S. market is 0.74; the average monthly rate of return remains at 1.45%. Thus, the U.S. market is given by point m_1 when the U.S. market is employed as the market portfolio and is given by point m_2 when the world market is employed as the market portfolio. In this specific example, m_2 is above both lines A and B. This finding indicates either that the market is not in equilibrium or that the data we employed are historical and, hence, that deviations from the SML are possible. (These deviations may or may not be statistically insignificant. To check such significance, however, we need more assets.)

Exhibit 9-9 shows that beta may change as a function of the selected market portfolio. However, by definition, the beta of the selected market portfolio is always 1. That is, if we use the SML with the U.S. market as the market portfolio, the beta of the U.S. market is equal to 1; if the SML is calculated with the world market, the beta of the world market is 1. However, the beta of the U.S. market calculated with

EXHIBIT 9-9   SML with Both the U.S. Market and the World Market as the Market Portfolio

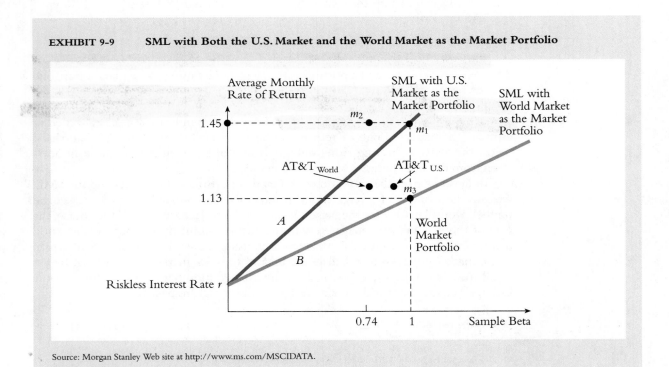

Source: Morgan Stanley Web site at http://www.ms.com/MSCIDATA.

other market portfolios—for example, the world market—may be different from 1. In our example, it is 0.74.

Take now the stock of an individual firm, say, AT&T stock. For a given set of data, AT&T has only one average rate of return but two betas—one beta that is calculated with the U.S. market as the market portfolio and one beta that is calculated with the world market as the market portfolio. Hence, two points correspond to AT&T: $AT\&T_{US}$ and $AT\&T_{world}$ (see Exhibit 9-9). If American investors diversified their portfolios only with the U.S. market, investing in AT&T would be considered a failure (at least it would have in the past), because AT&T is located below line A; the average rate of return on AT&T is below what is required by its risk. However, if American investors diversified internationally, investing in AT&T would be considered a success, because $AT\&T_{world}$ is above line B in Exhibit 9-9. The reason why investing in AT&T can be considered a success or a failure depending on the selected market portfolio is that the risk index of AT&T changes as the diversifying policy changes. AT&T's beta with the U.S. market as the market portfolio is not equal to AT&T's beta with the world portfolio as the market portfolio.

Why is the risk–return linear relationship called a *pricing* model, although no prices appear in Equation 9.8? Suppose that according to Equation 9.8, $E(R_i) = $ 15%, and the stock's expected price at the end of the investment period is $E(P_1) = $ \$115. Assuming no dividends, what is the current stock price? It must be $P_0 = \$100$, because 15% = (\$115 − \$100)/\$100. Suppose now that for some reason, the stock's beta increases so that $E(R_i)$ as implied by the CAPM increases to $E(R_i) = 20\%$. Assume that there is no change in the expected price at the end of the period; hence, $E(P_1)$ remains \$115. (One can also relax this assumption without affecting the analysis.) The current price (P_0) must now decrease until $E(R_i) = 20\% = (\$115 − P_0)/P_0$, or $(0.2 \cdot P_0) + P_0 = \$115$, or $P_0(0.2 + 1) = \$115$. Therefore, $P_0 = \$115/1.2 \cong \$95.83$. Thus, according to the CAPM, a change in $E(R_i)$ causes a change in the current price of the asset—hence the name capital asset *pricing* model. The expected return $E(R_i)$ as implied by the CAPM is also called the *required* rate of return, because it is the return that investors require in equilibrium as compensation for the risk exposure.

Given the SML relationship, what is the required (or expected) rate of return on an asset where beta is negative, say, -1? (See this chapter's Investment in the News.) The expected rate of return, according to Equation 9.8, is $ER_i = r + [E(R_m) − r](-1)$. This result is lower than r because $ER_m > r$, and it may even be negative. Does this result make sense? If an investor holds only the Rydex Ursa fund, the answer is no, because investors are expected to lose money. However, if the investor holds this fund with many other assets (for example, the Standard & Poor's index), this result does make sense. A fund with a negative beta stabilizes the whole portfolio's return (that is, reduces the portfolio's risk), so an investor will be willing to obtain a relatively low return on the fund.

9.5.5 The Risk Premium

The size of $E(R_i) − r$ is the risk premium required on the *i*th security—namely, the return the investor requires, on average, from the *i*th stock above and beyond what can be earned on the risk-free asset. Of course, the larger the risk of the ith asset, the larger the required risk premium. By the same token, $E(R_m) - r$ is the risk premium on Portfolio m, the market portfolio.

Exhibit 9-10 shows monthly returns for 20 years for two stocks and a value-weighted index of all securities on the NYSE and AMEX. It illustrates the monthly rates of return for two stocks: Commonwealth Edison (CWE), a regulated power company, and Dow Chemical, a chemical manufacturer. The lines in the exhibit are

EXHIBIT 9-10
The Risk Premium

Part a: Commonwealth Edison (CWE) Monthly Rates of Return Compared with the Market

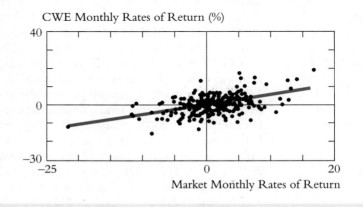

Part b: Dow Chemical Monthly Rates of Return Compared with the Market

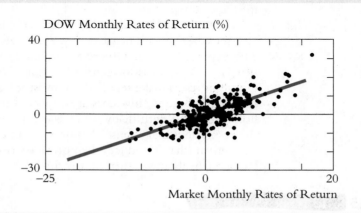

Source: Data from Center for Research on Security Prices.

characteristic lines. Notice that Dow is more sensitive to changes in the market than CWE is, because Dow has a higher beta (note the slope of the line). The one-month Treasury bill (annualized) rate of return for this period was 7.4%. As the previous discussion would suggest, Dow's average rate of return should be higher than CWE's in order to compensate for its higher risk. Indeed, the annualized rate of return for Dow was 16.3%, and for CWE it was 11%. Thus Equation 9.8 can be used to find the risk premiums:

$$E(R_i) - r = [E(R_m) - r]\beta_i$$

$$\text{CWE: } 11\% - 7.4\% = 3.6\%$$

$$\text{Dow: } 16.3\% - 7.4\% = 8.9\%$$

Thus, the larger the beta, the larger the risk premium, as is evident from Equation 9.8.

9.6 SYSTEMATIC AND UNSYSTEMATIC RISK

Investors can earn r by investing in the risk-free asset, and $[E(R_m) - r]\beta_i$ is the required risk premium for Asset i. Because $E(R_m) - r$ is common to all assets, β_i is the only factor that is specific to the ith asset in determining the required risk premium. Thus, the firm's only variance has almost no role in determining the risk premium. To elaborate, let us recall Equation 9.7:

$$R_{i_t} = \alpha_i + \beta_i R_{m_t} + e_{i_t}$$

The variance of R_i is as follows:[15]

$$\sigma_i^2 = \beta_i^2 \sigma_m^2 + \sigma_{e_i}^2 \qquad (9.9)$$

PRACTICE BOX	
Problem	A stock's beta is 2.0, and its mean rate of return is 15%. The expected rate of return on the market portfolio is 10%. What is the risk-free interest rate as implied by the CAPM formula?
Solution	We know that $$E(R_i) = r + [E(R_m) - r]\beta_i$$ Thus, $$0.15 = r + (0.10 - r)2.0$$ $$r = 0.05, \text{ or } 5\%$$

15. Because α_i and β_i are constant (α_i is the intercept of the line), their variances are zero. We take the variance of both sides to obtain Equation 9.9. Note that we also employ the rule variance $(ax) = a^2$ [variance (x)] where a is constant and use the fact that in regression analysis, by construction, $Cov(e_i, R_{m_t}) = 0$. Hence, we have only the two terms appearing in Equation 9.9, when $\sigma_{e_i}^2$ is the variance of e_i.

Thus, the variance σ_i^2 can be broken down into two terms. The first term, $\beta_i^2\sigma_m^2$, is the firm's **systematic risk** component, which represents the part of the stock's variance that is attributable to overall market volatility. The second term, $\sigma_{e_i}^2$, is the firm's **unsystematic risk** component, which represents the part of the stock's variance that is *not* attributable to overall market volatility. $\sigma_{e_i}^2$ is also called the variance of the error term e_i, and σ_{e_i} is its standard deviation. The unsystematic risk component is related to the firm's specific volatility. If all points fall exactly on the regression line (the error term e_i is zero for all points; see Exhibit 9-6a), then $\sigma_{e_i}^2 = 0$. The farther the points are from the regression line, the larger is $\sigma_{e_i}^2$, which measures the dispersion of the points around the regression line (see Exhibit 9-6a).

Note that β_i appears only in the systematic risk component. Therefore, we can conclude that only the systematic part of the firm's variance is relevant in determining expected rates of return and, hence, the required risk premium. The CAPM does not account for the component, $\sigma_{e_i}^2$, which implies that this risk is irrelevant because it can be eliminated by holding a well-diversified portfolio.

If we divide both sides of Equation 9.9 by σ_i^2, we have the following:

$$1 = \frac{\beta_i^2\sigma_m^2}{\sigma_i^2} + \frac{\sigma_{e_i}^2}{\sigma_i^2}$$

where the first term is the *proportion* of the total risk of a security that is systematic, and the second term is the proportion that is unsystematic.

Exhibit 9-11 illustrates the variance broken down into systematic and nonsystematic risk for five securities using monthly data over a 20-year period. Notice that the beta coefficient for Dow is 1.17, and for CWE it is 0.55. The exhibit also reports the proportions of systematic and unsystematic risk (where, of course, the sum of these two components is equal to 1). Firms like Commonwealth Edison that specialize in power production (which is highly regulated) have a low proportion of

EXHIBIT 9-11	Breakdown of Monthly Variances (market standard deviation = 0.047)				
	Dow	**CWE**	**Exxon**	**GE**	**IBM**
Alpha	0.002	0.004	0.007	0.001	−0.001
Beta	1.17	0.55	0.73	1.12	0.80
Standard deviation of stock, σ_i	0.076	0.055	0.053	0.067	0.059
Standard deviation of the error term, σ_{e_i}	0.05246	0.04854	0.04040	0.04145	0.04547
Proportion of systematic risk	52.4%[a]	22.1%	41.9%	61.7%	40.6%
Proportion of unsystematic risk	47.6%[b]	77.9%	58.1%	38.3%	59.4%

a. $[(1.17^2 \cdot 0.047^2)/0.076^2]100 \cong 52.4\%$.

b. $(0.05246^2/0.076^2)100 \cong 47.6\%$.

systematic risk. Alternatively, GE, which is a conglomerate, is very sensitive to market conditions and thus has a high proportion of systematic risk.

In Exhibit 9-11, the standard deviation of GE is 0.067 and that of CWE is 0.055. Hence, GE is riskier in terms of total risk (σ). However, the standard deviation of the error term for GE (0.04145) is *lower* than that for CWE (0.04854). Thus, the proportion of the total risk that can be diversified away is higher for CWE than it is for GE.

9.7 A PROOF OF THE CAPM[16]

Equation 9.8 claims that there is a *linear* relationship between the expected return and the risk of individual assets and portfolios alike. We now prove this claim. To derive the CAPM, we must make the following assumptions: (1) investors make their investment decisions according to the mean–variance rule, (2) investors incur no transaction costs that would prevent sufficient diversification to achieve Portfolio m, and (3) investors can borrow and lend at the riskless rate (r). Given these assumptions, the CAPM would place all risky individual assets and portfolios on line rb in Exhibit 9-8a, that is, on the SML. Indeed, if we show that all assets lie on the SML, Equation 9.8 holds, and so does the CAPM. The CAPM can be proven in the following two steps:

STEP 1

In the first step, we prove that the SML holds for all efficient portfolios whose returns are R_p. Thus, we claim that all points on line rb (see Exhibit 9-8a) are attainable by mixing Portfolio m, whose beta is equal to 1, and the risk-free asset.

To see this, construct a portfolio, R_p:

$$R_p = wr + (1 - w)R_m$$

where w is the investment weight in the risk-free asset and $(1 - w)$ is the investment weight in the market portfolio.

The expected return on this portfolio is

$$E(R_p) = wr + (1 - w)E(R_m)$$

and its beta is[17]

$$\beta_p = (1 - w)\beta_m = (1 - w) \cdot 1 = 1 - w \quad (\text{Recall that } \beta_m = 1)$$

---

16. For a detailed proof of the CAPM, see William F. Sharpe, "Capital Asset Prices: A Theory of Market Equilibrium," *Journal of Finance,* September 1964, pp. 425–442, and John Lintner, "Security Prices and Maximal Gains from Diversification," *Journal of Finance,* December 1965, pp. 587–615. Sharpe won the 1990 Nobel Prize in economics, in part because of this paper.

17. The beta of Portfolio p is given by the following:

$$\beta_p = \frac{Cov(R_p, R_m)}{\sigma_m^2} = \frac{Cov(wr + (1 - w)R_m, R_m)}{\sigma_m^2} = \frac{(1 - w)Cov(R_m, R_m)}{\sigma_m^2} = (1 - w)\sigma_m^2/\sigma_m^2 = 1 - w$$

Note that the covariance of r with R_m is zero, and $Cov(R_m, R_m)$ is simply the variance of R_m.

Substituting $w = (1 - \beta_p)$ and $(1 - w) = \beta_p$ in the equation for $E(R_p)$, we obtain the following:

$$E(R_p) = (1 - \beta_p)r + \beta_p E(R_m)$$

or

$$E(R_p) = r + [E(R_m) - r]\beta_p$$

Because r and $[E(R_m) - r]$ are the intercept and slope of the SML, the pair $[E(R_p), \beta_p]$ lies on the SML. By altering the investment proportion (w), we can select any point $[E(R_p), \beta_p]$ lying on the SML (line rb in Exhibit 9-8a).

STEP 2

We see from Step 1 that beta is a measure of the risk of a portfolio held in equilibrium. Thus, in Step 2 we consider the effect of individual assets held in a portfolio on the portfolio's risk (beta). We show that all assets, individual stocks, and portfolios must be in equilibrium on the SML.

To see why this claim holds, consider Asset A, whose beta is $\beta_A = 0.5$, which is located below the SML (see Exhibit 9-8a). No investor would be willing to hold Asset A, because by mixing Portfolio m and the risk-free asset, investors could achieve point A' (see Step 1 above). In the specific example with $\beta = 0.5$, the mix would be achieved by investing 50% in m and 50% in r. Because Asset A' has the same risk as Asset A ($\beta_{A'} = \beta_A = 0.5$) but a higher expected return, investors would prefer to sell Asset A and buy Asset A'.[18] As a result, the price of Asset A will go down and its expected rate of return will go up until, in equilibrium, point A shifts upward to line rb. Only when point A is located on line rb will equilibrium be restored and will there be no further incentive to sell Asset A and buy Asset A'.

By the same argument, no asset, such as Asset B, can be above line rb, because in this case, all investors would sell Portfolio m and hold this superior asset (see Exhibit 9-8a). The price of Portfolio m (or of the securities making up Portfolio m) will fall, and the price of Asset B will increase until equilibrium is restored, with all assets located on line rb. When all assets are on line rb, Equation 9.8 holds. This proves that in equilibrium, the linear relationship between expected return and risk (the SML) holds.

THE EQUAL PERCENTAGE CONTRIBUTION RULE (EPCoR)

The **equal percentage contribution rule (EPCoR)** sheds more light on the CAPM and provides an intuitive explanation for the optimum investment weights, as well as for the linear relationship implied by the CAPM. Recall that investors dislike

---

18. Portfolio m can be expressed as $R_m = \Sigma w_i R_i$, where w_i stands for the optimum diversification weights corresponding to Portfolio m. Therefore, the beta of Portfolio m is $\beta_m = \Sigma w_i \beta_i = 1$. Thus, the contribution of the ith stock to the portfolio's beta is $w_i b_i$. Because Assets A' and A have, by construction, the same beta (0.5), by switching weight from Asset A to Asset A' we do not change the portfolio risk while increasing its expected return (because $ER_{A'} > ER_A$). Therefore, Asset A cannot be in equilibrium below the line rb; as long as it is below line ra, the process of selling Asset A and buying Asset A' will continue, and the price of Asset A will continue to drop.

risk but like return. Stated another way, investors like a risk premium that is the average return in excess of the risk-free rate. The EPCoR implies that in equilibrium, all assets included in the portfolio should contribute the same percentage to both the portfolio risk and the portfolio risk premium. Thus, if AT&T accounts for 5% of the portfolio's risk, it should account for 5% of the portfolio risk premium. If it accounts for more—say, 10% of the risk premium and only 5% of the portfolio risk—the market is not in equilibrium, because there is an incentive to increase the investment weights of AT&T in the portfolio. By the same token, if IBM accounts for 10% of the portfolio risk, it must also account for 10% of the risk premium for the market to be in equilibrium.

To further illustrate the EPCoR, consider a market that is composed of only two stocks, Asset A and B. Suppose Asset A accounts for 90% of the portfolio risk premium and only 10% of the portfolio risk. Then, by definition, Asset B accounts for 10% of the portfolio risk premium and 90% of the portfolio risk (recall that the total contribution must be 100%). Obviously, Asset A has a better risk-return profile than Asset B, and all rational investors should decrease the weight of Asset B in their portfolios and increase the weight of Asset A. When the investment weights change, the prices of Assets A and B, as well as their contributions to the risk premium and risk, will also change. Suppose that after these changes, we find that Asset A accounts for 70% of the portfolio risk premium and 70% of the portfolio risk, and Asset B accounts for 30% of the portfolio risk premium and 30% of the portfolio risk. At this point, each asset is "working equally hard" for the investor, and there is no further incentive to change the portfolio composition. We say that the EPCoR holds, and the market is in equilibrium.

The CAPM implies that the EPCoR holds (and the EPCoR, in turn, implies that the CAPM holds). To see this, recall first that investors choose the risky portfolio m that maximizes the slope of the line ra (see Exhibit 9-3). Denote the investment weights that maximize this slope by w_i. Therefore, the portfolio return (R_m) is given by

$$R_m = \Sigma w_i R_i$$

With these optimum weights, the expected return on the market portfolio is

$$E(R_m) = \Sigma w_i E(R_i)$$

and the portfolio's beta is[19]

$$\beta_m = \Sigma w_i \beta_i = 1$$

19. The beta of any linear combination of random variables is equal to the linear combination of the betas. For example, consider $z = x + y$:

$$\beta_z = \frac{Cov(x + y, R_m)}{\sigma_m^2} = \frac{Cov(x, R_m)}{\sigma_m^2} + \frac{Cov(y, R_m)}{\sigma_m^2} = \beta_x + \beta_y$$

Hence, we get the beta of $\Sigma w_i R_i$ is $\Sigma w_i \beta_i$.

Thus, the ith asset contributes $w_i E(R_i)$ to the portfolio's expected return and $w_i \beta_i$ to the risk (portfolio's beta).

According to the CAPM, we have

$$E(R_i) = r + [E(R_m) - r]\beta_i$$

We subtract r from both sides, divide both sides by $E(R_m) - r$, and multiply by w_i in order to demonstrate that the CAPM implies that the following must hold in equilibrium:

$$\frac{w_i[E(R_i) - r]}{E(R_m) - r} = w_i \beta_i$$

Because the left-hand side of the previous equation is the percentage contribution of the ith asset to the market portfolio risk premium—recall that the risk premium is given by

$$\Sigma\, w_i[E(R_i) - r] = \Sigma\, w_i E(R_i) - \Sigma\, w_i r = E(R_m) - r \text{ (as } \Sigma\, w_i = 1)$$

and the right-hand side is the percentage contribution of the ith asset to the portfolio *risk* (recall that $\Sigma\, w_i \beta_i = \beta_m = 1$), the CAPM implies that the EPCoR holds.[20] Thus, according to the CAPM in equilibrium, each asset should work equally hard for the investor; it should account for the same percentage of the risk and of the risk premium. Connecting Theory to Practice 9.2 demonstrates how the CAPM (or alpha; see Section 9.8) is employed in portfolio selection.

CONNECTING THEORY TO PRACTICE 9.2
STOCK PICKS THAT ARE STOPPING THE PRESSES

One of the better-known newsletters is Louis Navellier's *MPT Review*. (MPT stands for modern portfolio theory, which was a buzz phrase back in 1987, when Navellier named his newsletter.) Following is a quotation by Louis Navellier that appeared in a 1994 *Smart Money* article.

ABOVE-AVERAGE RISK—MY FAVORITE MARGINS
I'm not worried about the market at all. Growth stocks corrected a lot in the fourth quarter as cyclical stocks took off. My stocks were so beaten up—we were down about 9 percent for the quarter, though we were up to 16.8 percent for the year—that I think a lot of the risk has been exhausted.

We look for inefficiently priced stocks. I calculate "alpha"—how much of a stock's return is independent of, or not correlated with, the market over the

(continued)

---

20. Because $\beta_m = \Sigma\, w_i \beta_i = 1$, $w_i \beta_i / \Sigma\, w_i \beta_i = w_i \beta_i / 1 = w_i \beta_i$ is the percentage contribution to the portfolio beta.

past year. I believe these high-alpha stocks will help us beat the market over the upcoming months.

Once I have this list, I do a lot of fundamental analysis on things like dividends, price-to-book ratio, earnings growth, earnings surprises and so on. I like my stocks to have positive revisions of earnings estimates by analysts.

We're also obsessed with buying stocks that have expanding profit margins. These stocks produce a lot of earnings surprises. Today, I like 230 stocks out of the 418 high-alpha ones. That's high. A year ago I had only 80; the economy was weaker then.

Part of finding market inefficiencies is just being one step ahead. I jump into a company as soon as it turns around rather than waiting for a few quarters of profits. I usually hold stocks for six to nine months. Unfortunately, the more aggressive you are the more you have to trade.

We are aggressive managers, but we like to be super-diversified. I can't do that in a $50,000 portfolio, because it wouldn't be cost-effective, but I've done the best I can. And I've stayed away from wild, crazy stocks.

My first pick is Armstrong World Industries, a linoleum and floor-covering company that is a classic example of profit-margin expansion. It had negative margins last fiscal year, but in its latest quarter the margins were 6.4 percent.

MAKING THE CONNECTION

This article shows that the main goal of investors is to find inefficiently priced stocks. If all stocks were correctly priced, stocks with abnormal returns would not exist in the market. Apparently, practitioners do not believe that the market is efficient. They use the CAPM (alpha and beta; see the discussion in Section 9.8) to locate candidates for investment. However, to make their final portfolio selection choices, practitioners also analyze earnings, dividends, and other variables.

9.8 USING THE CAPM FOR STOCK SELECTION

How are alpha (mentioned in Connecting Theory to Practice 9.2) and the CAPM employed in securities selection? If Equation 9.8 holds for all assets, it implies that all assets are located on the SML. In such a case, we say that the market is in equilibrium or that there are no inefficiencies in the market. The expected return on such stocks is exactly determined by their risk.

For example, if $E(R_m) = 15\%$, $r = 5\%$, and $\beta_i = 1.5$, then according to the CAPM, the expected return on the ith stock is (see Equation 9.8)

$$E(R_i) = 5\% + [(15\% - 5\%) \cdot 1.5] = 20\%$$

Thus, this stock lies on the SML. It is a good investment, although certainly not a bargain. However, what if we expect to have $E(R_i) = 25\%$, with no change in β_i? We say that this stock has a 5% **excess return** or **abnormal return** above and beyond the compensation for the risk involved in investing in such a stock (the return on the stock is more than expected by the CAPM, thus has an abnormal return). If the market is not in equilibrium, and if this excess return persists for a long time, we say that the market is *inefficient* (see the Preface to the book and Chapter 12). Of course, investors should grab such a stock.

This strategy is exactly the strategy suggested for picking stocks in Connecting Theory to Practice 9.2. The box refers to **alpha,** which exactly measures the excess return mentioned above; the higher the alpha, the higher the excess return. Thus, Connecting Theory to Practice 9.2 shows that practitioners employ the CAPM in selecting stocks.

According to the CAPM (see Equation (9.8)

$$E(R_i) - r = [E(R_m) - r]\beta_i$$

However, if there are excess returns in the market, there is a deviation from the line, and the equation becomes

$$[E(R_i) - r] = \alpha_i + [E(R_m) - r]\beta_i$$

where α_i is the deviation of the ith stock from the SML. Therefore, α_i is exactly what is referred to in Connecting Theory to Practice 9.2 as the "excess return."

In the previous example, α_i is 5%. Of course, in practice the expected return, $E(R_i)$, as well as β_i, is unknown and is estimated from historical data.[21] Connecting Theory to Practice 9.2 describes the process of estimating alpha using data from the past year and then determining high-alpha stocks. Stocks are then chosen for the portfolio from this high-alpha group.

Of course, if the CAPM is an accurate model and the market is efficient, this excess return will instantly disappear. The trick is to be the first one to discover the high-alpha stocks and buy them before everyone else does, thus forcing the stock prices up (recall the $100 bill found on the pavement—see the Preface).

It is also interesting to note that the suggested strategy does not rely solely on the CAPM. Once the high-alpha stocks are selected, fundamental analysis (which is discussed in Chapters 20 and 21) is used in choosing stocks from this group. Thus, practitioners feel that the CAPM is useful but has its shortcomings. They do not rely solely on the CAPM in making portfolio investment decisions.

---

21. In Equation 9.7, α_i can be estimated by running the regression of R_i on R_m. One can also run the regression of $R_i - r_t$ on $R_{m_t} - r_t$ and estimate alpha where these two variables are stated in terms of excess return in comparison with the risk-free interest rate. Connecting Theory to Practice 9.2 refers to alpha when excess returns are employed. Therefore, if $\alpha_i > 0$, a positive excess return is observed.

9.9 USING ALPHA AND BETA IN PRACTICE

Exhibit 9-12 shows that despite the shortcomings of the CAPM, practitioners use beta, as well as alpha, and consider these two parameters very informative. Thus, practitioners consider beta (and the CAPM) to be at least a useful risk index. The "Performance Overview" section of Exhibit 9-12 shows the profitability index (that is, rates of return on mutual funds for periods of various length). The table also provides risk-rating statistics. The "highs" and "lows" refer to funds with abnormal results. The CDA rating is a composite percentile rating from 1 to 99 based on a fund's performance over past market cycles.

In the following exhibit, two calculations of beta are presented. The first uses the regression line of the fund calculated using the S&P index. The other uses a category portfolio as a proxy for the market portfolio; a category portfolio is the average return on all funds (in the long-term growth class).

Alpha appears next; alpha is estimated by running a regression of $R_{i_t} - r_t$ on $R_{m_t} - r_t$ (see Footnote 21). It is interesting that alpha is reported in the risk segment of Exhibit 9-12. Actually, alpha is the *excess return* above and beyond the risk premium. Note that alpha is the return on an asset beyond the risk-free interest rate. Funds with a positive alpha outperformed the market.

The lower part of Exhibit 9-12 provides financial information, including the beta for each fund. Only the category beta is given in the detailed part of the table.

9.10 SHORTCOMINGS OF THE CAPM

We can test the CAPM by estimating Equation 9.8 with past data, substituting historical values for $E(R_i)$ and β_i. Of course, we do not expect to get an exact relationship, and we anticipate deviations from the line. Thus, it is possible to test the CAPM using the following equation:

$$\overline{R}_i = \gamma_0 + \gamma_1 \hat{\beta}_i + e_i$$

where $\overline{R}_i$ is the historical average return on the ith asset, γ_0 is the historical intercept, $\hat{\beta}_i$ is the historical estimate of the stock's beta, and e_i is the deviation from the line. The "hat" emphasizes that this is an estimate of the true beta. γ_0 and γ_1 are the regression coefficient (if the CAPM is true, we should have that $\gamma_0 = r$ and $\gamma_1 = [E(R_m) - r_f]$).

Many empirical studies have tested the CAPM. Most of them show that γ_1 is positive and significant (that is, there is a positive association between average return and risk). However, the fit is not as good as would be expected from the CAPM. (With individual stocks, R^2, which describes how well the model fits, was approximately 20%, which means that only 20% of this association could be explained by γ_1.) Recently, a study by Fama and French claimed that γ_1 is not significantly different from zero, which means that a positive association between beta and average return could not ever be found. In other words, Fama and French claim that beta is

EXHIBIT 9-12   The Use of Alpha and Beta in Practice

Performance Overview
General Bd–Investment Grade

Annualized Return	# Fds.	High	Low	Avg.
1-month	406	2.4	−2.4	0.3
Year-to-date	380	17.9	−4.8	7.4
12-month	378	16.4	−5.1	6.6
3-year	282	18.9	4.3	8.8
5-year	165	13.2	3.6	6.8
10-year	60	13.3	5.7	8.5

Risk and Rating Statistics	High	Low	Avg.
CDA rating	94	4	52
Beta (vs. S&P)	2.41	0.01	0.84
Beta (vs. category)	2.82	0.01	1.00
Standard deviation	10.06	0.12	3.52
Alpha	7.2	−3.6	−0.5
R^2	100	2	88

General Bd–Investment Grade Fund	This Month		1997 To Date		Latest 12 Months		Annualized Total Return Thru 11/30/97						Market Cycles				Cat Beta	CDA Rating
							3 Years		5 Years		10 Years		Up Mkt		Down Mkt			
	Pcnt	Rnk	Pcnt	Rnk	Pcnt	Rnk	Pcnt	Rnk	Pcnt	Rnk	Pcnt	Rnk	Pcnt	Rnk	Pcnt	Rnk		
1st Source Monogram Income	0.3	171	6.6	257	5.6	279	—	—	—	—	—	—	—	—	—	—	—	—
59 Wall Street Inflation Index Sec	0.4	117	3.0	378	2.5	376	6.4	261	4.9	163	—	—	—	—	—	—	0.61	—
AARP High Quality Bond Fund	0.2	242	7.0	216	5.9	246	9.1	118	6.8	76	8.3	37	74.1	45	3.0	45	1.08	61+
AHA Full Mat Fixed Income	0.5	59	8.7	66	7.5	84	9.9	63	7.6	37	—	—	82.9	29	1.6	74	1.25	25
AHA Limited Mat Fixed Income	0.2	311	5.7	313	5.6	278	7.2	227	5.6	137	—	—	58.4	83	3.1	43	0.47	90

Source: From CDA/Wiesenberger, *Mutual Funds Update*, November 30, 1997 (Rockville, Md.: CDA Investment Technologies, 1997), p. 90. Reprinted by permission.

not the appropriate risk index, which casts doubt on the validity of the CAPM. Other researchers disagree with this conclusion and show a positive relationship between average return and beta.[22] In particular, Amihud, Christensen, and Mendelson use an advanced econometric technique to show that expected return and beta are positively associated even when the same data set used by Fama and French is used. In their words, "beta is still alive and well."[23]

Roll showed that it is impossible to empirically test the CAPM.[24] Roll also showed that if beta is calculated with an efficient portfolio (a portfolio taken from the efficient frontier), then there is always a perfect positive association between average return and beta ($R^2 = 1$). Thus, the fact that empirical studies show less than a perfect linear association indicates only that an inefficient portfolio (a portfolio interior to the efficient frontier) has been selected as a proxy to the market portfolio. According to Roll, the only testable question is whether the market portfolio is mean-variance efficient—that is, whether the market portfolio lies on the frontier or not. However, such a test is technically impossible with existing computers, because it involves using thousands of securities to solve for the efficient frontier.

Roll and Ross claim that the empirical findings regarding the CAPM are very sensitive to the proxy of the market portfolio that is employed to calculate the beta of each individual security.[25] They claim:

This implies that an index proxy can conceivably be substantially inefficient and still produce a strong cross-sectional regression between expected returns and betas or it can conceivably be close to the efficient frontier and yet produce zero cross section relation.[26]

They conclude:

The empirical findings are not by themselves sufficient cause for rejection of the theory.[27]

Thus, some claim that beta is dead, and some claim that beta is alive and well. It seems that this controversy is not going to end soon. As Connecting Theory to Practice 9.2 showed, practitioners think that beta is alive but not well; therefore, they employ additional investment criteria and do not rely solely on the CAPM.

It is obvious that some of the assumptions of the CAPM do not hold. For example, there are transaction costs, and in general, the larger the number of shares bought, the lower the percentage paid in transaction costs. Investors, and in particular small investors, hold only a relatively small number of stocks in their portfolios; hence, they do not invest in Portfolio m.

22. For more details on studies showing a positive association between mean return and beta, see M. Miller and M. Scholes, "Rate of Return in Relation to Risk: A Reexamination of Some Recent Findings," in M. Jensen (ed.), *Studies in the Theory of Capital Markets* (New York: Praeger, 1972); H. Levy, "Equilibrium in an Imperfect Market: A Constraint on the Number of Securities," *American Economic Review* 68 (September 1978): 643–658; and Y. Amihud, B. J. Christensen, and H. Mendelson, "Further Evidence on the Risk-Return Relationship," working paper, Stanford University, 1992. An example of a study showing no association between risk and return is E. Fama and F. French, "The Cross-Section of Expected Stocks Returns," *Journal of Finance* 47 (1992): 427–466.

23. Amihud, Christensen, and Mendelson, p.1.

24. R. Roll, "A Critique of the Asset Pricing Theory's Test, Part I: On Past and Potential Testability of Theory," *Journal of Financial Economics* 4 (1977): 129–176.

25. R. Roll and S. Ross, "On the Cross-Section Relation between Expected Return and Betas," *Journal of Finance* 49 (March 1994): 101–122.

26. *Ibid.,* p.109.

27. *Ibid.,* p.115.

For the case in which there is only a limited number of stocks in the optimum portfolio, Levy, Markowitz, Merton, and Sharpe suggest an alternative model that is similar to the CAPM but that allows investors to hold a relatively small number of assets in their portfolios.[28] This model is called the **general capital asset pricing model (GCAPM);** it is general in the sense that once the transaction costs are eliminated from the model, the CAPM is obtained as a specific case of the GCAPM. Under this model, each investor holds a different portfolio; therefore, each portfolio has a different beta (which is measured against the portfolio held). The beta of the ith asset is obtained as a weighted average of all these betas.

In summary, the CAPM provides insight into the risk–return relationship, but it has its shortcomings.[29] An investor cannot rely solely on the CAPM, and practitioners realize this. Therefore, despite the wide use of the CAPM, as well as the use of beta as a measure of risk and alpha as a measure of excess return, practitioners require additional tools in choosing their investment portfolios. Indeed, practitioners use the CAPM as a screening tool to divide all stocks into high- and low-alpha groups. Their final investment decisions, however, rely on the analysis of dividends, price-to-book ratios, growth, earnings surprises, and so forth (see Connecting Theory to Practice 9.2).

SUMMARY

Identify the best investment opportunities with risk-free borrowing and lending. With risk-free borrowing and lending, the opportunity for investments expands as all investors become better off, many reaching a higher indifference curve.

Understand the capital market line (CML), which contains only efficient portfolios. An investor can mix any risky asset with a risk-free asset, creating a large set of investment opportunities all lying on the opportunity line. All investors, regardless of their indifference curves, will choose a portfolio from the opportunity line with the highest slope. This line is called the capital market line (CML). All portfolios lying on the CML are efficient, and all are composed of various mixes of the market portfolio and the risk-free asset.

Understand the separation property, which asserts that in Stage 1, all investors choose the same risky portfolio, and in Stage 2, investors borrow or lend according to their risk preferences. The portfolio selection procedure can be divided into two stages: (1) choose the best portfolio of risky assets, and (2) choose the optimal mix of the portfolio selected in Stage 1 with the risk-free asset. In Stage 1, no information regarding the indifference curve is needed. All investors choose the same portfolio (the market portfolio). In Stage 2, information on the indifference curve is needed.

28. For more details on the GCAPM, see H. Levy, "Equilibrium in an Imperfect Market: A Constraint on the Number of Securities in a Portfolio," *American Economic Review* 68 (1978): 643–658; Harry W. Markowitz, "Risk Adjustment," *Journal of Accounting, Auditing and Finance,* Winter/Spring, 1990; Robert C. Merton, "A Simple Model of Capital Market Equilibrium with Incomplete Information," *Journal of Finance* 42 (1987): 483–510; and W. F. Sharpe, "Capital Asset Prices with and without Negative Holdings," *Journal of Finance* 46 (June 1991): 489–510.

29. See H. Levy, "Risk and Return: An Experimental Analysis," *International Economic Review,* February 1997. This paper uses an investment experiment to show that both the CAPM and the GCAPM are not "dead" and can be used in risk-return equilibrium model analysis.

Understand why beta is the appropriate measure of risk. Beta—the slope of the characteristic line—is a risk measure that takes into account the variance of the asset under consideration, as well as the covariances with all other assets included in the portfolio. Beta is the correct risk measure of individual assets as well as portfolios.

Understand why the security market line (SML) and the capital asset pricing model (CAPM) describe the equilibrium relationship between risk and expected rate of return. In equilibrium, all assets, individual stocks, and portfolios lie on a straight line called the security market line (SML). According to the CAPM, the higher asset risk (beta) is, the higher the expected

rate of return will be; all assets lie on the SML. In equilibrium, all assets are correctly priced, and one cannot find "bargains." Any deviation from the SML implies that the market is not in the CAPM equilibrium.

Understand how practitioners who believe in market inefficiency use alpha and beta to select underpriced stocks. Practitioners use the CAPM's beta (systematic risk) as a measure of risk but believe that the market is not always in equilibrium. Therefore, they try to find underpriced stocks (that is, stocks that are located above the SML). These stocks are characterized by a relatively large alpha.

CHAPTER AT A GLANCE

1. The risky asset R_A and the risk-free asset with interest rate r can be used to obtain the opportunity line:

$$E(R) = r + \frac{[E(R_A) - r]}{\sigma_A}\sigma_R$$

2. When the slope of the opportunity line is maximized, the capital market line (CML) is obtained:

$$E(R) = r + \frac{[(E(R_m) - r)]}{\sigma_m}\sigma_R$$

where m is the market portfolio. This expected risk-return linear relationship is valid only for *efficient* portfolios.

3. *Separation property:* All investors select the same risky portfolio m, and each investor then decides individually how to mix Portfolio m with the risk-free asset. The first decision is objective (preference-free); the second decision is subjective (dependent on preference).

4. *Beta,* β_i, *a measure of systematic risk, is given by the following:*

$$\beta_i = \frac{Cov(R_i, R_m)}{\sigma_m^2}, \text{ where } -y < \beta_i < y$$

Assets can be classified according to their betas:

For risk-free assets,	$\beta_r = 0$.
For the market portfolio,	$\beta_m = 1$.
For defensive stocks,	$\beta_i < 1$.
For aggressive stocks,	$\beta_i > 1$.
For neutral stock	$\beta_i = 1$.

5. *The security market line (SML) is given by the following:*

$$E(R_i) = r + [E(R_m) - r]\beta_i$$

6. *The capital asset pricing model (CAPM) is the risk-return relationship given by the SML.* The CAPM applies to both individual securities and portfolios.

7. *An individual security's variance (σ_i^2) can be broken down into systematic and unsystematic risk:*

$$
\underset{\downarrow}{\sigma_i^2} \quad = \quad \underset{\downarrow}{\beta_i^2 \sigma_m^2} \quad + \quad \underset{\downarrow}{\sigma_{e_i}^2}
$$

$$\text{Security's Variance} \quad = \quad \text{Systematic Risk} \quad + \quad \text{Unsystematic Risk}$$

Only systematic risk is relevant in determining the required risk premium.

8. *The CAPM holds when the equal percentage contribution rule (EPCoR) holds. The EPCoR asserts that each asset contributes the same percentage to the portfolio risk premium as it contributes to the portfolio risk.*

KEY TERMS

Abnormal return   324
Aggressive stock   304
Alpha   324
Beta   301
Capital asset pricing model
  (CAPM)   311
Capital market line
  (CML)   298
Characteristic line   303

Defensive stock   304
Equal percentage contribution
  rule (EPCoR)   320
Excess return   324
General capital asset pricing
  model (GCAPM)   328
Indifference curve   290
Levered portfolio   296
Market portfolio   298

Neutral stock   304
Opportunity line   294
Security market line
  (SML)   311
Separation theorem   300
Systematic risk   318
Unsystematic risk   318
Utility   291

REVIEW

9.1 Describe the risk characteristics of Investors A, B, and C in terms of the following three indifference curves:

9.2 How does the shape of the efficient frontier change when the possibility of borrowing and lending at the risk-free rate is added? What is this

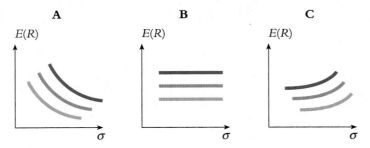

new line called? Are there any inefficient portfolios along this new line? Why or why not?

9.3 How is the efficient frontier improved when risk-free borrowing and lending is available?

9.4 Suppose you have two investments, A and B, where $E(R_B) = 10\%$, $E(R_A) = 11\%$, $\sigma_B = 15\%$, and $\sigma_A = 15\%$. Which investment lies on a higher indifference curve? Why?

PRACTICE

9.1 The rates of return on GM and on the market portfolio (R_m) for the last 4 years follow:

Year	GM	R_m
1	−5%	+10%
2	20	15
3	−2	−6
4	+30	+25

a. Calculate the beta.
b. Calculate the systematic and unsystematic risk, as well as the proportion of each in the variance of GM stock.

9.2 It is given that $E(R_m) = 10\%$, $\sigma_m = 10\%$, and $r = 5\%$. Draw the CML.

9.3 According to the CML, we have

$$E(R_p) = r + \frac{(E(R_m) - r)}{\sigma_m} \sigma_p$$

which holds for efficient portfolios (p). According to the SML, we have

$$E(R_p) = r + E(R_m) - r\beta_p$$

which holds for efficient portfolios as well as inefficient portfolios and individual assets. Show that for efficient portfolios, these two formulas are equivalent (hence, no contradiction arises).

9.4 Suppose there are two portfolios on the CML denoted by x and y. Calculate the correlation of x with y.

9.5 You have the following information: the stock is an aggressive stock, the systematic risk is 0.016, and the market portfolio has the following rates of return:

Year	Rate of Return
1	5%
2	20%
3	10%

Calculate the stock's beta.

9.6 It is given that $\beta_i = 1$, $E(R_1) - r = 10\%$, and $E(R_2) - r = 20\%$. (β_2 is unknown.) There are only two stocks in the market. You invest 50% in each stock. Are we in CAPM equilibrium? (Hint: Check whether the EPCoR holds.)

9.7 Suppose you receive the following rates of return on Assets X and Y:

Probability	X	Y
½	5%	3%
½	5%	20%

Calculate the expected rate of return and variance of each asset, as well as the covariance of X and Y. Explain your results.

9.8 Suppose you can invest in a risky portfolio where the expected return is $E(R_p) = 10\%$ and the standard deviation is $\sigma_p = 20\%$. You can lend and borrow as much as you wish at a risk-free rate of 0%. Derive and draw the opportunity line. (See Equation 9.4 in the text.)

9.9 Suppose you have the following two alternatives, and you can choose only one of the two:
a. Invest in Asset A with $E(R_A) = 20\%$ and $\sigma_A = 10\%$.
b. Invest in Asset B with $E(R_B) = 10\%$ and $\sigma_B = 10\%$.
If you choose Asset A, you are not allowed to borrow or lend. If you choose Asset B, you are allowed

to borrow and lend at 5%. Which alternative will you choose? Show graphically that the choice depends on your indifference curve.

9.10 a. Suppose there are only two stocks in the market. The portfolio is composed of ½ of Asset A and ½ of Asset B. The standard deviations are $\sigma_A = 10\%$ and $\sigma_B = 20\%$. The covariance is $Cov(R_A, R_B) = 0.02$. What is the percentage contribution of each asset to the portfolio variance?
b. Suppose that the means are $E(R_A) = 10\%$ and $E(R_B) = 10\%$, and the risk-free interest rate is 5%. Is the market in equilibrium? Does the CAPM hold with these parameters?

9.11 a. Prove that the beta of the market portfolio is equal to 1.
b. Calculate the beta of the market portfolio with the following data:

Year	Rate of Return on the Market Portfolio
1	5%
2	10
3	20

9.12 Suppose that in the regression line

$$R_{i_t} = \alpha_i + \beta_i R_{m_t} + e_{i_t}$$

all residuals are $e_{i_t} = 0$. "The beta, then, must be equal to 1." Evaulate this statement. Demonstrate your answer graphically.

9.13 a. Suppose there are two stocks, A and B, with $\beta_B = \beta_A$. "Then, if the CAPM holds, it must be true that $E(R_B) = 2E(R_A)$." Do you agree? Demonstrate your answer with $\beta_A = 1$, $\beta_B = 2$, $E(R_m) = 10\%$, and $r = 5\%$.
b. How would you change your answer to Part a if $r = 0$?

9.14 Suppose that the CAPM holds and $\beta_i = 0.9$, $E(R_i) = 10\%$, and $E(R_m) = 10.5\%$. Calculate the risk-free interest rate (r).

9.15 Suppose you have the following data for Stock A and the market portfolio:

Year	Rate of Return on Stock A	Rate of Return on the Market
1	5%	8%
2	3	-2
3	20	30

a. Calculate β_A.
b. Calculate σ_A^2.
c. Calculate the systematic and nonsystematic risk component. Discuss these risks in proportional terms.

9.16 Suppose you have the following figures:

Year	Stock A Return	Market Portfolio Return
1	10%	5%
2	5	2.5
3	20	10

a. Calculate the unsystematic risk component.
b. Calculate the correlation between R_A and R_m.
c. Prove that when the unsystematic risk is zero and the beta is positive, then the correlation coefficient is +1.

9.17 Suppose the rates of return on IBM and the market portfolio for the last 10 years are the following:

Year	Rate of Return on IBM	Rate of Return on the Market Portfolio
1	11%	12%
2	5	7
3	20	15
4	4	8
5	-5	-12
6	14	12
7	9	7
8	25	30
9	-35	6
10	3	10

a. Calculate the beta of IBM, and draw the characteristic line. Is IBM stock considered defensive or aggressive?

b. Calculate the systematic component and the un-systematic component of the total risk of IBM.

9.18 Suppose the market portfolio has the following parameters:

$$E(R_m) = 10\%, \text{ and } \sigma_m = 10\%$$

You hold an efficient portfolio with $\sigma_p = 20\%$, and the mean return on your portfolio is 15%.
a. Do you borrow or lend? How much?
b. What is the risk-free interest rate?

9.19 Suppose you have the following data for Exxon and the market portfolio:

Year	Exxon	Market Portfolio
1	−2%	−1%
2	10	5
3	40	20
4	20	10

a. Calculate the beta of Exxon.
b. For which risk-free rates are these figures consistent with CAPM equilibrium? Explain.

9.20 Suppose that the expected return on DuPont stock is 20%. If you believe that the SML holds and that markets are in equilibrium, if DuPont is twice as risky as the market and the risk-free rate is 4%, what is the expected return on the market portfolio?

9.21 Assume that the SML holds and that, accordingly, the expected return on CBS, Inc., stock should be 15%. You observe, however, that the return is 20%. Is this stock overvalued, undervalued, or correctly valued at its current price?

9.22 The following data regarding six alternate portfolios were published by *Barron's* in early 1998:

What Price Performance?

	Annual Total Return, 3 Years	Risk Rating
Blue Chip Growth	30.98%	0.62
Capital Appreciation	18.49	0.31
Equity Income	27.41	0.44

	Annual Total Return, 3 Years	Risk Rating
New Horizons	25.93	1.45
Value	32.43	0.54
Equity Index	30.75	0.77

Source: Lipper Analytical Services; Morningstar; Abby Schultz, "Like a Fox," *Barron's,* January 26, 1998, p. 17.

a. Assume that the risk rating is the portfolio's beta. Draw the six points in the average return–beta figure, where the average return is on the vertical axis and beta is on the horizontal axis.
b. Suppose that during these 3 years (1995 to 1997), the average rate of return on the market portfolio was 30%, and the riskless investment rate was 6%. Draw the security market line. Which of the six portfolios, in your view, reveals a good performance, and which reveals a bad performance in the last 3 years? Discuss your answer.

9.23 a. An American investor who wishes to invest in a global mutual fund considers investing in only one of the five global funds given in the table in the middle of page 334. Using the average annual return (see the column corresponding to 5 years after loads and taxes) and the standard deviation, which of the funds should be selected? (Assume a 6% annual risk-free interest rate).
b. Write down the CML formula corresponding to each of the funds and draw the CML, assuming that each of these formulas is considered as the market portfolio.

9.24 The following data are taken from Ibbotson for the years 1986 to 1996:

	Rates of Return	
Year	Corporate Bonds	S&P 500
1987	4.9%	9.9%
1988	5	10
1989	5.2	10.3
1990	5.2	10.1
1991	5.4	10.4
1992	5.5	10.3

(continued)

(continued)

Rates of Return		
Year	**Corporate Bonds**	**S&P 500**
1993	5.6	10.3
1994	5.4	10.2
1995	5.7	10
1996	5.6	10.7
Mean	5.35	10.22

Source: *Stocks, Bonds, Bills and Inflation* (Chicago: Ibbotson Associates, 1996).

Assume that the S&P index stands for the market portfolio.

a. Calculate the beta of corporate bonds and the beta of the S&P index.

b. Calculate the systematic and nonsystematic risk of corporate bonds and of the S&P index.

c. Repeat Parts a and b on the assumption that the market portfolio is composed of ½ of the S&P index and ½ of the corporate bonds.

Here's What You Get after Loads and Taxes[1]

Global/World	Returns Avg. Annual 5 Yr.	Returns Avg. Annual 1 Yr.	Return Avg. Annual 5 Yr.	Sales Load	Fees Annual Expenses	Risk Standard Deviation	Assets $ Millions
Oppenheimer Global A Manager: William L. Wilby	17.1%	19.5%	14.3%	5.75%	1.17%	14.2	$3,185
Templeton Growth I Manager: Mark G. Holowesko	17.6%	18.4%	14.1	5.75%	1.08%	11.3	$12,233
Fortis Global Growth A★ Manager: J. Byrd/S. Poling	14.9%	6.4%	13.8	4.75%	1.51%	15.7	$125
Founders Worldwide Growth Manager: Michael W. Gerding	14.1%	11.5%	13.5	None	1.53%	13.1	$347
Scudder Global Manager: Multiple Managers	14.3%	13.3%	13.5	None	1.34%	11.3	$1,532

★Fund will not declare capital gains Dec. 7–31, 1997.

1. Performance is through Nov. 14, 1997, and net of annual expenses, brokerage costs, and sales loads; also net of taxes, assuming the new 20% long-term rate for capital gains and income distributions.

Source: *Fortune,* December 29, 1997, p. 128.

CFA PROBLEMS

9.1 Identify and briefly discuss three criticisms of beta as used in the capital asset pricing model (CAPM).

9.2 Briefly explain whether investors should expect a higher return from holding portfolio A versus portfolio B under the capital asset pricing model (CAPM) (see the following table). Assume that both portfolios are fully diversified.

	Portfolio A	Portfolio B
Systematic risk (beta)	1.0	1.0
Specific risk for each individual security	High	Low

For Internet questions visit the Levy Investment Web site at http://levy-invst.swcollege.com.

YOUR TURN: APPLYING THEORY TO PRACTICE 9.1

SUPER DIVERSIFIERS: ADDING COMMODITIES TO YOUR PORTFOLIO WITHOUT ALL THE STOMACH-CHURNING

As last week's shakiness on Wall Street showed, it's nice to hedge your bets by having some investments that zig when the stock market zags. Of course, many investors believe they already are doing this when, for example, they divide their investments into three parts: stocks, bonds, and cash. But such conventional allocations represent "dinosaur diversification."

Source: Stanley W. Angrist, *Barron's*, November 3, 1997.

The Magic of Super Diversification

Over the long haul, an investor would have done better with a portfolio that included REITs [real estate investment trusts], small cap stocks, foreign equities, and commodities than one that held only cash, bonds, and S&P 500 stocks.

	Mr. Conservative		Mrs. Moderate		Ms. High Flyer	
	Super-diversified Portfolio	Conventional Asset Allocation	Super-diversified Portfolio	Conventional Asset Allocation	Super-diversified Portfolio	Conventional Asset Allocation
Stocks	10%	33%	20%	50%	20%	33%
Bonds	10	33	10	50	0	0
Cash	30	33	0	0	0	0
Small-cap	10	0	20	0	20	33
International stock	10	0	20	0	20	33
REITs	10	0	10	0	20	0
Real assets	20	0	20	0	20	0
Annual Performance (for selected years)						
1973	9.36%	−2.95%	1.23%	−7.89%	−0.21%	−20.16%
1974	1.64	−4.71	−7.72	−11.06	−10.29	−23.19
1977	9.41	−0.91	11.50	−3.93	13.81	12.09
1987	7.82	2.67	8.23	1.27	8.14	6.85
1990	2.42	3.61	−4.74	1.51	−6.89	−16.06
1994	3.01	−0.78	3.08	−3.13	4.18	4.14
1996	16.47	9.15	19.58	11.13	23.19	15.58
26-Year Performance (1971–1997, through September)						
Average Rate of Return	12.87%	10.55%	15.43%	12.02%	15.90%	15.45%
Risk	0.0589	0.0810	0.1026	0.1216	0.1104	0.1646

The following were used to obtain performance numbers: Stocks: Total return of the S&P 500. Small stocks: Dimentional Fund Advisors 9/10 Small Company Fund. International stocks: Morgan Stanley Europe Australasia Far East Index. Bonds: Total return of 20-year Treasury bonds. REITs: National Association of Real Estate Investment Trusts All Equity Index. Real assets: Goldman Sachs Commodity Index. Cash: 30-day Treasury bills. The standard deviation of annual returns was used as a proxy for risk.

(continued)

Questions

In your answers use the 26 years data.

1. Draw all six portfolios in the mean–standard deviation space. Which portfolios are in the efficient set? (Note that the rate of return in the table is an average rate of return, which is an estimate of the mean (or expected rate of return).

2. Assume that you can borrow and lend at the riskless rate of $r = 4\%$. Which portfolio dominates the other portfolios? Discuss your results, and show them graphically.

3. How would you change your results if you could borrow and lend at $r = 8\%$, and then at $r = 12\%$?

4. Suppose that you are Mrs. Moderate. Which portfolio will you choose with no riskless asset? Which one will you choose with a riskless asset whose interest rate is 4%? Explain your decision. Suppose your goal is to achieve an expected rate of return of 15.3%. Explain how you can achieve this.

SELECTED REFERENCES

Maginn, John L., and Donald L. Tuttle, eds. *Managing Investment Portfolios: A Dynamic Process.* 2d ed. (New York: Warren, Gorham & Lamont, 1990).

This book of readings covers many of the practical issues involved in applying the concepts developed in this chapter.

Rudd, Andrew, and Henry K. Clasing, Jr. *Modern Portfolio Theory: The Principles of Investment Management.* 2d ed. (Orinda, Calif.: Andrew Rudd, 1988).

This book is an applied approach to the risk-return relationships developed in this chapter.

SUPPLEMENTAL REFERENCES

Grundy, Kevin, and Burton Malkiel. "Reports of Beta's Death Have Been Greatly Exaggerated." *Journal of Portfolio Management,* Spring 1996, pp. 36–45.

Lintner, John. "Security Prices and Maximal Gains from Diversification." *Journal of Finance,* December 1965, pp. 587–615.

O'Neal, Edward S. "How Many Mutual Funds Constitute a Diversified Mutual Fund Portfolio." *Financial Analysts Journal,* March–April 1997, pp. 37–46.

Sharpe, William F. "Capital Asset Prices: A Theory of Market Equilibrium." *Journal of Finance,* September 1964, pp. 425–442.

LEARNING OBJECTIVES

After studying this chapter you should be able to:

1. Explain the single index model (SIM) and why it reduces the efficient frontier computations.

2. Explain the arbitrage pricing theory (APT), its assumptions, and the resulting linear relationship.

3. Compare and contrast the relationship between the CAPM and the APT.

PRACTICING WHAT THEY TEACH

Quantitative skills come in handy in lots of ways at Roll and Ross Asset Management. For starters, there's the office football pool: Staffers use regression analysis to make their weekly picks. Then there's the number-crunching required to allocate the check when Richard Roll goes out with his five-person staff to the Culver City Hamburger Hamlet for lunch. But mostly there are the workaday tasks of tracking the reactions of 15,000 stocks around the world to changes in key economic indicators and constructing portfolios that will respond positively to those changes according to the insights of a theory that only a Ph.D. could truly begin to grasp.

If what Roll and Ross does sounds like something out of a textbook on investments, it should, for this is the arbitrage pricing theory in action. Yale University professor Stephen Ross is the father of APT, and his longtime friend at the University of California at Los Angeles, professor Roll, is a leading interpreter of the theory. For years the two entertained the idea of putting APT to a real-world test, and in 1985 they got together with marketing expert Alan Yuhas to found Roll and Ross Asset Management. (Ross and Roll sounded too much like rock and roll, they decided.)

For an extracurricular activity—both Roll and Ross continue to teach—their venture has been a notable success, not only as a laboratory for APT but also as a commercial enterprise. Performance has been solid if unspectacular: R&R has returned 120 to 140 basis points per year over various client benchmarks. (Their method, Ross and Roll are quick to point out, is designed to impress over the long term.) And in roughly six years, R&R has come to manage, either directly or through joint ventures, some $7 billion. Nearly $5.5 billion of that is non-U.S. money, managed by two cross-border partnerships. What's more, the firm has just launched a third partnership.

Source: Stephen E. Clark, *Institutional Investor,* November 1991, pp. 92–97. This copyrighted material is reprinted with permission from *Institutional Investor,* 488 Madison Avenue, New York, N.Y. 10022.

Although the arbitrage pricing theory (APT) is a difficult concept to fully understand, it appears from this chapter's Investments in the News that when implemented correctly, this model can result in superior returns. The primary benefit of both the single index model (SIM) and the APT, which are both covered in this chapter, is additional flexibility relative to the CAPM model. The CAPM requires the use of the market portfolio, which is actually not observable. Recall that the market portfolio *must* include all assets. Neither the SIM nor the APT makes this stringent requirement. The APT is built on the concept that arbitrage does not exist for very long. When arbitrage opportunities do exist, a *few* large traders can take advantage of the opportunity and hence push prices back into equilibrium.

This chapter first examines the SIM, which was developed to reduce the numerical complexity of solving for the optimum portfolio on the efficient frontier. In addition, the SIM presents a simple case of arbitrage pricing and makes the development of the APT easier to understand.

10.1 THE SINGLE INDEX MODEL

The single index model (SIM), like other models, has some basic assumptions. This model is easier to work with than Markowitz's full covariance efficient frontier. Systematic and unsystematic risk can be broken down with the SIM. Specifically, the number of securities has an effect on these risks. The following sections will cover these topics.

10.1.1 Common-Factor and Firm-Specific Rates of Returns

The SIM has some basic assumptions about the way rates of return are generated. According to the SIM, two factors are responsible for a given stock's rate of return: the percentage change in the index (or the **common factor**) and changes related to firm-specific events. An index could be any variable that is correlated with security rates of return, such as the inflation rate, gross domestic product (GDP), or even the S&P 500 index.

The SIM assumes that the rate of return on Asset i, is given by

$$R_i = \alpha_i + \beta_i I + e_i \tag{10.1}$$

where R_i is the rate of return on Asset i, I is the percentage change in some index that is common to all stocks, and e_i is the changes in Asset i's rate of return related to firm-specific events. In the CAPM, the beta is related to the market portfolio, and hence I is the market portfolio. Like beta in the CAPM, in the SIM, β_i measures the sensitivity of the *i*th asset's return to changes in the index (I).

The SIM beta is formally calculated as follows:

$$\beta_i = \frac{Cov(R_i, I)}{\sigma_I^2} \tag{10.2}$$

For example, if $\beta_i = 2$ and I is the GDP, Equation 10.2 tells us that if the GDP goes up by 1%, R_i, on average, will go up by 2%. α_i is the intercept that measures the anticipated return when $I = 0$. The intercept term is calculated as

$$\alpha_i = \overline{R}_i - \beta_i \overline{I} \tag{10.3}$$

where $\overline{R}_i$ denotes the average rate of return on Asset i, and $\overline{I}$ denotes the average percentage change in the index.

The term e_i is the random deviation from the straight line given by $R_i = \alpha_i + \beta_i I$. It can be either above the line (positive) or below the line (negative), and it is zero on average.[1]

The straight line in Exhibit 10-1 has an intercept of α_i and a slope of β_i. If all points (R_i) are exactly on the line, then all deviations (e_i) are zero. However, in general, some points are located above the line and some below it. Hence, there are positive as well as negative deviations.

Note that the index (I) and the sensitivity factor (β_i) determine the average return on Asset i. For example, if the betas of all stocks are positive, we can predict that when the index (I) goes up, the stock returns of all stocks will go up on average, and when the index goes down, the rate of return will go down on average. Note that we say that *on average* the return will go up or down. This is different from saying

EXHIBIT 10-1
Illustration of the Deviations from the Line of the Single Index Model

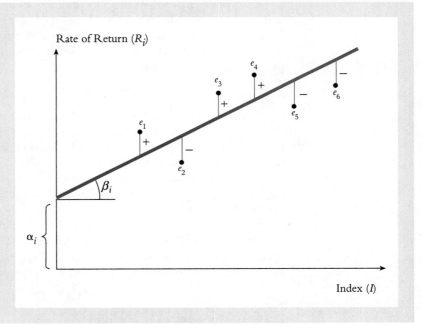

1. If the mean of e_i is not zero, we can always add the mean of e_i to α_i; then the mean of the deviations left are, by construction, zero. Also, when we run a regression to estimate β_i, the sample mean $\bar{e}_i$ is zero.

anything about the actual change in returns. In determining the actual rate of return, we must include a firm-specific event (e_i). It is possible for the index to go up but a firm-specific event to cause e_i to be negative. Therefore, the actual rate of return will go down.

For example, suppose the common index determining stock prices is the rate of return on S&P's 500 index, and the stock is IBM. Moreover, suppose $\alpha_{IBM} = 1\%$ and $\beta_{IBM} = 2$. The following relationship holds for IBM:

$$R_{IBM} = 1\% + 2I + e_{IBM}$$

Suppose that in a given year, $I = 10\%$ (namely, the S&P index goes up by 10%), and $e_{IBM} = 0$. (If no information regarding e_{IBM} is available, the best estimate is that $e_{IBM} = 0$.) Then the rate of return on IBM in this specific year is predicted to be

$$R_{IBM} = 1\% + (2 \cdot 10\%) + 0 = 21\%$$

Now suppose that I goes up by 12%. Would we predict the rate of return on IBM to go up? Absolutely:

$$R_{IBM} = 1\% + (2 \cdot 12\%) + 0 = 25\%$$

This is our best prediction when nothing is known about the firm-specific component (e_{IBM}). The *realized* return on IBM, however, can be larger or smaller than 25%, depending on the sign of the actual deviation of e_{IBM} from the straight line. For example, suppose that when the S&P index goes up by 12%, IBM also announces that it is unable to develop a new personal computer model. This **firm-specific news** (news that relates to the firm specifically and not to the whole market) will make e_i negative; hence, IBM stock will show an actual return lower than 25%. For example, if $e_{IBM} = -10\%$, we get

$$R_{IBM} = 1\% + (2 \cdot 12\%) - 10\% = 15\%$$

Thus, what determines the *actual* future return on each asset is the common index (I), as well as the firm-specific factor e_i. On average, we expect the firm-specific factor to be zero. In any given period, however, it can be either negative or positive, depending on whether the news is good or bad.

If an investor can predict the common index as well as the firm-specific news, the investor can predict the rate of return on the stock. Unfortunately, these types of predictions are hard to make.

Exhibit 10-2 demonstrates graphically the component of the return that is due to the common index and the component that is due to the firm-specific risk (e_i) for AT&T. We assume that $\alpha_{AT\&T} = 1\%$ and $\beta_{AT\&T} = 0.5$. If the index (say, the S&P 500) shows a return of 10%, then we expect *on average* that the return on AT&T will be 6%:

$$R_{AT\&T} = 1\% + (\frac{1}{2} \cdot 10\%) = 6\%$$

However, suppose that AT&T announces some positive information—for example, a new service that will greatly increase its profit. This firm-specific event will cause a deviation from our prediction that is based on the index only. For example,

EXHIBIT 10-2   **The Return Components: Common Factor and Firm-Specific Factor**

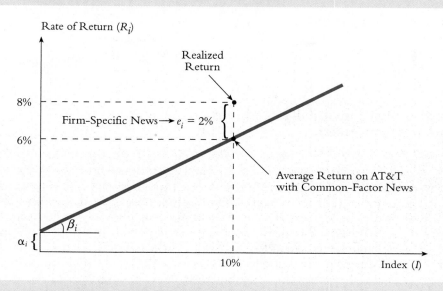

Realized Return = Average Return Due to Common Factor plus Firm-Specific Return.

the deviation (e_i) would be positive, say, 2% (see Exhibit 10-2).[2] Therefore, the realized rate of return, given the information on the index as well as AT&T–specific news, is

$$R_{AT\&T} = 1\% + (½ \cdot 10\%) + 2\% = 8\%$$

which can be rewritten in more general terms as follows:

$$R_i \quad = \quad \underset{\text{Constant}}{\alpha_i} \quad + \quad \underset{\substack{\text{Common-Factor} \\ \text{News}}}{\beta_i \cdot I} \quad + \quad \underset{\substack{\text{Firm-Specific} \\ \text{News}}}{e_i}$$

PRACTICE BOX	
Problem	The rate of return in a given year for Xerox is $R_i = 20\%$, $\beta_i = 2$, and $I = 5\%$. The firm-specific return is $e_i = 1\%$. What is the value of the constant term α_i?
	(continued)

2. Recall from Chapter 9, Equation 9.7 and following, that in practice, e_i is not directly observable; rather, it is derived from Equation 10.1 after all other parameters have been estimated.

Solution	We know from Equation (10.1) that

$$20\% = \alpha_i + (2 \cdot 5\%) + 1\%$$

and

$$\alpha_i = 20\% - (2 \cdot 5\%) - 1\% = 9\%.$$

10.1.2 Why the SIM Drastically Reduces the Amount of Computations

One of the benefits of the SIM in solving for optimum portfolios on the efficient frontier is the reduction in the number of inputs that must be estimated. Chapter 8 showed that in order to solve for the mean-variance efficient set, we have to minimize the portfolio's variance for a given mean return. The portfolio's variance, in turn, is a function of all possible covariances. If we have 100 stocks, for example, we first have to calculate the covariance of all possible pairs of the 100 assets. In this case, the number is $100!/(98! \cdot 2!) = 4{,}950$, which is quite a large number to handle.[3] The SIM is a simplified model that drastically decreases the necessary number of calculations of covariances. Using Equation 10.1, the covariance of Assets i and j is

$$Cov(R_i, R_j) = Cov(\alpha_i + \beta_i I + e_i, \alpha_j + \beta_j I + e_j)$$

The SIM assumes that Firm i's specific news is independent of Firm j's specific news. This means that if some success or failure occurs at IBM, it does not affect the chance of success or failure at AT&T. In statistical terms, this assumption implies that $Cov(e_i, e_j) = 0$. Also, the deviation from the lines for e_i is assumed to be independent of the common factor, namely, $Cov(I, e_i) = 0$. With these assumptions, the covariance of these two stocks is reduced to the following:[4]

$$Cov(R_i, R_j) = \beta_i \beta_j \sigma_I^2 \tag{10.4}$$

Thus, if we have 100 stocks and we estimate 100 values of β_i and σ_I^2, we get all possible covariances. Therefore, we have to estimate only 100 betas to get all 4,950 covariances needed without the assumptions of the SIM.[5] Thus, the assumptions of

---

3. All combinations of selecting 2 assets out of one hundred assets are given by the following formula:

$$C_2^{100} = \frac{100!}{(100-2)!2!}$$

where C_2^{100} denotes the combination of 2 taken from a population of 100, and ! denotes a factorial. For example, $4! = 4 \cdot 3 \cdot 2 \cdot 1 = 24$. If we know the weights, then there is no problem calculating the variance of the portfolio, because we simply calculate the variance of the given portfolio corresponding to the known weights. However, when we are trying to determine the optimal weights to select, we need all of these covariances.

4. Recall that α_i, α_j and β_i, β_j are constants, and that the deviation from the line e_i is assumed to be independent of the index level I. That is, $Cov(I, e_i) = 0$ and $Cov(I, I) = \sigma_I^2$. Therefore, $Cov(R_i, R_j) = Cov(\alpha_i + \beta_i I + e_i, \alpha_j + \beta_j I + e_j)$. Because α_i and α_j are constants, we have $Cov(R_i, R_j) = Cov(\alpha_i + \beta_i I + e_i, \alpha_j + \beta_j I + e_j)$. Because e_i and e_j are independent, it reduces to $Cov(R_i, R_j) = Cov(\beta_i I, \beta_j I)$, namely, $Cov(R_i, R_j) = \beta_i \beta_j \sigma_I^2$.

5. See Footnote 3.

the SIM, and in particular the assumption that $Cov(e_i, e_j) = 0$, greatly reduce the number of estimates needed for the derivation of the efficient frontier.

10.1.3 Systematic and Unsystematic Risk and Portfolio Size

How is risk broken down into its component parts (systematic and unsystematic risk) under the SIM? As we did with the CAPM, we examine the influence of the number of assets, n, in the portfolio on these risks. Suppose you invest a proportion of your wealth (w_i) in the ith stock. Then, using Equation 10.1, multiply both sides of the equation by w_i, and sum for all assets i ($i = 1, 2, \ldots, n$) to obtain the following:

$$\sum_{i=1}^{n} w_i R_i = \sum_{i=1}^{n} w_i \alpha_i + I \sum_{i=1}^{n} w_i \beta_i + \sum_{i=1}^{n} w_i e_i$$

Because $\Sigma w_i R_i$ is the return on the created portfolio, which we denote by R_p, and we further denote $\Sigma w_i \alpha_i = \alpha_p$ and $\Sigma w_i \beta_i = \beta_p$ (the portfolio intercept and portfolio beta), we can rewrite the previous expression as follows:

$$R_p \quad = \quad \alpha_p \quad + \quad \beta_p \cdot I \quad + \quad \sum_{i=1}^{n} w_i e_i$$

Return on = Portfolio + Portfolio Return + Portfolio Return
a Portfolio   Intercept   Due to   Due to
                              Market Factor   Firm-Specific
                                                              Factors

Note that α_p simply represents the time value of money and is equal to the risk-free interest rate. If $\beta_p = 0$, then the portfolio should earn on average only the risk-free rate; that is, there is no risk premium. Hence, in equilibrium, α_p is the risk-free interest rate. However, in practice, β_p is rarely equal to zero. $\beta_p \cdot I$ is the return component due to the common factor, and $\Sigma w_i e_i$ is the return component due to firm-specific risks. Recall that when the common factor (I) goes up or down, the portfolio's return also goes up or down, and the portfolio is a risky investment. Even if we hold a very large portfolio, our diversification cannot help eliminate this risk. For example, if I is the inflation rate, no matter how large our portfolio is, we cannot avoid the variability in the portfolio's return that is due to the variability of inflation; hence, the risk caused by this factor cannot be eliminated.

Therefore, the risk that is due to the common factor is called the **systematic risk** (common-factor risk); it is *undiversifiable risk* that cannot be eliminated, no matter how large the portfolio. This risk has the same interpretation as it did under the CAPM. The only difference lies in what the common factor is. In contrast, $\Sigma w_i e_i$ is the sum of all the individual firms' news. If the firms' specific news is independent, we expect some e_i to be positive and some to be negative, and on average to cancel each other out. In other words, on average, $\Sigma w_i e_i = 0$.

Examples of firm-specific news might be IBM's failure to develop a successful new computer, the development of the new drug Viagra by Pfizer Pharmaceuticals in 1998, or a fire that burned the assets of an uninsured factory. As you can see, these events are independent events, and for a large number of firms they tend to cancel each other. This is not true for small portfolios. For portfolios composed of a very large number of assets, however, one can safely assume that $\Sigma w_i e_i$ approaches zero. Therefore, the part of total risk that is due to the deviations e_i is called **unsystematic risk** (risk not related to the common factor) or *diversifiable risk*. This risk can be virtually eliminated if the investor holds a large portfolio of assets.

Exhibit 10-3 illustrates the relationship between the portfolio variance and its components, systematic and unsystematic risk. For example, if there are only two assets in the portfolio and the systematic risk is 10 and the unsystematic risk is 11, the portfolio variance is 21. By adding more assets to the portfolio, the variance of the unsystematic component, $\Sigma w_i e_i$, goes down (because the e_i of some assets cancels the e_i of others). For example, if systematic risk remains 10 in our example, then for $n = 30$, the unsystematic risk is reduced to only 1, and the portfolio variance is 11. For a very large n, the unsystematic risk is reduced to zero.

10.1.4 Risk and Expected Return with the SIM

Recall that our objective is to establish the appropriate relationship between risk and *expected* return. Refer back to Equation 10.1, and take the expected value of both sides to obtain

$$E(R_i) = \alpha_i + \beta_i \cdot E(I) + E(e_i) \tag{10.5}$$

EXHIBIT 10-3
Systematic and Unsystematic Risk as a Function of the Number of Assets in the Portfolio

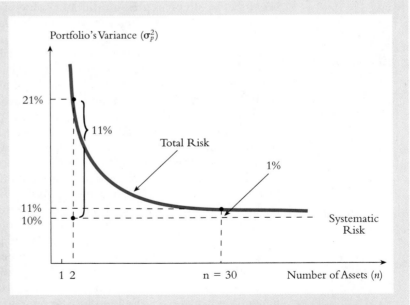

Unsystematic risk decreases as the number of assets (*n*) increases. Systematic risk is not affected by the number of assets (*n*).

Because α and β are fixed numbers, the mean of these numbers is the numbers themselves, and on average, the deviations from the line are zero, because $E(e_i) = 0$. Thus, the equation reduces to

$$E(R_i) = \alpha_i + \beta_i \cdot E(I)$$

or

$$\alpha_i = E(R_i) - \beta_i \cdot E(I)$$

Substituting this expression for α_i in Equation 10.1, we get

$$R_i = \{E(R_i) - [\beta_i \cdot E(I)]\} + (\beta_i \cdot I) + e_i$$

which can be rewritten as

$$R_i = E(R_i) + \beta_i[I - E(I)] + e_i \qquad (10.6)$$

This form of the SIM is exactly how the arbitrage pricing theory advocates that rates of return be generated. We now turn to the arbitrage pricing theory.

10.2   THE ARBITRAGE PRICING THEORY

The **arbitrage pricing theory (APT),** like the CAPM, is an equilibrium pricing model. (Arbitrage is a way to make a riskless profit from differences in the asset's price when this asset is traded on two or more markets.) The APT, developed by Stephen Ross, reaches conclusions similar to those of the CAPM (for example, linear relationships between risk and return, and the greater the risk, the greater the average return).[6] However, the APT is based on a different set of assumptions. Recall that in deriving the CAPM, we assumed that all investors make their investment decisions by a mean-variance rule. With this assumption, investors maximize the slope of the capital market line, seeking the highest expected return for a given level of standard deviation. In deriving the APT risk-return relationship, Ross does not assume risk aversion or rely on the mean-variance rule. Rather, he explains the linear relationship between expected return and risk as arising because there are *no* arbitrage opportunities in security markets. If investors can find a portfolio that earns a positive and *certain* return with a zero net initial investment, all investors will seek this attractive investment. As a result, the price of this investment will change until, in equilibrium, the positive return drops to zero, and such attractive investments vanish from the market. Indeed, when all such bargains vanish, investors have no arbitrage profit opportunities, and the linear risk-return relationship is very similar to the CAPM.

To better understand the concept of arbitrage opportunities, consider an investor who can create an investment that yields a positive future return and requires zero initial investment. That investor has an arbitrage opportunity. Investors would like such an investment independent of their preferences. Furthermore, the more

6. See S. A. Ross, "The Arbitrage Theory of Capital Asset Pricing," *Journal of Economic Theory* (December 1976), pp. 341–360.

money they can make from such an investment, the better off they are. To have an arbitrage opportunity the returns can be certain or uncertain, as long as with a zero investment the returns are nonnegative, and there is at least one positive potential return.

10.2.1 Examples of Arbitrage

Consider first the simplest case of arbitrage, where you can borrow $100 at Bank A at 5%, and you can deposit the money in a second fully insured Bank B to earn 6%. The cash flow from these two transactions is shown in Exhibit 10-4. In this simple example, you have a zero out-of-pocket investment at t_0 and a profit of $1 at the end of the year (t_1). If such a financial situation existed, it would be an arbitrage opportunity. If you could borrow an unlimited amount of money at 5% and lend it at 6%, the potential profit would be infinite. Such a case is called a *money machine;* one has a machine, so to speak, to create money.

Although in general such situations do not exist in the market, the simple example illustrates the concept of an arbitrage opportunity. You create a financial transaction such that with zero net investment, you earn a positive return. If such a situation exists, arbitrage profit is available, and the financial transaction by which this profit is achieved is called an **arbitrage** transaction.

A more realistic example, which is essential to the derivation of the APT, is short selling of securities. Recall that when investors sell a security short, they sell shares they do not own. The process of short selling is as follows: The investor borrows the shares from a broker and then sells the shares in the market to receive the proceeds from the sale. At some future date, the investor must buy the stocks in the market to replace the shares borrowed.

To illustrate how an investor can create an arbitrage profit using short-selling transactions, suppose you have three securities A, B, and C, with returns as given in Exhibit 10-5. For simplicity, assume that each share is trading at $100, so the profit or loss in dollars is also the percentage return on your investment. For example, making $10 on a $100 investment means a +10% rate of return. It is obvious from Exhibit 10-5 that Stock B does not always earn a better return than Stock A—Stock B yields a lower return in a recession and in a stable economy than does Stock A. In addition, Stock C does not always earn a better return than Stock A. Stock C yields a lower return than Stock A when the economy booms.

EXHIBIT 10-4 A Simple Case of Arbitrage with Bank Interest (in dollars)	Strategy	Time t_0	Strategy	Time t_1
	Borrow from Bank A	+$100	Withdraw your deposit from Bank B	+$106
	Deposit in Bank B	−100	Pay back Bank A	−105
	Net cash flow	0		+1

| EXHIBIT 10-5 | | Securities | | |
| Profit and Loss on an Investment | | | | |
State of the Economy	A	B	C
Recession	−$2	−$4	$0
Stable	6	4	10
Boom	10	16	6

Although neither Stock B nor Stock C is always better than Stock A, you can create a portfolio of B and C such that arbitrage opportunities are available. Recall that when an investor short sells an asset, the dollar profit to the short-seller is reversed. If the profit is −$2, this means the stock dropped by 2%. However, because the short-seller sells it today and returns the stock to the broker after buying it back at a lower price, the short-seller's profit is +$2. Suppose you borrow a share from the broker and sell it for $100. (The broker just lends you a share and hence you do not pay any money.) After a month, the stock drops to $98 (a −2% rate of return). You buy it back for $98, return the stock to the broker, and make a profit of +$2.

Holding a portfolio of Stocks B and C and selling short Stock A produces just such an arbitrage profit. Suppose you sell short two shares of Stock A for $200, take the $200 proceeds from the short sale, and buy one share of Stock C for $100 and one share of Stock B for $100. The return from the transaction in dollars is given in Exhibit 10-6. If a recession occurs, then stock A will lose −$2. However, you were short two shares of Stock A, and you have a gain of 2($2) = $4, as illustrated in the second column of Exhibit 10-6. Buying one share of Stocks B and C in a recession will result in a $4 loss on Stock B and no profit or loss on Stock C, as illustrated in the third column of Exhibit 10-6. A similar calculation shows a profit of $14 on Stocks B and C in a stable economy and a profit of $22 if the economy booms. Hence, the total net return from the arbitrage transaction is +$4 − $4 = $0 if recession occurs. Following similar logic, you have a $2 gain if either a stable or boom economy exists.

The initial investment on the transaction described in Exhibit 10-6 is zero (ignoring any trading costs), because the investor sells short two shares of stock A, gets the $200 proceeds, and invests $100 in Stock B and $100 in Stock C. The investor's future net return is always nonnegative regardless of the state of the economy. The investor gains either nothing (in a recession) or $2 (in a stable or boom economy). This is clearly an arbitrage opportunity. Why not double the transaction to $400 and make a potential profit of $4 (or $0), or invest $2,000 to make a profit of $20 (or $0), or even invest $1 million to make an arbitrage profit of $10,000 (or $0). The investor will continue to sell Stock A short and buy Stocks B and C to earn arbitrage profits.

With many such transactions in large amounts, there will be selling pressure on Stock A and buying pressure on Stocks B and C. Therefore, the price of Stock A will fall, and the price of Stocks B and C will go up until eventually no arbitrage opportunities are available. The market mechanism that eliminates the arbitrage

EXHIBIT 10-6   **Arbitrage Profit with Short Sales**

Cash Flow From Transaction

State of the Economy	Short Sale of Two Shares of Stock A	A Portfolio of One Share of Stock B and One Share of Stock C	Total Net Return from the Arbitrage Transaction
Recession	$2 \cdot \$2 = \$4$	$(1 \cdot -\$4) + 1 \cdot \$0 = -\$4$	$+\$4 - \$4 = \$0$
Stable	$2 \cdot (-\$6) = -\$12$	$(1 \cdot \$4) + (1 \cdot \$10) = \$14$	$-\$12 + \$14 = \$2$
Boom	$2 \cdot (-\$10) = -\$20$	$(1 \cdot \$16) + (1 \cdot \$6) = \$22$	$-\$20 + \$22 = \$2$

profit is as follows. Assume that as a result of the selling pressure on Stock A, its price falls from $100 to $90. Similarly, the price of Stock B rises to $105 due to buying pressure, and the price of Stock C likewise rises to $110. Selling two shares of Stock A will provide proceeds of only $2 \cdot \$90 = \$180$. This is not sufficient to buy one share of Stock B and one share of Stock C.

Suppose you split the $180 proceeds between Stocks B and C; hence, you buy only $\$90/\$105 \cong 0.857$ of a share of Stock B and $\$90/\$110 \cong 0.818$ of a share of Stock C. The proceeds in dollars given in Exhibit 10-6 are per one share; you now get a fraction of these proceeds, because you hold a fraction of Stocks B and C. This strategy would not result in an arbitrage profit. For example, if you have a boom in the economy, you lose $20 from short selling two shares of Stock A but gain from buying a fraction of Stock B [$\$16 \cdot (90/105) \cong \$13.71$] and from buying Stock C [$\$6 \cdot (90/110) \cong \$4.91$]. Thus, the net profit on such a transaction is $-20 + 13.71 + 4.91 = -\$1.38$. Note that the net profit is negative, implying that given the new market prices, this transaction no longer represents an arbitrage opportunity.

Investors will continue to search for another possible arbitrage opportunity, for example, splitting the $180 short sales proceeds in various proportions in Stocks B and C. If investors search for all possible financial transactions and find that none can guarantee a positive return in all states of the economy (returns can be zero in some states of the economy but positive at least for one state of the economy) with a zero investment, we say that arbitrage opportunities are not available.

When the prices of stocks are such that no arbitrage profit is available, the linear relationship between the mean return and risk of each asset is a main result of the APT. For example, if prices change such that a portfolio composed of short selling Asset A and holding Assets B and C (with zero initial investment) yields returns of $-\$2$ in recession, $+\$5$ in a stable economy, and $+\$4$ in a boom economy, we say that the arbitrage opportunity disappears because there is a chance of loss.

In practice, small investors may not get the proceeds from the short sale to take advantage of arbitrage opportunities, because the proceeds are held with the broker. However, large investors, particularly institutional investors, do get the short-sale proceeds. All investors do not have to make the arbitrage transaction; it is enough to have even one large investor who can create this money machine to move the stocks to the APT line—a property that makes the model more intuitively appealing than the CAPM. Connecting Theory to Practice 10.1 illustrates one type of arbitrage transaction that has become popular since the stock market minicrash in October 1989.

CONNECTING THEORY TO PRACTICE 10.1

PROGRAM TRADING*

NEW YORK-Program trading in the week ended Dec. 26 accounted for 15.3%, or an average 56.4 million daily shares, of New York Stock Exchange volume.

Brokerage firms executed an additional 41.5 million daily shares of program trading away from the Big Board, mostly on foreign markets. Program trading is the simultaneous purchase or sale of at least 15 different stocks with a total value of $1 million or more.

Of the program total on the Big Board, 10.7% involved stock index arbitrage, down from 22.3% the prior week. **In this strategy, traders dart between stocks and stock-index options and futures to capture fleeting price differences.**

Some 72.7% of program trading was executed by firms for their customers, while 24.5% was done for their own accounts, or principal trading. An additional 2.8% was designated as customer facilitation, in which firms use principal positions to facilitate customer trades. . . .

Of the five most active firms, BNP Securities, Salomon Smith Barney, and Susquehanna Brokerage Services each executes all or most of their program trading for customers as agent. Morgan Stanley split its program trading between its own accounts and those of its customers, while First Boston executed most of its program activity for its own accounts.

*Program trading is buying or selling a set of stocks all at the same time. It is usually executed by computer.

NYSE PROGRAM TRADING

Top 15 Firms	Volume (in millions of shares) for the week ending Dec. 26, 1997			
	Index Arbitrage	Derivative-Related[a]	Other Strategies	Total
BNP Securities	....	....	56.1	56.1
Morgan Stanley	3.4	....	15.4	18.8
Salomon Smith Barney	0.3	....	18.5	18.8
Susquehanna Bkrg Srvs	5.8	....	10.4	16.2
First Boston	3.3	....	11.4	14.7
Interactive Brokers	....	....	11.4	11.4

(continued)

Top 15 Firms	Volume (in millions of shares) for the week ending Dec. 26, 1997			
	Index Arbitrage	Derivative-Related[a]	Other Strategies	Total
W&D Securities	....	....	10.1	10.1
Donaldson Lufkin	....	....	9.7	9.7
NatWest	....	....	8.1	8.1
Lehman Brothers	0.3	1.2	6.6	8.1
Merrill Lynch	0.7	1.4	5.0	7.1
Smith Barney	....	....	6.7	6.7
Thomas Williams	0.7	....	5.7	6.4
Nomura Securities	3.9	....	2.3	6.2
Lawrence Helfant	....	....	5.7	5.7
Overall Total	24.2	2.6	198.8	225.6

a. Other derivative-related strategies besides index arbitrage.

Source: New York Stock Exchange, as cited in *The Wall Street Journal*, January 2, 1998, p. 29. Reprinted by permission of *The Wall Street Journal* © 1998 Dow Jones & Co., Inc. All Rights Reserved Worldwide.

MAKING THE CONNECTION

Arbitrage transactions cause the prices of securities to move toward equilibrium. The ability of money managers to trade vast sums of money or, as the above article indicates, to "dart between stocks and stock-index options and futures to capture fleeting price differences" between securities, is beneficial to small investors because it insures them that the securities will be trading close to their equilibrium price.

The dynamic nature of the securities markets creates arbitrage opportunities from time to time. Program trading, which hit record highs in 1997, is a recent example of how momentary disequilibrium opportunities are seized by money managers and thus restore price equilibrium.

10.2.2 The APT: Assumptions and Risk-Return Relationship

Recall that by the definition of an arbitrage opportunity, with a zero investment, the future return on the portfolio must be nonnegative. Ross employs this argument to derive the APT. To be more specific, he explores what asset prices should be in order to eliminate arbitrage opportunities, because prices change when arbitrage exists. The mean return and risk of each asset also change until arbitrage opportunities disappear. In short, when arbitrage transactions are available, the economy is not in equilibrium. This is why the APT is an equilibrium pricing model. Thus, the APT investigates the market equilibrium prices when all arbitrage transactions are eliminated. This section examines the assumptions and resulting model of the APT.

The assumptions underlying the APT follow:

1. Rates of return depend on some common factors and some "noise,"[7] which is firm specific. This dependency is called a *return-generating process*.
2. A very large number of assets exist in the economy.
3. Short sales are allowed, and the proceeds are available to the short–sellers.
4. Investors prefer more wealth to less.

According to the APT, the rates of return on Security i (R_i) in a given period (say, a month) are generated by the following process (see also Equation 10.6):

$$R_i = E(R_i) + \beta_i[I - E(I)] + e_i \qquad\qquad 10.7$$

where R_i is the rate of return on Security i $(i = 1, 2, \ldots, n)$, I is the value of the factor generating the return R_i (that is, the percentage change in some index), and $E(I)$ is the mean of this factor. Because only one factor is involved, this model is called the *one-factor model*. β_i is the coefficient measure of the sensitivity of changes in R_i as a result of changes in I.[8] e_i is "noise," or the deviation from the line that is firm specific; that is, whereas all firms have the same common factor I, each has a different e_i.

The assumed return-generating process is identical to the return process predicted by the SIM (see Equation 10.6). However, whereas the SIM's main purpose is to provide an easy way to calculate all possible pairs of correlations, the return-generating process given by Equation 10.7 is constructed for the purpose of deriving the risk-return linear relationship (similar to the CAPM); hence, further assumptions beyond the return-generating process are needed to derive the APT results.

The most important characteristic of this return-generating process is that I is a common factor to all risky assets, just as it is in the SIM. Because this factor is common to all assets, it cannot be diversified. The common factor could be the inflation rate in the economy, the unemployment rate, the interest rate on government bonds, the gross national product (GNP), or even the rate of return on the market portfolio R_m. Note that the APT uses $I - E(I)$ instead of simply I. This is called the "surprise" factor. For example, if we expect the inflation rate to increase on average by, say, $E(I) = 10\%$, and it actually increases by $I = 12\%$, we have a $+2\%$ surprise, or unexpected, factor. Thus, the APT measures the difference between expectations and actual outcome rather than simply actual outcome.

The larger an asset's beta, the larger the effect of the surprise on the asset's return. Another possible surprise is firm specific and is given by e_i, which is predicted to be zero before the firm-specific news is declared. As with the SIM, this firm-specific news could be the resignation of the chairman of General Motors, an increase in the dividends of AT&T, or a new drug discovery by Johnson & Johnson. Connecting Theory to Practice 10.2 gives examples of firm-specific news.

---

7. "Noise" in this case is the random variable e_i with zero mean.
8. Equation 10.7 should not be confused with the CAPM: $E(R_i) = r + [E(R_m) - r]\beta_i$.

CONNECTING THEORY TO PRACTICE 10.2

SURPRISE, SURPRISE! UNEXPECTED ANNOUNCEMENTS AFFECT STOCK PRICES

PART A: FIRE AT EXIDE PLANT EXPECTED TO AFFECT QUARTERLY EARNINGS

BLOOMFIELD HILLS, MICH.—Exide Corp. said it is in the "beginning stages" of determining the financial impact of a fire last week at its automotive-battery manufacturing plant in Bristol, Tenn., but expects the fire to have a significant impact on fourth-quarter earnings.

A spokeswoman for the maker of lead-acid batteries said a $1 million deductible on its insurance policy will reduce fourth-quarter earnings by three cents.

Source: *Wall Street Journal*, January 2, 1998, p.10. Reprinted by permission of *The Wall Street Journal* © 1998 Dow Jones & Co., Inc. All Rights Reserved Worldwide.

PART B: NETSCAPE REPORTS LOSSES, AND ITS SHARES TUMBLE

SAN FRANCISCO—Shares in the Netscape Communications Corporation lost more than a fifth of their value today after the company said it would report losses for both the fourth quarter and the year.

Netscape, a Mountain View, Calif., company best known for its Navigator software for browsing the World Wide Web, said it would reduce its workforce, close some offices, and refocus on corporate sales.

Netscape shares closed at $18.5625, down $4.8125, or nearly 21 percent, in heavy Nasdaq trading.

Source: *The New York Times*, January 6, 1998, p. C1. Copyright © 1998 by The New York Times Co. Reprinted by Permission.

PART C: CBS MARKETWATCH: EARNINGS SURPRISES

Adaptec Inc. shares plunged 40 percent on word the company expects a third-quarter profit of about 35 to 40 cents a share. The consensus estimate was 56 cents a share. Revenue for the quarter is estimated to be between $250 million to $255 million. Adaptec also expects a one-time charge and a change in accounting principles to reduce net income as much as $28 million, reducing earnings to about 21 to 23 cents a share. The technology company's shares dropped 14 3/8 to 21 9/16.

Source: http://cbs.marketwatch.com/news/current/surprises.htx? Source=htx/http2_mw

MAKING THE CONNECTION

From the previous examples, we see that the return on the market is a function of the "surprise" factor. Analysts estimate the firm's profits, and when the

(continued)

earnings are announced, positive or negative surprises are observed. For example, in Part a we see that because of a fire at Exide's Bristol, Tennessee, plant, quarterly earnings are expected to decline three cents. Upon this unexpected announcement, the stock price fell. In Part b, the lower-than-expected fourth-quarter and annual performances by Netscape resulted in a $4.8125-per-share drop in the firm's stock price. Note that these negative firm-specific surprises directly affect a firm's stock. Unpleasant surprises, such as lower earnings, result in stock price declines, whereas pleasant surprises result in increases in stock prices.

We will see that the APT assumes that rates of return on individual stocks are indeed affected by macroeconomic (or industry) surprises, as well as individual stock surprises. In other words, the realized return is rarely identical to the expected return. Macroeconomic and firm-specific announcements cause deviations from the expected return, and the bigger the surprises are, the bigger the deviations.

This return-generating process can be illustrated by a graphic demonstration of the returns of two firms, IBM with $\beta = 2$ and AT&T with $\beta = 0.5$. The common factor is assumed to be the inflation rate with an expected value of $E(I) = 10\%$. Estimating inflation to be 10% on average, investors in the market determine the expected rate of return to be 15% on AT&T and 25% on IBM. If there are no surprises $[I - E(I) = 0$ and $e_i = 0]$, these estimates will be the future *realized* returns on IBM and AT&T.

Suppose now that the market "surprises" investors, and inflation is announced to be 15%; hence, $I - E(I) = 15\% - 10\% = 5\%$. Then the return on the stocks with this surprise will be, for AT&T,

$$15\% + (0.5 \cdot 5\%) = 17.5\%$$

and, for IBM,

$$25\% + (2 \cdot 5\%) = 35\%$$

Thus, the surprise affects the two firms differently. Even though I is a common factor, the sensitivity to this factor is not the same for all stocks (their betas are not the same), and the larger the beta, the stronger the surprise effect on returns. Of course, in our example, if $I - E(I) < 0$, the return on IBM will decrease much faster than the return on AT&T.

Finally, suppose that AT&T has no firm-specific information ($e_i = 0$), whereas IBM announces a loss of $2.8 billion. Thus, IBM's bad news causes the return to decrease by 5%, or $e_i = -5\%$. The return on IBM will be only $25\% + 10\% - 5\% = 30\%$ (see Exhibit 10-7). The following table summarizes this example:

Company Return	Expected Return with No Surprises	Change in Return Due to Surprise in Inflation $I - E(I) = +5\%$	Change in Return Due to Firm-Specific News (e_i)	Total
AT&T	15%	$\beta_{ATT} [I - E(I)] = (\frac{1}{2})5\% = 2.5\%$	0%	17.5%
IBM	25%	$\beta_{IBM} [I - E(I)] = 2(5\%) = 10\%$	−5%	30%

PRACTICE BOX

Problem	When Hurricane Andrew hit the Florida and Louisiana coasts, it caused a big loss for many insurance companies. Is this a firm-specific surprise or a common-factor surprise?
Solution	If there were only one insurance firm in the country, then only this firm would be affected, and the loss due to the hurricane would be considered a firm-specific surprise. However, because there are many insurance firms, the loss would be considered an industry factor, which is a common factor rather than a firm-specific factor.

10.2.3 The Linear APT Relationship

To examine the relationship between risk and expected return implied by the APT, we first examine a unique portfolio that has a zero beta and requires no investment due to short selling.

ZERO BETA, ZERO INVESTMENT PORTFOLIOS MUST YIELD ZERO RETURN

The main result of the APT is the implied linear risk-return relationship. Suppose we invest a proportion of our wealth (w_i) in the ith asset. Then, by multiplying all

EXHIBIT 10-7
Illustration of Returns on IBM and AT&T with the APT

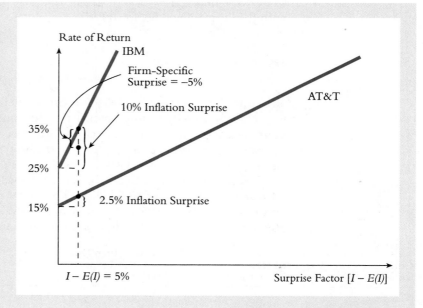

terms in Equation 10.7 by w_i and summing up for all n assets held in the portfolio, we get

$$\sum_{i=1}^{n} w_i R_i = \sum_{i=1}^{n} w_i E(R_i) + [I - E(I)]\sum_{i=1}^{n} w_i \beta_i + \sum_{i=1}^{n} w_i e_i \tag{10.8}$$

Because $\Sigma w_i R_i = R_p$ is the return on the created portfolio whose mean return is $\Sigma w_i E(R_i) = E(R_p)$, Equation 10.8 can be rewritten as follows:

$$R_p = E(R_p) + [I - E(I)]\sum_{i=1}^{n} w_i \beta_i + \sum_{i=1}^{n} w_i e_i \tag{10.9}$$

For a very large portfolio composed of many securities (that is, n is very large), the noise factors (e_i) tend to cancel each other, so we can safely assume that $\Sigma w_i e_i \cong 0$. Therefore, for a very large portfolio, Equation 10.9 can be rewritten as follows:

$$R_p = E(R_p) + [I - E(I)]\sum_{i=1}^{n} w_i \beta_i \tag{10.10}$$

where $\Sigma w_i \beta_i$ is the portfolio beta, which is actually the average of all the assets' betas weighted by their proportion (w_i) in the portfolio. Thus, the rate of return on a portfolio by the APT is equal to the expected return plus an adjustment for unanticipated changes in the common factor. Deviations of the portfolio return from what was expected is a function of the portfolio beta and the magnitude of the unanticipated change in the common factor.

Now suppose you can create a portfolio with *zero investment* and with *zero risk,* namely, $\Sigma w_i = 0$ and $\Sigma w_i \beta_i = 0$. Such a portfolio is called a **zero beta** *portfolio.* What should the return be on such a portfolio? According to Equation 10.10, the return must be $R_p = E(R_p)$, because the second term on the right-hand side is zero. Note that the rate of return on such a portfolio is equal to its mean [$E(R_p)$], and hence, there is *no variability in this return.* Because by assumption this is a zero investment portfolio, the expected return must be equal to zero; otherwise, we have an arbitrage opportunity. For example, if the zero beta, zero investment portfolio had positive dollar returns, then this would be a money machine. Alternatively, if this portfolio had negative dollar returns, then an investor could construct another portfolio with exactly opposite weights that would result in positive dollar returns.

THE LINEAR RISK-RETURN RELATIONSHIP

With no arbitrage opportunities and using the zero beta and zero investment portfolio, Ross demonstrated that the mean return on the ith asset, $E(R_i)$, is related to β_i in a linear fashion as follows:

$$E(R_i) = a_0 + a_1 \beta_i \tag{10.11}$$

where a_0 and a_1 are constant across securities. This result is very similar to the CAPM. Indeed, when we use the market portfolio as the index, we get $a_0 = r$, and $a_1 = E(R_m) - r$, with the APT and CAPM yielding the same result.

The basic idea behind Equation 10.11 can be illustrated with the following three stocks. (For simplicity, assume each stock has the same market price.)

	Stock		
	A	B	C
Mean Return, $E(R_i)$	8%	13%	?
Beta, β_i	1	2	3

Our goal is to select a mean rate of return on Stock C such that we can construct a zero investment, zero risk portfolio of Stocks A, B, and C with no arbitrage opportunities. Suppose we plot A and B and connect them by a straight line. What mean rate of return for Stock C will place it on line AB? We will show that when the mean rate of return of Stock C is determined such that no arbitrage exists, point C will be on the straight line connecting points B and A. Namely, all points are located on a straight line, which proves the APT linear relationship given by Equation 10.11.

If we select investment proportions $w_A = 1$, $w_B = -2$, and $w_C = 1$, then $\Sigma w_i = 1 - 2 + 1 = 0$ and $\Sigma w_i \beta_i = (1 \cdot 1) + (2 \cdot -2) + 3 \cdot 1 = 0$.[9] Thus, we constructed a zero investment and zero risk portfolio.

According to the requirement that the portfolio with zero beta and zero investment should not provide arbitrage profit, we must have[10]

$$R_p = E(R_p) = [w_A \cdot E(R_A)] + [w_B \cdot E(R_B)] + [w_C \cdot E(R_C)] = 0$$

or

$$1 \cdot 8\% - 2 \cdot 13\% + 1 \cdot E(R_3) = 0$$

Therefore, $E(R_C) = 26\% - 8\% = 18\%$. If $E(R_C) = 18\%$, there is no arbitrage profit. Let us elaborate. Suppose that $E(R_C) = 20\%$. Then we can earn the following on a portfolio with a zero risk and zero investment:

$$R_p = E(R_p) = 1 \cdot 8\% - 2 \cdot 13\% + 1 \cdot 20\% = 2\%$$

Hence, there are arbitrage opportunities. Holding such a portfolio creates a positive certain profit with no investment. This is impossible in equilibrium, because it

9. To obtain the weights, we solve two equations with two unknowns (w_1 and w_2):

$$w_1 + w_2 + (1 - w_1 - w_2) = 0$$

and

$$(w_1 \cdot 1) + (w_2 \cdot 2) + ((1 - w_1 - w_2) \cdot 3) = 0$$

Note that a negative weight implies short selling.

10. The equation claiming that $R_p = E(R_p) = 0$ is generally not true for only three stocks, because for three stocks, we would not expect that the sum of the error terms would actually be zero. We really need a large number of stocks to demonstrate the APT. Thus, here we assume that the sum of the error terms is zero (as if we had an infinite number of assets) but demonstrate the linear relationship by focusing on only three points. This greatly simplifies the demonstration.

constitutes a "money machine." Similarly, if $E(R_C)$ is lower than 18%—say, 15%—with zero investment and risk, we get a negative return of

$$R_p = E(R_p) = 1 \cdot 8\% - 2 \cdot 13 + 1 \cdot 15\% = -3\%$$

Then, by short selling such a portfolio with zero investment, we get a positive return, which is again a money machine.[11]

Now what is left to show is that the point given by $E(R_C) = 18\%$ and $\beta_C = 3$, which characterizes Stock C when there are no arbitrage opportunities, indeed lies on the same straight line as Stocks A and B, as asserted by the APT. Exhibit 10-8 demonstrates the straight line connecting points A and B with the relevant parameters taken from the example. The slope of the line is $[(13\% - 8\%)/(2 - 1)] = 5\%$, which is the line KB (the rise) divided by the line KA (the run). The intercept of this line can be found by inserting the parameters of point A (or point B) and employing the straight line formula with a slope of 5%:

$$E(R_i) = a_0 + (5\% \cdot \beta_i)$$

Because for Stock A we have $E(R_A) = 8\%$ and $\beta = 1$, we get $8\% = a_0 + (5\% \cdot 1)$; thus, $a_0 = 3\%$. The straight line connecting Stocks A and B is given by $E(R_i) = 3\% + (5\% \cdot \beta_i)$, where $a_0 = 3\%$ and $a_1 = 5\%$. Because one can pass a straight line

EXHIBIT 10-8
Illustration of No Arbitrage under the APT

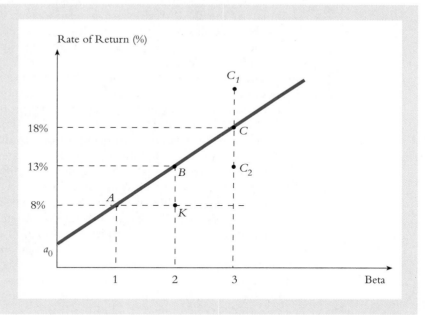

---

11. Recall that when you short sell a portfolio with zero initial investment, you get no proceeds from the short sale. If you hold a portfolio of two assets (say, $w_1 = +1$, $w_2 = -1$, and $\Sigma w_i = 0$), then by short selling it you get $w_1 = -1$, $w_2 = +1$, and again $\Sigma w_i = 0$. Thus, short selling a zero investment portfolio remains a zero investment strategy.

between any two points, these findings so far neither support nor refute the APT. The crucial test of the APT is whether Stock C with $E(R_C) = 18\%$ and $\beta_C = 3$, which are the necessary parameters to eliminate an arbitrage profit, also lies on the same line. To test this, we substitute 18% for $E(R_C)$ and 3 for β_C, and check whether there is an identity with this straight-line parameter:

$$18\% \overset{?}{=} a_0 + a_1 \cdot 3$$

Indeed, with $a_0 = 3\%$ and $a_1 = 5\%$, we have

$$18\% = 3\% + (5\% \cdot 3) = 18\%$$

which implies that the third point, corresponding to Stock C, also lies on the straight line. If $E(R_C)$ is greater than 18% (say, 20%), the point is above the line (see point C_1 in Exhibit 10-8). If $E(R_C)$ is lower than 18% (say, 16%), the point is below the line (see point C_2 in Exhibit 10-8).

Because a mean return of exactly 18% for Stock C eliminates an arbitrage possibility, and all three stocks lie on the same straight line, we conclude that when arbitrage opportunities are eliminated, we get the following linear relationship for the three stocks under consideration:

$$E(R_i) = a_0 + a_1\beta_i$$

where a_0 and a_1 are the intercept and the slope of the APT line, respectively. This is similar to the CAPM risk-return relationship. When arbitrage opportunities are available, not all stocks will lie on this line; hence, it will not describe the relationship between $E(R_i)$ and β_i. When all arbitrage opportunities vanish, all assets must lie on this straight line.

The APT linear relationship has been illustrated with three stocks, but the same principle holds with a portfolio having any number of stocks. As long as one of the stocks is not on the straight line, an arbitrage profit can be made. To eliminate such an arbitrage profit, all $[E(R_i), \beta_i]$ points must lie on the one straight line. We assumed a zero investment, zero beta portfolio to derive the APT, but the linear relationship derived holds for any type of investment, no matter what the beta is and, of course, for nonzero investments. For example, if $a_0 = 5\%$ and $a_1 = 10\%$, and the beta of Xerox is 2, on an investment in Xerox we expect to earn $5\% + (10\% \cdot 2) = 25\%$. Thus, every \$1 investment in Xerox is expected to grow to \$1.25. Similarly, if beta is zero, every dollar invested is expected to grow to \$1.05.

Let us now turn to the intuitive explanation of the linear risk-return relationship and to the meaning of the coefficients a_0 and a_1. First, because the APT assumes that a large portfolio is held, the variance of the unsystematic risk of each asset is not important.[12] This by no means implies that unsystematic risk does not exist. However, investors will not change the required risk premium from the assets, because this part of the risk is eliminated in a large portfolio. If two stocks have the same β, but one has a large unsystematic risk and the other has zero unsystematic risk, both will be priced the same and hence have the same average return.

---

12. Unsystematic and systematic risk have the same interpretation with the APT as with the SIM.

To find a_0 and a_1, first note that $a_0 = r$, the risk-free interest rate.[13] The reason is that when $\beta = 0$, there is no systematic risk (remember, only the systematic risk determines return), and to avoid arbitrage, the return on an investment with no variability (zero beta) must be equal to the risk-free rate.

The slope of the line (a_1) can be found in many ways. For example, take Asset A, which is on the line (See Exhibit 10-8). The slope of the line is given by $[E(R_A) - a_0]/\beta_A = [E(R_A) - r]/\beta_A = [E(R_A) - r]/1$ (where $\beta_A = 1$), and therefore the risk-return linear relationship is given by

$$E(R_i) = r + [E(R_A) - r]\beta_i$$

By the same token, for a_1 the slope is $[E(R_B) - r]/\beta_B$. However, because all these terms yield the same slope, the linear equation remains unchanged. Thus, shifting from one point to another does not change the slope. Hence, points with $\beta = 1$ can be selected (without loss of generality).

PRACTICE BOX

Problem

Suppose there are three assets on the APT straight line with the following parameters:

	A	**B**	**C**
Mean	5%	10%	15%
Beta	1	2	3

1. What are a_0 and a_1?
2. Show that every combination of the assets is also on the line.

Solution

1. The APT line can be written as

$$E(R_i) = a_0 + a_1\beta_i$$

As is, the slope of the line is given by the rate of change between any two of the assets. Thus,

$$\frac{10\% - 5\%}{2 - 1} = \frac{15\% - 10\%}{3 - 2} = \frac{15\% - 5\%}{3 - 1} = 5\%, \text{ or } 0.05$$

Then a_0 is given by

$$a_0 = E(R_i) - a_1\beta_i = E(R_i) - 0.05\beta_i$$

If we take Stock A, we get

$$a_0 = 0.05 - (0.05 \cdot 1) = 0.0$$

(continued)

---

13. Recall that we are still investing money; hence, we would want to be compensated for the time value of money, which would be the risk-free interest rate.

If we take Stock B, we get

$$a_0 = 0.1 - (0.05 \cdot 2) = 0.0$$

If we take Stock C, we get

$$a_0 = 0.15 - (0.05 \cdot 3) = 0.0$$

Thus, the APT line with these figures is given by

$$E(R_i) = 0 + 0.05\beta_i$$

2. Because the beta of a portfolio, β_p, and the mean of the portfolio, $E(R_p)$, are linear functions, we know

$$\beta_p = \sum_{i=1}^{n} w_i \beta_i$$

$$E(R_p) = \sum_{i=1}^{n} w_i E(R_i)$$

and any portfolio must also be on the line. For example, take a portfolio of ⅓ invested in each asset. Then

$$\beta_p = \frac{1 + 2 + 3}{3} = 2$$

$$E(R_p) = \frac{0.05 + 0.1 + 0.15}{3} = 0.1$$

This portfolio is also on the straight line, because $0.1 = 0 + (0.05 \cdot 2)$.

10.3 THE APT AND THE CAPM

When the common factor in the APT model is the market portfolio—for example, the S&P 500 index—then $a_1 = E(R_m) - r$, the risk premium of the market portfolio. In this instance, the APT and the CAPM yield the same results. To see this, select the market portfolio as the common factor, where the beta of the market portfolio is $+1$; it would be located on the line shown in Exhibit 10-8 (see point A).[14] The line can be found as follows: $a_0 = r$ and $a_1 = [E(R_m) - r]/1$. From Equation 10.11, $E(R_i) = r + [E(R_m) - r]\beta_i$, which is the well-known CAPM. Thus,

14. Recall that the beta of the market portfolio is defined as

$$\frac{Cov(R_m, R_m)}{\sigma_m^2} = \frac{\sigma_m^2}{\sigma_m^2} = 1$$

which is the covariance of the returns on the market with itself, which is the variance of the market divided by the variance of the market.

with the market portfolio as the common factor, if we assume that large portfolios are held and some specific return-generating process is driving returns, then we arrive at the same result as the CAPM. However, the CAPM and the APT rely on a completely different set of assumptions.

Recall that Chapter 9 (Section 9.7) identified the major assumptions of the CAPM. Primarily, the CAPM is built on the assumption that investors are risk-averse and follow the mean-variance rule. The APT does not require these assumptions. Thus, the APT is considered to be much less restrictive. That is, the APT can apply to markets where investors are *not* risk-averse or where more than portfolio mean and variance matter. The CAPM predicts that all investors will hold the same market portfolio; there is no such prediction with the APT.

The APT also can be extended to include more than one common factor in the return-generating process. The major disadvantage of the APT is that it fails to tell us exactly what the common factors are. Many researchers have attempted to establish the appropriate number of factors, as well as exactly which variables are the best to use as the factors. Similarly, if there is only one factor, the APT fails to tell what that factor is.

10.4 MULTIFACTOR APT MODEL

So far, we have assumed that only one factor, I, generates the return on the various assets. It is possible, however, that several macroeconomic factors generate the return on the assets, such as the inflation rate and the unemployment rate. Denoting the jth factor by I_j whose mean is $E(I_j)$, the multifactor model assumes that rates of return on the ith asset are generated by the following process:

$$R_i = E(R_i) + \beta_{i1}[I_1 - E(I_1)] + \beta_{i2}[I_2 - E(I_2)] + \ldots + \beta_{iK}[I_K - E(I_K)] + e_i$$

where there are K factors, and β_{ij} is the sensitivity of the return of the ith stock to the I_j factor ($j = 1, 2, \ldots, K$). The same no-arbitrage-opportunity approach can be used where we have zero investment ($\Sigma w_i = 0$) with zero betas for each of the above factors. Thus, $\Sigma w_i \beta_{i1} = 0$, $\Sigma w_i \beta_{i2} = 0$, and so forth, and there is no arbitrage opportunity. Following this procedure, we get a linear relationship similar to the one-factor APT of the following form:

$$E(R_i) = a_0 + a_1\beta_1 + a_2\beta_2 + \ldots + a_K\beta_K \qquad (10.12)$$

which is a generalization of the APT when K factors, rather than one factor, are generating the returns. a_0 is the rate of return expected if all betas are zero (the risk-free rate), a_1 is the market price of the risk related to factor i on a per-unit basis, and β_i is the sensitivity of the security to factor i.

In practice, the relevant risk factors are selected based on their historical influence on returns. For example, Berry, Burmeister, and McElroy suggest the following factors:

1. Unanticipated changes in bond default premiums (government bonds versus corporate bonds).
2. Unanticipated changes in the term structure (20-year government bonds versus one-month Treasury bills).
3. Unanticipated changes in inflation.
4. Unanticipated changes in the growth rate of corporate profits.
5. Unanticipated changes in residual market risk (the part of the S&P 500 return not explained by the previous four factors).[15]

Exhibit 10-9 illustrates the estimated betas for this APT model. Notice the wide variation of reported betas. The financial sector has the greatest sensitivity (in absolute value) to both default risk and term structure. The reason is that banks tend to lose money when default risk is high (-2.48 default beta) and tend to make money when the term structure is steeply sloped (1.00 term structure beta). Recall that bank assets are typically long-maturity loans, and bank liabilities are short-maturity deposits. Hence, a steeply sloped term structure implies that assets are earning a much higher rate than the bank must pay on liabilities.

EXHIBIT 10-9 **Estimated Betas** **for the APT** **Model Using Five** **Selected Factors**	**Sector Name**	**1. Default Premiums**	**2. Term Structure**	**3. Inflation**	**4. Corporate Profits**	**5. Market Risk**
	Cyclical	−1.63 [4][a]	0.55 [6]	2.84 [4]	−1.04 [2]	1.14 [3]
	Growth	−2.08 [2]	0.58 [4]	3.16 [3]	−0.92 [3]	1.28 [2]
	Stable	−1.40 [5]	0.68 [3]	2.31 [5]	−0.22 [7]	0.74 [6]
	Oil	−0.63 [7]	0.31 [7]	2.19 [6]	−0.83 [4]	1.14 [4]
	Utility	−1.06 [6]	0.72 [2]	1.54 [7]	0.23 [6]	0.62 [7]
	Transportation	−2.07 [3]	0.58 [4]	4.45 [1]	−1.13 [1]	1.37 [1]
	Financials	−2.48 [1]	1.00 [1]	3.20 [2]	−0.56 [5]	0.99 [5]

a. The numbers in square brackets report the rank order (absolute value) of the corresponding type of risk exposure across the seven economic sectors. Thus, for example, financials ranked first in exposure to default risk and term structure risk.

15. See Michael A. Berry, Edwin Burmeister, and Marjorie B. McElroy, "Sorting Out Risks Using Known APT Factors," *Financial Analysts Journal* (March–April 1988), pp. 29–42.

The remaining task in applying this five-factor model is to estimate the market price of risk for each factor. Although the market price of risk is difficult to estimate, this task is not impossible. Clearly, the multifactor APT model is much more flexible than the CAPM.

SUMMARY

Explain the single index model (SIM) and why it reduces the efficient frontier computations.   The single index model (SIM) and the arbitrage pricing theory (APT) were originally developed for different purposes, but they are very similar. The SIM was developed to reduce the computational problems in calculating the efficient frontier. The APT was developed as an alternative to the CAPM.

The SIM drastically reduces the inputs needed in solving for the optimum portfolios in the efficient frontier, because the covariances can be calculated as follows:

$$Cov(R_i, R_j) = \beta_i \beta_j \sigma_I^2$$

Thus, the investor only needs to estimate the betas for each stock rather than all possible covariances. This reduction is the result of the assumption that returns are generated by a single factor (say, I) and firm-specific factors. Specifically, the SIM assumes that

$$E(R_i) = \alpha_i + \beta_i E(I) + e_i$$

where $Cov(I, e_i) = 0$, and that for any two stocks, $Cov(e_i e_j) = 0$.

With the SIM, risk can easily be broken down into its systematic and unsystematic components. Systematic risk cannot be diversified; unsystematic risk can be diversified. With large portfolios, unsystematic risk can be virtually eliminated.

Explain the arbitrage pricing theory (APT), its assumptions, and the resulting linear relationship.   The primary assumption of the APT is that security returns are generated by a linear factor model. The APT is based on a no-arbitrage condition. That is, an investor should not be able to build a zero risk–zero investment portfolio that has positive returns. However, the APT assumes that there are many assets in the economy and that there is some specific return-generating process. In general, the expected return on a security under the APT with multiple factors is given by

$$E(R_i) = a_0 + a_1 \beta_1 + a_2 \beta_2 + \ldots + a_K \beta_K$$

where a_0 is the risk-free interest rate, β_i is the security's sensitivity to each factor, and a_i is the market price per unit of sensitivity.

Compare and contrast the relationship between the CAPM and the APT.   The APT is an alternate equilibrium pricing model that is built on different assumptions than the CAPM. Specifically, the APT does not assume that investors make decisions according to the mean-variance rule; also, investors do not have to be risk-averse.

CHAPTER AT A GLANCE

1. *The SIM is expressed as follows:*

$$R_i \quad = \quad \alpha_i \quad + \quad \beta_i I \quad + \quad e_i$$

| | Constant | Common-Factor News | Firm-Specific News |

The SIM also can be expressed as follows:

$$R_i = E(R_i) + \beta_i[I - E(I)] + e_i$$

2. *The one-factor APT return-generating process is expressed as follows:*

$$R_i = E(R_i) + \beta_i[I - E(I)] + e_i$$

which is identical to the SIM.

3. *The one-factor APT linear relationship is expressed as follows:*

$$E(R_i) = a_0 + a_1\beta_i$$

4. *The multifactor APT is expressed as follows:*

$$E(R_i) = a_0 + a_1\beta_1 + a_2\beta_2 + a_K\beta_K$$

KEY TERMS

Arbitrage   346
Arbitrage Pricing Theory
  (APT)   345

Common factor   338
Firm-specific news   340
Single Index Model (SIM)   338

Systematic risk   343
Unsystematic risk   344
Zero beta   355

REVIEW

10.1 Suppose there is only one stock, whose price is $100. The stock price at the end of the year will be as follows:

Stock Price at End of Year	
Boom	$115
Recession	$106

You have no money to invest, and there are no other stocks in the economy to short sell. However, you can borrow as much as you want from the bank at the risk-free rate of 6%.

a. Are there arbitrage opportunities? Explain the transaction you would carry out, if any.
b. How would you change your answer if you could lend at 6% but borrow from the bank at 8%?
c. How would you change your answer to Part a if you could borrow $1,000 at 6%, but you could borrow the next $1,000 at 7%? Do you have a money machine?

10.2 Suppose the stock price is $100, and its price at the end of this year is $105 if the economy contracts or $120 if the economy expands. You can borrow as much as you want at a 4% interest rate.
a. Do you have an arbitrage opportunity? Explain.
b. Do you have a money machine?
c. As a result of heavy purchasing of the stock, its price goes up. How much should the price rise to eliminate any arbitrage opportunities?

10.3 Suppose there are the following two stocks in the market, and they have the following prices at the end of the year:

	Stock A	Stock B
Boom	$120	$118
Recession	90	85

The current stock price is $100 for both Stock A and Stock B.

a. Do you have arbitrage opportunities? Explain the arbitrage transaction, as well as the profit involved.
b. Now suppose you pay a $0.5-per-share transaction cost for every transaction. Do you still have arbitrage opportunities, net of transaction costs?
c. Answer Part b when the short-sales transaction cost is $1 per share and the long-position transaction cost remains $0.5 per share.

10.4 a. According to the APT, if $\beta_i = 0$, this implies that the ith stock has no unsystematic risk. Evaluate this assertion.
b. According to the APT, if $\beta_i = 0$, this implies that the rate of return on the ith stock must be equal to the risk-free rate. Evaluate this assertion.

10.5 "Using the SIM, if two firms have the same alpha and the same beta, then both must have the same rate of return, R." Do you agree with this statement? Why or why not?

10.6 Suppose you have a large portfolio of firms that are all in the electronics industry. The portfolio return that is due to the firm-specific factors is $\Sigma w_i e_i$. Is the assumption that $\Sigma w_i e_i = 0$ reasonable? Why? How would your answer change if the firms were not all from the electronics industry?

10.7 A new stock market is established in an emerging capitalist country in the former Soviet Union. Only five stocks are traded in this country. In the United States, several thousands of stocks are traded. Do you think the APT will better explain the risk-return relationship in the former Soviet country or in the United States? Why?

10.8 Many small investors can short sell stocks, and they do not receive the proceeds from the short sales. Also, investors pay very large transaction costs on short sales. However, there are institutional investors who hold very large portfolios, can short sell stock, and have almost zero transaction costs. Under these conditions, do you think the APT might hold? Why?

PRACTICE

10.1 Suppose you have n stocks. You want to derive the efficient frontier. How many covariances do you have to calculate? Answer the question for alternate values of $n = 2, 4, 8, 12, 20, 50,$ and 100.

10.2 Refer to Question 10.1. Suppose you employ the single index model (SIM). How many covariances do you need? In light of your answer to this question, explain the advantage of the SIM over a direct calculation of all covariances.

10.3 The rate of return on Stock i (given by R_i) and the inflation rate (given by I) are as follows:

Year	R_i	I
1	−10%	+8%
2	+20	+3
3	+18	+4
4	+ 6	+5

a. Employ the SIM, and calculate α_i and β_i, assuming each year is equally likely.
b. Are all deviations from the line (e_i) equal to zero? Is the sum of all deviations (Σe_i) equal to zero? Is the average deviation ($\Sigma e_i/4$) equal to zero?

10.4 You have four stocks and one factor that is the market portfolio, denoted as R_m. The rates of return are as follows:

	Stocks				Market
Year	R_1	R_2	R_3	R_4	R_m
1	+10%	− 2%	− 5%	+ 1%	+ 8%
2	− 2	+ 8	+10	+20	+10
3	− 5	+10	+20	− 5	+12

a. Calculate directly all possible covariances of Stocks 1, 2, 3, and 4.
b. Employ the SIM to calculate all these covariances. Compare and analyze your results.

10.5 The rate of return on General Motors in a given year is 10%. The one-factor model is the S&P 500 index, which for the year $I = 20\%$. The intercept of the SIM line is $\alpha_i = 0$, and the deviation from the line $e_i = -10\%$. What is the β_i of General Motors?

10.6 You have the following three stocks with the following rates of return:

	Stocks		
State of the Economy	1	2	3
Above-average activity	+10%	+12%	+9%
Below-average activity	− 6	− 7	−2

You are allowed to short sell the stocks and get the proceeds from the sales. Each stock is traded for $100. Are there arbitrage opportunities? What arbitrage will you carry out, and what will your profit be?

10.7 Assume a one-factor model where the factor is the inflation rate. Investors expect next year's average inflation to be $E(I) = 5\%$. Given this information, the mean rate of return on Boeing is expected to be $E(R_i) = 10\%$. The actual inflation surprised the forecasters, and it is announced to be $I = 8\%$.
a. There is no firm-specific news. The firm's beta is 2. Calculate the actual rate of return on Boeing.
b. How would you change your answer to Part a if Boeing announced that Delta canceled its $2 billion order for aircraft and the firm-specific news drops the return by 2% ($e_i = -2\%$)?

10.8 Suppose you have the following three stocks with the following parameters:

	Stock A	Stock B	Stock C
Mean return	5%	10%	20%
Beta	1	2	3

Do you have any arbitrage opportunities in this market? Why or why not?

10.9 There are three stocks with the following parameters:

	Stock A	Stock B	Stock C
Mean return	10%	?	20%
Beta	1	4	2

a. What should be the mean return on Stock B to avoid arbitrage?
b. Find the value of a_0 and a_1 in the linear equation $E(R_i) = a_0 + a_1\beta_i$.

10.10 Suppose returns are generated by the SIM for two firms, Firm i and Firm j, and we have the following information: $\beta_i = 2$, $\beta_j = 4$, and $Cov(R_i, R_j) = 0.2$. Given that the residual covariance is zero, $Cov(e_i, e_j) = 0$, what is the variance of the common factor σ_I^2?

10.11 Use the SIM to evaluate the following statements:
a. "Suppose that for all stocks, $\alpha_i = 0$ and $\beta_i = 1$ ($i = 1, 2, \ldots, n$). Then $E(R_i)$ is constant for all stocks."
b. "Suppose that for all stocks, $\alpha_i = 0$ and $\beta_i = 1$ ($i = 1, 2, \ldots, n$). Then R_i is constant for all stocks."

10.12 Suppose you employ the SIM where the common factor is $I = R_m$, the market portfolio.
a. What should α_i be such that the results will be consistent with the CAPM?
b. How would you change your answer to Part a when the SIM is defined in terms of $R_i - \overline{R}$ as the dependent variable (instead of the R_i term) and $R_m - \overline{R}_m$ as the market factor?

10.13 Suppose that for each company, the firm-specific factor is determined by a flip of a coin. If a head shows up, then $e_i = +1\%$, and if a tail shows up, then $e_i = -1\%$. You invest $1/n$ in each of the n stocks. What can you say about $\Sigma w_i e_i$? How would your answer change if you toss the coin only once, and if heads show up, $e_i = +1\%$ for all stocks, and if tails show up, $e_i = -1\%$ for all stocks?

10.14 Suppose that in Equation 10.7 we have $I = E(I)$.
a. "This implies that the common factor has no variability."
b. "This implies that the stocks have no variability." Which of the two statements is correct? Explain.

10.15 Suppose $\beta_1 = 2$ and $\beta_2 = 1$. What investment strategy creates a zero beta portfolio?

10.16 Suppose you have only three stocks, $\beta_1 = 1$, $\beta_2 = 2$, and $\beta_3 = \frac{1}{2}$ as implied by the SIM. Also, it is known that $e_i = 0$ for the three stocks for all possible outcomes. Suggest an investment strategy that requires zero investment and also has a zero portfolio beta. How would you change your answer if $e_i \neq 0$?

10.17 In the SIM where the portfolio is denoted $R_p = \Sigma w_i R_i$, show that the beta of a portfolio (β_p) is nothing but a linear combination of all betas, specifically, $\beta_p = \Sigma w_i \beta_i$.

10.18 The table on the right provides the 10-year rates of return for the years 1986–1996.

Assume that the S&P 500 is used as the index in employing the single index model. Calculate directly the covariance between small stocks and bonds, and then calculate it once again using the single index model. Explain the difference in the two calculations and the difference in the results by analyzing the covariance of the error terms. (Hint: See Equation 10.4.)

Year	Corporate Bonds R_1	S&P 500 R_2	Small Stocks R_3	$R_1 \cdot R_3$
1987	4.9	9.9	12.1	59.29
1988	5	10	12.3	61.5
1989	5.2	10.3	12.2	63.44
1990	5.2	10.1	11.6	60.32
1991	5.4	10.4	12.1	65.34
1992	5.5	10.3	12.2	67.1
1993	5.6	10.3	12.4	69.44
1994	5.4	10.2	12.2	65.88
1995	5.7	10	12.5	71.25
1996	5.6	10.7	12.6	70.56
Mean	5.35	10.22	12.22	
Sum				654.12
Variance	0.0645	0.0496	0.0676	

Source: *Stocks, Bonds, Bills and Inflation, Annual Yearbook* (Chicago: Ibbotson Associates, 1997). Used with permission. © 1997 Ibbotson Associates, Inc. All Rights Reserved. [Certain portions of this work were derived from copyrighted works of Roger G. Ibbotson and Rex Sinquefield.]

For Internet questions visit the Levy Investment Web site at http://levy-invst.swcollege.com.

YOUR TURN: APPLYING THEORY TO PRACTICE
CALCULATING ASSET COVARIANCE BY THE SINGLE INDEX MODEL (SIM)

The following table provides the monthly rates of return on five portfolios for the year 1926 (the year in which Ibbotson Associates began listing rates of return):

Stocks, Bonds, and Bills—Monthly Data Series Returns in Decimal Form

Date	S&P 500 Total Return	Small Stock Total Return	Corporate Bond Total Return	Long-Term Government Bond Total Return	T-Bill Total Return
01/26	0.0000	0.0699	0.0072	0.0138	0.0034
02/26	−0.0385	−0.0639	0.0045	0.0027	0.0027
03/26	−0.0575	−0.1073	0.0084	0.0030	0.0030
04/26	0.0253	0.0179	0.0097	0.0076	0.0034
05/26	0.0179	−0.0066	0.0044	0.0014	0.0001
06/26	0.0457	0.0378	0.0004	0.0038	0.0035
07/26	0.0479	0.0112	0.0057	0.0004	0.0022
08/26	0.0248	0.0256	0.0044	0.0000	0.0025

(continued)

Date	S&P 500 Total Return	Small Stock Total Return	Corporate Bond Total Return	Long-Term Government Bond Total Return	T-Bill Total Return
09/26	0.0252	−0.0001	0.0057	0.0038	0.0023
10/26	−0.0284	−0.0227	0.0097	0.0102	0.0032
11/26	0.0347	0.0207	0.0057	0.0160	0.0031
12/26	0.0196	0.0332	0.0056	0.0078	0.0028

Source: *Stocks, Bonds, Bills and Inflation, Annual Yearbook* (Chicago: Ibbotson Associates, 1997). Used with permission. © 1997 Ibbotson Associates, Inc. All rights reserved. [Certain portions of this work were derived from copyrighted works of Roger G. Ibbotson and Rex Sinquefield.]

Assume that the S&P 500 is the index and that the other four assets are related to it, as suggested by the SIM. You are considering investing in these four assets (excluding the index). Answer the following questions.

Questions

1. How many parameters (for example, means, variances, and so forth) do you need to estimate in order to construct the efficient frontier from the four assets?

2. How many parameters do you need to estimate if you employ the SIM?

3. Answer Questions 1 and 2 for fifty assets under review rather than four. Discuss your results.

4. Use the data given for the year 1926 to estimate all the parameters needed to construct the efficient frontier. Do this twice, first by a direct calculation of the covariances and then by employing the SIM. Compare the results, and explain the source of any discrepancies. Which calculation method is more accurate? Which is easier to use?

SELECTED REFERENCE

Berry, Michael A., Edwin Burmeister, and Marjorie B. McElroy. "Sorting Out Risks Using Known APT Factors." *Financial Analysts Journal* (March–April 1988), pp. 29–42.

This paper is a nice application of the APT in practice.

SUPPLEMENTAL REFERENCES

Bansal, Ravi, David A. Hsieh, and S. Viswanathan. "A New Approach to International Arbitrage Pricing." *Journal of Finance* 48 (December 1993): 1719–1747.

Merton, Robert. "An Intertemporal Capital Asset Pricing Model." *Econometrica* 41 (September 1973): 867–880.

Roll, R. "A Critique of the Asset Pricing Theory's Tests, Part I: On Past and Potential Testability of the Theory." *Journal of Financial Economics* 4 (March 1977): 129–176.

Ross, S. A. "The Arbitrage Theory of Capital Asset Pricing." *Journal of Economic Theory,* December 1976, pp. 341–360.

Sharpe, William F. "A Simplified Model for Portfolio Analysis." *Management Science,* January 1963, pp. 277–293.

Shleifer, Andrei, and Robert W. Vishry. "The Limits of Arbitrage." *Journal of Finance,* March 1997, pp. 35–55.

CHAPTER 11

INTERNATIONAL INVESTMENT

LEARNING OBJECTIVES

After studying this chapter you should be able to:

1. Identify the risks and returns in international investment.

2. Explain how an investor can benefit from international diversification.

3. Describe the techniques used to predict exchange rates.

INTERNATIONAL INVESTING RAISES QUESTIONS ON ALLOCATION, DIVERSIFICATION, HEDGING

As Yogi Berra might say, the problem with international investing is that it's so darn foreign.

Currency swings? Hedging? International diversification? What's that?

- Foreign stocks account for some 60% of world stock-market value, so shouldn't you have 60% of your stock-market money overseas?

The main reason to invest abroad isn't to replicate the global market or to boost returns. Instead, "what we're trying to do by adding foreign stocks is to reduce volatility," explains Robert Ludwig, chief investment officer at money manager SEI investments.

Foreign stocks don't move in sync with U.S. shares and thus, they may provide offsetting gains when the U.S. market is falling. But to get the resulting risk reduction, you don't need anything like 60% of your money abroad.

- So, how much foreign exposure do you need to get decent diversification? "Based on the volatility of foreign markets and the correlation between markets, we think an optimal portfolio is 70% in the U.S., 20% in the foreign markets and 10% in the emerging markets," Mr. Ludwig says.

Why not put even more in foreign stocks? If your aim is to reduce a portfolio's risk level, "there are diminishing marginal benefits as the international equity exposure rises," explains Laurence Smith, a managing director with J.P. Morgan's investment management's subsidiary.

He argues that once you have a third of your stock portfolio in foreign shares, there's no point in putting more money abroad unless you believe that overseas markets will outperform U.S. equities.

Even with a third of your stock-market money in foreign issues, you may find that the risk-reduction benefits aren't all that reliable. Unfortunately, when U.S. stocks get really pounded, it seems foreign shares also tend to tumble.

Experts have suggested that investors can better diversify their U.S. portfolios if, instead of emphasizing large foreign companies, they favor emerging markets, smaller foreign concerns and stocks that are cheap based on value yardsticks, such as price-to-earnings or price-to-book value.

(continued)

369

"I do agree that there's a return advantage and a diversification benefit from emerging markets," Mr. Ludwig says. "But when people say that value stocks out-perform or small stocks outperform, I think they're extrapolating from a very small data series, and that's dangerous."

- Does international diversification come from the foreign stocks or the foreign currency?

"It comes from both in roughly equal pieces," Mr. Riepe says. "Those who choose to hedge their foreign currency raise the correlation with U.S. stocks, and so the diversification benefit won't be nearly as great."

Source: Jonathan Clements, "Getting Going," *Wall Street Journal,* July 29, 1997, p. C1. Reprinted by permission of *The Wall Street Journal* © 1997 Dow Jones & Co., Inc. All rights Reserved Worldwide.

This Chapter's Investments in the News indicates that foreign stocks account for 60% of the world stock market value; hence, they cannot be ignored. Like Chapter 8's Investments in the News, this article emphasizes that international diversification (without a hedge of foreign currencies) plays a key role in portfolio risk reduction.

This chapter expands investment opportunities to the international markets. It is true that international diversification has always been available, but the fast communication between markets today literally makes our world a single financial marketplace. Thus, it is easier nowadays to take advantage of the available opportunities that exist abroad. Some investors still do not exploit this opportunity, however. No matter how effective the lines of communication between countries, many investors consider investing internationally too risky. Part of the perceived risk results from a simple lack of information. Investors are more comfortable investing in domestic firms with which they are familiar, namely, firms from which they buy products on a daily basis.

Investing in foreign securities, however, has two significant risks: foreign exchange risk and political risk. Recall from Chapter 5 that rates of return on international investments are influenced by movements in foreign exchange. This risk is discussed in detail in this chapter. **Political risk,** discussed in Chapter 2, refers to the possibility that a country will take over a publicly held firm. This sometimes occurs when a country is at war or in severe economic crisis.

These risks are offset by important benefits. Three benefits of international investments discussed in this chapter follow:

1. *Portfolio risk reduction.* Investing in the international equity and bond markets enhances the gain from diversification. Because the correlations between some of these markets are not very high, the portfolio risk can be reduced with international investments.

2. *Enhancement of portfolio expected return.* Some of these economies are growing faster than others, which may offer the investor a higher potential return. For example, during the year ending on July 30, 1997, the rate of return in U.S. dollars was 68.85% in Finland, 54.225% in Mexico, and 47.98% in the United States.

3. *Exploiting riskless investment opportunities.* At times investors can find attractive international investment opportunities that are essentially riskless. For example, suppose an investor can borrow in the United States at 3% and lend (buy government bonds) in Germany at 8%. It is sometimes possible to trade certain international securities in such a way that a portion of the difference in interest rates can be captured at no risk.[1] (In most international markets and for most investors, these investment opportunities do not exist, because astute investors will exploit such opportunities so quickly that the unsophisticated, average investor will be too late.)

This chapter first shows the gains from international diversification in the stock and bond markets. It then analyzes some relationships among interest rates, inflation rates, and forward rates in the various markets—concepts that are helpful in identifying the investment opportunities just discussed.

11.1 RISKS AND RETURNS IN INTERNATIONAL INVESTMENTS

One compelling reason to consider investing internationally is the sheer size of international markets. Exhibit 11-1 illustrates the growth of international markets. In 1969, U.S. markets represented 80% of the world equity market. By 1996, the U.S. share had dropped to 49%. Thus, investors confining their investments to the United States in 1996 eliminated 51% of the marketplace. As the economies of the

EXHIBIT 11-1 Growth of World Stock Market Capitalization, 1969 to 1996

Country	Total Capitalization of Stock Markets, in Billions of U.S. Dollars, at Year-End			
	1969	1981	1991	1996
United States	598.7	1112.9	3702	6809
Japan	46.4	400.3	2996	3667
United Kingdom	NA	NA	954	1348
Germany	NA	NA	369	588
France	22.7	38.3	347	565
Switzerland	12.4	40.8	199	414
Canada	NA	NA	232	371
Hong Kong	1.5	40.9	119	311
Australia	31.6	59.6	137	262

(continued)

1. These securities are covered in Part 5 of this book.

EXHIBIT 11-1
(continued)

Country	Total Capitalization of Stock Markets, in Billions of U.S. Dollars, at Year-End			
	1969	1981	1991	1996
Italy	13.7	24.1	154	239
Sweden	5.4	17.6	104	201
Spain	12.1	16.7	120	162
Singapore	2.2	34.9	82	143
Mexico	1.8	9.5	NA	107
Denmark	1.0	4.3	45	61

Source: For all non-U.S. markets for 1969 and 1981, Sikorsky, and Nilly, "The Origin and Construction of the Capital International Indices," *Columbia Journal of World Business,* Summer 1982—copyright 1982. *Columbia Journal of World Business.* Reprinted with permission; for all countries for 1991 and 1996, Morgan Stanley Capital International Perspective; for the United States, 1969 and 1981 data are for the New York Stock Exchange only and are from the Center for Research in Security Prices at the University of Chicago as reported by Ibbotson and Brinson (1993), pp. 156–157. Used by permission. Web site at http://www.ibbotson.com,table2.htm.

Pacific rim countries have grown and European economies have remained stable (as a percentage of the world economy), more and more investors have begun to invest in these regions. Connecting Theory to Practice 11.1 presents the view of the chairman and chief executive officer of the New York Stock Exchange, Inc., Richard A. Grasso, regarding the impact that the international equity markets will have on the NYSE. With such a strong pull to international securities, it is essential for investors to understand the motivation for, and the potential gain from, global investing.

CONNECTING THEORY TO PRACTICE 11.1

EQUITY MARKET GLOBALIZATION: A VIEW FROM 11 WALL STREET

Remarks by Richard A. Grasso
Chairman and Chief Executive Officer
New York Stock Exchange, Inc.

Fordham University
January 13, 1997

I've spent a large portion of my adult life and all of my professional career working at the New York Stock Exchange. In my judgment, the Exchange is a few years into an entirely new realm, defined by an extraordinary set of

(continued)

changes in our operating environment. As a result of these changes, the New York Stock Exchange ten years from now will be remarkably different than it is today. Our challenge is to adapt successfully to these new developments.

Three facts illustrate the change in our operating environment in the past ten to fifteen years:

1. Two-thirds of the companies that we now trade on the New York Stock Exchange listed within the last dozen years;
2. In 1981 average daily volume was a bit under 47 million shares; last year it was 412 million shares;
3. In 1980 there were 38 non-U.S. companies on the NYSE list, half of which were from Canada. At year-end 1996, the non-U.S. list had grown to 290 companies from 42 countries around the world.

And the next ten to fifteen years will be even more remarkable. . . . Countries and companies are relying more each year on equity capital. Other sources of financing—governments, banks, and internal financing—are shrinking due to large government budget deficits, a world banking system reluctant to accept large credit risks, and the inability of internal funds to meet the needs of rapidly growing enterprises. Because local capital is often limited, especially in developing countries, reliance on equity has produced a shift toward raising international equity. . . .

The internationalization of capital markets is also being driven by a massive shift in the holdings of U.S. investors into non-U.S. equity. In 1983, the market value of U.S. equities comprised 53% of the world capitalization total; by December 1996, the U.S. portion, about $8.5 trillion, represents only forty-two percent. Although the United States continues to grow, the rest of the world grows faster. Additionally, the costs of acquiring and trading non-U.S. equities have declined for U.S. investors—a result of declining trading costs abroad and increased availability of non-U.S. equity on relatively low-cost U.S. public markets.

Source: http://www.nyse.com/public/thenyse/1d/1dix.htm. Reprinted by permission.

MAKING THE CONNECTION

The growth and popularity of international financial assets is cited as one of the three major factors facing the New York Stock Exchange over the next 10 years. As pointed out, costs of investing internationally are declining, and the growth in non-U.S. equities currently exceeds that of domestic equities. These facts, along with higher standards of financial statement disclosure, which will increase investor confidence, will undoubtedly continue to increase the demand for international investments.

11.1.1 Diversifying Internationally

Diversification is one of the driving forces behind global investment. By diversifying internationally, investors gain the opportunity for higher returns and the potential to reduce risk further than if they invested only domestically. This section begins by looking at risk reduction. It illustrates the gain from international diversification from the U.S. investor's viewpoint—namely, all local returns are translated into U.S. dollars. It also discusses the precise calculations involved.

Because international markets are not perfectly correlated with each other or with the U.S. market, investors can achieve reductions in risk beyond those achieved by investing in a variety of U.S. industries. Exhibit 11-2 illustrates the correlation of several countries' indexes from 1980 to 1995. These indexes represent how well a portfolio of stocks exclusively from a particular country would have performed relative to a portfolio of U.S. stocks. For example, Japanese stocks moved with the S&P 500 stock index only 6% of the time.

Exhibit 11-3 shows that international diversification helps stabilize a portfolio. In a hypothetical portfolio in which 80% was invested in U.S. stock and only 20% was invested in foreign stock, the return of the portfolio over the 20-year period ending December 31, 1996, was 14.62%, with a standard deviation of 13.09%. In contrast, a portfolio made up of 100% U.S. stocks would have realized only a 14.46% return and a 14.02% standard deviation.

EXHIBIT 11-2
Correlation of Returns
Percentage of Time U.S. and Selected Foreign Markets Moved in Sync, 1980 to 1995

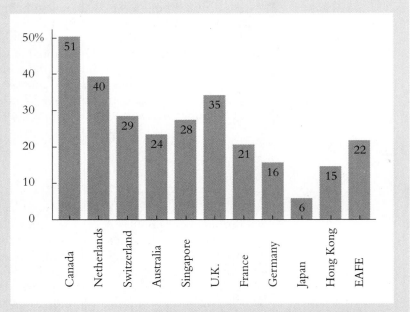

Source: InterSec Research Corp., as cited in Web site at http://www.troweprice.com/interspot/intlstck. html. Reprinted by permission.

EXHIBIT 11-3
Analysis of Various Portfolio Mixes
A diversified portfolio of foreign and U.S. stocks outperformed a portfolio invested only in U.S. stocks and helped reduce risk.

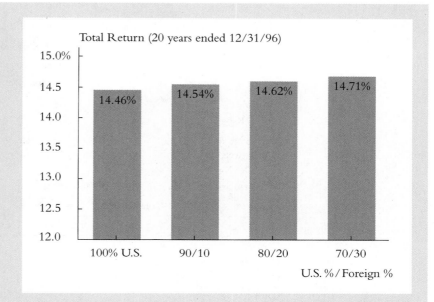

Total Return (20 years ended 12/31/96)

14.46%	14.54%	14.62%	14.71%
100% U.S.	90/10	80/20	70/30

U.S. % / Foreign %

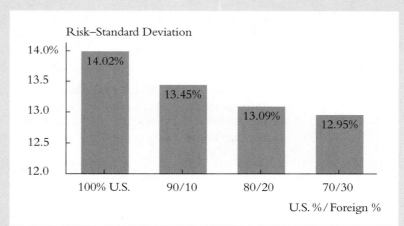

Risk–Standard Deviation

14.02%	13.45%	13.09%	12.95%
100% U.S.	90/10	80/20	70/30

U.S. % / Foreign %

Sources: T. Rowe Price—reprinted by permission; Standard and Poor's 500 index—reprinted by permission of Standard & Poor's, a division of The McGraw Hill Companies; Morgan Stanley Capital International (MSCI) Europe Australasia Far East (EAFE) Index. Web site at http://www.troweprice.com/interspot/intlstck.html.

These results can also be seen in Exhibit 11-4. Part a compares the mean rates of return and standard deviations of the individual country portfolios, as well as of an equally weighted portfolio across the four countries. In that portfolio, we assume investment in the same securities as in each country portfolio. The equally weighted portfolio's mean return is simply the average of the returns across countries. The standard deviation, or volatility, of the equally weighted portfolio, in

EXHIBIT 11-4
International
Index Data

(a) Means and Standard Deviations for Returns on World Equities from 1970 to 1995

	U.S. Currency	
	Mean	**Standard Deviation**
Canada	9.35%	17.01%
Germany	11.76	31.07
United Kingdom	12.93	31.56
United States	11.34	16.37
Equally weighted portfolio	11.35	18.1

(b) Correlation Coefficients from 1970 to 1995

	Correlation			
	Canada	**Germany**	**United Kingdom**	**United States**
Canada	1.0			
Germany	0.20	1.0		
United Kingdom	0.40	0.38	1.0	
United States	0.62	0.38	0.57	1.0

Source: Web site at http://www.ibbotson.com/table7.htm; calculated by the author from Morgan Stanley Capital International Perspective.

contrast, depends on the correlations between the individual assets (in this case, the country portfolios). Recall from Chapter 7 that to calculate the standard deviation of the portfolio, we first calculate the portfolio variance using the following formula (where we substitute $\sigma_i\sigma_j\rho_{i,j}$ for $\sigma_{i,j}$; see Equation 7.11'):

$$\sigma_p^2 = \sum_{i=1}^{n} w_i^2\sigma_i^2 + 2\sum_{i=1}^{n}\sum_{\substack{j=1 \\ j>1}}^{n} w_i w_j \sigma_i \sigma_j \rho_{i,j}$$

where i and j represent the individual country portfolios, in this case.

Exhibit 11-4b shows the correlations between some capital international indexes. The lack of perfect positive correlation demonstrates that risk can be reduced by investing internationally. The correlations between different stock *portfolios* within the United States are very high, typically in excess of 0.95. Thus, correlation coefficients such as 0.20 between Canada and Germany allow for significant risk reduction by international diversification. In fact, the standard deviation of the equally weighted portfolio is less than the standard deviation of most of the country portfolios (see Exhibit 11-4a). This portfolio standard deviation is calculated as follows:

$$\begin{aligned}
\sigma_p^2 = {} & (\tfrac{1}{4})^2(0.1701)^2 + (\tfrac{1}{4})^2(0.3107)^2 + (\tfrac{1}{4})^2(0.3156)^2 + (\tfrac{1}{4})^2(0.1637)^2 \\
& + 2(\tfrac{1}{4})(\tfrac{1}{4})(0.20)(0.1701)(0.3107) + 2(\tfrac{1}{4})(\tfrac{1}{4})(0.40)(0.1701)(0.3156) \\
& + 2(\tfrac{1}{4})(\tfrac{1}{4})(0.62)(0.1701)(0.1637) + 2(\tfrac{1}{4})(\tfrac{1}{4})(0.38)(0.3107)(0.3156) \\
& + 2(\tfrac{1}{4})(\tfrac{1}{4})(0.38)(0.3107)(0.1637) + 2(\tfrac{1}{4})(\tfrac{1}{4})(0.57)(0.3156)(0.1637)
\end{aligned}$$

$$= 0.001808376 + 0.006033406 + 0.00622521 + 0.001674856$$
$$+ 0.001321252 + 0.002684178 + 0.002158016 + 0.004657704$$
$$+ 0.002415926 + 0.00368104$$

$$= 0.032659961$$

and the standard deviation is about 0.181, or 18.1% (the square root of 0.32659961).

PRACTICE BOX

Problem

Suppose that a U.S. investor is considering diversifying internationally. This investor currently holds a widely diversified portfolio of U.S. stocks. Given the data in the following table (all returns have been converted to U.S. dollars), what is the expected rate of return and standard deviation of a portfolio that is equally weighted between the United States, Europe, and the Far East? What is the investor's gain from diversifying globally?

	Expected Return	Standard Deviation	Correlation United States	Europe	Far East
United States	9.6%	14.1%	1		
Europe	7.5%	12.7%	0.54	1	
Far East	11.2%	15.4%	0.32	0.21	1

Solution

From the previous discussion, the expected return of the portfolio, using Equation 7.2, is

$$E(R_p) = \sum_{i=1}^{n} w_i E(R_i)$$

$$= \tfrac{1}{3}(0.096) + \tfrac{1}{3}(0.075) + \tfrac{1}{3}(0.112)$$

$$= 0.094, \text{ or } 9.4\%, \text{ and the variance is}$$

$$\sigma_p^2 = (\tfrac{1}{3})^2 (0.141)^2 + (\tfrac{1}{3})^2 (0.127)^2 + (\tfrac{1}{3})^2 (0.154)^2$$
$$+ 2(\tfrac{1}{3})^2(0.127)(0.141)(0.54)$$
$$+ 2(\tfrac{1}{3})^2(0.141)(0.154)(0.32)$$
$$+ 2(\tfrac{1}{3})^2(0.127)(0.154)(0.21)$$

$$\cong 0.00221 + 0.00179 + 0.00264 + 0.00215 + 0.00154 + 0.00091$$

$$\cong 0.01124$$

Note that $w_i = w_j$ for all i and j. Thus, the portfolio standard deviation is

$$\sigma_p = \sqrt{0.01124} \cong 0.106, \text{ or } 10.6\%$$

(continued)

The gain from diversifying is a 24.8% [(14.1%−10.6%)/14.1%] reduction in the standard deviation with only a 2.1% [(9.6% −9.4%)/9.6%] reduction in the expected return.

Exhibit 11-5 illustrates risk reduction via international diversification in a slightly different manner. Recall that Chapter 8 illustrated the reduction in a portfolio's variance as the number of securities increased (see Exhibit 8-8). The same principle can be applied to international portfolios. Exhibit 11-5 illustrates the gain from diversifying both domestically and internationally. However, rather than measuring risk by the variance of the portfolio (as was done in Chapter 8), Exhibit 11-5 illustrates the risk reduction in percentage terms. That is, *percent risk* measures the percentage of the total risk of the average stock (measured by the standard deviation) remaining after diversifying.[2] Specifically, if σ_i denotes the standard deviation of the average stock and σ_p denotes the standard deviation of a portfolio of stocks, then percent risk can be expressed as

**EXHIBIT 11-5
Risk Reduction with
International Diversification**

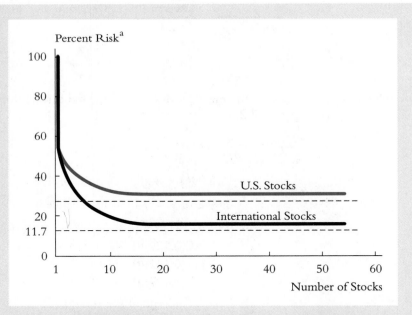

a. *Percent risk* represents the reduction in the standard deviation for the average stock as additional securities are added randomly (assuming they are equally weighted).

Source: Adapted with permission from Bruno Solnik, "Why Not Diversify Internationally Rather Than Domestically?" *Financial Analysts Journal,* July–August 1974, p. 50. © 1974, Association for Investment Management and Research, Charlottesville, Va. All rights reserved.

2. These results are based on a series of randomly diversified portfolios.

$$\text{Percent risk} = \left(\frac{\overline{\sigma}_i - \sigma_p}{\overline{\sigma}_i}\right)100$$

The larger the percent risk, the larger the gain from diversification, because the portfolio's standard deviation is small relative to the average standard deviation of the individual stocks.

If the average standard deviation across stocks is 35% and a portfolio of five stocks has a standard deviation of 20%, the percent risk reduction is

$$\text{Percent Risk} = \left(\frac{0.35 - 0.20}{0.35}\right)100 \cong 42.9\%$$

Thus, percent risk is a measure of risk corresponding to various levels of diversification. Note that percent risk declines as the number of stocks is increased for both domestic and international portfolios. Portfolios containing international securities, however, have a larger reduction in the percent risk than portfolios with just U.S. stocks.

One final way to illustrate the benefit from international diversification is with efficient frontiers. Exhibit 11-6a illustrates the improved efficient frontiers for bond portfolios with international investing. For example, a portfolio of U.S. bonds had a standard deviation of 5.5% and an average return of 4.3%. By adding international bonds and choosing a portfolio with weights such that point m is achieved, the average expected return increases to 9% with a corresponding increase in standard deviation of only 0.2% (or to a standard deviation of 5.7%). Thus, by diversifying internationally with bonds, a dramatic increase in average expected return is achieved with a negligible increase in standard deviation.[3]

Exhibit 11-6b focuses on international diversification in the equity market and illustrates several efficient frontiers derived from various combinations of country portfolios. Point F is a portfolio of U.S. equity securities, and the benefit to U.S. investors from international diversification is clear. Notice the significant gains in risk reduction and return enhancement by considering twenty-eight countries (curve aA). As in the bond market, the analysis of the equity market shows that there are considerable gains achieved by diversifying internationally.

Chapter 10 expands the investment universe by adding a risk-free asset. The current chapter expands the investment universe by allowing international diversification. Finally, these two expansions can be considered simultaneously: assuming a 5% interest rate in the United States, an American investor can shift from line I to line II. (See Figure 11-6b.)

Finally, Exhibit 11-6c illustrates efficient frontiers for an international bond portfolio, stock portfolio, and combined stock and bond portfolio. A global portfolio of both bonds and stocks results in an efficient frontier that is superior to the portfolios of either just bonds or just stocks. Overall, this is a strong case for global diversification across both bonds and stocks.

3. Based on Haim Levy and Zvi Lerman, "The Benefits of International Diversification in Bonds," *Financial Analysts Journal*, September–October 1988, pp. 56–64.

EXHIBIT 11-6   Various Efficient Frontiers

Part a: Efficient Bond Portfolio for a U.S. Investor
Diversifying across Thirteen Countries

Part b: Efficient Stock Portfolio for a U.S. Investor
Diversifying across Twenty-eight Countries
(riskless rate $r = 5\%$)

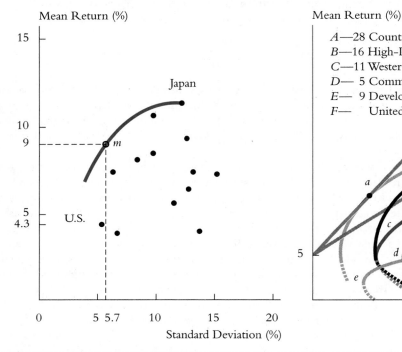

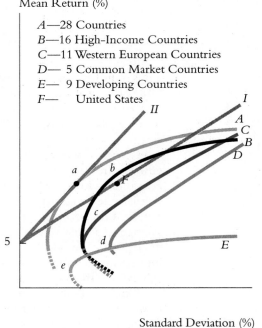

(continued)

11.1.2 Currency Risk

So far, this chapter has illustrated the gain to U.S. investors from international diversification. However, the text has not explained the role that exchange risk plays in such calculations. Recall from Chapter 5 (see Section 5.5) that the rate of return in foreign investments is influenced also by changes in the exchange rate. It is therefore important to factor those changes into rate-of-return calculations.

The rate of return on a foreign investment expressed in the domestic currency (R_D) is calculated as follows:

EXHIBIT 11-6
(continued)

Part c: Efficient Bond and Stock Portfolios for a U.S. Investor
Diversifying across Thirteen Countries

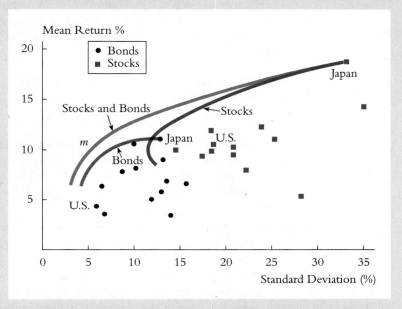

The dots denote bond portfolios from different countries, and the squares denote stock portfolios from different countries.

Source: Adapted with permission from Haim Levy and Zvi Lerman, "The Benefits of International Diversification in Bonds," *Financial Analysts Journal,* September–October 1988, pp. 56–64. © 1988, The Financial Analysts Federation, Charlottesville, Va. All rights reserved.

$$R_D = \frac{fx_n(DC/FC)}{fx_0(DC/FC)}(1 + R_L) - 1 = (1 + R_{fx})(1 + R_L) - 1 \qquad (11.1)$$

where $fx_n(DC/FC)$ is the exchange rate in domestic currency per foreign currency at time n, $fx_0(DC/FC)$ is the exchange rate in domestic currency per foreign currency at time 0, R_L is the rate of return in the stock market in the local currency, and R_{fx} is the rate of return on the foreign exchange. For example, suppose the rate of return on stocks in Canada was 11.5%, and the Canadian dollar becomes stronger. The percentage change in the foreign exchange rate between the United States and Canada is +3.5% in U.S. dollars per Canadian dollars. Namely, each Canadian dollar is worth, after the change in the exchange rate, 3.5% more in terms of U.S. dollars. Based on Equation 11.1, the rate of return to the U.S. investor in Canada—that is, in U.S. dollars—is

$$R_D = (1 + 0.035)(1 + 0.115) - 1 \cong 0.154, \text{ or } 15.4\%$$

PRACTICE BOX

Problem	Suppose that last year a U.S. investor bought a portfolio of U.K. stocks when the exchange rate was $2/£. There has been a gain of 20% on the stock portfolio measured in pounds, and the investor is considering selling her portfolio. If the current exchange rate is $1.5/£, what was the rate of return measured in U.S. dollars?
Solution	From Equation 11-1, in the problem [where $fx_n(\$/£) = 1.5$, $fx_0(\$/£) = 2$, and $R_L = 0.2$] we have

$$R_D = (^{1.5}\!/_2)\,(1 + 0.2) - 1 = -0.1, \text{ or } -10\%$$

or a loss of 10%. Hence, although the investor experienced a gain of 20% on the U.K. investment, that did not translate into a gain in U.S. dollars because the British pound weakened against the U.S. dollar. Namely, the investor paid $2 for each pound bought and received only $1.50 for each pound when the portfolio was sold.

Thus, a weaker dollar enhances the rate of return of a U.S. investor abroad, and the opposite occurs when the U.S. dollar becomes stronger. In the period from January 1, 1997, to July 30, 1997, the dollar was stronger in comparison to most currencies, which experienced a decrease in rates of return. The data in Exhibit 11-7 reflect the impact of the change in the exchange rates on rates of return in the bond markets.

Let us illustrate with the German bond market. An American investor who bought German bonds earned 4.06% in German marks. However, when he exchanged the marks for dollars, he received fewer dollars (because the dollar became

EXHIBIT 11-7 Total Ratios of Return on International Bonds		In Local Currency	In U.S. Dollar
	Japan	3.13%	1.67%
	Britain	7.55	2.51
	Germany	4.06	−12.32
	France	4.69	−11.73
	Canada	6.05	4.91
	Netherlands	4.00	−12.72
	Non-U.S.	4.78	−5.48
	World[a]	4.90	−2.02

a. Includes seventeen international government bond markets.

Source: *Wall Street Journal,* July 30, 1997, p. C13. Reprinted by permission of *The Wall Street Journal* © 1997 Dow Jones & Co., Inc. All Rights Reserved Worldwide.

stonger) and hence ended up with a negative rate of return of -12.32%. Equation 11.1 yields the following:

$$-0.1232 = (1 + R_{fx})(1.0406) - 1$$

Hence,

$$R_{fx} = \frac{0.8768}{1.0406} - 1 \cong -0.16$$

This means that the dollar gained about 16% of its value in comparison to the German mark during the first seven months of 1997.

What is the historical impact of changes in foreign exchange rates on actual rates of return? Exhibit 11-8 illustrates the foreign exchange rates for three countries in terms of U.S. dollars. It shows that the exchange rate of the German mark to the U.S. dollar has been the most volatile, with the dollar getting weaker in the years 1985–1988. A weaker U.S. dollar means that the U.S. dollar will buy fewer and fewer German marks. The exchange rate with the Canadian dollar and the British pound has been relatively stable. How have these exchange rates influenced actual returns? A look at each country in detail will help answer that question.

Exhibit 11-9 shows an index of German stocks valued both in German marks and in U.S. dollars. Note that the volatility of the foreign exchange translates directly into more volatile movements in the index when it is stated in U.S. dollars.

EXHIBIT 11-8
Exchange Rates of Various Countries against the U.S. Dollar, 1977 to July 1998

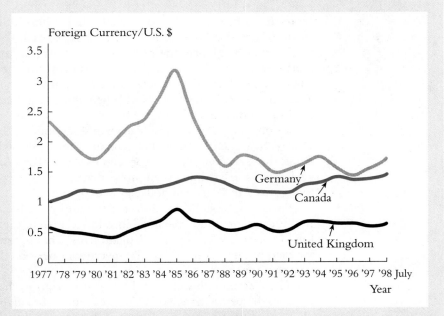

Source: http://www.triacom.com/archive/exchange.en.html.

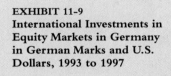

EXHIBIT 11-9
International Investments in Equity Markets in Germany in German Marks and U.S. Dollars, 1993 to 1997

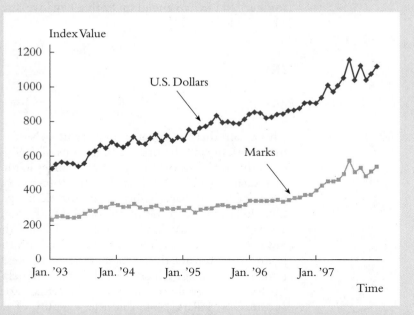

Source: Morgan Stanley Capital International indexes, Web site at http://www.ms.com./mscidata/perform/ind_lvl/ind=lvl=928000=Monthly.html.

Note that when the dollar depreciates (see 1985–1988, Exhibit 11-8), it enhances the return to the American investor.[4] That is, each German mark was worth more in U.S. dollars. Hence, the performance of an investment in Germany was greatly enhanced by the declining U.S. dollar. This phenomenon continued in the 1990s, and in December 1997, the exchange rate was less than 1.75 marks per 1 U.S. dollar. The opposite was true in 1998 when the dollar became stronger, reaching 1.79 marks per dollar on July 22, 1998.

Exhibit 11-10 shows the Canadian stock index. The exchange rate between the United States and Canada has remained relatively stable, as seen in Exhibit 11-8. Thus, the Canadian index (expressed in U.S. dollars) is not greatly influenced by the exchange rate. Exhibit 11-10 shows that the index expressed in U.S. dollars and the index stated in Canadian dollars move together.

Finally, Exhibit 11-11 illustrates the impact of the British pound exchange rate. In this case, the pound declined in value relative to the U.S. dollar, causing the portfolio to appreciate less in U.S. dollar terms. That is, fewer U.S. dollars were received for each pound at the end of the investment period relative to the beginning of the investment period.

These simple illustrations show that foreign exchange can have a major influence on the performance of U.S. investments abroad. Hence, changes in foreign ex-

4. Recall that domestic rates of return are determined by two factors, the rate of return in local currency and the percentage change in foreign exchange (see Equation 11.1).

EXHIBIT 11-10
International Investments in Equity Markets in Canada in Canadian Dollars and U.S. Dollars, 1993 to 1997

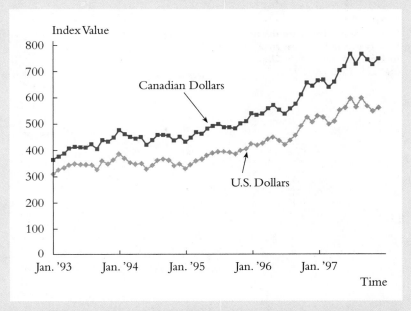

Source: Morgan Stanley Capital International indexes, Web site at http://www.ms.com./mscidata/perform/ind_lvl/ind=lvl=928000=Monthly.html.

change rates are a major variable to consider before investing globally. Investors can eliminate the foreign exchange risk by hedging with derivative securities or by a forward transaction, which will be discussed later in the chapter.

11.1.3 International Diversification: Various Points of View

As we have seen, the rate of return on international investments depends on both the securities' prices and foreign exchange fluctuations. Suppose that the rate of return on Japanese stocks, in yen, is +10%. An American investor and a German investor invest in Japan and earn this 10% in Japanese yen. Will the investors each receive the same rate of return of 10% in their own currencies? They will not; the 10% rate of return will be translated differently to dollars or German marks, because the dollar-yen and mark-yen fluctuations are generally different. Thus, an American investor and a German investor who face the same available international investment opportunities in local currencies will face different investment options once these returns are translated into their own domestic currencies—in our example, dollars and marks, respectively. Therefore, even if all experts agree on rate-of-return distributions in local currencies, the efficient frontier and the optimalinternational diversification depend on the investors' currency. What constitutes the optimal investment for the German investor may be a nonoptimal investment for the American investor, and vice versa.

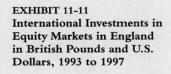

EXHIBIT 11-11
International Investments in
Equity Markets in England
in British Pounds and U.S.
Dollars, 1993 to 1997

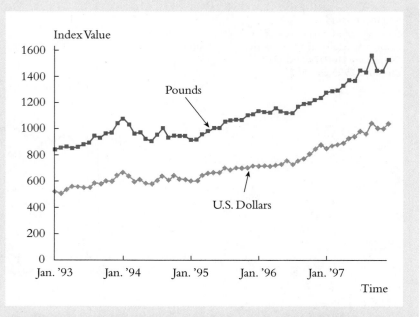

Source: Morgan Stanley Capital International indexes, Web site at http://www.ms.com/mscidata/perform/ind_lvl/ind=lvl=928000=Monthly.html.

To illustrate, take the monthly rates of return for the period October 1992 to October 1997 for Japan, the United States, the United Kingdom, and Germany from Morgan Stanley Capital International. Exhibit 11-12a shows the mean rate of return and the standard deviation when returns are calculated in German marks and U.S. dollars. Exhibit 11-12b shows the correlations between rates of return calculated in dollars (the American point of view) and in marks (the German point of view).

First note that if there were no foreign exchange fluctuations, there would be no difference between the German investor's point of view and the American investor's point of view in Part a of Exhibit 11-12. The differences are due to foreign exchange fluctuations. For example, the dollar mean rate of return on U.S. stocks is 1.37%. However, for the German investor who invests in the United States, the mean rate of return is 1.56%. This implies that the dollar becomes stronger on average, and the German investor earns in the U.S. stock market as well as gains from the foreign exchange fluctuations which were, on average, in the German investor's favor for this specific period.

By the same token, the standard deviations and correlations are also affected by the currency used by the investor. For example, investing in the United States is riskier for a German investor than for an American investor due to the added risk of currency fluctuations. Because all historical parameters needed to derive the efficient frontier are dependent on the investor's point of view (that is, the currency used), the mean-variance efficient frontier also will be dependent on the investor's point of view.

EXHIBIT 11-12   **Market Data Based on the Investor's Point of View (Currency Used)**

(a) Monthly Means and Standard Deviations

	German Investor's Point of View		American Investor's Point of View	
	Mean	**Standard Deviation**	**Mean**	**Standard Deviation**
Germany	1.43%	4.90%	1.27%	4.29%
Japan	0.46	6.73	0.31	6.45
U.K.	1.38	4.20	1.23	3.55
U.S.A.	1.56	4.76	1.37	3.10

(b) Correlations

	German Investor's Point of View				American Investor's Point of View			
	Germany	**Japan**	**U.K.**	**U.S.A.**	**Germany**	**Japan**	**U.K.**	**U.S.A.**
Germany	1	0.279	0.645	0.632	1	0.161	0.515	0.410
Japan	0.279	1	0.437	0.385	0.161	1	0.351	0.209
U.K.	0.645	0.437	1	0.722	0.510	0.351	1	0.498
U.S.A.	0.632	0.385	0.722	1	0.410	0.209	0.498	1

Source: Data from Morgan Stanley Capital International Web site at http://www.ms.com/mscidata.

Exhibits 11-13 and 11-14 illustrate the efficient frontier with and without short sales when German marks and U.S. dollars are the currencies used by the investor. Curves with similar shapes are obtained in both currencies, as well as very similar locations of the various countries (in terms of mean and standard deviations). However, the optimum investment portfolio is not the same from both investors' points of view. For example, see Exhibit 11-15, which shows the composition of the minimum variance portfolio (without short sales), denoted by MVP in Exhibits 11-13 and 11-14, in German marks and U.S. dollars. The investment proportions depend on the investor's point of view. The biggest difference is in the investment in the United States. The German investor would invest zero in the U.S. market, whereas the American investor would invest about 34% in the U.S. market.

The minimum variance portfolio also demonstrates how the portfolio composition is affected by the foreign exchange fluctuations (see point MVP in Exhibits 11-13 and 11-14). The same phenomenon holds with respect to the other portfolios on the frontier, regardless of whether short sales are allowed or not. This finding strongly implies that in considering the optimal international diversification, it is crucial that the investor take into account the foreign exchange fluctuations: what is good for the American investor is not necessarily good for the German or Japanese investor.

EXHIBIT 11-13
**Mean–Variance Frontier
in Dollars**

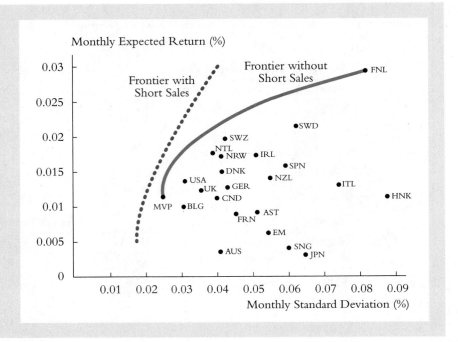

EXHIBIT 11-14
**Mean–Variance Frontier
in German Marks**

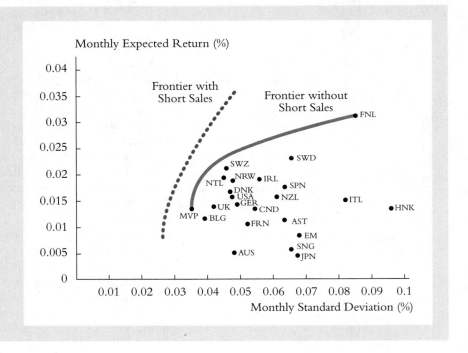

EXHIBIT 11-15 Composition of the Minimum Variance Portfolio, MVP (without short sales)	Asset Included on the Portfolio	German Investor's Point of View	U.S. Investor's Point of View
	Austria	13.7%	15.9%
	Belgium	41.5	33.6
	Denmark	8.6	4.9
	Ireland	—	0.1
	Italy	—	1.6
	Japan	4.3	1.6
	Switzerland	22.8	8.3
	United Kingdom	9.1	—
	United States	—	34.0
	Total	100%	100%

11.2 INTERNATIONAL PARITY RELATIONSHIPS[5]

Exchange rates are a key variable in determining returns from international investments. Investors rely on four parity relationships when they attempt to predict future exchange rates. A parity relationship is a mathematical expression that illustrates a hypothesized relationship between financial variables. This section covers purchasing power parity, the international Fisher relationship, foreign exchange expectations, and interest rate parity.

11.2.1 Purchasing Power Parity

Suppose that there is high inflation in one country (Country A) and no inflation in another country (Country B). Under these circumstances, the inhabitants of Country A will buy their products from country B. To do so, they will buy foreign currency, so the foreign exchange rate will be affected. Thus, differential inflation in two countries affects the foreign exchange rate.

Purchasing power parity is the relationship between two countries' inflation rates and their foreign exchange rates. This parity relationship is used to estimate exchange rates based on expected inflation rates. To clarify the appropriate relationship between inflation rates and exchange rates, suppose we have an internationally traded good (say, aluminum) with no trading restrictions. That is, suppose we can trade aluminum internationally with no transportation or other costs. As before, let *DC* denote domestic currency ($ in the following example) and *FC* denote foreign

---

5. This section is based on Chapter 1 of Bruno Solnik, *International Investments,* 2d ed. (Reading, Mass.: Addison-Wesley Publishing, 1991).

currency ($£$, the symbol for the British pound, in the following example). Thus, $P_{0,DC}$ denotes the price of aluminum in the domestic currency today, and $P_{0,FC}$ denotes the price of aluminum in the foreign currency today.

If we can trade internationally and costlessly, then we would expect aluminum to cost the same in either the local market or the foreign market, adjusted for the foreign exchange rate. That is,

$$P_{0,DC} = (\text{Foreign Exchange Rate Today}) \cdot P_{0,FC} \qquad (11.2)$$

where the foreign exchange rate today is in terms of domestic currency per foreign currency. For example, if aluminum was selling for $£0.65$ and the foreign exchange rate today was $\$1.5385/£$, then the price of aluminum in the United States should be

$$(\$1.5385/£)(£0.65) \cong \$1.00$$

If the cost of aluminum in the United States is any value other than $1, arbitrage profits can be made. For example, if the actual price in the United States is $1.01 (still assuming that transactions are costless), then we can buy aluminum in the United Kingdom for $£0.65$ (with dollars exchanged at $\$1.5385/£$) and sell it for $1.01, making a penny profit for each pound of aluminum; with a large volume of such transactions, an investor can be rich at no risk.

Now suppose that over the next year, the United States experiences 3% inflation, and the United Kingdom experiences 5% inflation. If inflation were the only influence on aluminum prices, we would expect the following prices for aluminum:

$$\begin{aligned} P_{1,DC} &= (1 + \text{Domestic Inflation Rate}) \cdot P_{0,DC} \\ &= (1 + 0.03)\$1 = \$1.03 \end{aligned} \qquad (11.3)$$

$$\begin{aligned} P_{1,FC} &= (1 + \text{Foreign Inflation Rate}) \cdot P_{0,FC} \\ &= (1 + 0.05)£0.65 = £0.6825 \end{aligned} \qquad (11.4)$$

To maintain equilibrium in the international markets with no possible arbitrage transaction, we know (according to Equation 11.2 but related to Period 1) that at the end of the year, we must have

$$P_{1,DC} = (\text{Foreign Exchange Rate in a Year}) \cdot P_{1,FC} \qquad (11.5)$$

In our case with aluminum, we must have

$$\$1.03 = (\text{Foreign Exchange Rate in a Year})(£0.6825)$$

Solving for the foreign exchange rate, we have

$$\text{Foreign Exchange Rate in a Year} = \$1.03/£0.6825 \cong \$1.5092/£$$

Thus, we see that the higher inflation rate in the United Kingdom has the effect of lowering the foreign exchange rate (the pound is said to depreciate).

We can extend this analysis of the relationship between inflation and exchange rates with aluminum prices to the general level of inflation, because other goods can also be exported and imported. Up to this point, we have assumed that the rates of inflation are known. In practice, however, we do not know what the actual foreign exchange rates or inflation rates will be in a year. Hence, the relationship is based on expected values. The relationship between expected foreign exchange rates and expected inflation rates, known as *purchasing power parity,* can be expressed as follows:

[1 + E(Foreign Inflation Rate)]/[1 + E(Domestic Inflation Rate)]
= E(Foreign Exchange Rate in a Year/Foreign Exchange Rate Today)

where E denotes the expected rate. That is, the ratio of 1 plus the expected inflation rate is equal to the expected return on foreign exchange. The expression just given can be hard to interpret, so most analysts use the following linear approximation:

$$E(s_{fx}) \equiv \frac{E[fx_1(FC/DC)]}{fx_0(FC/DC)} - 1 \cong E(h_{FC} - h_{DC}) \qquad (11.6)$$

where E is the expected rate, s_{fx} is the rate of return in the spot market for foreign exchange expressed in foreign currency per domestic currency,[6] $fx_1(FC/DC)$ is the foreign exchange rate at the end of the year, $fx_0(FC/DC)$ is the foreign exchange rate at the beginning of the year, and h is the inflation rate for one year. This equation basically says that the expected rate of return on foreign exchange is approximately equal to the difference in the expected inflation rates.

PRACTICE BOX

Problem

Suppose we observe that the expected inflation rate in Switzerland is 4%, and the expected inflation rate in the United States is 2% over the next year. If the current foreign exchange rate is SwF 1.53/$ (SwF stands for Swiss franc), what is the expected foreign exchange rate next year based on Equation 11.6?

Solution

From Equation 11.6 and the previous data, we have

$$\{E[fx_1(\text{SwF}/\$)]/(\text{SwF } 1.53/\$)\} - 1 \cong 0.04 - 0.02$$

Solving for $E[fx_1(\text{SwF}/\$)]$, we have

$$\{E[fx_1(\text{SwF}/\$)]/(\text{SwF } 1.53/\$)\} \cong 1 + 0.04 - 0.02$$

$$E[fx_1(\text{SwF}/\$)] \cong 1.02 \cdot (\text{SwF } 1.53/\$)$$

$$\cong \text{SwF } 1.5606/\$$$

Based on purchasing power parity, we would anticipate the dollar's getting stronger over the next year, rising to SwF 1.5606/$.

---

6. The spot market is where currency is exchanged today. However, usually there is a two-day settlement period. Hence, a trade made today in the spot market will actually result in currency trading in two days.

Let us see how well the approximation equation for purchasing power parity holds up using the data from the previous aluminum example. In the example,

$$fx_0(FC/DC) = 1/fx_0(DC/FC) = 1/(\$1.5385/\pounds) \cong \pounds0.65/\$$$

$$fx_1(FC/DC) = 1/fx_1(DC/FC) = 1/(\$1.5092/\pounds) \cong \pounds0.6626/\$$$

and we have

$$(\pounds0.6626/\$)/(\pounds0.65/\$) - 1 \cong 0.05 - 0.03$$

$$1.0194 - 1 \cong 0.02$$

$$0.0194 \cong 0.02$$

The precise figure is 2%, and the figure obtained by the approximation is 1.94%; hence, the approximation equation given by Equation 11.6 is very reasonable.

In principle, then, we should be able to look at the differences in expected inflation rates and get an estimate of future foreign exchange rates. In practice, however, there are two factors to consider. First, international trade is not costless, and there are actually significant trade barriers (such as tariffs). Second, purchasing power parity requires knowing the future inflation differential, but the actual inflation that will occur is unknown. Nevertheless, although far from perfect, purchasing power parity establishes a link between the foreign exchange market and the inflation differential that can be useful.

11.2.2 International Fisher Relationship

The **international Fisher relationship** establishes a link between nominal interest rates and inflation rates in different countries. Specifically, if we know the nominal interest rates in two countries, we can estimate expected inflation rates, which, as has been shown, can be used to estimate exchange rates.

We start with the observation that in the presence of inflation, investors will demand a premium in excess of their compensation for the time value of money to compensate themselves for the deterioration in the purchasing power of the currency. Investors wish to protect the purchasing power of their investment. Specifically, the nominal interest rate will be related to the real interest rate and expected inflation as follows:

$$(1 + \text{Nominal Rate}) = (1 + \text{Real Rate})[1 + E(\text{Inflation Rate})]$$

This is the same as Equation 5.9 in Chapter 5, with the distinction that this equation has expected inflation rather than historical inflation. This relationship holds regardless of which country an investor is in and thus is the same for interest rates in a foreign currency. Hence, in 1930, Fisher established the following relationship:[7]

---

7. See Irving Fisher, *The Theory of Interest* (New York: Macmillan, 1930). This relationship can be established by dividing the domestic relationship by the foreign counterpart.

$$\frac{(1 + \text{Domestic Nominal Rate})}{(1 + \text{Foreign Nominal Rate})} =$$

$$\frac{(1 + \text{Domestic Real Rate})}{(1 + \text{Foreign Real Rate})} \cdot \frac{(1 + \text{Domestic Inflation Rate})}{(1 + \text{Foreign Inflation Rate})}$$

Note that the inflation rates are actually expected inflation rates.

We would expect the real rate of interest to be the same. Otherwise, money would move from the country with the lower real rate to the country with the higher real rate. If we assume that the real rate of interest is the same in both countries, then the above expression can be approximated by the following equation:

$$R_{n,FC} - R_{n,DC} \cong E(h_{FC} - h_{DC}) \tag{11.7}$$

where R_n denotes the nominal interest rate on one-period bonds (default-free Treasury issues), and h denotes the inflation rate for one period. According to the international Fisher relationship, the difference between the nominal interest rates of two countries is approximately equal to the difference in the expected inflation rates. For example, if over the next year inflation is expected to be 5% in the United Kingdom and 3% in the United States, then we would anticipate approximately 2% difference in nominal 1-year interest rates.

11.2.3 Foreign Exchange Expectations

Foreign exchange expectations are estimated by the relationship between the current forward foreign exchange rate and the expected future foreign exchange rate. The **forward foreign exchange rate** is the exchange rate available today to exchange currency at some specified date in the future. The ability to convert one currency into another currency is critical for the successful management of international portfolios, because investors often know that they will have to exchange currencies at some future date.

For example, suppose a U.S. investor has a yen-denominated CD maturing in six months in Tokyo. In response to demand by investors to minimize the impact of currency swings on their portfolios, a forward market in foreign exchange has developed. A **forward foreign exchange contract** is a contract that obligates an investor to deliver a specified quantity of one currency in return for a specified amount of another currency. For example, if the U.S. investor has a 10-million-yen CD maturing in six months, the investor may enter into a forward foreign exchange contract to deliver 10 million yen in return for $100,000. With a forward foreign exchange contract, the investor has eliminated any future risk related to changes in exchange rate.

Because the forward foreign exchange rate reflects investors' expectations regarding the future exchange rate, it is commonly asserted that the forward rate is an unbiased estimate of the future spot foreign exchange rate. That is,

$$E[fx_1(DC/FC)] = F[fx_1(DC/FC)] \qquad (11.8)$$

where $F[fx_1(DC/FC)]$ denotes the forward foreign exchange rate today for foreign exchange at time 1, and $E[fx_1(DC/FC)]$ denotes the expected spot rate for foreign exchange at time 1.

If this assertion is true, then there is no benefit from bearing foreign exchange risk. On average, the return that is due to foreign exchange charges above or below the forward rate is zero. Thus, the expected return is zero for bearing foreign currency risk. Therefore, some argue that a risk offering no expected return should be hedged.

PRACTICE BOX	
Problem	Suppose you observe today that the Swiss forward foreign exchange rate in 1 year is SwF 1.58/\$ when the current spot rate is SwF 1.53/\$. What inferences can you draw regarding future expected foreign exchange rates between the United States and Switzerland?
Solution	Based on the foreign exchange expectations approach to forward foreign exchange rates, you would conclude that the U.S. dollar will strengthen against the Swiss franc. Specifically, the foreign exchange rate is expected to rise to SwF 1.58/\$ in 1 year. Note that this is what is expected to happen, not what will necessarily happen.

11.2.4 Interest Rate Parity

Assume that the interest rate is about 7% in Germany and less than 1% in Japan (the actual rates on July 30, 1997). It seems that an investor can take advantage of this situation and make a profit by borrowing money in Japan and investing it in Germany. Although such a transaction is default-free (because the investor buys German government bonds), it is not free from foreign exchange risk. The Japanese investor may earn the interest difference but may lose money when the marks are converted to yen when the loan has to be paid back. To avoid such a risk, the investor can lock in a transaction in the forward market that essentially allows the exchange of German marks for Japanese yen at the end of the period at an exchange rate that is determined today. If such a transaction with a forward risk protection yields a positive rate of return, it is an arbitrage position. The demand for such transactions will affect interest rates and forward exchange rates until the arbitrage profit vanishes, because in equilibrium arbitrage profit cannot exist.

To further illustrate this point, suppose that a Japanese investor borrows 1 million yen and invests them in Germany. The Japanese investor will invest 1 million yen $\cdot fx_0(FC/DC)$ marks and at the end of the year will obtain the following:

$$1 \text{ million yen} \cdot fx_0(FC/DC) \cdot (1 + R_{n,FC}) \text{ marks}$$

When this amount is sold in the forward market, the amount of yen obtained will be

$$1 \text{ million yen} \cdot fx_0(FC/DC)(1 + R_{n,FC})/F[fx_1(FC/DC)]$$

In equilibrium, when no arbitrage profit prevails, this must be equal to the amount of yen the borrower has to return to the lender in Japan, namely, 1 million yen $\cdot (1 + R_{n,DC})$. Thus, in equilibrium, the following must hold:

$$fx_0(FC/DC)(1 + R_{n,FC}) = F[f_{x1}(FC/DC)] \cdot (1 + R_{n,DC})$$

or

$$\frac{F[fx_1(FC/DC)]}{fx_0(FC/DC)} - 1 \cong \frac{1 + R_{n,FC}}{1 + R_{n,DC}} - 1 \cong R_{n,FC} - R_{n,DC}$$

Thus, no-arbitrage equilibrium is called interest rate parity.

Interest rate parity establishes a link between the forward foreign exchange rates and nominal interest rates where arbitrage profit does not exist. Specifically, interest rate parity can be expressed as follows:

$$F_{fx} \equiv \frac{F[fx_1(FC/DC)]}{fx_0(FC/DC)} - 1 \cong R_{n,FC} - R_{n,DC} \qquad (11.9)$$

where F_{fx} denotes the percentage difference in the forward foreign exchange rate relative to the prevailing current spot exchange rate. Thus, the percentage difference of the forward foreign exchange rate and the current exchange rate should be approximately equal to the prevailing difference between the nominal interest rates in the foreign and domestic countries. For example, if the British pound exchange rate with the U.S. dollar is currently at £0.67/\$, and the 1-year forward rate is at £0.7/\$, then we would expect the interest rate differential between the United Kingdom and the United States to be

$$(\text{£}0.7/\$)/(\text{£}0.67/\$) - 1 \cong 0.0448, \text{ or } 4.48\%$$

Specifically, we would anticipate that the British pound would weaken compared with the U.S. dollar by about 4.48%, according to interest rate parity.

Exhibit 11-16 helps clarify the interrelationships among the parity relationships discussed here. The exhibit shows that spot exchange rates, forward exchange rates, interest rates, and inflation in different countries are interrelated. However, these interrelationships are theoretical.

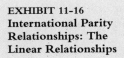

EXHIBIT 11-16
International Parity
Relationships: The
Linear Relationships

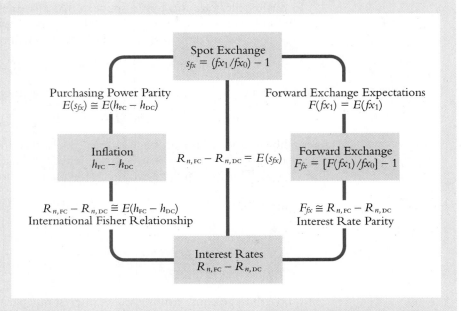

Note:

fx_1 is the foreign exchange rate in foreign currency per unit of domestic currency at the end of the period, fx_0 is the foreign exchange rate in foreign currency per unit of domestic currency at the beginning of the period, S_{fx} is the percentage change in the foreign exchange rate, h_{FC} is the inflation rate in the foreign country, h_{DC} is the inflation rate in the domestic country, $R_{n,FC}$ is the foreign yield on default-free bonds that mature in one period, $R_{n,DC}$ is the domestic yield on default-free bonds that mature in one period, $F(fx_1)$ is the forward foreign exchange rate, and F_{fx} is the percentage difference between the current foreign exchange rate and the forward foreign exchange rate.

Source: Based on Bruno Solnik, *International Investments*, 2d ed. (Reading, Mass.: Addison-Wesley Publishing, 1991), Exhibit 1.1, p. 9.

Exhibit 11-17 reveals the relevant comparisons for Japan and the U.S. Curve A denotes the inflation difference between Japan and the U.S.; $h_{Japan} - h_{U.S.}$, Curve B denotes the percentage change in foreign yen/dollar exchange rate, $f(x_1)/f(x_0) - 1$, and Curve C denotes the difference in the annual short-term interest $R_{n,Japan} - R_{n,U.S.}$. Of course, with ex-post data we employ the actual inflation rates and the actual foreign exchange rates rather than their corresponding expected values. However, on average, if the above theoretical relationships hold, we would expect all three graphs in Exhibit 11-7 to coincide or at least to be close to each other. This is not the case. For example, in the period 2/95–1/98, an American investor could borrow in Japan at a very low interest rate and deposit the money in the U.S. and make a profit, because the interest rate difference was much bigger than the percentage foreign exchange (compare graphs B and C). In the period January 1998– July 1998 the gain was enhanced because on top of the interest rates difference, the yen depreciated, providing a double source of profit for the American investor: interest rate differential as well as foreign currency profit. Thus, we see that the various relationships do not hold with actual ex-post data. They may hold with

EXHIBIT 11-17   The Inflation Difference, Interest Rate Difference, and Change in the Exchange Rate—Japan vs. U.S. 2.95–1.98

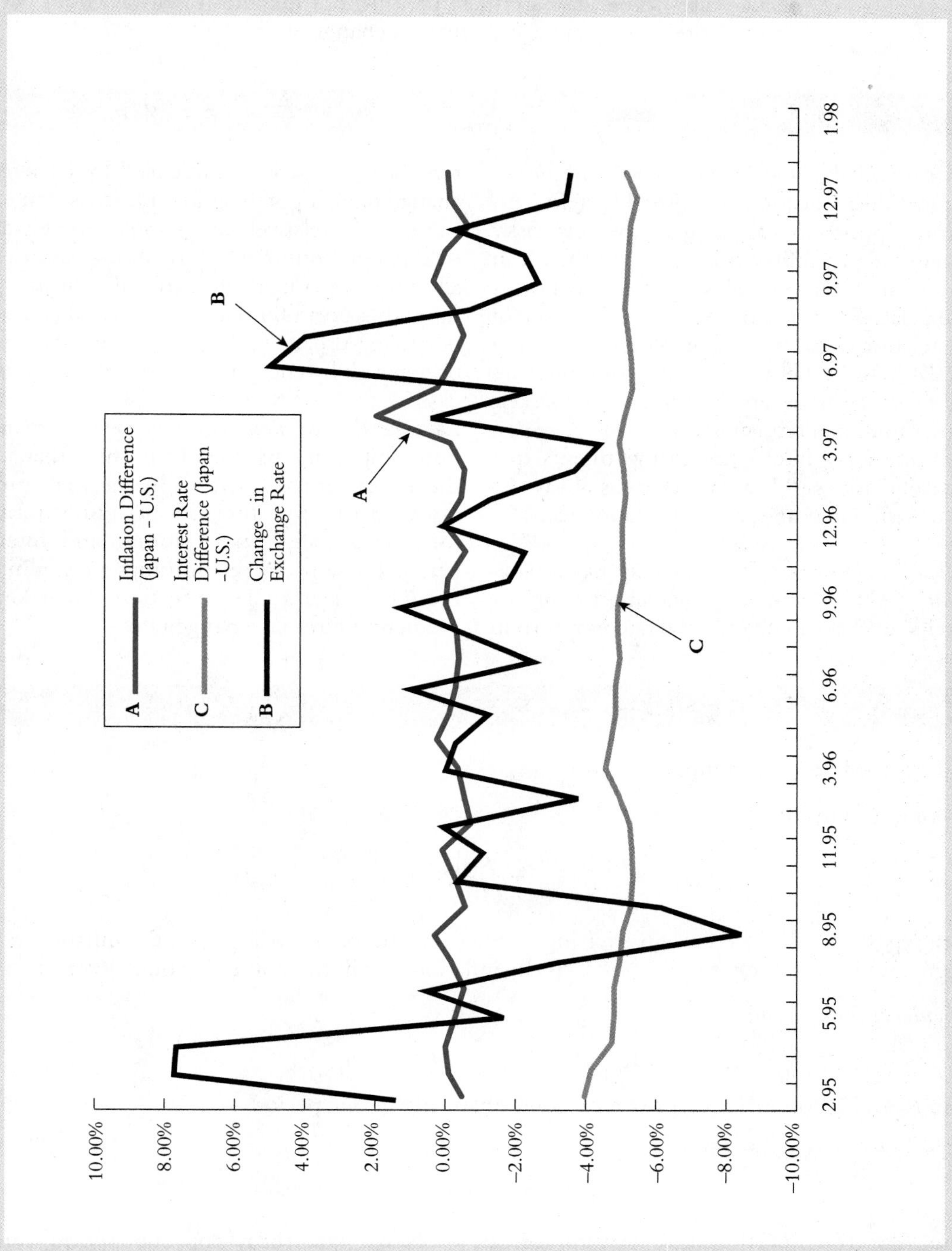

Source: International financial statistics.

expected unobserved value (see Exhibit 11-6) and they must hold with forward exchange rates (otherwise arbitrage prevails) but they do not always hold with actual ex-post foreign exchange and inflation changes.

SUMMARY

Identify the risks and returns in international investment. International diversification has several benefits. An international portfolio can actually be less risky than a domestic portfolio, with no loss in the mean rate of return. International securities are not as highly correlated as domestic securities. This lack of high correlation affords substantial diversification benefits. Moreover, because some economies are growing faster than others, international markets offer higher potential returns. At times investors can even find attractive international investments that are essentially riskless. However, there is always an element of risk when investing internationally.

Explain how an investor can benefit from international diversification. Although international investments involve foreign exchange risk (because rate of return in

foreign investment is influenced by changes in exchange rate), a potential for risk reduction exists because of the relatively low correlation between assets of different countries. Thus, an in- vestor can actually invest in riskier international securities and end up with a portfolio that is less risky than a domestic portfolio. Also, an investor can hedge the foreign exchange risk by engaging in forward transactions.

Describe the techniques used to predict exchange rates. Four important parity relationships that influence the international financial markets are purchasing power parity, the international Fisher relationship, foreign exchange expectations, and interest rate parity. These parity relationships are summarized in the Chapter at a Glance section. Their key goal is predicting future exchange rates.

CHAPTER AT A GLANCE

International Parity Relationships:

1. *Purchasing power parity:*

$$E(s_{fx}) \equiv \frac{E[fx_1(FC/DC)]}{fx_0(FC/DC)} - 1 \cong E(h_{FC} - h_{DC})$$

where $fx_1(FC/DC)$ is the foreign exchange rate at the end of the year, h_{FC} is the inflation rate in the foreign country for one period, and h_{DC} is the inflation rate in the domestic country for one period.

2. *International Fisher relationship:*

$$R_{n,FC} - R_{n,DC} \cong E(h_{FC} - h_{DC})$$

where R_n is the nominal interest rate of bonds maturing in one period.

3. *Foreign exchange expectations:*

$$E[fx_1(DC/FC)] = F[fx_1(DC/FC)]$$

where $F[fx_1(DC/FC)]$ is the forward foreign exchange rate today for one period, and $E[fx_1(DC/FC)]$ is the expected spot rate for foreign exchange in one period.

4. *Interest rate parity:*

$$F_{fx} \equiv \frac{F[fx_1(FC/DC)]}{fx_0(FC/DC)} - 1 \cong R_{n,FC} - R_{n,DC}$$

where $F[fx_1(DC/FC)]$ is the forward foreign exchange rate today for one period, $fx_0(FC/DC)$ is the foreign exchange rate today, and R_n is the nominal one-period interest rate (default-free).

KEY TERMS

Foreign exchange
   expectations   393
Forward foreign exchange
   contract   393

Forward foreign exchange
   rate   393
Interest rate parity   395
International Fisher
   relationship   392

Percent risk   378
Political risk   370
Purchasing power
   parity   389

REVIEW

11.1 "An investment in a security that is not in the investor's country will always have a higher standard deviation than the same investment made by a person in the country where the security is located." Evaluate this statement.

11.2 Suppose a U.S. investor places 80% in the U.S. market and 20% in the Japanese market. The investor also spends 80% of her money on U.S. products and 20% on imported goods from Japan. Which portfolio mean and variance is relevant for her—the one that is adjusted for the exchange rate changes or the one that is unadjusted? Why?

11.3 The nominal rates of return in local currency in the Canadian and U.S. markets are as follows:

Year	Canada	United States
1	10%	3%
2	8	7
3	−1	−2

Assume that international diversification is not allowed. Can we safely assert that the Canadian investors are better off?

PRACTICE

11.1 Suppose you are considering investing in bonds and have the following information:

	Mean	Standard Deviation	Correlation DBF	Correlation IBF
DBF	7.1%	8.3%	1	0.15
IBF	9.2%	10.4%	0.15	1

DBF denotes the Domestic Bond Fund, and IBF denotes the International Bond Fund. Assume that the risk-free rate is 4%. Graph the efficient frontiers in domestic currency for the following:

a. The Domestic Bond Fund with the risk-free rate.

b. The International Bond Fund with the risk-free rate.

c. The Domestic Bond Fund and the International Bond Fund with no risk-free rate.

d. All three—the Domestic Bond Fund, the International Bond Fund, and the risk-free rate. Assess the gain from diversification. What conclusions can you draw from these frontiers?

11.2 Suppose a U.S. investor earned 14.3% in the United Kingdom (before adjusting for exchange rate movements). If the U.S. investor earned 12.7% on this investment in U.S. dollars, what was the percentage change in the foreign exchange rate?

11.3 Suppose a U.S. investor earned 10.7% in the Swiss stock market when measured in Swiss francs. The exchange rate at the beginning of the investment was SwF 1.57/$. If the rate of return on this investment in U.S. dollars was −3.7%, what was the foreign exchange rate at the end of the investment period?

11.4 Suppose we observe that the expected inflation rate in France is 3% and the expected inflation rate in the United States is 9% over the next year. If the current foreign exchange rate is Fr 5.7/$, what is the expected foreign exchange rate next year?

11.5 Suppose that recently, the 1-year U.S. Treasury bill yield suddenly rose by ½% due to changes in monetary policy. If inflation expectations between the United States and Canada don't change, according to the international Fisher relationship, what will be the impact on the Canadian 1-year Treasury bill yield?

11.6 Based on the international parity relationships, what is the relationship between the inflation differential (the international Fisher relation) and the forward foreign exchange rate?

11.7 Suppose there is a total of only ten thousand financial securities in the world. Further assume that each security has a standard deviation of σ_0^2, and all securities are uncorrelated. What is the percentage reduction in variance from diversifying globally if only two thousand securities are located in the domestic country? Assume that the investments are equally weighted.

11.8 Suppose the rates of return in local currency on a portfolio of Japanese stocks and a portfolio of U.S. stocks are as follows:

Year	U.S. Portfolio (%)	Japanese Portfolio (%)	Exchange Rate ($/yen)
0			0.008503
1	10	0	0.008613
2	−5	20	0.008594
3	20	−1	0.008724

a. Calculate the annual rates of return to a U.S. investor who buys the Japanese portfolio.

b. Calculate the annual rates of return to a Japanese investor who buys the U.S. portfolio.

c. Calculate the variance and covariance in U.S. dollars and Japanese yen.

d. Suppose the Japanese investor diversifies by placing 50% of the investment in the U.S. portfolio and 50% of the investment in the Japanese portfolio. Also suppose the U.S. investor does the same. Calculate the mean and variance of these portfolios. Who gains more from this type of diversification? Analyze your results.

11.9 a. Referring to Question 11.8, assume that the exchange rate is fixed. The U.S. investor and the Japanese investor now have the same efficient frontier. Do you agree? Explain your answer.

b. Now suppose the risk-free rates in Japan and the United States are the same. Would the two investors have the same diversification policy? Explain.

11.10 Suppose you can borrow in U.S. dollars at 6% a year, and you can invest in the bank in Germany and earn 10% in German marks. Both positions are riskless. The current exchange rate is 1.62 marks per dollar. The 1-year forward rate is 1.61.

a. Are there arbitrage possibilities? If yes, show in detail what arbitrage you would conduct.

b. What should be the forward exchange rate such that there would be no arbitrage possibilities?

11.11 Suppose a U.S. investor can invest in U.S. Treasury bills and receive 4% a year and can also invest in German marks and get 8% a year. The current exchange rate is 1.62 marks per dollar. Suppose now the foreign exchange rate will be 1.58 one year from now with a probability of ½ and 1.80 with a probability of ½.

a. Calculate the mean and variance on the two alternative investments from a U.S. investor's viewpoint.

b. Calculate the mean and variance on the two alternative investments from a German investor's viewpoint.

c. What would be the exchange rate instead of 1.80 (but still with a probability of ½) such that the U.S. investor definitely would choose to invest in Germany?

11.12 Suppose Japan and the United States have the following estimated parameters of the stock market indices in local currency. The foreign exchange is fixed and the correlation is 1.0.

	Mean	Standard Deviation
Japan	15%	10%
United States	10	10

a. Who will gain from international diversification—the Japanese investor or the U.S. investor?

b. Who gains from international diversification if the correlation is −½?

c. Now suppose the foreign exchange rates are not fixed. Who will gain more?

11.13 Suppose there are three portfolios: Japan, United States, and United Kingdom. All have the same mean return (μ_0) and standard deviation (σ_0) in local currency. All correlation coefficients are zero.

a. What is the optimal diversification if the foreign exchange rate is fixed?

b. What is the optimal diversification, knowing that with foreign exchange fluctuations, we still have the same mean ($\mu_1 = \mu_0$) across all portfolios, but the standard deviations are doubled ($\sigma_1 = 2\sigma_0$)?

11.14 The following data regarding a U.S. portfolio and a German portfolio, stated in local currency, are estimated:

Probability	United States	Germany
½	10%	7%
½	20	12

As an American, you decide to own only one portfolio, either the U. S. or the German portfolio.

a. Which portfolio will you choose, knowing that the exchange rate is fixed at 1.62 marks per dollar?

b. Which portfolio will you choose when you are also allowed to borrow and lend at 4% in the United States?

c. How would your answer change if the exchange rate were 1.58 marks per dollar with a probability of ½ and 1.70 marks per dollar with a probability of ½? (Assume that the returns and exchange rates are uncorrelated.)

11.15 Suppose that a Japanese investor holds $1,000 in cash, and an American investor holds 120,000 yen in cash. The current exchange rate is 120 yen per dollar. At the end of the year, the yen is depreciated by 10%. Both investors convert their holdings to the local currencies. What is the rate of return to each investor? Is the average rate of return of the two investors zero? Explain.

11.16 An American investor considers diversifying internationally or investing locally. He considers buying a mutual fund (either local or international). He investigates two mutual funds with the following parameters (in U.S. dollars):

	U.S. Fund	International Fund
Expected rate of return	12%	10%
Standard deviation	18	8

a. Which fund should the investor select if he can borrow or lend at 6% in U.S. dollars (the riskless interest $r = 6\%$)? Use a graph to demonstrate your answer. (Hint: Use the capital market line (CML) formula, assuming that only one of these funds is held.)

b. How would you change your answer if the U.S. investor can borrow and lend at 8% in German marks?

11.17 a. The beta of IBM stocks is 1 when calculated with the U.S. market portfolio and 2 when calculated with the world market portfolio. The variance of IBM stocks is $\sigma_i^2 = 0.09$, and the nonsystemic risk is $\sigma_{ei}^2 = 0.01$. Calculate the variance of the U.S. and international market portfolios.

b. Suppose that the CAPM holds when the international market is the market portfolio. The market portfolio's mean rate of return in U.S. dollars is 0.15. The interest rate in U.S. dollars is $r = 6\%$. What is the expected rate of return on IBM stocks?

11.18 The following figure describes stock market indexes for the stock market in three Asian countries:

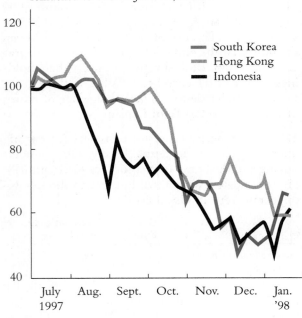

Key stock market indexes for selected Asian countries; reindexed to 100 on June 30, 1997

Source: *Wall Street Journal*, January 23, 1998, p. C14. Reprinted by permission of *The Wall Street Journal* © 1998 Dow Jones & Co., Inc. All Rights Reserved Worldwide.

Suppose this particular shape of downturn (and future uptrends) will continue in the future (that is, these markets move up and down simultaneously).

a. You are considering international diversification focusing in Asia. Do you have large risk reduction from diversification in such countries? Would you suggest adding one of these countries or all of them to your portfolio? Explain.

b. During the last month ending on January 23, 1998, the monthly rates of return in various regions in U.S. dollars were as follows:

Region	Rate of Return
Americas	22.72%
Latin America	5.5
Europe	21.54
Asia	−23.33

Source: *Wall Street Journal*, January 23, 1998, p. C14.

Suppose you wish to diversify your investment in four stocks. Given the information in the figure and assuming that you have no ability to predict which stock market will be up and which will be down next year, will you select four stocks from the Asia Pacific region? How would you change your answer if the rate of return last month in this region were +50%?

c. Suppose that you estimate the mean rate of return and the standard deviation in U.S. dollars on each stock to be $\mu = 10\%$, $\sigma = 30\%$, regardless of the region it is traded. The correlation of stocks within each region is $\rho = +0.8$, but the correlation between each two stocks taken from different regions is $\rho = +0.2$. Calculate the mean and portfolio variance on the following alternate conditions (assume the investment is equally divided among the four stocks):

1. All four stocks are taken from one region.
2. Three stocks are taken from one region, and one stock is taken from another region.
3. Two stocks are taken from one region, and two stocks are taken from another region.
4. Each of the four stocks is taken from a different region.

Show your portfolios graphically in the mean–standard deviation space.

11.19 The following excerpt discusses the three-month return ending September 30, 1997, when the South Asia stock markets crashed:

In the wake of devastating currency declines, the Southeast Asian stock markets are shuddering. Since early 1997, equity prices in Indonesia, Malaysia, the Philippines, Singapore, and Thailand have plunged as much as 55%. Now adventurous investors stand uncomfortably at the intersection of fear and greed: Optimists say these markets are cheap; pessimists counter that they deserve to be. So who's right? We asked experts on both sides. . . .[8]

See exhibit at the bottom of the page.

a. The total return in Indonesia was −42% in U.S. dollars, and the currency depreciates against the U.S. dollar by 24%. Calculate the rate of return to the U.S. investor and to the Indonesian investor who invest in Indonesia for this three-month period.

b. Repeat the same calculation for Thailand, with −32% depreciation and a −22% rate of return in U.S. dollars.

c. Explain what the relationship between currency depreciation, firms' bankruptcies, and the stock market is in these countries. (Hint: Firms in South Asia borrowed heavily in the international market.)

11.20 The rates of return in *local* currencies on an American stock and a German stock were as follows:

Year	American Stock	German Stock
1	20%	10%
2	10	5
3	30	15

Suppose that during Years 1 and 2, the foreign exchange rate was $1 = 2 marks; only in the middle of the third year has the rate changed to $1 = 1.5

Markets are down . . .

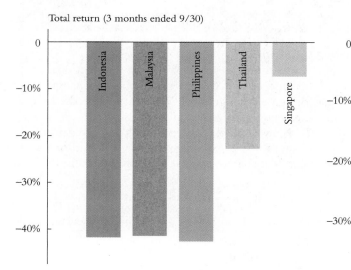

Total return (3 months ended 9/30)

and so are currencies

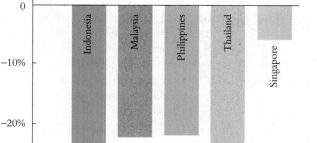

Change vs. the U.S. dollar (3 months ended 9/30)

Source: S. Velasco for *Fortune,* Morgan Stanley Capital International, and Bloomberg, as cited in Bethany McLean, "What's Next for Southeast Asia?" *Fortune,* November 10, 1997, p. 304. Reprinted from the November 10, 1997, issue of *Fortune* by special permission. © 1997, Time, Inc.

8. Bethany McLean, "What's Next for Southeast Asia?" *Fortune,* November 10, 1997, p. 304. Reprinted from the November 10, 1997, issue of *Fortune* by special permission. © 1997, Time, Inc.

marks; and this exchange rate remains up to the end of the third year.

a. Calculate the correlation between the two stocks in local currencies.

b. Calculate the correlation between the two stocks when the rates of return are calculated in U.S. dollars.

c. Calculate the correlation between the two stocks when the rates of return are calculated in German marks.

d. In your view, would the American and German investors hold the same diversified portfolio of these two stocks? Explain.

11.21 Suppose that an American investor is considering investing $10,000 in Japan in the Nikkei index for 1 year. The current exchange rate is 122 yen to a dollar. There is an equal chance that the Nikkei index will go up at the end of the year by 20% or go down by 10%. There is a probability of ⅓ that

the yen will be traded 1 year from now for each of the following exchange rates: 122 yen, 100 yen, or 140 yen. The probabilities of changes in the Nikkei index and in the exchange rate are independent.

a. Calculate the mean and standard deviation of the investor's portfolio in yen.

b. Calculate the mean and standard deviation of the investor's portfolio in dollars.

c. Suppose that the Nikkei index went down by 10%, and the exchange rate at the end of the year is 100 yen per dollar. Show the investor's cash flows on the $10,000 investment in the Nikkei index in dollars and in yen at the beginning and end of the year. Explain your results.

For Internet questions visit the Levy Investment Web site at http//levy-invst.swcollege.com.

YOUR TURN: APPLYING THEORY TO PRACTICE
INTERNATIONAL DIVERSIFICATION IN THE BOND MARKET

This case is based on the data given in the table in Chapter 8's Applying Theory to Practice. In this case, look only at the bond holdings in the various currencies. Suppose these portfolios are composed of government bonds with a 1-year maturity. The yield on the government bonds in local currency is as follows:

Dollar	5.67%
Yen	3.39
Sterling	6.39
DM	5.50
FFr	5/57
Others	5.40

Source: *The Economist*, January 15, 1994.

Because these bonds mature in 1 year, there is a zero variance for a 1-year holding period when returns are measured in the local currency.

Questions

1. Assume that you know with certainty that at the end of the year there will be no change in foreign exchange rates. What would be the best international investment diversification?

2. Now assume the following data regarding changes in the exchange rates by the end of the year. (All changes are in terms of U.S. dollars.)

	Expected Exchange Rate Relative to the U.S. Dollar	Standard Deviation of the Exchange Rate Relative to the U.S. Dollar
Yen	5%	8%
Sterling	−3	5
DM	2	4
FFr	1	2
Others	3	4

(continued)

Here 5%, for example, implies that the Japanese yen is worth 5% more in dollar terms at the end of the year relative to the beginning of the year. Assume also that all correlations between the foreign exchange rates are zero except for the correlation between the deutsche mark and the French franc, which is $\rho = 0.8$.

Calculate the mean and standard deviation of the rates of return (in dollars) of each of the investment strategies given in the table in Chapter 8's Applying Theory to Practice. Are there any international diversification policies that are observably inferior?

SELECTED REFERENCES

Eiteman, David K., Arthur I. Stonehill, and Michael H. Moffett. *Multinational Business Finance*. 6th ed. Reading, Mass.: Addison-Wesley Publishing, 1992.

This is an excellent introduction to the details involved in international corporate finance in general.

Investing Worldwide. Charlottesville, Va.: Association for Investment Management, various years.

This series of publications focuses on the various aspects of global investing.

Solnik, Bruno. *International Investments*. 2d ed. Reading Mass.: Addison-Wesley Publishing, 1991.

This book provides a thorough review of the issues surrounding international investments.

SUPPLEMENTAL REFERENCES

Black, Fischer, and Robert Litterman. "Global Portfolio Optimization." *Financial Analysts Journal* 48(September–October 1992), pp. 28–43.

Eichholtz, Piet, M.A. "Does International Diversification Work Better for Real Estate Than for Stocks and Bonds?" *Financial Analysts Journal,* January–February 1996, pp. 56–62.

Fisher, Irving. *The Theory of Interest*. New York: Macmillan, 1930.

International Monetary Fund. *International Financial Statistics Yearbook.* Various editions.

Levy, Haim, and Zvi Lerman. "The Benefits of International Diversification in Bonds." *Financial Analysts Journal,* September–October 1988, pp. 56–64.

Levy, Haim, and Marshall Sarnat. "International Diversification of Investment Portfolios." *American Economic Review,* September 1970, pp. 668–675.

Lofthouse, Stephen. "International Diversification." *Journal of Portfolio Management,* Fall 1997, pp. 53–56.

Peavy, John W. III. *Managing Emerging Market Portfolios*. Charlottesville, Va.: Association of Investment Management and Research, 1994.

Solnik, Bruno. *International Investment*. 3rd ed. Reading, Mass.: Addison-Wesley Publishing Company, 1996.

———. "Why Not Diversify Internationally Rather Than Domestically?" *Financial Analysts Journal,* July–August 1974.

Speidell, Lawrence S., and Vinod B. Bavishi. "GAAP Arbitrage: Valuation Opportunities in International Accounting Standards." *Financial Analysts Journal,* November–December 1992, pp. 58–66.

Speidell, Lawrence S., and Ross Sappenfield. "Global Diversification in a Shrinking World." *Journal of Portfolio Management* 19(Fall 1992), pp. 57–67.

CHAPTER 12

EFFICIENT MARKETS: THEORY AND EVIDENCE

LEARNING OBJECTIVES

After studying this chapter you should be able to:

1. Define an efficient market.

2. Identify the types of information related to each form of the efficient market hypothesis.

3. Compare investment strategies in efficient markets with investment strategies in inefficient markets.

4. Describe the findings of researchers who tested each form of the efficient market theory.

5. Define *anomaly,* and identify the common types of anomalies.

LUCK OR LOGIC? DEBATE RAGES ON OVER "EFFICIENT-MARKET" THEORY

For just over five years now, the Investment Dartboard column has pitted investment pros against the forces of chance, in the form of darts heaved at the stock listings. One aim has been to provide a lighthearted test of the "efficient-market theory." . . .

On the surface, the results clearly favor the professionals and go against the theory. Since the contest adopted its current rules in 1990, the pros have won 24 times, the darts 17 times. The average six-month gain for the pros, 8.4%, has been much better than the 3.3% gain achieved by the darts. (Those figures are price changes only, without dividends.)

But Burton Malkiel, an economics professor at Princeton University and a leading exponent of the efficient-market theory, says there's less than meets the eye in the pros' apparent success in the contest.

According to Prof. Malkiel, the pros' favorable showing can be explained by two factors. First, they are picking riskier, more volatile, stocks than the darts are. Second, they benefit from a favorable publicity effect on the day the article is published.

With Prof. Malkiel, Gilbert E. Metcalf, an assistant professor of economics at Princeton, recently wrote a paper analyzing the Dartboard contests from 1990 through 1992. The professors found that the pros' picks were about 40% more volatile—and therefore riskier—than the overall market. The dart stocks were only about 6% more volatile than the market.

In other words, the pros' selections tend to move up or down 14% for every 10% the overall market moves. Once you adjust for risk, the researchers say, the pros' margin shrinks to 0.4%, which is not statistically significant.

But that's not all. The researchers say the pros are riding the coattails of a strong "announcement effect" that causes the pros' picks to surge on the day they appear in this newspaper. Take away the announcement effect, they say, and the pros' superiority vanishes altogether. . . .

So, the great debate remains unsettled. Which, of course, allows the fun to continue.

Source: John R. Dorfman, "Luck or Logic? Debate Rages On over 'Efficient-Market' Theory," *Wall Street Journal,* © November 4, 1993, p. C1. Reprinted by permission of *The Wall Street Journal,* © 1993 Dow Jones & Co., Inc. All Rights Reserved Worldwide.

This chapter's Investments in the News shows that the same evidence can be interpreted in different ways. On the one hand, practitioners argue that the score is 24 to 17 (number of wins) or 8.4% to 3.3% (percentage gain achieved), both in favor of the practitioners. The practitioners argue that this is a clear victory. The academics, on the other hand, argue that by increasing the risk level, practitioners have positioned themselves to win more frequently. Hence, some academics perceive the evidence presented thus far as inconclusive.

Many successful managers do not believe in efficient market theory. The best summary of their strong view appeared in *Fortune:* "What do Sequoia Funds' William Ruane, Berkshire Hathaway's Charles Munger and Warren Buffett, and money manager Walter Schloss have in common? They don't believe in efficient markets. Says Buffett: 'I'd be a bum on the street with a tin cup if the market were efficient.' "[1]

This chapter considers ways investors can use information on stock prices to earn better returns. It looks at the information that investment professionals use to make their selections. The focus is on the way the markets process information and how that information influences security prices. Although this chapter focuses primarily on the stock market, the analysis is easily applied to the bond market and other markets.

In studying the impact of information on stock prices, we work with the *efficient market theory* (**EMT**).[2] Basically, the theory predicts that stock prices reflect all information that is relevant for the stock and that no investor can profit by earning an abnormal return (or an excess return after adjusting for risk) by trying to find buying or selling opportunities in the market. For example, if an investor could analyze the historical prices of IBM stock and develop a buy-sell rule that will yield a positive, risk-adjusted return, this would contradict the EMT. This chapter explores the various ways to interpret the EMT.

In general, academics support the EMT, whereas practitioners do not. Recently, however, some academics who preached for decades in support of the EMT have found empirical evidence favoring market inefficiency.[3] Because practitioners on Wall Street use investment strategies that rely on market *inefficiency,* Chapter 13 and Part 4 describe some widely used valuation methods that assume market inefficiency, at least to a certain degree.

Your own perception of the EMT will govern, in large part, the particular investment philosophy you adopt. The objective of this book is not to persuade you to adopt one school of thought over another but rather to give you the analytical tools needed to reach your own conclusions. This chapter examines the investment implications and appropriate strategies to use if markets are efficient or, alternatively, inefficient. It also surveys the available empirical evidence regarding market efficiency.

---

1. *Fortune,* April 3, 1995, p. 69, "Yes, You Can Beat the Market," by Terence P. Paré.
2. The EMT is also widely referred to as the *efficient market hypothesis* (EMH).
3. See Eugene F. Fama and Kenneth R. French, "The Cross-Section of Expected Stock Returns," *Journal of Finance* 47(June 1992): 427–466.

12.1 EFFICIENT MARKET DEFINED

How efficiently do markets process information? An investigation of the effect of information on security prices must begin with a definition of an efficient market. A well-functioning financial market in which prices reflect all relevant information is said to be an **efficient market.** Another way to state this is that the EMT claims that security prices reflect all relevant information; that is, the current market price of a security incorporates *all* relevant information. If a financial market is efficient, then the best estimate of the true worth of a security is given by its current market price.

In an efficient market, it is assumed that a large number of analysts are assessing the true value of firms. The analysts try to find stocks whose market prices are substantially different from their true values. If the analysts find such "mispriced" securities, they buy or sell them, driving the market price instantaneously toward the true value of the security. Thus, competition in the stock market pushes prices to their "true" value. Thus, stock prices change every day, every hour, even every second as new information flows into the marketplace.

To demonstrate how information influences stock prices, consider Tropicana, a corporation that produces citrus products in Florida. If analysts who study weather patterns anticipate a hard freeze that would be devastating to citrus crops, they will try to make large profits by selling short Tropicana stock. This selling pressure drives the stock price down toward its "true" value. Thus, the information changes the stock price. If doctors at a prominent research hospital release a study that shows that people who drink three glasses of orange juice a day reduce their risk of cancer, the price of orange juice stocks should rise because the demand for orange juice will increase. Thus, the results of trading by the weather predictors, which would force the stock price down, would be reversed by the actions of investors who think the demand for orange juice (and the profits of juice manufacturers) will rise. This constant assimilation of information causes the prices of securities to change as investors react to all relevant information.

Is the market efficient? Actually, it is almost impossible to purely test whether the market is efficient, which explains why there are no clear winners in the market efficiency dispute. Most of the tests of market efficiency are joint tests—that is, one is testing whether the model measuring returns is appropriate and the other whether markets are efficient. If the market is efficient, there are no "bargains" in the market, because all assets are correctly priced. In such a case, most of the work done by analysts who try to find bargains in the market is worthless. Thus, one of the reasons for the market efficiency dispute is that tests of market efficiency are *joint tests* of the assumed model *and* the market efficiency.

To illustrate, suppose that an analyst claims he observes the historical price movement of IBM stock, and based on these historical figures, he reaches the conclusion that IBM stock is a bargain (that is, it is underpriced). Suppose he buys IBM stock, and his annual realized rate of return on the stock is 12%. Can we then conclude that the market is inefficient? Did the analyst succeed in exploiting the information on historical prices to make an extraordinary return? To reach such a conclusion, we first need to find out the risk involved with the investment in IBM stock and figure out whether there is an abnormal return adjusted for this risk. For example, suppose that we use the CAPM and IBM's beta to estimate the expected rate of return on IBM to be 11%. In such a case, the analyst has an *extraordinary profit* of 1%. This extraordinary profit is also called an *abnormal return*. It seems that based on this result, we might claim that the market is inefficient. However, what if the CAPM is an incorrect model, and therefore the 11% estimate of the required expected return was wrong? Then we may come to the wrong conclusion regarding market efficiency, because we employed an incorrect model to measure the "normal" rate of return.

Thus, in testing for market efficiency, first we should estimate what should be the normal rate of return on an asset, which is also called the risk-adjusted rate of return. For that purpose, we need a model asserting what the risk is and what the corresponding risk premium should be. Then we compare the realized return by the analyst's investment policy to this normal return. If the realized return is significantly higher than the normal return, researchers generally assert that the market is inefficient, because the analyst made abnormal or *excess returns*.

However, by this procedure, we see that we have a *joint hypothesis* and therefore should conduct a joint test of the model and of market efficiency. To illustrate, suppose that the CAPM is wrong, and the variance of the rate of return, rather than beta, is the correct measure of risk. We may conclude that with this risk measure, the required rate of return is 12% in the IBM example. Now the analyst does not make any profit after adjusting for risk. Thus, testing market efficiency is based on a normal return as a benchmark. Because this normal return is deduced from some model, empirical tests are joint tests of the model and of market efficiency. Therefore, we cannot claim unequivocally that the market is efficient, even if empirical tests seem to reveal market efficiency (that is, that there are no abnormal returns).

12.2 WHAT CONSTITUTES THE APPROPRIATE INFORMATION SET?

A great deal of information is available in the stock market: historical stock prices, earnings and dividends, macroeconomic data, private information known only to insiders, and other information that seems irrelevant for stock valuation (for example, the age and eye color of a firm's chief executive officer). Exhibit 12-1 illustrates this idea. At one extreme, it might be argued that all information is useful in earning an abnormal return. An investor can use all available information and make an extraordinary profit. In other words, it pays to analyze available information in making a security selection.

At the other extreme, it might be argued that prices reflect *all* information that exists. That is, everything that can be known about a security is already incorporated in its price. For example, even the poor health of an important member of upper management would be reflected in the stock price. From this point of view, any data collection or economic analysis is a waste of time.

Clearly, these two extremes are irrational and probably irrelevant in price determination. However, somewhere between these two extremes lies a reasonable set of

**EXHIBIT 12-1
Continuum of
Appropriate
Information Sets**

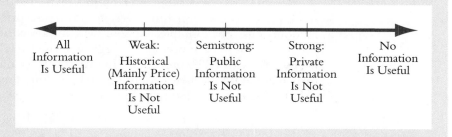

the information employed in determining stock prices. Along the journey across the continuum from "no information" to "all information" lie three milestones or information sets: historical, public, and private information. The efficient market theory, which describes the impact of information on the market prices of securities, can be analyzed in terms of these specific information sets and their impact on price determination. Thus, there are three forms of the efficient market theory: the weak, semistrong, and strong EMT.

12.2.1 Weak Form of the EMT

The first form of the efficient market theory is the **weak form of the EMT.**[4] According to the weak form of the EMT, today's stock prices reflect all information about the historical prices of the stock, so historical prices are not useful for investment decisions. However, other information—for example, historical earnings—may be useful in earning an abnormal profit. If this is true, then an investor could not use historical stock price information to find mispriced stocks and thus profit from buying or selling these stocks. The stock prices already would have adjusted for this information. Technical analysts try to use historical price information to locate mispriced stocks. Therefore, under the weak form of the EMT, we would not expect them to find opportunities that generate abnormal returns using these techniques. Investors would just earn the normal profit for the risk taken.

If the weak form of the EMT holds, and thus prices are independent of the pattern of historical stock prices, we say that price changes will appear to follow a random walk when examining just the historical series.[5] A **random walk** is a statistical concept that predicts that the next outcome in a series does not depend on its prior outcomes. A simple example that illustrates the random walk notion is the flipping of a coin. Although the first three tosses may be heads, heads, tails, these outcomes do not affect the probability of head or tail in the next toss. The result in the next toss has no memory; it does not depend on previous results.

4. See Roberts (1967), as quoted in Burton Malkiel, "Efficient Market Hypothesis," in John Eatwell, Murray Milgate, and Peter Newman (eds.), *The New Palgrave: Finance* (New York: Macmillan Press, 1989). In 1991 Fama suggested broadening this category to include other variables used in determining return predictability.

5. Technically, stocks, on average, will move up by the stock's expected return. Hence, the random walk concept is applied after adjusting for the expected return.

Because risky securities offer positive expected returns, we would anticipate stock prices to rise over time. Despite this trend, price changes may still follow a random walk. For example, suppose we have a security presently trading at $100. We know that in each period, the price will rise by 12% with a 75% probability, or fall by 10% with a 25% probability. In this case, three out of four times (75%) the return will be 12%, whereas only one out of four times (25%) the return will be −10%. The expected return in this case is

$$E(R) = 0.75(12\%) + 0.25(-10\%) = 6.5\%$$

Although the expected return is 6.5%, the particular outcome observed in a given year is random. Hence, even in this case, we say that the security follows a random walk.

Going back to the coin-tossing example, suppose you flip a biased coin with a probability of heads of ¾ and a probability of tails of ¼.[6] Do the results of the first three tosses affect the result of the next toss? Absolutely not. This process has no memory, and the probabilities are still ¾ for heads and ¼ for tails.

Exhibit 12-2 presents monthly rates of returns over a recent period for three stocks: Commonwealth Edison, General Electric (GE), and Dow Chemical. Can you spot any trends? It seems that monthly stock returns appear to follow a random walk.[7] Notice that although the next outcome for all three companies is unpredictable, it is apparent that Commonwealth Edison is less volatile than GE, and GE is less volatile than Dow Chemical. Hence, random walks can occur with varying magnitudes of volatility. Also note that these firms have more points above the zero horizontal line than below it, which reflects that on average, investors get a positive profit on such risky investments. There is one school of thought that the financial markets are not weak-form efficient (thus, they believe that they can learn from the historical data and improve their investment decisions). Trading strategies based on historical market data (mainly stock prices) are known as **technical analysis.**

12.2.2 Semistrong Form of the EMT

The second form of the efficient market theory is the **semistrong form of the EMT.** According to the semistrong form of the EMT, prices reflect all relevant publicly available information. In addition to historical stock prices, publicly available information includes financial statements, notes to the financial statements, and supplementary information required by accounting regulations. Publicly available information also includes other external financial and regulatory filings such as property taxes paid, as well as market-related data such as the level of interest rates and the stock's beta.

According to the semistrong form of the EMT, an investor could not earn abnormal returns on trading strategies built on publicly available information. Thus, if the market is semistrong efficient, a diligent study of financial statements is of no

---

6. A biased coin is typically heavier on one side. Hence, tossing it results in outcomes different from 50-50.

7. Of course, some quantitative methods are needed to measure the random walk, such as serial correlation, runs tests, and so forth. These quantitative methods are beyond the scope of this book.

EXHIBIT 12-2
Monthly Stock Returns
for Three Stocks

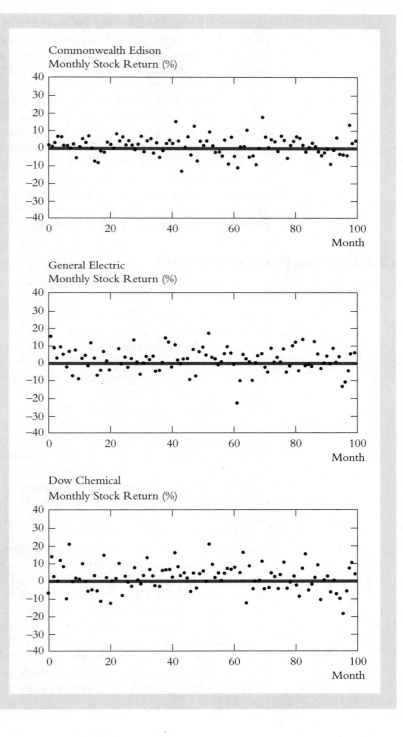

economic value. The idea behind this view is that once this information becomes public, all investors react instantaneously and push the price to reflect all public information. Thus, when you read the *Wall Street Journal* with your morning coffee and see some public information, such as a new drug discovery or a financial crisis in Asia, it is too late for you to earn an abnormal profit. The price at which you can buy or sell the stock already reflects this information.

In contrast to proponents of the semistrong form of the EMT, there are investors who think they can profit from a careful study of publicly available data—particularly accounting data. These investors practice **fundamental analysis** and use the information in financial statements and other public sources to identify mispriced stock. The two factors commonly employed to identify underpriced stock in a fundamental analysis are the price/earning (P/E) ratio and the market-to-book-value (M/B) ratio, where M is the market value (stock price) and B is the book value per share. These techniques will be discussed in Part 4.

12.2.3 Strong Form of the EMT

The third form of the efficient market theory is the **strong form of the EMT.** The strong form states that current prices already reflect all publicly and privately available information. Thus, the strong form includes all relevant historical price information and all relevant publicly available information, as well as information known only to a select few such as management, the board of directors, and private bankers. For example, suppose a member of the board of directors of Intel knows that the firm has decided to take over another firm. The board member's spouse then buys shares of Intel stock before the takeover becomes public information. This would be considered trading on inside information, and it is illegal.

If the strong EMT form were true, then insiders would not profit from trading on their information. As Connecting Theory to Practice 12.1 illustrates, however, the market is clearly not strong-form efficient, because there is money to be gained from trading on inside information (although such trading is illegal). Insiders who know about future takeovers or acquisitions can earn large profits, contradicting the strong-form market efficiency theory. However, it is illegal to trade on private information, and many inside traders have received prison sentences for doing so.

Exhibit 12-3 summarizes the discussion thus far from the viewpoint of an analyst. If an analyst believed that the weak form of the EMT was not true, then she should be able to earn abnormal returns based on historical price data, as well as public and private data. If an analyst believed that the weak form, but not the semistrong form, of the EMT was true, then he should be able to earn excess returns based on public and private data but not based on historical prices. If an analyst believed that the semistrong form, but not the strong form, of the EMT was true, then she should be able to earn excess returns only based on private information (which is illegal to trade upon). Finally, if an analyst believed that the strong form of the EMT was true, then no excess returns would be possible, no matter what information he could access. Clearly, investment strategy is directly linked to the analyst's view of the EMT.

EXHIBIT 12-3   Data Sources for Analysis According to an Analyst's View of the EMT

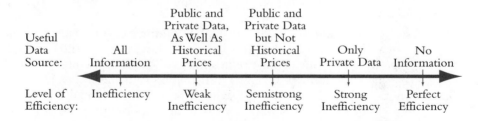

	All Information	Public and Private Data, As Well As Historical Prices	Public and Private Data but Not Historical Prices	Only Private Data	No Information
Useful Data Source:					
Level of Efficiency:	Inefficiency	Weak Inefficiency	Semistrong Inefficiency	Strong Inefficiency	Perfect Efficiency

CONNECTING THEORY TO PRACTICE 12.1

COURT ALLOWS BROADER MEANING OF INSIDER TRADING

WASHINGTON—People can be prosecuted for using inside information to buy or sell a company's stock even if they don't work for the company or owe it any legal duty, the Supreme Court ruled Wednesday.

The divided ruling upheld a legal tool for prosecuting cases where someone who is not a company insider uses confidential information—often another firm's secret takeover plans—to reap profits by buying the company's stock.

The justices reinstated the insider-trading convictions of former Minneapolis lawyer James O'Hagan. O'Hagan was convicted in 1994 of illegally earning more than $4.3 million by trading in Pillsbury stock after learning that a client of his law firm would attempt a takeover of Pillsbury.

Wednesday's decision reversed a lower court ruling that the Clinton administration said "opened a large loophole" in the ban on insider trading.

Insider trading ordinarily applies to transactions by people who have confidential information because they work for the company whose stock they are trading. Also, people who are tipped off by an insider can be prosecuted for insider trading.

But during the 1980s the Securities and Exchange Commission broadened its definition of insider trading to bar trading in a company's stock by someone who has confidential information but does not work for the company or owe it any legal duty.

O'Hagan's lawyer argued to the Supreme Court that because his client did not work for Pillsbury, he owed no legal duty to the company or its stockholders and therefore could not be prosecuted for insider trading.

(continued)

"It makes scant sense to hold a lawyer like O'Hagan a . . . violator if he works for a law firm representing the target of a tender offer, but not if he works for a law firm representing the bidder," Justice Ruth Bader Ginsburg wrote for the court.

"It is a fair assumption that trading on the basis of material, nonpublic information will often involve a breach of duty of confidentiality to the bidder or target company or their representatives," Ginsburg wrote.

Her opinion was joined by Justices John Paul Stevens, Sandra Day O'Connor, Anthony M. Kennedy, David H. Souter and Stephen G. Breyer.

Justice Antonio Scalia agreed with the majority that one of the two prosecution theories at issue in today's case should be upheld. But he contended the other, involving "misappropriation" of inside information, should not be applied to O'Hagan.

Chief Justice William H. Rehnquist and Justice Clarence Thomas dissented.

O'Hagan's law firm had been hired by a British company, Grand Metropolitan PLC, which was planning the takeover bid.

O'Hagan was convicted of 57 counts including securities fraud, mail fraud and fraudulent trading in connection with a takeover offer. He was sentenced to 18 months in prison.

The 8th U.S. Circuit Court of Appeals reversed the convictions. It said federal law does not allow a securities fraud conviction such as O'Hagan's to be based on "misappropriation" of inside information because it did not require deception or a breach of duty to the targeted company's shareholders.

The appeals court also threw out a separate SEC rule used to prosecute people for insider trading related to takeover offers. The court said a federal securities law does not let the SEC outlaw such transactions by people who do not owe a duty of trust to the targeted company.

The appeals court also reversed O'Hagan's mail fraud convictions, saying they were based on the securities fraud counts.

The case is U.S. vs. O'Hagan, 96-842.

MAKING THE CONNECTION

In 1996, the United States Supreme Court tightened the definition of insider trading. Next time you are on the golf course or tennis court and one of the players reveals that her company is in the process of negotiating a merger with another company, think twice before you act on this "tip." As the article states, "people who are tipped off by an insider can be prosecuted for insider trading."

12.3 INVESTMENT STRATEGY IN AN EFFICIENT MARKET

It seems reasonable that markets do process historical and public data with relative efficiency, and this is the view of many academic investment theorists. Thus, this section examines how to structure a successful investment strategy in the semistrong form of the EMT. It first examines how resources are allocated in this market. Next, it examines portfolio selection and the usefulness of employing the expected return-risk trade-off when markets are efficient. It also distinguishes between passive and active portfolio management strategies.

12.3.1 Resource Allocation and the EMT

If relatively more money is allocated to firms that have good capital budgeting projects and relatively less money is allocated to firms with poor projects, we say that money is allocated in the market in an effective manner. In efficient markets, resources are allocated to the various firms in an effective manner, because those firms with good prospects will be able to raise additional capital in the primary market on relatively good terms. That is, in constructing their portfolios, investors will allocate more money to those firms they deem a relatively good investment. For example, suppose IBM has a good new computer or Pfizer develops a new drug (like Viagra). When this information becomes public, investors will allocate more of their money to IBM, and its stock price will instantaneously go up.

Thus, a firm with good prospects will have a higher stock price and can issue stocks on better terms in the market. In contrast, a firm with poor prospects (one that is expected to go bankrupt) would be unable to raise money through either a stock issue or a bond issue. Thus, the information on the firm's prospects is reflected in the stock prices; the rosier the estimated future is, the higher the stock price.

This observation regarding the link between resource allocation and the EMT illustrates a seeming paradox. In order for markets to be efficient, new firm information should affect the stock price. Hence, some investors have to be paying attention to firm information. However, the EMT suggests there is no benefit to monitoring firm information. In practice, those with the least costly access to information capitalize on minor mispricing, which drives prices to reflect swiftly all relevant information. Hence, the practical application of the EMT focuses on trading costs and speed. This helps explain why some trading firms are willing to invest heavily in supercomputers and high-speed information highways. For most investors, however, the new information is worthless, because the price is instantaneously adjusted to reflect it.

12.3.2 Portfolio Selection and the EMT

Is there a contradiction between the EMT and portfolio selection? If financial markets are efficient under the semistrong form of the EMT, is there any need to burden ourselves with portfolio diversification? Under the semistrong form of the

EMT, the analysis conducted by technicians (who do technical analysis) and fundamentalists (who do fundamental analysis) will not generate excess returns. There are no "bargains" in the market, and stock selection techniques are worthless. What is left for portfolio managers is portfolio diversification, which pays off even in efficient markets.

To demonstrate this idea, suppose that two stocks, 1 and 2, each trade for $10. You flip two coins, one corresponding to each stock. If a head comes up, the stock price increases to $13; if a tail appears, the stock price falls to $9. Of course, these stock price changes conform to semistrong-form market efficiency, because the price changes are dependent on a random coin toss and do not depend on historical or public information. If you do not diversify between the two stocks, for your $10 investment, the future mean and variance of each stock is as follows:

$$\text{Mean: } (\tfrac{1}{2} \cdot \$13) + (\tfrac{1}{2} \cdot \$9) = \$11$$

$$\text{Variance: } \tfrac{1}{2}(13 - 11)^2 + \tfrac{1}{2}(9 - 11)^2 = 4, \text{ and } \delta = \$2.$$

Can you gain from diversification in such a market that obeys the EMT? The answer is yes. To see why, assume you invest $5 in Stock 1 and $5 in Stock 2. Because the two stocks are independent (you toss two coins, separately, one for each stock), you get the following returns:

Stock 1	Stock 2	Portfolio
$\tfrac{1}{2} \cdot \$13 +$	$\tfrac{1}{2} \cdot \$13 =$	$13 (with a probability of $\tfrac{1}{4}$)
$\tfrac{1}{2} \cdot \$13 +$	$\tfrac{1}{2} \cdot \$ 9 =$	$11 (with a probability of $\tfrac{1}{4}$)
$\tfrac{1}{2} \cdot \$ 9 +$	$\tfrac{1}{2} \cdot \$13 =$	$11 (with a probability of $\tfrac{1}{4}$)
$\tfrac{1}{2} \cdot \$ 9 +$	$\tfrac{1}{2} \cdot \$ 9 =$	$ 9 (with a probability of $\tfrac{1}{4}$)

where $\tfrac{1}{2}$ represents the proportion of investment in each stock ($5/$10 = $\tfrac{1}{2}$). The portfolio mean return is

$$(\tfrac{1}{4} \cdot 13) + (\tfrac{1}{4} \cdot 11) + (\tfrac{1}{4} \cdot 11) + (\tfrac{1}{4} \cdot 9) = \$11$$

which is exactly the same as investing in just Stock 1 or Stock 2 alone. Note, however, that the variance of the portfolio is lower:

$$\tfrac{1}{4}(13 - 11)^2 + \tfrac{1}{4}(11 - 11)^2 + \tfrac{1}{4}(11 - 11)^2 + \tfrac{1}{4}(9 - 11)^2 = 2 \text{ and } \delta \cong \$1.41$$

Thus, you reduce the risk by diversifying.

Some believe that the semistrong form of the EMT implies that all stocks are correctly priced, and therefore you can select stocks at random—for example, by throwing a dart at a list of stocks obtained from the financial pages (see this chapter's Investments in the News). This is not correct. Although you cannot predict which stock will go up and which will go down in the future, by diversification you can reduce your risk. If you ignore this diversification, you are exposing yourself to higher risk with no compensation in the form of a higher expected return. Note that in the previous example, your variance decreased through diversification, but your expected return remained the same, at $11.

The previous example can be extended to many assets with positive and negative correlations. For example, suppose you have a stock with a high variance but a low beta (for example, $\beta_i = 0.5$). According to the CAPM, the mean rate of return on the stock will be relatively low, because this stock has a low correlation with other securities, and hence portfolio risk is reduced. If you do not diversify and thus hold only one stock (or only a few stocks), you pay a relatively high price for the stock; you expose yourself to high risk and do not enjoy the benefits of the risk reduction possibilities that are due to the negative correlation.

In summary, if the semistrong form of the EMT holds, technical and fundamental analysis are economically worthless. However, portfolio analysis remains important; in fact, more effort should be allocated to portfolio analysis. If the market is inefficient, then both security analysis (to find "bargains" in the market) and portfolio analysis (to reduce risk) are economically important.

12.3.3 Passive versus Active Portfolio Management

Portfolio managers face two difficult tasks:

1. *How to diversify among the various assets.* Finding the desired investment proportions and adhering to them is called **passive investment strategy.**
2. *When to change the investment proportions in the various assets.* Managers try to predict whether the stock market or the bond market will be stronger, say, next month, and actively change the investment proportions according to their predictions. Such a management strategy is called **active investment strategy.** Managers may increase the proportion of stocks from 40% to 60% today, and reverse this proportion next month, reducing the stock proportion to 40% or even less.

If the market is efficient, only the passive management strategy is relevant, because according to the semistrong form of the EMT, publicly available information (for example, the budget deficit, the amount of money in the market, reported earnings by firms, or unemployment) is not useful in predicting whether stocks or bonds will be better in the future. In such a case, portfolio managers do not have "timing ability," or the ability to predict when is the best time to move from heavy bond investment to more stock investment or vice versa. Nearly all investors know that when interest rates go down, the stock market typically rallies. However, can they predict what the interest rate will be next month? If you believe in the semistrong form of the EMT, you cannot benefit from active investment strategies. The best investment strategy is simply to find some investment proportions and adopt a passive investment strategy; a portfolio manager should not try to outsmart the market.

Funds known as **index funds** do not engage in active rebalancing strategies. For example, the Vanguard Index 500 Portfolio holds stocks in the same proportions as the Standard & Poor's 500 stock price index. Thus, if you buy this fund, you really buy the index, and the manager does not make any attempt to outperform the S&P 500 index. Because index funds do not have a large turnover and do not need to spend money on economic analyses, they incur expenses of about 0.2%; for managed funds (funds that invest not just in indexes but in stocks, bonds, options, futures, currencies, etc., thus offering the investor the advantage of professional management), these fees are much larger (usually around 1.3%).

Despite the recent popularity of index funds, some fund managers do not believe in the EMT. They believe in active management strategies and think they can outperform the market.

Regardless of how they regard the efficiency of the financial markets, all investors must consider certain factors. Connecting Theory to Practice 12.2 shares what many believe is fundamental investment advice.

CONNECTING THEORY TO PRACTICE 12.2

REACHING ALL YOUR GOALS— WHY CHOOSING THE RIGHT MIX IS JOB #1

Here's an amazing statistic: according to some studies, almost 92% of your portfolio's return depends on how you allocate your money among various types of stock, bond, and money-market funds. Only 5% derives from adjusting that mix to changing market conditions. And a paltry 3% comes from the thing that most investors worry most about: picking top-performing stocks or funds.

To help you get the most out of your portfolio, check out the advice below and our five rules for smart asset allocation:

- *Why is asset allocation so important to your return?* Because different types of investments simply don't rise and fall at the same rate, according to researchers. By diversifying among funds that hold stocks, bonds, or cash, you can usually offset losses in one category with gains in another. . . .
- *How the pros allocate assets* . . . First, they look at the correlation between various asset classes. . . .
- *Rule #1: Identify your time horizon.* Nothing influences your allocation more than the number of years you have to reach your goal. For example, if you know you'll have to tap into your money within 5 years, volatility— the fluctuation in the value of your investments—should be your primary concern. The reason: With such a short time horizon, you run a big chance of having to sell investments when their prices are depressed or haven't had time to recover from a setback. . . .
- *Rule #2: Assess your risk tolerance.* If you lose sleep when stock prices dive—or worse yet, are apt to panic and sell—you might want to scale back on the equity allocation. . . .
- *Rule #3: Diversify, diversify, diversify.* To improve your returns while reducing risk, you must go beyond simply spreading your assets among the three broad asset classes of stocks, bonds and cash. . . .
- *Rule #4: Don't tinker with your mix.* Whatever your allocation, stay with it regardless of what happens in the markets. Trying to grab a little extra return

(continued)

by jumping into momentarily hot sectors rarely works—and could easily wipe out much of the benefits of your portfolio's diversification.
- *Rule #5: Re-balance your holdings once a year.* You can do this most easily by adding new money to the funds that have done worst, a strategy that forces you to buy more funds shares when their prices are beaten down.

Source: http://pathfinder.com/@@XN8KUAGIQAMAQPdH/money/features/fundguide/rightmix.html/#mainQ.

MAKING THE CONNECTION

There is no fail-safe magic formula for determining your optimal investment strategy, but there are factors that every investor must consider. For example, as the article points out, you must evaluate your tolerance for risk, identify your time horizon, and diversify your portfolio. These factors, along with others, apply regardless of your belief in the efficiency of the financial markets.

12.4 INVESTMENT STRATEGY IN AN INEFFICIENT MARKET

In an inefficient market, the appropriate investment strategy is different than when the market is efficient. The particular strategy to pursue depends on the level of efficiency (or inefficiency). Investors who believe in the weak form of the EMT but not the semistrong form might locate mispriced securities using fundamental analysis. Hence, the investors with the lowest cost per investment dollar for conducting fundamental analysis and those who are the best at analyzing the data will earn the greatest return.

Similarly, investors who do not believe in the weak form of the EMT would even benefit from some technical trading rules based on past historical prices, as well as fundamental analysis. Finally, investors who believe in the strong form of the EMT believe they cannot benefit even if they are insiders. Those who do not believe in the strong form of the EMT can earn abnormal profits. However, they have to consider the risk-return profile, where they risk being sent to prison!

12.5 EMPIRICAL EVIDENCE RELATED TO THE EMT

Does actual price behavior support the EMT? The existing evidence is vast; this text will survey just a few studies to answer this question.

However, before we look at the empirical tests of the various forms of market efficiency, it is worth noting another set of classifications that has been suggested by Fama.[8] His classifications are derived from the empirical tests conducted to figure

8. See Eugene F. Fama, "Efficient Capital Markets: 2," *Journal of Finance* 46(December 1991): 1575–1617.

out whether the market is efficient. The first category includes *tests for return predictability,* which includes historical prices and other variables such as dividends, interest rates, firm size, and so on. If one can use these variables to predict stock price or to make an abnormal return, we say that the market is inefficient. The second category includes *event studies,* which test whether an abnormal rate of return exists because of an announcement of an event such as an increase in dividends, or a merger. Once again, if one can make an abnormal return using this information, the market is inefficient. The third category includes *tests for private information,* which are similar to the tests for insider information discussed earlier.

This chapter will adhere to the original classifications of market efficiency. Nevertheless, keep in mind that these classifications are arbitrary and can be changed without changing the empirical tests for market efficiency. The names change, but not the content of the tests.

The objective of this section is to assess how efficient the market actually is in practice. To organize our investigation, we categorize the evidence according to how it is related to the three forms of the EMT (weak, semistrong, and strong).

12.5.1 Evidence Related to the Weak Form of the EMT

Many investment rules are based on historical prices. For example, one trading rule suggests buying stocks that are trading at their fifty-two week low. A large number of empirical studies have tested the weak form of the EMT; some are summarized in Exhibit 12-4. In general, the early research provides strong evidence in favor of markets' being weak-form efficient. More recent evidence has uncovered many **anomalies,** which are events that are not anticipated and that offer investors a chance to earn abnormal profits. (Researchers were so convinced that the EMT was true that they felt any contrary evidence must be an anomaly; some of these findings were referred to as *enigmas.*)

Two primary techniques are used to test the validity of the weak-form proposition: analysis of technical trading rules for abnormal rates of return and statistical tests on historical data to locate significant patterns.

ANALYSIS OF TECHNICAL TRADING RULES FOR ABNORMAL RATES OF RETURN

Technical trading rules can be examined to determine whether they generate abnormal rates of return after trading cost. (Technical trading rules are covered in detail in Chapter 13.) **Abnormal rates of return,** as defined earlier, are the rates of return that are above what we would expect to earn given the level of risk taken.

To calculate abnormal returns, we must first determine normal returns. We can use the CAPM, the SIM, or the APT to find normal returns. With the CAPM, recall that the expected return on Asset i (a security or a portfolio) is

$$E(R_i) = r + [E(R_m) - r]\beta_i \tag{12.1}$$

EXHIBIT 12-4   Summary of Evidence Related to the Weak Form of the Efficient Market Theory

Authors	Year	Assets Studied	Weak-Form Efficient?	Comments
Bachelier	1900	French securities	Yes	Tried to test whether the French government securities options and futures market was efficient
Roberts	1959	U. S. stocks	Yes	Found that stock prices resemble random patterns
Osborne	1959	U. S. stocks	Yes	Found that stock prices are similar to random movement of physical particles in water (Brownian motion)
Granger, Morgenstern	1963	U. S. stocks	Yes	Employed spectral analysis (a powerful statistical tool that identifies patterns), but still found no significant patterns
Fama	1965	U. S. stocks	Yes	Examined serial correlations and other statistical tools to check for patterns, and found no significant patterns
Fama, Blume	1966	U. S. stocks	Yes	Examined technical trading rules and found no abnormal profits
Solnik	1973	Stocks in 9 countries	Yes	Used serial correlations and found no profitable investment strategies
Merton	1980	U. S. stocks	No	Found that changes in variance are somewhat predictable from past data
French	1980	U. S. stocks	No	Identified a weekend effect
Keim	1983	U. S. stocks	No	Identified a January effect
Gultekin, Gultekin	1983	International markets	No	Identified seasonal patterns
Jaffe, Westerfield	1984	International markets	No	Identified seasonal patterns
Lehmann	1990	U. S. stocks	No	Identified reversal effects
Serletis, Sondergard	1995	Canadian stocks	Yes	Using tests of the 1980s, it was found that efficiency holds for Canadian stocks
Masih, Masih	1996	Daily spot exchange rates	No	Tested spot rates and found that they suggest violation of market efficiency
Yu	1996	East Asian exchanges	No	Found that exchange rates contain predictive power about stock movements in Hong Kong
McQueen, Thorley	1997	Gold	No	Found that prior returns on an equally weighted portfolio of gold stocks predict gold returns

where r is the risk-free interest rate, $E(R_m)$ is the expected rate of return on the market portfolio, and β_i is the beta coefficient (defined as $Cov(R_i,R_m)\sigma_m^2$. Thus, the normal expected rate of return is given by $E(R_i)$. The abnormal rate of return (AR_i) is defined as

$$AR_i = R_i - E(R_i) = R_i - \{r + [E(R_m) - r]\beta_i\} \tag{12.2}$$

or, in words,

$$\text{Abnormal Rate of Return} = \text{Actual Rate of Return} - \text{Normal Rate of Return}$$

where R_i is the realized or actual return on the ith stock. Because $E(R_m)$ and β_i are unknown parameters, they are usually estimated by using historical data. Hence, the normal return is estimated first, and then the abnormal return is estimated. This technique is commonly employed in the event studies explained next.

Many research studies of market efficiency examine the behavior of these abnormal rates of return over time. Researchers measure this using the **cumulative abnormal rate of return** (CAR_i), the sum of all abnormal rates of return for the whole investment period, which is calculated for a particular trading strategy as follows:

$$CAR_i = \sum_{t=1}^{m} AR_{i,t} \tag{12.3}$$

where m is the number of periods (which are usually days). If the cumulative abnormal rates of return are significantly positive, then we conclude that abnormal returns are possible following some strategy, and the EMT is wrong. An alternate conclusion would be that the risk of the portfolio was not appropriately estimated by its beta. Therefore, as discussed before, we face a joint hypothesis regarding EMT and the model used to measure the normal rate of return. In order to check whether the abnormal return is solely a consequence of the strategy used and not of the model used, we can use a technique called *event study*.

An event study is a technique to measure the impact of a particular event on a firm's stock price. It measures the response of the stock price to the event—for example an announcement of an increase in cash dividends. Suppose that a firm announces an increase in cash dividends, and the stock price on the same day goes up by 2%. Is it an abnormal profit? The answer is not clear, because many other economic phenomena that may affect the stock price may occur on the same day—an announcement of a decrease in the interest rate, a new peace treaty, and so on. The aim of event study methodology is to measure the increase in price that is solely due to the event itself.

Because β_i is unknown, we cannot directly employ Equation 12.2 to measure AR_i. Therefore, in an event study, we commonly employ the single index model (see Equation 10.1 in Chapter 10) when the factor is some stock index (for example, the S&P 500 index). The event date is denoted by t. Then the abnormal rate of return on day t (see Equation 12.2) is estimated by e_t, given by the equation

$$R_t = a + bR_{m,t} + e_t$$

Namely, the abnormal return is estimated by e_t, given by

$$e_t = R_t - a - bR_{m,t}$$

where R_t and $R_{m,t}$ are the rates of return on the announcement date of the firm's stock and on the market portfolio (for example, the S&P 500 index), respectively, and a and b are the intercept and the slope, respectively, of the regression line of R_t regressed against $R_{m,t}$. In order not to contaminate the estimates of a and b by the event itself, generally some period before the announcement date is taken—for example, sixty months (starting sixty-five months before the announcement date)—and a regression of R_t on $R_{m,t}$ is conducted in this period to estimate a and b. Also, because there may be leaks of information before the event and a continuing effect after the event, it is common to measure the abnormal return corresponding to a few days surrounding the event date as well.

To make sure that e_t measures the abnormal rate of return and not another economic factor occurring on the same date, many firms that increase the cash dividends from different dates in the past are included in the study. Thus, by having various periods, the effects of other economic factors tend to cancel each other. Thus, $\bar{e}_t$ is the estimate of the abnormal return, AR_i, across all firms on the various announcement dates (t). Having the average abnormal return ($\bar{e}_t$) of all the firms included in the study on the announcement date (which differ across firms but is still denoted by t) allows us to employ Equation 12.3 to calculate the average cumulative abnormal rate of return.

If the average abnormal return ($\bar{e}_t$) (or the average cumulative abnormal rate of return) is significantly different from zero, we say that the announcement itself provides an abnormal return, and the market is semistrong inefficient. If the average abnormal return is significant before the announcement date as well, we conclude that information was leaked before the announcement date. Finally, if the average abnormal return is significant after the event, we conclude that investors can earn an abnormal rate of return after the information is in the public domain for a few days, which strongly contradicts the market semistrong efficiency. However, do not forget that the event study has a joint test, and the commonly strong conclusion may be misleading, because the model employed to measure the normal return may be wrong!

The empirical evidence generally rejects the notion that abnormal returns are generated from simple trading rules. However, there are many trading rules, some of which are privately held; hence, not all rules have been tested.

STATISTICAL TESTS OF HISTORICAL DATA FOR SIGNIFICANT PATTERNS

A second way to test the validity of the weak form of the EMT is to conduct statistical tests on historical data to locate significant patterns. For example, autocorrelations or serial correlations can be examined to assess whether past returns had predictive power in determining future returns.[9] Alternatively, nonparametric tests

---

9. Autocorrelations or serial correlations look at how correlated past changes are with current changes. If past changes are highly correlated (positive or negative), they can be used to predict future changes.

can be employed to assess whether negative returns are followed by positive returns or vice versa.[10] Although some evidence suggests that weak patterns do exist, they are not strong enough to profit when transaction costs are taken into consideration.

Looking again at Exhibit 12-4, one pattern is clear. Early evidence appears to support the weak form of the EMT, but more recent evidence appears to reject it. Numerous patterns have been identified that suggest that markets do not even adhere to the weak form of the EMT. This evidence will be discussed in detail in Section 12.6.

PRACTICE BOX

Problem

Suppose you know that the expected daily rate of return of Morgan, Inc., common stock is 0.0453%. You also observe the following daily rates of return around Day 3. Assume that the firm announced an increase in dividends on Day 3.

Date	Rate of Return
1	−0.5%
2	0.3
3	5.0
4	3.0
5	0.05

Calculate the cumulative abnormal rates of return.

Solution

Given that $E(R_i) = 0.0453\%$, construct the following table:

Date	Rate of Return	$AR_{i,t}$	$CAR_{i,t}$
1	−0.5%	−0.5453%	−0.5453%
2	0.3	0.2547[a]	−0.2906[b]
3	5.0	4.9547	4.6641
4	3.0	2.9547	7.6188
5	0.05	0.0047	7.6235

a. 0.2547 = 0.3 − 0.0453.

b. −0.2906 = −0.5453 + 0.2547.

The main implication of these results is not that there was a 5% return on Day 3 when the dividends announcement is made. The main implication is that there was a 3.0% return the day after, which could have resulted in abnormal profits. Thus, investors can buy the stock at Day 3 and still make money at Day 4. This example illustrates the concept of abnormal returns. However, five observations of one security are not enough to draw any conclusions.

---

10. Nonparametric tests are statistical techniques that seek to determine whether patterns exist in a given set of data.

12.5.2 Evidence Related to the Semistrong Form of the EMT

When investigating whether the semistrong form of the EMT is true, researchers try to determine whether investors using fundamental analysis could earn abnormal returns. If these investors cannot not earn abnormal returns consistently, then the semistrong form is true. Exhibit 12-5 lists some studies of the semistrong form of the EMT and their conclusions.

The evidence related to the semistrong form of the EMT investigates information obtained through fundamental analysis. Part 4 of this book describes fundamental analysis techniques in great detail. Fundamental analysis focuses on the analysis of a firm's specific information and its stock prices. The most common information analyzed is the reported earnings per share (EPS). Thus, fundamental analysis seeks to determine whether there is a link between basic information about a company (such as earnings per share) and its stock price.

The key to understanding the relationship between earnings per share and stock prices lies in what was expected by the market. That is, we should ask, How different are the earnings from what was expected? Rendleman, Jones, and Latané used this measure to analyze the validity of the semistrong form of the EMT, examining

EXHIBIT 12-5		Summary of Evidence Related to the Semistrong Form of the Efficient Market Theory		
Authors	**Year**	**Assets Studied**	**Semistrong-Form Efficient?**	**Comments**
Fama, Fisher, Jensen, Roll	1969	U.S. stocks	Yes	Stock splits—no gains after announcements
Scholes	1972	U.S. stocks	Yes	Large secondary offerings—price decline is permanent when insiders are selling
Jaffe	1974	U.S. stocks	No	Insiders can profit from public information about insider trading
Ball	1978	U.S. stocks	No	Earnings announcement reactions take considerable time
Watts	1978	U.S. stocks	No	Reproduced work of Ball (1978) with better techniques and found same results
Dodd	1981	U.S. stocks	Yes	No abnormal profits after merger announcement
Rendleman, Jones, Latané	1982	U.S. stocks	No	Similar results to Ball (1978)
Roll	1984	Orange juice futures	Yes/No	Inefficient due to exchange limits; otherwise efficient

(continued)

EXHIBIT 12-5 *(continued)*

Authors	Year	Assets Studied	Semistrong-Form Efficient?	Comments
Seyhun	1986	U.S. stocks	Yes	Insiders cannot profit from public information about insider trading
Fama, French	1992	U.S. stocks	No	Investors can profit from information on the firm's size and the market-to-book-value ratio
Peterson	1995	U.S. stocks	Yes	Abnormal returns associated with "stock highlights" published by Valueline found consistent with EMT
Bernard, Seyhun	1997	U.S. stocks	No	Using a stochastic dominance approach to test market efficiency following earnings announcements showed the market is inefficient
Blose, Shieh	1997	U.S. stocks	No	Positive correlation found between Tobin's Q and stock price reaction to capital investment announcements, when Tobin's Q is defined as the ratio of the market value of the firm's assets to its replacement cost

the cumulative abnormal rates of return for ten groups of stocks.[11] The stock groups were constructed by rankings based on the following equation:

$$SUE = \frac{EPS - E(EPS)}{SEE} \tag{12.4}$$

where SUE = standardized unexpected earnings, EPS = earnings per share, E(EPS) = expected earnings per share,[12] and SEE = the standard error of the estimate. The denominator helps adjust for some industries' having more or less volatility than other industries. For example, utility firms have a fairly predictable EPS, whereas software firms have a very unpredictable EPS. Thus, a 5% difference in the actual EPS from the expected EPS may be interpreted as dramatic by investors in a utility firm's stock but interpreted as insignificant by investors in software companies. The SEE would be greater for the software firm, reducing the SUE. After adjusting for this difference in earnings volatility, ten groups of stocks were formed, where Group 1 represents firms with the lowest SUE, Group 2 represents firms with the

11. Rendleman, Richard J., Charles P. Jones, and Henry A. Latane, "Empirical Anomalies Based on Unexpected Earnings and the Importance of Risk Adjustments," *Journal of Financial Economics* 10(1982): 269–287.
12. E(EPS) is estimated by Rendleman, Jones, and Latané using an "extrapolative trend model with seasonal dummies." Basically, the forecasts were made based on projecting historical data.

next-to-lowest SUE, and so forth. Thus, Group 10 represents stocks with the highest SUE.

Exhibit 12-6 illustrates the results. Clearly, market prices react to unexpected earnings announcements as cumulative average excess returns move up or down due to the announcements. In contradiction to the EMT, however, the best (Group 10) and worst (Group 1) continue to move up and down, respectively, after the announcement. Thus, the information on the surprise in the past can be employed to make profits in the future. This is good evidence against the semistrong form of the EMT.

EXHIBIT 12-6
Cumulative Abnormal Rates of Return for Unexpected Earnings Announcements

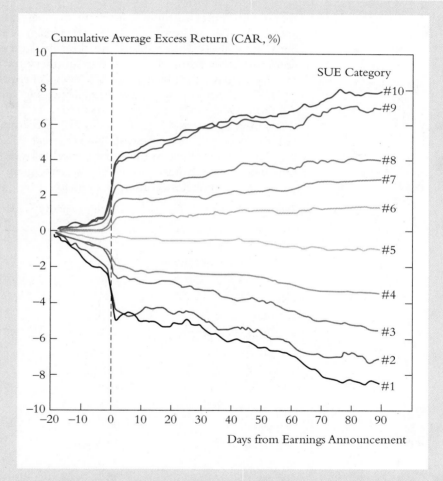

SUE stands for standardized unexpected earnings. Day 0 is the day when the quarterly earnings are announced. #1 is the lowest SUE, and #10 is the highest.

Source: Reprinted from *Journal of Financial Economics* 3 (November 1982), R. Rendleman et al., "Empirical Anomalies Based on Unexpected Earnings and the Importance of Risk Adjustment," p. 285, copyright 1982, with permission of Elsevier Science.

In response to this research, as well as other studies, the *Wall Street Journal* has now begun to publish "Quarterly Earnings Surprises." In Connecting Theory to Practice 12.3, Zacks Investment Service analyzes some of them. Because this phenomenon of surprises is now both well known and widely published, the abnormal returns should begin to vanish.

CONNECTING THEORY TO PRACTICE 12.3

ZACKS QUARTERLY EARNINGS UPDATE

As fourth quarter earnings report, we compare the reported earnings to the analysts' consensus estimates. An earnings surprise is the percentage difference between analysts' expectations and the actual earnings reported adjusted for continuing operations. Below is our summary for the 4th Quarter, covering the trading days from December 15, 1997 to February 11th, 1998. *4th Quarter '97 EPS Surprises are less positive than those in 4th Quarter '96.*

From December 15, 1997 to February 11, 1998, of the 2658 companies that reported quarterly earnings for the December quarter, *46.8% reported earnings above the Zacks' consensus estimate while 37.2% reported below the Zacks' consensus estimate.* During this same period last year, 2474 companies reported fourth quarter earnings with 56.9% reporting above consensus estimate and 31.3% reporting below consensus estimate.

Sector[a]	Earnings above Expectations	Earnings at Expectations	Earnings below Expectations
Consumer staples (134)	44.8%	12.7%	42.5%
Consumer discretionary (124)	54.8	12.1	33.1
Retail (137)	34.3	27.0	38.7
Medical (251)	43.4	22.3	34.3
Auto/tires/trucks (34)	61.8	11.8	26.5
Basic materials (174)	41.4	17.2	41.4
Industrial products (137)	48.9	14.6	36.5
Construction (74)	51.4	17.6	31.1
Multisector conglomerates (26)	50.0	11.5	38.5
Computer and technology (720)	50.8	15.6	33.6
Aerospace (26)	42.3	19.2	38.5
Oils/energy (115)	36.5	8.7	54.8
Finance (511)	45.6	16.8	37.6
Utilities (122)	46.7	4.1	49.2
Transportation (73)	56.2	15.1	28.8

[a] Number of companies reporting in.

Source: Web site at http://www.ultra.zacks.com/earn.html.

(continued)

> **MAKING THE CONNECTION**
>
> As the report shows, academic evidence related to quarterly earnings surprises has prompted practitioners to keep a closer watch on earnings announcements. Zacks Investment Service is only one of many firms that provide periodic earnings updates. Note that in many cases, as expected, the chance of negative earnings surprises (earnings below expectations) frequently equals the chance of positive earnings surprises (earnings above expectations).

12.5.3 Evidence Related to the Strong Form of the EMT

The evidence against the strong form of the EMT is irrefutable; some of this research is summarized in Exhibit 12-7. Several studies found that insiders can profit significantly from the valuable information they possess. Exactly where you draw

EXHIBIT 12-7   **Summary of Evidence Related to the Strong Form of the Efficient Market Theory**

Authors	Year	Assets studied	Strong-Form Efficient?	Comments
Cowles	1933	Money managers*	Yes	Professionals do not do any better than the market as a whole
Friend, Brown, Herman, Vickers	1962	Mutual funds*	Yes	Average mutual fund does not outperform market as a whole
Neiderhoffer, Osborn	1966	NYSE specialist	No	Specialists generate significant profits
Jensen	1968, 1969	Mutual funds*	Yes	Risk-adjusted performance of mutual funds is not any better
Scholes	1972	Insiders	No	Insiders have access to information not reflected in prices
Jaffe	1974	Insiders	No	Insiders can profit
Henriksson	1984	Mutual funds*	Yes	Before load fees but after other expenses, mutual funds do about average
Seyhun	1986	Insiders	No	Insiders can profit
Ippolito	1989	Mutual funds	No	Before load fees but after other expenses, mutual funds do slightly better than average
Liu, Smith, Syed	1990	U.S. stocks	No	Prices change with publication of articles in the "Heard on the Street" column in the *Wall Street Journal*

*Many assumed that money and mutual fund managers were in possession of inside information. Hence, examining the performance of mutual fund managers was a test of strong-form efficiency. The evidence suggests that mutual fund managers are not in possession of material inside information (or at least they cannot profit from it if they have it).

the line between private information and public information may influence your position on the strong form of the EMT. For example, Liu, Smith, and Syed (1990) found significant price changes on stocks discussed in the "Heard on the Street" column in the *Wall Street Journal*. When reporters find this information, is it private or public at that point? Clearly, after publication it is public information. However, reporters know this information before it is published, yet they are not insiders. Technically, however, it is inside information prior to publication.

Exactly who is an insider and when information moves out of the firm to the public are not always clear. Connecting Theory to Practice 12.4, "Cheat sheets" on initial public offerings (IPOs), is revealing. Clearly, whoever is first in the receiving line of potent inside information stands to benefit.

CONNECTING THEORY TO PRACTICE 12.4

"CHEAT SHEETS" ON IPOS RAISE FAIRNESS ISSUE

In the extraordinary bull market of the 1990s, it is no secret that many companies whose past results seem humdrum in prospectuses for their initial public stock offerings may nevertheless see their stock price soar after the IPO.

What is less well known is that one reason some stock offerings become red hot is the seemingly routine availability of "cheat sheets" that find their way to some big institutional investors while an IPO is being marketed.

Named for their similarity to the notes students sometimes sneak in to exams, Wall Street's version of cheat sheets contain one or more pages of information not found in the prospectus, such as earnings projections or comparisons with competitors.

Although the information they contain may play an important role in investors' decisions about whether to buy a stock offering, the companies often don't include them in the prospectus available to all investors because, among other reasons, they may hope to avoid legal liability if they miss their own rosy forecasts.

Securities-law experts say it is fine for brokers selling stock to use such material for their own internal purposes—but not to provide the raw material to their clients. The Securities Act of 1933 allows only prospectuses filed with and cleared by the Securities and Exchange Commission to be distributed to investors. Any other written material that is handed out to an investor could be considered an illegal prospectus.

"If any document is sent to a potential buyer, it had better be the prospectus," says Brian Lane, director of the SEC's division of corporate finance. "Sales literature may be considered an illegal prospectus and circulating it is not permitted during the quiet period" when the stock is being sold, he says. During this period, companies and their underwriters are limited in what they can say about the companies' business.

(continued)

Yet, investors and IPO watchers say many Wall Street firms give out cheat sheets to their best clients, no questions asked. "It's a widespread practice. They are given to preferred clients and once one client gets it, it gets passed around, says Robert Natale, director of equity research at Standard & Poor's.

In one instance last week, Lazard Freres, which was a co-manager on a $220 million IPO for investment banking firm Friedman, Billings, Ramsey Group, provided a six-page cheat sheet on the new offering to at least one client.

Source: Susan Pulliam, "'Cheat Sheets' on IPOs Raise Fairness Issue," in "Heard on the Street," *Wall Street Journal*, December 31, 1997, p. C1. Reprinted by permission of *The Wall Street Journal* © 1997 Dow Jones & Co., Inc. All Rights Reserved Worldwide.

MAKING THE CONNECTION

Just as the "cheat sheets" that some students might use to increase their grade on an exam might place other honest students at a disadvantage, so do the cheat sheets used by institutional investors place other investors at a potential disadvantage. Market efficiency is based on the premise that all information is available to all investors simultaneously. Clearly, providing additional information to select clients violates this premise.

If the strong form of the EMT is correct, then insiders should *not* be able to generate abnormal returns from their trading decisions. The evidence presented in this section is very convincing: insiders (but not mutual funds managers) can generate abnormal profits, and hence the strong form of the EMT is not supported. However, recall that it is illegal to trade on insider information.

12.6 MARKET ANOMALIES

The EMT has some widely known and well-documented violations. Recall that a market anomaly is any event that can be exploited to produce abnormal profits. Anomalies exist in any form of the EMT but in most cases relate to the semistrong form of the EMT.

Market anomalies imply market inefficiency. However, because all market efficiency tests are joint tests, it is possible that these anomalies are actually not anomalies but rather that we do not have a powerful model to explain them. This explanation is convincing particularly in cases where anomalies persist for a long time. Why don't they disappear, as investors are well familiar with them? Typically, these observations of anomalies have been extensively back tested by researchers— i.e., they have examined how historical prices behaved in response to some observation or some event. For the results of back testing to be significant, the pattern identified must persist for some time.

Exhibit 12-8 identifies four categories of anomalies: seasonal, event, firm, and accounting anomalies. **Firm anomalies** are anomalies that result from firm-specific

EXHIBIT 12-8   Summary of Market Anomalies

Anomaly	Description/Implication
Firm Anomalies	
Size	Returns on small firms tend to be higher, even on a risk-adjusted basis
Closed-end mutual funds	Returns on closed-end funds that trade at a discount tend to be higher
Neglect	Firms that are not followed by many analysts tend to yield higher returns
Institutional holdings	Firms that are owned by few institutions tend to have higher returns
Seasonal Anomalies	
January	Security prices tend to be up in January, especially the first few days (as well as the last days of December)
Week-end	Securities tend to be up on Fridays and down on Mondays
Time of day	Securities tend to be up in the first 45 minutes and the last 15 minutes of the day
End of month	Last trading day of the month tends to be up
Seasonal	Firms with highly seasonal sales tend to be up during high sales periods
Holidays	Returns tend to be positive on the last trading day before a holiday
Event Anomalies	
Analysts' recommendations	The more analysts recommending purchase of a stock, the more likely it will go down
Insider trading	The more insiders buying a stock, the more likely it is to go up
Listings	Security prices rise after it is announced that a firm will be listed on an exchange
Value Line rating changes	Security prices continue to rise after Value Line places a security in its #1 category
Accounting Anomalies	
P/E ratio	Stocks with low P/E ratios tend to have higher returns
Earnings surprises	Stocks with larger-than-anticipated earnings announcements tend to continue to rise even after the announcement
Price/sales ratio	If the price-to-sales ratio is low, then the stock tends to outperform
Price/book ratio	If the price-to-book-value ratio is low, then the stock tends to outperform
Dividend yield	If the dividend yield is high, then the stock tends to outperform
Earnings momentum	Stocks of firms whose growth rate of earnings is rising tend to outperform

characteristics. For example, small firms tend to outperform large ones on a risk-adjusted basis, an anomaly called the *size effect*. A similar anomaly is the *neglected firm effect:* the fewer the analysts tracking a particular security, the larger the average return. This anomaly may be an instance of the size effect, because neglected firms tend to be small.

13. Fama and French, "The Cross-Section of Expected Returns," *Journal of Finance* 47(1992): 427–465; Marc R. Reinganum, "The Anatomy of a Stock Market Winner," *Financial Analysts Journal,* March–April 1988, pp. 272–284.

Fama, French, and Reinganam analyze the market-to-book-value (M/B) ratio of stocks as a predictor of returns across securities.[13] The terms *book value* and *market value* relate to the book value and market value of the firm's equity. Fama and French classify all the stocks included in their sample into ten deciles, according to the M/B ratio. They found that the decile with the lowest M/B ratio had an average monthly rate of return of 1.65%, whereas the decile with the highest M/B ratio had a return on only 0.72% per month. Exhibit 12-9 shows their findings regarding the M/B anomaly.

A **seasonal anomaly** is an anomaly that depends solely on time. For example, the January anomaly (or January effect) is the tendency for stock prices to be abnormally up in January (and late December).

Exhibit 12-10 demonstrates the January effect for various assets for the periods 1926 to 1996 and 1987 to 1996. For the long period 1926 to 1996 (Exhibit 12-10a), the January effect is striking for small stocks, which had an average monthly rate of return of about 7% in January and less than 2% in most other months. For the S&P 500 index there is no January effect; a larger rate of return is recorded in July and August, and a similar rate of return is recorded in December. For the other assets categories (Treasury bills, long-term corporate bonds, long-term government bonds, and intermediate-term government bonds), there is no January effect.

EXHIBIT 12-9
Average Monthly Rate of Return as a Function of the Ratio of Market Value to Book Value

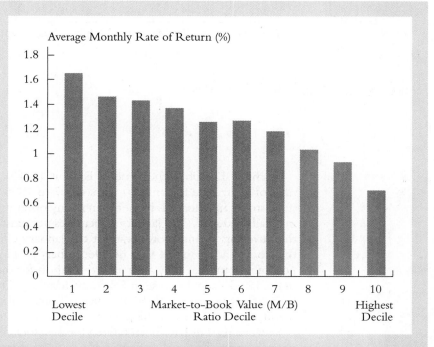

Source: Eugene F. Fama and Kenneth R. French, "The Cross Section of Expected Returns," *Journal of Finance* 47 (1992): 427–465.

EXHIBIT 12-10   The January Anomaly

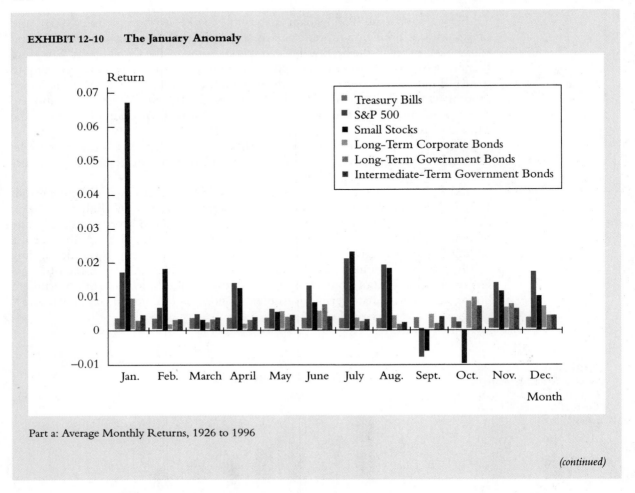

Part a: Average Monthly Returns, 1926 to 1996

(continued)

Exhibit 12-10b is the same as Exhibit 12-10a except that the averages of the rates of return are for only 10 years, 1987 to 1996. Although the rate of return on small stocks in January is higher than in any other month, the January effect was dramatically reduced. The January effect does not exist for the other assets. It is possible that investors, being more aware of the January effect in the recent period, bought the stocks earlier in the year (in December) in an attempt to gain in January. This possibility provides only a partial explanation for the reduction in the January effect in the last decade, because in February, May, and December there is also a relatively high rate of return on the S&P index and on small stocks, which is not explained by this argument. Whether the January effect disappears or not remains to be seen.

Several reasons have been offered for this stock price pattern. The size effect is the phenomenon that smaller firms tend to outperform larger firms on a risk-adjusted basis. Several studies have linked the January effect to the size effect. Although it is

EXHIBIT 12-10   *(continued)*

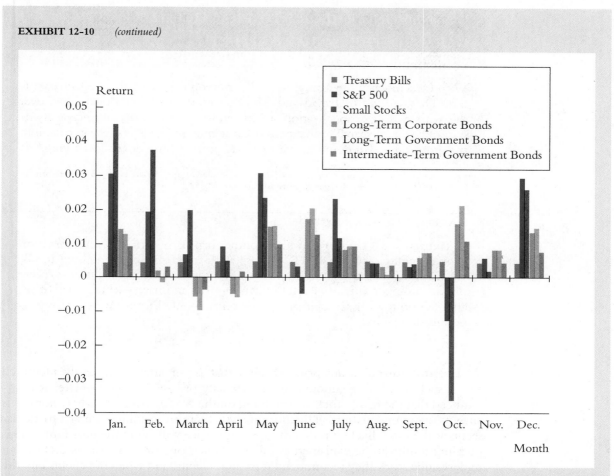

Part b: Average Monthly Returns, 1987 to 1996

unclear why, smaller firms have a much more pronounced January effect. There also is some empirical support for the January effect's being related to tax-loss selling in December. By selling in December stocks that have fallen during the year, an investor is able to realize losses that are deductible for income taxes. Connecting Theory to Practice 12.5 illustrates that Wall Street expects the January effect, which strongly contradicts the EMT.

Another anomaly is the week-end anomaly, the observation that securities tend to be up on Fridays and down on Mondays. This anomaly is even more pronounced on holiday week-ends.

CONNECTING THEORY TO PRACTICE 12.5

WARM TO THE JANUARY EFFECT
BUT NEW YEAR COMES EARLIER FOR SMALL-CAPS

With December in the offing, naturally everyone's bracing for the January Effect. That's a kind of David-and-Goliath pattern that's been established over the years as small capitalization stocks tend to outperform large-caps at the start of the new year. This happens because money managers swarm back into the group after abandoning it for year-end profit-taking or tax-loss selling.

Source: Sandra Ward, "Warm to the January Effect," *Barron's,* November 24, 1997. Reprinted by permission of Barron's, © 1997 Dow Jones & Co., Inc. All Rights Reserved Worldwide.

MAKING THE CONNECTION

In January, small firms, on average, outperform large firms. This observation strongly contradicts the EMT, because if this performance is known in advance, investors can earn money by investing in January in small stocks. Note that according to this article, not only is there an anomaly—where small firms, after adjusting for risk, yield an excess return—but also this size effect is pronounced in January.

Event anomalies are price changes that occur after some easily identified event, such as a listing announcement. Security prices of firms rise after it is announced that the firm's stock will be listed on the NYSE. Another event anomaly is analysts' recommendations. The more analysts there are recommending a particular security, the more likely it is that the security's price will fall in the near future. This puzzling result can be explained as follows. When one or two analysts discover an undervalued stock they recommend it to their clients, and when the clients buy the stock the price is driven up. This price increase attracts the attention of other analysts who subsequently recommend it, pushing the price even higher. This upward price pressure continues until some analysts start changing their buy recommendations to sell recommendations, and the price subsequently falls.

Finally, **accounting anomalies** are changes in stock prices that occur after the release of accounting information. For example, after an announcement of unusually high earnings, a firm's stock price continues to rise, as discussed earlier. Another accounting anomaly is the P/E ratio anomaly. Stocks with low price-to-earnings ratios tend to have higher returns. An anomaly that has attracted a lot of attention lately is the earnings momentum anomaly, in which stocks of firms whose growth rate of earnings has been rising tend to outperform other similar securities.

What can we conclude about market efficiency? As was stated at the beginning of the chapter, the purpose is not to place one position over another but rather to leave the final conclusion to the reader. The following are a few quotations that show what others have concluded:

In general, the empirical evidence in favor of the efficient market hypothesis is extremely strong.[14]

It's very hard to support the popular academic theory that the market is irrational [that is, that the EMT is true] when you know somebody who just made a twentyfold profit in Kentucky Fried Chicken, and furthermore, who explained in advance why the stock was going to rise. My distrust of theorizers and prognosticators continues to the present day.[15]

Event studies are the cleanest evidence we have on efficiency. . . . With few exceptions, the evidence is supportive.[16]

They [market inefficiencies] exist because we [practitioners] do not root out their basic causes. These causes are easy enough to identify, if one looks with enough dispassion and rigor. If the academics point to them, the rest of us can respond and . . . walk by.[17]

As you can see, disagreement regarding market efficiency still exists.

SUMMARY

Define an efficient market. A well-functioning financial market in which prices reflect all relevant information is said to be efficient.

Identify the types of information related to security prices in each form of the efficient market hypothesis. The efficient market theory (EMT) has three forms: the weak, the semistrong, and the strong forms. The weak form of the EMT states that stock prices reflect information revealed by the historical price sequence. The semistrong form of the EMT states that stock prices reflect all relevant publicly available information. The strong form of the EMT states that prices reflect all publicly and privately available information.

Compare investment strategies in efficient markets with investment strategies in inefficient markets. The existence of efficient capital markets has several important implications. Most important is that scarce resources are allocated in an efficient manner. Also, technical analysis is useless if at least the weak form of the EMT is true, and fundamental analysis is use-less if at least the semistrong form of the EMT is true. Finally, no matter what form of the EMT an investor adheres to, portfolio selection benefits still hold. Thus, even under the EMT, portfolio selection is still important.

Describe the findings of researchers who tested each form of the efficient market theory. Researchers have gathered empirical evidence related to the weak, semistrong, and strong forms of the EMT. The evidence against the strong form is the most conclusive; some insiders are clearly able to make abnormal returns. The evidence related to the weak and semistrong forms is mixed; some technical trading strategies and some fundamental trading strategies have generated abnormal returns in the past.

Define anomaly, and identify the common types of anomalies. An anomaly offers investors a chance to earn abnormal profits. Most of the anomalies that have been documented can be categorized in one of the following groups: firm, seasonal, event, or accounting anomalies.

14. Burton Malkiel, "Efficient Market Hypothesis," in John Eatwell, Murray Milgate, and Peter Newman (eds.), *The New Palgrave: Finance* (New York: Macmillan Press, 1989), p. 131.

15. Peter Lynch, *One Up on Wall Street* (New York: Penguin Books, 1989), p. 35.

16. Eugene F. Fama, "Efficient Capital Markets: 2," *Journal of Finance* 46(December 1991): p. 1602.

17. Dean LeBaron, "Reflections on Market Inefficiency," *Financial Analysts Journal* 39(May–June 1983): 16–17, 23. Reprinted in Charles D. Ellis (ed.), *Classics 2: Another Investor's Anthology* (Homewood, Ill.: AIMR and Business One Irwin, 1991), p. 239.

CHAPTER AT A GLANCE

1. *There are three forms of the EMT:*
   a. The weak form asserts that abnormal profits cannot be acquired from an analysis of historical stock prices.
   b. The semistrong form asserts that abnormal profits cannot be acquired from an analysis of public information.
   c. The strong form asserts that abnormal profits cannot be acquired from an analysis of public and private information.

2. *The EMT implies the following:*
   a. Resources are effectively allocated in the market.
   b. Technical (weak EMT) and fundamental analysis (strong EMT) is worthless.
   c. Portfolio selection is worthwhile, but timing is not.

3. *Empirical evidence suggests the following:*
   a. The weak form of the EMT is not completely supported because of anomalous results, such as the January effect.
   b. The semistrong form of the EMT is not completely supported because of large anomalous results, such as trading based on the size effect and the market-to-book-value ratio.
   c. The strong form of the EMT is not supported in most cases.

KEY TERMS

Abnormal rate of return 422	EMT 408	Random walk 411
Accounting anomaly 438	Event anomaly 438	Seasonal anomaly 435
Active investment strategy 419	Firm anomaly 433	Semistrong form of the
Anomaly 422	Fundamental analysis 414	EMT 412
Cumulative abnormal rate of	Index fund 419	Strong form of the EMT 414
return (CAR) 424	Passive investment	Technical analysis 412
Efficient market 409	strategy 419	Weak form of the EMT 411

REVIEW

12.1 Explain why it is important to determine how efficient the markets are.

12.2 Suppose you flip a fair coin. Whenever a head shows up, the stock price goes up by 10%. Whenever a tail shows up, the stock price drops by 5%. Are the stock rates of return following a random walk? Explain.

12.3 The rates of return on two stocks have the following values:

Day	Stock A	Stock B
1	+10%	+10%
2	−5	+10
3	+10	−5
4	−5	−5
5	+10	+10
6	−5	−5
7	+10	+10

Which stock's rates of return tend more to refute a random walk? Why?

12.4 A portfolio manager convincingly shows that whenever the market value of a stock divided by its book value is below 0.8, it is very likely that the stock price will go up. Whenever the ratio is above 1.2, the stock price tends to fall. Does this refute the EMT? If yes, which form of the EMT does it refute?

12.5 Suppose you can borrow at 6% and lend at 7%. The borrowing and lending is riskless. Is the mere availability of this borrowing and lending sufficient to reject the EMT?

12.6 Stock A is traded for $100, and stock B is traded for $200. Stock A will rise to $120 with a probability of ½ and fall to $90 with a probability of ½. Stock B will rise to $240 with a probability of ½ and fall to $180 with a probability of ½. These probabilities are independent of previous price changes and any other available information. The stock price changes are also independent of each other.
a. Are the stock price changes consistent with the EMT?
b. Would you diversify your portfolio between these stocks? In your opinion, how important is portfolio diversification in an efficient market?
c. How would you change your answer to Parts a and b if the stocks were negatively correlated?

12.7 Assume a stock price is $100. Every year there is a probability of ½ that the stock will go up 50% and a probability of ½ that the stock will go down by 20%. These probabilities are constant across years

and are not affected by any previous price information or publicly available information. The EMT holds.
a. Would you say that the stock's price next year is independent of previous price movements? Explain your answer.
b. Would you say that the stock's rate of return next year is independent of previous price changes? Explain your answer.

12.8 a. The rates of return of a given stock are serially correlated. Does this conform with the EMT?
b. The rates of return on two stocks are correlated. Does this conform with the EMT?

12.9 IBM reported $7 EPS for the second quarter—lower than expected. The stock price on the publication date (t_0) was $P_0 = \$90$. In the five days after the announcement, the prices were $P_1 = \$89$, $P_2 = \$88$, $P_3 = \$85$, $P_4 = \$84$, and $P_5 = \$83$. In this period the market went up. Does this evidence tend to support or refute semistrong efficiency? Why?

12.10 The market-to-book value (M/B) ratio of a given stock is as follows:

Quarter	M/B	Stock Price
1	1.2	$100
2	0.9	90
3	1.3	95
4	1.0	80

What can be learned from this regarding market efficiency?

PRACTICE

12.1 A firm's beta is 0.5. the riskless interest rate is 10%, and the mean annual rate of return on the market portfolio is 0.2. The annual rates of return on the firm's stock for five observations are $R_1 = 6\%$, $R_2 = 10\%$, $R_3 = 15\%$, $R_4 = 20\%$, and $R_5 = 10\%$. Calculate AR and CAR over this 5-year period.

12.2 Five firms announce an increase in dividends. On the announcement date the daily rate of return on these five stocks was $R_1 = 1\%$, $R_2 = 0\%$, $R_3 = 10\%$, $R_4 = 5\%$, and $R_5 = 3\%$, where the index $i = 1, 2, 3, 4,$ and 5 denotes the different firms. We are given the following additional information:

Firm	Beta	Daily Rates of Return on the Announcement Date	
		Market Portfolio	Risk-Free Rate
1	1	1%	0.013%
2	0.5	0.5	0.014
3	2	0.02	0.012
4	0.8	−1	0.009
5	1	2	0.010

Are there any abnormal returns on the dividend announcement date? Explain.

12.3 Four firms announce major stock repurchases. On the announcement date the daily rate of return on these four stocks was as follows: $R_1 = -3\%$, $R_2 = 2\%$, $R_3 = 12\%$, and $R_4 = -5\%$, where the index $i = 1, 2, 3$, and 4 denotes the different firms. We are given the following additional information:

Firm	Beta	Daily Rates of Return on the Announcement Date	
		Market Portfolio	Risk-Free Rate
1	1.2	1.5%	0.01%
2	0.4	0.5	0.014
3	2	0.02	0.009
4	0.8	3	0.015

Are there any abnormal returns on the stock repurchase announcement date? Explain.

12.4 IBM announced a loss of more than $2 billion in the third quarter of 1992. On the announcement date, IBM's stock price fell by 10%. Suppose that after the announcement date, the rate of return on IBM was as follows:

Days after announcement	+1	+2	+3	+4	+5	+6
Rate of return adjusted for risk	−1%	−0.5%	−2%	−1%	−3%	−6%

Does this result support the notion of the efficient market theory?

12.5 Suppose five firms announce they are going to split their stocks. On the announcement date you have the following *abnormal* returns:

Firm	Abnormal Return
1	−1%
2	2
3	3
4	0.5
5	4

a. Calculate the average abnormal return.
b. "Because Firm 1 has a negative abnormal return, we cannot conclude that a stock split announcement positively affects a particular stock's price." Evaluate this statement.

12.6 You observe the following abnormal returns on McDonnell Douglas, Inc., stock:

Day	Abnormal Return
1	0%
2	0.02
3	3
4	4
Announcement Date ⟶ 5	6
6	0.1
7	−0.1
8	0.5
9	−0.5
10	0

On Day 5 the firm announces that a big contract has been signed with the Department of Defense.
a. Calculate the cumulative abnormal return for Days 1 through 10.
b. What can we conclude from this price behavior?

12.7 Suppose five brokerage houses have the following returns on their stock selections for the past 5 years:

Brokerage House	5-Year Return
A	66%
B	67
C	61
D	59
E	62

The return on a random portfolio in the same 5-year period is 62%.

a. By how much, on average, did the brokerage houses outperform the random portfolio?

b. Suppose the brokerage houses charge, on average, 0.5% per year as a transaction fee. Would you give them your money to manage, or would you rather buy securities at random?

12.8 Many investment analysts expect Xerox, Inc., to have earnings of $10 per share. The firm announced $12 earnings per share. What is the standardized unexpected earnings if the standard error of the estimate was 0.05? (See Equation 12.4.)

12.9 Firm A announces an EPS of $10, whereas Firm B announces an EPS of $8 per share. The stock price of Firm A fell by 2%, and the stock price of Firm B went up by 4% on the announcement date. From this fact it is concluded that the lower the profit, the more positive is the market reaction. Do you agree?

12.10 There are two groups of firms. The first group consists of one hundred small firms with an average size of $100 million, and the second group consists of one hundred firms with an average size of $1 billion. The average rate of return and beta of these groups are as follows:

	Small Firms	Large Firms
Average annual return	18%	12%
Beta	1.3	0.9

The average rate of return on the market portfolio is $\overline{R}_m = 13\%$, and the risk-free interest rate is 3%. Are there abnormal returns to the small firms? Are there abnormal returns to the large firms? Discuss.

12.11 Suppose you are given the following information:

Year	Market-to-Book-Value Ratio	Rate of Return in the Following Year	
1	1.2	−20%	
2	1.1	−7	(continued)
3	0.9	18	
4	0.8	35	
5	1.3	−9	
6	1.5	−15	

Suppose you have the following two strategies:

- Buy a stock and hold it for 6 years (the buy-and-hold strategy).
- Buy a stock whenever the market-to-book-value (M/B) ratio < 1 and sell it whenever $M/B > 1$. When you sell the stock, you keep the proceeds in the bank, yielding 3% annually.

a. Given that the initial investment was $100, which policy yields a higher terminal wealth?

b. Do the return figures indicate that the market is efficient or inefficient? Why?

c. Repeat Parts a and b assuming you have a 2% transaction cost on each stock transaction.

12.12 "In an efficient market, the volatility of a security is totally unpredictable." Evaluate this statement, and use Exhibit 12-3 to defend your answer.

12.13 Using cumulative abnormal rates of return over time, describe the expected behavior of a stock before a major takeover when the following was true.

a. There was no insider trading, nor was any insider trading anticipated.

b. There was insider trading.

c. Some astute investors rightly viewed the company as being underpriced.

12.14 Suppose you had been studying event anomalies closely and had decided, based on Value Line rating changes evidence, to invest heavily in Value Line's Group #1 during the first half of 1992. Your experience, based on Value Line's selections, is that your portfolio was down 11.35% when the overall market was up 3.71%.[18] Explain this result in light of the well-documented superior historical performance of Group #1 stock.

18. Data based on an article by John R. Dorfman, "Value Line's Top Picks Flopped in 1st Half," *Wall Street Journal,* September 14, 1992, p. C1.

12.15 "One piece of evidence of inefficient markets can be found in the volume of trading activity. The volume of trading always increases before a takeover announcement." Evaluate this statement.

12.16 "If all stock prices are efficiently priced, then the best way to pick stocks is to choose them at random." Evaluate this statement.

12.17

Faced with this near-unanimous bullishness in a seemingly sky-high market, what is the investor to do? Try to avoid the problem by buying stocks in companies that are so good you will want to hold them through thick and thin. This buy-and-hold approach is the choice of most successful investors anyway. It would have served you well in the decline of 1973–74 and in the crash of 1987.

If you lack the temperament to ride out ups and downs, here's the best advice I can give: At the time of the purchase, set a one-year price target based on the valuation of the comparable stocks. Be prepared to reassess this target if conditions change. If nothing has changed in a year and the target has been reached, sell a portion of the holding.[19]

a. Do you think the author of the excerpt believes in market efficiency? Are the recommendations in the article necessarily inconsistent with weak-form, semistrong form, or strong-form market efficiency? Distinguish between the "buy-and-hold" recommendation and the "set a one-year" price.
b. Suppose that the stock price is $P_0 = \$100$. There is a chance of ¾ that it will go up by 30% next year and a ¼ chance that it will go down by 10%. The stock price follows a random walk, and the same probabilities are intact for the second year, too. Suppose that you follow the author's recommendation and set a target price of $120 to sell the stock. Assume that once a year you look at the price, and if it is above $120, you sell and put the money you receive in the bank to earn 3%. What is the distribution of returns after 2 years (that is, the end-of-second-year wealth) under the buy-and-hold policy and under the policy of selling above $120? Calcu-

late the mean and variance of the return on these two portfolios after 2 years.
c. Is there a rationale for the "target" pricing policy if you believe in the random walk theory?

12.18 The following article reports that a throw of darts (a random selection of stocks) beat the professional investors in a recent contest.

In a tumultuous stock market, a box of darts may be a good investment.

For the second time in a row, the forces of chance, as represented by Wall Street Journal staffers flinging darts at the stock tables, bested both a team of investment professionals and the Dow Jones Industrial Average in this column's stock-picking contest. The dart throwers posted an average investment gain of 6.5% in the period from July 8 through Dec. 31, 1997—which included the 554.26-point, or 7.2%, plunge in the Dow industrials on Oct. 27—compared with an average loss of 14.1% for the pros.

The industrial average itself, meanwhile, slipped 0.7% in the period.

"One thing this market has given us is some humility," says Robert Stovall of Stovall/Twenty-First Advisers, who notes that few mutual-fund managers beat the market indexes last year. "Many of the old rules don't apply.

Although the pros remain comfortably ahead of the darts when results of 91 contests since July 1990 are tallied, their margin over the industrial average is narrower.[20]

a. Suppose you repeat the dart selection many times. What do you expect the average rate of return on the dart portfolio to be relative to the average market portfolio rate of return (that is, the index of stocks)?
b. Suppose that the market is weak-form efficient but semistrong- and strong-form inefficient. Could the pros beat the darts portfolio in such a market?
c. Suppose that the market is efficient in all forms. In such a market, could the pros have a higher average rate of return than the dart portfolio when the contest is repeated many times? Suppose that this has indeed occurred. Suggest a method to ex-

---

19. R. S. Salomon, Jr., "Three to Sell Now," *Forbes,* August 11, 1997. Reprinted by Permission of *Forbes* magazine © Forbes, Inc., 1997.
20. Georgette Jasen, "Darts Again Beat Wall Street Pros," *Wall Street Journal,* January 15, 1998, p. C1. Reprinted by permission of *The Wall Street Journal* © 1998 Dow Jones & Co., Inc. All Rights Reserved Worldwide.

amine whether the pros have selectivity ability of stocks.

12.19 Read the following article, and answer the questions after it.

. . . The truth in question [is] that "asset allocation is everything," as one noted financial planner recently told us. We're not talking here about the benefits of diversifying risk by spreading investments among different asset classes. This is about performance—total return—and the importance of asset allocation in determining it.

The tale starts in 1986 when Gary Brinson, along with collaborators L. Randolph Hood and Gilbert Beebower, published a study about asset allocation in the Financial Analysts Journal. *Based on analysis of a decade of data from 91 pension funds, Brinson & Co. concluded that more than 90% of an investor's return is attributable to how you weigh assets among stocks, bonds, and cash. In other words, how much money you put into stocks as a group matters a lot more than which specific stocks you own. . . .*[21]

a. Suppose that the market is inefficient. You have some substantial ability (but not a perfect ability) to predict which stocks will go up and which will go down. Do you think you can benefit from asset allocation?

b. Suppose that you have no stock selectivity ability, but you do have some ability to predict whether the Federal Reserve will increase or decrease the interest rate. Do you think you can benefit from asset allocation in such a case?

c. Answer Parts a and b under the assumption that you have a perfect ability to predict what will be the rate of return on each stock and a perfect ability to predict what will be the change in the interest rate.

d. Suppose you have no ability to select stocks and no ability to predict macroeconomic factors (for example, interest rates, inflation, and so on). Is there a benefit from asset diversification in such an efficient market? Explain your answer.

e. Suppose that with no ability at all to predict the market, you diversify ⅓ in cash, ⅓ in bonds, and ⅓ in stocks. Suppose now that you have some ability to predict the interest rate, and you believe there is a 90% chance that the interest rate will go up and a 10% chance that it will go down. Explain how you will choose your asset allocation. (Just mention the direction of the changes and explain them).

12.20 The following article reports on the profit and split of Microsoft:

Microsoft Corp. split its common stock for the seventh time, lowering a psychological bar for owning one of the market's best-performing issues. . . .

Gregory Maffei, Microsoft's chief financial officer, said the split came in response to continued requests from investors who feel a lower per-share price makes the stock more accessible. Individual investors, who typically favor splits, only hold about 20% of Microsoft's shares; the rest are held by institutions and Microsoft employees, notably chairman Bill Gates, executive vice-president Steve Ballmer and co-founder Paul Allen.

Microsoft, because of its dominance in computer operating systems and other products, has had a remarkable run-up since its March 1986 initial stock offering. Adjusted for past splits, $10,000 invested in the IPO would be worth $2.4 million today, a company spokesman said.

The company announced its last split in December 1996. Six months later the stock was trading near pre-split levels, and reached a peak of 150¾ in July. Microsoft's stock price rose 2.55% yesterday, closing at $141.75, up $3.50, in Nasdaq Stock Market trading.[22]

a. Calculate the compounded annual rate of return since March 1986 (for simplicity, assume that 11 years passed from the date of the IPO until February 1998).

b. Explain why a split makes the stock more accessible to investors.

c. After the split announcement, Microsoft's stock went up by 2.5% in one day. Is this a "normal" or an "abnormal" rate of return (on the same day, the Dow Jones Industrial index rose by 0.12%)? Suggest an event study to examine whether splits have a positive effect on the stock price.

21. Maggie Topkis, "The Trouble with Asset Allocation," *Fortune,* October 13, 1997, p. 206. Reprinted from the October 13, 1997, issue of *Fortune* by special permission. © 1997, Time, Inc.

22. Don Clark, "Microsoft Sets Stock Split for February," *Wall Street Journal,* February 1998. Reprinted by permission of *The Wall Street Journal* © 1998 Dow Jones & Co., Inc. All Rights Reserved Worldwide.

CFA PROBLEMS

12.1 a. List and briefly define the three forms of the efficient market theory.

b. Discuss the role of a portfolio manager in a perfectly efficient market.

For Internet questions visit the Levy Investment Web site at http://levy-invst.swcollege.com.

YOUR TURN: APPLYING THEORY TO PRACTICE

THE INVESTOR'S PLAN OF ATTACK

1. Set your strategy. Remember your main advantage: You are not an institution. All stocks are fair game for investment—or short sale. Forget the conventional wisdom that growth-stock investing is just for the young. Even if you are approaching retirement, don't neglect the small-company stocks that offer the most growth potential.

2. Marshall your intelligence. Smart investors are never off duty. Your best ideas will come from your own backyard. Keep tabs on Wall Street research—but take it with a teaspoon of salt. Ask companies for annual and quarterly reports as well, and subject them to searing scrutiny.

3. Deploy your assets. Narrow your stock picks to a manageable number. In choosing the most promising companies, don't worry about diversification, and don't try to time the market. But wait until after quarterly earnings announcements to see if the latest profit report confirms your view of the company.

4. Monitor your positions. Don't just buy stock and stick it in a drawer. Keep tabs. If the news starts turning sour, and the company can't give a satisfactory explanation, sell. If your stock is rising, don't take profits until it begins to weaken.

The National Association of Investors Corp. is the umbrella organization of 9,200 clubs of individual investors nationwide. Each club in the network maintains a portfolio whose results are reported to the NAIC. The numbers are impressive.

The returns belie the clubs' stodgy image. The average club in the 1992 survey earned a 13.9% annual return over its life. Even more noteworthy is that 69% of them have beaten or matched the S&P 500 since they have been investing.

Source: "How Savvy Fund Investors Tally the Risk," by John Meehan. Reprinted from the October 2, 1989, issue of *Business Week* by special permission, copyright © 1989 by McGraw-Hill, Inc.

Questions

1. a. A young investor invests for 2 years, and an older investor invests for 1 year. The stock price that currently stands at $100 is expected to change during the next 2 years as shown in the following exhibit:

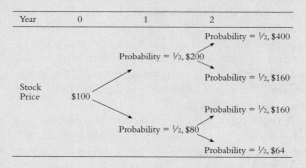

Calculate the expected rate of return for the young investor and for the older investor. Does the behavior of the stock price conform to a random walk?

b. What are the probabilities of the young investor's and the older investor's incurring a loss?

c. For the past 60 years the average annual rate of return on "small stocks" has been 17%, whereas the average annual rate of return on the Standard

(continued)

& Poor's index has been 12%. "This implies that mainly small stocks are bargained, and therefore the market is inefficient." Evaluate this assertion.

d. Suppose that if the stock price is $200 in the first year, the probability of getting $400 in the second year is ¾ and the probability of getting $160 is ¼. If the price in the first year is $80, the probabilities are as shown in Part a. Is the market efficient? Does the behavior of the stock price conform to a random walk?

2. The average annual return of an individual investors' club in a 1992 survey was 13.9%. Moreover, 69% of the investors surpassed the S&P index. As suggested by the "Investors' Plan of Attack," an investor's portfolio should consist of small stocks and growth stocks. Suppose the average rate of return on a typical mutual fund is 11.9% and on the S&P 500, it is 15.6%. Assume that the beta of a typical individual's portfolio is 1.2, the beta of the S&P 500 is 1, and the beta of the mutual fund is 0.8. Let the annual risk-free interest rate be 5.6%. Who were the best stock-pickers in the market? Discuss your results.

3. Point 2 of the "Investors' Plan of Attack" recommends analyzing firms' annual and quarterly reports. Suppose that on February 10, 1998, you receive IBM's annual report and observe a 20% increase in the EPS during 1997, and this 20% increase is much higher than what investors expected. Would you rush to the stock market to buy the stock? The mean annual rate of return on IBM stock before this information was released was 12%. In view of the 1997 annual report, what would be your estimate of the mean rate of return if the market were semistrong efficient? Explain.

4. Suppose you believe in the EMT, and you have no tips regarding next year's stock price. Point 3 of the "Investors' Plan of Attack" urges you not to try to time the market and not to worry about diversification. Suppose you have two independent stocks, each with a mean return of 10% and a standard deviation of 5%. As recommended, you do not worry about diversification and invest in only one of these stocks. Another investor does

diversify and invests 50% of his wealth in each of the two stocks. Which investment strategy is optimal? Discuss your answer.

5. Suppose you do not believe in the EMT, and you accept that the mean return on one stock is 10% with a standard deviation of 5%. You receive a tip regarding another stock. You also analyze the annual earnings of this firm and come to the conclusion that the mean return is 20% (rather than 10%) with a standard deviation of 5%. "In view of these market tips, you have nothing to gain from diversification, and you should put all your money in the stock with the mean return of 20%." Evaluate this recommendation.

6. a. Point 4 of the "Investors' Plan of Attack" suggests that "if your stock is rising, don't take profits until it begins to weaken." Is this recommendation in line with the principle of market efficiency? Discuss.

b. The price of a given stock varies over five days as follows:

Day	Price
1	$100
2	101
3	102
4	103
5	101

The probability of the stock price going up on any given day is ⁴⁄₇, and the probability of it going down is ³⁄₇. With these probabilities, you think that the stock is fairly priced and therefore decide to keep it. With a higher probability of a decline in the stock price, you would sell the stock. You follow the recommendation given in the "Investors' Plan of Attack" and sell the stock on Day 5. In doing so, what assumption are you making about the probability of the stock price going down on Day 6 (is the probability larger or smaller than ³⁄₇)? What is your prediction of the stock price on Day 6 if the behavior of the stock price conforms to a random walk? Would you sell your stock if it conformed to a random walk?

SELECTED REFERENCES

Malkiel, Burton. "Efficient Market Hypothesis." In John Eatwell, Murray Milgate, and Peter Newman (eds.). *The New Palgrave: Finance.* New York: Macmillan Press, 1989.

This book is a concise review of the efficient market hypothesis.

Moy, Ronald L., and Ahyee Lee. "A Bibliography of Stock Market Anomalies." *Journal of Financial Education,* November 1991, pp. 41–51.

This article is a good place to begin examining the empirical evidence related to market anomalies.

Rendleman, Richard J., Jr., Charles P. Jones, and Henry A. Latane. "Empirical Anomalies Based on Unexpected Earnings and the Importance of Risk Adjustments." *Journal of Financial Economics* 10 (1982): 269–287.

This paper is one of many that address the quarterly earnings surprise anomaly.

SUPPLEMENTAL REFERENCES

Ariel, Robert A. "A Monthly Effect in Stock Returns." *Journal of Financial Economics* 18 (March 1987): 161–174.

Bachelier, L. *Theorie de la speculation: Annales de l'Ecole Normale Superieure.* Translated by A. J. Boness in P. H. Cootner (ed.). *The Random Character of Stock Market Prices.* Cambridge, Mass.: MIT Press, 1967.

Ball, R. "Anomalies in Relationships between Securities' Yields and Yield-Surrogates." *Journal of Financial Economics* 6 (June–September 1978): 103–126.

Bernard, Victor L., and Jacob K. Thomas. "Evidence That Stock Prices Do Not Fully Reflect the Implications of Current Warnings for Future Earnings." *Journal of Accounting and Economics* 13 (December 1990): 305–340.

Bhardwaj, R. K., and L. D. Brooks. "The January Anomaly: Effects of Low Share Price, Transaction Costs, and Bid-Ask Bias." *Journal of Finance* 47 (January 1992): 553–575.

Chan, K. C., and Nai-fu Chen. "Structural and Return Characteristics of Small and Large Firms." *Journal of Finance* 46 (September 1991): 1467–1484.

Cochrane, John H. "Volatility Tests and Efficient Markets: A Review Essay." *Journal of Monetary Economics* 27 (June 1991): pp. 463-485.

Connolly, Robert A. "An Examination of the Robustness of the Weekend Effect." *Journal of Financial and Quantitative Analysis* 24 (June 1989): 133–169.

Cowles, A., and H. E. Jones. "Some Posteriori Probabilities in Stock Market Action." *Econometrica* 5, no. 3 (1937): 280–294.

Fama, E. "The Behavior of Stock Market Prices." *Journal of Business* 38, no. 1 (1965): 34–105.

Fama, Eugene F. "Efficient Capital Markets: 2." *Journal of Finance,* December 1991, pp. 1575–1617.

Fama, Eugene F., and Kenneth R. French. "The Cross-Section of Expected Stock Returns." *Journal of Finance* 47 (June 1992): 427–466.

Fama, E., L. Fisher, M. Jensen, and R. Roll. "The Adjustment of Stock Prices to New Information." *International Economic Review* 10, no. 1 (1969): 1–21.

Granger, D., and O. Morgenstern. "Spectral Analysis of New York Stock Market Prices." *Kyklos* 16 (1963): 1–27.

Haugen, Robert A., and Jorion Philippe. "The January Effect: Still There after All These Years." *Financial Analysts Journal*, January–February 1996, pp. 27–31.

Huberman, Gur, and Shmuel Kandel. "Market Efficiency and Value Line's Record." *Journal of Business* 63 (April 1990): 187–216.

Jegadeesh, Narasimhan. "Evidence of Predictable Behavior of Security Returns." *Journal of Finance* 45 (July 1990): 881–898.

Jersen, Gerald R., Robert R. Johnson, and Jeffrey M. Mercer. "New Evidence on Size and Price to Book Effects." *Financial Analysts Journal,* November–December 1997, pp. 37–42.

Kendall, M. "The Analysis of Economic Time Series, 1: Prices." *Journal of the Royal Statistical Society* 96, no. 1 (1953): 11–25.

Lakonishok, Josef, and Edwin Maberly. "The Weekend Effect: Trading Patterns of Individual and Institutional Investors." *Journal of Finance* 45 (March 1990): 231–243.

Liu, Pu, Stanley D. Smith, and Azmat A. Syed. "Stock Price Reactions to the *Wall Street Journal's* Securities Recommendations." *Journal of Financial and Quantitative Analysis* 25 (September 1990): 399–410.

Merton, R. "On Estimating the Expected Return on the Market: An Exploratory Investigation." *Journal of Financial Economics* 8, no. 4 (1980): 323–361.

Ogden, J. P. "Turn-of-Month Evaluations of Liquid Profits and Stock Returns: A Common Explanation for the Monthly and January Effects." *Journal of Finance* 45 (September 1990): 1259–1272.

Roll, R. "Orange Juice and Weather." *American Economic Review* 74, no. 5 (1974): 861–880.

Seyhun, H. N. "Can Omitted Risk Factors Explain the January Effect? A Stochastic Dominance Approach." *Journal of Financial and Quantitative Analysis* 28 (June 1993): 195–212.

LEARNING OBJECTIVES

After studying this chapter you should be able to:

1. Describe a technical analyst's view of the market.

2. Explain how technical analysts use charts to make inferences about future prices.

3. Identify the basic tools used by technical analysts.

4. Describe some popular technical indicators.

INVESTMENTS IN THE NEWS

TECHNICIANS TURN BEARISH ON U.S. STOCKS

Stock-market technical analysts are turning bearish. As recently as a few months ago, most "technicians" confidently predicted further gains for stocks. But today, many of them see their electrocardiograms of the market flashing warning signals, and expect a stock-market decline in the next six months.

For example, money managers' cash levels—a sign of latent buying power—are the lowest on record. And the advance-decline line, a measure of the breadth of a stock market's advance, appears weak.

"The first six months of 1994 look less than thrilling," says Stan Weinstein, editor of the Professional Tape Reader and Global Trend Alert newsletters in Hollywood, Florida. He wouldn't be surprised if big stocks fell 10% or so. Hot little stocks like Synopsis, Snapple, and Starbucks could "take it on the chin big time" and fall a lot further, he says.

"Market risk is increasing," says Andrew Addison, editor of the Addison report in Franklin, Massachusetts. He thinks stocks might edge up a bit further in the next month or two, then drop 10% on the New York Stock Exchange and more on the Nasdaq Stock Market.

Source: "Technicians Turn Bearish on U.S. Stocks," *Wall Street Journal Europe,* December 14, 1993, p. 13. Reprinted by permission of *The Wall Street Journal,* © 1993 Dow Jones & Co. Inc. All Rights Reserved Worldwide.

Technical analysis in stock selection is based on graphs and charts rather than on fundamental values such as dividends, sales, and earnings. Although many analysts dispute the value of this method of analysis, it is widely used on Wall Street. Therefore, no matter how investors view the effectiveness of technical analysis, they should know how it works. Moreover, because many Wall Street traders follow the rules of technical analysis, this method may actually push prices up, at least in the short run. Thus, investors unfamiliar with technical analysis might miss such a rally, however economically unjustified it is.

Investors who practice fundamental analysis make investment decisions based on such economic factors as the firm's earnings, the firm's growth rate of dividends, the cash available, the P/E ratio, and the strength of the firm's balance sheet. Investors using **technical analysis,** in contrast, rely on historical technical figures related to the firm or the whole economy. For example, a technical analyst would evaluate the amount of short selling, the volume of trading, or the past price behavior of a stock.

If we assume that markets are perfectly efficient, all this historical information (regardless of whether it is macroeconomic data, accounting data, or market data) should already be reflected in the stock price. Adherents of the EMT would argue that these data cannot be used to improve the investment performance. Nevertheless, there are many market professionals whose sole task is to examine historical market data to predict future price behavior. Technical analysts believe that their analysis enables them to beat the market consistently and that their activities help move prices back into equilibrium. The existence of technical analysts suggests one of the following:

1. The market is inefficient, or at least there are many investors who believe it is not efficient.
2. Even if the market is efficient and thus, *on average,* technical analysts cannot earn abnormal profits, it is possible that some, for a time, *consistently* earn abnormal profits.

This chapter introduces some of the key concepts used by technical analysts. First, it discusses the main justification for using technical analysis and provides reasons why technical analysis may be useful. Next, the main tools used by technical analysts, such as charts and technical indicators, are discussed and illustrated. Although the focus is on stocks, many of these tools are applied to bonds, currencies, commodities, and other financial assets.

13.1 IN DEFENSE OF TECHNICAL ANALYSIS

The underlying premise of technical analysis is that financial prices are determined by investors' attitudes. Investors' attitudes are influenced by many factors, some rational and some irrational. Hence, formal rational models of financial prices will never fully reflect or explain the behavior of financial prices. However, technical analysts assume that human nature is fairly static; that is, when current investors face situations similar to those faced by investors in the past, they will behave in a similar fashion. Therefore, technical analysts believe that the study of historical price patterns and relationships of prices with other variables provides clues as to how the market will behave in the future.

Martin J. Pring, president of the International Institute for Economic Research and a well-respected technical analyst, defines *technical analysis* this way:

The technical approach to investment is essentially a reflection of the idea that prices move in trends which are determined by the changing attitudes of investors toward a variety of economic, monetary, political, and psychological forces. The art of technical analysis—for it is an art—is to identify trend changes at an early stage and to maintain an investment posture until the weight of the evidence indicates that the trend has reversed. . . .

Since the technical approach is based on the theory that the price is a reflection of mass psychology ("the crowd") in action, it attempts to forecast future price movements on the assumption that crowd psychology moves between panic, fear, and pessimism on one hand and confidence, excessive optimism, and greed on the other. . . . [T]he art of technical analysis is concerned with identifying these changes at an early phase, since these swings in emotion take time to accomplish. Studying these market trends enables technically oriented investors to buy or sell with a degree of confidence, on the principle that once a trend is set in motion it will perpetuate itself.[1]

Pring thus views technical analysis as the art of being able to identify trends early.

In their popular book on technical analysis, Robert D. Edwards and John Magee define technical analysis as

the study of the action of the market itself as opposed to the study of the goods in which the market deals. Technical analysis is the science of recording, usually in graphic form, the actual history of trading (price changes, volume of transactions, etc.) in a certain stock or in "the averages" and then deducing from that pictured history the probable future trend.[2]

Whether technical analysis is an art (as Pring believes) or a science (as Edwards and Magee suggest), it is clear that it deals with making inferences about future price trends based on historical price information and other related data.

Is there any empirical evidence to support the usefulness of technical analysis? Recently, researchers have discovered patterns in security prices. For example, by monitoring stock price movements, Bruce N. Lehmann noted that when a stock price experienced a sizable fall one week, the next week the stock would bounce back, and when a stock price experienced a sizable rise one week, the next week the stock would fall back.[3] These trends do not always occur, but historically they have occurred with sufficient frequency to create many profit opportunities.

Narasimhan Jegadeesh also found predictable patterns in stock prices for monthly returns over a long period (1934 to 1987).[4] Specifically, Jegadeesh found strong evidence that the stocks with large losses in one month are likely to experi-

1. See Martin J. Pring, *Technical Analysis Explained* (New York: McGraw-Hill, 1991), pp. 2–3.
2. See Robert D. Edwards and John Magee, *Technical Analysis of Stock Trends*, 6th ed. (New York: New York Institute of Finance, 1992), p. 4.
3. See Bruce N. Lehmann, "Fads, Martingales, and Market Efficiency," *Quarterly Journal of Economics*, February 1990, pp. 1–28.
4. See Narasimhan Jegadeesh, "Evidence of Predictable Behavior of Security Returns," *Journal of Finance* 45 (July 1990): 881–898.

ence a significant reversal in the next month. Also, stocks with large gains in one month are likely to experience a significant loss in the next month. Finally, Jegadeesh documents clear seasonal patterns, a finding that supports the January effect mentioned in Chapter 12.

This evidence in favor of technical analysis is a direct challenge to the traditional view that markets are efficient and technical analysis is useless. Earlier research by Eugene F. Fama found evidence that markets are efficient.[5] Alternatively, more recent research identifies patterns in historical stock prices.[6] This more recent empirical evidence gives merit to the use of technical analysis.

13.2   CHARTING

To the technical analyst, the chart is the place to find clues regarding the future price direction of an asset. Technical analysis use several different charts, including bar charts, point-and-figure charts, and candlestick charts. All these charts are based on historical prices. Thus, the users of these charts obviously do not believe in weak-form market efficiency.

13.2.1 Bar Charts

Bar charts are charts that illustrate each day's (or week's or month's) high, low, and closing price movements for a specified time period. Exhibit 13-1 shows a bar chart of Coca-Cola Company stock price for one week (August 4 to 8, 1997), and Exhibit 13-2 presents the data used to plot it. For example, on Tuesday the high for Coke was $68.8125; the low was $68, which was also that day's closing price. In Exhibit 13-1, the straight lines give the distance between the high and low prices, and the protruding horizontal nubs designate the closing prices.

Technical analysts use bar charts to determine trends and to observe when these trends will reverse themselves. The **trendline** is a line drawn on a bar chart to identify a trend where the angle of this line will indicate if it is an up or down trend line. For example, Exhibit 13-3 shows both an up trendline and a down trendline.

In Exhibit 13-3a, an up trendline is drawn to touch the lowest prices over several days. Exhibit 13-3b shows a down trendline drawn to touch the two highest prices over several days.

Historical price data are used to draw trendlines. However, the precise manner in which technical analysts draw up and down trendlines is an art. That is, there is no widespread agreement about what criteria to use to establish when a trend has begun or about exactly how to draw the trendlines. Also, the number of days to check in order to select from the two lowest points is arbitrary.

---

5. See Eugene F. Fama, "Efficient Capital Markets: A Review of Theory and Empirical Work," *Journal of Finance* 25 (1970): 383–417.
6. See, for example, Eugene F. Fama and Kenneth R. French, "Permanent and Temporary Components of Stock Prices," *Journal of Political Economy* 98 (1988): 247–273; Kenneth R. French and Richard Roll, "Stock Return Variances: The Arrival of Information and Reaction of Traders," *Journal of Financial Economics* 17 (1986): 5–26; and Andrew W. Lo and A. Craig MacKinlay, "Stock Market Prices Do Not Follow Random Walks: Evidence from a Simple Specification Test," *Review of Financial Studies* 1 (1988): 41–66.

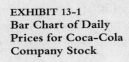

EXHIBIT 13-1
Bar Chart of Daily Prices for Coca-Cola Company Stock

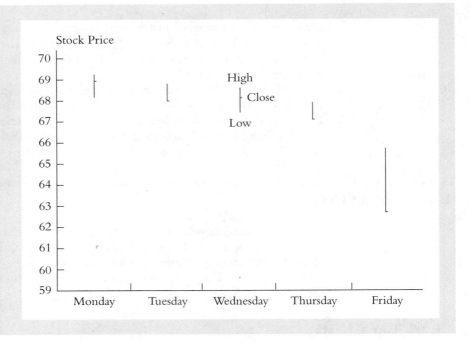

Once analysts have drawn a trendline, they follow stock prices to identify changes in the trend. Exhibit 13-3a examines historical prices over the last *n* days and uses the lowest two points to draw the up trendline. Of course, other criteria could have been used.

A trendline is said to be penetrated when market prices move across it. This penetration is viewed as a sell signal for an up trendline and a buy signal for a down trendline. When a trendline is penetrated by a "sufficient" magnitude, technical analysts say the trend has changed.

A **channel** is a pattern formed when two lines are drawn on a bar chart. Exhibit 13-4 illustrates up and down trend channels. An up trend channel (Exhibit 13-4a) is formed by first drawing the up trendline (the lower line) and then drawing another line near the two recent highs but also parallel with the up trendline. The line above

	Day	**High**	**Low**	**Close**
EXHIBIT 13-2 **Daily Prices for Coca-Cola Company (August 4 to 8, 1997)**	Monday	69.25	68.125	68.9375
	Tuesday	68.8125	68	68
	Wednesday	68.625	67.4375	68.125
	Thursday	67.9375	67.125	67.125
	Friday	65.75	62.6875	62.6875

EXHIBIT 13-3
Trendlines in Technical Analysis

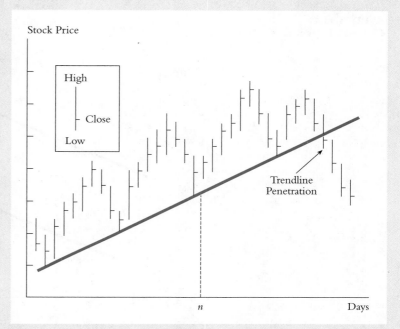

Part a: Penetration of an
Up Trendline

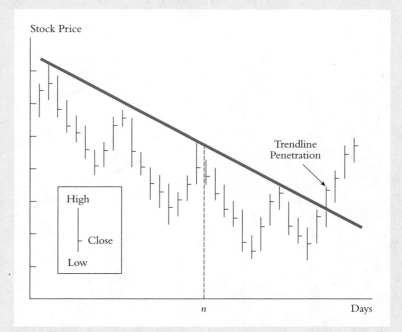

Part b: Penetration of a
Down Trendline

Source: Thomas A. Meyers, *The Technical Analysis Course* (Chicago: Probus Publishing, 1989), pp. 102, 103. Reprinted with permission of The McGraw–Hill Companies.

EXHIBIT 13-4
Channels in Technical Analysis

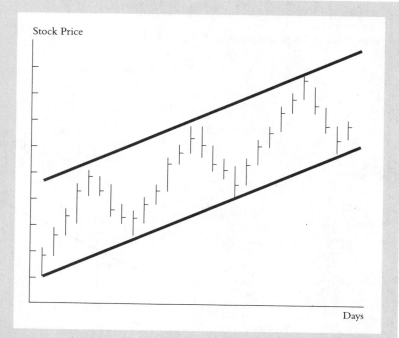

Part a: Up Trend Channel

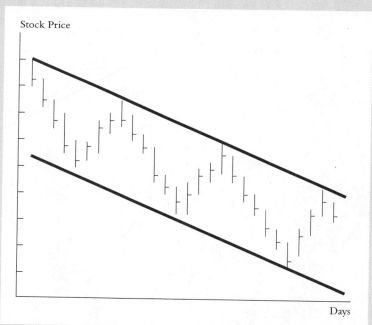

Part b: Down Trend Channel

Source: Thomas A. Meyers, *The Technical Analysis Course* (Chicago: Probus Publishing, 1989), pp. 109–110. Reprinted with permission of The McGraw-Hill Companies.

the bar chart cannot touch the two recent highs, because channels require that the two lines be parallel. The down trendline is drawn in a similar fashion (see Exhibit 13-4b).

Technical analysts believe that if stock prices do not reach the upper line of an up trend channel during a rally, then the price will fall below the lower trendline. They also assert that if stock prices do not reach the lower line of a down trend channel as prices fall, then the price will rise above the down trend channel.

Technical analysts also use bar charts to establish patterns of support and resistance (see Exhibit 13-5). The idea behind these patterns is that within a certain price range, demand and supply factors influence a security's price movement. When prices rise, a number of sellers enter the market, causing the stock prices to fall. This downward price movement is known as **resistance.** Resistance is the upper bound on prices due to the quantity of willing sellers at that price level. When prices fall, a number of buyers enter the market, causing the stock prices to rise. This upward price movement is known as **support.** Support is the lower bound on prices due to the quantity of willing buyers at that price level.

For example, in Exhibit 13-5a, at the first resistance level, a sufficient number of shareholders are willing to sell, which keeps the price from rising above this resistance level. Once the resistance level is broken, the price moves up until supply exceeds demand and the rising price is hindered. Some technical analysts would buy when the resistance level is broken (point *A* in Exhibit 13-5a) and sell when another higher resistance level is established (point *B* in Exhibit 13-5a). Technical analysts try to profit by buying when demand exceeds supply and then subsequently selling when supply exceeds demand.

Support works in the same way, except buyers are willing to buy more shares when prices fall. Exhibit 13-5b shows how support and resistance are used in a declining market. Some technical analysts would short sell when the support level is broken (point *A* in Exhibit 13-5b) and buy back once another lower support level is established (point *B* in Exhibit 13-5b).

13.2.2 Point-and-Figure Charts

In contrast to bar charts, which look at stock price behavior over time, **point-and-figure charts** attempt to identify reversals in the direction of stock prices without consideration of time. Exhibit 13-6 is a point-and-figure chart constructed with daily closing prices. Notice that the chart is a series of Xs and Os positioned on a grid (see Exhibit 13-6a). The Xs represent price increases of $2 or more, and the Os represent price decreases of $2 or more. For example, in Exhibit 13-6b, the stock price initially was at $18, and its first $2 move was up. Therefore, an *X* was placed in the first column by $20. Over the next few days the stock finally surpassed the $22 mark (without first falling below $18), so another *X* was placed in the first column at $22. Once again the stock rose to $24, so yet another *X* was added in the first column. After the price reached $24, the stock price fell more than $2. To show this, an *O* was placed in the second column on the row at $22. In this case, the price continued to fall to $16.

All of the trendline analysis, channels, and support and resistance information used in bar charts also can be applied to point-and-figure charts. Compare the general

EXHIBIT 13-5
Support and Resistance in Technical Analysis

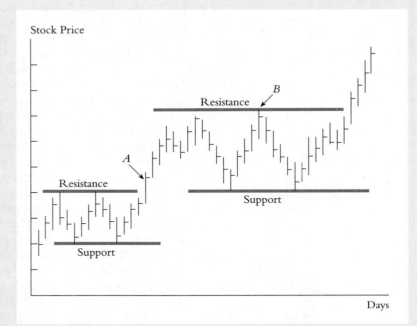

Part a: Rising Support and Resistance

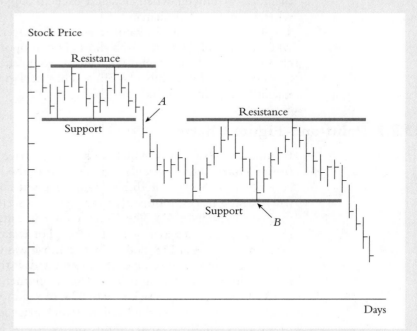

Part b: Declining Support and Resistance

Source: Thomas A. Meyers, *The Technical Analysis Course* (Chicago: Probus Publishing, 1989), pp. 120, 121. Reprinted with permission of The McGraw-Hill Companies.

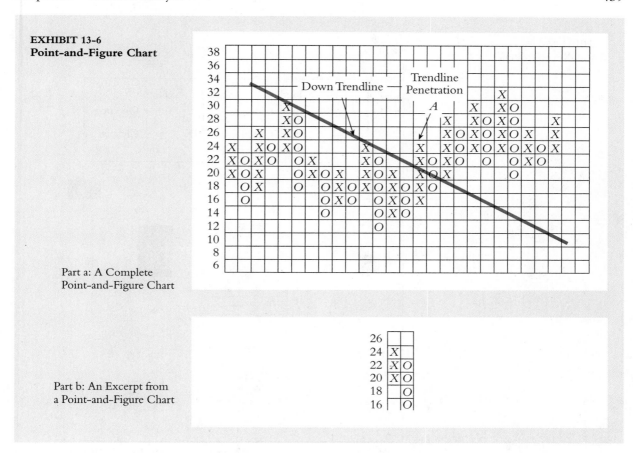

EXHIBIT 13-6
Point-and-Figure Chart

Part a: A Complete
Point-and-Figure Chart

Part b: An Excerpt from
a Point-and-Figure Chart

pattern in Exhibit 13-6 with Exhibits 13-1, 13-3, 13-4, and 13-5. Clearly, bar charts and point-and-figure charts look generally similar. Thus, technical rules developed for bar charts are also applied to point-and-figure charts. For example, some technical analysts would draw a down trendline, as illustrated in Exhibit 13-6a. Point A shows a trendline penetration, and the technical analyst might view this as a bullish sign for this stock. Hence, point-and-figure charts are another popular tool of the technical analyst.

13.2.3 Candlestick Charts

The **candlestick chart,** another tool of the technical analyst, was developed in Japan and has been used there for a long time. Only recently has the candlestick chart become popular in the United States and other countries. Exhibit 13-7 shows a candlestick chart of the daily price data from Exhibit 13-8. The only piece of data used for candlestick charts that is not included in bar charts is the opening price. Each observation on a candlestick chart is based on a day's opening, high, low, and

EXHIBIT 13-7
A Candlestick Chart

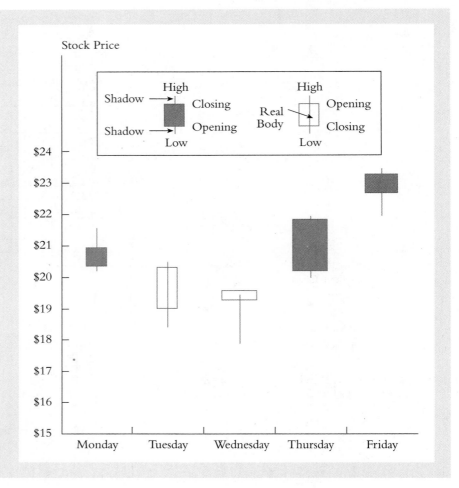

EXHIBIT 13-8	**Day**	**Open**	**High**	**Low**	**Close**
Daily Prices	Monday	$20.375	$21.5	$20.25	$20.875
for Borland	Tuesday	20.25	20.5	18.125	19
International Inc.	Wednesday	19.5	19.5	17.75	19.25
	Thursday	20.25	22	20	21.875
	Friday	22.5	23.125	21.375	23

closing prices. The candlestick chart is similar in many ways to the bar chart in that it maps the price movement over time. For each day, the chart contains a **candle-stick line.** There are two parts to the candlestick line. The **real body** is the broad part consisting of the difference between the opening and closing prices, and the **shadows** are the vertical thin lines above and below the real body. If the opening price is above the closing price, then the real body is shaded dark. Alternatively, if the opening price is below the closing price, then the real body is not shaded. Candlestick charts can also be constructed with intraday data, weekly data, and so forth.

PRACTICE BOX

Problem

Examine the following data for Merck stock prices. Suppose that on Day 6 a technical analyst analyzed the data for Days 1 through 6. What would the analyst most likely conclude? If the analyst had acted on that conclusion, would the action have been profitable?

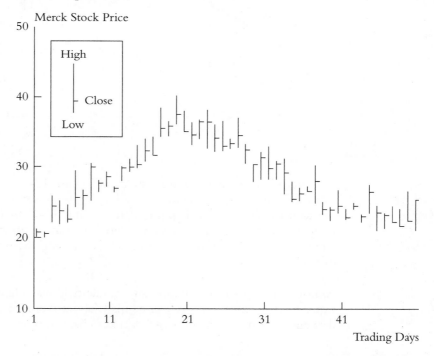

Solution

The technical analyst most likely would have identified an up trendline, as shown in the following chart. Notice that the trendline connects the two lowest points. In this particular case, the technical analysis would have proven to be very profitable. Suppose that Merck was purchased at $25 on Day 7 after the up trendline was established on Day 6. Merck was then sold at $32 on Day 24 after the up trend was violated on Day 23, and the sell signal was given on Day 23 (see the following chart). Hence, a profit of $7 per share (a rate of return of $7/$25 = 0.28, or 28%) was achieved over a period of eighteen days.

(continued)

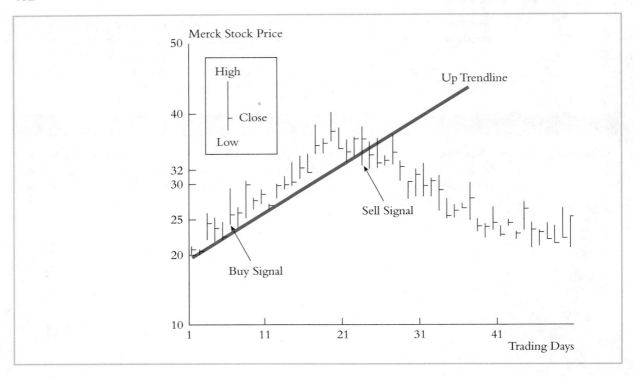

The symbol shown for Wednesday in Exhibit 13-7 is called a *hammer* in a down market (hammering out a base) and a *hanging man* in an up market (the market is going to leave the investor hanging).[7] In Exhibit 13-7, Wednesday's result would be interpreted as a hammer and is considered by some technical analysts as a buy signal. There are many other interpretations of candlestick charts that are beyond the scope of this book.[8]

Although bar, point-and-figure, and candlestick charts have vastly different applications, certain generalizations can be made about them. Exhibit 13-9 summarizes the data and the time horizon of each kind of chart, as well as its applications.

EXHIBIT 13-9 Summary of Charts		**Bar Chart**	**Point-and-Figure Chart**	**Candlestick Chart**
	Data Used	High, low, close	Close	Open, high, low, close
	Time Horizon	Days	None	Days
	Applications	Trendlines (channels, support, resistance)	Trendlines (channels, support, resistance)	Depends on pattern and shapes

7. Based on Steve Nison, *Introduction to Japanese Candle Charts* (New York: Merrill Lynch, Pierce, Fenner & Smith, 1991), p. 3.
8. The interested reader can find several books on candlestick charts. The technical analysis books in this chapter's Selected References and Supplemental References all discuss candlestick charts.

13.3 THEORETICAL BASIS OF TECHNICAL ANALYSIS

Technical analysts use certain tools with their charts to discern the future path of asset prices. Most interpretation of charts finds its roots in the Dow Theory. This section examines the basic tenets of the Dow Theory, as well as some of the other tools used by technical analysts.

13.3.1 Dow Theory

Most approaches to technical analysis assume that financial prices follow some sort of market cycle model. That is, overall prices tend to move through long trends of either rising or falling prices. Exhibit 13-10 illustrates a model of a market cycle. In theory, every 4 to 4½ years, the market moves through a complete cycle. The broad double line, known as the **primary trend** cycle, represents this 4-to-4½-year cycle. Technical analysts assert that such broad trends appear in currencies, stocks, bonds, commodities, and other financial assets. The solid black line that has more wave is known as the **intermediate trend,** which has a much shorter duration (from 3 weeks to 6 months). Finally, the **short-term trend,** denoted by the dotted line, documents much more volatility and is more erratic.

The first person to note these trends was Charles Dow (the founder of the Dow Jones news service), around 1900. The theory became known as the **Dow Theory,** and Charles Dow became known as the grandfather of technical analysis. In its original form, the Dow Theory asserted that a bull market is established when both the

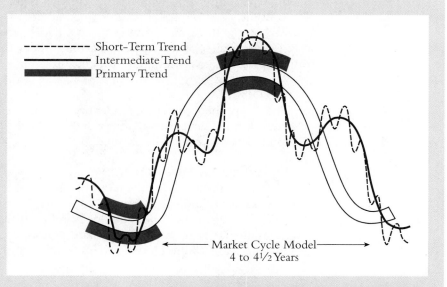

EXHIBIT 13-10
The Market Cycle Model of Technical Analysis

- - - - - - - - - Short-Term Trend
——————— Intermediate Trend
■■■■■■■ Primary Trend

Market Cycle Model
4 to 4½ Years

Source: Martin J. Pring, *Technical Analysis Explained* (New York: McGraw-Hill, 1991), p. 14. Reprinted with permission of The McGraw-Hill Companies.

Dow Jones Industrial Average and the Dow Jones Transportation Average are moving up. A bear market is established when the two indexes are moving down. The basic tenets of the Dow Theory can be summarized as follows:

1. No additional information is needed for the stock market outside of data on stock indexes.
2. The financial market has three distinct types of movements: the primary trend, the intermediate trend, and short-term trends.
3. There is usually a positive relationship between a trend and the volume of shares traded.

The Dow Theory has been extended and reworked in many different ways. Most technical analysis theories originate from it. Connecting Theory to Practice 13.1 shows that the Dow Theory is still a popular technical tool.

CONNECTING THEORY TO PRACTICE 13.1

ADHERENTS OF THE DOW THEORY ON STOCK TRENDS DISAGREE OVER WHEN THE BULL MARKET WILL END

NEW YORK—Followers of the venerable Dow Theory are feuding again about the stock market.

The stock market is in a bull trend, nobody disputes that. But advocates of the 90-year-old Dow Theory—which seeks to identify stock market trends using two key Dow Jones stock market averages—can't agree on the next important turning point, when the bull market is going to end.

While stock market theories come and go, the Dow Theory lives on. It's based on the stock market writings of Charles Dow, a founder of Dow Jones & Co., publisher of the *Wall Street Journal*. Today fervent believers in the Dow Theory are relatively few, but many investors still keep an eye on it.

"A TOOL"
"The Dow Theory is a tool to identify" broad stock market trends, says Hugh Johnson, chief investment officer at First Albany. "And the one thing you should never do is ignore the trend." . . .

"CORPORATE DINOSAURS"
Other analysts don't like the theory because of the weight it gives to the Dow Jones Industrial Average. Peter Canelo, chief investment strategist at County NatWest, suggests that the Dow Jones industrials are weighted down by old-line industrial companies—"corporate dinosaurs," he calls them—that don't adequately reflect the growing role of technology and service companies in the nation's economy.

(continued)

"The problem with the Dow Theory is that the Dow Jones Industrial Average has become grossly misrepresentative of the whole stock market," Mr. Canelo says. "Even if you think Dow Theory has some usefulness, I'm not sure the Dow industrials is the index you want to use for confirmations." . . .

But defenders of the Dow Theory are adamant. Mr. Evans [Richard Evans, a Flossmoor, Illinois, investment adviser who writes about Dow Theory] contends that Dow Theory isn't meant as an early warning tool. Rather, it is a safety valve that helps investors participate in upward trends and avoid major losses during the downward swings.

"If the Dow Theory signals a bear market after a 10% to 15% decline, sure, it may be late," Mr. Evans says. "But what if the market is going down another 40%? What the theory can do is help people avoid really big losses."

Source: Steven E. Levingston, "Adherents of the Dow Theory on Stock Trends Disagree Over When the Bull Market Will End," *Wall Street Journal*, February 1, 1993, p. C1. Reprinted by permission of *The Wall Street Journal*, © 1993, Dow Jones & Co., Inc. All Rights Reserved Worldwide.

MAKING THE CONNECTION

This article shows that the Dow Theory is still followed fervently by a few analysts, but many investors are wary of it. Because the Dow Jones Industrial Average is composed of mainly industrial stocks, many analysts believe that it is no longer representative of U.S. stocks. Thus, some analysts have taken the theory and applied it to a broader-based index, such as the S&P 500. In any event, because many investors still believe it is a credible theory, it is important for investors to be aware of it.

Two of the more popular tools derived from the Dow Theory are moving averages and relative strength.

13.3.2 Moving Averages

One of the most popular tools of technical analysis is the **moving average.** A simple moving average is built by taking the arithmetic average of a stock price over the past predetermined number of days and graphing these results over a period of time. For example, Exhibit 13-11 gives the closing prices of a stock for twenty days. The five-day moving average is found by taking closing prices for the past five days, adding them up, and dividing by 5. For example, on August 8, the five-day moving average can be calculated as

$$(68.9375 + 68 + 68.125 + 66.5625 + 62.6875)/5 = 66.8625$$

and on August 11, the earliest day (8/4) is dropped, and the most recent one (8/11) is added. This process continues across the entire data set. Exhibit 13-12 illustrates graphically the five-day moving average.

EXHIBIT 13-11 Calculating a Five-Day Simple Moving Average for Coca-Cola Company

Date	Closing Price	Five-Day Total (A)	Five-Day Simple Moving Average (A/5)
8/4/97	$68.9375		
8/5/97	68		
8/6/97	68.125		
8/7/97	66.5625		
8/8/97	62.6875	$334.3125	$66.8625
8/11/97	63.75	329.125	65.825
8/12/97	60.9375	322.0625	64.4125
8/13/97	60.4375	314.375	62.875
8/14/97	60.125	307.9375	61.5875
8/15/97	58.75	304	60.8
8/18/97	60.375	300.625	60.125
8/19/97	60.8125	300.5	60.1
8/20/97	61.5	301.5625	60.3125
8/21/97	60.5625	302	60.4
8/22/97	60.6875	303.9375	60.7875
8/25/97	59.6875	303.25	60.65
8/26/97	59	301.4375	60.2875
8/27/97	58.625	298.5625	59.7125
8/28/97	58.25	296.25	59.25
8/29/97	57.3125	292.875	58.575

Source: *Daily Stock Price Record* (New York: Standard and Poor's, 1997), p. 117. Reprinted by permission of Standard & Poor's, a division of The McGraw-Hill Companies.

Most technical analysts use moving averages for longer time periods. For example, one popular approach is that if the Dow Jones Industrial Average is above its two-hundred-day moving average, then security prices should rise, and if it is below its two-hundred-day moving average, then security prices should fall. Many technical analysts use moving averages in an attempt to identify the primary, intermediate, and short-term trends.

Moving averages can also be used with individual stocks. For example, if a particular stock's price has been falling, then the moving average will typically be above the bar chart. If the stock's price subsequently rallies, breaking through the moving average line from below, technical analysts view this as a bullish sign. Alternatively, if a particular stock's price has been rising, then the moving average will typically be below the bar chart. If the stock's price subsequently falls, breaking through the moving average line from above, technical analysts view this as a bearish sign. As with other technical analysts' tools, there are many possible interpretations of moving averages.

EXHIBIT 13-12
A Five-Day Simple Moving Average Based on the Closing Price for Hypothetical Data
The bar chart is based on high, low, and closing prices.

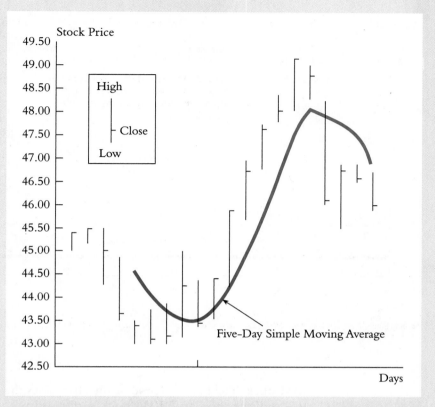

Source: Thomas A. Meyers, *The Technical Analysis Course* (Chicago: Probus Publishing, 1989) p. 137. Reprinted with permission of The McGraw-Hill Companies.

13.3.3 Relative Strength

Many technical analysts use **relative strength** to assess a security. Relative strength measures the relationship between two historical series of financial assets' data (the rate at which one asset falls or rises relative to the second asset). Although relative strength can be expressed in various ways, it is typically expressed as a ratio of the price performance of one asset or index to the price performance of another asset or index. For example, a technical analyst might use relative strength to compare the overall market performance as measured, for example, by the S&P 500 with the performance of a certain stock. This relative strength index (RSI) can range from 0% to 100%.[9] A high RSI value means that industry stock prices have been outperforming the market.

Exhibit 13-13 gives prices of IBM stock and the RSI level for this stock during the period July 1995–August 1996. The top curve of the chart shows the price of

9. The actual numerical calculation is complex. RSI is widely available from data and analysis services such as Bloomberg.

EXHIBIT 13-13   **The Relative Strength of IBM Stock (July 1995–August 1996)**

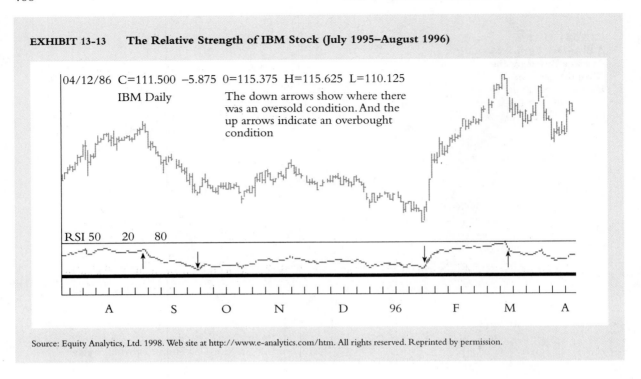

04/12/86 C=111.500 –5.875 0=115.375 H=115.625 L=110.125

IBM Daily   The down arrows show where there
                   was an oversold condition. And the
                   up arrows indicate an overbought
                   condition

RSI 50   20   80

A   S   O   N   D   96   F   M   A

IBM stock. The bottom curve of the chart gives the RSI value for IBM. Thus, the RSI indicates how well IBM stock performed relative to the other stocks (represented by some stock index like the S&P 500). Exhibit 13-13 shows that it is possible that the price of the stock will rise sharply while its RSI value will fall (see March 1996), due to a sharper rise in the S&P 500 index price.

Some technical analysts believe that high RSI values indicate a sell signal, and low RSI values indicate a buy signal. Many analysts are now using the RSI value of 20 for buy signals and 80 for sell signals (see Exhibit 13-13). Alternatively, some technical analysts believe "the trend is your friend." That is, high values of RSI indicate a buy signal, because trends are believed to be persistent. In this view, an investor would sell only after the RSI value had fallen substantially. There are many sources for obtaining relative strength values, including *Investor's Business Daily* and most data services, such as Bloomberg.

13.4 TECHNICAL INDICATORS

At the very heart of technical analysis are charts that use technical indicators to interpret trends. Technical indicators typically draw from additional historical market-related data, such as volume of trading. Several technical indicators are believed to be leading indicators of future security price movements. These indicators can be classified as **breadth indicators,** which highlight overall market strength or weakness, and **sentiment indicators,** which highlight traders' opinions about the market. Because technical analyses rely on historical prices as well as other information (for example, volume), these methods are based on the semistrong inefficiency model of the market.

13.4.1 Breadth Indicators

Breadth indicators include the advance–decline line, volume, and new high/new low indicators. The **advance–decline line** is the number of advancing issues (stocks whose prices have gone up from the previous day) minus the number of declining issues (stocks whose prices have gone down from the previous day) on a particular day plus the cumulative total from the previous day (so trends can be monitored). Exhibit 13–14 provides some stock data from the NYSE Composite Index, a value-weighted index of all stocks traded on the NYSE. On January 12, 1998, advances (1,343) were lower than declines (1,710) by 367. Hence, the advance–decline line would be reduced by 367 on January 12. The advance–decline line on Day t (ADL_t) is the number of the advancing issues on Day t (A_t) minus the number of declining issues on Day t (D_t) plus the cumulative total from the previous day (ADL_{t-1}). That is,

$$ADL_t = A_t - D_t + ADL_{t-1}$$

In this case, if $ADL_{1/11} = 1,500$, we have

$$ADL_{1/12} = 1,343 - 1,710 + 1,500 = 1,133$$

EXHIBIT 13-14 NYSE Composite Index Daily Breadth	Daily	Jan. 12	Jan. 13	Jan. 14	Jan. 15	Jan. 16
	Issues traded	3,495	3,465	3,469	3,469	3,471
	Advances	**1,343**	**2,136**	**1,877**	**1,350**	**2,133**
	Declines	**1,710**	**864**	**1,080**	**1,608**	**854**
	Unchanged	442	465	512	511	484
	New highs	86	106	129	109	165
	New lows	191	42	34	50	27
	Blocks	14,964	13,822	12,452	12,264	13,730
	Total (000)	815,076	761,348	707,540	676,613	783,384

Source: "NYSE Composite Daily Breadth," *Barron's,* January 19, 1998, p. MW100. Reprinted by permission of Barron's, © 1998 Dow Jones & Co., Inc. All Rights Reserved Worldwide.

On January 13, 14, and 16, the advances led the declines, so the advance-decline line would rise on each of these days by the difference between advances and declines. Most technical analysts view a falling advance-decline line in a rising market as bearish and a rising advance-decline line in a falling market as bullish.

PRACTICE BOX

Problem	Assuming the advance-decline line had a value of 1,500 on January 11, use the data in Exhibit 13-14 to calculate the advance-decline line for January 12 through 16.
Solution	From the text, we know that

$$ADL_t = A_t - D_t + ADL_{t-1}$$

and we can construct the following table:

Date	A_t	D_t	ADL_t
Jan. 11			1,500
Jan. 12	1,343	1,710	1,133
Jan. 13	2,136	864	2,405
Jan. 14	1,877	1,080	3,202
Jan. 15	1,350	1,608	2,944
Jan. 16	2,133	854	4,223

Thus, the advance-decline line rose during the week of January 12, 1998.

Many breadth indicators are based on trading volume, because technical analysts interpret changes in trading volume as indicators of the size of future price changes in securities. Most financial media report the volume of trading in individual securities. For example, a sharp rise in volume of a stock whose price has been rising is interpreted as a signal of even more dramatic price increases in the future. Alternatively, a sharp rise in volume of a stock whose price has been falling is interpreted to signal even more dramatic price declines in the future.

Technical analysts also monitor trading volume for groups of stocks. For example, changes in the total volume of trading for stocks in the Dow Jones Industrial Average would be interpreted in the same manner as increases in the volume of an individual stock. Technical analysts also monitor the relative changes in volume. For example, when the volume of the smaller, over-the-counter stocks goes up as compared with the larger NYSE stocks, technical analysts interpret this trend as increased speculative activity—investors choosing riskier OTC stocks—that usually occurs at market tops. Connecting Theory to Practice 13.2 illustrates how practicing technical analysts interpret volume changes.

CONNECTING THEORY TO PRACTICE 13.2

HEAVY VOLUME AND LAGGING BLUE CHIPS MAY POINT TO COMING DECLINE IN STOCKS

NEW YORK—The warning flags are flying.

The heavy trading volume on both the New York Stock Exchange and the Nasdaq over-the-counter market in recent weeks signal that chances are growing for a sharp drop in stock prices, say some analysts.

"All the volume right now is an amber warning light for a few months down the road," says Jack Solomon, a technical analyst at Bear Stearns.

"[High volume with a declining Dow Jones Industrial Average] indicates to me that the market is at a point of inefficiency where there's more supply of stock than demand," [says A.C. Moore, a portfolio manager and stock market strategist in Santa Barbara, California].

Other analysts say that danger also lurks in the feverish trading in small stocks on the over-the-counter market. Over-the-counter trading volume has exceeded Big Board volume in eight of the past 12 weeks. And now, ironically, it's rising small-stock prices along with that heavy trading volume that is the threatening combination. It suggests that speculators are accounting for a large portion of the trading.

"When Nasdaq volume exceeds NYSE volume, it signals excessive speculation in the marketplace, which usually occurs at market highs," says Bernadette Murphy, director of technical analysis at money-management firm M. Kimelman & Co.

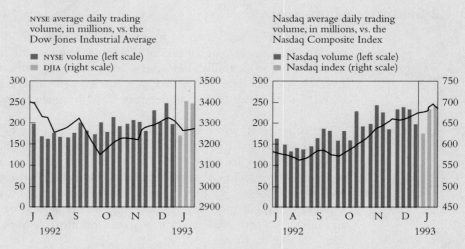

NYSE average daily trading volume, in millions, vs. the Dow Jones Industrial Average

■ NYSE volume (left scale)
■ DJIA (right scale)

Nasdaq average daily trading volume, in millions, vs. the Nasdaq Composite Index

■ Nasdaq volume (left scale)
■ Nasdaq index (right scale)

Source: Steven E. Levingston, "Heavy Volume and Lagging Blue Chips May Point to Coming Decline in Stocks," *Wall Street Journal,* January 18, 1993, p. C1. Reprinted by permission of *The Wall Street Journal* © 1993 Dow Jones & Co., Inc. All Rights Reserved Worldwide.

(continued)

MAKING THE CONNECTION

The heavy volume of trading has many technical analysts concerned, especially because the Dow Jones Industrial Average has declined. High volume and declining market prices indicate that there are more sellers than buyers in the marketplace. If the supply imbalance persists, then clearly market prices will continue to fall. It is unclear, however, whether lower market prices will induce a large number of buyers back into the marketplace.

The last category of breadth indicators to be described is related to the number of stocks hitting new fifty-two-week highs when compared with the number of stocks hitting new fifty-two-week lows (see Exhibit 13-14). Breadth is typically measured as the ratio of new highs to new lows. Hence, from Exhibit 13-14, breadth would be calculated as follows:

Date	Jan. 12	Jan. 13	Jan. 14	Jan. 15	Jan. 16
Breadth	$86/191 \cong 0.45$	$106/42 \cong 2.52$	$129/34 \cong 3.79$	$109/50 \cong 2.18$	$165/27 \cong 6.11$

When the breadth is declining in a rising market, it is thought to be a signal that the bull market is stalling. Hence, many technical analysts keep an eye on the trend in the ratio of new highs to new lows.

13.4.2 Sentiment Indicators

Sentiment indicators attempt to gauge the overall mood, or sentiments, of investors. One measure of sentiment is a comparison of the number of stock market newsletters that are bullish with the number of those that are bearish. Technical analysts typically believe that on average, stock market newsletters are wrong. Hence, when the majority of newsletters are bearish, analysts interpret this as a bullish sign.

Another sentiment indicator is based on the quantity of **odd-lot trading.** Recall that an odd lot is any transaction that is less than 100 shares (the trading in multiples of 100 is known as a *round lot*). Odd-lot trading is typically done by small investors, who, technical analysts believe, are usually wrong. Hence, technical analysts see odd-lot buying that exceeds odd-lot selling as a bearish signal, because they believe that small investors typically buy at the wrong time. One source for the amount of odd-lot trading is the market laboratory section related to stocks in the financial weekly *Barron's*.

Another sentiment indicator is the **put/call ratio,** which is found by dividing the volume of put option trading by the volume of call option trading (see Chapters 23 and 24). Technical analysts view excessive put buying as a bearish signal and excessive call buying as a bullish signal. Investors buy put options, which give them the right to sell stocks in the future, when they believe that stock prices will fall. Alternatively, investors buy call options, which give them the right to buy stocks in the future, when they believe that stock prices will rise. Therefore, when the volume of put buying exceeds the volume of call buying, it indicates that option buyers in the aggregate are bearish.

Finally, technical analysts also monitor the amount of short selling done by specialists. Recall that the specialist is the market maker on the NYSE. Specialists typically have superior information regarding a stock (they have the limit book—see Chapter 3) and are perceived as particularly good speculators. Hence, when specialists are selling short, it is a signal that the stock may decline. Specialists are also perceived as insiders, and investors want to mimic specialists' trading activities. Specialist short selling indicates a bearish view on a stock; hence, technical analysts would view increases in specialist short positions as bearish.

SUMMARY

Describe a technical analyst's view of the market. Technical analysts believe that prices reflect investors' attitudes, which at times may not be entirely rational. Thus, technical analysts believe that by studying historical market data they can find clues regarding the future direction of security prices.

Explain how technical analysts use charts to make inferences about future prices. Technical analysts plot market data on charts, such as bar charts, point-and-figure charts, and candlestick charts. The charts display historical information that enables technical analysts to extrapolate trends into the future.

Identify the basic tools used by technical analysts. Most technical analysis procedures originate from the Dow Theory, which is based on the idea that prices tend to move in primary, intermediate, and short-term trends. These trends are assessed using such tools as moving averages and relative strength. Moving averages are obtained by averaging the most recent past price data. Relative strength measures the price performance of one portfolio or index against another.

Describe some popular technical indicators. Two popular technical indicators are the breadth and sentiment indicators. The breadth indicators include the advance-decline line, volume, and new high/new low indicators. The advance-decline line measures the number of stocks that rose compared with the number of stocks that fell. Sentiment indicators include stock market newsletters, odd-lot trading, the put/call ratio (a measure based on the volume of put and call option trading), and specialist short selling.

CHAPTER AT A GLANCE

1. *The basic charts used by the technical analyst include the following:*
    a. The bar chart.
    b. The point-and-figure chart.
    c. The candlestick chart.

2. *The analytical tools used by the technical analyst include the following:*
  a. Moving averages.
  b. Relative strength.
  (These tools are derived from the Dow Theory.)

3. *The technical indicators used by the technical analyst include the following:*
  a. Breadth indicators.
    (1) Advance–decline line.
    (2) Volume.
    (3) New high/new low indicators.
  b. Sentiment indicators.
    (1) Stock market newsletters.
    (2) Odd-lot trading.
    (3) Put/call ratio.
    (4) Specialist short selling.

KEY TERMS

Advance–decline line   469
Bar chart   453
Breadth indicator   469
Candlestick chart   459
Candlestick line   460
Channel   454
Dow Theory   463
Intermediate trend   463

Moving average   465
Odd-lot trading   472
Point-and-figure chart   457
Primary trend   463
Put/call ratio   472
Real body   460
Relative strength   467
Resistance   457

Sentiment indicator   469
Shadow   461
Short-term trend   463
Support   457
Technical analysis   451
Trendline   453

REVIEW

13.1 Compare and contrast technical analysis and fundamental analysis.

13.2 Classify each of the following activities as either technical analysis or fundamental analysis.
a. Examining the "quality" of earnings.
b. Computing a percentage balance sheet.
c. Calculating the relative strength of the basic materials sector.
d. Identifying an up trendline on a bar chart.
e. Examining the debt/equity ratio of a firm.
f. Calculating the put/call ratio.

13.3 What is the assumption on which technical theories are typically built?

13.4 "All empirical research suggests that technical analysis is totally useless." Evaluate this statement.

13.5 Can a technical pattern that is statistically significant be economically insignificant? Explain.

PRACTICE

13.1 Given the following price data, draw a bar chart.

Day	High Price	Low Price	Closing Price
0	$53⅛	$50½	$51⅜
1	52	48⅛	49¾
2	53⅞	51¼	52½
3	54	52⅛	54
4	55⅜	54⅜	54⅞
5	54¾	52⅛	52¼
6	56⅞	55	56¾
7	58½	57	57⅛
8	59⅜	57½	58½
9	60⅛	59⅜	60
10	61	60½	61

13.2 Given the historical data of Johnson and Johnson, Inc. (J&J), in the following exhibit, chart a down trendline based on the highest two points in the first twenty days. What trading signal would have been produced, and would it have been profitable?

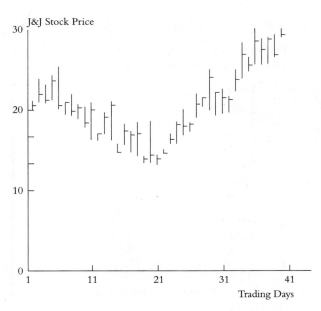

13.3 Given the data in Question 13.1, draw a point-and-figure chart using $1 gains and losses to determine when Xs and Os occur.

13.4 Given the following data for the past ten days, calculate the five-day moving average for Days 5 through 10.

Day	High Price	Low Price	Closing Price
1	$14⅞	$13¾	$14¼
2	15½	14⅞	15
3	17½	16⅛	16⅞
4	19	16⅛	18⅝
5	20½	17⅜	18⅜
6	18⅞	17¾	18⅝
7	22½	19½	21
8	22	20⅞	21⅞
9	25½	20⅜	24⅜
10	22¾	19⅞	22½

13.5 Assuming that the advance-decline line for stocks in the NYSE Composite had a value of 1,237 on Day 0, calculate the advance-decline line for each of the following days. (Complete the table, and discuss your results.)

Day	Index Value	Advancing Issues	Declining Issues
0			
1	250.13	1,055	1,199
2	248.37	1,757	580
3	251.87	1,143	1,194
4	252.11	757	1,410
5	253.98	969	1,197
6	254.54	722	1,418
7	255.01	938	1,193
8	254.39	906	1,260
9	257.72	645	1,460
10	260.18	862	1,230

13.6 Suppose the beta of a stock is 1.0, and the average rate of return over the past 20 years on the market portfolio was 12%. A technical analyst claims to have a method that signals buy and sell decisions. Over 10 years, she has made on average a return of 15% by trading in this stock.
a. In your view, does the technical analyst have a method with which to buy and sell successfully?
b. How would you change your answer if the beta of the stock were 2.0 and the risk-free interest rate were 4%?

13.7 Suppose you have the following bar chart showing the recent history of stock prices, and you already own the stock.

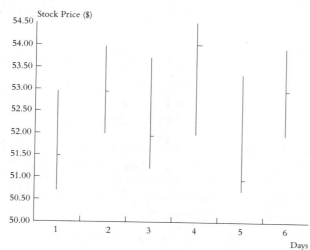

a. What is the trendline if it is based on the lowest two points in the first three trading days? When would you sell the stock?
b. How would your answer change if the trendline were drawn based on the first five days?

13.8 A stock price is at $100. Suppose it goes up every day by $⅛ (the lowest point = highest point = closing price). You want to draw a trendline.
a. Does it make a difference whether you take the lowest two points in the first five days or the lowest two points in the first twenty days?
b. How would you change your answer if the stock price went up every day by ⅛%?

13.9 Suppose you have the following prices:

Day	High Price	Low Price	Closing Price
1	$102	$ 98	$ 99
2	100	95	98
3	102	95	97½
4	101	100	100⅜

a. Make a freehand drawing of the resistance and support lines.
b. Suppose that on Days 5, 6, and 7, the prices hit a high of $95 and a low of $90. Would you buy or sell the stock?

13.10 Suppose you have the following prices of a given stock:

Day	Price
1	$100
2	99
3	97
4	96
5	93
6	96
7	99

Draw the point-and-figure chart for price moves of $2.

13.11 Suppose you are given the following data on the Dow Jones Industrial Average:

Day	Index
1	3,000
2	3,105
3	3,227
4	3,197
5	3,201
6	3,097
7	3,005
8	2,995
9	3,326
10	3,576

a. Calculate the three-day moving average for Days 3 through 10.

b. Suppose the index on Day 11 is above the three-day moving average. Would this signal a buy or sell decision?

13.12 Suppose we are given the following data on advancing issues and declining issues:

Day	Advancing Issues	Declining Issues
1	1,086	509
2	854	1,237
3	966	902
4	1,234	792
5	950	1,189

Assuming that the advance-decline line had a value of 1,887 on Day 0, calculate the advance-decline line for Days 1 through 5.

13.13 Suppose we are given the following information on new highs and new lows in the market:

Day	New High	New Low
1	70	20
2	80	10
3	60	30
4	85	15
5	100	8

a. Assess the breadth of the market each day.
b. Suppose the market was rising during these days. Would you buy or sell the stocks?

13.14 A specialist short position in Xerox stock is as follows:

Day	Position
1	1,000
2	1,200
3	1,300
4	1,800
5	2,000

Would you buy or sell the stock based on this information alone? Why?

13.15 Suppose you had the following information on the volume of put and call option trading:

Day	Put Volume	Call Volume
1	1.32	0.95
2	1.03	0.99
3	0.98	1.30
4	0.99	1.20
5	0.95	1.35

Compute the put/call ratio. What would you conclude based on this technical index?

13.16 The following table summarizes one measure of market sentiment as of January 19, 1998:

Investors' Intelligence

	Last Week	Two Weeks Ago	Three Weeks Ago
Bulls	46.3%	45.9%	47.6%
Bears	35.0	36.9	35.2
Correction	18.7	17.2	17.2

Source: *Barron's,* June 19, 1998, p. MW107.

Explain the bulls-bears sentiment. What can be learned from changes in the proportions of bulls and bears? Analyze the changes in these proportions as given in the table.

13.17 The bar chart at the top of page 478 shows the Dow Jones Industrial Averages up to January 18, 1998.
a. Explain this bar chart by referring to the two days with the highest gap between the high and low prices (about Day 50 on the chart).
b. Suppose that every ten days, you examine the data to figure out whether there is a trend. You connect two points during these ten days with the lowest (or highest) prices. Describe your investment policy, which follows from the technical rule introduced here (analyze only the first twenty days, that is, two decision dates).

13.18 In its "Charting the Market" section, *Barron's* analyzes a few firms every week. The exhibit at the bottom of page 478 shows four firms. Based on the bar charts showing the last five days, what would you recommend for each of these four firms (buy, sell, or hold) when you decide to establish the

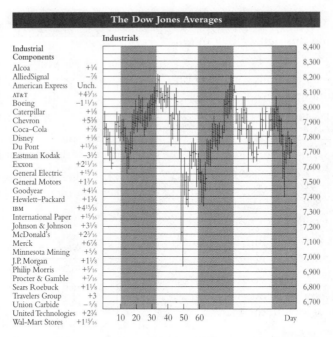

The Dow Jones Averages

Industrial Components	
Alcoa	+1/4
AlliedSignal	−7/8
American Express	Unch.
AT&T	+4 5/16
Boeing	−1 11/16
Caterpillar	+1/8
Chevron	+5 5/8
Coca-Cola	+7/8
Disney	+1/8
Du Pont	+13/16
Eastman Kodak	−3 1/2
Exxon	+2 11/16
General Electric	+15/16
General Motors	+1 3/16
Goodyear	+4 1/4
Hewlett-Packard	+1 3/4
IBM	+4 15/16
International Paper	+15/16
Johnson & Johnson	+3 1/8
McDonald's	+2 3/16
Merck	+6 7/8
Minnesota Mining	+5/8
J.P. Morgan	+1 1/8
Philip Morris	+5/16
Procter & Gamble	+7/16
Sears Roebuck	+1 1/8
Travelers Group	+3
Union Carbide	−5/8
United Technologies	+2 3/4
Wal-Mart Stores	+1 15/16

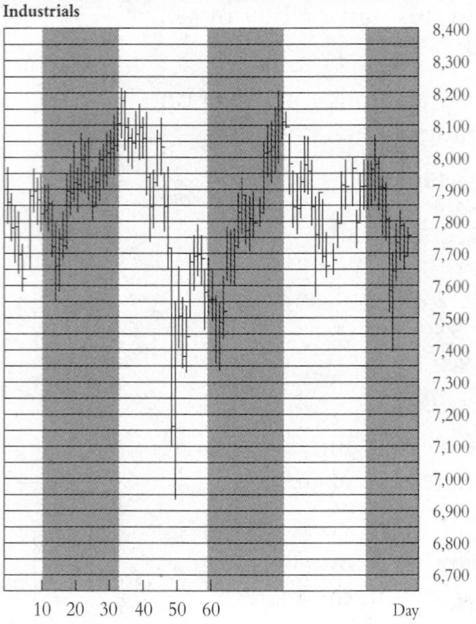
Industrials
8,400
8,300
8,200
8,100
8,000
7,900
7,800
7,700
7,600
7,500
7,400
7,300
7,200
7,100
7,000
6,900
6,800
6,700
10 20 30 40 50 60
Day

Source: *Barron's,* January 19, 1998, p. MW5. Reprinted by permission of *Barron's,* © 1998 Dow Jones & Co., Inc. All Rights Reserved Worldwide.

McCLATCHY NEWSPAPERS

MNI (NYSE) • 25 7/8 • −5/16

► The Sacramento publisher agreed to sell the magazine and book-publishing business of recently acquired Cowles Media to Primedia, formerly known as K-III Communications, for $175 million and $25 million in assumed debt.

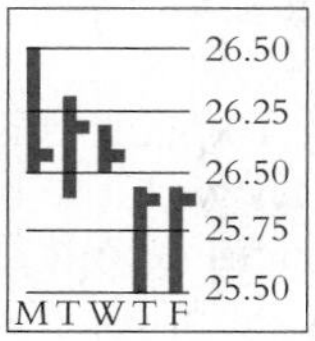
26.50
26.25
26.50
25.75
25.50
M T W T F

INTEL

INTC (NNM) • 7 13/16 • +2 15/16

► The chip maker announced new 266- and 166-megahertz mobile Pentium processors with MMX technology intended to boost performance and lessen power needs in portable personal computers.

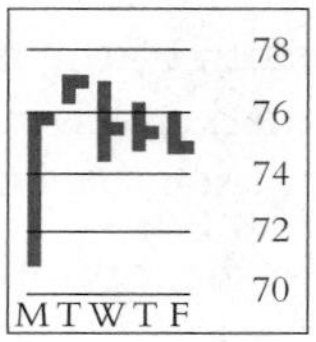
78
76
74
72
70
M T W T F

US OFFICE PRODUCTS

OFIS (NNM) • 17 11/16 • +1 13/16

► The company announced a restructuring that includes a $1 billion share buyback, a $270 million equity investment from a private firm and the spinoffs of four divisions.

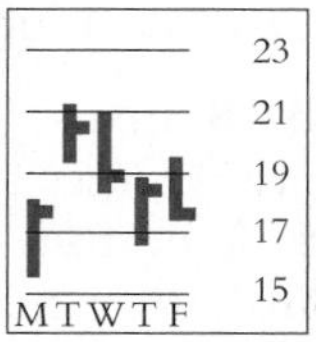
23
21
19
17
15
M T W T F

GENERAL NUTRITION

GNCI (NNM) • 34 7/8 • +3 1/2

► The retailer of nutritional and health-care products expects to report strong sales. Analysts forecast a fourth-quarter same-store sales gain in excess of 7%–8%, following a 10.1% increase in the third quarter.

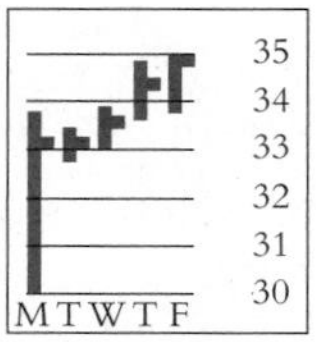
35
34
33
32
31
30
M T W T F

Source: *Barron's,* January 19, 1998, p. MW20. Reprinted by permission of *Barron's,* © 1998 Dow Jones & Co., Inc. All Rights Reserved Worldwide.

trendlines based on only two days (with the lowest or highest prices during these five days)? Explain your answer.

13.19

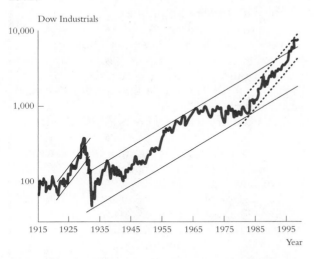

Dow Industrials

Source: "The Free Market Timer," as reprinted in William I. Ferree, Jr., *Barron's*, February 23, 1998, p. R47. Reprinted by permission of Barron's, © 1998 Dow Jones & Co., Inc. All Rights Reserved Worldwide.

Based on this exhibit, answer the following questions:
a. Explain what a channel is. How many channels are drawn in the chart?
b. In the channel of 1920s, the Dow Index broke the upper trendline. What does this signal mean to technical analysts? What actually happened?
c. Suppose that the recent channel of the 1980s and 1990s is similar to the 1920s channel. What are the implications?

For Internet questions visit the Levy Investment Web site at http://levy-invst.swcollege.com.

YOUR TURN: APPLYING THEORY TO PRACTICE
VOODOO OR SCIENCE?

Academics often scorn technical analysis as voodoo. But many money managers and individual investors put faith in it. And almost every brokerage house boasts an in-house technical analyst.

Here's a look at some technical indicators that analysts are focusing on right now.

Advance-Decline Line. The A-D line, as technicians call it, is a cumulative total of the number of advancing stocks minus the number of declining ones. The starting point is arbitrary. Suppose that on Monday 1,100 stocks rise on the New York Stock Exchange, while 900 stocks fall. But on Tuesday, decliners outnumber gainers by a margin of 1,075 to 925. In that case, the A-D line would begin at 200 on Monday, but the cumulative total would fall to 50 after Tuesday's net 150 decliners.

This is a measure of what market professionals call "breadth." It indicates whether an advance is broad-based, or limited to a few leading stocks, such as the blue-chip cyclicals that dominate the Dow Jones Industrial Average. Lately, breadth hasn't looked too good. The daily A-D line peaked in mid-October.

Cash Levels. Indata tracks more than 1,300 institutional portfolios at pension funds, mutual funds, banks, insurance companies and the like. Between them, these portfolios include more

(continued)

than $370 billion in assets. Cash levels, often thought to represent buying power in reserve, are down to 3.7%. That's the lowest since Indata started keeping track in 1979.

Volume. October and November were the second- and third-busiest trading months ever. On the New York Stock Exchange, each of this year's first 11 months rank among the top 13 on record, with more than five billion shares traded every month.

Technicians are divided over what the high volume means. Alfred Goldman of A.G. Edwards in St. Louis says the heavy trading is positive, showing "a high level of desire to be in this market." Richard Arms of Arms Cos. in Albuquerque, New Mexico, says it's a negative, because "a high amount of volume was unable to move the market" very far.

Highs and Lows. In a long-running bull market that still has steam left in it, technicians expect to see sizeable numbers of stocks hitting new 52-week highs, and few stocks hitting new lows. But in November, new lows sometimes outnumbered new highs.

Source: "Technicians Turn Bearish on U.S. Stocks," *Wall Street Journal Europe*, December 14, 1993, p. 13. Reprinted by permission of *The Wall Street Journal Europe* © 1993 Dow Jones & Co., Inc. All Rights Reserved Worldwide.

Questions
1. The table below shows the advances and declines on the NYSE.

Calculate the cumulative advances–declines for the days January 24 through 28. The market went down on January 24 and 25 and went up on January 26, 27, and 28. As a technician who believes in the advance-decline line, what conclusion would you draw from the data based on each of the days January 24 through 28? Explain your answer.
2. Calculate the ratio of new highs to new lows for each of the days January 24 through 28. What conclusion regarding the market trend would you conclude from these statistics on the ratio of new highs to new lows?
3. The last line of the table reports the volume of trading. The volume increased on January 25, decreased on January 26, increased on January 27, and decreased again on January 28. Analyze the volume and price changes on these days. Can you draw any conclusions regarding the future trend?

NYSE Composite Daily Breadth

	Jan. 24	Jan. 25	Jan. 26	Jan. 27	Jan. 28
Issues traded	2,759	2,752	2,751	2,752	2,753
Advances	934	883	1,172	1,329	1,324
Declines	1,206	1,202	888	784	770
Unchanged	619	667	691	639	659
New highs	105	64	61	102	149
New lows	34	49	30	12	8
Blocks	6,811	7,544	7,088	7,852	7,528
Total volume of trades (1,000)	368,523	394,499	371,878	413,871	380,333

Source: "NYSE Composite Daily Breadth," *Barron's*, January 31, 1994, p. 152. Reprinted by permission of *Barron's*, © 1994 Dow Jones & Co., Inc. All Rights Reserved Worldwide.

SELECTED REFERENCES

Edwards, Robert D., and John Magee. *Technical Analysis of Stock Trends.* 6th ed. Boston: New York Institute of Finance, 1992.

This book on technical analysis was first published in 1948 and covers the basic position of the Dow Theory.

Kroll, Stanley, and Michael J. Paulenoff. *The Business One Irwin Guide to the Futures Markets.* Homewood, Ill.: Business One Irwin, 1993.

This book provides a detailed look at technical analysis as it is used in the futures market.

Meyers, Thomas A. *The Technical Analysis Course.* Chicago: Probus Publishing, 1989.

This book provides the basic information needed to understand technical analysis.

Morris, Gregory L. *CandlePower: Advanced Candlestick Pattern Recognition and Filtering Techniques for Trading Stocks and Futures.* Chicago: Probus Publishing, 1992.

This book provides a detailed look at candlestick charting techniques.

Pring, Martin J. *Technical Analysis Explained.* New York: McGraw-Hill, 1991.

This book presents a modern look at technical analysis.

SUPPLEMENTAL REFERENCES

Brown, David P., and Robert H. Jennings. "On Technical Analysis." *Review of Financial Studies* 2, no. 4 (1989): 527–551.

Clarke, Roger G., and Statman Meir. "Bullish or Bearish." *Financial Analysts Journal,* May–June 1998, pp. 63–72.

Fama, Eugene F. "Efficient Capital Markets: A Review of Theory and Empirical Work." *Journal of Finance* 25 (1970): 383–417.

Fama, Eugene F., and Kenneth R. French. "Permanent and Temporary Components of Stock Prices." *Journal of Political Economy* 98 (1988): 247–273.

French, Kenneth R., and Richard Roll. "Stock Return Variances: The Arrival of Information and Reaction of Traders." *Journal of Financial Economics* 17 (1986): 5–26.

Jegadeesh, Narasimhan. "Evidence of Predictable Behavior of Security Returns." *Journal of Finance* 45 (July 1990): 881–898.

Lehmann, Bruce N. "Fads, Martingales, and Market Efficiency." *Quarterly Journal of Economics,* February 1990, pp. 1–28.

Lo, Andrew W., and A. Craig MacKinlay. "Stock Market Prices Do Not Follow Random Walks: Evidence from a Simple Specification Test." *Review of Financial Studies* 1 (1988): 41–66.

Nison, Steve. *Introduction to Japanese Candle Charts.* New York: Merrill Lynch, Pierce, Fenner & Smith, 1991.

CHAPTER 14

INVESTMENT COMPANIES AND MUTUAL FUNDS

LEARNING OBJECTIVES

After reading this chapter you should be able to:

1. Compare and contrast closed-end and open-end funds.

2. Contrast the benefits and costs of investing in mutual funds.

INVESTMENTS IN THE NEWS

THE TERMINATOR

Despite their discounts, closed-end bond funds are lousy buys. Well, almost all are.

"This is Capital Gain, over," says George Karpus into his two-way ship-to-shore radio. He is maneuvering his 34-foot boat from Lake Ontario to the Genesee River. . . .

"Bonds are a science, stocks are an art," says Karpus. . . . Science tells him that the best action is in closed-end bond funds. "To me, if you delve into it, it's very difficult to force yourself to go out and buy the bonds themselves." That's because most sell at a discount: Why pay retail when you can get a 10% discount?

Yet even with discounts of 10% some closed-end bond funds aren't good buys. Their discounts can be so overwhelmed by high expenses that an investor would be better off in a cheap Vanguard fund.

That is, unless the closed-end bond fund has a termination date. Termination dates are a feature of a breed of closed-end bond funds called term trusts. Wall Street issued $11.6 billion of them in the early 1990s.

It's now payback time. At least 9 term trusts have terminated already, and some 31 more are expected to terminate during the period between this fall and 2009. Karpus likes them because many are trading at discounts to their termination price. "They're a layup. A slam dunk. It's Michael Jordan on your basketball team."

Source: Mary Beth Grover, "The Terminator," *Forbes,* August 11, 1997, p. 130. Reprinted by Permission of *Forbes* Magazine © Forbes Inc., 1997.

FUND SURVEY: ENOUGH ALREADY

The way things are going, there will be more funds than stocks. You can even buy one that invests only in funeral stocks.

Take three popular investment ideas:

- Index funds, which mechanically track a group of stocks;
- Sector funds, which allow you to make a bet on one industry;
- Performance histories, which are what this annual fund survey is all about. . . .

(continued)

The mutual fund industry is booming, with $4 trillion in assets. That's a good thing, reflecting as it does a strong economy and a rebirth of saving. It is not necessarily a good thing that close to 10,000 funds vie for your attention, many of them, moreover, with two, three, or even four different classes of shares. The whole idea of a mutual fund was to save individuals the difficult task of picking stocks. Now it's almost as tough to pick funds.

You may be tempted to throw up your hands. How can you begin to sort through all the options?

Source: William P. Barrett, "Enough Already": Fund Survey, *Forbes*, August 25, 1997, p. 159. Reprinted by Permission of *Forbes* magazine © Forbes Inc., 1997.

This Chapter's Investments in the News claims that there are bargains—discount closed-end bond funds that terminate their assets on a predetermined future date (term trusts). The chapter discusses closed-end funds as well as open-end funds (also known as *mutual funds*) and explains the meaning of discounts. The text examines the different types of mutual funds, as well as the costs and benefits of investing in these types of securities.

Mutual funds are a popular investment vehicle because they provide an easy way for small investors to profit in the financial markets. Small investors are aware of the benefits of diversification, and the variety of mutual funds currently available offers something for everyone. Furthermore, the returns on more traditional securities, such as bank certificates of deposit, have declined, so investors seeking higher returns have moved to mutual funds.

An **investment company** is an organization that takes a pool of investors' money and invests it in securities according to a stated set of objectives. Like other publicly held companies, investment companies start by selling shares to a group of investors. These companies do not invest in plant and equipment; they invest in securities. Thus, investment company managers manage a portfolio of securities on behalf of their shareholders. The primary benefits that these portfolio managers provide, especially for small investors, are diversification and professional management.

14.1 TYPES OF FUNDS

Investment companies run two types of funds. **Mutual funds** (also known as **open-end funds**) are able to issue new shares on a daily basis. Specifically, supply and demand for mutual fund shares governs how many shares are outstanding at any point in time. When an investor buys shares of a mutual fund, the purchase is made directly from the mutual fund that issues new shares. When an investor sells shares of a mutual fund, the sale is made directly with the mutual fund, which redeems the old shares. **Closed-end funds** (also known as **investment trusts**) are not able to issue new shares daily.[1] The investor who wishes to purchase shares of a closed-end fund must find a willing seller, whereas an investor can purchase shares of an open-end fund directly from the investment company. Most closed-end company shares trade on an exchange such as the NYSE or the AMEX. Thus, shares are traded with other investors. From time to time, closed-end investment companies do issue new shares in the same manner as other corporations. A new type of closed-end fund is the term trust, which has a termination date (see this chapter's "Investments in the News"). Wall Street issued $11.6 billion in term trusts in the early 1990s.

In the recent past, closed-end funds have been very popular with investors. For example, between 1969 and 1984 only thirty seven closed-end funds were issued. However, between 1985 and 1996 over five hundred funds were issued. By the end of 1994 the assets of closed-end funds exceeded $116 billion.[2] Recall from Chapter 3 that the world bond and stock market total value is approximately $40 trillion (see Chapter 3, Exhibits 3-13 and 3-14). Thus, overall closed-end funds represent only a small fraction of world markets.

Mutual funds have experienced similar growth. Exhibit 14-1 shows that total net assets and the total number of funds grew dramatically between 1940 and 1996. (Note that Exhibit 14-1 includes only funds that are members of the Investment Company Institute; it excludes money market mutual funds.)

How can we account for the dramatic increase over time in individual investment in funds rather than in the purchase of individual securities? Theoretically, in an efficient market, individuals should be able to invest in individual securities at no greater cost than they would incur investing in funds managed by someone else (called managed funds). Thus, there would be no apparent benefit from using in-

EXHIBIT 14-1 The Growth of Mutual Funds (1940 to 1996)	Year	Total Net Assets ($ in Millions)	Number of Funds	Growth in Net Assets	Growth in Funds
	1996	$3,540	6,270	523%	165%
	1990	568	2,362	879	331
	1980	58	548	22	54
	1970	47.6	356	180	121
	1960	17	161	580	64
	1950	2.5	98	525	44
	1940	0.4	68		

Source: Data derived from CDA/Wiesenberger Investment Companies Service, *Investment Companies Yearbook* (Rockville, Md.: CDA/Wiesenberger, 1997), p. 14.

1. The terminology is particularly confusing in international markets. For example, in Great Britain, mutual funds are called *unit trusts*. Also, it is common practice to refer loosely to both closed-end and open-end companies as *mutual funds*. This book holds to the strict definition and uses *mutual fund* to refer only to open-end companies.
2. See CDA/Wiesenberger Investment Companies Service, *Investment Companies Yearbook* (Rockville, Md.: CDA/Weisenberger, 1997), p. 14.

vestment companies. However, it is not costless to gather information and manage a portfolio, particularly with internationally diversified funds. Clearly, investment companies have the benefit of economies of scale. One manager can do the analysis and portfolio management for hundreds of investors. Also, by investing in a mutual fund, small investors can achieve a diversification level with investment companies that would be hard to achieve otherwise.

Generally, investing involves double taxation; a firm pays corporate tax, and then stockholders pay personal income tax on dividends received or capital gains tax on capital appreciation. Theoretically, investment in a mutual fund could involve triple taxation. Recall that a corporation normally pays corporate income tax, and shareholders pay income tax on dividends and capital gains tax on any stock appreciation (see Chapter 2, Appendix A). If investment companies bought stock of corporations and paid taxes, the shareholder would have triple taxation: the corporate tax, the investment company tax, and the shareholder's tax. The Internal Revenue Service (IRS) makes sure this does not happen. The IRS allows an investment company to be classified under Regulation M of the IRS as a **regulated investment company;** such a designation allows the company to avoid taxation on the capital gains, dividends, and interest income it receives. The investment company is acting as a conduit through which the investor's money flows, so capital gains and ordinary income should *not* be triple taxed (the **conduit theory**). Thus, there is no major tax disadvantage to buying mutual fund shares. (Note, however, that investors do pay tax on income once they receive it.)

Investment companies must meet specific requirements of the IRS to avoid such triple taxation. An investment company must pass almost all of its capital gains and ordinary income on to its shareholders; that income is taxed according to each individual shareholder's tax bracket. To be classified as a regulated investment company, "the fund must meet such requirements as 98% minimum distribution of interest and dividends received on investment and 90% distribution of capital gains net income. Shareholders must pay taxes even if they reinvest their distributions."[3]

The increased popularity of investment companies is also due to the strong overall market performance, tax law changes, and ERISA laws. The strong bull market of the late 1980s and the 1990s has resulted in growth in fund size just because the underlying securities have increased in value. Recent tax law changes have made holding financial assets relatively more attractive than real estate. Finally, the Employee Retirement Income Securities Act (ERISA) provides regulatory support for building retirement savings by employees.

14.1.1 Closed-End Funds (Investment Trusts)

Closed-end funds were first developed in Europe in the 1820s and became very popular in Great Britain in the nineteenth century. They were the most popular form of investment company in the United States until the stock market crash of 1929. Only recently have closed-end funds once again become popular.

---

3. John Downes and Jordan Elliot Goodman, *Dictionary of Finance and Investment Terms,* 2d ed. (New York: Barron's Educational Series, 1987), p. 334.

Closed-end funds issue a specified number of shares, after which no additional shares are issued, unless a special public issue is conducted. Therefore, the behavior of closed-end funds is much like that of common stock. As a particular fund becomes popular, demand rises and so does the market value of the closed-end fund shares. Investors do not trade the closed-end fund shares directly with the investment company; they trade in the secondary market.

Closed-end funds are easier to manage than open-end funds. After the initial issue, the portfolio manager does not have to be concerned with day-to-day liquidity needs of the shareholders. Unlike open-end funds, which allow investors to redeem their shares at any time and which consequently must have funds available to provide for possible redemption, closed-end funds do not need to have a large amount of liquid funds available. Closed-end funds are typically diversified portfolios of publicly traded securities that meet specific investment objectives.

Exhibit 14-2 summarizes the different categories of closed-end funds. It is clear from this exhibit that closed-end funds have many investment objectives. For example, some closed-end funds are portfolios of securities issued in a single country.

The Monday edition of the *Wall Street Journal* lists information on closed-end funds gathered by Lipper Analytical Services, Inc., a mutual fund data and analysis company. (*Barron's* also carries this information.) As Exhibit 14-3 shows, this listing includes the fund's name and the stock exchange on which it is traded; *N* denotes the NYSE, *A* denotes the AMEX, *O* denotes the NASDAQ, *C* denotes the Chicago Stock Exchange, and *T* denotes the Toronto Stock Exchange. The vast majority of the closed-end funds trade on the NYSE.

The pricing of closed-end funds differs from the pricing of individual securities in that there are quotes for both a market price and an estimate of the current value

EXHIBIT 14-2 **Categories of** **Closed-End Funds** **as Classified by** **Lipper Analytical** **Services, Inc.**	**Category**	**Description**
	General equity	Invests primarily in domestic equities
	Specialized equity	Limits investments to a specific industry
	World equity	Invests in equities worldwide
	Convertible securities	Invests primarily in convertible bonds and convertible preferred stock
	Dual purpose	Two funds based on one portfolio; one fund receives the capital gains, and the other fund receives any income
	Loan participations	Invests primarily in commercial loans
	Bond	Invests primarily in corporate and government bonds
	World income	Invests in bonds worldwide, seeking high cash flow
	National municipal	Invests in tax-free bonds nationally
	Single state municipal	Invests in tax-free bonds issued in only one state to get state and local tax benefits

EXHIBIT 14-3
A Sample of Closed-End Funds as Reported in the Monday Edition of the *Wall Street Journal*

CLOSED-END FUNDS

Friday, January 30, 1998

Closed-end funds sell a limited number of shares and invest the proceeds in securities. Unlike open-end funds, closed-ends generally do not buy their shares back from investors who wish to cash in their holdings. Instead, fund shares trade on a stock exchange. The following list, provided by Lipper Analytical Services, shows the ticker symbol and exchange where each fund trades (A: American; C: Chicago; N: NYSE; O: Nasdaq; T: Toronto; z: does not trade on an exchange). The data also include the fund's most recent net asset value, its closing share price on the day NAV was calculated, and the percentage difference between the market price and the NAV (often called the premium or discount). For equity funds, the final column provides 52-week returns based on market prices plus dividends. For bond funds, the final column shows the past 12 months' income distributions as a percentage of the current market price. Footnotes appear after a fund's name. a: the NAV and market price are ex dividend. b: the NAV is fully diluted. c: NAV, market price and premium or discount are as of Thursday's close. d: NAV, market price and premium or discount are as of Wednesday's close. e: NAV assumes rights offering is fully subscribed. v: NAV is converted at the commercial Rand rate. w: Convertible Note-NAV (not market) conversion value. y: NAV and market price are in Canadian dollars. All other footnotes refer to unusual circumstances; explanations for those that appear can be found at the bottom of this list. N/A signifies that the information is not available or not applicable.

Fund Name (Symbol)	Stock Exch	NAV	Market Price	Prem /Disc	52 week Market Return
General Equity Funds					
Adams Express (ADX)	♣N	28.68	24 3/8	− 15.0	27.5
Alliance All-Mkt (AMO)	N	31.76	30 1/4	− 4.8	58.2
Avalon Capital (MIST)	O	15.42	15	− 2.7	30.4
Baker Fentress (BKF)	♣N	21.76	18 1/16	− 17.0	16.6
Bergstrom Cap (BEM)	A	156.61	140 1/4	− 10.4	30.7
Blue Chip Value (BLU)	♣N	9.56	10 1/8	+ 5.9	35.6
Central Secs (CET)	A	28.35	30 1/4	+ 6.7	22.1
Corp Renaissance (CREN)-cp	O	8.39	5 7/8	− 30.0	−20.3
Engex (EGX)	A	11.97	9 15/16	− 17.0	−13.6
Equus II (EQS)	♣A	28.52	25 1/8	− 11.9	53.0
Gabelli Equity (GAB)	N	11.55	11 11/16	+ 1.2	37.6
General American (GAM)	♣N	28.73	25 5/16	− 11.9	30.9
Librty AllStr Eq (USA)-g	♣N	13.30	13 3/8	+ 0.6	29.6
Librty AllStr Gr (ASG)	♣N	12.83	12 5/16	− 4.0	37.5
MFS Special Val (MFV)	N	14.44	19 5/16	+ 33.7	19.3
Morgan FunShares (MFUN)-c	O	13.31	11 1/2	− 13.6	25.1
Morgan Gr Sm Cap (MGC)	♣N	11.12	10 3/16	− 8.4	17.6
NAIC Growth (GRF)-c	C	10.99	14 15/16	+ 35.9	31.6
Royce Value (RVT)-q	♣N	16.67	14 15/16	− 10.4	30.5
Royce,5.75 '04Cv-wq	N	126.58	114 1/2	− 9.5	19.8
Salomon SBF (SBF)	N	18.49	17 1/4	− 6.7	19.7
Source Capital (SOR)	N	50.23	52 7/8	+ 5.3	29.9
Tri-Continental (TY)	♣N	32.44	26 7/8	− 17.2	22.5
Zweig (ZF)	♣N	12.11	13 1/8	+ 8.4	30.5

of all securities within the fund. This estimate of current value, called the **net asset value (NAV),** is listed in the third column of Exhibit 14-3. Specifically, it is the current market value of all securities held by the fund less any net liabilities divided by the total number of shares outstanding. Net asset value is adjusted for liabilities to better represent the true value of a share in a closed-end fund, just as the book value of equity for a normal corporation is assets minus liabilities. One liability is securities purchased but not yet paid. (On most security exchanges there is a three-day settlement period between the time securities are purchased and their payment date.) Other liabilities include accrued fees, options that have been written, dividends payable, and other accrued expenses.

The fourth column in Exhibit 14-3 shows the current market prices for the closed-end funds, which may differ from the NAV. The fifth column gives the premium or discount. The **premium** is the percentage difference between the current market price (CMP) and the NAV (dividing by the NAV) if the difference is positive. If the difference is negative, it is called the **discount.** For example, the Adams Express Fund was trading on Friday, January 30, 1998, for $24\frac{3}{8}$; hence, the discount was

$$\text{Premium (Discount)} = \frac{CMP - NAV}{NAV} = \frac{\$24\frac{3}{8} - \$28.68}{\$28.68} = -0.150 \qquad (14.1)$$

or a 15.0% discount.

The final column in Exhibit 14-3 shows the fifty-two-week rate of return from investing in a closed-end equity fund. Although the rates of return for some categories of closed-end funds are typically highly correlated, this is not true for world equity funds. The returns here depend on factors influencing a particular country's stock market.

An examination of any current financial data of closed-end funds reveals that the NAV differs from the fund's current value in the marketplace. As illustrated in Exhibit 14-3, on January 30, 1998, the Adams Express Fund had a net asset value of $28.68 per share and a market value of $24\frac{3}{8}$ per share. That is, the value of the underlying assets was higher than the current market value. There is no guarantee, however, that these premiums or discounts will move toward zero once the shares are purchased. The differences could increase.

Let us examine the concept of NAV in more detail. Mathematically, NAV can be expressed as

$$NAV = \frac{\sum_{i=1}^{n} Q_i P_i - Liab}{N} \qquad (14.2)$$

where Q_i is the quantity of shares of Security i held by the fund, P_i is the market price of Security i, $Liab$ includes any net liabilities of the fund, and N is the number of outstanding shares of the fund.

For example, suppose Select Value Fund (Sel Valu), a closed-end fund, consists of two securities: 1,000 shares of Security A, which is currently trading for $50, and 2,000 shares of Security B, which is currently trading for $40. If the fund has $50,000 in net liabilities and 4,000 shares outstanding, then its NAV is

$$NAV = \frac{(1,000 \cdot \$50) + (2,000 \cdot \$40) - \$50,000}{4,000} = \$20$$

Exhibit 14-4 illustrates a typical balance sheet of a closed-end company. The value of the marketable assets of this fund is

$$\text{Investments} + \text{Cash} = \$1,136,893,216 + \$99,486 = \$1,136,992,702$$

The fund's net liabilities are

$$\text{Total Net Liabilities} - \text{Other Assets}$$
$$= \$4,345,982 - (\$496,458 + \$2,248,998 + \$3,368,220) = -\$1,767,694$$

Thus, the net asset value is

$$NAV = [\$1,136,992,702 - (-\$1,767,694)]/\$48,036,528 = \$23.71$$

New closed-end fund offerings tend to sell initially at a premium and then decline to discounts.[4] Several reasons that have been suggested for this price change. One reason IPOs of closed-end funds initially trade at a premium is the successful marketing efforts of retail brokerage firms; Wall Street is very good at generating demand for a new product. Second, Lee, Shleifer, and Thaler document that IPOs of closed-end funds tend to occur when other closed-end funds overall are trading at a premium or at a small discount.[5] Whatever the reason for the initial premium, on average, it eventually disappears. Thus, it may be wiser to avoid new issues. One strategy is to purchase only closed-end funds that are selling for at least a 10% discount in the hope that the amount of the discount will decline and you will profit. You can also earn a higher current yield for an investment of 90% of net asset value, because you still receive income on 100% of net assets (excluding expenses). Stock funds tend to trade at higher discounts (on average, 12%) than do bond funds (on average, 4%).[6] Although there are years when seasoned closed-end funds trade, on average, at a premium, the most typical case is that they are sold at a discount, which is sometimes quite large.

Closed-end funds trading at large premiums are very risky. Consider, for example, a closed-end mutual fund investing in Chinese stocks that is traded at premium. If China's emerging stock market fell, for example, you could lose on the closed-end funds in two ways. First, the market value of the portfolio would fall; second, the premium over net asset value probably would also fall. Hence, closed-end funds have their own unique risks. (See Connecting Theory to Practice 14.1 for a historical perspective on the risks associated with foreign investments.)

4. See Seth C. Anderson and Jeffery A. Born, "The Selling and Seasoning of Closed-End Investment Company's IPOs," *Journal of Financial Services Research* 2 (Summer 1989): 131–150. Anderson and Born argue that the poor return performance of closed-end IPOs is due to falling NAVs. Similar results are reported by Kathleen Weiss, "The Post-Offering Price Performance of Closed-End Funds," *Financial Management* 18 (Autumn 1989): 57–67; John M. Peavy, "Returns on Initial Public Offerings of Closed-End Funds," *Review of Financial Studies* 3 (1990): 695–708; Seth C. Anderson, Jeffery A. Born, and T. Randolph Beard, "An Analysis of Bond Investment Company IPOs: Past and Present," *Financial Review* 26 (May 1991): 211–222; and Charles C. Lee, Andrei Shleifer, and Richard H. Thaler, "Closed-End Mutual Funds," *Journal of Economic Perspectives* 4, no. 4 (1990): 153–164.

5. See Charles C. Lee, Andrei Shleifer, and Richard H. Thaler, "Investor Sentiment and the Closed-End Fund Puzzle," *Journal of Finance* 46 (March 1991): 75–109.

6. See Thomas J. Herzfield, *Wall Street Journal*, September 19, 1988, p. 53. His study covered a 10-year period through 1987.

EXHIBIT 14-4   **Statement of Assets and Liabilities: An Example (December 31, 1996)**

Assets

Investments at value;

Non-controlled affiliate, Petroleum & Resources Corporation (cost $22,153,015)	$ 39,808,558	
Common stocks and convertible securities (cost $638,789,329)	1,043,558,641	
Short-term investments (cost $53,526,017)	53,526,017	$1,136,893,216
Cash		99,486
Receivables:		
Investment securities sold		496,458
Dividends and interest		2,248,998
Prepaid expenses and other assets		3,368,220
Total Assets		1,143,106,378

Liabilities

Investment securities purchased	1,931,489
Open option contracts at value (proceeds $543,020)	518,750
Accrued expenses	1,895,743
Total Liabilities	4,345,982
Net Assets	$1,138,760,396

Net Assets

Common Stock at par value $1.00 per share, authorized 75,000,000 shares; issued and outstanding 48,036,528 shares	$ 48,036,528
Additional capital surplus	661,729,190
Undistributed net investment income	2,173,294
Undistributed net realized gain on investments	4,372,259
Unrealized appreciation on investments	422,449,125
Net Assets Applicable to Common Stock	$1,138,760,396
Net Asset Value Per Share of Common Stock	$23.71

Source: Adams Express Company, 1996 Annual Report.

CONNECTING THEORY TO PRACTICE 14.1

SHOULD YOU BE A BULL IN CHINA'S SHOP?

Wait for the Correction Before You Invest.

Sure, investment options may look dull here in the U.S., but Wall Street has the answer: China! Fired by visions of a populous nation awakening to economic freedom and by newspapers' breathless accounts of the country's new millionaires, Wall Street firms have rolled out several mutual funds that invest exclusively in China. With stocks on one of the country's two exchanges up by 50.6 percent so far this year, China is the place to be, say brokers.

Or is it?

It's easy to see why some investors have been willing to put all their chips on China. The loosening of restrictions on entrepreneurs in the southern Guangdong province has triggered an economic boom. That region's gross domestic product is growing at nearly 12 percent a year, among the fastest growth rates in the world.

But Chinese citizens who are benefiting from the surging economy have little to buy in the way of consumer goods, so they're pouring money into the financial markets. Fueled by that torrent of cash, the Shenzhen exchange has climbed 28.6 percent since the end of last year, and the Shanghai exchange soared by more than 50 percent.

These heady figures are part of the trouble, though. American investors can't buy any Chinese stock they want. And the stocks they *can* buy haven't risen nearly as much as the securities that the Chinese can invest in.

The Chinese government also has been trying to slow the economy's breakneck pace by raising interest rates. The last time it did so, the ensuing recession sent hundreds of students and dissatisfied workers marching into Tiananmen Square in June of 1989. The killings that resulted not only ended the nascent democratic movement, they brought down the curtain on a decade-long financial market boom.

No one is expecting a similar disaster now, but the chances of a slow-down—and possibly a recession—are high. A significant political risk also looms. When long-time leader Deng Xiao-ping dies, a power struggle between the economic reformers and the old-style hard-liners is likely to erupt.

Most importantly, though, China's stock markets are simply too speculative right now. We think investors should wait for the Chinese and Hong Kong stock markets to undergo a correction, which many fund managers believe could happen in the next few months. While China's prospects over the long run look great, there are too many risks to getting in now. If you're determined to participate in a racy overseas stock market, you're far better off getting into an international mutual fund that specializes in emerging markets.

(continued)

Above all, don't put your money into one of the three closed-end China funds until their prices fall to a discount below their net asset value. Because closed-end funds issue a finite number of shares, their share prices are especially affected by big swings in demand for the fund. Investors' appetite for China mutual funds, for example, has driven share prices way above what the stocks in the portfolios are currently worth (see table).

Investors who prefer open-end funds should keep an eye on the Eaton Vance China Growth Fund. Managed from Hong Kong by Robert Lloyd George, great-grandson of Britain's former prime minister, the fund has nearly half of its assets in Hong Kong stocks, and a 4.75 percent load.

The most conservative approach, however, is to skip the funds that load all their eggs into one basket and put your money in a fund that spreads its assets throughout the Pacific Rim or other emerging foreign markets. Two of the better offerings: Merrill Lynch Pacific and Lexington Worldwide Emerging Markets.

With their overview of the world's most excitable markets, managers of such funds have something that is in short supply among China fund managers: perspective. That's what caused William Stack, co-manager of Lexington Worldwide, to pull out of China recently and reduce holdings in Hong Kong. All the more reason, we think, to hurry up and wait.

Source: Virginia Munger Kahn, "Should You Be a Bull in China's Shop?" *Smart Money,* August 1993, p. 44. Reprinted with permission of Virginia Munger Kahn. © 1993 by Smart Money, a joint venture of the Hearst Corp. and Dow Jones & Co., Inc. All rights reserved.

SEC–Registered China Funds

Investors scrambling to invest in China have driven the price of all four of the region's mutual funds sharply higher. Shares of the three closed-end funds are trading for more than the net asset value (NAV) of their portfolios.

Fund	Average Total Return (12/31/92–4/30/93)		Premium over NAV (5/14/93)
China Fund Inc.	NAV	9.58%	+15.18%
	Share	28.85	
Greater Fund Inc.	NAV	15.75	+2.6
	Share	30.30	
Jardine Fleming China Region Fund Inc.	NAV	14.82	+1.4
	Share	27.93	
Eaton Vance China Growth Fund[a]	NAV	21.02	N/A

[a]Open-end mutual fund.

Source: Lipper Analytical Services, Inc.

(continued)

MAKING THE CONNECTION

As with most securities, there is a difference of opinion regarding investment in closed-end funds invested in China. On the one hand, the economic potential in China is enormous. On the other hand, there are risks, and the closed-end shares are all trading above the NAV. Some advisers believe that China's stock market will undergo a correction, implying that share prices will fall. As demand for China's stock falls, closed-end share prices will probably fall and trade at a discount to the NAV. Incidentally, Deng Xiao-Ping died in 1996, and no power struggle took place between economic reformers and old-style hard-liners.

If the markets are efficient, then why do closed-end funds trade, on average, at a discount? How do we explain the fact that closed-end funds sometimes trade at a premium? The following are four major explanations that have been offered for why funds trade at a discount or premium:[7]

1. *Unrealized capital appreciation.* When investors purchase closed-end funds, they acquire the tax liabilities for stocks held in the portfolio that have risen but not yet been sold. When the stocks are subsequently sold, the new investors may pay taxes on the realized gains even though the price appreciated before the closed-end fund was purchased. Specifically, the capital gains tax burden falls on the investors who are holding the closed-end fund shares when the security within the closed-end fund is sold. Very little empirical evidence has been found to support this explanation.

2. *Management fees and transaction costs.* The costs of running a closed-end fund are paid from fund earnings. This reduction in return that is due to management costs, as well as transaction costs, may account for the discounts observed. There is strong empirical evidence that the degree of discounts is positively correlated with expenses of closed-end equity funds.[8]

3. *Performance of the fund.* The percentage difference from NAV can be attributed to how well the closed-end fund has performed in the past. If the fund's management has generated superior returns in the past, then the fund should trade at a premium. Alternatively, if the fund's management has performed poorly in the past, then the fund will trade at a discount. Crawford and Harper found an inverse relationship between fund income and discounts that supports this proposition.[9]

---

7. For an excellent summary and synthesis of closed-end fund empirical evidence, see Seth C. Anderson and Jeffery A. Born, *Closed-End Investment Companies Issues and Answers* (Boston: Kluwer Academic Publishers, 1992). Other reasons offered include the capital gains distribution policy, diversification level, illiquid assets in the fund, availability of foreign investment, lack of available information, and overall investor sentiment.

8. See Seth C. Anderson and Jeffery A. Born, "The Effects of Market Imperfections on Asset Pricing and Risk: An Empirical Examination," *Journal of the Midwest Finance Association* 16 (1987): 1–17; and Seth C. Anderson and Jeffery A. Born, "Market Imperfections and Asset Pricing," *Review of Business and Economic Research* 23 (Spring 1987): 14–25.

9. See Peggy J. Crawford and Charles P. Harper, "An Analysis of the Discounts on Closed-End Mutual Funds," *Financial Review* 20 (August 1985): 30–38.

4. *Turnover.* Closed-end funds, which trade frequently (have high turnover), incur higher transaction costs, which are paid in the form of lower returns. Hence, there should be a direct relationship between **turnover** (the volume of shares traded as a percentage of total shares listed on an exchange during a day or year) and discounts, where the higher the turnover, the higher the observed discount. Anderson and Born, however, find no significant empirical relationship between turnover and discounts.[10]

If a closed-end fund is selling at a discount, by changing its format to an open-end fund, the shareholders immediately gain. Connecting Theory to Practice 14.2 describes a case where this process took place.

CONNECTING THEORY TO PRACTICE 14.2

AT CLOSED-END FUNDS, A BIG PUSH TO OPEN UP CONVERSIONS CAN MEAN WINDFALLS FOR SHAREHOLDERS

Last week, investors in T. Rowe Price Associates' New Age Media voted themselves a healthy profit just by changing the legal format of the fund.

It was the most recent example of a change that is sweeping the closed-end fund business, an arcane corner of the nation's mutual fund industry. It has been spurred by professional investors who are seeking profits and assisted by the Securities and Exchange Commission, which has vowed to make funds more responsive to investors.

The T. Rowe Price investors received their windfall by voting to turn their closed-end fund into a traditional mutual fund, called open-end because the sponsoring company can sell an unlimited number of shares and must buy them back from shareholders who want to bail out. The price of an open-end fund's shares is usually equal to the pro-rata value of its portfolio, plus any sales charges.

Closed-end funds, by contrast, issue a fixed number of shares; investors buy from or sell to other investors, usually through a stock exchange. This means there are two factors that can determine the value of closed-end shares: the value of the assets in the portfolio and the level of demand among investors for the shares of the fund.

Low interest among investors often leads to closed-end funds' trading at a discount to the value of the securities in their portfolios. Analysts attribute a lack of demand for such funds to the fact that they often invest in securities that are hard to trade, including those that are offered by smaller companies or those in emerging markets. They also receive little marketing support from brokers, and relatively few investors understand how they work.

(continued)

---

10. See Seth C. Anderson and Jeffrey A. Born, "The Effects of Market Imperfections on Asset Pricing and Risk: An Empirical Examination," *Journal of the Midwest Finance Association* 16 (1987): 1–17.

> While a discount of about 5 percent is considered normal, discounts topping 15 percent of net asset value are not rare. Recently, discounts on many funds have hovered at about 5.9 percent, according to Lipper Analytical Services.
>
> Source: Sharon R. King, "At Closed-End Funds, A Big Push to Open Up Conversions Can Mean Windfalls for Shareholders," *New York Times,* July 27, 1997. Copyright © 1997 by The New York Times Co. Reprinted by Permission.

MAKING THE CONNECTION

If the assets held by the fund implies that NAV = $100, and the share price is traded for $80, a big discount prevails. By changing the fund's status to an open-end fund, each share must be worth $100, and a $20 gain per share is immediately obtained. This explains the pressure to open closed-end funds, which are sold at a discount.

14.1.2 Open-End Funds (Mutual Funds)

Unlike closed-end funds, mutual funds (or open-end funds) can issue additional shares and buy shares when investors wish to sell. Thus, a mutual fund trades directly with investors. The share price is directly related to the net asset value. Mutual funds can be broadly classified as either no-load or load. As mentioned in Chapter 2, a **load** is a sales commission paid by the investor. **No-load mutual funds** do not add any sales commissions to the fund price. Other funds carry a sales commission (load), and hence the offer price is higher than the NAV.

Each mutual fund is required by law to provide a prospectus to investors. The prospectus contains information regarding the fund's objectives, fund expenses, historical performance, risks, who should invest, and who is managing the fund.

The Investment Company Act of 1940 requires every mutual fund to state its specific investment objectives in the prospectus. For example, the Fidelity Puritan Fund (FPURX) prospectus contains the following statement regarding its investment principles and risk:

Puritan seeks as much income as possible, consistent with preservation of capital, by investing in a broadly diversified portfolio of high-yielding securities, such as common stocks, preferred stocks, and bonds. The fund also considers the potential for growth of capital.

FMR manages the fund to maintain a balance between stocks and bonds. When FMR's outlook is neutral, it will invest approximately 60% of the fund's assets in stocks and other equity securities and the remainder in bonds and other fixed-income securities. FMR may vary from this target if it believes stocks or bonds offer more favorable opportunities, but will always invest at least 25% of the fund's total assets in fixed-income senior securities (including debt securities and preferred stock).

The fund has the flexibility to pursue its objective through any type or quality of domestic or foreign security. FMR varies the proportions invested in each type of security based on its interpretation of economic conditions and underlying security values.[11]

11. From *The Fidelity Puritan Fund,* prospectus dated September 26, 1997, p. 9.

By reading a mutual fund's prospectus, an investor can easily determine its objective—in other words, which type of fund it is. Exhibit 14-5 illustrates how Lipper Analytical Services, Inc. (LAS), categorizes the different mutual funds as they are reported in the *Wall Street Journal*.

LAS maintains performance averages for each category. These averages can be used to compare how a particular fund is doing relative to other funds of the same

EXHIBIT 14-5
Mutual Funds—Classification

MUTUAL FUND OBJECTIVES

Categories compiled by The Wall Street Journal, based on classifications by Lipper Analytical Services Inc.

STOCK FUNDS

Capital Appreciation (CP): Seeks rapid capital growth, often through high portfolio turnover.
Growth (GR): Invests in companies expecting higher than average revenue and earnings growth.
Growth & Income (GI): Pursues both price and dividend growth. Category includes S&P 500 Index funds.
Equity Income (EI): Tends to favor stock with the highest dividends.
Small Cap (SC): Stocks of lesser-known, small companies.
MidCap (MC): Shares of middle-sized companies.
Sector (SE): Environmental; Financial Services; Real Estate; Specialty & Miscellaneous.
Global Stock (GL): Includes small cap global. Can invest in U.S.
International Stock (IL) (non-U.S.): Canadian; International; International Small Cap.
European Region (EU): European markets or operations concentrated in Europe.
Latin America (LT): Markets or operations concentrated in Latin America.
Pacific Region (PR): Japanese; Pacific Ex-Japan; Pacific Region; China Region.
Emerging Markets (EM): Emerging market equity securities (based on economic measures such as a country's GNP per capita).
Science & Technology (TK): Science, technology and telecommunications stocks.
Health & Biotechnology (HB): Health care, medicine and biotechnology.
Natural Resources (NR): Natural resources stocks.
Gold (AU): Gold mines, gold-oriented mining finance houses, gold coins or bullion.
Utility (UT): Utility stocks.

TAXABLE BOND FUNDS

Short-Term (SB): Ultrashort obligation and short, short-intermediate investment grade corporate debt.
Short-Term U.S. (SG): Short-term U.S. Treasury; Short, short-intermediate U.S. government funds.
Intermediate (IB): Investment grade corporate debt of up to 10-year maturity.
Intermediate U.S. (IG): U.S. Treasury and government agency debt.
Long-Term (AB): Corporate A-rated; Corporate BBB-rated.
Long-Term U.S. (LG): U.S. Treasury; U.S. government; zero coupon.
General U.S. Taxable (GT): Can invest in different types of bonds.
High Yield Taxable (HC): High yield high-risk bonds.
Mortgage (MG): Ginnie Mae and general mortgage; Adjustable-Rate Mortgage.
World (WB): Short world multi-market; short world single-market; global income; international income; Emerging-Markets debt.

MUNICIPAL BOND FUNDS

Short-Term Muni (SM): Short, short-intermediate term municipal debt; Short-intermediate term California; Single states short-intermediate municipal debt.
Intermediate Muni (IM): Intermediate-term municipal debt including single-state funds.
General Muni (GM): A variety of municipal debt.
Single-State Municipal (SS): Funds that invest in debt of individual states.
High Yield Municipal (HM): High yield low credit quality.
Insured (NM): California insured, New York insured, Florida insured, all other insured.

STOCK & BOND FUNDS

Balanced (BL): A balanced portfolio of both stocks and bonds with the primary objective of conserving principal.
Stock/Bond Blend (MP): Multi-purpose funds such as balanced target; convertible; flexible income; flexible portfolio; global flexible and income funds that invest in both stocks and bonds.

Source: *Wall Street Journal*, January 2, 1998, p. 34. Reprinted by permission of *The Wall Street Journal*
© 1998 Dow Jones & Co., Inc. All Rights Reserved Worldwide.

group. Exhibit 14-6 illustrates how these averages are reported for general equity funds in *Barron's*. The first column gives the total net asset value of all funds of a particular type. The second column gives the number of mutual funds of that type. The remaining columns give the cumulative rate of return over selected time periods. The performances of these funds are very similar, partly because all equities are influenced by the same general factors.

Exhibit 14-7 illustrates these data for two mid-sized company growth stocks, Fidelity Investment's Over-the-Counter (OTC) Fund and Vanguard's Select Value (SelValu) Fund, that are reported daily in the *Wall Street Journal*. MC denotes stock of middle-sized companies (see Exhibit 14-5). Certain key information is provided daily: the fund name, investment objective, NAV, NAV change, and the percentage return year-to-date. On Friday, three additional columns give analytical data to help investors make informed decisions (see Exhibit 14-7). For example, the maximum initial sales charge and the total expense ratio are given. The maximum initial sales

EXHIBIT 14-6   Lipper Mutual Fund Performance Averages

LIPPER MUTUAL FUND PERFORMANCE AVERAGES

Weekly Summary Report: Thursday, July 9, 1998
Cumulative Performances With Dividends Reinvested

Net Asset	No. Funds		12/31/97- 07/09/98	07/02/98- 07/09/98	06/11/98- 07/09/98	04/09/98- 07/09/98	07/10/97- 07/09/98
General Equity Funds:							
113,646.2	267	Capital Appreciation	+ 15.40%	+ 1.50%	+ 6.51%	+ 2.06%	+ 21.13%
648,595.0	1,070	Growth Funds	+ 17.93%	+ 1.41%	+ 6.35%	+ 3.55%	+ 24.30%
91,043.6	341	Mid Cap Funds	+ 12.65%	+ 1.38%	+ 5.50%	+ 0.41%	+ 20.59%
148,719.5	647	Small Cap Funds	+ 7.33%	+ 0.66%	+ 4.10%	− 3.31%	+ 16.39%
4,978.8	54	Micro Cap Funds	+ 7.62%	+ 0.36%	+ 2.38%	− 3.99%	+ 20.81%
593,041.5	800	Growth and Income	+ 14.02%	+ 0.59%	+ 4.03%	+ 1.21%	+ 21.27%
136,962.5	94	S&P 500 Objective	+ 19.99%	+ 1.08%	+ 5.92%	+ 4.59%	+ 28.11%
151,458.9	232	Equity Income	+ 10.37%	+ 0.03%	+ 2.43%	− 0.44%	+ 19.13%
1,888,446.0	3,505	Gen. Equity Funds Avg.	+ 13.76%	+ 0.97%	+ 5.00%	+ 0.98%	+ 21.26%
		Securities Market Indexes					
Value		**U.S. Equities:**					
460.00		Russell 2000 Index P	+ 5.26%	+ 0.37%	+ 3.52%	− 4.17%	+ 15.24%
590.23		NYSE Composite P	+ 15.46%	+ 0.76%	+ 4.37%	+ 2.05%	+ 23.93%
1,343.76		S&P Industrials	+ 19.83%	+ 0.77%	+ 5.62%	+ 4.66%	+ 24.86%
1,158.56		S&P 500 P	+ 19.39%	+ 1.06%	+ 5.85%	+ 4.31%	+ 26.79%
9,089.78		Dow Jones Ind. Avg. P	+ 14.94%	+ 0.71%	+ 3.15%	+ 1.06%	+ 15.25%
Value		**International Equities:**					
1,644.70		Nikkei 225 Average P	+ 7.79%	− 0.15%	+ 9.54%	− 0.54%	− 16.74%
6,035.50		FT S-E 100 Index	+ 17.53%	+ 1.44%	+ 1.96%	− 1.15%	+ 26.59%
6,028.19		DAX Index	+ 41.85%	+ 2.08%	+ 0.00%	+ 13.37%	+ 50.99%
		Fund Management Companies					
Value:							
3,301.21		Stock-price Index	+ 13.34%	+ 0.80%	+ 3.07%	− 4.61%	+ 29.55%

Source: Lipper Analytical Services, Inc., as cited in *Barron's*, July 13, 1998, p. MW74. Reprinted by permission of *Barron's*, © 1998 Dow Jones & Co., Inc. All Rights Reserved Worldwide.

charge is the highest percentage commission allowable for selling shares, which is 3% for the OTC Fund. The total expense ratio is the total operating expenses of the fund divided by the total funds invested. Exhibit 14-7 shows that the SelValu Fund expenses are only 0.75%, whereas the OTC Fund expenses are 0.85%. Thus, the investor can see that the OTC Fund has two strikes against it: it has a 3% sales fee and a higher expense ratio.

Before the OTC Fund is eliminated from consideration, however, the investor should examine how the funds have historically performed. The final column ranks the fund's performance as compared with other funds having the same objectives. For example, as of Friday, the OTC Fund has earned 11.3% over the past year, whereas SelValu Fund has earned 3.5%. These performances afforded both funds a C rating. Funds are rated from A to E depending on the quintile in which the fund's return lands. An A rating means the fund is in the top 20% of the funds within the same category; a B rating means the fund is in the next 20% range, and so on. Thus, a C rating is about average, and a D rating is below average.

Although historical performance is no guarantee of future performance, at least it shows that in the past, investors who held the OTC Fund for a long time did better than those who held SelValu. This makes it more difficult to choose the best fund. For example, it is possible that the OTC Fund has higher sales charges but also makes better portfolio selection decisions in the long run. In this case, investors would have to read the prospectus carefully and evaluate their own objectives to make a good decision.

Most mutual funds are members of a group of mutual funds known as a **family of funds.** For example, the SelValu Fund (Select Value) is one of several investment companies operated by the Vanguard Group of Investment Companies. Exhibit 14-8 lists the Vanguard family of funds. The Vanguard Group offers a range of funds, from index funds (funds with names starting with *Idx* or *Indx*) to a fund that invests in junk bonds (HYCorp).

One benefit of a family of funds is the ease with which investors can reallocate their investment dollars among funds in a family. *Barron's* publishes data on each fund's income and dividend payments.

A final category of mutual funds is *money market mutual funds.* These funds invest in debt securities of very short maturities. Most money market funds allow investors to write checks on the balance invested in the fund. Hence, these funds are highly liquid. Money market funds typically invest in U.S. government debt, commercial paper, bank certificates of deposit, repurchase agreements, banker's acceptances, and other short-term securities. Money market funds have very little risk and have many restrictions on how they can invest shareholders' money. For example, the SEC requires money market funds to invest solely in commercial paper in the top two grades as evaluated by Moody's or Standard & Poor's. By the end of 1996, there were 1,032 different money market mutual funds (28% of the total number of the different fund categories) with combined assets of over $900 billion.[12]

---

12. CDA/Wiesenberger Investment Companies Service, p. 20.

EXHIBIT 14-7   **Data for Two Mutual Funds as Provided by the *Wall Street Journal* during the Week of February 9 through February 13, 1998**

		NASD Data				Lipper Analytical Data		
Day	Fund	Investment Objective	NAV	NAV Change	% Return YTD	Maximum Initial Charge	Total Expense Ratio[a]	Rank
Monday	OTC	MC	36.33	+0.34	+ 8.6			
	SelValu	MC	12.49	+0.06	+ 1.7			
Tuesday	OTC	MC	36.21	−0.12	+ 8.3			
	SelValu	MC	12.46	−0.03	+ 1.5			
Wednesday	OTC	MC	36.88	+0.67	+10.3			
	SelValu	MC	12.62	+0.16	+ 2.8			
Thursday	OTC	MC	37.04	+0.16	+10.7			
	SelValu	MC	12.68	+0.06	+ 3.3			
Friday	OTC	MC	37.23	+0.19	+11.3	3.00	0.85	C
	SelValu	MC	12.71	+0.03	+ 3.5	0.00	0.75	C

[a]Annualized.

INDEX FUNDS

Index funds are funds that simply replicate a given index. For example, S&P index funds simply invest in the stocks and weights that compare with the S&P 500 index. Thus, these funds, so to speak, sell the S&P 500 index to their customers with relatively very little management fees; for example, the Vanguard Group of funds, a leading index fund, charges only 0.2% annually as a management fee. However, index funds hold no cash (because they replicate the S&P 500 index); hence, stocks held by the fund must be sold whenever investors redeem shares. This characteristic can cause difficulties for the fund's management and place some annoying obstacles in the way of nervous investors seeking quick redemptions. For example, index funds do not allow investors to sell shares by a telephone call, and they charge a redemption fee for shares held for less than a given period, say, six months. For example, T. Rowe Price Associates charges 0.5% for shares held less than six months. Fidelity Investment charges 0.5% for shares held less than ninety days, and Dreyfus Corporation, a 1.2 billion S&P 500 index fund, charges a 1% redemption fee for shares held less than six months.[13]

Apart from daily information on a fund, from time to time a survey conducted of hundreds of mutual funds, comparing and ranking them by performance in an up and down market, is reported (where A is the highest grade given). Usually a

13. For more details on index funds, see Jeff Benjamin, "Index Funds May Not Be So Easy to Exit," *Wall Street Journal,* July 21, 1997, p. C23.

EXHIBIT 14-8 An Illustration of a Family of Funds

MUTUAL FUNDS

52 Week High	52 Week Low	Fund Name	Week's High	Week's Low	Close NAV	Wk's Chg.	% Return 1-Wk	% Return YTD	3-Yr	Latest Dividend Income+Cap. gains	Record Date	12 MTH Inco. Divs.	12 MTH Cap. Gain
		Van Wagoner Funds:											
14.35	8.81	EmgGro n	10.34	10.22	10.22	−.06	−.6	+.7	...	....	....	....	....
13.88	8.79	MicroCap n	10.54	10.45	10.45	−.03	−.3	+4.6	...	....	....	....	....
14.74	9.35	MidCap n	11.67	11.51	11.65	+.19	+1.7	+9.2	...	....	....	....	....
12.18	7.84	PostVent np	10.65	10.57	10.64	+.08	+.8	+21.2	...	....	....	....	....
		Vanguard Fds:											
10.67	10.18	AdmIT n	10.60	10.58	10.59	...	+.1	+4.5	+22.6	.0539	5-31-98	.6389	....
11.33	10.22	AdmLT n	11.33	11.27	11.28	−.04	+.2	+6.2	+30.6	.0566	5-31-98	.6655	.006
10.18	10.04	AdmST n	10.12	10.12	10.12	...	+.1	+3.3	+19.1	.0474	5-31-98	.5811	.006
24.38	19.25	AssetA n	24.38	24.26	24.35	+.21	+.9	+16.6	+90.8	.54+1.01	12-11-97	.74	1.01
10.88	10.58	CAInsIT n	10.75	10.75	10.75	+.01	+.2	+2.2	+21.5	.0418	5-31-98	.4948	....
11.71	11.29	CAInsLT n	11.52	11.52	11.52	...	+.2	+2.6	+24.9	.0495	5-31-98	.5844	.0689
13.00	11.15	Convt n	12.41	12.33	12.36	+.03	+.2	+6.4	+47.7	.11	3-26-98	.54	1.12
25.09	21.13	EqInc n	24.73	24.49	24.54	−.03	−.1	+10.9	+99.7	.14	3-26-98	.67	.89
61.76	51.25	Explorer n	57.49	57.27	57.29	+.25	+.4	+3.6	+48.8	.25+5.85	12-18-97	.25	5.85
11.53	11.06	FL InsLT n	11.35	11.35	11.35	...	+.1	+2.6	+23.9	.047	5-31-98	.5565	....
10.53	10.26	GNMA n	10.45	10.43	10.44	−.01	0.0	+3.7	+24.8	.0579	5-31-98	.7108	.002
31.18	23.61	GroInc n	31.18	30.80	31.06	+.47	+1.5	+21.4	+124.3	.01+.54	5-31-98	.42	2.86
8.21	7.96	HYCorp nr	8.13	8.12	8.13	+.01	+.3	+5.1	+36.6	.0566	5-31-98	.6839	....
16.53	13.53	HznAgGr nr	15.62	15.47	15.59	+.11	+.7	+6.8	...	.14+1.08	12-26-97	.14	1.08
12.23	9.28	HznCpOp nr	12.07	11.95	12.01	+.12	+1.0	+17.7	...	.045	12-26-97	.045	....
11.25	9.97	HznGAA r	11.25	11.20	11.20	−.03	−.3	+8.9	...	.75+.54	12-26-97	.75	.54
13.89	11.29	HznGlbEq nr	13.44	13.27	13.27	−.07	−.5	+10.8	...	.23+.44	12-26-97	.23	.44
10.91	10.77	STCorpIst n	10.84	10.83	10.84	+.01	NA	NA	NA	.0577	5-31-98	.4786	....
19.74	15.31	IntlGr n	19.16	18.92	18.92	+.08	+.4	+15.4	+41.6	.21+.52	12-18-97	.21	.52
27.28	21.19	IntlVal n	27.01	26.34	26.34	−.28	−1.1	+18.2	+26.9	.01+.42	3-26-98	.70	2.68
10.13	9.75	iTCorp n	10.03	10.01	10.01	...	+.1	+4.3	+23.5	.0537	5-31-98	.6368	.026
10.87	10.39	ITTsry n	10.80	10.78	10.80	+.01	+.2	+4.4	+22.3	.0542	5-31-98	.6425	....
14.54	13.19	LIFECon n	14.54	14.50	14.52	+.07	+.5	+10.3	+52.8	.11	3-26-98	.57	.19
18.48	15.52	LIFEGro n	18.48	18.38	18.41	+.15	+.8	+15.5	+77.7	.26+.29	12-26-97	.38	.29
13.13	12.16	LIFEInc n	13.09	13.08	13.09	+.04	+.3	+7.8	+41.8	.14	3-26-98	.64	.10
16.58	14.49	LIFEMod n	16.58	16.51	16.54	+.11	+.7	+13.0	+65.5	.30+.215	12-26-97	.49	.215
9.48	8.83	LT Corp n	9.40	9.35	9.35	−.03	−.2	+5.3	+30.9	.0501	5-31-98	.6065	.153
11.00	9.92	LTTsry n	11.00	10.94	10.95	−.03	−.2	+6.1	+30.2	.0546	5-31-98	.6413	....
20.62	15.95	Morgan n	20.62	20.38	20.60	+.40	+2.0	+19.7	+109.7	.01+.37	3-26-98	.16	2.42
11.07	10.74	MuHiYd n	10.95	10.94	10.95	...	+.1	+2.9	+24.3	.0485	5-31-98	.5895	.0518
12.82	12.35	MuInIg n	12.58	12.58	12.58	...	+.1	+2.4	+23.1	.0563	5-31-98	.6639	.0811
13.56	13.21	MuniInt n	13.38	13.38	13.38	...	+.1	+2.3	+19.3	.0563	5-31-98	.6642	.0517
11.46	11.07	MuLong n	11.28	11.27	11.28	+.01	+.2	+2.6	+24.6	.0499	5-31-98	.5843	.0575
10.83	10.69	MuLtd n	10.77	10.77	10.77	...	+.1	+2.2	+14.9	.0395	5-31-98	.4644	....
15.62	15.55	MunSht n	15.59	15.58	15.59	...	+.1	+2.1	+12.5	.053	5-31-98	.6169	.0061
12.03	11.59	NJ InsLT n	11.84	11.84	11.84	...	+.1	+2.6	+21.5	.0513	5-31-98	.6025	.0109
11.35	10.90	NYInsLT n	11.17	11.17	11.17	...	+.2	+2.7	+23.1	.0484	5-31-98	.5677	.0169
12.06	11.58	OHInsLT n	11.87	11.87	11.87	...	+.1	+2.6	+22.6	.0504	5-31-98	.5947	....
11.57	11.16	PAInsLT n	11.39	11.39	11.39	...	+.1	+2.7	+22.5	.051	5-31-98	.5983	....
10.65	9.90	Prefd n	10.47	10.45	10.46	−.06	−.6	+5.2	+36.6	.16	3-26-98	.65	....
45.03	37.43	Prmcp n	45.03	44.49	45.03	+.93	+2.1	+14.6	+93.0	.01+.28	3-26-98	.21	1.42
13.87	11.63	SelValu n	12.85	12.60	12.60	−.24	−1.9	+2.6	...			.33	1.17
27.07	21.50	SPEnrg n	24.01	23.29	23.29	−.91	−3.8	−7.2	+64.1	.02+.06	3-26-98	.33	1.17
10.14	6.04	SPGold n	6.91	6.61	6.61	−.10	−1.5	−4.9	−43.2	.02	3-26-98	.14	....
87.39	69.27	SPHlth n	87.39	87.01	87.32	+.78	+.9	+23.4	+139.2	.07+1.21	3-26-98	.81	2.69
14.58	12.78	SP ReItInPr r	13.47	13.25	13.38	+.21	+1.6	−3.2	...	.11	3-26-98	.76	.05
16.32	13.12	SPUtil	15.72	15.62	15.63	−.06	−.4	+7.3	+64.6	.16+.15	3-26-98	.58	.41
19.23	16.22	STAR n	19.11	19.03	19.04	+.08	+.4	+11.0	+70.7	.34+1.20	12-26-97	.59	1.20
10.91	10.75	STCorp n	10.84	10.83	10.84	+.01	+.2	+3.5	+20.6	.0567	5-31-98	.6663	....
10.22	10.10	STFed n	10.17	10.16	10.17	+.01	+.2	+3.5	+19.6	.0502	5-31-98	.6031	....
10.31	10.16	STTsry n	10.25	10.25	10.25	...	+.1	+3.3	+18.7	.047	5-31-98	.5794	....
42.83	33.82	TrUS n	42.83	42.38	42.83	+.84	+2.0	+20.1	+105.9	.01+1.14	3-26-98	.44	8.61
16.16	14.14	TxMBal nr	16.16	16.06	16.15	+.16	+1.0	+11.2	+55.6	.08	3-26-98	.38	....
24.44	18.87	TxMCAp nr	24.44	24.14	24.40	+.47	+2.0	+20.9	+102.1	.17+.02	12-26-97	.17	.02
25.17	18.87	TxMGl r	25.17	24.91	25.12	+.39	+1.6	+21.0	+121.8	.06	3-26-98	.29	....
36.54	26.82	USGro n	36.54	36.18	36.54	+.70	+2.0	+27.3	+128.6	.27+.89	12-18-97	.27	.89
23.01	20.09	Wellsly n	22.72	22.55	22.55	−.09	−.4	+6.9	+53.5	.28+.24	3-26-98	1.20	1.52
32.27	27.68	Welltn n	32.16	31.91	31.91	−.01	0.0	+9.9	+73.3	.22	3-26-98	1.14	1.57
19.98	16.03	Wndsr n	19.14	18.87	18.87	−.02	−.2	+11.9	+77.4	.12+2.88	12-11-97	.32	2.88
33.40	25.76	WndsII	33.40	33.13	33.16	+.11	+.3	+16.6	+119.8	.46+2.19	12-11-97	.66	2.19

Source: *Barron's*, July 13, 1998, p. MW78. Reprinted with permission of *Barron's*, © 1998 Dow Jones & Co., Inc. All Rights Reserved Worldwide.

fund's performance is checked relative to a benchmark unmanaged portfolio. For example, Exhibit 14-9 provides a small sample of the survival funds table from *Forbes*. These are global funds, mutual funds that can invest in stocks and bonds throughout the world (see top of Exhibit 14-9). Each global fund can be compared with these

EXHIBIT 14-9   Global Stock Funds

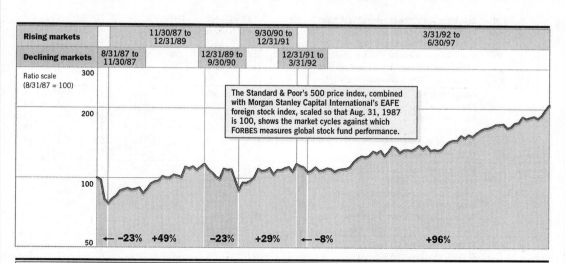

The Standard & Poor's 500 price index, combined with Morgan Stanley Capital International's EAFE foreign stock index, scaled so that Aug. 31, 1987 is 100, shows the market cycles against which FORBES measures global stock fund performance.

MARKET PERFORMANCE		Fund/distributor	Annualized total return 8/31/87 to 6/30/97	3-year	$10,000 grew to (aftertax)[1]	Assets 6/30/97 ($mil)	Weighted average P/E	Foreign investment %	Maximum sales charge	Annual expenses per $100
Up ▲	Down ▼									
		BLENDED DOMESTIC AND FOREIGN STOCK INDEX	10.9%	18.7%						
		FORBES GLOBAL STOCK FUND COMPOSITE	5.8%	13.7%			25.5	61.7%		$1.55
■ C	■ C	AIM Global Utilities Fund-A/AIM	— *	17.0%	$15,444	$248	15.4	34%	5.50 %	$1.17
A	F	Alliance Global Small Cap-A/Alliance	7.3 %	19.1	15,161	121	29.4	50	4.25	2.51
■ D	■ C	American Century Global Gold[2]/Amer Century	— *	−6.8	7,927	335	35.5	77	none	0.62
C	A	Blanchard Global Growth/Federated	6.4	11.6	12,934	65	14.1	49	none	2.41
■ D	■ D	Blanchard Precious Metals/Federated	— *	−1.1	8,467	62	46.0	62	none	2.32
		Brinson Global Equity/Chase	— *	17.4	15,331	110	26.6	51	none	0.95 a
		Brinson Global Fund/Chase	— *	15.9	14,605	613	26.4	41	none	0.96
		Calvert World Values–Intl-A[3]/Calvert	— *	10.9	13,220	228	25.0	99	4.75	1.79 a
		Capital World Growth & Income/American Funds	— *	21.1	16,855	6,655	21.5	68	5.75	0.85
		Colonial Global Equity-A/Colonial	— *	17.2	14,893	107	20.4	74	5.75	1.58
D	C	Colonial International Horizons-A[4]/Colonial	0.1	13.7	13,953	65	20.9	54	5.75	1.61
		Dean Witter Global Div Growth[5]/Dean Witter	— *	17.5	15,288	3,574	23.5	70	5.00 b	1.75
		Dean Witter Global Utilities[5]/Dean Witter	— *	13.5	14,305	373	20.9	67	5.00 b	1.82

Three-year return 6/30/94 through 6/30/97. ■ Fund rated for two periods only; maximum allowable grade A. *Fund not in operation or did not meet asset minimum for full period. a: Net of absorption of expenses by fund sponsor. b: Includes back-end load that reverts to distributor. [1]Hypothetical three-year return for upper-middle-income investor after federal tax on distribution; no deduction for load or for tax on unrealized gains. [2]Formerly Benham Global Gold. [3]Formerly Calvert World Valuest–Global Equity. [4]Reflects performance of Colonial Advance Strategies Gold prior to June 1992 merger. [5]Converted to multiclass format July 28, 1997.
Sources: Forbes; Lipper Analytical Services; Morningstar, Inc.

Rules, page 162. Distributor table, page 257.

(continued)

EXHIBIT 14-9   *(continued)*

C	C	Dean Witter World Wide Investment[1]/Dean Witter	6.0 %	5.9%	$11,521	$437	27.8	74%	5.00 %b	$2.36
C	A+	Dreyfus Global Growth/Dreyfus	11.1	11.8	13,315	98	31.9	72	none	1.39
		Dreyfus Premier Global Investing-A/Dreyfus	— *	12.3	13,212	141	29.4	78	5.75	1.31
		Dreyfus Premier Worldwide Growth-A[2]/Dreyfus	— *	25.2	19,428	298	25.3	34	5.75	1.25 a
A+	B	EV Traditional WW Health & Sciences/Eaton Vance	15.8	31.5	21,243	131	41.1	53	4.75	2.06 a
■ C	■ A	Fidelity Advisor Natural Resources-T[3]/Fidelity Adv	— *	19.0	16,307	674	21.6	17	3.50	1.46 a
		Fidelity Global Balanced/Fidelity	— *	9.6	13,000	74	26.0	74	none	1.47 a
D	A	Fidelity Select–American Gold/Fidelity	1.1	1.4	10,204	279	47.1	63	3.00	1.42 a
		Fidelity Worldwide Fund/Fidelity	— *	13.4	14,129	1,184	21.2	81	none	1.19 a
B	D	First Investors Global Fund-A/First Inv	8.6	15.2	14,408	299	24.4	75	6.25	1.83
		Fortis Global Growth-A/Fortis	— *	20.9	17,674	157	33.4	52	4.75	1.43
■ A	■ A	Founders Worldwide Growth/Founders	— *	16.8	15,484	347	30.9	73	none	1.55
		Franklin Global Health Care-I/Franklin	— *	31.5	21,822	200	21.4	15	4.50	1.14
		Fremont Global Fund/Fremont	— *	15.0	14,049	677	15.0	38	none	0.85
		Gabelli Global Telecommunications/Gabelli	— *	14.7	14,676	109	23.5	56	none	1.72
		Global Utility Fund-A/Prudential	— *	15.4	14,432	303	17.9	55	5.00	1.24
		GT Global Financial Services-A/GT Global	— *	16.5	15,461	58	17.6	49	4.75	2.40 a
		GT Global Growth & Income-A/GT Global	— *	14.5	14,463	734	20.0	69	4.75	1.66
■ A	■ B	GT Global Health Care-A/GT Global	— *	24.9	18,004	586	19.2	8	4.75	1.84
		GT Global Infrastructure-A/GT Global	— *	13.0	14,216	110	20.4	65	4.75	2.25
		GT Global Natural Resources-A/GT Global	— *	13.4	14,389	117	27.0	44	4.75	2.30
		GT Global Telecommunications-A/GT Global	— *	9.8	12,547	1,804	31.0	69	4.75	1.79
B	D	GT Global Worldwide Growth-A/GT Global	8.0	9.5	12,472	163	24.2	65	4.75	1.80
B	D	Hancock Global Fund-A/Hancock	6.6	13.1	13,398	141	26.8	55	5.00	1.89
		Hancock Global Rx-A/Hancock	— *	27.4	20,356	97	36.5	5	5.00	1.75
		IDEX Global-A/InterSecurities	— *	23.4	17,894	253	28.5	89	5.50	2.09
		IDS Global Growth-A/Amer Express	— *	8.5	12,293	1,216	29.5	85	5.00	1.37
D	D	Invesco Strategic–Gold/Invesco	-4.3	0.4	9,307	179	37.0	76	none	1.22
		Janus Worldwide Fund/Janus	— *	24.7	18,425	9,221	31.1	88	none	0.95
		Keystone Fund of the Americas-A/Evergreen	— *	22.6	17,886	128	29.4	95	4.75	1.83
■ B	■ C	Keystone Global Opportunities-A/Evergreen	— *	11.3	13,585	452	28.4	58	4.75	1.62
D	C	Keystone Precious Metals/Evergreen	-1.7	-5.0	8,463	134	38.4	73	4.00 b	2.33
D	B	Lexington Goldfund/Lexington	-2.6	-3.9	8,522	84	29.7	33	none	1.60
■ C	■ D	Lord Abbett Global–Equity-A/Lord Abbett	— *	9.2	12,448	88	26.4	76	5.75	1.56
		Mentor Perpetual Global-A/Mentor	— *	16.0	15,214	118	24.0	66	5.75	2.01
■ B	■ B	Merrill Lynch Global Allocation-D/Merrill	— *	15.2	14,201	13,934	24.2	38	5.25	1.10 a
B	B	Merrill Lynch Global Holdings-D/Merrill	8.3	12.4	13,579	524	30.7	80	5.25	1.63
C	A	Merrill Lynch Global Resources-D/Merrill	3.4	9.7	13,013	205	27.6	70	5.25	1.27
		Merrill Lynch Global Utility-D/Merrill	— *	15.6	14,730	371	19.3	62	4.00	1.07
B	C	Merrill Lynch Healthcare-D/Merrill	9.8	26.6	18,923	374	15.9	26	5.25	1.65
B	C	Merrill Lynch Technology-D/Merrill	13.7	10.0	12,466	699	17.7	6	5.25	1.55
C	B	MFS World Equity-A/MFS	9.5	18.2	15,322	407	25.0	60	5.75	1.67
		MFS World Growth-A/MFS	— *	15.7	14,792	541	33.1	58	5.75	1.54 a

Three-year return 6/30/94 through 6/30/97. ■ Fund rated for two periods only; maximum allowable grade A. *Fund not in operation or did not meet asset minimum for full period. a: Net of absorption of expenses by fund sponsor. b: Includes back-end load that reverts to distributor. [1]Converted to multiclass format July 28, 1997. [2]Formerly Premier Growth Fund. [3]Formerly Fidelity Advisor Global Resources.
Sources Forbes; Lipper Analytical Services; Morningstar, Inc.

two unmanaged benchmark portfolios (Forbes Global Stock Fund Composite and Blended Domestic and Foreign Stock Index). The graph shows the up and down period, and the funds are ranked relative to the performance of the unmanaged portfolio in these two time categories (August 30, 1987, to June 30, 1997, and the last three years). Note that some funds do not have a sales charge (load), whereas others have as much as a 5.75% sales charge. Consider an investor who invests for 1 year in Calvert World Values. The fund earns 10.9% on an annual basis, but if the 4.75% sales charge is deducted, a very low rate of return is left. Therefore, investors who buy such a fund share must invest for a relatively long period; the load will then be spread out over many years and will not substantially affect the returns.

14.2 BENEFITS AND COSTS OF INVESTING IN MUTUAL FUNDS

Mutual funds hold securities that in principle, the individual investor can buy directly. Then why do investors buy mutual funds rather than owning the individual assets directly? There are obviously some benefits from buying funds rather than individual assets. This section examines the benefits and costs of investing in mutual funds.

14.2.1 Benefits of Investing in Mutual Funds

The use of mutual funds provides several benefits, from increasing a society's supply of capital to free checking accounts. The following are the main benefits:

1. *Diversification.* Mutual funds offer investors an easy way to diversify. Because of the large pool of money that a mutual fund is able to attract, it is not difficult for fund managers to diversify widely among a range of different securities.

   Exhibit 14-10 lists the largest securities held by the Fidelity Magellan Fund and illustrates the fund's high level of diversification. Notice that even the largest security holding is just over 2% of the portfolio. Clearly, this level of diversification would be difficult for the small investor to achieve, especially because most of these securities are international firms. However, mutual funds may not have the optimal level of diversification. For example, most mutual funds have restrictions on their investments. The State Farm Balanced Fund (STFBX), for one, will not invest more than 75% of its funds in common stock.[14]

2. *Professional management.* Many individual investors do not wish to devote the time that is necessary to learn how to participate in financial markets. Some investors do not have the necessary skills, particularly in analyzing international stocks. Hence, they would rather entrust their savings to someone who has been professionally trained. Using mutual funds is one way to obtain a professional

14. Rockville, Md.: CDA/Wiesenberger Investment Companies Service, p. 1181.

EXHIBIT 14-10
Fidelity Magellan
Fund (FMAGX);
Fund Category:
Long-Term
Growth

Top Equity Holdings (as of 9/19/96)

Stock	% of Portfolio Holdings
Caterpillar Inc.	2.27%
Intel Corporation	2.23
Chrysler Corporation	1.99
General Motors Corporation	1.71
Royal Dutch Pete Company	1.68
CSX Corporation	1.45
International Business Machines	1.45
Deere and Company	1.40
General Electric	1.33
Exxon Corporation	1.26

Portfolio Composition (as of 12/31/96)

Stocks	89.6%
Bonds	3.8
Preferred	0.0
Convertibles	0.0
Cash	6.6

Sector Weightings (as of 12/31/96)

Basic industries	10.8%
Capital goods & technology	27.2
Consumer cyclicals	18.3
Consumer non-cyclicals	4.9
Energy	13.5
Finance	9.5
Transportation	6.0
Utilities	7.3
Miscellaneous	2.4

Source: CDA/Wiesenberger Investment Companies Service, *Investment Companies Yearbook* (Rockville, Md.: CDA/Wiesenberger, 1996), p. 793. Reprinted with permission.

money manager to make asset allocation and security selection decisions on your behalf, and without your consultation. Exhibit 14-10 illustrates the value of professional management. Can you imagine the complexity involved in evaluating all the different securities? Most small investors would not wish to conduct such an enormous amount of research.

3. *Reduced trading costs (or the gain from diversification).* Because of their sheer size, mutual funds enjoy a considerable reduction in the cost of trading securities. This characteristic leads some investors to select mutual funds over individual securities. Consider the transaction costs facing a small investor with just enough resources to buy two securities, A and B, in round lots. Exhibit 14-11 illustrates the optimum portfolio for this investor (point *O*). Although the market portfolio lies on the more steeply sloped capital market line, this portfolio is not

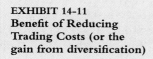

EXHIBIT 14-11
Benefit of Reducing Trading Costs (or the gain from diversification)

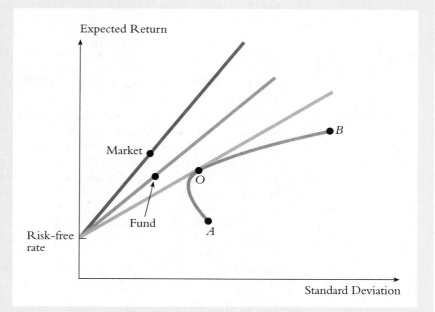

achievable by the individual because of trading costs. To diversify widely would require investing in odd lots, which is very expensive; the trading costs alone would wipe out any benefits from diversification. If a fund can position itself on a higher opportunity line, then the investor would prefer the fund over individual portfolio management. Mutual funds allow investors to achieve a better risk-return trade-off than they could otherwise have obtained. Investors should buy the mutual fund as long as it provides a higher line, after all costs are considered, than one that goes through point *O* (see Exhibit 14-11).

4. *Systematic accumulation and withdrawal plans.* Many mutual funds offer the advantage of either directly withdrawing funds from, or regularly depositing funds into, the investor's personal bank checking account. (Many investors make monthly deposits, but some use other time periods.) These plans are beneficial for those who lack the financial discipline to save voluntarily or for retired individuals who need the monthly income. For example, a retired couple who is traveling around the world could have money directly deposited from the mutual fund to their bank account each month.

5. *Checking accounts.* Many mutual funds offer investors the ability to write checks and deposit monies into the mutual fund just as they would into a bank checking account. However, because of the physical location of the mutual fund office, deposits are usually made by mail. Typically, there are dollar limits on the check withdrawals (for example, the withdrawal must exceed $250.00). The idea is to limit the volume of checks written (and hence the cost of processing them).

6. *Switching services.* Most families of funds allow investors to switch between individual funds by telephone. Hence, if an investor's money is invested in a stock fund and she believes it would be better for the money to be in a bond fund, she can reallocate her wealth with one phone call. This affords a high level of flexibility to the individual investor. Typically, these switching services are free or available at a very reasonable cost. An investor holding individual securities would not have this flexibility.

7. *Security custody and bookkeeping.* Mutual funds eliminate the need to store the physical securities to keep track of an investor's trading activities. Most mutual funds also keep detailed records of investors' trading activities and related tax consequences. Hence, each year at tax time the mutual fund will determine the specific tax liabilities, ordinary income, and capital gains.

8. *Increasing an economy's capital supply.* One of the often overlooked benefits of mutual funds is that by providing an attractive investment vehicle to the small investor, mutual funds are increasing the amount of capital available to firms. Without an efficient means to participate in the financial markets, individuals and families might decide to consume their income rather than save it in a poor-yielding bank savings account. Mutual funds provide a reasonable method for small investors to participate and hence increase an economy's savings rate.

With all of these benefits, one may wonder why everyone doesn't invest in mutual funds. Mutual fund investments also have costs, and investors must weigh them against the benefits when making investment decisions.

14.2.2 Costs of Investing in Mutual Funds

Investors incur several costs when they use mutual funds:

1. *Load.* Open-end funds are classified as either load or no-load funds. Load funds are sold in the over-the-counter market by broker-dealers who do not receive an up-front sales commission. Instead, a load is added to the net value of the asset at the time of the purchase. A load is a fee paid to the seller of mutual funds. Recall, for example, that Fidelity Investment's OTC Fund carried a 3% load. A 3% load means that for every dollar invested in the OTC Fund, 3 cents goes to the salesperson (the broker-dealer) and only 97 cents is actually invested in the fund. If an investor bought a mutual fund for only 1 year and it earned 10%, the load would take about 30% of the earnings, resulting in a gain of only 7%. However, over a long period of time, this cost would decline on a percentage basis.[15] For many years the typical load was 8½%, but it is currently about 4½% to 5%. Many load funds do not have an up-front load but rather impose a back-end load, which customers pay if they sell the fund shares within a stated period of time (for example, 5 years). The shares of a no-load fund, in contrast, are

---

15. However, a load is still costly over time in absolute dollar terms. For example, for 25 years a $10,000 investment in the load fund would be worth ($10,000 · 0.97)(1 + 0.1)^{25} = $105,096.65, which is a 9.866% annual rate of return [($105,096.65/$10,000)$^{1/25}$ − 1]. The no-load fund, with the same 10% annual rate of return, would be worth $10,000(1 + 0.1)^{25} = $108,347.06, or $3,250.41 more. Thus, this load would result in the investor's losing $3,250.41, but only 0.134% on an annual percentage basis.

bought directly from the funds, thus saving the load payment. Note that dealers of closed-end funds obtain their income from commission fees, just as they do in any other stock transaction.

2. *Management fees.* Whether or not a mutual fund has a load, every mutual fund incurs costs in its day-to-day management. These costs are passed directly on to mutual fund shareholders. Recently, the OTC Fund reported management expenses of 0.85% of assets under management, and the SelValu Fund reported 0.75%. Recall that the OTC Fund is actively managed, whereas the SelValu Fund is passively managed.

3. *12b-1 fees.* On October 28, 1980, the SEC adopted Rule 12b-1, allowing mutual funds to pay selling expenses directly rather than charging investors a load. At issue is whether selling expenses are part of the ongoing expenses of the fund or are a one-time expense that is charged at the purchase date. The 12b-1 rule is in contrast to a long-standing rule that prohibits funds from paying selling expenses directly, due to the conflict of interest. Fund managers have to decide whether to invest in securities or to pay a sales force. From the time of the passage of Rule 12b-1, many funds have opted to use 12b-1 fees to pay selling and advertising costs. Typically, 12b-1 fees are less than 0.70%. By March 1996, 5,168 funds had adopted 12b-1 fees.[16] Fund managers in favor of 12b-1 fees argue that these fees provide a more efficient mechanism for paying selling expenses.

    Several academic studies, including those by Ferris and Chance and Trzcinka and Zweig, find that 12b-1 fees tend to be higher than fees of funds without 12b-1 fees, and that there is no difference in the average performance of 12b-1 funds and funds without 12b-1 fees.[17] (If anything, the evidence suggests that 12b-1 funds actually underperform funds without 12b-1 fees.)

4. *Transaction costs.* Mutual fund investors must pay for the trading costs incurred by the fund's management. Even though the trading costs may be lower for each share traded, mutual funds can still incur substantial costs from active trading. These costs are typically reported as part of the management fee. If the mutual fund manager is an active trader, then the fund will have higher transaction costs. Because of the obvious link between the volume of trading and transaction costs, these costs are usually measured by the fund's turnover. Turnover is usually defined as the value of securities purchased (or sold—whichever is less) divided by the average NAV for a given period. A related measure is the *expense ratio.* The expense ratio is the cost (including operating expenses and management fees) as a percentage of the NAV incurred by the mutual fund. For example, the Kemper Diversified Income fund, a growth fund, had a turnover ratio of 310% in 1996, whereas the Northeast Investors Trust Fund, an index fund, had only a 32% turnover in 1996. It is not surprising to find that the Kemper Diversified Income fund had an expense ratio of 0.66%.[18] Over time, high turnover has two

16. See Charles Trzcinka and Robert Zweig, *An Economic Analysis of the Cost and Benefits of S.E.C. Rule 12b-1,* Monograph 1990-1 (New York: Salomon Brothers Center for the Study of Financial Institutions, Leonard N. Stern School of Business, New York University, 1990); and J. R. Brandstrader, "Insatiable: 12b-1 Fees Taking Bigger Bite Out of Returns," *Barron's,* October 6, 1997, p. F13.
17. See Stephen P. Ferris and Don Chance, "The Effect of 12b-1 Plans on Mutual Fund Expense Ratios: A Note," *Journal of Finance,* September 1987, pp. 1077–1082; and Trzcinka and Zweig, *An Economic Analysis, ibid.*
18. Rockville, Md.: CDA/Wiesenberger Investment Companies Service, pp. 916,1015.

negative effects. First, capital gains will be realized, subjecting the investor to capital gains tax. Second, higher turnover will result in higher expenses, thus lowering returns.

5. *Higher income tax rate.* According to the 1997 U.S. tax laws, the capital gains tax rate is 20% if a security is held for at least eighteen months. Otherwise, the ordinary income tax rates apply. In a mutual fund with a relatively high turnover, assets are held for less than eighteen months, so investors may be subjected to an income tax rate as high as 39.6% (versus 20%). This is a big disadvantage for some funds and always compares negatively with direct investment in stocks.

6. *Accounting, distribution, and other miscellaneous costs.* Each mutual fund incurs costs related to the day-to-day affairs of running a business. The mutual fund must conform to acceptable accounting procedures and must be audited. Most funds issue monthly statements to shareholders in order to report trading activities of the account, as well as price performance of the fund. Numerous other minor expenses are incurred, such as in fulfilling staffing requirements and obtaining office space. Recently, the SmCap Fund reported miscellaneous expenses of 0.04%, and the OTC Fund reported 0.33%. Again, the actively managed portfolio is incurring higher expenses.

7. *Suboptimal investment.* An often overlooked cost of investing in mutual funds is the fact that the asset allocation strategy may not be optimal for a particular investor. For example, consider a fund that allocates a significant portion of its assets in the retail industry. If an investor is an employee of a retail firm, such as WalMart, then the investor probably owns WalMart stock through an employee benefits program. By purchasing a fund that has a large portion of its assets in retail stocks such as WalMart, the investor will be overallocated in the retail industry. Optimally, the investor would want a fund that invests less in the retail industry. (However, other investors may want just the opposite.)

It is difficult to find a mutual fund that has the appropriate asset allocation for each individual. This is especially true because a fund's management may alter the asset allocation of the fund at any time. Hence, even if an investor finds the ideal fund, the asset allocation may change tomorrow, resulting in a suboptimal allocation for that investor.

One solution to the problem of suboptimal investment is to invest in specialized funds. Many families of funds offer industry-specific mutual funds. For example, Vanguard offers specialized funds in energy, gold, health care, services, technology, and utilities. With specialized funds, the mutual fund investor can control the asset allocation decision directly. Thus, investors can diversify across specialty funds to achieve their desired level of diversification.

A second cost related to suboptimal investment is overdiversification. For example, if an investor is already well diversified, then purchasing a widely diversified mutual fund will not provide any further substantial benefit. The investor may be able to achieve a higher level of diversification by judicious selection of individual securities.

8. *The disadvantage of being too big.* Sometimes being too big forces a mutual fund either to pick stocks it does not want or to hold too much cash. Both factors reduce the fund's return. Connecting Theory to Practice 14.3 illustrates this problem.

CONNECTING THEORY TO PRACTICE 14.3

MAGELLAN, THE FLAGSHIP OF FIDELITY, WILL CLOSE TO MOST NEW INVESTORS

Move Will Blunt Criticism of Fund's Size but Cost Firm a Lot of Revenue

A '97 Investment Comeback

BOSTON—Fidelity Magellan Fund, the $62.9 billion investment pool whose performance once led the bull market, is closing its doors to new customers.

According to people familiar with the matter, Fidelity Investments will announce shortly that Magellan will no longer sell shares to anyone other than current shareholders or members of retirement plans that carry Magellan on their menu of investment choices. . . .

Magellan, which has 4.3 million shareholders, is the world's largest mutual fund. But without new shareholders, it may lose that position to the $45 billion Vanguard Index 500 Portfolio, a fast-growing fund that seeks to mimic the performance of the Standard & Poor's 500 index. Fidelity and Vanguard Group, based in Valley Forge, Pa., are bitter rivals; having the largest fund confers prestige and generates attention, both of which can translate into fund sales.

The decision to shutter Magellan reflects strategic and management shifts at Fidelity, whose business has shifted away from individual, or "retail," clients and toward institutions such as big retirement plans. It also reflects the philosophy of Mr. Stansky, who believes in staying more or less fully invested in the stock market. A reduced inflow of money means Mr. Stansky won't often face a choice of buying stocks he isn't wild about or leaving the money uninvested and thus raising his "cash" level. He also may be less likely to have to sell to meet redemptions, since shareholders will hesitate to bail out completely knowing they can't get back in.

Shutting the fund to most new investors cuts off a huge source of potential revenue for Fidelity, a unit of FMR Corp. Fidelity receives a 3% sales commission for new money moved into Magellan, except what comes from retirement-plan accounts. (About 70% of new money now does come from such plans.) Fidelity also gets an annual management fee of 0.47% of each $1 for the entire portfolio, or about $245.4 million for the fiscal year ended March 31. The fund's overall expense ratio is 0.66%.

Source: James S. Hirsch, "Trimming Its Sails," *Wall Street Journal,* August 27, 1997. Reprinted by permission of *The Wall Street Journal* © 1997 Dow Jones & Co., Inc. All Rights Reserved Worldwide.

MAKING THE CONNECTION

When the Magellan fund closes its doors to new investors, Fidelity loses the 3% sales commission and the annual management fee of 0.47%. This only emphasizes the cost of a mutual fund's being too big and the need to purchase stocks it really does not want. This is a clear disadvantage of open-end funds.

In light of all these costs of investing in mutual funds, some investors have decided to pick their own stocks. Connecting Theory to Practice 14.4 provides reasons why Richard Ranny, a private investor, decided to invest in stocks rather than mutual funds. In conclusion, mutual funds may or may not be appropriate for particular investors, depending on how the associated costs and benefits affect each individual.

CONNECTING THEORY TO PRACTICE 14.4

WITHOUT PORTFOLIO: THE CASE FOR PICKING YOUR OWN STOCKS

No-load mutual funds are undeniably good for the individual investor. They're easy to purchase, give instant diversification and have excellent liquidity.

Despite these laudable qualities, I believe that long-term investors—especially those who have to pay yearly income taxes—should hold individual stocks, rather than funds. . . .

Here are some of my reasons for favoring stocks over funds:

- Investors in individual stocks avoid the annual expenses and management fees charged by the funds. Equity funds normally impose yearly expense and management fees ranging from 0.3% (for an index fund) to 1.5% or more. Though this may seem to be trifle, it's a significant drag on long-term returns. For example, $100,000 invested for 25 years at 10% per year will grow to $1,205,695. But if one were to slice off, say, 0.8 of a percentage point in fees from the annual return, that $100,000 would grow to $988,707 in the same span.
- Holders of individual stocks retain control over whether, and when, to take capital gains and losses. This is a powerful tax-planning tool. In contrast, fund shareholders have little or no such control, at least when it comes to the issues the fund owns, rather than shares of the fund itself.
- The purchaser of an open-end mutual fund is usually purchasing a hidden future tax liability.

   Funds often have a tax basis that, in reality, is much lower than what an investor pays for its shares. As the mutual fund sells its appreciated stocks, this tax liability is passed on to you, even if you don't sell any shares of the fund.
- The portfolio turnover rate of an open-end fund isn't totally controlled by the portfolio manager. If the market sours and investors get nervous, excessive redemptions can force a fund to sell stocks. The disadvantages of this phenomenon are passed on to the remaining shareholders. Those who hold individual issues will never be forced to sell, even if others are panicking.
- One apparent advantage of a no-load mutual fund is that the buyer or seller pays no commission, whereas purchasers of individual issues pay brokers' commissions.

(continued)

However, a mutual fund does pay commissions on its purchases and sales of stocks. The long-term investor in a fund will pay his proportionate share of any commissions it incurs.

- The diversification benefit of a mutual fund can easily be matched by the individuals.
- Many people choose funds, rather than stocks, because they believe a professional portfolio manager must be far better at picking stocks than they ever could be. Alas, if they only knew how close to "average" most fund managers really are! In any given year, about two-thirds of fund managers lag the market.

The individual investor, if he chooses his stocks purely at random from a well-diversified list representative of the market, will likely do better than the average fund.

Source: Richard Ranney, "Without Portfolio: The Case for Picking Your Own Stocks," *Barron's,* April 12, 1993, p. 13. Reprinted with permission of Barron's, © 1993 Dow Jones & Co., Inc. All Rights Reserved Worldwide.

MAKING THE CONNECTION

The choice between using mutual funds or investing directly is difficult. The author of this article clearly favors direct investing for a variety of reasons. The rapid growth of the mutual fund industry, however, shows that there must be compelling reasons to favor mutual funds. Annual expenses and fees clearly add up over time. However, mutual funds alleviate the need to determine which individual stocks should be purchased and sold. Thus, investors must carefully weigh the various issues before deciding whether to invest directly or to use mutual funds.

SUMMARY

Compare and contrast closed-end and open-end funds. A closed-end fund rarely issues more shares after the original issue; open-end (mutual) funds continue to issue more shares, as well as redeem outstanding shares at the request of investors. Closed-end funds can trade at either a premium or a discount from the net asset value (NAV). One benefit of buying closed-end funds is the ability to purchase them at a discount from the funds' intrinsic net asset value. Mutual funds can be purchased at net asset value plus a load, if there is one. Mutual funds are sold at net asset value and can expand or contract according to investors' demands.

Contrast the benefits and costs of investing in mutual funds. The benefits of mutual funds include diversification, professional management, reduced trading costs, systematic accumulation and withdrawal plans, checking accounts, switching services, security custody and bookkeeping, and increasing an economy's capital supply. Costs of investing in mutual funds include the load; management fees; 12b-1 fees; transaction costs; higher tax burdens if a mutual fund has a relatively high turnover that forces shareholders to pay regular income tax rather than capital gains; accounting, distribution, and other miscella-neous costs; and suboptimal investment costs. Each investor must weigh these benefits and costs before deciding whether to use mutual funds.

CHAPTER AT A GLANCE

1. *Net asset value is computed as follows:*

$$NAV = \frac{\sum_{i=1}^{n} Q_i P_i - Liab}{N}$$

where Q_i is the quantity of shares of Security i held by the fund, P_i is the market price of Security i, *Liab* includes any net liabilities of the fund, and N is the number of outstanding shares of the mutual fund.

2. *Closed-end funds can trade at a premium or a discount, which is expressed as follows:*

$$Premium\ (Discount) = \frac{CMP - NAV}{NAV}$$

where CMP is the closed-end fund's current market price, and NAV is the closed-end fund's net asset value.

3. *Explanations for why closed-end funds tend to trade at a discount or at a premium include the following:*
   a. Unrealized capital appreciation.
   b. Management fees and transaction costs.
   c. Performance of the fund.
   d. Turnover.

4. *Benefits of using mutual funds include the following:*
   a. Diversification.
   b. Professional management.
   c. Reduced trading costs.
   d. Systematic accumulation and withdrawal plans.
   e. Checking accounts.
   f. Switching services.
   g. Security custody and bookkeeping.
   h. Increasing an economy's capital supply.

5. *Costs of using mutual funds include the following:*
   a. Sales fee or load.
   b. Management fees.
   c. 12b-1 fees (where funds pay selling expenses).
   d. Transaction costs (reported typically as part of the management fee).
   e. For mutual funds with a higher turnover rate, possible need to pay income tax rather than capital gains tax.
   f. Accounting, distribution, and other miscellaneous expenses.
   g. Suboptimal investment (suboptimal asset allocation and overdiversification).

KEY TERMS

Closed-end fund 483	Investment trust 483	Open-end fund 483
Conduit theory 485	Load 495	Premium 488
Discount 488	Mutual fund 483	Regulated investment
Family of funds 498	Net asset value (NAV) 487	company 485
Investment company 483	No-load mutual fund 495	Turnover 494

REVIEW

14.1 Compare and contrast open-end and closed-end funds.

14.2 What is the conduit theory?

14.3 Suppose mutual funds have to pay taxes, and shareholders also must pay taxes. Is this double or triple taxation? Explain.

14.4 Can mutual funds be sold at a discount? At a premium? Explain.

14.5 What are the main advantages of investing in mutual funds versus direct investment? What are the main disadvantages?

PRACTICE

14.1 Suppose a mutual fund charges a load of 4%. You would like to invest for six months. Would you buy this fund? What if you would like to invest for 10 years? Why does the length of the investment holding period influence this decision?

14.2 Suppose a mutual fund has the following assets and liabilities:

Stocks	$100,000
Bonds	200,000
Accounts payable	20,000

There are 1,000 shares outstanding.
a. What is the NAV?
b. Suppose the firm sells another 100 shares. It has a 3% load. What is the selling price?

14.3 Ford Motor Corporation has $100 billion in assets, and a closed-end fund has $100 million in assets. Which of these two firms will sell for the largest discount or premium? Why?

14.4 Suppose Dave wants to invest for 1 year, and Jane wants to invest for 10 years. Both purchase a mutual fund that earns 10% a year and charges a 3% load. What is the annualized rate of return for Dave and Jane? Who is hurt more by the load? Why? (Assume each has a $1,000 investment.)

14.5 Suppose the return on the S&P 500 index is 12%. A mutual fund has a group of experts who can earn 15%. The load is 2%, and the management fee is 1.5%. Suppose you can buy the S&P 500 index. Which of these two investments would you prefer?

14.6 Suppose a mutual fund has the following rates of return:

Year	Rate of Return	Rate of Return on S&P 500
1	−2%	12%
2	0	8
3	30	10
4	20	20
5	15	15

a. Calculate the mean and variance of the rates of return on the mutual fund and the S&P 500.

b. Assume that the load is zero and the risk-free interest rate is 3%. Which portfolio would you prefer? (Hint: Draw the opportunity lines.)

c. Repeat Part b, but this time the fund charges a 3% load, and you are investing for 1 year only.

14.7 Suppose the rates of return on two stocks and one mutual fund you are considering buying are as follows:

Year	Stock A	Stock B	Mutual Fund
1	10%	15%	25%
2	0	10	15
3	20	-20	-1
4	10	60	35

If you decide to buy stocks, then you will diversify equally between the two stocks. If the risk-free rate is 3%, would you buy the mutual fund or the stocks? Explain.

14.8 Suppose a closed-end fund is sold at a 10% premium. The value of the shares held is $100 million, and there are 1 million shares outstanding. Also, net liabilities are $100,000. What is the current market price of this closed-end fund?

14.9 Suppose the NAV is $10, and there are 10,000 shares traded. The fund has net liabilities of $20,000. What is the market value of all the assets the mutual fund holds?

14.10 Suppose a mutual fund holds 100,000 shares of National Health, Inc., which is trading at $48 per share, and 200,000 shares of Ford Motor, which is trading at $54 per share. There are 70,000 shares outstanding. The firm's NAV is $200. What is the fund's net liabilities?

14.11 A mutual fund invests in the exact composition of the market index (say it is the S&P 500 index). However, the fund has a much smaller size than the market value of the index. Will the fund have the same beta as the index? Explain how the different size influences the calculation of beta.

14.12 Closed-End Fund A holds only money market securities, and Closed-End Fund B holds stocks.

For which fund would a higher deviation be expected between NAV and the share's actual market price? Why?

14.13 An open-end fund is charging you a 5% load and is making, on average, 10% on its investment. What is your net annual rate of return if you invest for n years, where $n = 1, 2, 5, 10, 50$, and 100? Draw a graph, and explain your results.

14.14 Suppose an open-end fund offers you either a 5% load and a ½% 12b-1 fee or a zero load and a 2% maintenance fee. Also, assume the fund is earning 10% on its investments. Which alternative would you choose? What is the critical number of years you would wish to invest such that you would be indifferent between these two alternatives?

14.15 Suppose an open-end fund holds a lot of Intel stock. In a recent year, Intel split its stock 2-for-1. How does this split affect the NAV?

14.16 You consider either investing in one of the seven mutual funds in the table at the top of page 515 or diversifying directly in two stocks (AT&T and General Motors).

a. Draw the seven funds in the mean–standard deviation space when the mean is based on the 5-year average *before* tax and load.

b. Assume that the after-tax mean rate of return on AT&T is 14% per year, and the standard deviation is 13%. The corresponding numbers for General Motors are 15% and 25%, respectively. Draw the efficient frontier obtained from these two stocks on the assumption that the correlation between the return on these two stocks is +0.8. (In your answer, construct eleven points on the frontier, with $w_1 = 0, 0.1, \ldots, 1$, where w_1 is the investment proportion in AT&T, and $1 - w_1$ is the investment proportion in General Motors.)

c. Which investment policy (that is, investing in the two stocks or investing in one of the mutual funds) is the best one if the risk-free interest rate is $r = 6\%$? Show your answer graphically.

d. How would you change your answer to Part c if the correlation between AT&T and General Motors were -0.8?

	Returns	Here's What You Get after Loads and Taxes[a] ↓ Return	Fees		Risk	Assets
	Avg. Annual 5 yr.	Avg. Annual 5 yr.	Sales Load	Annual Expenses	Standard Deviation	$ Millions
Balanced Group Avg. →	12.8%	10.9%				
Flag Investors Value Builder A Manager: Hobart C. Buppert III	17.8%	15.9%	4.50%	1.27%	9.0	$382
Dodge & Cox Balanced Manager: Multiple managers	16.2%	15.1%	None	0.56%	8.4	$5,307
Greenspring Manager: Charles v.K. Carlson	16.5%	14.7%	None	1.04%	6.7	$170
Gabelli/Westwood Balanced Manager: S. Byrne/P. Fraze	17.7%	14.6%	None	1.32%	8.3	$70
Eclipse Balanced[b] Manager: W. McCain/J. Sabella	15.1%	13.3%	None	0.80%	7.6	$86
Vanguard Balanced Index Manager: Multiple Managers	14.1%	13.3%	None[c]	0.20%	8.1	$1,172
Van Eck/Chubb Total Return Manager: M. O'Reilly/R. Witkoff	15.6%	13.0%	5.00%	1.08%	9.7	$47

a. Performance is through Nov. 14, 1997, and net of annual expenses, brokerage costs, and sales loads; also net of taxes, assuming the new 20% long-term rate for capital gains and income distributions.

b. Fund will not declare capital gains Dec. 7–31, 1997.

c. Telephone exchange privileges available only on IRA accounts.

Source: *Fortune*, December 29, 1997, p. 130. Reprinted from the December 29, 1997, issue of *Fortune* by special permission. © 1997, Time, Inc.

e. How would you change your answer if you could diversify in many stocks rather than in only two? Show graphically the possible answers to this question.

14.17 The table at the top of page 516 presents the performance of ten mutual funds.
a. Calculate the average annual compounded rate of return on each fund for the past 3 years.
b. Suppose that there is a 2% sales load and 0.3% annual expense. How will this affect the annual rate of return for a 1-year investment and for a 3-year investment?
c. Suppose that the rate of return on the S&P 500 for the 3 years is 122%. Would it be rational for an investor to buy the Vanguard Index 500? Explain

the gain to investors who hold mutual funds in an imperfect market (when transaction costs prevail).

14.18 The following article explains the pros and cons of investing in bond funds relative to direct investment in bonds.

Secret to Smart Fixed-Income Investing: Keep Your Costs Down

You make money in bonds one penny at a time. If costs are important in equity investing, they are more so with bonds.

Look at the arithmetic. A long Treasury yields 6%, or maybe 3% to 4% net of inflation. An efficient Treasury fund will peel a quarter of a point off this return. A bad fund will gobble up a full percentage

Fund	Net Assets (billions)	Investment Objective	3-Year Return	1-Year Return	One-Week Return
Fidelity Magellan	$63.77	Growth	86.00%	19.70%	–0.45%
Vanguard Index 500	49.36	S&P Index	119.20	25.57	–0.54
Investment Co of Amer	39.72	Growth & Income	97.24	23.22	–0.25
Washington Mutual Inv	38.25	Growth & Income	120.06	26.37	–0.20
Fidelity Growth & Income	36.66	Growth & Income	108.80	25.20	–0.37
Fidelity Contrafund	30.81	Growth	99.22	14.60	–0.07
Vanguard Windsor II	24.38	Growth & Income	118.73	22.95	–0.43
Amer Century 20th Cent Ultra	22.42	Growth	89.88	14.38	–0.19
Fidelity Equity Income	21.18	Equity Income	102.08	22.93	–0.60
Fidelity Adv Growth Opp T	21.01	Growth	98.22	23.35	–0.64

Through Thursday   **Source: Lipper Analytical Services**

Source: Lipper Analytical Services, as cited in *Barron's,* January 19, 1992, p. MW83. Reprinted by permission of *Barron's,* © 1992 Dow Jones & Co., Inc. All Rights Reserved Worldwide.

point or more. Look at it this way: That cost-heavy fund is eating up more than 15% of what your bonds yield. The world is full of naive bond fund investors. Almost half of the 3,700 bond funds tracked by Morningstar charge in excess of 1% annually. . . .

Last thing to think about: Would you be better off owning bonds directly?

If you might need the money in a hurry, the answer is no. For transaction costs, a no-load fund cannot be beat: It costs nothing but a phone call to get in and out.

What if you are reasonably confident of holding the bonds to maturity? Direct ownership can save a few bucks. For a nominal $49, a discount place like Charles Schwab will fill out the paperwork and get you the same terms institutions get at Treasury auctions. Or buy second-hand T bonds in the open market.

If you take the latter route, watch those markups. On a $50,000 Treasury trade through a discount broker, the stated commission may be only $50 (or even $0), but you pay perhaps $250 in the form of a markup over the wholesale value of the bonds. It would cost you another $250 in the form

of a markdown to get rid of the bonds before maturity. On a $10,000 purchase you are going to lose at least 1% every time you buy or sell. . . .

[See table on page 517.]

Source: Thomas Eastman, "Buying a Bond Fund," *Forbes,* December 1, 1997, pp. 312–313. Reprinted by Permission of *Forbes* magazine © Forbes Inc. 1997.

a. Suppose you decide to invest $50,000 either directly in bonds or by buying a bond fund. The fund is a no-load fund; however, it charges 0.28$ per $100 investment as annual expenses (see Vanguard Fixed Income L-T Corp. Fund in the table on page 517). The commission for buying bonds directly is $50, and the markup on such a direct purchase is $250 for a buy transaction and $250 for a sell transaction. The yield on the bond, as well as on the fund before all these costs, is 6.9%. What is the rate of return on your investment in the fund and the rate of return if you invest directly in bonds when you invest for the following periods?

(1) One month.
(2) One year.
(3) Five years.

Discuss your results.

A Penny Saved Is a Penny Earned

Performance UP —markets—	DOWN	Fund	Investment style	Total return[1] 3-year annualized	latest 12-month	SEC yield %	Assets[2] ($mil)	Duration[3] (years)	Annual expenses per $100
Taxable									
A	D	Vanguard Fixed Inc— L–T Corp	Long–Term	13.0	12.1	6.9	3,505	9.0	0.28
A	D	Dodge & Cox Income	Long–Term	10.8	9.2	6.5	660	5.3	0.50
B	C	Standish Fixed Income	Medium–Term	10.7	9.4	6.7	3,017	4.7	0.38
B	C	Vanguard Bond Index— Total Bond Market	Medium–Term	10.0	8.9	6.4	4,535	4.6	0.20
D	A	Vanguard Fixed Income— S–T Corp	Short–Term	7.7	6.7	6.1	4,532	1.9	0.25
D	A	Vanguard Bond Index— S–T Bond	Short–Term	7.7	6.8	5.9	477	2.3	0.20
A+	F	Vanguard Fixed Income— L–T US Treasury	US Treasury	13.2	11.3	6.3	916	9.1	0.25
A	D	Vanguard Fixed Income— I–T US Treasury	US Treasury	9.8	7.9	6.1	1,372	4.7	0.25
Municipal									
A	C	Vanguard New York Insured T-F	One-State	9.6	7.7	4.7	1,100	6.8	0.20
F	A+	USAA Tax-Exempt— Short–Term	Short–Term	5.8	5.6	4.2	852	2.4	0.41
F	A+	Vanguard Muni Bond— Ltd Term	Short–Term	5.5	5.0	4.1	1,951	2.6	0.21

All funds are no-load.

[1] As of Oct. 30.

[2] As of Sept. 30.

[3] Weighted average.

[4] Distributor may impose redemption fee whose proceeds revert to the fund.

Source: Thomas Eastman, "Buying a Bond Fund," *Forbes*, December 1, 1997, pp. 312–313. Reprinted by Permission of *Forbes* magazine © Forbes Inc. 1997.

b. You are considering investing in either Vanguard Bond Index—Total Bond Market, or Vanguard Muni Bond. The pretax and pretransaction costs yields are 6.4%, and 4.1%, respectively (see the table). Ignoring the annual expenses, calculate the after-tax yield, assuming a 39.6% income tax. Which of the two funds will you select?

For Internet questions visit the Levy Investment Web site at http://levy-invst.swcollege.com.

YOUR TURN: APPLYING THEORY TO PRACTICE
THE DISCOUNT INDICATOR

Bargains in closed-end funds these days are as rare as champagne at a frat party. That says something about both values in the funds and the over-all state of the market.

In times past investors could buy closed-ends at attractive discounts to their underlying assets. In late 1974, for example, as the market was hitting bottom, such excellent funds as Diebold Venture (now Bergstrom) Capital and Source Capital were being given away for no more than half their liquidating value. As recently as five years ago the discount on domestic equity funds averaged a fat 13%. Today it's a measly 2%.

Investors wise enough to buy when the discounts were wide made money two ways. First, the funds' portfolios rose along with the entire stock market. Second, the funds' share prices climbed to a higher percentage of the portfolio values.

The double whammy cuts both ways, though. What happens in a bear market? Closed-end buyers lose two ways. The portfolio declines in value, and the fund share prices shrink to a smaller percentage of the underlying portfolio's value.

Take a closed-ender with net asset value of $25 a share and selling at a 2% discount—price $24.50 a share. Now suppose the market drops 40% and takes the net asset value down the same amount. The asset value drops to $15. But now suppose the discount on the closed-end fund widens at the same time from 2% to 20%. In a market that is down 40%, the holder of the closed-end shares is down more than 50%.

There's risk in closed-end shares when the discounts narrow or disappear. Closed-end dis-

counts aren't a perfect market-timing signal—nothing is—but their present state should give investors pause. The last time discounts were as thin as 2% was in December 1986, before the October 1987 crash.

Another bearish signal is the very number of closed-ends available. The New York Stock Exchange lists 297 closed ends—1 in 9 listings—up from 170 at the end of 1991. Not since 1929 have there been this many closed-end funds on the market. The 1920s bash, of course, ended in the hangover of the century. Of the roughly 400 closed-end funds that were born in the Roaring Twenties, just a half dozen or so have survived until today.

Historically, closed-end discounts have trended with the market, narrowing as price/earnings ratios increase (see chart). The more expensive stocks become, the more money investors are willing to pay for the funds that hold them.

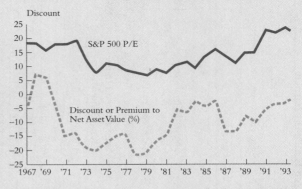

Source: Mary Beth Grover, "The Discount Indicator," *Forbes,* June 21, 1993, p. 207. Reprinted by Permission of *Forbes* magazine © Forbes, Inc., 1993.

(continued)

Questions

1. "The variance of rates of return on closed-end mutual funds is larger than the variance of the S&P index, since in a bear market it goes down more than the index, and in a bull market it goes up more than the index." Discuss this assertion.

2. Refer to the paragraph that begins, "Take a closed-ender. . . ." Assume that the data in the article is correct. Calculate the rate of return on the shares of a closed-end mutual fund. What would the rate of return on an open-end mutual fund be if it held the market portfolio?

3. "It is claimed that the closed-end discount isn't a perfect market signal but the present state of the discount should give investors a pause. What signal does the size of the discount give, and why?

4. The discount was 2% in 1986 (before the 1987 crash). It was 2% in 1993. What does the writer conclude regarding a possible crash in 1993?

5. In 1969 a closed-end fund was sold at a premium of about 5%. Suppose the fund can sell all its assets with 1% transaction costs and without affecting the prices of the assets sold. Would the fund's investors be better off following such a liquidation? What is the percentage profit (loss)? How would your answer change if the fund sold at a 10% discount?

6. Suppose that when the S&P is up by 10%, a closed-end fund is up by 12%, and when the S&P is down by 10%, that closed-end fund is down by 12%. The probability of a 10% increase is ⅔, and the probability of a 10% decrease is ⅓. Calculate the mean and variance of the rate of return on the S&P index and the closed-end fund. Are your results consistent with the article? Explain.

SELECTED REFERENCES

American Association of Individual Investors. *The Individual Investor's Guide to No-Load Mutual Funds.* Chicago: International Publishing, various issues.

Anderson, Seth C., and Jeffery A. Born. *Closed-End Investment Companies: Issues and Answers.* Boston: Kluwer Academic Publishers, 1992.

Cappiello, Frank, W. Douglas Dent, and Peter W. Madlem. *The Complete Guide to Closed-End Funds.* Chicago: International Publishing, 1990.

CDA/Wiesenberger Investment Companies Service. *Mutual Funds Panorama.* Boston: Warren Gorham & Lamont, various issues.

Fredman, Albert J., and George Cole Scott. *Investing in Closed-End Funds: Finding Value and Building Wealth.* New York: New York Institute of Finance, 1991.

Investment Company Institute. *Mutual Fund Fact Book.* Washington, D.C.: Investment Company Institute, various issues.

Morningstar's *Mutual Fund Sourcebook.* Chicago: Mutual Fund Sourcebook, various issues.

Standard & Poor's/Lipper, *Mutual Fund Profiles.* New York: Standard & Poor's, various issues.

SUPPLEMENTAL REFERENCES

Anderson, Seth C., and Jeffery A. Born. "The Effects of Market Imperfections on Asset Pricing and Risk: An Empirical Examination." *Journal of the Midwest Finance Association* 16 (1987): 1–17.

Anderson, Seth C., and Jeffery A. Born. "Market Imperfections and Asset Pricing." *Review of Business and Economic Research* 23 (Spring 1987): 14–25.

Anderson, Seth C., and Jeffery A. Born. "The Selling and Seasoning of Closed-End Investment Company's IPOs." *Journal of Financial Services Research* 2 (Summer 1989): 131–150.

Anderson, Seth C., Jeffery A. Born, and T. Randolph Beard. "An Analysis of Bond Investment Company IPOs: Past and Present." *Financial Review* 26 (May 1991), 211–222.

Brauer, Greggory A. " 'Open Ending' Closed-End Funds." *Journal of Financial Economics* 13, no. 4 (December 1984): 491–507.

Brauer, Greggory A., and Eric C. Chang. "Return Seasonality in Stocks and Their Underlying Assets: Tax-Loss Selling versus Information Explanations." *Review of Financial Studies* 3, no. 2 (1990): 255–280.

Crawford, Peggy J., and Charles P. Harper. "An Analysis of the Discounts on Closed-End Mutual Funds." *Financial Review* 20 (August 1985): 30–38.

diBartolomeo, Dan, and Erik Witkowski. "Mutual Fund Misclassification: Evidence Based on Style Analysis." *Financial Analysts Journal,* September–October 1997, pp. 32–43.

Ferris, Stephen P., and Don Chance. "The Effect of 12b-1 Plans on Mutual Fund Expense Ratios: A Note." *Journal of Finance,* September 1987, 1077–1082.

Hendricks, Darryll, Jayendu Patel, and Richard Zeckhauser. "Hot Hands in Mutual Funds: Short-Run Persistence of Relative Performance, 1974–1988." *Journal of Finance* 48, no. 1 (March 1993): 93–130.

Lee, Charles C., Andrei Shleifer, and Richard H. Thaler. "Investor Sentiment and the Closed-End Fund Puzzle." *Journal of Finance* 46 (March 1991): 75–109.

Lee, Charles C., Andrei Shleifer, and Richard H. Thaler. "Closed-End Mutual Funds." *Journal of Economic Perspectives* 4, no. 4 (1990): 153–164.

O'Neal, Edward S. "How Many Mutual Funds Constitute a Diversified Mutual Fund Portfolio?" *Financial Analysts Journal,* March–April 1997, pp. 37–46.

Peavy, John M. "Returns on Initial Public Offerings of Closed-End Funds." *Review of Financial Studies* 3 (1990): 695–708.

Trzcinka, Charles, and Robert Zweig. *An Economic Analysis of the Cost and Benefits of S.E.C. Rule 12b-1.* Monograph 1990-1. New York: Salomon Brothers Center for the Study of Financial Institutions, Leonard N. Stern School of Business, New York University, 1990.

Weiss, Kathleen. "The Post-Offering Price Performance of Closed-End Funds." *Financial Management* 18 (Autumn 1989): 57–67.

LEARNING OBJECTIVES

After studying this chapter you should be able to:

1. Calculate portfolio performance using four performance indexes.

2. Summarize the empirical evidence regarding portfolio managers' performance.

3. Identify some problems with measuring portfolio managers' performance in practice.

4. Evaluate performance attribution as a means of identifying the sources of performance.

U.S. EQUITY FUNDS

As explained in our Best Buy introduction, we weight costs equally with past performance in these rankings of U.S. stock funds. Within each category, funds are listed in descending order of a combined cost/performance score.

You might be wondering: How can we cavil at an extra percentage point or two of overhead costs when good funds have been earning 15% or 20% a year? The answer: Because so much of what passes for investment skill these days is nothing but the dumb luck of a wildly bullish market.

If you have any doubts about how much of your fund's earnings are due to chance rather than to skill, compare them with those of an index fund. There are very few actively managed stock funds that have beaten the Vanguard Index 500 fund over the past 20 years.

Source: James M. Clash, "Best Buys: Fund Survey," *Forbes*, August 25, 1997. Reprinted by Permission of *Forbes* Magazine © Forbes Inc., 1997.

Mutual funds charge annual expenses (given as a percentage of assets), and some funds have sales charges. Investors are ready to pay these sums in the hope that the funds' professional managers are able to pick stocks smartly. This chapter's "Investments in the News" article states that this is not the case and that very few actively managed stock funds have beaten the unmanaged Vanguard Index Trust–500 Portfolio fund. Indeed, if the efficient market hypothesis discussed in Chapter 12 is correct, we would expect that on average, a professional money manager would be unable to earn abnormal profits. However, investors do evaluate and select portfolio managers based on their past performances. Are these selection criteria valid? We could find some managers who do better than an unmanaged portfolio like the S&P 500 and some who do worse. As investors, we would obviously like to be able to identify the above-average managers, and only hope that their performance continues to reap positive returns.

Portfolio managers could earn abnormal returns if they were able to select underpriced assets and to time movements into and out of the market. Managers face a risk-return trade-off in selecting assets. On the one hand, managers seek to maximize their expected return on the portfolio, and on the other hand, they seek to reduce the risk. Typically, pursuing higher expected returns requires taking a higher risk. Any analysis of a manager's ability must evaluate the manager's asset selection skills and ability to successfully time when to buy and sell, and then weigh these characteristics against the risk of the portfolio.

Regardless of the difficulties in measuring a portfolio manager's performance, many groups, such as institutional investors, benefit from information on historical returns. The two main customers of performance information are the fund managers and potential investors:

1. *Managers.* The compensation committee of the portfolio manager needs performance information. If a portfolio manager consistently outperforms an unmanaged portfolio of equivalent risk, the manager should receive a bonus. If the manager consistently underperforms an unmanaged portfolio of equivalent risk, then the manager probably should be replaced.
2. *Investors.* Investors seeking an appropriate mutual fund or choosing a financial planner can use performance information to help them make a selection. If the market is inefficient, then the best manager of the past may also turn out to be a successful performer in the future. If the market is efficient, past performance cannot be used to predict future performance, *on average.* However, investors may find a few good managers who have consistently outperformed the market and who will continue to do so in the future. Finding these superior managers is not easy, however.

Other people and organizations can benefit from this information as well. Corporate financial officers need to evaluate the managers of their corporate pension plans. Government agencies need to be able to assess the performance of public pension fund managers. Large money management firms need good evaluation tools to assess their employees' performance. Bank trust departments need these tools to evaluate the performance of their various trust accounts.

This chapter surveys the existing techniques for evaluating managers and the portfolios they manage. This evaluation requires a yardstick to measure a portfolio's performance. After all, a portfolio's registering a high return of 20% does not necessarily indicate that it was well managed. For example, what if every other fund earned in excess of 25% for the same period? The focus of this chapter is on measuring a portfolio's performance relative to the benchmark portfolio or relative to its risk.

The discussion of performance measurement techniques begins with calculations used to quantify risk. The risk–return trade-off is then reduced to a single measure known as a **performance index.** After describing four performance indexes, the chapter discusses some of the challenges encountered in applying these measures. It concludes with a discussion of performance attribution. The portfolio manager must make many decisions on asset allocation in building a portfolio, and performance attribution attempts to rate each of the portfolio manager's decisions.

15.1 HOW TO MEASURE RISK

To develop a measure of performance quality, we must quantify risk and return. Specifically, we need to find the risk and return of a portfolio—in this case, a mutual fund. Return is easy to quantify; it can be estimated with rate-of-return methods described in Chapter 5. However, the appropriate measure of risk is not as obvious.

Chapters 6 through 8 discussed models to find the risk and return of individual assets and portfolios. Chapter 9 introduced the capital market line, which gives the trade-off between expected return and standard deviation when there is a risk-free asset. In this case, the appropriate risk measure is the standard deviation of the portfolio, because the implicit assumption is that no other assets are held apart from this portfolio, so risk is the *total risk* of the portfolio (as opposed to the systematic risk).

Suppose an investor's financial holdings are well diversified, and apart from the mutual fund under consideration whose performance is being measured, the investor holds many other assets. In this case, the appropriate measure of risk is no longer the standard deviation. The investor's concern should be how the fund investment will influence the overall performance of the holdings, so the appropriate measure of risk is beta.

Standard deviation and beta stand at two extremes. Standard deviation is the appropriate measure of risk when the investor holds no other assets besides the mutual fund. Beta is the appropriate measure of risk of the mutual fund when the investor holds the entire market portfolio. In practice, neither extreme is realistic. However, if an investor has very limited holdings, then standard deviation may prove to be a more accurate measure of risk. If an investor has a wide array of holdings outside of this particular mutual fund, then beta may be a more accurate measure of risk.

For example, it is reasonable for an investor owning only one mutual fund to measure its risk by its standard deviation. Investors who put their money in mutual funds generally trust that a fund will provide some level of diversification and hence do not buy numerous mutual funds. In contrast, the risk level of an individual stock—for example, IBM—is better measured by beta, because investors normally diversify into other stocks. Investors holding stock of IBM probably also hold other stocks to diversify their portfolios.

Let's consider an example using three mutual funds: one that mirrors the market and two that are actively managed. We assume that the Vanguard Index Trust–500 Portfolio is an adequate proxy for the market portfolio and hence has a beta of 1. This fund is a passively managed index fund that seeks to mimic the performance of the S&P 500 stock index. Exhibit 15-1a lists the historical return information for a 5-year period. All three funds have similar objectives: they seek growth and income. The returns in Exhibit 15-1a reveal no clear-cut preference for one fund over another. Fund B experienced the worst year, at −5.0%, in Year 5. Vanguard had the best year, at 31.4%, in Year 4. Fund A has a return higher than the other two funds' returns in Year 2.

Exhibit 15-1b shows the mean return, standard deviation, and betas of these three funds. Fund A had the lowest average return, the lowest standard deviation, and the lowest beta. The Vanguard fund was at the other extreme, with the highest average return, the highest standard deviation, and the highest beta. Fund B was in the middle on both risk and return. Over the 5 years shown, which of these funds achieved the superior performance? Is it the Vanguard fund, because it had the highest return on average? Perhaps it was Fund A with the lowest risk measures.

To illustrate further, suppose you wish to invest for 1 year, and you believe that the distribution of *ex-post* performance will be repeated in the future.[1] You do not

EXHIBIT 15-1 **Basic Statistics** **on Three Mutual** **Funds**	Part a: Actual Annual Rates of Return on Three Mutual Funds after Fees with Reported Betas			
	Year	**Fund A**	**Fund B**	**Vanguard Index Trust–500 Portfolio**
	1	16.3%	15.4%	18.3%
	2	8.6	3.1	4.7
	3	8.7	17.9	16.2
	4	23.6	28.7	31.4
	5	−3.3	−5.0	−3.3

Part b: Mean Return, Standard Deviation, and Beta Based on Part a

	Fund A	**Fund B**	**Vanguard Index Trust–500 Portfolio**
Mean return	10.78%	12.02%	13.46%
Standard deviation	10.03%	13.17%	13.33%
Beta	0.64	0.85	1.0

1. Recall that ex-post data are historical data used to make inferences about the future.

know which observation will be selected, but you know the set of possible outcomes. Which fund would you select? Performance indexes provide a method of comparing funds with different risk–return characteristics. Thus, finding the best performer is what we hope performance indexes will tell us. We will use the data from Exhibit 15-1 in the next section when we construct performance measures.

15.2 PERFORMANCE INDEXES

Analysts use four main performance measures or indexes. Each performance index is based on a different set of assumptions about portfolio risk.

15.2.1 Sharpe's Performance Index (PI_S)

For portfolios, as for mutual funds, **Sharpe's performance index** is a performance index that uses standard deviation as the appropriate risk measure.[2] Recall that Chapter 9 developed the capital market line (CML), which is a linear relationship between the expected return, $E(R_i)$, and standard deviation, σ_{R_i}:

$$E(R_i) = r + \frac{[E(R_m) - r]}{\sigma_m} \sigma_{R_i} \qquad (15.1)$$

where r is the risk-free interest rate, $E(R_m)$ is the expected return on the market portfolio, and σ_m is the standard deviation of the market portfolio.

Of course, we do not know the values of the parameters $E(R_i)$ and σ_{R_i}, and we estimate them by using the *ex-post* data. We denote these estimates by $\overline{R}$ and $\hat{\sigma}_{R_i}$ [rather than $E(R_i)$ and σ_{R_i}].[3] We normally assume that $\overline{R}$ and $\hat{\sigma}$ are the best estimates of $E(R_i)$ and σ_{R_i}. Hence, we use the historical CML as our estimate of the CML.

Exhibit 15-2a illustrates a historical CML. The average short-term interest rate over this period was approximately 5%. Note that both Fund A and Fund B lie below the CML. On the line denoted *A* in Exhibit 15-2a are all possible combinations of Fund A with borrowing or lending of the risk-free asset. Line *B* similarly denotes all possible combinations of Fund *B* with borrowing and lending. The line denoted CML represents all possible combinations of the market portfolio (approximated by Vanguard) and the risk-free asset.

Recall from the analysis of indifference curves that the steeper the line is, the higher the average return for a given level of risk (see Chapter 9). Hence, the Vanguard fund outperformed both Fund A and Fund B. That is, the set of all borrowing or lending combinations of the risk-free asset and the Vanguard fund produces a

2. See William F. Sharpe, "Mutual Fund Performance," *Journal of Business,* January 1966, pp. 119–138.

3. The symbol $\overline{R}$ is used when estimating the average return based on history, and $E(R_i)$ denotes the population parameter, which is unobservable. $\hat{\sigma}$ denotes the historical standard deviation estimate, whereas σ is a population parameter, which is unobservable.

EXHIBIT 15–2
The Capital Market Line and the Lines Corresponding to Two Other Mutual Funds

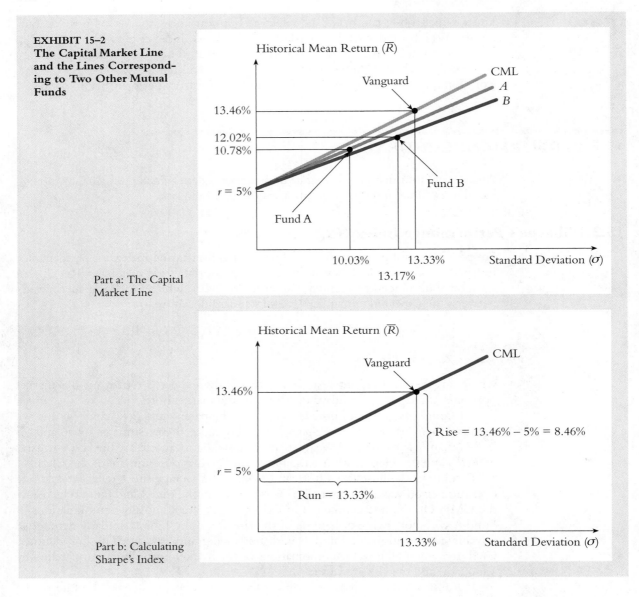

Part a: The Capital Market Line

Part b: Calculating Sharpe's Index

CML that is steeper than the line that would be produced by either Fund A or Fund B and the risk-free asset.

An investor would prefer the fund that produces a line with the steepest slope. Hence, Sharpe suggests that when portfolios rather than individual securities are held, and only one portfolio is owned, the slope of the lines given in Exhibit 15-2a is an appropriate performance index. Specifically, Sharpe's index $(PI_{S,i})$ for each Portfolio i is given as follows:

$$PI_{S,i} = \frac{\overline{R}_i - r}{\hat{\sigma}_{R_i}} \qquad (15.2)$$

where $\overline{R}_i$ is the average historical rate of return on Portfolio i, $\hat{\sigma}_{R_i}$ is the standard deviation of returns on Portfolio i, and the risk-free rate for this period is given by r, 5%. As the numerator and the denominator are given in percentages, Sharpe's index is a pure number.

Exhibit 15-2b illustrates graphically Equation 15.2 for the Vanguard fund. Specifically, Sharpe's index is the "rise over the run," or slope, of the line where the denominator of Equation 15.2 (the run) is $\hat{\sigma}_{R_i} = 13.33\%$, and the rise is $E(R_{Vanguard}) - r = 13.46\% - 5\% = 8.46\%$. The rise measures the additional return expected for taking the risk related to the Vanguard fund. The risk-free rate is compensation for the time value of money (see Exhibit 15-1). Hence, Sharpe's index for the Vanguard fund is calculated as follows:

$$PI_{S,Vanguard} = \frac{13.46\% - 5.0\%}{13.33\%} \cong 0.635$$

In a similar manner, we can calculate Sharpe's performance indexes for the other two funds:

$$PI_{S,Fund\ A} = \frac{10.78\% - 5.0\%}{10.03\%} \cong 0.576$$

$$PI_{S,Fund\ B} = \frac{12.02\% - 5.0\%}{13.17\%} \cong 0.533$$

Assuming that standard deviation is the appropriate risk measure, we can conclude by Sharpe's performance index that the best-performing fund for this period is Vanguard, followed by Fund A. Fund B came in last, with the lowest Sharpe's index value.

PRACTICE BOX

Problem

The following data are for two bond funds over a recent 5-year period. Using Sharpe's index, which fund performed the best? (Assume that the risk-free rate was 6%.)

	T. Rowe Price New Income Fund	Vanguard Investment Grade Income Fund
Average return	8.9%	9.75%
Standard deviation	4.6	6.1

(continued)

Solution   Equation 15.2 yields the following:

$$PI_{S,\text{T. Rowe Price}} = \frac{8.9\% - 6.0\%}{4.6\%} \cong 0.63$$

$$PI_{S,\text{Vanguard}} = \frac{9.75\% - 6.0\%}{6.1\%} \cong 0.61$$

Thus, although the Vanguard's fund achieved higher returns, it failed to outperform the T. Rowe Price fund on a risk-adjusted basis. Hence, the T. Rowe Price fund performed the best according to Sharpe's index.

15.2.2 Treynor's Performance Index (PI_T)

In 1965, Treynor evaluated portfolio performance based on the security market line (SML).[4] **Treynor's performance index** is the appropriate index to use in order to measure the performance of one specific portfolio while many other assets are also held in another portfolio. Recall from Chapter 9 that the security market line is the linear relationship between the expected return of a specific asset and its beta. Specifically, the SML was defined as follows:

$$E(R_i) = r + [E(R_m) - r]\beta_i$$

where $E(R_i)$ is the expected return on the specific asset (or portfolio), and β_i is the beta of the asset.

As with the CML, investors prefer the SML to be steeper. Of course, when the market is in equilibrium, all assets should lie on the SML. In actuality, however, some funds will be above the line, and some funds will be below the line. Investors seek to achieve the highest return for a given beta or the lowest beta for a given return. Exhibit 15–3a illustrates the three mutual funds plotted using values from Exhibit 15–1. Fund A lies above the SML and hence "beat the market"; that is, Fund A outperformed the market on a risk-adjusted basis.

Treynor suggested using the slope of the SML as a benchmark to assess performance. Treynor's performance index for a given portfolio, i, ($PI_{T,i}$), follows:

$$PI_{T,i} = \frac{\overline{R}_i - r}{\hat{\beta}_i} \tag{15.3}$$

where $\hat{\beta}_i$ is the historical beta, calculated with historical rates of return, that is the best estimate of the beta. Exhibit 15–3b illustrates the calculations required for the Vanguard fund. This fund has a beta of 1.0, because we use this fund as a proxy for the market portfolio. Treynor's index compares the slope of the Vanguard fund with

4. Jack Treynor, "How to Rate Management of Investment Funds," *Harvard Business Review,* January–February 1965, pp. 63–75.

EXHIBIT 15-3
The Security Market Line and the Lines Corresponding to Two Other Mutual Funds

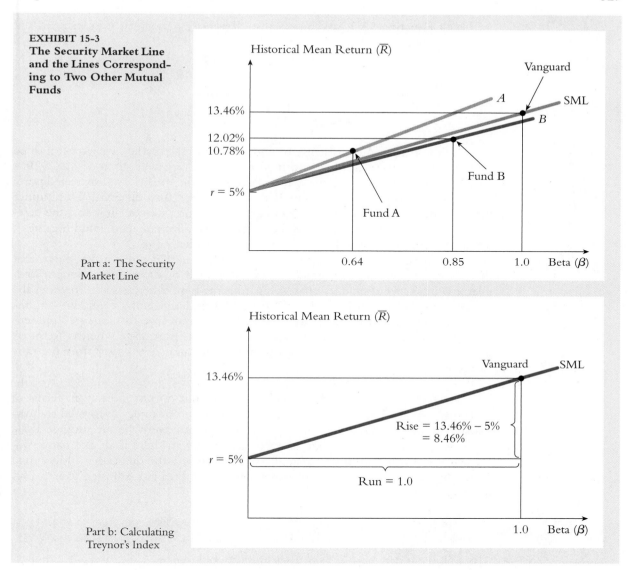

Part a: The Security Market Line

Part b: Calculating Treynor's Index

the slopes of other lines measuring other portfolios. Again, because this is a slope, we calculate the "rise over the run." Mathematically, we calculate the following for Vanguard:

$$PI_{T,Vanguard} = \frac{13.46\% - 5\%}{1.0} = 8.46\%$$

Note that because the numerator is given in percentages and beta is a pure number, Treynor's index is given in percentages.

Using Equation 15.3, we can calculate Treynor's performance indexes for the other two funds:

$$PI_{T,Fund\ A} = \frac{10.78\% - 5.0\%}{0.64} \cong 9.03\%$$

$$PI_{T,Fund\ B} = \frac{12.02\% - 5.0\%}{0.85} \cong 8.26\%$$

If a fund neither outperforms nor underperforms the market, we expect it to lie on the SML—just as the Vanguard fund does—and to have a slope of 8.46%. If a fund has a line with a higher slope, it outperformed the market or unmanaged portfolio. The opposite is true for a line with a lower slope than the SML. Thus, under the assumption that beta is the appropriate risk measure, we conclude that the best-performing fund for this period was Fund A, followed by Vanguard. Fund B came in last again, with the lowest Treynor's performance index value.

A comparison of the results of Sharpe's index and Treynor's index shows that the choice of risk measure, standard deviation, or beta affects the rankings. With Sharpe's index, we concluded that Vanguard is the best, whereas with Treynor's index, we concluded that Fund A is the best. This finding is not a contradiction, because different results could be appropriate for different investors. Sharpe's index is more relevant for investors who do not hold any other portfolios, whereas Treynor's index is more relevant for investors who hold many other assets apart from the mutual fund.

The Treynor and Sharpe indexes rank portfolios but do not indicate in terms of percentage return by how much a fund outperformed or underperformed the unmanaged portfolio. Thus, it is hard to understand intuitively the meaning of a PI_T of, for example, 8.26% per one unit of risk. However, there is an alternative performance index based on beta that allows us to answer the question, "How much better did the fund do in terms of percentage return on a risk-adjusted basis?" This method is *Jensen's performance index*.

PRACTICE BOX

Problem

The following data are for two stock funds over a recent 5-year period. Using Treynor's index, which fund performed the best? (Assume that the risk-free rate was 6%.)

	Financial Industrial Fund	Dreyfus New Leaders Fund
Average return	8.3%	8.8%
Beta	1.05	0.88

(continued)

Solution	Equation 15.3 yields the following:

$$PI_{T,Financial} = \frac{8.3\% - 6\%}{1.05} \cong 2.19\%$$

$$PI_{T,Dreyfus} = \frac{8.8\% - 6\%}{0.88} \cong 3.18\%$$

Because Treynor's index for Dreyfus is larger, we conclude that the Dreyfus fund outperformed the Financial Industrial fund.

15.2.3 Jensen's Performance Index (PI_J)

In 1968, Jensen suggested a performance measure based on the capital asset pricing model that could assess, on a risk-adjusted, percentage basis, how well a mutual fund performed.[5] Recall from Chapter 9 that the CAPM equilibrium relationship between risk and return is as follows:

$$E(R_i) = r + [E(R_m) - r]\beta_i$$

Jensen's performance index examines the difference between the returns actually earned during the evaluation period and the returns expected using the CAPM. We can use historical rates of return to estimate $E(R_i)$, $E(R_m)$, and β_i by $\overline{R}_i$, $\overline{R}_m$, and the ex-post $\hat{\beta}_i$. We then substitute the estimates for the parameters in the CAPM. With ex-post data, we may not have a straight line; hence, we write

$$\overline{R}_i = r + (\overline{R}_m - r)\hat{\beta}_i + \alpha_i$$

where α_i is the deviation from the line. Indeed α_i is Jensen's performance index, which we denote by PI_J.[6] If $\alpha_i > 0$, we say that the fund earns more than is expected given its risk; the opposite holds for $\alpha_i < 0$. Thus, Jensen's performance index, α_i, is as follows:

$$PI_{J,i} = \overline{R}_i - [r + (\overline{R}_m - r)\hat{\beta}_i] \tag{15.4}$$

We find the following performance measures using Jensen's index on the three funds we have been tracking:

---

5. C. Michael Jensen, "The Performance of Mutual Funds in the Period 1945–1964," *Journal of Finance,* May 1968, pp. 389–415.

6. Formally, Jensen suggested running the following regression:

$$R_{i,t} - r_t = \hat{\alpha}_i + \hat{\beta}_i(R_{m,t} - r_t) + e_{i,t}$$

Taking the average for both sides, we get

$$\overline{R} - \overline{r} = \hat{\alpha}_i + \hat{\beta}_i(\overline{R}_m - \overline{r}) + \overline{e}_i$$

where the last term, ($\overline{e}_i$) is zero. Therefore,

$$\hat{\alpha}_i = \overline{R}_i - \overline{r} - \hat{\beta}_i(\overline{R}_m - \overline{r})$$

$$PI_{J,\,Fund\,A} = 10.78\% - [5\% + (13.46\% - 5\%)0.64] \cong 0.366\%$$

$$PI_{J,\,Fund\,B} = 12.02\% - [5\% + (13.46\% - 5\%)0.85] = -0.171\%$$

$$PI_{J,\,Vanguard} = 13.46\% - [5\% + (13.46\% - 5\%)1.0] = 0.0\%$$

These performance measures are expressed in percentages. Fund A earns an excess return of 0.366% compared with what it should earn given its beta. Notice that Jensen's performance index is zero for Vanguard. This is not a coincidence. We chose Vanguard as our market portfolio, hence $\beta = 1$ and $\overline{R}_m - [r + (\overline{R}_m - r)1] = 0$. We find that the results using Jensen's measure are similar in some respects to the results using Treynor's measure. This, too, is no coincidence: Both Treynor's and Jensen's indexes use beta as their risk measure. As such, they both yield the same "beat-the-market" assessment. That is, if Treynor's index for a fund indicates that it outperformed the market portfolio, then we know that Jensen's index must yield the same result.[7] This does not mean that Treynor's and Jensen's indexes give the same fund rankings. In fact, the rankings generally will differ. That is, if, for example, we evaluate one hundred funds, both measures may show that twenty-six funds outperformed the market portfolio and seventy-four funds underperformed the market portfolio. However, Jensen's measure may show that Fund 5 was the best, whereas Treynor's measure may rank Fund 18 as the best.

A benefit of Jensen's index is its intuitive interpretation. We can conclude that Fund A outperformed the Vanguard fund by 36.6 basis points (or 0.366%) and that Fund B underperformed the Vanguard fund by 17.1 basis points (or 0.171%). Jensen's measure allows an investor to determine by how much one fund outperformed or underperformed another fund. Statistical tests can also be run to determine the significance of these results.

PRACTICE BOX

Problem

Using the data given in the previous Practice Box, use Jensen's index to determine how the Financial Industrial Fund and Dreyfus New Leaders Fund performed. (Assume that the average return on the market was 10.8% for this period, and the risk-free interest rate was 6%.)

Solution

Equation 15.4 yields the following:

$$PI_{J,Financial} = 8.3\% - [6\% + (10.8\% - 6\%)1.05] = -2.74\%$$

$$PI_{J,Dreyfus} = 8.8\% - [6\% + (10.8\% - 6\%)0.88] \cong -1.42\%$$

Again, the Dreyfus fund performed better than Financial Industrial, because $PI_{J,Dreyfus} > PI_{J,Financial}$. Nevertheless, both funds failed to outperform the market portfolio.

---

7. We ignore here the technical difficulties encountered with negative beta portfolios. Negative beta portfolios are very rare.

15.2.4 Performance Indexes with APT (PI_A)[8]

In principle, the notion of Jensen's performance measure can be applied within the arbitrage pricing theory (APT) framework (see Chapter 10).[9] That is, the difference between the actual average return earned and the return expected under some single-factor or multifactor pricing model can be estimated. The basic idea of the **APT performance index** is to examine the difference between the actual average rate of return earned during the evaluation period compared with the average rate of return that is expected based on the APT. For example, after considering all risk factors, if the required expected rate of return is 10% but the fund actually earned 12%, it outperformed 2% by the APT measure.

The extension of Jensen's performance index to the APT framework has the advantage of showing instantly by how much one fund outperformed the benchmark of another fund. In the simple illustration just given, the fund outperformed by 2%. Thus, the index is

$$\overline{R}_i - \hat{R}_{APT_i} = 12\% - 10\% = 2\%$$

Finally, statistical tests can also be run to determine whether the difference between the actual return and the expected return is statistically different from zero.

15.2.5 Summary of Performance Indexes

Four different methods can be used to assess the relative performance of a portfolio: Sharpe's index, Treynor's index, Jensen's index, and the APT index. Sharpe's index uses the standard deviation as a risk measure and the slope of the lines that are similar to the CML. Sharpe's index is relevant only when the standard deviation of the portfolio is the appropriate risk measure—that is, when there are no other assets held apart from the portfolio under consideration. Treynor's and Jensen's indexes use beta as a risk measure. Both indexes assume that only the market portfolio affects risk, but unlike Sharpe's index, they assume that other assets are held in the portfolio apart from the assets under consideration. For investors who are only interested in whether they "beat the market," Treynor's index is relevant. For investors who want to compare their performance with that of other fund managers, Jensen's index is relevant. Finally, the APT-based index is similar to Jensen's index except that it uses the APT instead of the CAPM as the equilibrium model. In the APT, one or more factors are assumed to determine the risk—for example, the market portfolio, inflation, the GNP, and so forth (see Chapter 10).

8. For more discussion of this concept, see John L. Maginn and Donald L. Tuttle (eds.), *Managing Investment Portfolios: A Dynamic Process,* 2d ed. (New York: Warren, Gorham & Lamont, 1990), pp. 14–22; Richard Roll and Stephen Ross, "The Arbitrage Pricing Theory Approach to Strategic Portfolio Planning," *Financial Analysts Journal,* May–June 1984, pp. 14–26; Richard A. Brealey, "Portfolio Theory versus Portfolio Practice," *Journal of Portfolio Management,* Summer 1990, pp. 6–10; William F. Sharpe, "Asset Allocation: Management Style and Performance Measurement," *Journal of Portfolio Management,* Winter 1992, pp. 7–19; and Ronald N. Kahn, "Bond Performance Analysis: A Multi-factor Approach," *Journal of Portfolio Management,* Fall 1991, pp. 40–47.

9. Because the single-index model can be viewed as a special case of the APT, it is implicitly also covered here.

Of the three mutual funds just examined, none is clearly superior. If standard deviation is the appropriate risk measure, then the Vanguard fund is superior by Sharpe's index. If beta is the appropriate risk measure, then Fund A is superior by Treynor's and Jensen's indexes.

Note that the choice between PI_S and the pair PI_T and PI_J depends on whether you hold only the asset under consideration or you hold many other assets in addition. The choice between these indexes and the APT index depends on your belief about the process generating the returns. If, for example, you believe that apart from the market portfolio, inflation also affects prices, you should select the APT index. Connecting Theory to Practice 15.1 illustrates how the financial community uses historical data to evaluate and rank funds.

CONNECTING THEORY TO PRACTICE 15.1
A HAPPY FEW MANAGE TO BEAT THE S&P

Drat Coca-Cola and Gillette! Curses on Microsoft and Intel.

That's what a lot of money managers are muttering these days.

Money managers on average continue to trail behind the Standard & Poor's 500-stock index, the gauge most managers use to judge themselves, according to Thomson Investment Software. For the first six months of the year, the average manager is up 16.9%, while the index of 500 big stocks is up 20.6%.

A lot of managers won't buy the big, reliable growth stocks that dominate the S&P 500, viewing them as unoriginal, overly popular, and excessively priced. For example, Coca-Cola sells for about 42 times the past four quarters' earnings, and Gillette for about 53 times earnings.

Yet such stocks have shown continuing strength. No wonder S&P index funds, low-cost investment vehicles that simply replicate the index, have outperformed most managers. What hurts most is that they've done it while charging fees that are paltry compared with those most managers charge. Many index funds charge 0.2% of assets in annual fees, compared with as much as 1% or more for many money managers.

Nevertheless, some managers have managed to beat the market. The accompanying table shows the best performing managers over the six months, one year and three years ended, June 30. It uses estimates prepared by Thomson Investment Software of Boston and CDA Investment Technologies of Rockville, Md. Both companies are units of Thompson Corp., Toronto.

Source: "A Happy Few Manage to Beat the S&P," *Wall Street Journal*, July 22, 1997, p. C1. Reprinted by permission of *The Wall Street Journal* © 1997 Dow Jones & Co., Inc. All Rights Reserved Worldwide.

(continued)

Money-Manager Scorecard

Estimated stock-market performance of the best-performing U.S. money-management firms in periods ended June 30, 1997. Currently, 944 managers are tracked.

MANAGER	STOCKS HELD (millions)	LOCATION	PERFORMANCE SIX MONTHS	PERFORMANCE ONE YEAR	PERFORMANCE THREE YEARS
BEST FOR SIX MONTHS					
GW Capital	$119	Bellevue WA	32%	42%	111%
Orion Capital	324	New York	29	32	78
Capital International	2109	Los Angeles	28	23	16
BEST FOR ONE YEAR					
Ruane Cunniff	5197	New York	28	53	135
ABN/Amro Chicago Bank Fund	296	Chicago	24	51	112
Cheswick Investment Co.	291	Greenwich CT	24	50	194
BEST FOR THREE YEARS					
Cheswick Investment Co.	291	Greenwich CT	24	50	194
Oak Associates	3924	Akron OH	13	32	190
Gamble Jones Holbrook & Bent	612	Pasadena, CA	28	48	149
AVERAGE MANAGER			17	30	106
S&P 500 STOCK INDEX			21	35	113

Source: Thomson Investment Software and CDA Investment Technologies, as cited in "A Happy Few Manage to Beat the S&P," *Wall Street Journal*, July 22, 1997, p. C1. Reprinted by permission of *The Wall Street Journal* © 1997 Dow Jones & Co., Inc. All Rights Reserved Worldwide.

MAKING THE CONNECTION

According to the article, the average of 944 funds managers lagged behind the S&P index in the last six months, the last 1 year, and the last 3 years. The S&P index funds, which have low costs (annual fees of only 0.2% of assets), outperformed most managers. However, a few funds were able to select the winning stocks and outperform the S&P index (see, for example, Cheswick Investment Company).

How should these results be interpreted? First, for an investor who held Cheswick Investment Company in the last 3 years, there is no question that this was the best ex-post (historical) performer. Can we say that the fund will be the best in the next 3-year period? Not necessarily, especially if we believe in market efficiency. Is an investor who has invested in the fund for the past six months happy with the fund's performance? As the table shows, this fund is not on the six-month honor roll list. Thus, 3-year performance with no risk adjustment is meaningless for analyzing performance, even on an ex-post basis, as long as the investment horizon is less than 3 years.

In short, ex-post performance with no risk adjustment is irrelevant even for ex-post investors unless they invested precisely for the period for which the returns are reported (for example, 3 years).

15.3 EMPIRICAL EVIDENCE OF THE PERFORMANCE OF MUTUAL FUNDS

Most research on the performance of mutual funds shows that they fall behind the market as a whole. That is, mutual funds on average consistently underperform the market (see Connecting Theory to Practice 15.1).

Sharpe examined the performance of thirty-four open-end mutual funds from 1954 through 1963. He found that the major differences in their returns resulted from the expenses incurred by each mutual fund. Furthermore, as measured by Sharpe's index, the majority of these funds failed to outperform the Dow-Jones Industrial Average based on Sharpe's index. This led Sharpe to conclude the following:

The burden of proof may reasonably be placed on those who argue the traditional view—that the search for securities whose prices diverge from their intrinsic values is worth the expense required.[10]

Jensen examined the performance of 115 mutual funds for the 10-year period 1955 through 1964. Applying Jensen's index, he concludes,

The evidence on mutual fund performance . . . indicates not only that these 115 mutual funds were on average not able to predict security prices well enough to outperform the buy-the-market-and-hold policy, but also that there is little evidence that any individual fund was able to do significantly better than that which we expected from mere random chance.[11]

More recently, Cumby and Glen examined a sample of fifteen U.S.–based international mutual funds from 1982 through 1988.[12] Using Jensen's index, they found no evidence that these funds outperformed a broad, international equity index. That is, the market portfolio selected was an internationally diversified portfolio. It is interesting to note that they did find some evidence that the funds outperformed when a U.S.–based market portfolio is used. That is, international mutual funds tend to do better when the risk is calculated with a domestic portfolio. The excess performance using a U.S.–based index is easily attributable to the gains in diversification with international securities. The international portfolio is less correlated with the domestic portfolio, resulting in considerable gains from diversification.

Eun, Kolodny, and Resnick also examined the performance of international mutual funds.[13] Their results are very interesting:

According to the Sharpe performance measure, the majority of international funds outperformed the S&P 500 Index during the ten-year period of 1977–1986. Most of them, however, failed to outperform the MSCI [Morgan Stanley Capital International] World Index.[14]

---

10. See William F. Sharpe, "Mutual Fund Performance," *Journal of Business,* January 1966, p. 138.

11. See C. Michael Jensen, "The Performance of Mutual Funds in the Period 1945–1964," *Journal of Finance,* May 1968, p. 415.

12. Robert E. Cumby and Jack D. Glen, "Evaluating the Performance of International Mutual Funds," *Journal of Finance,* June 1990, pp. 497–521.

13. Cheol S. Eun, Richard Kolodny, and Bruce G. Resnick, "U.S.–Based International Mutual Funds: A Performance Evaluation," *Journal of Portfolio Management,* Spring 1991, pp. 88–94.

14. *Ibid.,* p. 93.

Thus, international mutual funds tend to outperform the S&P 500. However, if the market portfolio is a global one, such as the Morgan Stanley Capital International World Index, the mutual funds did not outperform this index. This result supports earlier work by Lehman and Modest,[15] who demonstrate that the choice of a market portfolio is critical to the inferences drawn. Hence, the choice of a market portfolio is critical to analyzing a fund's historical performance.

Lehman and Modest also compare the performance of 130 mutual funds from 1968 through 1982 using the APT-based approach. The performance of the mutual funds was found to be very sensitive to the method of constructing the APT portfolio. Lehman and Modest also found considerable differences in performance measures based on the CAPM and the APT.

Blake, Elton, and Gruber examined bond funds using several different single- and multiple-index models of performance measurement.[16] They found that overall, bond funds underperformed the relevant indexes. It is interesting to note that they found a direct relationship between the size of the underperformance and the expense ratio. The higher the expenses charged by a fund, the greater the degree of underperformance, which is consistent with the previously reported results of Sharpe. Also, Blake, Elton, and Gruber found underperformance of bond funds using a wide array of performance measures.

Exhibit 15-4 shows the percentage of pension funds outperformed by the passive S&P 500 index during the past two decades using rate of return as the performance benchmark. The majority of pension plans are consistently outperformed by the S&P 500. For example, in 1991, almost 60% of pension funds were outperformed by the S&P 500 index. Thus, the argument in favor of following an investment strategy that passively mimics the S&P 500 appears strong.[17]

15.4 TIMING THE MARKET

Another portfolio management strategy that is employed by money managers is an attempt to time the market, that is, to decide when to move into and out of different asset categories. In recent years, newsletters advising investors when to move into and out of stocks have proliferated. Exhibit 15-5 provides some interesting insights into the quantity and quality of this advice. In 1980 there were only fourteen mutual fund market–timing newsletters, and by the early 1990s there were over a hundred.[18] How have these newsletters performed their stated task? Exhibit 15-5 shows clearly that they have failed miserably.

15. Bruce N. Lehman and David M. Modest, "Mutual Fund Performance Evaluations: A Comparison of Benchmarks and Benchmark Comparisons," *Journal of Finance* 42 (June 1987): 233–265.

16. See Christopher R. Blake, Edwin J. Elton, and Martin J. Gruber, "The Performance of Bond Mutual Funds," *Journal of Business* 66, no. 3 (July 1993): 371–403.

17. An alternative explanation would appear to be that most funds take less risk than the S&P 500. However, most studies of fund performance on a risk-adjusted basis find similar results to those of Exhibit 15-4.

18. Exhibit 15–5 shows that there were fourteen newsletters in 1980 and eighty-five at the start of 1989. However, the source cited in the exhibit goes on to state that there were over a hundred newsletters in the early 1990s.

EXHIBIT 15-4   Percentage of Pension Funds Outperformed by the S&P 500 Index, 1971–1991

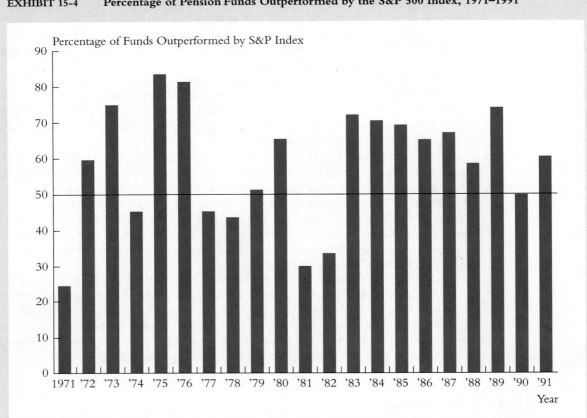

Source: Adapted with permission from John C. Bogle, Sr., "Is a Long-Term Time Frame for Investing Affordable or Even Relevant?" in the *Investing for the Long Term* seminar proceedings. Copyright 1992, Association for Investment Management and Research, Charlottesville, Va. All rights reserved. Data originally from SEI (1971–78) and INDATA (1979–90).

EXHIBIT 15-5   Performance of Mutual Fund Timing Newsletters

Period	Number of Newsletters	Advisors Outpacing Market	Advisors Falling Short	Median Timing Return	Market Return
June 30, 1980–June 30, 1990	14	4	10	+271.5	+336.9
Jan. 1, 1989–June 30, 1990	85	8	77	+17.1	+31.5

Source: Adapted with permission from John C. Bogle, Sr., "Is a Long-Term Time Frame for Investing Affordable or Even Relevant?" in the *Investing for the Long Term* seminar proceedings. Copyright 1992, Association for Investment Management and Research, Charlottesville, Va. All rights reserved. Data from M. Hulbert, *The Hulbert Financial Digest* (New York: Institute of Finance, 1991).

To sum up, the performance of mutual funds does not reveal that the funds' managers have special knowledge in security selection. However, some have argued that the miserable performance of mutual funds can be attributed to problems with the performance indexes, not with the performance of the funds. We next look at some of the common problems with performance indexes.

15.5 A WORD OF CAUTION ABOUT PERFORMANCE INDEXES IN PRACTICE

Several problems arise when we attempt to apply performance measures in practice. First, performance evaluation is a historical exercise by its very nature; a performance index tells us how well a manager did in the past. Our concern, however, is how well the manager will do in the future. Although we use historical data to make current decisions that will affect future performance, the link between past performance and future performance may be weak (see Connecting Theory to Practice 15.2).

CONNECTING THEORY TO PRACTICE 15.2

WHAT MONEY MANAGERS REALLY SELL

More than $2 trillion now is invested in pension funds in the U.S. These funds are expected to grow safely until workers retire and need their benefits. Money managers—banks, insurance companies and investment counselors—compete to manage these funds for corporations by promising to beat, typically by 2% to 4%, the Standard & Poor's index of 500 stocks.

In an effort to improve performance, most money managers actively pick stocks. Unfortunately, the managers don't beat the market. On average, fund managers have underperformed the market by 1.3% a year. When the funds are weighted by size, the degree of underperformance jumps to 2.6%. And that doesn't take into account the fees that the managers charge; they can amount to 0.5% a year.

. . . [T]here doesn't seem to be much consistency of performance over one-year periods. A manager who outperformed the market in one year might very well underperform it in the following year. But giving discretion to outside managers gives the treasurer's office other people to blame.

The treasurer, if he wanted, could place all the money in an index fund. Index funds are carefully designed to duplicate the performance of the market. This would deny the treasurer the pleasure of beating the market, but at least he wouldn't have the pain of underperforming it.

But treasurers, by and large, don't like passive management. As the authors [of a recent study by Josef Lakonishok, Andrei Shleifer, and Robert Vishny]

(continued)

state, "Passive management reduces the demand for services produced by (the treasurer's office) and thus reduces the size of its empire." Those in charge of the plan must do some work to preserve their positions.

Source: Lindley H. Clark, Jr., "What Money Managers Really Sell," *Wall Street Journal*, July 2, 1992, p. A8. Reprinted by permission of *The Wall Street Journal*, © 1992 Dow Jones & Co., Inc. All Rights Reserved Worldwide.

MAKING THE CONNECTION

This article reiterates the historically poor performance of fund managers, as well as the lack of consistency in performance of funds from year to year. This lack of consistency over time greatly reduces the effectiveness of performance measures. However, it is clear that if a fund consistently charges too much for its services, over time it will be outperformed by a similar fund with lower fees. Also note that performance measures are widely used in practice. Skillful practitioners use performance measures while at the same time understanding their limitations.

Another problem in using performance measures is appropriately measuring risk for a money manager who actively trades. Specifically, what is the appropriate comparison or benchmark portfolio for the manager? Jeffery V. Bailey puts it this way:

Good benchmarks increase the proficiency of performance evaluation, highlighting the contributions of active managers, and enhance plan sponsors' ability to control risk. Bad benchmarks obscure the contribution of managers and can lead to inefficient allocations of plan assets. Yet, despite the importance of benchmark quality, and the advances that have been made in the construction and application of customized benchmarks, benchmark quality has remained a neglected issue. [19]

For example, an active money manager may hold 80% stocks, 15% bonds, and 5% cash one day and then 50% stocks, 45% bonds, and 5% cash the next. [20] If the stock portfolio is riskier than the bond portfolio, then the riskiness of the overall portfolio (namely, beta) clearly has changed. There are ways to handle the problem, but they are very difficult to implement.

For example, if beta is the appropriate risk measure, then we can calculate the betas of the stocks, bonds, and cash portfolios and adjust the overall portfolio beta. That is, rather than compute the beta based on the historical behavior of the portfolio, we can compute the beta based on the allocations among stocks, bonds, and cash. Recent research using this approach has documented that professional money

---

19. From the abstract of Jeffery V. Bailey, "Evaluating Benchmark Quality," *Financial Analysts Journal,* May–June 1992, p. 33.
20. Such radical changes in allocations are now straightforward with the use of futures contracts (see Chapter 22).

managers with poor year-to-date returns at the end of the third quarter tend to have increased equity risk exposure during the fourth quarter of the calendar year.[21] Apparently, managers tend to "go for broke" by increasing their betas in the fourth quarter if they have not been doing well in the first part of the year. This higher risk strategy will either dramatically improve the year-end performance or dramatically reduce the year-end performance. Thus, by calculating the portfolio beta as a weighted average of the securities' beta, we can detect changes in risk level as soon as portfolio changes are made.

Performance measures based on beta may be ambiguous, however. Roll has argued that beta itself is not a clear measure of risk.[22] For example, if we use a different proxy for the market than the S&P 500 index, the betas may change, and we may arrive at different portfolio rankings. Moreover, if we employ the mean-variance efficient portfolio to calculate beta, all assets will show the same performance when adjusted for risk; this casts doubt on the Jensen and Treynor performance measures. Also, the calculated beta changes over time and depends on the time intervals used to compute rates of return. Thus, beta itself is not stable and depends on the market proxy used to calculate it.[23]

Finally, overall performance indexes provide no clues about which activities within the portfolio manager's domain are generating the superior (or inferior) performance; thus, it is not clear what the portfolio manager is doing well or not so well.

15.6 PERFORMANCE ATTRIBUTION

Portfolio managers generally make two types of decisions: a) the investment proportions in various asset classes (bonds, stocks, cash) and b) the selection of individual securities out of these classes. Assessing the performance of the activities that make up portfolio management is known as **performance attribution.** If a manager is doing well in one area and badly in another, performance attribution will identify areas where the manager can improve or identify tasks that should be taken from the manager and given to somebody else.

Performance attribution seeks to take the overall rate of return on a fund and break it down into its component parts, such as asset allocation and security selection. To attribute performance, we just need to analyze the various management decisions.

---

21. Based on Robert Radcliffe, Robert Brooks, and Haim Levy, "Active Asset Allocation Decisions of Professional Equity Managers," *Review of Financial Services* 2, no. 1 (1992/1993): 21–40.

22. See Richard Roll, "Ambiguity When Performance Is Measured by the Security Market Line," *Journal of Finance,* September 1978, pp. 1051–1069; Richard Roll, "Performance Evaluation and Benchmark Errors, 1" *Journal of Portfolio Management,* Summer 1980, pp. 5–12; Richard Roll, "Performance Evaluation and Benchmark Errors, 2," *Journal of Portfolio Management,* Winter 1981, pp. 17–22; and Richard Roll and Stephen Ross, "The Arbitrage Pricing Theory Approach to Strategic Portfolio Planning," *Financial Analysts Journal,* May–June 1984, pp. 14–26.

23. Also, Roll shows that if an efficient portfolio is employed to calculate beta, Jensen's measure will be zero also in the sample for all portfolios (see Richard Roll, "A Critique of the Asset Pricing Theory's Tests, 1: On Past and Potential Testability of the Theory," *Journal of Financial Economics,* March 1977, pp. 129–176). Thus, the different performances that we observe may only indicate that an inefficient market portfolio was employed to calculate beta.

Exhibit 15-6 illustrates the four layers of decisions that are typically made in the **top-down approach** used by portfolio managers. First, the portfolio manager decides what percentage of the portfolio will be stocks, bonds, and cash. This decision is known as **asset allocation.** (Other categories, such as real estate, also could be included.) For example, the manager may decide to place 40% of the portfolio in stocks, 30% in bonds, and 30% in cash. Using the notation w_a, the asset allocation proportion (or weight), we have $w_{a,Stocks} = 0.40$, $w_{a,Bonds} = 0.30$, and $w_{a,Cash} = 0.30$.

EXHIBIT 15-6   Flow Chart of the Top-Down Money Management Process

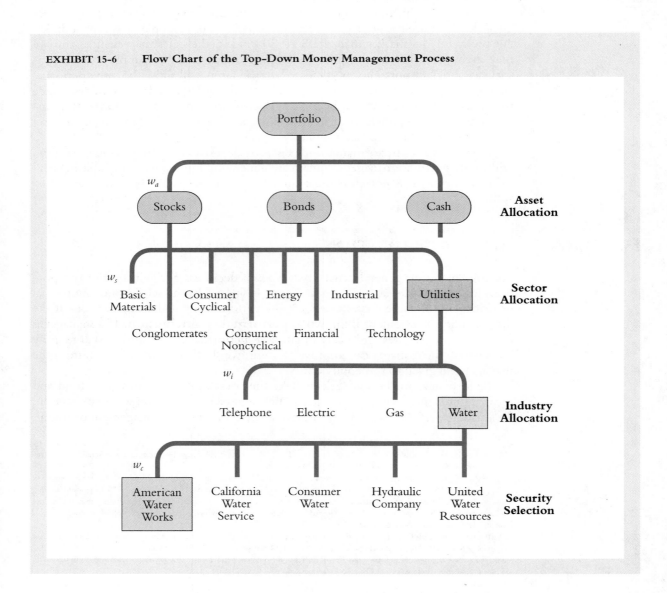

Next, the manager must decide how to allocate the 40% portion of stocks into various sectors, such as basic materials, conglomerates, and so forth. The sectors shown in Exhibit 15-6 are based on sector definitions provided in the *Wall Street Journal*. The decision to place 10% of the stock portion in utilities (denoted $w_{s,Utilities}$ = 0.10), for example, is known as the **sector allocation** decision (how much of an asset to place in a specific sector). The sum of all the sector weights (w_s) will equal 100%. Hence, sector weights denote the portion of the stocks held given to a certain sector category.

The next decision managers make is how to allocate each of the sector portions into various industries. For example, the utilities sector can be broken down into four basic industries: telephone, electric, gas, and water. The **industry allocation** is the allotment of investment dollars given to a sector's industry components. For example, the manager may decide to allocate 30% of the utilities sector to the water industry (denoted $w_{i,Water}$ = 0.30, where i denotes *industry*).

At this point, the manager is ready to select individual securities. For example, of the allocation given to the water industry, what portion should be invested in American Water Works (AWW)? This decision is known as **security selection.** The manager may decide to place 15% of the water industry allocation into American Water Works (denoted $w_{c,AWW}$ = 0.15, where c denotes *company*).

To attribute performance among the various management decisions, an index portfolio is needed for comparison. This index portfolio plays the role of a benchmark portfolio. The fund manager knows that the fund's performance will be compared with this benchmark portfolio. For example, suppose the fund outperformed the index portfolio by 250 basis points. Senior management wants to be able to determine which decisions generated the excess returns. Was it the asset allocation decision to have less in stocks? Was it the sector allocation decision, the industry allocation decision, and/or the security selections? The answer can be determined through the process of performance attribution.

15.7 INDEXING AND INTERNATIONAL DIVERSIFICATION

In response to the historically poor performance of mutual funds overall, many managers and investors are turning to indexing. Investors who follow an indexing strategy invest in a passively managed mutual fund that mirrors the market and incurs minimal expenses. If you are a manager or an individual investor who concludes that you have no ability to pick stocks or to time the market, you should consider diversifying according to an index.

If you desire to expand globally, you should diversify in various countries. Obviously, you cannot diversify directly in all stocks available in the world. However, you can buy most of them indirectly by buying existing index funds in these countries. The advertisement of the Vanguard Group shown in Connecting Theory to Practice 15.3 demonstrates how this is done.

CONNECTING THEORY TO PRACTICE 15.3

AT LAST. A SIMPLE STRATEGY FOR INTERNATIONAL INVESTING. USE THE POWER OF INDEXING

Over 55% of the world market capitalization is currently *outside* the U.S. Which means, international stocks open up another whole world of growth and opportunity for investing.

The Vanguard Total International Fund offers a simple indexing strategy for investing in these international markets, providing broad diversification at the lowest costs.

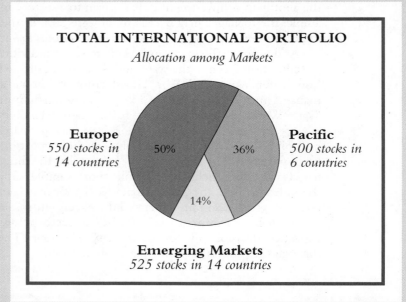

TOTAL INTERNATIONAL PORTFOLIO
Allocation among Markets

Europe
*550 stocks in
14 countries*
50%

Pacific
*500 stocks in
6 countries*
36%

14%

Emerging Markets
525 stocks in 14 countries

Chart based on 5/31/97 composition of the MSCI-EAFE Select EMF index. Hong Kong, Malaysia and Singapore are represented in both the Pacific and Emerging Markets portions of this Portfolio.

Source: Morgan Stanley Capital International, as cited in *Forbes*, August 25, 1997.

INDEXING MEANS DIVERSIFICATION

You can add an important international component to your portfolio with one simple investment.

The Vanguard Total International Fund is the most diversified international stock fund available. It invests in Vanguard's existing European, Pacific

(continued)

and Emerging Markets Index Funds and holds more than 1500 stocks in 31 different countries.

Source: An advertisement of Vanguard Group taken from *Forbes*, August 25, 1997. Reprinted with permission of Vanguard Group.

MAKING THE CONNECTION

The Vanguard advertisement shows the Vanguard Group's policy: buy existing indexes of various countries for an unmanaged international portfolio. This policy admits a lack of ability to time the market or to pick stocks but recognizes the importance of diversification, and in particular international diversification, in risk reduction.

SUMMARY

Calculate portfolio performance using four performance indexes.   Performance indexes provide a method of comparing funds with different risk-return characteristics. Four performance indexes used to rank portfolio performance are Sharpe's index, Treynor's index, Jensen's index, and an index based on the arbitrage pricing theory (APT). Sharpe's performance index compares fund performance where the standard deviation measures the risk, whereas Treynor's performance index compares fund performance where beta serves as the measure of risk. Sharpe's index is appropriate for portfolios in isolation, and Treynor's index is appropriate for portfolios in the context of the entire market portfolio. Jensen's performance index is also based on beta as a risk index, but it gives performance measure results in terms of rates of return. Because Treynor's and Jensen's indexes are based on the CAPM framework, they both give the same assessment of overperformance or underperformance in relation to the market, but the indexes can give different rankings within the two groups based on performance.

Summarize the empirical evidence regarding portfolio managers' performance.   The empirical evidence consistently finds that professional portfolio managers lag behind the market as a whole in performance. Even after adjusting for risk, which is measured in a variety of ways, managers are underperforming the market.

Identify some problems with measuring fund managers' performance in practice.   Problems with measuring the performance of fund managers include the fact that historical performance is not an accurate forecast of future performance; difficulties in measuring the risk of actively traded accounts; difficulties in measuring beta and in identifying the relevant market portfolio against which beta should be calculated; and the lack of clues as to what activities are generating the performance.

Evaluate performance attribution as a means of identifying the sources of performance.   Performance attribution breaks down a fund's excess return into component parts. The component parts correspond with the four layers of decisions that are typically made through a top-down portfolio management approach. The layers are the asset allocation decision, the sector allocation decision, the industry allocation decision, and security selection.

CHAPTER AT A GLANCE

1. *Overall performance indexes:*

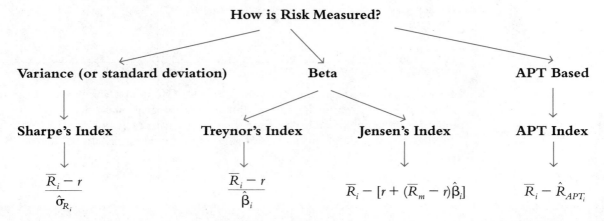

where $\overline{R}$ is the realized average rate of return and $\hat{R}_i$ is the required rate of return from the relevant model. Treynor's and Jensen's indexes generally give different rankings but the same assessment of overperformance or underperformance.

2. *Problems in the use of performance indexes in practice:*
   a. Historical performance is used to infer future performance.
   b. It is difficult to measure the risk of actively traded accounts.
   c. Beta is not stable and depends on the choice of market index.
   d. Overall performance indexes cannot identify what activities of the portfolio manager resulted in the performance.

3. *Performance attribution:*
   Performance attribution determines which levels of decisions caused observed excess returns:
   Level 1: Asset allocation.
   Level 2: Sector allocation.
   Level 3: Industry allocation.
   Level 4: Security selection.

KEY TERMS

APT performance index   533
Asset allocation   542
Industry allocation   543
Jensen's performance
  index   531
Performance attribution   541
Performance index   523
Sector allocation   543
Security selection   543
Sharpe's performance
  index   525
Top-down approach   542
Treynor's performance
  index   528

REVIEW

15.1 How should risk be measured for a specific asset? Explain the pros and cons of the alternative risk measures.

15.2 "Sharpe's index gives the same ranking for any risk-free interest rate." Evaluate this statement, and defend your answer graphically.

15.3 How does one "beat the market" according to the following?
a. Sharpe's index.
b. Treynor's index.
c. Jensen's index.

15.4 In general, what does the empirical evidence suggest about the historical performance of mutual funds?

15.5 If you were a pension fund manager who was proud of the history of your pension fund management, how would you respond to the evidence presented in Exhibit 15-4?

15.6 Discuss some of the practical problems with employing performance measures in practice.

PRACTICE

15.1 The rates of return on two mutual funds (A and B) and on the market portfolio are as follows. Assume the risk-free rate $(r) = 5\%$.

Year	Fund A	Fund B	Market
1	25%	15%	12%
2	10	8	8
3	8	6	7
4	−3	4	5
5	7	8	6

a. Which fund performed better according to Sharpe's index? How did the funds compare with the market portfolio?
b. Which fund performed better according to Treynor's index? How did the funds compare with the market portfolio?
c. Which fund performed better according to Jensen's index? How did the funds compare with the market portfolio?

15.2 What is the relationship between Treynor's index and Jensen's index with regard to ranking portfolios? Show your results analytically.

15.3 Suppose $\sigma_m = 17\%$, $\overline{R}_m = 12.5\%$, and $r = 6\%$. If a mutual fund's performance is just equal to the market, determine the following for the fund:

a. Sharpe's index.
b. Treynor's index.
c. Jensen's index.

15.4 Suppose we are given the following information for five mutual funds ($r = 7\%$, and the average rate of return on the market was 12%):

Fund					
	A	**B**	**C**	**D**	**E**
$\overline{R}$	12.5%	15%	8%	10%	18%
σ_{R_i}	22.1%	25%	30%	8%	34%
β_i	1.17	1.2	0.6	1.1	1.25

a. Rank these funds by Sharpe's, Treynor's, and Jensen's indexes. Discuss your findings.
b. Now suppose the risk-free rate is 4%. Recalculate Part a, and discuss any differences.

15.5 Suppose you can invest directly in either a mutual fund or a portfolio of a few stocks. You pay 1% transaction costs on a direct investment and a 4% management fee to the mutual fund. (Assume that costs are incurred only on purchases; for example, the return on the mutual fund in Year 1 will be 8% rather than 12%.)

The rates of return before transaction costs are as follows:

Year	Mutual Fund	Direct Investment
1	12%	11%
2	10	11
3	−2	−6
4	18	17

Assume that the risk-free rate is $r = 4\%$.

a. Which investment is better, according to Sharpe's index, before transaction costs?

b. Which investment is better, according to Sharpe's index, after transaction costs?

c. Compare your results for Parts a and b graphically in the expected return–standard deviation space.

15.6 Suppose for two stocks, A and B, we have

$$E(R_A) = 2E(R_B), \text{ and } \sigma_A = 2\sigma_B$$

a. Show that Sharpe's index for Stock A must be larger than Sharpe's index for Stock B.

b. Show that if $r = 0$, Sharpe's index for Stocks A and B is the same.

15.7 Two mutual funds have the following rates of return:

Year	Fund A	Fund B	Market Portfolio
1	10%	12%	12%
2	−5	−4	0
3	30	25	10

a. Calculate $\bar{R}_A$, $\bar{R}_B$, σ_A, σ_B, β_A, and β_B.

b. Suppose $PI_{S,A} = PI_{S,B}$. What must be the interest rate (r)?

c. Suppose $PI_{T,A} = PI_{T,B}$. What must be the interest rate (r)?

15.8 Suppose $E(R_m) = 2r$. Treynor's index for the market portfolio is 0.1. What is the interest rate (r)?

15.9 Suppose you know that the interest rate (r) equals 4%. A portfolio's mean return is 3%.

a. Is it possible that according to Sharpe's index, the managers would have successfully beaten the market?

b. Is it possible that this performance will be considered successful according to Treynor's index?

15.10 Suppose Jensen's alpha is $\alpha = 0.05$, and the portfolio beta is $\beta = 2$. Also assume that $R_m = 0.1$ and $r = 0.05$. What is Treynor's index?

15.11 A mutual fund has the following rates of return:

Year	R_i	R_m
1	10%	8%
2	15	12
3	−3	3

Assume that the interest rate is $r = 3\%$ and is constant across years.

a. Calculate Sharpe's index.

b. Calculate Treynor's index.

15.12 There are two mutual funds, A and B. It is known that the rates of return of Fund A and Fund B are related as follows:

$$R_A = 2R_B$$

a. "If the interest rate is zero, then Treynor's index for Fund A must be twice Treynor's index for Fund B."

b. "If the interest rate is positive $(r > 0)$, then Treynor's index for Fund A is twice as large as Treynor's index for Fund B."

Do you agree with these two statements? Why or why not?

15.13 Suppose that two mutual funds have the following returns:

Year	Fund A	Fund B	Market Portfolio
1	5%	7%	5%
2	−3	−1	2
3	4	6	10

Assume that the interest rate is $r = 3\%$.

a. Calculate Sharpe's index.

b. Calculate Treynor's index.

c. Can you prove that $PI_{S,B} > PI_{S,A}$ and/or $PI_{T,A} > PI_{T,B}$ without using calculations?

15.14 Suppose the real interest rate is 2%, and the nominal interest rate is 6%. Here are the nominal rates of return on two portfolios, as well as the inflation rate:

Year	Nominal Rates of Return		
	A	B	Inflation
1	5%	15%	2%
2	10	10	4
3	14	5	6

a. Calculate PI_S for the two portfolios in nominal terms.
b. Calculate PI_S for the two portfolios in real terms.
c. Compare and explain the results in Parts a and b.

15.15 The rates of return on IBM, the S&P 500, and the world market portfolio are as follows:

Year	IBM	S&P 500	World Market Portfolio
1	−5%	7%	8%
2	30	9	14
3	15	12	12

a. Calculate the beta of IBM with the S&P 500, and alternatively with the world market portfolio. In your view, which is more relevant?
b. Assume that $r = 2\%$. Calculate PI_S and PI_T with the two market portfolios. Analyze your results.

15.16 A pure equity firm has the following rates of return:

Year	Rate of Return	Rate of Return on Market Portfolio
1	10%	7%
2	2	3
3	20	15

Assume that the interest rate is $r = 3\%$.
a. Calculate the beta and the performance indexes of Sharpe and Treynor.
b. Suppose you pay 25% tax on your rate of return. Calculate the after-tax beta and performance indexes. Discuss your results.

15.17 Suppose two firms, A and B, are ranked identically by Sharpe's index. Also, we know that

$\overline{R}_A = 10\%$, $\hat{\sigma}_A = 0.05$, $\overline{R}_B = 0.20$, and $\hat{\sigma}_B = 0.1$. Solve for the risk-free rate, r.

15.18 Express Jensen's index (PI_J) as a function of Treynor's index. Explain the relationship.

15.19 Suppose that Fund A has a higher expected return and a lower standard deviation than Fund B. "In such a case, Fund A must perform better than Fund B according to Sharpe's index." Is this assertion correct?

15.20 Suppose you buy Mutual Fund A with expected return $\overline{R}_A$ and standard deviation $\hat{\sigma}_A$. Now you lever yourself such that for each $1 invested from your own money, you borrow $1 at the risk-free interest rate, r. How will the borrowing influence the following?
a. Sharpe's index.
b. Treynor's index.
c. Jensen's index.

15.21 Two mutual funds have identical means, identical betas, and identical standard deviations. The returns on these two funds are independent, implying a correlation coefficient of zero. Suppose you invest 50% in each fund. Can you benefit from such diversification based on the following?
a. Sharpe's index.
b. Treynor's index.

15.22 Recall from Chapter 10 that the equilibrium relationship between risk and return under the APT was expressed as follows:

$$E(R_i) = a_0 + a_1\beta_1 + a_2\beta_2 + \ldots + a_K\beta_K$$

where a_0 is the risk-free interest rate, β_i is the security's sensitivity to each factor, and a_i is the market price per unit of sensitivity paid for taking this factor risk. Thus, the performance index based on the APT is expressed as follows:

$$PI_{A,i} = \overline{R}_i - (a_0 + a_1\hat{\beta}_1 + \ldots + a_K\hat{\beta}_K)$$

Suppose you believe that the stock market is driven by a three-factor APT model: (1) inflation, (2) gross domestic product (GDP), and (3) oil prices. You estimate that $r = 3.7\%$, $a_1 = 4.2\%$, $a_2 = 1.7\%$, and a_3

= 0.5%. You also estimate the following parameters for three funds:

	Fund A	Fund B	Fund C
β_1	0.1	0.3	0.2
β_2	0.5	0.7	−0.2
β_3	3.1	1.2	4.0
$\overline{R}$	12.1%	10.4%	8.7%

How did these funds perform according to the performance index based on the APT?

15.23 Answer this problem based on the equation for the performance measure of the APT, $PI_{A,i}$ given in Question 15.22. Suppose we believe that returns on securities are generated by two factors that can be approximated by the S&P 500 index and the inflation rate.[24] Suppose we estimate $a_i = a_{Inflation} = 1.2\%$, and $a_m = a_{S\&P\ 500} = 8.46\%$. Also, suppose the beta coefficients for inflation ($\hat{\beta}_i$) are as follows for the three mutual funds discussed in this chapter:

$$\hat{\beta}_{i,Fund\ A} = 0.5, \ \hat{\beta}_{i,Fund\ B} = -0.5, \text{ and } \hat{\beta}_{i,Vanguard} = 0.8$$

Calculate the APT performance measure for each fund. Discuss these results.

15.24 Suppose we have determined the following information regarding the Babson Value Fund and the Bartlett Basic Value Fund:

	Babson Value Fund	Bartlett Basic Value Fund
$\beta_{Inflation}$	0.8	−1.2
β_{Market}	1.0	0.75
Average return	9.2%	6.9%

Also, we have estimated the market price of risk to be $a_{Inflation} = 2.3\%$ and $a_{Market} = 4.7\%$. The risk-free rate was 4.5%. Which fund outperformed using the APT-based index discussed in Question 15.22?

15.25 Suppose we know that the risk-free rate is 5%, Sharpe's performance index for an international portfolio (in dollars) is $PI_{S,I} = 0.125$, and Sharpe's performance index for a domestic portfolio is $PI_{S,D} = 0.1$. If we have a target rate of return of 10%, what is the percentage reduction in the

standard deviation obtained by moving from the domestic fund to the international fund?

15.26 The table at the top of page 551 reports the rate of return and risk of five mutual funds.
a. Assuming a 5% riskless interest rate, calculate the share's performance ratio for each of the funds, where the average rate of return is *before* loads and taxes. Draw your results in the mean–standard deviation space. What fund performed best during these 5 years?
b. Repeat Part a, this time when the average rate of return is *after* loads and taxes.
c. Analyze Parts a and b. Does the ranking of funds change? Explain why or why not.

15.27 The bar graph at the bottom of page 551 illustrates the performance of the Dow Jones Industrial Average and the S&P 500, as well as the average performance of mutual funds for the year 1997 and the past 3, 5, and 10 years before 1997.
a. Focus on the 10-year annual average returns. Suppose that the riskless annual interest rate is $r = 6\%$ and that all three investments lie on the security market line (SML). Assume also that the beta of the S&P 500 is equal to 1; that is, the S&P 500 is assumed to be the market portfolio. Based on these assumptions, calculate the beta of the Dow Jones Industrial Index and the beta of "Mutual Funds."
b. Nowadays, you can buy a share of a trust that buys the Dow Jones Industrial or the S&P 500 (called Diamonds and Spiders, respectively). The units of these trusts are traded, like any other stocks, on the American Stock Exchange. Alternatively, you can buy the average mutual fund whose return is given in the bar graph. What is the maximum fee (as a percentage of the investment) that the investor could pay on buying Spiders and still get the same rate of return as on the mutual funds? Answer this question separately for a 1-year investment (1997) and a 3-, 5-, and 10-year investment.

For Internet questions visit the Levy Investment Web site at http://levy-invst.swcollege.com.

---

24. We assume, for simplicity, that these factors are uncorrelated.

	Returns	Return ↓	Fees		Risk
Here's What You Get after loads and taxes[a]					
	Avg. Annual 5 yr.	Avg. Annual 5 yr.	Sales Load	Annual Expenses	Standard Deviation
Strong Corporate Bond[b]	11.2%	9.6%	None	1.00%	5.6
Smith Barney Investment Grade Bond B	10.4%	8.7%	4.50%[c]	1.54%	10.8
Vanguard Preferred Stock	10.0%	8.4%	None	0.39%	5.9
Managers Bond	9.7%	7.9%	None	1.36%	7.6
Ivy Bond A	9.6%	6.7%	4.75%	1.56%	5.3

a. Performance is through Nov. 14, 1997, and net of annual expenses, brokerage costs, and sales loads; also net of taxes, assuming the new 20% long-term rate for capital gains and income distributions.

b. Fund will not declare capital gains Dec. 7–31, 1997.

c. Deferred sales charge, which declines over time.

Source: *Fortune,* December 29, 1997, p. 132. Reprinted from the December 29, 1997, issue of *Fortune* by special permission. © 1997, Time, Inc.

Dow for the Common Man

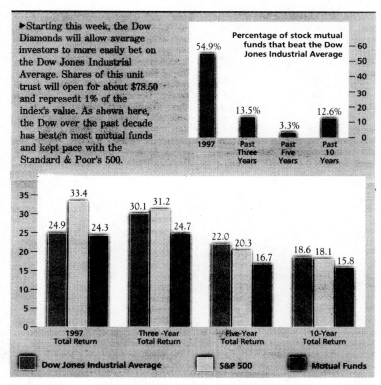

Source: Andrew Bary, "Trading the Dow," *Barron's,* January 19, 1998, p. 18. Reprinted by permission of Barron's, © 1998 Dow Jones & Co., Inc. All Rights Reserved Worldwide.

YOUR TURN: APPLYING THEORY TO PRACTICE
MEASURING THE PERFORMANCE OF SMALL STOCKS AND CORPORATE BONDS

The following are the monthly rates of return for 2 years, 1927 and 1996, on a portfolio of small stocks, a portfolio of corporate bonds, and a portfolio of long-term government bonds, along with the rates of return on the market portfolio (S&P 500 index).* In 1927 there was an uptrend in the stock market, and in 1996 there was a downturn.

1927

Month	S&P 500 Total Return	Small Stock Total Return	Corporate Bond Total Return	Long-Term Government Bond Total Return
1	−0.0193	0.0296	0.0056	0.0075
2	0.0537	0.0547	0.0069	0.0088
3	0.0087	−0.0548	0.0083	0.0253
4	0.0201	0.0573	0.0055	−0.0005
5	0.0607	0.0734	−0.0011	0.0109
6	−0.0067	−0.0303	0.0043	−0.0069
7	0.0670	0.0516	0.0003	0.0050
8	0.0515	−0.0178	0.0083	0.0076
9	0.0450	0.0047	0.0149	0.0018
10	−0.0502	−0.0659	0.0055	0.0099
11	0.0721	0.0808	0.0068	0.0097
12	0.0279	0.0316	0.0068	0.0072

1996

Month	S&P 500 Total Return	Small Stock Total Return	Corporate Bond Total Return	Long-Term Government Bond Total Return
1	3.44	0.28	0.14	−0.11
2	0.96	3.69	−3.73	−4.83
3	0.96	2.28	−1.30	−2.10
4	1.47	8.48	−1.60	−1.65
5	2.58	7.49	0.05	−0.54
6	0.41	−5.82	1.72	2.03
7	−4.45	−9.43	0.10	0.18
8	2.12	4.76	−0.70	−1.39
9	5.62	2.91	2.59	2.90
10	2.74	−1.75	3.61	4.04
11	7.59	2.88	2.63	3.51
12	−1.96	2.04	−1.86	−2.56

*Note that in 1927 the average return on some assets was below the riskless interest rate. The monthly risk-free interest rate was 0.2% in 1929 and 0.42% in 1996.

(continued)

Suppose there are three mutual funds. Fund A specializes in small stocks, Fund B specializes in corporate bonds, and Fund C specializes in government bonds. Assume that the returns given in the above tables apply to these three mutual funds.

Questions

1. Rank the performance of these three funds by the Sharpe, Treynor, and Jensen measures. Rank each year separately. Discuss your results.

2. A new fund is considering investing ¼ of its assets in the S&P index and ¼ in each of the other three assets reported in the table. Assuming that each of the years represents the rate of return distribution, calculate all three performance measures for each year separately. Summarize all the performance measures in a table. Analyze the results.

3. Compare your results for each year. Are the performance measures meaningful for an asset with average returns below the riskless interest rate? In light of your results, explain why, in order to measure the performance of funds, we need a relatively long period of time rather than just 1 year. (Hint: Note that if the mean return is smaller than the risk-free interest rate, with Treynor's and Sharpe's indexes we obtain a paradoxical result: the higher the risk [σ or β], the better the performance.)

SELECTED REFERENCES

American Association of Individual Investors. *The Individual Investor's Guide to No-Load Mutual Funds.* Chicago: International Publishing Corporation, various issues.

This publication is a good source of information on no-load mutual funds.

Bogle, John C. "Selecting Equity Mutual Funds." *Journal of Portfolio Management,* Winter 1992, pp. 94–100.

This article is a good review of the issues involved in selecting actively versus passively managed mutual funds.

Karnosky, Denis S., and Brian D. Singer. *Global Asset Management and Performance Attribution.* Char-

lottesville, Va.: The Research Foundation of the Institute of Chartered Financial Analysts, 1994.

This monograph is a detailed presentation of one method of assessing performance attribution of a global portfolio.

Maginn, John L., and Donald L. Tuttle (eds). *Managing Investment Portfolios: A Dynamic Process.* 2d ed. New York: Warren, Gorham & Lamont, 1990.

See especially Chapter 7 for a detailed discussion of asset allocation.

SUPPLEMENTAL REFERENCES

Allen, Gregory C. "Performance Attribution for Global Equity Portfolios." *Journal of Portfolio Management,* Fall 1991, pp. 59–65.

Ankrim, Ernest M., and Chris R. Hensel. "Multicurrency Performance Attribution." *Financial Analysts Journal,* March–April 1994, pp. 29–35.

Blake, Christopher R., Edwin J. Elton, and Martin J. Gruber. "The Performance of Bond Mutual Funds." *Journal of Business* 66, no. 3 (July 1993): 371–403.

Cumby, Robert E., and Jack D. Glen. "Evaluating the Performance of International Mutual Funds." *Journal of Finance,* June 1990, pp. 497–521.

Eun, Cheol S., Richard Kolodny, and Bruce G. Resnick. "U.S.–Based International Mutual Funds: A Performance Evaluation." *Journal of Portfolio Management,* Spring 1991, pp. 88–94.

Grinblatt, Mark, and Sheridan Titman. "Performance Measurement without Benchmarks: An Examination of Mutual Fund Returns." *Journal of Business* 66 (January 1993): 47–68.

Halpern, Philip. "Investing Abroad: A Review of Capital Market Integration and Manager Performance." *Journal of Portfolio Management* 19 (Winter 1993): 47–57.

Hodgos, Charles W., Walton R. L. Taylor, and James A. Yoder. "Stocks, Bonds, the Sharpe Ratio, and the Investment Horizon." *Financial Analysts Journal,* November–December 1997, pp. 74–80.

Jensen, C. Michael. "The Performance of Mutual Funds in the Period 1945–1964." *Journal of Finance,* May 1968, pp. 389–415.

Kahn, Ronald N. "Bond Performance Analysis: A Multi-factor Approach." *Journal of Portfolio Management,* Fall 1991, pp. 40–47.

Khorana, Ajay, and Edward Nelling. "The Performance Risk, a Diversification of Sector Funds." *Financial Analysts Journal,* May–June 1997, pp. 62–73.

Lehman, Bruce N., and David M. Modest. "Mutual Fund Performance Evaluations: A Comparison of Benchmarks and Benchmark Comparisons." *Journal of Finance* 42 (June 1987): 233–265.

Roll, Richard. "Ambiguity When Performance Is Measured by the Security Market Line." *Journal of Finance,* September 1978, pp. 1051–1069.

Roll, Richard. "A Critique of the Asset Pricing Theory's Tests, 1: On Past and Potential Testability of the Theory." *Journal of Financial Economics,* March 1977, pp. 129–176.

Roll, Richard. "Performance Evaluation and Benchmark Errors, 1." *Journal of Portfolio Management,* Summer 1980, pp. 5–12.

Roll, Richard. "Performance Evaluation and Benchmark Errors, 2." *Journal of Portfolio Management,* Winter 1981, pp. 17–22.

Roll, Richard, and Stephen Ross. "The Arbitrage Pricing Theory Approach to Strategic Portfolio Planning." *Financial Analysts Journal,* May–June 1984, pp. 14–26.

Sharpe, William F. "Asset Allocation: Management Style and Performance Measurement." *Journal of Portfolio Management,* Winter 1992, pp. 7–19.

Sharpe, William F. "Mutual Fund Performance." *Journal of Business,* January 1966, pp. 119–138.

Treynor, Jack. "How to Rate Management of Investment Funds." *Harvard Business Review,* January–February 1965, pp. 63–75.

CHAPTER 16

INTEREST RATES AND BOND VALUATION

LEARNING OBJECTIVES

After studying this chapter you should be able to:

1. Construct and interpret a yield curve.

2. Use the bond pricing equation to find bond prices and bond yields.

3. Summarize the theories that explain the shape and level of yield curves.

4. Describe the behavior of the spread over Treasuries.

5. Describe the impact of the call feature and the convertible feature on bond prices.

INVESTMENTS IN THE NEWS

BOND PROS: WHERE TO RIDE OUT A JITTERY MARKET

Bond pros are jittery. The bull market culminated in late 1993 with the 30-year Treasury bond yielding 5.75%. Since then, bonds have been relatively flat, trading between 6.25% to 7.25% for the past two years. But within that range, you can still get some stomach-churning volatility. In fact, with the U.S. economy deep into one of the longest economic expansions on record, any news even slightly hinting at rising inflation can send the market into a tizzy. On October 8, when Federal Reserve Board Chairman Alan Greenspan said the economy "has been on an unsustainable track," bond prices plunged, pushing the long-bond yield up 15 basis points, to 6.37%, in one day. Days before, tensions between Iran and Iraq sparked fear of rising oil prices and another yield upsurge.

Source: Amy Dunkin (ed.), Personal Business, *Business Week,* November 3, 1997, p. 174. Reprinted from the November 3, 1997, issue of *Business Week* by special permission, © 1997 by The McGraw-Hill Companies Inc.

ZEROING IN

Merrill Lynch's chief investment strategist, Charles Clough, believes interest rates will continue to decline in coming months, falling as much as 100 basis points by year-end. Reasons: low inflation and a slowing economy.

If you agree, put some money into long-term, zero-coupon Treasurys. These bonds pay no interest but make one payment of principal at maturity. They're issued at a deep discount to their maturity value and increase in price as they mature. In a declining-rate scenario, they give a darn good bang for the buck.

Mark Lay, who helps run MDL Capital Management's $400 million fixed-income fund, recommends Treasurys maturing on Nov. 15, 2022. Currently yielding 6.65% to maturity, bonds that will be worth $100,000 in 2022 cost only $19,105 today. Lay believes interest rates will fall at least 50 basis points in the next six months, giving a 33% return by year-end. Clough also likes zeros; in his scenario, they'd return 62%. For even bigger returns, buy Treasurys on margin: pros suggest leverage of no more than 40%. If interest rates do nothing? The zeros will go up almost 7% a year.

Source: Caroline Waxler (ed.), Money and Investments: Streetwalker, *Forbes,* August 11, 1997, p. 134. Reprinted by Permission of *Forbes* magazine © Forbes Inc., 1997.

As the first article in this chapter's Investments in the News discussed, for example, trading bonds with yields to maturity between 6.25% and 7.25% creates a high trading volatility. When the economy expands and there is a hint of rising inflation, the bond yield goes up. Before 1970, interest rates were relatively stable, and investing in bonds was straightforward. A typical investor would buy a bond and hold it to maturity. Because interest rates were fairly stable, an investor could accurately predict the future price of a bond. For example, if you purchased a 5-year, 3% annual coupon bond with $1,000 par value, you would collect $30 coupon payments each year for 5 years and receive $1,000 par value when the bond matured.[1] If current interest rates were 3%, then the market price would initially be $1,000. Because interest rates were expected to remain relatively stable, the bond's market value over the 5-year period would be expected to remain around $1,000.

The climate for investing in bonds changed dramatically in the 1970s. Holding bonds became much more risky, because high and volatile inflation resulted in high and volatile nominal interest rates. If you purchased a 5-year, $1,000 par, 3% coupon bond for $1,000 and interest rates shot up to 10%, then the value of your bond would decline. Who would pay $1,000 for a bond yielding 3% when there were comparable kinds of assets yielding 10%? No one would, and thus the bond would decline in value.

This chapter and the next focus on the risk and return associated with investing in bonds and on managing an investment in bonds in a climate of volatile interest rates. This chapter discusses the meaning of a bond yield (called *yield to maturity,* or *yield* for short), how bond yield is related to inflation, and why a relatively small change in yield may induce "stomach-churning volatility." This chapter also introduces techniques that investors use to determine a bond's value in an environment with volatile interest rates. Because interest rates have such a dramatic impact on bond values, the chapter begins with an overview of why interest rates change. It also demonstrates how the rates of return discussed in Investments in the News are calculated. Techniques used to value bonds and the risks that bond investors face also are covered.

This book uses the terms *price* and *value* interchangeably. It is implicitly assumed that the bond market is efficient. That is, the intrinsic bond value is equal to its market price. Although there may be disagreement on whether the bond market is efficient, this assumption is a clear starting point for understanding bonds' market prices. Thus, unless explicitly indicated, in this text a bond's market price is the same as its value.

16.1 INTEREST RATE CHANGES

Interest rates are the price of money. If you consider money a commodity like any other good, interest rates are determined by the supply and demand for money. Changes in the supply and demand for money cause interest rates to vary. The actors

---

1. Recall from Chapter 2 that bonds are fixed-income securities that offer periodic coupon payments plus a promise of the payment of the par value at maturity.

in the economy—individuals, businesses, governments, and foreign investors—influence the supply and demand for money.

Consumer behavior has a direct impact on interest rates. The amount individuals are willing to save, which is also part of the money supply, is determined in part by interest rates, the individuals' current incomes, and wealth levels. Higher savings result in a greater supply of money and hence a lower interest rate. The relationship between the amount people save and interest rates is not immediately transparent, however. An increase in interest rates may be an incentive for people to save, because their savings earn a higher rate of return. Investors substitute, so to speak, consumption today for savings that allow for future consumption—a phenomenon called the *substitution effect*. Alternatively, an increase in interest rates may actually result in a decrease in savings, because people now have to save less in order to achieve a fixed level of consumption in the future—a phenomenon called the *income effect*. There is also a **wealth effect,** the phenomenon that an increase in interest rates implies a decrease in current wealth levels, which may affect people's investment behavior. For example, if you hold a bond portfolio and the interest rate goes from 8% to 10%, then the value of your portfolio goes down.

Money is demanded by groups similar to those who supply it: individuals, businesses, governments, and foreign borrowers. For example, an increase in the demand for home mortgages will cause interest rates to rise. An increased demand for loans by businesses will also cause rates to rise.

Exhibit 16-1 illustrates the demand and supply for, say, 1-year loans as a function of the interest rate. The curve *S,* the supply function for funds, is generally upward

EXHIBIT 16-1
Demand and Supply for Loans as a Function of Interest Rate

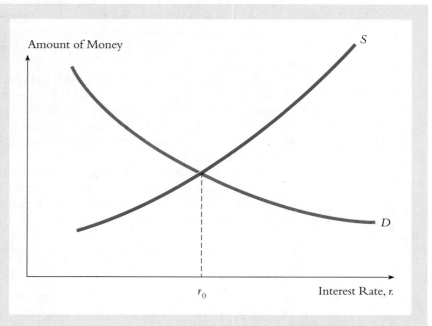

sloping, because the higher the interest rate, the more individuals are ready to save (lend) money. (Firms and government agencies also can save money, but typically individuals are the source of savings.) Curve D, the demand function for funds, is downward sloping: the lower the interest rate, the more individuals, firms, and government agencies are willing to borrow. As corporate finance classes explain, the lower the interest rate, the lower a firm's cost of capital, the more projects are expected to have positive net present values, and the more the firm is willing to borrow.

The intersection of the two curves in Exhibit 16-1 determines the equilibrium interest rate; at this interest rate (r_0), the market is in equilibrium, because the amount individuals are willing to lend is equal to the amount that firms, government agencies, and individuals are willing to save.

By similar analysis, borrowers and lenders of money of other maturities (say, 2 years, 3 years, and so forth) determine the interest rate for other maturities; hence, the market generally has various interest rates for various maturities. Although the demand and supply is for money, we can consider the demand and supply for various maturities as the demand and supply for various products; hence, various equilibrium interest rates may be observed.

16.2 THE YIELD CURVE

When individuals or organizations demand or supply funds, their needs with respect to the length of time the money is borrowed or lent generally vary. Investors want to loan money for varying lengths of time. Borrowers have similar differences in the time needed for capital projects. Thus, there are loans of different maturities (such as 1 month, 1 year, or 10 years), and as a result, different interest rates may prevail, corresponding to the different maturities (as discussed earlier). In reality, interest rates are not constant, and interest rates depend on how long someone wants to borrow or lend money.

A bond represents borrowing by the bond's issuer and saving by the bond's purchaser. The interest earned on a bond if held to its maturity is called the **yield to maturity.** The demand and supply for bonds with given coupons and par values determine their market prices. A bond's market price, in turn, determines the yield to maturity, which is the percentage profit for the bond buyer and the percentage cost to the bond seller.

Yield to maturity is the annualized discount rate that makes the present value of future cash flows just equal to the current price of the bond. Mathematically, it is calculated from the value of y (that is, the internal rate of return of the bond) in the following equation:

$$P = \sum_{t=1}^{n} \frac{C}{(1 + y)^t} + \frac{Par}{(1 + y)^n} \tag{16.1}$$

where C is the coupon payment each period, n is the number of periods to maturity, Par is the face value of the bond (payment at maturity), and P is the current market price of the bond.

If coupons are paid annually, then y is the yield to maturity. If coupons are paid semiannually, then the yield to maturity is $(1 + y)^2 - 1$. Thus, the yield to maturity is given on an annual basis.

From Equation 16.1, it seems that lenders should choose to lend for maturity n with the highest yield to maturity y, because by such a lending policy they obtain the highest annual interest rate (that is, the highest internal rate of return on their investment). Although this is a tempting conclusion, it is generally wrong, because the lending and borrowing decisions are not only functions of the yield but also a function of the risk of such borrowing—lending activities that vary across savers as well as borrowers. The following discussion will elaborate on this point.

The yield curve generally refers to the yield on government bonds, which are default-free. Even in the absence of a risk of bankruptcy, as the time to maturity (n) changes, the yield to maturity (y) that solves Equation 16.1 may change. The **yield curve** is the relationship between the yield to maturity and the time to maturity. That is, ideally C and Par are held constant, and P and y change as n changes.

Exhibit 16-2 illustrates some recent yield curves for U.S. Treasury securities. Exhibit 16-2a shows the yield curve for U.S. Treasury securities on August 5, 1997, when the yield curve was upward sloping. The horizontal axis is time to maturity (n), and the vertical axis is yield to maturity (y). Exhibit 16-2b shows a flat yield curve observed on December 29, 1989, and Exhibit 16-2c shows an *inverted* yield curve observed on December 31, 1980, where the yield decreases as the maturity increases. These graphs show that the yield curve can have a wide variety of shapes.

For zero-coupon bonds with n years to maturity, the yield to maturity is given by the value y that solves the following equation:

$$P = \frac{Par}{(1 + y)^n} \qquad (16.1')$$

For a perpetuity bond with an annual coupon of $\$C$, the yield to maturity is given by the value y that solves the equation:

$$P = \frac{C}{y}$$

To facilitate the following discussion, we refer to y as the yield to maturity, meaning that it is the annualized value.

Analysts seek to determine why bonds of different maturities have different yields to maturity (or why equilibrium interest rates are different for different maturities). That is, they try to determine what factors influence the shape of the yield curve. The next section explains these factors.

Investing in the bond market is not without risks. These risks are a function of the time to maturity of the bond relative to the investor's time horizon. In addition to their preferences for bonds with different maturities according to the length of time they need (or can lend) the money, borrowers and lenders have different expectations of changes in future interest rates.

EXHIBIT 16-2
Examples of Actual
Yield Curves
These curves are based only on
the most actively traded issues.
Market yields on coupon issues
due in less than three months
are excluded.

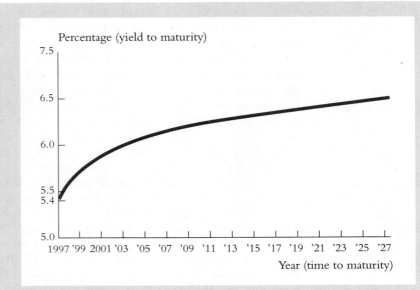

Part a: Upward-Sloping Yield
Curve—Yields of Treasury
Securities, August 5, 1997
(based on closing quotations)

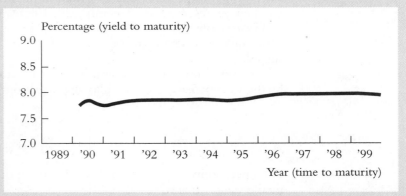

Part b: Flat Yield Curve—
Yields of Treasury Securities,
December 29, 1989 (based
on closing bid quotations)

(continued)

The lender must choose between investing in short-term bonds or long-term bonds. Consider the choices facing young parents who want to invest or lend their money to insure that their children will have funds to attend college in 15 years. Should the parents invest in short- or long-term bonds? Changing interest rates complicate this decision. If the parents invest over a short period, then they may have to reinvest the money in the near future at a different interest rate, which may be lower. This risk of declining interest rates is known as **reinvestment risk**—the risk to bondholders that in the future they will not be able to reinvest the cash flows they receive from their investment at the same rate they receive today.

If long-term lenders expect an increase in interest rates in the future, they should lend for the short term only and reinvest later at a higher interest rate. By

EXHIBIT 16-2
(continued)

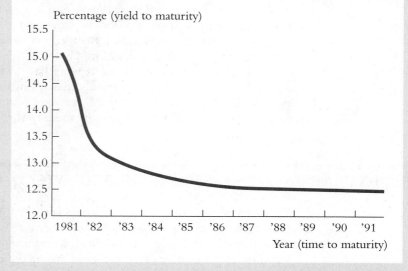

Part c: Inverted Yield Curve—
Yields of Treasury Securities,
December 31, 1980 (based on
closing bid quotations)

Source: *U.S. Treasury Bulletin* (Washington, D.C.: Department of the Treasury, various issues).

purchasing long-term bonds, they might miss out on the higher rates should interest rates go up. Long-term bonds would be a poor investment choice when interest rates rose, because the bond's price would decline as a result of an increase in the interest rate. The longer the length to maturity of a bond, the greater the risk exposure to large price declines. To see this, return to Equation 16.1. As y increases, then the larger is n, the larger is the decline in P thus the larger is the loss to the investor who holds these bonds. This exposure to price declines is known as **price risk.** Bond investors experience price risk because increases in interest rates decrease a bond's price. The opposite effect occurs if the investor expects interest rates to fall. In this case, the lender could benefit by investing in long-term bonds and locking in the current higher interest rate.

To summarize, price risk is the negative effect of changes in interest rates on a bond's value; that is, when rates rise, bond prices fall. Reinvestment risk is the negative effect of a decline in interest rates on the cash flows received when those cash flows must be reinvested at a lower interest rate; that is, when interest rates fall, the interest rate available for future investment of cash flows is lower.

Let's turn to the borrower's viewpoint. Assume that a borrower—maybe a corporation—needs money for long-term investment in profitable capital projects. The corporation faces the choice of either borrowing for a short-term or a long-term period. If a corporation chooses a short-term bond, it may have to refinance the bond at higher interest rates. Note that this is exactly opposite to the problem faced by lenders. If the corporation chooses the long-term bond and interest rates fall, the corporation is paying a higher borrowing rate than would have been required if the financing had been short term.

So far, we have assumed that the lender wanted to invest for a long-term period and the borrower needed the money for a long-term period. In reality, lenders and borrowers want to lend and borrow for varying lengths of time. In addition, the needs of borrowers and lenders change over time. These varied needs within the economy create the demand and supply for bonds of varying maturities. Also, individual long-term borrowers and lenders have different preferences regarding risk and different expectations regarding changes in future interest rates. These are the factors that influence the shape of the yield curve. The next section discusses the various hypotheses regarding the role these factors have in determining the shape of the yield curve.

16.3 EXPLAINING THE SHAPE OF THE YIELD CURVE

The behavior of the yield curve, which is also known as the **term structure of interest rates,** has certain well-known patterns. First, short-term yields are generally more variable than long-term yields. Second, the yield curve is *usually* upward sloping. Third, inverted or declining yield curves typically occur when the overall level of interest rates is relatively high.

It is not surprising that gleaning information from the shape of the yield curve is difficult. It is interesting to note that in November 1988, the yield curve was essentially flat. Connecting Theory to Practice 16.1a illustrates the varied opinions about what the shape of the yield curve means. Connecting Theory to Practice 16.1b illustrates how the yield curve actually changed in response to changes in the supply of bonds with specific maturities.

Several hypotheses have been developed in an attempt to explain different yield curve shapes. This section reviews each hypothesis and briefly highlights its strengths and weaknesses. However, first it is necessary to define and explain several concepts related to bonds that are used in the explanation of the shape of the yield curve.

CONNECTING THEORY TO PRACTICE 16.1a

CURVE ON YIELDS POSES DILEMMA FOR BOND BUYER

NEW YORK—Why would anyone buy 30-year Treasury bonds right now when they can earn nearly the same return on short-term issues that aren't as susceptible to price declines?

Investors are confronting that dilemma because of an unusual development in the bond market—a "flat yield curve."

The yield curve is bond market jargon for the difference between short-term and long-term interest rates. Normally, investors get a significantly higher yield when they buy long-term bonds. That's supposed to compensate them for the risk of holding bonds for many years while interest rates could gyrate.

(continued)

The flat yield curve right now may provide a good opportunity to buy long-term bonds. The shape of the yield curve occasionally predicts the direction of the economy, the course of interest rates and inflation. For some bond specialists, a flattening of the yield curve is a signal to buy bonds or even stocks.

"The flatness of the curve is typical of what you see late in the business cycle," said John M. Stuckey, Jr., a vice president at Citibank. "It's certainly telling you that it's time to be alert to the prospect [of buying longer-term bonds.]"

A CONTRARIAN ARGUMENT

The prospect of falling rates may seem a convincing argument against owning long-term bonds—or stocks, too. If you can earn such high rates on short-term government backed issues, why take the risk of owning stocks or locking up your money in long-term bonds? Paradoxically, some bond specialists argue just the opposite. They contend that the unusual configuration [a flat yield curve] of interest rates today may represent a classic market signal that long-term interest rates will fall and bond prices will rally. But so far, the evidence isn't clear.

Source: Tom Herman and Matthew Winkler, "Curve on Yields Poses Dilemma for Bond Buyer," *Wall Street Journal*, November 14, 1988, p. C1. Reprinted by permission of *The Wall Street Journal*, © 1988 Dow Jones & Co., Inc. All Rights Reserved Worldwide.

Flatter Yield Curve   U.S. Treasury Yield Curve

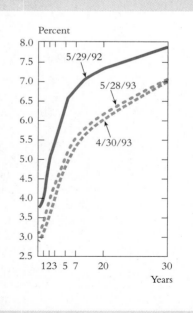

Source: "Flatter Yield Curve," *Wall Street Journal*, November 14, 1988, p. C1. Reprinted by permission of *The Wall Street Journal*, © 1988 Dow Jones & Co., Inc. All Rights Reserved Worldwide.

Source: "U.S. Treasury Yield Curve," *Barron's*, May 31, 1993, p. 38. Reprinted by permission of *Barron's*, © 1993 Dow Jones & Co., Inc. All Rights Reserved Worldwide.

CONNECTING THEORY TO PRACTICE 16.1b

BOND PRICES CONTINUE THEIR DECLINE AS TREASURY PREPARES SALE OF $38 BILLION IN NEW SECURITIES

NEW YORK—Anticipation of this week's Treasury sale of $38 billion of new securities pressured the bond market yesterday, extending Friday's market rout.

The benchmark 30-year Treasury bond was down $13/32$ point, or about $4 for a bond with a $1,000 face value, at $101^{27}/_{32}$. Its yield rose to 6.47% from 6.44% late Friday, as bond yields move in the opposite direction as prices. . . .

. . . Treasury's third-quarter refunding package includes $16 billion of three-year notes to be sold today; $12 billion of 10-year notes set for tomorrow; and $10 billion of 30-year bonds due to be sold Thursday.

In when-issued trading, three- and 10-year notes and bonds are bid at yields of 6.02%, 6.20% and 6.45%, respectively. Friday, those issues were bid to yield 5.98%, 6.16% and 6.41%.

Source: Credit Markets, *Wall Street Journal*, August 5, 1997, p. C21. Reprinted by permission of *The Wall Street Journal* © 1997 Dow Jones & Co., Inc. All Rights Reserved Worldwide.

MAKING THE CONNECTION

The first article was written in 1988, when the yield curve was almost flat (see the upper curve in the graph labeled "Flatter Yield Curve.") As this article shows, investors' expectations vary regarding future changes in interest rates. For some investors, a flat yield curve implies that buying long-term bonds is recommended, whereas for other investors the opposite is true. In this case, hindsight reveals that buying long-term bonds would have been profitable, because 30-year Treasury bond yields fell from about 9% (see the "Flatter Yield Curve" graph) to about 7%, producing a large capital gain (see the "U.S. Treasury Yield Curve" graph) over this time period. The first article shows that expectations about future interest rates heavily influence lending and borrowing decisions and, thus, the demand and supply of bonds for various maturities. The demand and supply, in turn, influence the shape of the yield curve.

The second article illustrates how an increase in supply affects the shape of the yield curve. A large sale of 3-, 10-, and 30-year Treasury notes will push the yield down on these three maturities. For other maturities, the yield is unaffected and is even greater on August 5 relative to the previous day. Thus, for a given demand, a change in supply will determine the yield.

16.3.1 Spot Rates, Forward Rates,
Forward Contracts, and Holding Period Rates

The **spot rate** is the yield to maturity of a zero-coupon bond that has a stated maturity, where zero-coupon bonds are sold at a discount from their par value and pay no coupons. For example, if a 1-year bond is trading at $90.9 with $100 par value, we say the spot rate is about 10%, or [($100 − $90.9)/$90.9] · 100.

The **forward rate** is the yield to maturity of a zero-coupon bond that an investor agrees to purchase at some future specified date. For example, an investor agrees today to purchase *in 1 year* at $89.286 a bond that has 1 year to maturity with a par value of $100. In this case there is no cash flow today, and in 1 year the investor will pay $89.286 for the bond (regardless of its current market price in a year) and will receive $100 two years from today (or 1 year from the bond purchase date). The forward rate is about 12%, or [($100 − $89.286)/$89.286] · 100. The forward rates can be used in interpreting the information contained in the yield curve, as will be shown later.

A concept related to the forward rate is the **forward contract,** which is an agreement between a buyer and a seller to trade something in the future at a price negotiated today. A forward contract is *obligatory* to both the buyer and the seller. For example, a forward contract to buy $1 million of par value of Treasury bills at a 6% discount rate (which determines the bond's price) in six months obligates the buyer to purchase the T-bills at a 6% discount rate; it also obligates the seller to sell the T-bills at the same price. Suppose T-bills are selling for a 7% discount rate in six months when the forward contract matures and the buyer delivers the bills. This means that the T-bills have a lower market price. Recall that when interest rates are up, bond prices are down, (that is, there is an inverse relationship between bond prices and yields). The seller will profit from this transaction, and the buyer will lose, because the buyer is obligated to purchase the T-bills at 6% despite the fact that a 7% rate is available in the market. At a 7% rate, the buyer could purchase the T-bills at the lower market price, but the buyer must buy them at the 6% rate (a higher price) to comply with the forward contract. A range of actively traded forward contracts are available in interest rates, currencies, and energy products (such as crude oil or natural gas).

The forward interest rates can be derived from the spot rates of bonds with various maturities.[2] To see this, consider the numerical example in Exhibit 16-3. The data in the table are spot and forward rates for annually compounded, zero-coupon bonds.[3] A yield curve plotted from these data would be upward sloping from 5% for 1-year bonds to 6.45% for 5-year bonds.

Now suppose we wish to invest for 2 years. Consider the following investment strategies:

Strategy 1. Invest in a 2-year zero-coupon bond and earn 5.8%.

---

2. A market exists for contracts based on forward interest rates. These contracts are known as forward rate agreements, and they are traded in the over-the-counter market primarily between banks.

3. The following analysis could be conducted with coupon-bearing bonds but would be slightly more complex.

EXHIBIT 16-3	Maturity (in years, n)	Spot Rate (R_m)	Forward Rate (f_n)ᵃ
Spot and Forward Rates for Annually Compounded, Zero–Coupon Bonds	1	5%	—
	2	5.8	6.606%
	3	6.3	7.307
	4	6.4	6.701
	5	6.45	6.650

a. $f_2 = (1 + R_2)^2/(1 + R_1) - 1 = (1 + 0.058)^2/(1 + 0.05) - 1 \cong 0.06606$

$f_3 = (1 + R_3)^3/(1 + R_2)^2 - 1 = (1 + 0.063)^3/(1 + 0.058)^2 - 1 \cong 0.07307$

$f_4 = (1 + R_4)^4/(1 + R_3)^3 - 1 = (1 + 0.064)^4/(1 + 0.063)^3 - 1 \cong 0.06701$

$f_5 = (1 + R_5)^5/(1 + R_4)^4 - 1 = (1 + 0.0645)^5/(1 + 0.064)^4 - 1 \cong 0.06650$

Strategy 2. Invest in a 1-year zero-coupon bond and earn 5%. Also enter into a 1-year forward rate agreement (FRA) to invest in 1 year.

What interest rate on the FRA will make Strategies 1 and 2 equivalent?

It will be the forward rate that results in an overall annual rate of return of 5.8% for 2 years. To see this, consider investing $1 in each bond, and let R_i denote the spot rate and f_i denote the forward rate for each year, $i = 1, 2$.

Strategy 1. $\$1(1 + R_2)^2 = \$1(1 + 0.058)^2 = \$1.119364$
Strategy 2. $\$1(1 + R_1) = \$1(1 + 0.05) = \$1.05$. Then invest $1.05 in the FRA.

The forward rate that makes Strategies 1 and 2 equivalent is $\$1.05(1 + f_2) = \$1.119364$, or $f_2 = 0.06606$, or 6.606%. Thus, in equilibrium we have

$$(1 + R_2)^2 = (1 + R_1)(1 + f_2)$$

Note that if f_2 is higher than 6.606%, all investors will be better off not buying the 2-year bond. Its price will fall, and R_2 will go up until the equation $(1 + R_2)^2 = (1 + R_1)(1 + f_2)$ holds. The opposite is true if f_2 is smaller than 6.606%. Similarly, for a 3-year period there are three alternative strategies:

Strategy 1. Invest in a zero-coupon bond with 3 years to maturity and earn 6.3%.
Strategy 2. Invest in a 1-year zero-coupon bond, enter into a 1-year FRA to invest in 1 year, and enter again into a 1-year FRA to invest in 2 years.
Strategy 3. Invest in a 2-year zero-coupon bond and enter into a 1-year FRA to invest in 2 years.

Following the same analysis as before, the return on all of these strategies must be the same. Hence, we arrive at the following equilibrium:

$$(1 + R_3)^3 = (1 + R_1)(1 + f_2)(1 + f_3)$$

However, because in equilibrium, as we have seen before, $(1 + R_2)^2 = (1 + R_1)$ $(1 + f_2)$, this can be rewritten as

$$(1 + R_3)^3 = (1 + R_2)^2(1 + f_3)$$

and for the given spot rates R_2 and R_3, f_3 can be determined.

This type of analysis could be conducted for n periods in order to arrive at the following general expression of equilibrium:

$$(1 + R_n)^n = (1 + R_1)(1 + f_2)(1 + f_3) \ldots (1 + f_n) \tag{16.2}$$

or

$$(1 + R_n)^n = (1 + R_{n-1})^{n-1}(1 + f_n) \tag{16.2'}$$

We can use Equation 16.2' to calculate the equilibrium forward rate. If we know that the 4-year spot rate is 6.4% and the 5-year spot rate is 6.45%, then we can solve for the forward rate over the fifth year as follows:

$$(1 + 0.0645)^5 = (1 + 0.064)^4(1 + f_5)$$

Solving for f_5, we find the forward rate to be 6.65% (see Exhibit 16-3).

From Equation 16.2 we see that spot interest rates can be thought of as a portfolio of agreements for forward contracts. If the yield curve is upward sloping, then the implied forward rates are higher than the short-term spot rate. Indeed, in the example, we have an upward-sloping yield curve, and we found $f_5 > R_4$, which confirms this assertion. Similarly, if the yield curve is downward sloping, then the implied forward rates are lower than the short-term spot rate. For a flat yield curve, the forward rates are equal to the spot rate.

PRACTICE BOX

Problem

Suppose the 10-year spot interest rate was 8%, and the 11-year spot interest rate was 7.9%. What is the equilibrium forward rate for the eleventh period?

Solution

Using Equation 16.2' and solving for f_n, we have

$$f_n = \frac{(1 + R_n)^n}{(1 + R_{n-1})^{n-1}} - 1$$

Substituting for the spot interest rates, we have

$$f_n = \frac{(1 + R_{11})^{11}}{(1 + R_{10})^{10}} - 1 = \frac{(1 + 0.079)^{11}}{(1 + 0.08)^{10}} - 1 \cong \frac{2.3080}{2.1589} - 1 \cong 0.069$$

or 6.9%. Once again, notice that the forward rate is less than the 10-year spot rate because the 11-year spot rate is less than the 10-year spot rate.

The final bond-related concept pertinent to the slope of the yield curve is the **holding period rate,** the rate of return earned on a bond by holding it for the next period (see Chapter 5). This rate is different from the yield to maturity, because the price of the bond changes over time. Falling bond prices may cause the holding period rate to be negative. The holding period rate is uncertain, whereas the yield to maturity is a fixed number, given the price.

These basic bond and interest rate concepts can help investors understand the various hypotheses that have been developed to explain yield curves. The discussion begins with the expectations hypothesis.

PRACTICE BOX

Problem

A bond is sold for $1,000 at the beginning of the year and is traded at $950 at the end of the year. The bond pays a coupon of $20 at the end of the year. What is the holding period rate of return for this year?

Solution

Recall from Chapter 5 that the interim rate of return was defined as

$$R = \frac{EMV - BMV + I}{BMV}$$

where EMV denotes the ending market value, BMV denotes the beginning market value, and I denotes the cash flow or income from the asset. In this case, $EMV = \$950$, $BMV = \$1,000$, and $I = \$20$. Hence,

$$R = \frac{\$950 - \$1,000 + \$20}{\$1,000} = \frac{-\$30}{\$1,000} = -0.03, \text{ or } -3\%$$

16.3.2 The Expectations Hypothesis

The expectations hypothesis, as its name implies, predicts that investors' expectations determine the course of future interest rates. There are two main competing versions of this hypothesis: the local expectations hypothesis and the unbiased expectations hypothesis.

The **local expectations hypothesis (LEH)** states that all bonds (similar in all respects except for their maturities) will have the same expected holding period rate of return. That is, a one-month bond and a 30-year bond should, on average, provide the same rate of return over the next period. Thus, by this hypothesis, if you wish to invest for one month, on average, you get the same rate of return if you buy a one-month bond and hold it to maturity or buy a 30-year bond and sell it after one month. The LEH doesn't specify the length of the next period.

Empirical evidence consistently rejects this hypothesis. Specifically, holding period returns on longer-term bonds are, on average, significantly different than holding period returns on shorter-term bonds. On average, the holding period rates of return on longer-term bonds are higher and have higher volatility. Hence, longer-term bonds offer greater rewards, yet have higher risk. The LEH doesn't match our observations that investors are risk averse and require higher returns, on average, to take the higher risk related to long-term bonds. Investor risk aversion implies, in turn, that the yield curve, *on average,* will be upward sloping.

The **unbiased expectations hypothesis (UEH)** states that the current implied forward rates are unbiased estimators of future spot interest rates. Therefore, if the yield curve is upward sloping, the UEH states that the market expects the spot rates to rise. For example, from Exhibit 16-3 and the UEH, our best estimate in Year 1 of Year 2's spot rate is for it to rise to 6.606% (the implied forward rate). In contrast, if the yield curve is downward sloping, the UEH states that the market expects rates to fall.

The empirical evidence consistently shows that forward rates are biased predictors of future interest rates. Specifically, forward rates generally overestimate future spot rates.[4] This evidence leads to the next hypothesis, the liquidity preference hypothesis.

16.3.3 The Liquidity Preference Hypothesis

The **liquidity preference hypothesis (LPH)** states that the yield curve should normally be upward sloping, reflecting investors' preferences for the liquidity and lower risk of shorter-term securities. In its purest form, the LPH is not supported by observation of the historical behavior of the term structure. In fact, on numerous occasions the yield curve has been inverted.

Note that an inverted yield curve does not necessarily contradict the LPH when that hypothesis is combined with the UEH. If nothing is known regarding the future (but interest rates can go up or down with an equal probability), then an upward-sloping yield curve should be expected. Suppose, however, that inflation is so high that it pushes the interest rate to 15% (which in fact occurred in 1980, when interest rates were very high, as shown in Exhibit 16-2c). Thus, for short-term bonds, the yield is 15%. However, no one expects this rate of inflation to continue at such a high level for a long period. Hence, for 10-year bonds the yield is only 12.5%, and we observe a decreasing yield curve. Taking these yields and dividing them by the expected inflation rate, the yield curve can be stated in *real* terms. The resulting real yield curve may be increasing and consistent with the LPH. Thus, the LPH may hold even if there is a decreasing nominal yield curve.

A combination of the UEH and the LPH is therefore a possible explanation of the shape of the yield curve. That is, both hypotheses, when combined, may be valid. Specifically, the UEH may account for part of the shape of the yield curve, with the LPH accounting for the rest. Exhibit 16-4 illustrates this idea. "Yield Curve by UEH" is based on expectations. For example, analysts could be surveyed

---

4. See Eugene F. Fama, "Forward Rates as Predictors of Future Spot Interest Rates," *Journal of Financial Economics,* October 1976, pp. 361–377; Eugene F. Fama, "The Information in the Term Structure," *Journal of Financial Economics,* December 1984, pp. 509–528; and Haim Levy and Robert Brooks, "An Empirical Analysis of Term Premiums Using Stochastic Dominance," *Journal of Banking and Finance,* May 1989, pp. 245–260.

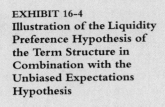

EXHIBIT 16-4
Illustration of the Liquidity Preference Hypothesis of the Term Structure in Combination with the Unbiased Expectations Hypothesis

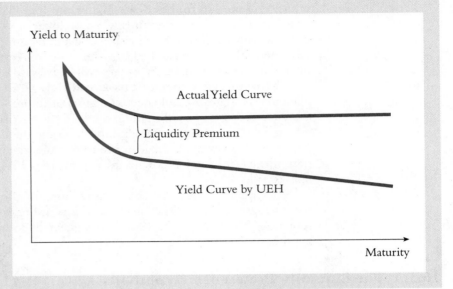

about their expectations for the future course of interest rates. Suppose the market is anticipating a sharp decline in interest rates over the next few years, and therefore the forward rates are declining with time. The UEH would suggest a downward-sloping yield curve, as shown in Exhibit 16-4. However, the LPH may cause the curve to be less steep (see "Actual Yield Curve" in Exhibit 16-4) because of risk premiums that have to be offered to investors to induce them to take the risk of investing in longer-term securities. If the risk premium increases as the length to maturity increases, the gap between these two curves increases.

The difference between the yield curve under the UEH and the actually observed yield curve is sometimes called the **liquidity premium.** This name reflects the idea that shorter-term bonds have greater marketability than long-term bonds. Unfortunately, it is very difficult to estimate the magnitude of the liquidity premium, because it changes over time. Thus, breaking down the existing term structure into its component parts—expectations and liquidity premiums—is virtually impossible. However, these theoretical hypotheses help explain why the yield curve has the shape it does.

16.3.4 The Market Segmentations Hypothesis

The last hypothesis, the **market segmentations hypothesis (MSH),** evaluates the yield curve from a slightly different perspective. This hypothesis states that bonds of different maturities trade in separate segmented markets. (For example, banks tend to participate exclusively in the short-maturity bond markets, whereas insurance companies tend to participate exclusively in the long-maturity markets.) The yield curve shape is a function of these different preferences. Thus, as Exhibit

16-1 demonstrated, the supply and demand preferences of participants within each maturity segment determine the equilibrium interest rate without regard to the equilibrium interest rate in neighboring maturities. Also, speculators will take risky positions across the term structure if it gets out of perceived equilibrium.

A modified version of the MSH, the **preferred habitat hypothesis,** states that different participants have preferred locations on the yield curve, but with sufficient incentive they can be induced to move. Thus, segmentation in the bond market affects the term structure, because short-term bonds that are riskless for banks may be risky for insurance firms, which have long-term obligations. If a bank invested in long-term bonds, it would be taking considerable price risk. If an insurance company invested in short-term bonds, it would be taking considerable reinvestment risk. Different segments have different risk premiums, but they are ready to take less preferable bonds once the price of the bonds falls below a certain level.

In summary, no theory provides a complete description of what we actually observe. Each hypothesis offers insight into what may drive the current shape of the yield curve. Expectations and risk clearly play a role in determining the shape of the yield curve.

16.4 OTHER MEASURES OF BOND YIELDS

This text uses the term *yield* to mean *yield to maturity.* Among investors and in the financial media, the term *yield* has various meanings. This section introduces five different definitions of *yield*.

The **coupon yield** or **nominal yield** is the promised annual coupon rate. For example, if the annual coupon payment is $120 and the par value is $1,000, then the coupon or nominal yield is 12%.

Current yield is found by taking the stated annual coupon payment and dividing it by the current market price of the bond. Current market prices for bonds can be found in any financial newspaper or through a broker. A 12% coupon bond selling at $900, for example, has a current yield of $120/$900 ≅ 13.33% (where $120 is 12% of $1,000 par).

The yield to maturity is a more complex yield and represents the internal rate of return of a bond investment, as discussed earlier. That is, it is y that solves the standard bond-pricing equation (Equation 16.1, repeated here):

$$P = \sum_{t=1}^{n} \frac{C}{(1 + y)^t} + \frac{Par}{(1 + y)^n}$$

A careful analysis of this equation illustrates several interesting relationships. For example, the yield to maturity on long-term bonds is close to the current yield. The value of a perpetual bond (a bond with no maturity date that pays a steady stream of cash flows, denoted by C) is just $P = C/y$. For longer maturities, because of discounting, the value of $Par/(1 + y)^n$ is zero, and the value of a perpetuity of C is simply

$$P = \sum_{t=1}^{\infty} \frac{C}{(1+y)^t} = \frac{C}{y}^5$$

Also, the yield to maturity on a short-term bond is close to the coupon yield, be-cause the bond's price will be close to its par value. The yield to maturity is the pre-cise rate of return earned on the bond investment if interest rates do not change, the bond is held to maturity, and the coupons are reinvested at the yield to maturity.

The **yield to call** is similar to the yield to maturity, except it assumes that the bond will be called at the first possible call date. The call feature allows a firm to es-sentially buy back bonds at a specified price. In this case, instead of using the par value at maturity as the final payment, we use the amount to be paid to bondholders when the bond is called. Specifically,

$$P = \sum_{t=1}^{nc} \frac{C}{(1+y)^t} + \frac{Call\ Price}{(1+y)^{nc}} \qquad (16.3)$$

where nc is the number of coupon payments until the first call date. Note that if C is paid semiannually, then y is the semiannual yield, and the annual yield is $(1+y)^2 - 1$.

This call price is typically in excess of the par value. For example, the call price may be set at par plus 1 year's interest. However, the investor is not assured that the bonds will in fact be called on this date.

Finally, the **realized yield** refers to the holding period rate of return actually generated from an investment in a bond. It is the return found after the bond has matured and all risks have been resolved. The calculation of this rate of return was explained in Chapter 5.

When referring to yield, be careful to specify exactly which yield calculation you mean. The most common yield quoted is the yield to maturity. However, there are no set standards in interest rate quotations, and as the previous discussion shows, the yield calculation does make a difference in the returns.

PRACTICE BOX

Problem

Calculate the five different yields given the following information. The bond is a 2-year, 8% annual coupon, and it has $1,000 par. The bond is currently trading for $1,030 and is callable at $1,050 (without interest included) in 1 year. After 1 year the bond is trading for $1,010 (without interest).

Solution

The current yield is

$$C/P = \$80/\$1,030 \cong 7.77\%$$

(continued)

---

5. The British consol bond is a bond that is never redeemed. For this bond, $y = C/P$.

The coupon or nominal yield is

$$C/Par = \$80/\$1,000 = 8.0\%$$

The yield to maturity is found using software or a handheld calculator by solving the following equation:

$$\$1,030 = \sum_{t=1}^{2} \frac{\$80}{(1+y)^t} + \frac{\$1,000}{(1+y)^2}$$

Using a financial calculator, we get 6.36%.

The yield to call is found by solving this equation:

$$\$1,030 = \sum_{t=1}^{1} \frac{\$80}{(1+y)^t} + \frac{\$1,050}{(1+y)^1} = \frac{\$1,130}{1+y}$$

Thus, the yield to call is 9.71%.

Finally, assuming that the bond has not been called, the realized yield if the bond was actually held for 1 year is

$$R = (\$1,010 + \$80)/\$1,030 - 1 \cong 5.83\%$$

Thus, we see that none of the yields are the same.

16.5　PRICING BONDS IN PRACTICE

The quoted prices of bonds may differ from their present value or economic value. However, some modification, which is described in this section, can help the investor interpret the quoted prices. Exhibit 16-5a shows the basic cash flows paid (down arrows) and received (up arrows) by a bond investor and Exhibit 16.5b shows precisely these cash flows for an 8% semiannual bond. There is a cash outflow when the bond is purchased and cash inflows when coupon payments and the par value are received. Bond valuation is based on standard present value analysis.

The price of a bond can be expressed as the present value of its coupon payments plus the present value of the par value, discounted at the yield to maturity (y) as expressed in Equation 16.1. For example, a 10% annual coupon, $1000 par bond with a yield to maturity of 12% and 30 years to maturity is worth

$$P = \sum_{t=1}^{30} \frac{\$100}{(1+0.12)^t} + \frac{\$1,000}{(1+0.12)^{30}} \cong \$838.90$$

Of course, as the market interest rate changes, the yield to maturity changes, and the bond prices change to adjust to the new yield to maturity. The longer the maturity, the more sensitive the bond price to changes in yield.

Exhibit 16-6 lists the prices of several bonds, all with 10% coupon rates, for various interest rates. At yields of 10%, all the bonds are priced at $1,000. Note in

EXHIBIT 16-5
Cash Flow Characteristics of Bonds

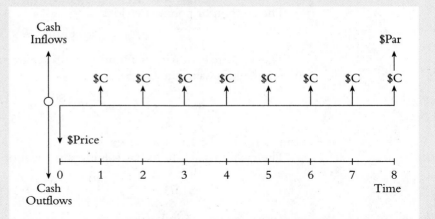

Part a: General Diagram of the Cash Flows Related to Bonds

$Price is the current market price of the bond, $C is the periodic coupon payment, and $Par is the bond's par value.

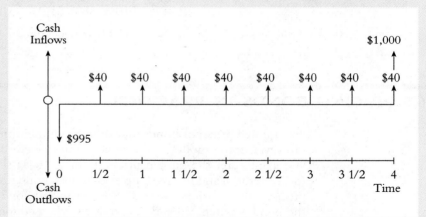

Part b: Diagram of the Cash Flows of an 8%, Semiannual, 4-Year Bond

Exhibit 16-6a that longer-term bonds experience greater fluctuations in price than do shorter-term bonds. For example, when yields rise from 10% to 12%, 1-year bonds drop $17.86 (or $1,000 − $982.14), whereas bonds with no stated maturity (*n* approaches infinity) drop $166.67 (or $1,000 − $833.33).

Exhibit 16-6b illustrates the percentage change (or rate of return) on a bond if it originally had a 10% yield to maturity and then immediately rose to 12%, stayed the same, or dropped to 8% with equal probability. A couple of interesting properties can be observed.[6] First, longer-term bonds have a higher standard deviation of rates of return than do shorter-term bonds. Second, for the same absolute change in in-

6. These properties and others will be more formally developed in Chapter 17.

EXHIBIT 16-6
Bond Prices and
Changes in Yield
to Maturity

Part a: Bond Prices for 10% Coupon Bonds, Par Value of $1,000

	Yield to Maturity (y)		
Years to Maturity	**12%**	**10%**	**8%**
1	$982.14	$1,000.00	$1,018.52
10	887.00	1,000.00	1,134.20
30	838.90	1,000.00	1,225.16
Infinity	833.33	1,000.00	1,250.00

Part b: Percentage Changes, Mean, and Standard Deviation (assuming 12%, 10%, and 8% are equally likely)

	Yield to Maturity				
Years to Maturity	**12%**	**10%**	**8%**	**Mean**	**Standard Deviation**
1	−1.79	0.00	1.85	0.02[a]	1.49[b]
10	−11.30	0.00	13.42	0.71[c]	10.10
30	−16.11	0.00	22.52	2.14	15.84
Infinity	−16.67	0.00	25.00	2.78	17.12

a. $\frac{1}{3}(-1.79\%) + \frac{1}{3}(0.00\%) + \frac{1}{3}(1.85\%)$, because we assume each outcome to be equally likely.

b. $[\frac{1}{3}(-1.79 - 0.02)^2 + \frac{1}{3}(0.00 - 0.02)^2 + \frac{1}{3}(1.85 - 0.02)^2]^{1/3} = 1.49\%$.

c. The mean and standard deviations of the other bonds are calculated in a similar manner.

terest rates, a rate decline produces a larger gain than a rate increase produces losses. For example, the 10-year bond gained 13.42% on a rate decline, whereas it lost only 11.30% on a rate increase. The result is a positive expected rate of return.

Exhibit 16-7 illustrates these observations. Notice that the 10-year bond and the perpetual bond have the same price when rates are 10%. The reason is that by assumption, they are 10% coupon-bearing bonds, and when the coupon yield equals the yield to maturity the bonds will trade at par. However, when rates change, the perpetual bond price is more sensitive. Also, when rates fall, prices move up by a greater amount than when rates rise and prices fall. Hence, perpetuities are more risky. As you will see in more detail in Chapter 17, longer-maturity bonds are more sensitive to changes in yield than are shorter-maturity bonds.

Appendix 16A provides a simple equation for bond pricing that is easier to work with in spreadsheets (see specifically Equation 16A.2). In practice, bonds pay coupons more frequently than annually, and we are not always exactly at a coupon payment date. Appendix 16B presents a more general equation for the valuation of bonds at any date, not necessarily on the coupon date. Appendix 16C discusses the various compounding methods used in the bond market.

Now we are ready to examine how the rates of return (or realized yields) are calculated in the second article of this chapter's Investments in the News ("Zeroing In"). On August 11, 1997, a November 15, 2022, bond was trading for $19,105,

EXHIBIT 16-7
The Relationship between Bond Prices and Yield to Maturity for Bonds of Different Maturities

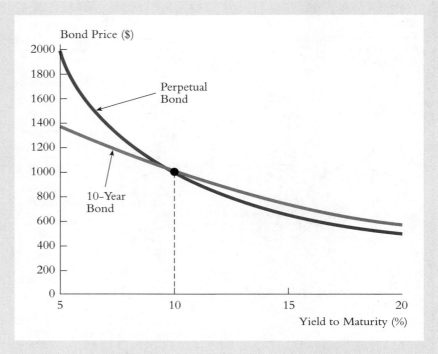

with a yield to maturity of 6.65% and a par value of $100,000. Recall that this is a zero-coupon bond with about 25 years to maturity. (Actually, it is 25.25 years and 4 days, but for simplicity we ignore the 4 days.)

Given the yield to maturity, the bond price is

$$P = \frac{\$100,000}{(1.0665)^{25.25}} \cong \$19,678.45$$

(Note that the $19,678.45 is different from the published figure of $19,105, probably due to a typo in the Investments in the News article.) Now suppose that the yield drops to 6.15% (or 50 basis points). The price of the bond will rise to

$$P = \frac{\$100,000}{(1.0615)^{25}} \cong \$22,490.55$$

16.6 SPREADS OVER TREASURIES

So far this chapter has discussed only one type of risk: the risk associated with changes in the interest rate and its effect on the price of a bond. With government bonds this is the only real risk investors face. With corporate bonds, however, there is an additional risk factor: the risk of default. The risk of default applies to both the firm's failure to pay the coupon payments and the par value at maturity. Thus, there is no guarantee that bond issuers will honor their commitments. The uncertainty over whether the lender will make coupon and principal payments is called *default risk,* and it causes the yields to maturity for corporate bonds to exceed those for Treasury bonds. This difference is known as the *spread over Treasuries,* and it is a measure of default risk.

The analyses of bond pricing and yield to maturity in the previous sections were based on the assumption that the bond's coupon and par value would be paid in a timely way. For U.S. Treasury securities, this is a reasonable assumption. However, for corporate bonds, there exists a significant risk of default. If investors believe there is a possibility the bond issuer will default, they will demand a higher yield to maturity on corporate bonds than on Treasury bonds with similar characteristics.

16.6.1 Bond Ratings

At least four independent firms assess the credit risk of a bond issue. The most familiar rating services are Moody's Investors Service, Standard & Poor's, Fitch Investors Services, and Duff and Phelps. **Credit risk** is the risk that the interest or principal will not be paid as agreed. The firms that assess this risk are known as **rating agencies,** because they seek to "rate" bonds on a scale from low credit risk to high credit risk. Corporations issuing bonds pay a rating fee ranging from a few thousand dollars to over $50,000.

Exhibit 16–8 lists the categories the rating agencies use. The highest-rated bonds are known as *prime-rated bonds* (Aaa by Moody's and AAA by the other three firms). These bonds are referred to as triple A and are perceived to have very little credit risk. They are described as being of high **credit quality,** indicating a low risk of default. The next level down in credit quality is a high-quality rating, or double A (Aa by Moody's and AA by the other three firms). The main difference between double A and triple A is the amount of cushion available to avoid default. Double A bonds have a smaller cushion, but are still very strong and have relatively low credit risk. Double A and triple A bonds are sometimes called **high-grade** bonds.

Single A bonds are the third level down on the rating scale, indicating slightly higher credit risk than double A. These bonds are referred to as *upper-medium-grade* bonds, and they may suffer under circumstances such as an economic downturn in the firm's industry.

The next rating category is *medium-grade bonds,* which is denoted as Baa by Moody's and BBB by the other three firms. These bonds are more vulnerable to default if the firm encounters hard times.

Triple A through triple B bonds fall under the classification of **investment grade.** Many professionally managed funds are restricted to investing solely in investment grade securities. For example, the Vanguard Bond Market mutual fund must invest in investment grade bonds.[7] Because of these restrictions, firms strive to keep the ratings on their bonds at or above triple B in order to maintain greater demand for their bonds and hence also maintain a lower required yield to maturity.

---

7. See *The Individual Investor's Guide to No-Load Mutual Funds,* 10th ed., 1991, p. 433.

EXHIBIT 16-8		Bond Rating Categories by Company			
Category	Moody[a]	S&P[b]	Fitch[b]	DP[b]	Description
Prime	Aaa	AAA	AAA	AAA	Best quality, extremely strong
High quality	Aa	AA	AA	AA	Strong capacity to pay
Upper medium	A	A	A	A	Adequate capacity to pay
Medium	Baa	BBB	BBB	BBB	Changing circumstances could affect the ability to pay
Speculative	Ba	BB	BB	BB	Has speculative elements
Speculative	B	B	B	B	Lacks quality
Default	Caa	CCC	CCC	CCC	Poor standing
Default	Ca	CC	CC		Highly speculative
Default		C	C		Low quality, may never repay
Default		D	DDD[c]	DD	In default
			DD		
			D		

Moody = Moody's Investors Services, Inc.; S&P = Standard & Poor's, Inc.; Fitch = Fitch Investors Services, Inc.; and DP = Duff and Phelps.

a. Applies numerical modifiers 1, 2, and 3 to indicate relative position within rating category. For example, Baa will be Baa-1, Baa-2, or Baa-3.

b. Uses + or − to indicate relative position within the rating category. For example, BBB will be either BBB+, BBB, or BBB−.

c. Different degrees of default, with D being worse than DD and DDD.

Bonds rated below investment grade (below triple B) are referred to as **speculative grade bonds** or **junk bonds.** At the upper end of speculative grade bonds are Ba, BB, or double B. These bonds are considered to have "major ongoing uncertainties." That is, these bonds face considerable risks in an economic downturn. Single B bonds are slightly more risky than double B. Bonds in categories CCC and below are bonds nearing default or in default. Also, triple C and double C sometimes refer to bonds that are subordinated to bonds holding B ratings that are not already in default (the term **subordinated bonds** means bonds that stand behind senior bonds in the credit line in the event of default). Junk bonds are discussed in detail later in the chapter.

To enhance the credit quality of their bonds (to improve the rating and reduce the interest cost), firms agree to abide by certain restrictions and requirements that are spelled out in the **bond indenture** agreement. The bond indenture is a legal agreement between the bond issuer and the bondholders covering all the terms of the issue. It includes such stipulations as type of bond issued and amount of the issue, sinking fund provisions, restrictions on financial ratios, and call features.

Some bonds are secured with collateral and are thus called **secured bonds.** Mortgage bonds are an example of secured bonds. In the event of default, the bondholder takes possession of the underlying collateral (which may be in the form of land, buildings, or even equipment). Unsecured bonds, known as **debentures,** are only backed by the "full faith and credit" of the issuing firm.

A **sinking fund** is money put into a separate custodial account that is used to reduce the outstanding principal through repurchases. An independent third party manages the sinking fund. The effect of a sinking fund is to reduce the likelihood of default at the time of bond maturity.

Restrictions on financial ratios are established in an effort to insure that the firm has the ability to meet its interest payments, as well as its sinking fund requirements. For example, there may be a restriction that requires the current ratio (the ratio of current assets divided by current liabilities) to be greater than 2. The purpose of this restriction is to insure that the issuing firm has the liquidity necessary to make the bond's coupon payment. Indeed, financial analysts examine the financial ratios of some items taken from the firm's financial statements as indicators of the firm's financial strength. (We discuss this in detail in Chapter 21.)

Many firms like to have the option of calling their bonds back and refinancing them if interest rates fall. Typically, this call feature requires paying a bonus above the par value. The size of the bonus varies across bonds and even during the life of a bond, but it is typically about 1 year's interest. This call feature gives added flexibility to the issuing firm.

The rating agencies take these four restrictions into account. However, the quality of the ratings done by these firms is questionable. Connecting Theory to Practice 16.2a illustrates the growing concern about the quality of credit ratings and exactly what they mean. Connecting Theory to Practice 16.2b shows some upgradings and downgradings of bonds. However, the economic value of upgrading and downgrading is questionable. Are the changes too late? In particular, some people claim that when downgrading occurs, it is too late; the market already knows the firm is in trouble, and the bond's price has already fallen. Thus, if the market reacts to the financial stress of a firm before the rating agencies downgrade the firm's bond, what service do the rating agencies provide?

CONNECTING THEORY TO PRACTICE 16.2a

VALUE OF BOND RATINGS QUESTIONED BY A GROWING NUMBER OF STUDIES

Investors put a lot of faith in bond ratings. But a growing body of research indicates that ratings provide an incomplete and often outdated guide to credit quality.

The studies note that ratings do provide one valuable service: distinguishing between investment-grade bonds and low-rated "junk" bonds. Beyond that, however, the research:

(continued)

- Questions the significance of the assorted letter grades or notches separating one investment grade bond from another.
- Finds that there is less correlation than might be expected between ratings and the likelihood of default.
- Indicates that ratings don't tell investors much about other measures of risk like volatility and market performance.

"Ratings provide information, albeit with a lag, to investors who don't have the resources to investigate a firm," says Jerome Fons, an economist at the Federal Reserve Bank of Cleveland. "But there are questions about [their] usefulness."

"There's been numerous examples of the rating agencies' failure to warn investors of potential problems," says Robert Dennis, president of Massachusetts Financial Services Inc.'s managed municipal bond trust. "During all the major crises in the market, the rating agencies caught on after the fact."

A RECORD DEFAULT

Perhaps the best-known incident involved the record $2.25 billion of bonds sold in the late 1970s and early 1980s for two nuclear power plants built by the Washington Public Power Supply System. The ratings firms assigned the debt single-A plus and single-A1 ratings,[8] indicating a strong capacity to pay interest and principal.

In May 1981, analysts at Merrill Lynch Capital Markets Inc. and Drexel Burnham Lambert Inc. predicted the power plants would never be built. The rating agencies downgraded the debt soon after, but it remained investment-grade. It wasn't until seven months later, when the power plants were canceled, that Moody's and S&P assigned the debt junk status. The bonds went into default in June 1982, the biggest default in the history of the municipal market.

But bond ratings don't indicate whether debt might be downgraded. Since a move by S&P or Moody's to downgrade a bond can erode its price, the two companies "can't act until facts are conclusive," says Richard Ciccarone, senior research analyst of Van Kampen Merritt Inc., an Illinois municipal-bond firm.

Adds Mary Stearns Broske, a professor of finance at Oklahoma State University who conducted a 25-month study of corporate bonds: "Ratings aren't predictors of the future likelihood of bonds to default or an indicator of the way they perform in the market."

Source: Alexandra Peers, "Value of Bond Ratings Questioned by a Growing Number of Studies," *Wall Street Journal,* September 16, 1987, p. 37. Reprinted by permission of *The Wall Street Journal,* © 1987 Dow Jones & Co., Inc. All Rights Reserved Worldwide.

8. The single-A plus rating was assigned by Standard & Poor's, and the single-A1 rating was assigned by Moody's.

CONNECTING THEORY TO PRACTICE 16.2b

MOODY'S BOND-RATING CHANGES

Upgrade	From	To
USG Corp		
sen sec	Ba2	Ba1
sen unec	Ba2	Ba1
sub shelf	B1	Ba3
Downgrade	**From**	**To**
Clark Equipment		
sen unsec	A3	Baa1
Ingersoll Rand		
sen unsec	A2	A3

Note: See Exhibit 16-8 for an explanation of numerical modifiers.

Source: *Barron's,* September 22, 1997, p. MW116. Reprinted by permission of *Barron's,* © 1997 Dow Jones & Co., Inc. All Rights Reserved Worldwide.

MAKING THE CONNECTION

When a firm's risk of bankruptcy changes, Moody's (as well as other financial firms) changes the firm's bond rating. When the bond becomes less risky, its price goes up, and its yield goes down. The opposite occurs when the bond becomes more risky and hence is downgraded.

There is evidence that bond rating changes follow a pattern. Specifically, a bond that is downgraded once is much more likely to be downgraded a second time. Exhibit 16-9 presents some recent evidence of this phenomenon. Note that 64.4% of bond rating changes are downgrades. Of the bonds downgraded, a whopping 71.8% are downgraded a second time. For BBB bonds, the probability of a change in either direction is almost even after a first downgrade. After an up-grade, a bond's next ratings change is more likely to be another upgrade, but this is not significant (with the exception of AA bonds). The investment implication is that if a bond experiences a downgrade (except for the original rating of BBB), then you should consider selling the bond, because it is a good candidate for yet another downgrade. Recall from Connecting Theory to Practice 16.2a that bond prices fall when they are downgraded.

In an effort to provide timely information on bond ratings, S&P has developed a tool called CreditWatch.[9] When a firm is placed on CreditWatch, investors know

---

9. CreditWatch is a service that alerts subscribers to the S&P bond rating agency that a particular security is being closely examined for a rating change.

EXHIBIT 16-9   **Bond Rating Change Experience, 1970 to 1985**

	First Rating Change		First Rating Change Is Down, Then the Next Rating Change Is		First Rating Change Is Up, Then the Next Rating Change Is	
Rating	Downgrade	Upgrade	Down	Up	Down	Up
AAA	100.0%	0.0%	78.6%	21.4%	N/A	N/A
AA	83.5	16.5	80.8	19.2	91.8%	8.2%
A	57.1	42.9	65.6	34.4	45.9	54.1
BBB	43.8	56.2	54.3	45.7	40.5	59.5
NIG	50.0	50.0	72.0	28.0	42.9	57.1
Total	64.4	35.6	71.8	28.2	49.6	50.4

NIG—not investment grade.

Source: Reprinted with permission from Edward I. Altman and Duen Li Kao, "The Implications of Corporate Bond Ratings Drift," *Financial Analysts Journal*, May–June 1992, p. 71. Copyright 1992, Association for Investment Management and Research, Charlottesville, Va. All rights reserved.

that a potential rating change may be forthcoming. With this information, bond investors may reallocate their holdings of these bonds. For example, if a firm decides to increase its financial leverage, it may not be able to meet future debt obligations. Therefore, the risk of bankruptcy increases, and the firm may be moved to the CreditWatch list.

Rating agencies are used throughout the world. Rating agencies also evaluate the ability of governmental units, such as the Republic of Italy or Mexico, to meet their financial obligations.

16.6.2 Bond Ratings and Spreads over Treasuries

We have seen that bond ratings influence bond prices and, consequently, bond yields. The spread over Treasuries for similar bonds varies over time. For example, Exhibit 16-10 gives the yield to maturity for 10-year corporate bonds rated Baa by Moody's and for 10-year Treasury bonds from 1986 to 1996. The difference in yield between Baa bonds and Treasuries has changed over time.

The investor who was considering purchasing Baa bonds would want to know if the yields on Treasury bonds were expected to rise and also if the credit spreads (spreads over treasury bonds due to different ranking) were expected to widen. A combination of both of these concerns could result in a sharp rise in yields and thus a sharp fall in prices.

For example, in 1989, the economy was strong, with the gross domestic product (GDP) growing at 7.7% per annum.[10] Yields on 10-year Treasury bonds were 8.49%, and the spread was 0.79%; by 1995, the economy had slowed, and the GDP

10. The growth rate of the GDP is a measure of economic health. The higher the growth in the GDP, the healthier the economy.

EXHIBIT 16-10   **Credit Spreads of 10-Year Corporate Bonds Rated Baa (by Moody's) and 10-Year Treasury Bonds**

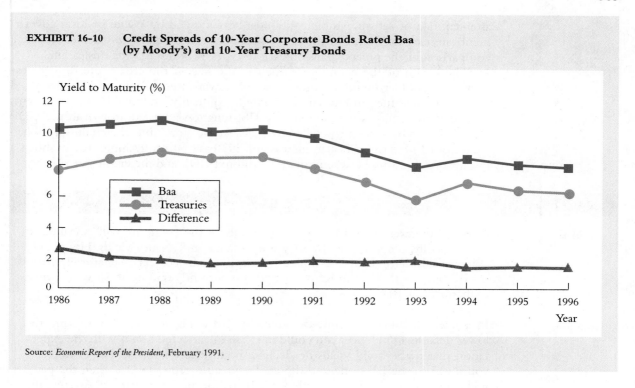

Source: *Economic Report of the President*, February 1991.

was only 4.6% per annum. Treasury bond yields were at 6.57%, and the spread was 1.97%. The increase in the spread reflects the market's demanding a premium for an increase in the risk of bankruptcy during a recessionary period.

Another example corresponds to years 1978–1982, when the interest rate rises sharply and bondholders incur relatively large losses. An investment in 10-year Treasury bonds at $1,000 par in 1978 would have fallen to $824 in 1982 because of the increase in interest rates.[11] This is a 17.65% loss. Because the spread also widened, an investment in Baa bonds at a $1,000 par in 1978 would have fallen to $764, a 23.57% loss.[12] Thus, the widening of the spread from 1.08% in 1978 to 3.11% in 1982 resulted in an additional 5.92% loss.

GDP experienced more stability from 1986 to 1995. In this period, GDP growth remained positive every year, with little variation in the credit spread (see Exhibit 16-11b).

The yield to maturity published in the financial media is the pretax yield. Because investors pay income tax on regular interest and capital gain tax on realized profit from the sale of the bonds, the published yields do not reflect the investor's

---

11. The value $824 was calculated using the standard bond pricing equation with the bond now being a six-year bond (four years have elapsed), and the yield to maturity has risen.

12. These computations are based on semiannual bonds with 10 years to maturity initially (Treasury bonds with 8.41% coupon and Baa bonds with 9.49% coupon) and then six years to maturity left in 1982 to calculate the losses.

after-tax rate of return. Municipal bonds (bonds issued by a state or local government) are exempt from income tax, whereas all other bonds are taxable. Hence, a comparison of the pretax yields on various types of bonds may be misleading.

The health of the economy influences the size of the credit spread. In recessions, bondholders tend to move out of lower-rated bonds into higher-rated bonds—a phenomenon known as "the flight to quality." Exhibit 16-11 documents this flight to quality. For example, in 1978, inflation-adjusted growth in the GDP was 6.1%, and by 1982 it had fallen to −3%. At the same time, the credit spread had risen from 1.08% to 3.11%, an increase of 203 basis points. Exhibit 16-11a shows a negative relationship between inflation-adjusted GDP and the credit spread.[13]

PRACTICE BOX

Problem	After conducting extensive analysis, you believe the economy will continue to grow steadily, accompanied by very little change in Treasury yields. How could you profit from this belief (assuming it turns out to be correct)? Specifically, there is a BB bond with 30 years to maturity that is currently trading at par with a yield to maturity of 10%.
Solution	In a strengthening economy, the credit spread tends to decline, reflecting the lower default risk. Hence, you could invest in lower-rated bonds with the expectation that if the bond yields do decline, bond prices will rise. For example, if you invest in the BB bond and the credit spread narrows by 2%, then the price will appreciate by $225.16. (See Exhibit 16-6a for the 30-year bond. At 10%, the bond trades at par of $1,000, and at 8%, the bond trades for $1,225.16.)

Exhibit 16-12 provides the yields on utility bonds, long-term Treasury bonds, and municipal bonds. It shows that the yield on municipal bonds is smaller than the yield on Treasury bonds. This phenomenon is quite common. For example, on September 22, 1997, the yield to maturity on Florida Ports Financing was 5.52%, whereas the yield to maturity on U.S. Treasury bonds (with the same 30 years to maturity) was 6.36%. Does this mean that municipals are less risky than government bonds? The reason municipals offer such low yields is that they are exempt from Federal income tax—not because their risk is lower than that of Treasury bonds.

From Chapter 2 recall that

$$R_{AT} = R_{BT}(1 - T)$$

where R_{AT} is the rate of return after taxes, R_{BT} is the rate of return before taxes, and T is the income tax rate.

Thus, the implied before-tax rate of return when $T = 31\%$ and $R_{AT} = 6.06\%$ (Year 8 in Exhibit 16-12) is

$$R_{BT} = R_{AT}/(1 - T) = 6.06\%/(1 - 0.31) \cong 8.78\%$$

---

13. The correlation for this time period was −0.52, indicating a very strong negative relationship.

EXHIBIT 16-11
Credit Spread of Changes in Gross Domestic Product

Part a: The Credit Spread between Baa (by Moody's) and 10-Year Treasuries and Inflation-Adjusted Growth in Gross Domestic Product (1965–1990)

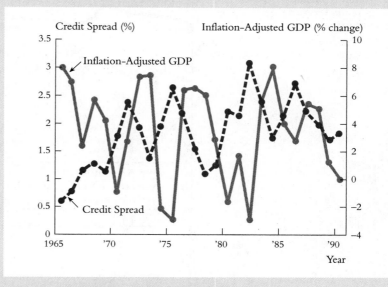

Source: *Economic Report of the President,* February 1991, p. 301.

Part b: The Credit Spread between Baa (by Moody's) and 10-Year Treasuries and Inflation-Adjusted Growth in Gross Domestic Product (1986–1995)

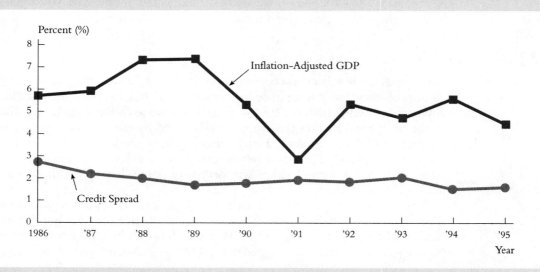

Source: *Economic Report of the President,* 1997, p. 301.

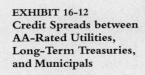

EXHIBIT 16-12
Credit Spreads between
AA-Rated Utilities,
Long-Term Treasuries,
and Municipals

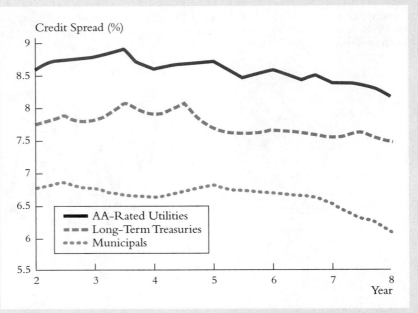

Source: Merrill Lynch Securities Research, as cited in *Wall Street Journal,* August 3, 1992, p. C17. Reprinted by permission of *The Wall Street Journal,* ©1992 Dow Jones & Co., Inc. All Rights Reserved Worldwide.

which exceeds both the Treasury bonds with 8 years to maturity (at 7.48%) and the AA bonds (at 8.14%). Hence, we see that as expected, municipals have significantly higher before-tax yields, which reflect the default risk premium.

16.6.3 Junk Bonds

Junk bonds are lower-rated corporate bonds. About 25% of the junk bond market consists of bonds that were once investment grade but have had their credit rating downgraded below BBB (or Baa). These are known as **fallen angels.** Another 25% of the junk bond market consists of bonds issued by corporations that initially do not carry a high credit rating. Finally, about 50% of the junk bond market is composed of bonds issued in major restructurings, such as leveraged buyouts. This segment of the junk bond market was primarily composed of bonds issued in the period 1986 to 1989.[14]

Exhibit 16-13 illustrates the growth of the junk bond market, as well as the subsequent growth of default rates. It was not until 1987 that the junk bond market exceeded $100 billion in par value. By 1989, however, it exceeded $200 billion. Notice that the default rates lagged behind this phenomenal growth by a few years.

14.   Edward I. Altman, "Revisiting the High-Yield Bond Market," *Financial Management,* Summer 1992, pp. 78–92.

EXHIBIT 16-13 Historical Default Rates for Junk Bonds	Calendar Year	Par Value Outstanding (in billions $)	Par Value in Default (in billions $)	Default Rate (%)
	1991	209	18.9	9.0
	1990	210	18.4	8.7
	1989	201	8.1	4.0
	1988	159	3.9	2.5
	1987	137	1.8	1.3
	1986	93	3.2	3.4
	1985	59	0.99	1.7
	1984	41.7	0.034	0.83
	1983	28	0.3	1.1
	1982	18.5	0.58	3.1
	1981	17.4	0.027	0.16
	1980	15.1	0.2	1.48
	1979	10.7	0.02	0.19
	1978	9.4	0.12	1.27

Source: Years 1978 to 1988 from Edward I. Altman, *The High-Yield Debt Market: Investment Performance and Economic Impact* (Homewood, Ill.: Dow Jones–Irwin, 1990), p. 45; years 1989 to 1991 from Edward I. Altman, "Revisiting the High-Yield Bond Market," *Financial Management*, Summer 1992, p. 82, Exhibit 4.

Clearly, the high default rates in the early 1990s were a result of excessive optimism in the late 1980s.

Although junk bonds have a considerable amount of default risk, they have one very attractive feature. Their yields are relatively high, which implies a high realized rate of return if bankruptcy does not occur. For example, the yield to maturity on September 22, 1997, was 10.71% on Globastar LP and as high as 31.30% on Grand Union.[15] Because these bonds are so sensitive to the overall health of the issuing firm, each bond's price moves more with information related to the firm than with changes in overall interest rates. It turns out that a diversified portfolio of junk bonds with a relatively low correlation is many times less volatile than a diversified portfolio of U.S. Treasury securities. Recall from our portfolio analysis that securities that have low correlations can be used to form portfolios with relatively low overall volatility.

16.6.4 Inflation-Indexed Bonds

Some countries that suffer from relatively high inflation issue bonds whose principal and interest are linked to the cost of living index (indexed bonds). For example, if a

15. See *Barron's*, September 22, 1997, p. W1161.

bond's face value is $1,000 and there was 10% inflation in the first year after the bond was issued and 20% inflation in the second year, then the bond's face value is adjusted to

$$\$1,000(1.1)(1.2) = \$1,320$$

Similarly, the interest coupon payments are adjusted for inflation.

Recently, the U.S. Treasury issued inflation-adjusted securities. The yield to maturity on such bonds is smaller than the yield to maturity on nonindexed bonds; however, these two yields are not comparable: one is real yield, whereas the other is nominal yield. For example, the yield to maturity on August 19, 1997, was 3.528% on indexed bonds that mature in the year 2007, whereas the yield to maturity was about 6.25% on Treasury bonds with a similar maturity. The difference between these two yields reflects the expected annual inflation. The higher the inflation, the bigger is the expected difference between the nominal and real yields.

16.6.5 International Bond Markets

Recall from Chapter 3 (Exhibit 3-12) that U.S. bonds account for approximately half of the global corporate bond market. As investors strive to achieve returns in excess of Treasuries, one popular strategy is a global bond portfolio. Although the potential returns are great, however, there are several risks (such as an exchange risk—see Chapter 11 for a description of the risks involved in international investing).

The global bond market has its own terminology. For example, *yankee bonds* are issued by foreign corporations and foreign banks that pay in U.S. dollars. Hence, yankee bonds are an efficient way to diversify default risk. If you allocate a portion of your bond portfolio to yankee bonds, when the United States goes into a severe recession you may not suffer as great a loss if these foreign corporations are not hit as hard.

As the financial markets become increasingly interrelated, corporations seeking the lowest funding costs are issuing bonds in different countries. These bonds, referred to as *Eurobonds,* are not related in any way to Europe. Eurobonds are sold to investors outside of the issuing corporation's country. For example, *Samurai bonds* are yen-denominated Eurobonds offered by non-Japanese firms.

The primary benefits of international bonds, from the investor's point of view, are enhanced returns and diversification. Because of supply and demand imbalances, many international bonds have yields to maturity higher than comparable domestic securities even after adjusting for exchange risk. Also, international bonds are not perfectly correlated. Thus, it is possible to build an international bond portfolio that has a higher expected return and a lower volatility than a domestic bond portfolio. See Chapter 11 for more details on international investing.

Exhibit 16-14 illustrates the yield to maturities and the realized rates of return on international government bonds. A few interesting conclusions can be drawn from this exhibit. First, the yield curve is upward sloping in three countries, whereas in the United Kingdom it is almost flat, with a 7% yield.

Second, on long-maturity bonds, the biggest difference in the yield is between the United Kingdom (about 7% yield) and Japan (about 2.9% yield).

EXHIBIT 16-14   International Government Bonds

Prices in local currencies, provided by Salomon Brothers Inc.

	Coupon	Maturity (Mo./yr.)	Price	Change		Yield[a]	Coupon	Maturity (Mo./yr.)	Price	Change		Yield[a]
Japan (3 p.m. Tokyo)							*Germany* (5 p.m. London)					
#112	5.00%	9/98	104.782	−	0.006	0.59%	3.50%	12/98	99.780	+	0.076	3.63%
#143	6.30	9/01	119.800	+	0.034	1.31	5.25	2/01	102.573	+	0.130	4.38
#163	4.40	9/03	114.990	+	0.058	1.79	6.25	3/04	105.808	+	0.250	5.11
#188	3.20	9/06	107.896	+	0.080	2.23	6.00	7/07	102.657	+	0.320	5.55
#30	3.70	9/15	111.138	+	0.132	**2.90**	6.25	1/24	98.736	+	0.450	6.25
United Kingdom (5 p.m. London)							*Canada* (3 p.m. EDT)					
	6.00%	3/98	98.219	−	0.015	6.98%	4.00%	3/99	99.910	+	0.150	4.05%
	7.00	11/01	99.784	+	0.082	7.04	7.00	9/01	106.550	+	0.280	5.17
	8.00	6/03	104.475	+	0.148	7.04	7.50	12/03	110.023	+	0.375	5.58
	7.25	12/07	101.751	+	0.373	7.00	7.25	6/07	109.645	+	0.443	5.93
	8.75	8/17	118.526	+	0.554	**7.01**	8.00	6/23	118.350	+	0.450	6.52

a. Equivalent to semi-annual compounded yields to maturity

Total Rates of Return on International Bonds
In percent, based on Salomon Brothers' World Government Bond Index

	Local Currency Terms						U.S. Dollar Terms					
Mos	Index Value–a 12/31	1 Day	1 Mo	3 Mos		Since	Index 12/31	Value–a	1 Day	1 Mo		Since 3
Japan	233.55	+ 0.08	+ 1.30	+ 3.08	+	**3.87**	499.27	− 0.49	− 0.61	+ 0.96	+	**2.40**
Britain	385.37	+ 0.30	+ 0.82	+ 2.13	+	**7.70**	536.00	+ 0.35	− 3.01	+ 0.47	+	**1.38**
Germany	253.41	+ 0.22	− 0.18	+ 1.38	+	**3.81**	438.46	0.00	− 1.91	− 5.75	−	**12.21**
France	366.52	+ 0.28	0.00	+ 1.81	+	**4.40**	576.09	+ 0.02	− 1.50	− 5.42	−	**11.64**
Canada	405.36	+ 0.34	+ 0.95	+ 4.45	+	**6.23**	384.50	+ 0.40	− 0.05	+ 3.06	+	**4.83**
Netherlands	265.03	+ 0.24	− 0.19	+ 1.45	+	**3.65**	459.77	+ 0.03	− 1.95	− 5.84	−	**12.63**
Non-U.S.	299.58	+ 0.17	+ 0.46	+ 2.50	+	**4.83**	477.54	− 0.14	− 1.52	− 2.22	−	**5.43**
World[a]	315.63	+ 0.20	+ 0.49	+ 2.89	+	**4.82**	386.76	0.00	− 0.82	− 0.26	−	**2.09**

a. Includes 17 international government bond markets   NA=Not Applicable   a-Dec 31, 1984=100

Source: *Wall Street Journal*, August 19, 1997, p. C17. Reprinted by permission of *The Wall Street Journal* © 1997, Dow Jones & Co., Inc. All Rights Reserved

Why not issue bonds in Japan at 2.9% a year and lend in the United Kingdom at 7% a year and make a profit? This tempting transaction does not guarantee an arbitrage profit. The reason is that the difference in the yields represents different expected inflation rates in these two countries, which in turn reflects an expectation that the British pound will depreciate against the Japanese yen. When the investor converts the British pound back to Japanese yen (because the investor needs to pay back the loan), she may find that she lost money on what seems to be an arbitrage transaction.

A third conclusion can be drawn from the lower part of Exhibit 16-14. The realized return since December 31, 1996, was (in local currency) only 3.87% in Japan and 7.7% in the United Kingdom. However, the tables turn when the realized returns are compared in U.S. dollars: the realized return is 2.4% in Japan and only 1.38% in the United Kingdom, a change in the ranking of profitability that is due to the depreciation of the British pound relative to the Japanese yen.

Fourth, the striking results are for Germany, France, and the Netherlands: a positive return in local currency of about 3% to 6% a year turns out to be a negative return of about 5% to 12% in U.S. dollars. Thus, an American investor who invested in these foreign bonds earned in local currency but lost when the foreign currency was converted back to dollars. Thus, international investing should be done cautiously. The investor can enjoy the high return on international bonds with no risk only if she invests in additional transactions to hedge against the foreign exchange risk. These transactions could be forward contracts or foreign exchange options.

16.7 THE IMPACT OF EMBEDDED OPTIONS

Issuers often add provisions to bonds to protect themselves from interest rate changes or to make the bonds more attractive to investors. Many features in corporate bond issues are essentially options. Recall from Chapter 2 that an option gives its holder the right, but not the obligation, to do something in the future. Both callable and convertible bonds contain option-like features. The option to call a bond and the option to convert a bond to stock dramatically change the fundamental price behavior of bonds.

16.7.1 The Call Feature

Most corporate bonds issued in the United States are callable by the issuing firm. That is, the issuer has the right to buy the bonds back at a stated redemption price. The bondholders face the risk that the bonds will be called at a time when they would prefer to hold them.

For example, in 1979, Duke Power Company issued a 10⅛% coupon bond at $1,000 par that had a stated maturity of March 1, 2009.[16] The bonds were rated Aa by Moody's and thus contained little credit risk.

Suppose these bonds were purchased with the idea of holding them until 2009. As interest rates fell in the late 1980s and early 1990s, these bonds should have experienced a dramatic rise in price, except they were callable at 105.65% of par, or $1,056.50. Thus, even though yields on comparable bonds reached the mid-8% level,

---

16. From Moody's, *Corporate Bond Guide* (New York: Moody's Investors Service, 1991), p. 69.

these bonds never rose much above $1,056.50. Thus, the call provision put a ceiling on the possible profit due to a fall in interest rates. On December 23, 1991, Duke Power Company called the bonds back and paid $1,056.50 (plus accrued interest).

The investor then had the problem of what to do with the $1,056.50 proceeds per bond. Unfortunately, the investor had to replace a 10⅛% coupon bond with an 8½% bond (the yield available at the time), resulting in an annual coupon loss of 1⅝%, or $16.25 (0.01625 · $1,000), per bond per year.

Exhibit 16-15 illustrates the impact of the call feature on bond price behavior with respect to yield to maturity, assuming everything else about the bonds is the same (maturity, coupon, and so forth). If the callable and the noncallable bonds were priced the same, which bond would you rather own? You would prefer the noncallable bond, of course, because you could gain more if there were a large increase in price because of falling interest rates. Thus, for similar bonds, a noncallable bond is always worth more. Indeed, Exhibit 16-15 demonstrates this property. The exhibit also shows that as yields to maturity get progressively higher, the difference in prices gradually declines. An investor would not expect too great a threat from a call feature at 105% of par when the bond is trading at, say, 70% of its par value. Thus, the market value of the call feature declines as yields to maturity rise.

Exhibit 16-15 also highlights the divergence in price when interest rates fall. Specifically, the callable bond usually does not trade much above the price at which the firm can call the bonds. Notice the left-hand side of Exhibit 16-15. As rates fall, the noncallable bond's price continues to rise. However, the callable bond levels off at the value of the bond if it were called.

Why, then, do investors buy callable bonds? The reason is that issuing firms offer "sweeteners" in the form of higher coupon rates in return for the call feature. The

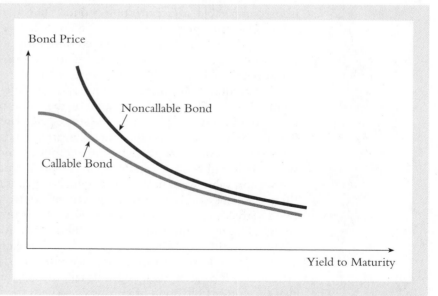

EXHIBIT 16-15
The Impact of the Call Feature on Bond Prices

issuing firm of callable bonds offers the investor a higher yield to maturity. However, should the yield to maturity fall, the investor will miss out on a sizable run-up in price. Once again there is a trade-off between risk (the call feature) and return (the higher initial yield to maturity).

Why do firms issue callable bonds? The call feature allows firms some flexibility in their financing policies. In particular, the firm is not locked into an expensive debt issue. When interest rates fall, the bonds can be refinanced at a lower rate.

16.7.2 The Conversion Feature

When firms want to reduce their required coupon rate, they sometimes offer to make their bonds convertible to common or preferred stock. One advantage from the issuing firm's viewpoint is that it will issue new common stock at a relatively high price when the conversion takes place in the future. Typically, the conversion price (which equals the par value of the bond divided by the conversion ratio) is set significantly above the current common stock price. If the firm raised capital through a new issue of common stock, it would have to offer the new issue at a price slightly less than the current stock price. Therefore, convertible bonds provide a way to achieve, albeit in the future, an equity issue at a higher price.

Consider the Cray Research Inc. (makers of supercomputers) $6\frac{1}{8}\%$ coupon, semiannual convertible bonds, maturing February 1, 2011, with a rating of Baa-2 by Moody's. The conversion ratio is 12.82, which means that for every bond converted, the firm will issue 12.82 shares of common stock. Thus, the conversion price is about $78 (*Par/Conversion Ratio* = $1,000/12.82).

On July 24, 1992, the bonds closed at $73\frac{1}{2}\%$ of par, and the common stock closed at $29\frac{3}{8}$. These bonds offer a yield to maturity of approximately 9%. At the time, the Cray Research bonds offered a yield to maturity that was indistinguishable from comparable nonconvertible bonds. The conversion feature had very little value. The stock price must rise by 165.53% before the conversion price is reached [($78 − $29\frac{3}{8}) / $29\frac{3}{8}]. Thus, these bonds offer a strong 9% yield to maturity, and they also contain an "equity kicker." If the common stock price goes up considerably, then these bonds will likewise rise.

Convertible bond price behavior is quite different from the price behavior of regular bonds. The conversion value is the value of the bond if it is immediately converted into stock. Hence, as the stock price rises, so does the conversion value. The reason for the loss on the Cray Research bonds is that the common stock price lost over 50% of its value. (The supercomputer industry is very sensitive to recessions.) If it had been a straight bond, its price would have gone up; however, the conversion value went down more, which explains the loss. Exhibit 16-16 illustrates this price behavior. Notice that the straight (nonconvertible) bond is almost insensitive to stock price changes except when the firm's stock price gets very low. The straight line represents the value of the bond if it is converted into stock. This value is known as the *conversion value*, which equals the conversion ratio times the current stock price. Clearly, as the stock price rises, so does the conversion value. Thus, when Cray Research stock began its fall, the convertible bond followed suit. Notice that the convertible bond price always exceeds the straight bond price, even for low

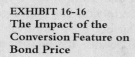

**EXHIBIT 16-16
The Impact of the
Conversion Feature on
Bond Price**

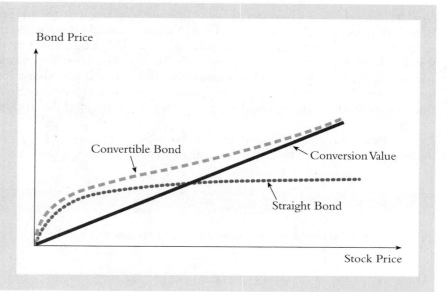

stock prices, because the ability to convert the bonds to stock is always worth something (although it may not be worth very much at low stock prices). The higher price of convertible bonds relative to straight bonds implies that their yield is also higher.

SUMMARY

Construct and interpret a yield curve. The yield to maturity is the interest earned on a bond if held to its maturity. A yield curve is a relationship between a bond's time to maturity and its yield to maturity. The yield curve provides some clues regarding the future course of interest rates.

Use the bond pricing equation to find bond prices and bond yields. When the bond's price is given, the yield to maturity can be computed, thus indicating the bond's future cash flows. There is an inverse relationship between yield to maturity and bond prices.

Summarize the theories that explain the shape and level of yield curves. The local expectations hypothesis (LEH) states that the holding period rates of return

are the same regardless of the time to maturity. The unbiased expectations hypothesis (UEH) states that forward rates are unbiased predictors of future spot rates. The liquidity preference hypothesis (LPH) states that investors have a preference for securities with shorter maturities; hence, longer-term bonds will have a higher yield to maturity. The market segmentations hypothesis (MSH) is based on investors and borrowers having specific preferences regarding time to maturity. Supply and demand in these segments of the yield curve will govern the yield to maturity. Finally, the preferred habitat hypothesis is similar to the MSH except that investors and borrowers can be induced to change their maturity preference when yields to maturity are sufficiently different.

Describe the behavior of the spread over Treasuries.
Bond rating agencies classify the credit risk inherent in bonds. Over time, the additional yield required for bearing this credit risk—the spread over Treasuries—varies. During economic downturns, the spread over Treasuries widens to compensate investors for the additional risk of default.

Describe the impact of the call feature and the convertible feature on bond prices. The call feature causes bond prices not to rise as much as a comparable non-callable bond when interest rates fall. The option to call a bond held by the issuer becomes more valuable when interest rates fall, because the bonds can be refinanced at a lower rate. The conversion feature causes bonds to behave like the underlying stock after the stock price has risen sufficiently.

CHAPTER AT A GLANCE

1. *The bond pricing equation for semiannual coupon-bearing bonds follows:*

$$P = \sum_{t=1}^{n} \frac{C}{(1 + y)^t} + \frac{Par}{(1 + y)^n}$$

where n is the number of coupon payments, C is the coupon payment each period, y is the semiannual yield to maturity, and *Par* is the face value of the bond. The annual yield to maturity is equal to $(1 + y)^2 - 1$.

2. *The hypotheses developed to explain yield curves include the following:*
    a. Local expectations hypothesis (LEH)—holding period rates of return are the same (no matter which bond is purchased).
    b. Unbiased expectations hypothesis (UEH)—forward rates are unbiased predictors of future spot rates.
    c. Liquidity preference hypothesis (LPH)—investors prefer shorter maturities.
    d. Market segmentations hypothesis (MSH)—the term structure is segmented.
    e. Preferred habitat hypothesis—the term structure is segmented, but investors will move to obtain better rates.

3. *The different types of yields follow:*
    a. Coupon yield or nominal yield = C/Par.
    b. Current yield = C/P, where C = the coupon payment and P = the current price.
    c. Yield to maturity = y, the discount factor, resulting in zero NPV for the bond.
    d. Yield to call = y resulting in zero NPV for the bond (assuming it is called).
    e. Realized yield = actual rate of return earned on the bond for a given holding period.

KEY TERMS

Bond indenture 578	Current yield 571	Forward rate 565
Coupon yield 571	Debenture 579	High grade 577
Credit quality 577	Fallen angel 586	Holding period rate 568
Credit risk 577	Forward contract 565	Investment grade 577

Junk bond   578

Liquidity preference hypothesis (LPH)   569

Liquidity premium   570

Local expectations hypothesis (LEH)   568

Market segmentations hypothesis (MSH)   570

Nominal yield   571

Preferred habitat hypotheses   571

Price risk   561

Rating agency   577

Realized yield   572

Reinvestment risk   560

Secured bonds   578

Simple interest   609

Sinking fund   579

Speculative grade bond   578

Spot rate   565

Subordinated bond   578

Term structure of interest rates   562

Unbiased expectations hypothesis (UEH)   569

Wealth effect   557

Yield curve   559

Yield to call   572

Yield to maturity   558

REVIEW

16.1 What sparked the changes in bond management in the 1970s?

16.2 What determines the equilibrium level of interest rates?

16.3 If interest rates rise, will individuals save more or less? Explain your answer.

16.4 Describe some historical characteristics of the U.S. Treasury yield curve.

16.5 Identify and discuss the various theories related to the behavior of the yield curve.

16.6 Assuming a flat yield curve and a bond that is trading at par, why does the yield to call exceed the yield to maturity?

16.7 "The stock market seems risky these days. I am going to put my money in safe, 30-year U.S. Treasury bonds." Evaluate this statement.

16.8 Because of financial stress, the bonds of Intelo have been downgraded by Moody's from A to BBB. What is the predicted effect on the bonds' price? What is the predicted effect on the bonds' yield to maturity?

16.9 Suppose the only information you had regarding the current health of a country's economy was its credit spread between triple-B bonds and Treasury bonds. Specifically, the spread had recently widened considerably. What would you infer?

PRACTICE

16.1 Suppose you are given the following information:

Maturities	Spot Rates	Forward Rates
1	8%	—a
2		7.8%
3	7.2	
4		6.0
5	5.0	

a. Recall that forward rates involve an interest rate starting at some future point in time. Hence, most practitioners say the forward rate during the first period is just the one-period spot rate, which in this case is 8%.

a. Complete the table assuming the rates are for annual, zero-coupon bonds.

b. If the unbiased expectations hypothesis (UEH) is strictly true, what is the market forecast for the one-year spot rate in one year?

16.2 Describe the empirical evidence regarding patterns in bond rating changes. Is this evidence consistent with the efficient market hypothesis?

16.3 The maturity of a bond is one year ($n = 1$), the annual coupon is $C = \$100$, the par value is

$1,000, and the market value is $P = \$950$. Calculate the yield to maturity.

16.4 The yield on a one-year municipal bond is 6.4%, and the yield on a one-year Treasury bond is 7.5%. Ignoring default risk, if the tax rate is $T = 31\%$, which bond would you prefer? Why?

16.5 "If the yield to maturity is zero, no matter what the maturity is, the par value of the bond must be equal to its market value." Evaluate this statement. Is there a specific type of bond for which this is true?

16.6 Suppose you are the chief financial officer of a large life insurance company. Looking at mortality tables, you estimate that you will have to pay the insured families $100 million in each of the next five years and $900 million in Year 6. What kind of bonds would you seek to make these payments? Would it make a difference whether the yield curve is flat or upward sloping?

16.7 Short-term bonds traded in the United States, like Treasury bills, are often referred to as the risk-free asset. In what respect are they risk-free?

16.8 What asset would you consider to be riskier, three-month Treasury bills or a 30-year Treasury bond that matures in three months?

16.9 Looking at the international financial statistics, we find that the interest paid to U.S. banks on loans to some Latin American countries is about 30% per year. The interest within the United States is only 10%.
a. How can you explain the difference in interest rates if the loans are made in local currency?
b. How can you explain the difference in interest rates when the loan is made in U.S. dollars? After all, it is said, the government cannot go bankrupt. Why do U.S. banks receive such a high interest rate on foreign loans?

16.10 In some countries, the inflation rate is fairly high. Suppose you are a citizen of such a country where inflation next year is *estimated* to be 10%.
a. Which investment is risk-free: a bond paying 2% above the cost of living index or a bond paying a fixed 12% interest?

b. Calculate the mean and variance of the rate of return on your investment by assuming that the inflation will be 8%, 10%, and 12% with an equal probability of ⅓. Do the calculations in nominal and real terms.

16.11 "If the yield curve is flat, then all forward rates must be equal to zero." Evaluate this statement. Demonstrate your answer with a numerical example.

16.12 Suppose you wish to hold a bond for one year. The current price is $1,000, and a coupon of $50 is paid at the end of each year. Assume the yield to maturity is 10%.

Immediately after you buy the bond, the yield to maturity will be either 5%, 10%, or 15%, with equal probability. For each of the following possible bonds with maturities of 1, 5, and 10 years, conduct the following analysis.
a. Calculate in percentages the profit or loss that is due to the possible changes in the interest rate.
b. Calculate the mean rate of return, as well as the standard deviation. Which bond is the most profitable? Why? Which bond is the riskiest?
c. Are the data regarding the three bonds consistent with the liquidity preference hypothesis (LPH)?

16.13 The interest rate for depositors in the United States is 4%, and in Germany it is 9%. "As an American, you would be better off putting your money in German bonds." Do you agree?

16.14 Suppose you can borrow in the United States at 6% and lend in Germany at 10%. The exchange today is 1.6 German marks per dollar. What should be the maximum forward exchange rate, such that for any forward exchange rate below this maximum, arbitrage profit can be made? Explain carefully how you carry out this arbitrage.

16.15 *Did somebody say "new era"? In financial history, that idea has invariably gotten popular just in time for a crash. And after October's Fall fall, the idea of a stock market crash no longer seems quite so funny.*

As we showed in the issue of Nov. 17, the real (inflation-adjusted) cumulative total return (capital gains plus dividends) on stocks is now significantly above its two-century 6.5%-to-7% long-run growth trend, according to Wharton professor Jeremy J. Siegel's calculations. Our latest reading shows stocks are about 40% above trend. There's nothing magic about trend lines, but it stands to reason that at some point stocks will either pull back toward it, or—best case—drift sideways until the trend catches up.

Things look more promising for the bond market. Our chart shows that the cumulative real total return for long-term government bonds grew at 4.9% per year, on average, until about 1913. After that, the growth trend moderated, to 0.9% or thereabouts.

Source: Peter Brimelow, "Stocks versus Bonds," *Forbes,* December 1, 1997, p. 49; research by Edwin S. Rubenstein, Hudson Institute. Reprinted by Permission of *Forbes* magazine © Forbes Inc., 1997.

a. What is the value of a $1 investment in bonds at the end of 113 years of investment (up to about 1913; see the article) when the annual real rate of return is 4.9%? What is the value of a $1 investment in stock at the end of 113 years with an annual real rate of return of 7%?

b. Suppose that the rate of return on bonds will be adjusted in the years 1998 to 2005 so it will be on the trend line at the end of 2005 (that is, average earnings of 4.9% a year for the whole period from 1801 to 2005). What should be the annual real rate of return on bonds during these 7 years? Explain your calculation.

c. From the figures given in the article, can you calculate the annual inflation rate for the whole period from 1801 to 1997? Explain.

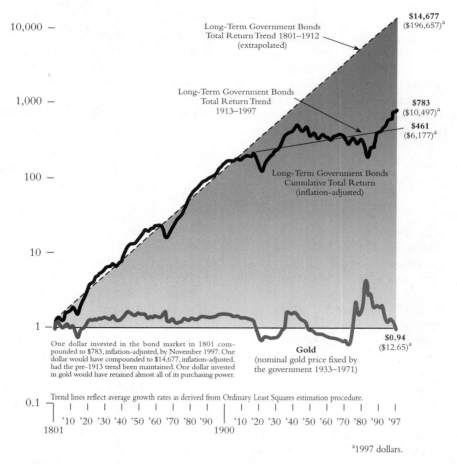

Source: Jeremy J. Siegel, "Stocks for the Long Run," updated data provided by author; Peter Brimelow, "Stocks versus Bonds," *Forbes,* December 1, 1997, p. 49. Reprinted by Permission of *Forbes* magazine © Forbes Inc., 1997.

16.16 *While stocks may struggle for the next four to six months, investors should be rewarded for taking the risk with a 1998 return of 15%–20%, most of which will be received in the second half. Psychology has become pessimistic, creating the first contrarian buy for stocks since last April. The political sex scandal has combined forces with the Asian flu to create a sharp rise in investor fear. Bonds are very attractive with rates near 6%. Long rates are likely to fall to 5% in 1998 as Asia exports her disinflation to the U.S.*

Source: Paul Rabbitt, "CIBC Oppenheimer's Q-Market Strategy" *Barron's,* February 2, 1998, p. 58.

a. Explain why the crisis in Asia may export "disinflation" to the United States and why this situation may induce a decrease in the interest rate in the United States.

b. Suppose that the current yield on long-term bonds is 6%. Assume that the par value of a bond is $1,000 and the annual coupon is $60 paid semiannually. Calculate the capital gain if the long-term interest drops to 5% under the assumption that *n* years are left to maturity, where *n* = 1, 5, 10, 20.

16.17 *Still there's a long road to travel. South Korean debt prices remain far underwater. For example, Korea Development Bank's 7¼% bonds due in 2006 traded at 100—face value—in early October before plummeting to the low 60s in December. They've slowly bounced off their lows and now are quoted around 83. But investors are still looking at a 17-point—or $170—loss per $1,000 bond.*

Looking back, it seems amazing that all three agencies had solid investment-grade ratings on Korea's debt as recently as October. In fact, it wasn't until December, with Korea's currency and prospects collapsing, that the ratings plummeted to their current junk-bond status (see chart).

Back on September 1, 1,000 won would have fetched more than one U.S. dollar. Recently it would have brought less than 60 American pennies. As the Korean currency's value plunged, so did Korea's debt ratings. But investors wonder why the rating agencies didn't begin their downgrading until the debacle was well under way.

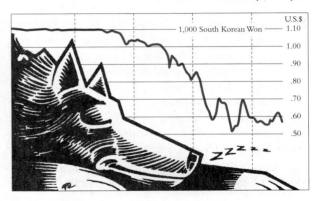

South Korean Sovereign Ratings	Sept	Oct	Nov	Dec	Jan
Moody's	A1	A1	A3	Ba1[a]	Ba1
S&P	AA−	A+	A−	B+[a]	B+
FitchIBCA	AA−	AA−	A	B−[a]	B−

a. Ratings were downgraded twice in December.

Source: Jaqueline Doherty, "Costly Lessons," *Barron's,* January 26, 1998, p. 22.

a. In looking at the graph, do you think that the rating agencies fulfilled their job successfully? Explain.

b. The 7¼% bonds due in 2006 were traded at 100—face value—in early October and at, say, 64 in December 1997. Assuming exactly 6 years to maturity left, calculate the yield to maturity in December 1997.

c. Assume that the investor fixes the bond price such that the *expected* rate of return in October 1997 (7¼%) is equal to the expected rate of return in December 1997. Assume that in October 1997, there was a zero probability of bankruptcy. What is the estimate of the probability of a bankruptcy of the Korea Development Bank during the period 1997–2006 as estimated in December 1997 (that is, the probability that the bank is unable to return dollar payment because of a lack of foreign currency)? Assume that in the case of a bankruptcy, the investor loses all the investment.

CFA PROBLEMS

16.1 The following are the average yields on U.S. Treasury bonds at two different points in time:

Term to Maturity	Yield-to-Maturity	
	January 15, 19xx	May 15, 19xx
1 year	7.25%	8.05%
2 years	7.50	7.90
5 years	7.90	7.70
10 years	8.30	7.45
15 years	8.45	7.30
20 years	8.55	7.20
25 years	8.60	7.10

a. Assuming a pure expectations hypothesis, define a forward rate. (The unbiased expectations hypothesis is sometimes referred to as the pure expectations hypothesis.) Describe how you would calculate the forward rate for a three-year U.S. Treasury bond two years from May 15, 19XX, using the actual term structure shown in the table above.

b. Discuss how each of the three major term structure hypotheses could explain the January 15, 19XX, term structure shown in the foregoing table.

c. Discuss what happened to the term structure over the time period and the effects of this change on 2-year and 10-year U.S. Treasury bonds.

d. Assume that you invest solely on the basis of yield spreads, and in January 19XX, you acted upon the expectation that the yield spread between 1-year and 25-year U.S. Treasuries would return to a more typical spread of 170 basis points. Explain what you would have done on January 15, 19XX, and describe the results of this action based on what happened between January 15, 19XX, and May 15, 19XX.

For Internet questions visit the Levy Investment Web site at http://levy-invst.swcollege.com.

YOUR TURN: APPLYING THEORY TO PRACTICE
ENHANCING PORTFOLIO RETURN WITH CONVERTIBLE BONDS

This is a time for extreme prudence, because we are not on an automatic conveyer belt to growth in the world.
—Bond Manager Kenneth Lipper

Lipper, 52, practices prudence by concentrating clients' money—and his own—in intermediate-term fixed-income securities. That way, he gets a much better yield than in money market instruments but avoids the inflation risk inherent in long-term bonds and the tremendous market risk inherent in stocks after a decade-old bull market.

This does not mean that Lipper expects Armageddon. What he expects, as he put it in a recent interview, is a "relatively low-inflation environment with slow economic growth." If he were certain that inflation would be subdued for a long time, it would make sense to buy long-term noncallable bonds. Not being certain, he buys shorter-term bonds. Consider Lipper's hedged convertible bond strategy, accounting for half his funds under management. The hedging turns these equity-like instruments into something half as risky as stocks, because he shorts the underlying stock or buys a put on it. Objective: a 15% annualized return "if these companies continue to pay interest on the bonds and the stock does nothing."

The biggest part of this profit is the result of capturing the spread between the coupon on the bond and the lower dividend rate on the common. Take, for example, Bank of New York

(continued)

7½% bonds due in 2001, which recently had a current yield of 4.9%. This yield is about 210 basis points more than the cash dividend on the common stock. Clever, darned clever. Follow a hypothetical example:

Say you own $1 million of convertible bonds trading at par, convertible into 10,000 shares of stock. The $90 stock yields 3%. The bond, meanwhile, yields 5%. Look at the bond as a way of buying the stock and buying at the same time the right to collect an enhanced dividend for a while. In this case, the $1 million bond position is convertible into $900,000 worth of stock. The extra $100,000 paid by the bond buyer entitles him to collect $50,000 a year rather than the $27,000 collected by the owner of a corresponding amount of common. Even with some dividend increases likely on the common, the bond buyer can earn back his $100,000 premium in a little more than four years.

In this case, Lipper would short 7,500 shares of the stock. By borrowing back the proceeds of the short sale from the broker, he reduces his net investment in the position to about a third of the bond's price. His profit, before some transaction costs, is roughly equal to the spread between the bond's coupon and the much smaller sum he'd owe to cover the dividend on the shorted stock.

Risk? Not much. If the bond drops in price, the stock is likely to drop faster; profits on the short position should cover the loss on the bonds. If the stock goes up, he loses on his short position, but should make it up from the rise in the bonds' value.

What makes Lipper so sure we'll have a slow-growth, low-inflation economy, the kind where his strategy should flourish? He thinks Federal Reserve Chairman Alan Greenspan has made a tacit pact with the White House. Greenspan will shut up about Clinton's tax-and-spend program and Clinton will not try to interfere with Greenspan's inflation fighting. Lipper puts it somewhat more delicately: "The price of Greenspan's support for Clinton's economic program allows him to keep a tight rein on inflation." That's hardly a prescription for a continuation of the bull market. But with inflation kept down and the economy sluggish, bonds are bound to flourish.

Source: Robert Lenzner, "Haven for Scared Money," *Forbes,* June 21, 1993, pp. 154–155. Reprinted by Permission of *Forbes* Magazine, © Forbes Inc., 1993.

Convertibles

Issue/Coupon and Maturity	Price	Shares on Conversion	Conversion Premium (%)	Current Yield		Break-even Time (years)	Fixed Income Value ($)	S&P Rating
				Convert (%)	Stock (%)			
Bank of New York/ 7½s of '01	153	25.58	11.8	4.9	2.8	4.4	94	BBB+
Chubb Capital/6s of '98	117½	11.63	17.0	5.1	2.0	4.7	92	AA
Ford/$4.20 conv pfd	89	1.63	5.6	4.7	3.1	2.8	54	A−
Home Depot/4½s of '97	135¼	25.81	14.2	3.3	0.2	4.4	87	A−
National Bank of Detroit/ 7¼s of '06	114	32.90	13.6	6.4	3.5	4.3	94	A+
Pennzoil[a] 6½s of '03	118½	11.89	17.8	5.5	3.9	NM	86	BBB

Prices as of May 24. All of the convertible positions are 70% to 100% hedged.

a. Convertible to shares of Chevron.

NM: Not meaningful.

Source: Lipper and Co.

(continued)

Questions

1. Using the example given in the article, calculate the conversion ratio and the conversion price. (The par value of each bond is $1,000.)

2. The article claims that for the extra $100,000 investment in bonds, you collect $50,000 a year rather than the $27,000 collected by the owner of a corresponding amount of common stock. Calculate the internal rate of return on the incremental $100,000 investment in bonds when the maturity is seven years.

3. a. Suppose Lipper is wrong, and the economy is hit by 8% annual inflation. The yield on the bonds goes up from 5% to 13%. (Note: The coupon remains the same, and the bond's price drops to adjust to the new yield.) Suppose the stock price drops to $80, and it is *certain* that it will not exceed $95 at the end of the year. Calculate the capital gain or loss on the investment suggested by Lipper. (Do not include the short position yet.) Assume that the bond matures in one year.

b. Suppose now that there is no inflation, but the stock's price rises from $90 to $150 at the end of the year. What would be the rate of return on an investment in the convertible bonds? On the stocks? Which would you prefer? Again, assume that the bond matures in one year.

In light of your answers to Parts a and b, explain why Lipper's strategy flourishes in "a rela-

tively low-inflation environment with slow economic growth."

4. Assume now that you follow Lipper's strategy: buy $1 million bonds, short 7,500 shares at $90 apiece, and use the proceeds to finance a portion of the bond's purchase. Dividends on the short sale are transferred back to the broker. You hold your portfolio for one year. Assume that conversion is possible only at the end of the first year. Thus, the bond is evaluated in the rest of the years (Year 2 onward) as a straight bond. Calculate the rate of return on your net investment under the following scenarios:

a. Because of rapid inflation (an oil crisis), the yield on the bonds increases from 5% to 10%. The bond's maturity is seven years, and the stock price stays at $90. Is this scenario consistent with the assertion that "if the bond drops in price, the stock is likely to drop faster"?

b. The yield on bonds increases from 5% to 10%, and the stock price drops from $90 to $60.

c. The stock price increases from $90 to $150, and the yield on the bonds decreases from 5% to 1%.

d. There is low inflation and slow economic growth. The stock price increases by the end of the year from $90 to $92, and the yield to maturity remains 5%. Calculate the rate of return on the strategy suggested by Lipper.

SELECTED REFERENCES

Altman, Edward I. *The High-Yield Debt Market: Investment Performance and Economic Impact.* Homewood, Ill.: Dow Jones–Irwin, 1990.

This is an exhaustive book of readings related to the junk bond market.

Altman, Edward I., and Duen Li Kao. "The Implications of Corporate Bond Ratings Drift." *Financial Analysts Journal,* May–June 1992, pp. 64–75.

This article examines in detail the corporate ratings drift.

Cottle, Sidney, Roger F. Murray, and Frank E. Block. *Graham and Dodd's Security Analysis.* 5th ed. New York: McGraw-Hill, 1988.

This reworking of a classic applies the basic principles of security analysis in determining security value.

Geanuracos, John, and Bill Millar. *The Power of Financial Innovation.* New York: Harper Business, 1991.

This book provides interesting insights into the global bond markets and has an emphasis on derivative securities.

Livingston, Miles. *Money and Capital Markets: Financial Instruments and Their Uses.* Englewood Cliffs, N.J.: Prentice Hall, 1990.

This book covers thoroughly many of the technical aspects of bond pricing and theories of term structure.

SUPPLEMENTAL REFERENCES

Altman, Edward I. *The High-Yield Debt Market: Investment Performance and Economic Impact.* Homewood, Ill.: Dow Jones–Irwin, 1990.

Altman, Edward I. "Measuring Corporate Bond Mortality and Performance." *Journal of Finance,* September 1989, pp. 909–922.

Altman, Edward I. "Revisiting the High-Yield Bond Market." *Financial Management,* Summer 1992, pp. 78–92.

Altman, Edward I. "Setting the Record Straight on Junk Bonds." *Journal of Applied Corporate Finance,* Summer 1990, pp. 82–95.

Asquith, Paul, David W. Mullins, Jr., and Eric D. Wolff. "Original Issue High-Yield Bonds: Aging Analysis of Defaults, Exchanges and Call." *Journal of Finance,* September 1989, pp. 923–952.

Best, Peter, Alistair Byrne, and Antli Ilmanen. "What Really Happened to U.S. Bond Yield." *Financial Analysts Journal,* May–June 1998, pp. 41–49.

Blume, Marshall E., and Donald B. Keim. "Realized Returns and Defaults on Low-Grade Bonds: The Cohort of 1977 and 1978." *Financial Analysts Journal,* March–April 1991, pp. 63–72.

Blume, Marshall E., and Donald B. Keim. "The Risk and Return of Low-Grade Bonds: An Update." *Financial Analysts Journal,* September–October 1991, pp. 85–89.

Cornell, Bradfors. "Liquidity and the Pricing of Low-Grade Bonds." *Financial Analysts Journal,* January–February 1991, pp. 63–67, 74.

Fabozzi, Frank J. (ed.). *The New High-Yield Debt Market: A Handbook for Portfolio Managers and Analysts.* New York: HarperCollins, 1990.

Fama, Eugene F. "Forward Rates as Predictors of Future Spot Interest Rates." *Journal of Financial Economics,* October 1976, pp. 361–377.

Fama, Eugene F. "The Information in the Term Structure." *Journal of Financial Economics,* December 1984, pp. 509–528.

Fons, Jerome S., and Andrew E. Kimball. "Corporate Bond Defaults and Default Rates 1970–1990." *Journal of Fixed Income,* June 1991, pp. 36–47.

Fridson, Martin S., and Christopher Garman. "Determinants of Spreads on New High Yield Bonds." *Financial Analysts Journal,* March–April 1998, pp. 28–39.

Fridson, Martin S., Michael A. Cherry, Joseph A. Kim, and Stephen W. Weiss. "What Drives the Flows of High-Yield Mutual Funds?" *Journal of Fixed Income,* December 1992, pp. 47–59.

Lederman, Jess, and Michael P. Sullivan (eds.). *The New High-Yield Bond Market: Investment Opportunities, Strategies and Analysis.* Chicago: Probus Publishing, 1993.

Levy, Haim, and Robert Brooks. "An Empirical Analysis of Term Premiums Using Stochastic Dominance." *Journal of Banking and Finance,* May 1989, pp. 245–260.

Ma, Christopher K., Ramesh Rao, and Richard L. Peterson. "The Resiliency of the High-Yield Bond Market: The LTV Default." *Journal of Finance,* September 1989, pp. 1085–1097.

Ryan, Patrick J. "Junk Bonds—Opportunity Knocks?" *Financial Analysts Journal,* May–June 1990, pp. 13–16.

Appendix 16A Simple Equations for Bond Pricing

In this appendix we develop bond valuation formulas that can easily be programmed in a spreadsheet. Since we present bond pricing equations that can be placed in a single cell of a spreadsheet, sensitivity analysis (like the graphs presented in this chapter and the next) can be performed easily.

When we have a bond that never matures (for example, the British Consol or preferred stock), we can employ the *Geometric Series Theorem,*[17] which states that the present value of an infinite stream of $1 payments discounted at y is worth $\$1/y$. That is,

$$P_p = \sum_{t=1}^{\infty} \frac{1}{(1+y)^t} = \frac{1}{y} \qquad (16A.1)$$

where P_p is the price of a perpetual bond or perpetuity (a bond with no maturity), and y is the yield to maturity.

Thus, a perpetuity, which is a security that offers an infinite stream of cash flows (such as preferred stock or consol bonds), is worth the payment amount divided by the yield to maturity.

Using the Geometric Series Theorem, the n period bond pricing equation can be rewritten as[18]

$$P = C \left\{ \frac{1}{y} - \frac{1}{y} \left[\frac{1}{(1+y)^n} \right] \right\} + \frac{Par}{(1+y)^n}$$

Factoring $1/y$, we have

$$P = \frac{C}{y} \left[1 - \frac{1}{(1+y)^n} \right] + \frac{Par}{(1+y)^n} \qquad (16A.2)$$

Using Equation 16A.2 we can compute the bond prices in Table 16.2(a). For example, the price of a $1,000 par, 10% coupon bond with 30 years to maturity when yield to maturity is 12% is

$$P_{30\text{-year, }12\% \text{ yield}} = \frac{\$100}{0.12} \left[1 - \frac{1}{(1+0.12)^{30}} \right] + \frac{\$1,000}{(1+0.12)^{30}}$$

$$= \$833.3333(1 - 0.03338) + \$33.37792 \cong \$838.90$$

17. Formally, the Geometric Series Theorem states

$$\sum_{t=1}^{\infty} ax^t = a\frac{x}{1-x}$$

where $x < 1$. In the case of bonds, $x = 1/(1+y)$.

18. The first summation sign of Eq. 16A.1 can be viewed as two infinite series, one starting today less one starting at period n.

Equation 16A.2 applies to annual coupon bonds at a coupon payment date. Using a similar approach for the more popular semiannual bonds and also finding the price at times other than the coupon payment date, we have the following bond pricing equation.[19]

$$P = \left(1 + \frac{y}{2}\right)^f \left\{ \frac{2C}{y} \left[1 - \frac{1}{\left(1 + \frac{y}{2}\right)^n} \right] + \frac{Par}{\left(1 + \frac{y}{2}\right)^n} \right\} \qquad (16A.3)$$

where

f is the fraction of the semiannual period since the last coupon payment,

n is the number of coupon payments,

C is the semiannual amount of coupon paid, and

y is the annualized yield to maturity.

For example, consider using closing prices observed on October 4, 1994 for the 9% coupon, November 15, 1996, U.S. Treasury notes with ask yield of 6.00% and quoted asked price of 105.27. The coupon is paid semiannually on May 15 and November 15. Thus, we have the following inputs.

$C = \$45$, namely $\frac{1}{2} \cdot 0.09 \cdot \$1{,}000$

$y = 0.06$

$n = 5$, number of coupon payments left from October 4, 1994 up to November 16, 1996

$f = 142/184 \cong .77$, where 142 is the number of days from May 15 through October 4 and 184 is the number of days from May 15 through November 15.

$Par = \$1{,}000$

Working through Equation 16A.3 we have

$$P = \left(1 + \frac{0.06}{2}\right)^{142/184} \left\{ \frac{2 \cdot \$45}{0.06} \left[1 - \frac{1}{\left(1 + \frac{0.06}{2}\right)^5} \right] + \frac{\$1{,}000}{\left(1 + \frac{0.06}{2}\right)^5} \right\}$$

19. Writing Equation 16A.3 in this manner facilitates developing spreadsheet applications because the price of the bond can be input in a single cell of a spreadsheet. The alternative way to express this same price is as given in Equation 16.1. Equation 16.1 cannot be easily programmed into spreadsheets.

$$\cong 1.023074\left[\$1,500\left(1 - \frac{1}{1.159274}\right) + \frac{\$1,000}{1.159274}\right]$$

$$= 1.023074(\$206.0867 + \$862.6088)$$

$$= \$1,093.35$$

APPENDIX PRACTICE

16A.1 Suppose you hold two bonds with the following characteristics:

Bond	C^a	y	f	n	Par
A	$50	10%	0.4	40	$1,000
B	$40	8%	0.4	10	$1,000

a. Recall that C denotes the semiannual coupon amount.

a. Based on Equation 16A.3, calculate the price and accrued interest of each bond.

b. Based on detailed economic forecasts, you anticipate the following four possible scenarios for the next year:

Scenario	Probability	Bond A Yield	Bond B Yield
1	⅛	12%	10%
2	⅜	11%	9%
3	⅜	9%	7%
4	⅛	7%	6%

Calculate the bond prices next year under these scenarios.

c. Compute the rates of return for both bonds under all four scenarios (ignore the interest earned on reinvested coupons).

d. Calculate the mean and standard deviation of these rates of return.

e. Calculate the correlation coefficient between the rates of return on bonds A and B. Would there be any advantage to diversifying? Explain.

16A.2 Consider using closing prices observed on October 4, 1994 for the 9% coupon, November 15, 1996, U.S. Treasury notes with ask yield of 6.00% and quoted asked price of $105.27. Reconcile the reported yield to maturity with the reported price.

16A.3 If the par value is equal to the market value of the bond, the coupon yield (C/Par) must be equal to the IRR on the bond no matter what the maturity is. Do you agree?

Appendix 16B Incorporating Accrued Interest and Partial Periods

In this appendix we illustrate how to calculate the bond price by a variation of Equation 16A.3 and show how accrued interest affects the value of the bond. We also explain the difference between the quoted price of a bond and its value, namely, the amount of cash one has to pay when one buys the bonds.

Suppose that for the popular semiannual bonds we need to price bonds on days other than a coupon payment date; the following bond pricing equation then is required.[20]

20. Equation 16B.1 can be written in a manner that facilitates developing spreadsheet applications because the price of the bond can be input in a single cell of a spreadsheet. See Appendix 16A (Equation 16A.3) for this formulation.

$$P = \sum_{t=1}^{n} \frac{C}{\left(1 + \dfrac{y}{2}\right)^{t-f}} + \frac{Par}{\left(1 + \dfrac{y}{2}\right)^{n-f}} \qquad (16B.1)$$

where

f is the fraction of the semiannual period since the last coupon payment,

n is the number of coupon payments (namely, if we have four years with semiannual coupons, then $n = 8$),

C is the semiannual amount of interest paid, and

y is the annualized yield to maturity.

The factor, f, reflects the fact that two bonds that are entitled to the same future coupons and par value are not priced the same. This can happen if one bond pays its next coupon in a week and the other pays its coupon in five months. Thus, the closer the next coupon the larger f, and the smaller the discount factor the larger the bond price.

Suppose $n = 4$ and we evaluate the bond exactly one second *after* the last coupon was paid. Then $f = 0$ and Equation 16.5 is

$$P = \sum_{t=1}^{4} \frac{C}{\left(1 + \dfrac{y}{2}\right)^{t-0}} + \frac{Par}{\left(1 + \dfrac{y}{2}\right)^{n-0}}$$

Now suppose three months have elapsed and we want to price this bond. Then, since three months is one-half of a half year ($f = \frac{1}{2}$) we get

$$P = \sum_{t=1}^{4} \frac{C}{\left(1 + \dfrac{y}{2}\right)^{t-1/2}} + \frac{Par}{\left(1 + \dfrac{y}{2}\right)^{n-1/2}}$$

Thus, we see that incorporating the fractional periods alters the original formulation in a minor way. Note that for a given number of remaining coupons, the closer we are to the next coupon payment date, the larger the value of f, and, as expected, the price of the bonds goes up since there is less discounting.

Let us illustrate this calculation with a U.S. Treasury note used in Appendix 16A. Consider using closing prices observed on October 4, 1994, for the semiannual 9% coupon note that matures on November 15, 1996. The time line for this bond shows that the last coupon was paid on May 15, 1993, and the next coupon will be paid on November 15, 1993 (see chart at top of page 607).

The yield was 6.00%, and the quoted price was 105.27. The ask yield is the yield to maturity based on the asked price and is reported in the financial press. Thus, we have the following inputs.

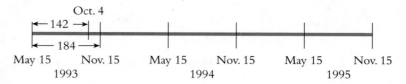

$C = \$45$ namely, $\frac{1}{2}(0.09 \cdot \$1,000)$

$y = 0.06$

$n = 5$, number of coupon payments left

$f = 142/184$, where 142 is the number of days from May 15, 1994, to October 4, 1994, and 184 is the number of days from May 15 through November 15, 1994.

$Par = 1,000$

Working through Equation 16B.1 we have

$$P = \sum_{t=1}^{5} \frac{\$45}{\left(1 + \dfrac{0.06}{2}\right)^{t - 142/184}} + \frac{\$1,000}{\left(1 + \dfrac{0.06}{2}\right)^{5 - 142/184}}$$

$$= \frac{\$45}{\left(1 + \dfrac{0.06}{2}\right)^{1 - 142/184}} + \frac{\$45}{\left(1 + \dfrac{0.06}{2}\right)^{2 - 142/184}} + \frac{\$45}{\left(1 + \dfrac{0.06}{2}\right)^{3 - 142/184}}$$

$$+ \frac{\$45}{\left(1 + \dfrac{0.06}{2}\right)^{4 - 142/184}} + \frac{\$45 + \$1,000}{\left(1 + \dfrac{0.06}{2}\right)^{5 - 142/184}}$$

Calculating the present value of each component, we get

$$P = \$44.6974 + \$43.3955 + \$42.1316 + \$40.9045 + \$922.2256$$

$$= \$1,093.35$$

This is slightly different from what we calculated in Appendix 16.A, due to rounding.

Note that if we made this calculation one second before November 15, 1994, $f = 184/184 = 1$ and $t - f = 1 - 1 = 0$ (when $t = 1$), and we immediately get the $45. On the other hand, if we make the calculation one second after May 15, 1994, $f = 0/182$ and $t - f = 1$ ($n = 4$), and we get a simple discounting with no correction for f.

How do we reconcile this result with the quoted asked price of 105.27 reported in the *Wall Street Journal*? The answer is accrued interest. Bond prices are quoted without accrued interest, whereas the pricing formula incorporates accrued interest. To get the quoted price we have to deduct accrued interest. Accrued interest is found by multiplying the fraction of the semiannual coupon period that has elapsed (f) times the coupon amount (C). Therefore, the quoted price will be as follows.

Quoted Price $= P -$ Accrued Interest

$$= P - f \cdot C$$

$$= \$1,093.35 - [(142/184) \cdot \$45]$$

$$= \$1,093.35 - (0.77 \cdot \$45)$$

$$= \$1,093.35 - 34.65 = \$1,058.70$$

Again, how can we reconcile this with the 105.27 quoted price? Bonds are quoted based on $100 par and in 32nds. Converting the ask quote we have

$$\text{Actual Quoted Price} = 10(105 + 27/32) = \$1,058.44$$

(where 10 is a figure that makes the bonds based on $1,000 par rather than $100 par). The remaining differences are attributed to the rounding of the yield to maturity.

Figure 16B-1 illustrates the effect of accrued interest on the market value of a bond. This pattern has important ramifications to bondholders. The bond value goes up (assuming no other changes) as each semiannual coupon payment approaches (and maturity gets shorter—moving from right to left). The bond value is increasing due to the accruing of interest. In this case, the quoted price remains the same because we assumed no change in interest rates, and bonds are quoted without accrued interest. To avoid the gyrations in price due simply to the accruing of interest, prices are quoted without accrued interest, and thus changes in bond prices better reflect changes in market conditions. When a coupon payment is made, the economic value of the bond declines by the amount of the coupon payment, but the quoted price does not change. When trading bonds, we need to account for both the quoted price as well as accrued interest.

FIGURE 16B-1
The Effect of Accrued Interest on the Market Value of a Bond

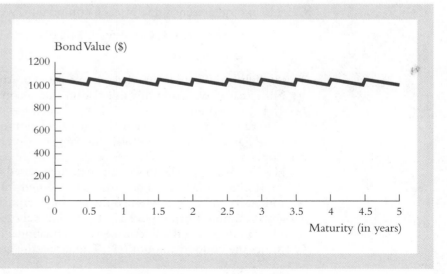

APPENDIX PRACTICE

16B.1 The yield to maturity on a bond is 6%, the maturity is five years, and it has a par value of $1,000. If the current market price of the bond is $900, what is the annual coupon, C?

Appendix 16C Methods of Compounding Interest Rates

Suppose one bank tells you that you can borrow at 10% a year compounded annually and another bank lends to you at 9.5% compounded quarterly. Which bank offers you a better deal? The different methods used to compute interest and quote bond prices make bond management difficult. At one time you probably thought computing interest was straightforward. Interest is just equal to the principal or initial price (P) times the interest rate (R) times the time (t). That is, **simple interest** (*Int*) is calculated as follows:

$$Int = P \cdot R \cdot t$$

For example, if you borrow $10,000 at 8% for two years, do you have to pay $Int = $10,000 \cdot 0.08 \cdot 2 = $1,600$ in interest? If the lender agrees to be paid by the simple interest method then you pay $1,600 in interest; the total loan amount to be repaid is $11,600 ($10,000 borrowed + $1,600 interest).

If the lender specified that interest is compounded annually, then the loan amount or Par value (*Par*) to be repaid is

$$Par = P(1 + R)^t = $10,000(1 + 0.08)^2 = $11,664$$

Notice in this case you have to pay an additional $64 ($11,664 − $11,600) in interest due to compounding (for a review of compounding, see Appendix 1A). In effect, the $64 is the interest earned in the second year on the $800 interest payment made at the end of the first year.

If the lender specified multiple compounding within one year, then the loan amount to be repaid is

$$Par = P\left(1 + \frac{R}{n_p}\right)^{t \cdot n_p}$$

where n_p is the number of compounding periods within one year. For example, using the data above for the two-year loan, if the compound frequency is monthly, then the loan amount to be repaid is

$$Par = $10,000\left(1 + \frac{0.08}{12}\right)^{2 \cdot 12} = $11,729$$

Unfortunately, the differences in compounding methods are not the only characteristics separating the various methods actually employed in practice. Exhibit 16C-1 provides a brief summary of the most common compounding methods.

EXHIBIT 16C-1   Different Compounding Methods Used in the Bond Market

Compound Method[a]	Pricing Equation[b]	Securities Using This Method
Discount (d)	$P = Par_d \left(1 - \dfrac{dt}{360} \right)$	U.S. Treasury bills
Add-on or Money Market (m)	$P = \dfrac{Par_m}{1 + \dfrac{mt}{360}}$	Eurodollar CDs
Bond equivalent (r)	$P = \dfrac{Par_r}{1 + \dfrac{rt}{365}}$	Makes discount or add-on rate comparable to semiannual rates
Annual (a)	$P = \dfrac{Par_a}{[1 + a]^{t/365}}$	Not widely used outside of academia
Semiannual (y)	$P = \dfrac{Par_y}{\left(1 + \dfrac{y}{2} \right)^{2t/365}}$	U.S. Treasury bonds, corporate bonds
Daily[c] (b)	$P = \dfrac{Par_b}{\left(1 + \dfrac{b}{365} \right)^{t}}$	Bank securities and mortgages
Continuous (c)	$P = Par_c \cdot e^{-c(t/365)}$	Bank securities like CDs are used with options

a. The letters in parentheses denote the interest rate, which is expressed in decimal terms.

b. P represents the current price or the amount of the original loan, Par represents the Par value of the bond or the amount that has to be paid back at the end of the period (the subscript just denotes the compounding method), t is the number of calendar days in the loan period, and d, m, r, a, y, b, and c all represent quoted interest rates by various methods.

c. Sometimes 360 is used instead of 365.

Source: Based, in part, on Miles Livingston, *Money & Capital Markets Financial Instruments & Their Uses.* (Englewood Cliffs, NJ: Prentice Hall, 1990), p. 201.

Clearly, in order to compare the various rates quoted on different bonds, you must know which compounding method is being used.

For example, suppose you wanted to invest $50,000 for six months (more specifically, 182 days) in a safe investment. A previously issued U.S. Treasury bond with six months to maturity is offering 6% semiannual yield. A bank offers a 6%, six-month CD where interest is compounded daily on a 360-day basis. Which would you prefer, ignoring your preferences for cash flow and transaction costs?

From Exhibit 16C-1, we know the compound method for U.S. Treasury bonds is semiannual yield (y), and for daily, 360-day CDs is the daily yield (denoted by b) with 360 rather than 365. Because we assume that the initial investment is the same, the security prices, P, are the same for all expressions. Hence, the appropriate pricing equations are

$$P = \frac{Par_y}{\left(1 + \dfrac{y}{2}\right)^{2t/365}} \qquad \text{Treasury bond}$$

$$P = \frac{Par_b}{\left(1 + \dfrac{b}{360}\right)^{t}} \qquad \text{360-day CDs}$$

Since we invested \$50,000 in both contracts in this example, our preference will depend on which security will have the largest payoff at the end. Restating both equations in terms of par value and recalling that these are six-month securities ($t = 182$), we have

$$Par_y = P\left(1 + \frac{y}{2}\right)^{2t/365} \qquad \text{Treasury bond}$$

$$Par_b = \left(1 + \frac{b}{360}\right)^{t} \qquad \text{360-day CDs}$$

where

Par_y is the amount paid back at the end of the period with semiannual compounding,

Par_b is the amount paid back at the end of the period with compounding on a daily basis with a 360-day year,

P is the price paid today,

y is the semiannual compounding interest rate, and

b is the compounding on a daily basis with a 360-day year.

In our example, $y = b$ and is 6%. Computing the future value of these two investments, we have

$$Par_y = \$50,000\left(1 + \frac{0.06}{2}\right)^{2 \cdot 182/365} = \$51,496$$

$$Par_b = \$50,000\left(1 + \frac{0.06}{360}\right)^{182} = \$51,540$$

Thus, although the quoted rates are the same, the proceeds from the investment in the bank CD are \$44 higher, indicating a clear preference for the bank CD. We see that the quoted interest rate must be accompanied by a statement regarding how interest is being compounded, or else the rate is not precise.

APPENDIX PRACTICE

16C.1 There are many different ways to quote interest rates. Suppose you were quoted a rate of 7% on an add-on basis (or money market yield) for a 30-day security. What is the bond equivalent yield for this security?

16C.2 U.S. Treasury bills are quoted on a discount basis. A 180-day bill is offering a discount yield of 4.1%. What is the comparable semiannual yield?

CHAPTER 17

BONDS—ANALYSIS AND MANAGEMENT

BOND'S DURATION IS HANDY GUIDE ON RATES

Suppose you buy a 10-year Treasury note today at a yield to maturity of 6%, and interest rates shoot up to 8%. What happens to your investment?

A. You lose money.
B. You make money.
C. Nothing happens.
D. All of the above.

The answer: D. All of the above.

How is that possible? The trick is how long you hold the investment.

In the short run, you lose money. Since interest rates and bond prices move inversely to one another, higher rates mean the value of your bond investment withers when rates go up. For a 10-year Treasury yielding 6%, a two percentage-point rise in rates would cause the value of your principal to sink by roughly 14%, according to Capital Management Sciences, a bond research company.

However, if you hold the note, rather than selling it, you'll get to reinvest the interest received from it at the new, higher 8% rate. Over time, this higher "interest on interest" adds up, allowing you not only to offset your initial loss of principal but also to profit more than if rates had never moved at all.

Over 10 years, for instance, a Treasury note with an initial yield of 6% would produce a total return—price change plus interest—of 6.5% a year if you could reinvest the interest payments at 8%, according to Capital Management Sciences. That compares with an average return of 6% if rates remain unchanged. If rates dropped, so that the reinvestment rate declined to 4%, the 10-year return would average just 5.5% a year.

Perhaps the best way to judge a bond's interest-rate sensitivity is to get a handle on its "duration." Duration is one measure of a bond's life. It's that sweet spot, somewhere between the short term and the long term, where a bond's return remains practically unchanged, no matter what happens to interest rates.

Source: Barbara Donnelly Granito, "Bond's Duration Is Handy Guide on Rates," *Wall Street Journal,* April 19, 1993, p. C1. Reprinted by permission of *The Wall Street Journal,* © 1993 Dow Jones & Co., Inc. All Rights Reserved Worldwide.

LEARNING OBJECTIVES

After studying this chapter you should be able to:

1. List the basic principles of bond pricing.

2. Explain how duration is used to minimize interest rate risk.

3. Explain how immunization techniques protect bond portfolios from interest rate risk.

4. Describe active bond management strategies.

After reading Chapter 16, you might have answered "A" to the question posed by Granito in this chapter's Investments in the News, yet she explains that the other answers are also possible. The goal of this chapter is to analyze the risk associated with changes in the interest rate and to find out how investors can develop strategies to minimize interest rate risk—the risk faced by a bond investor when market interest rates change. The investigation begins with a look at basic factors that influence bond prices. The fundamental properties of bond price behavior are called *bond pricing principles*. The bond pricing principles are used to explain convexity and duration (more advanced tools in interest rate risk management) and to build effective bond portfolios.

17.1 BOND PRICING PRINCIPLES

This chapter's investigation of bond pricing principles begins with the basic bond pricing equation. The price of a bond is the present value of all future coupon payments plus the par value discounted to the present at the required rate of return. Therefore, the price of a bond can be expressed as follows:

$$P = \sum_{t=1}^{n} \frac{C}{(1 + y)^t} + \frac{Par}{(1 + y)^n} \qquad (17.1)$$

where n is the number of coupon payments left, C is the coupon paid each period, and y is the *periodic* yield to maturity. (For example, if this is a semiannual bond with a yield to maturity of 10%, then $y = 5\%$.) Equation 17.1 can be used to identify specific relationships among the factors that determine bond prices. These bond pricing principles will be used to develop more advanced tools used in interest rate risk management.

17.1.1 Principle 1: Bond Prices
Change with the Passage of Time

The first bond pricing principle is that the price of a bond—not just its quoted price but also its value including accrued interest—changes with the passage of time. That is, bond prices change as the number of coupon payments left (n) changes. Exhibit 17-1 illustrates the change in bond price that occurs with three different assumed yields to maturity. All three bonds are characterized by a 10% semiannual coupon rate, $1,000 par value with 20 years to maturity. For simplicity, assume the yield to maturity does not change over the 20-year period.

These bonds differ in their yield to maturity; they have 8%, 10%, and 12% yields to maturity. These various yields could be due to differences in risk. The 10% yield bond is the essentially flat line at the par value. This bond's price moves up because of the accruing of interest. At a coupon payment date, the price drops back to $1,000. When a bond has a coupon rate of 10% and a yield to maturity of only 8%,

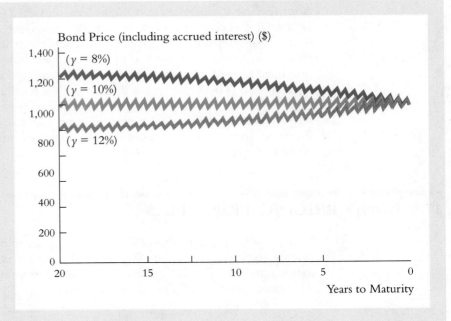

it trades at a premium above par, because the coupon rate is higher than the yield to maturity. That is, the price is greater than the par value. As time to maturity becomes shorter, there are fewer coupon payments to be paid, and the premium declines. Indeed, this bond's price drifts downward over time, and it is redeemed at the par value. Similarly, a bond trading at a discount (when $C = 10\%$ and $y = 12\%$) drifts upward over time. Hence, bond prices change with the passage of time. Of course, the 10% yield, 10% coupon-paying bond has a par value equal to the bond price; the price drifts neither upward nor downward, hence is flat, apart from the small spikes reflecting the accruing of interest.

Investors analyzing a particular bond must assess the trade-off between a bond's current price and its coupon rate. Premium bonds with high coupon rates experience declining prices in the future, whereas discount bonds with low coupon rates experience rising prices in the future. Neither kind of bond is always preferred; rather, the best bond depends on an investor's holding period and expectations regarding the future direction of interest rates.

17.1.2 Principle 2: Bond Prices Are Inversely Related to the Yield to Maturity

After a bond is issued, the interest rate in the economy may change (for example, because of a change in the rate of inflation), and thus the yield on bonds changes. As discussed in Chapter 16, for a given coupon rate, bond prices are inversely related to the yield to maturity. Exhibit 17-2 illustrates this relationship for a $1,000 par bond having a 20-year length to maturity and a 10% semiannual coupon rate. The resulting curve is convex—that is, it is curved away from the origin. As yields to maturity fall below 10%, the price rises at an increasing rate; as yields to maturity rise above 10%, the price falls at a decreasing rate.

The data in Exhibit 17-3 also show the convex relationship graphed in Exhibit 17-2. Consider the data for a bond with 20 years to maturity. Notice that the decline in the bond price becomes smaller for each 2.5% incremental increase in the yield. For example, when the yield rises from 5% to 7.5%, the price falls by $371 ($1,628 − $1,257). However, when the yield rises from 12.5% to 15%, the price falls only $133 ($818 − $685). The explanation for this result is that the percentage change in interest rates from 5% to 7.5% (a 50% increase) is much greater than the percentage increase from 12.5% to 15% (a 20% increase). Thus, the price-yield relationship is convex—i.e., it has the kind of curve shown in Exhibit 17.2.

17.1.3 Principle 3: The Longer the Maturity, the More Sensitive the Bond's Price to Changes in the Yield to Maturity

The relationship between bond prices and changes in yield to maturity is different for various bond maturities. Specifically, for a given coupon at a given yield to maturity,

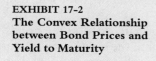

EXHIBIT 17-2
The Convex Relationship between Bond Prices and Yield to Maturity

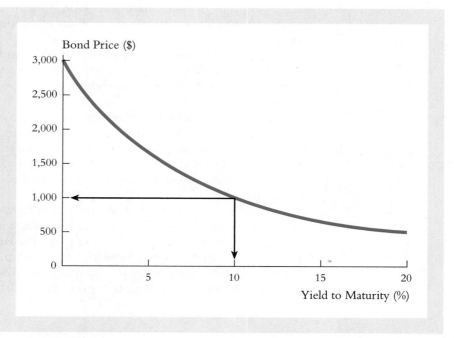

		Yield to Maturity				
Years to Maturity		**5%**	**7.5%**	**10%**	**12.5%**	**15%**
1		$1,048	$1,024	$1,000	$977	$955
2		1,094	1,046	1,000	957	916
3		1,138	1,066	1,000	939	883
4		1,179	1,085	1,000	923	854
5		1,219	1,103	1,000	909	828
10		1,390	1,174	1,000	859	745
15		1,523	1,223	1,000	832	705
20		**1,628**	**1,257**	**1,000**	**818**	**685**
25		1,709	1,280	1,000	810	676
30		1,773	1,297	1,000	805	671
∞		2,000	1,333	1,000	800	667

EXHIBIT 17-3 Bond Prices for Different Maturities and Yields to Maturity

the prices of longer-maturity bonds are more sensitive than the prices of short-maturity bonds to changes in the yield to maturity.[1] Exhibit 17-4 illustrates the differences in price for bonds having 10-year, 20-year, and 30-year maturities. (Here $n = 20$, 40, and 60, where n is the number of coupon payments with semiannual coupons.)

Notice that all three bonds trade at par (the coupon rate on all three bonds is 10%) when the yield to maturity is 10%. Thus, we assume the coupon rate is constant and consider the effect of different maturities (n) for changing yields to maturity. As yields change in either direction from $y = 10\%$, the 30-year ($n = 60$) bond's price experiences the largest price change. In contrast, the 10-year ($n = 20$) bond experiences the least amount of price change. Notice in Exhibit 17-3 that when the yield falls from 10% to 5%, the price of the 30-year bond rises to $1,773, whereas the price of the 10-year bond rises to only $1,390. We can conclude that short-term bonds are less volatile than long-term bonds for equivalent changes in yield to maturity.

The explanation for the shape of the lines in Exhibit 17-4 is straightforward: the longer an investor is locked in a contract (the bond's maturity) that pays, say, 10% a year when the market interest rate is only 8%, the larger the gain in present value terms (the price of the bond). Similarly, the longer the investor is locked in a contract that pays 10% when the market interest rate is 12%, the larger the loss. This explains the effect of the bond's maturity on its price demonstrated in Exhibit 17-4.

1. This is true as long as the coupon is unchanged. If two bonds have different coupons, their duration rather than their maturity measures the sensitivity of the bonds' price to changes in the interest rate. See the discussion later in the chapter.

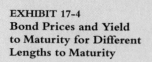

EXHIBIT 17-4
Bond Prices and Yield to Maturity for Different Lengths to Maturity

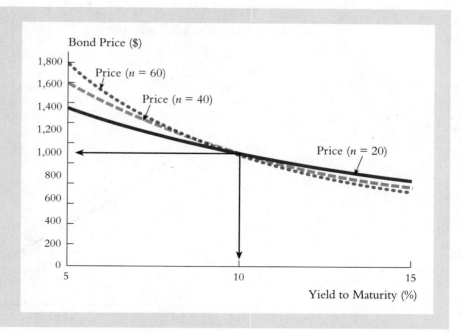

PRACTICE BOX

Problem

Suppose you have a bond with $n = 10$ years to maturity that pays an annual coupon of $100 every year. The bond's price is $1,000, and the par value is $1,000. Determine the bond's price for the following changes in yield to maturity: +2.5%, +5.0%, +7.5%, −2.5%, −5.0%, and −7.5%. Draw the price-yield relationship. Is it convex?

Solution:

Using Equation 17.1, the following bond prices can be determined when $n = 10$, $Par = \$1,000$, and $C = \$100$:

Yield to Maturity	Price
2.5%	$1,656.40
5.0	1,386.09
7.5	1,171.60
10.0	1,000.00
12.5	861.59
15.0	749.06
17.5	656.87

(continued)

The price-yield relationship is as follows:

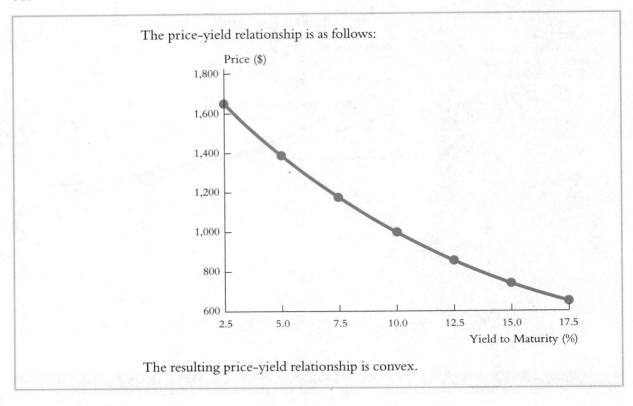

The resulting price-yield relationship is convex.

17.1.4 Principle 4: The Sensitivity of the Price of a Bond to Changes in the Yield to Maturity Increases at a Decreasing Rate with the Length to Maturity

Although longer-term bonds are more sensitive to changes in yield to maturity, this sensitivity declines for longer maturities. Exhibit 17-5 compares the price difference between 5-year and 10-year bonds with the price difference between 25-year and 30-year bonds for various yields to maturity. Initially the bonds had 10% yields. Now check the price difference of two bonds when the interest rates change (Exhibit 17-3). Note that the price difference between a 5-year bond and a 10-year bond, with a yield to maturity of 15%, is $83 ($828 − $745), whereas the price difference between a 25-year bond and a 30-year bond is only $5 ($676 − $671). Notice that when moving from a 30-year bond to a perpetuity, the price difference for a 5% yield to maturity is $227 ($2,000 − $1,773), whereas when moving from a 1-year bond to a 10-year bond, the price difference is $342 ($1,390 − $1,048). In Exhibit 17-5, the black line represents the price *difference* between 10% coupon bonds that have 5 and 10 years to maturity—namely, $P(\text{10-year}) - P(\text{5-year})$. The colored line represents the price difference between 10% coupon bonds that have 25 and 30 years to maturity: $P(\text{30-year}) - P(\text{25-year})$. Thus, the price difference is much more sensitive to changes in yield to maturity for shorter-term bonds.

EXHIBIT 17-5
Difference between Bond Prices for Different Yields to Maturity for Bonds of Different Maturities

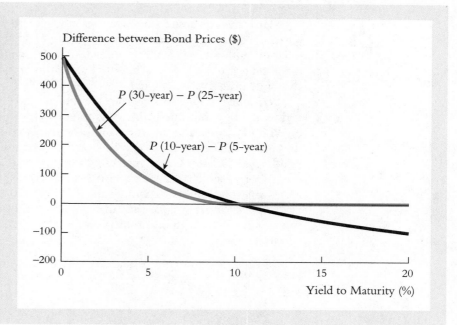

What can we learn from this pattern? Suppose that you are considering investing in either relatively short-term bonds (5 to 10 years to maturity) or long-term bonds (25 to 30 years to maturity). You expect changes in the interest rate, but you are uncertain of the direction of the changes. It is recommended that you devote more analysis to whether to invest in 5-year or 10-year bonds than to 25-year bonds or 30-year bonds (see Exhibit 17-5). The reason is that any error in your decision has a greater impact for relatively short horizons. Connecting Theory to Practice 17.1 describes an investor's assessment of time to maturity with an analysis of the Tennessee Valley Authority's (TVA's) decision to make an initial public offering of 50-year bonds. The article gives the TVA's prediction of how investors will compare 50-year bonds with 30-year bonds. William Gross's response illustrates his knowledge of this bond pricing principle.

CONNECTING THEORY TO PRACTICE 17.1

TVA IS MULLING SALE OF 50-YEAR BONDS

NEW YORK—The Tennessee Valley Authority [TVA], the big federally owned electric utility, said yesterday it is considering selling $1 billion of 50-year bonds. It would be the first 50-year bond issue in decades, traders said.

But will anyone want to buy a 50-year bond?

(continued)

Many analysts aren't sure whether a 50-year bond has much of a market when the federal government is running big budget deficits and the long-term inflation outlook is difficult to predict. One lingering fear in the market is that the deficit, projected to reach $400 billion this year, will one day lead to runaway inflation.

Yet some big investors say they are intrigued by the idea of a 50-year bond and would buy the issue if the price was right.

"I don't know why anyone would want a 50-year bond unless it provided a substantial amount of extra yield" when compared with 30-year Treasury bonds, said William Gross, managing director of Pacific Investment Management Corp., which manages $35 billion in bonds, mostly for pension funds. Mr. Gross concedes that although the price of a 50-year bond probably would not be much more volatile than that of a 30-year bond, he nevertheless would want to get paid for the extra interest-rate risk of owning a security with such a long maturity.

Source: Constance Mitchell and Terence Donnelly, "TVA Is Mulling Sale of 50-Year Bonds," *Wall Street Journal*, March 27, 1992, p. C1. Reprinted by permission of *The Wall Street Journal*, © 1992 Dow Jones & Co., Inc. All Rights Reserved Worldwide.

MAKING THE CONNECTION

In 1992, long-term interest rates were fairly low. Thus, the TVA believed it was a good time to raise $1 billion in capital with a debt issue. Normally, organizations like the TVA would issue 30-year bonds, and investors would require a yield to maturity slightly above the 30-year U.S. Treasury rate. The TVA, thinking that rates would probably never be this low again, wanted to issue 50-year bonds instead.

From the bond pricing principle on the relationship of price to time to maturity, we know that the price behavior of a 50-year bond will be very similar to that of a 30-year bond. Because the risk of 50-year bonds is not that much greater than the risk of 30-year bonds, the additional yield demanded by investors may not be very great. Although these bonds may not be appealing to some investors, such as William Gross, other investors, such as life insurance companies, may find 50-year bonds attractive.

It turns out that these bonds were issued easily and were very popular with investors. Hence, the TVA was able to extend the maturity of a $1 billion issue by 20 years without having to offer much of an additional yield.

17.1.5 Principle 5: There Is a Linear Relationship Between a Bond's Coupon Rate and Its Price

A bond price can be formulated as a line in relation to the bond's coupon payment. As will be described below, this linear relationship is useful in creating a portfolio of bonds and in taking advantage of arbitrage opportunities in the bond market. Equation 17.1 can be rearranged to express the bond price as a linear function of the coupon payment:

$$P = aC + b \qquad (17.2)$$

where

$$a = \sum_{t=1}^{n} \frac{1}{(1 + y)^t}$$

and

$$b = \frac{Par}{(1 + y)^n}$$

Equation 17.2 shows that there is a *linear* relationship between the bond's price and its coupon rate. Assuming a par value of $1,000 (which is common), the parameters a and b of the straight line given in Equation 17.2 are functions of the yield (y) and the number of years (n). Suppose we have two bonds with the same length to maturity (n) and yield to maturity (y) but different coupon rates. We can determine that the larger the coupon (C), the larger the bond price. For example, the prices of two bonds having the same length to maturity and the same yield to maturity but with coupons C_1 and C_2 will be P_1 and P_2. Exhibit 17-6 illustrates the relationship between price and coupon for bonds with the same yield and maturity. For

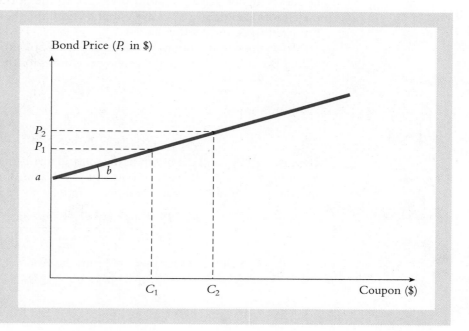

EXHIBIT 17-6
The Linear Relationship between Bond Price and Coupon

given data on y and n, you can plot the line directly by calculating the values of a and b. Moreover, by moving along the line and changing the coupon, you can find any bond price as long as y and n remain unchanged.

PRACTICE BOX

Problem

Suppose you are monitoring the U.S. Treasury bond market, and you notice the following information about three bonds with identical maturities. The par value of the three bonds is $1,000.

Bond	Coupon (%)	Yield to Maturity (%)
A	3	5
B	5	4.5
C	7	5

Are there opportunities for arbitrage profits?

Solution

Note that Bonds A and C have the same yield to maturity. This observation can be used to identify opportunities for arbitrage profits as long as these yields to maturity are available. Because the yield to maturity of Bonds A and C is 5%, any combination of the two still yields 5%. If we can create a portfolio from Bonds A and C that provides the same coupon as Bond B, we can profit by short selling Bond B and buying the portfolio of bonds, because the future cash flows are the same (the same coupon and par value). Also, the yield of Bond B is lower, which implies a higher price for Bond B relative to the portfolio, and hence the arbitrage profit. Namely, we get more money from the short sale than what we need for investing in the portfolio.

To elaborate, suppose we consider investing 50% in Bonds A and C and short selling Bond B. We denote the pricing equations for these bonds as follows:

$$P_A = a_A C_A + b_A$$
$$P_B = a_B C_B + b_B$$
$$P_C = a_C C_C + b_C$$

Because $y_A = y_C$ and the bonds have identical maturities, we know that $a = a_A = a_C$ and $b = b_A = b_C$. If we invest 50% ($w_A = 0.5$) in Bond A and 50% ($w_C = 0.5$) in Bond C, the value of the bond portfolio is

$$P = \underline{w_A \cdot P_A + w_C \cdot P_C} = \underline{w_A \cdot a_A \cdot C_A + w_C \cdot a_C \cdot C_C + w_A \cdot b_A + w_C \cdot b_C}$$

$$\downarrow \qquad\qquad\qquad\qquad \downarrow$$

Value of Investment = From the Above Linear Equations

(continued)

Therefore,

$$P = a(w_A \cdot C_A + w_C \cdot C_C) + b(w_A + w_C)$$

Because $w_A + w_C = 1$ and $w_A \cdot C_A + w_C \cdot C_C = 0.5 \cdot 3\% + 0.5 \cdot 7\% = 5\%$, we have "synthetically" created a 5% coupon bond (or portfolio of bonds) with a yield to maturity of 5% (recall that both bonds initially had 5% yields to maturity). Bond B has the same coupon rate as the portfolio, but a lower yield to maturity of 4.5%. Thus, Bond B will sell at a higher price. If we short sell Bond B and use the proceeds to buy the portfolio previously described, we will capture the difference in prices between Bond B and the portfolio. The gain from the arbitrage will depend on the maturity of the bonds. (If we assume 10-year bonds, then the gain will be $40. The $40 gain reflects the price of a 4.5% yield bond minus the price of a 5% yield bond, i.e., $1,040 − $1,000.) At the same time, all future cash flows required from short selling Bond B will be provided by the portfolio (the 5% coupon payments and the par value). Thus, the net future cash flow is zero at all dates, and the current cash flow is positive, which implies that an arbitrage profit is feasible. In equilibrium, this profit will vanish, because the price of Bond B will fall, and the price of Bonds A and C will rise. However, quick investors can benefit from a temporary disequilibrium in the bond market.

Note that we decided to invest 50% in Bond A and 50% in Bond C, thus making the average coupon rate 5%, the same as with Bond B. If Bond C had had a coupon rate of 8%, we would have had to invest different proportions in Bonds A and C to get 5%. Specifically, we would have to solve

$$5\% = w_C \cdot 8\% + (1 - w_C)3\%$$

which works out to be an investment of 40% in Bond C and 60% in Bond A. Thus, in this case there is an opportunity for arbitrage profits.

Exhibit 17-7 presents a numerical example demonstrating the relationship between the percentage change in the bond price and the change in the yield to maturity for various coupon levels. The percentage change in the bond's price for given changes in yield is lower for higher-coupon bonds. For example, for the 5% coupon bond, when the yield to maturity falls from 5% to 0%, the percentage change is 100% [($2,000 − $1,000)/$1,000]. Recall that for a 5% coupon, 20-year bond, you receive $50 · 20 = $1,000 in coupon payments. Hence, with 0% yields, the price of the bond is $2,000 ($1,000 interest plus the $1,000 par value). For a 15% coupon bond, the percentage bond change is 77% for the same change in the yield from 5% to 0%.

Thus, if you were anticipating a decline in interest rates, you would buy lower-coupon bonds. (Compare any given line in the table.) The reason for this decision is that for lower-coupon bonds, you receive your payments further in the future, and changes in interest rates will have a greater impact. Alternatively, for higher coupon rates you are "paid back" sooner, and hence changes in rates do not have as great an impact.

EXHIBIT 17-7		Coupon Rate					
The Effect of Changes in Yield to Maturity for Different Coupon Levels for 20-Year, Semiannual Bonds		5%		10%		15%	
	Annual Yield to Maturity	Price	Change[a]	Price	Change[a]	Price	Change[a]
	0	$2,000	100%	$3,000	84%	$4,000	77%
	5	1,000	75	1,628	63	2,255	58
	10	571	54	1,000	46	1,429	43
	15	370	39	685	34	1,000	32
	20	267		511		756	

a. *Change* means the percentage change in the price for a given change in the yield to maturity. Thus, the percentage figures correspond to a decline from 20% yield to 15% yield, then to a decline from 15% to 10%, and so on. Because we start with a 20% yield, all percentage changes are positive.

In summary, bond prices change just with the passage of time; that is, they "drift" toward their par value. Bond prices also are inversely related to changes in interest rates, and this relationship is more pronounced for longer maturities. However, the percentage change in bond prices in response to changes in yields declines for longer and longer maturities. Bond prices are also linearly related to coupon rates, which allows for arbitrage trading and the synthetic creation of the coupon an investor desires. Of course, in equilibrium the arbitrage profit vanishes. Finally, the higher the coupon rates, the less sensitive the bond is to changes in yield to maturity.

Hence, if we forecast a decline in overall yields, we will first want to move into long-term bonds, because their prices appreciate more than short-term bonds. We will want long-term bonds in order to experience greater appreciation. In addition, we will want to invest in low-coupon bonds—perhaps synthetically creating the coupon level we desire—because the lower the coupon rate, the higher the capital gain on bonds due to a decrease in the interest rate.

17.2 DURATION AND CONVEXITY

Duration and convexity are useful tools in the process of managing interest rate risk. These advanced interest rate risk management tools are based on the various bond pricing principles discussed in the previous section.

A bond's risk stems mainly from possible changes in interest rates. Bond portfolios' duration corresponds to the investment holding period at which the bond portfolio's interest risk is minimized. Is there a way to reduce or eliminate this interest-rate risk? To answer this question, let's look at the impact of a change in bond price when interest rates rise.

An increase in interest rates reduces the price of a bond, a phenomenon known as the **price effect.** However, when interest rates rise, investors can make more money on the new opportunities offering a higher interest rate. Investors who own a coupon bond can reinvest the coupon payments at a higher rate even though the bond's price falls. Thus, a rise in the interest rate results in a higher reinvestment rate for the coupon payments, a phenomenon known as the **reinvestment effect.** (This reinvestment effect does not exist for zero-coupon bonds.) In contrast, a fall in interest rates causes bond prices to rise. Reinvestment opportunities offer less attractive rates. In this case, the price and reinvestment effects have the opposite effect on bond investments than they do when market interest rates rise.

The holding period determines whether the price effect is greater than the reinvestment effect, regardless of the direction of the change in market interest rates. An investor who plans to hold the bond for only one day would be concerned exclusively with the price effect. For a one-day holding period, the investor does not reinvest any cash flow and therefore does not gain or lose from the reinvestment effect. However, if an investor plans to hold the bond until it matures, then only the reinvestment effect matters. The higher the coupon rate, the greater the reinvestment effect. (Because the investor will receive the par value of the bonds at maturity, assuming no default risk, there is no concern about the path the price takes to maturity, and the investor is concerned solely with the reinvestment of the coupons.) Finally, if an investor holds the bond until it matures and it pays no coupon, the investor is not concerned with either the price effect or the reinvestment effect. Thus, the planned holding period and the bond's dispersion of future cash flows are crucial in measuring the effect of changes in the interest rate.

To illustrate how to evaluate price and reinvestment effects, suppose you purchase a four-year annual coupon bond that pays $100 each year, has a yield to maturity of 10%, and has a par value of $1,000. Because the coupon rate equals the yield to maturity, you know the bond is currently trading at $1,000. Suppose interest rates immediately jump to 12% after you purchase the bond. Are you glad or disappointed? If your holding period is only a day, you will be disappointed, because the price will fall to $939.25—a loss of about 6.1%. If you hold the bond for two years (and rates do not change again), then your $1,000 investment will be worth $100 coupon payment at the end of Year 2 plus $100(1 + 0.12) = $112 for the coupon payment paid at the end of the first year (reinvested at 12% for one year) plus $966 (the price of a two-year, 10% coupon bond with a 12% yield). The total value of the bond holding at the end of the second year is thus $1,178 ($100 + $112 + $966), for an annualized rate of return of 8.5%[($1,178/$1,000)$^{1/2}$ − 1]. If you hold the bond for four years, at the end of the fourth year the bond holdings will be worth

$$\$1,000 + 100 + \$100 \cdot (1 + 0.12) + \$100 \cdot (1 + 0.12)^2$$
$$+ \$100 \cdot (1 + 0.12)^3 = \$1,477.90$$

The annualized rate of return is 10.26% [($1,477.93/$1,000)$^{1/4}$ − 1], which exceeds the original 10% yield. Here we see the benefits of the additional interest with no loss due to the increase in interest rate.

Thus, for a one-day holding period, you are worse off. For a four-year holding period, you are better off. The opposite is true if interest rates decline rather than increase. Because you do not know in advance the direction of the changes in the interest rate, you are exposed to interest rate risk. Can you eliminate this risk? Yes, you can. Somewhere between a holding period of one day and a holding period of the maturity of the bond, you would intuitively anticipate a holding period where the price effect and the reinvestment effect just offset one another. At this holding period, you should have little, if any, interest rate risk. When rates rise, you benefit enough from the reinvestment effect to just offset the cost encountered from the price effect, provided that indeed you hold the bonds for a predetermined period.

Let us examine the offsetting of price and reinvestment effects with an example. Exhibit 17-8a lists information about three default-free bonds. The yield curve is upward sloping, because the yield of the shortest-maturity bond (Bond A) is less than the yield of the middle-maturity bond (Bond B), which is less than the yield of the lowest-maturity bond (Bond C); $y_A < y_B < y_C$.

Suppose you have money to invest, and you definitely know that you will need the money back in exactly 4 years. What is relevant for you is the final change in your wealth at the end of 4 years. This is crucial in selecting your investment strategy. If you select Bond A, you incur considerable reinvestment risk; this bond matures in 1 year, and you will have to reinvest the cash available at the end of the first year in another bond at an unknown rate. (For simplicity, assume that you reinvest in 1-year bonds three times.) If you select Bond C, which has a 10-year maturity, you incur considerable price risk, because you will have to sell the bond after 4 years. The price at the end of 4 years is greatly affected by the prevailing interest rates at that time (this bond will have 6 years left to maturity). What about Bond B? In 4 years, Bond B will have only 1 year left to maturity, so it will have some price risk. However, you have 4 years in which to incur reinvestment risk. Recall that these risks have offsetting effects.[2]

Exhibit 17-8b contains the annual holding period rates of return (compounded semiannually) for these three bonds under three different scenarios. Assume that the yield curve either immediately shifts down by 3%, stays the same, or immediately shifts up by 3% (see Column 1). A 3% shift down means that Bond A now has a yield to maturity of 6% (9% − 3%). Also examine three alternate holding periods: 1 year, 4 years, and 7 years. The yield curve shift is assumed to be immediate and permanent. Also, assume that the coupons received are reinvested in the identical yield to maturity of the bond prevailing when the coupons are received. That is, coupons from the 10-year bond are reinvested in the same 10-year bond.[3]

Exhibit 17-9 gives the detailed calculations of one cell in Exhibit 17-8; it calculates the rate of return of about 10.7% for Bond B when rates fall by 3%.

---

2. Exhibit 17–8 assumes that interest rates change only once—immediately after the bond is purchased. In practice, interest rates change every day. However, this type of analysis remains very helpful, and it is widely used.

3. For simplicity, ignore any potential changes that may occur as the bond's maturity shortens. That is, assume that the initial yield to maturity is earned over the life of the bond.

EXHIBIT 17-8
Illustration of Duration and Its Impact on a Bond's Volatility

Part a: Parameters of Three Semiannual, Default-Free, $1,000 Par Bonds

Bond	Coupon Rate	Yield to Maturity	Years to Maturity	Market Price
A	9%	9%	1	$1,000
B	10.68	10.68	5	1,000
C	11	11	10	1,000

Part b: Annualized Holding Period Annual Rates of Return

		Holding Period		
Yield to Maturity	Bond	1 Year	4 Years	7 Years
	A	8.94%	6.73%	6.42%
Decline of 3%	B	20.05	10.705	9.40
	C	28.22	12.88	10.77
	A	9.00	9.00	9.00
No change	B	10.68	10.68	10.68
	C	11.00	11.00	11.00
	A	9.06	11.26	11.58
Rise of 3%	B	2.02	10.704	11.97
	C	−3.74	9.42	11.37

Part c: Mean and Standard Deviation of Annual Rate of Return, Assuming Each Scenario Is Equally Likely

		Holding Period		
	Bond	1 Year	4 Years	7 Years
	A	9.00%[a]	9.00%	9.00%
Mean	B	10.92	10.70	10.69
	C	11.83	11.10	11.05
	A	0.05[b]	1.85	2.11
Standard deviation	B	7.36	0.01	1.05
	C	13.06	1.41	0.25

a. The mean for Bond A is ⅓(8.94%) + ⅓(9.00%) + ⅓(9.06%) = 9.00%.

b. The variance for Bond A is ⅓(8.94% − 9.00%)² + ⅓(9.00% − 9.00%)² + ⅓(9.06% − 9.00%)² = 0.0024; the standard deviation is $(0.0024)^{1/2} \cong 0.05\%$.

| EXHIBIT 17-9 | | Illustration of the Rate-of-Return Calculation for the 10.68% Coupon Bond Held for 4 Years with a Rate Decline of 3% | | | | |

| | Value of Coupons Due to the First 4 Years ($) | | | | Value of Coupon of the 5th Year and Par Value ($) | |
Time to Cash Flow	Semiannual Coupon[a]	Future Value[a] (at the end of the 4th year) of Coupon	Time to Cash Flow	Cash Flow	Present Value[b] (at the end of the 4th year) of Coupon and Par
0.5	53.40	69.5175	4.5	53.4	51.4253
1.0	53.40	66.9467	5.0	1053.4	976.9311
1.5	53.40	64.4710		Total	1028.3564
2.0	53.40	62.0869			
2.5	53.40	59.7909			
3.0	53.40	57.5799			
3.5	53.40	55.4506			
4.0	53.40	53.4000			
	Total	489.2435			

a. The coupons are reinvested at $(10.68\% - 3\%) = 7.68\%$, and on a semiannual basis at $7.68\%/2 = 3.84\%$. For example, $53.4(1.0384) \cong 55.4506$. Similarly, $53.40 interest for 7 half-year periods is worth $53.40(1.0384)^7 \cong \$69.5175$.

b. Calculated at 3.84% on a semiannual basis. For example, $1,053.4/(1.0384)^2 \cong 976.9311$.

There are two parts to Exhibit 17-9. The first three columns are used to calculate the future value of the coupons received out to 4 years. A 10.68% coupon bond with a par value of $1,000 has a semiannual coupon payment of $53.4, or $0.1068 \cdot \frac{1}{2} \cdot 1,000$. The second part of this table—the last three columns—is used to calculate the present value of the cash flows received after the fourth year. The value after 4 years is $1,517.60, or $489.2435 + \$1028.3564$. Hence, the semiannual rate of return is $(\$1,517.60/\$1,000)^{1/8} - 1 = 0.0535$, or 10.7% on an annual basis $(0.0535 \cdot 2)$, which is approximately 10.68%, the original coupon yield. Note that the precise annual yield is $(1.0535)^2 - 1 = 0.10986$, or about 10.986%. However, because practitioners commonly switch from semiannual yields to annual yields, ignoring the compounding effect, we adhere to their simple method of calculating the figure shown in Exhibit 17-8b.

Notice that if there is no change in the yield to maturity, then the holding period rate of return exactly equals the initial yield to maturity. If yields fall 3%, then for a 1-year holding period the 10-year bond experiences a rate of return of 28.22% due to the large appreciation in price. (See the previous discussion on bond prices and maturity.) However, the 1-year bond actually has a rate of return of 8.94% less than the original 9%, because the semiannual coupon had to be reinvested at 6% rather than 9%. If yields rise by 3%, exactly the opposite effect occurs for the 1-year holding period.

Exhibit 17–8b shows that for the 7-year holding period, the reinvestment effect is more prevalent. For example, if rates fall by 3%, then the 1-year bond (Bond A) has to be reinvested at a lower rate. Hence, the rate of return is 6.42%.

Notice what happens at Year 4 for Bond B. The rates of return under all three scenarios are almost identical, at around 10.7%. Exhibit 17–8c presents the mean and standard deviation, assuming the yield curve shifts are equally probable. Notice that the standard deviation for *only* Bond B for a 4-year holding period was almost 0. The reason for this result is that at 4 years, the price effect and reinvestment effect just offset each other for a 5-year bond.

In summary, investors with a well-defined holding period should be able to invest in a bond or construct a bond portfolio that will have minimal overall interest rate risk. Investors accomplish this result by balancing the price effect against the reinvestment effect.

To find the investment strategy that minimizes the interest rate risk, we need to consider the bond's **duration.** The concept of duration takes into account the fact that the bond's par value is paid at maturity, whereas coupon payments are paid during the life of the bond. Duration is a weighted average of the timing of these various cash flows. The concept of duration and its definition was suggested first by Macaulay in 1938. (See the Selected References at the end of the chapter.)

Duration is also the holding period that balances the price effect against the reinvestment effect. As we will see, the duration of a 5-year bond is 4 years. Recall that if an investor has a bond with a 10-year maturity, he does not wait 10 years to receive his money back (he may receive some of it earlier as coupon payments). Duration is similar to the average number of years investors have to wait to get their money back. It is not a simple average, because the farther away the cash inflow, the less weight investors give it, because it has a lower present value in comparison to the same amount of money received earlier.

The formal definition of *duration* is a present value-weighted average of the number of years investors wait to receive cash flows. The duration is calculated as follows:[4]

$$D = \sum_{t=1}^{T} t w_t \qquad (17.3)$$

where the weight w_t is given by $w_t = PV(CF_t)/P$, and $PV(CF_t)$ is a present value,

$$PV(CF_t) = \frac{CF_t}{(1 + y)^t}$$

and CF_t is the cash flow received (coupon payment or both coupon and Par) at time t, P is the current market price of the bond, y is the periodic yield to maturity, and T is the bond's time to maturity (i.e., the number of periods to maturity measured generally in years or half years—see next examples).

---

4. Appendix 17A contains an alternative expression for duration that is easier to program in spreadsheets.

Because $P = \Sigma PV(CF_t)$, we see that duration is a weighted average of the time t when cash flows are received [where $PV(CF_t)/P$ serves as the weight]. Note that for a zero-coupon bond there is only one future cash flow; hence, $P = PV(CF_t)$, and the duration is just the time to maturity. Moving from a zero-coupon bond to a coupon-paying bond, the duration declines.

Exhibit 17-8 shows that the duration of the 5-year bond with ten semiannual coupon payments [where $C = \$53.40$ (10.68% on a semiannual bond), y is approximately equal to $0.1068/2$, and $Par = \$1,000$] is as follows:

$$D = \sum_{t=1}^{10} t \left[\frac{CF_t \Big/ \left(1 + \dfrac{0.1068}{2}\right)^t}{\$1,000} \right]$$

$$= \left[\frac{1}{\$1,000} \sum_{t=1}^{10} \frac{t \cdot C}{(1.0534)^t} + \frac{1}{\$1,000} \cdot \frac{10 \cdot Par}{1.0534^{10}} \right]$$

$$= \left\{ 0.001 \left[\frac{1 \cdot 53.4}{(1.0534)^1} + \frac{2 \cdot 53.4}{(1.0534)^2} + \cdots + \frac{10 \cdot 53.4}{(1.0534)^{10}} \right] \right.$$

$$\left. + \frac{1}{\$1,000} \cdot \frac{10 \cdot \$1,000}{1.0534^{10}} \right\}$$

$$\cong 0.001(\$2,057.588) + 5.944 = 8$$

It is not surprising that the duration for Bond B equals exactly eight semiannual periods, or the 4-year holding period. Similar calculations reveal that the duration for the 1-year bond is 0.98 of a year, and the duration for the 10-year bond is 6.3 years.

Exhibit 17-10 shows the duration for the 5-year bond. For holding periods shorter than 4 years, the price risk is more dominant than the reinvestment risk. This price risk declines for longer holding periods, as it is being offset by the benefits of reinvestment. For holding periods longer than 4 years, the reinvestment risk is more dominant. This reinvestment risk increases for longer holding periods because the benefits of the price effect are declining. For a 4-year holding period, the two risks almost offset each other; hence, σ is almost zero. Duration is the mathematical procedure to find the minimum point, as is illustrated in Exhibit 17-10.

PRACTICE BOX

Problem

Calculate the duration of the following two bonds. Bond A is a 2-year, zero-coupon bond trading at $850 ($Par = \$1,000$). Bond B is a 2-year, 5% annual coupon bond trading at par ($Par = \$1,000$).

(continued)

**EXHIBIT 17-10
Duration as a Measure
of the Holding Period
That Minimizes Interest
Rate Risk Measured as
the Standard Deviation
of Rates of Return
(The holding period is
assumed to be 4 years.)**

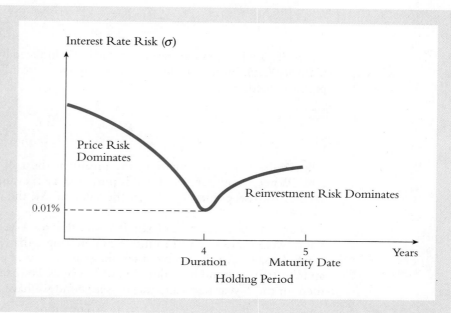

| Solution | Equation 17.3 shows the following for Bond A: |

$$D = 2(\$850/\$850) = 2 \text{ years } [\text{Note that } CF_t = Par \text{ and } PV(CF_t) = P.]$$

For Bond B, Equation 17.3 shows the following:

$$D = \left[\sum_{t=1}^{2} t \left(\frac{CF_t/1 + 0.05)^t}{\$1,000} \right) \right] = \frac{1}{\$1,000} \left[1 \left(\frac{\$50}{1 + 0.05} \right) + 2 \left(\frac{\$1,050}{(1 + 0.05)^2} \right) \right]$$

$$\cong \frac{1}{\$1,000} (\$47.619 + \$1,904.762) \cong 1.95 \text{ years}$$

Thus, the coupon payments are shown to reduce the value of duration.

Duration has another application. Duration is a direct measure of the sensitivity of a bond's rate of return to changes in the yield to maturity. Thus, duration can be used as a measure of the overall sensitivity or riskiness of a bond or a bond portfolio. The following can be shown mathematically (using the derivative of the bond price with respect to yield):[5]

5. This relationship is based on taking a Taylor series of the relationship between price and yield to maturity. See any standard calculus book for more information on the Taylor series.

$$D \cong \frac{\Delta P}{P} \cdot \frac{(1 + y)}{\Delta y} = -R(\Delta y) \cdot \frac{(1 + y)}{\Delta y}$$

where $R(\Delta y)$ is the rate of return on the bond induced by a given change in yield to maturity (Δy). Note that this is just an approximation. Rearranging the above expression yields

$$R(\Delta y) \cong \frac{D \Delta y}{(1 + y)} \qquad (17.4)$$

Clearly, the larger the duration, the greater is the risk due to changes in interest rates. When using duration for this purpose, Δy is assumed to be a small constant, such as 10 basis points. The larger the value of Δy, the less accurate is the approximation.[6]

For example, we saw in Exhibit 17-8b that for 1-year holding periods, 10-year bonds were more sensitive to interest rate changes than were 1-year bonds. We can reach the same conclusion by observing that the 1-year bond has a duration of 0.98, and the 10-year bond has a duration of 6.3 years. For example, if we let $\Delta y = +1\%$, then for the 1-year bond and the 10-year bond we have (from Equation 17.4)

$$R_{1\text{-}year}(0.01) \cong -\frac{0.98 \cdot 0.01}{1 + 0.09} = -0.009$$

$$R_{10\text{-}year}(0.01) \cong -\frac{6.3 \cdot 0.01}{1 + 0.11} = -0.0568$$

Hence, for short holding periods, the 1-year bond is less risky than the 10-year bond. Recall that using duration as a measure of price sensitivity is just one function of duration. Duration is also used to identify the holding period at which interest rate risk is minimized.

Duration and maturity are widely used by investment analysts. Exhibit 17-11 provides a small portion of a more extensive table from *Forbes* that reports the maturity and duration of funds specializing in bonds. Because these funds hold various bonds, the weighted average of the maturity and duration of the various bonds is reported, where the weight of each bond is the proportion of its value in the fund's assets. Obviously, the maturity is longer than the duration (with the exception of funds that hold non-coupon-paying bonds, a cash in which the maturity is equal to its duration).

17.2.1 Duration Principles

The following are well-known duration principles.

Principle 1.   Duration normally declines over time, a pattern called the **duration drift.** Because duration declines over time, for a given investment period, the bonds portfolio should be rebalanced to minimize the risk.

---

6. This characteristic will lead to one useful application of convexity discussed later.

EXHIBIT 17-11   Taxable Bond Funds Survey

Market Performance Up	Down	Fund/Distributor	5-Year Annualized Total Return	Yield %	Assets 6/30/97 ($mil)	Weighted Average Maturity (years)	Duration (years)	Maximum Sales Charge	Annual Expenses per $100
		Lehman Brothers Municipal Bond Index	7.1%	5.4%					
		Forbes Municipal Bond Fund Composite	6.5%	5.2%					$0.72
C	C	AAL Municipal Bond-A/AAL	6.6%	4.7%	$431	18.2	9.0	4.00%	$0.89
A	D	AARP T-F Income—Insured Genl Bond/Scudder	6.6	4.8	1,696	11.0	7.2	None	0.66
D	B	AIM Municipal Bond-A/AIM	6.3	5.2	314	12.5	4.5	4.75	0.80
D	A	AIM Tax-Free Intermed Shares/AIM	5.7	4.7	186	4.6	3.6	1.00	0.56
B	C	Alliance Muni Income—Calif-A/Alliance	7.2	5.4	699	26.4	9.6	4.25	0.77[a]
A+	D	Alliance Muni Income—Natl-A/Alliance	7.2	5.4	604	26.5	8.0	4.25	0.69[a]
A	D	Alliance Muni Income—New York-A/Alliance	6.9	5.5	309	27.0	9.4	4.25	0.64
C	A	Amer Century-Benham Calif Muni Hi-Yld/Amer Century	7.7	5.7	191	20.8	7.2	None	0.50
A	D	Amer Century-Benham Calif T-F Ins/Amer Century	7.1	5.2	188	18.1	8.0	None	0.48
D	A	Amer Century-Benham Calif T-F Inter/Amer Century	6.2	4.8	431	8.3	5.4	None	0.47
F	A+	Amer Century-Benham Calif T-F Ltd/Amer Century	4.6	4.2	122	3.7	2.7	None	0.49
B	C	Amer Century-Benham Calif T-F L-T/Amer Century	7.2	5.3	303	19.4	7.7	None	0.47

(continued)

EXHIBIT 17-11 *(continued)*

Market Performance		Fund/ Distributor	5-Year Annualized Total Return	Yield %	Assets 6/30/97 ($mil)	Weighted Average		Maximum Sales Charge	Annual Expenses per $100
Up	Down					Maturity (years)	Duration (years)		
C	C	Atlas California Muni Bond-A/ Atlas	6.3%	4.8%	$180	19.6	6.9	3.00%	$0.96
D	A	Bernstein California Muni/ Bernstein	5.7	4.3	366	6.5	4.9	None	0.67
		Merrill Lynch Corporate/ Govt Bond Index	7.3	6.8					
		Forbes Taxable Bond Composite	6.7	6.1					0.71
F	A+	Smith Breeden—Short Dur Govt/ Smith Breeden	5.4	5.2	111	0.5	0.5	None	0.78[a]
C	B	Spartan Ginnie Mae/Fidelity	6.3	6.7	492	7.2	4.3	None	0.65
C	C	Spartan Government Income/ Fidelity	6.0	6.5	256	8.5	4.8	None	0.60
		Spartan Investment Grade Bond/ Fidelity	—★	6.3	469	8.2	4.7	None	0.60[a]
D	B	Spartan Limited Maturity Govt/ Fidelity	5.8	6.8	686	4.6	3.0	None	0.65
		Spartan Short-Term Bond/ Fidelity	—★	6.4	267	2.2	1.7	None	0.61
		SSGA Yield Plus/Russell	—★	5.4	779	NA	0.3	None	0.38
C	C	Stagecoach GNMA Fund-A/ Stagecoach	6.3	6.8	151	9.2	4.3	4.50	0.82[a]
B	C	Standish Fixed Income/Standish	7.7	7.1	2,874	8.6	5.1	None	0.38
B	C	SteinRoe Income Fund/ Stein Roe	8.4	7.1	376	7.6	5.2	None	0.83

Five-year return 6/30/92 through 6/30/97.

★Fund not in operation or did not meet minimum for full period.

a. Net of absorption of expenses by fund sponsor.

Source: *Forbes*; Lipper Analytical Services; and Morningstar, Inc.; as cited in Fund Survey, *Forbes*, August 25, 1997, p. 236. Reprinted by Permission of *Forbes* Magazine © Forbes Inc., 1997.

However, duration does not decline at the same speed as time. For example, from the previous discussion, we know that the duration of a zero-coupon bond is equal to its time to maturity. Thus, duration will decline with the passage of time, requiring the portfolio to be periodically adjusted to keep the duration equal to the desired holding period. After 4 years, the 5-year bond in Exhibit 17-8, will have a duration of almost 1 year; therefore, if the holding period remains 4 years, the bond portfolios employing duration-based strategies must be rebalanced periodically.

Principle 2.   Normally, duration is inversely related to yield to maturity. For higher yields, the present value of more distant cash flows will be discounted by a greater amount. Hence, those cash flows will receive less weight, resulting in a lower duration. Recall that duration is the present value–weighted average of the number of years investors wait to receive cash flows.

Principle 3.   Normally, duration is directly related to the length to maturity. Like zero-coupon bonds, most bonds exhibit the characteristic of having longer durations for longer maturities. This fact does not mean that longer-term bonds always have longer durations, because duration is affected by more than just maturity.

Principle 4.   Normally, duration is inversely related to the level of coupon payments. The higher the coupon level, the greater the weight given to the earlier cash flows (the coupon payments). Hence, the greater the coupon payments, the shorter the duration. Principles 3 and 4 are useful when an investor is altering the bond portfolio's duration. The investor who wishes to lengthen the duration should move to lower-coupon and longer-maturity bonds.

Principle 5.   The duration of a bond portfolio, D, is equal to the weighted average of the durations of the individual bonds, where the weights are determined by the market value of the bonds.[7]

$$D = \sum_{i=1}^{n} w_i D_i \qquad (17.5)$$

where $w_i = MV_i/MV$, MV_i is the market value of the portfolio holding of Bond i, MV is the market value of the total bond portfolio, D_i is the duration of Bond i, and n is the number of bonds in the portfolio. Therefore, an investor who wants a

---

7. To see that Equation 17.5 is appropriate, for simplicity we use zero-coupon bonds. Recall that the duration of a zero-coupon bond is its maturity. Denote by t_i the maturity of the ith bond. If we let each cash flow of a bond be represented as a zero-coupon bond, then the duration of a bond (a portfolio of zero-coupon bonds, and thus $MV = P$) can be represented as follows:

$$D = \sum_{i=1}^{n} w_i D_i = \sum_{i=1}^{n} \frac{MV_i}{MV} D_i = \sum_{i=1}^{n} \frac{PV(CF_i)}{P} t_i$$

where D_i is the duration of each cash flow, and thus $D_i = t_i$ for zero-coupon bonds, and n is the number of various bonds in the portfolio. We can treat a bond portfolio as one bond with numerous cash flows (each discounted at the individual bond's appropriate discount rate).

5-year duration (to manage the interest rate risk) can mix several bonds to achieve this goal. Thus, duration can be used to manage the interest rate sensitivity of bond portfolios.

PRACTICE BOX

Problem

Suppose you are considering an investment in two bonds. Bond A has a duration of 8 years and a market price of $950, and Bond B has a duration of 4 years and a market price of $1,050. How should you invest $10,000 in these bonds if you have a desired holding period of 7 years and wish to minimize interest rate risk?

Solution

The duration of the bond portfolio can be found using Equation 17.5:

$$D = w_A D_A + w_B D_B = w_A D_A + (1 - w_A)D_B$$

Substituting for w_A yields

$$D = (MV_A/MV)D_A + (1 - MV_A/MV)D_B$$

Solving for MV_A yields

$$MV_A = [MV(D - D_B)]/(D_A - D_B)$$

Using the data given in the problem yields

$$MV_A = [\$10,000(7.0 - 4.0)]/(8.0 - 4.0) = \$7,500$$

Hence, $7,500 should be invested in Bond A, and $2,500 ($10,000 − $7,500) should be invested in Bond B.

Generally, duration increases with maturity. For zero-coupon bonds, duration increases linearly with maturity, because duration is equal to maturity. Curve 1 in Exhibit 17-12 describes this relationship for zero-coupon bonds.

Curve 2 describes a bond that pays an annual coupon. In such a case, the duration is shorter than the yield to maturity; hence, curve 2 is completely below curve 1.

According to Principle 3, it is tempting to believe that the duration always increases with the years to maturity. This idea is not necessarily true, because there is a coupon effect (Principle 4) that may offset the years to maturity effect. To clarify this idea, consider a 3% coupon bond whose yield is 15%. As the years to maturity increase, at the beginning the duration also increases. However, beyond some critical point, the weight of the par value drastically decreases (recall that it is discounted at 15%), and the weight of the coupons increases (in particular, the weight of the early coupons, which are not so heavily discounted). Hence, the duration may decrease. This type of relationship is described by curve 3.

In summary, the five principles state clearly the separate effect of each factor on duration. However, when more than one factor is changed simultaneously (for example, for a given yield, the coupon decreases and the maturity increases), the rela-

EXHIBIT 17-12
The Relationship of Duration to Years to Maturity

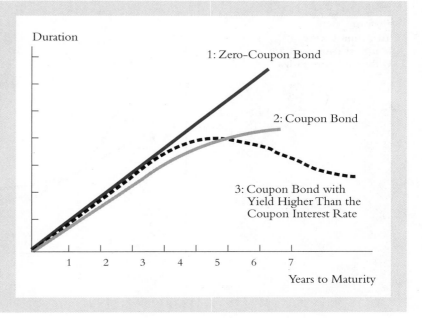

tionship between duration and years to maturity is more complex, as illustrated by curve 3 in Exhibit 17-12.

As has been illustrated, duration is not a precise measure of interest rate sensitivity (see Equation 17.4). Also, the use of duration as an interest rate risk minimization tool requires some very restrictive assumptions. For example, interest rate risk is minimized against instant and small changes in interest rates. Due in part to these weaknesses, an additional measure known as *convexity* has been developed.

17.2.2 Convexity

Convexity is a measure of the curvature of a bond's price-yield relationship. Duration can be used to measure the slope of a line tangent to the convex price-yield relationship.[8] Exhibit 17-13 illustrates two bonds with identical durations but different convexities. If the yield to maturity of both bonds is y_0, then the bonds have the same price, P_0. We do not make the assumption that these bonds have the same maturity or the same coupon. The only assumption we make is that these two bonds have the same slope of the price-yield relationship at y_0 and the same duration (notice

---

8. Recall from Equation 17.4 (after rearrangement of the terms) that duration can be approximated by

$$D \cong -\left(\frac{\Delta P}{\Delta y}\right)\left[\frac{(1 + y)}{P}\right]$$

and the first term is the slope of the price-yield relationship. Thus, if two bonds have the same price (P), the same yield (y), and the same duration (D), they must have the same slope, as described in Exhibit 17-13.

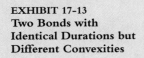

EXHIBIT 17-13
Two Bonds with
Identical Durations but
Different Convexities

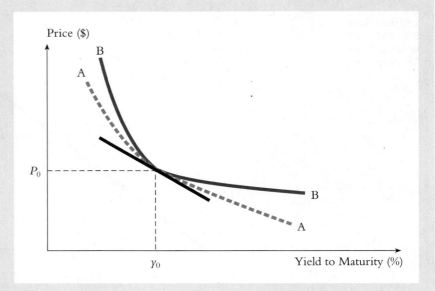

that $P_A = P_B = P_0$). Hence, all investors prefer Bond B, because no matter which direction yield to maturity goes, Bond B will always be worth more than Bond A. Thus, not only should investors be concerned about minimizing interest rate risk with duration, but also they should strive to maximize convexity to capitalize on large changes in interest rates.

In general, we would not expect to find two bonds like Bond A and Bond B. Investor demand for Bond B will drive its price up and therefore lower its yield to maturity. Investor preference for higher convexity results in higher prices for highly convex bonds, and thus they have lower yields to maturity. The higher the convexity, the more curvature there is in the price–yield relationship. For example, in Exhibit 17-13, Bond B has a higher convexity than Bond A.

As with bond prices and duration, there are some basic principles related to convexity:

Principle 1.   Convexity is inversely related to yield to maturity. Recall from Exhibit 17-2 that the curvature was greater for lower yields than for higher yields.
Principle 2.   Convexity is inversely related to the coupon. Recall from Exhibit 17-10 that the curvature was flatter for higher-coupon bonds.
Principle 3.   Convexity is positively related to duration. Recall from Exhibit 17-4 that the curvature is greater for longer-maturity bonds (which in this case also have longer durations).

These principles are useful for bond management. For example, if you wanted to lengthen duration and raise the convexity, you could move to lower coupon–

bearing bonds. Recall from duration Principle 4 that duration is normally inversely related to the coupon level. Convexity Principle 2 indicates that convexity is also inversely related to coupon. Hence, by selling high-coupon bonds and buying lower-coupon bonds of the same maturity, you can both lengthen the duration and increase the convexity.

The tools of duration and convexity can be used in bond portfolio management. Because these techniques are used primarily by institutional portfolio managers, we refer to *bond managers* rather than *bond investors.*

17.3 IMMUNIZATION

A bond manager who has a well-defined holding period can identify all the potential portfolios with the duration equal to the holding period and adopt the portfolio with the highest convexity. For example, a life insurance company may have a rather long holding period. Hence, it would seek a portfolio with a long duration. Strategies such as this one are known as **immunization strategies;** they try to neutralize the adverse effects of changes in yield to maturity while still benefitting, if possible, from changes in interest rates. This section discusses two categories of immunization strategies: income immunization and price immunization.

17.3.1 Income Immunization

Consider the problems facing a manager of a company's pension plan. Recall from Exhibit 17-7 that the smaller the coupon, the larger the percentage change in the bond's price in response to a given change in the bond's yield. The pension fund will need to pay out money to its clients based on their age; hence, the cash outflow can be accurately predicted. Having sufficient liquid assets in the portfolio to meet cash disbursements is critical to the pension manager's success. The manager can invest in bonds that minimize the probability that insufficient funds will occur in the future. The technique to achieve this goal is called *immunization.*

Income immunization strategies insure that adequate resources are available to meet perceived cash disbursement needs. One appealing strategy is to invest in a bond portfolio that has coupon payments and principal payments that exactly meet the future cash needs. This approach is known as a **cash matching strategy.** A cash matching strategy is very restrictive and allows very little flexibility. Cash matching may eliminate many otherwise attractive bonds because they do not have the desirable cash flow properties.

An alternative approach is known as a **duration matching strategy,** which allows for a variety of potential portfolios so long as the duration of the liability stream equals the duration of the bond portfolio. However, this approach has a potential problem, too. To meet liquidity needs, bond managers may have to sell bonds at temporarily depressed prices. For example, one way to construct a portfolio with the needed payment stream would be to purchase only zero-coupon bonds that had a maturity exactly equal to the duration of the pension liability stream. Although this is a duration matching strategy (recall that the duration of a zero–coupon bond is its maturity), it will not prove useful for the pension manager, because next year's cash disbursements must be paid by selling bonds that may be depressed because of a temporary rise in interest rates. Of course, such a problem would be avoided in the unrealistic case where a pension fund would have only one payout to its pension holders at the maturity of the bond.

By combining the benefits of cash matching strategies with the benefits of duration matching strategies, the **horizon matching strategy** has been developed. In a horizon matching strategy, the manager designs a portfolio that is cash matched over the short horizon and duration matched over the long horizon. For example, the manager could cash match over the next 4 years to avoid having to sell in a bear market and duration match the remaining liabilities. Thus, the horizon matching strategy provides the liquidity benefits of cash matching, as well as the flexibility of duration matching.

For example, suppose a pension plan must pay out $1 million in benefits in each of the next 5 years and then pay out $2 million for the next 20 years. The pension manager using the horizon matching strategy would invest in zero-coupon bonds with par values of $1 million that mature in each of the next 4 years (or any equivalent strategy that assures $1 million in cash each year) and then duration match the remaining liabilities.

PRACTICE BOX

Problem

Suppose the liabilities of a pension plan have a duration of 5 years. Also suppose there are two bond portfolios in which the pension manager could invest. Bond Fund A has a duration of 11 years, and Bond Fund B has a duration of 1 year. How can the money manager employ the duration matching strategy?

Solution

Recall from Equation 17.5 that

$$D = \sum_{i=1}^{n} w_i D_i$$

The manager has to determine what portion to place in Fund A and Fund B such that the pension assets have a duration of 5.0. Specifically, $5 = w_1 + w_2 11 = w_1 + (1 - w_1)11$. Thus, $5 = w_1 + 11 - 11w_1$. Solving for w_1 yields $w_1 = 0.6$, or 60%, and thus $w_2 = 40\%$. The manager should place 60% of the assets in Fund A and 40% in Fund B.

All three income immunization strategies insure that sufficient resources are available to meet the future income needs of the pension plan. However, these strategies ignore the impact of changes in yield to maturity on the current market value of the portfolio. The current market value of the portfolio is a critical concern for bank portfolio managers who must maintain certain levels of capital for regulatory reasons. Also, the performance of fund managers is commonly judged by the market value of the assets managed. Managers who are concerned with the preservation of the original market value of the portfolio must consider the price immunization techniques discussed next.

17.3.2 Price Immunization

Price immunization includes those strategies that insure that the market value of assets always exceeds the market value of liabilities by a specified amount. For example, there is a push in the banking industry toward "market value" or "current value" accounting. Market value accounting seeks to restate the assets and liabilities to their current market value so investors can assess the true worth of the equity. Thus, there is a strong incentive for managers of financial institutions to insure that the difference between the market value of their assets and the market value of their liabilities does not decline.

Price immunization strategies use convexity. For example, the pension plan previously described seeks to develop a portfolio that is not only duration matched but also has the convexity of its assets exceeding the convexity of its liabilities. Exhibit 17-14 illustrates this bond portfolio strategy. It assumes that the pension fund was adequately funded such that the market value of the bond portfolio (assets) equaled the present value of the portfolio's future payments (liabilities). As long as the convexity of the assets exceeds the convexity of the liabilities, the market value of the difference will grow with changes in interest rates. Also, the greater the convexity, the greater will be the gains from changes in interest rates. Hence, in this case we say the pension fund is price immunized.

**EXHIBIT 17-14
Convexity of Assets
and Liabilities**

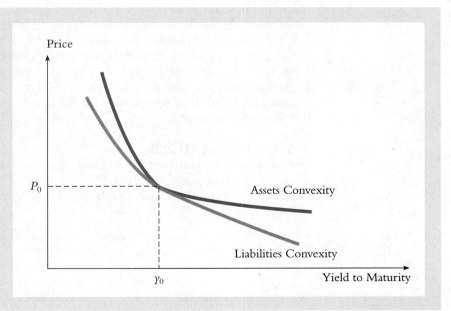

17.4 PASSIVE VERSUS ACTIVE BOND MANAGEMENT STRATEGIES

Up to this point in the discussion, the role of security selection to enhance the value of bond portfolios has been ignored. This section integrates security selection into bond management.

The immunization strategies already discussed can be passive or active (see Chapter 12). In a passively managed bond portfolio, the manager attempts to mimic a bond index. Recall that if the bond market is efficient, and thus all bonds are fairly priced, then the process of selecting bonds could be managed passively. Alternatively, active management implicitly assumes that the bond market is *not* efficient and, hence, that there are excess returns to be pursued.

Passive bond management requires few financial resources and uses little time. Passive bond managers can devote most of their energy to refining the immunization technique they adopt. Connecting Theory to Practice 17.2 illustrates a technique for passive bond management.

CONNECTING THEORY TO PRACTICE 17.2

BUILDING A BOND LADDER IS SAFE WAY TO INCREASE YIELD

With long-term bonds now yielding more than twice as much as money-market funds, investors may be tempted to pour most of their savings into long-term issues.

Resist that temptation. A much safer approach, according to many investment managers, is a strategy known as bond "laddering."

Building a bond ladder means buying bonds scheduled to come due at several different dates in the future, rather than all in the same year. For example, an investor might buy similar amounts of bonds due in one year, two years, three years, and so on out to 10 years. It is known as "laddering" because each group of bonds represents a rung on the investment maturity ladder. (See the table on the next page.)

THE $50,000 LADDER

Investors who want to build a ladder all at once have to be prepared to buy bonds in the secondary market. Marshall Front of Stein Roe & Farnham says this portfolio could be put together for $50,000, but that investors would get better yields on larger purchases.

Source: Tom Herman, "Building a Bond Ladder Is Safe Way to Increase Yield," *Wall Street Journal,* September 1, 1992, p. C1. Reprinted by permission of *The Wall Street Journal,* © 1992 Dow Jones & Co., Inc. All Rights Reserved Worldwide.

(continued)

Face Amount	Issue	Recent Yield to Maturity
$10,000	4.250% Treasury due 8/31/94	4.17%
$10,000	4.625% Treasury due 8/15/95	4.71%
$10,000	5.625% Treasury due 8/31/97	5.63%
$10,000	7.875% Treasury due 11/15/99	6.29%
$10,000	6.375% Treasury due 8/15/02	6.63%
$50,000	Average	5.49%

MAKING THE CONNECTION

Bond laddering is a typical passive bond management strategy. It requires no economic forecasting or ongoing asset allocation decisions. Once the portfolio is established, one simply waits until the shortest-term bond expires. On expiration, the proceeds are invested in the longest-term bond designed for the ladder.

17.4.1 Contingent Immunization

Active bond managers are faced with a dilemma. How can they pursue active bond management strategies without exposing a bond fund to excessive interest rate risk? One solution is known as contingent immunization. **Contingent immunization** is an investment strategy designed to accommodate both the desire of bond managers to pursue active strategies and the desire to minimize the effect of adverse movements in interest rates. A bond manager using this approach pursues timing strategies or duration mismatches in an attempt to profit from forecasted moves in interest rates. Alternatively, a bond manager may actively trade bonds that are believed to be mispriced by selling overpriced bonds and buying underpriced bonds.

The bond manager can act unimpeded as long as the performance is good. However, when she begins to experience relatively poor performance, she must move toward immunizing strategies. As performance continues to decline, the manager continues to move more quickly toward an immunized portfolio. Hence, the pension fund can establish a "floor" on the active manager's performance. If the active manager performs well, then there are very few restrictions regarding exposure to interest rate risk. As the active manager's performance declines, there are increasing restrictions. Specifically, the manager must increasingly immunize the bond portfolio.

17.4.2 Popular Active Bond Management Strategies

There are many different speculative bond management strategies. One strategy involves selling bonds that are believed to be relatively overpriced and buying bonds with similar characteristics that are believed to be relatively underpriced. This strategy is called a **substitution swap.**[9] Another strategy, called a **pure yield pickup swap,** involves moving to bonds with a higher yield to maturity, which also typically implies longer-duration bonds. Speculating on the spread between two different bond markets, such as Eurodollar bonds[10] and domestic bonds, is known as an **intermarket spread swap.** Finally, a **rate anticipation swap** involves positioning a bond portfolio such that maximum gains are achieved if a perceived rate change occurs. Connecting Theory to Practice 17.3 presents a mutual fund's prospectus, which explains how these swaps were used.

CONNECTING THEORY TO PRACTICE 17.3

VANGUARD'S INVESTMENT GRADE BOND FUND

In the Investment Grade Bond Portfolio, we used the weakness in the market to add to bond positions and reduce cash reserves. The average maturity is now 24.8 years, up from 21.9 years six months ago. The Portfolio's duration is now 9.1, up from 8.6 on January 31. Swaps were made into issues that provide better call protection, improving the sustainability of the Portfolio's income. Utility investments were reduced in favor of industrial issuers, as the possibility of event risk now appears to be lower. We maintain nearly 20% of the Portfolio in U.S. government securities, which provide excellent quality, liquidity, and call protection. The average quality of our corporate holdings is between "A" and "Aa." The Portfolio is well diversified with over 60 different corporate issuers. It is aggressively structured to provide solid returns if interest rates trend lower, as we expect over the next year.

Source: *Semi-Annual Report of the Vanguard Fixed Income Securities Fund,* July 31, 1990, p. 2.

MAKING THE CONNECTION

This report indicates that the managers of Vanguard's Investment Grade Bond Portfolio pursue active bond management strategies. Clearly, these managers believe they have superior forecasting abilities. Specifically, they are forecasting lower interest rates and a stronger economy. Their reference to "event risk" shows a concern about a severe recession. Public utility bonds are safer than industrial bonds in recessions. Of course, industrial bonds offer a higher yield. Believing that interest rates will "trend lower" and the economy will strengthen, the managers lengthened the duration and accepted more default risk with industrial bonds.

---

9. The names given to these active strategies originated in Sidney Homer and Martin L. Leibowitz. *Inside the Yield Book: New Tools for Bond Market Strategy* (Englewood Cliffs, N.J.: Prentice Hall, 1972).

10. Recall that Eurodollar bonds are bonds that pay in U.S. dollars but are issued outside the United States.

The overall objective of active bond management is to make superior selections of bonds. In an efficient market this is impossible, of course, so what is left are immunization strategies. Superior selection can be achieved by superior foresight regarding the future of overall interest rates or by superior foresight regarding the credit quality of individual bonds. This chapter has discussed changes in a bond's price that are due to changes in the interest rate. Managers, therefore, try to predict the future market interest rate. However, sometimes the interest rate in the economy falls, and prices increase. Also, the price of specific bonds may decline because of firm-specific circumstances, such as financial distress. This condition may result in heavy losses. Unless they are buying only government bonds, managers should also analyze the risk of bankruptcy of a specific firm's bonds. For example, when Wang Laboratories filed for Chapter 11 bankruptcy, the price of its bonds fell 50%. Specifically, bond managers do not want to be caught holding bonds when a firm is declining in credit quality.

SUMMARY

List the basic principles of bond pricing.   The price of a bond is the present value of all future coupon payments plus the par value discounted to the present at the required rate of return (the yield to maturity). Bond prices change with just the passage of time. Bond prices are inversely related to the yield to maturity. Longer-term bonds are more sensitive to changes in yield to maturity. The sensitivity to changes in yield to maturity increases at a decreasing rate with maturity. There is a linear relationship between a bond's coupon rate and its price. Finally, higher-coupon bonds are less sensitive to changes in yield to maturity than lower-coupon bonds.

Explain how duration is used to minimize interest rate risk.   A bond portfolio's duration corresponds to the holding period at which the portfolio's interest-rate risk is minimized. Duration can also be used as a measure of relative bond price volatility. Convexity is a measure of the curvature of a bond's price-yield relationship. When everything else is the same, bond investors prefer higher convexity.

Explain how immunization techniques protect bond portfolios from interest rate risk.   Immunization tech-

niques protect both income streams and the current market value of the assets and liabilities from the effects of changing interest rates. Income immunization protects future income needs. Income immunization strategies include cash matching, duration matching, and horizon matching. Price immunization uses convexity and seeks to protect current market values.

Describe active bond management strategies.   The overall objective of active bond management strategies is to make superior bond selections. Prudent bond trading strategies require the ability to forecast future events such as changing interest rates and overall economic activity. Default risk should always be of utmost concern. Contingent immunization is an investment strategy designed to accommodate both the desire of bond managers to trade actively and the desire of investors to minimize interest rate risk. Several bond trading strategies are designed to enhance returns, including substitution swaps, pure yield pickup swaps, intermarket swaps, and rate anticipation swaps.

CHAPTER AT A GLANCE

1. *The following are the basic principles of bond pricing:*
    a. Bond prices change with just the passage of time.
    b. Bond prices are inversely related to the yield to maturity.
    c. Longer-term bonds are more sensitive to changes in yield to maturity.
    d. The sensitivity to changes in yield to maturity increases at a decreasing rate with maturity.
    e. There is a linear relationship between coupon and price.
    f. Higher-coupon bonds are less sensitive to changes in yield to maturity than are lower-coupon bonds.

    Duration is computed as follows:

$$D = \sum_{t=1}^{T} tw_t$$

    where w_t is the weight and is equal to $PV(CF_t)/P$, P is the bond's price, $PV(CF_t)$ is the present value of the cash flow obtained in year t, and T is the bond's time to maturity.

2. *The basic duration principles follow:*
    a. Duration normally declines with the passage of time.
    b. Duration is normally inversely related to yield to maturity.
    c. Duration is normally directly related to maturity.
    d. Duration is normally inversely related to the level of coupon payments.
    e. The duration of a bond portfolio is equal to the weighted average of the durations of the individual bonds, where the weights are determined by the market value of the bonds.

3. *The basic convexity principles follow:*
    a. Convexity is inversely related to yield to maturity.
    b. Convexity is inversely related to the coupon.
    c. Convexity is positively related to duration.

4. *Immunization mitigates adverse effects of changes in yield to maturity.*
    a. Income immunization (cash matching, duration matching, and horizon matching) protects future income needs.
    b. Price immunization, which employs convexity, protects current market values.

5. *Active bond management includes the following:*
    a. Contingent immunization.
    b. Swaps (substitution, pure yield pickup, intermarket spread, and rate anticipation).

KEY TERMS

Cash matching strategy   639
Contingent immunization   643
Convexity   637

Duration   629
Duration drift   632
Duration matching strategy   639

Horizon matching
   strategy   640
Immunization strategy   639

Income immunization
   strategy   639
Intermarket spread swap   644

Price effect   625
Price immunization   641
Pure yield pickup swap   644

Rate anticipation swap   644
Reinvestment effect   625
Substitution swap   644

REVIEW

17.1 Suppose you have two similar bonds. Bond A is callable, and Bond B is not. However, Bond A offers a higher coupon such that both bonds are currently priced the same. Show graphically how these two bonds' prices will behave for different yields to maturity.

17.2 Exhibit 17-10 illustrates the trade-off between price risk and reinvestment rate risk for various holding periods.
a. How would this graph change if a 4-year, zero-coupon bond were used?
b. How would this graph change if a very high coupon bond were used (but the bond still had a duration of 4 years)?

17.3 Several income immunization strategies were discussed in this chapter. Rank each immunization strategy from the least flexible to the most flexible. Explain your rankings.

17.4 "If the yield to maturity is zero, then the duration must also be zero." Evaluate this statement.

17.5 "Two bonds have the same market price, the same yield to maturity, the same par values, and the same maturity. Thus, the two bonds must have the same duration." Evaluate this statement. If you agree, then prove it. If you do not agree, then provide an example refuting this statement.

17.6 Which bond will have a shorter duration, a bond that is callable or the same bond that is not callable? Explain.

17.7 Suppose you have a bond with a yield to maturity of 5% and a duration of 4 years. Suddenly inflation escalates. How would this affect duration?

17.8 Suppose a new medicine has been invented that immunizes people against cancer. How should this invention influence the investment policy of the bond portfolio managers of life insurance companies? Explain your answer.

PRACTICE

17.1 Suppose you invest in a 10-year, 8% semiannual coupon bond, $1,000 par, with a yield to maturity of 6%.
a. What is the price of the bond?
b. Show graphically the path of the bond's price over time if the yield to maturity remains the same.

17.2 The following table gives the bond prices for 5-year and 30-year bonds for various yields to maturity. What inferences can be drawn from this information?

Years to Maturity	Yield				
	5%	7.5%	10%	12.5%	15%
5	$1,219	$1,103	$1,000	$909	$828
30	1,773	1,297	1,000	805	671

17.3 Suppose you were given the following information on three semiannual Treasury bonds with the same maturity:

Bond	Coupon	Price
A	8%	$1,000
B	7⅝	?
C	7	975

What is the price of Bond B? (Hint: Arbitrage profits do not exist in equilibrium.)

17.4 Using Equation 17.3, calculate the duration of a 3-year, 8% annual coupon bond that is trading at par. (Assume $1,000 par.)

17.5 Using the bond in Question 17.4, conduct sensitivity analysis on the coupon and yield to maturity. Specifically, calculate the duration for the following conditions:
a. The coupon is 9% rather than 8%.
b. The yield to maturity is 9% rather than 8%.

Compare your results with those for Question 17.4.

17.6 Suppose you owned four different bonds with the following characteristics:

Bond	Market Value of Holdings	Duration
A	$14,327	1.27 years
B	$56,490	8.74 years
C	$19,467	5.66 years
D	$37,592	6.72 years

What is the duration of the bond portfolio?

17.7 Suppose you have an $n = 10$-year bond with a par value of $1,000 and an annual coupon of $50. The market price of the bond is $900.
a. Calculate the bond's duration.
b. How will the duration change if the coupon is paid at the beginning of each year rather than at the end of the year? (Assume that the yield to maturity remains the same.)

17.8 Suppose you owned a 10-year bond with a par value of $1,000 and a market value of $1,000 with a coupon of $50 paid at the end of each year.
a. What is the yield to maturity?
b. Calculate the market bond price for yields to maturity of 2.5%, 5%, 7.5%, 10%, 12.5%, 15%, 17.5%, and 20%. Draw the market price of the bond as a function of the interest rate. Is there a convex relationship?

17.9 Suppose you have two bonds with the following characteristics: for Bond A, $P_A = \$900$ and $D_A = 8$ years; for Bond B, $P_B = \$1,100$ and $D_B = 15$ years. You have a holding period of 12 years. What bond portfolio mix will suit your holding period, assuming you wish to minimize interest rate risk? (Assume a $500,000 portfolio.)

17.10 There are five bonds, each of which has a duration of 4 years. Your holding period is 2 years. "By diversifying between these four bonds, you can reduce the portfolio duration to 2 years." Do you agree with this statement? Defend your answer.

17.11 Suppose you can invest in a 10-year, fixed-coupon bond whose yield to maturity is 10%. The expected inflation rate is 5% per year. A firm offers a bond with a 5% yield to maturity, 10-year maturity, and coupons and principal linked to the cost of living index. Which bond has a longer duration? Explain.

17.12 You are considering investing in two bonds, both with 10 years to maturity. Bond A is a zero-coupon bond with a 10% yield to maturity. Bond B pays $50 coupons annually, and its yield to maturity is 12%. (Assume $1,000 par.)
a. Calculate the market price of each bond, as well as its duration.
b. If you buy one bond of Bond A and one bond of Bond B, what is the yield to maturity and the duration of your portfolio?
c. How would you change your answer if you bought two bonds of Bond A and two bonds of Bond B? Explain your answer.
d. How would you change your answer in Part b if you bought ten bonds of Bond A and one bond of Bond B? Compare and discuss your results.

17.13 In the early 1990s there was a steep upward-sloping yield curve with a 3% yield to maturity on 1-year bonds and a 7% yield to maturity on 15-year bonds. Suppose a bank borrowed at 3% (sold short-term CDs) and invested in long-term bonds yielding 7%. This policy would produce large profits for the bank as long as rates stayed the same. What do you think of this policy?

17.14 A consol bond never matures. It pays a coupon of 50 British pounds every year. The current market price for the bonds is 1,000 pounds.
a. Calculate the consol's duration and yield to maturity.
b. How would you change your answer to Part a if the market price of the bond was 500 pounds? 1,500 pounds? Explain your results.

17.15 A government bond with 2 years to maturity is traded for $1,000 (which is also its par value). The coupon is $90 per year. There is a 31% income tax on the interest. Foreign investors are taxed, and American investors are not taxed. Calculate the yield to maturity and the duration from the American point of view, as well as the foreign investor's point of view. Explain your results.

17.16 A 2-year bond traded in the United States has a yield to maturity of 10%. A Japanese investor would like to purchase the bond. The investor has to convert yen to dollars to make this investment. Will the Japanese investor's yield to maturity and duration measured in yen be the same as the American investor's yield to maturity and duration? Explain.

17.17 Referring to the data in Question 17.16, suppose the yen appreciated by 2% a year relative to the dollar. From the American investor's point of view, we know that the yield to maturity is 10%, the maturity is 2 years, and the coupon is $50 per year. What is the duration of the bond in yen? Explain.

17.18 The following is taken from *Barron's* Bond section:

U.S. Zero-Coupons

Maturity	Type	Bid[a]	Asked	Fri. Chg.	Ask Yld.
Feb. 08	C_i^b	55:22	55:27	−24	5.88
Nov. 27	C_i	17:20	17:25	−20	5.88

a. 55:22 means $55^{22}/_{32}$, etc.

b. C_i = stripped coupon interest.

Source: *Barron's*, January 26, 1998, p. MW59.

Assume that there are 10.1 years to maturity for the first bond and $29^{10}/_{12}$ years to maturity for the second bond.
a. Check the yield calculations to verify the 5.88% reported yield.
b. What is the duration of these two bonds? Explain.
c. Draw the convexity curves of these two bonds (calculate it for alternate yields of 4½%, 5%, 5½%, 6%, 6½%, and 7%). Analyze your results.

17.19 The following is taken from *Barron's* Bond section:

U.S. Notes and Bonds

Rate	Mo./Yr.	Bid	Asked	Fri. Chg.	Ask Yld.
5	Jan. 00n	101:23	101:25	−7	5.41
6⅝	Feb. 27n	108:22	108.04	−53	6.03

n = notes.

Source: *Barron's*, Jan. 26, 1998, p. MW59.

a. Recalculate the yield to maturity of the second bond (6.03%).
b. Calculate the duration of the first bond (use an annual coupon of 5% and YTM = 5.41% per year).
c. You wish to invest for 10 years. The interest rate for all maturities went up by 1% immediately after you bought the bond on January 26 (namely, it went up to 7.03), and it remains at this level until you sell your bond 10 years hence.
(1) What is the capital loss on the bond? (Assume that coupons are paid annually.)
(2) Compare the terminal wealth of your investment in the bond under the assumption that you reinvest the coupons at the new interest rate. In light of your results, discuss the price risk and the reinvestment risk of the bond.

17.20 The following table presents various bonds issued by the Inter-American Development Bank:

Rate	Mat.	Bid	Asked	Yld.
Inter-Amer. Devel. Bank				
9.45	9-98	102:14	102:17	5.30
7.13	9-99	102:24	102:27	5.31

(continued)

Rate	Mat.	Bid	Asked	Yld.
8.50	5-01	108:04	108:08	5.69
6.13	3-06	101:20	101:26	5.84
6.63	3-07	104:26	105:00	5.91
12.25	12-08	146:02	146:10	6.30
8.88	6-09	120:20	120:28	6.27

Source: *Barron's*, January 26, 1998, p. MW60.

a. Assume 10 years to maturity and coupons paid annually. Calculate the yield to maturity of the 12.25% coupon bond, and compare it with the reported 6.30% yield.

b. Calculate the duration of this bond. (Assume a 6.3% interest rate.)

c. Suppose that the bank that issued the bond could issue it on the issuing date either at a 12.25% yield or at a 14% yield but callable at 110. Assume that the bond was issued 5 years ago and reached the 110 level 4 years ago. Ignoring the discounting factor, describe the cash flow to the bank and to the investor under these two alternatives. How much could the bank save on callable bonds up to January 1998?

CFA PROBLEM

17.1 Barney Gray, CFA, is director of fixed-income securities at Piedmont Security Advisors. In a recent meeting, one of his major endowment clients suggested investing in corporate bonds yielding 9%, rather than U.S. government bonds yielding 8%. Two bond issues—one U.S. Treasury and one corporate—were compared to illustrate the point. (Assume that today's date is June 1, 1991, the date of the actual CFA exam on which this question appeared.)

U.S. Treasury bond	8% due 6/15/2010	Priced at 100
AJAX Manufacturing	9.5% due 6/15/2015	Priced at 105
Rated AAA		
Callable @ 107.5 on 6/15/1995		

Gray wants you to prepare a response based on his expectation that long-term U.S. Treasury interest rates will fall sharply (at least 100 basis points) over the next three months.

Evaluate the return expectations for each bond under Gray's scenario, and support an evaluation of which bond would be the superior performer. Discuss the price-yield measures that affect your conclusions.

For Internet questions visit the Levy Investment Web site at http://levy-invst.swcollege.com

YOUR TURN: APPLYING THEORY TO PRACTICE

WILL YOU RIDE DOWN THE YIELD CURVE OR TAKE THE "HAIRCUT" ON YIELD?

Be forewarned: It will cost you to ride down the yield curve toward the shorter, safer end. A U.S. Treasury due in two years pays 4%; one due in 25 yields 7%. But any investor who survived the early 1980s knows what long bonds do if interest rates spike up. They spike down; 25-year Treasurys lose about 20% of their value if interest rates jump up 2 percentage points. There's lots of risk in going out a couple of decades to get that extra 3%. If you're nervous about the future—and who isn't these days—you might stay short and take the haircut on yield.

(continued)

Below, we update the Best Buy rankings published in our annual mutual funds guide (Aug. 31, 1992) for taxable, shorter-term bond funds. Best Buys combine good "risk-adjustment performance" over the past five years with low expenses and loads. Funds are shown in descending order of their cost/performance ranking. . . .

Why are Ginnie Mae funds, which own mortgage pools due in up to 30 years, on a list of shorter funds? Optional mortgage prepayments turn what looks like a 30-year investment into something that behaves more like a 2-to-8 year investment. We have eliminated one Best Buy Ginnie Mae fund, Vanguard's, from today's list because it is more rate-sensitive than most.

Junk funds are the one category still weighted 50/50 on cost and performance; portfolio skill matters more in results here. Some junk bonds with long maturities have the interest-rate sensitivity of shorter investments. If you are worried more about inflation than a depression, junk is a very attractive alternative to long Treasurys. You get higher interest without exposing yourself to the rate risk of very long-term bonds.

Source: "Chicken Bond Funds." *Forbes,* June 21, 1993, p. 156. Reprinted by Permission of *Forbes* magazine, © Forbes Inc., 1993.

Best Buys in Shorter-Term Bond Funds

Fund	5-Year Annualized Total Return	SEC Yield	Annual Expenses per $100	Maximum Sales Charge	Assets 3/31/93 ($mil)	Minimum Initial Investment[a]	Performance Up Markets	Down Markets
Short-term								
Vanguard Fixed Inc— Short-Term Corp. Tel.: 800-835-1510	9.6%	4.86%	$0.27	None	$2,942	$3,000	D	A
Scudder Short Term Bond Fund Tel.: 800-225-2470	9.7	6.68	0.78[b]	None	2,910	1,000	D	A
N & B Limited Maturity Bond Tel.: 800-877-9700	8.7	4.60	0.65[b]	None	298	5,000	D	A
Fidelity Short-Term Bond Port Tel.: 800-544-8888	8.8	5.90	0.75	None	1,870	2,500	D	A
Intermediate-term								
Vanguard Bond Index Fund Tel.: 800-835-1510	10.6	6.06	0.20	None	1,170	3,000	B	C
Columbia Fixed Income Securities Tel.: 800-547-1707	11.2	5.81	0.66	None	292	1,000	A	D
Fidelity Intermediate Bond Fund Tel.: 800-544-8888	9.7	6.23	0.58	None	1,568	2,500	C	B

(continued)

Best Buys in Shorter-Term Bond Funds

Fund	5-Year Annualized Total Return	SEC Yield	Annual Expenses per $100	Maximum Sales Charge	Assets 3/31/93 ($mil)	Minimum Initial Investment[a]	Performance	
							Up Markets	Down Markets
T Rowe Price New Income Fund Tel.: 800-638-5660	9.8	5.99	0.84	None	1,529	2,500	C	C
Ginnie Mae								
Benham GNMA Income Tel.: 800-321-8321	10.8	6.84	0.59	None	1,153	1,000	B	B
AARP Inc Trust— GNMA & US Treasury Tel.: 800-225-2470	9.8	6.18	0.72	None	6,060	500	D	B
Fidelity Ginnie Mae Tel.: 800-544-8888	10.0	6.31	0.81	None	959	2,500	C	B
T Rowe Price GNMA Fund Tel.: 800-638-5660	10.1	7.33	0.79	None	912	2,500	C	B
Junk								
Fidelity Capital & Income Fund Tel.: 800-544-8888	12.5	6.04	0.83	None	2,037	2,500	B	B
Merrill Lynch Corp —High Income-A Tel.: 800-637-3863	13.8	9.08	0.59	4.00%	1,508	1,000	C	A
Federated High Yield Trust Tel.: 800-245-5000	12.1	9.13	0.77[b]	None	389	25,000	B	C
Vanguard Fixed Income—High Yield Tel.: 800-835-1510	10.1	8.64	0.34	None	2,384	3,000	D	A

a. Most funds have lower minimum requirements for IRAs and automatic savings plans.

b. Net of absorption of expenses by fund sponsor.

Questions

1. Explain why the 5-year annualized total returns reported in the table are much higher than the yields to maturity on the bonds.

2. Suppose the yield curve remains stable. The yield to maturity on a 25-year bond is 7% and on a 24-year bond, 6%. Show the profit from "riding

(continued)

the yield curve," that is, investing in the 25-year bond and selling it 1 year later.

3. Suppose that now there is a probability of $\frac{1}{3}$ that the yield curve will remain at the same level, a $\frac{1}{3}$ probability of the curve's shifting upward by 3%, and a $\frac{1}{3}$ probability of the curve's shifting downward by 3%. You are considering whether to invest for 1 year in the 25-year bond or whether to purchase a 1-year bond at a yield of 4%. Calculate the mean and variance of the rates of return on each of these two investment policies. Can you explain why some investors would prefer to take a "haircut on yield"?

4. Repeat Question 3, but this time let the probability of the upward shift be $\frac{9}{10}$ and the probability of the downward shift be $\frac{1}{10}$. Discuss your results.

5. The Ginnie Mae fund has a 30-year maturity and pays an annual coupon of $68; its yield to maturity is 8%, and its face value is $1,000. Calculate the current market price and duration of the bond.

Suppose now that the interest rate decreases from 8% to 6%. Explain the claim in the article that "optional mortgage prepayments turn what looks like a 30-year investment into something that behaves more like a 2-to-8 year investment."

6. Suppose that the yield on a 30-year junk bond is 9.13%. The yield on a short-term 5-year bond is 5.90%. Suddenly, inflation (accompanied by rapid expansion) hits the economy. The yield on the short-term bond goes up from 5.90% to 7.90%, and the yield on the junk bond goes up from 9.13% to 9.20%. Calculate the capital loss on these two bonds, assuming that before the inflation, the two bonds sold at par, which is $1,000.

In light of your results, explain the article's argument that "some junk bonds with long maturities have the interest-rate sensitivity of shorter investments. If you are worried more about inflation than a depression, junk is a very attractive alternative to long Treasurys." (Hint: Consider the risk of bankruptcy.)

SELECTED REFERENCES

Bierwag, G. O. *Duration Analysis: Managing Interest Rate Risk.* Cambridge, Mass.: Ballinger, 1987.

This book focuses on duration and how it is used to manage interest rate risk.

Fabozzi, Frank J. *Fixed Income Mathematics.* Chicago: Probus Publishing, 1988.

This book addresses the fundamentals of the relationship between bond prices and underlying variables. The specific focus is on duration and convexity.

Fabozzi, Frank J., and T. Dessa Fabozzi. *Bond Markets, Analysis and Strategies.* Englewood Cliffs, N.J.: Prentice Hall, 1989.

This book is similar to Fabozzi's Fixed Income Mathematics *but also gives specific institutional details of the Treasury, corporate, and municipal bond markets.*

Homer, Sidney, and Martin L. Liebowitz. *Inside the Yield Book: New Tools for Bond Market Strategy.* Englewood Cliffs, N.J.: Prentice Hall, 1972.

This path-breaking book in the area of bond management developed the taxonomy of active trading strategies.

Macaulay, Frederick R. *Some Theoretical Problems Suggested by the Movements of Interest Rates, Bond Yields, and Stock Prices in the United States since 1856.* New York: National Bureau of Economic Research, 1938.

This monograph first developed the idea of duration.

SUPPLEMENTAL REFERENCES

Barber, Joel R., and Mark L. Copper. "Is Bond Convexity a Free Lunch?" *Journal of Portfolio Management,* Fall 1997, pp. 113–119.

Bierwag, Gerald O., Iraj Fooladi, and Gordon S. Roberts. "Designing an Immunized Portfolio: Is M-Squared the Key?" *Journal of Banking and Finance* 17, no. 6 (December 1993): 1147–1170.

Christensen, Peter Ove, and Bjarne G. Sorensen. "Duration, Convexity, and Time Value." *Journal of Portfolio Management* 20, no. 2 (Winter 1994): 51–60.

Dybrig, Philip H., and William Marshall. "Pricing Long Bonds: Pitfalls and Opportunities." *Financial Analysts Journal,* January–February 1996, pp. 32–39.

Kahn, Ronald N. "Bond Managers Need to Take More Risk." *Journal of Portfolio Management,* Spring 1998, pp. 70–76.

Kritzman, Mark. "What Practitioners Need to Know . . . about Duration and Convexity." *Financial Analysts Journal* 48, no. 6 (November–December 1992): 17–20.

Longstaff, Francis A., and Eduardo S. Schwartz. "Interest Rate Volatility and Bond Prices." *Financial Analysts Journal* 49, no. 4 (July–August 1993): 70–74.

Mehran, Jamshid, and Ghassem Homaifar. "Analytics of Duration and Convexity for Bonds with Embedded Options: The Case of Convertibles." *Journal of Business, Finance and Accounting* 20, no. 1 (January 1993): 107–113.

Thomas, Lee, and Ram Willner. "Measuring the Duration of an Internationally Diversified Bond Portfolio." *Journal of Portfolio Management,* Fall 1997, pp. 93–101.

Appendix 17A Computational Equation for Duration

This appendix develops a duration equation that can be placed in a single cell of a spreadsheet; hence, sensitivity analysis can easily be performed. The approach developed here is primarily beneficial for students who want to analyze duration using a spreadsheet.

The following equation is flexible enough to accommodate compounding other than just semiannual compounding. The computational equation for duration, which can easily be programmed into spreadsheets, is as follows:

$$D = \frac{C\left[\left(1 + \frac{y}{np} - f\frac{y}{np}\right)\left(1 + \frac{y}{np}\right)^n - \left(1 + \frac{y}{np}\right) - \frac{y}{np}(n - f)\right] + \left(\frac{y}{np}\right)^2 Par(n - f)}{C\frac{y}{np}\left[\left(1 + \frac{y}{np}\right)^n - 1\right] + \left(\frac{y}{np}\right)^2 Par} \tag{17A.1}$$

where C is the coupon payment in dollars per period, f is the fraction of the coupon period elapsed since the last payment, n is the total number of remaining coupon payments, Par is the par value of the bond, and np is the number of coupon payments per year (for example, mortgages are typically paid monthly, so $np = 12$).

Although Equation 17A.1 looks messy, it is much easier to program into a spreadsheet than is Equation 17.3, because Equation 17.3 requires setting up summations of differing lengths. For example, the spreadsheet to compute a 30-year, semiannual coupon bond requires 60 cash flows to be discounted. Equation 17A.1 can be placed in a single cell and used for a bond of any maturity (as well as any payment frequency).

For example, according to Exhibit 17–8, the inputs for the 5-year bond are as follows: $C = \$53.40$, or $1{,}000 \cdot 0.1068 \cdot \frac{1}{2}$; $y = 0.1068$; $f = 0$; $np = 2$ (semiannual bond); $Par = 1{,}000$; and $n = 10$ (5-year bond with two payments per year). Thus,

$$D = \frac{\$53.4\left[\left(1 + \dfrac{0.1068}{2}\right)\left(1 + \dfrac{0.1068}{2}\right)^{10} - \left(1 + \dfrac{0.1068}{2}\right) - \dfrac{0.1068}{2}(10)\right] + \left(\dfrac{0.1068}{2}\right)^2 1{,}000(10)}{53.4\dfrac{0.1068}{2}\left[\left(1 + \dfrac{0.1068}{2}\right)^{10} - 1\right] + \left(\dfrac{0.1068}{2}\right)^2 1{,}000}$$

Working through the calculations yields $D = 4.0$ years.

CHAPTER 18

COMMON STOCKS— VALUATION

LEARNING OBJECTIVES

After studying this chapter you should be able to:

1. Explain how investors use stock valuation models.

2. Describe the assumptions underlying the constant dividend growth model.

3. Value firms that are presently experiencing supergrowth.

4. Explain when the P/E ratio can be used safely.

INVESTMENTS IN THE NEWS

RATING YOUR BROKER'S STOCK PICKS

The five-year performance champ in the study is Paine-Webber with an estimated 314.8% return on its "Performance Portfolio." Performance has been cooler lately, however; the firm was in the bottom half of the rankings for the latest 12 months.

Michael Culp, research director, says the firm's focus is "mostly on growth stocks—companies that can deliver double-digit earnings gains the next couple of years." To make the recommended list, the company should have a price/earnings ratio of less than the growth rate, Mr. Culp says. For example, a company whose earnings are expected to grow 15% a year should sell for a P/E ratio of less than 15.

Mr. Culp singles out three stocks as illustrating the kind of thing Paine Webber is looking for. One is Chase Manhattan, the banking giant that is "a restructuring play." Another is Boston Scientific, a maker of surgical instruments, which is showing strong international growth. . . .

Then there's Applied Materials, which makes wafer-fabrication systems for the semi-conductor industry.

Source: "Rating Your Broker's Stock Picks," *Wall Street Journal,* August 15, 1997, p. C.23. Reprinted by permission of *The Wall Street Journal* © 1997 Dow Jones & Co., Inc. All Rights Reserved Worldwide.

How do you pick a stock? This chapter's Investments in the News emphasizes selecting growth stocks. Moreover, Michael Culp, of Paine Webber, uses two criteria: P/E ratio and growth. If a company has a P/E ratio of less than 15 and its earnings grow at 15% or more, it is on the recommended buy list. We will come back to this recommendation after a study of the meaning of P/E ratios and the various sources of growth in earnings.

This chapter and Chapter 19 introduce methods investors use to value stocks. Most of the methods described are based on economically sound investment rules. In particular, discount rates are used to evaluate a stock's future cash flows. In addition to valuation methods based on discounted cash flows, the P/E ratio is also discussed. This widely used valuation measure (see Investments in the News), which is based on past performance, often appears in the financial press. Thus, investors should understand its predictive power and limitations.

Investors should hold portfolios composed of many assets. Indeed, this is an assumption of the capital asset pricing model (CAPM). This chapter evaluates stocks in isolation and estimates the present value of all expected future cash flows corresponding to the stock under consideration. Does this contradict the CAPM, which advocates that each stock should be evaluated only in a portfolio context? It does not contradict the CAPM, because the discount rate that we use to evaluate an individual stock's future cash flows is determined in the marketplace, and it takes into account the firm's specific risk as well as the covariance with other assets. For example, if Du Pont has zero correlation with the market portfolio and Apple Computer has a positive correlation with the market portfolio, other things being equal, Apple Computer will probably have a higher discount rate.

As will be explained later in the chapter, in calculating the present value of future dividends we must assume some discount rate. The **discount rate** is the required rate of return by investors, given the riskiness of the stock. If investors hold only Du Pont, then the variability of future dividends determines the value of the discount rate (k). If, as in the CAPM, investors hold many assets in their portfolios, then the betas (or the covariances) of the future income from the stock with the market portfolios determine the discount rate. Thus, the valuation method presented in this chapter does not contradict the portfolio analysis studied in the previous chapters, and in particular, it does not contradict the CAPM.

For a given discount rate, valuation models are developed based on the future average cash flow. This chapter assesses whether investors should discount earnings, dividends, or the future stock price. Also, it analyzes how retained earnings and the firm's reinvestment policy affect the stock price.

18.1 USES OF STOCK VALUATION MODELS

Why should stock valuation models be studied? Many investors and business owners rely on the stock values obtained from the valuation models described in this chapter to make investment decisions. This section looks at typical applications of model-generated stock values to demonstrate how the stock valuation models are used in practice.

18.1.1 Assessing Investment Opportunities

The most important use of valuation models is in selecting stocks for investment. How can you tell if a share of General Motors stock currently priced at $20 is a good investment? Is the stock underpriced? Is it overpriced? The ability to correctly value securities is essential to successful investing. For example, if you value Amoco stock at $100 and the current market price is $55, this valuation suggests you should buy Amoco stock. Of course, you should actually buy the stock only after rigorously testing your model and gaining confidence in its valuation capabilities.

Many investment theorists believe that changes in stock prices, particularly short-run changes in stock prices, cannot be predicted. They feel that no stock valuation model can locate underpriced or overpriced stock. Even though you may not believe stock valuation models can locate mispriced stocks, you must include other people's opinions in your assessment of stock prices. After all, if a group of believers in a particular model of stock valuation predict that prices will move in a given direction, their actions could affect stock prices even though there is no economic foundation for this price change. For example, adherents of the "Super Bowl indicator" will buy stocks after an NFL win and thus push stock prices higher (statistics reveal that after an NFL win, the stock market tends to rise significantly more than after an NFL loss). You may not agree with these investors, but you could benefit from knowing the direction the market will take based on their actions. If you weren't aware of their valuation model, you might miss a stock market rally. Indeed, the famous economist John Maynard Keynes describes the stock exchange as a place where successful investing is the art of what people think other people think about stock prices.[1]

18.1.2 Valuing a Common Stock Issue

When a firm goes public, it needs some method to estimate the value of its stock. Suppose you own a successful family firm that needs additional capital to expand internationally. You decide to issue stock to the public. (Recall that this is called an IPO.) When you make this decision, there is no market price for your shares. To determine the selling price of your firm's stock, you need a way to value your equity. Even if you believe the market price of common stock equals the value of the stock, you need to employ a stock valuation model, because at the time of the first public offering there is no market price for the shares. By the same token, an underwriter who insures your issue needs some valuation model in order to decide the firm's economic value to be insured.

18.1.3 Estimating the Appropriate Discount Rate

You studied the concept of a firm's cost of capital or discount rate in your course on the principles of finance. The evaluation of an investment project requires an estimate of the firm's cost of capital. The cost of equity is a major component in the

---

1. See John Maynard Keynes, *The General Theory of Employment and Money* (New York: Harcourt Brace, 1936), p. 156.

cost of capital. Financial managers can use stock valuation models to calculate the cost of equity.

18.1.4 Understanding the Financial Media

Articles and reports in the financial media use terms from stock valuation models: *growth rate, supergrowth firms, price/earnings ratios,* and so forth. By studying stock valuation models, you will know what these terms mean and how to apply them.

Many stock valuation models exist. The following sections explain how the different methods should be used and under what situations all these methods yield the same results.

18.2 THE DISCOUNTED CASH FLOW PRINCIPLE

Many stock valuation models have their roots in the discounted cash flow (DCF) principle, which states that the current value of any asset is the present value of all its future cash flows. Thus, when you work with discounted cash flows, you must both forecast future cash flows and estimate the appropriate discount rate to use in your calculations. By using a stock valuation model based on the discounted cash flow principle, you can determine whether the stock is undervalued or overvalued.

A stock is an asset whose future expected cash flows are CF_1, CF_2, ... , CF_n, where the subscript $i = 1, 2 \ldots n$ denotes the year in which the cash flow is obtained. The value of the stock is simply the discounted value of all these cash flows (see Appendix 18A). To illustrate how to value a given stock, suppose you forecast that Ford Motor Company will pay a $4 cash dividend per share at the end of the next year and a $5 cash dividend per share at the end of the second year. Furthermore, you estimate that you will be able to sell the shares of Ford 2 years from now for $130. Because these are only estimates, they are uncertain; and like any uncertain cash flow stream, you discount the cash flows at a discount rate (k), which is composed of the risk-free interest rate (time value of money) and a risk premium.[2] Suppose the discount rate is $k = 15\%$. The current stock price as published in the *Wall Street Journal* is $P_0 = \$100$. Should you buy the Ford stock? Like any other capital budgeting project, your decision rules are these (where PV is the present value of the expected cash flows):

If $PV > P_0$, buy the stock ($NPV > 0$).
If $PV < P_0$, do not buy the stock ($NPV < 0$).
If $PV = P_0$, you are indifferent whether to buy or not to buy the stock ($NPV = 0$).

These decision rules can be applied to all valuation models presented in this chapter.

To continue the example, the present value of Ford's $4 dividend paid at the first year is $3.48 (see Exhibit 18-1). At the end of the second year, $5 dividends are

---

2. For simplicity, we ignore the effects of inflation.

EXHIBIT 18-1 Present Value of $4 Dividend in Year 1 and $5 Dividend and $130 Stock Price in Year 2

	Beginning of the First Year (t_0)	End of the First Year (t_1)	End of the Second Year (t_2)
Expected dividends		$4	$5
Expected price			$130
Total expected cash flow		$4	$135
Discount factor for each year		1/1.15	$1/1.15^2$
Contribution to present value		$4/1.15 \cong \$3.48$	$\$135/1.15^2 \cong \$102.08$
Present value of the total cash flows		$3.48 + \$102.08 = \$105.56$	

paid; however, the stock is also expected to be sold at $130, making the total expected cash flow $135, with a discounted value of $102.08. Therefore, the present value of all expected cash flows is $PV = \$105.56$. Because $105.56 is greater than the current price ($P_0 = \$100$), the net present value ($NPV = PV - P_0 = \$105.56 - \$100 = \$5.56$) is positive. If you expect these cash flows, you should buy the stock.

Who, then, sells Ford stock? Other investors in the market may have different predictions of the cash flows and hence a different future stock price. Suppose another investor believes, as you do, that the dividends will be $4 next year and $5 in 2 years, but unlike you, this investor believes that at the end of the second year the Ford stock will be selling only at $120. Even if this investor also uses a 15% discount rate, the present value of these cash flows is $98, as shown in Exhibit 18–2.

Suppose the second investor owns Ford stock. Because the present value is $98, which is less than the current stock price ($P_0 = \$100$), this investor should sell the stock for $100. Indeed, every day investors trade Ford stock and almost all other stocks. Investors who believe a stock is undervalued ($P_0 < PV$) buy the stock, and investors who believe a stock is overvalued ($P_0 > PV$) sell their stock. Because investors have differing opinions, the stock of Ford, as well as the stocks of other firms, changes hands. However, note that in both cases, the stock valuation method employed is based on the discounted cash flow principle.

EXHIBIT 18-2 Present Value of $4 Dividend in Year 1 and $5 Dividend and $120 Stock Price in Year 2

	Beginning of the First Year (t_0)	End of the First Year (t_1)	End of the Second Year (t_2)
Expected dividends		$4	$5
Expected price			$120
Total expected cash flow		$4	$125
Discount factor for each year		1/1.15	$1/1.15^2$
Contribution to present value		$4/1.15 \cong \$3.48$	$\$125/1.15^2 \cong \$94.52$
Present value of the total cash flows		$3.48 + \$94.52 = \$98.00$	

When investors buy and sell stocks, they affect the stocks' prices. When no one wants to execute any more transactions, the present value of cash flows for all investors who hold the stock (or those considering buying it) must be equal to the market stock price (P_0). To illustrate, assume that for some investors, $PV = \$120$ and $P_0 = \$100$. Then investors with $PV = \$120$ will continue to buy the stock. The market price will go up until $PV = P_0$—a point where, on this day with the present available information, no more transactions are desired. Similarly, if $PV < \$100$, investors will sell the stock, and the price will go down until $PV = P_0$.

The stockholder is entitled to an infinite stream of cash dividends. This infinite cash flow determines the stock's value. When the cash flow is cash dividends, stock valuation models based on the discounted cash flow principle are called **dividend discount models (DDMs).** However, in practice, investors do not hold the stock for an infinite period. How does this fact affect the valuation procedure? How does it affect the stock's price? In the examples in Exhibits 18-1 and 18-2, we assumed that investors hold the stock for 2 years, get two annual dividends, and then sell the stock. Now we will see that the valuation result does not change whether investors hold the stock for 1 year or for 10 years. We show that the holding period does not affect the value of the stock. To see this, we generalize the results for Ford Motor Company to any security held for any length of time.

To be more specific, suppose an investor invests for, say, 1 year and receives at the end of the first year a dividend of d_1. Then the investor sells the stock for P_1, where P_1 is the expected stock price at the end of the first year. The market is in equilibrium, namely, $PV = P_0$. How are P_0, P_1, and d_1 related? Because the current stock price is nothing but the discounted cash flows from future dividends and the stock sale, the stock price (P_0) is given by

$$P_0 = \frac{d_1}{1 + k} + \frac{P_1}{1 + k} \tag{18.1}$$

where k is the investor's required rate of return (given the stock's risk). However, what if the investor considers holding the stock for 2 years and then selling it? The investor would get dividend d_1 at the end of the first year; would get d_2 at the end of the second year; and would sell the stock for P_2 at the end of the second year, where P_2 is the expected stock price 2 years from now.

For this investment policy we have by the DCF principle: stock price (P_0^*) is given by

$$P_0^* = \frac{d_1}{1 + k} + \frac{d_2}{(1 + k)^2} + \frac{P_2}{(1 + k)^2} \tag{18.1'}$$

Would the DCF from the 2-year holding period yield a price (P_0^*) that is different from the value P_0 given in Equation 18.1? The answer is no. Regardless of how many years' dividends one wishes to incorporate into the DCF equation, the present value remains constant at P_0. In other words, P_0 in Equation 18.1 must be equal to P_0^* of Equation 18.1'. To see why this is so, consider the stock price *at the end of the first year* (P_1) for an investor who buys the stock *at the end of the first year* and holds it for 1 year. The investor invests P_1, receives a dividend at the end of the second year (d_2), and sells the stock for an expected price of P_2. For such an investment that takes place at the end of the first year, the DCF principle determines that

$$P_1 = \frac{d_2}{1 + k} + \frac{P_2}{1 + k} \tag{18.2}$$

Substituting P_1 from Equation 18.2 into Equation 18.1 reveals that

$$P_0 = \frac{d_1}{1 + k} + \frac{\dfrac{d_2}{1 + k} + \dfrac{P_2}{1 + k}}{1 + k}$$

which can be simplified as

$$P_0 = \frac{d_1}{1 + k} + \frac{\dfrac{d_2 + P_2}{1 + k}}{1 + k}$$

or

$$P_0 = \frac{d_1}{1 + k} + \frac{d_2 + P_2}{(1 + k)^2} \tag{18.3}$$

However, because the DCF on the right-hand side of Equation 18.3 is identical to the DCF of Equation 18.1', we have $P_0 = P_0^*$. Thus, no matter how many annual dividends are discounted, the DCF, and therefore the stock value, remains the same.

We conclude from this discussion that no matter if we assume holding the stock for 1 year and selling it for P_1, or holding the stock for 2 years and selling it at the end of the second year for P_2, the stock price, which is the *PV* of the two alternative cash flows (given by Equations 18.1 and 18.3), remains the same, at P_0.

Note that by substituting P_1 from Equation 18.2 into Equation 18.1, we get the discounted value of two annual dividends rather than one. Continuing this method, we can substitute for P_2 in Equation 18.3, then for P_3, and so forth, and we can continue this process indefinitely. Every such substitution adds more dividends to the cash flow. We finally determine that the stock price (P_0) is nothing but the DCF of all future dividends:

$$P_0 = \frac{d_1}{1 + k} + \frac{d_2}{(1 + k)^2} + \frac{d_3}{(1 + k)^3} + \ldots = \sum_{t=1}^{\infty} \frac{d_t}{(1 + k)^t} = \sum_{t=1}^{n} \frac{d_t}{(1 + k)^t} + \frac{P_n}{(1 + k)^n} \tag{18.4}$$

where d_t is the dividend paid at the end of Year t, and n is the number of future dividend payments. Thus, if we discount all future dividends, or the n future dividends plus P_n, we get the same stock price, P_0.

PRACTICE BOX

Problem

Suppose you know that Zoom, Inc., is going to pay $5 in dividends at the end of next year and $6 in dividends at the end of Year 2, and you estimate a price of the stock at the end of Year 2 of $110. Suppose the required rate of return (k) is 12%.

1. What is the stock price today (P_0) based on Equation 18.3?
2. What is the price at the end of Year 1 (P_1) based on Equation 18.2?
3. What is the price today (P_0) based on Equation 18.1?

Solution

1. Based on Equation 18.3 and the data given in the problem,

$$P_0 = \frac{\$5}{1 + 0.12} + \frac{\$6 + \$110}{(1 + 0.12)^2} \cong \$96.94$$

2. Based on Equation 18.2,

$$P_1 = \frac{\$6}{1 + 0.12} + \frac{\$110}{1 + 0.12} \cong \$103.57$$

3. Based on Equation 18.1,

$$P_0 = \frac{\$5}{1 + 0.12} + \frac{\$103.57}{1 + 0.12} = \$96.94$$

We see that the price today is independent of whether we discount based on the Year 1 price or the Year 2 price.

Regardless of whether you use Equation 18.1, 18.3, or 18.4, you will get the same value for the discounted cash flows (P_0). The intuitive explanation of this fact is that in Equation 18.1 we discount the price P_1. However, P_1 is nothing but the discounted dividends paid in Year 2 plus the discounted value of the price, P_2. Continuing this process, we find that the stock price (P_0) is nothing but the discounted value of *all* future dividends plus the discounted value of the stock price at the end of the nth year, $P_n/(1 + k)^n$. As n approaches infinity, however, the present value of the stock approaches zero, and we can ignore the price of the stock for dividend-paying firms.[3]

Some investors may claim that they definitely will not hold the stock for an infinite number of years. Moreover, they may claim that they intend to hold the stock for a few years, and hence Equation 18.4, which discounts an infinite series of dividends, is irrelevant for them. As has just been demonstrated, if these investors employ an equation that assumes holding the stock for 1 year and then selling the stock, or holding the stock for 2 years and then selling it, or for that matter holding the

---

3. Of course, we assume that the firm pays dividends such that the denominator, $(1 + k)^n$, grows faster than the stock price. Otherwise, the stock price would be infinite.

stock for any finite number of years, the same result is obtained if the DCF principle (which relies on an infinite stream of dividends) is used. Thus, a stock valuation formula (see Equation 18.4) should be based on all future dividends. However, the same value is also obtained when the investment is assumed to be for n years only. In such a case, the current stock price is the present value of the n year's cash dividends plus the present value of the stock price that is sold after n years. Therefore, Equation 18.4 can safely be employed for stock valuation even if the stock will be held only for a short period. Therefore, from now on this chapter simply assumes that the stock price is nothing but the DCF of all future dividends. It also employs an equation that assumes an infinite holding period or, interchangeably, the DCF of any finite number of dividends plus the discounted value of the stock price when sold.

As will be shown, the DCF principle is the foundation on which several valuation models are built. The next section describes a dividend discount model that incorporates a simple growth rate of dividends into the investor's assessment of a given stock.

18.3 THE CONSTANT DIVIDEND GROWTH MODEL

When stock valuation is based on future dividends, it is called the *dividend discount model* because it discounts cash dividends. When the dividends grow at a constant rate every period, it is called the constant dividend growth model. The **constant dividend growth model** is the most common valuation model used to determine both stock values and the firm's cost of equity. This model determines the stock price by the first-year dividend (d_1), the discount rate (k), and the growth rate (g).

The model assumes that the firm pays a constant percent of its earnings as dividends and the rest of the earnings are retained in the firm. It also assumes that the firm's earnings per share, dividends per share, and—as a result—the stock price are expected to grow every year by a *constant* growth rate denoted by g, where g is expressed as a percentage:[4]

$$P_1 = P_0(1 + g) \tag{18.5}$$

Substituting P_1 from Equation 18.5 into Equation 18.1 yields the following:

$$P_0 = \frac{d_1}{1 + k} + \frac{P_0(1 + g)}{1 + k} \tag{18.6}$$

---

4. Note that

$$P_0 = \frac{d_1}{1 + k} + \frac{d_1(1 + g)}{(1 + k)^2} + \cdots$$

and after a year,

$$P_1 = \frac{d_1(1 + g)}{1 + k} + \frac{d_1(1 + g)^2}{(1 + k)^2} + \cdots$$

because the dividend grows annually by g. Because the numerators all grow by g, the stock price grows by g, and $P_1 = (1 + g)P_0$.

Multiplying both sides of Equation 18.6 by $(1 + k)$ yields

$$P_0(1 + k) = d_1 + P_0(1 + g)$$

or

$$P_0(1 + k) - P_0(1 + g) = d_1$$

which can be further simplified as follows:

$$P_0(k - g) = d_1$$

The last equation can be written as the constant dividend growth model:[5]

$$P_0 = \frac{d_1}{k - g} \tag{18.7}$$

The constant dividend growth model given by Equation 18.7 asserts that the value of the stock (P_0) is nothing but the first-year dividend per share (d_1) divided by the discount rate (k) minus the constant growth rate (g). Obviously, the greater the growth rate (g), other things being the same, the larger the discounted future dividends will be, resulting in a greater stock price (P_0). One nice feature of this model is that all future dividends do not have to be estimated directly. We need only estimate g.

Note that this formula holds only when the growth rate (g) is smaller than the discount factor (k). If $g > k$, dividends grow faster than the discount rate, and the DCF of an infinite stream of dividends yields an infinite price. Also, $g = k$ is not possible; it results in an infinite price. Because an infinite stock price does not exist in the market, we safely assume that $g < k$, or at least that $g > k$ cannot continue forever. The case where $g > k$ for a limited period of time is discussed later in the chapter.

18.4 SOURCES OF GROWTH

Very few firms fit neatly into the assumptions needed to derive the constant dividend growth model. This section examines the sources of growth and how to effectively apply the constant dividend growth model. It also explains when this basic valuation model is not appropriate.

Usually, the earnings per share (EPS) and dividends per share (DPS) grow simultaneously. However, if the dividend policy changes over time, the dividends and earnings may reveal a different growth rate. This discussion focuses on the cases where both the EPS and the DPS grow at the same rate. Suppose we observe in a given year a change in the growth rate of the DPS, say, an increase from 5% to 9%. Does this increase imply that the stock's price should also increase? To answer the question, we need to have a closer look at the potential sources of the growth in the firm and, in particular, the sources of possible changes in the firm's growth rate.

5. This model was originally developed by M. J. Gordon, "Dividends, Earnings and Stock Prices," *Review of Economics and Statistics* 41 (May 1959): 99–105.

The DPS grows by (1) reinvestment of the retained earnings, even in normal-profit projects, and (2) undertaking projects with extraordinary profits. Let us elaborate on these two sources of growth. These two sources of growth do not have the same impact on the stock price.

18.4.1 Source 1: Reinvestment of Earnings

Consider a firm with no extraordinarily profitable projects. Such firms are **normal-growth firms.** Given the riskiness of such firms, the stockholders require, say, $k\%$ return per year on their investment. Suppose the firm reinvests the retained earnings in projects yielding $k\%$, exactly as required by the stockholders. Can the firm's earnings and dividends grow in such a case? Yes, they can, because the firm pays only a portion of its earnings as dividends and has some cash left to reinvest in the firm. Moreover, paying less dividends and increasing the dollar amount invested in profitable projects leads to higher future earnings. A firm pursuing this dividend policy will achieve growth in earnings and dividends. In this case, the increase in investment is financed by internal sources, namely, by cutting the current dividends. The lower the portion of earnings paid out as dividends, the greater the firm's future growth rate.

18.4.2 Source 2: Opportunities for Extraordinary Profits

When firms have opportunities for extraordinary profits, they can increase the growth rate of the EPS and the DPS with no change in their dividend policy—that is, without reducing the current dividends. Firms with these opportunities are **supergrowth firms.** Such a firm reinvests the retained earnings in projects yielding more than $k\%$, which is the required rate of return by the stockholders, given the risk of the firm. Because the firm earns extra profits on these projects, it experiences increased growth in sales, earnings, and dividends. It should be emphasized that the firm's profit increases with *no* change in risk; hence, the required rate of return by investors remains $k\%$.

It might seem as though supergrowth firms will always have a larger growth rate than normal-growth firms, but this is not always true. To illustrate, consider the following example. One firm may reinvest 90% of its profit at the required rate of return k and grow at $g = 10\%$, whereas another firm may reinvest only 20% of its profit in projects with extraordinary profits (those with a rate of return greater than k) and grow only at $g = 8\%$. The relatively low growth rate of the second firm results from the low proportion of the earnings retained. However, the firm with a 10% growth rate is classified as a normal-growth firm, whereas the firm with an 8% growth rate is classified as a supergrowth firm. In other words, the actual growth rate is determined by the rate of return on reinvested earnings, as well as the proportion of earnings reinvested in the firm. However, only the first factor—the profit on projects—determines whether the firm is classified as a normal-growth or a supergrowth firm.

Growth rates play a major role in stock valuation models based on the DCF principle. To examine whether an increase in g affects the stock price, the following sections analyze situations facing normal and supergrowth firms. They show that an increase in the growth rate caused by a cut in dividends changes the future dividends but does not lead to an increase in the stock price, whereas an increase in the growth of dividends due to the availability of extraordinarily profitable projects does cause an increase in the stock price.

18.4.3 Normal–Growth Firms

Let us look first at Exhibit 18-3. Year 0 stands for the current time, and P_0 is the current price. Similarly, Year 1 stands for the end of the first year. Here, a normal-growth firm's earnings per share is $10, and the firm distributes $5 per share as dividends. The firm earns 10% on its investments, and the stockholder's required cost of equity is $k = 10\%$. The current stock price is P_0. In the second year the earnings grow to $10.5, because $5 per share earned in the first year is reinvested at 10%, yielding an additional $5 \cdot 0.1 = \$0.5$ earnings per share. Because by assumption, the firm distributes 50% of its earnings as dividends, in the second year it pays dividends of $5.25, or ½($10.5), per share. Thus, the earnings, dividends, and hence the firm's stock price (see Equation 18.5) grow from the first year to the second year at a 5% growth rate.

EXHIBIT 18-3
The Growth Rate in Dividends, Earnings, and Stock Prices for Normal-Growth Firms

Part a: Growth Rate of $g = 5\%$ with $5 First-Year Dividends

Year	EPS	DPS	Stock Price
0			P_0
1	$10	$5	$P_0(1.05)$
2	$10.5	$5.25	$P_0(1.05)^2$
3	$11.025	$5.5125	$P_0(1.05)^3$
.	.	.	.
.	.	.	.
.	.	.	.

Part b: Growth Rate of $g = 9\%$ with $1 First-Year Dividends

Year	EPS	DPS	Stock Price
0			P_0
1	$10	$1	$P_0(1.09)$
2	$10.9	$1.09	$P_0(1.09)^2$
3	$11.881	$1.1881	$P_0(1.09)^3$
.	.	.	.
.	.	.	.
.	.	.	.

By this process the earnings, dividends, and stock price are expected to continue to grow at this rate in all other years. For example, the earnings of the second year are $10.5(1.05) = 11.025. Similarly, the dividend grows at 5%; hence, in the second year, the DPS is $5.25(1.05) = 5.5125.

Let us generalize these results. Denoting by b the proportion of the EPS retained in the firm (that is, not distributed as dividends) and by R the rate of return on the reinvested monies in the firm, then the growth rate is given by $g = b \cdot R$. Thus, if $b = 0.50$ and $R = 10\%$, the growth rate is $g = 0.5 \cdot 0.10 = 0.05$, or 5%, as the previous example reveals.

Employing Equation 18.7, the stock price (P_0) corresponding to the example in Exhibit 18–3a is given by

$$P_0 = \frac{d_1}{k - g} = \frac{\$5}{0.10 - 0.05} = \frac{\$5}{0.05} = \$100$$

Note that although this firm earns 10% on its investment, the growth rate is only 5%, because only 50% of the EPS is retained. Exhibit 18–3a shows that a normal-growth firm will experience the same growth in EPS, DPS, and its stock price.

Exhibit 18–3b still assumes a normal-growth firm—namely $k = 10\%$, and the firm reinvests 90% of its retained earnings in projects yielding 10%. The only difference between this case and the previous case is that the firm distributes only $1 (out of $10) as cash dividends and reinvests the retained earnings of $9 per share. The $9 per share is invested in projects yielding, as before, 10%; therefore, the dollar return on this reinvestment of the retained earnings is $0.90 (given by $9 \cdot 0.1 = \$0.90$) per share.

Let us continue these computations for the second year; 10% of the EPS, or $0.1 \cdot 10.9 = \$1.09$, is paid out as dividends in the second year. What is left is once again reinvested at 10%. Because the growth rate is 9% for all years, the EPS in the third year is $10.9 \cdot 1.09 = \$11.881$, and the DPS is $1.09 \cdot 1.09 = \$1.1881$; this growth rate continues forever. Note that in Exhibit 18–3b, we have $b = 0.9$ and $R = k = 10\%$; hence, the growth rate is $g = b \cdot R = 0.9 \cdot 0.10 = 0.09$, or 9%. Comparing Parts a and b of Exhibit 18–3, it is easy to see that by decreasing the dividends that are paid to the stockholders in the first year, more money is left to be reinvested. Hence, earnings and dividends grow at a growth rate of $g = 9\%$, in comparison with only $g = 5\%$ growth rate (see the previous two examples). Therefore, when only 10% of earnings is paid out as dividends, the stock price at the end of the first year (P_1) should grow at 9% over the original price (P_0). Note that the increase in the stock price is not due to the availability of extraordinary projects. The firm reinvests, as before, in projects yielding 10%. However, by cutting the dividends from $5 per share to $1 per share, the dollar volume of the investment in projects increases, and hence the dividend growth increases.

Does the increase in the growth rate by moving from 5% to 9% affect the current stock price (P_0)? To answer this question, use Equation 18.7 in the case described in Exhibit 18–3b to obtain

$$P_0 = \frac{d_1}{k - g} = \frac{\$1}{0.10 - 0.09} = \frac{\$1}{0.01} = \$100$$

From this result, you can see that an increase in the growth rate of the dividends *does not* increase the current stock price (P_0). It is true that in Part b of Exhibit 18-3, the future dividends grow at a faster rate than in Part a (9% versus 5%). However, for the faster-growth case (9%), there is also a lower dividend base—a $1 first-year dividend versus a $5 first-year dividend. These two factors exactly cancel each other, and the stock price remains unchanged, at $P_0 = \$100$. The price ($P_1$) at the end of the first period increases faster in Part b than in Part a because as less dividends are consumed, the money is kept in the firm. This higher stock price does not mean that the investor is better off, however. Although the investor gets more dividends and hence the price (P_1) is lower, the investor's total wealth is unaffected.

The intuitive economic explanation for this result is that stockholders require a $k = 10\%$ return on their investment. If the firm invests the retained earnings at 10%, then by investing more or less (that is, by changing the dividend level), the stockholders cannot be worse off or better off. The reason is that the NPV of cash flows created by a 10% profit, discounted at 10%, is zero; therefore, no change in the current stock price occurs, and the stock price is unchanged at $P_0 = \$100$.

To illustrate this argument, suppose you invest for 2 years in one of the two alternate firms given in Exhibit 18-3. If the firm pays out 50% of its earnings as dividends, at the end of 2 years you obtain $P_0(1.05)^2 = \$110.25$ plus the second-year dividend of $5.25 and the $5 dividend received in the first year. Assuming you can invest for a year at 10%, its value at the end of the first year is $5(1.1) = \$5.50$. You obtain $121 altogether. Now suppose that the firm pays out only 10% of its earnings as dividends. At the end of 2 years you obtain $P_0(1.09)^2 = \$118.81$ plus $1.09 (the second-year dividend) plus the first-year dividends that you can invest at 10%, $1(1.1) = \$1.10$—again, $121 altogether. As you see, the sum is the same in both cases; hence, the current price will be the same. P_0 is the sum in both cases.

PRACTICE BOX

Problem

The stock of Commonwealth Edison, Inc. (CWE), a power company, trades at $25, will pay $1.50 in dividends next year (d_1), and has a required rate of return of 9.5%. CWE is a normal-growth firm.

1. What is the implied growth rate of dividends?
2. If CWE lowers its dividend by 10%, what is the percentage change in the growth rate of dividends?

Solution

1. From Equation 18.7, solve for g:

$$P_0(k - g) = d_1$$

$$(k - g) = \frac{d_1}{P_0}$$

$$g = k - \frac{d_1}{P_0}$$

(continued)

Thus,

$$g = 0.095 - \frac{\$1.50}{\$25} = 3.5\%$$

2. A 10% decline in dividends will result in a dividend payment next year of $1.35 ($1.50 · 0.9). For a normal-growth firm, the change does not affect the price, which remains at $25. Hence, because CWE is a normal-growth firm,

$$g = 0.095 - \frac{\$1.35}{\$25} = 4.1\%$$

and the percentage change in the growth rate is 17.14%, or (4.1% − 3.5%)/3.5%. Therefore, growth rates are very sensitive to dividend policy.

18.4.4 Supergrowth Firms

In Exhibit 18-4, the change in the growth rate is due to the availability to the firm of extraordinarily profitable projects. Suppose the stockholders still require $k = 10\%$ (the risk of the firm does not change), but the firm can invest its retained earnings at 18% rather than 10%. Suppose the firm pays $5 per share in the first year as a cash dividend, and $5 per share is reinvested at 18%. In this case, the second-year EPS will be $10 + ($5 · 0.18) = $10.90. The second-year dividend, assuming that 50% of earnings are paid as dividends, is $d_2 = \frac{1}{2}(\$10.9) = \$5.45$. Similarly, the EPS and dividends grow at 9% in all other years.[6] Once again, the general formula can be applied to validate this 9% growth rate. In this example, $b = 0.5$, the reinvestment rate is $R = 18\%$, and hence $g = 0.5 \cdot 0.18 = 0.09$, or 9%.

Because dividends and earnings grow at $g = 9\%$ per year, the stock price should also grow at 9% per year. Equation 18.7 in this case yields:

EXHIBIT 18-4 The Growth Rate in Dividends, Earnings, and Stock Prices for a Supergrowth Firm: 9% with $5 First-Year Dividends	Year	EPS	DPS	Stock Price
	0			P_0
	1	$10	$5	$P_0(1.09)$
	2	$10.90	$5.45	$P_0(1.09)^2$
	3	$11.88	$5.94	$P_0(1.09)^3$
	.	.	.	.
	.	.	.	.
	.	.	.	.

6. Reinvestment at 18% of 50% of the EPS induces a growth rate of 18% · ½ = 9%.

$$P_0 = \frac{d_1}{k - g} = \frac{\$5}{0.10 - 0.09} = \frac{\$5}{0.01} = \$500$$

Unlike the comparison of stock prices corresponding to Exhibit 18-3a and Exhibit 18-3b, a comparison of stock prices corresponding to Exhibit 18-3a and Exhibit 18-4 (in both cases, 50% of earnings is paid as dividends) reveals a dramatic jump in the current stock price (P_0), from $100 to $500. How can we account for this large price increase? By shifting from Exhibit 18-3a to Exhibit 18-3b, we see that the change in the growth rate (from 5% to 9%) is due to a change in the dividend policy. The firm reduces its dividend and reinvests more in projects (at 10%); hence, the growth rate increases from 5% to 9% at the expense of a reduction in the base dividend from $5 to $1. As a result, no gain in the stock price is achieved, and it remains $P_0 = \$100$. However, in the comparison of Exhibit 18-3a and Exhibit 18-4, the growth rate increases, once again, from 5% to 9%, not at the expense of a reduction in the base dividend, which is kept in the first year at $d_1 = \$5$. The increase in the growth rate is due to an increase in the project profitability (from 10% to 18%) with no change in the firm's risk. This is an economic gain, so the price increase from $100 to $500 is a reaction to the newly available profitable projects and is not due to an increase in the dollar volume invested.

The key difference between the normal-growth and the supergrowth firms is that with the normal-growth firm, both the stockholders and the firm can reinvest at $k = 10\%$. The supergrowth firm, in contrast, can reinvest at 18%, whereas stockholders can reinvest the dividends at only 10%. The availability of projects with a positive NPV induces an increase in the stock price from $100 to $500.

In summary, Exhibit 18-3 shows normal-growth firms with different dividend policies. Exhibit 18-4 represents a supergrowth firm, which can reinvest money at a rate of return greater than the minimum rate required by the stockholders. A change in the growth rate of a firm that is due to a change in the proportion of earnings paid as dividends not accompanied by an increase in project profitability does not affect the stock price (see Exhibit 18-3). A change in the growth rate that is induced by the availability of more profitable projects, as expected, affects the stock valuation and thus the investors' view on whether a stock is overpriced or underpriced.

18.4.5 Supergrowth Firms for a Limited Time Period

The large increase in the stock price, from $100 to $500, should not come as a surprise. The price jump might seem to be very large and not justified by an increase in the projects' profitability from 10% to 18%. However, recall that this extra profit (18% rather than 10%) is assumed by the constant dividend growth model to continue forever on all earnings retained. Thus, the present value of the extra profit (18% − 10%) on all retained earnings is $400; hence, the stock price increases from $100 to $500.

Does it make sense to expect that the company can reinvest its earnings at 18% but investors require only 10% on their investment? The answer is absolutely yes. To see why, consider a firm that discovers a new drug (e.g., the recent Viagra pill) and is granted a patent on this new drug. The firm earns an 18% rate of return rather than the 10% it would make without this new drug. However, the firm's risk does not change, and the required rate of return by the stockholders remains 10%. Because the firm makes 18%, investors will buy the stock, so the price will go up until the rate of return on the stock is 10%.

Because the firm in this case invests at a rate of return higher than that required by the stockholders ($k < R$), it is a supergrowth firm. However, this supergrowth cannot continue forever, as Equation 18.7 assumes. Most firms face a limited number of years of supergrowth. Competition restricts the future growth of the firm. When one firm has an extraordinary profit, competitors will enter the market. Prices of the product, as well as its profitability, then go down. When Apple and IBM first entered the personal computer market, for example, prices were very high, and these firms enjoyed extra profits. After a few years, many competitors were attracted to this profitable business, the prices of personal computers fell dramatically, and the extra profit disappeared. Firms such as IBM and Apple are supergrowth firms for a few years. When the accelerated growth levels off, they become normal-growth firms, with earnings and dividends growing at normal, rather than abnormal, rates.

Firms involved in the research and development of a new drug often achieve supergrowth for a limited period. If a firm's research is successful, the firm can obtain a patent on the drug for a limited number of years, during which supergrowth prevails. After the patent expires, competitors will be allowed to produce the drug, and the original firm becomes a normal-growth firm. The constant dividend growth model thus needs to be adjusted to reflect this nonconstant growth.

Let's consider the general method of evaluating a stock characterized by a supergrowth rate for only a limited period of time. Suppose that at the end of the first year, the dividend is $d_1 = \$5$ per share, and the firm indeed can reinvest the retained earnings from the first year in a very profitable project with a positive NPV. This high rate of return is only for 1 year. (If it is for more than 1 year, a similar, but more complex, analysis applies.) The earnings retained from all subsequent years are invested at the firm's normal rate of 10%. In this case, the growth rate is not constant. Thus, Equation 18.7 cannot be employed to evaluate the stocks, because this equation is appropriate only for *constant*-growth cash flows. In this specific example the supergrowth lasts only 1 year, so we can apply Equation 18.1′. P_0 is thus given by

$$P_0 = \frac{d_1}{1 + k} + \frac{d_2}{(1 + k)^2} + \frac{P_2}{(1 + k)^2} \qquad (18.8)$$

(Recall that $P_0^* = P_0$. See the above discussion of Equations 18.1–18.1′.)

Let us employ the data in Exhibit 18-5. In this example, the dividend for the first year is $d_1 = \$5$. We assume that earnings and dividends grow for 1 year at 9% (the second year) and that beginning with the second year, dividends and earnings grow only at the normal growth of 5%. Therefore, for given dividends of $d_1 = \$5$, $d_2 = \$5(1.09) = \$5.45$, $d_3 = \$5.45(1.05) \cong \$5.72$, and so on. (All future dividends after the second year grow at 5%.) Because $d_1 = \$5$ (see Exhibit 18-5) and $k = 10\%$ (by assumption), if you know P_2, you can easily solve for P_0. P_2 can be found by using

	Year	EPS	DPS	Stock Price
EXHIBIT 18-5 **Supergrowth Firm for 1 Year and Normal Growth Thereafter:** **Growth Rate of** g_1 **= 9% for the First Year and** g_2 **= 5% after the First Year with $5 First-Year Dividends**	0			P_0
	1	$10	$5	$P_0(1.09)$
	2	$10.90	$5.45	$P_0(1.09)(1.05)$
	3	$11.44	$5.72	$P_0(1.09)(1.05)^2$
	.	.	.	.
	.	.	.	.
	.	.	.	.

the constant dividend growth model, because after the second year the firm will grow at the normal and constant rate. According to Equation 18.7,

$$P_2 = \frac{d_3}{k - g} = \frac{\$5.72}{0.10 - 0.05} = \frac{\$5.72}{0.05} = \$114.40$$

where $d_3 = \$5.72$, which is $d_1 = \$5$ growing at 9% in the second year and at 5% in all the years from the third year on (see Exhibit 18-5). Recall that P_2 is nothing but the present value of all dividends obtained in the third year and thereafter; hence, P_2 is the present value of $d_3, d_4, \ldots$. Because the growth rate after Year 2 is constant at 5% (normal growth), using Equation 18.7 to solve for P_2 is appropriate. Therefore, Equation 18.8 yields the following:

$$P_0 = \frac{d_1}{1 + k} + \frac{d_2}{(1 + k)^2} + \frac{P_2}{(1 + k)^2} = \frac{\$5}{1.1} + \frac{\$5.45}{1.1^2} + \frac{\$114.40}{1.1^2}$$

$$\cong \$4.55 + \$4.50 + \$94.55 = \$103.60$$

Hence, because of the supergrowth of d_2 in comparison with d_1, the stock price increases from $100 to only $103.60. This result is quite different from the large jump of $400 in the stock price that occurred before, when the extra profit of 18%, and hence the supergrowth of 9%, were assumed to continue forever.

From this example it can safely be concluded that the longer the number of years a firm can enjoy extraordinary profits (or the slower the competitors are), the bigger the jump in the stock price due to the availability of these profitable projects.

This example assumed supergrowth for 1 year and normal growth thereafter. The valuation formula can be generalized for a stock with a supergrowth for n years and normal growth thereafter. For example, if a firm has a patent that protects it for $n = 7$ years, it has supergrowth for 7 years. After 7 years, competitors produce the protected product, and the growth rate is expected to go down. The firm steps into a second economic cycle characterized by a normal growth rate.

In summary, a firm's dividends can grow because of a reduction in dividends paid, or by the firm's reinvesting funds in profitable projects. A firm that has extraordinarily profitable projects (projects with positive NPVs) is called a *supergrowth firm*.

Otherwise, it is a *normal-growth firm,* regardless of the actual growth rate. Most su-pergrowth firms cannot enjoy this extraordinary investment opportunity forever; hence, a supergrowth firm model for a limited time period seems to be the most rel-evant stock valuation model to value the stock of supergrowth firms. With accurate valuation models that realize that supergrowth cannot continue forever, investors are better able to assess the reasonableness of current stock prices.

18.5 CONSTANT DIVIDEND GROWTH MODEL VALUATION WHEN ALL THE EARNINGS ARE PAID AS CASH DIVIDENDS

If a firm is a normal-growth firm and distributes all its earnings as cash dividends, the stock price (P_0) is nothing but the present value of an annuity discounted at k%. As an example, assume $EPS = \$10$, and hence $d_1 = \$10$. However, because all EPS is distributed as dividends, the firm does not grow, and next year's profit, as well as dividends, will be constant at $10.[7] In this case,

$$P_0 = \frac{d}{1+k} + \frac{d}{(1+k)^2} + \frac{d}{(1+k)^3} + \cdots = \sum_{t=1}^{\infty}\frac{d}{(1+k)^t} = \frac{d}{k}$$

Using the data in Exhibit 18–3a yields the following:

$$P_0 = 10/0.1 = \$100$$

This is exactly the value obtained before, when some of the profit was retained and reinvested in the firm, as long as these retained earnings were invested at $k = 10\%$ and not in extraordinarily profitable projects ($k = 18\%$).

PRACTICE BOX

Problem

A firm pays a $5 dividend per share and has a growth rate of 10% for 4 years. The growth rate is only 5% from then on. If the discount rate is a constant $k = 8\%$, what is the stock price today?

Solution

The value of this common stock in 4 years (P_4) will be based on the standard constant dividend discount model:

$$P_4 = \frac{d_5}{k - g_2} = \frac{d_4(1 + g_2)}{k - g_2}$$

$$= \frac{d_0(1 + g_1)^4(1 + g_2)}{k - g_2} = \frac{\$5(1 + 0.1)^4(1 + 0.05)}{0.08 - 0.05} \cong \frac{\$7.6865}{0.03}$$

$$\cong \$256.2167$$

(continued)

[7]. The firm reinvests the depreciation, which makes it possible to create the perpetuity of $10 per share.

where $d_0(1 + g_1)^4 = d_4$, or the dividend paid at the fourth year, and g_2 is the growth rate from the fifth year and following. The present value of this stock price plus the present value of the dividends for the first 4 years is

$$P_0 = \frac{d_0(1 + g_1)^1}{(1 + k)^1} + \frac{d_0(1 + g_1)^2}{(1 + k)^2} + \frac{d_0(1 + g_1)^3}{(1 + k)^3} + \frac{d_0(1 + g_1)^4 + P_4}{(1 + k)^4}$$

$$= \frac{\$5.5}{(1 + 0.08)^1} + \frac{\$6.05}{(1 + 0.08)^2} + \frac{\$6.655}{(1 + 0.08)^3} + \frac{\$7.3205 + \$256.2167}{(1 + 0.08)^4}$$

$$\cong \$5.0926 + \$5.1869 + \$5.2830 + \$193.7077 \cong \$209.27$$

18.6 FINDING THE COST OF EQUITY CAPITAL WITH THE CONSTANT DIVIDEND GROWTH MODEL

Valuation models can be used for purposes other than finding overvalued and undervalued securities. Recall from your first finance course that the discount rate (k) is the required cost of equity capital by the stockholders, given the firm's risk. The constant dividend growth model can be used to estimate the cost of equity. In this case we assume the stock price to be the "correct" or equilibrium market price and solve for the unknown value (k). According to the constant dividend growth model,

$$P_0 = \frac{d_1}{k - g}$$

which can be rewritten as

$$k = \frac{d_1}{P_0} + g \qquad\qquad (18.9)$$

Because d_0 and P_0 are observed in the market, we can estimate the expected growth rate (g), then $d_1 = d_0(1 + g)$ can be calculated, and we can solve for the required cost of equity by the stockholders, which is simply the expected rate of profit on equity. In the example that corresponds to the constant dividend growth model (with no supergrowth) described by Exhibit 18-3a, we get $d_1 = \$5$, $P_0 = \$100$, and $g = 5\%$. Hence,

$$k = \frac{d_1}{P_0} + g = \frac{\$5}{\$100} + 0.05 = 0.05 + 0.05 = 0.10$$

or 10%. Therefore, investors who determine the stock price in the market are expecting (or requiring) to earn 10% on this investment. Given the risk of the stock, if an investor's required rate of return is greater than 10%, then the investor should avoid this investment. However, if the investor's required rate of return is lower than 10%, then this stock is an attractive investment.

The firm's managers, in contrast, can use the market stock price as the market's equilibrium price and from this deduce the market's required rate of return (k). The firm can use this value to estimate the weighted average cost of capital, which is the appropriate discount rate used in project evaluation. Thus, the valuation formulas for stocks discussed in this chapter can be used by investors to estimate the price of a stock, as well as by a firm's management to estimate the firm's cost of equity capital. Chapter 19 discusses how historical data can be used to estimate the growth rate (g).

18.7 PICKING STOCKS USING THE P/E RATIO

In an article published in *Fortune* on April 13, 1995, practitioners describe a method for selecting securities that can beat the market. They conclude, "To put the wind at your back when picking stocks, start with these value strategies. Over a 21-year period, portfolios loaded with stocks selling at low P/Es, low price to cash flow, and cheap market to book value die best." What is the P/E ratio, and how does it measure the profitability of stocks?

Price/earning (P/E) ratios for every firm (also known as *P/E multiple* or simply the "multiple") are published by most economic media (for example, *Wall Street Journal* and *Barron's*). Although the P/E ratio is not based on the DCF principle, it is widely quoted and published. For example, see the analysis from *Forbes* of fashion design firms and the financial data given in Exhibit 18-6. Recent price information and estimates of P/E ratios illustrate the importance that practitioners attribute to the P/E ratio in comparative analysis of the economic value of stocks.

This section discusses under what circumstances the P/E ratio conveys valuable information, and it warns against potential misuse of the P/E ratio. Unlike the "Super Bowl method," the P/E ratio does have some economic basis. The section covers the predictive power and limitations of the P/E ratio.

The P/E ratio published in the *Wall Street Journal* is the previous day's closing stock price divided by the last reported four quarters of EPS (denoted E). For example, if the closing stock price is $P = \$100$ and annual EPS is $10, then $P/E = \$100/\$10 = 10$. This P/E ratio shows that an investor has to wait 10 years to recover the $100 initial investment in the stock. Similarly, a P/E ratio of 5 implies that an investor has to wait 5 years to recover an investment. Note that P is the current price (namely, P_0), but it is denoted as P and not P_0 in the P/E ratio.

As with the payback method of project evaluation,[8] if the investor is willing to wait 7 years to recover the initial investment and the payback is 5 years, he should buy the stock. If the payback is longer than 7 years—say, 10 years—the investor should not buy the stock.

Investment analysts, when recommending buying stock, talk about the relatively low **multiples,** a term they use synonymously with *P/E ratios.* They use either the

---

8. The payback method is an investment criterion that counts the number of years until the initial investment is recovered. If the payback period is smaller than a predefined cutoff point, then the project is accepted.

EXHIBIT 18-6
Special Focus:
P/E Ratio

The S&P 500 index is up 29% since the beginning of the year, but fashion design firms have not followed suit. On average these stocks have lost 20% since December 1996. Based on the 1997 consensus earnings estimates the first four fashion companies listed below look cheap; the remaining four are still not bargains.

Good Looks Aren't Everything

Company	Recent Price	1997 Est P/E
Designer Holdings	$ 7.06	8
Farah	7.06	13
Guess	9.69	8
Salant	2.88	6
Donna Karan International	11.94	36
Gucci[a]	64.13	19
Mossimo	7.50	107
Phillips-Van Heusen	14.25	20

a. American Depositary Receipt

Source: Worldscape via OneSource Information Services and IBES Express, as cited in Eric S. Hardy, "Money and Investment: Good Looks Aren't Everything," *Forbes*, August 25, 1997, p. 265. Reprinted by Permission of *Forbes* magazine © Forbes Inc., 1997.

P/E ratio expressed in years or its reciprocal, the E/P ratio, in a percentage figure to evaluate the investment profitability. The P/E rule says that if the P/E ratio is too low, the market will rise, and if the P/E ratio is too high, the market will fall. Connecting Theory to Practice 18.1 illustrates the popularity of the P/E ratio, as well as its divergent interpretations by market professionals.

Are analysts justified in using the P/E ratio? Is the P/E ratio consistent with the present value of dividends model (see Equation 18.7)? The following discussion explores when the P/E rule can safely be used.

It has been stated that what is relevant for investment valuation is the future cash flows. However, in the P/E calculation, E is the last (past) EPS, not the future EPS or the future dividends. When you buy a stock, though, you buy it for the future, not for the past earnings. It is also not a cash flow to the investor. Therefore, using the E/P ratio (or the P/E ratio), which is based on past earnings, is conceptually wrong. However, in the following cases, the E/P ratio yields a precise measure of profitability that is equal to the one implied by the constant dividend growth model, which probably accounts for its popularity:

1. Constant earnings, when all earnings are distributed as cash dividends.
2. Constant growth in earnings and dividends, as long as the firm has a normal growth rate (and not a supergrowth rate) and every year it pays out a fixed proportion of its earnings as dividends.

Suppose the EPS and the DPS are constant at $10, and the stock price is $P = 100. Therefore, $E/P = d_1/P = \$10/\$100 = 10\%$. In this case, the E/P ratio is 10%, which is equal to $d_1/P + g$, because $g = 0$ and $d_1/P = 10\%$. This is a trivial case, because the past earnings are equal to the future earnings (and dividends); therefore, by looking at past earnings rather than future dividends, no harm is done. However, cases in which all earnings are distributed as dividends are rare; hence, the more realistic case is one in which some fixed portion of earnings is distributed as dividends.

Let us turn to more relevant cases by illustrating the two cases in Exhibit 18-3. These two cases have the following cost of equity:

$$\text{(a)} \quad k = \frac{d_1}{P_0} + g = \frac{\$5}{\$100} + 0.05 = 0.05 + 0.05 = 0.10$$

$$\text{(b)} \quad k = \frac{d_1}{P_0} + g = \frac{\$1}{\$100} + 0.09 = 0.01 + 0.09 = 0.10$$

Thus, the future profitability to the investor, using the constant dividend growth model, which is the correct method, is expected to be 10%. Indeed, $E/P = 0.10$ in both cases, as $\$10/\$100 = 0.10$. However, employing the P/E ratio (or the E/P ratio) for supergrowth firms is misleading. Comparing Exhibits 18-3a and 18-4 yields

$$\text{For normal-growth firm:} \quad \frac{E}{P_0} = \frac{\$10}{\$100} = 0.10$$

$$\text{For supergrowth firm:} \quad \frac{E}{P_0} = \frac{\$10}{\$500} = 0.02$$

Using the P/E ratio (or its reciprocal E/P ratio), we get a precise figure for a normal-growth firm but a distorted figure for supergrowth firms. (Note that $k = 10\%$, not 2%—see Exhibit 18-4.)

CONNECTING THEORY TO PRACTICE 18.1

STOCKS ARE IN A STRATOSPHERE, BY SOME MEASURES— VALUATION METER INDICATES PRICES OFF THE CHARTS

Have stock-market investors gone crazy?

Less than four months after October's precipitous plunge in stock prices, culminating in the largest-ever one-day point decline in the Dow Jones Industrial Average Oct. 27, stock-market indexes have rocketed to a string of records. . . .

According to statistics compiled by the *Wall Street Journal,* stocks in Standard & Poor's 500-stock index now trade at 26.1 times their operating earnings over the past four quarters. That's up from price/earnings multiple of 20.7 at this time last year, and a mere 15.9 in 1995. Meanwhile, the dividend

(continued)

yield—the amount of annual income thrown off by the stocks in the S&P 500—has plunged to only 1.51% of stock prices, an all-time low. . . .

The Dow industrials' P/E ratio as of last night was 22.2, up from 19.4 a year ago.

Source: Suzanne McGeen, "Stocks Are in a Stratosphere, by Some Measures," *Wall Street Journal,* March 4, 1998, p. C1. Reprinted by permission of *The Wall Street Journal* © 1998 Dow Jones & Co., Inc. All Rights Reserved Worldwide.

MAKING THE CONNECTION

This article shows that investors look closely at the P/E ratio. The P/E ratio for the S&P 500 was 26.1, significantly higher than it had been in 1995. Some professional managers argue that such a P/E ratio signals a time to reduce stock exposure, whereas others, including Jeffrey Applegate, U.S. market strategist for Lehman Brothers, is quoted elsewhere in this article as saying, "I think we're in a place we've never been before, and where most of the risks that can reasonably be anticipated have been mostly digested by the market." Even if the P/E ratio lacks a rigorous theoretical foundation, it is important to realize that other investors make major financial decisions based on it. These financial decisions could easily result in changes in security prices and, hence, changes in the value of a portfolio.

Thus, although both firms—one with a normal growth rate and one with a supergrowth rate—yield the same rate of return of 10%, looking at the E/P ratio as an indicator of profitability leads to an error: 10% for the normal-growth firm and only 2% for the supergrowth firm. The reason for the bias is that for the supergrowth firm, the future earnings, which grow at an accelerated rate, are ignored in the E/P calculation, because that calculation is fully based on current (or past) earnings.

To stress the possible distortion of the P/E ratio, suppose the P/E of Advo Inc. is 70. Namely, $E/P = 1/70 \cong 1.43\%$. Does that mean that the investor's required rate of return on equity is only 1.43%? No, it does not, because investors can earn a higher certain income by buying U.S. Treasury bills. However, there are two possible interpretations of this low figure: (1) the firm is a supergrowth firm, so the P/E ratio is misleading as discussed above, or (2) the current EPS is low and does not represent the future average EPS. Thus, a random deviation in the EPS in a particular year leads to a biased P/E ratio. Which of these two interpretations is correct can be known only by carefully studying the firm's income statement. Finally, there is a technical disadvantage to the P/E ratio. When the EPS values are negative, they are undefined.

Now we can analyze the recommendation regarding stock selection given in this chapter's Investments in the News. Suppose that you consider investing in stocks of two firms, both in the same industry. Hence, they have the same risk and the same discount rate of $k = 10\%$. Consider the following relevant data for these two firms:

	Firm A	Firm B
EPS	$10	$10
DPS	$1	$8
Price of stock	$70	$100
Rates of return on retained earnings (R)	9%	15%
Proportion of EPS retained in the firm (b) is 0.9		
Growth rate (g) = bR	8.1%	3%
P/E ratio	7	10

An investor using the criteria for picking stocks given in Investments in the News would prefer Stock A over Stock B, because Stock A has a lower P/E ratio and a higher growth rate. Moreover, according to the criteria in this article, Stock A should be accepted ($P/E < g$), and Stock B should be rejected ($P/E > g$). Let us see if this recommendation is consistent with the dividend cash flow valuation formulas in this chapter.

Employing Equation 18.7, we find the following values of Stock A and Stock B:

Value of Stock A: $d_1/(k - g) = \$1/(0.1 - 0.081) = \$1/0.019 \cong \$52.63$

Value of Stock B: $d_1/(k - g) = \$8/(0.1 - 0.03) = \$8/0.07 \cong \$114.29$

Thus, the reverse is true: Stock A should be rejected because its price is higher than its discounted cash flows, and Stock B should be bought because the value of its discounted cash flows is higher than its market price. Thus, what is wrong with the recommendation given in Investments in the News? It simply ignores the source of growth in EPS: Firm A reinvests 90% of its earnings in the firm and thus has 8.1% growth. This growth is achieved in spite of the fact that the money is reinvested in projects with negative NPV whose rate of return (9%) is smaller than the cost of capital (10%). Firm B, in contrast, reinvests at 15%. It is a supergrowth firm, which explains its relatively high value of $114.29. However, because it reinvests only 20% of its earnings, its growth rate is relatively low. Thus, looking at the P/E ratio and g, as the article recommends, and ignoring the source of the growth rate (g) is simply misleading. If both firms have the same retention ratio (that is, both distribute the same percentage of their earnings as dividends), then the growth rate (g) indeed reflects the reinvestment rate, and the higher the growth rate, the higher the rate of return on the investment undertaken by the firm. This example illustrates the risk of using the P/E ratio for firms that are not normal-growth firms.

The *Wall Street Journal* publishes the P/E ratio in which P is the current price and E is the last published EPS. However, Exhibits 18-3a and 18-3b show that $d/p + g = E/p$; that is, for normal-growth firms, the constant dividend growth model and the reciprocal of the P/E ratio provide the same rate of return. However, it is important to note that the two methods provide the same result only when E is the next year's EPS, that is, the future EPS (see Exhibits 18-3a and 18-3b). Indeed, the financial media sometimes publish not only the P/E ratio with last year's earnings per share, E, but also the P/E ratio where E is next year's EPS. A sample of such ratios is given in Exhibit 18-7, which provides the P/E ratio for the 1997 EPS and the

EXHIBIT 18-7   The P/E Ratio for Firms on the Dow Jones Index 1997–1998

▶ Among the Dow stocks that bargain-hunters are eyeing: GM, Sears, Boeing, Merck and Kodak.

Company	Price 10/30	1997 P/E	1998 P/E	Change Since Dow Peak	1997 Change	Dividend Yield	Comments
AT&T	48³/₁₆	18	16	· 23.4%	16.8%	2.7%	Best stock in Dow since August.
AlliedSignal	35¹¹/₁₆	17	15	−23.0	6.5	1.5	Misses earnings, first time in six years.
Alcoa	72³/₁₆	15	10	−17.9	13.2	1.4	Asian slowdown crimps aluminum demand.
American Express	76³/₄	18	16	−9.0	35.8	1.2	Strong results on card, investment units.
Boeing	47	63	19	−19.4	−12.0	1.2	Production woes clobber earnings.
Caterpillar	52¹/₈	12	12	−10.9	38.5	1.9	Asian infrastructure spending waning?
Chevron	80¹/₄	18	18	0.1	23.5	2.9	High hopes for Kazakhstan oil fields.
Coca-Cola	56¹/₂	38	32	−17.1	7.4	1.0	Fears of slower earnings growth.
Disney	80⁵/₈	29	25	−0.2	15.6	0.7	Defensive play in jittery market.
Du Pont	56¹/₄	15	14	−18.2	19.5	2.2	Soft prices weigh on chemical king.
Eastman Kodak	59¹¹/₁₆	17	13	−12.1	−25.6	3.0	Worst '97 Dow performer. Rebound ahead?
Exxon	60¹¹/₁₆	19	20	−6.5	23.9	2.7	Rock-solid oil giant. Global reach.
General Electric	63¹/₄	25	22	−8.7	27.9	1.6	CEO Jack Welch keeps delivering.
General Motors	66	8	8	3.5	18.4	3.0	Earnings hold up in tough auto market.
Goodyear	62³/₁₆	13	11	−4.0	21.1	1.9	Leading tire maker, modest P/E.
Hewlett-Packard	60¹¹/₁₆	21	18	−13.7	20.8	0.9	Suffers from investors' technology jitters.
IBM	96	16	14	−11.0	26.8	0.8	Strong performer. Huge buyback program.
Intl Paper	46³/₈	47	16	−19.4	14.5	2.2	Asian fears dim hopes for 1998.
Johnson & Johnson	56¹/₂	23	20	−9.2	13.6	1.6	Solid but unspectacular.
McDonald's	44¹/₂	19	17	−15.0	−1.8	0.7	Needs to revive U.S. business.
Merck	88	23	20	−13.7	11.3	2.0	Competitive threats, patent worries.
Minn. Mining (3M)	92	23	20	−4.0	11.1	2.3	Solid 3Q earnings lift this laggard.
J.P. Morgan	110	14	13	−4.5	12.6	3.2	Overseas exposure, high costs limit gains.
Procter & Gamble	67¹/₄	26	23	−9.6	25.0	1.5	Can growth rate be sustained?
Sears	41	12	11	−36.6	−11.0	2.3	Credit-card program a mess.
Travelers	69⁷/₁₆	17	15	−0.8	53.0	0.7	Street just loves CEO Sandy Weill.
Union Carbide	46¹/₂	10	11	−17.3	13.8	1.9	Profits seen falling in '98.
United Tech	67¹⁵/₁₆	17	15	−17.7	5.6	1.8	New doubts on earnings outlook.
Wal-Mart	34³/₄	23	20	−9.4	52.8	0.8	Big winner in '97 after tough five years.

P/E ratio for the 1998 EPS (the next year) for the firms that make up the Dow Jones Industrial Index.

In summary, investors should always rely on a stock valuation method that takes into account the discounted future dividends. However, the P/E ratio (or the E/P ratio) can be safely used for stock valuation (and for estimating the cost of equity) in the following two cases: (1) when all earnings are paid as cash dividends, and the dividends (and earnings) are constant across all years; and (2) when some constant percentage of the earnings is paid as cash dividends every year, and dividends grow over the years at a constant and normal growth rate—that is, the firm does not face an extraordinarily profitable project.

In practice, for each individual firm, the P/E ratio may give a distorted figure. However, on average for the whole economy or for some industries, investors can look at the P/E ratio to determine whether the stock market is relatively attractive or unattractive. Also, P/E ratios are used to identify the supergrowth firms. Assuming that the past years' earnings of a firm were typical, an unusually high P/E ratio indicates that investors view this firm as one with supergrowth potential.

Another useful application of P/E ratios is valuing stock of companies that pay no dividends. When a firm has never paid a cash dividend, how are we to use the DCF principle? In general, we estimate the future date when cash dividends will be paid and then apply the DCF principle to arrive at a current value. However, this exercise is very difficult. An easier approach is to determine the appropriate P/E ratio for this type of firm and estimate the price by multiplying the P/E ratio times the current EPS. For example, suppose the appropriate P/E ratio for Microsoft is estimated to be 30, indicating that it is a supergrowth firm. If the current EPS is $3.5, then Microsoft's stock would be valued at $(P/E) \cdot (EPS) = 30(\$3.5) = \$105$.

Although the P/E ratio is not based on the DCF principle, its ease of use has made it attractive for many investors. Appendix 18A and Appendix 18B suggest two additional methods for valuing the stock of nondividend-paying firms: the free cash flow model and the economic value–added model.

SUMMARY

Explain how investors use stock valuation models. Stock valuation models can be useful for several purposes. The two most important uses are for assessing investment opportunities and for estimating a firm's cost of equity. Stock valuation models are also useful for determining stock prices in initial public offerings. A sound valuation method must rely on discounted future dividends. Whereas the current dividend is known, future dividends can only be estimated. Therefore, we say that the stock price is the present value of all *expected* dividends.

A valuation formula should be based on the discounted cash flow (DCF), hence it discounts all future dividends. However, the same value is also obtained when the investment is assumed to be for *n* years only. In such a case, the current stock price is the present value of the *n* years' cash dividends plus the present value of the stock price that is sold after *n* years.

Describe the assumptions underlying the constant dividend growth model. The most popular valuation model is the constant dividend growth model, which assumes that every year the firm pays a constant percentage of its earnings as dividends, and the rest of the earnings are retained in the firm. Normal-growth firms invest the retained earnings at the required cost of equity, hence the percentage of profits retained in the firm does not affect the current stock price.

Value firms that are presently experiencing supergrowth. Although the constant dividend growth model can be employed for normal-growth and supergrowth firms, economic logic and historical data tell us that constant supergrowth cannot continue forever. (IBM, for example, was a symbol of supergrowth, but faced a decline in profit and even had negative earnings in 1992 and 1993.) Therefore, in the case of a supergrowth firm, a more reasonable assumption is that the supergrowth will last only for a given number of years. Then competitors will reduce the firm's growth, and after this supergrowth period, normal growth will characterize the firm. In any case, no matter whether the firm experiences normal growth or supergrowth after this initial period of supergrowth the valuation formula changes, but the valuation is still based on the discounted value of future dividends. One task facing an analyst is how long the supergrowth will last.

Explain when the P/E ratio can be used safely. The popular use of the P/E ratio as an investment criterion is not based on the principle of discounted future cash flows; hence, it is conceptually wrong. However, the use of the P/E ratio yields the same results as the use of the present value of future dividends in two cases: (1) all earnings are paid as cash dividends, and these dividends (and earnings) are constant across all years; and (2) some constant percentage of the earnings is paid as cash dividends every year, and dividends grow at a constant and normal growth rate. For supergrowth firms, the P/E ratio leads to misleading results and sometimes even to absurd results. Thus, the P/E ratio should be used with great care.

CHAPTER AT A GLANCE

1. *Stock valuation models are mainly employed by the following:*
   a. Investors.
   b. A firm estimating its cost of equity.
   c. An underwriter and a firm evaluating a stock in an initial public offering.

2. *The following are two popular valuation formulas:*

$$P_0 = \sum_{t=1}^{n} \frac{d_t}{(1 + k)^t} + \frac{P_n}{(1 + k)^n} \qquad\qquad P_0 = \sum_{t=1}^{\infty} \frac{d_t}{(1 + k)^t}$$

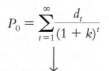

Assumes holding the stock for *n* years and then selling it

Assumes holding the stock for an infinite number of years

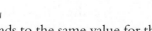

Leads to the same value for the stock price (P_0)

(where d_t is the dividend paid in Year *t*, *k* is the investors' required rate of return, and P_n is the stock price at Year *n*)

(where d_1 is the dividend paid next year and *k* is the investors' required rate of return)

3. *Valuation by the constant dividend growth model for normal-growth firms is as follows:*

$$P_0 = \frac{d_1}{k - g}$$

where d_1 is the next year's expected dividend and g is the growth rate of dividends ($k > g$).

4. *A constant dividend growth model with normal growth yields the following:*

$$\frac{E}{P} = \frac{d}{P} + g$$

$$\downarrow \qquad\qquad \downarrow$$

Reciprocal of the price/earnings
ratio = expected return on equity
(where P is the current stock price)

KEY TERMS

Constant dividend growth
   model   664
Discount rate   657

Dividend discount model
   (DDM)   661
Multiple   676

Normal-growth firm   666
Supergrowth firm   666

REVIEW

18.1 Can a stock's price be negative? (Hint: Use Equation 18.1 to explain your answer.)

18.2 If the growth rate of dividends is $g = k$, and this is expected to continue for an infinite number of years, then the stock price will be infinity. Do you agree?

18.3 a. "For a growth firm, when both the discount rate (k) and the growth rate (g) increase by +1%, this will not affect the stock price."
b. "If one of the values, k or g, goes up by +1% and the other goes down by −1%, this will not affect the stock price."
    Which quotation is correct? Explain why the quotations in Parts a and b are accurate or inaccurate.

18.4 Suppose you are given the following information regarding Firm A:

Year	EPS	DPS
1	$10	$ 2
2	11	6
3	12	10
4	13	12

Based on these figures, you want to estimate the growth rate of future dividends (g). Would you use the EPS or the DPS?

18.5 Suppose you are considering two firms, A and B. For Firm A, $P/E = 100$, and for Firm B, $P/E = 2$. Would you say that Firm A is overvalued and

Firm B is undervalued? Explain the possible factors that may cause this large difference in the P/E ratio.

18.6 "Some firms have never paid dividends in the past. Therefore, according to the dividend discount model, the stock price should be zero." Evaluate this assertion.

PRACTICE

18.1 Suppose a stock whose market value is $P_0 = \$100$ will pay an expected dividend of $10 per share at the end of each year in the next 2 years. At the end of the second year, the stock price will be either $110 or $140 with equal probability. Given the uncertainty, you decide to discount the expected cash flow at a cost of capital of $k = 15\%$.
a. Would you buy the stock?
b. How would you change your answer if the stock price would be either $70 or $150 with equal probability, where for this type of risk the discount rate is $k = 20\%$?

Assume that when the stock is riskier, the average dividend is also riskier.

18.2 One investor owns a stock whose market price is $P_0 = \$100$. He expects to get in the future, on average, $15 per year as a dividend for an infinite number of years. His discount rate is 16%. Another investor agrees with the expected cash flow of $15 a year but attaches less uncertainty to these cash flows. Hence, her discount rate is $k = 14\%$. Do you think these two investors would make a financial transaction? Explain what transaction would take place.

18.3 The price of the stock of Mars Macro Systems, Inc., is $100, and the firm pays all its earnings as dividends of $10 per share. The managers of Mars Macro Systems announce that because of new competition in the market, from now on the dividends (and earnings) will be only $8 per share.
a. What do you expect the new stock price of Mars Macro Systems will be?
b. What will be the stock price when in addition to the decrease in earnings, the market believes the

profits of Mars Macro Systems are now more uncertain than before?

18.4 Suppose the stock price is $P_0 = \$50$, and the dividend per share next year is $d_1 = \$2$. The discount rate is $k = 10\%$. What is the expected stock price (P_1) one year from now?

18.5 You expect to get a dividend per share of $d_1 = \$10$ next year and of $d_2 = \$15$ two years from now. The stock price 2 years from now is expected to be $P_2 = \$120$, and the current stock price is $P_0 = \$100$. What is the equilibrium discount rate?

18.6 A stock, on average, pays $10 per share every year, and the stock price 2 years from now is $110. The risk-free interest rate is $r = 5\%$. Can you determine the maximum value of the stock? Explain.

18.7 Suppose you use Equation 18.7 to calculate the stock price (P_0). Also, it is known that $d_1 = \$10$. The firm decides to change its dividend policy and pay not d_1 but rather zero at the first year, to invest this cash flow, and to pay all the cash flows from this investment (in addition to the previous d_2) at Year 2. How will this affect the stock price if $k = 10\%$ and the firm reinvests d_1 at 5%? What if the firm reinvests at $k = 15\%$? At $k = 10\%$?

18.8 In 1990, the stock of IBM traded for $P_0 = \$100$ with $d_1 = \$6$ per share, $k = 12\%$, and $g = 6\%$ (see Equation 18.7). Because of sharp competition in the computer industry and mismanagement, the market revised the estimate of the growth rate, making it only 4%. What should be the effect on the stock price?

18.9 Suppose the dividend at the end of the first year is $d_1 = \$10$. The growth rate will be $g_1 = 8\%$ for the next n years and then, from $n + 1$ forever, the growth rate will be $g_2 = 5\%$. The discount rate is $k = 10\%$.
a. What is the stock price if $n = 1$?
b. What is the stock price if $n = 10$?
c. What is the stock price if $n =$ infinity?

18.10 A normal-growth firm has earnings of $10 per share and dividends of $5 per share. The discount rate is $k = 10\%$.
a. What is the stock price?
b. What is the multiplier, P/E?

18.11 One stock offers $10 a year from the next year to infinity. Another stock offers $5 next year and a growth rate of 10% a year.
a. In what year will the dividends from both firms be equal?
b. What stock will have a higher price if the discount rate for both is $k = 10\%$?

18.12 Suppose Firm A is a normal-growth firm. The firm's dividend policy is to maintain a dividend growth rate that is 50% of the firm's cost of equity *(k)*. It is given that the stock price is $100, and $d_1 = \$10$. What is the firm's cost of equity (k)?

18.13 The P/E ratio of a normal-growth firm is $P/E = 10$. The dividend is $d_1 = \$10$, and the stock price is $20. What is the growth rate (g)?

18.14 Suppose you employ the CAPM to estimate the stockholder's required cost of capital. The firm's beta is 2, the market risk premium is 10%, and the risk-free rate is 3%. The dividend on the firm's stock was $10 per share, which is estimated to grow in the future at 2% a year indefinitely. What is the present value of all future dividends?

18.15 In 1993, IBM cut its quarterly dividends per share from more than 50 cents to 25 cents. Suppose the annual dividends next year will be $1. IBM stock was trading for about $40. Assuming a 10% cost of capital, what is the market's long-term estimate of the growth rate of dividends for IBM?

18.16 A firm's stock price is $50, and its EPS is $5. The firm changes its accounting procedures (for example, changes its method of valuing inventory). As a result, the EPS went up to $7. How should this change affect the P/E ratio? How should it affect the present value of dividends? How should it affect the stock price?

18.17 Demonstrate that if a firm pays out a constant proportion of its earnings as dividends and reinvests its retained earnings at the cost of capital (k), then the dividend model and the P/E ratio (actually the inverse E/P ratio) yield the same value for the stock.

18.18 Suppose the average P/E ratio in the United States was about 20 in the early 1990s. In Japan the average P/E ratio was about 50. Does this fact mean that the Japanese stock market should be considered expensive and the U.S. market inexpensive?

18.19 "Any comparison of P/E ratios in a given country may be meaningful. However, an international comparison of P/E ratios may yield paradoxical results, because various countries have various accounting reporting standards." Discuss this assertion.

18.20 Suppose that as an underwriter you would like to evaluate an IPO. From data on the last 10 years, you see that the firm's EPS grew at 10% a year. The dividends fluctuated, because the firm changed its payout ratio every year. The current EPS is $10. The firm is a normal-growth firm, and you estimate its cost of equity to be about 10%.
a. Suppose that as an underwriter, you have zero expenses and zero profits. What is the maximum price you would offer for this firm?
b. Suppose that the firm issues 1 million shares. You need 5% of the issue as an insurance fee and 10% of the issue for expenses and profit. What is the maximum price you would offer for shares of this firm?

18.21 The following is an excerpt from *Fortune:*

When Goldman Sachs' crack research chief Steven Einhorn issued a bullish stock market report recently, he didn't prattle on about the usual S&P 500 benchmarks—P/E ratios, dividend yields, and the like. Instead, he based his forecast on a single measure: economic value added, or EVA.

It was just the latest evidence that EVA has moved from buzzword to financial phenomenon. As a performance measure, as an analytic tool, and as a management discipline, EVA is cropping up all over: Community hospitals harness EVA to improve efficiency. Lots of money managers use it to pick stocks. Even the U.S. Postal Service employs EVA to help run its operations. One thing that makes EVA so popular is that at its core, it is an almost embarrassingly basic concept. Take a company's after-tax operating profit. Subtract the cost of capital used to make that profit. Bingo—you've got EVA. It tells us how efficient management is at turning investor money—capital—into profits.

In practice it's useful to make adjustments in the calculation. For example, Stern Stewart, the consulting firm that trademarked the term, doesn't amortize goodwill, and it capitalizes R&D expenditures instead of expensing them. These and other adjustments are attempts to wring out accounting distortions.

Investors like EVA because it's a running score showing how well managers are performing their primary task, creating wealth. When a company uses EVA to set compensation, it seems to be a powerful tool that gets managers to deploy capital for maximum gain. For a bigger picture, look at market value added, or MVA, a cousin of EVA that in effect shows how good (or bad) an EVA performance investors expect of a company in the future. Simply put, MVA is the total market value of a company, minus all the money that has ever been invested in it: the cash investors could get out of the company today minus the cash that has been put in. To calculate it you add up all the capital that has been invested in a company—including debt and equity offerings, bank loans, and retained earnings—then subtract this from the current market value of the company's securities, both stocks and bonds.

As you might suspect, the red-hot stock market made 1996 a humdinger of a year for MVA. (The rankings,

Who creates value? Taken from a list of 1,000 companies ranked by MVA [market value added], here's how the 200 largest, based on market capitalization, stack up.

What market value added means to you: MVA, in effect, shows the difference between the capital investors have put into a company and the money they can take out.

Wealth predictor: EVA is after-tax net operating profit minus cost of capital. A growing EVA is a good sign that a stock will soar.

The real story: Does the return on capital exceed the cost of capital? If so, then the company is using investors' money wisely.

MVA Rank[a]								
1997	1996[b]	1992[b]	Company[c]	Market Value Added ($ millions)	Economic Value Added ($ millions)	Capital ($ millions)	Return on Capital	Cost of Capital
1	1	4	Coca-Cola	$124,894	$2,442	$10,814	36.0%	9.7%
2	2	6	General Electric	$121,874	$2,515	$53,567	17.7%	12.7%
3	5	14	Microsoft	$ 89,957	$1,727	$ 5,680	47.1%	11.8%
4	12	74	Intel	$ 86,481	$3,605	$17,483	36.4%	13.6%
5	3	2	Merck	$ 78,246	$1,688	$22,219	23.0%	14.5%

a. Calculations are based on figures as of the previous year-end.

b. Historical rankings reflect alterations due to mergers and other financial changes.

c. The rankings exclude electric utilities, banks, and financial and real estate firms.

which can be complicated to figure, are as of Jan. 1, 1997.) Nothing sizzled like technology. Microsoft, No. 5 on last year's list, doubled its MVA to almost $90 billion, muscling aside such giants as Philip Morris and Merck to grab the No. 3 spot. Intel did a similar trick, sprinting from No. 12 to No. 4. Note that Intel's EVA is more than twice that of Microsoft, yet Intel still trails the Redmond, Wash., giant in MVA. Why? As Stern Stewart senior VP Al Ehrbar explains, "The market expects Microsoft's economic value to grow even faster than Intel's in the future."

Though not quite as dramatic, energy companies of various stripes benefited from rising oil prices and—critically—from their disciplined capital spending over the past several years. Exxon, which boasts the most capital of any company on our list, moved from No. 9 to No. 7, Chevron from No. 39 to No. 29, and Texaco from No. 78 to No. 60.

Coca-Cola held on to its premier spot in the rankings. But our updated flash figures, which reflect stock prices as of Aug. 31, 1997, show the effects of this summer's nasty blue-chip selloff: While Coke's MVA has risen slightly, General Electric sidestepped that rout and has seen its MVA rise to a stunning $163.6 billion. It was just $121.9 billion at the beginning of the year.

Our MVA hospital list? Kmart, Union Pacific, and International Paper are among those that have fallen furthest in rank in the past five years. But don't sniff at such laggards as potential investments. Remember that MVA reflects the market's expectations, and beating the market means betting it's wrong. Many of our cellar dwellers, including Ford Motor (No. 998) and Champion International (No. 988), are restructuring to boost market value. Wall Street may not be convinced, but the list's tag end is not a bad place to look if you're shopping for bargains.

In practice it is useful to make an adjustment in the economic value added (EVA) calculation. For example, Stern Stewart, the consulting firm that trademarked the term EVA, doesn't amortize goodwill, and it capitalizes R&D expenditures instead of expensing them. . . .

Source: Article and table from Richard Teitelbaum, "America's Greatest Wealth Creators," *Fortune*, November 10, 1997, pp. 265–266. Reprinted from the November 10, 1997, issue of *Fortune* by special permission. © 1997, Time, Inc.

a. Write a formula for the economic value added (EVA) of the capital invested in a firm (see the definition in the article).

b. The average rate of return on Microsoft's investment is $R = 47.1\%$. Given its cost of capital of 11.8% and the information on the EVA, what is the "adjusted" invested capital of Microsoft? By how much does it differ from the reported capital in the article?

c. Microsoft is making 47.1% on its invested capital, but the required cost of capital on such an investment (given its risk; see Chapter 9) is only 11.8%. Do you think Microsoft should pay cash dividends to the stockholders?

d. Do you think Microsoft will ever pay cash dividends? What is the economic rationale for your answer?

18.22 The table in Problem 18.21 shows that the EVA of Coca-Cola is $2,442 million. The EVA of General Motors (not reported in the table) is −$3,527 million. Do these data imply that Coca-Cola stock should be bought and General Motors stock should be sold? Explain.

18.23 The table on page 689 shows the P/E ratio for the firms composing the Dow Jones Industrials as of January 5, 1997. The P/E ratio is calculated twice—once with the 1997 EPS and once with the future 1998 EPS.

a. Assume a normal-growth firm with a constant growth in dividends. Which of the following two P/E ratio criteria is consistent with the dividend discount model: (1) the P/E ratio corresponding to the 1997 EPS or (2) the P/E ratio corresponding to the 1998 EPS?

b. The P/E ratio for 1997 for Boeing is reported as 74.2 (see table). Explain why the 74.2 P/E ratio does not measure the true worth of the investment in Boeing stock.

c. The P/E ratio of IBM is 14.9 (based on the 1998 EPS). In the sixties the P/E ratio of IBM was about 60. How can you explain the big difference? Is it possible that the difference is due to the splits in IBM stock during these years? Is it possible that the difference can be explained by the inflation and deterioration in the value of the dollar?

Consensus Operating Earnings Estimates for Dow Industrials

Company	1997 EPS[a]		97 P/E[b]	1998 EPS[a]		98 P/E[b]
	4 Wks Ago	Cur		4 Wks Ago	Cur	
AT&T	2.70	2.70	22.7	2.93	2.99	20.5
Alcoa	4.72	4.62	15.2	7.16	7.01	10.0
Allied Signal	2.06	2.06	18.8	2.38	2.38	16.3
Amer. Express	4.16	4.16	21.5	4.74	4.74	18.8
Boeing	**.67**	**.66**	**74.2**	**2.45**	**2.46**	**19.9**
Caterpillar	4.35	4.35	11.1	4.60	4.61	10.5
Chevron Corp	4.55	4.59	16.8	4.44	4.37	17.6
Coca Cola	1.68	1.67	39.9	1.73	1.70	39.2
Disney	2.83	2.83	35.0	3.51	3.50	28.3
Dupont	3.62	3.62	16.6	3.90	3.89	15.4
East. Kodak	3.48	3.48	17.4	4.09	4.14	14.6
Exxon Corp	3.13	3.14	19.5	3.07	3.04	20.1
Gen'l Elec	2.50	2.50	29.4	2.84	2.85	25.7
Gen'l Motors	7.83	7.83	7.8	8.10	8.01	7.6
Goodyear	4.71	4.71	13.5	5.21	5.21	12.2
Hewlett-Pack	2.96	2.95	21.1	3.61	3.61	17.3
IBM	6.18	6.18	16.9	7.02	7.01	14.9
Int'l Paper	1.08	1.03	41.9	2.68	2.29	18.8
Johnson & J	2.47	2.47	26.7	2.79	2.78	23.7
McDonalds	2.37	2.36	20.2	2.61	2.61	18.3
Merck	3.82	3.82	27.7	4.42	4.42	24.0
Minn Minn	4.05	3.95	20.8	4.62	4.39	18.7
Morgan (J.P.)	7.81	7.48	15.1	8.44	8.33	13.6
Phillip Morris	2.96	2.94	15.4	3.36	3.32	13.6
Proc & Gamb	2.61	2.61	30.6	2.93	2.93	27.2
Sears Roebuck	3.40	3.31	13.7	3.72	3.63	12.5
Travelers	2.75	2.75	19.6	3.24	3.25	16.6
Union Carbide	4.49	4.50	9.5	3.93	3.94	10.9
United Tech.	4.11	4.11	17.7	4.74	4.74	15.4
Wal-Mart	1.54	1.54	25.6	1.75	1.75	22.5
Median			19.5			17.4
DJ Industrials	420.84	418.17	18.9	482.30	477.88	16.5

a. Earnings estimates are for calendar years.

b. Based on latest earnings estimate.

Source: First Call 800-448-2348, as cited in *Barron's,* January 5, 1998, p. MW97. Reprinted by permission of *Barron's,* © 1998 Dow Jones & Co., Inc. All Rights Reserved Worldwide.

CFA PROBLEMS

18.1 Eastover Company (EO) is a large, diversified forest products company. Approximately 75% of its sales are from paper and forest products, with the remainder from financial services and real estate. The company owns 5.6 million acres of timberland, which is carried at a very low historical cost on the balance sheet.

Peggy Mulroney, CFA, is an analyst at the investment counseling firm of Centurion Investments. She is assigned the task of assessing the outlook for Eastover, which is being considered for purchase, and comparing it with another forest products company in Centurion's portfolios, Southampton Corporation (SHC). SHC is a major producer of lumber products in the United States. Building products, primarily lumber and plywood, account for 89% of SHC's sales, with pulp accounting for the remainder. SHC owns 1.4 million acres of timberland, which is also carried at a very low historical cost on the balance sheet. In SHC's case, however, that cost is not as far below current market as Eastover's is.

Mulroney recalled from her CFA studies that the constant-growth dividend discount model (DDM) was one way to arrive at a valuation for a company's common stock. She collected the following current dividends and stock price data for Eastover and Southampton (see Table a at the bottom of the page).

a. Using 11% as the required rate of return (that is, the discount rate) and a projected growth rate of 8%, compute a constant-growth DDM value for Eastover's stock, and compare the computed value for Eastover with its stock price indicated in the table. Show your calculations.

Mulroney's supervisor commented that a two-stage DDM may be more appropriate for companies such as Eastover and Southampton. Mulroney believes that Eastover and Southampton could grow more rapidly over the next 3 years and then settle in at a lower, but sustainable, rate of growth beyond 1994. (This CFA exam question was given in 1992. Assume that it is year-end 1991.) Mulroney's estimates are indicated in Table b at the bottom of the page.

b. Using 11% as the required rate of return, compute the two-stage DDM value of Eastover's stock, and compare that value to its stock price indicated in the previous table. Show your calculations.

c. Discuss two advantages and three disadvantages of using a constant-growth DDM. Briefly discuss how the two-stage DDM improves upon the constant-growth DDM.

For Internet questions visit the Levy Investment Web site at http://levy-invst.swcollege.com.

a. Current Information

	Current Share Price	Current Dividends per Share	1992 EPS Estimate	Current Book Value per Share
Eastover (EO)	$ 28	$ 1.20	$ 1.60	$ 17.32
Southampton (SHC)	48	1.08	3.00	32.21
S&P 500	415	12.00	20.54	159.83

b. Projected Growth Rates

	Next 3 Years (1992, 1993, 1994)	Growth beyond 1994
Eastover (EO)	12%	8%
Southampton (SHC)	13	7

YOUR TURN: APPLYING THEORY TO PRACTICE
SARA LEE—VALUATION, GROWTH RATE, AND COST OF EQUITY

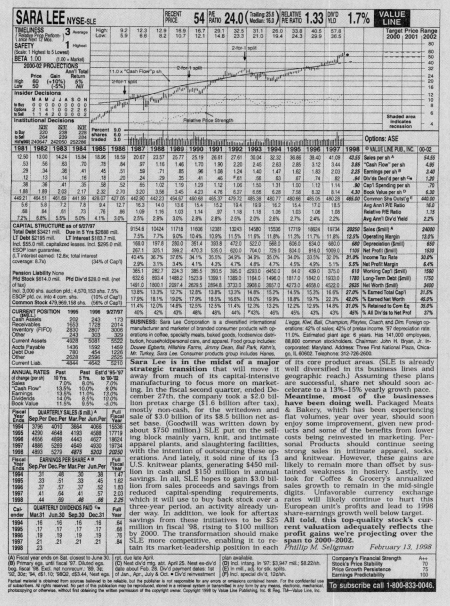

(continued)

Questions

Note: Because this *Value Line* was published in February 1998, in your answer use the EPS or DPS estimates up to 1997 (ignore the 1998 estimate). The share price of Sara Lee at the end of 1997 was $50⅛.

1. The rate of return on the market portfolio is $\overline{R}_m = 12.5\%$, and the risk-free interest rate is 3.25%. Employ the CAPM to estimate Sara Lee's cost of equity.

2. Use the results of Question 1 and the data given in the table to estimate the growth rate (g) at the end of 1997.

3. Calculate the average annual growth rate in EPS and DPS for Sara Lee during the period 1988 to 1997, and compare your results with the estimate obtained in Question 2.

4. The firm has a fairly stable dividend payout ratio of approximately .45. Given the results in Question 2 regarding the growth rate, what is your estimate of the share price at the end of 1998? Compare your estimate with the *Value Line* share price projection.

5. The P/E ratio is 24. What is the implied rate of return to the Sara Lee shareholder? Is this result consistent with *Value Line*'s projected rates of return? How can you explain the differences? In light of the previous analysis, can an investor safely employ the P/E ratio of Sara Lee as an investment tool? Does the P/E ratio have any economic meaning? Explain your answer.

SELECTED REFERENCES

Leibowitz, Martin L., and Stanley Kogelman. "The Growth Illustration: The P/E 'Cost' of Earnings Growth." *Financial Analysts Journal,* March–April 1994, pp. 36–48.

This paper shows in detail some of the problems related to using the P/E ratio.

Tuttle, Donald L., et al. *Equity Security Analysis and Evaluation.* Charlottesville, Va.: Association for Investment Management and Research, 1993.

This series of papers focuses on various approaches to valuing stocks. The models presented range from using financial statement analysis to factor models.

SUPPLEMENTAL REFERENCES

Bower, Richard S. "The N-Stage Discount Model and Required Return: A Comment." *Financial Review* 27, no. 1 (1992): 141–149.

Danielson, Morris G. "A Simple Valuation Model and Growth Expectation." *Financial Analysts Journal,* May–June 1998, pp. 50–57.

Fouse, William L. "Allocating Assets across Country Markets." *Journal of Portfolio Management* 18, no. 2 (1992): 20–27.

Gehr, Adam K., Jr. "A Bias in Dividend Discount Models." *Financial Analysts Journal* 48, no. 1 (1992): 75–80.

Good, Walker R. "When Are Price/Earnings Ratios Too High—or Too Low?" *Financial Analysts Journal,* July–August 1991, pp. 9–12.

Gordon, M. J. "Dividends, Earnings and Stock Prices." *Review of Economics and Statistics* 41 (May 1959): 99–105.

Horvath, Philip A. "A Further Comment on the N-Stage Discount Model and Required Return." *Financial Review* 28, no. 2 (1993): 273–277.

Kahn, Sharon. "What (Global) Dividend Discount Models Say Now." *Global Finance* 6, no. 2 (March 1992): 71–73.

Appendix 18A   Free Cash Flow Model (FCFM) for Normal-Growth Firms

A normal-growth firm is a firm that reinvests at the required cost of capital; that is, R (the reinvestment rate) $= k$ (the cost of capital). Because most firms are normal growth firms, it is important to find a valuation method for the stocks of these firms, even if they do not pay regular dividends. To this issue, we address this appendix. As dividends are the relevant cash flows to the stockholders, conceptually the use of the present value of all future dividends is the only correct method for stock valuation. (If the firm pays cash to the stockholders not in the form of a dividend, then this cash flow is also relevant.) Moreover, even if a stock is held for a relatively short period of time and the investor's cash flow is composed of dividends plus the cash flow from selling the stock, these cash flows can be rewritten as the present value of all expected future dividends (see Section 18.2).

Regardless of whether dividends grow at a constant rate or not, and regardless of whether dividends are paid for some years or not, given a series of expected future dividends of d_1, d_2, d_3, . . . , the present value of this dividend series can be calculated to obtain the value of the stock. To illustrate, suppose that a firm declares that it will not pay cash dividends, and that at the end of the tenth year it will liquidate all its assets and distribute the cash flow to the stockholders. From the investor's point of view, the obtained cash flow at the tenth year can be considered as divided, d_{10}. Therefore, in such a case, $PV = d_{10}/(1 + k)^{10}$, where d_{10} is the tenth-year expected liquidation value per share, k is the discount rate, and PV is the present value of d_{10}.

Conceptually, therefore, only future dividends or future cash flows to the stockholders are relevant for stock valuation. However, estimating these expected future cash flows is difficult. If the firm regularly pays a given portion of its earnings as cash dividends and the dividend per share, DPS, grows at a constant rate, then dividends are generally expected to grow at a constant rate. In such a case, investors can apply the simple constant dividend growth model as a specific case of the present value of future dividends to evaluate the stock. As we have seen, in the case of a normal-growth firm (where the reinvestment rate by the firm is equal to the cost of equity, k; see Section 18.3), also the P/E ratio can be employed for picking stock where E is *next year's* expected EPS. Namely, if the P/E ratio is smaller than some cutout ratio, the stock is considered to be undervalued.

It should be emphasized that the P/E ratio is similar to discounting a constant annual earnings series, E (next year's EPS), even though the EPS is predicted to grow over time (see Section 18.7). However, the dividend discount model is the only correct valuation method. If dividends grow at a constant rate (normal growth or supergrowth), then the dividend discount model provides a method to estimate the future dividends; it is a relatively simple valuation model to apply. The P/E ratio, as a method used to decide whether the stock is undervalued or overvalued, leads to the same decision as the constant dividend growth model only if the dividend payout ratio is constant over time, the dividends grow at a constant rate, and the firm is a normal–growth firm. Otherwise, the P/E ratio may be a misleading rule for decision making.

In practice, however, relying on future dividends presents an estimation and valuation problem for firms that do not pay cash dividends, firms that pay irregular dividends, and firms that change their payout ratio over time. For example, how can we evaluate firms like Microsoft, which as of 1998 had never paid cash dividends and had announced no intention to do so in the future? We need not even go to the extreme case of a firm like Microsoft, however, to show the difficulty in employing the dividend discount model, as Connecting Theory to Practice 18.2 illustrates.

CONNECTING THEORY TO PRACTICE 18.2

MAN FROM THE PRU BANKS ON NEW IMAGE

Next year the Prudential will celebrate its 150th anniversary confident of its position as Britain's largest insurer, although no longer quite the dominant force it was between the wars when one in three adults was a client. While its market share has decreased to 10 percent in Britain, that is still more than 6 million customers.

Fact File: Prudential

How much is it worth?	£13.3 billion
How many does it employ?	22,187
1997 earnings per share[a]	32.3p
1997 dividends per share[a]	19p
Share price now	668.5p
Share price 12 months ago	476.5p

Breakdown of sales:

Prudential UK	£3,569m
Jackson National Life (US)	£2,462m
Prudential Asia	£88m
Other international	£543m

(continued)

	5-year record				
	92	93	94	95	96
Operating profit (£bn)	402	629	693	804	873
Earnings per share (p)	14.1	22	26.3	28.7	34.1
Net dividend per share (p)	11.9	13.2	14.4	15.7	17.3

a. Forecasts for 1997 profits from the Estimates Directory.

Source: Heather Cannon, "Man from the Pru Banks on New Image," *The Observer*, October 12, 1997, p. 14. Copyright 1997 by *The Observer*. Reprinted with permission.

MAKING THE CONNECTION

The EPS of Prudential grows faster than its DPS. The reason is that the payout ratio decreased from $11.9/14.01 \cong 84.9\%$ in 1992 to $17.3/34.1 \cong 50.7\%$ in 1996. Thus, the constant dividend growth model cannot be used to evaluate this stock.

Evaluating a stock by the constant dividend growth model first requires an estimate of the future growth rate of the dividends. The natural step is to measure this growth rate in the past and use the constant dividend growth model to evaluate the stock. However, a look at the EPS and DPS of Prudential makes it obvious that this method is not applicable in this specific case, because the dividend payout ratio changes over time. The P/E method is also inappropriate in this case because, as already discussed, the P/E ratio can be employed only when the constant dividend growth model applies and the firm is a normal-growth firm. Thus, what valuation model can be used in cases like Microsoft or Prudential, whose future expected dividends are unknown?

The free cash flow model (FCFM) applies in such cases. The FCFM is a method of estimating the value of a stock even if dividends have not been paid in the past or if dividends are paid irregularly. In most cases, the FCFM provides the same value of the stock as the present value of unknown expected dividends. However, the FCFM does not require an estimate of the future dividends, which are hard to forecast. The value of the stock is calculated as if the future expected dividends were known, even though in fact they are not known.

Before defining *free cash flow* (FCF), a definition of the firm's cash flow (CF) from operations is in order. The firm's annual cash flow is the cash flow received from operations in a given year, after interest and taxes have been paid. For simplicity, assume that all the firm's expenses and revenues are for cash (this issue will be discussed later). Then the cash flow from operations is simply the earnings plus the depreciation, denoted by D_p. We add the depreciation to the earnings, because depreciation is not a cash outflow. Thus,

$$CF = EPS + D_p$$

where *CF*, *EPS,* and D_p are all per one share.

The CF has a clear-cut definition and is easy to measure, but the definition of the FCF, which we need for stock valuation, is more ambiguous. The most common definition of FCF is the cash flow the firm has after deducting the capital expenditure needed to maintain the ongoing operation of the firm *at its current level*. To illustrate, suppose the firm's CF is $50 million. It needs to invest $10 million to maintain its operation at the current level, but it invests $20 million because it wants to expand. After deducting the cash outlay on investment, the firm actually has only $30 million; however, according to the previous definition, its FCF is $40 million. It could distribute $40 million as dividends without affecting its current level of operation. If the firm needs to reinvest the depreciation to maintain the current level of operation (a reasonable assumption), then (once again assuming that all operations are for cash) the FCF equals the EPS, because

$$FCF = CF - D_p = EPS + D_p - D_p = EPS$$

To find the value of the stock, we need to discount the FCF per share.

Thus, if we adopt the FCFM as the model for stock valuation, the value of the stock is simply the present value of the EPS. In other words, the EPS is the maximum amount the firm can pay as dividends without affecting its current level of operation. As is shown later in this appendix, next year's expected FCF (or EPS) is relevant for stock valuation, and any increase in the FCF in the future should be ignored; otherwise we will not get the correct value of the stock. Thus, the stream of *hypothetical* dividends (or FCF, which is actually not paid) is as follows:

	Year			
	1	2	3	...
Hypothetical dividends	EPS	EPS	EPS	...

where EPS = FCF is the *next year's* earnings per share, and the present value of the FCF is EPS/k, where k is the appropriate discount rate.

Note that EPS and FCF are based on next year's estimate of the EPS and should be kept constant in the discounting process, even though we know that in fact the EPS (and the FCF) grows over time (because the EPS is retained, and even if deposited in the bank will add income to the firm). This principle is illustrated in the next practice box.

PRACTICE BOX

Problem   Suppose that the EPS next year is $10. The firm invests the depreciation in such a way that it can maintain its operation at the current level forever. The discount rate is $k = 10\%$.

(continued)

1. What is the value of the stock if the entire $10 per share is paid as cash dividends each year?
2. What is the value of the stock if the firm does not pay dividends in the first year and invests this $10 in a perpetuity at k? (Assume that from Year 2 and thereafter, all earnings are paid as dividends.)
3. Assume that the characteristics in Part b apply, and we discount the future EPS rather than next year's EPS. What is the PV of all future earnings?

Solution

1. The value of the stock is given by the present value of the $10 annual dividends: $10/0.1 = $100.
2. If dividends are not paid in the first year, then the next $10 is invested, yielding $10 \cdot 0.1 = $1 in each of the following years. Thus, $11 will be paid from Year 2 onward, and the present value of future dividends is as follows:

$$\frac{0}{1.1} + \frac{\$11}{(1.1)^2} + \frac{\$11}{(1.1)^3} + \ldots = \frac{1}{1.1}\left[\frac{\$11}{1.1} + \frac{\$11}{(1.1)^2} + \ldots\right] = \frac{1}{1.1}\left(\frac{\$11}{0.1}\right) = \$100$$

We see that by the DDM the value of the stock is $100 regardless of the dividend policy of the firm. Thus, even though earnings (and dividends) will be $11 per share in the future (from Year 2), the value of the stock can be obtained by dividing *the next year's earnings ($10) by the discount rate and ignoring the future growth in earnings.*

3. In this case, the PV of earnings is given by

$$\frac{\$10}{1.1} + \frac{\$11}{(1.1)^2} + \frac{\$11}{(1.1)^3} + \ldots = \frac{\$10}{1.1} + \$100 \cong \$109.09$$

which is higher than the true value as obtained by the DDM.

The Practice Box illustrates that the dividend discount model implies that we can either discount all future dividends or simply discount the next year's EPS (i.e., $10 in our example) and ignore the future growth in EPS. (This is correct for normal-growth firms.) Both methods yield the same PV, because under our assumption that all operations are done for cash, the FCF can be estimated by the EPS. Therefore, we conclude that according to the FCFM, we should rely only on next year's EPS and ignore the future growth in EPS. Although the firm will have $11 free cash flow from Year 2 and thereafter, we look at the next year's FCF of $10 and assume it will be at this level forever. Thus, using the FCFM, we discount the maximum dividends the firm could pay next year, not the dividends it actually will pay. The fact that stockholders did not get the $10 in the first year does not affect the value of the stock, because it is offset by the fact that the $10 is invested by the firm, and more will be paid to the stockholders in the future. Thus, assuming that the $10 was obtained in Year 1 (even though no cash was distributed to the stockholders) and ignoring the increase in future earnings (or FCF) that is due to the reinvestment of the retained earnings, the same present value of future cash flows (see the previous Practice Box) is obtained.

In other words, the example just given reveals that the following two hypothetical cash flows have the same present value of $100:

1. $10, $10, $10, . . .   ("next year's" FCF)
2. $ 0, $11, $11, . . .   (future DPS)

Thus, although the second scenario represents the cash flows to the stockholder and the first scenario does not, we can switch from Scenario 2 to Scenario 1 without changing the present value. This is exactly what the FCFM does. It relies on next year's FCF (or EPS) ($10) and ignores the growth in next year's FCF (+$1). If we discount the future FCF, rather than next year's FCF, we get an overvaluation, as in Part c of the previous Practice Box.

Because we do not know the cash flow given by Scenario 2 or when the firm will stop reinvesting its earnings and start to pay cash dividends (for example, the firm may also skip the $11 in Year 2 and pay more dividends from Year 3 onward), we can use the FCF given by Scenario 1 to calculate the value of the stock. Thus, by using the FCFM, we can get the PV of future dividends without knowing what these dividends will actually be. This is true as long as the firm reinvests at k.

Finally, we assume that the EPS is cash obtained by the firm. This is not necessarily so, however, because firms sell on credit and take credit from their customers. Furthermore, there are some other differences between EPS and CF per share because of the accounting principles, which are not based on cash flow. If there are substantial differences between the EPS and the FCF per share, the FCF per share rather than the EPS is the relevant figure to discount. Also, the firm may need to invest more or less than its accounting depreciation to maintain its operation at the current level. An adjustment for this investment should also be considered, so the FCF may differ from the EPS. These adjustments to the cash flow bases are relatively easy to incorporate. Regardless of these adjustments, we discount the next year's expected cash flow and ignore its increase in the future—an increase that is due to the fact that retained earnings are reinvested in the firm. Thus, to get the correct value of the stock, we implicitly assume that all free cash flows are distributed as dividends, and therefore there is no growth in these cash flows.

Another version of the FCFM commonly employed by practitioners discounts the firm's gross operating cash flow, which is the cash flow before interest and taxes are paid. This method avoids the distorting effects of changing taxes and debt over time. (Note that when the proportion of debt changes, the cost of equity [k] also changes, which complicates the analysis.) By discounting the gross free cash flow, the value of the firm that belongs to the stockholders, bondholders, and the Internal Revenue Service (taxes) is obtained. Connecting Theory to Practice 18.3 shows how practitioners use the FCFM to evaluate stocks.

CONNECTING THEORY TO PRACTICE 18.3

SEEKING SHELTER

Value stocks gain appeal in times of trouble, and sometimes they soar.

Playing for Cash

The stocks listed here stand out for their 20%-plus returns, as measured by comparing their operating cash flows to their adjusted stock prices. The stocks also look appealing when their free cash flow, which includes the effects of capital spending, is compared with the adjusted stock price. Adjustments to the stock price are made to factor in each company's debt and its cash on hand.

Company/ Symbol	Recent Price	Adjusted Price	Gross Operating Cash Flow[a]	Operating Cash Flow/ Adjusted Price	Free Cash Flow[a]	Free Cash Flow/ Adjusted Price
AMR (AMR)	$110.50	$139.20	$33.33	24%	$24.90	18%
Ann Taylor (ANN)	13.88	17.03	3.96	23	2.98	18
Guess? (GES)	8.50	11.83	2.70	23	1.99	17
HomeBase (HBI)	9.88	10.60	3.92	37	2.29	22
Inland Steel (IAD)	19.00	31.69	7.99	25	4.80	15
LaSalle RE Hldg (LSH)	33.75	29.48	8.57	29	8.57	29
LTV (LTV)	12.25	7.22	4.10	57	1.29	18
Magellan Health Svcs (MGL)	28.25	30.65	6.42	21	4.96	16
National Presto (NPK)	38.31	8.34	1.77	21	1.54	18
National Steel B (NS)	16.75	17.38	6.55	38	3.00	17
Southern Peru Copper (PCU)	16.13	14.57	3.82	26	2.19	15
Terra Ind (TRA)	12.06	17.93	5.18	29	3.48	19
Union Texas Petroleum (UTH)	22.00	27.60	7.01	25	4.80	17
USX-US Steel (X)	32.06	38.61	10.11	26	6.66	17
Yellow (YELL)	25.25	30.61	6.96	23	5.10	17

a. Per share.

Source: Oppenheimer, as cited in Jay Palmer, "Seeking Shelter," *Barron's,* November 3, 1997, p. 22. Reprinted by permission of *Barron's,* © 1997 Dow Jones & Co., Inc. All Rights Reserved Worldwide.

(continued)

MAKING THE CONNECTION

As can be seen from this article, practitioners employ both cash flow and free cash flow. The cash flows are divided by the "adjusted price" to get a percentage figure. Because the firm may have debt and equity, and the gross CF belongs to both parties (as well as to the IRS), the stock price is adjusted to reflect this fact. The more debt the firm has, the higher the adjusted stock price.[9] Also, if the firm holds cash not needed for current operations, the stock price is adjusted for this factor, too. If the firm does not have debt and does not have cash that is not needed for the current operations, then the adjusted price is equal to the market price of the stock.

In summary, for a normal-growth firm whose operations are solely for cash, the PV of all future dividends is equal to the PV of the EPS, provided next year's expected EPS is used and the future growth in EPS due to reinvestment of retained earnings is ignored. Because under this simplistic assumption the FCF is equal to the EPS, discounting the next year's expected FCF also leads to the correct valuation model, which is the PV of all future expected dividends. Thus, the FCF (or the EPS) can be used to evaluate a normal-growth firm even if no dividends have been paid in the past. Using the FCFM, there is no need to forecast when the firm will start paying dividends or whether the firm's payout rate will change in the future.

Finally, the FCFM assumes that all operations are for cash, and the depreciation is what the firm needs to invest to maintain its operation at the current level. Otherwise, some adjustments are needed in employing the FCFM. Because the accounting principles are not on a cash basis, the EPS is not precisely the FCF per share, and a more accurate method to estimate the FCF is needed. The FCF is estimated by taking the CF from operations and subtracting the capital expenditure needed for the firm to maintain its current level of operation. A final adjustment is very tricky. The capital expenditures must be carefully analyzed and added back to the CF if they are not necessary for the firm's continuing operation at its current level. For example, if Microsoft invests all its earnings because it expands, it does not mean that Microsoft does not have FCF. The FCF in this case is all that is invested for growth rather than for maintaining current operations.

A final note on supergrowth firms: These firms generally invest more than what is needed to maintain the current operation of the firm at the present level because they are able to project positive net prevent value.

---

9. Suppose that the stock price is $100, the firm has $20 debt per share, and $2 cash per share is held (where the cash is not needed to maintain the firm's operations). Then the adjusted price is $P = \$100 + \$20 - \$2 = \$118$.

Appendix 18B Picking Stocks with EVA

The economic value–added (EVA) model is a relatively new tool for project evaluation, as well as for stock valuation (that is, for picking stocks). A brief description of this method is given in the advertisement shown in Exhibit 18B-1. Note that there is even The EVA Company, which provides consultations to firms on how to employ EVA.

In project evaluation, EVA is defined as $EVA = (1 - T)EBIT - kI$, where T is the corporate tax rate, EBIT is the earnings before interest and taxes due to the project, k is the weighted average cost of capital (WACC), and I is the investment in the project. Calculating the PV of EVA provides a measure of the economic wealth created (or destroyed) by the project. Practitioners can use this method to evaluate the whole value of the firm, but in that case I is the invested capital in the firm rather than the cash outlay on the marginal project.

**EXHIBIT 18B-1
EVA as an Equity
Valuation Tool**

Use It Because It Works!

"EVA® — Economic Value Added — is a company's after-tax profit less the cost of the operation's *total* capital. Not just the cost of debt, but the cost of equity capital as well. At CS First Boston, we use EVA as our primary equity valuation tool because it works.

"EVA helps us understand a company's financial strategies. EVA, as Stern Stewart calculates it, avoids the cash flow distortions you get using earnings per share. EVA makes our analysts account for investments in both fixed and working capital. With EVA, we ask better questions about sales, profit margins, cash tax rate and competitive advantage.

PICKING STOCKS WITH EVA
"Most important, EVA is a framework to quantify investor expectations. When you understand those expectations and put them in the appropriate relationship to stock price, you get better stock selection. Our analysts use EVA very effectively to pick stocks.

"Investors value a company in terms of cash flow, risk and duration. Only EVA captures all these elements. Statistically, EVA 'explains' half the movement in stock prices, which is a lot better than return on equity and far better than earnings per share. EPS doesn't help you predict stock prices. EVA does.

© All rights reserved for Stern Stewart & Co. EVA® is a registered trademark of Stern Stewart & Co.

WHAT'S THE MARKET SAYING?
"As a CEO, you need a sense of whether the market's expectations about future performance and yours are in line. And if they're not, you need to identify the reasons and take steps. If you believe the market is undervaluing your stock, you can buy back shares, you can tell the story differently, you can spin off operations into IPOs, or you can divest the underperformers.

"When EVA is the framework for a total management system, it can help shape most corporate decisions — from a company acquisition to project financing or budgeting. Using EVA as the basis for incentive compensation, line managers are paid to bring greater value to the true bottom line.

"EVA, looked at as both an evaluation and management tool, can help you make the market assessment, then help you manage for increased value."

For more information, contact Al Ehrbar at Stern Stewart & Co. at (212) 261-0600. Stern Stewart developed EVA® and has helped more than 200 companies to implement its EVA framework for financial management and incentive compensation.

Stern Stewart & Co.
THE EVA COMPANY®

Source: *Fortune*, September 8, 1997. Reprinted with permission of Stern Stewart & Co.

Suppose that the value of the firm as estimated by the discounted EVA is V. Then, by subtracting the debt and dividing by the number of outstanding shares, we can evaluate the stock and make a comparison with the market price. We can then figure out whether the stock is underpriced or overpriced. An alternative way to evaluate the stock with EVA is simply to look at the EPS (the after-tax profit that belongs to the stockholders) and compare it with the stockholder's investment (simply the stock's price). However, in this case the EPS should be discounted by the cost of equity, not by the WACC. The advantage of this method is that it precisely measures the stockholder's investment—the stock price—whereas the previous method, which relies on EBIT rather than EPS, has some problems measuring the investment capital in the firm (I).

To illustrate, suppose that you consider buying a stock. For you, then, the investment is P, where P is the stock price. The earnings per share (EPS) is the profit that belongs to each share. Therefore, your EVA is

$$EVA = EPS - kP$$

where P is your investment, and k is the required discount rate by the stockholder, given the risk of the firm. By the EVA principle, again using the perpetuity formula, the net present value of all future earnings is given by

$$\frac{EPS}{k} - P \text{ or } PV - P$$

If the PV of all future EVAs is greater than the stock price (that is, $PV > P$), the stock is undervalued and should be bought. Thus, the EVA, in principle, is no different from the simple stock evaluation methods discussed in Chapter 18. In cases where the EPS can be used to evaluate the cash flow (CF) to each share, then the present value of the earnings per share is EPS/k, and if it is greater than the stock price P, the stock should be purchased. If there are differences between the cash flow and the EPS, the EPS can be adjusted to obtain next year's estimate of the cash flow per share, and EVA yields the same results as the FCFM, as well as the PV of future dividends. Thus, if measured correctly, the present value of the EPS, the present value of FCF, EVA, and the present value of future dividends provide the same results.

SUPERGROWTH FIRMS

For supergrowth firms, some adjustment is needed. The NPV (per share) of the extraordinarily profitable projects must be added to obtain the value of the stock.

Supergrowth firms invest at R, where $R > k$ (k is the cost of capital). For supergrowth firms the FCF can be estimated by two alternate methods: (1) by deducting the investment necessary to maintain the current level of operation or (2) by deducting the actual investment. Using the first method, the NPV of all projects with extraordinary profit ($R > k$) must be added to the value of the firm.

METHOD 1

Deduct from the CF only the investment needed to maintain the current level of operations, and add the NPV of all extraordinarily profitable projects. This FCF definition has a measurement problem: Suppose that a firm invests $1 billion a year. How can this amount be divided between the investment necessary to guarantee the firm's operation at its current level and the investment to extend the operations? This measurement difficulty applies to normal-growth and supergrowth firms alike. Supergrowth firms (which are a small portion of all firms) have another estimation problem: How can the NPV of all projects with extraordinary profits be estimated?

METHOD 2

FCF can be defined as it was before, with one change: the *actual* investment taken by the firm is deducted rather than the investment necessary to maintain the firm's operations at the current level. If Microsoft invests all of its retained earnings, then the FCF by this definition will be zero. However, the supergrowth period that characterizes Microsoft will end, extraordinarily profitable projects will not be available, and the FCF will be very large. Conceptually, there is nothing wrong with this approach. However, it is very difficult to estimate when the FCF will be available in the future and at what amount. These things actually depend on factors that are very hard to predict, including macroeconomic factors and new competition in the market.

CHAPTER 19

COMMON STOCK SELECTION

LEARNING OBJECTIVES

After studying this chapter you should be able to:

1. Identify some characteristics of a stock market winner, based on the analysis of Marc Reinganum.

2. Explain how an analyst views the stock valuation process.

3. Identify the risks that are relevant in stock investment.

4. Describe how to estimate *g* and *k* of the constant dividend growth model in practice.

5. Explain why dividend discount models must be used with caution.

FINDING THE COMMON DENOMINATOR OF WINNING STOCKS

What do winning stocks have in common?

Investment specialists have come up with a wealth of divergent, sometimes contradictory answers over the decades. Now, new academic research raises questions about some widely held beliefs, and gives additional perspective on others.

Among other things, it suggests that two of the most popular strategies with individual investors may not be the best way to select winning stocks.

Many investors credit their success to picking small-cap issues (the shares of companies with low stock-market capitalization)[a] and those with low price-earnings ratios (the price of a company's stock divided by its per-share earnings). But neither criterion would have pointed investors to the winning stocks featured in a recent study by Marc Reinganum, a finance professor at the University of Iowa.

"The fascinating thing is that there are strategies independent of these variables that earn very, very good performance," he says. "In other words, there is more than one way to skin the investment cat."

Prof. Reinganum's findings provide scant comfort for contrarian investors who try to beat the market by picking stocks that are out-of-favor with the mainstream investment community. More than half of the winning stocks were selling at close to two-year highs before their prices took off.

So what did work? The winners ranked high on several factors that are part of some classic investment approaches. These include a number of fundamental measures: a per-share price that is less than the company's book per-share value (its assets minus its liabilities, divided by the number of shares outstanding); year-to-year increases in earnings over the past five years; earnings that have been increasing at an accelerating pace; and simply having pre-tax profits. They also included some technical indicators, which attempt to predict future stock-price movements from historical price changes.

a. Market capitalization is calculated by multiplying the stock price times the number of shares outstanding. It is a measure of firm size. Small-cap issues, therefore, are stocks of relatively small firms.

Source: Barbara Donnelly, "Funding the Common Denominator of Winning Stocks," *Wall Street Journal,* June 15, 1988. Reprinted by permission of *The Wall Street Journal,* © 1988 Dow Jones & Co., Inc. All Rights Reserved Worldwide.

(continued)

THREE WINNING STRATEGIES

To put the wind at your back when picking stocks, start with these three value strategies. Over a 21-year period, portfolios loaded with stocks selling at low P/Es, low price to cash flow, and cheap market to book value did best.

Source: Terence P. Pare, "Yes, You Can Beat the Market," *Fortune*, April 3, 1995, p. 51.

As the articles in this chapter's Investments in the News point out, the search for clues on which stocks to purchase is never ending. This chapter's objective is to examine selection criteria for individual stocks—from the viewpoint of both individual investors and professional managers.

This chapter assumes that there are investors and portfolio managers who believe there are winners in the stock market. The chapter first looks at qualities that winning stocks seem to possess and examines the way investment professionals view the stock valuation process. Even if a financial analyst has a valuation method that has the capability of identifying winners in the stock market, this process is not risk-free, because this ability is based on averages. In some cases, the analyst is wrong. The analyst still needs to consider portfolio risk and diversification even when applying the valuation methods. Therefore, the chapter next turns to the sources of risk for investments in common stock and observes how duration can immunize stock investors from this risk. One of the methods of identifying winners is the dividend discount model. Therefore, the chapter extends the earlier investigation of the dividend discount model. It discusses how to estimate the inputs to this model. The chapter concludes with an interpretation of the use of the dividend discount model and its results.

19.1 THE ANATOMY OF A STOCK MARKET WINNER[1]

If investors believe they can find stocks that are winners, how can they locate these opportunities? The first step would be to identify characteristics of superior-performing common stocks. Marc Reinganum investigated stock selection strategies to determine their accuracy in picking winners, and he identified several common characteristics of superior stocks after examining 222 stocks that doubled in price.

One common stock selection strategy is following the trading activities of money managers. When Reinganum investigated this strategy, he found that the trading activities of money managers such as investment advisers, banks, mutual funds, and insurance companies did not predict the doubling of the stock price.

---

1. This title and section are based on Marc Reinganum, "The Anatomy of a Stock Market Winner," *Financial Analysts Journal*, March–April 1988, pp. 16–27.

However, these investors were buying as the prices went up. That is, the percentage of a common stock held by institutional money management groups increases during the price run-ups.

The valuation measure that proved most significant in locating winning stocks was the price-to-book ratio (the stock price divided by the accounting equity value per share).[2] Over 80% of the 222 stocks sold below 1.0 one quarter before the beginning of the price increase.

What is interesting in Reinganum's research are the variables that were not significant. For example, the average beta of the 222 stocks was 1.14, and fewer than five of the stocks had a beta greater than 2.0. Thus, the stock price doubled not because of a large beta. Only nine stocks had an initial price of less than $10. A low price/earnings ratio (P/E) ratio also was not a significant predictor. (Recall, however, from Chapter 10 that small-company stock and stock with low P/E ratios tend to outperform the overall market.)

Many investors rely on earnings per share (EPS) or other measures of profitability when selecting stocks. Reinganum found several of these measures to be significant. Specifically, 216 out of 222 stocks had positive pretax profits. Also, on average, quarterly earnings were accelerating. Stocks with **accelerating earnings** not only have earnings that are growing but also have a growth rate that itself is increasing.[3] One final observation was that more than 80% of these 222 stocks were selling within 15% of their previous 2-year *highest* prices before they increased in value.

In summary, the characteristics common among stocks that double in price are a price-to-book ratio less than 1.0, a positive pretax profit, accelerating earnings, and a trading price near the stock's previous 2-year high. Although there is no guarantee that these variables will remain important in the future, it is helpful to see what variables have and have not been significant in the past. When investors select stocks, they now can evaluate these particular characteristics.

19.2 HOW ANALYSTS VIEW THE STOCK VALUATION PROCESS[4]

How do professionally trained security analysts evaluate common stocks? A survey of members of the Financial Analysts Federation sheds some light on this question.[5] This section examines how analysts value stocks in their pursuit of selecting winners.

The survey of the Financial Analysts Federation focused on the investment horizon that security analysts have. The investment horizon determined the characteristics the analysts used to select superior stocks. The survey results overwhelmingly

---

2. The price-to-book ratio was also found by Fama and French to be significant in identifying overperforming stocks. See Eugene F. Fama and Kenneth R. French, "The Cross-Section of Expected Stock Returns," *Journal of Finance* 47 (June 1992): 427–466.

3. This idea is equivalent to pressing down on the accelerator of an automobile. Not only are you moving, but also the speed at which you are moving is increasing.

4. This selection is based on Lal C. Chugh and Joseph W. Meador, "The Stock Valuation Process: The Analysts' View," *Financial Analysts Journal,* November–December 1984, pp. 41–48.

5. The Financial Analysts Federation is now a part of the Association for Investment Management and Research.

indicated that analysts examine the long-run economic and financial outlook of the company. In the long-run (more than 1 year), analysts attached the greatest importance (in this order) to (1) expected changes in EPS, (2) expected return on equity, and (3) prospects of the relevant industry. In the short run (less than 1 year), analysts attached the greatest importance (in this order) to (1) prospects of the relevant industry, (2) expected change in EPS, and (3) general economic conditions.

Arriving at the valuation of these factors, and in particular the valuation of changes in EPS, requires a detailed analysis of the firm. Based on their survey results, Chugh and Meador conclude the following:

No single operating ratio from the company's financial statements, nor any single product or market event, captures for the analyst the long-term prospective value of the stock. Analysts appear to view a company in its entirety—its history, capabilities and position in the industry. . . . [Analysts] attached more importance to the regularity of new product introduction and product refinement, for example, than to anticipated introduction of a new product. . . . [Analysts also] look to qualitative factors such as quality and depth of management, market dominance and strategic credibility to validate quantitative financial and economic variables.[6]

The analysts indicated that the quality and depth of a company's management was an important criterion in assessing a stock's value. Is the firm run by one superstar, or are there numerous highly qualified people managing the firm? How can analysts measure something like this? Analysts assess the quality and depth of management. The most relevant assessment media are (1) the performance record of management; (2) interviews, meetings, and presentations of management to analysts; and (3) evidence of management's strategic planning and ability to meet stated objectives.

Exhibit 19-1 illustrates the stock valuation process as inferred from the results of the survey of the Financial Analysts Federation. Standard information sources are combined with assessment media to develop predictors of financial performance. The predictors of financial performance are combined with the environment in which the firm operates to develop a systematic, or well-ordered, view of the company. From this systematic view, analysts develop long-term financial performance forecasts of EPS and return on equity (ROE, or net income/book value of equity). Finally, based on these long-term forecasts of EPS and ROE, analysts arrive at the value of the common stock.

19.3 MANAGING A STOCK PORTFOLIO

When security analysts actually analyze a stock, they seek a thorough understanding of the risks and rewards of this investment to understand the stock's impact on a managed portfolio. Their systematic view of the company includes a clear exposition of the various risks. This section briefly examines the various risks that analysts

---

6. Chugh and Meador, pp. 42, 43.

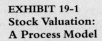

**EXHIBIT 19-1
Stock Valuation:
A Process Model**

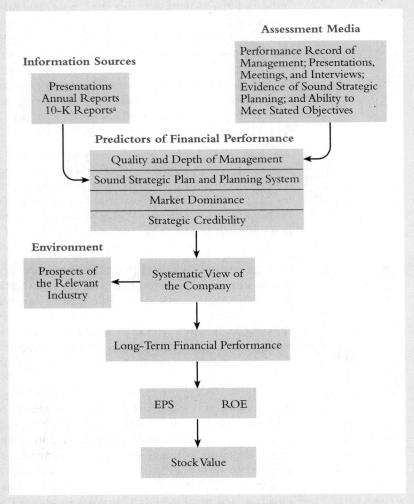

a. 10-K reports are annual reports of publicly held firms filed with the SEC.

Source: Excerpted with permission from Lal C. Chugh and Joseph W. Meador, "Break the Barrier between You and Your Analyst," *Financial Executive,* September 1984, p. 19. Reprinted with permission from *Financial Executive,* Sept./Oct. 1984, copyright 1984 by Financial Executives Institute, 10 Madison Avenue, P.O. Box 1938, Morristown, NJ 07962-1938. (973)898-4600.

consider and looks at equity duration and the role it plays in assessing risk based on the investment horizon.

If the market is perfectly efficient, then all stocks are correctly priced, and no model can predict stocks that will have abnormal returns or be winners. In addition, if historical returns are perfectly representative of future returns, simply using the portfolio theory given in Chapter 8 to find the best portfolio combination would suffice. Note, however, that if we believe that markets are efficient, this does not mean we cannot construct an optimal portfolio, as has been discussed.

Because no one knows the future rates of return, the best estimate is to use ex-post rates of return or some subjective figures and then to construct optimal portfolios. However, some professional investors and academicians claim that there are some characteristics of some stocks (for example, small stocks) that predict to some extent future returns. Thus, these characteristics can be used to predict winners in the stock market. However, an investor who holds this view will not select stocks that will win with certainty. This investor's chances of picking a winner do increase, but due to the risk involved the investor should still diversify in other assets to reduce the risk of a major loss.

For example, suppose there are two stocks, A and B, with mean returns of 10% and standard deviations of 10%. A research analyst predicts that Stock A will be a winner. You then revise your estimate for Stock A—say, to a mean return of 15% and maybe even a standard deviation of 5% (but not a standard deviation of zero). Hence, you still diversify between Stocks A and B. The information that Stock A will be a winner will probably cause you to increase your investment proportion in Stock A, but you still diversify. The only case in which you ignore the benefits of diversification and invest only in Stock A is when its standard deviation is zero. However, no one, not even those who strongly believe they have the ability to locate winners, makes such a claim.

Recall that the objective of this book is to design a portfolio that is on the efficient frontier (see Parts 2 and 3 of this book). Thus, we should view risk from the perspective of the portfolio as a whole and should evaluate risk with measures such as beta. When examining the risk-return characteristics, we are interested in the impact of the stock on the whole portfolio. Hence, we should be concerned with covariances, not only with variances.

One problem in building efficient portfolios is the ability of historical estimates of values like beta to adequately predict actual future performance. For example, if we develop estimates of betas based on history, how sure are we that these estimates fairly represent a stock's sensitivity to market forces in the future?

One practical way to insure an adequate level of diversification is not to diversify solely based on statistical parameters. For example, an investor could make sure the portfolio is adequately diversified across various asset classes, such as stocks and bonds. Second, an investor could examine how the entire portfolio is diversified across sectors such as energy and construction. Investors who invest in several firms would not want to hold large amounts of, say, Exxon bonds and large amounts of Mobil Oil stock unless they were very bullish on energy. Finally, an investor should pay attention to how well diversified the portfolio is among different industries. Diversification can be qualitative as well as quantitative. That is, diversification can be achieved qualitatively by selecting stocks from various sectors, in addition to using such quantitative methods as calculating the efficient frontier.

Obviously, investors use these quantitative and qualitative methods to increase their expected return and to reduce risk. What are the risks of investing in common stocks?

19.3.1 Sources of Risk for Common Stock

The sources of risk that affect common stock prices include the following:

1. *Business risk.* **Business risk** is the possibility that projects undertaken by a firm will not be profitable. Clearly, if management cannot run its firm profitably, this shortcoming will have adverse effects on the firm's share price. The assessment of the risk from internal factors requires an evaluation of the operating efficiency of the firm. Are any unnecessary operations being conducted? Does the firm use the most efficient mix of labor and capital? Is there enough research and development (R&D)? Are expenditures on R&D optimal? Firms with a large amount of R&D are more risky than firms without such investments, because the success of R&D is uncertain. All these factors affect the firm's profitability, as well as its riskiness.

   Firms also face risk from the environment in which they operate. Even the most efficient firm can run into business difficulties in a depressed industry. When gasoline prices rose during the oil crisis of the mid-1970s, for example, people drove less and bought fewer cars. As a result, automobile industry stocks declined as automakers' profits fell.

   Thus, the more sensitive the firm's profit is to changes in prices and macroeconomic factors, the larger the firm's business risk. Naturally, the business risk of a utility firm that supplies water is smaller than the business risk of a mining company.

2. *Financial risk.* **Financial risk** measures the riskiness of the firm's capital structure. Firms with a large amount of debt are riskier than firms that are financed mostly with equity. For example, the rash of leveraged buyouts in the late 1980s sparked numerous defaults in the early 1990s, as was discussed in Chapter 16. In general, the larger the proportion of debt obligations the firm holds, the greater the financial risk. The ability to make interest and principal payments is critical to avoiding default.

3. *Systematic risk.* **Systematic risk** is the movement in securities that results from economic changes that affect the entire market. Beta is a measure of systematic risk. Recall that beta measures how sensitive a stock's price is to changes in the overall market (see Chapter 9). Beta is affected by the financial leverage; generally, an increase in the proportion of debt (leverage) increases beta.

4. *Agency risk.* The owners of a corporation (the stockholders) hire managers to handle day-to-day decisions. There is a risk that these managers—agents of the owners—will not act in the best interest of the owners. This risk is called **agency risk.** For example, a manager may open a branch office in Hawaii for his/her personal benefit rather than opening an office in a colder region closer to the firm's manufacturing or sales base, which is a better choice from the stockholder's point of view. Clearly, this type of behavior is not in the best interest of shareholders.

   In response to agency risk, many firms have tried to align the interests of management with the interests of shareholders:

   More and more companies are trying to imbue top managers with shareholders' interests by forcing them to buy and hold company shares, often the equivalent of one to five times base pay. These shares may be acquired at a discount or through stock options.

Last year, 16 percent of the biggest corporations required top executives to hold stock, up from 10 percent in 1990, according to William M. Mercer Inc., benefits consultants in New York. Companies requiring stock ownership include Borden, Eastman Kodak and General Motors. The policies usually affect the 20 to 100 most senior managers, Mercer said.[7]

By forcing managers to hold a large number of shares, shareholders hope that management will act to maximize the stock price and hence reduce the conflict of interest between stockholders and management. Managers may not favor this requirement, however, because it forces them to be less than optimally diversified. However, the financial benefits from the job may very well offset any loss experienced from a portfolio that lacks adequate diversification.

5. *Regulatory risk.* **Regulatory risk** is the possibility that government agencies will change the way a firm operates. For example, a firm could decide to locate a division near a navigable river, only to later have legislators pass new regulations that prohibit the operation of the firm's new $10 million facility.

6. *Inflation risk.* Future inflation is unknown, and the effect of inflation on stock prices is also unknown. This inflation induces uncertainty, which is called inflation risk. We have shown that inflation adversely affects bond prices. However, it also has an impact on stock prices, even though the influence of inflation on common stock prices is not as direct as it is on bond prices. If inflation caused both the investor's required rate of return and the dividend growth rate to increase, then it is possible that the stock price would remain unchanged.

We illustrate the impact of inflation on stock prices, or **inflation risk,** through a modified version of the constant dividend growth model. Suppose we let h_g represent the added growth rate of dividends because of inflation and let h_k represent the increase in the investor's required rate of return because of inflation. With these definitions, the constant dividend growth model can be written as follows:[8]

$$P_0 = \frac{d_1(1 + h_g)}{k(1 + h_k) - g(1 + h_g)} \qquad (19.1)$$

Do we expect h_g to be equal to h_k? Not necessarily. If the cost of living index is expected to grow by 10%, h_k will grow by 10%, because investors would like to be able to buy the same amount of goods. However, what if the firm produced, for example, tires for cars, and the prices of tires went up by less than 10%? The firm's profits would go up by less than 10%, and h_g would be less than h_k.

Clearly, if $h_k = h_g$, then the price of the stock will remain unchanged. When inflation has a greater impact on the cost of capital (k), then stock prices are expected to fall. However, when inflation has a greater impact on the growth

---

7. From Susan Scherveik, "Executives May Be Asked to Buy and Hold," *New York Times,* April 30, 1994, p. 37.

8. This type of model was developed by T. Estep and N. Hanson, "The Valuation of Financial Assets in Inflation," Salomon Brothers Stock Research Paper, 1980. This type of model was empirically tested by Yaman Asikoglu and Metin R. Ercan, "Inflation Flow-Through and Stock Prices," *Journal of Portfolio Management,* Spring 1992, pp. 63–68. The authors found that the relationship between h_k and h_g varied considerably among industries.

rate of dividends (g), stock prices are expected to rise. Because inflation generally does not have the same effect on g as on k, inflation causes additional uncertainty. This uncertainty is another source of risk.

7. *Interest rate risk.* The interest rate may affect the stock price. Any change in the interest rate in the future may induce a change in the stock price. Those possible changes are called *interest rate risk.* Because investors can substitute between investing in bonds and stocks, stock prices, in general, are influenced by interest rates. For example, we would anticipate that the investor's required rate of return from equity is positively related to interest rates. (As interest rates rise, investors can earn more in the bond market, typically with less risk.) Hence, rising interest rates typically cause the cost of capital (k) to go up; therefore, $k - g$ will rise, and $P_0 = d_1/(k - g)$ will decline. As explained above, the risk of such a decline due to an increase in the interest rate is called **interest rate risk**. Although in most cases when interest rates rise, stock prices fall, the relationship between interest rates and common stock prices is not as strong as that between interest rates and bond prices.

Although the relationship between interest rates and common stock prices is difficult to assess, the relationship between the investor's required rate of return and common stock prices is clear [recall that $P_0 = d_1/(k - g)$]. When k rises, the stock price typically falls [because $k - g$ gets larger, implying that $d_1/(k - g)$ gets smaller], which is termed *price risk*. However, the dividend yield changes when prices change, which is termed *reinvestment risk*. Thus, as with bonds, the idea of duration can be applied to stock portfolios, as will be discussed shortly.

19.3.2 Market Signals of a Crash: An Analyst's View

Connecting Theory to Practice 19.1 reveals what analysts believe are market signals of a high chance of a forthcoming crash. Low dividend yield, high price/book ratio, and high P/E ratio (not mentioned specifically in this article, but the graph included in the article reveals the importance of this factor) are the main factors analysts use to predict market trends.

However, recall once again that even if some factors have some predictability, it is not a perfect predictability. Hence, investors should not necessarily sell all their stock when such factors indicate that the chance of a forthcoming crash increases.

CONNECTING THEORY TO PRACTICE 19.1
VERTIGO

The S&P 500 has more than doubled since the beginning of 1995, an average gain of 33%, a freakish performance given that the average annual price gain since 1926 is only 7%. At its current value of 4.0, the price/book ratio is almost three times the historic norm. The ratio of stock prices to corporate sales

(continued)

is even higher than it was just before the crash of 1929. The S&P 500's yield of 1.6% is so low that stock prices would have to fall to less than half their current levels to bring the yield up to its historical average.

If you sell, you will probably pay almost confiscatory capital gains taxes. If you did get out, you would have to hope that you will know when to get back in because, long range, stocks are still the best investment for most people. It's pretty tough to be a good market timer, both getting out near the top and getting back in near the bottom.

Still, you feel dizzy. Fortunately, there are steps you can take, short of selling everything, to relieve those feelings of vertigo. They won't immunize you against a correction, just lessen the damage enough so that you can sleep at night.

IS A CRASH AROUND THE CORNER?

You can't predict a market top, any more than you can predict the weather. But you can lay odds. And this graph of market results since 1931 shows odds for a good return on the stock market over the next 5 years are not good. The market's trailing 5-year P/E is now around 26.

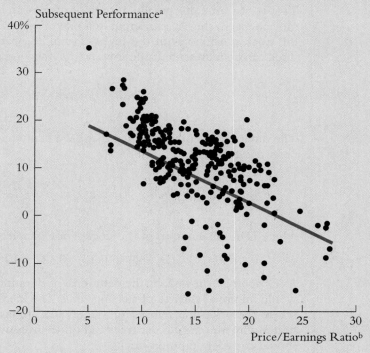

a. Annualized total return on S&P 500 over the following 5 years.

b. Ratio of price to average earnings over the previous 5 years.

Source: James M. Clash and Mary Beth Grover, "Vertigo," *Forbes,* August 25, 1997, pp. 114–116. Reprinted by Permission of *Forbes* magazine © Forbes Inc., 1997.

(continued)

19.3.3 Duration of Common Stock

As with bonds, attention should also be given to the anticipated holding period of the portfolio of common stock. Recall from the Chugh and Meador survey that analysts focus on different factors when their investment horizon is short term versus long term. In an effort to understand the relationship between holding period and returns, most of the analyses of duration have been extended to common stocks. That is, at least conceptually, a stock portfolio can be "immunized" against adverse movements in the investor's required rate of return (k) by equating the duration of the stock portfolio with the investor's holding period. Recall that the price of a stock can be represented as follows by the dividend discount model (DDM):

$$P_0 = \frac{d_1}{k-g} \tag{19.2}$$

The duration of common stock that has a constant growth of dividends can be expressed as follows:[9]

$$D_s = \frac{1+k}{k-g} \tag{19.3}$$

where D_s is the duration of the stock. For example, if $k = 14\%$ and $g = 10\%$, then

$$D_s = (1 + 0.14)/(0.14 - 0.10) = 28.5 \text{ years}$$

As Chapter 17 showed, by the definition of duration, a holding period of 28.5 years would minimize the risk of a change in k. The 28.5-year holding period is the point where the price and reinvestment rate risks are just offset.[10] This analysis demonstrates why insurance companies and other investors who have long-term horizons should consider common stocks.

---

9. The duration is defined as

$$D_s = \sum_{t=1}^{y} t \, \frac{d_0(1+g)^t}{(1+k)^t} \Big/ P_0$$

Recall that $t = 1, 2, \ldots$, hence D_s can be broken down into a progressive series whose sum is given by Equation 19.3.

10. Recall that this application of duration assumes that the discount rate changes only once (as soon as the stock is purchased).

Suppose another firm has the same d_1 and k but a higher growth rate ($g = 11\%$). Then the duration of the firm's stock is

$$D_s = (1 + 0.14)/(0.14 - 0.11) = 38 \text{ years}$$

Thus, the common stock of this firm has a longer duration. This makes sense, because with a higher growth rate, relatively more cash flow is obtained in the more distant future, which increases the duration.

Duration can be approximated by the reciprocal of the dividend yield. That is,

$$D_s = \frac{1 + k}{k - g} \cong \frac{1}{k - g}$$

From the DDM,

$$P_0 = \frac{d_1}{k - g}$$

we find that

$$D_s = \frac{1}{k - g} = \frac{P_0}{d_1}$$

which is the reciprocal of the dividend yield (except it uses d_1 rather than d_0). For example, as the July 6, 1998, *Wall Street Journal* reports, Texaco's dividend yield (d_1/P_0) is 2.9%, implying a duration of $1/0.029 \cong 34.48$ years. For utility firms, which typically have dividend yields of about 6%, the duration is about $1/0.06 = 16.67$ years.

Investors with a clear understanding of the various risks related to a stock and the stock's duration are in a good position to assess how a stock will influence the riskiness of their portfolios. Hence, they will be able to make better decisions regarding stock selection.

PRACTICE BOX

Problem

Suppose a normal-growth firm has a dividend yield based on next year's dividend of 5% (d_1/P_0). If the firm is expected to pay $0.98 in dividends next year, compute the following:

1. The stock price.
2. The stock's duration.

Solution

1. We know that $d_1/P_0 = 0.05$ and $d_1 = \$0.98$. However, because $P_0 = d_1/(k - g)$, then $d_1/P_0 = k - g = 5\%$. Thus, $P_0 = d_1/0.05 = \$0.98/0.05 = \$19.60$.
2. According to Equation 19.2, $k - g = d_1/P_0 = 0.05$. Thus, the duration is $D_s \cong 1/0.05 = 20$ years. Thus, the duration for a normal-growth firm is simply the reciprocal of the dividend yield (based on next year's estimated dividends).

19.4 ESTIMATING DIVIDEND DISCOUNT MODEL INPUTS

So far in this text, the DDM has been developed as a theoretical valuation model and its use explained. When investors use this model to select stocks, however, they cannot simply work with assumed levels of g and k. They must estimate these values. This section illustrates how investors can make these estimates. Actually applying the DDM and employing the concept of duration requires estimating two critical parameters: the investor's required rate of return (k) and the growth rate of dividends (g).

19.4.1 Estimating the Dividend Growth Rate (g)

The appropriate growth rate (g) for the DDM can be estimated by extrapolating the past dividend payments. If d_t represents the annual dividend payment at the end of year t, then g is represented by

$$d_t = d_0(1 + g)^t \qquad (19.4)$$

where d_t represents the dividend paid in year t, and d_0 represents the dividend paid t years ago. Solving for g yields the following:[11]

$$g = \left(\frac{d_t}{d_0}\right)^{1/t} - 1 \qquad (19.5)$$

This method for estimating g is known as the *point estimate method,* because only two dividend payments (points in time) are used. The growth rate estimated by this method is very sensitive to the selected starting and ending year. Actually, it depends on only two observations, d_0 and d_1. For example, if CSX, Inc. (a transportation company), paid a $1.52 dividend in 1998 and a $0.95 dividend in 1988, the growth rate for this 10-year period would be

$$g = \left(\frac{\$1.52}{\$0.95}\right)^{1/10} - 1 = (1.6)^{1/10} - 1 \cong 0.048$$

or about 4.8%. However, if we select a 5-year period and suppose that the dividends paid in 1993 were $1.16, then the growth rate would be

$$g = \left(\frac{\$1.52}{\$1.16}\right)^{1/5} - 1 \cong (1.3103)^{1/5} - 1 \cong 0.055$$

or about 5.5%.

Although these growth rates may not appear to be very different, the impact on the respective stock prices is significant. For example, if we assume that $k = 9\%$, then the estimated prices with growth rates of 4.8% and 5.5%, respectively, are

---

11. By dividing by d_0 to get $d_t/d_0 = (1 + g)^t$, taking the $1/t$th root, and subtracting 1, we get Equation 19.5. When the firm changes its payout ratio, sometimes it is better to use the EPS series rather than the DPS series to estimate growth rates.

$$P_0 = \frac{d_0(1 + g)}{k - g} = \frac{\$1.52(1 + 0.048)}{0.09 - 0.048} \cong \$37.93$$

$$P_0 = \frac{d_0(1 + g)}{k - g} = \frac{\$1.52(1 + 0.055)}{0.09 - 0.055} \cong \$45.82$$

Thus, a 0.7% (5.5% − 4.8%) difference in our estimate of g results in a $7.89 ($45.82 − $37.93) difference in the stock price. The estimation procedure is therefore very sensitive to the choice of the dividend growth estimation period. For example, do we use the past 5 years or the past 10 years? The choice of the initial period may be crucial to the estimated growth rate. However, in selecting the initial period and the estimation period we should keep in mind that the objective is to find the best estimate of *future* dividend growth.

Another problem with this method is that it ignores the dividend payments made during the interim periods. For example, our future estimates for CSX would not be different if we knew that instead of gradually increasing dividends, there were no dividend payments between 1988 and 1998, which of course constitutes a major drawback. Thus, we would need to refine our analysis to incorporate the information contained in the interim periods. Appendix 19A presents the following estimation equation, which relies on all dividends rather than only on the dividends of the first and the last years:

$$g = \exp\left\{\frac{cov[\ln(d), t]}{\sigma_t^2}\right\} - 1 \qquad (19.6)$$

where $\ln(d)$ is the natural logarithm of dividend payments, t is a counter for time (years), σ_t^2 is the variance of the counter for time, cov is the variance, and exp stands for *exponential* (that is, "e to the power of").

This method of estimating g is known as the *regression method,* because it is based on linear regression. Recall from our calculation of beta that

$$cov(\ln(d), t) = \frac{1}{n}\sum_{i=1}^{n}\ln(d_i)t_i - \overline{\ln(d_i)}\ \overline{t}_i$$

and

$$\sigma_t^2 = \frac{1}{n}\sum_{i=1}^{n}t_i^2 - \overline{t}_i^2$$

where $\overline{\ln(d_i)}$ is the average of the $\ln(d_i)$, and $\overline{t}_i$ is the average of t_i.

Exhibit 19-2 illustrates the data required to estimate g using Equation 19.6:

$$g = \exp(0.46/10) - 1 = 4.7\%$$

Thus, the regression estimate of the growth rate of dividends over the past 10 years is 4.7%. In this particular case, the regression approach resulted in an estimate very close to the case with only two points, because in our hypothetical example of CSX, Inc., CSX has paid steadily increasing dividends over this 10-year period. In the case of a steady increase in dividends with a sharp fall in the last year, the two methods yield quite different estimates.

An alternative method for estimating the dividend growth rate is to use consensus forecasts of future earnings per share (EPS). The growth rate of dividends in year t can be estimated by taking the return on equity ($ROE_t = EPS_t/BVPS_{t-1}$, where BVPS is the book value per share in year $t - 1$) and multiplying it by the estimated payout ratio (b). That is,

$$g = b \cdot ROE_t = b \cdot (EPS_t/BVPS_{t-1})$$

This method of estimating g is known as the *accounting method*, because it is based on accounting data. There are several sources for obtaining estimates of future EPS. For example, Zack's Earnings Estimates, I/B/E/S, and Value Line are information services that provide these figures.[12]

For example, assume that the predicted EPS for 1999 for CSX was $5.40, and the book value per share was $37.95.[13] Suppose we estimate the payout ratio to be around $b = 30\%$. This would mean that dividends are estimated to grow at $g = 0.3$ ($5.40/$37.95) $\cong 4.3\%$. Note that this estimate is within the range of our other estimates.

EXHIBIT 19-2 **Hypothetical** **Illustration for** **Estimating** g **for CSX, Inc.**	Year	Dividend	t (years)[a]	$\ln(d)$[b]	$t \cdot \ln(d)$[c]	t^{2c}
	1988	$ 0.95	0.00	−0.05	0.00	0
	1989	0.99	1.00	−0.01	−0.01	1
	1990	1.04	2.00	0.04	0.08	4
	1991	1.13	3.00	0.12	0.37	9
	1992	1.16	4.00	0.15	0.59	16
	1993	1.18	5.00	0.17	0.83	25
	1994	1.24	6.00	0.22	1.29	36
	1995	1.28	7.00	0.25	1.73	49
	1996	1.40	8.00	0.34	2.69	64
	1997	1.43	9.00	0.36	3.22	81
	1998	1.52	10.00	0.42	4.19	100
	Sum	$13.32	55.00	2.01	14.98	385
	Average	$1.21	5.00	0.18	1.36	35

a. Starting t at zero is arbitrary. It is easier to compute the statistics with low numbers, however.

b. The reported numbers are rounded. However, the product $t \cdot \ln(d)$ is calculated with the precise numbers of $\ln(d)$.

c. The covariance between $\ln(d)$ and t is given by

$$cov[\ln(d), t] = 1.36 - (0.18 \cdot 5.0) = 0.46$$
$$\sigma_t^2 = 35 - 5^2 = 10$$

12. I/B/E/S denotes the Institutional Brokerage Estimate System.
13. These predictions were made in mid-1998.

PRACTICE BOX

Problem

Calculate the growth rate of dividends (g) for CSX from 1994 through 1998 using the data in Exhibit 19-2.

Solution

We need to construct a table similar to Exhibit 19-2 for the years 1994 through 1998:

Year	Dividend	t (years)	$\ln(d)$[a]	$t \cdot \ln(d)$[a]	t^2
1994	$1.24	0.00	0.22	0.00	0
1995	1.28	1.00	0.25	0.25	1
1996	1.40	2.00	0.34	0.67	4
1997	1.43	3.00	0.36	1.07	9
1998	1.52	4.00	0.42	1.67	16
Sum	$6.87	10.00	1.59	3.66	30
Average	$1.37	2.00	0.32	0.73	6

a. See Footnote b in Exhibit 19-2.

Thus, the covariance is

$$cov[\ln(d), t] = 0.73 - (0.32 \cdot 2.00) = 0.09$$

and the variance of t is

$$\sigma_t^2 = 6 - 2^2 = 2$$

From Equation 19.6 we get the following (the exponential, e, is on most calculators):

$$g = e^{(0.09/2)} - 1 = e^{(0.045)} - 1 \cong 4.60\%$$

We can also calculate g using industry and company analysis, which is described in Chapter 21.

19.4.2 Estimating the Investors' Required Rate of Return (k)

The first way to calculate the investors' required rate of return is to use the DDM itself to estimate k, as demonstrated in Chapter 18:

$$k = \frac{d_1}{P_0} + g \qquad (19.7)$$

Based on our calculation of g using historical hypothetical data for CSX (and assuming that CSX was trading for $62 per share at this time), we could estimate

$$k = \frac{\$1.52(1 + 0.047)}{\$62} + 0.047 \cong 0.0727$$

If the one-year Treasury bill rate is 6% at the time of this estimation, this estimate is probably too low. Why would we risk our money in stock for 7.27% when we could earn just a little less than that in U.S. Treasuries? Of course, g is only an estimate, and in this case the estimate is probably lower than the true future growth rate.

We also can use the capital asset pricing model (CAPM) to estimate k:

$$k = r + \beta[E(R_m) - r] \tag{19.8}$$

Suppose CSX's beta is 1.25, according to Value Line. If we use $r = 6\%$ as before (which implicitly adjusts for expected inflation) and estimate $E(R_m)$ to be 10%, then

$$k_{CSX} = 0.06 + 1.25(0.10 - 0.06) = 0.11, \text{ or } 11\%$$

A third method is to estimate the historical average rate of return on the common stock. This average rate of return is a proxy of what investors will require in the future. For example, suppose the average rate of return on CSX common stock over the past 10 years is 15.6%. Thus, we could estimate the investor's required rate of return for the future as 15.6%.

A fourth method uses the yield to maturity of a firm's long-term bonds. Because common stocks are riskier than bonds, we must add a positive premium of approximately 4%. For example, assume CSX has a 9½% coupon bond that matures in 24 years. The bond's yield to maturity is presently 9%. Thus, we could estimate k as 13% (9% + 4%). This approach has the benefit of being forward looking, because the yield to maturity incorporates expectations about the market, as well as expectations about the firm's prospects. However, the addition of a risk premium is arbitrary.

Finally, you'll recall from Chapter 18 that there are circumstances when the E/P ratio (the reciprocal of the P/E ratio) is an appropriate estimate of k. For CSX, E/P = \$4.50/\$62 $\cong$ 0.073, or 7.3%. This appears to be too low relative to the other estimates, because CSX is a supergrowth firm. Discussing all these methods to estimate k, note that no one method is always appropriate to estimate k and g. Part of the skill in acquiring security is knowing which method to use at what time.

19.5 IMPLEMENTING DIVIDEND DISCOUNT MODELS

Dividend discount models (DDM) can be used to select stocks. By estimating g and k, investors can calculate the present value of the future dividends. Under a DDM, if the present value is greater than the current market price, the stock is considered to be a bargain. When used carefully, DDMs seem to have promise in selecting stocks. In fact, researchers have evaluated the performance of DDMs; they have tested how effective a DDM is in forming portfolios of undervalued and overvalued securities. The evidence presented here includes three-stage DDMs. The three-stage DDM is very similar to the life cycle of a supergrowth firm discussed in Chapter 18, except that rather than having two growth stages, it has three growth stages.

Sorensen and Williamson examined the no-growth, constant growth, super-growth, and three-stage growth models as to their ability to select stocks that outperform the market.[14] They found that employing DDMs resulted in portfolios that outperformed the market. When comparing the various models, Sorenson and Williamson found a very interesting result:[15]

Portfolio returns improved considerably, however, as the complexity of the model used to rank them increased. The top-ranked portfolio from the three-period dividend discount model, for example, had an annual return 3.5 per cent greater than the return on the top-ranked portfolio from the P/E model.

Ability to discriminate between under and overperformance also increased with model complexity. The portfolio ranked best and worst by the P/E method differed in return by 22.26 per cent; this difference increased to 35.63 per cent when the three-period model was used for ranking.

Although the empirical studies provide support for DDMs, they should be used in practice with caution.

A close examination of the DDMs (and related models) reveals several baffling problems.[16] The purpose of this section is not to destroy confidence in DDMs but to identify some of the weaknesses of these models. Most of these weaknesses are shared by other valuation models (for example, the model that uses historical data to predict the future; see later in the chapter).

19.5.1 DDM Assumptions

If we use a DDM to identify undervalued (or overvalued) stocks, we are assuming that although a stock is not now appropriately valued, someday soon its value will return to its appropriate level. If we apply the DDM to a stock, we might find that it is worth $120 when it is currently trading at $90. In this case, we would buy the stock, hoping that it would soon go to its DDM value of $120. That is, the DDM would be of no use if the stock did not revert back to its fair value soon, where fair value is based on the DDM.

A second assumption of DDMs is that the discount rate (k) is constant over time. In practice, this may not be the case. For example, many analysts believe that firms go through a life cycle as they move from infancy to maturity. Most firms have a rapid-growth phase, when they pay no dividends; then an expansion phase, when they begin to pay dividends; and finally a maturity phase, when they exhibit little or no growth. A DDM incorporates the changing dividends as the firm progresses through its life cycle. When discounting dividends through these different phases, why should we believe that the investor's required rate of return remains the same? After all, the risk of the firm also changes over the life cycle, so k should change with the firm's life cycle. Intuitively, we would anticipate that k would be lower

14. See Eric H. Sorensen and David A. Williamson, "Some Evidence on the Value of Dividend Discount Models," *Financial Analysts Journal*, November–December 1985, pp. 60–69.

15. Sorensen and Williamson (see Footnote 14) estimate supergrowth rates using earnings forecasts and assume a constant payout ratio, as well as extrapolating the past. They use the CAPM to estimate the appropriate discount rate. For the constant growth DDM, Sorenson and Williamson assume that g is based solely on future earnings estimates. They also assume that $k - g = 5.75\%$ for all firms (based on their originally calibrating their model to the S&P 500.)

16. The following sections are based in part on John J. Nagorniak, "Thoughts on Using Dividend Discount Models," *Financial Analysts Journal*, November–December 1985, pp. 13–15.

when the firm is in maturation, because less risk is involved. Thus, to estimate value accurately, we need to allow for both changes in dividends and changes in the investor's required rate of return.

When the CAPM approach to estimating k is used, there is a potential conflict. The DDM is an infinite-period model, whereas the CAPM is a single-period model. For example, changes in expected inflation over the next 5 years would not be included in CAPM-based estimates over the next year. Hence, how can we justify using results from within a single-period framework over an infinite period? This conflict potentially can be avoided by the judicious selection of input parameters. Recall from Equation 18.1 and the discussion that followed in Chapter 18 that it does not matter whether you discount future dividends or the future price. Thus, the DDM can be used as a single-period model where the price in one period is estimated using the infinite-period DDM.

19.5.2 Proper Inputs

The DDM is a forward-looking equation, yet most analysts rely on history to establish initial estimates. They combine history with current events to estimate future events. One difficult job of an analyst is to make the appropriate alterations to historical estimates.

The alterations should include management's current strategy. Clearly, such alterations require skills in evaluating things that are not quantifiable. For example, assessing the current quality of management and the impact it will have on the current stock price is difficult to quantify.

A final difficulty lies in establishing how long it will take for a firm to move from one phase to another. For example, how long can a firm remain in the supergrowth phase? How can this be estimated? Although not entirely impossible, it is a difficult task. Perhaps this is one reason analysts are paid so well.

19.5.3. Interpreting the Results of a DDM Calculation

After the exercise of calculating stock values based on the DDM has been completed, what can you do with the results? For example, suppose you determine that a stock is 10% undervalued according to the DDM. What should you do? At first glance, you may say, "Buy it, of course!" The answer, however, is not that clear-cut. For example, the factors that caused the price to be 10% undervalued may well drive it to be 20% undervalued before it begins to turn around. Thus, the timing decision is very tricky.

A second problem is determining whether the stock is really mispriced or whether you are just missing some crucial information. You must address why the stock is mispriced. Understanding the forces driving the mispricing (for example, institutional selling because of a legal constraint) will be helpful in assessing the appropriate action to take when mispricing actually occurs.

The final problem is determining how to assess the performance of the DDM. The critical question is whether the predicted DDM performance leads to abnormal profit (or to a profit adjusted for risk). If so, it will be a valuable tool for the analyst. Thus, we need a statistical tool to evaluate the extra profit made if we employ this method on many investments. One can, for example, employ the CAPM on many decisions made by the DDM and test whether the return on such a portfolio is significantly higher than the return on a random portfolio with the same risk. The DDM as an investment tool may lead to a successful result (or profit) on some stocks and to a failure (loss) on other stocks.

SUMMARY

Identify some characteristics of a stock market winner, based on the analysis of Marc Reinganum.   Stock market winners, according to a study by Marc Reinganum, have a price-to-book ratio that is less than 1.0, positive pretax profits, and accelerating earnings. These qualities do not guarantee a winner, but they are attributes of many winning stocks.

Explain how an analyst views the stock valuation process. An analyst examines the long-run economic and financial outlook of the company, focusing on the expected change in EPS, the expected return on equity, and the prospects of the relevant industry. The analyst also considers the quality and depth of management based on its ability to successfully develop sound strategic plans and implement them. The analyst may be wrong with his valuation. Therefore, our investment risk remains, and investors still should diversify, because returns are uncertain, and the stock selection process does not eliminate the need for diversification. However, when a winner is identified, its mean increases, and a higher investment proportion should be allocated to this stock.

Identify the risks that are relevant in stock investment. Investment in common stock has seven sources of risk: business risk, financial risk, systematic risk, agency risk, regulatory risk, inflation risk, and interest rate risk. Investors who understand a stock's risks are better able to select stocks that are appropriate for their portfolios. A change in the stockholder's required rate of return, *k,* is another source of risk. By matching the portfolio duration to the investment horizon, one can minimize the risk exposure where duration is defined—as it is in bonds—as the weighted average number of years corresponding to the cashflows from the stock. The duration of a stock was analyzed, with a focus on the role of the investor's holding period.

Describe how to estimate g and k of the constant dividend growth model in practice.   Methods for estimating g include the point estimate method, the regression method, and the accounting method. Methods for estimating k include the DDM method, the CAPM method, using historical stock returns, the yield to maturity method, and using the inverse of the P/E ratio. No one method is always appropriate for estimating k and g. Part of the skill a security analyst acquires is knowing which method to use at what time.

Explain why dividend discount models must be used with caution.   Some empirical results indicate that dividend discount models can be used to build stock portfolios that outperform the market. However, analysts must be cautious when actually implementing DDMs. Using DDMs to identify mispriced stocks implicitly assumes that stocks are not correctly priced at present and that they will one day soon move toward the correct price. Also, DDMs assume that the discount rate is constant over time, which is not necessarily true. Combining the CAPM (a single-period model) with DDMs (infinite-period models) is difficult at best. Analysts doing so must modify historical parameter estimates in light of current conditions.

CHAPTER AT A GLANCE

1. *The purpose of security analysis is to find undervalued stocks.*

2. *Per-share price less than the per-share book value, increases in earnings, and the acceleration in this increase are the key factors predicting winners in the stock market.*

3. *The DDM can be employed to find undervalued stocks.*

4. *Sources of risk for common stock:*
   a. Business risk.
   b. Financial risk.
   c. Systematic risk.
   d. Agency risk.
   e. Regulatory risk.
   f. Inflation risk.
   g. Interest rate risk.

5. *The duration of a common stock according to the DDM follows:*

$$D_s = \frac{1 + k}{k - g}$$

6. *Methods for estimating* g *include the following:*
   a. Point estimate:

$$g = \left(\frac{d_t}{d_0}\right)^{1/t} - 1$$

   b. Regression estimate:

$$g = \exp\left\{\frac{cov[\ln(d), t]}{\sigma_t^2}\right\} - 1$$

   c. Accounting estimate:

$$g = b \cdot ROE$$

7. *Methods for estimating* k *include the following:*
   a. DDM estimate:

$$k = \frac{d_1}{P_0} + g$$

   b. CAPM estimate:

$$k = r + \beta[E(R_m) - r]$$

   c. Average of historical rates of return.
   d. Positive premium above the yield to maturity of a firm's long-term bonds.
   e. The reciprocal of the P/E ratio, or earnings divided by the price.

KEY TERMS

Accelerated earnings   706
Agency risk   710
Business risk   710

Financial risk   710
Inflation risk   711
Interest rate risk   712

Regulatory risk   711
Systematic risk   710

REVIEW

19.1 The following table gives the percentage growth rates in two firms' earnings per share over a recent 5-year period:

Year	Firm A	Firm B
1	1.0	7
2	3.4	6.8
3	5.3	7.4
4	6.9	5.4
5	8.6	7.6

Which firm has experienced the phenomenon known as *accelerating earnings?* Explain your answer.

19.2 Compare and contrast the business risk and financial risk of common stock.

19.3 A firm issues bonds and uses the proceeds to repurchase 15% of its stocks. What happens to the business risk? What happens to the financial risk?

19.4 "Suppose a firm has zero business risk. Then its financial risk must also be equal to zero." Evaluate this statement, and demonstrate your opinion with a hypothetical example.

19.5 Firm A employs a manager whose contract is renewed once every 2 years and firm B employs a manager whose contract is renewed once every 10 years. Which firm is exposed to a greater agency risk? Explain why.

19.6 Suppose a firm went public by selling 60% of its shares. However, the family who originally founded the firm still holds 90% of the controlling vote. What risk would outside investors be concerned about? Why?

19.7 "If the business risk is zero, then beta must also be zero." Evaluate this statement. Distinguish in your answer between efficient and inefficient markets.

19.8 "Suppose beta is equal to 1.0. Then in the CAPM framework, an increase in the interest rate, other things being equal, does not affect the cost of capital (k)." Do you agree? Prove your answer.

19.9 "For a given cost of equity (k), the lower the growth rate of dividends (g), the lower the stock's duration." Evaluate this statement, and defend your evaluations.

19.10 Firm A pays dividends of $1 this year and $10 the year after. Firm B reverses this pattern by paying $10 this year and $1 next year. Both firms will pay the same dividends thereafter. Which stock has the longer duration? Why?

PRACTICE

19.1 Suppose National Health Corporation will pay dividends in 1 year of $0.75 ($d_1 = \$0.75$), its required rate of return is $k = 11.5\%$, and its growth rate of dividends is $g = 5\%$. The stock follows the constant dividend growth model.

a. What is the value of the common stock?
b. Inflation is now thought to occur such that investors increase their required rate of return by 5%. What is the added growth rate in dividends because of this inflation if the stock price remains unchanged?

c. What will happen to the stock price if the added growth rate in dividends because of inflation is greater than or less than the result found in Part b?

19.2 "The duration of a common stock is approximately the price-to-dividend ratio." Evaluate this statement.

19.3 Suppose you were given the following historical information regarding CWE, Inc., common stock:

Year	Dividend
1	$3.00
2	1.50
3	1.75
4	2.10
5	2.50

a. Estimate the historical growth rate of dividends using Equation 19.5 and Years 1 and 5, as well as Years 2 and 5. Discuss your results.

b. Suppose you know that because of an unusual catastrophe, CWE, Inc., cut its dividend at the end of Year 1. You do not believe that such an event will happen again. Estimate the historical growth rate of dividends using the regression method.

19.4 Suppose you believe that a stock followed the constant dividend growth model and the CAPM. Suppose you estimate the following parameters: $d_0 = \$1$, $g = 3\%$, $\beta = 1.2$, $E(R_m) = 11\%$, and $r = 4\%$.
a. What is the value of the common stock?
b. If the Federal Reserve Bank increases interest rates to 5% (and this does not influence any of the other parameters), what will happen to the stock's value?

19.5 Suppose that with no inflation, a stock's price is evaluated by Equation 19.1 and is valued at $P_0 = \$100$. Now inflation of 10% is expected. The firm's dividend growth rate will be 10% because of this inflation. However, the cost of capital will increase at a fraction of this rate, such that $1 + h_k = 2(1 + h_g)$. What will be the new stock price after these changes, when it is known that originally $k = 2g$?

19.6 You have the following series of data:

Year	Dividends per Share	Earnings per Share
1	$0.50	$1
2	0.35	1.1
3	0.25	1.21
4	0.25	1.331

You wish to estimate the growth rate (g). Which series of data should you use, DPS or EPS? Why? Calculate the growth rate using point estimates for Years 1 and 4 based on these two series, and defend your answer.

19.7 Suppose you have the following series of dividends per share:

Year	Dividends per Share
1	$1
2	2
3	3
4	4
5	1

Use the point estimate approach and the regression approach to estimate the growth rate (g). How can you explain the differences? Which method is preferable?

19.8 Based on the CAPM, the cost of capital (k) is estimated as

$$k = r + \beta[E(R_m) - r]$$

where $\beta = 1$ and $k = 15\%$. The firm decides to increase its leverage (financial risk). Would this affect the cost of equity (k)? If so, in which direction? Explain what parameters change in this equation to account for this change in k.

19.9 Suppose the stock price is consistent with both the constant dividend growth model and the CAPM (Equation 19.8). Also, the dividend yield (using next year's dividend) is equal to the interest rate (r). It is known that g is 10%, and $E(R_m) - r = 5\%$. What is the firm's beta?

19.10 A firm invests $100, all financed by equity (100 shares each at $1). Its EPS and DPS for the next 3 years are estimated to be the following:

Year	EPS	DPS
1	$0.10	$0.05
2	0.12	0.06
3	0.144	0.072

a. Estimate the growth rate (g).

b. Now suppose that $50 of the investment is financed by 5% coupon bonds and $50 of the investment is financed by stocks. Thus, the number of shares outstanding is 50. Calculate the new value of g. (Ignore taxes.)

c. Assume that the stock price is unaffected by the leverage and remains at $1. Calculate the cost of capital (k) before and after the leverage.

19.11 Suppose two assets, A and B, are uncorrelated and to the best of your knowledge have the following means and standard deviations:

Asset	Mean	Standard Deviation
A	10%	10%
B	10	10

a. Find the optimum mean-variance diversification. Draw the efficient frontier.

b. Suppose now that a financial analyst predicts that Asset B is a winner. (Suppose it has a low price-to-book ratio.) As a result, you revise your estimate as follows:

Asset	Mean	Standard Deviation
A	10%	10%
B	20	2

Would you still diversify? Assuming the risk-free rate of 5%, draw the efficient frontier. Explain.

19.12 The past rates of return on two stocks are the same, and therefore they have the same mean, standard deviation, and beta. However, Stock A is a small firm with a low price-to-book ratio of 0.8, whereas Stock B is a large firm with a price-to-book ratio of 2.0. In which stock would you invest more? Why?

19.13 Suppose Firms A and B have the following percentage revenue per dollar of investment:

Year	Firm A	Firm B
1	10%	−8%
2	12	12
3	−8	5
4	5	10

Assume that the share price is $1 for both firms.

a. Which firm has a greater business risk?

b. Firm A is a pure equity firm, and Firm B financed 50% of its investments by equity and 50% by bonds. Which firm has a higher financial risk? Why?

19.14 Suppose you are given the following historical data:

Year	EPS	DPS
1	$1	$0.5
2	2	1
3	1	0.5
4	2	1

The firm got a new contract that guarantees an EPS of $1.50 a year for the next 100 years. The DPS will not change during these 100 years. The cost of capital is $k = 10\%$. Use the constant dividend growth model to evaluate the stock.

19.15 Suppose you classify ten stocks according to their price-to-book ratio and get the following rates of return:

Stock	Low Price-to-Book Ratio	High Price-to-Book Ratio
1	10%	7%
2	−5	0
3	20	5
4	10	17
5	10	−1

Analyze these data. In particular, calculate the mean and standard deviation across stocks of each group. If you had to choose one group, which group would you choose? Defend your choice.

19.16 Suppose a firm had dividends per share as follows:

Year	DPS
1	$1
2	0.5
3	0.6
4	0.7

The firm split its stock 2-for-1 in Year 2. It also paid a stock dividend of 10% in Year 3. Calculate the growth rate of dividends using the point estimate method.

19.17 "If the dividend is $2 and the stock price is $100, no one would buy the stock, because its dividend yield is 2% lower than the going 4% interest rate." Evaluate this assertion.

19.18 Suppose the dividend next year is $10, the cost of capital is 10%, and the current price is $150.
a. What is *g*?
b. Suppose there is now permanent 10% inflation that affects only the dividends. What will be the effect of this type of inflation on the stock price? Assume that the cost of capital remains at 10%. How would you change your answer if the cost of capital also increases by the inflation rate?

19.19 a. The stock price is $100, and the firm pays all of its earnings as cash dividends. It expects constant earnings of $10 forever. Calculate the internal rate of return on the investment in this stock. (Hint: See Appendix 1A.)
b. What will be the internal rate of return on the investment if the firm distributes 50% of its earnings as cash dividends and reinvests the retained earnings at 10%? Write out the next 5 years' dividend payments. Compare and discuss your results.

19.20 The table on page 729 provides the list of twenty-five stocks that made up an aggressive portfolio (called the "Magic 25") as recommended in November 1996 based on a forecast for 1997 and the rates of return up to September 16, 1997. The graph shows the performance of some indexes for the corresponding period.
a. In how many stocks out of the twenty-five were the experts right in their recommendations, and in how many of the stocks were they wrong?

b. Suppose that you consider investing in the S&P 500 (Spiders, whose rate of return was about 28% during the period) or the recommended list. In how many stocks on the recommended list would you make a higher rate of return than on a random portfolio (that is, the S&P 500)? Do the experts have predictability ability if the number of successes out of the twenty-five stocks is considered?
c. During this period, the rate of return on the Dow Jones Industrial Average was about 22%, on the S&P 500 about 28%, and on the Nasdaq about 33%. Suggest a method to examine whether the recommended list outperformed these unmanaged indexes overall. (Hint: Incorporate risk into the analyses).

19.21 *What do these companies have in common? They are smallish, with market values under $600 million; they are manufacturers; and they pay nice dividends. They are all in the portfolio of the Stratton Small-Cap Yield fund.*

This fund has scarcely been noticed, having attracted only $37 million in assets. But it is going to be. Over the past three years Frank Reichel has guided this pip-squeak to a 25.8% compound annual return, four points ahead of the Russell 2000 index of small-company stocks. . . .

A lot of the action in small companies is in technology stocks, but Reichel's favorites tend to be older, sleepier companies trading at low price/earnings multiples. The choice makes eminent sense if you happen not to like volatility. On infamous Oct. 27, when the Dow crashed 554 points and the Russell took a 6.2% beating, Small-Cap Yield lost just 3.4%.

Reichel, 33, a Wharton M.B.A., joined Stratton Management Co. in Plymouth Meeting, Pa. 11 years ago. . . .

For his fund Reichel first screens the 2,700 actively traded small companies for the 600 or so with yields higher than the Russell 2000 (currently 1.3%). His next criterion is another value measure. He wants to see a company trading at a lower multiple of cash flow (in the sense of net income plus depreciation and amortization) than its competitors, yet enjoying prospects for greater earnings growth.

That's an unusual combination, but it does occur.

Source: James M. Clash, "Small Fries—with Dividends, Please," *Forbes,* December 1, 1997, p. 310. Reprinted by Permission of *Forbes* magazine © Forbes Inc., 1997.

The Magic 25

Stock	Start Price 11/18/96	Recent Price 9/16/97	Gain/Loss	Rating	Investor Relations
Activision (ATVI)	$12.13	$14.50	+19.6%	Buy	310-473-9200
ACT Networks (ANET)	32.00	12.81	−60.0	Sell	805-388-2474
Advanced Digital Info. (ADIC)	11.00	18.75	+70.5	Buy	206-881-8004
Ballantyne of Omaha (BTN)	10.92	18.43	+68.8	Buy	402-453-4444
Bio-Technology General (BTGC)	9.22	13.75	+49.1	Buy	908-632-8800
Bio Time (BTIM)	16.59	33.13	+99.7	Buy	510-845-9535
Cognos (COGNF)	35.00	33.13	−5.3	Buy	613-738-1440
Horizon Health (HORC)	17.17	24.25	+41.3	Hold	214-991-0112
Human Genome Sciences (HGSI)	37.00	38.63	+4.4	Buy	301-309-8504
I-Flow (IFLO)	4.25	4.47	+5.2	Buy	714-553-0888
Informix (IFMX)	20.63	9.56	−53.7	Sell	415-926-6300
JetForm (FORMF)	18.88	16.75	−11.3	Buy	613-230-3676
Lone Star Technologies (LSS)	16.75	48.00	+186.6	Hold	214-386-3981
Network Appliance (NTAP)	34.75	51.25	+47.5	Buy	415-428-5100
Nice Systems (NICEY)	21.00	46.38	+120.9	Hold	212-752-0504
Periphonics (PERI)	20.00	13.75	−31.3	Sell	516-468-9000
Physician Comp. Network (PCNI)	8.63	6.88	−20.2	Sell	201-490-3111
Qlogic (QLGC)	18.25	44.50	+143.8	Buy	714-438-2200
Stratasys (SSYS)	18.13	16.13	−11.0	Hold	612-937-3000
Syncor International (SCOR)	10.13	16.75	+65.4	Buy	818-886-7400
Theragenics (THRX)	21.31	45.25	+112.3	Hold	770-381-8338
Thermo Electron (TMO)	37.50	40.25	+7.3	Buy	617-622-1111
THQ (THQI)	7.63	12.75	+67.2	Buy	818-591-1310
UroMed (URMD)	11.00	5.03	−54.3	Buy	617-433-0033
Wandel & Goltermann (WGTI)	21.00	11.75	−44.1	Hold	919-941-5730

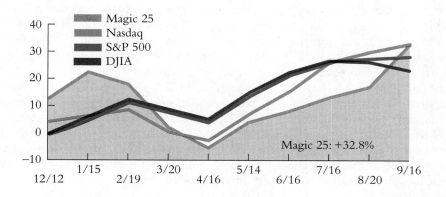

Source: *Individual Investor*, November 1997, p. 28. Copyright 1997 *Individual Investor*. Reprinted with permission.

a. What are the criteria by which Frank Reichel selects the stock to be included in the portfolio?

b. Suppose that all firms are normal-growth firms, which pay a constant proportion of their profit as cash dividends. The dividend grows at a constant growth rate per year. Is the P/E multiplier a good stock selection criterion in such a case? Is the amount of dividend paid relevant for stock selectivity in such a case?

c. Suppose that you have two firms, A and B, with a normal growth. For Firm A, $P = 100$ and $E = 10$. For firm B, $P = 90$ and $E = \$10$. The depreciation per share of Firm A is \$5; for Firm B it is \$1. Which stock is preferred by the multiple of cash flow? Is the choice justified? Discuss your answer. (Hint: The assets of Firm A, a firm in the electronics industry, are depreciated over 2 years, whereas the assets of Firm B, a firm in the machinery for cars industry, are depreciated over 10 years.)

d. Is Reichel's stock selection criterion, based on the multiple of cash flow, consistent with the free cash flow method discussed in Chapter 18 (see Appendix 18A)? Explain your answer.

e. Over the past 3 years, Reichel made a 25.8% compound annual rate of return. Calculate the monthly uncompounded rate of return. Then, based on these thirty-six monthly rates, suggest a method to examine whether Reichel's stock selection criteria yielded an abnormal rate of return. (Hint: Use beta and the CAPM.)

For Internet questions visit the Levy Investment Web site at http://levy-invst.swcollege.com.

YOUR TURN: APPLYING THEORY TO PRACTICE

ACE STOCK PICKER NAMES SOME TACTICS THAT WORK IN THIS YEAR'S MARKET

In a market that has punished many stock pickers this year, which stock-picking methods are working?

Let's ask Richard Bernstein, ace number-cruncher at Merrill Lynch. Of the two dozen methods he tracks, few are working especially well this year, including two old favorites and a couple of oddballs.

One venerable technique enjoying renewed success is picking stocks with low P/E ratios—that is, low stock prices compared to per-share earnings. The tactic goes all the way back to Benjamin Graham in the 1930s, and has worked well ever since, with occasional lapses. Mr. Graham, with David Dodd, was co-author of the investment classic "Security Analysis." An unusually long and severe lapse happened in 1989 and 1990, but low P/E investors have been doing dandy since then.

Another popular method—in use for about a decade—is buying stocks on which analysts are raising their earnings estimates. This tactic produced rotten results in the first half of 1992, but is generating nice gains so far this year.

The low-P/E approach is the only one that has done well both year-to-date and during the previous six years. "It's the longest-lasting" stock selection method around, says Grace Messner, head of the investment strategy committee at Wilmington Trust.

And it deserves to be, she says, because its underlying rationale makes sense. Low-P/E investors, by definition, are buying unpopular stocks about which other investors are worried. That means they are taking extra risk and according to investment theory, should be compensated for that risk.

(continued)

WHAT'S WORKING IN STOCK SELECTION

Stocks displaying the attributes listed below have outperformed the overall market. Figures are average price changes for 50 stocks in the S&P 500 that best embody each attribute.

The following lists five investment strategies (and the S&P 500) and the return they achieved in two periods.

Current Year (through April)	Return
Wide estimate dispersion	9.2%
Favorable estimate revisions	9.0
Big variation in past earnings	8.9
Low price/earnings ratio	8.5
High dividend yield	8.4
S&P 500-stock index	1.0

Past Six Years (1987–1992)	Return
Low price/earnings ratio	122.3%
High relative strength	122.3
Low price/cash flow	116.8
Low debt/equity	106.0
High projected five-year growth	100.5
S&P 500-stock index	79.9

Source: *Wall Street Journal Europe,* May 21–22, 1993, p. 11. Reprinted by permission of *The Wall Street Journal,* © 1993 Dow Jones & Co., Inc. All Rights Reserved Worldwide.

Questions

1. Suppose you wish to use the low-P/E investment criterion and are willing to revise your portfolio every year. Assume that you include only ten stocks in your portfolio out of a total of one hundred available stocks. Describe a possible investment strategy.

2. During the years 1987 to 1992, by how much did the low-P/E investment strategy outperform the S&P 500 stock index on an annual basis?

3. Using the figures from Question 2, can we unequivocally conclude that the market is inefficient? Explain.

4. Why, in your view, would a wide dispersion of financial analysts' forecasts regarding a stock's earnings imply a high mean return? Does this contradict or support the idea of market efficiency?

5. Why would a large variation in earnings imply a high return? Does this support or reject the notion of market efficiency?

6. Suppose the annual risk-free interest rate for the years 1987 to 1992 was 7%. If the CAPM holds, what would the beta of each of the five investment strategies be for the period 1987 to 1992? Draw all the portfolios on the security market line (SML). How would you decide whether to adopt one of the above investment strategies? What additional information would you need? Assume that the holding period of all investors is 1 year.

7. Assume that the betas that you solved for in Question 6 are the true betas. What would the estimated return on each strategy be during a year when the S&P index declined by 10%? Assume an annual risk-free interest rate of 7%. Discuss your results.

SELECTED REFERENCES

Farrell, James L., Jr. "The Dividend Discount Model: A Primer." *Financial Analysts Journal,* November–December 1985, pp. 16–25.

This is an informative review of DDMs and their applications.

Fouse, William L. "Allocating Assets across Country Markets." *Journal of Portfolio Management,* Winter 1992, pp. 20–27.

Fouse finds support for using DDMs in deciding how to allocate assets across countries.

Kahn, Sharon. "What (Global) Dividend Discount Models Say Now." *Global Finance*, March 1992, pp. 71–73.

This is a good article on how DDMs are used in country comparisons.

Rozeff, Michael S. "The Three-Phase Dividend Discount Model and the ROPE Model." *Journal of Portfolio Management*, Winter 1990, pp. 36–42.

This research paper examines two 3-phase DDMs. The researchers found that the DDM that is based on the growth of return on equity works better.

Sorensen, Eric H., and David A. Williamson. "Some Evidence on the Value of Dividend Discount Models." *Financial Analysts Journal*, November–December 1985, pp. 60–69.

This research paper examines the value added to a portfolio's construction based on the DDM. The authors found that the more complex the model, the better the performance.

SUPPLEMENTAL REFERENCES

Higgins, Huong N. "Analyst Forecasting Performance in Seven Countries." *Financial Analysts Journal*, May–June 1998, pp. 58–62.

Rohweder, Harold C. "Implementing Stock Selection Ideas: Does Tracking Error Optimization Do Any Good?" *Journal of Portfolio Management*, Spring 1998, pp. 49–59.

Appendix 19A Estimating the Growth Rate of Dividends

This appendix uses the regression method for estimating the growth rate of dividends. According to Equation 19.4,

$$d_t = d_0(1 + g)^t$$

where d_t is the dividend paid in year t. Recall that linear regression analysis is based on many observations. However, the relationship between dividend payments and time as expressed in Equation 19.4 is not linear. We can make this relationship linear by taking the natural log of both sides. Specifically,[17]

$$\ln(d_t) = \ln(d_0) + t \cdot \ln(1 + g) \tag{19A.1}$$

which resembles a standard linear regression equation ($y = \alpha + \beta_x$), where $y = \ln(d_t)$, $\alpha = \ln(d_0)$, $\beta = \ln(1 + g)$, and $x = t$. From our analysis of beta in Chapter 9, we know that

---

17. Recall that $\ln(ax) = \ln(a) + \ln(x)$, and $\ln(x^a) = a\ln(x)$.

$$\hat{\beta} = \frac{cov(y, x)}{\sigma_x^2} = \frac{cov[\ln(d), t]}{\sigma_t^2} \qquad (19A.2)$$

Substituting Equation 19A.2 for $\ln(1 + g)$ yields

$$\hat{\beta} = \ln(1 + g) = \frac{cov[\ln(d), t]}{\sigma_t^2}$$

Taking the exponential of both sides of the previous equation yields

$$1 + g = \exp\left\{ \frac{cov[\ln(d), t]}{\sigma_t^2} \right\}$$

Finally, solving for g yields

$$g = \exp\left\{ \frac{cov[\ln(d), t]}{\sigma_t^2} \right\} - 1 \qquad (19A.3)$$

CHAPTER 20

MARKET AND INDUSTRY ANALYSIS

LEARNING OBJECTIVES

After studying this chapter you should be able to:

1. Identify and describe the macroeconomic variables that measure economic health.

2. Describe the impact of government fiscal and monetary policy on investment decisions.

3. Describe the measures used to value the stock market as a whole.

4. Evaluate market sectors and specific industries.

THE DOLLAR'S DECLINE HAS AN UPSIDE

As the great dollar debacle of 1995 unnerves markets from Brazil to Belgium, traders, government officials, and ordinary folks are all left with the same question. Why did the dollar drop? What's next? What does this mean to me?

Source: Andrew E. Serwer, "The Dollar's Decline Has an Upside," *Fortune*, April 3, 1995, p. 10.

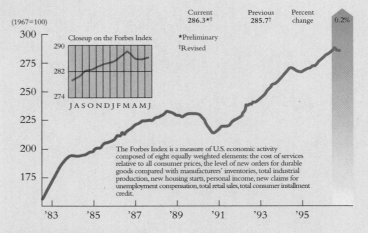

The Forbes Index is a measure of U.S. economic activity composed of eight equally weighted elements: the cost of services relative to all consumer prices, the level of new orders for durable goods compared with manufacturers' inventories, total industrial production, new housing starts, personal income, new claims for unemployment compensation, total retail sales, total consumer installment credit.

THE FORBES INDEX

Inflation has totaled 1.4% (annualized) so far this year. Will it stay down? Yes, says Richard Berner, chief economist at Mellon Bank. "The dollar's strength limits U.S. companies' ability to raise prices, and there is still a lot of excess global capacity, particularly in Southeast Asia," he says. If Berner is right, long Treasurys yielding 6.5% are pretty tempting for long-term investors. Berner expects economic growth of 3.5% (annualized) in the second half of 1997.

Source: Shlomo Z. Reifman, ed., "The Forbes Index," *Forbes*, August 11, 1997, p. 40. Reprinted by Permission of *Forbes* Magazine, © Forbes Inc., 1997.

Investors analyze a specific firm using the firm's financial and market data. However, no less important is the analysis and forecast of the strength of the economy or the industry in which the firm operates. The Forbes index is one measure of the U.S. economy's activity (see this chapter's Investments in the News). The larger the increase in this index, the stronger the economy.

The Forbes index reveals past behavior, but what is relevant for investors is the forecast of the index. For example, citing economic factors, Richard Berner predicted in August 1997 an economic growth of 3.5% (annualized) for the second half of 1997. Investors can use such forecasts to analyze the future economy and thus decide whether to invest in equity or in the bond or cash markets. Thus, the purpose of market and industry analyses is to indicate whether investors should invest in equity, in bonds, or in cash; these analyses also help investors choose particular industries in which to invest.

This chapter examines the major principles related to evaluating the overall health of a country's economy. It also looks at the role that government policy plays in economic health.

Why should investors analyze the whole economy, or even a given industry, when they are interested only in evaluating stocks or bonds? After all, investors are interested in the potential earnings of a specific firm, not the whole economy. Investors buy individual stocks, not industries or whole economies. Thus, it may seem that macroeconomic analyses are not of much value to individual investors. However, this is not the case.

It is well known that the majority of the variation in a stock price can be explained by movements in the overall market.[1] Therefore, this chapter examines economic factors that influence the entire market, and hence also affect the prices of individual stocks. After accounting for market movements, the environment in which a firm operates—the firm's sector and industry—also explains a significant portion of a stock's price movement. Thus, the chapter examines how to analyze sectors and industries. Chapter 21 explains how to analyze individual companies, which is typically done *after* economic, sector, and industry analysis.

Investors would like to have macroeconomic or industry indicators that could be used to predict the stock market. Unfortunately, in many cases the stock market is too quick and responds ahead of most other economic indicators. This characteristic, of course, is not useful for the investor.

This chapter first reviews some basic economic principles and their influence on financial markets. It then establishes the necessary links between the economy and financial markets. Next it focuses on valuing the overall stock market, specifically by examining book value, dividends, and earnings of broad stock market indexes. The chapter concludes with an overview of how to assess the relative value of market sectors and industries.

---

1. See, for example, B. F. King, "Market and Industry Factors in Stock Price Behavior," *Journal of Business* 39 (January 1966): 139–190.

20.1 MACROECONOMIC EVALUATION

A vibrant and growing economy needs a well-functioning capital market. In turn, when the economy is growing and firms are profitable, investors are willing to invest and thus provide the needed funds for capital expansion. All firms are influenced by the economic environment in which they operate. Therefore, the ability to forecast the overall economy is a key to being a successful portfolio manager.

However, the most important key is the ability to find economic factors that change before the stock market changes, not after the stock market changes. Identifying these economic factors enables the investor to buy stocks before stock prices rise or to sell them before they drop. Unfortunately, it is very difficult to identify such factors, because the stock market is a leading index (it reacts first) relative to most other economic indicators. Nevertheless, forecasting long-term economic trends and government policy may be beneficial for long-run investors who consider investing in stocks or bonds.

This section reviews several economic series that indicate the overall strength of the economy. It first reviews the concept of gross domestic product and other measures of economic health. It also reviews the most popular economic indicators used to forecast future economic trends. Finally, it examines various government policies, especially those of the Federal Reserve, and their role in stimulating economic activity.

20.1.1 Understanding Gross Domestic Product

The most widely used measure of the health of the overall economy is the **gross domestic product (GDP).** The GDP is typically measured both quarterly and annually, and the government issues preliminary estimates throughout the year. The GDP, or the *nominal GDP,* as it is sometimes called, is the value of all goods and services produced in an economy in a particular time period. The GDP is measured in dollars. Because inflation changes the value of dollars, economists adjust GDP values to include the effects of inflation. This inflation-adjusted measure, called the **real GDP,** allows economists and investors to compare the GDP over time, ignoring the impact of inflation. In the United States, statistics on the GDP and related measures of economic health are produced by the Bureau of Economic Analysis of the U.S. Department of Commerce.

A problem in measuring total output is how to count goods and services produced in a domestic country (say, the United States) by foreigners and how to count goods and services produced by nationals (say, Americans) in a foreign country. The solution to this problem is to have two measures of economic activity. Gross national product (GNP) counts goods and services produced by U.S. nationals in a foreign country but does not include goods and services produced by foreigners in the domestic country. Thus, a factory built in Spain by U.S. citizens would count in the U.S. GNP but not in Spain's GNP. The GDP counts goods and services produced within the country's borders, ignoring who produced it. Thus, the factory built in

Spain by U.S. citizens would count as part of Spain's GNP but not as part of the U.S. GDP.

One key to the successful use of macroeconomic data in investment analysis is an understanding of exactly how these data are published. Investors attempting to establish relationships between macroeconomic data and financial markets need to consider the revision process of reported macroeconomic data. Quarterly estimates of the GDP are first released during the last few days of the month following the end of the quarter. For example, for the first quarter ending March 31, the **advanced estimate** of the GDP is released at the end of April (see Exhibit 20-1). **Preliminary estimates** are released a month later (May, in our example), followed by a **revised estimate** after another month (June, in our example). Finally after another month (in July, in our example), **benchmark revisions** are made covering the past 3 years. Thus, advanced estimates may be altered several times before a final GDP figure is established because of improvements in data collected over the particular time period. Thus, when examining historical data to establish relationships between financial markets and macroeconomic data, be sure to incorporate revised figures. The final reported GDP may be significantly different from the initial advanced estimate. Investors should make future investment decisions based not only on advanced estimate figures but also on the revised estimate.

The GDP has four components: consumption, investment, government spending, and net trade (exports less imports). The GDP is traditionally expressed as

$$GDP = C + I + G + (X - M) \qquad (20.1)$$

where C is consumption, I is investment, G is government spending, and $(X - M)$ is net trade (i.e., export minus import). In this equation, investment (I) includes spending for new capital goods and increases in corporate inventory, not financial investments. Investors watch the different components of the GDP closely, because some components tend to provide better information regarding the direction of the

EXHIBIT 20-1
The Procedure for Reporting the GDP

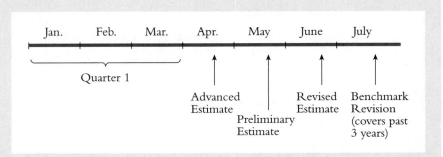

Source: W. Stansbury Carnes and Stephen D. Slifer, *The Atlas of Economic Indicators* (New York: HarperCollins Publishers, 1991), p. 39.

economy in the future. For example, in 1997, C = $5,488.1 billion, I = $1,240.9 billion, G = $1,452.7 billion, X = $958.0 billion, and M = $1,058.8 billion.[2] Thus,

$$GDP = \$5,488.1 + \$1,240.9 + \$1,452.7 + (\$958.0 - \$1,058.8) = \$8,080.9$$

where all figures are in billions.

To compare real GDPs, economists divide the GDP by the inflation rate.[3] Real GDP is equal to nominal GDP divided by a "deflator." The deflator was arbitrarily set to 100% in 1987. Because inflation has occurred since 1987, the deflator has grown to account for the effects of inflation since 1987. For example, in 1997 the implicit deflator (ID) was 200%. Thus (in billions),

$$Real\ GDP = \frac{C + I + G + (X - M)}{ID} \tag{20.2}$$

$$[\$5,488.1 + \$1,240.9 + \$1,452.7 + (\$958.0 - \$1,058.8)]/2.0$$
$$= \$8,080.9/2.0 \cong \$4,040.5$$

PRACTICE BOX

Problem

Suppose we estimate the real GDP for next year at $4,357 billion. We also estimate consumption to be C = $4,076 billion, investment to be I = $822 billion, government spending to be G = $1,347 billion, and the implicit deflator to be ID = 142.7%. Based on these estimates, what would we forecast for net trade (the difference between exports and imports) $(X - M)$?

Solution

Recall from Equation 20.2 that

$$Real\ GDP = \frac{C + I + G + (X - M)}{ID}$$

Substituting our estimates yields the following (in billions):

$$\$4,357 = [\$4,076 + \$822 + \$1,347 + \$(X - M)]/1.427$$

Solving for $(X - M)$ yields

$$\$4,357 \cdot 1.427 = \$6,245 + \$(X - M)$$

Rearranging yields the following:

$$\$(X - M) = (\$4,357 \cdot 1.427) - \$6,245 \cong -\$27.6$$

Thus, we are forecasting imports to exceed exports by $27.6 billion.

2. Data from http://www.bea.doc.gov/bea/dn/niptbl-d.htm#Table 2, Part B.
3. There are two methods for adjusting the GDP for inflation. The implicit deflator measures both price changes and changes in spending patterns. That is, spending pattern changes can influence the implicit deflator. Thus, the implicit deflator is not a pure measure of inflation. Rather, it is a measure of how people change their spending habits in response to inflation. The fixed-weight deflator is a pure measure of inflation, because as its name implies, the weight given to each component of the GDP remains constant. Most analysts adopt the implicit deflator to maintain a precise measure of the effect of inflation on the GDP.

Several measures of economic activity provide clues on the magnitude and direction of the real GDP. Exhibit 20-2 lists some of these measures, what component of the GDP they influence, and when these measures are announced. For example, the number of cars sold is announced every two weeks about three days following the end of the second week. Clearly, car sales represent consumption, and they help give early clues as to whether consumers are loosening their purse strings. Consumers tend to purchase cars when they have confidence in the overall economy.

The value of these published economic measures depends heavily on how soon they are available. Car sales, for example, are very valuable, because they are published after only three days (as well as biweekly). Factory orders are not as valuable, because they are published only several months after the order day.

EXHIBIT 20-2	Measuring Inflation and Components of the GDP and When They Are Reported		
Component	**Percentage of GDP**	**Economic Measures**	**When Available**[a]
Consumption	69%	Car sales	After 3 days (biweekly)
		Retail sales	11th–14th
		Personal income/expenditures	22nd–31st
Investment	13	Housing starts/building permits	16th–20th
		Durable goods orders	22nd–28th
		New home sales	28th–4th
		Construction spending	1st (2 months prior)
		Factory orders/business inventories	30th–6th (2 months prior)
Government spending	19	Public construction	1st (2 months prior)
Net exports	−0.5	Merchandise trade balance	15th–17th (2 months prior)
GDP[b]	100[c]	Purchasing managers' index	1st
		Employment	1st–7th
		Industrial production capacity	14th–17th
Inflation		Producers price index	9th–16th
		Consumer price index	15th–21st

a. Unless otherwise stated, the dates refer to the following month. See page 15 of the source.

b. A negative figure implies that exports are smaller than imports.

c. The sum is not exactly 100% because of rounding.

Source: W. Stansbury Carnes and Stephen D. Slifer, *The Atlas of Economic Indicators* (New York: HarperCollins Publishers, 1991).

20.1.2 The Business Cycle and Economic Indicators

A **business cycle** is a period of expansion and contraction of aggregate economic activity measured by the real GDP. When the economy expands, stock prices rise, because firms are relatively profitable. The opposite is true in periods of contraction. Thus, predicting the business cycle is relevant for investors in the security market. Exhibit 20-3 illustrates the stages of a business cycle. The black line moving up through time represents long-run growth. As economic activity contracts, the real GDP dips below this growth rate. It reaches a low point known as the **trough.** Eventually the economy expands until it reaches the high point of the business cycle, known as the **peak.** An economy is in an **expansion** phase between a trough and before a peak; it is in a **contraction** phase after a peak and before a trough. Because business cycles do not occur regularly or predictably, they are difficult to forecast. Even harder is predicting how financial markets will react to changes in the business cycle.

Because financial markets and business cycles are related, investors can be hurt if they forecast a business cycle incorrectly. For example, if an investor bought stocks that tend to move with the business cycle, known as *cyclical stocks,* and the economy suddenly deteriorated, then these stocks probably would incur substantial losses for the investor.

The National Bureau of Economic Research has constructed measures of business activity known as *composite indexes,* which are made up of selected economic data that vary depending on the purpose of the composite index. The three main

EXHIBIT 20-3
A Business Cycle

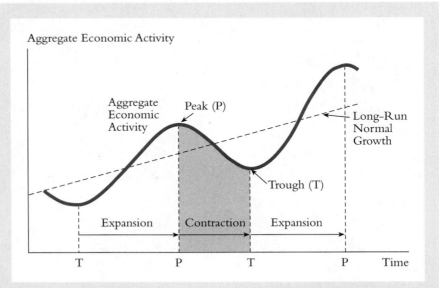

Source: Andrew B. Abel and Ben S. Bernanke, *Macroeconomics,* fig. 9.1—p. 291. © 1995 by Addison-Wesley Publishing Co., Inc. Reprinted by permission of Addison Wesley Longman.

indexes (also called indicators—a technical measurement used to forecast the market's direction) are the leading, coincident, and lagging indexes. **Coincident indicators** are indicators that are supposed to move directly with the business cycle. **Leading indicators** and **lagging indicators** are indicators that are supposed to lead and lag behind the business cycle. For example, the composite index of eleven leading indicators is a weighted average of eleven economic statistics that are supposed to lead the business cycle. Exhibit 20-4 gives these eleven components. Each index is given a specific reference number that helps analysts keep track of how a particular index or a composite index is constructed. Thus, each index can be identified uniquely by its number. For example, the average weekly hours worked in manufacturing is Series 1.

From time to time, the composition of these composite indexes is changed. We see from Exhibit 20-4 that the eleven series making up the leading index are statistics that would be expected to change first with changes in the business cycle. For example, Series 1, the average weekly hours worked by manufacturing labor, would tend to rise as businesses perceived that the economy was entering an expansion phase and demand was rising. It is interesting to note that Series 19, the index of stock prices (which is actually the Standard & Poor's 500 index), is one of the best-performing leading indicators of the business cycle.

20.1.3 Fiscal and Monetary Policy

The government uses fiscal policy and monetary policy to influence the level of real GDP in the economy and to promote GDP growth, relatively full employment, and stable prices. The government can also intervene to avoid bankruptcy trends. For example, in November 1997, the fourth largest investment house in Japan declared bankruptcy. The Nikkei index dropped sharply, igniting fear of a bankruptcy chain reaction. The Japanese government immediately announced a reform plan to avoid the chain reaction, and the Nikkei index recovered in response to this plan. Thus, governments, in implementing their policies, can affect the business environment as well as the stock market.

THE FEDERAL GOVERNMENT AND FISCAL POLICY

Fiscal policy refers to the taxation and spending policies of the government designed to achieve GDP growth, relatively full employment, and stable prices. Governments can stimulate growth in real GDP with tax incentives for investment. For example, a reduction in the corporate capital gains tax rates may motivate businesses to make capital expenditures. This increase in investment directly increases the GDP. Personal tax rates also affect the stock market. For example, if investors had been able to forecast that the Clinton administration would reduce the capital gains tax from 28% to 20% (or even to 18% for a 5-year holding period) in 1997, before this information was public or even before it was publicly discussed, they could have made money by purchasing stocks, because such an announcement usually induces an increase in stock market prices. Fiscal policy seeks to find the optimal strategy that maximizes GDP growth and employment and at the same time maintains stable prices.

EXHIBIT 20-4   **Business Cycle Indicators and Their Components**

Series	Type of Index Component	Explanation
	Leading Index Components	
1	Average weekly hours, manufacturing	Length of work week increases with perceived future demand
5	Average weekly initial claims on unemployment insurance	Claims decline as an economy rebounds
8	Manufacturers' new orders, consumer goods and materials	New orders increase with a stronger economy
32	Vendor performance, slower deliveries	A stronger demand will result in slower deliveries
20	Contracts and orders for plant and equipment	New orders increase as the business outlook brightens
29	Index of new private housing units	People build houses based on the forecast of future prospects
92	Change in manufacturers' unfilled orders, durable goods	Unfilled orders indicate future GNP growth
99	Change in sensitive materials prices	The demand for certain materials increases as an economy expands
19	Index of stock prices, 500 common stocks	Stock prices are based on forecasted *future* performance
106	Money supply, M2 (M1, M2, and M3 are three measures of the money supply as defined by the Federal reserve. M1 represents all money that can be converted to cash immediately; M2 includes M1 plus savings accounts and time deposits; M3 is M2 plus the money market funds held by institutions)	Economies are sensitive to the quantity of money available
83	Index of consumer expectations, University of Michigan	Consumers with bright expectations will spend more
	Coincident Index Components	
41	Employees on nonagricultural payrolls	The number of persons employed moves with the business cycle
51	Personal income less transfer payments	Employee pay moves directly with the business cycle
47	Index of industrial production	Production moves directly with the demand for goods
57	Manufacturing and trade sales	Sales move directly with the business cycle
	Lagging Index Components	
91	Average duration of unemployment	Length of unemployment declines after an economy rebounds
77	Ratio of manufacturing and trade inventories to sales	After an economy rebounds, sales increase and inventories decline
62	Change in labor cost per unit of output	Labor costs rise after an economy rebounds
109	Average prime rate charged by banks	Interest rates rise in response to business demand for funds
101	Commercial and industrial loans outstanding	Borrowing increases after an economic rebound
95	Ratio of consumer installment credit outstanding to personal income	People borrow a greater percentage of their income *after* an economic recovery
120	Change in Consumer Price Index for services	Price levels tend to rise only after an economy is expanding

The government can affect the unemployment rate in various ways. The most popular employment statistic monitored by governments is the **civilian unemployment rate,** which is the number of unemployed persons as a percentage of civilians working or actively seeking work. For example, in December 1997 there were 6.7 million unemployed people in the United States, and the size of the civilian labor force was 136.297 million. The civilian unemployment rate was

$$(6.7 \text{ million}/136.297 \text{ million})100 \cong 4.9\%$$

One method of stimulating a sluggish economy is for the government to hire unemployed persons to perform various tasks, such as building roads. Without tax increases, however, this government spending will produce **budget deficits**. Similar to a personal budget deficit, a governmental budget deficit occurs when a government spends more in a given period than it takes in as tax revenues. Budget deficits make prices unstable. If budget deficits are financed by printing money—something the United States has yet to do—the result is inflation. If budget deficits are financed by borrowing money, there is less capital for business investment.

Assessing the fiscal soundness of a country's government is a critical task for international portfolio analysis, as well as analysis of domestic portfolios. Even good companies have difficulty remaining profitable if they operate in a country whose government is irresponsible. Hence, one key assessment criterion for international investment is the integrity of the foreign government's fiscal policy.

THE FEDERAL RESERVE BANK AND MONETARY POLICY

In 1913, Congress created the Federal Reserve Bank (the Fed) to carry out monetary policy. **Monetary policy** refers to actions by a central bank to control the supply of money and interest rates that directly influence the financial markets. Like fiscal policy, monetary policy aims to achieve growth in the real GDP, relatively full employment, and stable prices. The Fed's primary focus is on interest rates and money supply. Additionally, the Fed acts as a lender of last resort (when there is a cash drain on a bank) and guards against severe currency depreciation. The Fed will lend to banks, for example, when there are unusually large withdrawals. It will also try to support its currency in volatile foreign exchange markets. Generally, when the Fed announces an interest rate increase, the stock market falls; similarly, an interest rate decrease is accompanied by an increase in stock prices. Thus, analyzing the Fed's policy and being able to predict it ahead of time can turn out to be very profitable.

The Fed regulates the volume of bank reserves, affects the pace of money creation, and sets the percentage of funds that banks are required to hold as reserves. It rarely uses bank reserves as a policy tool in its efforts to manipulate the economy. **Bank reserves** are the percentage of deposits that banks must hold in noninterest-bearing assets (cash). Reserve requirements set by the Fed are one of the key tools in deciding how much money banks can lend. The higher the reserve requirement, the tighter the money, and therefore the slower the economic growth. In a **recession,** the Fed can decrease the reserve requirement to stimulate the economy. The tool used most often by the Fed to alter the money supply is its **open market operations** (these are activities by which the Federal Reserve Bank of New York carries out the instructions of the Federal Open Market Committee, which intends to regulate the money supply in the market). By buying and selling U.S. Treasury securities directly in the bond market, the Fed can expand or contract the volume of bank reserves.

Exhibit 20-5 illustrates how the Federal Reserve system influences economic activity. Note that changes in bank reserves influence both the money supply and interest rates, which in turn influence both economic activity and inflation.

The Fed also establishes the **bank discount rate,** which is the rate the Fed charges banks when they borrow directly from it. Indirectly, the bank discount rate influences other interest rates. The amount borrowed varies widely and is seasonal. The **federal funds rate** is the rate charged for reserves borrowed between banks. The bank discount rate and the federal funds rate are highly correlated.

The ability of a central bank such as the Fed to maintain stable prices and stable interest rates is a key ingredient in providing an environment conducive to running business profitably. Thus, investors need to assess the current abilities of Federal Reserve Bank authorities, as well as compare central bank operations across countries.

20.2 THE ECONOMY AND THE FINANCIAL MARKETS

This section examines the relationship between the overall economy and the bond and stock markets. An economy experiencing real growth in GDP will have a strong

EXHIBIT 20-5
The Actions of the Federal Reserve Bank and Its Influence on the Economy
Open market operations occur when the Federal Reserve buys or sells U.S. Treasuries to influence the reserves held by banks.

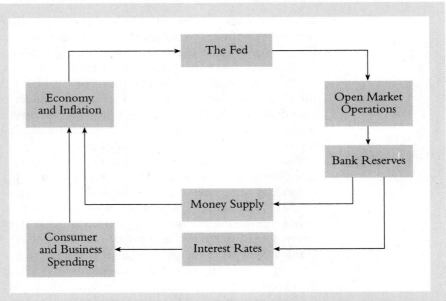

Source: "The Actions of the Federal Reserve and Its Influence on the Economy" from *The Atlas of Economic Indicators* by W. Stansbury Carnes and Stephen D. Slifer, Copyright © 1991 by HarperCollins Publishers, Inc. Reprinted by permission of HarperCollins Publishers, Inc.

stock market. A strong economy implies that firms are working near capacity and profit margins are high. These higher earnings suggest higher stock prices. A productive country will also experience a strong demand for its currency as outside investors convert their currency and invest in the vibrant economy. A strong economy also implies a threat of some inflation, which is not favorable for the bond market. When firms are operating at capacity, the ability to raise prices (and to spark inflation) is always a consideration. Higher inflation translates into higher interest rates, which means falling bond prices.

Although we can make the intuitive link between the economy and the financial markets, what is the empirical evidence for such a link? Let's look at the actual experience of the United States.

20.2.1 Bond Market

Exhibit 20-6 shows the relationship between real GDP and the bond markets. Specifically, the exhibit compares changes in real GDP with the nominal yield to maturities on Aaa-rated bonds. There is no general pattern in these trends. For example, the economy moved into a recession (negative growth rates of real GDP) in the early 1980s and the real GDP fell, but bond yields rose. The higher risk of default sent bond prices down, resulting in higher yields. Also in the early 1980s, increasing inflation lowered the real GDP, as well as caused yields to rise. By the mid-1980s, inflation was more stable; the exhibit shows a direct relationship between real GDP and bond yields, with both falling. Thus, the yield to maturity is affected by both inflation and the risk of default. In a recession the risk of default goes

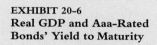

EXHIBIT 20-6
Real GDP and Aaa-Rated
Bonds' Yield to Maturity

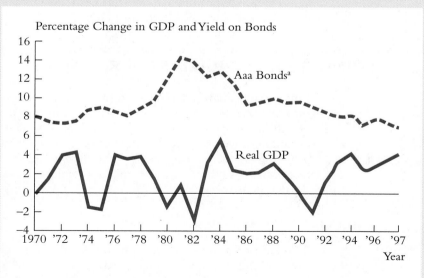

Percentage Change in GDP and Yield on Bonds

[a]The yield for the last year corresponding to April 1995.

up; this increases the yield to maturity. However, inflation may go up or down. When inflation is up (in the early 1980s) in a recession, the two forces of inflation and default risk join each other, and bond prices plummet. When the inflation and the economy are down (in the early 1990s), there are conflicting forces, and bond prices are relatively stable.

20.2.2 Stock Market

The link between the stock market and real GDP growth is even less clear. However, there are several possible links between the business cycle and the stock market.

One link between the business cycle and the stock market is based on earnings. In an expansion phase, firms typically have wider profit margins and hence are able to pay higher dividends or reinvest in projects with positive NPVs. Either way, investors are being well served, and stock prices tend to rise.

Another link between the business cycle and the stock market, as already explained, is based on interest rates. Falling interest rates at the end of recessions tend to lift stocks. When the interest rate falls, the cost of capital (which is made up of the interest rate plus a risk premium) also falls. Recall from the constant dividend growth model that if the cost of capital (k) declines, then stock prices (P_0) rise.

The stock market tends to move before the GDP, and although we would like to predict the stock market moves by looking at GDP changes in earlier periods, we cannot. The stock market is one of the best leading indicators of trends in real GDP, so tracking the GDP to get a preview of stock market trends is not of much use to an investor.

Exhibit 20-7 shows the relationship between real GDP and the U.S. stock market. There is a positive relationship between real GDP and the stock market; the stock market tends to lead the real GDP.

20.3 VALUING THE OVERALL STOCK MARKET

Once analysts have established an overall view of the future direction of the economy, they can assess how the overall stock market compares with this view. For example, if an analyst believes that an economy is headed for an extended expansionary period and overall valuation measures of the stock market indicate that the market valuation is low, then the analyst will have a bullish view of stocks in general. This section reviews three measures of the overall stock market's value: book value, dividends, and earnings.

20.3.1 Book Value

The ratio of a stock's price to its book value is sometimes used to predict up and down trends in the stock market. Book value is the accounting measure of the net worth of a firm. Indexes are constructed for book value in the same manner as for market value of stock. For example, a value-weighted index would sum up the book

EXHIBIT 20-7
Real GDP and the Stock
Market as Measured by the
Morgan Stanley Capital
International U.S. Stock
Index

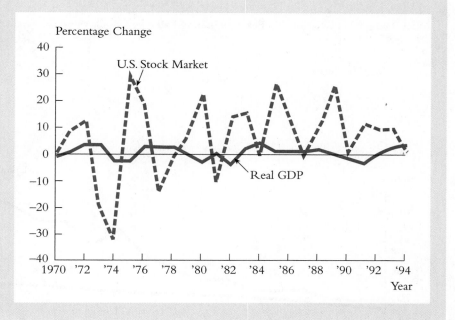

values of each firm rather than multiplying the number of shares times the stock price (see Chapter 5). Exhibit 20-8 illustrates the book value and the market value of the S&P 400 over the past forty years.[4] In the recent past, the difference between the market value and book value narrowed during recessions and widened during growth periods.

In general, when the market value is sufficiently larger than the book value, the stock market is considered to be overpriced and is predicted to fall. When the market value is sufficiently smaller than the book value, the stock market is considered to be underpriced and is predicted to rise. Fama and French found the relationship between price-to-book ratio and subsequent average returns to be very strong.[5] Hence, there is empirical support for monitoring book value in relation to market value to tell us when we might expect the overall market to rise or fall.

Using the long-term relationship between book value and market value alone, we would conclude that in the early 1990s, the U.S. stock market was overpriced. One counterargument to this conclusion is that accounting conventions, which in the United States do not adjust assets to inflation, severely understated the value of the assets on the books in the early 1990s.

---

4. The S&P 400, an index of four hundred industrial stocks, is one of the most widely used indexes for assessing the stock market as a whole. The S&P 500 includes the S&P 400, forty financial stocks, forty utility stocks, and twenty transportation stocks.
5. See Eugene F. Fama and Kenneth R. French, "The Cross-Section of Expected Stock Returns," *Journal of Finance* 47 (June 1992): 427–465.

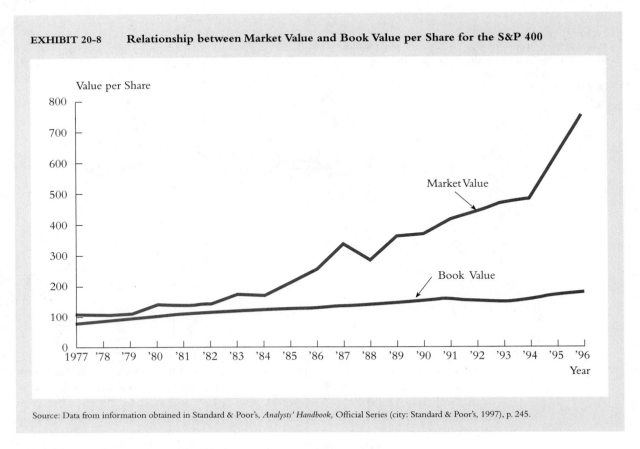

EXHIBIT 20-8   Relationship between Market Value and Book Value per Share for the S&P 400

Source: Data from information obtained in Standard & Poor's, *Analysts' Handbook,* Official Series (city: Standard & Poor's, 1997), p. 245.

20.3.2 Dividends

Dividends are a second tool used in appraising the overall stock market. Dividing the stock market index per share by the dollar dividend paid per share on an index such as the S&P 500 indicates how many years an investor has to wait until the investment is recovered by the paid dividends. The dividend divided by the price is called the dividend yield. For example, in August 1998 the dividend yield was 1.4%. Normally, this value is compared with the interest rate to see which investment has higher cash flows. When the ratio of the price divided by the dividend is high, it generally indicates that the stock market is overpriced, and shifting to bonds is recommended. Exhibit 20-9 illustrates an overpriced stock market in the 1990s. Specifically, the graph plots the dividend yield as well as the price/earnings (P/E) ratio, which is discussed in the next section. As the stock market of the 1990s rose (and dividends remained virtually constant), the dividend yield decreased. However, not everyone interpreted this as bad news for the stock market, as Connecting Theory to Practice 20.1 illustrates.

**EXHIBIT 20-9
The S&P 500 P/E
Ratio, as a Measure
of the Overall
Market**

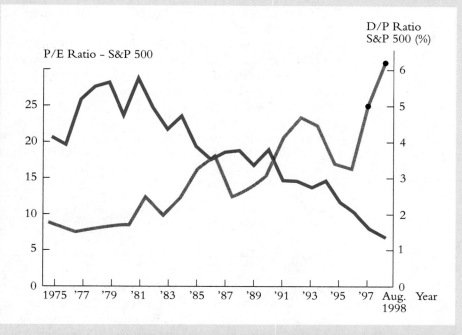

CONNECTING THEORY TO PRACTICE 20.1

LOW DIVIDEND YIELD MAY NO LONGER BE THE RED FLAG FOR STOCKS IT ONCE WAS

NEW YORK—Is the low dividend yield on stocks the red flag it once used to be?

After decades of stock market analysis, many strategists have concluded that when the Standard & Poor's 500-stock Index is yielding less than 3%, stock prices are dangerously high. Eventually, they argue, the yield rises, either because companies boost their dividends or, more ominously, stock prices fall back to more reasonable levels.

The dividend yield has been flashing a bright red danger signal since last October [1992]. And last week's powerful stock market rally pushed the dividend yield even further into the danger zone. With the S&P 500 at 448.93, the dividend yield now stands at 2.79.

"Whenever the dividend yield has gotten below 2.85%, we've had 'accidents,'" says David Shulman, chief market strategist at Salomon Brothers.

(continued)

But there's a growing tendency among analysts to dismiss the dividend yield as a valuation tool.

"When investors are looking forward to earnings growth, dividend growth is not so important," says Abby Cohen, stock market strategist at Goldman Sachs.

She notes that the yields on bonds and other competing investments are at the lowest level in years. That makes stocks, even with their low yield, very attractive, she says. "You can't look at dividend yields in a vacuum," she says. "The dividend yield at 3% when the Treasury bill rate is at 2.97% is different than when the dividend yield is 3% and the T-bill rate is 12%."

"I don't think the dividend yield is necessarily a sign that we are at the end of the bull market," says Peter L. Bernstein, who heads a financial consulting firm that bears his name.

Source: Anita Raghavan, "Low Dividend Yield May No Longer Be the Red Flag for Stocks It Once Was," *Wall Street Journal*, February 8, 1993, p. C1. Reprinted by permission of *The Wall Street Journal*, © 1993 Dow Jones & Co., Inc. All Rights Reserved Worldwide.

MAKING THE CONNECTION

When the overall stock market rallies to extreme highs or falls to extreme lows, analysts begin to question the validity of their measurement tools. With the dividend yield at 2.79%, why hasn't the overall stock market begun to decline? At these crucial points in time, analysts have one of two choices. Either they stick with their measurement tools and sell stocks, or they reassess the validity of the measurement tools themselves. David Shulman at Salomon Brothers remains faithful to the tool and is concerned about the market's falling, whereas Abby Cohen at Goldman Sachs tosses out the tool and believes the market will rise further.

This article was published in 1993. Who was right? By December 1997, the S&P 500 had risen to 963, and the dividend yield continued to decline to 1.6. Thus, at least in this specific case, the warning signal of low dividend yield in February 1993 was wrong, and Cohen and Peter Bernstein were correct.

20.3.3 Earnings

Some experts claim that the P/E ratio is a good indicator of whether the stock market is overpriced or underpriced. Recall that a high P/E ratio means a low E/P ratio, or a low profit on investment. Exhibit 20-9 gives the P/E ratio in the period 1975–1996 for the S&P 500. The P/E ratio climbed from 10 in 1975 to about 23 in 1992 and then fell to a level of about 20 in 1996. In June 1997 the P/E was 24.35, and it continued to rise in 1998 to a level of 31.73 on June 24, 1998. Hence, either earnings must rise or prices must fall.

Connecting Theory to Practice 20.2 illustrates how the P/E ratio of the Dow was interpreted in 1998.

CONNECTING THEORY TO PRACTICE 20.2

ARE STOCKS OVERVALUED? NOT A CHANCE

The Dow Jones Industrial Average has returned more than 200% over the past five years, and the past three have set an all-time record. So it's hardly surprising that many observers worry the stock market is overvalued. One of the most popular measures of valuation, the ratio of a stock's price to its earnings per share (P/E)—is close to an all-time high. The P/E of the average stock on the Dow is 22.5, meaning that it costs $22.50 to buy $1 in profits or conversely, that an investor's return (earnings divided by price) is just 4.4%, vs. 5.9% for long-term Treasury bonds.

Yet Warren Buffet, chairman of Berkshire Hathaway Corp. and the most successful large-scale investor of our time, told shareholders in a March 14 letter that "there is no reason to think of stocks as generally overvalued" as long as interest rates remain low and businesses continue to operate as profitably as they have in recent years.

Source: James K. Glassman and Kevin A. Hassett, "Are Stocks Overvalued? Not a Chance," *Wall Street Journal*, March 30, 1998, p. A18 Reprinted by permission of *The Wall Street Journal*, © 1998 Dow Jones & Co., Inc. All Rights Reserved Worldwide.

MAKING THE CONNECTION

The point made in this article, although subtle, demonstrates the essence of the risk and return associated with common stocks. Investing in either stocks or bonds results in cash flows to an investor. However, with bonds, the cash flows are fairly simple to determine. With stocks, the cash flows are dividends, and they should increase with profits. As profits grow over time, then cash flows to an investor will increase over time. The price of the stock will rise as well. The last paragraph of the article points out that as long as businesses continue to increase profits, then stocks are not overvalued at their current levels.

20.4 INDUSTRY ANALYSIS

There are periods when stocks of some industries flourish or drop significantly more than the whole market. The task of industry analysis is to forecast the activities of these specific industries. Recall from Chapter 15, on performance attribution, that the overall market can be classified into sectors and then industries. A sector is a classification that is broader than an industry. Exhibit 20-10 lists the sectors and industry classifications as reported in the *Wall Street Journal*.

EXHIBIT 20-10   Dow Jones Industry Groups

Basic Materials

Aluminum

Other non-ferrous

Chemicals

Chem-commodity

Chem-specialty

Forest products

Mining, diversified

Paper products

Precious metals

Steel

Independent

Conglomerates

Overseas Trading

Plantations

Consumer, Cyclical

Advertising

Airlines

Apparel

Clothing/Fabrics

Footwear

Auto manufacturers

Auto parts & equip

Casinos

Home construction

Home furnishings

Consumer electronics

Other furnishings

Lodging

Media

Broadcasting

Publishing

Recreation products

Entertainment

Other rec products

Toys

Restaurants

Retailers, apparel

Retailers, broadline

Retailers, drug-based

Retailers, specialty

Consumer, Non-Cycl

Beverages

Consumer services

Cosmetics

Food

Fishing

Other food

Food retailers

Health care

Household products

Durable

Non-durable

Medical supplies

Pharmaceuticals

Tobacco

Energy

Coal

Oil drilling

Oil cos, major

Oil cos, secondary

Oilfield equip/svcs

Pipelines

Financial

Banks, all

Major int'l

Regional banks

U.S. east

U.S. central

U.S. south

U.S. west

Diversified financial

Insurance, all

Full line

Life

Property/Casualty

Real estate

Savings & loan

Securities brokers

Industrial

Air freight

Building materials

Containers & pkging

Elec comps & equip

Factory equipment

Heavy construction

Heavy machinery

Industrial, diversified

Marine transport

Pollution control

Other industrial svcs

Railroads

Transportation equip

Trucking

Technology

Aerospace/Defense

Commu-w/AT&T

Commu-wo/AT&T

Computers w/IBM

Computers wo/IBM

Diversified technology

Industrial technology

Medical/Bio tech

Advcd med devices

Biotechnology

Office equipment

Semiconductors

Software

Utilities

Electric

Gas

Telephone

Water

The goal of sector and industry analysis is to determine the relative attractiveness of the different sectors and industries. Specifically, an analyst wants to determine the risk-return trade-offs and important factors that will affect future performance. Once these factors have been identified, the analyst will seek to forecast future trends in each sector or industry. This exercise will shed light on future prospects.

Sector and industry analysis is an important element in successful investing. Although the overall market may be going up, a particular industry may decline. Thus even though you are bullish on the overall stock market, you must carefully assess the strengths and weaknesses of each industry. Connecting Theory to Practice 20.3 illustrates what happens when investors ignore industry analysis.

20.4.1 The Industrial Life Cycle

Many analysts believe that industries go through **life cycles.** A life cycle is a discernible pattern for an industry in which it is first born, then goes through an expansion phase of rapid growth, and finally reaches a period of maturation. Each industry is unique in how it progresses through each phase. Some industries, such as the biotechnology industry, develop rapidly; others, such as the natural gas industry, develop slowly. It is important for analysts to understand where in the industrial life cycle a particular industry is located, as future prospects depend on the remaining life of the industry.

External forces greatly influence a particular industry's progression through its life cycle. Political and regulatory changes influence the growth or decline of a given industry. For example, environmental legislation has spurred the growth of industries engaged in reducing pollution and cleaning toxic waste sites. Social and demographic forces also play an important role. For example, as the U.S. population grows older with the aging of the baby boomers, the pharmaceutical industry probably will experience stronger sales.

20.4.2 Demand and Supply Analysis

When analyzing a particular industry, it is helpful to break down the analysis based on factors that influence demand for the industry's products, as well as factors that influence the supply of the industry's raw materials. Analysts focus on real and nominal growth rates of the factors, as well as overall trends and cyclical variation.

On the demand side, analysts try to identify who the end users of products are and how they may change their behavior in the future. Analysts are ever watchful for technological innovations that may have dramatic influences on demand for an industry's products. For example, a recent technological innovation is the ability to send interactive television signals via telephone wires. If this technology develops, the cable television industry will suddenly have as a competitor the telephone industry, which already has a direct connection to most homes.

On the supply side, analysts try to identify the degree of concentration within an industry. The **concentration ratio** is a measure of how much of the industry is dominated by the largest firms. How do these firms compete? Is the competition

CONNECTING THEORY TO PRACTICE 20.3

BIOTECHS ON THE BLINK

Bea Amaral wanted to make a lot of money fast. So in January, the 54-year-old mother of one from Raynham, Mass., dipped into her savings, pulled out $60,000 and spent it all on shares of Cytogen, a little-known but highflying biotechnology company developing a drug to help detect cancer.

She giddily paid $30 each for 2,000 shares—even though the stock had risen 164% in 13 months. The day she bought, a Food and Drug Administration panel recommended Cytogen's drug, OncoScint, for full approval. "I thought it would go up, up, up," Amaral says of the stock. But it went down, down, down instead. Wednesday, the stock closed at $15½, handing Amaral a paper loss of about $29,000 or nearly 50%, in four months.

Behind this years' sell-off [of biotechs]:

1. Bad news. Biotechnology stocks have always been newsdriven. Lately, bad news has dominated.
2. A new focus. Investors stayed with biotech, medical, drug, food and other recession-resistant stocks through the economic downturn. But since January, cyclical stocks—those that tend to rebound fastest as the economy recovers—have been the rage. To buy auto and manufacturing stocks, many investors sold the previous favorites. "Investors want to be at the right place at the right time," says Joyce Lonergan, analyst at Cowen & Co.
3. Speculative bust. Let's face it: A lot of people bought biotech stocks just because the group was hot—often not bothering to read a prospectus or find out if a company had competition.

Source: "Biotechs on the Blink," by James Kim, *USA Today,* April 23, 1992, p. B1. Copyright 1992, *USA Today.* Reprinted with permission.

MAKING THE CONNECTION

Amaral's first mistake was to ignore the benefits of diversification. Second, she failed to analyze the biotechnology industry. She purchased a biotechnology stock very near the peak of the stocks in that industry (see the exhibit on page 755).

A little analysis would have revealed that the biotechnology industry was trading at all-time highs and that the fundamentals such as earnings were not there to justify it. Therefore, it is important to carefully analyze industries before making investment decisions.

As the graph and table show, from January to May 1992, the stocks of biotechs fell by an average of 47%; as shown in the table, many of these stocks fell by much more than that. In this period, there was no crash in the overall market; on the contrary, the Dow Jones Industrial Average rose by 2.5%. This article indicates that sometimes the economic (and psychological) conditions

(continued)

are in favor of some industries and against other industries. An investor should analyze each industry separately, because industries, just like economies, experience cyclical behavior.

BIOTECHS ON THE BLINK
A key indicator of biotech stocks nearly tripled as investors enthused over the many wonder drugs in development. But a dizzying fall began in January as key drugs failed to win approval.

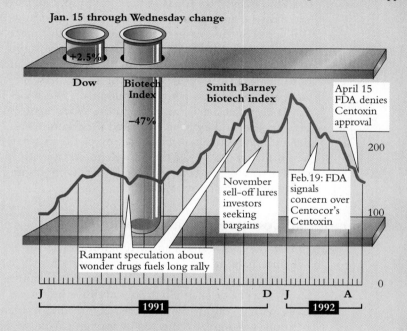

HOW BIOTECH STOCKS HAVE FALLEN

Stock	Stock Peak (price, date)	Wed. Close	Chng.
Centocor	$60¼, 1/8	$13⅜	−78%
US Bioscience	$42½, 1/7	$10¼	−76%
MGI Pharma	$24⅝, 1/14	$7	−72%
Immune Response	$62¾, 11/12	$21	−67%
Immunex	$65½, 2/4	$26¼	−60%
Icos	$19¾, 8/14	$7⅞	−60%
Repligen	$29, 10/22	$12	−59%
Xoma	$31, 4/17/91	$13¼	−57%
Immunogen	$24, 1/17	$10½	−56%
Chiron	$77½, 10/31	$38½	−50%
Medimmune	$53½, 11/12	$26½	−50%

Source: James Kim, "Biotechs on the Blink," *USA Today*, April 23, 1992, p. B1. Copyright 1992, *USA Today*. Reprinted with permission.

based on price, quality, or warranties? For example, software firms and airline firms are both notorious for their price-cutting wars. Clearly, when a group of firms is willing to cut its prices enormously to gain market share, this could have an adverse impact on share prices.

20.4.3 Industry Profitability

Industry analysts try to assess the future profitability of an industry. They use supply and demand analysis in an effort to understand how these different factors interact. Will any cost factors get out of control? Will price wars erupt that will seriously dampen profitability? What technological innovations are on the horizon that may redefine the entire industry? Will future governmental regulations dramatically alter how a particular industry functions? These are some of the important questions that analysts must address when examining an industry.

Analysts seek to forecast the future short-term and long-term profitability for an industry. Once they have estimated the future earnings potential, they can translate that estimate into an overall valuation of the industry. For example, analysts who believed that the outlook for the telephone systems industry was particularly bright relative to where stocks in this industry were trading would want to increase their holdings of telephone stocks.

20.4.4 International Competition and Markets

Industry analysis cannot afford to ignore international competition. As trade barriers fall, international trade will increase, which may have a dramatic impact on any given industry. Is there another country with a comparative advantage for a particular industry? For example, labor-intensive industries will be greatly affected by free trade with a country with a relatively inexpensive labor supply. International competition is also greatly affected by foreign exchange rates. In 1995 the dollar reached its lowest exchange rate in comparison with the Japanese yen and the German mark. (See the second article in this chapter's Investments in the News.) In August 1998, just the opposite occurred, when the dollar reached 147 yen. As Chapter 11 explained, foreign exchange movements can result in foreign firms' being able to sell their goods at lower dollar prices. Thus, people considering international investment should take into account the possibility of changes in foreign exchange rates.

SUMMARY

Identify and describe the macroeconomic variables that measure economic health.   The key measure of economic health is the gross domestic product (GDP). The GDP is composed of consumption, investment, government spending, and net trade. Real GDP (GDP adjusted to include the effects of inflation) is used, because inflation changes the value of dollars. Analysts attempting to establish relationships between macroeconomic variables such as GDP and financial markets must incorporate a complex revision process into their analysis. Relationships that may appear based on final estimates of GDP may not appear based on advanced estimates of GDP.

Describe the impact of government fiscal and monetary policy on investment decisions.   Fiscal and monetary policy are key tools governments use to achieve GDP growth, relatively full employment, and stable prices. Fiscal policy includes taxation and spending policies, whereas monetary policy includes actions taken by a central bank, such as controlling the money supply and manipulating interest rates. The effectiveness of a government is a key factor to consider when analyzing a country's financial market. Governments use both fiscal and monetary policies to stimulate economic growth, which directly affects financial markets.

Describe the measures used to value the stock market as a whole.   The three key measures of an overall stock market are book value, dividends, and earnings. It is useful to compare the P/E ratio, dividend yield, and the book value over time to establish reasonable historical ranges. With these ranges established, investors can assess the relative value of the overall stock market.

Evaluate market sectors and specific industries.   A careful assessment of market sectors and specific industries helps investors allocate their portfolios effectively. A significant portion of a stock's volatility can be attributed to its industry. Thus, analysts seek to determine the future prospects within sectors and industries.

CHAPTER AT A GLANCE

1. *The GDP is the primary measure of economic health. The GDP is composed of the following:*
   a. Consumption.
   b. Investment.
   c. Government spending.
   d. Net trade.

2. *Government policies influence economies in various ways:*
   a. Fiscal policy, taxation, and spending policies can be used to stimulate the economy in recessions.
   b. Monetary policy and actions by a central bank, such as the Federal Reserve Bank in the United States, can be used to stimulate or cool down economies.

3. *The economy and financial markets are usually related in the following ways:*
   a. When GDP is up, accompanied by inflationary pressure on interest rates, the bond market is down.
   b. When GDP is up, the stock market is up.

4. *The stock market's current value can be assessed by comparing it with the following:*
   a. The book value.
   b. The dividend yield.
   c. The P/E ratio.

KEY TERMS

Advanced estimate 737	Budget deficit 743	Coincident indicator 741
Bank discount rate 744	Business cycle 740	Concentration ratio 753
Bank reserves 743	Civilian unemployment	Contraction 740
Benchmark revision 737	rate 743	Expansion 740

Federal funds rate 744	Leading indicator 741	Preliminary estimate 737
Fiscal policy 741	Life cycle 753	Real GDP 736
Gross domestic product	Monetary policy 743	Recession 743
(GDP) 736	Open market operations 743	Revised estimate 737
Lagging indicator 741	Peak 740	Trough 740

REVIEW

20.1 Recently, Germany dramatically increased its interest rate. How should this increase affect the U.S. stock market? How should it affect the U.S. bond market?

20.2 Suppose the consumption in the United States increased by $10 billion, and this increase was in imported goods. How would this influence the GDP?

20.3 Suppose the Federal Reserve Board reduced the interest rate, and at the same time the price of bonds went down. Is this result what was predicted by macroeconomic analysis? If not, how can you explain this result?

20.4 Suppose another oil crisis is predicted in the near future. How will this crisis affect car industry stocks? How will it affect food industry stocks? Explain your answer.

20.5 Some analysts claim that portfolio holdings of auto stocks, such as GM and Ford, as well as holdings of oil stocks, such as Exxon and Mobil, would be a good hedge against an oil crisis. Does this make any sense?

20.6 The price-to-book ratio is 40 in Japan and 25 in the United States. Do these ratios mean that there is a higher probability of a stock market crash in Japan? Explain your answer.

20.7 In some countries the book value of assets is adjusted every year to inflation. In the United States such an adjustment is not done. In your view, how would this adjustment affect the price-to-book ratio?

PRACTICE

20.1 A financial analyst who analyzed CBM Corporation concludes that its earnings are expected to grow at 10% every year for the next 10 years. The analyst highly recommends buying this stock. After a week, the Federal Reserve increases the interest rate from 4% to $4\frac{1}{2}$%. The S&P 500 index drops by 8%. CBM drops by 4%. Explain these outcomes.

20.2 Suppose that for each $\frac{1}{4}$% increase in the interest rate, the stock market falls by 5%. Today the Dow Jones Industrial Average is at 3,000 points, and the interest rate is at 4%. What would be the predicted value of the Dow if interest rates went up to 6%? What if interest rates fell to 2%?

20.3 You use the constant dividend discount model, $P_0 = d_1/(k - g)$. For two firms, Sirop Oil Corporation and Food Limited, you find that $d_1 = 1, $k = 12$%, and $g = 7$%. Thus, $P_0 = $1/(0.12 - 0.07) = 20. Because of a recent war, investors become more uncertain about oil prices; hence, the oil industry becomes more risky. However, the war has no effect on the food industry. Assuming that the risk-free interest rate is 5% and the risk premium doubled for the oil industry, how would this uncertainty affect the price of Sirop Oil Corporation's stock? What will happen to the price of Food Limited's stock?

20.4 Suppose you have the following series for the market-to-book value and rates of return on the S&P 400 index:

Year	Rate of Return	Ratio of Market to Book Value
1		1.3
2	−10%	2.0
3	−30	1.0
4	+5	0.8
5	+20	0.8

What can you learn from this series?

20.5 Suppose you have the following series of price-to-dividend ratios and rates of return on the S&P 400 index:

Year	Rate of Return	Ratio of Price to Dividends
1		20
2	+10%	30
3	−15	40
4	−20	10

Analyze these numbers. What can be learned about the relationship between the series in Questions 20.4 and 20.5?

20.6 Suppose the interest rate is 4% in both Japan and the United States. Now suppose Japan decreases its interest rate to 3%, but no change is made in the U.S. interest rate. How is this change expected to affect the following?
a. The Japanese stock market.
b. The Japanese bond market.
c. The U.S. stock market.
d. The U.S. bond market.

20.7 Suppose the ratio of the market price to dividends is 34. Suppose that in real terms, future dividends will not increase and will remain at the same level. The short-term interest rate is 3.6%. Is this possible? If not, what should happen in the future as advocated by the "bulls," and what should happen in the future as advocated by the "bears"?

20.8 Suppose we estimate the real GDP for next year at $5,241 billion. We also estimate consumption to be $C = \$3,765$ billion, investment to be $I = \$822$ billion, government spending to be $G = \$1,347$ billion, and net trade (exports − imports) to be −$24 billion. Based on these estimates, what would we forecast for the implicit deflator?

20.9 Recall from Chapter 9 that according to the CAPM,

$$E(R_i) = r + [E(R_m) - r]\beta_i$$

For the utilities industry, beta is 0.6. For the electronics industry, beta is 2.0. For the S&P 500 stock index, beta is 1.0. Suppose the Federal Reserve increased the interest rate from 4% to 5%. Assume that the expected return on the market portfolio is fixed at 12% and that the industry betas are unchanged.
a. Find the expected return for the utilities industry, the electronics industry, and the S&P 500 before the change in interest rates.
b. How will the change in interest rates affect each of the three groups?
c. Suppose that as a result of the increase in the interest rate, investors shift from the stock market to the bond market, and stock prices fall. The lower stock prices result in a 16% increase in the expected return of the market portfolio. How will this affect the expected return of each of the three groups?
d. Assume that the future earnings of the firms do not change. Suppose that the price of each group was $100 before the interest rate change. Calculate by how much the price of each group will change in Part c.

20.10 Suppose you employ the constant dividend growth model to a firm and find that $d_1 = \$10$, $g = 5\%$, and $k = 10\%$. Thus, the market price is $\$10/(0.1 - 0.05) = \$200$. Your research department concludes that the firm will discover a new drug, and g will be 7% rather than 5%.
a. What is the value of the stock? Would you buy it?
b. Suppose the Federal Reserve suddenly increases the interest rate, and this affects the discount rate (k). For all firms in the economy, k increases by 4%.

For this particular firm, k rises from 10% to 14%. How will this change in Federal Reserve policy affect your decision to buy or not buy the stock?

20.11 A 1-year bond is trading for $1,000, and the coupon is $50 paid annually. The face value is $1,000, and the maturity is 1 year. A stagflation (inflation along with a recession) erupts. The inflation was zero before and is now predicted to be 3%. The risk of bankruptcy increases from 0% to 10% on a yield-to-maturity basis. By how much will the bond price fall if investors demand the same average real rate of return as they had before? Do the calculations separately for inflation and recession, as well as for both.

20.12 Suppose you have the following two alternatives (A and B):

	Change in GDP		Rates of Return	
Year	A	B	A	B
1	5%			20%
2	0	5%	20%	−10
3	1	0	−10	5
4		1	5	

a. Analyze the two sets of figures.
b. What set, A or B, is typical in the market? What set would investors like to have?

20.13 Suppose the government taxes consumers by taking 4 cents from each dollar of gas sold. The total taxes raised is $10 billion, and consumers reduce their spending by $5 billion. The government spends all of this $10 billion on developing a space station. What is the net change in GDP?

20.14 A low-dividend yield is predicted by practitioners as a sign of a bear market. Analyze the following figures:

Year	Dividend Yield	Interest Rate
1	6%	12%
2	5	8
3	4	6
4	2.9	2.5

Do analysts necessarily expect a crash in the stock market in Year 4? Explain your answer.

20.15 Suppose a firm has total assets of $100 million and liabilities of $20 million. There are 40 million shares outstanding. The price-to-book ratio is 2.0. What is the current stock price?

20.16 How will your results in Question 20.15 be affected by a 2-for-1 split if the split results in a price-to-book ratio of 2.2?

20.17 Suppose that when the dividend yield is 5% and the price-to-book ratio is 1, the probability of a stock market crash is zero. However, for each 1% drop in the dividend yield and each 0.5 increase in the price-to-book ratio, the probability of a crash increases by 5%.
a. What is the probability of a crash when the dividend yield is 3%?
b. What is the probability of a crash when the price-to-book ratio is 2.5?
c. What is the probability of a crash when the dividend yield is 3% and the price-to-book ratio is 2.5? (Assume that one factor does not affect the additional probability of the other factor.)

20.18 The following exhibit shows the relationship between the 10-year bond yield and the S&P 500 index up to 1996.

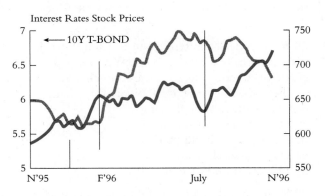

Source: Web site at http://www.lcef.org/welkfolder

a. In your view, are these two series positively or negatively correlated? Explain.
b. Suppose that you have *no* stock selectivity ability. However, you expect the Federal Reserve to decrease the interest rate, and hence the 10-year bond yield to drop to 5.50%. What action will you take?

CFA PROBLEMS

20.1 Adam's research report continued as follows:

"With a business recovery already under way, the expected profit surge should lead to a much higher price for Universal Auto stock. We strongly recommend purchase."

a. Discuss the business cycle approach to investment timing. (Your answer should describe actions to be taken on both stocks and bonds at different points over a typical business cycle.)

b. Assuming that Adam's assertion is correct—that a business recovery is already under way—evaluate the timeliness of his recommendation to purchase Universal Auto, a cyclical stock, based on the business cycle approach to investment timing.

For Internet questions visit the Levy Investment Web site at http://levy-invst.swcollege.com.

YOUR TURN: APPLYING THEORY TO PRACTICE

THE BIG PICTURE—WHAT MACROECONOMIC AND POLITICAL FACTORS SHOULD BE CONSIDERED IN SELECTING THE TYPE OF INVESTMENT?

The Seventies was the decade of the tangible assets, the Eighties and early Nineties of financial assets. What are the prospects for the balance of the Nineties?

THE BIG PICTURE

One of the crucial decisions an investor must make is how to allocate his assets. Most people choose from a narrow range of possibilities, dividing their money among such financial instruments as stocks, bonds and cash, or real estate. Now and then an individual may also decide to sink money into more esoteric—and less liquid—investments such as a barrel of oil or a rare work of art.

Since these different types of investment do not move in unison, it matters a great deal how you allocate your money among them. The short- and long-term performance of one particular group of assets I have tracked for many years is summarized in the table below. If you did not load up on this winter's winners, take heart—in the long run, the value of all these assets has increased—at least in nominal terms.

The long-term performance data are expressed in compound annual growth rates. To understand the power of reinvesting, note that the 12.2% compound growth in stocks means that $1 invested in stocks in 1973 would be worth $10 today. The arithmetic of compound interest also means that what appear to be small differences in growth rates actually translate into large disparities in the terminal value of an investment. Thus, the 2.4-percentage-point difference between the 20-year growth rate of stocks and bonds means that $1 invested in bonds would be worth roughly one-third less than the same investment in stocks.

Broadly speaking, every period confronts an investor with the necessity of choosing between financial and tangible assets. An investor who correctly positions a portfolio from one period to the next stands to reap considerably greater returns than an investor who does not adjust his mix of investments.

What are the key factors that drive the performance of these two broad classes of assets? Roughly speaking, they can be summarized as follows:

(continued)

Factors favoring financial assets:
1. Declining inflationary expectations
2. Peace and democracy
3. Declining tax rates
4. Deregulation and a shrinking public sector
5. Increased confidence

Factors favoring tangible assets:
1. Rising inflationary expectations
2. Political instability
3. Rising tax rates
4. Increased regulation and a growing public sector
5. Rising anxiety

Although these factors are qualitative, some general discussion of these factors in the 1993 environment is still possible.

From the above list, one can conclude that financial assets are not a good hedge in an inflationary period while tangible assets are.

Inflation is the most critical factor on this list. The direction and stability of prices affect the future value of money, and the future value of money is what investing is all about. The Consumer Price Index is included in the table of returns to help owners of these assets decide whether they are winning or losing in terms of purchasing power.

Source: R. S. Salomon Jr., "The Big Picture," *Forbes,* July 5, 1993, p. 139. Reprinted by Permission of *Forbes* magazine, © Forbes Inc. 1993.

Investment Clues from the Past

Asset	20–Year Return[a]	Rank	10–Year Return	Rank	5–Year Return	Rank	1–Year Return	Rank
Stocks	12.2%	1	14.8%	1	15.1%	1	11.6%	2
Bonds	9.8	2	13.2	2	13.1	2	14.8	1
Stamps	9.6	3	(1.7)	11	0.5	11	8.8	4
3-month Treasury bills	8.8	4	7.3	4	6.6	4	3.3	8
Diamonds	8.5	5	5.9	5	4.3	5	1.5	11
Oil	7.5	6	(4.7)	12	1.7	9	(6.3)	12
Gold	6.9	7	(1.0)	9	(4.2)	12	9.6	3
Housing	6.7	8	4.4	7	3.7	7	1.8	10
Consumer Price Index	6.1	9	3.8	8	4.2	6	3.3	7
Chinese ceramics	5.8	10	7.6	3	9.8	3	(7.5)	13
U.S. farmland	5.4	11	(1.2)	10	2.1	8	2.3	9
Foreign exchange	3.4	12	5.6	6	1.7	10	6.2	6
Silver	2.7	13	(10.1)	13	(8.5)	13	8.4	5

a. Corresponds to years 1973 to 1993.

Source: Salomon Brothers Inc.; Diamonds, The Diamond Registry; Basket of U.S. stamps, Scott Inc.; Chinese ceramics, Sotheby's; Oil, American Petroleum Institute; Housing, National Association of Realtors; U.S. farmland (excluding income), U.S. government statistics. Note: Old Masters were excluded because current data were unavailable. "Investment Clues from the Past," *Forbes,* July 5, 1993. Reprinted by Permission of *Forbes* magazine, © Forbes, Inc., 1993.

(continued)

Questions

Use the data in the table to answer the following questions:

1. Suppose that in 1973 you invest $1,000 in each of the assets appearing in the table. What is the terminal value of each asset in 1993? What is the terminal value of your total investment? What is the terminal value in real terms? Why may a small difference in reported returns amount to a large difference in terminal wealth?

2. a. Discuss each of the five factors favoring financial assets and each of the five factors favoring tangible assets.

b. Suppose that we expect a drop in the inflation rate. Would you invest in bonds or stocks? Why? If you chose bonds, would you buy long-term or short-term bonds?

3. When the article was written (in 1993), we could have observed the following:

a. Inflation rates were very low and were expected to remain so—oil prices were especially low. Telephone and airline companies slashed prices as a result of increased competition.

b. The Cold War era had ended. Although there were regions experiencing political unrest, the probability of a superpower confrontation had declined.

c. President Bill Clinton had raised taxes and would do so again.

d. The government's role in the economy under President Clinton's administration was expected to shrink.

(1) Given these predictions, would you concentrate your investments in financial or tangible assets? If you would choose financial assets, would you invest in airline and oil stocks or auto manufacturing firms?

(2) Explain the relationship between the industries selected and the reason given for the decline in inflation expected in the future.

SELECTED REFERENCES

Abel, Andrew B., and Ben S. Bernanke. *Macroeconomics.* Reading, Mass.: Addison-Wesley Publishing, 1992.

This is a good introductory textbook on macroeconomics.

Baker, H. Kent. *Improving the Investment Decision Process—Better Use of Economic Inputs in Security Analysis and Portfolio Management.* Charlottesville, Va.: Association for Investment Management and Research, 1992.

This series of presentations ranges from global economic analysis to selecting fixed-income securities. The material provides interesting insights into making the connection between economic forecasts and portfolio management.

Carnes, W. Stansbury, and Stephen D. Slifer. *The Atlas of Economic Indicators.* New York: HarperCollins Publishers, 1991.

This is a good overview of economic indicators related to the GDP.

SUPPLEMENTAL REFERENCES

Balog, James (ed). *Industry Analysis—The Health Care Industry.* Charlottesville, Va.: Association for Investment Management and Research, 1993.

Black, Fischer. "The ABCs of Business Cycles." *Financial Analysts Journal,* November–December 1981, pp. 75–80.

Council of Economic Advisers. *Economic Report of the President.* Washington, D.C.: U.S. Government Printing Office, various issues.

Fama, Eugene F., and Kenneth R. French. "The Cross-Section of Expected Stock Returns." *Journal of Finance* 47 (June 1992): 427–465.

Ingene, Charles A. (ed.). *Industry Analysis—The Retail Industry.* Charlottesville, Va.: Association for Investment Management and Research, 1993.

King, Benjamin F. "Market and Industry Factors in Stock Price Behavior." *Journal of Business* 39 (January 1966): 139–190.

McFall, R. Lamm, Jr. "Asset Allocation Implication of Inflation Protected Securities." *Journal of Portfolio Management,* Summer 1998, 93–101.

Petrie, Thomas A. (ed.). *Industry Analysis—the Oil and Gas Industries.* Charlottesville, Va.: Association for Investment Management and Research, 1993.

Porter, Michael E. *Competitive Advantage: Creating and Sustaining Superior Performance.* New York: Free Press, 1985.

Treynor, Jack. "Bulls, Bears, and Market Bubbles." *Financial Analysts Journal,* March–April 1998, pp. 69–74.

U.S. Bureau of the Census. *Statistical Abstract of the United States.* Washington, D.C.: U.S. Government Printing Office, various issues.

CHAPTER 21

FINANCIAL STATEMENT ANALYSIS

"WE WERE GREAT!"—EXCEPT FOR . . .

The cover of ConAgra's 1997 Annual Report, just out for its fiscal year ended in May, shows a Healthy Choice "grilled glazed pork"—also a pretty apt description of one financial rendering inside the report. This hard-to-swallow stuff leads off the chairman's letter, signed by CEO Philip Fletcher and President Bruce Rhode, and says, "ConAgra's 17 consecutive years of earnings per share growth at a compound rate better than 14% is unequaled by any major food company in the United States, and probably in the world." Alongside is the inevitable chart, reproduced below, showing a steadily ascending staircase of earnings.

Hello! Slide to the small print under the chart. It says that the earnings record "excludes" an accounting change in 1993 (for retiree health benefits) and also "excludes" no fewer than three years of nonrecurring charges, in 1983, 1984, and 1996. Meaning that bottom-line earnings didn't climb steadily at all. The worst year was 1996, when the nonrecurring charges, most of them for a "restructuring" expected to lop off a number of plants and 6,300 employees, amounted to $508 million. That wallop reduced ConAgra's per share earnings from $2.06 in 1995 to $0.79 in 1996.

At least we know that ConAgra didn't lop off the part of the company, nor the employees, that grill and glaze those numbers.

LEARNING OBJECTIVES

After studying this chapter you should be able to:

1. Name the three financial statements commonly used in security analysis, and describe which accounting values require scrutiny by investors.

2. Explain how analysts interpret earnings per share.

3. Identify the most important ratios used in financial statement analysis, and discuss how they are used.

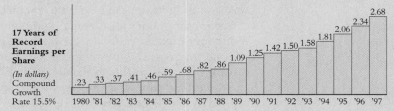

17 Years of Record Earnings per Share

(In dollars) Compound Growth Rate 15.5%

1980	'81	'82	'83	'84	'85	'86	'87	'88	'89	'90	'91	'92	'93	'94	'95	'96	'97
.23	.33	.37	.41	.46	.59	.68	.82	.86	1.09	1.25	1.42	1.50	1.58	1.81	2.06	2.34	2.68

Operating results as actually reported. Excludes accounting change in 1993, non-recurring charges in 1983, 1984 and 1996.

Source: Carol J. Loomis, "We Were Great!—Except for . . . ," *Fortune,* October 13, 1997, p. 28. Reprinted from the October 13, 1997, issue of *Fortune* by special permission. © 1997, Time, Inc.

YES, YOU CAN BEAT THE MARKET

Investors will appreciate most a study by Josef Lakonishok at the University of Illinois, Andrei Shleifer of Harvard and Robert Vishny of the University of Chicago. . . . Lakonishok's team classified stocks by four measures: the ratio of market value to book value, price to cash flow, price to earnings and growth rate for sales. . . .

The news from the halls of academia will likely drive successful value investors, who have always bought and sold according to these principles.

Source: Terence P. Pare, "Yes, You Can Beat the Market," *Fortune,* April 3, 1995, p. 52.

Financial statement analysis is widely used by security analysts. Financial statements include information such as earnings per share (EPS) and dividends per share (DPS), which are commonly employed to estimate the future growth rate of the firm—an essential ingredient for stock valuation (see Chapters 18 and 19). The first article in this chapter's Investments in the News points out that analysts should also carefully read "the small print under the chart." What seems to be a smooth, nice, stable growth may in fact not be so. Thus, although financial statements provide a good deal of essential information, these statements should be read carefully to check whether the figures are manipulated or not. The investor's objective in using financial statement analysis is to identify problems or opportunities with companies such as ConAgra *before* other investors see them.

This chapter describes the information that investors can obtain from financial statement analysis. Although this text has stressed that investors should use economic earnings or market values rather than accounting earnings in assessing the value of a stock, there are many benefits in studying the reported accounting data contained in a company's financial statements. Moreover, some crucial information appears only in a firm's financial statements. In some cases, the analyst can try to adjust the accounting figures, thereby avoiding the distortion of figures based on historical rather than market values.

The following are some uses of financial statement analysis:

1. Investors can compare accounting earnings for firms in an industry to locate firms with below- (or above-) average performance.
2. Investors can compare accounting earnings over time for a specific firm to detect future problems.
3. Accounting values can be used to predict future economic values.
4. Accounting values for earnings and dividends can be used as inputs to dividend discount models.
5. Bond investors can use financial statements to assess the risk that a firm will go bankrupt or be unable to make scheduled interest payments or repay principal.
6. Accounting values may predict future rates of return in the stock market, as implied by the second article in this chapter's Investments in the News.

This chapter first reviews the role and function of basic accounting statements. Next, it looks in detail at one of the most important accounting figures—the earnings per share. Specifically, it focuses on how to determine the quality of the reported earnings per share. The chapter concludes with a review of some important ratios used by securities analysts.

21.1   FINANCIAL STATEMENTS

Financial statements contain the basic accounting data that help investors understand a firm's financial history. Firms provide three major financial statements for investors:

1. *The income statement.* The **income statement** reports the firm's sales, cost of goods sold, other expenses, earnings, and so forth during a given accounting period, quarter, or year.
2. *The balance sheet.* Unlike the income statement, the **balance sheet** provides a "snapshot" of the firm's assets and liabilities at a given moment, for example, on December 31, 1998.
3. *The statement of cash flows.* The **statement of cash flows** is based on actual cash inflows and outflows rather than on accrual accounting. From this statement analysts can learn about the sources of a firm's cash flow and how these cash flows are used to pay for capital expenditures, dividends, interest expenses, and so forth.

21.1.1 Financial Accounting Concepts

Accountants follow specific rules when collecting, organizing, and reporting financial information about a company. The concepts and assumptions that form the framework for these rules are listed in Exhibit 21-1. Most of these concepts are probably already familiar to you.

In adhering to these concepts, managers may report values on financial statements for items or activities that overstate or understate their economic worth.

EXHIBIT 21-1   **Basic Accounting Concepts**

Concept	Explanation
Business entity	Entity is separate from owners.
Going concern	Statement reflects an ongoing firm (not liquidation).
Monetary	Events are measured only in monetary terms.
Accounting period	Flow of activity is divided into periods.
Consistency	Statement reports similar transactions in the same way.
Historical cost	Transactions are measured in price paid (not value today).
Realization	Revenues are realized when services or goods are exchanged, not when cash is exchanged.
Matching costs and revenues	Statement uses accrual accounting method that attempts to match costs and revenues to when they are incurred rather than when they are paid.
Dual aspect	Assets = Liabilities + Owners' Equity.
Reliability of evidence	Transactions are based on evidence.
Disclosure	Statement provides enough information so that informed readers will not be misled.
Conservatism	Accountant is skeptical and estimates value on the low side.
Materiality	Statement reports items that have "significant" economic value.
Substance over form	Accounting emphasizes economic substance of events, not legal form.

Source: Based in part on Leopold A. Bernstein, *Financial Statement Analysis: Theory, Application, and Interpretation,* 4th ed. (Homewood, Ill.: Irwin, 1989).

Managers assume that the business entity—an enterprise separate from its owners—is a going concern. Under the going concern assumption, managers value amounts that will be paid or received at their future expected values. For example, accounts receivable are reported as the amount expected to be eventually received. The reporting procedure for accounts receivable ignores the time value of money. In the balance sheet, accounts receivable due in three months are valued in the same way as accounts receivable due in six months.

Financial statements record only events that are measurable in monetary terms. However, not all events affecting a firm's value are monetary. For example, a scientific breakthrough by an employee can be converted into profit in the years ahead, but it is not included as an asset on the balance sheet.

Firms are required to report their financial data in a consistent fashion. For example, they cannot constantly change their method of valuing inventory. A firm adopts one method and sticks with it. However, if there are changes, they should be reported in the footnotes to the financial statements.

Most accounting statement items are valued using historical cost, not current market value. This method can result in dramatic differences between the recorded value of an asset on the balance sheet and its actual current market value. Thus, a security analyst must be very cautious when using accounting statements for the purpose of establishing market value. In most cases, valuing assets and liabilities at historical cost is an obvious source of problems for investors. Investors want to know the value of the assets and liabilities today, not what price was paid for them in the past. For example, an eastern Florida railroad company may not have much growth potential in moving cargo, but if it holds many acres of land on the east coast of Florida that were bought 40 years ago, then it may be a valuable company in terms of the market value of its assets.

When accountants apply the concept of conservatism to value assets and revenues, they may underestimate their actual worth. Similarly, they may overestimate liabilities and expenses. Firms apply conservatism in different degrees, which may make it difficult for investors to compare similar firms or the performance of the same firm in different years. This problem is described in Connecting Theory to Practice 21.1.

CONNECTING THEORY TO PRACTICE 21.1

AS IBM'S WOES GREW, ITS ACCOUNTING TACTICS GOT LESS CONSERVATIVE

To all outward appearances, International Business Machines Corp. ran into trouble with startling speed.

Even its harshest critics have been stunned by its nearly $5 billion of losses last year, its first layoffs in half a century and an unprecedented purge of top executives. Its stock has lost more than $70 billion in market value since it

(continued)

peaked in 1987. And the crisis has sparked a once-unthinkable move: IBM turned to an outsider, Louis V. Gerstner, to rescue it.

Now, considerable evidence suggests that IBM may have helped delay its day of reckoning with some surprisingly aggressive accounting moves. The moves didn't violate any laws or cause the company's fundamental business problems. Some, though not all, of the moves were fully disclosed to the public.

But some finance experts say that just as IBM's business started to sour, its accounting became markedly less conservative. "Since the mid-1980s, IBM has been borrowing from the future to bolster today's profits, says Thornton O'glove, a frequently critical San Francisco accounting expert and former publisher of the *Quality of Earnings* newsletter.

In an interview late last year, Daniel Gough, a former IBM accounting manager, said he and his colleagues were under pressure to make more liberal interpretations of IBM's sales policies. "It amazed me to see how aggressive IBM became to help bolster a revenue stream that was slowing down significantly," he said. Mr. Gough concedes that he left IBM last year unhappily. He said it was because he didn't approve of its accounting policies; an IBM spokesman declines to comment on why Mr. Gough left. But Mr. Gough's concern was echoed in the 1988 memo by Price Waterhouse's Mr. Chandler.

For example, Mr. Chandler wrote, IBM's computer shipments to dealers "are recorded as sales at time of shipment" even though the dealers have the right to return the computers. He worried that some revenue from such shipments would be "difficult to defend at very best." In some cases, he found, IBM was recording revenue when it shipped products merely to its own warehouses. "This seems clearly inappropriate," he wrote.

Footnotes in IBM's 1984 annual report show that it began overhauling its accounting tactics to spread the costs of factories and other investments far into the future, instead of recording them in the short term. IBM also reduced the estimated cost of its retirement plans, which then would take a smaller chunk out of each year's earnings. The accounting changes themselves were standard practice at many companies and hardly a secret; IBM's annual report disclosed them.

Mr. O'glove, the auditing expert, calculates that in 1984 the accounting changes were responsible for 26% of IBM's profit gain. That year profits surged by $1.73 a share, to $10.77; so that 26% amounts to 45 cents a share. In 1985, earnings fell 10 cents a share, but without the accounting changes, Mr. O'glove says, they would have dropped 86 cents a share.

Although IBM has never specified how much the accounting changes affected its earnings, it says Mr. O'glove's numbers are "way off." It also cites a 1985 accountants' survey showing that 70% of U.S. companies were spreading investment costs into the future, just as IBM did. And as for lowering its retirement-plan costs, IBM says its financial advisers predicted that the plan's

(continued)

invested assets would start earning a higher return—and thus the cost to the company would drop. "We strongly disagree that our actions were anything but appropriate," IBM says.

Source: Michael W. Miller and Lee Berton, "As IBM's Woes Grew, Its Accounting Tactics Got Less Conservative," *Wall Street Journal*, April 7, 1993, p. A1. Reprinted by permission of *The Wall Street Journal*, © 1993 Dow Jones & Co., Inc. All Rights Reserved Worldwide.

MAKING THE CONNECTION

Managers desire to show their firm's performance in the best possible light on financial statements, so they sometimes "stretch" accounting rules. To spot problems before share prices fall, as in the case of IBM, the astute investor must be aware of variations in the application of accounting concepts. The ability to identify subtle shifts in accounting policies may give investors the information they need to make wise investment choices. Financial statement analysis could provide investors the edge needed to be successful. Analyzing the financial statement and realizing the firm's true profit would be beneficial.

IBM's stock price fell sharply in the early 1990s, and only when a new CEO was hired did the EPS indeed go up, from −$14.02 in 1993 to +$10.24 in 1996. The EPS of IBM for 1998 was $6.50. Thus, smart investors would not avoid selling the stock on time despite IBM's delaying the drop in reported earnings. Thus, the analysis of accounting figures is very important.

The following sections will examine in detail the three financial statements: the balance sheet, the income statement, and the statement of cash flows. They use the financial statements of Pfizer, Inc., a leading drug company, to identify the information contained in financial statements and to show how investors can interpret these data. Pfizer discovers, develops, manufactures, and sells pharmaceuticals, medical devices, surgical equipment, and health care products. Probably the most well-known drug produced by Pfizer is Viagra, which was introduced to the market in 1998.

21.1.2 Balance Sheet

A balance sheet shows the assets, liabilities, and equity of a firm on a specific date. The balance sheet is based on the following:

$$\text{Assets} = \text{Liabilities} + \text{Owners' Equity}$$

The information contained in the balance sheet helps answer questions such as these: What is the size of the firm? Are most assets current or fixed? How is the capital being invested? What is the firm's capital structure?

When analyzing a balance sheet, investors look for patterns. Do any significant patterns emerge over time? Is a particular firm deviating significantly from others within its industry? Good financial statement analysis will always look beyond the numbers. However, the numbers often suggest which areas require further investigation.

Exhibit 21-2 presents Pfizer's balance sheet, which contains data for 3 years. Notice that Pfizer holds a large portion of its assets in current assets and property, plant, and equipment. One risk a company like Pfizer has is that some inventory may become obsolete or outdated. A new drug discovery, for example, may result in the need to destroy the stock of existing drugs.

Probably the most notable changes in the balance sheet are the reduction in cash and cash equivalents in 1995 relative to 1994. Also, accounts receivable have risen. This increase in accounts receivable may signal lower credit standards in an effort to sell more products. In 1996, Pfizer reported an increase in its cash ($1,150 million versus $403 million in 1995) and an increase in accounts receivable and inventory. These increases may indicate a much greater sales volume (as we will soon discover from the income statement). On the liability side, the most notable change is the increase in total current liabilities, which is very modest.

EXHIBIT 21-2 **Pfizer 1996 Annual Report: Quarterly Consolidated Balance Sheet (in millions, except per-share data)**

	December 31		
	1996	1995	1994
Assets			
Current Assets			
Cash and cash equivalents	$ 1,150	$ 403	$ 1,458
Short-term investments	487	1,109	560
Accounts receivable, less allowances for doubtful accounts: 1996—$58; 1995—$61; 1994—$44	2,252	2,024	1,665
Short-term loans	354	289	361
Inventories			
Finished goods	617	564	528
Work in process	695	579	535
Raw materials and supplies	277	241	202
Total inventories	1,589	1,384	1,265
Prepaid expenses, taxes and other assets	636	943	479
Total current assets	6,468	6,152	5,788
Long-term loans and investments	1,163	545	829
Property, plant and equipment, less accumulated depreciation	3,850	3,473	3,073
Goodwill, less accumulated amortization: 1996—$115; 1995—$79; 1994—$48	1,424	1,243	326
Other assets, deferred taxes and deferred charges	1,762	1,316	1,083
Total assets	$14,667	$12,729	$11,099

(continued)

EXHIBIT 21-2   *(continued)*

	December 31		
	1996	**1995**	**1994**
Liabilities and Shareholders' Equity			
Current Liabilities			
Short-term borrowings, including current portion of long-term debt	$ 2,235	$ 2,036	$ 2,220
Accounts payable	913	715	525
Income taxes payable	892	822	731
Accrued compensation and related items	436	421	419
Other current liabilities	1,164	1,193	931
Total current liabilities	5,640	5,187	4,826
Long-term debt	687	833	604
Postretirement benefit obligation other than pension plans	412	426	433
Deferred taxes on income	253	166	212
Other noncurrent liabilities	671	564	661
Minority interests	50	47	39
Total liabilities	7,713	7,223	6,775
Shareholders' Equity			
Preferred stock, without par value; 12 shares authorized, none issued			
Common stock, $.05 par value; 1,500 shares authorized; issued: 1996—689; 1995—685; 1994—681	34	34	34
Additional paid-in-capital	1,728	1,235	651
Retained earnings	8,017	6,859	5,945
Currency translation adjustment and other	145	163	196
Employee benefit trust	(1,488)	(1,170)	(749)
Treasury stock, at cost: 1996—44; 1995—48; 1994—52	(1,482)	(1,615)	(1,753)

See Notes to Consolidated Financial Statements, which are an integral part of these statements.

Source: Web site at http://www.pfizer.com/pfizerinc/inv. . .annual/1996/financials/consbal.html.

A financial analyst should investigate these changes. Are the changes in cash and marketable securities a signal that something is wrong, or are they due to a temporary demand for cash? Why are accounts receivable increasing? To answer these questions, the analyst must look at the explanations to the balance sheet that are normally part of the financial statements. If satisfied by the explanations, the analyst can conclude that this is a firm with very low *long-term* liabilities. Hence, it is mostly an equity firm with regard to its long-term financial policy. Thus, Pfizer has relatively little financial risk. Also, Pfizer seems quite stable, because this firm has had no drastic changes in the past few years. Most balance sheet items have grown steadily over time. It seems that creditors are quite safe, because most of them are short-term creditors, and the current liabilities are covered by the current assets.

One valuable exercise is to convert the balance sheet items to market values. Many clues as to the current market values of various balance sheet items are hidden in the financial statements. The analyst must diligently search through the reported financial statements to find these clues. This exercise helps the analyst assess the current stock price and whether it is reasonable. The following sections examine selected balance sheet items.

INVENTORY EVALUATION: FIFO, LIFO, AND AVERAGE COST

Inventory is a relatively large item on the balance sheet; it can represent more than 50% of the assets of department stores such as J. C. Penney or Sears. Financial analysts, therefore, should carefully analyze changes in a firm's inventory level.

Recall that the balance sheet reports assets at book value or historical cost, not at market value. How can an investor convert book values of assets and liabilities to their corresponding market values? Sometimes the book values equal the market values of the assets. For most firms, however, this is not the case. In particular, the book value of the stock is generally different from its market value. To convert the balance sheet from book value to market value, the analyst must make several adjustments. For example, receivables are listed at the amount anticipated to be collected. Clearly, the current market value is lower.

The "Notes to Financial Statements" section of most annual reports discusses how inventories, raw materials, work in progress, and finished goods are carried on the balance sheet. For example, a recent annual report of Pfizer, Inc., includes the following:

Inventories are valued at cost or market, whichever is lower. Except as noted below, raw materials and supplies are valued at average or latest actual costs and finished goods and work in process are average actual costs.

Substantially all of the Company's U.S. sourced pharmaceuticals, animal health and specialty chemicals inventories are valued utilizing the last-in, first-out (LIFO) method.

The concept of conservatism applies to inventory valuation. Inventory is valued at cost or market, whichever is *less*. Pfizer uses the last-in, first-out (LIFO) method to value certain U.S. product inventories. Alternative methods to LIFO for valuing inventories are the first-in, first-out (FIFO) and the average cost methods. Although LIFO is the most popular, it tends to understate inventories during inflationary periods.

Let us compare these three methods with a simple example.[1] Suppose we are given the following information regarding the inventory of EMI/Micro Computer Retailers, Inc., a computer hardware mail order firm:

---

1. For a more detailed discussion of valuing inventories, see Leopold A. Bernstein, *Financial Statement Analysis: Theory, Application, and Interpretation,* 4th ed. (Homewood, Ill.: Irwin, 1989).

			Total Cost
Inventory on January 1	100	PCs at $1,000	$100,000
First Purchase in Year	300	PCs at $900	$270,000
Second Purchase in Year	200	PCs at $800	$160,000
Total available for sale	600	PCs	$530,000
Inventory on December 31	50	PCs	

To better understand inventory accounting methods, we examine the impact of each method on the income statement. A more thorough examination of the income statement is covered below. Our interest here is in the appropriate value for ending inventory, because ending inventory valuation plays a critical role in determining the cost of goods sold on the income statement. Recall that the cost of goods sold can be calculated as follows:

Cost of Goods Sold = Beginning Inventory + Purchases − Ending Inventory

The value of beginning inventory is given as $100,000, and two purchases were made totaling $430,000 [(300 · $900) + (200 · $800)]. The problem of calculating ending inventory remains.

With the FIFO method, the goods first placed in inventory are the ones sold first. Thus, the ending inventory would be valued at the cost of the latest purchases. In our example, the ending inventory by the FIFO method would be $40,000 (50 · $800), and the cost of goods sold would be $490,000 ($530,000 − $40,000).

The LIFO method bases the cost of goods sold on the most recent costs incurred. To illustrate, think of inventory as a pile of sand. The last goods purchased are poured onto the inventory pile, and any sales are taken from the top of the pile. Based on the LIFO method, the ending inventory would be $50,000 (50 · $1,000), and the cost of goods sold would be $480,000 ($530,000 − $50,000). If prices go up because of inflation, the cost of goods sold by the LIFO method will be higher than by the FIFO method. Indeed, the goal of the LIFO method is to better align the revenues with current costs during inflation. (See the next Practice Box.)

The average cost method spreads cost fluctuations over time. A weighted-average cost is employed in valuing inventories and charging cost of goods sold. Thus, the average cost of all purchases and beginning inventories is $883.33 (total cost/number of units = $530,000/600). Thus, the ending inventory would be valued at $44,166.50 (50 · $883.33), and the cost of goods sold would be $485,833.50 ($530,000 − $44,166.50).

The following table summarizes the results of the three inventory accounting methods. Clearly, the method used influences both the cost of goods sold reported on the income statement and the ending inventory carried on the balance sheet.

	FIFO	**LIFO**	**Average Cost**
Ending Inventory	$ 40,000	$ 50,000	$ 44,166.50
Cost of Goods Sold	490,000	480,000	485,833.50

A firm's adoption of an inventory valuation practice is accompanied by some tax considerations. In the previous example, the LIFO method would report the lowest cost of goods sold and hence result in the highest reported earnings. This method subjects the firm to higher taxes. For tax reasons, therefore, this firm would want to adopt the FIFO method, which would result in lower reported earnings.[2]

Firms are not allowed to constantly switch their inventory accounting practices. This switching would violate the basic accounting concept of consistency. Although the Internal Revenue Service does allow firms to change inventory accounting policies, the firm must document valid reasons for the switch. The following Practice Box illustrates a more traditional inventory example that has rising prices (assumed to be due to inflation).

PRACTICE BOX

Problem

Suppose you are given the following information about Birmingham Steel Tubing Retailers, Inc.:

		Total Cost ($)
Inventory on January 1	1,000 tubes at $500	500,000
First Purchase in Year	3,000 tubes at $550	1,650,000
Second Purchase in Year	3,000 tubes at $600	1,800,000
Third Purchase in Year	2,000 tubes at $650	1,300,000
Total available for sale	9,000 tubes	5,250,000
Inventory on December 31	3,000 tubes	

What is the value of the ending inventory and the cost of goods sold by the FIFO, LIFO, and average cost methods? Which method is preferred for tax purposes?

Solution

By the FIFO method, the ending inventory is $(2,000 \cdot \$650) + (1,000 \cdot \$600) = \$1,900,000$. Recall that according to the FIFO method, the first tubes in are assumed to be sold first, so the inventory remaining is the inventory acquired by the third purchase and 1,000 of the tubes acquired by the second purchase. The cost of goods sold is $\$5,250,000 - \$1,900,000 = \$3,350,000$.

By the LIFO method, the ending inventory is $(1,000 \cdot \$500) + (2,000 \cdot \$550) = \$1,600,000$. Recall that according to the LIFO method, the last tubes in are assumed to be sold first so the inventory remaining is the original inventory plus 2,000 of the tubes acquired by the first purchase. The cost of goods sold is $\$5,250,000 - \$1,600,000 = \$3,650,000$.

By the average cost method, the average cost of tubes available for sale is $\$5,250,000/9,000 \cong \$583.33$. Thus, the ending inventory is valued at $3,000 \cdot \$583.33 = \$1,749,990$, and the cost of goods sold is $\$5,250,000 - \$1,749,990 = \$3,500,010$.

(continued)

---

2. A recently enacted U.S. tax policy requires that firms be consistent in their use of inventory valuation methods. The method used for tax purposes must be the method used for financial reporting.

The LIFO method gives the highest cost of good sold. Hence, it will produce the lowest taxable profits (as the following table illustrates), so it is preferred for tax reasons. However, the LIFO method also results in the lowest reported earnings to shareholders. (The table assumes that each tube was sold for $700, and the income tax rate is 31%.)

Income Statement	FIFO	LIFO	Average Cost
Sales	$4,200,000	$4,200,000	$4,200,000
Cost of Goods Sold	3,350,000	3,650,000	3,500,010
Earnings before Tax	850,000	550,000	699,990
Tax	263,500	170,500	216,996.90
Net Income	586,500	379,500	482,993.10

Inventory is at the very heart of most corporations. High inventories are an early warning sign that a firm is unable to sell its products. In early 1998, for example, Compaq Computers announced that it was significantly reducing the retail price of its computers because of low inventory turnover (slow sales). Many times, when inventory rises considerably during a quarter, analysts react very negatively and dump the stock, believing that trouble lies ahead for the firm. Inventory is a closely watched item on the balance sheet.

PLANT AND EQUIPMENT

Property, plant, and equipment (PPE) is reported on the balance sheet at cost less depreciation. Investors seek current values for these assets. For older firms, this value is especially difficult to determine. For example, a firm may have a physical plant that has been fully depreciated but is worth hundreds of millions of dollars. Investors might have to work with other sources to find estimates of the current values for these assets. One source is the property tax assessments for the firm. Although this information is publicly available, it is usually difficult to acquire. (It is buried in some public tax collector's office.) Another method to determine the value of the firm's property is by examining how much the firm pays for fire insurance. A value for the property can be inferred from fire insurance expenses. Firms may or may not provide this information.

INTANGIBLES

Most analysts exercise a great deal of conservatism when assessing the market value of reported intangibles. Intangibles include goodwill, patents, copyrights, trademarks, franchises, licenses, and organization and development expenses. Many of these assets are placed on the financial statements as a result of mergers and buyouts.

The basic problem with evaluating intangibles stems from its accounting treatment. For example, Procter and Gamble has developed strong brand names internally, and these costs have been expensed through the income statement. The value of these brand names does not appear on the balance sheet. Alternatively, RJR Nabisco has acquired strong brand names through outside purchases. When purchased, RJR Nabisco records the costs as intangibles, and they are reported on the balance sheet. Thus, the uninformed investor could easily reach radically different conclusions when comparing these two firms.[3]

LIABILITIES

On the liability side of the balance sheet, current liabilities are typically listed at what will be paid rather than at their present value. Hence, the analyst must discount the current liabilities to determine their market value. To assess the market value of long-term debt, the analyst should adjust the debt for changes in interest rates. For example, if a firm issued 30-year bonds at 6.5% and rates moved up to 12%, the market value of the 30-year bonds is much less than what the firm received (hence, the firm has benefited from this issue).

EQUITY

An analyst can adjust equity to market value fairly easily by taking the number of shares outstanding and multiplying it by the current market price. Unlike accounting requirements, the exercise of converting the balance sheet to market value does not require assets to exactly equal liabilities and owners' equity. In fact, the differences that arise are the basis on which analysts determine whether to buy or sell the firm's stock.

PRACTICE BOX

Problem

Suppose a firm's current assets are $100 million, and current liabilities are $50 million. The long-term liabilities are $25 million. The firm issued 10 million shares whose current market price is $2 per share. Based on the book value, is this stock underpriced or overpriced? Why?

Solution

Even if we completely ignore the firm's fixed assets, the firm can use the current assets to pay all its liabilities and still have $100 million − $50 million − $25 million = $25 million left. Because there are only 10 million shares, the firm can liquidate itself and pay $2.5 per share ($25 million/10 million). Thus, based on this information, the stock trading for $2 is underpriced. However, before buying it, we should learn who manages the firm, how much of the profit is taken in compensation to managers, if there is any pending litigation, and so forth.

---

3. For an in-depth discussion of this problem as well as others, see Peter H. Knutson, *Financial Reporting in the 1990s and Beyond* (Charlottesville, Va.: Association for Investment Management and Research, 1993).

21.1.3 Income Statement

The income statement shows the flow of sales, expenses, and earnings during a specified period. The income statement is also known as the profit and loss (P&L) statement. It provides a summary of the revenues, cost of goods sold, and expenses of a firm for an accounting period.

The income statement helps investors assess the abilities of management. Specifically, the income statement demonstrates how profitably the firm operated over a period of time. Related to profitability is management's ability to control expenses.

The information contained in the income statement helps answer several questions that investors have: What were the primary sources of income, cost of goods sold, and expenses? What is the value of research and development? Does research and development produce income? What is the "true" earning power of the firm, where "true" implies actual benefits accruing to the firm? In particular, by comparing several years, what is the trend in revenues, market share, and profits? Answers to these questions are found in part in the income statement.

Exhibit 21-3 shows the income statement of Pfizer. The expense categories are cost of sales; selling, informational, and administrative expenses; and research and development expenses.

Investors seek to identify trends over time, as well as across industries. Most items that appear on the income statement are stable, with reasonable growth every year. Nevertheless, there is a significant rise in earnings in 1996 (from $1,573 million to $1,929 million, an increase of more than 22.5%). The main item responsible for this increase is the increase in net sales from $10,021 million in 1995 to $11,306 million in 1996. In 1996 Pfizer managed to sell 15% more than in 1995 without a similar increase in the cost of sales. This item increased only 0.55% relative to 1995 and is the main reason for the more than 22.5% increase in 1996 net income. Also notice that Pfizer managed to increase its net income by 22.63%.

We observe that Pfizer spends a significant amount on research and development ($1,684 million in 1996). Note that the R&D expense is 87% of the company's net profit in 1996. What is the value of this research and development? Can we assume that just because a firm like Pfizer spends hundreds of millions of dollars on R&D that this expenditure will necessarily add value to the firm? Are actual costs of R&D the best way to measure the usefulness of R&D expenditures? What is the best way to value R&D? R&D is one of the most difficult expense items to assess.[4] Investors view R&D expenses differently than accountants do. Typically, R&D is treated as an expense and does not appear on the balance sheet. Depending on the type of R&D, investors may view R&D as an asset-generating expense. For example, because of its R&D expenditures, Pfizer will be marketing several drugs over the next few years. Investors view these future drugs as income-generating assets and incorporate this information into their analysis. The introduction of Pfizer's Viagra in 1998 is an example of how years of R&D can translate into success.

---

4. Accounting policies require the expensing of research and development outlays when they occur (except for assets that have alternate uses, which are placed on the balance sheet as intangibles).

EXHIBIT 21-3   **Consolidated Statement of Income**
Pfizer, Inc., and Subsidiary Companies (in millions, except per-share data)

	Year Ended December 31		
	1996	1995	1994
Net sales	$11,306	$10,021	$7,977
Costs and expenses			
Cost of sales	2,176	2,164	1,722
Selling, informational and administrative expenses	4,366	3,855	3,184
Research and development expenses	1,684	1,442	1,126
Other deductions—net[a]			
Income from continuing operations before provision for taxes on income and minority interests	2,804	2,299	1,830
Provision for taxes on income	869	738	549
Minority interests	6	7	5
Income from continuing operations	1,929	1,554	1,276
Discontinued operations—net of taxes on income	—	19	22
Net income	$ 1,929	$ 1,573	$1,298
Earnings per common share			
Income from continuing operations	$ 2.99	$ 2.47	$ 2.05
Discontinued operations—net of taxes on income	—	.03	.04
Net income	$ 2.99	$ 2.50	$ 2.09
Weighted average shares used to calculate per share amounts	644	630	620

See Notes to Consolidated Financial Statements, which are an integral part of these statements.

a. Interest expense was $165 million in 1996 and $193 million in 1995.

Source: Web site at http://www.pfizer.com/pfizerinc/inv...annual/1996/financials/consinc.html.

It might seem that if the firm did not spend money on R&D, this savings would dramatically increase the profit. Although this is true in the short run, in the long run, without R&D Pfizer would not have new products to offer, and its future earnings would decline. R&D expenditures are not necessary for some types of firms, but for Pfizer, which is in the pharmaceutical industry, they are essential.

Another major expense that requires close scrutiny is depreciation. The way an asset changes in value over time can be considerably different from how it is expensed on the income statement. Compounding the problem is the fact that firms can depreciate certain assets by different methods. Just like inventory valuation, there are different methods to determine depreciation expense. Inflation also further distorts the difference between an asset's economic value and accounting value.

Thus, some analysts attempt to determine the appropriate economic depreciation in trying to assess a firm's actual earnings abilities.

21.1.4   Statement of Cash Flows

Accounting principles are very different from valuation methods. By accounting principles a firm may be profitable, yet by valuation methods it could be near bankruptcy. Suppose Boeing sells 747 jumbo airplanes for $500 million each. The production costs, which are all paid in cash, are $470 million. Would Boeing be profitable? Your answer depends on the method you use to evaluate this firm. An accountant would report on the income statement $30 million in earnings for each plane sold. Suppose now that the planes are sold not for cash but on credit for 1 year. Does this affect accounting earnings? No, the earnings will be reported in the year of the transaction as $500 million in revenues, even though the $500 million has not yet been received. Thus, the $500 million will be on the balance sheet as accounts receivable. Now suppose that the appropriate annual discount rate is 10%. Clearly, $500 million received 1 year from now is worth only $500 million$/(1 + 0.10) \cong$ $454.5 million (recall the time value of money). Because it cost $470 million to produce the planes, Boeing actually loses in economic terms (or in market value), even though the accounting statement shows a profit.

Although the reported earnings can be adjusted to reflect the true economic earnings, such distortions can be identified in the statement of cash flow that is also reported by the firm. In our example, if there are accounts receivable of $500 million, this sum will not be written as cash flow this year but rather in the next year, when they are actually received.

The statement of cash flows tells us all the sources of cash for the firm (including borrowing or a new issue of stock) and how the firm uses this cash for expenses, investment, paying dividends, and so forth. The statement of cash flows has three components: operating activities, investing activities, and financing activities. Operating activities include almost all items in the income statement, as well as balance sheet items that directly relate to earnings activities. Investing activities include buying or selling securities or revenue-generating assets, as well as activities related to lending money. Financing activities include activities related to borrowing money, as well as transactions related to owners' equity. The statement of cash flows is beneficial in assessing the ability of the firm to pay future dividends, fund future growth, and service its debts.

The statement of cash flows documents the flow of cash through the firm during an accounting period. There are two methods for reporting the cash flows. The **direct method** shows the cash receipts and payments from operations. This approach gives the analyst a better understanding of how cash moves through a firm. The most popular method of reporting the cash flows, however, is the **indirect method,** which takes net income and adjusts for noncash items in order to convert it to cash from operations. The indirect method reconciles net income with cash from operations. For example, Exhibit 21-4 presents Pfizer's statement of cash flows, which starts with net income and reconciles the change in the cash asset account on the balance sheet.

EXHIBIT 21-4   **Statement of Cash Flows for Pfizer, Inc. (in millions of dollars)**

	Year Ended December 31		
	1996	**1995**	**1994**
Operating Activities			
Net income	$1,929	$1,573	$1,298
Adjustments to reconcile net income to net cash provided by operating activities:			
Depreciation and amortization of intangibles	430	374	292
Deferred taxes	75	(12)	32
Other	14	76	(5)
Changes in assets and liabilities, net of effect of businesses acquired and divested:			
Accounts receivable	(255)	(290)	(160)
Inventories	(149)	(25)	(111)
Prepaid and other assets	(208)	(171)	(12)
Accounts payable and accrued liabilities	66	320	168
Income tax payable	23	88	121
Other deferred items	142	(112)	(135)
Net cash provided by operating activities	2,067	1,821	1,488
Investing Activities			
Acquisitions, net of cash acquired	(451)	(1,521)	—
Purchases of property, plant and equipment	(774)	(696)	(672)
Proceeds from the sale of a business	353	—	—
Purchases of short-term investments	(2,851)	(2,611)	(1,356)
Proceeds from redemptions of short-term investments	3,490	2,185	1,245
Purchases of long-term investments	(820)	(151)	(162)
Purchases and redemptions of short-term investments by financial subsidiaries	(11)	(30)	44
Decrease in loans and long-term investments by financial subsidiaries	52	330	21
Other investing activities	75	151	40
Net cash used in investing activities	(937)	(2,343)	(840)
Financing Activities			
Proceeds from issuance of long-term debt	636	502	40
Repayments of long-term debt	(804)	(52)	(4)

(continued)

EXHIBIT 21-4 *(continued)*

	Year Ended December 31		
	1996	1995	1994
Financing Activities *(continued)*			
Increase/(decrease) in short-term debt	$ 259	$ (444)	$1,030
Stock option transactions	280	205	64
Purchases of common stock	(27)	(108)	(511)
Cash dividends paid	(771)	(659)	(594)
Other financing activities	45	37	37
Net cash (used in)/provided by financing activities	(382)	(519)	62
Effect of exchange rate changes on cash and cash equivalents	(1)	(14)	19
Net increase/(decrease) in cash and cash equivalents	747	(1,055)	729
Cash and cash equivalents at beginning of year	403	1,458	729
Cash and cash equivalents at end of year	$1,150	$ 403	$1,458

Source: Web site at http://www.pfizer.com/pfizerinc/inv. . .annual/1996/financials/consinc.html.

For example, the net earnings of Pfizer in 1996 were $1,929 million. However, this does not mean that the firm obtained $1,929 million in cash inflows. Cash inflows could be more or less. For example, the firm had depreciation of $430 million. This is not a cash outflow but an accounting allocation. Therefore, we add it to the $1,929 million. If there are no more adjustments, this means that the cash inflow will be $1,929 million + $430 million = $2,359 million.

In practice, we see from Exhibit 21-4 that the cash flow calculations are more complex. The firm makes these adjustments to get a net cash inflow from operations in 1996 of $2,067 million. Similarly, the net cash flow from investing activities was −$937 million, and from financing activities it was −$382 million. Of course, when the firm takes a loan it increases the cash flow, and when the firm pays dividends it decreases the cash flow (see Exhibit 21-4).

PRACTICE BOX	
Problem	Suppose a firm reported net income of $20 million. The depreciation for the period was $10 million, and the firm paid $5 million in dividends. Finally, the firm raised $2 million in long-term debt. What was the net cash flow for the firm?

(continued)

Solution	Starting with net income, we would add in depreciation, deduct dividend payments, and add in the long-term debt. Hence, the cash flow was

$$\$20 \text{ million} + \$10 \text{ million} - \$5 \text{ million} + \$2 \text{ million} = \$27 \text{ million}$$

It is interesting to see from this analysis that the firm has a policy of repurchasing its stocks. Stock buybacks can be interpreted by investors in one of two ways. Either management has run out of projects with positive NPVs and seeks to give investors capital gains rather than taxable dividends, or management believes the stock price is significantly underpriced. Instead of raising money by issuing more stock, Pfizer is using cash to repurchase its stocks. Because Pfizer's policy has been consistent for the past few years, it probably reveals significant information. It is possible that management thinks that its stock is underpriced, and it is a good investment to repurchase the stock. Also, this repurchasing signals a strong cash balance, because the repurchase is not financed by borrowing but from the firm's past earnings. The repurchasing may also mean that the firm lacks other profitable (NPV > 0) investment opportunities. It clearly indicates strong confidence in the stock by management and may be based on some positive information that management knows but investors do not.

21.2 EARNINGS PER SHARE (EPS)

Recall from Chapter 19 (see Exhibit 19-1) that analysts determine stock values from EPS and ROE estimates based on their systematic analysis of the company. Earnings per share, the firm's net income divided by the number of shares outstanding, plays a critical role in the way analysts form valuation estimates. This section focuses exclusively on EPS and issues related to assessing its accuracy.

How does the reported EPS differ from the actual earning ability of the firm? Reported EPS measures the past performance of the firm. Earning power, in contrast, refers to earnings per share that are sustainable in the future and that do not depend on accounting techniques. Many analysts use the income statement and reported EPS as a means to estimate the future earnings ability of a firm. When trying to arrive at the actual earning ability of a firm, the analyst must make several adjustments. For example, earnings attributable to nonrecurring items, such as the sale of a subsidiary, should not be expected to be repeated. Therefore, they should not be included in the EPS calculation.

As standard deviation measures dispersion around the mean, analysts seek to measure their uncertainty surrounding a reported EPS number. Although methods vary widely, analysts assess how much the actual operating earnings differ from the reported EPS. Many analysts have devised ranking systems that are referred to as *quality of earnings.* Low quality implies that the reported EPS number differs greatly from the firm's actual operating earnings.

As analysts pore over financial statements, they seek information on the quality of earnings. They ask several questions about quality. For example, when managers can select among different accounting procedures, do they select conservative or liberal procedures? Can a firm actually pay out the reported EPS, or is it not yet fully realized? Recall the preceding example of Boeing, where the $500 million in sales are in accounts receivable, so they cannot be paid as dividends. Over time, does the firm have stable earnings, or are the earnings volatile? How hard is it to forecast future earnings? Exhibit 21-5a summarizes these and other issues involved in assessing quality. Analysts seek to establish their level of confidence—similar to standard deviation—in the reported EPS figure.

Along with measures of quality, analysts have devised checklists for review, or red flags to look for, when assessing the quality of earnings. The first item on the checklist is typically the audit report. Auditors write a letter—known as the *independent auditor's report*—to shareholders and the board of directors, giving an opinion on the fairness of management's financial statements. If the auditor has reservations about the financial statements, then the auditor will express them in this letter. The independent auditor's report is a part of the annual report to shareholders required by the Securities and Exchange Commission. A sample checklist appears in Exhibit 21-5b.

21.3 RATIO ANALYSIS[5]

Ratio analysis is a method used to compare financial trends both between firms and for a given firm over time. Ratio analysis is useful in converting raw financial statement information into a form that makes it easy to compare firms of different sizes. Ratio analysis helps to identify the risk and return potential for a given firm.

Ratios are typically categorized into three groups: profitability ratios, liquidity ratios, and debt ratios. Profitability ratios measure the earning power of the firm. ROE (Net Income/Shareholders' Equity) and EPS (Net Income/Shares) are two popular profitability ratios. Liquidity ratios measure the ability of the firm to pay its immediate liabilities. For example, the current ratio (Current Assets/Current Liabilities) addresses the ability of the firm's current assets to pay for the firm's current liabilities. Because it is difficult to pay bills with inventory, analysts have devised other ratios, such as the *quick ratio,* which is similar to the current ratio except that inventory and other nonmarketable assets are first deducted from current assets. It is a "quick" way to assess a firm's ability to meet current liabilities. Debt ratios measure the financial risk of a firm by evaluating the firm's ability to pay its debt obligations over time. For example, the fixed charge coverage ratio, which is given by

$$\left[\frac{\text{(Income before Tax + Interest Expense)}}{\text{(Interest Expense + Leasehold Payments)}}\right]$$

5. Based on Sidney Cottle, Roger F. Murray, and Frank E. Block, *Graham and Dodd's Security Analysis,* 5th ed. (New York: McGraw-Hill, 1988).

**EXHIBIT 21-5
Issues When
Assessing
the Quality
of Earnings**

Part a: Measures of Quality

High Quality	Low Quality
Conservative accounting	Liberal accounting
Earnings are distributable	Earnings are not realized
Stable earnings	Volatile earnings
Recent earnings good forecast of future	Recent earnings poor forecast of future
Related to ongoing business	Nonrepeatable earnings
Reflect prudent, realistic view	Not economically realistic
No balance sheet surprises	Overstated balance sheet
Earnings are from operations	Earnings are from financing
Earnings are domestic	Earnings are offshore
Earnings are understandable	Complex earnings

Part b: Red Flags Related to Quality of Earnings

1. Long audit report
2. Reductions in managed costs, such as advertising
3. Changes in accounting policies
4. Increase in accounts receivable
5. Increase in intangible assets
6. One-time sources of income
7. Decline in gross margin percentage—price competition, high costs, or product mix is changing
8. Reduction in reserves for contingencies
9. Increase in borrowings
10. Increase in deferred tax portion of tax expense
11. Increase in unfunded pension liabilities
12. Low cash and marketable securities
13. Peak short-term borrowings at year end
14. Slowdown in inventory turnover

Source: David F. Hawkings, *Corporate Financial Reporting and Analysis,* 2nd ed. (Homewood, Ill.: Dow Jones–Irwin, 1986).

assesses how many times interest expense and leasehold payments can be paid with current income.

Exhibit 21-6 lists the top five ratios for each category in order of importance based on the survey of chartered financial analysts (CFAs) quoted in Connecting Theory to Practice 21.2. The computation required for each ratio is shown in the second column of the exhibit and is illustrated briefly with Pfizer data in the third column.

EXHIBIT 21-6   **Ratios by Category[a]**

Ratio	Equation	Pfizer Example
Profitability		
Return on equity	Net Income/Shareholders' Equity	$1,929/6,954 \cong 27.7\%$
Earnings per share	Net Income/Shares	$1,929/644 \cong \$2.99$
Net profit margin	Net Income/Net Sales	$1,929/11,306 \cong 17.06\%$
Return on assets	Net Income/Total Assets	$1,929/14,667 \cong 13.15\%$
Return on total invested capital	(Net Income + Interest on Long-Term Debt)/Total Capitalization	$(1,929 + 165)/$ $(6,954 + 687) = 27.4\%$
Liquidity		
Quick ratio	(Current Assets − Inventory − Other Current Assets)/Current Liabilities	$(6,468 - 1,589 - 636)/5,640$ $\cong 0.752$
Current ratio	Current Assets/Current Liabilities	$6,468/5,640 \cong 1.147$
Days' sales in inventory	(Inventories/Net Sales)365	$(1,589/11,306) \cdot 365 \cong 51.3$
Cash	(Cash + Marketable Securities)/Current Liabilities	$(1,150 + 487)/5,640 \cong 0.29$
Inventory turnover	Cost of Goods Sold/Ending Inventory	$(2,176/1,589) \cong 1.37$
Debt		
Fixed charge coverage	(Income before Tax + Interest Expense)/(Interest Expense + Leasehold Payments[b])	$(2,804 + 165)/(165 + 0) \cong 17.99$
Times interest earned	(Income before Tax + Interest Expense)/Interest Expense	$(2,804 + 165)/165 \cong 17.99$
Debt to equity	Total Liabilities/Shareholders' Equity	$7,713/6,954 \cong 1.11$
Degree of financial leverage	(Income before Tax + Interest Expense)/Income before Tax − [Preferred Dividends/(1 − Tax Rate)]	$(2,804 + 165)/(2,804 - 0) \cong 1.06$
Debt to assets	Total Liabilities/Total Assets	$7,713/14,667 \cong 0.526$

a. In order of importance according to a survey by Charles Gibson, *Financial Analysts Journal,* May–June 1987, pp. 74–76. Excerpted with permission from *Financial Analysts Journal.* Copyright 1987, Association for Investment Management and Research, Charlottesville, Va. All rights reserved. All numbers are in millions and taken from previous tables, except where noted.

b. Leasehold payments figures are in footnotes to the Annual Report.

CONNECTING THEORY TO PRACTICE 21.2

HOW CHARTERED FINANCIAL ANALYSTS VIEW FINANCIAL RATIOS

Financial analysts in the United States, United Kingdom and New Zealand have consistently given the corporate annual report the highest ranking as the most important source of information. Of 10 items included in annual reports,

(continued)

these analysts selected the income statement as the most important and the balance sheet as the second most important.

Financial statements obviously play a major role in a fundamental approach to security analysis. Among the items of potential interest to analysts are financial ratios relating key parts of the financial statements. . . .

The surveyed analysts gave the highest significance ratings to profitability ratios. Return on equity after tax was given the highest significance by a wide margin. Four of the next five most significant ratios were also profitability ratios—earnings per share, net profit margin after tax, return on equity before tax and net profit margin before tax.

The price-earnings ratio—categorized by the analysts as an "other" measure—received the second-highest significance rating. . . .

Apparently, the analyst first wants to know about profitability and what is being paid for these profits before turning to debt and liquidity. He likely places more emphasis on debt than on liquidity because debt represents a longer-term position than liquidity.

Source: Charles Gibson, "How Chartered Financial Analysts View Financial Ratios." Excerpted with permission from *Financial Analysts Journal,* May–June 1987, pp. 74–76. Copyright 1987, Association for Investment Management and Research, Charlottesville, Va. All rights reserved.

MAKING THE CONNECTION

This survey found that financial analysts focus heavily on accounting profitability. Recall that the ability of firms to produce dividends and capital gains in the future is what gives stock its value. The ability to make timely interest payments does not compare with the ability of the firm to be profitable. However, once a firm's profitability has been assessed, financial analysts turn to the ability of the firm to meet its current and future financial obligations.

Exhibit 21-7 shows some selected ratios over time for Pfizer, along with its industry averages. We see that the ROE has declined over time. However, Pfizer has remained above its industry averages for every year. Pfizer's above-average performance is due in part to its more aggressive use of financial leverage. For example, the current ratio for Pfizer is consistently at or below its industry averages. This indicates that other firms have more current assets available to pay for their current liabilities. We see also that Pfizer's debt-to-equity ratio is higher than its industry averages. Pfizer has more financial risk than its competitors. However, by taking this risk, Pfizer has outperformed other firms in the pharmaceutical industry based on ROE (except for the setback in 1991).

Two other ratios currently receiving a lot of attention are the price/earnings (P/E) ratio and the market-to-book (M/B) ratio. These two ratios combine one market value and one accounting value.

EXHIBIT 21-7	Ratio	Company/Industry	1996	1995	1994
Comparison of Pfizer with Its Industry for Selected Ratios	Return	Pfizer	27.7	28.6	30.0
		Industry	17.4	16.9	17.6
	Current	Pfizer	1.1	1.2	1.2
		Industry	1.4	1.4	1.2
	Debt to equity	Pfizer	111	131	157
		Industry	54.1	50.6	52.6

Source: Leo Troy, *Almanac of Business and Industrial Financial Ratios* (Englewood Cliffs, N.J.: Prentice-Hall, various editions).

The P/E ratio is the price per share divided by the most recent earnings per share and is called the *earnings multiplier*. If a firm has a low multiple, it is considered to be a bargain. However, an investor should check the firm's financial statement before buying its stock. If the firm is under financial distress, the low price may indicate a forthcoming bankruptcy rather than a "bargain," and therefore the stock is not a good investment. However, a low P/E ratio accompanied by a strong operation and cash surplus can be an indicator of a "bargain." Thus, here the financial statement analysis complements the analysis of the market data.

The M/B ratio is the market value of equity per share (that is, the stock price) divided by the book value of equity per share. If the market value of equity is $12 and the book value is only $10, then the M/B ratio is 1.2 ($12/$10). In general, a ratio greater than 1 implies that the stock is overpriced, and a ratio less than 1 implies that it is underpriced. Indeed, researchers have shown that by looking at the M/B ratio in one period, an investor can earn excess rates of return in the next period by buying portfolios with an M/B much lower than 1.[6]

Percentage financial statements help analysts make sense out of the many numbers contained in the balance sheet and income statement. **Percentage financial statements** (also known as **common size statements**) are the balance sheet and income statement converted to percentages. Specifically, each item in the balance sheet is converted to a percentage of total assets (or total liabilities and equity), and each item in the income statement is converted to a percentage of net sales. With this information an analyst can easily see how the relative composition of the financial statement is changing over time. Exhibits 21-8 and 21-9 provide this information based on Pfizer's financial statements.

These percentage financial statements reveal the amazing consistency of Pfizer over the past few years. For example, inventories have remained around 10% or 11% of assets, and accounts receivable has stayed at 15% for these 3 years. Net property, plant, and equipment has remained between 26% and 27% for these 3 years. The

6. See Eugene F. Fama and Kenneth R. French, "The Cross-Section of Expected Stock Returns," *Journal of Finance* 47 (June 1992): 427–465. See also the second article in this chapter's Investments in the News.

EXHIBIT 21-8 Percentage Balance Sheet for Pfizer, Inc.	**Year**	**1996**	**1995**	**1994**
	Assets			
	Cash	7.84%	3.2%	13.1%
	Marketable Securities	3.33%	8.7%	5.0%
	Receivables	15.4%	15.9%	15.0%
	Inventories	10.83%	10.9%	11.4%
	Other Current Assets	6.7%	9.6%	7.6%
	Total Current Assets	**44.10%**	**48.3%**	**52.1%**
	Property, Plant, and Equipment	26.3%	27.3%	27.7%
	Other Investments	7.9%	4.3%	7.5%
	Intangibles	9.7%	9.8%	2.9%
	Deposits, Other Assets	12.0%	10.3%	9.8%
	Total Assets	**100%**	**100%**	**100%**
	Liabilities			
	Accounts Payable	6.2%	5.6%	4.7%
	Accrued Expenses	3.0%	3.3%	3.8%
	Income Taxes	6.1%	6.5%	6.6%
	Other Current Liabilities	7.9%	9.4%	8.4%
	Total Current Liabilities	**38.5%**	**40.7%**	**43.5%**
	Deferred Taxes on Income	1.7%	1.3%	1.9%
	Long-Term Debt	4.7%	6.5%	5.4%
	Other Long-Term Liabilities Plus Minority Interest and Postretirement Benefit Obligations	7.7%	8.2%	10.2%
	Total Liabilities	**52.6%**	**56.7%**	**61.0%**
	Common Stock Net	2.3%	0.3%	0.3%
	Capital Surplus	11.8%	9.7%	5.9%
	Retained Earnings	54.7%	53.9%	53.6%
	Treasury Stock	(10.1)%	(12.7)%	(15.8)%
	Other Liabilities	1.0%	1.3%	1.8%
	Employee Benefit Trust	(10.1)%	(9.19)%	(6.75)%
	Shareholders' Equity	**47.4%**	**43.3%**	**39.0%**
	Total Liabilities and Net Worth	**100%**	**100%**	**100%**

cost of goods sold has declined (from 21.6% in 1994 to 19.25% in 1996); selling, general, and administrative expenses have steadily decreased (from 39.91% in 1994 to 38.61% in 1996). Finally, we see that Pfizer is committed to research and development, and this expense is stable at around 14% to 15%.

EXHIBIT 21-9		1996	1995	1994
Percentage	Net Sales	100.00%	100.00%	100.00%
Income	Cost of Goods	19.25%	21.60%	21.60%
Statement for	Gross Profit	80.75%	78.40%	78.40%
Pfizer, Inc.	R&D Expenses	14.90%	14.40%	14.11%
	Selling, General, and Administrative	38.61%	38.47%	39.91%
	Other Deductions—Net	2.44%	2.60%	1.44%
	Income before Tax	24.80%	22.93%	22.94%
	Tax and Minority Interests	7.74%	7.43%	6.94%
	Net Income	17.06%	15.50%	16.00%

PRACTICE BOX

Problem

Suppose you are analyzing two firms with the following attributes. Which firm is more attractive? Why?

	Firm A	Firm B
P/E ratio	3	3
EPS growth rate last year	+10%	−20%
Debt-to-equity ratio	0.30	0.70
Sales	$100 million	$100 million
Cash on balance sheet	$20 million	$2 million

Solution

The low P/E ratio is a sign of a good investment. However, it also may be a sign of bankruptcy. We see from the financial data that Firm A is strong. Firm A has a low debt-to-equity ratio, shows a +10% growth rate in EPS, and holds a lot of cash. It is probably underpriced. These are not characteristics of Firm B, whose low P/E ratio probably indicates a good chance of bankruptcy.

The next practice box discusses some of the ratios used by practitioners.

PRACTICE BOX

What's the best way to measure a stock's value? Without hesitation, many investors would say, "Earnings." And earnings are certainly a good place to start. But looking at earnings alone can obscure some virtues and vices among publicly

(continued)

traded companies. That's why some of the world's savviest investors, corporate raiders included, prefer to look at a company's cash flow, a measure that strips away the sometimes-distortive effects of taxes and interest as well as depreciation taken for plant, property and equipment.

"Reported earnings really are an accounting fiction, avers Michael Metz, chief investment strategist at Oppenheimer & Co. "The single most important factor making a company attractive is its ability to generate discretionary cash flow: That is cash flow in excess of what's needed to conduct its business.

Companies with strong cash flow generally don't need to pour huge sums into building new plants or investing new products. That means there is plenty of cash left to reward shareholders through aggressive stock buybacks and higher dividends, which in turn lead to higher stock prices. To find such opportunities, Oppenheimer periodically screens the stock market in search of companies that look attractive on a cash-flow basis. The accompanying table lists 20 of the more than 100 companies that now make the brokerage firm's cut. The pared-down list includes some well-known companies, like Apple Computer, Dow Chemical, Phelps Dodge, and UAL, parent of United Airlines, as well as firms in such currently unfashionable industries as chemicals and steel. . . .

"We're focusing on the excess cash flow these companies can generate over the next two to four years, assuming the economy stays on a moderate growth track, and what they can do with the cash in terms of buying back stock or increasing dividends," Freeman says.

To make the Oppenheimer list (on the next page), a company's cash flow, which Oppenheimer defines as earnings before interest, taxes and depreciation, has to be at least 20% of the company's "adjusted" stock price. Put another way, a company's adjusted stock price can't be more than five times cash flow.

The *adjusted stock price* is generated by taking the stock price, adding in debt and preferred stock, and then subtracting out cash on the balance sheet. In adjusting the stock price for debt and cash, Oppenheimer looks at companies the way potential buyers do, because a purchaser must assume a company's debts but gains use of any cash in the till. Two companies may have the same stock price, but the one that has less debt and more cash is probably the more attractive of the two.

Oppenheimer also looks at free cash flow, which is cash flow less capital spending. It then generates a ratio of free cash flow to the adjusted stock prices. To make the grade, companies must have a ratio of 15% or better, about double the market average.

Metz thinks free cash is the better of the two valuation methods because it reflects the capital spending needed to keep companies competitive. Oppenheimer uses financial data for the twelve months ended June 30 for most of its calculations.

Oppenheimer's analysis is a bit like screening the stock market for companies with low price/earnings ratios, but Metz points out that many companies with

(continued)

CASH MACHINES

These companies generate hefty cash flow. Stock prices are adjusted by subtracting cash on the balance sheet and adding in debt. The higher the level of free cash flow relative to the adjusted share price, the better.

Company	Recent Price	Adj. Price	Gross Oper. Cash Flow[a]	Oper. Cash Flow/ Adj. Pr.	Free Cash Flow[a]	Free Cash Flow/ Adj. Price
AK Steel Corp	$ 31.00	$ 30.84	$ 13.13	43%	$ 8.59	28%
Amdahl	9.31	3.67	1.79	49	1.15	31
America West	13.75	18.67	4.93	26	2.90	16
Apple Computer	36.63	28.69	7.62	27	6.42	22
Cummins Engine	35.25	38.29	11.87	31	5.80	15
Cyrk	11.00	5.04	2.26	45	1.68	33
Dow Chemical	67.88	74.13	18.44	25	13.12	18
Georgia Gulf	33.50	41.92	10.19	24	8.60	21
Inland Steel	22.75	38.48	9.83	26	7.27	19
McClatchy News	19.50	15.56	3.60	23	2.52	16
Methanex	6.63	7.02	4.29	61	3.45	49
National Presto	41.00	13.42	3.31	25	2.95	22
Phelps Dodge	63.88	66.58	17.88	27	12.33	19
Rexene	9.38	17.58	8.24	47	6.31	36
Sterling Chem	8.13	10.42	5.21	50	4.60	44
Thiokol	34.63	37.49	7.74	21	5.88	16
UAL	177.38	370.82	117.63	32	55.93	15
USG	28.75	48.62	9.74	20	7.54	16
Wellpoint Hlth	31.13	10.08	3.94	39	3.69	37
Western Digital	15.50	9.31	3.56	38	2.45	26

a. Per share.

Source: Oppenheimer & Co.

low P/Es don't generate a lot of cash because they need to invest heavily to keep pace with rivals, while some companies with high P/Es have light capital expenditures and heavy depreciation, and therefore are significant cash generators. . . .

Source: Andrew Bary, "Cash in the Till," *Barron's*, November 6, 1995, p. 17. Reprinted by permission of *Barron's*, © 1995 Dow Jones & Co., Inc. All Rights Reserved Worldwide.

The following are selected data taken mainly from Micron Corporation's financial statements for 1997 (in millions of dollars):

(continued)

Earnings before Interest and Taxes (Operating Expense)	8,239
Depreciation	1,150
Interest Payment	1,522
Cash Holding ("cash in the till")	5,124
Capital Spending	2,500
Preferred Stocks	
Outstanding Debt	12,000

Additional Information

Number of outstanding shares	572,003,382
Current stock price (January 1, 1998)	$68

Problem

Read the excerpt from "Cash in the Till," and answer the following questions (use the data given about Micron):

a. Calculate the following two ratios for Micron Corporation: operating cash flow/adjusted stock price and free cash flow/adjusted stock price. In your answer, use Oppenheimer's definitions of *operating cash flow* and *free cash flow*. Would Micron be an attractive stock according to Oppenheimer's criteria?

b. Suppose that the capital spending every year is equal to the annual depreciation. Evaluate Michael Metz's assertion that "reported earnings really are an accounting fiction." In your calculation, compare reported earnings to free cash flow.

c. Suppose again that the annual capital spending is roughly equal to the annual depreciation. Also, suppose that in the last 10 years, the capital spending was about $2,500 million each year. Assume now that in 1997, the capital spending jumps to $6,150 million rather than $2,500 million. Recalculate the free cash flow/adjusted stock price ratio. Would Micron be on Oppenheimer's list? Discuss your results.

d. Micron sells for cash only. The management of Micron is considering selling for ninety-days' credit, because it believes this policy would boost sales. It is estimated that the new policy would cause the following changes in Micron's assets composition (in millions of dollars):

	Selling for Cash	Selling for Credit
Cash	5,124	500
Receivables	0	4,624
Total	5,124	5,124

One board member opposes the move because Micron would then be deleted from Oppenheimer's list; hence, the firm's value would go down, which contradicts the goal of the firm (that is, maximizing the stockholders' wealth). Carry out the relevant calculations, and discuss the board member's claim.

(continued)

e.   Micron's board of directors discusses the possibility of using $4,000 million of its cash for a stock repurchase at the market price of $68 per share. A board member claims, "With this operation the firm will have less cash. This will increase the adjusted stock price and decrease the ratio of free cash flow to adjusted stock price below 15%. The stock then will be deleted from the pro recommended list. Therefore, the stock repurchase is not recommended." Evaluate the board member's claim. Carry out the necessary calculations to support your answer.

SUMMARY

Name the three financial statements commonly used in security analysis, and describe which accounting values require scrutiny by investors.   The primary financial statements used in security analysis are the balance sheet, income statement, and statement of cash flows. The balance sheet presents the book value of assets and how the assets were financed. Many analysts convert the balance sheet into current market values. Important items to examine include inventory, property, plant and equipment, and intangibles. The methods of valuing these assets vary among firms in an industry, because they may use different accounting methods.

The income statement examines the flow of assets through the firm over a period of time. The income statement presents the sales, expenses, and profits of the firm over a stated time period (usually a quarter or a year). Two major items that require close scrutiny are research and development and depreciation expense.

The statement of cash flows examines the flow of cash through a firm, specifically the sources of cash (financings and retained earnings) and the uses of cash (dividends, inventory, and physical plant).

Explain how analysts interpret earnings per share. Earnings per share is the net income of the firm divided by the number of shares outstanding. Analysts studying a firm's financial statements look for clues on how to assess the quality of the reported earnings number. For example, analysts assess whether the firm uses conservative or liberal accounting methods. Also, analysts seek to determine whether the earnings could actually be paid as dividends (as opposed to just accounting earnings that are not distributable). Analysts also examine specific items to identify red flags regarding the quality of earnings.

Identify the most important ratios used in financial statement analysis, and discuss how these ratios are used. Ratios allow investors to compare companies of various sizes. There are three major categories of ratios: profitability, liquidity, and debt. Profitability ratios measure the earning power of the firm. Liquidity ratios measure the ability of the firm to pay its immediate liabilities. Debt ratios measure the financial risk of a firm.

CHAPTER AT A GLANCE

1. *Accounting Statements*
    a.   Balance sheet—book value of assets and how they were financed.
    b.   Income statement—flow of business, its revenues, expenses, and profits.
    c.   Statement of cash flows—flow of cash.

2. *Ratio analysis includes the following:*
   a. Profitability ratios:

   Return on Equity $=$ Net Income/Shareholders' Equity

   EPS $=$ Net Income/Number of Shares

   Net Profit Margin $=$ Net Income/Net Sales

   Return on Assets $=$ Net Income/Total Assets

   Return on Total Invested Capital $=$ (Net Income $+$ Interest on Long-Term Debt)/
   $\qquad\qquad\qquad\qquad\qquad\qquad$ Total Capitalization

   b. Liquidity ratios:

   Quick $=$ (Current Assets $-$ Inventory $-$ Other Current Assets)/Current Liabilities

   Current $=$ Current Assets/Current Liabilities

   Days' Sales in Inventory $=$ (Inventories/Net Sales)365

   Cash $=$ (Cash $+$ Marketable Securities)/Current Liabilities

   Inventory Turnover $=$ Cost of Goods Sold/Ending Inventory

   c. Debt ratios:

   Fixed Charge Coverage $=$ (Income before Tax $+$ Interest Expense)/
   $\qquad\qquad\qquad\qquad\quad$ (Interest Expense $+$ Leasehold Payments)

   Times Interest Earned $=$ (Income before Tax $+$ Interest Expense)/Interest Expense

   Debt to Equity $=$ Total Liabilities/Shareholders' Equity

   Debt to Assets $=$ Total Liabilities/Total Assets

KEY TERMS

Balance sheet   767
Common size statement   788
Direct method   780
Financial statement   766

Income statement   767
Indirect method   780
Percentage financial
   statement   788

Ratio analysis   784
Statement of cash flows   767

REVIEW

21.1 Suppose you were assigned the task of assessing the fair value of a manufacturing plant in Phoenix, Arizona, as part of a security analysis. Discuss ways of determining the property value without talking with the management of the firm.

21.2 Explain the role of research and development (R&D) within a corporation. How is it treated on the financial statements? Does more research and development automatically mean good things for shareholders? Discuss your answer.

21.3 Suppose Amoco Inc. changed its accounting auditors five times over the past 5 years. Is this a good or bad signal? Explain.

21.4 Suppose firms are allowed to report their income statement up to three months after the accounting period. These three months correspond to the reporting period. There are two groups of firms: Group A publishes the financial statements within a month of the end of the reporting period, and Group B publishes the financial statements at the very end of the reporting period. Which group would you anticipate had good news to report?

21.5 Suppose you analyze the auto industry and find the following current ratios: Ford = 1.1, Chrysler = 1.2, General Motors = 0.6, and Honda = 0.98. Which firm would you try to get more information on? Why?

21.6 When IBM started facing problems, it "was recording revenue when it shipped products merely to its own warehouses" (see Connecting Theory to Practice 21.1). How does such an accounting practice affect reported earnings and reported cash flows?

21.7 Which of the following activities affect the firm's balance sheet accounts, and which activities do not?
a. The firm issues $1 million in stock and uses the money to redeem $1 million in bonds.
b. The firm issues $1 million in bonds and uses the money to buy a new building.
c. The firm issues $1 million in bonds and keeps the money in cash.
d. The firm uses $1 million of current assets to pay $1 million of current liabilities.
e. The firm borrows an additional $1 million on a short-term basis and uses the money to pay long-term debt.
f. The economy experiences overall 10% inflation during the year. (All prices rise by 10%.)
g. Bad debts of $1 million are realized.

PRACTICE

21.1 Suppose you are given the following information about the inventory of FRM, Inc., a maker of heating elements:

		Total Cost
Inventory on January 1	30 elements at $750	$ 22,500
First Purchase in Year	85 elements at $780	$ 66,300
Second Purchase in Year	55 elements at $850	$ 46,750
Total available	170 elements	$135,550

a. Calculate the value of inventory at the end of the year by the FIFO, LIFO, and average cost methods if there are sixty elements in inventory on December 31.
b. Calculate the cost of goods sold given the information in Part a by each inventory method.
c. If FRM, Inc., sold each element for $900 and is in a 27% average tax bracket, what was the net income reported by each inventory method? (Assume no other costs.)

21.2 Suppose you know that a firm has $1,259 million in cash and marketable securities, $3,981 million in accounts receivable, and $8,551 million in total current assets.
a. If inventory is the only other current asset account, what is its balance sheet value?
b. How sensitive are inventories to management manipulation?
c. What are some red flags to examine when assessing the legitimacy of reported inventories?

Questions 21.3 through 21.5 are based on the data for RFS, Inc., on page 797.

21.3 Calculate the profitability, liquidity, and debt ratios given in Exhibit 21-6 for each of the 4 years. Assess the results. (Assume no preferred stock and no leasehold payments. Also assume that interest expense is 7% of outstanding long-term debt.)

Balance Sheet for RFS, Inc. (in millions of $)

	Year			
	4	3	2	1
Assets				
Cash	73	90	108	120
Marketable Securities	37	56	69	85
Receivables	74	57	51	48
Inventories	21	17	15	12
Other Current Assets	36	35	32	28
Total Current Assets	**241**	**255**	**275**	**293**
Net Property, Plant, and Equipment	96	91	84	81
Other Noncurrent Assets	18	1	0	0
Intangibles	10	26	20	15
Total Assets	**365**	**373**	**379**	**389**
Liabilities				
Accounts Payable	41	44	43	38
Accrued Expenses	56	30	28	25
Income Taxes	2	22	15	10
Other Current Liabilities	9	15	14	12
Total Current Liabilities	**108**	**111**	**100**	**85**
Long-Term Debt	12	16	18	20
Other Long-Term Liabilities	17	0	0	0
Total Liabilities	**137**	**127**	**118**	**105**
Common Stock Net	0.3	0.2	0.2	0.2
Capital Surplus	225	133	120	115
Retained Earnings	5	113	100	75
Other Liabilities	−2	0	41	94
Shareholder's Equity	**228**	**246**	**261**	**284**
Total Liabilities and Net Worth	**365**	**373**	**379**	**389**
Net Sales	483	457	378	321
Cost of Goods	104	109	113	95
Gross Profit	**379**	**348**	**265**	**226**
R&D Expenditures	60	66	59	57
Selling, General, and Administrative Expenses	307	174	111	98
Income before Nonoperating Income	12	108	95	71
Nonoperating Income	−137	10	−4	0.3
Income before Tax	**−125**	**118**	**91**	**71.3**
Provisions for Income Taxes	14	−13	0	0
Net Income	**−111**	**105**	**91**	**71.3**
Shares Outstanding (in millions)	26	23	13	12

21.4 Convert both the balance sheet and income statement for RFS, Inc., into percentage financial statements. Discuss any issues revealed about RFS, Inc.

21.5 Suppose you are considering investing in RFS, Inc., stock, and the price is $100 per share. Analyze the income statement and, in particular, the P/E ratio, the growth rate in earnings, and so forth. What is the single most important item for which you would like to get more information?

21.6 "The firm has accounts receivable of $10 million that are due in 1 year and $20 million that are due in six months. Therefore, on the balance sheet, the accounts receivable will be

$10 million + $20 million/2 = $20 million

Do you agree? Explain your answer.

21.7 The firm estimates that with a probability of 10%, the bad debt will be $1 million, and with a probability of 90%, there will be no bad debt. What will be the bad debt reported on the financial statements by the principle of conservatism?

21.8 Suppose a firm's revenues are $100,000. The inventory at the beginning of the year is $50,000, which is composed of 50,000 units at $1 per unit. The firm bought 50,000 additional units during the year, but this time, because of inflation, the cost was $1.2 per unit. The corporate tax rate is 36%. Assume that the firm has 40,000 units in ending inventory.
a. Assuming that the cost of goods sold is the only expense, calculate the following values according to the three inventory evaluation methods:
   (1) The firm's tax payment.
   (2) The firm's reported earnings.
   (3) The firm's cash flows.
b. As a firm manager, what method would you choose?
c. How would you change your answer to Part b if investors select stocks according to the P/E ratio?

21.9 The firm's total book value of assets is $100 million, and total liabilities are $50 million. The firm has issued 1 million shares, and the market price per share is $55. Calculate the market-to-book ratio.

21.10 Suppose you are given the following information regarding Galactoca, Inc.:

Net Income	$100 million
Depreciation	$20 million
Allocation for Bad Debts	$5 million
Stock Repurchases	$10 million
Investments on New Project	$30 million

Based solely on these figures, what is the net cash flow for this period?

21.11 Assume that a firm sells computers on 180 days' credit. Sales are $100 million, and expenses are $95 million. What is the accounting income? What is the economic income based on cash flow? (Assume that the appropriate discount rate is 7% per annum, and ignore default risk.)

21.12 Assume that you are given the following information about ABC, Inc.:

Year	Sales	Inventory
1	$100	$20
2	105	23
3	99	27
4	103	30

Is there anything alarming about these data?

21.13 Assume that the firm's historical stock price and EPS are as follows:

Year	EPS	Stock Price
1	$10	$100
2	10	95
3	9.5	70
4	9.0	65
5	9.0	40
6	9.0	30

Is there anything alarming in these data?

21.14 Suppose two firms, Firm A and Firm B, have the following characteristics:

	Stock Price	EPS	Bond's Rating
Firm A	$100	$20	C
Firm B	10	2	AAA

Using the P/E ratio, which investment seems to be a bargain, and for which firm may bankruptcy be forthcoming?

21.15 A firm has current assets of $10 million and current liabilities of $1 million. Thus, the current ratio is 10. Evaluate each of the following assertions about the firm:
a. "Therefore, the firm is very strong, and the stock is a buy recommendation."
b. "Therefore, the firm is strong, and it is worth lending the firm money for the long run."
c. "Therefore, the firm is very strong, and it is worth lending the firm money for the short run."

21.16 Suppose that a firm's net income is $100 million. The accounts receivable increases by $20 million, the depreciation is $10 million, the cost of goods sold is $20 million, and accounts payable increases by $2 million. Interest paid was $5 million, and dividends were $5 million. What is the net cash flow of this firm?

21.17 A firm's current liabilities were $50 million, and its current assets were $60 million. The firm has $40 million of inventory, of which $30 million has become worthless.
a. What is the current ratio?
b. What is the quick ratio?
c. Which ratio is more relevant in this case: the current ratio or the quick ratio?

For Internet questions visit the Levy Investment Web site at http://levy-invst.swcollege.com.

YOUR TURN: APPLYING THEORY TO PRACTICE
WHAT IF BEN GRAHAM HAD HAD A PC?

He might be scouring the databases for value stocks.
Ben Graham is the father of value investing and the author, along with David Dodd, of the value investor's bible, *Security Analysis.* Among his famous pupils: Warren Buffett, the billionaire "sage of Omaha." Graham's precepts are still sound, but his research methods could use some updating—Graham, after all, pored over annual reports and the *Standard & Poor's Stock Guide* to find his bargains. These days, a little computer know-how can eliminate the eyestrain. To see what Graham might turn up in today's market, I decided to test his techniques using state-of-the-art technology.

First, some background. Graham was conservative. He tried to find companies that were bargains because they were temporarily in trouble or out of favor. But he also wanted to make sure his company of choice had solid assets. The distillation of his wisdom is a set of 10 questions, summarized in the table on the following page, that he and James Rea prepared shortly before Graham's death in 1976.

The ideal stock would receive all "yes" answers. In the real world, that rarely happens. But some affirmative answers are more important than others. Graham, for example, adored companies that could answer "yes" to question five

(continued)

What to Buy: Graham's Guidelines

Reward Measures

1. Is the P/E less than half the reciprocal of the yield on triple-A corporate bonds? (At a current yield of 7.25%, that means a P/E of 6.9 or better.)

2. Is the P/E less than 40% of the average P/E over the past five years?

3. Is the dividend yield more than two-thirds the triple-A corporate-bond yield? (This now requires a dividend yield of 4.8% or higher.)

4. Is the price less than two-thirds of book value?

5. Is the price less than two-thirds of net current assets?

Risk Measures

1. Is the debt-to-equity ratio less than 1?

2. Are current assets more than twice current liabilities?

3. Is total debt less than twice net current assets?

4. Is the 10-year average EPS growth rate greater than 7%?

5. Were there no more than two years out of the past 10 with earnings declines greater than 5%?

Source: *Fundamentals of Investments* (Englewood Cliffs, N.J.: Prentice-Hall, 1993).

on the reward measures. Such companies sell for less than liquidation value—where cash, receivables and inventory exceed current liabilities and long-term debt. In theory, an investor gets the underlying business for free.

Not surprisingly, companies rarely get this cheap. Still, when I scanned MarketBase's 5,780-company universe on my PC, I found 70 companies selling for less than the value of their net current assets. I then eliminated companies that are not currently profitable and those that posted annual losses in more than two of the past five years. Then I tried to isolate companies with problems that might wipe out equity. What if inventory is worthless or receivables can't be collected? You can approach an answer to that question by showing inventory as a percentage of total equity (see table on page 801).

It's easy to see why investors have soured on some of these stocks. G-III and USA Classic both sell sports-oriented leisure wear—often to teenagers. That's a difficult market today. Astrosystems, Espey Manufacturing and Sunair make sophisticated electronic gear—the kind the Pentagon is buying less of these days. Advanced Marketing distributes books to warehouse clubs, which are suffering from sales declines.

But other stocks seem to be getting a bum rap. The future seems bright at New Jersey–based TransNet, which distributes computer gear and has just won a big contract, and at Equinox Systems, which offers products that help link PCs.

Think carefully before buying any of these stocks, though. Most of these companies are tiny; TransNet, for instance, has a market value of only $5.8 million. A little buying could have a major impact on prices. Remember, too, the value of diversification. Graham recommended owning

(continued)

Nine Stocks Ben Graham Might Buy Today

Company	Ticker Symbol	Industry	Price as of Jan. 14, 1994	Price/ Earnings	Net Current Assets	Ratio of Inventory to Equity	Revenue (millions of dollars)
Advanced Marketing	ADMS	Distribution	$4.88	8.78	0.78	2.16	$269.3
Astrosystems	ASTR	Electronic equipment	4.25	16.29	0.62	0.13	14.6
Equinox Systems	EQNX	Computer equipment	4.00	7.24	0.88	0.20	21.0
Espey Manufacturing	ESP	Electronic equipment	14.50	13.53	0.88	0.32	15.9
G-III	SJM	Apparel	4.38	25.88	0.88	0.83	123.2
Penobscot Shoe	PSO	Shoes	5.50	11.79	0.87	0.22	13.4
Sunair	SNR	Electronic equipment	2.25	10.97	0.94	0.52	5.9
TransNet	TRNT	Distribution	1.16	14.50	0.84	0.35	30.3
USA Classic	USCL	Apparel	4.75	20.83	0.97	0.70	76.3

Source: Data from Market Base. Paul Sturm, "What if Ben Graham Had a PC?" *SmartMoney*, March 1994. © 1994 by *SmartMoney*, a joint venture of the Hearst Corporation and Dow Jones & Company, Inc. All Rights Reserved.

a portfolio of net-current-assets companies to spread the risks—which can be significant.

Source: Paul Sturm, "What If Ben Graham Had a PC?" *SmartMoney*, March 1994. © 1994 by *SmartMoney*, a joint venture of the Hearst Corporation and Dow Jones & Co., Inc. All Rights Reserved.

The table on page 802 presents selected data for Eastman Kodak (EK). (Note that the publication date is March 1998; therefore, 1998 and 1999 data are estimates only.)

Questions

1. Answer each of the ten questions from "What to Buy: Graham's Guidelines," using the data on Eastman Kodak. For your calculations, use 1997 as the last year. (1998 is only an estimate.)

2. How can you explain that in 1997 the EPS of EK increased, whereas the sales per share fell drastically? Is this a good or a bad sign from the potential investor's point of view? In answering this question, refer also to the net profit margin data.

3. What can be concluded from the capital spending per share?

4. How would you use the following information?

a. The board of directors has asked the chairman of Eastman Kodak to resign.

b. Eastman Kodak has asked the Commerce Department to impose steep tariffs on competing goods imported from Japan.

c. Taking the information in Parts a and b as well as Ben Graham's ten questions into account, do you think that Eastman Kodak should be on the buy list or the sell list?

(continued)

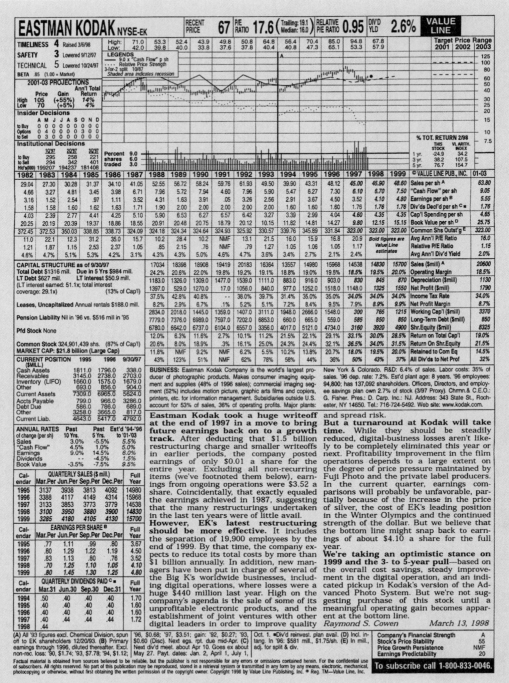

Source: *Value Line*, March 13, 1998, p. 13. © 1998 Value Line Publishing, Inc. Reprinted with permission.

SELECTED REFERENCES

Bernstein, Leopold A. *Financial Statement Analysis: Theory, Application, and Interpretation.* 4th ed. Homewood, Ill.: Irwin, 1989.

This excellent accounting book focuses on helping the user of accounting information interpret the information.

Cottle, Sidney, Roger F. Murray, and Frank E. Block. *Graham and Dodd's Security Analysis.* 5th ed. New York: McGraw-Hill, 1988.

This reworking of a classic applies the basic principles of security analysis in determining security value.

Klarman, Seth A. *Margin of Safety: Risk-Averse Value Investing Strategies for the Thoughtful Investor.* New York: Harper Business, 1991.

This book addresses security analysis from a very practical point of view. Specifically, it discusses how to find underpriced securities to achieve long-term success in investing.

Knutson, Peter H. *Financial Reporting in the 1990s and Beyond.* Charlottesville, Va.: Association for Investment Management and Research, 1993.

This is a position monograph on the relationship between financial analysis and financial reporting that attempts to express the collective views of the membership of the Association for Investment Management and Research. This monograph is an excellent synthesis of this subject.

Lynch, Peter. *One Up on Wall Street.* New York: Penguin Books, 1989.

This national best-seller by the person who managed Fidelity Magellan (a very successful stock mutual fund) is helpful in teaching investors to use information that is not necessarily provided by Wall Street to spot investment value.

SUPPLEMENTAL REFERENCES

Bernstein, Leopold A. "A Financial Analysts' Guide to Accounting Quality." *Business Credit* 94, no. 2 (February 1992): 11–13.

Dennis, Michael C. "Understanding Cash Flow Statements." *Business Credit* 96, no. 1 (January 1994): 40–42.

Evans, Frank C. "Analyzing a Financial Statement." *Management Review* 82, no. 11 (November 1993): 52–53.

Jennings, Ross, Marc J. Leclery, and Robert B. Thomson II. "Evidence on the Usefulness of Alternative Earnings per Share Measures." *Financial Analysts Journal,* November–December 1997, pp. 24–33.

Jensen, Gerald R., Robert R. Johnson, and Jeffrey M. Mercer. "New Evidence on Size and Price/Book Effects in Stock Returns." *Financial Analysts Journal,* November–December 1997, pp. 34–42.

"Market Focus: All the World's a Ratio." *Economist* 322, no. 7747 (February 22, 1992): 72.

Miller, Barry. "Cause-and-Effect Ratio Analysis Adds Decision-Making Value to Credit Scoring Models." *Business Credit* 96, no. 2 (February 1994): 27–29.

Penman, Stephen H. "Financial Statement Information and the Pricing of Earnings Changes." *Accounting Review* 67, no. 3 (July 1992): 563–577.

Shivaswamy, Melkote, James P. Hobun, Jr., and Keishiro Matsumoto. "A Behavioral Analysis of Financial Ratios." *Mid-Atlantic Journal of Business* 29, no. 1 (March 1993): 7–25.

Speidell, Lawrence S., and Vinod B. Bavishi. "GAAP Arbitrage: Valuation Opportunities in International Accounting Standards." *Financial Analysts Journal* 48 (November–December 1992): 58–66.

Woelfel, Charles J. "Analysis Looks behind the Numbers." *Business Credit* 95, no. 2 (February 1993): 4–5.

CHAPTER 22

FORWARD AND FUTURES CONTRACTS

LEARNING OBJECTIVES

After studying this chapter you should be able to:

1. Explain the terminology of futures contracts.

2. Describe the process of buying and selling futures.

3. Explain margin and mark to market amounts.

4. Describe the basic strategies involving futures contracts.

5. Calculate futures values using the futures pricing equations.

INVESTMENTS IN THE NEWS

COMMODITIES AND FINANCIAL FUTURES

Commodities, or futures, contracts originally called for delivery of physical items, such as agricultural products and metals, at a specified price at a specified future date. Increasingly, these contracts have come to apply also to Treasury bills, notes and bonds, certificates of deposit, major market indices and major currencies. Our futures options list includes only the week's most actively traded options with a minimum trade volume of 500 contracts.

Source: *Barron's,* July 6, 1998, p. MW84.

CHICAGO'S TWO FUTURES EXCHANGES AGREE TO CONSOLIDATE THEIR CLEARINGHOUSES

Chicago's two futures exchanges reached a tentative agreement to merge back-office operations.

After more than 20 hours of negotiations at an industry conference in Boca Raton, Fla., last week, the Chicago Board of Trade and the Chicago Mercantile Exchange agreed to combine clearing entities, the divisions that process and financially back trades. . . .

A unified clearinghouse between the two largest U.S. futures exchanges is aimed at cutting costs by reducing staff and increasing standardization. "Bringing the Chicago exchanges together with their clearing firms . . . is a great achievement," that will enhance the futures business in the U.S., said Laurence Mollner, chairman of the Futures Industry Association.

Source: Aaron Lucchetti, "Chicago's Two Futures Exchanges Agree to Consolidate Their Clearing Houses," *Wall Street Journal,* March 23, 1998, p. C15. Reprinted by permission of *The Wall Street Journal,* © 1998 Dow Jones & Co., Inc. All Rights Reserved Worldwide.

USING DERIVATIVES BY DOW

Dow decided to use derivatives to hedge strategic and competitive risks out as long as three years.

A visitor to Dow's out-of-the-way headquarters in Midland, Mich., finds finance-department trainees seated at trading desks behind computers that rival those of any of the major banks. Like traders anywhere, Dow's youngsters shout into telephones, stare into blinking trading screens, pore over new feeds and try

(continued)

to outguess the markets. They use the whole gamut of derivatives—futures, swaps, options and hundreds of elaborate mathematical combinations thereof—all in an effort to protect the company's bottom line from currency moves, interest-rate spikes, oil-price volatility, taxes and the myriad shocks capital is heir to.

Hedging with derivatives has become so important that companies can be taken to court if they don't hedge. A class-action suit filed in 1991 against Compaq complained that the company "lacked sufficient and adequate foreign-currency hedging mechanisms."

Source: Gregory J. Millman, "The Risk Not Taken," *Barron's,* May 1, 1995, p. 46. Reprinted by permission of *Barron's,* © 1995 Dow Jones & Co., Inc. All Rights Reserved Worldwide.

Derivatives are financial assets whose price is derived from the price of another asset, hence the name "derivative." The derivative market is very colorful. There are options, futures, forward contracts, options on futures, and many more complicated assets (see, for example, Exhibit 22-4 later in the chapter). As mentioned above, the derivatives have one thing in common: their price is derived from another asset, called the *underlying asset,* which can be oil, wheat, German marks, a stock index, and so on. The derivatives can be employed to reduce risk or as speculative investments that drastically enhance risk. If you gamble and are wrong in the position you take (for example, you predict the stock index will fall, but it actually rises), you may lose a good deal. To mention just one example, Barings Bank collapsed in 1995 after losing more than a billion dollars in the futures market.

The main categories of derivatives are futures and forward contracts and options contracts. Futures and forward contracts are distinctly different from options contracts. With an options contract the buyer has the *right* to buy some asset, such as common stock, in the future, whereas with futures and forward contracts the buyer is *obligated* to buy some asset in the future. Because futures and forward contracts are obligatory, they are often considered risky. Therefore, many state legislatures prohibit placing retirement money in futures and forward contracts.

This chapter introduces futures contracts and describes how traders can gain or lose from investments in futures. It surveys the different futures markets and their organizational structures, and in particular the role that margin plays in reducing default risk. It also looks at several investment strategies that employ futures contracts, including hedging, speculating, arbitrage, and portfolio diversification. The pricing of derivative assets is not a simple task. Indeed, Robert Merton and Myron Scholes were awarded the 1997 Nobel Prize in economics mainly for their contribution in the area of derivatives.

The chapter begins with a discussion of forward contracts, which are the simplest contracts used to hedge (or increase) risk. A knowledge about forward contracts and their limitations is the basis for an understanding of more complicated contracts, such as futures and options. Futures are discussed in this chapter, whereas options and options on futures are discussed in the next two chapters.

22.1 FORWARD CONTRACTS

In conducting a cash transaction, a buyer pays cash when the seller delivers goods. In contrast, when engaging in a **forward contract,** the buyer and the seller agree to exchange goods for cash at some future date (say, January 1 of the next year), at a predetermined price. The short position means that the investor has to deliver the good while long position means that the investor has a commitment to receive the good. Thus, the seller of the contract is in a **short position,** whereas the buyer is in a **long position.** Various forward contracts can be made, but the most common are foreign exchange forward contracts.

Exhibit 22-1 reports data on forward contracts. For example, on November 24, 1997, 1 U.S. dollar could be traded for 1.738 German marks (DM). That was the *current exchange rate* for cash transactions, also called the *spot rate.* The *forward exchange rate*—or, simply, the *forward rate*—between these two currencies depended on the delivery date. If you wished to buy or sell dollars for delivery one month later, on December 24, 1997, you could close a deal for 1.7346 DM per dollar. If you wished a delivery date six months later (May 24, 1997), the forward rate was 1.7213 DM per dollar. The following Practice Box demonstrates how forward contracts can be used to hedge foreign currency risk.

PRACTICE BOX	
Problem	A U.S. investor buys agricultural machinery in the United States for $1 million and sells it to a Japanese client. The U.S. investor pays in cash but sells the machines to the Japanese client on six months' credit terms. The sale is for 120 million yen.

a. The discount rate is 5% for the six-month period. What will be the NPV if the future exchange rate remains at 126.40 yen per dollar?
b. What will be the NPV if the exchange rate six months from now is 80 yen per dollar? If it is 130 yen per dollar?
c. Suppose also that the forward rate six months from now is 113.86 yen per dollar. Show how the U.S. investor can guarantee a positive NPV by using a forward contract.

(continued)

EXHIBIT 22-1 Spot and Forward Exchange Rates against the Dollar		Closing	1 Month	3 Months	6 Months
	Germany (DM)	1.738	1.7346	1.7230	1.7213
	Japan (Y)	126.40	125.86	124.63	122.99

Source: *Barron's,* November 24, 1997, p. MW97. Reprinted by permission of *Barron's,* © 1997 Dow Jones & Co., Inc. All Rights Reserved Worldwide.

Solution   a. The investor will receive 120 million yen six months from now at the exchange rate of 126.40 yen per dollar. The investor will receive about $0.949 million (120 million yen/126.40 yen per dollar).

If the investor invests $1 million today, the NPV of this transaction is as follows:

$$\frac{\$0.949 \text{ million}}{1.05} - \$1 \text{ million} \cong -\$96,190.48$$

In reality the loss would be even larger, because in June 1997 (about six months after the publication of the exchange rate given in Exhibit 22-1), the exchange rate was 140 yen to the dollar. This means that the investor gets about $0.857 million, and the loss would be

$$\frac{\$0.857 \text{ million}}{1.05} - \$1 \text{ million} = -\$183,809.95$$

b. If the exchange rate six months from now is 80 yen per dollar, the investor will receive $1.5 million (120 million yen/80 yen per dollar = $1.5 million). The NPV is

$$\frac{\$1.5 \text{ million}}{1.05} - \$1 \text{ million} \cong \$428,571$$

If the exchange rate is 130 yen per dollar, the investor will receive about $0.923 million (120 million yen/130 yen per dollar). The NPV is

$$\frac{\$0.923 \text{ million}}{1.05} - \$1 \text{ million} \cong -\$120,879.12$$

With no hedging, the investor may profit ($428,571) or may lose ($120,879) if there are adverse changes in the foreign currency exchange rate.

c. The investor cannot know the future exchange rate. Moreover, the investor does not want macroeconomic factors such as international trade or government monetary policy to interfere with her operation. Therefore, the investor can hedge the risk by buying a forward contract to sell yen at a predetermined price six months from now.

Suppose the investor buys a contract to sell 120 million yen at 113.86 yen per dollar six months from now. The investor will receive about $1,053,925.87 (120 million yen/113.86 yen per dollar). The NPV is

$$\frac{\$1,053,925.87}{1.05} - \$1 \text{ million} \cong \$3,738.93$$

If the investor uses a forward contract, she eliminates foreign currency risk.

The preceding Practice Box demonstrates how an investor can completely eliminate foreign exchange risk by using forward contracts. In this specific case, the U.S. investor's profits may even increase in comparison with a transaction at the current exchange rate. However, if the forward rate were higher—say, 128 yen per dollar—the investor's profit would decline relative to a transaction at the current exchange rate.

Who is taking this risk? You buy a forward contract from your bank. Does this mean that the bank is exposed to the risk? No, it does not; the bank is operating as a mediator. It finds another customer (say, a Japanese investor who exports to the U.S. on credit) who wishes to sell dollars six months from now. Both sides eliminate risk through the transaction. This risk reduction is in effect as long as neither of the parties defaults.

Forward contracts have a major deficiency. If prices fall sharply, one party has a strong incentive to default. For example, suppose Cone Mills has a forward contract to buy cotton from Cotton Corporation in July at 76.4 cents per pound. Suppose the current price of cotton is 75 cents per pound, but it falls in July to 40 cents per pound. Cone Mills can buy cotton in July at 40 cents in the market, but it is committed to pay 76.4 cents per pound to Cotton Corporation. Cone Mills has a strong incentive to default—to walk away from this transaction. Firms and institutions that know and trust each other engage in forward transactions. When such trust does not exist, a firm needs a financial tool that minimizes the incentive to default. This is exactly what a futures contract does.

22.2 FUTURES CONTRACTS

Futures contracts exist on a wide variety of items: agricultural products (corn, oats, wheat, livestock and meat, coffee, orange juice, cotton, and sugar), metals and petroleum (gold, silver, and crude oil), and financial assets (various currencies, Treasury bonds, and various stock indexes). Like a forward contract, a **futures contract** can be used to hedge risk. Both contracts commit buyer and seller to exchange goods for cash at some future date at a predetermined price. The futures contract, however, has the following differences: it is traded on a financial exchange, it offers more flexibility in its delivery date, and its cash flows differ.

22.2.1 Characteristics of Futures Contracts

Futures contracts are traded on organized exchanges, whereas forward contracts are not. Therefore, the prices of futures contracts are reported daily in the financial media, as shown in Exhibit 22-2. Because they have an organized market, futures contracts are more liquid than forward contracts; buyers of futures contracts can "net out" their position by *selling* a similar futures contract. For example, a buyer who has a July contract to buy cotton and a July contract to sell cotton would not have to make a delivery of cotton.

EXHIBIT 22-2   **Futures Contracts for Orange Juice (15,000 lb; cents per lb)**

| Season's | | | Week's | | | | |
High	Low	Month	High	Low	Sett	Net Chg.	Open Int.
119.75	69.10	Jan 98	86.50	78.05	81.65	−0.5	22,836
100.25	22.2	Mar 98	89.15	81.30	84.60	−0.4	13,301
97.50	75.3	May 98	91.90	84.50	88.00	−0.1	3,337
105.00	78.25	Jul 98	94.75	87.60	90.75	−0.35	1,765
99.15	80.80	Sep 98	96.50	90.00	93.00	−0.6	834
99.90	83.40	Nov 98	99.25	91.80	94.80	−1.30	890
102.50	85.50	Jan 99	100.65	93.00	97.30	−1.30	187

Fri. to Thurs. sales 29,668

Total open interest 43,269

Each contract is for 15,000 outstanding pounds of orange juice.

Source: *Barron's*, November 24, 1997, p. MW97. Reprinted by permission of *Barron's*, © 1997 Dow Jones & Co., Inc. All Rights Reserved Worldwide.

The second difference between forward and futures contracts relates to delivery dates. Forward contracts specify precise delivery dates. With futures contracts, the seller can choose any delivery date during the specified *delivery month*. If the seller of a July cotton futures contract notifies the exchange clearinghouse that he will deliver the cotton on July 15, the clearinghouse notifies one of the contract buyers to be ready to receive the cotton in a few days. (The clearinghouse selects one of the many July buyers at random.) Choosing the delivery date at any day during the month gives the seller some flexibility.

The third difference between forward and futures contracts is in their cash flows. With forward contracts, one party delivers the product and the other pays cash for it on the delivery date. Futures contracts, in contrast, are marked to market on a daily basis. With a **mark-to-market** cash settlement, cash flows in and out (between buyer and seller) on a daily basis whenever there are changes in the futures contract prices. As will be explained later, this mark-to-market daily cash settlement drastically reduces the risk of default. It was noted earlier that forward contracts should be conducted between "friends" who trust each other. In contrast, futures contracts can be executed between strangers, because the incentive to default is relatively small. This feature makes futures contracts the better financial tool.

Exhibit 22-3 demonstrates the cash flows to the buyer and the seller of a futures contract. Suppose that on November 26, 1998, Cone Mills buys a July 1999 futures contract at 90.75 cents per pound. If it had been a forward contract, then on July 16 the buyer would pay $13,612.5 (90.75 cents per pound · 15,000 pounds) per contract. Instead, with a futures contract, cash flows are involved each time the price

EXHIBIT 22-3	Cash Flows to Buyer and Seller of Cotton Futures Contracts: Mark-to-Market Daily Cash Settlements			
Closing Price (cents per pound)	**November 24** 90.75	**March 1** 93.75	**May 1** 90.25	**July 16** 90.25
Buyer	Buyer purchases cotton futures contracts at 90.75 cents per pound.	Buyer receives 3 cents per pound from the clearing-house within one business day.	Buyer must pay the clearinghouse 3.50 cents per pound within one business day.	Buyer pays 90.75 cents per pound and receives the cotton.
Seller	Seller sells futures contracts at 90.75 cents per pound.	Seller pays the clearinghouse 3 cents per pound within one business day.	Seller receives from the clearinghouse 3.50 cents per pound within one business day.	Seller receives 90.25 cents per pound of cotton and delivers the cotton to the buyer within one business day.
Buyer's cash flow per 15,000-pound contract	—	3 cents per pound · 15,000 pounds = $450	3.50 cents per pound · 15,000 pounds = −$525	−90.25 cents per pound · 15,000 pounds = −$13,537.5
Seller's cash flow per 15,000-pound contract	—	−$450	$525	$13,537.5

changes. For simplicity, assume the price changes only twice. (In reality, the price is likely to change daily, and the same technique for determining the cash flow would be used on a daily basis.) Suppose that on March 1 the price rises to 93.75 cents. The seller, who loses from such an increase (because she is committed to sell at a lower price), must pay 3 cents per pound to a clearinghouse that, in turn, pays the sum to the buyer. Then, on May 1, the price drops to 90.25 cents, and the buyer pays the clearinghouse 3.50 cents per pound, which is passed along to the seller. Assuming no further changes in price, the buyer pays the seller 90.25 cents per pound on July 16, and the seller delivers the cotton. The total cash flow paid by the buyer for all dates is $13,612.5 ($450 − $525 − $13,537.5). This amount is exactly what the buyer would have paid in a forward contract. Similarly, the seller receives $13,612.5, just as she would have received in a forward contract.

However, there are two differences between the cash flows of forward and futures contracts. The first difference is that in futures contracts, the interim cash flows cannot be ignored, and the present value of interim cash flows in a futures contract may be different from the present value of cash flows in a forward contract. The more important difference is that the incentive to default is lower with futures contracts, because the daily losses are not very large. With forward contracts all losses are accumulated to one payment on the delivery date, producing a stronger incentive to default.

Exhibit 22-3 presents the mark-to-market cash flows between the buyer and the seller. However, on top of these cash flows, each trader establishes a margin account typically of 5% to 10% of the contract value that is paid to the clearinghouse. The margin is a security account consisting of near-cash securities to insure that traders are able to satisfy their obligations under futures contracts. Because both parties are exposed to possible losses, both must post a margin. However, because the margin is in terms of interest-earnings securities, it does not impose a substantial cost on the traders.

Continuing the previous example, Cone Mills has hedged its risk against an increase in the price of cotton by buying a futures contract at 90.75 cents per pound. But what happens if the price of a pound of cotton falls to 40 cents? Cone Mills is locked into this transaction and must pay 90.75 cents per pound. Is there a way for Cone Mills to hedge possible increases in the cotton price while also enjoying the lower price of cotton if the price falls? As will be shown later on, options can provide Cone Mills a hedge against price increases and a benefit if the price falls. However, because there are no free lunches in the market, these options cost money. We devote the next two chapters to options.

22.2.2 Reading Financial Data on Futures

The financial media provide data on futures contracts. Exhibit 22-4 shows trading information for various futures contracts. The major types of futures contracts are (1) grains and oilseeds, (2) livestock and meat, (3) food and fiber, (4) metals and petroleum, (5) currencies, (6) interest rates, and (7) stock indexes.

Many financial institutions find interest rate futures useful in managing their exposure to changes in interest rates. Multinational corporations and international investors use currency futures to manage their exposure to changes in foreign exchange rates. Equity investors find stock index futures useful when managing the systematic risk of their portfolios. If investors have adverse exposures, they can invest in futures contracts to help offset these exposures.

The format for reporting futures trading information is to give the opening price at the beginning of the day followed by the high and low for the day. (See the top of Exhibit 22-4.) Next, the settle price and the change from the previous day are given. For example, the futures contracts for December 1998 delivery of corn opened at 221 cents, reached a high of 222¾ cents during the day and a low of 220 cents. December 1998 corn contracts settled at 220½ cents, down ¾ cent from the previous day. The **settle price** is an average of the trading prices that occur during the last few minutes of the day. After this, the contract's lifetime high and low are given, followed by the open interest. December 1998 corn has been as high as 299½ and as low as 220 cents per bushel. Open interest on this contract is 159,606. **Open interest,** which is reported in the last column, is the number of contracts outstanding. It is half of the total number of positions both purchased and sold (which are the same). Note that each corn futures contract is for 5,000 bushels of corn.

A futures contract, as has been discussed, is mark to market. Profits and losses are taken daily. When we purchase a stock for $100 per share and sell it in 1 year at $110, we have a profit of $10, which we receive at the end of the year. With futures

EXHIBIT 22-4   **Futures Prices as Reported in the Financial Press for August 5, 1998**

Wednesday, August 5, 1998

Open Interest Reflects Previous Trading Day.

GRAINS AND OILSEEDS

CORN (CBT) 5,000 bu.; cents per bu.

	Open	High	Low	Settle	Change	Lifetime High	Low	Open Interest
Sept	213	214½	211	211½	− 2	301	211	85,934
★ Dec	221	222¾	220	220½	− ¾	299½	220	159,606
Mr99	232¼	233½	231¼	231¾	− ¼	305	231	38,735
May	240	240½	238¾	239½	....	299	238½	11,113
July	244¼	245¾	244	244¾	+ ¼	312	243¾	16,454
Sept	248½	248¾	248¼	248½	....	280	248¼	1,661
Dec	254	254	253	254	+ ½	291½	252¾	6,308
Dc00	261	261	255	258	− 6	279½	255	172

Est vol 55,000; vol Tue 319,983, +2,048.

OATS (CBT) 5,000 bu.; cents per bu.

	Open	High	Low	Settle	Change	Lifetime High	Low	Open Interest
Sept	105½	106	101½	101¾	− 3½	177	101½	3,749
Dec	115	115	110¼	110½	− 3½	177½	110¼	8,826
Mr99	123	123	119	119	− 3¾	166½	119	1,871

Est vol 1,200; vol Tue 14,549, −3.

SOYBEANS (CBT) 5,000 bu.; cents per bu.

	Open	High	Low	Settle	Change	Lifetime High	Low	Open Interest
Aug	564	564	555	555½	− 9	745	555	8,562
Sept	550½	551	542½	543¼	− 8¼	723	542½	16,467
Nov	547¾	548½	538½	541¼	− 6½	717	538½	78,730
Ja99	555	557¾	548½	551	− 6¾	701½	548½	10,878
Mar	567½	567¾	559	560¾	− 7	694	559	8,781
May	573½	574	568	569	− 6	671	568	2,385
July	582	582	576	576¼	− 6¾	728	576	4,432
Nov	590½	591½	586	587¾	− 3¾	680	586	2,409

Est vol 46,000; vol Tue 45,626; open int 132,708, −1,444.

WHEAT (CBT) 5,000 bu.; cents per bu.

	Open	High	Low	Settle	Change	Lifetime High	Low	Open Interest
Sept	247	248¾	246	246¾	− ½	403	246	45,270
Dec	263	265	262½	263¼	....	417	262½	52,409
Mr99	278½	280¼	278	278¾	....	384½	278	19,024
May	289	289¼	287½	287½	− ½	355	287½	3,365
July	300	300	297½	299	....	389	297½	7,334

Est vol 13,500; vol Tue 19,782; open int 127,628, −920.

LIVESTOCK AND MEAT

CATTLE-FEEDER (CME) 50,000 lbs.; cents per lb.

	Open	High	Low	Settle	Change	Lifetime High	Low	Open Interest
Aug	68.10	69.42	68.10	69.37	+ 1.45	83.25	65.77	7,300
Sept	67.95	69.05	67.90	69.05	+ 1.50	83.05	65.60	3,527
Oct	68.15	69.20	68.10	69.20	+ 1.50	83.00	65.77	5,187
Nov	70.20	71.05	69.80	70.95	+ 1.40	83.60	67.60	2,472
Ja99	71.15	72.20	71.05	72.05	+ 1.35	81.75	68.60	1,150
Mar	70.90	72.20	70.85	72.10	+ 1.40	79.55	69.00	233
May	72.00	72.10	71.80	72.10	+ 1.35	76.25	69.05	116

Est vol 3,887; vol Tue 4,498; open int 20,037, −538.

CATTLE-LIVE (CME) 40,000 lbs.; cents per lb.

	Open	High	Low	Settle	Change	Lifetime High	Low	Open Interest
Aug	60.35	61.32	60.35	61.32	+ 1.50	72.15	57.82	18,257
Oct	61.00	61.97	60.80	61.97	+ 1.50	74.05	58.42	39,367
Dec	62.10	63.35	62.00	63.35	+ 1.50	74.20	59.80	16,168
Fb99	64.00	65.32	63.70	64.95	+ 1.12	73.50	61.95	9,382
Apr	65.70	67.20	65.45	66.27	+ .52	73.25	63.77	3,843
June	64.50	64.85	63.80	64.37	+ .37	70.20	62.50	926

Est vol 14,894; vol Tue 20,347; open int 88,011, −3,415.

FOOD AND FIBER

COCOA (CSCE)-10 metric tons; $ per ton.

	Open	High	Low	Settle	Change	Lifetime High	Low	Open Interest
Sept	1,560	1,570	1,552	1,553	− 1	1,836	1,456	22,314
Dec	1,600	1,609	1,590	1,592	....	1,863	1,510	24,745
Mr99	1,642	1,649	1,633	1,633	+ 1	1,901	1,605	13,348
May	1,665	1,665	1,660	1,661	+ 2	1,911	1,653	5,403
July	1,689	1,689	1,689	1,688	+ 2	1,850	1,675	1,748
Sept	....	....		1,714	+ 2	1,858	1,695	1,677
Dec	....	....		1,742	+ 2	1,885	1,740	4,750
Mr00	....	....		1,770	+ 2	1,910	1,747	2,099

Est vol 5,849; vol Tu 9,085; open int 76,084, −953.

METALS AND PETROLEUM

COPPER-HIGH (Cmx.Div.NYM)-25,000 lbs.; cents per lb.

	Open	High	Low	Settle	Change	Lifetime High	Low	Open Interest
Aug	74.50	74.50	73.70	73.60	+ .20	102.00	71.35	1,658
Sept	73.75	75.20	73.15	74.00	+ .10	102.10	71.20	20,911
Oct	74.00	75.10	74.00	74.20	+ .10	99.40	72.00	2,138
Nov	74.60	74.75	74.25	74.35	+ .05	98.80	72.85	1,566
Dec	74.15	75.70	74.15	74.65	+ .05	102.00	72.30	13,563

Ja99	75.10	75.10	74.90	74.95	+ .15	96.80	73.40	1,835
Feb	75.00	75.00	75.00	75.10	+ .15	94.60	73.60	923
Mar	75.55	75.90	75.50	75.25	+ .05	98.20	73.30	3,708
Apr	....	....		75.45	+ .05	96.00	73.80	902
May	76.10	76.10	75.85	75.60	+ .05	98.50	73.70	2,018
June	76.00	76.00	76.00	75.70	+ .05	91.00	74.40	744
July	76.10	76.40	76.10	75.80	+ .05	95.75	74.20	2,008
Aug	76.30	76.30	76.30	75.85	+ .05	90.50	74.25	583
Sept	76.30	76.30	76.30	75.90	+ .05	94.60	74.35	1,513
Oct	76.30	76.30	76.30	75.95	+ .05	90.00	74.75	381
Nov	76.30	76.30	76.30	76.00	+ − .05	86.90	75.00	383
Dec	76.50	76.50	76.15	76.05	+ .05	86.00	74.70	1,645

Est vol 8,000; vol Tu 8,855; open int 56,559, −900.

GOLD (Cmx.Div.NYM)-100 troy oz.; $ per troy oz.

	Open	High	Low	Settle	Change	Lifetime High	Low	Open Interest
Aug	288.10	289.50	287.60	288.20	− .60	403.80	284.50	3,368
Oct	291.10	292.40	289.00	289.70	− .70	367.80	285.00	11,325
Dec	293.20	294.80	291.10	291.80	− .70	505.00	286.80	98,847
Fb99	293.50	293.50	293.30	293.60	− .70	349.50	290.80	13,825
Apr	296.00	296.00	296.00	295.60	− .70	351.20	291.50	8,974
June	296.90	296.90	296.90	297.50	− .70	520.00	294.50	12,373
Aug	....	....		299.30	− .70	327.00	298.80	1,997
Oct	....	....		301.10	− .70	304.70	301.50	218
Dec	304.50	304.50	302.90	302.80	− .70	506.00	299.50	7,356
Fb00	....	....		304.50	− .70	312.00	310.60	315
Apr	....	....		306.30	− .70	307.00	307.00	490
June	....	....		308.00	− .70	473.50	309.50	7,303
Dec	....	....		313.20	− .70	474.50	311.50	4,882
Ju01	....	....		318.30	− .70	447.00	347.00	2,212
Dec	....	....		323.30	− .70	429.50	320.00	4,672
Ju02	....	....		328.60	− .70	385.00	335.00	1,460
Dec	....	....		333.90	− .70			215

Est vol 23,000; vol Tu 46,951; open int 179,832, +2,141.

SILVER (Cmx.Div.NYM)-5,000 troy oz.; cnts per troy oz.

	Open	High	Low	Settle	Change	Lifetime High	Low	Open Interest
Aug	....	....		539.5	− 4.8	536.0	529.0	2
Sept	545.0	550.0	538.5	540.5	− 4.8	728.0	453.0	40,165
Dec	549.0	553.0	541.5	544.0	− 4.7	734.0	448.5	26,465
Mr99	550.0	550.0	543.5	546.0	− 4.5	690.0	473.0	4,789
May	....	....		547.6	− 4.5	656.0	493.0	1,703

Est vol 13,000; vol Tu 14,072; open int 81,012, +730.

GAS OIL (IPE) 100 metric tons; $ per ton

	Open	High	Low	Settle	Change	Lifetime High	Low	Open Interest
Aug	108.00	110.00	105.25	109.50	+ .50	182.00	105.25	23,896
Sept	111.75	113.75	109.50	113.75	+ 1.00	184.00	109.50	24,784
Oct	116.50	118.00	114.25	118.00	+ 1.00	179.75	114.25	21,099
Nov	119.50	122.55	118.50	121.75	+ .50	175.00	118.50	14,091
Dec	123.50	125.50	122.00	125.00	+ .75	162.00	122.00	35,547
Ja99	126.50	128.00	125.00	127.75	+ .75	160.50	125.00	12,574
Feb	128.00	128.75	127.50	130.50	+ 1.00	186.00	12750	10,118
Mar	130.25	132.00	129.75	132.25	+ 1.00	148.75	129.75	6,180
Apr	131.75	131.75	131.75	134.00	+ 1.00	149.25	131.75	4,103

Est vol 30,000; vol Tu 23,453; open int 168,983, −1,173.

CURRENCY

JAPAN YEN (CME)-12.5 million yen; $ per yen (.00)

	Open	High	Low	Settle	Change	Lifetime High	Low	Open Interest
Sept	.6928	.7014	.6928	.6981	+ .0040	.8695	.6887	137,071
Dec	.7070	.7083	.7055	.7072	+ .0040	.8445	.6987	2,806
Mr99	....	....		.7163	+ .0040	.8315	.7077	1,918
June	.7250	.7250	.7240	.7255	+ .0040	.7800	.7181	649

Est vol 15,260; vol Tue 27,832; open int 142,444, +3,427.

DEUTSCHEMARK (CME)-125,000 marks; $ per mark

	Open	High	Low	Settle	Change	Lifetime High	Low	Open Interest
Sept	.5646	.5678	.5645	.5667	+ .0018	.5944	.5425	106,944
Dec	.5691	.5698	.5684	.5696	+ .0018	.5840	.5496	746
Mr99	....	....		.5721	+ .0018	.5775	.5540	70

Est vol 18,683; vol Tue 14,798; open int 107,880, +455.

CANADIAN DOLLAR (CME)-100,000 dlrs.; $ per Can $

	Open	High	Low	Settle	Change	Lifetime High	Low	Open Interest
Sept	.6603	.6617	.6590	.6594	− .0009	.7463	.6590	67,123
Dec	.6611	.6621	.6595	.6600	− .0009	.7400	.6595	4,654
Mr99	.6620	.6620	.6610	.6600	− .0009	.7247	.6608	1,193
June	....	....		.6612	− .0009	.7170	.6615	309

Est vol 5,066; vol Tue 7,451; open int 73,331, +1,001.

BRITISH POUND (CME)-62,500 pds.; $ per pound

	Open	High	Low	Settle	Change	Lifetime High	Low	Open Interest
Sept	1.6318	1.6380	1.6306	1.6328	+ .0010	1.6870	1.5690	39,660
Dec	1.6260	1.6274	1.6240	1.6252	+ .0010	1.6760	1.5630	836
Ju99	....	....		1.6106	+ .0010	1.6460	1.5960	130

Est vol 4,375; vol Tue 10,576; open int 40,629, −1,478.

(continued)

EXHIBIT 22-4　　*(continued)*

INTEREST RATE

TREASURY BONDS (CBT)-$100,000; pts. 32nds of 100%

	Open	High	Low	Settle	Change	Lifetime High	Low	Open Interest
Sept	123-19	123-30	123-06	123-17	− 1	124-14	103-22	835,571
Dec	123-12	123-13	122-31	123-09	− 1	124-00	103-13	205,260
Mr99	....	....	....	123-01	− 1	123-20	103-04	38,910
Sept	....	....	....	122-13	− 1	121-26	115-11	3,767

Est vol 450,000; vol Tue 499,252; open int 1,083,528, +25,527.

TREASURY BONDS (MCE)-$50,000; pts. 32nds of 100%

	Open	High	Low	Settle	Change	Lifetime High	Low	Open Interest
Sept	123-18	123-21	123-06	123-12	− 15	124-07	118-07	14,834

Est vol 6,000; vol Tue 14,887, −1,261.

TREASURY NOTES (CBT)-$100,000; pts. 32nds of 100%

	Open	High	Low	Settle	Change	Lifetime High	Low	Open Interest
Sept	114-03	114-09	113-30	114-04	+ 2	114-22	110-25	475,914
Dec	114-04	114-05	113-31	114-05	+ 2	114-21	111-11	69,998
Mr99	....	....	....	114-08	+ 2	113-29	112-04	476

Est vol 99,999; vol Tue 111,479; open int 546,388, +3,907.

5 YR TREAS NOTES (CBT)-$100,000; pts. 32nds of 100%

	Open	High	Low	Settle	Change	Lifetime High	Low	Open Interest
Sept	09-275	09-315	09-245	109-29	+ 2.5	110-05	108-09	268,749
Dec	110-00	110-00	109-27	109-31	+ 3.0	110-00	108-30	27,936

Est vol 58,000; vol Tue 57,425; open int 296,685, +2,973.

2 YR TREAS NOTES (CBT)-$200,000, pts. 32nds of 100%

	Open	High	Low	Settle	Change	Lifetime High	Low	Open Interest
Sept	104-11	04-125	04-092	04-115	+ 1.7	04-175	03-225	43,018

Est vol 5,000; vol Tue 4,293; open int 44,510, +56.

30-DAY FEDERAL FUNDS (CBT)-$5 million; pts. of 100%

	Open	High	Low	Settle	Change	Lifetime High	Low	Open Interest
Aug	94.490	94.490	94.485	94.485	....	94.830	94.220	6,024
Sept	94.47	94.48	94.47	94.48	+ .01	94.64	94.30	4,237
Oct	94.50	94.51	94.50	94.51	+ .01	94.60	94.32	2,964
Nov	94.49	94.51	94.49	....	+ .01	94.60	94.27	3,824
Dec	94.48	94.48	94.48	....	+ .01	94.59	94.25	985
Ja99	94.46	94.46	94.46	94.46	+ .02	94.55	94.25	922
Feb	....	....	....	94.54	+ .02	94.55	94.31	279

Est vol 1,974; vol Tue 1,331; open int 19,318, +162.

EURODOLLAR (CME)-$1 million; pts of 100%

	Open	High	Low	Settle	Chg	Yield Settle	Chg	Open Interest
Aug	94.32	94.32	94.31	94.32	....	5.68	....	14,004
Sept	94.33	94.33	94.32	94.33	....	5.67	....	468,896
Oct	94.29	94.30	94.29	94.30	+ .01	5.70	− .01	6,330
Nov	94.29	94.31	94.29	94.31	+ .01	5.69	− .01	1,015
Dec	94.31	94.32	94.30	94.32	+ .01	5.68	− .01	395,434
Ja99	94.36	94.38	94.36	94.37	+ .01	5.63	− .01	1,589
Mar	94.38	94.39	94.36	94.38	+ .01	5.62	− .01	345,490
June	94.36	94.38	94.35	94.37	+ .01	5.63	− .01	299,807
Sept	94.36	94.36	94.32	94.34	+ .02	5.66	− .02	224,218
Dec	94.22	94.22	94.19	94.20	+ .01	5.80	− .01	200,250
Mr00	94.27	94.27	94.24	94.26	+ .02	5.74	− .02	160,427
June	94.23	94.24	94.22	94.23	+ .01	5.77	− .01	145,102
Sept	94.21	94.22	94.20	94.21	+ .01	5.79	− .01	98,000
Dec	94.14	94.15	94.12	94.13	....	5.87	....	81,467
Mr01	94.17	94.18	94.16	94.17	....	5.83	....	71,405
June	94.15	94.16	94.14	94.15	....	5.85	....	59,436
Sept	94.14	94.15	94.13	94.14	....	5.86	....	48,467
Dec	94.08	94.08	94.06	94.07	....	5.93	....	43,521
Mr02	94.11	94.12	94.10	94.11	....	5.89	....	47,140
June	94.10	94.10	94.08	94.09	....	5.91	....	45,950
Sept	94.09	94.09	94.07	94.08	....	5.92	....	47,330
Dec	94.01	94.01	94.00	94.01	....	5.99	....	36,984
Mr03	94.04	94.05	94.03	94.04	− .01	5.96	+ .01	32,851
June	94.03	94.03	94.02	94.02	− .01	5.98	+ .01	26,408
Sept	94.00	94.00	94.00	94.00	− .01	6.00	+ .01	16,536
Dec	93.92	93.92	93.92	93.92	− .01	6.08	+ .01	9,775
Mr04	93.95	93.95	93.95	93.95	− .01	6.05	+ .01	8,108
June	93.92	93.92	93.92	93.92	− .01	6.08	+ .01	8,533
Sept	93.91	93.91	93.89	93.90	− .01	6.10	+ .01	6,612
Dec	93.84	93.84	93.82	93.82	− .02	6.18	+ .02	7,848
Mr05	93.87	93.87	93.85	93.85	− .02	6.15	+ .02	5,757
June	93.83	93.83	93.82	93.82	− .02	6.18	+ .02	5,428
Sept	....	....	....	93.80	− .02	6.20	+ .02	3,981
Dec	....	....	....	93.73	− .02	6.27	+ .02	3,178
Mr06	....	....	....	93.76	− .02	6.24	+ .02	5,455
June	....	....	....	93.73	− .02	6.27	+ .02	3,695
Sept	....	....	....	93.71	− .02	6.29	+ .02	4,383
Dec	....	....	....	93.63	− .03	6.37	+ .03	4,764
Mr07	....	....	....	93.66	− .03	6.34	+ .03	3,960
June	93.66	93.66	93.64	93.64	− .03	6.37	+ .03	4,140
Sept	....	....	....	93.61	− .03	6.39	+ .03	4,799
Dec	93.56	93.56	93.54	93.54	− .03	6.46	+ .03	3,819
Mr08	....	....	....	93.57	− .03	6.43	+ .03	3,756
June	93.56	93.56	93.54	93.54	− .03	6.46	+ .03	1,088

Est vol 339,401; vol Tue 460,774; open int 3,017,136, −20,383.

INDEX

DJ INDUSTRIAL AVERAGE (CBOT)-$10 times average

	Open	High	Low	Settle	Chg	High	Low	Open Interest
Sept	8545	8610	8380	8605	+ 100	9418	7150	15,126
Dec	8630	8700	8475	8690	+ 100	9515	7677	1,585
Mr99	8707	8775	8575	8775	+ 100	9586	8575	743

Est vol 20,000; vol Tue 25,604; open int 17,567, +1,442.
Idx prl: High 8574.85; Low 8361.92; Close 8546.78 +59.47

S&P 500 INDEX (CME)-$250 times index

	Open	High	Low	Settle	Chg	High	Low	Open Interest
Sept	107400	109100	106000	108850	+ 14.50	119940	879.20	364,028
Dec	109100	110300	107100	110000	+ 14.50	121210	890.85	16,119
Mr99	110400	111300	108400	111130	+ 14.80	122500	902.85	3,883
June	111680	112430	109500	112290	+ 15.10	123810	914.85	1,706
Dec	113300	114950	112100	114470	+ 11.70	126390	981.40	642

Est vol 159,111; vol Tue 180,187; open int 386,457, +5,870.
Idx prl: High 1084.80; Low 1057.35; Close 1081.44 +9.32

OTHER FUTURES

Settlement prices of selected contracts. Actual volume (from previous session) and open interest of all contract months.

	Vol.	High	Low	Settle	Net Change	Lifetime High	Low	Open Interest
BRAZILIAN REAL (CME) 100,000 Braz. reais; $ per reais.								
Sep	9	....	.85250	....	.85320	.85040		6,043
BRITISH POUND/DEUTSCHEMARK (FINEX)								
125,000 British Pounds; Marks per Pound								
Sep	100	2.8875	2.8860	2.8818	− .0075	3.0020	2.7550	3,281
CALIFORNIA OREGON BORDER ELECTRICTY (NYM)								
736 mwh; .01 per mwh								
Sep	176	41.00	39.00	39.78	+ .13	43.50	22.00	4,045
CORN (MCE) 1,000 bu.; cents per bu.								
Sep	497	214¼	211¼	211½	− 2	300½	211¼	12,378
FRENCH FRANC (CME)-FFr 500,000; $ per Fr. Franc								
Sep	43	.16900	.16860	.16900	+ 00040	.17786	.16320	2,682
FLAXSEED (WPG) 20 metric tons; Can. $ per ton								
Sep	131	315.50	315.50	315.50	....	365.50	313.00	6,301

EXCHANGE ABBREVIATIONS
(for commodity futures and futures options)

CBT-Chicago Board of Trade; CME-Chicago Mercantile Exchange; CSCE-Coffee, Sugar & Cocoa Exchange, New York; CMX-COMEX (Div. of New York Mercantile Exchange); CTN-New York Cotton Exchange; DTB-Deutsche Terminboerse; FINEX-Financial Exchange (Div. of New York Cotton Exchange; IPE-International Petroleum Exchange; KC-Kansas City Board of Trade; LIFFE-London International Financial Futures Exchange; MATIF-Marche a Terme International de France; ME-Montreal Exchange; MCE-MidAmerica Commodity Exchange; MPLS-Minneapolis Grain Exchange; NYFE-New York Futures Exchange (Sub. of New York Cotton Exchange); NYM-New York Mercantile Exchange; SIMEX-Singapore International Monetary Exchange Ltd.; SFE-Sydney Futures Exchange; TFE-Toronto Futures Exchange; WPG-Winnipeg Commodity Exchange.

---

contracts, however, gains and losses are taken daily based on the settle price. Thus, if we buy a futures contract at \$2.07 and the next day it rises to \$2.09 (the settle price), we will receive \$0.02 (without having to sell the contract). If the next day the settle price is \$2.05, then essentially the contract buyer would have to pay \$0.04 (\$2.09 − \$2.05) to the seller of the futures contract. This simplified description ignores the role of margin, which is discussed in detail later in the chapter. Because futures contracts are mark to market, large traders are tempted to drive prices up at the end of the day if they are long on futures contracts. The higher the price at the end of the day, the more profit futures buyers receive. Thus, settle prices were developed to avoid manipulation of futures prices at the end of the day. Using settle prices rather than the last trade of the day makes it much more difficult to move the price. Trading does not occur at the settle price; the settle price is an average of the trading prices occurring during the last few minutes of trading. Typically, the settle price is close to the price of the last trade of the day.

Open interest is used as a measure of the liquidity of a futures contract. Higher open interest indicates that more buyers and sellers exist, which typically means a high volume of trading activity. The more trading activity there is, the easier and cheaper it will be to enter into a futures contract.

Most futures traders close their position rather than actually deliver or take delivery of the specified asset. A corn farmer in Iowa, for example, will find it more convenient to close his Chicago delivery futures contract than to actually deliver corn to Chicago. Observe that the contract with the nearest maturity usually has less open interest. (In Exhibit 22-4, see the futures contracts with August maturities, such as soybeans, copper-high, gold, and silver). This confirms the previous statement that most futures investors close or offset their positions rather than hold them to maturity. Futures traders offset their positions when they take an opposite position from the position held. For example, suppose an investor purchased 10 contracts of March 1999 (Mr99) corn on the Chicago Board of Trade (CBT). The investor can offset this position by selling 10 contracts of March 1999 corn on the CBT. The 10 contracts sold will automatically negate the 10 contracts initially purchased. Thus, the investor now has no position at all in CBT March 1999 corn futures contracts. This action will reduce open interest only if both buyers and sellers are offsetting.[1] If one seller sells to a new trader, the open interest remains the same.

When futures markets originally developed, physical delivery of the underlying commodity was required. For example, the investor who bought corn futures contracts actually purchased the required quantity of corn. Over time, however, market participants pressed for cash settlement instead. **Cash settlement** is the exchange of cash at the expiration of the futures contract based on the value of the spot asset rather than the actual exchange of the physical asset. For example, it is much easier to make a cash settlement for an S&P 500 futures contract than to actually deliver five hundred different securities (with different quantities of each security). Thus, the S&P 500 futures contract is strictly a cash-settled futures contract.

---

1. Each futures contract is actually two contracts: a contract between the buyer and the clearinghouse and a contract between the seller and the clearinghouse. Hence, when both buyer and seller are offsetting a position, the clearinghouse has no position with either buyer or seller, and the open interest declines.

22.3 BUYING AND SELLING FUTURES CONTRACTS

This section examines the process by which a futures trade is executed, the function of clearinghouses, and the margin requirements for an investment in futures.

22.3.1 Trading a Futures Contract

All trading on futures exchanges is conducted by **futures commission merchants (FCMs),** who are equivalent to stock brokers. The typical order follows the sequence given in Exhibit 22-5a. First, the buyer and seller contact their brokers, who usually are futures commission merchants (Step 1 in Exhibit 22-5a). A broker that is not an FCM typically works through an FCM. The FCM contacts its floor brokers

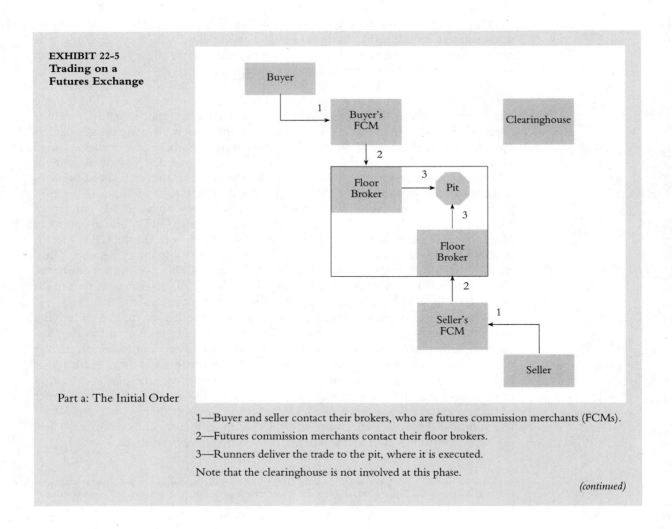

EXHIBIT 22-5
Trading on a Futures Exchange

Part a: The Initial Order

1—Buyer and seller contact their brokers, who are futures commission merchants (FCMs).

2—Futures commission merchants contact their floor brokers.

3—Runners deliver the trade to the pit, where it is executed.

Note that the clearinghouse is not involved at this phase.

(continued)

regarding the buy or sell orders (Step 2). A **floor broker** handles orders for several FCMs. Floor brokers are distinguished from **locals,** who trade solely for their own accounts. The floor brokers have the trade executed in the **pit,** the part of the futures exchange where all buying and selling of futures contracts take place (Step 3). If a buyer wants to acquire December corn futures at $2.21 per bushel and a seller wants to sell December corn futures at $2.22, then no transaction will take place. It is not until the buyer and seller reach a price acceptable to both that a transaction takes place.

Once the buyer and seller reach a mutually acceptable price, the trade can occur. The clearinghouse now enters the picture to effect the trade. Exhibit 22-5b shows the path of activity once the transaction has been made in the pit. The exact terms of the trade are sent back to the floor broker, who then contacts both the FCM and the clearinghouse.

EXHIBIT 22-5
(continued)

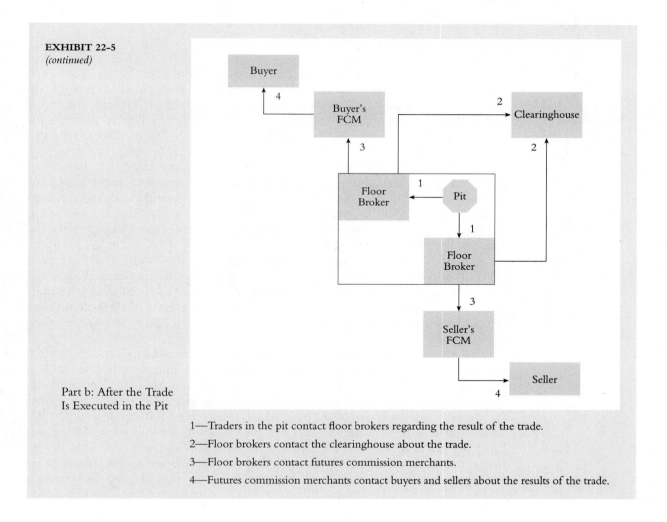

Part b: After the Trade
Is Executed in the Pit

1—Traders in the pit contact floor brokers regarding the result of the trade.

2—Floor brokers contact the clearinghouse about the trade.

3—Floor brokers contact futures commission merchants.

4—Futures commission merchants contact buyers and sellers about the results of the trade.

22.3.2 The Clearinghouse

The clearinghouse plays a key role in futures trading. As with an options contract, the clearinghouse guarantees both sides of a futures contract. The clearinghouse not only helps eliminate default risk but also guarantees the quality of the goods delivered. Most commodity futures contracts have a specified quality level, and the clearinghouse makes sure that a commodity of the appropriate quality is delivered.

The clearinghouse also facilitates the exchange of daily cash flows between the winners and the losers. It makes sure that both the buyer and the seller of futures contracts provide adequate collateral.

The clearinghouse thus plays three vital roles:

1. *Banker.* The clearinghouse provides for the exchange of profits and losses.
2. *Inspector.* The clearinghouse insures good product delivery.
3. *Insurer.* The clearinghouse guarantees that each trader will honor the contract.

22.3.3 Margin Requirements

Margin monies are required by the clearinghouse to reduce the default risks related to futures trading. Recall from Chapter 3 that initial and maintenance margins are required for investors who borrow money to purchase stock. In the same way, initial and maintenance margins are required for both buyers and sellers of futures contracts. The actual margin requirements change frequently, but they are usually significantly lower than margins for stocks.

Exactly how do margin requirements work? The initial margin is the monies placed with the clearinghouse when the trade is initially executed. For example, investors who buy futures contracts must place the initial margin with the clearinghouse. If prices move in the investors' favor, then the gains are received daily. However, if prices fall, the investor does not have to post more margin until the maintenance margin level is reached.

Exhibit 22-6 illustrates an example of margin cash flow. On Day 1 the futures price experiences a modest decline. There are no cash flows between the broker and the client. On Day 4 the maintenance margin is hit, so the client must post additional monies (because the client is a buyer) to bring the value of the account back to the initial margin level. On Day 5 there is a gain that the client can take out of the account immediately.

Exhibit 22-7 shows how the margin account has changed over a six-day period. For simplicity, assume that this trader sold one S&P 500 futures contract at 924.5 in the morning of October 29 and that the initial margin is $14,000. Each S&P 500 futures contract is cash settled based on 500 times the index. By the end of October 29, the S&P 500 had risen by 1 point, which results in a $500 loss. Recall that this investor is short one futures contract that pays at 500 times the index. We see that this $500 loss reduces the margin balance to $13,500, but there is no margin call. When the price rises to 929.50 on July 7, the cumulative losses now have reduced the margin account so it is below the maintenance margin of $12,000. In this case, a margin call of $2,500 is issued to restore the account balance to $14,000. In this

**EXHIBIT 22-6
Margin Cash Flow
over Time**

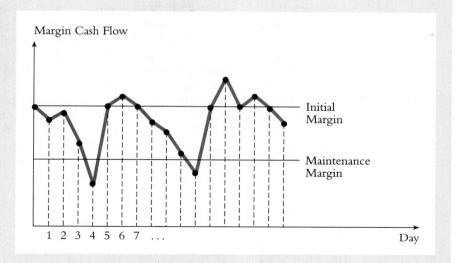

simple case the investor closes the futures position at exactly the original trade price for a net gain of zero. The margin account on July 9 is $2,500 greater than it was at the time of the initial investment because of the margin call.

Margin requirements for futures contracts are the subject of controversy. Stock traders have to post margin of at least 50%, whereas futures traders in the S&P 500

EXHIBIT 22-7   Calculating Margins for a Short Position in One S&P 500 Futures Contract[a]

Day	Futures Price	Daily Gain (Loss)	Cumulative Gain (Loss)	Margin Account Balance	Margin Call
	$924.5			$14,000	
July 1	925.5	$(500)[b]	$(500)	13,500	
July 2	923.5	1,000	500[c]	14,500[d]	
July 3	926.5	(1,500)	(1,000)	13,000	
July 7	929.5	(1,500)	(2,500)	11,500	$2,500
July 8	928.5	500	(2,000)	14,500	
July 9	924.5	2,000	0	16,500	

a. The initial margin is $14,000, and the maintenance margin is $12,000. Each S&P 500 futures contract is for 500 times the index. The contract is entered on July 1 at 924.5 and closed on July 9 at 924.5.

b. $500 = 500(925.5 − 924.5)$.

c. $500 = (500) + 1,000$.

d. The investor could withdraw $500, but we assume there was no withdrawal.

index have to post margin at only approximately 5% to 10%. Thus, investors can take a larger speculative position with futures contracts than with the stocks themselves. This ability to take more speculative positions with futures contracts has some people concerned, because the high leverage in futures contracts may induce sharp changes in the futures prices. Actually, some people blame the 1987 stock market crash on the high leverage in this market.

Margin requirements have a direct bearing on the rate of return realized by a futures trader. Because margin requirements on futures contracts are lower than they are for stocks, investors are allowed greater leverage than that allowed by margin trading on the underlying securities, which in turn affects the returns. Consider the following example. Suppose the S&P 500 index is at 934.67, and the nearest-maturity S&P 500 futures contract is trading at 934.20. Also suppose the futures margin is 5% of the contract, and the security margin is 50%. One unit of the S&P 500 futures contract would require a margin deposit of $46.71 ($0.05 \cdot 934.20$), and one unit of the S&P 500 index contract would require $467.335 ($0.50 \cdot 934.67$). Now suppose that *both* markets rise by 10%; hence, the futures contract is at $1,027.62 ($1.1 \cdot 934.20$), and the S&P 500 index is at 1,028.374 ($1.1 \cdot 934.67$). The rate of return on the futures contract is

$$R_{Futures} = \text{Profit/Investment} = (1{,}027.62 - 934.20)/46.71 = 200\%$$

The rate of return on the S&P 500 is[2]

$$R_{S\&P\ 500} = \text{Profit/Investment} = (1{,}028.137 - 934.67)/467.335 = 20\%$$

Now suppose that *both* markets fall by 10%; hence, the futures contract is at 840.78 ($0.9 \cdot 934.20$), and the S&P 500 index is at 841.203 ($0.9 \cdot 934.67$). In this case, the rate of return on the futures contract is

$$R_{Futures} = (840.78 - 934.20)/46.71 = -200\%$$

and the rate of return on the S&P 500 is

$$R_{S\&P\ 500} = (841.203 - 934.67)/467.335 = -20\%$$

Clearly, the highly leveraged trading in futures contracts increases the volatility of returns. In this example, the rates of return are magnified by a factor of 10.

Futures margins are different from stock margins. Recall that the margin requirement for a stock is essentially a down payment for a security to be owned. The investor who trades on margin has all the rights and privileges of an outright owner. This is not true with futures contracts. When a stock is purchased, the new owner assumes control over the voting rights, whereas with futures contracts only price risk is transferred. Also, because of daily mark to market, the need for enormous collateral on futures contracts is minimized. A futures margin is just a performance bond that insures that both parties will fulfill their obligations.

---

2. Investors can buy the S&P index. Securities based on the S&P 500 now trade on the American Stock Exchange and are known as *spiders*.

PRACTICE BOX

Problem   Suppose a futures contract on palladium, a platinum alloy used as a catalyst and in dental products, is trading at $90 per troy ounce, and each contract is for 100 troy ounces. The margin requirement is $675 per contract, and the spot market price is $95. Compute the rate of return both on buying one futures contract and on a cash purchase of 100 troy ounces if palladium rises to $108 per troy ounce or falls to $72 per troy ounce at the expiration of the futures contract.

Solution   Recall that the rate of return is profit divided by investment. For the futures contract, then,

$$R_{Futures} = 100(\$108 - \$90)/\$675 = 267\% \quad \text{Price Goes Up}$$

$$R_{Futures} = 100(\$72 - \$90)/\$675 = -267\% \quad \text{Price Goes Down}$$

For the cash purchase, note that the price at the expiration of the futures contract must be equivalent to the price in the spot market. A futures contract that will expire immediately is the same as a spot market purchase. Therefore,

$$R_{Cash} = 100(\$108 - \$95)/\$9,500 = 13.7\% \quad \text{Price Goes Up}$$

$$R_{Cash} = 100(\$72 - \$95)/\$9,500 = -24.2\% \quad \text{Price Goes Down}$$

where $\$9,500 = 100 \cdot \$95$.

Thus, futures contracts are much more volatile than spot market purchases, because futures contracts allow for highly leveraged transactions.

Connecting Theory to Practice 22.1 discusses the conflict of interest of block traders and floor brokers in futures contracts.

CONNECTING THEORY TO PRACTICE 22.1

CFTC WEIGHS BLOCK TRADES OF CONTRACTS

The Commodity Futures Trading Commission is considering whether to allow block trades of commodity contracts on futures exchanges.

Such large trades, which take place in private transactions between two big dealers and are then cleared by the exchange, are popular in the stock market, but aren't permitted in the futures exchanges, where all orders to buy or sell must pass through a trading floor. Big brokerage firms and institutional money managers say that allowing block trades on the futures exchanges would simplify their business and cut costs while allowing large sums of money to change hands without disrupting the markets. . . .

(continued)

But floor brokers at the futures exchanges, who would lose the opportunity to bid on a piece of such large transactions if they occurred off the exchange floor, aren't happy at all and the management of the exchanges echoes their views.

Source: Aaron Lucchetti, "CFTC Weighs Block Trades of Contracts," *Wall Street Journal*, March 30, 1998, p. C1. Reprinted by permission of *The Wall Street Journal*, © 1998 Dow Jones & Co., Inc. All Rights Reserved Worldwide.

MAKING THE CONNECTION

The commodities market, like all markets, is forever evolving. The pros and cons of each change must be weighed. In this case, the needs of institutional investors must be weighed against the possible disadvantage to individual investors. The article points out that permitting large block transactions on the floor of the exchange will hurt individual investors by changing the playing field. (Recall from Chapter 3 that a large block transaction represents orders for 10,000 shares or more.) This issue arises in many of the changes that occur in the financial market.

22.4 INVESTMENT STRATEGIES WITH FUTURES CONTRACTS

Investors use futures contracts in four strategies: hedging, speculating, arbitrage, and portfolio diversification. Hedging strategies use futures contracts to transfer price risk. Speculative strategies are based on some prior belief about the future course of asset prices. If investors believe that stocks will rise, then they buy index futures contracts. If they are wrong in their belief, as occurred with Nicholas Leeson of Barings bank, their loss can be devastating. (Mr. Leeson traded on the derivatives for speculative reasons. He was wrong in guessing the market direction, inducing a loss of more than $1 million to Barings bank.) Hedgers use futures contracts to offset an existing long or short position, whereas speculators seek to profit by exposing themselves to more risk. Arbitrage strategies involve synthetically creating a particular asset and trading the synthetic asset against the underlying asset. A synthetic security is a portfolio of securities that have payoffs identical to some other security. For example, a synthetic six-month wheat futures contract will have payoffs identical to those obtained by trading a six-month wheat futures contract. Portfolio diversification strategies use futures like any other assets to combine with a portfolio in order to gain further diversification. The benefit of futures is that they can be used to create correlations with the portfolio that are otherwise difficult to obtain. For example, a portfolio that has sold stock index futures contracts will be highly negatively correlated with a stock portfolio. (Unfortunately, however, the expected rate of return in equilibrium will be about equal to the risk-free interest rate.) This section discusses each of these four strategies.

If we ignore the effects of mark to market, then the payoff diagrams for buying and selling futures contracts and holding them to maturity are represented by Exhibit 22-8. Mark to market may have a minor influence on the value of a futures contract. When a futures contract matures, it will be worth the price of the underlying asset. A futures contract at expiration is the same as a spot contract at that date. Specifically, at maturity,

$$F_t = S_t$$

where F_t is the value of the futures contract at maturity, and S_t is the value of the underlying asset at t.

Exhibit 22-8a shows that a trader profits or loses from buying futures when the underlying asset price changes. The gain equals the payoff of owning the underlying asset. The losses are limited by the underlying asset price, which at most can drop to zero. Suppose you buy a futures contract on corn for $F_0 = \$2.07$ per bushel. If at maturity the spot corn price (S_t) is exactly $2.07 per bushel, you will have no profit or loss on the trade. Suppose, however, that the spot price is $S_t = \$2.17$ per bushel at maturity. Then you can buy the corn for $F_0 = \$2.07$ per bushel with the futures contract and sell the corn for $S_t = \$2.17$ per bushel in the spot market,

EXHIBIT 22-8   Payoff Diagrams for Futures Contracts

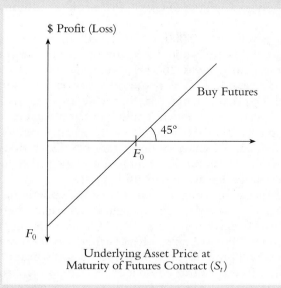

Part a: Buyer of a Futures Contract

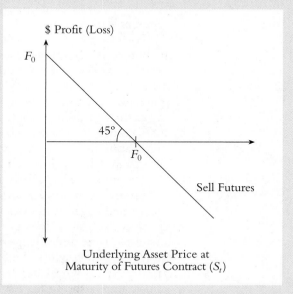

Part b: Seller of a Futures Contract

profiting $0.10 per bushel (or $500 per contract, because each corn futures contract is for 5,000 bushels). Hence, in this case, for every dollar increase in the spot price at maturity, there is an additional dollar profit per bushel on the futures contract. In the same way, if the spot price is $1.97 at maturity and you have an obligation to buy at $2.07, you buy it for $2.07, sell for $1.97, and lose $0.10 per bushel. Therefore, the line in Exhibit 22-8a is at a 45-degree angle, passing through point $F_0 = S_t$, where neither loss nor profit occurred. Because the most that can be lost is F_0, the line stops at the intersection with the vertical axis.

A similar example illustrates the dollar profits and losses from selling a futures contract. The payoff diagram is similar to short selling stock (see Exhibit 22-8b). Suppose you sell a futures contract on corn for $F_0 = \$2.07$ per bushel; there will be no profit or loss on the trade. Now suppose that the spot price is $S_t = \$2.17$ per bushel at maturity. Then you must sell the corn for $F_0 = \$2.07$ per bushel with the futures contract and buy the corn for $S_t = \$2.17$ per bushel in the spot market, resulting in a loss of $0.10 per bushel. For every dollar increase in the spot price at maturity, there is an additional dollar loss. In the same way, if the spot price is $S_t = \$1.97$ at maturity and you sell at $F_0 = \$2.07$ with the futures contract and buy for $S_t = \$1.97$, you gain $0.10 per bushel, if the price of the underlying asset at maturity is $2.07 per bushel. Therefore, the line has a negative 45-degree angle, passing through the point $F_0 = S_t$.

22.4.1 Hedging

One reason for trading futures contracts is to transfer price risk from an entity that has the price risk to another party who is willing to take it. Price risk arises in many different settings.

For example, suppose a firm purchases 100,000 MMBtu (million British thermal units) of natural gas each month. There is about a six-month lag between the time prices rise and the point the firm can pass the price increase on to its customers. Clearly, this firm could face significant risk if the price of natural gas rose. Therefore, the firm could lock in the price of natural gas for the next six months using natural gas futures contracts. Specifically, the firm could buy ten natural gas futures contracts, where each contract is for 10,000 MMBtu. The firm benefits by eliminating the influence of natural gas price swings on its earnings. Firms that are heavily in debt are attracted to hedging with futures contracts, because this strategy helps them avoid large losses in earnings that are due to rising prices.

Futures contracts are particularly useful when the quantity of the underlying assets to be hedged is known. When the quantity to be hedged is uncertain, there is quantity risk. How does an investor hedge when there is uncertainty regarding the quantity of the underlying asset at risk? For example, wheat farmers are not sure exactly how much wheat the harvest will produce. A farmer who hedges wheat price risk by selling wheat futures could face very bad consequences. Suppose a farmer anticipating a spring harvest of 100,000 bushels of wheat hedges the price risk by selling 20 March wheat futures contracts (each for 5,000 bushels) at $3.495 per bushel on the Chicago Board of Trade. If a drought occurs, the farmer will have nothing to harvest. The price of wheat also rises dramatically during droughts. Suppose in this case that wheat prices rise $2 per bushel, to $5.495. The farmer would take a total loss on the wheat and face a loss of $200,000 [100,000($3.495 − $5.495)] in futures contracts. (Recall that if an investor sells wheat futures and prices rise, then the investor loses.) Futures contracts should be used as hedging vehicles only when the quantity to be hedged is fairly certain. When there is quantity risk, option contracts can be used. (This topic will be discussed in Chapter 23.)

PRACTICE BOX

Problem

The settle price for the December natural gas futures contract is $2.295. Suppose a firm that purchases 100,000 MMBtu of natural gas monthly buys ten December futures contracts. Calculate the gains or losses for the firm if futures prices rise 30% or fall 30%.

Solution

The settle price for the December natural gas futures contracts is

$$F_{Dec} = 2.295$$

If the futures price rises by 30%, then the price will be 1.3 · $2.295 = $2.9835. If the futures price falls by 30%, then the price will be 0.7 · $2.295 = $1.6065. Hence, if a firm purchases ten contracts at 10,000 units each, it profits as follows:

Futures Profit on Price Rise = 10 · 10,000($2.9835 − $2.295) = $68,850

This profit would offset losses on the increased purchase price of natural gas. However, if prices fall, the futures contract will experience losses of

Futures Loss on Price Fall = 10 · 10,000($1.6065 − $2.295) = −$68,850

This loss in the futures market will offset gains that would be experienced in the spot market from falling prices. Thus, using futures contracts reduces volatility.

22.4.2 Speculating

There are many ways to speculate with futures contracts. Central to speculation is some belief about future prices. For example, if you believe that Treasury bond prices are going to fall (because of a perceived increase in interest rates), then you can speculate by selling Treasury bond futures contracts.[3] The basic element of a speculative strategy is the acceptance of additional price risk because of a belief that it will be profitable. If one is wrong in his/her belief, the loss from speculation could be very large.

---

3. Alternatively, you could short sell U.S. Treasury bonds, but this requires a considerable amount of capital. Recall that futures trading margin requirements are much lower than the securities market.

22.4.3 Arbitrage

Arbitrage is different from speculation, because typically there is little or no price risk accepted with arbitrage. Recall that an arbitrageur attempts to synthetically create an asset and trade the synthetic asset against the actual asset. The objective is to design a portfolio with no investment and positive cash flows in the future or positive cash flows today with no liabilities in the future. For example, with Major Market Index (MMI) futures contracts, investors can synthetically take a position in the portfolio of twenty stocks in the MMI by buying an appropriate number of futures contracts.[4] Hence, an arbitrageur can monitor two portfolios—the synthetic portfolio with futures and the actual portfolio of twenty stocks—and buy and sell when discrepancies appear.

22.4.4 Portfolio Diversification

Recently, futures contracts have been used to gain additional portfolio diversification benefits. Many portfolio managers recognize the tremendous benefits available from finding securities that are not highly correlated. Recall that the lower the correlation between assets, the greater the overall risk reduction potential. Hence, portfolio managers have found that a carefully crafted portfolio of futures contracts can provide decent returns, as well as diversification benefits. Connecting Theory to Practice 22.2 further illustrates the idea of using futures to diversify a portfolio.

CONNECTING THEORY TO PRACTICE 22.2
INSTITUTIONS BUY FUTURES TO CUT RISKS

More pension funds and other fuddy-duddy institutional investors are putting money into volatile futures markets for a surprising reason: They want to reduce risk in their investment portfolios.

The trick to lowering risk, modern portfolio theorists say, is diversifying. That means adding types of investments whose values don't move in lockstep with assets already in a portfolio. Futures fit this description nicely.

Over the past five years, returns from stocks rose or fell in line with bonds in a loosely associated way. But movements of futures contracts, as represented by an index of futures pools (portfolios) were found to be almost totally unrelated to returns on stocks and bonds.

One company that decided to test this theory, on the advice of a consultant, is McCormick Paint Works Co. in Rockville, Md. The company put 6% of its $4.4 million profit-sharing plan into a futures pool that used more than one money manager.

(continued)

---

4. The MMI is a price-weighted index of twenty blue chip stocks. It is very similar to the Dow Jones Industrial Average, which has thirty stocks. See Chapter 5.

For example, in the third quarter the futures portion of McCormick's profit-sharing plan appreciated by 9.4% while the portion devoted to U.S. stocks sank 8.6% and international stocks fell 7.1%. Overall, the futures portion reduced the decline in its total portfolio by about half a percentage point.

Source: Stanley W. Angrist, "Institutions Buy Futures to Cut Risks," *Wall Street Journal,* December 10, 1990, p. C1. Reprinted by permission of *The Wall Street Journal,* © 1990 Dow Jones & Co., Inc. All Rights Reserved Worldwide.

MAKING THE CONNECTION

One reason futures pools (portfolios) had returns that were unrelated to stocks and bonds is that many pools are invested in commodity futures, whose prices do not move in the same direction as the financial markets. Another reason for the diversification benefits is that many pools have managers who are actively buying and selling futures contracts. Hence, one week a pool's manager may be selling the MMI and the next week buying the MMI. Thus, the position held is very dynamic and not necessarily correlated with stock markets.

22.5 PRICING FUTURES CONTRACTS

This section develops general pricing models for futures contracts. Futures prices rarely equal the current value of the spot asset. Most of the time, futures prices have a definite pattern when compared across maturities (see Exhibit 22-4). How can we explain the pattern of the settle prices? How can we explain the fact that early-maturity futures of the S&P 500 index are less than the S&P 500 index value? This section develops a method of valuing futures contracts. First, however, the concept of the basis must be introduced.

22.5.1 The Basis

To help us examine futures prices over time, Exhibit 22-9 provides historical graphs of spot and futures prices of the Dow Jones indexes during 1997. Notice that sometimes the futures price exceeds the current spot price by a large amount, sometimes the difference is negligible, and sometimes the current spot price exceeds the futures price. How can these different patterns be explained? The arbitrage pricing of futures, which will be discussed here, helps explain the difference in futures prices and spot prices.

The difference between the current spot price and the current futures price is known as the **basis.** The basis is totally different from the concept of a basis point. Specifically,

$$\text{Basis} = \text{Spot Price} - \text{Futures Price}$$

$$B_{0,t} = S_0 - F_{0,t}$$

EXHIBIT 22-9
Spot and Futures Prices in 1997
for the Dow Jones Indexes

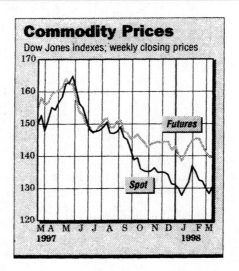

where $B_{0,t}$ denotes the basis using a futures contract maturing at time t, S_0 is the current spot price, and $F_{0,t}$ is the current futures price of a futures contract maturing at t. For example, according to Exhibit 22-4, the basis for each of the S&P 500 futures contracts follows:

$$B_{0,\text{Sep}} = S_0 - F_{0,\text{Sep}} = 1081.44 - 1088.50 = -7.06 \text{ September '98}$$

$$B_{0,\text{Dec}} = S_0 - F_{0,\text{Dec}} = 1081.44 - 1100.00 = -18.6 \text{ December '98}$$

$$B_{0,\text{Mr99}} = S_0 - F_{0,\text{Mr99}} = 1081.44 - 1111.30 = -29.86 \text{ March '99}$$

$$B_{0,\text{June}} = S_0 - F_{0,\text{June}} = 1081.44 - 1122.90 = -41.46 \text{ June '99}$$

Thus, we observe that the basis decreases with the maturity of the futures contract.

Arbitrage-based pricing uses existing assets to design zero-risk portfolios from which the equilibrium futures price can be determined. We turn now to determining the equilibrium futures price for stock index futures contracts, assuming a zero-risk portfolio is created.

22.5.2 Pricing Stock Index Futures

What should the value of a futures contract be prior to maturity? Let us look in detail at an S&P 500 index futures contract. The S&P 500 index futures contract is cash settled. Recall that the S&P 500 is a value-weighted index of five hundred common stocks. If we actually invested in the S&P 500 index, our rate of return would be higher than the S&P 500 index, because we would receive the cash dividends (which are not included in the S&P 500 index calculation).

Consider the following strategy: borrow $S_0 + m$, where m is the margin required on one futures contract, and S_0 is the current stock price. The borrowing is for a predetermined period, e.g., one month. Hence, the future cash flow is $-(S_0 + m)(1 + r)$, where r is the interest rate for the relevant borrowing period. At the end of the period it is the expiration date of the contract at which the spot price is equal to the futures price. Buy one stock for S_0; hence, the future cash flow is $S_T + D$, where S_T is the stock price at the end of the period, and D is the cash dividend paid at the end of this period. Sell one futures contract; hence, you pay today a margin of m, on which you earn interest and get in the future $m(1 + r)$. In addition, your cash flow on the futures is $F_0 - S_T$, where F_0 is the current price.

As Exhibit 22-10 reveals, the total cash flow today is by construction of the financial strategy zero. To avoid an arbitrage profit, the future cash flow must be also zero, namely,

$$F_0 - S_0(1 + r) + D = 0$$

or

$$F_0 = S_0(1 + r) - D$$

Because D/S_0 is the dividend yield, we obtain

$$F_0 = S_0(1 + r) - S_0\frac{D}{S_0} = S_0(1 + r - d) \qquad (22.1)$$

where $D/S_0 \equiv d$ is the dividend yield.[5]

The futures price is a function of the current index value, the risk-free interest rate, the dividend yield, and the time to maturity. Intuitively, the futures price is equal to the spot price times the cost of carrying the spot asset. That is, if the S&P

EXHIBIT 22-10 Determining the Equilibrium Price of Stock Index Futures	Strategy	Cash Flow Today ($)	Cash Flow at the End of One Period ($)
	Borrow $(S_0 + m)$	$S_0 + m$	$-(S_0 + m)(1 + r)$
	Buy stock for S_0	$-S_0$	$S_T + D$
	Sell one futures contract	$-m$	$(F_0 - S_T) + m(1 + r)$
	Net position	0	$F_0 - S_0(1 + r) + D$

5. If we have annualized and continuing compounded dividend and interest, the equation can also be rewritten as

$$F_0 = S_0 e^{(r - d)t}$$

where t is a fraction of year between the two periods, and $r - d$ is the total rate of return on the stock less the dividend rate of return components—that is, the rate of return that is due to capital gains only.

500 index is purchased by borrowing at the risk-free interest rate, the cost of financing for the relevant period is r. However, actually owning the securities in the S&P 500 gives investors a dividend flow that reduces these financing costs. For this reason, Equation 22.1 is often referred to as the **cost of carry model.** Thus, observing S_0 and r and estimating d, the price of the futures, $\bar{r}_0$, is given by

$$F_0 = S_0(1 + r - d)$$

Notice that if $r > d$, then $r - d > 0$ and $F_0 > S_0$.[6] It is interesting to note that the expectation regarding future prices does not enter the equation for futures pricing except through S_0.

Other futures contracts can be priced using a similar approach. The only differences lie in the cost of owning (or carrying) the underlying asset. In the case of the S&P 500, the cost of owning the S&P 500 is the risk-free rate (the financing cost) less the dividend yield (the cash flow from the asset). For example, assume that the dividend yield on the MMI is 3%, and the risk-free interest rate is 5%. Also assume that the MMI is currently at 345, and six-month futures are trading at 355. Thus, $355 > 345(1 + 0.05 - 0.03) = 351.9$, and an arbitrage profit is available. Consider the following trading strategy that follows Exhibit 22-10. Buy the underlying MMI (either by direct purchase of the underlying securities or by purchasing a mutual fund that mimics the MMI); sell one futures contract that would require interest-bearing margin; and finally, borrow the margin as well as the MMI price ($345). Thus, the initial cash flow will be zero. From Exhibit 22-10 we know that this strategy produces a positive cash flow (for zero investment) in the future of $355 - 345(1 + 0.05 - 0.03) = 3.51$ per unit of the MMI on this transaction.

Note that this activity will drive the futures price down and the index value up. The arbitrageur plays an important role in making the securities market efficient by trading on price discrepancies. The arbitrageur does take some risks, such as the risk of misestimating the dividend yield or the current interest rate.

22.5.3 Pricing Currency Futures

Currency futures are used by firms having exposure to foreign exchange risk. If a U.S. company sells its goods in the United Kingdom, it receives British pounds in exchange for its products. Because exchange rates fluctuate, the value of the pound in dollars might vary from the time the goods are exchanged until payment is made. To minimize the effects of foreign exchange risk on the value of the products sold, the firm might want to sell British pound futures today to hedge adverse movement in the exchange rate between dollars and pounds.

Currency futures can be evaluated in much the same way as index futures, except the cost of carry is the difference between the domestic risk-free rate (r) and the foreign risk-free rate, r_f. Exhibit 22-11 illustrates the financial strategy by which one can derive an equilibrium price for futures of foreign currency. The primary

---

6. The exact reverse is true if $r < d$.

EXHIBIT 22-11 Determining the Equilibrium Price of Foreign Currency Futures	Strategy	Cash Flow Today ($)	Cash Flow at Expiration ($)
	Borrow 1 German mark (convert to local currency)	S_0	$-S_1(1 + r_f)$
	Lend $(S_0 - m)$ in the United States	$-(S_0 - m)$	$(S_0 - m)(1 + r_L)$
	Purchase futures position to buy $(1 + r_f)$ marks for F_0 dollars	$-m$	$(1 + r_f)(S_1 - F_0) + m(1 + r_L)$
	Net position	0	$S_0(1 + r_L) - F_0(1 + r_f)$

difference between currency futures and index futures is that with currency futures, the foreign risk-free rate is earned, whereas in the index futures calculation, the dividend yield is earned. Note that the futures contract is unaffected by the foreign risk-free rate. However, when the spot currency is purchased, it is assumed to be invested in the foreign risk-free rate.

Exhibit 22-11 suggests some financial transactions, the cost of these transactions today, and the cash flows at contract expiration. Once again, a margin of m dollars is assumed on future transactions. This example uses German marks for the foreign currency and U.S. dollars for the local currency.

First we borrow 1 German mark, which at the current exchange rate (S_0) provides a cash flow of S_0 dollars. For example, if the exchange rate is 2 German marks to 1 dollar, then borrowing 1 German mark will provide $0.50, where S_0 is 0.50, or the exchange rate for 1 German mark. Then we have to pay $(1 + r_f)$ German marks, where r_f is the foreign exchange rate that the German bank charges for the relevant transaction period. However, because in 1 year the exchange rate will be $\$S_1$ per 1 German mark, the cash payment in dollars will be $\$S_1(1 + r_f)$.

We lend $S_0 - m$ in the United States to obtain in the future $(S_0 - m)(1 + r_L)$, where r_L is the interest in local currency for the relevant period. Finally, we purchase futures to buy $(1 + r_f)$ marks; today we pay a margin of m, and next year we get an interest of $m(1 + r_L)$ plus a profit on the future transaction of $(1 + r_f)(S_1 - F_0)$.

With no arbitrage profit, the cash flow at the end of the period must be zero. Therefore,

$$F_0 = \frac{S_0(1 + r_L)}{1 + r_f} \tag{22.2}$$

where S_0 and F_0 are the spot and futures prices of one asset of foreign currency in terms of a local currency.[7]

---

7. With annualized continuous interest rates, this formula can be written as

$$F_0 = S_0 e^{(r_L - r_f)t}$$

where t is the time, usually given as a fraction of a year.

PRACTICE BOX

Problem

Suppose you are an arbitrage trader in the Swiss franc foreign exchange. After a major move in exchange rates, you observe the following information: $S_0 =$ $0.65/SwF (the foreign exchange rate between U.S. dollars and Swiss francs), $F_0 =$ $0.64/SwF (foreign exchange futures price), $r_L =$ 3% (the annual U.S. risk-free rate), $r_f =$ 6% (the annual Swiss risk-free rate), and $t = \frac{1}{2}$ year. Are these prices in equilibrium? How will you profit if they are not in equilibrium?

Solution

To see if these prices are in equilibrium, calculate the theoretical futures price, and compare it with the actual futures price. Thus,

$$F_0 = \frac{S_0(1 + r_L)^{\frac{1}{2}}}{(1 + r_f)^{\frac{1}{2}}} = (\$0.65/\text{SwF}) \cdot \left(\frac{1.03}{1.06}\right)^{\frac{1}{2}} = 0.6407/\text{SwF}$$

which is greater than the current futures price of $0.64/SwF. Thus, the futures price is too low relative to the spot price, so in this case, the arbitrage trade suggested in Exhibit 22-11 would result in the following cash flow today (see "Net position" in the exhibit):

$$S_0(1 + r_L) - F_0(1 + r_f) = (\$0.65/\text{SwF})(1.03)^{\frac{1}{2}}$$
$$- (\$0.64/\text{SwF})(1.06)^{\frac{1}{2}} \cong 0.0007$$

This strategy will result in a positive cash flow of 0.0007 and no cash flow in the future. (Note that both the buyer and the seller of futures contracts must place margin.)

PRACTICE BOX

Problem

Assume that the British pound December 1997 futures contract settled at $1.6664/£ and the March 1998 contract settled at $1.6604/£. What is the implied interest rate difference for this period between the pound and the dollar? (Assume that the yield curve is flat in both countries.)

Solution

We know from Equation 22.2 that

$$F_{\text{Dec97}} = S_0\left(\frac{1 + r_L}{1 + r_f}\right)^{t_1} \tag{1}$$

$$F_{\text{Mar98}} = S_0\left(\frac{1 + r_L}{1 + r_f}\right)^{t_2} \tag{2}$$

(continued)

Dividing Equation 2 by Equation 1 yields

$$F_{\text{Mar 98}}/F_{\text{Dec 97}} = \left(\frac{1 + r_L}{1 + r_f}\right)^{(t_2 - t_1)}$$

Because these contracts are three months apart, we know that $t_2 - t_1 = \frac{3}{12}$. Substituting for the futures prices yields the following:

$$1.6604/1.6664 \cong 0.9964 = \left(\frac{1 + r_L}{1 + r_f}\right)^{\frac{1}{4}}$$

Thus,

$$\left(\frac{1 + r_L}{1 + r_f}\right) \cong 0.9857, \text{ or } r_L - r_f \cong -1.43\%$$

The implied interest rate difference between the United States and England is about -1.43%.

The use of currency futures is just one tool available to hedge foreign exchange risk. Other tools include currency options, currency forward contracts, currency swaps, and currency futures options. We turn now to pricing commodity futures contracts.

22.5.4. Pricing Commodity Futures

Exhibit 22-12 reveals a transaction with commodity futures. To price commodity futures, we need to consider storage costs and insurance costs, denoted by C, along with interest. Here S_0 is the current price of the commodity, and F_0 is the price of the futures of the commodity. S_T is the future price of the commodity, and m is the margin required on the futures transaction. Once again, no arbitrage profit implies the following:

$$F_0 = S_0(1 + r) + C \tag{22.3}$$

EXHIBIT 22-12 Determining the Equilibrium Price of Commodity Futures	Transaction	Cash Flows Today	Cash Flow at Expiration
	Buy asset at price S_0	$-S_0$	$S_T - P_C$
	Borrow $S_0 + m$	$S_0 + m$	$-S_0(1 + r) - m(1 + r)$
	Short futures position	$-m$	$F_0 - S_T + m(1 + r)$
	Net cash flow	0	$F_0 - S_0(1 + r) - C$

Recall that the investor who owned the S&P 500 received dividends, so the financing cost was reduced by the benefit of the dividends. With commodities, storage costs are an additional cost to carrying the asset.

The ability to value futures contracts is useful in many ways. Investors are able to assess whether the current futures prices are reasonable. Also, even when futures are not being traded, futures prices contain useful information. Knowing what it would cost to enter a futures contract is useful when performing project analysis.

SUMMARY

Explain the terminology of futures contracts.   A futures contract is a marketable obligation to deliver a specified quantity of a particular asset on a given day (or during a given period). A forward contract is similar to a futures contract, except a forward contract is not marketable.

Describe the process of buying and selling futures.   All trading in futures contracts is handled by futures commission merchants (FCMs). The clearinghouse guarantees performance by both sides of the futures contract. It insures that the futures contract buyer will deliver and the futures contract seller agrees to accept delivery.

Explain margin and mark to market amounts.   Margin is required by the clearinghouse to reduce the default risk related to futures trading. The initial margin amount is usually higher than the maintenance margin. With futures contracts, profits and losses are taken daily through a process known as mark to market. When a losing position reduces the margin account balance below the required maintenance margin, then a margin call is placed to replenish the margin account to its initial margin level.

Describe the basic strategies involving futures contracts.   Four strategies use futures contracts: hedging, speculating, arbitrage, and portfolio diversification. Hedging strategies use futures contracts to offset an existing risk exposure, whereas speculating seeks to profit by taking more risk. Arbitrage strategies are based on equal pricing between various markets. Some investors now view a portfolio of futures contracts as a separate asset class that can be used to diversify an investment portfolio.

Calculate futures values using the futures pricing equations.   The difference between the current spot price and the current futures price is known as the basis. The basis can be explained for most futures contracts based on the ability to implement arbitrage trading strategies. The futures price depends on the current spot price, the risk-free interest rate, the time to expiration of the futures contract, and the cost of carrying the underlying asset (which includes dividends). The owner of the stock index portfolio receives the dividend yield, the owner of the currency receives the foreign interest rate, and the owner of the commodity has to pay the cost of storing it.

CHAPTER AT A GLANCE

1. *The futures pricing equations follow:*

$$F_0 = S_0(1 + r - d) \qquad \text{Stock Indexes}$$

$$F_0 = \frac{S_0(1 + r_L)}{(1 + r_f)} \qquad \text{Currencies}$$

$$F_0 = S_0(1 + r) + C \qquad\qquad \text{Commodities}$$

where F_0 is the current futures price, S_0 is the current spot price, r is the risk-free domestic interest rate, d is the dividend yield, r_f is the foreign interest rate, and C is the storage cost, and where r, d, r_f, and C reflect the relevant time period to the contract expiration.

KEY TERMS

Basis 827	Futures commission merchant	Mark to market 810
Cash settlement 815	(FCM) 816	Open interest 812
Cost of carry model 830	Futures contract 809	Pit 817
Floor broker 817	Local 817	Settle price 812
Forward contract 807	Long position 807	Short position 807

REVIEW

22.1 If the open interest was 162,022 on the S&P 500 December contract, and the futures price fell by 2.45 points on a given day, what was the total gain or loss over all long positions? (Each contract is 500 times the index.)

22.2 "Because futures prices of different maturities all move together, it doesn't matter which maturity is used when hedging. They all work about the same." Evaluate this statement using just the data given in Exhibit 22-4.

PRACTICE

22.1 Suppose the initial margin is $12,000 for an S&P 500 index futures contract, and the maintenance margin is $10,000. Each S&P 500 index futures contract is for 500 times the index value. Suppose that on Day 0 you purchased one futures contract at 418 points. Describe the cash flow to and from your account, given the following ten days of settle prices. Assume there is no withdrawal from the account, and the surplus remains in the new account.

Day	Settle Price	Day	Settle Price
0		6	$422
1	$420	7	417
2	425	8	410
3	418	9	415
4	415	10	420
5	419		

22.2 Suppose you have $12,000 to invest. You believe that the stocks in the S&P 500 index are going to appreciate by 20% over the next three months. However, they may also depreciate by 20%. Discuss the relative merits of the following three strategies:
a. Invest $12,000 in SP DRS (pronounced "spiders"), which are depository receipts for the S&P 500. These securities were designed to track the S&P 500. Assume that this investment perfectly tracks the value of the S&P 500 index.
b. Borrow an additional $12,000 (assuming a 50% initial stock margin), and buy SP DRS for $24,000. (Assume, for simplicity, that the interest rate is zero.)
c. Buy one S&P 500 index futures contract with three months to maturity with an initial futures margin of $12,000. Assume that the futures price and the spot price are the same, at 420.

Be sure to address the consequences of (1) the S&P 500's appreciating by 20%, as well as (2) the S&P 500's depreciating by 20%. (Assume that the initial futures price is the same as the SP DRS value on a per-unit basis.)

22.3 Assume that the spot price of gold is $340 per troy ounce. Suppose also you observe the following gold futures prices:

Time to Maturity (in years)	Futures Price (in troy ounces)
¼	$344.28
½	348.61
¾	353.00
1	357.43

a. Calculate the basis for each futures contract.
b. If the risk-free interest rate is 3%, what is the implied storage cost of gold (in percent) for 1 year?

22.4 If the current Canadian foreign exchange rate is $0.805/Can $ (that is, U.S. dollars per Canadian dollar) and the six-month futures foreign exchange rate is $0.80/Can $, what is the implied difference in interest rate between the United States and Canada?

22.5 Suppose the NYSE Composite Index closed at 342.02. If the dividend yield is 2% for six months and the current six-month risk-free rate is 4%, what is the equilibrium value of a six-month futures contract on the NYSE Composite?

22.6 Suppose you are the chief financial officer at Yummie Chocolate Company (YCC) and have just entered a contract to deliver a large amount of chocolate candy to McDonald's Corporation in six months. You know that your firm will be purchasing 1,000 metric tons of cocoa in five months. A five-month futures contract on cocoa is trading at $1,000 per metric ton, and each contract is for 10 metric

tons. If the cost of cocoa is $1,000 per metric ton in five months, you anticipate a profit of $100,000.
a. Map the profit and loss from this contract with the fast-food chain with respect to future cocoa prices.
b. Graphically illustrate the profit and loss from purchasing one five-month cocoa futures contract.
c. How could you completely hedge the cocoa price risk? Demonstrate your results graphically.
d. Discuss the costs and benefits to YCC of hedging with futures contracts.

22.7 Suppose a fourth-generation cattle rancher in Texas has an amazing ability to forecast the future price of live cattle. This ranch usually has 8,000 cattle with an average weight of 500 pounds per head. The rancher has made considerable money from buying and selling cattle at the local auction.
a. What alternative is available for the cattle rancher to speculate on live cattle?
b. Suppose the current price of live cattle is $0.85 per pound. How is this rancher affected by changes in live cattle prices? Draw a diagram for the different hypothetical prices.
c. Suppose the rancher believed that in six months, live cattle would be trading at $1.00 per pound. How could the rancher speculate with futures contracts?
d. Discuss the consequences of the rancher's buying 100 six-month futures contracts on live cattle at $0.82 per pound. (Each live cattle futures contract is for 40,000 pounds.) Draw the profit and loss line on (1) the futures contracts, (2) the value of the cattle on the ranch, and (3) a combination of both (1) and (2).

22.8 The price of September futures on German marks is $0.555; the spot is $0.5548. The annual interest rate in the United States is 5%. Use the futures price and the spot price to estimate the annual interest rate in Germany.

CFA PROBLEMS

22.1 Michelle Industries issued a Swiss franc–denominated 5-year discounted note for SwF 200 million. The proceeds were converted to U.S. dollars to purchase capital equipment in the United States. The company wants to hedge this currency exposure and is considering the following alternatives:

a. At-the-money Swiss franc call options.

b. Swiss franc forwards.

c. Swiss franc futures.

Contrast the essential characteristics of each of these three derivative instruments. Evaluate the suitability of each in relation to Michelle's hedging objective, including both advantages and disadvantages.

22.2 Chris Smith of XYZ Pension Plan has historically invested in the stocks of only U.S.–domiciled companies. Recently, he has decided to add inter-

national exposure to the plan portfolio. Rather than select individual stocks, Smith decides to use Nikkei futures to obtain his Japanese portfolio exposure. The Nikkei index is now at 15,000, with a 2% dividend yield. The Japanese risk-free interest rate is 5%. Calculate the price at which Smith can expect a six-month Nikkei futures contract to trade. Show all your work.

For Internet questions visit the Levy Investment Web site at http://levy-invst.swcollege.com.

YOUR TURN: APPLYING THEORY TO PRACTICE
FUTURES PRICES

Index Futures COMEX
Chicago Mercantile Exchange: S&P 500 Index

Seasons's			Week's				
High	Low		High	Low	Settle	Net Change	Open Interest
480.15	434.30	Mar	480.15	470.70	478.75	+5.15	184,482
481.00	448.00	Jun	481.00	471.75	479.80	+5.25	5,051
482.40	460.00	Sep	482.40	473.15	481.00	+5.05	886
484.00	429.70	Dec	484.00	474.80	482.50	+5.15	1,717

Last spot 478.70, up 3.97.

Fri. to Thurs. sales 264,321.

Total open interest 192,136

Source: *Barron's*, January 31, 1994, p. 146. Reprinted by permission of *Barron's*, © 1994 Dow Jones & Co., Inc. All Rights Reserved Worldwide.

Questions

1. Suppose you invest in the March futures. You buy one contract of the S&P 500 index. (Recall that a contract consists of 500 units.) The margin is 5.9%. How much money do you need to invest? (Assume you buy the futures at the settle price.) How much do you need to invest if you buy 500 units of the S&P spot index (that is, a portfolio of these 500 stocks), if the margin on buying stocks is 50%?

Assume that the investment required, less the margin payment, is borrowed at zero interest rate. Use this assumption in the questions below as well.

2. Suppose you consider buying, at $t = 0$, either a portfolio (the S&P index) or the S&P 500 March futures. Assume that both the S&P futures index and the spot index go up by 2% in each of the next two days ($t = 1$ and $t = 2$). At the end

(continued)

of the second day you plan to sell your financial assets. Show the cash flow of each investment. Calculate the IRR on each investment.

3. Suppose now that there is a crash, and in one day the spot price, as well as the futures price, goes down by 5%. Using the margin rates previously cited, calculate the one-day rate of return on each of two alternative investments.

4. Suppose there is a 60% chance that both the futures and spot prices will go up by 5% and a 40% chance that they will go down by 5%. Calculate the mean rate of return and the standard deviation on each of these two investments. (Hint: Don't forget the margin requirement.) Which investment has a higher mean? Which investment has a higher risk?

5. If the investment is done on 100% margin, the long-run mean annual rate of return on the S&P (spot rate) is 14%, and the standard deviation is 20%. Suppose these figures apply also to the futures index. Calculate the mean rate of re-

turn and standard deviation with 50% margin on the spot index investment and 5.9% margin on the futures index investment. Once again, assume borrowing at zero interest rate.

6. Connecting Theory to Practice 22.2 claims that institutions buy futures to cut risk.

a. Suppose you are a manager for a mutual fund that holds a portfolio that is very similar to the S&P index. What will be the effect of buying S&P futures on your portfolio mean return and risk?

b. Connecting Theory to Practice 22.2 claims that "returns from stocks rose or fell in line with bonds in a loosely associated way." Therefore, investors add an "index of futures pools" (which includes many commodities) to stabilize portfolio return. Discuss this statement, and explain why bonds and stocks may be positively correlated. Also explain how a financial institution can eliminate the risk involved with the leverage effect of futures (as discussed in Question 5).

SELECTED REFERENCES

Chance, Don M. *An Introduction to Options and Futures.* 2nd ed. New York: Dryden Press, 1991.

Duffie, Darrell. *Futures Markets.* Englewood Cliffs, N.J.: Prentice-Hall, 1989.

Tucker, Alan L. *Financial Futures, Options and Swaps.* New York: West, 1991.

SUPPLEMENTAL REFERENCES

Ehrhardt, M. C., J. V. Jordan, and R. A. Walking. "An Application of APT to Futures Markets: Test of Normal Backwardation." *Journal of Futures Markets* 7,1 (February 1987): 21–34.

Green, J., and E. Saunderson. "No Room at the Top." *Risk,* February 1998.

Institute of Chartered Financial Analysts. *CFA Readings in Derivative Securities.* Charlottesville, Va.: Institute of Chartered Financial Analysts, 1988.

Kaufman, P. J. *Handbook of Futures Markets: Commodity Financial, Stock Index, and Options.* New York: Wiley, 1984.

Robertson, Malcolm J. *Directory of World Futures and Options.* Englewood Cliffs, N.J.: Prentice-Hall, 1990.

Stein, J. L. *The Economics of Futures Markets.* City: Blackwell, 1986.

Tyson-Quah, K. "Clearing the Way." *Risk,* August 1997.

LEARNING OBJECTIVES

After studying this chapter you should be able to:

1. Name the benefits of modern option contracts.

2. Understand the buying and selling of put and call options.

3. Explain the risk of holding naked options.

4. Describe the role of clearing corporations.

5. Explain how margin requirements on option writers protect buyers from default.

6. Use payoff diagrams to determine the value of an option upon expiration.

7. Identify profitable option strategies based on beliefs about future asset price movements.

THE $1 BILLION LESSON OF NICHOLAS LEESON*

Like many financial institutions, Barings Futures in Singapore originally set out to employ derivatives in a low-risk, but very profitable, arbitrage strategy. In this particular instance, Leeson and his team bought and sold Japanese stock index futures and options on both the Osaka and Singapore (Simex) exchanges, taking their profits out of the price differentials between the two markets. . . . He had it wrong. . . . By the time Leeson threw in the towel and fled to Singapore, his losses were reportedly over $800 million. . . .

Source: Erick Schonfled, *Fortune,* April 3, 1995, p. 42. Reprinted from the April 3, 1995, issue of *Fortune* by special permission. © 1995, Time, Inc.

WHAT ARE DERIVATIVES, AND HOW COULD YOU LOSE $382 MILLION WITH THEM?

Derivatives can be bafflingly complex, but most are simple. A derivative is a financial instrument that *derives* its value (thus the name) from an underlying security or index. Most derivatives are straightforward bets. You bet that interest rates are going up (or down). Like a Super Bowl bet, they usually cost nothing to enter into. (The people who write the contracts—banks or brokerage houses—build their profit into the equation.) The loss—or gain—to the person who uses the derivative comes later, when the derivative is wound up. Since derivatives don't cost the user anything to begin with, they need not appear on the balance sheet.

Source: Scott Woolley, "Derivatives Are a Sensible Way to Manage Risk," *Forbes,* August 11, 1997, p. 43. Reprinted by Permission of *Forbes* magazine © Forbes Inc., 1997.

*Author Note: Nick Leeson worked at Barings Bank. His activities led to the downfall of his employer. On February 27, 1995, Barings, via Leeson, had national positions of more than $30 billion while the total capital of the bank was only $0.615 billion.

A **derivative security** is any asset that derives its value from another asset. A derivative security is also called a **contingent claim,** because its claim is contingent on the value of the underlying security. Derivative securities can alter the risk-to-return profile of an investor's portfolio; thus, if misused, these securities can cause major losses. (See the first article in this chapter's Investments in the News.)

The basic concepts of derivatives are very simple. Derivatives are like a bet on a Super Bowl game. However, as the second article in Investments in the News shows, such bets can be very risky and may induce big losses to investors. Moreover, if derivatives are merely bets, why are they of interest to investors or firms? Derivatives are important for several reasons. First, they can be employed by both investors and firms to hedge risk. Second, derivatives can affect the accounting appearance of financial statistics as well as the real cash flows.[1] Thus, investors who wish to speculate rather than to hedge risk should know the implied future cash flow of such a bet.

Although derivatives can be considered as a simple bet, putting a value on such bets is complicated. How can investors determine the worth of a "ticket" to play such a bet? This chapter examines the basic cash flow of options. The next chapter studies the role derivatives play in reducing risk, as well as the pricing of derivatives.

An **option** is a legal contract that gives its holder the right to buy or sell a specified amount of an underlying asset at a fixed or predetermined price. There are two basic types of options: call options and put options. A **call option** gives its holder the right to buy a specified amount of the underlying asset during some period in the future at a predetermined price. If you hold a call option on IBM common stock and the option expires in three months with a predetermined price of $100, then you have the right to buy IBM stock for $100 on or before the expiration date, regardless of the current market price. Similarly, a **put option** gives its holder the right to sell a specified amount of the underlying asset during some period in the future at a predetermined price. Although puts and calls can be based on the same underlying asset, such as shares of IBM, they are separate securities.

Put and call options trade on a vast array of underlying assets, including common stocks, Treasury bills, Treasury notes, Treasury bonds, futures contracts, commodities, stock indexes, and interest rates.

23.1 THE DEVELOPMENT OF MODERN OPTION TRADING

The earliest record of option trading is attributed to the ancient Greek philosopher, mathematician, and astronomer Thales around 550 B.C.[2] In one account, Thales is said to have purchased call options (or something similar to call options) on the use of olive presses to benefit from his belief that the next olive harvest was going to be

---

1. Indeed, last June the Financial Accounting Standards Board (FASB) proposed that derivatives be "mark to market" and put directly into the company balance sheet and income statements. Thus, any gain or loss on derivatives will be treated according to their current value ("mark to market") and will be reported, even if the asset is not realized. See Scott Woolley, "Derivatives Are a Sensible Way to Manage Risk," *Forbes,* August 11, 1997, p. 43.

2. For a detailed history of options, see Chapter 1 of Options Institute (ed.), *Options: Essential Concepts and Trading Strategies* (Homewood, Ill.: Business One Irwin, 1990), as well as Diogenes Laertius, *Lives of the Philosophers,* vol. 1, pp. 22–44.

extremely good. When his prediction came to pass and a good harvest occurred, Thales exercised his call options and subsequently leased the olive presses to farmers at a considerable profit. A second account states that Thales anticipated a bad harvest and subsequently cornered the market by buying contracts giving him the right to buy olives in the future at a predetermined price. Although some scholars question whether Thales was the individual who participated in these transactions, the historical evidence does show that options trading existed centuries ago.[3]

Option contracts (or *privileges,* as they were first called) began to appear in the United States in the 1790s, shortly after the Buttonwood Tree Agreement—the agreement that established the New York Stock Exchange. In the late nineteenth century, Russell Sage, the grandfather of modern option trading, organized a system for trading put and call options on an over-the-counter market. Sage also introduced the idea of put-call parity—a concept that will be discussed in Chapter 24.

On the theoretical side, Louis Bachelier developed an option pricing model in his Ph.D. dissertation, which he defended on March 29, 1900, at the Academy of Paris. Bachelier's option pricing model is similar to an equation developed later and used in physics to measure how heat moves through a substance. Bachelier's work was not well received by his dissertation chairman, however, because at that time speculation was neither a popular nor a palatable topic. It was not until the early 1950s, when Paul Samuelson rediscovered Bachelier's work, that his contribution gained much attention.[4]

Although options have been around for a long time, organized option trading did not occur until the passage of the Investment Act of 1934, which legalized option trading. Option trading was regulated by the Securities and Exchange Commission (SEC), and the Put and Call Brokers and Dealers Association was established in the early 1940s to assist option traders in their efforts to develop a market. However, during this period, option contracts had several limitations, including the following:

1. The lack of standardized contracts—each transaction required a custom-designed contract.
2. The lack of transferability between investors—it was difficult to get out of an options position.
3. The requirement that the option holder had to take physical delivery of the underlying asset.
4. The risk associated with the lack of collateral required by the seller of the option.
5. The lack of market makers, which made transacting in options more difficult.

To address these five concerns, the Chicago Board of Trade (CBOT) created the Chicago Board Options Exchange (CBOE). The CBOE began option trading on April 26, 1973, at 10:00 AM eastern standard time. Initially, sixteen call options were

---

3. See Frederick Copleston, S. J., *A History of Philosophy,* vol. 1, *Greece and Rome* (Garden City, N.Y.: Image Books, 1985), pp. 22–24.
4. See P. A. Samuelson, "Rational Theory of Warrant Pricing," *Industrial Management Review* 6(Spring 1965): 13–31.

traded on common stocks (that is, the underlying assets were common stocks). Since 1973, the growth of the option market has been explosive. Exhibit 23-1 summarizes the key events in development of the option market.

23.2. BUYING AND SELLING OPTIONS

This section shows how investors buy and sell options. In the explanations of the transactions, the vocabulary used by option traders to describe the process is introduced.

23.2.1 The Option Buyer

An **option buyer** is the purchaser of an option contract. Recall that a call option gives its holder the right to buy the underlying asset at a predetermined price. Thus, if you bought a call option on Compaq common stock, by **exercising** the option contract, you would be purchasing Compaq common stock at a predetermined

EXHIBIT 23-1	Modern History of Option Trading
Year	**Activity**
1973	Chicago Board Options Exchange (CBOE) started, trading sixteen call options. Thus, they introduced a standardized option contract for the first time. Black and Scholes publish seminal option pricing paper
1975	American Stock Exchange (AMEX) and Philadelphia Stock Exchange (PHLX) start trading options
1976	Pacific Stock Exchange starts trading options
1977	Put options start trading; CBOE seeks approval to trade nonstock options
1979	U.S. Labor Department decalres that option use is not a breach of fiduciary duty Comptroller of Currency eases restrictions on bank trust departments' use of options
1980	Volume of option trading exceeds New York Stock Exchange (NYSE) stock volume
1982	Kansas City Board of Trade starts trading the options on Value Line Composite Average Chicago Mercantile Exchange (CME) starts trading the options on the S&P 500 New York Futures Exchange starts trading the options on the NYSE Composite Index CBOE starts trading options on U.S. Treasury bonds PHLX starts trading options on foreign exchange rates
1983	CBOE starts trading CBOE 100 stock index options
1984	International Money Market at the CME starts trading futures options (option contracts whose future value depends on the value of a futures contract) on foreign exchange
1985	CME starts trading Eurodollar futures options; NYSE introduces option trading
1989	Osaka Stock Exchange starts trading Nikkei 225 options
1996	NYSE sells option business to CBOE
1997	CBOE begins trading options on the Dow (DJX options)

price. This predetermined price is the **strike price,** or **exercise price.** Likewise, if you bought a put option on Compaq common stock, by exercising the option contract, you would be selling Compaq's stock at the strike or exercise price. The buyer who holds an option—whether a call or a put option—takes a **long position in an option** (the buyer owns the option and has the right to receive any income from the underlying asset, as defined by the option contract).

23.2.2 The Option Seller

To purchase call and put options, there must be people willing to sell the options. Option sellers are called **option writers,** and they can write both call and put options. The option writer is the person from whom the option buyer purchases the option contract. Options trade between individual investors—the option writer and the option buyer. The option writer is obligated to honor the terms of the option contract if the buyer decides to exercise the option. The option writer takes a **short position** in an option (thus the writer has agreed to sell the underlying asset, as defined by the option contract).

It is worthwhile to distinguish an option writer and a short seller. A short seller of a stock sells stock that is not owned but rather is borrowed from a broker. Therefore, the short seller has an obligation to eventually repurchase the actual shares of stock so that the borrowed stock can be returned to the broker. An option writer, in contrast, may or may not have to actually supply or acquire the underlying asset.

23.2.3 The Option Contract

Some actual figures and possible transactions in call and put options will demonstrate how an option contract works. The relevant information on option prices is reported in several sources, including on-line services, satellite communications, newspapers, and television. This section briefly explains how to read option quotes in newspapers such as *Barron's* and the *Wall Street Journal.*

Consider the example of Compaq in Exhibit 23-2. The first column has the option name in abbreviated form, along with the closing price of the underlying security, which in this case is a stock. Compaq stock closed at $63^{11}/_{16}$ on this date. The option prices listed under call and put last prices headings are the prices for the last trade of the day, which could have been hours before the closing time—4:15 PM eastern standard time. The option prices are given on a per-share basis, although option contracts are written in multiples of 100 shares. The second column gives the strike price (or exercise price) for the options. This column also includes the expiration date. The third column presents the type of option. Call options are identified either by "c" or no symbol at all, and "p" stands for put option. The fourth column gives the number of option contracts traded (sales volume) on November 24, 1997. To demonstrate how to read an option quote, look at the bold Jan 60 put option. The Jan 60 strike price of the put option for Compaq last traded at $3\frac{1}{2}$. Because each option contract is for 100 shares of the stock, the cost of one option contract is $100 \cdot \$3.5 = \$350$.

EXHIBIT 23-2   **Compaq Option Price Quotes as Reported in** *Barron's*

Company/ Exch Close	Strike Price		Sales Vol	Open Int	Opt Exch	Week's High	Low	Last Price	Net Chg
Compaq	Jan 50	p	1695	2324	PC	$1\frac{1}{8}$	$\frac{3}{4}$	1	$-\frac{5}{8}$
$63\frac{11}{16}$	Dec 55	p	1579	2678	PC	$1\frac{3}{8}$	$\frac{5}{8}$	$\frac{13}{16}$	$-\frac{13}{16}$
$63\frac{11}{16}$	Nov 60	p	2636	7033	PC	$\frac{5}{8}$	$\frac{1}{16}$	$\frac{1}{16}$	$-1\frac{3}{16}$
$63\frac{11}{16}$	Nov 60		6178	5282	PC	$7\frac{7}{8}$	$1\frac{3}{4}$	$3\frac{1}{2}$	$-\frac{1}{8}$
$63\frac{11}{16}$	Dec 60	p	5802	6176	PC	$2\frac{11}{16}$	$1\frac{1}{4}$	2	$-1\frac{1}{4}$
$63\frac{11}{16}$	Dec 60		4455	4137	PC	$9\frac{1}{2}$	$5\frac{5}{8}$	$6\frac{1}{8}$	$-\frac{3}{8}$
$63\frac{11}{16}$	**Jan 60**	**p**	**1514**	**5502**	**PC**	**4**	**$2\frac{1}{2}$**	**$3\frac{1}{2}$**	**$-1\frac{1}{8}$**
$63\frac{11}{16}$	Jan 60		1432	4936	PC	11	$7\frac{1}{2}$	$8\frac{1}{8}$	$+\frac{3}{8}$
$63\frac{11}{16}$	Nov 65	p	22750	17017	PC	$2\frac{1}{8}$	$\frac{3}{16}$	$1\frac{1}{2}$	$-1\frac{3}{4}$
$63\frac{11}{16}$	Nov 65		22780	16055	PC	$3\frac{3}{8}$	$\frac{1}{16}$	$\frac{1}{16}$	$-\frac{13}{16}$
$63\frac{11}{16}$	Dec 65	p	3888	4955	PC	$4\frac{1}{2}$	$2\frac{7}{8}$	4	$-1\frac{5}{8}$
$63\frac{11}{16}$	Dec 65		7509	11199	PC	$5\frac{7}{8}$	3	$3\frac{1}{4}$	$-\frac{3}{8}$
$63\frac{11}{16}$	Jan 65		3138	8430	PC	8	5	$5\frac{1}{4}$	...
$63\frac{11}{16}$	Nov 70	p	7400	13700	PC	7	3	$6\frac{1}{4}$	-1
$63\frac{11}{16}$	Nov 70		15293	19850	PC	$\frac{11}{16}$	$\frac{1}{16}$	$\frac{1}{16}$	$-\frac{1}{8}$
$63\frac{11}{16}$	Dec 70	p	2904	12046	PC	$7\frac{3}{4}$	5	7	$-1\frac{3}{4}$
$63\frac{11}{16}$	Dec 70		7699	10384	PC	$3\frac{3}{8}$	$1\frac{7}{16}$	$1\frac{9}{16}$	$-\frac{1}{4}$
$63\frac{11}{16}$	Jan 70		4360	13414	PC	$5\frac{3}{8}$	$3\frac{1}{4}$	$3\frac{3}{8}$	...
$63\frac{11}{16}$	Apr 70		2377	4784	PC	$9\frac{3}{8}$	$6\frac{7}{8}$	7	$-\frac{1}{4}$
$63\frac{11}{16}$	Nov 75	p	2135	11284	PC	$11\frac{5}{8}$	$7\frac{1}{4}$	$11\frac{1}{8}$	$-1\frac{3}{4}$
$63\frac{11}{16}$	Nov 75		2562	25432	PC	$\frac{1}{8}$	$\frac{1}{16}$	$\frac{1}{16}$	...
$63\frac{11}{16}$	Dec 75		6144	6864	PC	$1\frac{3}{4}$	$\frac{5}{8}$	$\frac{11}{16}$	$-\frac{3}{16}$
$63\frac{11}{16}$	Jan 75		3632	13941	PC	$3\frac{1}{2}$	$1\frac{15}{16}$	$2\frac{1}{8}$	$-\frac{1}{8}$
$63\frac{11}{16}$	Apr 75		1443	6955	PC	$7\frac{3}{8}$	5	$5\frac{1}{4}$	$-\frac{1}{4}$
$63\frac{11}{16}$	Jan 80		1795	14833	PC	$2\frac{1}{4}$	$1\frac{1}{16}$	$1\frac{1}{4}$	$-\frac{1}{8}$
$63\frac{11}{16}$	Dec 85		2465	2157	PC	$\frac{1}{2}$	$\frac{1}{16}$	$\frac{1}{16}$	$-\frac{1}{4}$

Source: *Barron's*, November 24, 1997, p. MW94. Reprinted by permission of Barron's © 1997 Dow Jones & Co., Inc. All Rights Reserved Worldwide.

The **expiration date** (or **maturity date**) of an option contract is the date on which the option expires or ceases to exist if the option contract is not exercised. For most stock options, the expiration date is the Friday before the third Saturday of the expiration month. For example, a December 1997 stock option matured on December 16, which was the Friday before the third Saturday. Options on underlying assets other than stocks, such as interest rate options, have unique expiration dates. Eurodollar futures options expire on the Monday preceding the third Wednesday of the contract month. If the third Wednesday of March is March 16, then the March contract expires Monday, March 14.[5]

The cost of purchasing an option contract is called the **option premium.** Specifically, the option premium is the price that the option buyer pays to the writer of the option. For example, if an option buyer pays $5¼ for the call option (Compaq Jan 65; see Exhibit 23-2), the total premium would be $525 ($5.25 · 100), because each option contract is for 100 shares. This $525 premium is not just a good faith deposit or a down payment but rather a nonrefundable fee. The *option price* refers to the current market price of the option. The option premium and the option price are the same at the time of the option transaction ($525 in the above example). However, after the time of purchase, the option premium is $525, whereas the option price can change with current market conditions. For example, if the stock price rallies, the option price may rise to $600 per contract, whereas the option premium is still $525. The option premium refers to the option price when first traded, not the current market price.

A distinction is made between when an option contract is initiated and when the contract is closed. An **opening transaction** occurs when a new position is established. A **closing transaction** occurs when an already established position is eliminated. For example, suppose you purchased one Compaq Jan 65 call to open on July 29 for a premium of $5¼ per share. After two months you decide to sell one Compaq Jan 65 call for a market price that happens to be $6 per share. The opening transaction takes place when you purchase the Compaq Jan 65 call. When you sell the call option, the transaction will be closed. Hence, after selling the options, you have no option position, and you have $¾ per-share profit ($6 − $5¼) before transaction costs. Therefore, after the sale of one Compaq 65 call on September 2, you would have no outstanding position, because the sale of the previous purchase is offsetting.

Another distinction related to option contracts involves when the contract can be exercised: European-style versus American-style options. **European-style options** can be exercised only on specific dates. For example, contracts that can be exercised only on the last day of the contract, such as foreign exchange options, are traded on the Philadelphia Stock Exchange. **American-style options,** in contrast, can be exercised any time on or before the expiration date of the contract. The holder of an American option has the freedom to decide when, if ever, the option contract will be exercised. Note that these terms do not refer to, or even reflect, geographic location (that is, Europe or the United States). Most stock options are American-style options, and many index options and interest rate options are European-style options.

Exhibit 23-3 illustrates quotes on long-term options on individual stocks, as well as options on various financial products: options on various indexes (for example, S&P 100 and S&P 500), foreign currency, and interest rates. As an example of

---

5. Another concept associated with options is the *option cycle,* which is the procedure with which new option contracts initiate trading. Some contracts have monthly cycles (say, each month for the next six months), and other contracts have quarterly cycles (say, each quarter for the next 2½ years, such as Eurodollar futures options). Some contracts are a combination of both monthly and quarterly cycles. Before actually trading options, investors must investigate which contracts are available.

EXHIBIT 23-3 Various Listed Option Quotations

LONG-TERM EQUITY OPTIONS

Company Exch Close	Strike Price			Sales Vol	Open Int	Opt Exch	Week's High	Week's Low	Last Price	Net Chg
AT&T	Jan 00	30		325	1447	CB	16 3/4	16	16	− 1/2
43 3/16	Jan 99	35	p	760	4146	CB	1 5/8	1 3/8	1 1/2	+ 1/8
43 3/16	Jan 99	40		811	5706	CB	10	8 1/4	8 3/8	−1 1/8
43 3/16	Jan 99	45		309	6780	CB	6 7/8	5 3/8	5 3/8	−1
AMD	Jan 99	30		523	1708	PC	11 1/4	6 1/2	8 1/4	−1 7/8
29 13/16	Jan 99	30	p	1052	3708	PC	7 1/2	5 3/4	5 3/4	+ 5/8
29 13/16	Jan 99	35		380	1936	PC	9	5	6 7/8	−1 7/8
29 13/16	Jan 99	35	p	862	2614	PC	10 1/2	8 3/4	8 3/4	+2
29 13/16	Jan 99	40		314	1675	PC	7 3/8	4	5	−1 1/2
29 13/16	Jan 99	40	p	1160	1628	PC	14 1/2	13	13 1/4	+2
29 13/16	Jan 99	45	p	506	648	PC	18 1/2	16 1/4	16 1/4	...
Aetna	Jan 00	100	p	1158	1150	AM	23 1/2	21 1/8	23 1/2	+7
AmExp	Jan 00	90		306	445	XC	17 1/8	16 1/2	16 5/8	+3 3/8
AppleC	Jan 00	35		300	5061	XC	3 5/8	3 3/8	3 3/8	− 3/8
Ascend	Jan 00	30		471	416	XC	17 1/2	4 1/4	14 1/2	−3 5/8
32 11/16	Jan 00	30	p	357	403	XC	9 1/8	7 3/4	8 1/4	+ 1/2
32 11/16	Jan 99	30		1039	3543	XC	14 1/4		11 3/8	−3 3/8
32 11/16	Jan 99	30	p	444	2160	XC	7 1/2	5 7/8	6 5/8	+ 5/8
32 11/16	Jan 99	35		675	545	XC	12 1/4	8 5/8	9 5/8	−2 3/4
32 11/16	Jan 00	40		1064	3182	XC	13 7/8	10 1/8	11	−2 3/4
32 11/16	Jan 99	40		724	3417	XC	9 3/4	7	7 3/4	−2 1/4
32 11/16	Jan 99	45		436	3985	XC	8 3/8	5 3/4	6 1/4	−2 3/8
32 11/16	Jan 00	60		700	2024	XC	8 1/2	6 1/4	7	−2 1/8
32 11/16	Jan 99	60		996	4056	XC	5	3 1/4	3 1/2	−1 3/4
BankTr	Jan 99	100		306	537	PC	29 1/2	28 1/4	29 1/2	+2 1/4
Boeing	Jan 99	50		337	4602	XC	12	9 1/4	10 3/8	−1 3/8

LONG-TERM INDEX OPTIONS

Company Exch Close	Strike Price			Sales Vol	Open Int	Opt Exch	Week's High	Week's Low	Last Price	Net Chg
S&P100	Dec 97	60	p	433	35196	CB	1/16	1/16	1/16	...
92.81	Dec 97	65	p	595	17993	CB	1/8	1/16	1/16	−3/16
92.81	Dec 98	70	p	305	3893	CB	1 5/8	1 3/8	1 1/2	+1/16
92.81	Dec 97	70	p	930	14785	CB	1/4	3/16	3/16	...
92.81	Dec 97	72 1/2	p	1025	4293	CB	5/16	3/16	3/16	−3/16
92.81	Dec 97	80	p	633	9177	CB	13/16	1/2	1/2	− 1/2
92.81	Dec 98	95	p	1003	3992	CB	8 1/2	7 1/2	7 1/2	−2 7/8
SP500	Jun 99	1075	p	515	739	CB	120	111 7/8	112 1/2	...
SP500 2Yr	Jun 98	725	p	311	4637	CB	16 3/4	16 1/2	16 3/4	−3 1/4
965.03	Jun 98	800	p	503	635	CB	29 1/2	29	29	+1 3/4
965.03	Dec 97	800	p	421	4801	CB	24	20	22	−8 1/2
965.03	Jun 98	850	p	400	4900	CB	41 1/8	37 3/4	37 3/4	−4 3/4
965.03	Dec 97	850	p	3862	5374	CB	34 3/4	32 1/2	32 1/2	−4
965.03	Dec 97	925		1250	2381	CB	124 3/4	121	124 1/4	− 1/4
965.03	Jun 98	950		300	4562	CB	137 1/4	136 3/4	136 3/4	+1 3/4
965.03	Jun 98	995		400	900	CB	113	113	113	...
SPX500	Dec 98	75	p	438	15188	CB	1 3/4	1 3/8	1 5/8	...
96.50	Dec 98	85	p	390	8694	CB	3 3/4	2 7/8	3 3/8	− 1/4

INTEREST RATE OPTIONS

CBOE

Yields									
30yrTN	Dec	60		75	6.04	6.04	6.04	− 2.00	322.56
30yrTN	Dec	65		20	4.04	4.00	4.00	− 1.00	322.56
30yrTN	Dec	75		221	1.16	1.00	1.00	− 0.04	322.56
Interest Rate									
IRX	Oct	50	p	61	1.02	0.26	0.26	...	50
IRX	Dec	50	p	102	0.16	0.16	0.16	...	50
IRX	Jun	47 1/2	p	50	1.08	1.08	1.08	...	47 1/2
IRX	Jun	50	p	10	2.04	2.04	2.04	...	50
Total Call Vol			659	Call Open int					3,534
Total Put Vol			964	Put Open int					3,163

CBOE INTEREST OPTIONS

Friday, August 15, 1997

10 YEAR TREASURY YIELD OPTION (TNX)

Total call volume 0 Total call open int. 253

Total put volume 400 Total put open int. 246

TNX levels: High 63.08; Low 62.44; Close 62.48, −.13

30 YEAR TREASURY YIELD OPTION (TYX)

Strike Price	Calls-Last Aug	Calls-Last Sep	Calls-Last Oct	Puts-Last Aug	Puts-Last Sep	Puts-Last Oct
62 1/2	3 3/8	....	....	....	....	....
65	....	1 5/8	....	....	....	1 1/8
67 1/2	....	....	7/8	1 5/8	2 1/4	....
70	....	....	5/16	....	4	4 1/2

Total call volume 493 Total call open int. 3,434

Total put volume 398 Total put open int. 3,252

TYX levels: High 66.21; Low 65.52; Close 65.57, +0.00

FOREIGN CURRENCY OPTIONS

Philadelphia Exchange

50,000 Australian Dollars-cents per unit.										
ADollr	Dec	74 1/2		5	500	0.06	0.06	0.06	...	72.85
31,250 Brit. Pounds-cents per unit.										
BPound	Dec	172	p	1	282	2.19	2.15	2.15	...	161.55
BPound	Oct	157	p	3	92	0.02	0.02	0.02	...	161.55
BPound	Oct	158	p	2	260	0.02	0.02	0.02	...	161.55
BPound	Oct	164		2	294	0.02	0.02	0.02	...	161.55
BPound	Dec	163		17	1536	0.38	0.30	0.31	...	161.55
50,000 Canadian Dollars-cents per unit.										
CDollr	Oct	72 1/2		31	1302	0.07	0.05	0.05	...	72.89
CDollr	Oct	73		5	340	0.02	0.02	0.02	...	72.89
CDollr	Dec	73		5	794	0.09	0.08	0.09	− 0 01	72.89
CDollr	Dec	73 1/2		3	885	0.09	0.05	0.09	− 0.02	72.89
62,500 German Marks-European Style.										
DMark	Oct	55 1/2		1	225	0.27	0.27	0.27	− 0.02	56.90
DMark	Oct	55 1/2	p	1	475	0.01	0.01	0.01	...	56.90
DMark	Oct	56	p	7	1120	0.05	0.03	0.03	...	56.90
DMark	Dec	56		1	271	0.34	0.27	0.27	+ 0.09	56.90
DMark	Dec	56	p	1	365	0.13	0.11	0.13	− 0.04	56.90
62,500 German Marks-cents per unit.										
DMark	Oct	55 1/2	p	7	133	0.02	0.02	0.02	...	56.90
DMark	Oct	56	p	12	1033	0.05	0.03	0.04	− 0.04	56.90
DMark	Oct	56 1/2	p	35	2391	0.09	0.04	0.04	...	56.90
DMark	Nov	55	p	1	158	0.05	0.05	0.05	...	56.90
DMark	Dec	53	p	7	1639	0.02	0.02	0.02	− 0.02	56.90
DMark	Dec	53 1/2	p	12	500	0.04	0.03	0.04	...	56.90
DMark	Dec	54	p	16	3844	0.05	0.04	0.05	− 0.01	56.90
DMark	Dec	55	p	2	1545	0.09	0.06	0.09	+ 0.02	56.90
DMark	Dec	56 1/2	p	12	1157	0.20	0.16	0.16	...	56.90
DMark	Mar	54	p	10	2521	0.09	0.08	0.09	− 0.03	56.90
DMark	Mar	56	p	3	270	0.21	0.19	0.20	− 0.11	56.90
DMark	Mar	57		2	430	0.34	0.28	0.28	− 0.09	56.90
DMark	Mar	57	p	4	311	0.34	0.29	0.34	− 0.04	56.90
250,000 French Francs-European Style										
FFranc	Oct	16 3/4	p	1	750	0.20	0.10	0.20	+ 0.04	169.24
62,500 German Mark-Japanese Yen cross.										
GMk-YJn	Oct	69		1	160	0.05	0.05	0.05	...	69.49
GMk-YJn	Dec	66	p	1	160	0.09	0.09	0.09	...	69.49
6,250,000J.Yen-100ths of a cent per unit.										
JYen	Dec	80 1/2	p	2	1979	0.19	0.13	0.19	+ 0.02	81.87
JYen	Dec	84	p	1	870	0.52	0.40	0.51	+ 0.04	81.87
JYen	Dec	81	p	2	2004	0.22	0.15	0.22	+ 0.03	81.87
JYen	Dec	82	p	1	2353	0.29	0.29	0.29	...	81.87
62,500 Swiss Francs-European Style.										
SFranc	Oct	68	p	1	160	0.05	0.04	0.05	...	69.02
62,500 Swiss Francs-cents per unit.										
SFranc	Mar	68		1	178	0.59	0.59	0.59	...	69.02
Total Call Vol				13,291	Call Open int					162,212
Total Put Vol				19,555	Put Open int					158,635

Source: *Barron's*, October 6, 1997, p. MW79—reprinted by permission of *Barrons*, © 1997 Dow Jones & Co., Inc.; All Rights Reserved Worldwide; and *Wall Street Journal*, August 18, 1997, p. C15—reprinted by permission of *The Wall Street Journal*, © 1997 Dow Jones & Co., Inc. All Rights Reserved Worldwide.

an option on an index, the quote of an S&P 100 index put option (December 1998) with a strike price of $95 is $7½ (see "Last Price"). As an example of a quote on options on foreign currency, the call option to buy a German mark until March 1998 with a strike price of 57 American cents per German mark costs 0.28 cents. (The current exchange rate is 56.90 cents per 1 German mark.)

To illustrate options on interest rates, note that the 30-year Treasury note's last quoted price is $65.57. There is a call option to buy the bond at $62½. The market price of this August 1997 call is $3⅜ (see CBOE Exhibit 23-3). Note that an immediate exercise of the option yields $65.57 − $62½ = $3.07. The call is traded for $3⅜, and the difference between $3⅜ and $3.07 reflects the chance that if the interest rate goes down before the end of August, the bond's price will go up, and the call option holder will have more profit. Note that these options are really on bonds, but they are called interest rate options because investors are gambling (or hedging) on changes in interest rates. A change in interest rate induces a change in the bond's price, and hence a change in the option's price.

23.2.4 Investing in Options versus Investing in Stock

Suppose Bill Ups, an eternal optimist, believes the price of Compaq stock will rise sharply over the next three months. Compaq stock is currently trading at $63.6875 per share. How can Bill profit from his hunch? He could simply buy Compaq stock: one round lot (100 shares) would cost him $6,368.75 ($63.6875 · 100). Alternatively, he could buy call options on Compaq stock at a much lower initial cost. He would profit if his prediction was correct. For example, if a three-month call option was $5.25 with a strike price of $65, he would pay only $525 to take a long position in 100 call options on shares of Compaq.[6] If Compaq rose to $75, then a 100 long position of call options in Compaq will result in a profit of $1,000 [($75 − $65) · 100]. The profit on options is taxable; the tax calculation is explained in Appendix 23A. A $1,000 profit on a $525 investment results in a rate of return of 190% [($1,000/$525) · 100]. The rate of return from merely buying the stock is only about 17.8% [($7,500 − $6,368.75)/$6,368.75]. Clearly, Bill would rather have the 190% rate of return. Thus, call options provide a low-cost way of taking large positions in stock at a lower cost than buying the stock directly.

Now suppose Jane Downs, an eternal pessimist, believes Compaq's stock price will fall over the next six months. Short selling the stock is risky, requires margin money, and may not be allowable for regulatory reasons (depending on the nature of the invested funds).[7] Rather than short sell stock, Jane could buy a put option. Recall that a put option gives its holder the right to sell the underlying asset at a predetermined price. Put options cost less than the margin required to short sell the stock, and the loss is limited to the purchase price of the put. Thus, the optimist on the future price of an asset buys call options, and the pessimist buys put options.

---

6. Each stock option contract is for 100 shares. Option prices are quoted on a per-share basis.
7. See Chapter 3.

For example, the price of a six-month put option is $2 with a strike price of $60. Jane would pay only $200 to take a short position in 100 shares of Compaq. If Compaq fell to $50, then the put option would have a profit of $1,000 [($60 − $50)100]. A $1,000 profit on a $200 investment results in a rate of return of 500% [($1,000/$200)100]. Clearly, investors bearish on Compaq's stock would be attracted to put options.

With such tremendous gains available to option buyers, why would anyone wish to write options? The primary benefit is that option writers receive the option premium. If the asset price moves against the option buyer, then there are no future costs to the option writer.

PRACTICE BOX

Problem

Consider the call option price for Genentec, Inc., of $2 with the strike price of $25. The stock price never goes above $20 before the maturity (the expiration date) of the option. What is the profit or loss to the call writer? What is the profit or loss to the call buyer? What is the call option worth at expiration? Why? What is the premium? (Recall that each option contract is for 100 shares, and the option price is quoted on a per-share basis.)

Solution

Because the stock price never exceeds the strike price, the call option expires worthless. (You would not wish to buy a stock at a price higher than it is currently trading in the market.) The call writer will keep the entire option premium of $2 · 100 = $200. The call buyer will lose the entire option premium of $200.

23.2.5 The Underlying Asset and the Option

Options are categorized by the relationship that exists between the current market price of the underlying asset and the option's exercise price. Let S_0 represent the current market price of the generic underlying asset (for example, the stock price) and X represent the option exercise price. An **in-the-money option** is an option that would generate a positive cash flow if it were exercised now. That is, a call option is an in-the-money option if the market price of the underlying asset is greater than the strike price ($S_0 > X$) of the option contract. If the option is American style, an investor could exercise the call option, pay X dollars for the stock, and turn around and sell the stock for S_0, generating a positive cash flow of $S_0 − X$. For put options, an in-the-money option is an option in which the price received for exercising the option (X) is greater than the current price of the stock ($X > S_0$). An **out-of-the-money option** is the exact opposite of an in-the-money option. That is, for calls, $X > S_0$; for puts, $X < S_0$. In the case of out-of-the-money options, there is no incentive to exercise the put or call. **At-the-money options** occur when the current price of the stock is exactly equal to the exercise price $S_0 = X$.

Sometimes option traders refer to *deep in-the-money options* or *deep out-of-the-money options*. The word *deep* emphasizes that the distance between S_0 and X is relatively large. For example, for a deep in-the-money call option, S_0 is much higher than X. In the case of deep out-of-the-money call options, S_0 is much lower than X.

A call option written when the investor does not own the underlying asset is a **naked position**. A **covered position** is a call option written when the underlying asset is already owned. Writing a call option without owning the underlying asset is very risky and hence exposes the writer to great risk. The consequences of naked option trading is demonstrated in the first article in this chapter's Investments in the News, in which the naked position of Nicholas Leeson ultimately led to the bankruptcy of Barings Bank.

Clearly, investing in options can be very risky. Connecting Theory to Practice 23.1, however, demonstrates another use of options—hedging to reduce losses. Obviously, understanding the risk and return structure of options is crucial in a decision to invest in options.

CONNECTING THEORY TO PRACTICE 23.1

NEW TOOLS FOR THE OPTIONS CROWD

These days, many investors seem to think about the derivative sort of like pornography: They can't really define what it is but they're pretty sure it's nothing they should look at. "When we say to some of our clients, 'We'd like to talk to you about derivatives,' many of them say, 'Talk to someone else. I'm not into that stuff,' " says Robert McBain, head of global equity derivatives at Bank of America in San Francisco.

That's changing. In the wake of a bull market that's created legions of stock option millionaires in Silicon Valley and elsewhere, the much-maligned derivative is finding new life as, of all things, a tool for individual stockholders who are worried about risk. Specifically, a growing number of banks' private banking units (which focus on wealthy clients) are peddling what's called a zero-cost dollar, a derivative tailored for individual investors. . . .

Mark Munoz, head of U.S. equity derivatives of Bank of America, explains the collar solution this way: You simultaneously sell a call option (the right to buy the stock at a particular price) and buy a put option (the right to sell the stock at a particular price). The simultaneous transactions form the "collar." The put protects the investor on the downside—typically limiting losses to about 10% of the stock's market price—so if your stock is trading at $50, you're protected for any losses below $45 if, for example, a broad correction knocks the stock for a loop. On the other hand, the call means you give up a portion of the upside potential if, say, a sweet bid from WorldCom drives the share price up. (The bank determines the collar's ceiling.)

(continued)

But there's another advantage: Because the terms of these contracts are usually at least one year and your holdings are stabilized, you can now use your position as collateral and borrow against it, a procedure called monetizing. . . .

Source: Shaifali Puri, *Fortune,* November 10, 1997, p. 308. Reprinted from the November 10, 1997, issue of *Fortune* by special permission. © 1997, Time, Inc.

MAKING THE CONNECTION

When options were first introduced, their risk and return structure was often misunderstood. This led to large losses because of the inappropriate use of options by investors. (You may recall, for example, the case of derivatives being blamed in the bankruptcy of a California school system.) As the article points out, however, options can be used to hedge against large losses.

23.3 OVERVIEW OF OPTION MARKETS

Option trading occurs on exchanges, over the counter, and directly between buyers and sellers. There are many different exchanges on which options are traded. The most active option exchanges are the Chicago Board Options Exchange (CBOE), the American Stock Exchange (AMEX), the Chicago Board of Trade (CBOT), the Philadelphia Stock Exchange (PHLX), the Chicago Mercantile Exchange (CME), and the Pacific Stock Exchange (PSE). On the CBOE alone, the total volume of contracts traded increased over 23% in 1 year (1996 to 1997; see Exhibit 23-4).

Option transactions are similar to stock transactions. For example, if John Q decides to buy call options on Compaq, he would call his broker and state his desires. The broker would communicate this order to the appropriate option exchange, where the trade would occur with either an investor wanting to sell call options on Compaq or with the market maker (see Chapter 3).

The **Options Clearing Corporation (OCC)** maintains the records of option trades and is one of the major clearing corporations (organizations that facilitate the validation, delivery, and settlement of security transactions). The OCC is owned

EXHIBIT 23-4 Option Contract Volume on the CBOE	Date	Call Volume	Put Volume	Total Volume
	12/1/95	326,385	239,526	565,911
	12/2/96	375,228	200,637	575,865
	12/1/97	443,900	264,396	708,296

and backed by several exchanges (such as the CBOE, AMEX, NYSE, and PHLX). Hence, the OCC is a very creditworthy corporation. It issues all option contracts and guarantees both sides of the contracts. Thus, the option buyer does not have to evaluate the credit risk of the option writer. Also, all option contracts have standardized features that make them easier to resell, thus enhancing the option contract's liquidity. The OCC provides a prospectus for each contract, which details the regulations related to trading options and processes all transactions related to option trading.

Suppose that you purchase a call option with an exercise price of $50. The stock price subsequently increases to $200. Who guarantees that the call writer will pay you the difference (that is, $200 − $50 = $150)? The OCC requires that the call writer (as well as all other option writers) provide collateral, known as margin. The margin requirements, which are explained in detail in Appendix 23B, insure that the option writer will pay the option buyer if the events indeed occur in the buyer's favor.

23.4 OPTION VALUES AT EXPIRATION

This section examines the value of options at expiration. In this examination, it is helpful to use graphs with lines that plot the future possible values of the underlying asset. These graphs, called *payoff diagrams,* are used in Section 23.5 to compare the objectives of different option-based trading strategies. This section first examines option values and then explains the mechanics of payoff diagrams.

23.4.1 Option Prices: Intrinsic and Time Value Components

Option prices can be broken down into two components: intrinsic value and time value. The **intrinsic value** of an option is the value of the option if it is immediately exercised (assuming it is an American-style option) or zero. That is, the intrinsic value for calls (IV_c) is[8]

$$IV_c = \max(0, S_0 - X) \tag{23.1}$$

The intrinsic value for puts (IV_p) is

$$IV_p = \max(0, X - S_0) \tag{23.2}$$

As the stock price changes, the intrinsic value of the option may change as well. It remains zero if the option remains out of the money. The **time value** of an option is whatever value an option currently has above its intrinsic value. Even if an option is out of the money, the chance that the stock price may change and the option may

---

8. Note that max(a, b) means to take the larger of a or b. For example, if y = max(a, b) and if $a > b$, then $y = a$.

end up in the money gives the option time value. Most often, the term *time value* refers to discounting future cash flows. When related to options, time value has a different meaning. It is the value of the option related to the chance that the option may go in the money (or further in the money, if it is already in the money).

Let c_0 and p_0 represent the call and put premiums, respectively. Then the time value of a call (TV_c) is

$$TV_c = c_0 - IV_c \tag{23.3}$$

The time value of a put (TV_p) is

$$TV_p = p_0 - IV_p \tag{23.4}$$

Clearly, from the definition of *time value* and *intrinsic value,* we can represent option prices as follows:

$$c_0 = IV_c + TV_c = \max(0, S_0 - X) + TV_c \tag{23.5}$$

and

$$p_0 = IV_p + TV_p = \max(0, X_0 - S_0) + TV_p \tag{23.6}$$

For example, suppose the current price of GNE stock now is \$28 ($S_0 = \$28$). If the current price of a GNE July 25 call is \$6½ ($c_0 = 6½$, $X = 25$), then the call's intrinsic value is \$3 ($IV_c = \$28 - \$25 = \$3$), and the time value is \$3½ ($TV_c = \$6½ - \$3 = \$3½$). If the GNE July 25 put is trading at \$¾, then the put's intrinsic value is \$0 [$IV_p = \max(0, 25 - 28) = \$0$], and the time value is \$¾ ($TV_p = \$¾ - \$0 = \$¾$).

PRACTICE BOX

Problem

Suppose you are given the following option quotes for United Airlines:

Option & NY Close	Strike Price	Calls			Puts		
		Oct.	Nov.	Dec.	Oct.	Nov.	Dec.
114	110	4¼	7½	8¼	⅜	2¼	3
114	115	⅞	3⅞	5	1¾	4½	5¼
114	120	⅛	2	2½	6⅛	7¾	8¼

Compute the intrinsic value and time value for each option.

Solution

The intrinsic value is the dollar amount of an in-the-money option. For calls only, the 110 strikes are \$4 in the money. For puts, the 115 strikes are \$1 in the

(continued)

money, and the 120 strikes are $6 in the money. Thus, we can construct the following table for intrinsic value:

Intrinsic Value

Strike Price	Calls			Puts		
	Oct.	Nov.	Dec.	Oct.	Nov.	Dec.
110	4	4[a]	4	0	0	0
115	0	0	0	1	1	1
120	0	0	0	6	6[b]	6

a. $IV_c = \max(0, S_0 - X) = \max(0, \$114 - \$110) = \$4$.

b. $IV_p = \max(0, X - S_0) = \max(0, \$120 - \$114) = \$6$.

The time value is nothing but the option value minus the intrinsic value. We can construct the following table of time value:

Time Value

Strike Price	Calls			Puts		
	Oct.	Nov.	Dec.	Oct.	Nov.	Dec.
110	$\frac{1}{4}$	$3\frac{1}{2}$[a]	$4\frac{1}{4}$	$\frac{3}{8}$	$2\frac{1}{4}$	3
115	$\frac{7}{8}$	$3\frac{7}{8}$	5	$\frac{3}{4}$	$3\frac{1}{2}$	$4\frac{1}{4}$
120	$\frac{1}{8}$	2	$2\frac{1}{2}$	$\frac{1}{8}$	$1\frac{3}{4}$[b]	$2\frac{1}{4}$

a. $TV_c = c_0 - IV_c = \$7\frac{1}{2} - \$4 = \$3\frac{1}{2}$.

b. $TV_p = p_0 - IV_p = \$7\frac{3}{4} - \$6 = \$1\frac{3}{4}$.

23.4.2 Payoff Diagrams

A **payoff diagram** is a graph that illustrates (1) the relationship among the values of securities (the value line), (2) the dollar profit or loss (the P/L line), or (3) both the value line and the P/L line.[9] To illustrate, let us consider buying stock in Apple Computer Corporation. Exhibit 23-5a shows the various possible values of Apple's stock at some future date, which will be the option expiration date. This 45-degree line is called the *value line* (not to be confused with the information service company Value Line, Inc.). The value line will have a value of $70 on the vertical axis when the stock, at expiration, is $70. Thus, the relationship on the horizontal and vertical axes is one to one.

9. Payoff diagrams can be used to illustrate option contracts that are for 100 shares or to illustrate an option on a single share. For simplicity, we illustrate payoff diagrams for an option on a single share. Payoff diagrams also ignore the ability to exercise early on American-style options.

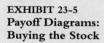

EXHIBIT 23-5
Payoff Diagrams:
Buying the Stock

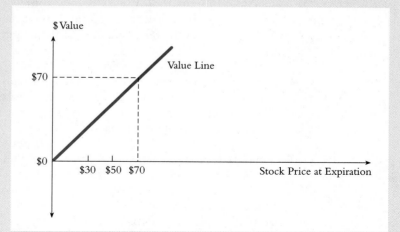

Part a: Value Line for Buying Stock

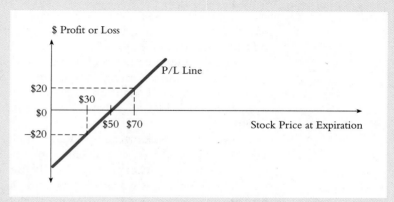

Part b: P/L Line for Buying Stock
(Initial Stock Price = $50)

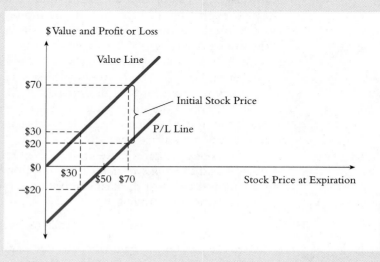

Part c: Payoff Diagram for
Buying Stock

Now suppose that Apple stock was purchased for $50 per share. Exhibit 23-5b shows the profit or loss at the option expiration date. This 45-degree line, called the *P/L line,* crosses the horizontal axis at the original purchase price of $50. When Apple stock is at $70, the investor has a $20 ($70 − $50) profit; when Apple stock is at $30, the investor has a $20 ($50 − $30) loss.

Exhibit 23-5c shows both the value line and the P/L line. In the option markets, one or both of these lines are referred to as a *payoff diagram.* When examining complex option strategies, there are times when it is helpful to analyze value lines and times when it is helpful to analyze P/L lines. Notice in Exhibit 23-5c that the difference between the value line and the P/L line is the original purchase price of the stock. For example, when the stock price goes to $70, the value line is at $70 and the P/L line is at $20, for a difference of $50 ($70 − $20).

Exhibit 23-6 is based on the same data, except the investor is short selling the stock. As illustrated in Exhibit 23-6a, the value line is a −45-degree line starting at zero. If Apple stock ends up at $30, then it will cost $30 to buy it back. If the investor initially sold the stock for $50 and bought it back for $30, the investor will have a $20 ($50 − $30) profit, as illustrated by the P/L line in Exhibit 23-6b. The payoff diagram shown in Exhibit 23-6c is simply the combination of the value line and the P/L line. Once again, the difference between these two lines is −$50. Notice that the difference between buying and short selling the stock is graphically equivalent to a mirror image, where the mirror is placed on the horizontal axis. For example, the P/L line for buying the stock when the stock is at $70 is $20, whereas the P/L line for short selling the stock is −$20 (see Exhibits 23-5b and 23-6b).

Now let us consider a call option on Apple with a strike price of $50 ($X = \$50$) and a call price of $5 ($c_0 = \$5$). The value line in Exhibit 23-7a illustrates the value of the call option at its expiration date. If the stock price falls below $50 at expiration, then the option is worthless. For example, if the stock price is selling for $30 at maturity, the call price is $0; its intrinsic value is zero. If the stock price rises above $50 at expiration, the option is in the money and has a positive price. Specifically, for every dollar the stock is above $50, the option is worth an additional dollar. If the stock price rises to $70 at expiration, then the call option has a value of $20 ($70 − $50), because at expiration we receive the right to buy the stock for $50 when its market value is $70. Hence, we buy the stock via the option contract for $50 and sell the stock received for $70, profiting $20. Thus, the value line is zero on the horizontal axis up to the strike price. At the strike price it becomes a positive 45-degree line. From the value line we see clearly that a call option is very profitable when the underlying stock price goes up.

If an option expires in the money, then it has intrinsic value. The option investment is said to *break even* if the proceeds from the exercise of the option at expiration are just equal to the original option premium. Specifically, we break even on the call option investment if

$$IV_{c,t} = \max(S_t - X, 0) = c_0$$

where *t* represents the maturity date. For example, when the stock price at maturity date is $S_t = \$55$ and $X = \$50$, then $IV_{c,t} = c_0 = \$5$, and we just break even.

EXHIBIT 23-6
Payoff Diagrams:
Short Selling the Stock

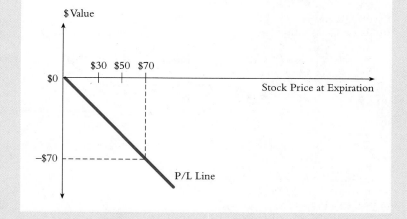

Part a: Value Line for Short
Selling Stock

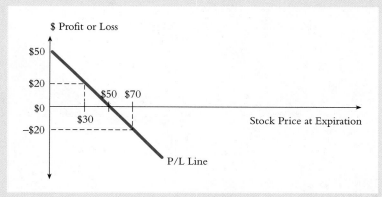

Part b: P/L Line for Short
Selling Stock

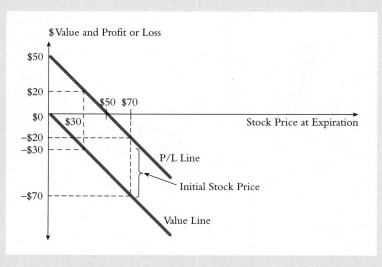

Part c: Payoff Diagram for Short
Selling Stock

EXHIBIT 23-7
Payoff Diagrams:
Buying a Call Option

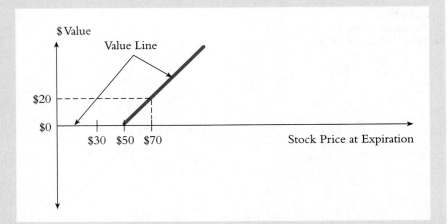

Part a: Value Line for Buying
a Call Option (Strike Price
= $50, Call Price = $5)

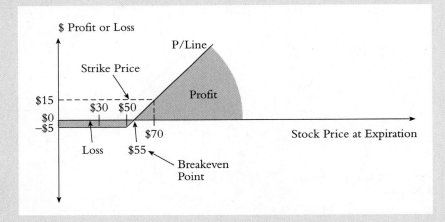

Part b: P/L Line for Buying
a Call Option ($c_0 = $5, X
= $50)

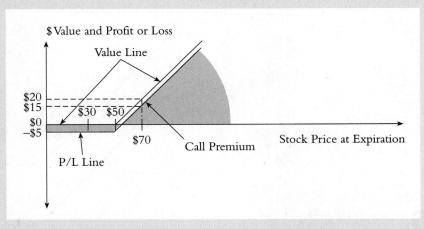

Part c: Payoff Diagram for
Buying a Call Option ($c_0 =
$5, X = $50)

Exhibit 23-7b illustrates the P/L line for this $5 call, at a strike price of $50. If the stock price falls below $50 at expiration, then the option is worthless, and the investor loses the $5 option premium. For every dollar the stock rises above $50, the investor makes an additional dollar. With a $5 premium, the stock must rise to $55 in order to break even on the contract. For every additional dollar above $55, the option provides an additional dollar of profit. Hence, if the stock price reaches $70 at maturity, then the profit from this option is $15 [$70 − ($50 + $5)].

Exhibit 23-7c combines both the value line and the P/L line. We see that the P/L line lies below the value line by exactly the purchase price of the call option. If the value line is shifted down by $5 (the amount of the premium), it matches the P/L line exactly. This makes sense, because the dollar profit or loss line is nothing but the price line minus the $5 investment on the call.

PRACTICE BOX

Problem

We know that for call options, the higher the strike price, the lower the value of the call premium. (For example, the right to buy stock at $110 will be worth less than the right to buy the same stock at $100.) Demonstrate the difference between three call options with different strike prices using the value line, as well as the P/L line. (X_L is low strike price, X is middle strike price, and X_H is the high strike price.)

Solution

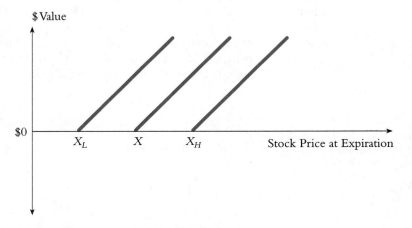

The value lines will be 45-degree lines moving up from the different strike prices. The P/L lines will be the same 45-degree lines shifted down by the cost of the call options. (Remember that the lower strike options will command a higher price.) Thus, if we denote the call prices by $C_{0,L}$, C_0, and $C_{0,H}$ corresponding to X_L, X, and X_H, we have the following:

(continued)

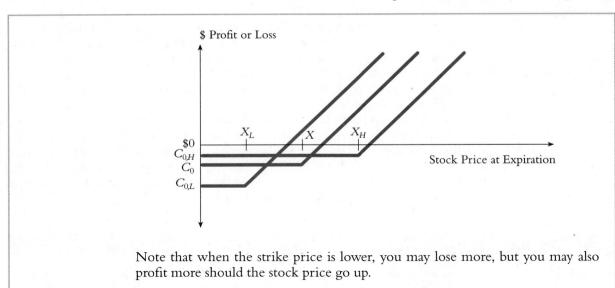

Note that when the strike price is lower, you may lose more, but you may also profit more should the stock price go up.

We now examine the value of a call option at expiration from the call writer's point of view. Exhibit 23-8 illustrates the payoff diagram of writing a call option on Apple stock with a strike price of $50 and a call premium ($c_0$) of $5. Recall that when you short a call, you receive the cash flow c_0, which is the call premium. The value of this short call position at expiration can be described as a -45-degree line going out from the horizontal axis at the strike price. The P/L line is similar, except it is shifted up by the $5 premium, because you receive the $5 from writing each call. For example, if the stock price falls to $30, then the call writer keeps the call

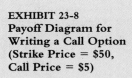

**EXHIBIT 23-8
Payoff Diagram for
Writing a Call Option
(Strike Price = $50,
Call Price = $5)**

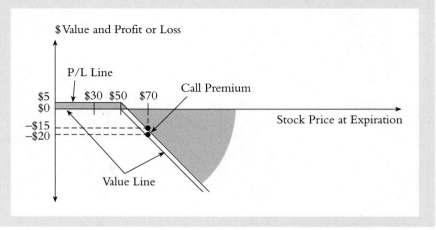

premium of $5 and has no obligations at maturity, because the option buyer will not exercise the call option. However, if the stock price rises to $70 at maturity, then the writer loses $20 at expiration and has a dollar loss of $15 ($-$20 + 5). Clearly, call writers face large liabilities when the stock price rises sharply.

Exhibits 23-7c and 23-8 are mirror images of each other if the mirror is placed along the stock price axis. Hence, for every dollar made in the option market, there is a dollar lost. This implies, in principle, that option trading is a "zero-sum game" —for every winner there must be a loser.

In a similar fashion, Exhibit 23-9 presents the value and P/L lines for buying a put option. Recall that buying a put option, in the case of stocks, gives the buyer the right to sell a stock at the strike price. Hence, a put option is more valuable as the price of the stock declines. In contrast, the value of the put option at expiration is zero if the put option expires out of the money (when the stock price is above $50, in this case). The value at expiration is a 45-degree line rising as the stock price falls below $50 ($-$45-degree line), because for each $1 drop in the stock price, the value of the put option at maturity increases by $1.

The dollar P/L line is merely shifted $5 down from the value at expiration line, because the buyer of the put option in this example pays $5 for the put. For puts, the breakeven point is

$$IV_{p,t} = \max(X - S_t, 0) = p_0$$

$p_0 = 5, so the breakeven point corresponds to $S_t = 45, because $50 - $45 = $5. For example, if the stock price rises to $70 at maturity, the put option is worth $0, and the dollar loss is $5 (the put price). If the stock price falls to $30 at maturity, the put option is worth $20 ($50 - 30), and the dollar profit will be $15 ($20 - 5). Thus, buying a put option is similar to buying a call option, except money is earned when the stock price falls. The put payoff diagram can be viewed as the mirror image

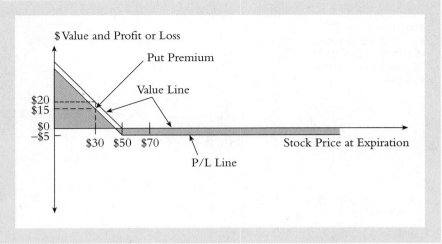

EXHIBIT 23-9
Payoff Diagram for Buying a Put Option (Strike Price = $50, Put Price = $5)

of the call payoff diagram, except the mirror is placed vertically on the strike price. (Note there is no requirement that the put price equal the call price. We adopted these values to simplify the discussion.)

Exhibit 23-10 presents the value and P/L lines for writing put options. Recall that put writing obligates an investor to buy a stock from the put buyer at a specified price. Hence, as the stock price falls, the put buyer will want to exercise the option and sell stock at $X. Therefore, the put writer loses as the stock price declines. Note that from the put writer's viewpoint, the P/L line is above the value line, because by writing the put, the option writer receives the put price, which in our example is $5. Of course, the put price can be different from $5 (say, $3); then we add $3 to the value line to get the P/L line. The lines in Exhibit 23-10 are the mirror image of those in Exhibit 23-9, where the mirror is placed on the horizontal axis.

23.5 INVESTMENT STRATEGIES USING OPTIONS

Options differ from most other securities because dollar profits and losses are asymmetric. For option buyers, losses are limited to the purchase price (which is relatively low), but profits are virtually unlimited. Purchasing stocks, in contrast, exposes investors to large losses, as well as large gains. Because of the asymmetric profit opportunities in options, investment strategies can be implemented for almost any prediction of the future stock price behavior. Moreover, there may be more than one investment strategy that permits an investor to profit from a given prediction for the stock market; investors can receive almost the same future cash flow by implementing different combinations of puts, calls, and underlying assets. For example, investors who are very bullish on a stock could (1) buy a call option or (2) buy both the underlying stock and a put option (illustrated later in this section).

EXHIBIT 23-10
Payoff Diagram for Writing a Put Option (Strike Price = $50, Put Price = $5)

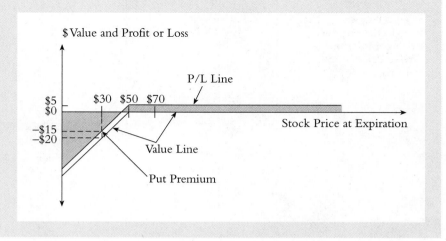

Both strategies will result in similar payoffs and achieve the stated goal with only minor differences.

There are two primary categories of complex option strategies: the spread and the straddle. A **spread** involves holding both long and short positions on the same type of option (for example, calls on Exxon), but the options have different expiration dates and exercise prices. A **straddle** involves either buying or selling both puts and calls on the same underlying asset with the same exercise price and expiration date. This section first describes two basic option-based strategies: protective put buying and covered call writing. It then describes the bull spread strategy.

Another spread strategy, the put ratio backspread, is discussed in Appendix 23C, along with the straddle.

23.5.1 Protective Put Buying

This section reviews several strategies using the data for Exxon stock listed in Exhibit 23-11.

Suppose you purchase Exxon stock for $50 per share and become concerned that its price might fall dramatically in the near future. However, you also believe there is a strong chance that Exxon stock will double in the near future. (For example, there is a chance that an expensive offshore drilling site might yield gains and a chance the site is worthless.) You do not know for sure which of your beliefs will be realized. What can you do? If you sell the stock, you might miss out on a run up in price. One solution to this problem is to buy out-of-the-money put options on Exxon stock. Having the stock and at the same time buying a put option is called **protective put buying.**

Exhibit 23-12a graphs the P/L lines of both buying the stock and buying a $45 strike, $1.50-per-share put option. Recall that a put option will benefit investors when the stock price falls. If the stock price remains at $50 per share, then the investor has no profit or loss on the stock and has a $1.5-per-share loss on the put option, because it expired out of the money. At a stock price of $45, the investor has a total loss of $6.5, because the stock position has a loss of $5 ($50 − $45) and the put position is still not in the money, resulting in a $1.5-per-share loss. Notice in Exhibit 23-12a, however, that below a $45 stock price, for every additional dollar lost on the

EXHIBIT 23-11 Exxon Stock Data	Strike Price	Call Price	Put Price
	$X_L = \$45$	$C_{0,L} = \$8$	$p_{0,L} = \$1\frac{1}{2}$
	$X = \$50$	$C_0 = \$5$	$p_0 = \$3\frac{1}{2}$
	$X_H = \$55$	$C_{0,H} = \$3$	$p_{0,H} = \$6\frac{1}{2}$

Current stock price is $S_0 = \$50$.

L stands for a lower strike price, and H stands for a higher strike price.

EXHIBIT 23-12
Payoff Diagrams: Buying a Stock and a Put Option

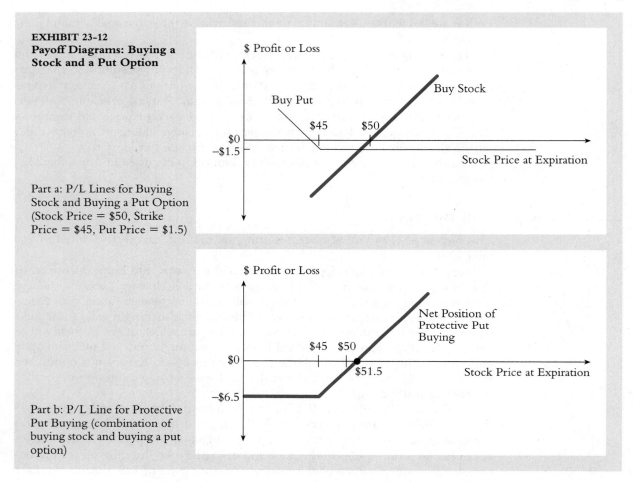

Part a: P/L Lines for Buying Stock and Buying a Put Option (Stock Price = $50, Strike Price = $45, Put Price = $1.5)

Part b: P/L Line for Protective Put Buying (combination of buying stock and buying a put option)

stock position, the put position gains a dollar, resulting in no overall change in the protective put buying portfolio. Above a $45 stock price, for every additional dollar gained on the stock position, the put position does not change, resulting in a dollar gain for the protective put buying portfolio. Exhibit 23-12b illustrates the net position for protective put buying. Note that for a stock price of $51.5, the net profit is zero, as $1.5 is earned on the stock but the investor loses $1.5, which is the premium on the put option.

Notice that the net position is very similar to the P/L line derived when simply buying a call option. The only actual difference between protective put buying and buying a call option relates to the timing of cash flows and the required discounting of these cash flows. Payoff diagrams ignore the time value of money.

It should be clear that by purchasing a put option, investors can dramatically alter the risk-return profile of their investments. With put options, investors can set a floor on their losses.

23.5.2 Covered Call Writing

Now suppose you purchased Exxon stock for $50 per share, wanted to generate additional cash flow, and did not believe that Exxon's stock price had much potential for a substantial rise. What could you do? One solution to this problem is to write out-of-the-money call options on Exxon stock. Having the stock and writing a call option is called **covered call writing.**

Exhibit 23-13 illustrates the P/L lines of both buying the stock and writing a $55 strike, $3-per-share call option. Recall that a call buyer benefits when the stock price rises; hence, a call writer suffers a loss in this case. If the stock price rises to $55 (the strike price), the investor has a $5 ($55 − $50) gain in the stock and a $3 (the call premium) gain on the call option, because it expired at the money. Notice in Exhibit 23-13a that above a $55 stock price, for every additional dollar gained on the stock position, the call option position loses a dollar. Hence, the profit is greatest

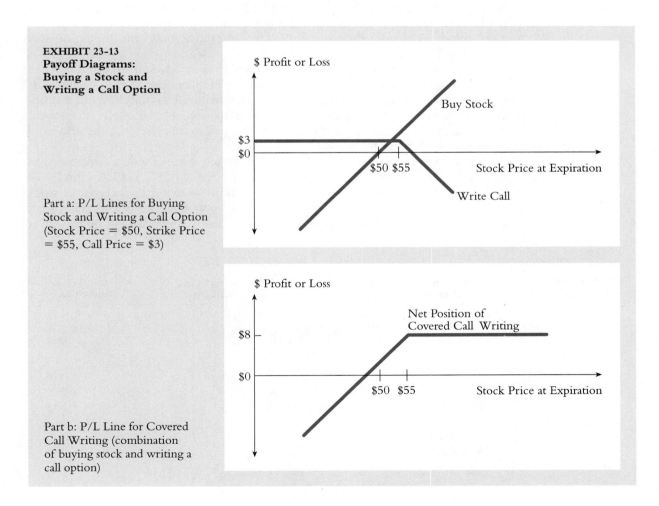

EXHIBIT 23-13
Payoff Diagrams:
Buying a Stock and
Writing a Call Option

Part a: P/L Lines for Buying
Stock and Writing a Call Option
(Stock Price = $50, Strike Price
= $55, Call Price = $3)

Part b: P/L Line for Covered
Call Writing (combination
of buying stock and writing a
call option)

at $8 ($5 from the stock and $3 from selling the option). Below a $55 stock price, for every additional dollar reduction in the stock position, the call position's cash flow does not change. Hence, the net position loses a dollar.

Exhibit 23-13b illustrates the net position of covered call writing. Notice that the net position is very similar in its shape to the P/L line derived when just writing a put option. Again, the actual differences relate to the timing of the cash flows. Covered call writing dramatically alters the risk-return profile of a stock position; it sets a ceiling on the potential gain. Investors are willing to accept this ceiling in return for receiving the call premium.

23.5.3 Bull Spread

Suppose you know that Exxon will release its quarterly earnings soon. You expect earnings to be slightly better than anticipated, so you expect a slight run up in the stock price. You are also concerned that there may be a large negative earnings surprise. What can you do? Buying the stock would expose you to enormous potential losses. A bull spread is appropriate in this case.

A **bull spread** is an option strategy designed to allow investors to profit if prices rise but to limit investors' losses if prices fall. A bull spread can be employed whenever an investor is either slightly bullish or bullish with uncertainty. (Recall that being bullish means you expect the stock price to rise.) For example, an investor employing a bull spread buys a call option with a low strike price (X_L) and sells a call option at a high strike price (X_H).

Let us examine this bull spread. Consider buying one call with a strike price of X_L ($45) at $8 and selling one call with a strike price of X_H ($55) at $3. Exhibit 23-14 shows the dollar profits and losses on the options at maturity for various stock prices. Note that the higher the strike price, the lower the price of the call. Also, if the stock price falls below $45, the most you can lose is $5 (an $8 loss on the call at

EXHIBIT 23-14 Profits and Losses for a Bull Spread	Stock Price at Expiration (S_t)	Long Call[a] at X_L = $45	Short Call[b] at X_H = $55	Bull Spread[c]
	$40	−$ 8	$ 3	−$5
	45	−8	3	−5
	50	−3	3	0
	55	2	3	5
	60	7	−2	5
	70	17	−12	5

a. Profit on long call: $\max(0, S_t - X_L) - C_{0,L}$.

b. Profit on short call: $-\max(0, S_t - X_H) + C_{0,H}$.

c. Total profit is the sum of the profit on the call and the profit on the put.

X_L plus a \$3 gain on the call at X_H). If the stock price falls to, say, \$40 at maturity, both options expire out of the money. You lose \$8 on the \$45 strike call and make \$3 on the \$55 strike call. Therefore, you lose only \$5 on the bull spread. If you had just purchased the stock and the stock price fell to \$40, you would stand to lose \$10 (\$50 − \$40). Hence, with the bull spread, you have less risk. Unfortunately, you also have limited your potential return. The most you can gain is \$5 if the stock price exceeds \$55. To illustrate this claim, suppose the stock price rose to \$70. The low strike price call value would be \$25 (\$70 − \$45), and the profit on this option would be \$17 (\$25 − \$8). The high strike price call is \$15 in the money (\$70 − \$55); thus, the writer would lose \$12 (−\$15 + \$3), so the total profit would be \$17 − \$12 = \$5. For each additional dollar over \$55, you have a \$1 increase in the loss on being short the call at X_H. Also, you have a \$1 increase in the gain on being long the call at X_L. Therefore, the net additional profit from the stock price increase is zero, and the maximum profit is \$5 in this particular example.

The payoff diagram for a bull spread is shown in Exhibit 23-15. Notice that the investor profits if the price rises even slightly (which is not true if the investor merely purchases a call option, because the investor first has to recoup the call premium).

Once again we see that there is no free lunch. If you have a bull spread, you limit your losses, but you also limit the potential for large gains. Determining whether this strategy is optimal for an investor depends on the investor's risk preferences and future stock price expectations. Options offer a wider array of potential payoff patterns than an investor could earn solely from investments in stock.

There is more than one way to implement a bull spread strategy. To be more specific, a bull spread strategy can be achieved by the following possible investments:

1. Buy a call at X_L, and sell a call at X_H.
2. Buy a put at X_L, and sell a call at X_H.
3. Buy a call at X_L, sell a put at X_H, and sell short the stock.
4. Buy a put at X_L, sell a call at X_H, and buy the stock.

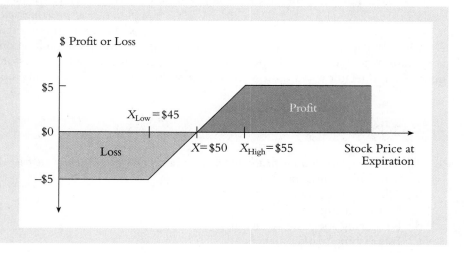

EXHIBIT 23-15
Payoff Diagram
for a Bull Spread

Some other investment strategies with options are discussed in detail in Appendix 23C and in the Problems at the end of the chapter.

SUMMARY

Name the benefits of modern option contracts. Although options have been around for a long time, they were not actively traded until 1973. In that year the Chicago Board Options Exchange introduced an option contract that was standardized, was transferable, and provided insurance against defaults of option writers. Since 1973, the growth of option trading has been phenomenal.

Understand the buying and selling of put and call options. An option buyer has the right, but not the obligation, to exercise the option in the future. A call option buyer has the right to buy stock in the future at a stated price, whereas a put option buyer has the right to sell stock in the future at a stated price. An active secondary market allows option investors to get out of an option trade if they so desire and accept the current market price.

Explain the risk of holding naked options. Writing a call option without owning the underlying asset is very risky and hence exposes the writer to great risk. The $1 billion lesson of Nicholas Lesson from Barings Bank illustrates the risk of holding naked options.

Describe the role of clearing corporations. Clearing corporations protect option buyers from the consequences of a default by an option writer. They also issue option contracts, maintain appropriate records, and process all the necessary financial transactions.

Explain how margin requirements on option writers protect buyers from default. Option clearing corporations require option writers to post and maintain adequate collateral to cover potential losses. The OCC issues all options contracts and guarantees both sides of the contracts. The OCC is owned by several exchanges, such as the CBOG, AMEX, and NYSE.

Use payoff diagrams to determine the value of an option upon expiration. The value of an option at expiration is its intrinsic value. With this observation, investors can examine a wide array of alternative risk-return tradeoffs using payoff diagrams. A payoff diagram is a graphical means of illustrating (1) the relationship among the values of securities (the value line), (2) the dollar profit or loss (the P/L line), or (3) both the value line and the P/L line.

Identify profitable option strategies based on beliefs about future asset price movements. Protective put buying sets a floor on potential losses, whereas covered call writing sets a ceiling on potential gains. Bull spreads are used when investors believe that the stock price will rise by a small amount.

CHAPTER AT A GLANCE

1. *The CBOE established the first liquid option market in 1973 by doing the following:*
   a. Standardizing contracts.
   b. Allowing for easy resale.
   c. Not requiring physical delivery.
   d. Requiring adequate collateral.
   e. Establishing market makers.

2. *The value of a call and put option at maturity can be graphically represented as follows:*

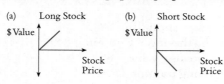

3. *The intrinsic value of options is expressed as follows:*

$$IV_c = \max(0,\ S_0 - X) \quad \text{(Calls)}$$

$$IV_p = \max(0,\ X - S_0) \quad \text{(Puts)}$$

4. *The time value of options is expressed as follows:*

$$TV_c = c_0 - IV_c \quad \text{(Calls)}$$

$$TV_p = p_0 - IV_p \quad \text{(Puts)}$$

5. *The P/L lines of a call and put option at maturity can be graphically represented as follows:*

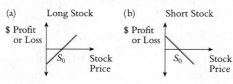

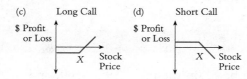

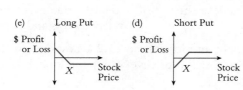

KEY TERMS

American-style option   846
At-the-money option   849
Bull spread   866
Call option   841
Closing transaction   846
Contingent claim   841
Covered call writing   865
Covered position   850
Derivative security   841
European-style option   846
Exercise   843
Exercise price   844

Expiration date   845
In-the-money option   849
Intrinsic value   852
Long position in an
   option   844
Maturity date   845
Naked position   850
Opening transaction   846
Option   841
Option buyer   843
Option premium   846
Option writer   844

Options Clearing Corporation
   (OCC)   851
Out-of-the-money option   849
Payoff diagram   854
Protective put buying   863
Put option   841
Short position   844
Spread   863
Straddle   863
Strike price   844
Time value   852

REVIEW

23.1 Why was option trading thin between 1934 and 1973?

23.2 Why was 1973 such a pivotal year in option trading history?

23.3 What is the difference between an opening option transaction and a closing option transaction?

23.4 What is the difference between European-style options and American-style options?

23.5 If $S_0 = \$100$ and $X = \$90$, are puts in the money or out of the money? What about calls?

23.6 Can option prices be negative? Explain your answer.

23.7 If $S_0 = \$120$ and $X = \$130$, what is the intrinsic value of puts and calls? Given that the call price is c_0 and the put price is p_0, write the time value of the put and call in terms of p_0 and c_0.

23.8 Is it possible that a put and a call option on the same stock with the same strike price would have the same time value? Could they have the same intrinsic value?

23.9 Using payoff diagrams, describe the difference between being long a call at the money and being short a put at the money.

23.10 "A call buyer who buys a call for $c = \$10$ does not need to deposit any initial margin." Do you agree with this assertion? Explain.

23.11 Describe in nonfinance terms (to your non-business major friend) what could be the motivation behind selling naked positions in options.

PRACTICE

Questions 23.1 through 23.5 are based on the information about Microsoft in the table at the top of page 871.

23.1 Draw the payoff diagram (profit and loss line only) for long July calls for all three strike prices

($95, $100, and $105) on one graph. Be sure to identify the exact breakeven point. Describe the relative costs and benefits of each strategy.

23.2 Draw the payoff diagram (profit and loss line only) for long July puts for all three strike prices

Microsoft's Option Data

Option & NY Close	Strike Price	Calls—Settle			Puts—Settle		
		June	July	October	June	July	October
$100\frac{3}{4}$	$ 95	$5\frac{7}{8}$	$8\frac{3}{4}$	$12\frac{3}{8}$	$ \frac{1}{16}$	$2\frac{3}{8}$	$ 5\frac{1}{2}$
$100\frac{3}{4}$	100	$1\frac{5}{8}$	$5\frac{1}{2}$	$10\frac{3}{8}$	$\frac{3}{4}$	$4\frac{1}{8}$	$7\frac{5}{8}$
$100\frac{3}{4}$	105	$\frac{1}{8}$	$3\frac{1}{4}$	$8\frac{5}{8}$	$4\frac{1}{2}$	$6\frac{3}{4}$	$11\frac{1}{8}$

($95, $100, $105) on one graph. Be sure to identify the exact breakeven point. Describe the relative costs and benefits of each strategy.

23.3 Create two tables similar to the one given for Microsoft, except one table has the time value, and the other table has the intrinsic value. What general inferences can you draw about time value from your table?

23.4 Using the data in the section of the text on bull spreads, show the payoff diagram for the other two strategies given in the text.

23.5 Suppose the stock price is $100 and the call price is $5 with a strike price of $105. What is the profit or loss on the following two strategies when the stock price goes up to $110 *and* when the stock goes down to $90?
a. Write a call option.
b. Write a covered call option; that is, write a call and buy a stock.

23.6 Suppose the call price is $c_0 = \$10$, the stock price is $100, and the strike price is $X = \$95$.
a. Calculate the initial margin for selling a call option.
b. Suppose now that the stock price goes up to $120, and the call price falls to $1. What is the maintenance margin required?

23.7 Refer to the following table. Suppose you buy a call option for $6\frac{3}{4}$ that matures in June with a strike price of $65.

Pfizer Stock Price	Strike Price	Calls—Settle June
$69\frac{1}{2}$	65	$6\frac{3}{4}$
$69\frac{1}{2}$	70	$3\frac{1}{2}$
$69\frac{1}{2}$	75	$1\frac{3}{4}$

a. What is your dollar profit if the stock price in June is $70? What if it is $50?
b. Calculate the rate of return.

23.8 Referring to the following table, suppose you buy a put option for $1\frac{5}{8}$ that matures in June with a strike price of $65.

Pfizer Stock Price	Strike Price	Puts—Settle
$69\frac{1}{2}$	65	$1\frac{5}{8}$
$69\frac{1}{2}$	70	$3\frac{1}{2}$
$69\frac{1}{2}$	75	$6\frac{3}{4}$

a. What is your dollar profit if the stock price in June is $70? What if it is $50?
b. Calculate the rate of return.

23.9 Referring to the data in Problem 23.10, suppose that in June the stock price falls to $60. Calculate your dollar profit and rate of return for the following strategies:
a. Buy one stock for $69\frac{1}{2}$ and one put option with a June maturity and a strike price of $65.
b. Buy one stock and two put options with a June maturity and a strike price of $65.

23.10 Repeat Problem 23.11, but this time in June the stock price jumps to $75. Compare and analyze the results of Problems 23.8 and 23.9.

23.11 The following table provides quotations on Boeing stock (current stock price is $44\frac{7}{16}$):

Maturity Date	Strike	Type	Price
Feb	40	p	$\frac{1}{4}$
Feb	45	p	$1\frac{3}{4}$
Feb	45	c	$1\frac{1}{8}$

(continued)

Maturity Date	Strike	Type	Price
Feb	50	c	⅛
Feb	60	c	⅛
Mar	50	c	½
May	45	p	2⅞
May	45	c	3
May	50	c	1⅛
May	55	c	7¹⁄₁₆

Source: *Barron's*, January 26, 1998, p. MW94. Reprinted by permission of *Barron's*, © 1998 Dow Jones & Co., Inc. All Rights Reserved Worldwide.

a. For each of the put and call options, calculate the intrinsic value and the time value. Analyze your results, emphasizing how the options' maturity date and strike price affect these two components.
b. From the point of view of the options buyer, draw value lines and P/L lines of the Feb 45 and May 55 call options of Boeing. Draw all of the value lines on one graph and all of the P/L lines on one graph.
c. Repeat Part b from the option writer's point of view.

CFA PROBLEMS

23.1 An institutional bond portfolio manager wants to increase the return on his existing holding of $1.0 million par value government 11% bonds due June 1, 2006. The current market price of the bonds is 111. The manager has decided on June 1, 1986, to implement a covered option-writing program on the portfolio. The available option information follows in the table below. The standard deviation of the price of government 11% bonds due 2006 over six-month holding periods has been 10%.

a. Design a "straddle" option-writing strategy for the manager.[10]
b. Calculate the breakeven market prices for the underlying government bond as a result of the "straddle" option-writing strategy.
c. Comment on the potential for a "straddle" option-writing strategy to add return to the portfolio.

For Internet questions visit the Levy Investment Web site at http://levy-invst.swcollege.com.

Options on Government 11% Bonds Due 2006 Expiring in 1986	Current Market Price of Option	Par Value of Bonds on Underlying Option	Option Commission per $100 Par Value
December 112 CALLS	$1.65	$25,000	.05
December 109½ PUTS	$2.25	$25,000	.05

YOUR TURN: APPLYING THEORY TO PRACTICE
OPTION-STOCK HEDGES: A STRATEGY FOR CATERPILLAR

Thirteen months ago, this Department outlined an IBM option-stock hedge suggested by Skip Becker of Northbrook, Ill. Becker, of H.P. Becker & Co., purchased IBM at 50, bought one January 1994 45-strike call for each 100 shares, and sold two January 55s, bringing in cash equal to the cost of the in-the-money 45.

As Becker put it then, "If the stock moves up 10%, your return will be 34%, including divi-

(continued)

10. The use of the word *straddle* here is archaic. The strategy intended here is now referred to as a bull spread.

dends; if it moves down 10%, you'll lose 6%." At prices up to 65 (a 34% gain, with dividends, on the $50 stock), the options strategy offered superior gain potential to the shares alone, with less exposure to a big move down, because the investor is long only half as many shares. By last January's expiration, Big Blue had risen 10%, to 55¼, so Becker's clients realized the maximum possible gain—and demonstrated that properly structured options strategies can be more conservative than investment in shares alone.

Last week, Cowen's Harrison Roth set up a computer program to search for similar opportunities. That black box pointed to Caterpillar. With CAT trading at 114 Thursday, the August 110 call was offered at 10½. Sale of two August 120s, on their 5⅜ bid, would more than cover the cost of the 110. For someone considering purchase of 200 CAT versus buying 100 shares and the call option spread, the math (including dividends) is that the option approach outperforms return on capital on the share purchase alone, up to 130 at August expiration. "If the stock goes to 120 and you're called on the two 120s sold," says Roth, "you'll make 10 points on the spread and six points on the covered write of the stock bought at 114 and delivered for 120. Plus $30 in dividends, so you'll make $1,630 on $11,400. That's a little over 14% in six months." And that ignores the net credit for putting on the options spread.

Source: "Option-Stock Hedges: A Strategy for Caterpillar," *Barron's Market Week,* March 14, 1994, p. MW17. Reprinted by permission of *Barron's,* © 1994 Dow Jones & Co., Inc. All Rights Reserved Worldwide.

Questions

In the following questions, consider the following two investment strategies for investing in CAT:

a. Buy 200 shares of CAT.

b. Buy 100 shares of CAT, buy 100 August 110 calls, and sell 200 August 120 calls.

The dividend for the six months is $0.30 per share. The call option transactions are in units of 100 shares.

1. Compare the rates of return on the two strategies for the following stock price ranges: $P < \$110$, $\$110 < P < \$120$, and $P > \$120$. It is claimed that up to a price of $130 per share, Strategy b outperforms Strategy a. Do you agree? Show your calculations, and find the precise price for which the two strategies yield the same rate of return.

2. Explain why the return on Strategy b is fixed at about 14% when the stock price is greater than $120.

3. Calculate the rate of return on the two strategies for the following stock prices on the expiration date: $P = \$80$, $\$90$, $\$100$, $\$110$, $\$114$, $\$120$, $\$130$, $\$140$, and $\$150$. Graph your results with the stock price on the horizontal axis and the rate of return on the vertical axis. You will have one curve for each strategy.

4. Suppose you estimate that there is a high probability that the stock price will fall in the range of $100 to $130. Which strategy would you choose? Discuss your results.

5. Explain the following quote from the article: "And that ignores the net credit for putting on the options spreads."

SELECTED REFERENCES

Chance, Don M. *An Introduction to Options and Futures.* 2d ed. New York: Dryden Press, 1991.

This text provides a good introduction to options and other derivative securities.

Hull, John C. *Options, Futures, and Other Derivative Securities.* 2d ed. Englewood Cliffs, N.J.: Prentice-Hall, 1993.

This text presents a more advanced introduction to options and other derivative securities.

SUPPLEMENTAL REFERENCES

Black, Fischer, and Myron Scholes. "The Pricing of Options and Corporate Liabilities." *Journal of Political Economy* 81(May–June 1973): 637–654.

Bookstaber, Richard M. *Option Pricing and Investment Strategy*. 3d ed. Chicago: Probus Publishing, 1991.

Cox, John C., Stephen A. Ross, and Mark Rubinstein. "Option Pricing: A Simplified Approach." *Journal of Financial Economics* 7 (September 1979): 229–263.

Cox, John C., and Mark Rubinstein. *Options Markets*. Englewood Cliffs, N.J.: Prentice-Hall, 1985.

Fabozzi, Frank J. (ed.). *The Handbook of Fixed-Income Options Pricing, Strategies & Applications*. Chicago: Probus Publishing, 1989.

Figlewski, Stephen, William L. Silber, and Marti G. Subrahmanyam (eds.). *Financial Options from Theory to Practice*. Homewood, Ill.: Business One Irwin, 1990.

Gibson, Rajna. *Option Valuation Analyzing and Pricing Standardized Option Contracts*. New York: McGraw-Hill, 1991.

Konishi, Atsuo, and Ravi E. Dattatreya (eds.). *The Handbook of Derivative Instruments*. Chicago: Probus Publishing, 1991.

McLean, Stuart K. (ed.). *The European Options and Futures Markets*. Chicago: Probus Publishing, 1991.

Merton, Robert. "Theory of Rational Option Pricing." *Bell Journal of Economics and Management Science* 4 (Spring 1973): 141–183.

Options Institute (ed.). *Options: Essential Concepts and Trading Strategies*. Homewood, Ill.: Business One Irwin, 1990.

Robertson, Malcolm J. *Directory of World Futures and Options*. Englewood Cliffs, N.J.: Prentice-Hall, 1990.

Smith, Clifford W., Jr., and Charles W. Smithson. *The Handbook of Financial Engineering*. New York: Harper Business, 1990.

Smith, Clifford W., Jr., Charles W. Smithson, and D. Sykes Wilford. *Managing Financial Risk*. New York: Harper & Row, 1990.

Tsiveriotis, K., and N. Chriss. "Pricing with a Difference." *Risk,* February 1998.

Appendix 23A Taxes

The tax consequences of option trading depend on a number of factors, such as the tax status of the investor, the underlying interest involved, whether the option is exercised or not, if the position is a covered or uncovered position, and whether the position is subject to a closing transaction. Taxes are usually paid in the year in which the position is closed. As with all tax laws, however, there are exceptions. For example, index options are mark to market (gains and losses are taxed even if the position is still held) at year-end for tax purposes.[11] As a result, the paper profits and losses are taxed in each year (as opposed to waiting until an offsetting position is taken, as is true with options on individual stocks, such as IBM, AT&T, and so forth).

11. Mark to market is discussed in Chapters 3 and 22.

Suppose you purchased an index option for $500 in June of Year 1 that matures in June of Year 2 (see Exhibit 23A-1a). On December 31, the index option is worth $1,100; thus, you have taxable income of $600 ($1,100 − $500) even if you do not sell it. Now further suppose that in Year 2 the option expires worthless. In this case, you have a tax loss of $1,100 ($500 purchase price + $600 gain in Year 1) in Year 2.

As Exhibit 23A-1 shows, with options on individual stocks, taxes are paid when the options are sold. However, when options on individual stocks are exercised, the option premium is used to adjust the cost basis, and no taxes are paid until the underlying asset is sold. For example, suppose you paid $8 per share for an option on ABC with a strike price of $120. At the expiration date you exercise your option and purchase ABC at $120. Your cost basis is $128 + commission (see Exhibit 23A-1b). Hence, taxable gains will occur only if ABC is subsequently sold for a price above $128 plus commissions.

Appendix 23B Margin Requirements

Suppose an investor purchased 100 call option contracts for $5 per share (the total cost would be $50,000 = $5 · 100 shares per contract · 100 contracts), and the stock was in the money $20 on the expiration date (that is $S_0 − X = 20). Then the 100 option contracts would be worth $200,000 ($20 · 100 shares per contract · 100 contracts). Will the call writer pay cash to the OCC as a result of the price increase?

Clearing corporations such as the OCC protect themselves against option writers' defaulting by requiring writers to provide collateral known as *margin*. Margin

EXHIBIT 23A-1 Example of Tax Liabilities from Option Trading with 28% Tax Bracket	Part a: Index Options		
	Date	**Action**	**Option Value**	**Cash Flow**
	June, Year 1	Buy 1 index option	$500	−$500
	December, Year 1	Mark to market for tax purposes	1,100	−168[a]
	June, Year 2	Option matures out of the money	0	308[b]

a. −$168 = 0.28($1,100 − $500). Tax on paper gain at year end.

b. $308 = 0.28 · $1,100. Tax credit on loss of the $1,100.

Part b: Stock Cost Basis via Call Option

Action	Cost per Share
Buy call option ABC 120	$8 + Commission
Exercise option	$120
Cost basis for future tax calculation	**$128 + Commission**

requirements reduce the incentive of the option writers to default on their obligations. If the writer has posted a substantial amount of collateral, then the writer is less likely to default. The risk of default is intimately related to the volatility of the underlying asset. The more volatile the asset, the higher the risk of default by option writers. For example, in the crashes of October 1987, 1989, and 1997, there were several defaults by option writers. (However, do not forget that option buyers were protected by the guarantees provided by option clearinghouses such as the OCC.)

The risk of default is limited to option writers. The Federal Reserve Board (the regulatory body for U.S. option transactions) does not allow options to be purchased on margin (by borrowing money). The Federal Reserve Board regulates margin requirements through Regulation T, which covers the extension of credit to customers by security brokers, dealers, and members of the national securities exchanges. Regulation T establishes initial margin requirements and defines which securities are eligible to be traded on margin. The brokerage firms have the discretion to require higher margins if they wish. Option buyers must pay for the option in full; this totally eliminates the possibility of default by the option buyer. Thus, option buyers could never default on the contract, because option contracts give the option buyers the *right,* but not the obligation, to do something in the future. Specifically, an option buyer at most could lose the option premium, but the buyer had to pay that up front.

The *initial margin* is money that option writers send to the OCC when they initially sell the specific options. The *maintenance margin* is the dollar amount that must be kept at the OCC throughout the life of the contract. The maintenance margin changes as asset prices change.

Exhibit 23B-1 compares the initial and maintenance requirements for margin accounts for different types of contracts traded on the CBOE. Recall that margin accounts are required to keep securities (or cash) on deposit with the broker as collateral. In the options market, margin implies the money deposited by the option writer as collateral for the potential future liability. As Exhibit 23B-1 illustrates, margin requirements are complex and differ across different types of securities and purposes (long, short, and spreads). Margin requirements change with market conditions.

As an illustration, consider writing one call option on the S&P 100 stock index. The option contract is actually for 100 times the index. Index options are *cash settled,* which means that cash, rather than securities in the amount of the intrinsic value of the options, is exchanged at expiration. For example, if the index rises to 470 and the strike price is 370, the index call writer must pay $10,000 [100($470 − $370)].

The formula for finding the margin requirement of the option writer based on Exhibit 23B-1 (see "Short Position"—"Index" row and "Initial Margin" column) is as follows:[12]

$$\text{Margin} = \max(A, B)$$

---

12. See Footnote 8.

EXHIBIT 23B-1   .   Initial and Maintenance Margin Requirements

Position	Option Type	Initial Margin	Maintenance Margin
Long puts or long calls	Index, equities, interest rates	Pay for option in full	None required
Short puts or short calls (This means to "write" the options.)	Index (for example, stock index options)	The highest of the option price + 15% of index − out-of-the-money amount, if any, or the option + 10% of index	Same as initial margin
Short puts or short calls (This means to "write" the options.)	Equities (for example, stock options)	The highest of the option price + 20% of equity − out-of-the-money amount, if any, or the option + 10% of equity value	Same as initial margin
Short puts or short calls (This means to "write" the options.)	Interest rates (for example, options on Treasury bonds)	The highest of the option price + 3.5% of underlying asset − out-of-the-money amount, if any, or the option + $\frac{1}{2}$% of underlying asset	Same as initial margin
Spreads[a]	Index, equities, interest rates	Difference in exercise prices + long option value	Same as initial margin

a. A spread is both long and short on options of the same type but has different expiration dates and exercise prices.

Source: Chicago Board Options Exchange, *Margin Manual* (Chicago: CBOE, 1989).

where

$$A = c_0 + (0.15 \cdot 15 \cdot 100 \cdot \text{Index}_0) - [100 \cdot \max(0, X - \text{Index}_0)]$$

$$B = c_0 + (0.10 \cdot 100 \cdot \text{Index}_0)$$

where c_0 is the call price (per 100 units), and $100 \cdot \max(0, X - \text{Index}_0)$ is the out-of-the-money amount. For example, suppose we observe the S&P index at 365, along with a call option with a strike price of $370 and a call price of $900. In this example,

$$A = \$900 + (0.15 \cdot 100 \cdot \$365) - \max[0, 100 \cdot (\$370 - \$365)]$$
$$= \$900 + \$5,475 - \$500 = \$5,875$$

$$B = \$900 + (0.10 \cdot 100 \cdot \$365) = \$900 + \$3,650 = \$4,550$$

Hence, the margin is

$$\text{Margin} = \max(\$5,875, \$4,550) = \$5,875$$

To write one call option contract on the S&P index, we are required to post margin of $5,875. This margin is quite a bit more than the possible proceeds of

$900. The reason is that if stock prices rise, the option writer must pay the option buyer the difference between the index value and the exercise price. Exhibit 23B-1 shows that for short positions in options, the maintenance margin is the same as the initial margin. The equations for both A and B above are directly influenced by the value of the index. As the index rises, so does the margin required. For example, if the index rises to 375 and the call price rises to $1,500, then the required maintenance margin is

$$A = \$1,500 + (0.15 \cdot 100 \cdot \$375) - \max[0, 100 \cdot (\$370 - \$375)]$$
$$= \$1,500 + \$5,625 - 0 = \$7,125$$

$$B = \$1,500 + (0.10 \cdot 100 \cdot \$375) = \$1,500 + \$3,750 = \$5,250$$

Hence, the margin required is

$$\text{Margin} = \max(\$7,125, \$5,250) = \$7,125$$

Thus, the option writer must place additional monies as margin. Specifically, $7,125 − $5,875 = $1,250 more must be placed as margin.

PRACTICE BOX

Problem

Determine the required initial margin on selling an IBM call option contract that has a market value of $3 per share and is $5 out of the money; the stock is selling at $95.

Solution

From Exhibit 23B-1 for equities, we can develop the following expression:

$$\text{Margin} = \max(A, B)$$

where

$$A = c_0 + (0.20 \cdot 100 \cdot S_0) - [100 \cdot \max(0, X - S_0)]$$
$$B = c_0 + (0.10 \cdot 100 \cdot S_0)$$

Recall that each contract is for 100 options, and $c_0 = \$300$, $S_0 = \$95$, and $X - S_0 = \$5$. Therefore,

$$A = \$300 + (0.20 \cdot 100 \cdot \$95) - [100 \cdot \max(0, \$5)]$$
$$= \$300 + \$1,900 - \$500 = \$1,700$$

$$B = \$300 + (0.10 \cdot 100 \cdot \$95) = \$300 + \$950 = \$1,250$$

Therefore,

$$\text{Margin} = \max(\$1,700, \$1,250) = \$1,700$$

Thus, selling a call option valued at $300 will require $1,700 in collateral.

PRACTICE

23B.1 Suppose the index is exactly at the money, $S_0 = X$. The call price on the index is $c_0 = \$10$, and the S&P 500 index is 365.

a. What is the initial margin required to sell a naked call option?

b. How would you change your answer if the call is out of the money, where $X = 380$, $S_0 = 365$, and $c_0 = \$10$?

c. What if the call is way out of the money ($X = 500$, $S_0 = 365$, and $c_0 = \$10$)?

Appendix 23C   Other Option Strategies

PUT RATIO BACKSPREAD

The *put ratio backspread* is employed whenever an investor is significantly bearish (predicts price declines) but believes there is a chance that the prediction is wrong and that the stock will move up. For example, if a possible takeover is announced, the investor would expect the stock price to rise. If an investor believes that the takeover will not go through, however, she may expect that the stock price will fall. The investor is concerned, however, that she could be wrong. In this situation, the investor might decide to hold a position called a *put ratio backspread*. This position may result in a profit, but it also limits the losses. The put ratio backspread can be implemented with the following two positions:

1. Write one put option at X_H (\$55), receiving \$6½.
2. Buy two put options at X (\$50), paying \$7 (2 · \$3½).
    (See Exhibit 23C-1 for the relevant prices.)

Exhibit 23C-1 illustrates the profits and losses at different stock prices at maturity. Let us move from a stock with a high stock price to one with a low stock price. For stock prices more than X_H, we gain \$6½ on Position 1 and lose \$7 on Position 2 (2 · \$3½). Therefore, we lose only \$½ if we are wrong. Between X_H and X, every dollar loss on the stock price results in a dollar loss on the portfolio. At $S_0 = X$, the portfolio value is −\$5½. For every dollar below X, we gain \$2 on Position 2 and lose \$1 on Position 1. We break even at \$44½ and gain \$1 for every dollar below \$44½. For example, if the stock price falls to \$30, then the put option sold will lose \$18½ (−\$25 + \$6½), and the two puts bought will gain \$33 [(2 · \$20) − (2 · \$3½)]. Exhibit 23C-2 shows these results graphically.

EXHIBIT 23C-1 Profits and Losses for a Put Ratio Backspread (Price of a put with $X = \$55 = \$6.5$, and price of a put with $X = \$50 = \$3.5$)	Stock Price at Expiration (S_t)	Short Put[a] at $X_H = \$55$	Two Long Puts[b] at $X = \$50$	Put Ratio Backspread[c]
	$ 0	$-\$48\frac{1}{2}$	$93	$44\frac{1}{2}$
	30	$-18\frac{1}{2}$	33	$14\frac{1}{2}$
	44.5	-4	4	0
	45	$-3\frac{1}{2}$	3	$-\frac{1}{2}$
	46	$-2\frac{1}{2}$	1	$-1\frac{1}{2}$
	47	$-1\frac{1}{2}$	-1	$-2\frac{1}{2}$
	48	$-\frac{1}{2}$	-3	$-3\frac{1}{2}$
	49	$\frac{1}{2}$	-5	$-4\frac{1}{2}$
	50	$1\frac{1}{2}$	-7	$-5\frac{1}{2}$
	51	$2\frac{1}{2}$	-7	$-1\frac{1}{2}$
	52	$3\frac{1}{2}$	-7	$-3\frac{1}{2}$
	53	$4\frac{1}{2}$	-7	$-2\frac{1}{2}$
	54	$5\frac{1}{2}$	-7	$-1\frac{1}{2}$
	55	$6\frac{1}{2}$	-7	$-\frac{1}{2}$
	60	$6\frac{1}{2}$	-7	$-\frac{1}{2}$
	70	$6\frac{1}{2}$	-7	$-\frac{1}{2}$

a. Profit on short put: $-\max(0, X_H - S_t) + p_{0,H} = -\max(0, \$55 - S_t) + \$6.5$.

b. Profit on two long puts: $2 \cdot \max(0, X - S_t) - 2 \cdot p_{0,X} = 2 \cdot \max(0, \$50 - S_t) - 2 \cdot \$3.5$.

c. Total profit is the sum of the profit on the short put at X_H and two long puts at X.

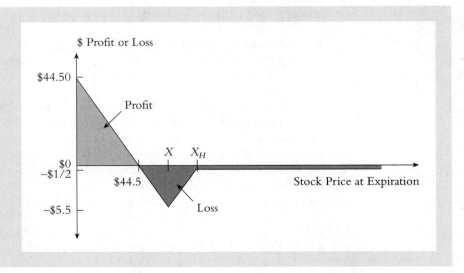

EXHIBIT 23C-2 Payoff Diagram of a Put Ratio Backspread

STRADDLE

At times an investor believes something dramatic will happen to the stock price, but he is not sure exactly which direction it will go. For example, the company might make a major research and development announcement. A straddle is a suitable strategy for investing under these circumstances .

A straddle requires buying or selling both puts and calls on the same asset, with the same exercise price and expiration date. Investors employing a long straddle purchase options, and those using a short straddle sell options. Let us consider a straddle with at-the-money Exxon options.

As is shown in Exhibit 23C-3, buying an at-the-money call ($X = \$50$) costs $5 per share, and buying an at-the-money put costs $3½ per share. The exhibit illustrates the profits and losses for different possible stock prices at maturity. The most that can be lost is $8½ when the stock price remains at $50, and both options have no value at maturity. When the stock moves either up or down, the long straddle increases in value, as illustrated graphically in Exhibit 23C-4. At a stock price of either $58.5 or $41.5, the breakeven on the total profit on the position exactly equals $8.5, which is the cost of the put and the call that were bought.

Notice how useful diagrams are in examining the costs and benefits of different strategies. Many other possible strategies could be created for which payoff diagrams would be useful illustrations. Exhibit 23C-5 illustrates just a few of these strategies and how they might be generated. The "Expected Direction of Stock" in Exhibit 23C-5 is the direction that will produce the largest profits for the particular strategies. "Neither" in this column indicates that the largest gains will be produced if the stock price does not move or moves only slightly. The "Profit Potential Limited" column indicates whether large profits are possible. The "Loss Potential Limited"

EXHIBIT 23C-3 Profits and Losses for an At-the-Money Long Straddle	Stock Price at Expiration Date (S_t)	Long Call[a] at $X = \$50$	Long Put[b] at $X = \$50$	Long Straddle[c]
	$ 0	−$5	$46½	$41½
	30	−5	16½	11½
	41.50	−5	5	0
	45	−5	1½	−3½
	50	−5	−3½	−8½
	55	0	−3½	−3½
	58.50	3½	−3½	0
	60	5	−3½	1½

a. Profit on call: $\max(0, S_t - X) - c_0 = \max(0, S_t - \$50) - \$5$.

b. Profit on put: $\max(0, X - S_t) - p_0 = \max(0, \$50 - S_t) - \$3.5$.

c. Total profit is the sum of the profit on the call and the profit on the put.

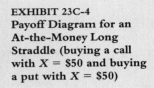

EXHIBIT 23C-4
Payoff Diagram for an At-the-Money Long Straddle (buying a call with $X = \$50$ and buying a put with $X = \$50$)

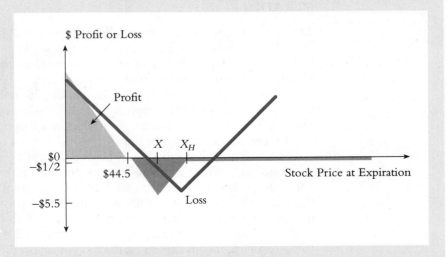

column addresses whether the strategy produces the potential for large losses. The "Option Position" columns provide one of many explicit trading strategies that could be implemented under the named strategy. For example, the long call strategy could clearly involve X_H (high strike price).[13]

Let us briefly discuss a few of these strategies. A *long butterfly strategy* has the characteristic of modest losses if prices move up or down dramatically and gains only when the price remains the same. A *short butterfly* is the exact opposite: modest gains if prices move up or down dramatically and losses only when the price remains the same. A *long straddle* produces big gains if prices move up or down and big losses if the price remains unchanged. A *long strangle* produces big gains if prices move up or down dramatically and modest losses if the price remains relatively unchanged. Ratio spreads are asymmetric and similar to Exhibit 23C-1 except that only modest gains are possible. The *call ratio spread* exposes you to large losses when prices rise, and the *put ratio spread* yields large losses when prices fall. Ratio backspreads are asymmetric, as shown in Exhibit 23C-1. A *call ratio backspread* produces a payoff diagram similar to Exhibit 23C-2 except that the big gains are produced when the prices rise.

---

13. Because of space limitations and for clarity, only one potential trading strategy is provided here.

EXHIBIT 23C-5   **Option Strategies: Costs, Benefits, and Possible Structure**

Strategy Name	Expected Direction of Stock	Profit Potential Limited	Loss Potential Limited	Option Position			
				Calls— Long	Calls— Short	Puts— Long	Puts— Short
Long call	Up	No	Yes	X_H	—	—	—
Short call	Down	Yes	No	—	X_H	—	—
Long put	Down	No	Yes	—	—	X_L	—
Short put	Up	Yes	No	—	—	—	X_L
Bull spread	Up	Yes	Yes	X_L	X_H	—	—
Bear spread	Down	Yes	Yes	X_H	X_L	—	—
Long butterfly	Neither	Yes	Yes	$X_L + X_H$	2 at X	—	—
Short butterfly	Either	Yes	Yes	2 at X	$X_L + X_H$	—	—
Long straddle	Either	No	Yes	X	—	X	—
Short straddle	Neither	Yes	No	—	X	—	X
Long strangle	Either	No	Yes	X_H	—	X_L	—
Short strangle	Neither	Yes	No	—	X_H	—	X_L
Call ratio spread	Neither	Yes	No (+)[a]	X_L	2 at X	—	—
Put ratio spread	Neither	Yes	No (−)	—	—	X_H	2 at X
Call ratio backspread	Either	No (+)	Yes	2 at X	X_L	—	—
Put ratio backspread	Either	No (−)	Yes	—	—	2 at X	X_L

a. No (+) indicates that potential is not limited on the positive side. No (−) indicates that potential is not limited on the negative side.

PRACTICE

23C.1 Develop the long butterfly strategy using Microsoft October call options (see Question 23.2). Repeat this exercise with July call options. Discuss the differences.

23C.2 Develop the put ratio spread strategy using Microsoft October puts (see Question 23.2). Repeat this exercise with July puts. Discuss the differences.

CHAPTER 24

VALUING OPTIONS

LEARNING OBJECTIVES

After studying this chapter you should be able to:

1. Identify option boundaries and put-call parity.

2. Use the Black–Scholes option pricing model (BSOPM) to value call and put options.

3. Understand how portfolio insurance works with a stock portfolio.

4. Describe options on futures contracts.

INVESTMENTS IN THE NEWS

TRICK OR TREAT? RISK MANAGEMENT TOOLS MAY BE THE RISK

In the panic of October 1997, investors forgot the dirty word of October 1987: "derivatives." . . .

"I think the big time bomb out there is the pervasive nature of derivatives," declares Metz. "The dimensions are absolutely staggering. The chance of someone not meeting an obligation could have a snowball effect."

Maybe it's time to listen. Especially now, when investors seem lulled by this Lotus-land economy and lured more and more to leverage. Sanctioning this scene somewhat is the new respectability conferred on the derivatives market in the past few months as Dow Jones & Co., publisher of *Barron's*, licensed derivative products on its venerable Industrial Average, and the Nobel Foundation granted its prize in economics to the team that developed the definitive pricing model for derivatives. . . .

The truth is that things can go terribly wrong terribly quickly trading derivatives. As Kyle Rosen, portfolio manager and options strategist at Santa Monica, Calif.-based hedge fund Strome Sussking Investment Management puts it, "Black-Scholes works great when the markets are quiet, but when turmoil hits, it gets thrown out the window."

Prices explode too fast, as they did Monday, for anyone to sit patiently plugging numbers into a model. And the quickest reflexes in the world can't change things, particularly if accurate quotes aren't available, as was the case during the fast-moving markets, and if it takes more than an hour to open trading in an option, such as it did on the Philadelphia Stock Exchange on Tuesday and Thursday in Dell Computer.

Source: Sandra Ward, *Barron's*, November 3, 1997, p. MW17. Reprinted by permission of *Barron's*, © 1997 Dow Jones & Co., Inc. All Rights Reserved Worldwide.

Robert Merton and Myron Scholes received the 1997 Nobel Prize in economics mainly for their work in the options field and, in particular, in pricing options. Fischer Black, who is a co-author of the Black-Scholes option pricing model, did not live to share the Nobel Prize for his contribution to the breakthrough option pricing model. The article in this chapter's Investments in the News asserts that the Black-Scholes option pricing model works very well when the markets are quiet but not when turmoil hits.

This chapter covers the pricing of options and how investors can detect whether an option is underpriced or overpriced. Option pricing heavily relies on the no-arbitrage argument—that is, in equilibrium, no arbitrage profit prevails.

Understanding the price behavior of options requires a knowledge of options arbitrage. When there are arbitrage opportunities available, they do not last long. With the lightning-fast computer technology available today, investors need to be quick to exploit arbitrage opportunities. Arbitrage is basically a "free lunch," which occurs rarely and does not last very long (see Chapter 10).

Although there are many possible definitions of arbitrage, this text focuses on two popular definitions. An arbitrage opportunity exists when either (1) a portfolio can be constructed at zero cost (by selling some securities short) that has future positive cash flows but absolutely zero probability of negative cash flows or (2) a portfolio can be constructed for a negative cost (that is, the investor receives money today) that has no risk of future losses. In equilibrium, arbitrage opportunities do not exist. The existence of arbitrage profit thus represents disequilibrium. Option prices are determined for the most part by option traders' eliminating arbitrage opportunities.

Some investors look for arbitrage opportunities, and others invest in options such as protective put buying to reduce risk (see Chapter 23). In Europe, only a small number of pension funds and insurance companies use options to protect their assets, but the use of options is predicted to grow rapidly there. Indeed, options have a wide range of useful applications, including managing currency risk, interest rate risk, commodity price risk, security price risk, and portfolio insurance. Finally, some investors invest in derivatives simply to speculate. This action may be very profitable but also may be disastrous. As you consider the costs and benefits of employing options in portfolio management, it is critical that you understand basic option price behavior.

This chapter examines the pricing of European-style options (that is, options where early exercise is not allowed). First, the chapter examines the option pricing boundaries that all option prices must satisfy. Option prices remain within the boundaries because of arbitrage forces in the market. The chapter then discusses the Black-Scholes pricing approach to determining the equilibrium price of an option. Finally, it examines a risk management strategy called *portfolio insurance,* which uses this approach.

Most of the illustrations in this chapter relate to pricing stock options. However, the same principles demonstrated in this chapter apply to pricing options on any underlying asset, such as stock index options, futures, or foreign currency options.

24.1 OPTION BOUNDARIES

Option boundaries provide a helpful first step in the quest to understand option price behavior. Option boundary conditions represent the range where we would anticipate finding option prices. Option prices must satisfy certain boundaries; otherwise, investors could make an infinite profit at no risk. (This arbitrage activity would push the option price inside these bounds.) Clearly, an infinite-profit opportunity would be desirable if it could be found. The derivation of option prices is based on the assumption that there are sophisticated investors in the market. Whenever these investors see arbitrage opportunities, they exploit them. This trading activity causes prices to change until the arbitrage profits disappear and option prices lie within the designated boundaries.

Exhibit 24-1a is a hypothetical closed market quote sheet for a market maker in Microsoft options. How are we to make sense out of all these numbers? Are these reasonable prices? Are they overpriced? Are they underpriced? Finding option boundaries helps to answer these questions.

EXHIBIT 24-1   Closing Price Options Based on Microsoft

Part a: Closing Price Quotes

		Calls			Puts		
Stock Price	Strike Price	31 Day	91 Day	182 Day	31 Day	91 Day	182 Day
100	90	10.80	12.85	15.47	0.42	1.74	3.26
100	95	6.76	9.39	12.31	1.35	3.21	4.97
100	100	3.70	6.57	9.62	3.27	5.33	7.16
100	105	1.74	4.41	7.38	6.30	8.11	9.80
100	110	0.70	2.84	5.57	10.24	11.47	12.86

Part b: Lower Bounds

		Calls			Puts		
Stock Price	Strike Price	31 Day	91 Day	182 Day	31 Day	91 Day	182 Day
100	90	10.37	11.09	12.16	0.0	0.0	0.0
100	95	5.39	6.15	7.28	0.0	0.0	0.0
100	100	0.41	1.21	2.40	0.0	0.0	0.0
100	105	0.0	0.0	0.0	4.57	3.73	2.48
100	110	0.0	0.0	0.0	9.55	8.67	7.36

The closing price quotes are based on the Black-Scholes option pricing model discussed later in this chapter. They assume a 5% interest rate and a standard deviation of 30%.

An arbitrageur would like to find option prices that are either too high or too low. The analysis in this section establishes ways of assessing the validity of option market prices. The section first examines call option boundaries and then put option boundaries.

24.1.1 Call Option Boundaries

For a call option, there is both an upper and a lower boundary for the current call price. If the call price is above the upper boundary or below the lower boundary, then an arbitrageur will be able to make money with no risk. This section first examines call option boundaries and then describes what happens when option prices get outside of them.

LOWER BOUNDARY

The prices of a European-style call option (c_0) must lie above the following boundary:[1]

$$c_0 \geq \max\left[0, S_0 - \frac{X}{(1 + r)^t}\right] \tag{24.1}$$

where S_0 is the price of a security or underlying asset today; X is the strike or exercise price; t is the time to maturity until the expiration date (in fraction of years); and r is the annual risk-free interest rate, which is assumed to be constant. Exhibit 24-1b presents the lower boundaries where r is assumed to be 5%. Notice that all of the closing call prices are above the lower boundary. For example, the quote on the 91-day call with a strike price of 95 is 9.39, whereas its lower boundary is max[0, $100 - 95/(1 + 0.05)^{91/365}] \cong 6.15$ (see Equation 24.1). However, the amount by which the option price is above the lower boundary varies. (See 31-day calls with strike prices of 105 and 110 in Exhibit 24-1a.) If the option is about to expire ($t = 0$), then the discounting factor $[1/(1 + r)^t]$ equals 1.0, because $(1 + r)^0 = 1$. Hence, when $t = 0$,

$$c_t = \max(0, S_t - X) \tag{24.2}$$

Notice that this is an equality, not an inequality, because at maturity the option is worth its intrinsic value (there is no time value left).

To see why Equation 24.2 holds at maturity, recall that if the option matures out of the money ($S_t < X$), then the call option buyer has no incentive to exercise the stock. [Why buy the stock at X when you can buy it at $S_t(S_t < X)$?] If the option matures in the money ($S_t > X$), then at maturity, buying the stock is equivalent to buying the option and immediately exercising it. Hence, $S_t = c_t + X$, or $c_t = S_t - X$.

---

1. We use the term *price* rather than *premium* because these boundaries apply throughout the life of the option, not just on the initial purchase date.

Prior to maturity ($t > 0$), however, we need to consider a more complicated strategy to establish the inequality given in Equation 24.1. The trading strategy presented in Exhibit 24-2 will establish the lower boundary by examining cash flows at date 0 and maturity date t. (We assume that any trade opened at 0 is closed at t.) Note that we separate the future into two possibilities: $S_t \geq X$ and $S_t < X$. More information on the exact value of S_t is not needed.

Column 1 of Exhibit 24-2 identifies the exact trading strategy to adopt at Time 0 (today). As a cash flow table, Columns 2, 3, and 4 contain dollar cash inflows if positive ($+$) and outflows if negative ($-$). Column 2 shows the dollar cash flows today from following the trading strategy in Column 1. (Recall that when you short sell the stock, you receive money.) The net cash flow at the bottom of this column is found by summing the cash flows in the "Today" column (the required investment). The question mark (?) indicates that we investigate whether the investment will be positive, zero, or negative if arbitrage profits are absent. Columns 3 and 4 depict the cash flow when $S_t \geq X$ (Column 3) and when $S_t < X$ (Column 4).

According to Exhibit 24-2, if the cash flow today (0) is positive (that is, the question mark in the exhibit is positive, $? > 0$), then an arbitrage profit opportunity (sometimes called a *money machine*) prevails. That is, we are able to generate a positive cash flow today with no risk of future loss (and possibly a positive future cash flow). The last column of this table is positive by assumption ($S_t < X$). Thus, to avoid this arbitrage or money machine, we must find the cash flow today to be negative. Therefore, we must have, in equilibrium,

$$-c_0 + S_0 - \frac{X}{(1 + r)^t} \leq 0$$

which implies that

$$c_0 \geq S_0 - \frac{X}{(1 + r)^t}$$

EXHIBIT 24-2 The Lower Boundary for Call Options: A Cash Flow Table		Cash Flows		
			At Expiration	
	Trading Strategy	Today (0)	$S_t \geq X$	$S_t < X$
	Buy one call option	$-c_0$	$S_t - X$	0
	Sell short one share of stock	$+S_0$	$-S_t$	$-S_t$
	Lend $X/(1 + r)^t$	$-X/(1 + r)^t$	X	X
	Net cash flow	$-c_0 + S_0 - X/(1 + r)^t = ?$	0	$X - S_t$ (positive)

c_0 = the current call price, S_0 = the current stock price, S_t = the stock price at expiration, X = the strike price, r = the risk-free interest rate, and t = the time to maturity in fractions of a year.

How do the actions of the arbitrageur influence market prices? If $-c_0 + S_0 - X/(1 + r)^t$ is positive, everyone will want to buy call options, short sell the stock, and borrow to create this money machine. These actions will push the price of the call up and the price of the stock down until the cash flow is nonpositive. Also, because of limited liability of an option, the option price cannot be negative ($c_0 \geq 0$). Recall that the option buyer does not have to exercise the options. We can conclude that the inequality given in Equation 24.1 holds.

UPPER BOUNDARY

Using similar arguments, we can demonstrate that the price of a European-style call option must lie below the underlying stock price:

$$c_0 \leq S_0 \tag{24.3}$$

Intuitively, we would not pay more for an option to buy a security than we would pay for the underlying security if we purchased it directly. For example, why should we pay $100 for the right to buy the stock when we could buy it in the market for $S_t = \$90$? Thus, a call option is always worth less than the underlying security on which the option is written.

Exhibit 24-3 illustrates the boundaries for call options. Note that if we have an American-style call option and it is exercised, the value is $S_0 - X$. Because $c_0 > S_0 - [X/(1 + r)^t] > S_0 - X$, it never pays to exercise the call option before maturity. (You are better off selling the option.) Thus, the boundaries of European-style call options also apply to American-style options.

EXHIBIT 24-3
Call Option Boundaries[a]

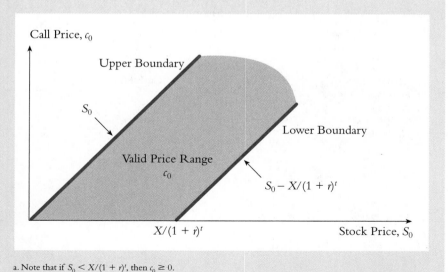

a. Note that if $S_0 < X/(1 + r)^t$, then $c_0 \geq 0$.

24.1.2 Put Option Boundaries

LOWER BOUNDARY

As with call options, European-style put options have pricing boundaries. The lower boundary for the put price (p_0) is

$$p_0 \geq \max\left[0, \frac{X}{(1+r)^t} - S_0\right] \tag{24.4}$$

The trading strategy employed to demonstrate the lower boundary of a put option consists of three parts: (1) borrowing the amount $\$X/(1+r)^t$, (2) buying one share of stock, and (3) buying one put option. Exhibit 24-4 illustrates the cash flows. The next-to-last column of this table is nonnegative by assumption ($S_t \geq X$). Therefore, if the cash flow today (0) is positive (? > 0), then this is an arbitrage opportunity. We are able to generate a positive cash flow today with no risk of future loss (and possibly a positive future cash flow). Thus, to avoid this arbitrage, we must find the cash flow today to be negative. We must have

$$-p_0 + X/(1+r)^t - S_0 \leq 0$$

which implies

$$p_0 \geq X/(1+r)^t - S_0$$

If we observe that $-p_0 + X/(1+r)^t - S_0$ is positive, everyone will want to buy put options, buy the stock, and lend to create this money machine. Buying the stock and the put option will drive the stock price and the put price up, and eventually any arbitrage profits will vanish.

EXHIBIT 24-4 The Lower Boundary for Put Options: A Cash Flow Table

Trading Strategy	Cash Flows Today (0)	At Expiration $S_t \geq X$	$S_t < X$
Buy one put option	$-p_0$	0	$X - S_t$
Borrow $\$X/(1+r)^t$	$+X/(1+r)^t$	$-X$	$-X$
Buy one share of stock	$-S_0$	$+S_t$	$+S_t$
Net cash flow	$-p_0 + X/(1+r)^t - S_0 = ?$	$S_t - X$ (positive)	0

p_0 = the current put price, S_0 = the current stock price, S_t = the stock price at expiration, X = the strike price, r = the risk-free interest rate, and t = the time to maturity in fractions of a year.

As with call options, the put price is zero at expiration if the option is out of the money [or its intrinsic value $(X - S_t) < 0$]. Therefore, at the expiration date,

$$p_t = \max(0, X - S_t) \tag{24.5}$$

UPPER BOUNDARY

The most you can lose from writing a put option (or earn by buying a put option) is the strike price (see Equation 24.5). This occurs when the stock price falls to zero. Because this loss occurs at maturity and not on the day the put option is purchased, the put option price must be below the discounted value of the strike price:

$$p_0 \leq \frac{X}{(1 + r)^t} \tag{24.6}$$

Why would you pay more for an option than the present value of its maximum payoff? The answer is that you would not. For example, a 1-year put option with a strike price of $100 at a 5% risk-free rate has an upper boundary of $95.24 [$100/$(1 + 0.05)^1$]. Investors will not pay more than $95.24 for a put option that gives them the right to make at most $100 one year from now.

Exhibit 24-5 illustrates the boundaries for put options. Again, the valid range of prices is still wide. We must investigate option pricing further to find out whether

EXHIBIT 24-5
Put Option Boundaries[a]

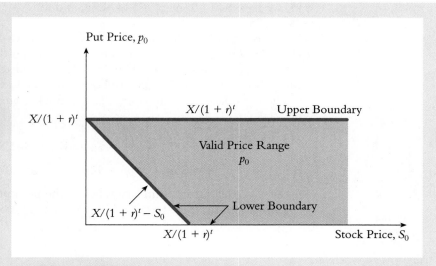

a. Note that if $S_t > X/(1 + r)^t$, then $p_0 \geq 0$.

we can make a more precise assertion regarding the option price. We turn now to examine the relationship between stock, put option, and call option prices.

PRACTICE BOX

Problem

Based on the following information from *Barron's,* verify that the closing prices of Borland's put and call options satisfy the boundary conditions. The time to maturity is one month ($t = \frac{1}{12}$), Borland's stock price is \$41⅞, and the annual risk-free interest rate is 3%. Are there any arbitrage opportunities?

Expiration Date and Strike Price	Closing Price (\$)
Borland Oct 40 call	3¾
Borland Oct 40 put	1¾
Borland Oct 45 call	1⅝
Borland Oct 45 put	4¼
Borland Oct 50 call	½
Borland Oct 50 put	8¼

Source: *Barron's,* January 5, 1998, p. MW81.

Solution

Clearly, none of these prices approaches the upper bounds (\$41⅞ for calls and \$40, \$45, and \$50 discounted for one month at the risk-free rate for puts). We now examine the lower bounds. The discount factor is $1/(1 + r)^t = 1/(1 + 0.03)^{1/12} = 0.9975$. Thus, for $X = \$40$, we have $\$40 \cdot 0.9975 = \$39.9$; for $X = \$45$, we have $\$45 \cdot 0.9975 = \$44.8875$; and for $X = \$50$, we have $\$50 \cdot 0.9975 = \$49.875$.

Let us consider calls first. When $X = \$40$, we have a lower boundary of $\$41.875 - \$39.9 = \$1.975$, which is lower than the closing price of \$3¾. When $X = \$45$, we note that $\$44.8875 > \$41.875$, and the lower boundary is zero. This is also true when $X = \$50$. In both cases, the lower boundary holds.

The boundaries for puts (using Equation 24.4) are as follows:

$$X = \$40 \qquad p_0 = 0$$

$$X = \$45 \qquad p_0 = \$44.8875 - \$41.875 = \$3.0125$$

$$X = \$50 \qquad p_0 = \$49.875 - \$41.875 = \$8.0$$

We see that each lower boundary is below the put option prices. Thus, based on these observations, there are no arbitrage opportunities.

Unlike with the call options analysis, with put options there may be value associated with an early exercise. Thus, American-style put options may have a higher value than European-style put options. To illustrate, suppose that you buy a put option on a firm that is under financial distress, and its stock price is, say, 1 cent. If the strike price is, say, $10, you had better exercise your right, get the cash flow (of $10 less 1 cent), and deposit the money in the bank to earn interest on this cash flow. The interest received may be more than the maximum additional profit from holding the put option (1 cent at most if the stock price drops to zero) until maturity. Thus, unlike with call options, with put options there is economic value for the possibility of an early exercise. We therefore expect the market value of American-style put options to be higher than the market value of similar European-style put options.

24.1.3 Put-Call Parity

Put-call parity is very useful in establishing pricing relationships between securities such as calls and puts. The notion of **put-call parity (PCP)** was first published by Russell Sage in the late nineteenth century. Put-call parity establishes an exact relationship among the current stock price, the call price, and the put price. In other words, put-call parity establishes the relationship among the underlying security, the risk-free interest rate, and call and put options that have the same strike price. Given any three of the following four securities—(1) the underlying security, (2) zero-coupon bonds (borrowing or lending),[2] (3) a call option, and (4) a put option—we can *synthetically* create the fourth. That is, by creating a portfolio of three assets, we can duplicate the cash flow of the fourth asset. Put-call parity can be written as follows:

$$c_0 = S_0 - \frac{X}{(1 + r)^t} + p_0 \tag{24.7}$$

or

$$0 = -c_0 + S_0 - \frac{X}{(1 + r)^t} + p_0 \tag{24.8}$$

Again, we assume that any trade opened at Time 0 is closed at the option maturity date (t). Exhibit 24-6 establishes the validity of Equation 24.8 (and, hence, Equation 24.7).

As in Exhibit 24-2, the first column of Exhibit 24-6 identifies a trading strategy adopted at Time 0 (today). The other three columns show the relevant cash flows. The net cash flows are simply the sum of all cash flows from the investment. For example, the net cash flow in Column 2 represents the required investment today (if negative) or the cash inflow to the investor (if positive).

Exhibit 24-6 shows that the future net cash flow from this portfolio is zero regardless of the future stock price. (That is, the sums of Columns 3 and 4 are zero.) Hence, from capital budgeting, we know that the discounted value of these payoffs

2. Buying a zero-coupon bond is equivalent to lending money, and selling a zero-coupon bond is equivalent to borrowing money.

EXHIBIT 24-6
Put–Call Parity:
A Cash Flow Table

Trading Strategy	Cash Flows		
		At Expiration	
	Today (0)	$S_t \geq X$	$S_t < X$
Buy one call option	$-c_0$	$S_t - X$	0
Sell short one share of stock	$+S_0$	$-S_t$	$-S_t$
Lend $X/(1+r)^t$	$-X/(1+r)^t$	X	X
Sell (write) one put option	$+p_0$	0	$-(X-S_t)$
Net cash flow	$-c_0 + S_0 - X/(1+r)^t + p_0$	0	0

c_0 = the current call price, p_0 = the current put price, S_0 = the current stock price, S_t = the stock price at expiration, X = the strike price, r = the risk-free interest rate, and t = the time to maturity in fractions of a year.

(which are zero) is definitely zero (regardless of the discount rate used). Therefore, the cash flow today must be zero, or else there exists a "money machine." If the net cash flow today is positive, everyone would want such an investment; the demand for the call options would increase their price, selling short the stock would decrease the price of the stock, and selling the put would decrease the put price. This selling will continue until the cash flow at Time 0 is zero and any arbitrage profit vanishes.

PRACTICE BOX

Problem

Using the information in the previous problem on Borland, evaluate whether the put–call parity holds when the strike price is $X = \$40$.

Solution

From Equation 24.7 we know that

$$c_0 - p_0 = S_0 - \frac{X}{(1+r)^t}$$

and we have $c_0 = \$3\frac{3}{4}$, $p_0 = \$1\frac{3}{4}$, $S_0 = \$41\frac{7}{8}$, $X = \$40$, $r = 3\%$, and $t = \frac{1}{12}$. We need to evaluate whether the following equality exists:

$$\$3.75 - \$1.75 \overset{?}{=} \$41.875 - \$39.9$$

$$\$2 \neq \$1.975$$

Thus, put–call parity does not hold precisely. However, it would probably be impossible to profit from this discrepancy because of transaction costs. In practice, put–call parity holds very closely.

24.2 BLACK-SCHOLES OPTION PRICING MODEL (BSOPM)

The Black-Scholes option pricing model (BSOPM) was developed in the now famous paper published by Fischer Black and Myron Scholes in 1973 in the *Journal of Political Economy*. It is interesting to note that many elements of the BSOPM were contained in Bachelier's 1900 dissertation. The BSOPM was distinct from other, similar models proposed in the late 1960s and early 1970s in that the option price does not depend on the expected returns of the underlying stock. Moreover, the model is based on a creation of a fully hedged position; thus, the riskless asset is employed to discount the future cash flows.

To better understand the usefulness and limitations of the BSOPM, let us examine the primary assumptions required for the BSOPM to be developed:

1. The market is frictionless.
2. Investors are price takers.
3. Short selling is allowed, with full use of the proceeds.
4. Borrowing and lending occur at the risk-free rate, which is continuously compounded.
5. Stock price movements are such that past price movements cannot be used to forecast future price changes.

A **frictionless market** is a market where trading is costless; there are no taxes, bid–ask spreads, brokerage commissions, and so forth. The second assumption means that no single investor can significantly influence prices. As discussed in Chapter 3, short selling is selling stock that you do not own with the understanding that you will return stock to the lender in the future.

The first three assumptions are identical to the first three assumptions in the binomial option pricing model, which is discussed in Appendix 24A. The assumption that the risk-free interest rate is compounded continuously is made for convenience and conforms with standard practice.[3] The fifth assumption determines the stock price distribution. The assumption that the stock price movement in the future cannot be predicted from the past is used by Black and Scholes, when obtaining the BSOPM.[4]

24.2.1 Call Options

Black and Scholes used the assumptions just listed and the same no-arbitrage argument given in the binomial option pricing model (see Appendix 24A) to develop a model for pricing call options. At first glance, the BSOPM looks difficult. However,

---

3. See Appendix 24C for a detailed discussion of continuously compounded interest rates.

4. For more details on this assumption, see any derivatives securities book, such as Don Chance, *An Introduction to Options and Futures,* 2d ed. (New York: Dryden Press, 1991).

a familiarity with the symbols and steps required to systematically solve pricing problems, as well as software packages, makes the BSOPM easier to use.

The BSOPM for call options is as follows:[5]

$$c = SN(d_1) - Xe^{-r_c t}N(d_2) \tag{24.9}$$

where

$$d_1 = \frac{\ln(S/X) + [r_c + (\sigma^2/2)]t}{\sigma\sqrt{t}} \tag{24.10}$$

$$d_2 = \frac{\ln(S/X) + [r_c - (\sigma^2/2)]t}{\sigma\sqrt{t}} = d_1 - \sigma\sqrt{t} \tag{24.11}$$

$N(d)$ is the cumulative area of the **standard normal distribution.**[6] For example, if $d_1 = 1.645$, then using the normal distribution, the cumulative areas up to 1.645 are 95% (see Exhibit 24-5 and Exhibit 24B-1 in Appendix 24B). Hence, $N(d_1) = 0.95$. Thus, the area under the normal curve right to d_1 is 0.05. Suppose that $\sigma = 24.5\%$, or 0.245, and $t = 1$. Then $d_2 = d_1 - \sigma\sqrt{t} = 1.645 - 0.245 = 1.400$, and the cumulative area up to $d_2 = 1.400$ is about 92%. Hence, $N(d_2) \cong 0.92$, and the area right of d_2 is about 0.08. Thus, the area between d_2 and d_1 is about 3%, or 0.03.

The other parameters of Equations 24.10 and 24.11 are as follows: $\ln(\ )$ is the natural logarithm; σ is the continuously compounded, annualized standard deviation of stock returns; r_c is the continuously compounded, annual risk-free interest rate; t is the time to maturity as a fraction of a year (with some software, we need to plug in t as the number of days to expiration); X is the strike price; S is the current stock price; and e is the base of natural logarithms and is equal to 2.7128. Thus, we need five variables (σ, r_c, t, X, and S) to calculate the price of a call option using the BSOPM.

The most difficult aspect of numerically calculating a call price is calculating $N(d_1)$ and $N(d_2)$ [represented as $N(d)$]. Exhibit 24B-1 in Appendix 24B provides the value of $N(d)$ for various values of d and thus eliminates the most painful aspect of option pricing.

Calculating the call option price is easy with the available software. All we have to do is to insert S, X, σ, r_c, and t. (In some software, t is given in days to expiration—for example, 182 days—rather than as a fraction of a year.) c then appears on the screen. However, tables with $N(d_1)$ and $N(d_2)$ are also available. We can use them along with a calculator to derive c. Appendix 24B demonstrates how tables of $N(d)$ are used to calculate c. For example, suppose we are given the following parameters:

---

5. Unless otherwise indicated, we drop the subscripts. That is, $c = c_0$, $S = S_0$, and $p = p_0$ from here on, because we are no longer in a two-period model.

6. $N(d)$ is the area under the standard bell or normal curve up to point d. $N(d)$ can be solved using a computer or be estimated with standard statistical tables, as discussed below.

$S = \$100.0$, $X = \$100.0$, $\sigma = 30\%$, $r_c = 7\%$, and $t = 182$ days (about ½ year). The use of a software package reveals that $c = \$10.06$. Using Appendix 24B, we get $c = \$10.13$ rather than $\$10.06$, because we extrapolate and hence do not get the exact price.

24.2.2 Put Options

The appropriate formula for put options can be found using the BSOPM for call options and put-call parity. Rearranging Equation 24.7 (with continuous compounding rather than discrete compounding) yields the following:

$$p = c - S + Xe^{-r_c t} \tag{24.12}$$

However, we can price a put option without explicitly writing the call price by substituting into Equation 24.12 the call option pricing equation (Equation 24.9):

$$p = SN(d_1) - Xe^{-r_c t}N(d_2) - S + Xe^{-r_c t}$$

Rearranging,

$$p = Xe^{-r_c t}[1 - N(d_2)] - S[1 - N(d_1)] \tag{24.13}$$

which can also be expressed as follows:[7]

$$p = Xe^{-r_c t}N(-d_2) - SN(-d_1) \tag{24.14}$$

Using the previous data and Equation 24.6, we can calculate the put price:

$$p = 100.0 \cdot e^{-0.07/2} \cdot (1.0 - 0.5235) - 100.0(1.0 - 0.6068)$$

$$= 100.0 \cdot 0.9656 \cdot 0.4765 - 100.0 \cdot 0.3932$$

$$p = 46.01 - 39.32 = \$6.69$$

Thus, the Black-Scholes put price is approximately $\$6.69$. Using the above parameters directly and 182 days to expiration, the computer program reveals that $p = \$6.74$. (See Section 24.2.5 for an explanation about the difference in these two prices).

24.2.3 Estimating Inputs to the BSOPM

There are five input parameters in the BSOPM: S, X, t, r_c, and σ. The current stock price (S) is easily obtainable by calling a broker or contacting an information service, such as Reuters or Telerate. The strike price (X) is specified in the options contract and published in the financial media, such as the *Wall Street Journal* and *Barron's*.

---

7. In general, $N(-d) = 1 - N(d)$ because of the symmetry of the normal distribution.

Time to maturity (t) is the fraction of the year remaining until the option expires. There is some debate on whether the year should be measured in business days (days when the market is open, which is approximately twenty days per month) or calendar days. The consensus appears to be calendar days. Hence, if there are seventy three calendar days before expiration, then $t = 73/365 = 0.20$ (assuming that the year is not a leap year[8]).

The risk-free interest rate (r_c) is slightly more difficult to estimate. We know that we should use fixed-income securities that are default-free, such as U.S. Treasury bills. Thus, the appropriate rate to employ is the continuously compounded yield to maturity closest to the option maturity date. For example, if the option is for $t = \frac{1}{5}$ of a year, then we want a Treasury bill that pays \$1 in $\frac{1}{5}$ of a year that is trading now for P_B (the price of the bill). Mathematically, we have the following relationship:

$$P_B = 1 \cdot e^{-r_c \cdot \frac{1}{5}} = e^{-r_c/5}$$

or

$$\ln(P_B) = -r_c/5$$

and, solving for r_c,[9]

$$r_c = -\frac{\ln(P_B)}{t} = -\frac{\ln(P_B)}{\frac{1}{5}} \tag{24.15}$$

Thus, for the observed price P_B, we can solve for r_c. Appendix 24C elaborates on the relationship between the discrete and continuous interest rates.

The last and most difficult parameter to estimate is the volatility of stock returns, which is measured by σ. There are several methods to estimate volatility, including the use of historical return data. Recall that the standard deviation of returns is calculated based on the following equation:

$$\sigma = \sqrt{\frac{1}{n} \sum_{t=1}^{n} (R_t - \overline{R})^2} \tag{24.16}$$

where R_t is the continuously compounded rate of return (see Appendix 24C for a detailed numerical example). Appendix 24D further explains the calculation of σ in the BSOPM.

---

8. Recall that a leap year has 366 days and occurs every 4 years: 1996, 2000, 2004, and so on.

9. Unfortunately, U.S. Treasury bills are quoted on a 360-day year and on a discount basis. That is, the prices are not widely reported. Calculating the continuously compounded interest rate based on the discount rate reported requires using the following formula:

$$r_c = \frac{\ln\left[1 + d \cdot t\left(\frac{365}{360}\right)\right]}{t}$$

where d is the quoted discount rate (in decimals) for bills (the average between the bid and asked rate), t is the fraction of the year, and ln is the natural log function. For example, suppose $t = 0.2$ and $d = 5\%$, or 0.05. In this case,

$$r_c = \frac{\ln\left[1 + 0.05 \cdot 0.20\left(\frac{365}{360}\right)\right]}{0.20} = 0.051$$

An alternative method is estimating the implied volatility of stock returns by basically turning the BSOPM around and finding the volatility that gives the current option price. However, this procedure assumes that the call price is given as observed in the market. Calculating the implied volatility is difficult, but software that computes these values swiftly is available.

24.2.4 Sensitivity Analysis of the BSOPM

We are now ready to employ the BSOPM to enhance our understanding of option price behavior. Exhibit 24-7a shows the call price as it relates to the ratio of the stock price divided by the strike price (S/X, a measure of moneyness). *Moneyness* is a term that describes whether the option is in the money or out of the money. Note that at expiration, the call price is either 0 or $S - X$. However, before the expiration date, the Black-Scholes formula shows the call price by a curved line that lies between the upper and lower bounds. Clearly, the call price is positively related to this ratio. Exhibit 24-7a also has the boundary conditions discussed earlier (see Equations 24.1 and 24.3). The exhibit shows that when the stock price either rises or falls by a large amount, the call option converges to its lower boundary.

Exhibit 24-7b presents a similar graph of the relationship between the put price and the S/X ratio. For puts, the relationship is negative. Again, the put price converges to the lower boundary for low or high stock prices.

Exhibit 24-7c presents the relationship of option pricing with the time to maturity. It illustrates time decay, which is the erosion of the time value of an option price that is due solely to the elapse of time.

Exhibit 24-7d illustrates the critical importance of volatility on option prices. Option prices are very sensitive to estimates of volatility (which are hard to obtain). For example, based on the initial estimates of $S = X = \$100$, $r_c = 5\%$, $t = 1$, and $\sigma = 30\%$, the BSOPM call price is \$13.58, and the put price is \$8.70. If it is subsequently determined that volatility is actually $\sigma = 25\%$, then the BSOPM call price is \$11.72, and the put price is \$6.85, yielding a decline in option price of 16% [(\$13.58 − \$11.72)/\$11.72] and 27% [(\$8.70 − \$6.85)/\$6.85], respectively. Hence, it is critical to have a valid estimate of volatility before trading options.

24.2.5 Empirical Evidence Regarding the BSOPM

How accurate is the BSOPM in determining option prices? We can calculate the theoretical value of an option as predicted by the BSOPM and compare it with the observed market call price. If there is no significant deviation, we say that there is no bias, and the model works well. Several empirical studies have tested this model. Generally, these tests support the BSOPM. In general, the BSOPM performs well for longer terms (three months to 1 year) and for at-the-money options. With extremely high or low volatilities, the BSOPM does not perform well. Most of the known mispricings by the BSOPM are not consistent across time. For example, highly volatile stock options may be found to be overpriced by the BSOPM during one 5-year period and underpriced during a different 5-year period.

EXHIBIT 24-7
The Sensitivity of Option Prices to Changes in Underlying Parameters

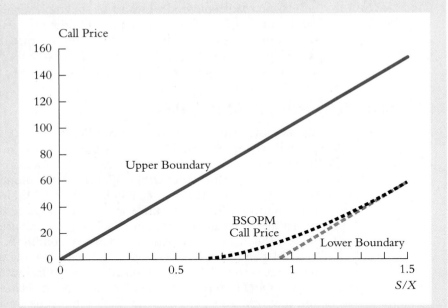

Part a: Sensitivity Analysis of the Call Price with Respect to Moneyness (S/X)

The parameters selected were $r_c = 5\%$, $\sigma = 30\%$, and $t = 1$ year.

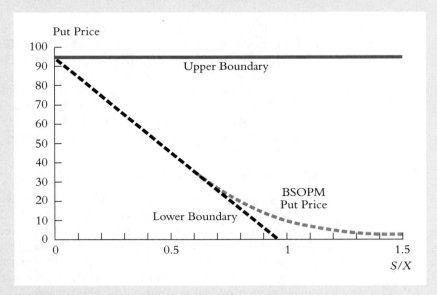

Part b: Sensitivity Analysis of the Put Price with Respect to Moneyness (S/X)

The parameters selected were $r_c = 5\%$, $\sigma = 30\%$, and $t = 1$ year.

(continued)

EXHIBIT 24-7
(continued)

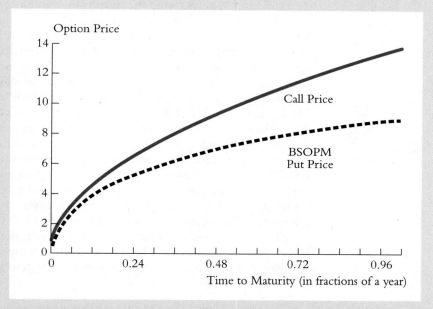

Part c: Sensitivity Analysis
of Time Decay

The parameters selected were $r_c = 5\%$, $\sigma = 30\%$, and $S = X = \$100$. Thus, when no time remains, both put and call options are worthless, because $S - X = X - S = 0$.

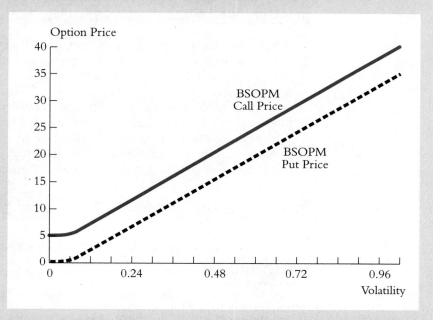

Part d: Sensitivity Analysis
of Volatility

The parameters selected were $r_c = 5\%$, $t = 1$ year, and $S = X = \$100$. Thus, when the standard deviation is zero, the options are valued at their lower boundaries [calls at $S - X/(1 + r)$ and puts at zero, because $X/(1 + r) - S < 0$].

Black and Scholes found that buyers tend to pay too much for call options; they determined that the BSOPM tends to overprice options with high variance and to underprice options with low variance.[10] Gultekin, Rogalski, and Tinic found similar results, as well as finding that the BSOPM overestimates values of in-the-money options and underestimates values of out-of-the-money options.[11] Chiras and Manaster found that adjusting for dividends and improving the way implied volatilities are estimated improve the performance of the BSOPM in predicting actual prices.[12] Macbeth and Merville found that the BSOPM predicted prices less than the market for in-the-money options and predicted prices greater than the market for out-of-the-money options.[13] The bias is more pronounced for shorter-term options. More recently, Long and Officer investigated the relationship between mispricing in the BSOPM and the volume of trading. Their evidence indicates that call options that are heavily traded are priced more efficiently and have lower mispricing errors than do thinly traded options.[14] Connecting Theory to Practice 24.1 further illustrates the nature of problems that arise in the use of the BSOPM.

Although researchers have found some biases, the BSOPM remains one of the best models in all of finance for explaining a security's price behavior. The BSOPM is better able to explain the variation in option prices than the CAPM can explain the variation in stock prices.

CONNECTING THEORY TO PRACTICE 24.1

THE HOLES IN BLACK-SCHOLES

When we calculate option values using the Black-Scholes model, and compare them with option prices, there is usually a difference. It is rare that the value of an option comes out exactly equal to the price at which it trades on the exchange.

One possible reason for the difference between value and price is that we have made a mistake in figuring the value. We may be looking at the wrong date, or using a volatility estimate that we meant to use for a different stock, or using a stock price that was reported incorrectly. Leaving aside errors like these, there are three reasons for a difference between value and price: we may

(continued)

10. See Fischer Black and Myron Scholes, "The Valuation of Option Contracts and a Test of Market Efficiency," *Journal of Finance* 27(May 1972): 399–418.

11. See N. Bulent Gultekin, J. Rogalski, and Seha M. Tinic, "Option Pricing Model Estimates: Some Empirical Results," *Financial Management* 11(Spring 1982): 58–69.

12. See D. Chiras and S. Manaster, "The Informational Content of Option Prices and a Test of Market Efficiency," *Journal of Financial Economics*, June 1978, pp. 213–234.

13. See J. Macbeth and L. Merville, "An Empirical Examination of the Black-Scholes Call Option Pricing Model," *Journal of Finance,* December 1979, pp. 1173–1186.

14. See D. Long and D. Officer, "The Relation between Option Mispricing and Volume in the Black-Scholes Option Model," *Journal of Financial Research* 20(Spring 1997): 1–12.

have the correct value, and the option price may be out of line; we may have used the wrong inputs to the Black-Scholes formula; or the Black-Scholes formula may be wrong. Normally, all three reasons play a part in explaining a difference between value and price.

If the option price is out of line with value, it may be possible to trade profitably using the formula. Some people would say, however, that transaction costs will wipe out any possible trading profits in options no matter what formula is used.

The main input that may be wrong is the volatility. The stock price may be observed at a different time from the option price, or the interest rate we use may be outdated. These errors can be detected and corrected if they are large enough to make correction worthwhile. The volatility of the stock over the life of the option, though, must be estimated.

Different people will make different volatility estimates. An option price that is higher than the value we figure may signal that others in the market have higher volatility estimates than we do. Sometimes the market's estimate will be closer, and sometimes ours will be closer.

Source: Fischer Black, *From Black-Scholes to Black Holes* (London, England: Risk Publishing, 1992), pp. 51–56. Reprinted with permission.

MAKING THE CONNECTION

This excerpt suggests four reasons why the numerical result of the BSOPM may differ from the observed market price:

1. There is a computational error.
2. Observed market prices are out of line.
3. The wrong inputs were used.
4. The BSOPM is wrong.

Investors trading options must use caution when applying the BSOPM. Just because differences are observed between the BSOPM values and market price does not mean investors should immediately trade. However, once potential biases have been investigated, the BSOPM provides a solid basis for decision making related to options.

24.3 APPLICATIONS OF THE BSOPM

With the BSOPM, we can now accurately estimate option prices. In addition to finding arbitrage opportunities, which seem to be difficult to locate, we can use the information generated by the model for other investment strategies. This section describes some of those applications.

Today options are employed by firms and individuals. Investing abroad involves foreign currency risk, and buying options on foreign currency can eliminate this risk (although not without cost). Similarly, manufacturers that need raw material and are afraid of a price rise in the future can protect themselves with derivatives. However, this section focuses on the point of view of an investor who buys a share or a portfolio of shares. It first discusses portfolio insurance, which is one of the most important uses of put options. It also discusses convertible securities and warrants.

24.3.1 Valuing Portfolio Insurance Using the BSOPM

One benefit of the BSOPM is the ability to estimate the cost of engaging in various risk management strategies. Recall that protective put buying is the strategy of buying puts on the underlying portfolio and is one form of portfolio insurance. **Portfolio insurance** is any strategy in which the maximum loss is set or determined in advance.

Suppose you are a portfolio manager responsible for a $100,000,000 stock portfolio that closely resembles the Standard & Poor's 500 (S&P 500) stock index. Because of an unprecedented rise in stock prices, you are concerned that recent gains will be lost in another "crash" like the ones that occurred in October 1987, October 1997, and August 1998. Of course, if you wanted to guarantee no loss at all, you would have to pay a high price for the insurance. For example, you might buy a put option on your portfolio with a strike price of $100,000,000. Then, no matter what the value of your portfolio became, you would be guaranteed to have a value no less than your original $100,000,000 minus the cost of the put option.

More realistically, suppose you allow for some loss—say, not more than 10%. Suppose it is now August, and you are considering "insuring" your portfolio risk for 182 days. How much should such a put option cost? If current interest rates are around 7% and the S&P 500 index has a volatility of 20%, how much should the insurance cost? Without option pricing analysis, this would be a difficult problem to solve.

Because this type of portfolio insurance is nothing more than buying a put option, you can employ the BSOPM for puts. The inputs are $S = \$100,000,000$, $X = \$90,000,000$ (or 10% loss),[15] $r_c = 7\%$, $\sigma = 20\%$, and $t = 182$ days (or about ½ year).

Using a software package, you find that according to the BSOPM, the insurance policy should cost $1,127,709.50. Hence, the fair value for this insurance policy is $1,127,709.50, or about 1.1% of the portfolio value. Thus, if there is a crash in the market and the market value of your portfolio goes down to $70,000,000, you sell the put option for $20,000,000 (which is $90,000,000 less $70,000,000). After the

---

15. An alternative approach to pricing this option would be to first calculate the value of the option on a per-unit price of the S&P 500 index. Then multiply the per-unit price by the number of contracts needed. For example, if the S&P 500 is currently at 400, the appropriate strike price would be 360 (0.9 · 400). This portfolio would need 250,000 units ($100,000,000/400). Each option contract is actually for 500 times the index, so the number of contracts needed is 500 (250,000/500).

cost of the put option, you have \$88,872,290.50 (\$90,000,000 − \$1,127,709.50). If, in contrast, the value of the portfolio goes up to \$110,000,000, the option expires worthless. What is left is \$108,872,290.50 (\$110,000,000 − \$1,127,709.50). Thus, you have established a floor on your losses at the cost of some of the gains if prices rise.

24.3.2 Convertible Securities

Recall from Chapters 2 and 16 that a convertible bond is a bond that can be converted into stock by the bondholder. Hence, a convertible bond is equivalent to an ordinary bond with a call option on the stock. Mathematically, the value of a convertible bond (CB) can be expressed as follows:

$$CB = SB + CVO$$

where SB denotes the value of a comparable straight bond, and CVO denotes the value of the option to convert the bonds.

In practice, valuing the option to convert is very complicated. First, this option is sensitive to overall interest rates; recall that the BSOPM assumes a constant risk-free rate. Clearly, this assumption cannot be made with options on bonds, because bonds are issued for relatively long terms, and over a relatively long period the interest rate changes (sometimes drastically). Second, the decision of whether to exercise this option to convert is complicated by the relationship between dividend payments on the stock and coupon payments on the bond. Third, the conversion ratio (the number of stocks received for each bond converted) of many convertible bonds varies over time.

Finally, most convertible bonds are also callable. A callable, convertible bond is equivalent to a straight bond plus a conversion option minus the callable option; that is, the call feature is equivalent to the bondholder's being short a call option. The firm holds the right to buy the bonds back at a stated price. Mathematically, the value of a callable, convertible bond can be expressed as follows:

$$CCB = SB + CVO - CLO$$

where CCB denotes a callable, convertible bond, and CLO denotes the option the firm holds to call the bonds.

Callable, convertible bonds are sensitive to interest rates, as well as stock prices. If interest rates fall, the firm may call the bonds, which sets a ceiling on the value of the bonds. However, if the stock price rises, then the convertible bonds will likewise rise. When callable, convertible bonds are called, bondholders have the right to convert the bonds into stocks rather than redeem the bonds to the firm. When firms want to alter their balance sheet to reduce their debt, they often call convertible bonds. If stock prices appreciate, bondholders wishing to get the most for their bonds will convert them to stock, resulting in a firm with more equity and less debt. Hence, callable, convertible bonds are an attractive tool for firms that want added flexibility in managing their capital structure.

24.3.3 Valuing Warrants

A *warrant* is usually issued with a bond or preferred stock and gives the owner the right to buy a specified number of shares of common stock at a stated price during a specified number of years. Thus, warrants are essentially call options on common stock. Warrants typically have longer times to maturity. Sometimes they have no stated maturity, in which case they are perpetual warrants. Warrants are used by firms as an added sweetener when raising capital through a bond or preferred stock issue.

It is important to note one subtle difference between call options and warrants. When a call option is exercised, the firm whose stock is being purchased is not involved. With a warrant, however, the firm itself actually issues more shares. Hence, warrants have a dilutive effect on the proportional ownership of outstanding shares—a fact that causes a warrant to be priced slightly lower than a call option.

24.3.4 Options on Futures Contracts

A fairly recent development is the trading of options on futures contracts. Exhibit 24-8 shows the quotation of some of the various options on futures. When an investor exercises a call option on a future, he or she receives a long position in the future contract.

Options on futures were developed in response to the problem of hedging when there is quantity risk, as in the case of the wheat farmer who is uncertain about how much wheat will be harvested. Buying options does not require that a farmer actually deliver the wheat. The farmer will have the right to deliver the wheat and will do so only if prices are favorable.

Another benefit of options on futures is that exercising an option on futures requires only accepting a futures contract, not taking physical possession of the physical asset itself, for example, wheat. For example, if the wheat farmer had purchased a call option on wheat futures, then the farmer could exercise the option and receive a long position in the futures contract. For most hedgers as well as speculators, this feature is preferable to having to take physical delivery of the wheat.

A final benefit is that the farmer will receive the benefit of rising wheat prices and has hedged the risk of falling wheat prices. Recall that hedging with options allows you to insure the risk without eliminating the potential for gain if prices move in your favor. The wheat farmer who had purchased put options on wheat futures would be out only the premium of the put option, which would be much less than the loss on selling futures contracts. If the harvest had been large and prices had fallen, the farmer would benefit from the put option and lose from selling wheat.

There are times when selling options is preferable to selling futures. For example, a grain elevator company (a company with a large inventory of wheat) may sell call options on wheat futures when it thinks the price is too high. If the company is correct, it will be able to keep the option premium, because the option buyer will not exercise if the price falls. If the company is wrong, then the only cost will be

EXHIBIT 24-8 Futures Options Trading

FUTURES OPTIONS

CBOT

Month	Strike	Vol	Open Int	Week's High	Week's Low	Sett	Pt Chg	Future Sett
10 YR. TREASURY				**$100,000 prin, pts & 64ths of 100 pct**				
Aug 98 p	111	1270	3735	-01	-01	-01	– -01	114-01
Aug 98 c	112	1832	458	...	...	2-04	+ -15	114-01
Aug 98 p	112	2102	5998	-07	-01	-02	– -03	114-01
Aug 98 c	113	1313	3958	...	...	1-09	+ -08	114-01
Aug 98 p	113	7214	10179	-18	-06	-07	– -10	114-01
Aug 98 c	114	9490	9793	-35	-20	-28	...	114-01
Aug 98 p	114	2541	3015	-26	-25	-26	– -17	114-01
Aug 98 c	115	5278	11995	-12	-07	-08	– -02	114-01
Aug 98 c	116	800	510	-03	-02	-02	– -01	114-01
Sep 98 c	105	600	150	...	...	9-02	+ -18	114-01
Sep 98 p	106	800	181	...	...	-01	...	114-01
Sep 98 p	107	800	200	...	...	-01	...	114-01
Sep 98 p	108	1877	2296	-01	-01	-01	...	114-01
Sep 98 p	109	4212	25366	-01	-01	-01	...	114-01
Sep 98 p	110	1600	19580	...	...	-02	...	114-01
Sep 98 c	111	1400	1200	...	...	3-04	+ -16	114-01
Sep 98 p	111	1478	20046	-06	-05	-03	– -03	114-01
Sep 98 c	112	2954	9919	2-09	2-03	2-09	+ -12	114-01
Sep 98 p	112	4875	20620	-14	-10	-08	– -06	114-01
Sep 98 c	113	2402	32205	1-24	1-02	1-22	+ -07	114-01
Sep 98 p	113	14698	29135	-33	-19	-20	– -11	114-01
Sep 98 c	114	12953	41556	-49	-37	-46	+ -03	114-01
Sep 98 p	114	4626	15019	1-05	-42	-45	– -14	114-01
Sep 98 c	115	10011	47520	-26	-18	-21	...	114-01
Sep 98 c	116	3006	26258	-10	-08	-08	– -01	114-01
Sep 98 c	117	800	3761	-04	-03	-03	– -01	114-01
Dec 98 p	107	1200	300	...	...	-02	– -01	113-30
Dec 98 p	108	1200	25601	...	...	-04	– -01	113-30
Dec 98 p	109	1200	13662	...	...	-07	– -02	113-30
Dec 98 p	110	2000	5629	-11	-10	-11	– -04	113-30
Dec 98 p	111	1200	9051	...	...	-20	– -06	113-30
Dec 98 p	112	1025	9410	...	...	-33	– -09	113-30
Dec 98 c	113	6650	11872	...	...	1-48	+ -09	113-30
Dec 98 c	114	6031	16505	1-15	1-02	1-12	+ -05	113-30
Dec 98 p	114	1120	1406	1-23	1-14	1-16	– -15	113-30
Dec 98 c	115	4050	10390	-54	-41	-50	+ -04	113-30
Dec 98 c	116	2000	10600	...	...	-30	+ -01	113-30
Dec 98 p	116	2600	650	...	...	2-32	– -18	113-30
Dec 98 c	117	6000	11130	...	...	-18	+ -01	113-30
Dec 98 c	119	1200	300	...	...	-06	...	113-30
Dec 98 c	120	1192	300	...	...	-04	+ -01	113-30
Mar 99c	114	1000	80	...	...	1-35	+ -04	113-31
Total Call volume		58,884	**Call Open int**			268,255		
Total Put volume		46,453	**Put Open int**			233,335		
5 YR. TREASURY				**$100,000, pts & 64ths of 100 pct**				
Aug 98 p	10800	2000	500	...	...	-01	– -01	109-55
Aug 98 p	10850	1204	4675	...	...	-02	– -03	109-55
Aug 98 c	10900	2000	875	...	...	-59	+ -13	109-55
Aug 98 p	10900	3461	4451	...	...	-04	– -06	109-55
Aug 98 c	10950	1830	1877	...	...	-33	+ -07	109-55
Aug 98 p	10950	1437	2029	...	...	-10	– -12	109-55
Aug 98 c	11000	5585	5207	...	...	-15	+ -02	109-55
Aug 98 c	11050	1826	601	...	...	-06	...	109-55
Aug 98 c	11100	1750	2075	...	...	-02	...	109-55
Aug 98 c	11150	1600	400	...	...	-01	...	109-55
Sep 98 p	10650	800	1380	...	...	-01	...	109-55
Sep 98 p	10700	800	5165	...	...	-01	– -01	109-55
Sep 98 p	10750	800	6788	...	...	-02	– -01	109-55
Sep 98 c	10800	2400	525	...	...	1-57	+ -16	109-55
Sep 98 p	10800	850	7457	...	...	-03	– -03	109-55
Sep 98 c	10850	520	405	...	...	1-28	+ -13	109-55
Sep 98 p	10850	1920	4822	...	...	-06	– -05	109-55
Sep 98 p	10900	800	11321	...	...	-11	– -08	109-55
Sep 98 c	10950	3705	12599	...	...	-43	+ -07	109-55
Sep 98 p	10950	3545	6624	...	...	-20	– -12	109-55
Sep 98 c	11000	1701	14032	...	...	-25	+ -03	109-55
Sep 98 c	11050	1901	24634	...	...	-13	+ -01	109-55
Sep 98 c	11100	851	7977	...	...	-06	+ -01	109-55
Sep 98 c	11150	1600	1255	...	...	-03	...	109-55
Sep 98 c	11200	2000	561	...	...	-01	– -01	109-55
Dec 98 p	10700	8400	2000	...	...	-07	– -04	109-57
Dec 98 p	10750	2000	1000	...	...	-10	– -05	109-57
Dec 98 c	10900	5800	3400	...	...	1-24	+ -10	109-57
Dec 98 c	11000	4000	1900	...	...	-52	+ -07	109-57
Dec 98 p	11000	4000	1750	...	...	-58	– -14	109-57
Dec 98 c	11250	1300	325	...	...	-08	...	109-57
Total Call volume		18,499	**Call Open int**			95,740		
Total Put volume		8,222	**Put Open int**			66,572		
SOYBEAN OIL				**60,000 lbs- cents per lb**				
Aug 98 p	2500	1698	2896	0.57	0.15	0.20	–0.07	25.82
Aug 98 p	2550	969	2411	0.85	0.40	0.41	–0.05	25.82
Aug 98 c	2700	855	1250	0.40	0.19	0.23	–0.19	25.82
Aug 98 c	2800	674	4347	0.15	0.10	0.11	–0.14	25.82
Aug 98 p	3100	800	60	...	...	5.20	+0.17	25.82
Sep 98 c	2550	1037	450	1.10	1.00	1.18	–0.27	25.96
Sep 98 c	2600	614	1746	1.05	0.65	0.98	–0.22	25.96
Sep 98 p	2950	1400	125	...	...	3.78	+0.18	25.96
Sep 98 p	3100	800	400	...	...	5.17	+0.22	25.96
Oct 98 c	2800	572	759	0.55	0.43	0.62	–0.03	26.05
Dec 98 p	2450	1100	1696	0.50	0.48	0.50	+0.12	26.13
Dec 98 p	2550	1224	1347	1.00	0.85	0.95	+0.19	26.13
Dec 98 p	2950	800	75	...	...	3.78	+0.38	26.13
Mar 99p	2650	536	148	...	...	1.60	+0.25	26.32
Mar 99c	2800	600	310	...	...	0.94	–0.31	26.32
Total Call volume		5,713	**Call Open int**			52,868		
Total Put volume		4,752	**Put Open int**			34,408		
SOYBEANS				**5,000 bu, cents per bushel**				
Aug 98 c	475	623	1827	159½	141¾	151¾	– 20	626¾
Aug 98 p	550	573	1685	1¼	½	½	– ⅛	626¾
Aug 98 p	575	4918	8568	4½	1½	2	...	626¾
Aug 98 c	600	1012	2222	38	22	32⅞	–18⅛	626¾
Aug 98 p	600	4948	5592	13	4¾	5¾	– ¼	626¾
Aug 98 c	625	3124	5478	24½	13	18	– 17	626¾
Aug 98 p	625	3269	4697	26½	13½	16¼	+ 1¼	626¾
Aug 98 c	650	5167	7703	14½	6¾	9¾	–13¼	626¾
Aug 98 p	650	1026	2646	46	30	33⅜	+ 4⅞	626¾
Aug 98 c	675	3605	6518	11	3¾	5	–10½	626¾
Aug 98 c	700	3095	6002	5½	2½	2¾	– 7¼	626¾
Aug 98 c	725	2529	4224	3½	1½	1⅝	– 5½	626¾
Aug 98 c	750	2499	4770	3	1	1⅛	– 3⅞	626¾
Aug 98 c	775	966	1911	3	¾	¾	– 2¾	626¾
Aug 98 c	800	565	3692	1½	½	½	– 2	626¾
Sep 98 p	575	3623	4567	12½	7¾	8⅞	+ 1⅞	610¼
Sep 98 c	600	1237	2790	40	27	29	– 25	610¼
Sep 98 p	600	2021	3335	26	16	19	+ 5	610¼
Sep 98 c	625	1163	3866	30	19	20	– 21	610¼
Sep 98 c	650	2273	6258	25	11½	12¾	– 17	610¼
Sep 98 c	675	3483	3836	17	8	9	–13½	610¼
Sep 98 c	700	3884	4753	13	5½	6	– 11	610¼
Sep 98 c	725	3412	3284	16	4½	4¾	– 9¼	610¼
Sep 98 c	750	647	2370	7	3½	3⅝	– 7⅜	610¼
Sep 98 c	775	892	1167	6	2¾	3	– 5½	610¼
Sep 98 c	800	1025	2578	5	2	2⅜	– 4⅜	610¼
Nov 98 c	450	521	33	166¾	151	152	– 34	602
Nov 98 p	500	717	3315	2½	1¼	1½	...	602
Nov 98 p	525	1252	3808	5½	3	3⅞	+ ½	602
Nov 98 p	550	2925	7305	12	7	9½	+ 2¾	602
Nov 98 c	575	590	2920	59	44	45½	–28¾	602
Nov 98 p	575	3870	7606	22	14	18½	+ 4½	602
Nov 98 c	600	1327	4636	45	32	33¼	–25¾	602
Nov 98 p	600	3947	8087	35	24½	31¼	+ 7¾	602
Nov 98 c	625	3920	11140	36	23	24	–21½	602
Nov 98 p	625	1374	4639	50	38	46½	+11¾	602
Nov 98 c	650	5660	9045	27	16½	17¼	–18¾	602
Nov 98 p	650	642	2578	68¾	57	64¾	+14¾	602
Nov 98 c	675	4614	6060	21	12	13¼	–15¾	602
Nov 98 c	700	4068	9588	17	9½	10¼	–13¼	602
Nov 98 c	725	1583	4122	13	7	8	–10½	602
Nov 98 c	750	1379	7073	10	6	6½	– 9	602
Nov 98 c	800	3356	6253	7	3¾	4⅛	– 5⅞	602
Nov 98 c	850	1290	4185	5	2½	2⅝	– 4⅜	602
Nov 98 c	900	2014	4370	3½	1¾	1¾	– 3	602
Nov 98 c	1000	812	1494	2	⅞	⅞	– 1⅝	602
Mar 99p	550	800	212	...	...	13¾	+ 5¼	617¼
Jul 99 c	750	1780	500	...	...	27	– 6	624
Total Call volume		75,729	**Call Open int**			164,925		
Total Put volume		36,314	**Put Open int**			78,463		

(continued)

EXHIBIT 24-8 *(continued)*

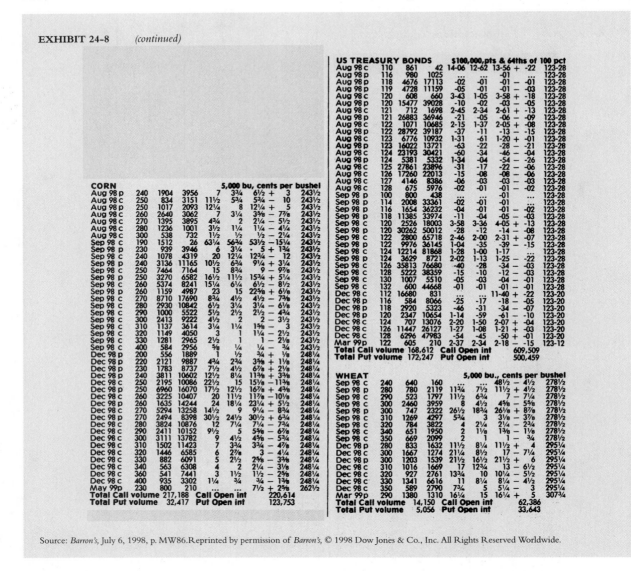

CORN — 5,000 bu, cents per bushel

Aug 98 p	240	1904	3956	7	3¾	6½	+ 3	243½
Aug 98 c	250	834	3151	11½	5¾	5¾	− 10	243½
Aug 98 p	250	1017	2093	12¼	8	12¼	+ 5	243½
Aug 98 c	260	2640	3062	7	3¼	3⅝	− 7⅞	243½
Aug 98 c	270	1395	3895	4¾	2	2¼	− 5½	243½
Aug 98 c	280	1236	1001	3½	1¼	1¼	− 4¼	243½
Aug 98 c	300	538	732	1½	½	½	− 2¼	243½
Sep 98 c	190	1512	26	63¼	56¾	53½	−15¼	243½
Sep 98 p	230	939	3946	6	3¼	5	+ 1¾	243½
Sep 98 c	240	1078	4319	20	12¼	12¾	− 12	243½
Sep 98 p	240	3136	11165	10½	6¾	9¼	+ 3¼	243½
Sep 98 c	250	7464	7164	15	8¾	9	− 9⅞	243½
Sep 98 p	250	3270	6582	16½	11½	15¾	+ 5¼	243½
Sep 98 c	260	5374	8241	15¼	6¼	6½	− 8½	243½
Sep 98 p	260	1159	4987	23	15	22⅝	+ 6⅛	243½
Sep 98 c	270	8710	17690	8¾	4½	4½	− 7⅜	243½
Sep 98 c	280	2930	10842	6½	3¼	3¼	− 6⅛	243½
Sep 98 c	290	1000	5522	5½	2½	2½	− 4¾	243½
Sep 98 c	300	2413	9222	4½	2	2	− 3½	243½
Sep 98 c	310	1137	3614	3¼	1¼	1⅝	− 3	243½
Sep 98 c	320	1149	4050	3	1	1¼	− 2½	243½
Sep 98 c	330	1281	2965	2½	1	1	− 2⅛	243½
Sep 98 c	400	584	2956	⅝	¼	¼	− ¾	243½
Dec 98 p	200	556	1889	1	½	¾	+ ⅛	248¼
Dec 98 p	220	2121	9887	4¾	2¾	3⅝	+ 1⅛	248¼
Dec 98 p	230	1783	8737	7½	4½	6⅞	+ 2⅛	248¼
Dec 98 p	240	3811	10602	12½	8¼	11⅜	+ 3⅜	248¼
Dec 98 c	250	2195	10086	22½	15	15⅛	−11⅜	248¼
Dec 98 p	250	6960	16070	17½	12½	16⅞	+ 4⅜	248¼
Dec 98 c	260	3225	10407	20	11½	11⅞	−10⅛	248¼
Dec 98 p	260	1635	14244	24	18¼	23¼	+ 5½	248¼
Dec 98 c	270	5294	13258	14½	9	9¼	− 8¾	248¼
Dec 98 p	270	2494	8398	30½	24½	30½	+ 6¾	248¼
Dec 98 c	280	3824	10876	12	7¼	7¼	− 7¾	248¼
Dec 98 c	290	2411	10152	9½	5	5⅝	− 6⅞	248¼
Dec 98 c	300	3111	13782	9	4½	4⅝	− 5¾	248¼
Dec 98 c	310	1502	11423	7	3¾	3¾	− 4⅞	248¼
Dec 98 c	320	1446	6585	6	2⅞	3	− 4¼	248¼
Dec 98 c	330	882	6091	5	2½	2⅝	− 3⅜	248¼
Dec 98 c	340	563	6308	4	2	2¼	− 3⅛	248¼
Dec 98 c	360	541	7441	3	1½	1½	− 2⅝	248¼
Dec 98 c	400	935	3302	1¼	¾	¾	− 1⅜	248¼
May 99p	230	800	210	...	...	7½	+ 2⅝	262½

Total Call volume 217,188 **Call Open int** 220,614
Total Put volume 32,417 **Put Open int** 123,753

US TREASURY BONDS — $100,000,pts & 64ths of 100 pct

Aug 98 c	110	861	42	14-06	12-62	13-56	+ -22	123-28
Aug 98 p	116	980	1025	...	...	-01	...	123-28
Aug 98 p	118	4676	17113	-02	-01	-01	− -01	123-28
Aug 98 p	119	4728	11159	-05	-01	-01	− -03	123-28
Aug 98 c	120	608	660	3-43	1-05	3-58	+ -18	123-28
Aug 98 p	120	15477	39028	-10	-02	-03	− -05	123-28
Aug 98 c	121	712	1698	2-45	2-34	2-61	+ -13	123-28
Aug 98 p	121	26883	36946	-21	-05	-06	− -09	123-28
Aug 98 c	122	1071	10685	2-15	1-37	2-05	+ -08	123-28
Aug 98 p	122	28792	39187	-37	-11	-13	− -15	123-28
Aug 98 c	123	6776	10932	1-31	-61	1-20	+ -01	123-28
Aug 98 p	123	16022	13721	-63	-22	-28	− -21	123-28
Aug 98 c	124	23193	30421	-60	-34	-46	− -04	123-28
Aug 98 p	124	5381	5332	1-34	-04	-54	− -26	123-28
Aug 98 c	125	27861	23896	-31	-17	-22	− -06	123-28
Aug 98 c	126	17260	22013	-15	-08	-08	− -06	123-28
Aug 98 c	127	4146	8386	-06	-03	-03	− -03	123-28
Aug 98 c	128	675	5976	-02	-01	-01	− -02	123-28
Sep 98 p	100	800	438	...	...	-01	...	123-28
Sep 98 p	114	2008	33361	-02	-01	-01	...	123-28
Sep 98 p	116	1654	36232	-04	-01	-01	− -02	123-28
Sep 98 p	118	11385	33974	-11	-04	-05	− -03	123-28
Sep 98 c	120	2526	18003	3-58	3-36	4-05	+ -13	123-28
Sep 98 p	120	30262	50012	-28	-12	-14	− -08	123-28
Sep 98 c	122	2800	65718	2-46	2-00	2-31	+ -07	123-28
Sep 98 p	122	9976	36145	1-04	-35	-39	− -15	123-28
Sep 98 c	124	12214	81868	1-28	1-00	1-17	...	123-28
Sep 98 p	124	3629	8721	2-02	1-13	1-25	− -22	123-28
Sep 98 c	126	35813	76680	-40	-28	-34	− -03	123-28
Sep 98 c	128	5222	38359	-15	-10	-12	− -03	123-28
Sep 98 c	130	1007	5510	-05	-03	-04	− -01	123-28
Sep 98 c	132	600	44668	-01	-01	-01	− -01	123-28
Dec 98 c	112	16680	831	...	...	11-40	+ -22	123-20
Dec 98 p	116	584	8066	-25	-17	-18	− -05	123-20
Dec 98 p	118	2920	5323	-46	-31	-34	− -07	123-20
Dec 98 p	120	2347	10654	1-14	-59	-61	− -10	123-20
Dec 98 c	124	707	13076	2-20	1-50	2-07	+ -04	123-20
Dec 98 c	126	11447	26127	1-27	1-08	1-21	+ -03	123-20
Dec 98 c	128	6296	47983	-54	-45	-50	+ -01	123-20
Mar 99p	122	605	210	2-37	2-34	2-18	− -15	123-12

Total Call volume 168,612 **Call Open int** 609,509
Total Put volume 172,247 **Put Open int** 500,459

WHEAT — 5,000 bu., cents per bushel

Sep 98 c	240	640	160	...	...	48½	− 4½	278½
Sep 98 p	280	780	2119	11¾	7½	11½	+ 4½	278½
Sep 98 c	290	523	1797	11½	6¾	7	− 7¼	278½
Sep 98 c	300	2460	3959	8	4½	4⅝	− 5⅝	278½
Sep 98 p	300	747	2322	26½	18¾	26⅛	+ 8⅞	278½
Sep 98 c	310	1269	4297	5¾	3	3⅛	− 3⅞	278½
Sep 98 c	320	784	3822	4	2¼	2¼	− 2¾	278½
Sep 98 c	340	651	1950	2	1⅛	1⅜	− 1⅛	278½
Sep 98 c	350	669	2099	2	1	1	− ¾	278½
Dec 98 p	280	833	1632	11½	8¼	11½	+ 4	295¼
Dec 98 c	300	1667	1274	21¼	8½	17	− 7¼	295¼
Dec 98 p	300	1203	1539	21½	16½	21½	+ 6	295¼
Dec 98 c	310	1016	1669	17	12¾	13	− 6½	295¼
Dec 98 c	320	927	2761	13¾	10	10¼	− 5½	295¼
Dec 98 c	330	1341	6616	11	8¼	8¼	− 4½	295¼
Dec 98 c	350	589	2790	7¾	5	5¼	− 3	295¼
Mar 99p	290	1380	1310	16¼	15	16¼	+ 5	307¾

Total Call volume 14,150 **Call Open int** 62,386
Total Put volume 5,056 **Put Open int** 33,643

Source: *Barron's,* July 6, 1998, p. MW86.Reprinted by permission of *Barron's,*

that it must sell the wheat at the strike price (which it initially thought was high anyway). Thus, the only loss in this case is an opportunity loss of selling the inventory of wheat at an even higher price. Also, a cereal producer (a buyer of wheat) may consider selling put options on wheat futures if the producer believes wheat prices to be low. If the cereal producer is correct and wheat prices rise, it keeps the put option premium. If it is wrong and wheat prices fall further, it must buy the wheat at the exercise price, which it thought was initially low.

Pricing options on futures is similar to pricing stock options.[16] The futures option pricing model for call options can be expressed as follows:

$$c = e^{-rt}[F_0 N(d_1) - XN(d_2)] \qquad (24.17)$$

where $d_1 = \dfrac{\ln(F_0/X) + (\sigma^2/2)t}{\sigma\sqrt{t}}$ and $d_2 = d_1 - \sigma\sqrt{t}$.

The value of a futures put option can be expressed as follows:

$$p = e^{-rt}[XN(-d_2) - F_0 N(-d_1)] \qquad (24.18)$$

The volatility in this case is the volatility of the futures contract. Also notice that d_1 is slightly different.

SUMMARY

Identify option boundaries and put-call parity. An analysis of option boundaries is the first step toward understanding the behavior of option prices. The call option's lower boundary is zero or the current stock price minus the discounted strike price, whichever is greater. The call option's upper boundary is simply the current stock price. The put option's lower boundary is zero or the discounted strike price minus the current stock price, whichever is greater. The put option's upper boundary is simply the discounted exercise price. Put-call parity establishes an exact relationship among the current stock price, the call price, and the put price.

Use the Black-Scholes option pricing model (BSOPM) to value call and put options. The BSOPM is dependent on five parameters. Four of them—stock price, strike price, time to maturity, and risk-free interest rate—are readily available. The fifth parameter, the volatility (or standard deviation), has to be estimated. The BSOPM is very sensitive to estimates of volatility, which are difficult to obtain.

Understand how to insure a portfolio with options. Put options insure the downside risk of a stock portfolio; they set a floor on potential losses. Hence, the BSOPM is a useful tool in assessing the risk related to portfolio management.

Describe options on futures contracts. Options on futures contracts are very similar to stock options. However, when an investor exercises a call option on a futures contract, the investor receives a long position in the futures contract. Options on futures contracts are calculated like options on stock, except the formula is slightly different.

16. Recall from Equation 22.1 the relationship between futures prices that can be expressed as $S_0 = F_0 e^{-(r-d)\cdot t}$ for index options. If this expression is substituted into the BSOPM, we get the above results.

CHAPTER AT A GLANCE

1. *The following are option boundary conditions:*
   Lower boundary of calls:

$$c_0 \geq \max\left[0,\ S_0 - \frac{X}{(1+r)^t}\right]$$

   Upper boundary of calls:

$$C_0 \leq S_0$$

   Lower boundary of puts:

$$p_0 \geq \max\left[0,\ \frac{X}{(1+r)^t} - S_0\right]$$

   Upper boundary of puts:

$$p_0 \leq \frac{X}{(1+r)^t}$$

   where c_0 is the call price at Time 0, p_0 is the put price at Time 0, S_0 is the stock price at Time 0, X is the strike price, r is the annual risk-free interest rate, and t is the time to maturity expressed in fractions of a year.

2. *Put-call parity:*

$$c_0 = S_0 - \frac{X}{(1+r)^t} + p_0$$

3. *The Black-Scholes option pricing model (BSOPM) follows:*

$$c = SN(d_1) - Xe^{-r_c t}N(d_2) \qquad \text{(Calls)}$$
$$p = Xe^{-r_c t}N(-d_2) - SN(-d_1) \qquad \text{(Puts)}$$

   where

$$d_1 = \frac{\ln(S/X) + [r_c + (\sigma^2/2)]t}{\sigma\sqrt{t}}$$
$$d_2 = d_1 - \sigma\sqrt{t}$$

   $N(d)$ is the cumulative area of the standard normal distribution, which can be approximated using Exhibit 24B-1; σ is the continuously compounded, annualized standard deviation of stock returns; r_c is the continuously compounded, annual risk-free interest rate; S is the current stock price; X is the strike price; and t is the time to maturity as a fraction of a year.

4. *The futures options pricing model follows:*

$$c = e^{-rt}[F_0N(d_1) - XN(d_2)] \qquad \text{(Calls)}$$
$$p = e^{-rt}[XN(-d_2) - F_0N(-d_1)] \qquad \text{(Puts)}$$

where

$$d_1 = \frac{\ln[F_0/X + (\sigma^2/2)]t}{\sigma\sqrt{t}}$$

$$d_2 = d_1 - \sigma\sqrt{t}$$

KEY TERMS

Frictionless market   895   Put-call parity (PCP)   893   Standard normal
Portfolio insurance   904   distribution   896

REVIEW

24.1 Prove that $c_0 \leq S_0$ is the call price's upper boundary, using an arbitrage table.

24.2 Prove that $p_0 \geq \max[0, X/(1 + r)^t - S_0]$ is the put price's lower boundary, using an arbitrage table.

24.3 Prove that $p_0 \leq X/(1 + r)^t$, the put price's upper boundary, using an arbitrage table.

24.4 Is the value of $N(d_1)$ always greater than the value of $N(d_2)$? Explain.

PRACTICE

24.1 Suppose you work for an express mail service that will purchase 10,000,000 gallons of gasoline in three months. Assume that a gallon of gas costs $1.00 wholesale, and you wish to guarantee a maximum price of $1.10. Also, you feel that gasoline price volatility is about 25%, and the six-month interest rate is 7% (annualized). Assuming that the BSOPM is valid, how much would it cost to hedge 10,000,000 gallons of gas with options? What is the appropriate option strategy? (Assume that a gas option contract exists on an exchange.)

24.2 What is the price of a call option if $S_0 = \$25$, $X = \$20$, $r = 10\%$, $t = \frac{1}{2}$, and the put option value is $p = \$1.50$? (Make whatever assumptions are necessary.)

24.3 Suppose the interest rate decreases from 5% to 1%. How should this affect the lower boundary of a

call option when $S_0 = \$100$, $X = \$80$, and $t = \frac{1}{2}$. How will this affect the lower boundary for a put option?

24.4 Based on the following information from *Barron's*, verify that the closing prices of Coke's put and call options satisfy the boundary conditions. The time to maturity is five months ($t = \frac{5}{12}$), Coke's stock price is $41\frac{7}{8}$, and the annual risk-free interest rate is 3%.

Expiration Date and Strike Price	Closing Price
Coke May 40 call	$3\frac{3}{4}$
Coke May 40 put	$1\frac{1}{2}$
Coke May 45 call	$1\frac{3}{8}$
Coke May 45 put	$4\frac{1}{4}$

24.5 Suppose there are puts and calls on IBM stock with the same strike price and the same maturity.

You observe that $c_0 = p_0$, and the interest rate for the period remaining until expiration is 5%. Is the call option in the money, at the money, or out of the money? Is the put option in the money or out of the money? Explain.

24.6 Suppose $\sigma = 35\%$, $S_0 = \$100$, $X = \$100$, $r_c = 5\%$, and $t = \frac{1}{2}$. Calculate the Black-Scholes call and put option prices.

24.7 Suppose the standard deviation is $\sigma = 35\%$, $S_0 = \$58$, $X = \$55$, $r_c = 4\%$, and $t = \frac{1}{2}$. Calculate the Black-Scholes call and put option prices.

24.8 Suppose the standard deviation is $\sigma = 30\%$, $S_0 = \$100$, $X = \$100$, $r_c = 5\%$, and $t = \frac{1}{2}$. Calculate the Black-Scholes call and put option prices.

24.9 Use the data in Question 24.8, but suppose the standard deviation is increased by 1% to $\sigma = 30.3\%$. What are the Black-Scholes call and put option prices? Compare your result with that of Question 24.8.

24.10 Use the data in Question 24.8, but suppose the stock price is increased by 1% to $101. What are the Black-Scholes call and put option prices? Compare your result with that of Question 24.8.

24.11 Use the data in Question 24.8, but suppose the strike price is increased by 1%, to $101. What are the Black-Scholes call and put option prices? Compare your result with that of Question 24.8.

24.12 Use the data in Question 24.8, but suppose the time to maturity is increased by 1%, to 0.505

of a year. What are the Black-Scholes call and put option prices? Compare your result with that of Question 24.8.

24.13 Use the data in Question 24.8, but suppose the risk-free interest rate is increased by 1%, to 5.05%. What are the Black-Scholes call and put option prices? Compare your result with that of Question 24.8.

24.14 Suppose you manage a portfolio of $100 million. You estimate that there is a probability of 20% that the portfolio value will go to $80 million next year and a probability of 80% that it will go to $120 million. If the value is less than $90 million, you will be fired. How can you protect yourself with put options?

24.15 Using the data given in Question 24.14 and the following information, calculate the cost of insuring this $100 million portfolio (assuming it mimics the S&P 500 index). The index is at 435, the strike price is 390, the time to maturity is ½ year, the standard deviation is 14%, and the current risk-free rate is 3.5%.

24.16 On January 26, 1998, *Barron's* reported the prices for the put and call options on the stock of Sears in the table at the bottom of the page. Assume that there are *exactly* three months to the expiration date of the options and that the annual risk-free interest rate is 5%. Assuming that the call price is the equilibrium price, what should be the put price according to put–call parity? How do you explain the difference from the reported put price?

Company Exch Close	Strike Price		Sales Vol	Open Int	Opt Exch	Week's		Last Price	Net Chg
						High	Low		
$46\frac{5}{16}$	Apr 45	p	1243	1755	CB	3	$2\frac{3}{8}$	$2\frac{1}{2}$	$-\frac{1}{4}$
$46\frac{5}{16}$	Apr 45		1146	1974	CB	4	$2\frac{3}{8}$	$3\frac{1}{4}$	$+\frac{1}{4}$

Source: *Barron's*, January 26, 1998, p. MW14. Reprinted by permission of *Barron's*, © 1998 Dow Jones & Co., Inc. All Rights Reserved Worldwide.

24.17 The following quotations are for options on IBM stock:

Option/Strike		Exp.	–Call– Vol.	Last	–Put– Vol.	Last
IBM	80	Jan	225	19 7/8	24	1/16
100	80	Feb	...	...	301	3/4
100	80	Apr	76	22 5/8	257	1 3/8
100	85	Jan	454	15 1/4	263	1/8
100	90	Jan	133	9 7/8	1045	1/4
100	90	Feb	75	12 7/8	289	2
100	95	Jan	630	5 3/4	3513	5/8
100	95	Feb	75	8 3/4	862	3 3/8
100	95	Apr	114	10 3/4	734	4 7/8
100	95	Jul	41	13 3/8	700	6 5/8
100	100	Jan	4482	2 3/16	5829	2 1/8
100	100	Feb	1190	5 5/8	822	5 1/2
100	100	Apr	341	8	217	6 3/4
100	105	Jan	4643	1/2	1541	5 1/2
100	105	Feb	1027	3 3/8	169	8
100	105	Apr	419	5 7/8	71	9 7/8
100	110	Jan	735	1/16	255	10
100	110	Feb	1007	1 15/16	113	12
100	110	Apr	533	3 7/8	103	12 5/8
100	115	Apr	269	2 3/4	...	...

Source: *Wall Street Journal,* January 13, 1998, p. c18. Reprinted by permission of *The Wall Street Journal,* © 1998 Dow Jones & Co., Inc. All Rights Reserved Worldwide.

a. The annual risk-free interest rate is 5%. Use the six call options for April ($t = 3\frac{1}{2}$ months) to calculate the implied standard deviation of the IBM stock. Analyze the results. (Hint: Assume that the call option quotations conform with the Black-Scholes formula, and use a computer program to solve for the implied σ).
b. For April 1998 with a 100 strike price, calculate the Black-Scholes call option price on the assumption that $\sigma = 30\%$ and the annual risk-free interest rate is 5%. Compare this price with the market quotations.

24.18 *Developing an investment strategy using options is like piloting a ship. The captain can point his vessel in what he believes is the right direction, but without the proper navigational aids, he'll probably spend more time and energy reaching his destination than he should. Purchasing and writing options contracts also requires navigation tools. Formulas and computer programs are as valuable to an investor as a map and compass [are] to the sea captain . . .*

A byproduct benefit of Black-Scholes is that in calculating the theoretical value, another value is generated, known as the delta or hedge ratio—the percentage relationship between the price movements of the underlying security and the option. Using this, it's easy to determine a change in the theoretical value from a move in the stock price.

For example, a call with a delta of 0.60 will gain or lose 60 cents in theoretical value on a one-point move in the underlying stock. The delta for a put contract is normally a negative number, denoting the inverse relationship between the stock price and the option. The absolute values of the delta of a put contract and the delta of the corresponding call contract will add up to 1. A long call and a short put will result in a total one-point gain or loss if the underlying security rises or falls by one point. The value of the hedge ratio and the theoretical value change as one or more of the variables, including days-till-expiration, change.

Source: Scott H. Fullman, "Using Black-Scholes: It's Not Just for Pros and Nobel Laureates," *Barron's,* January 5, 1998, p. MW15. Reprinted by permission of *Barron's,* © 1998 Dow Jones & Co., Inc. All Rights Reserved Worldwide.

$N(d_1)$, which appears in the Black-Scholes formula (see Section 24.2), is the hedge ratio or delta referred to in the article. Use a computer software program to answer the following questions:
a. Suppose that for both a put and a call option, we have the following parameters: $S = \$100$, $X = \$100$, $\sigma = 30\%$, $r = 7\%$, and $t = \frac{1}{2}$. Calculate the put and call values of options on the stock.
b. Suppose that the stock price (S) changes to \$101. Calculate the new price of the call and the put. What is "delta" for each of these two options? Does the sum of the absolute values add up to 1, as the article claims?
c. Repeat the calculations in Part b for a change in the stock price to \$99.
d. Repeat Parts a, b, and c when $t = 0$ (that is, we are at the expiration date), and the change in price occurs just at the expiration date.

For Internet questions visit the Levy Investment Web site at http://levy-invst.swcollege.com.

YOUR TURN: APPLYING THEORY TO PRACTICE
OPTION VALUATION: DOES IT WORK IN PRACTICE?

The following table lists call and put option prices on the British FTSE 100 Stock Index (Financial Times Stock Exchange 100 Stock In-dex—a weighted index of 100 stocks traded in the London Stock Exchange):

FTSE 100 Share Index

Strike Price	Call—Settle				Put—Settle			
	Mar	Apr	May	Jun	Mar	Apr	May	Jun
2400	—	—	—	838	—	—	—	3.5
2500	—	—	—	739	—	—	—	4.5
2600	—	—	—	642	—	—	—	5.5
2700	539	—	—	546	0.5	—	—	8.5
2750	489	—	—	—	0.5	—	—	—
2800	439	436	442	452	0.5	4	6.5	13
2850	389	386	395	—	0.5	5	8.5	—
2900	339	336	350	361	0.5	6	13	21
2950	289	288	305	—	0.5	7	18	—
3000	239	242	265	277	1	11	28	37
3050	189	197	222	238	1	15	35	49
3100	140	156	184	202	2	24	47	62
3150	91	119	147	167	3	37	60	76
3200	45	85	118	138	10	54	80	97
3250	15	58	89	109	33	76	101	118
3300	3.5	37	68	88	73	106	130	147
3350	1	23	48	68	121	143	161	176
3400	0.5	13	34	53	171	83	197	211

Source: "Option Valuation: Does It Work?" *Wall Street Journal Europe*, March 15, 1994. Reprinted by permission of *The Wall Street Journal*, © 1994 Dow Jones & Co, Inc. All Rights Reserved Worldwide.

Each point in this table represents £25. However, for simplicity, we assume that each point represents £1, which does not alter the results. The short-term annual risk-free interest rate on British pounds is 5.50%. The FTSE 100 Stock Index on March 15, 1994, was 3233.4. The standard deviation of the annual rate of return, calculated on a continuous basis (see Appendix 24C), is 25%. Use the data from the table to answer the following questions.

Questions

1. Analyze the prices of options given in the table. In particular, discuss the economic explanation of the fact that most call option prices decrease as the strike price increases, and most put option prices increase as the strike price increases. Are there any other trends in the table?

2. Note that the March put option price is 1 for strike prices of both 3000 and 3050. The follow-

(continued)

ing arbitrage transaction is suggested: Sell the put option with a 3000 strike price, and buy the put option with a 3050 strike price. Then, with zero net investment, you will have made a sure profit. Analyze this suggestion for the following future (namely, March) index values: 2500, 3000, 3010, 3020, 3030, 3040, 3050, 3500, and 4000. Is there a reason why investors might not adopt this strategy?

The following questions relate to the same options. Assume that 3¼ months are left to expiration.

3. For a strike price of 3000, does the June call option conform with the upper boundary price? The lower boundary price? Repeat this question for the June put option.

4. Assume that put–call parity holds. Estimate the risk-free interest rate based on the June options. Estimate the risk-free interest rate for strike prices of 2800, 3000, and 3400. Compare and discuss your results.

5. Calculate the Black-Scholes call and put values for the June options for the following strike prices: 2800, 3000, and 3400. Compare your results with the put and call prices reported in the table. Analyze your results.

6. This table is typed exactly as it appeared in the *Wall Street Journal Europe*. However, it seems that there is a typographical error. Can you find it? Why, in your view, is it a typographical error? Suppose you have no further information, and you would like to correct this "error" without looking at other sources. How would you do it?

SELECTED REFERENCES AND SUPPLEMENTAL REFERENCES

See Chapter 23.

Appendix 24A Binomial Option Pricing Model

Option boundaries are useful in explaining option prices, but sometimes they are too wide, and a more precise method of valuing an option is needed. The binomial option pricing model (BOPM) is an elegant and relatively simple way to price options. It is called *binomial* because as with the binomial distribution in statistics, it is assumed that only two future stock prices (outcomes) are possible.

Like any pricing model, the BOPM is based on several assumptions:

1. The market is frictionless.
2. Investors are price takers.
3. Short selling is allowed, with full use of the proceeds.
4. Borrowing and lending at the risk-free rate is permitted.
5. Future stock prices will have one of two possible values.

The BOPM for call (or put) options is developed in six steps.

STEP 1: DETERMINE STOCK PRICE DISTRIBUTION

Assume that the price of a stock can change from its current level of S_0 to only one of two possible future values, S_u or S_d, where u implies that the stock went up, and d implies that the stock went down. To express the future value of the stock in terms of its current value, we set $S_u = u \cdot S_0$ and $S_d = d \cdot S_0$, where u and d are constants. We assume that $d < 1 + r < u$.[17] Graphically, we have

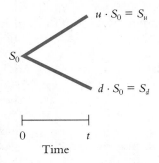

For example, assume that we have the following information: $S_0 = \$100.0$, $X = \$100.0$, $u = 1.10$, $d = 0.95$, and $r = 0.05$. With these data,

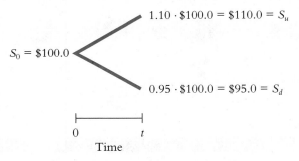

At expiration, the stock price will be either $110 or $95. However, as we shall see later in this discussion, we can determine the equilibrium value of an option in this case without knowing the probabilities that S_u or S_d will occur. Thus, unlike the derivation of boundaries, where the stock price can have any value (S_t), at the expiration date in this case we must assume only two possible outcomes, S_u and S_d. Once again, there is no free lunch. If we want to get a more precise value for the option, we must introduce more assumptions.

STEP 2: DETERMINE PRICE DISTRIBUTION

Given Step 1, we can now calculate the value of the call option *at expiration*. Specifically, the value of an option at expiration is just the dollar amount it is in the

---

17. If $d > 1 + r$, then the stock will always yield more than the risk-free rate. In this case, everyone would borrow at r and invest in stock, yielding an arbitrage profit. If $u < 1 + r$, then the stock will always yield less than the risk-free rate. In this case, everyone would short sell the stock and lend at r, yielding an arbitrage profit.

money. (See Equation 24.2 and the related discussion.) That is, we can describe the call price distribution as follows:

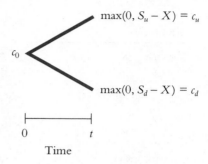

$$\max(0, S_u - X) = c_u$$

c_0

$$\max(0, S_d - X) = c_d$$

0   t

Time

The data from our example yield the following:

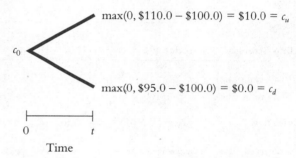

$$\max(0, \$110.0 - \$100.0) = \$10.0 = c_u$$

c_0

$$\max(0, \$95.0 - \$100.0) = \$0.0 = c_d$$

0   t

Time

STEP 3: CREATE A HEDGED PORTFOLIO

In this step, we construct a portfolio of a call option and a stock. However, we cannot yet determine the proportions of these two assets in the portfolio. In Step 4, we tailor this portfolio to provide a future cash flow that is known with certainty—hence, the term *hedged portfolio.* Recall that the objective is to determine the call option price. This objective can be met by constructing a hedged portfolio. Consider the following strategy and the resultant cash flows depicted in Exhibit 24A-1.

A hedged portfolio is constructed by first selling (that is, writing) one call option. This action results in a positive cash flow today of the option price ($+c_0$), but it requires paying out the option value (if any) at expiration ($-c_u$ or $-c_d$); see Exhibit 24A-1). Next, an unspecified number of shares (h_c) of stock are purchased. (The amount h_c will be specified in Step 4.) The proceeds from the sale of the shares will be either $h_c \cdot S_u$ or $h_c \cdot S_d$. The net cash flows are then found by adding together the component cash flows within this trading strategy.

STEP 4: SOLVE FOR h_c

h_c is the number of shares we must buy for each *one* call option we write (or sell). At the start of Step 4, we have net cash flows today (0) and at expiration (t) that depend

EXHIBIT 24A-1   Hedged Portfolio for a One-Period Binomial Model to Price a Call Option

Part a: A Cash Flow Table

Trading Strategy	Cash Flows		
	Today (0)	At Expiration	
		$S_t = S_u = \$110$	$S_t = S_d = \$95$
Write one call option	$+c_0$	$-c_u$	$-c_d$
Buy h_c share of stock	$-h_c \cdot S_0$	$+h_c \cdot S_u$	$+h_c \cdot S_d$
Net cash flow	$+c_0 - h_c \cdot S_0 = ?$	$-c_u + h_c \cdot S_u$	$-c_d + h_c \cdot S_d$

Part b: An Example in Which $S_0 = \$100$, $X = \$100$, $u = 1.10$, $d = 0.95$, $r = 5\%$, and $h_c = \frac{2}{3}$

Trading Strategy	Cash Flows		
	Today (0)	At Expiration	
		$S_t = S_u = \$110$	$S_t = S_d = \$95$
Write one call option	$+c_0$	$-\$10$	$\$0$
Buy $\frac{2}{3}$ share of stock	$-(\frac{2}{3})\$100$	$+(\frac{2}{3})\$110$	$+(\frac{2}{3})\$95$
Net cash flow	$+c_0 - (\frac{2}{3})\$100 = +c_0 - \$66.67$	$-\$10 + (\frac{2}{3})\$110 = \$63.33$	$-\$0 + (\frac{2}{3})\$95 = \$63.33$

c_0 = the current call price, S_0 = the current stock price, S_t = the stock price at expiration, S_u = the stock price at expiration when it goes up, S_d = the stock

on two unknown variables—the call price at 0 (c_0) and h_c, called the *hedge ratio*. It is a ratio because we are finding the number of shares of stock to buy for each call option we write in order to eliminate future risks. That is, we find the ratio of calls written to stocks purchased, which makes our future cash flows certain. We take the net cash flows of the hedged portfolio when S_u occurs and set that net cash flow equal to the net cash flows when S_d occurs:

$$-c_u + h_c \cdot S_u = -c_d + h_c \cdot S_d$$

In such a case, the portfolio's cash flow is certain, whether the stock's price rises or falls. Because all values are known apart from h_c, we can solve for h_c:

$$h_c \cdot S_u - h_c \cdot S_d = c_u - c_d$$
$$h_c(S_u - S_d) = c_u - c_d$$
$$h_c^* = (c_u - c_d)/(S_u - S_d)$$

where h_c^* represents the selected hedge ratio. Substituting uS_0 for S_u and dS_0 for S_d, we have

$$h_c^* = \frac{c_u - c_d}{S_0(u - d)} \qquad (24A.1)$$

Hence, the hedge ratio can be computed using data known at Time 0. Using the data in the example, we have

$$h_c^* = [\$10 - \$0.0]/[\$100(1.1 - 0.95)] = {}^{10}\!/_{15} = {}^2\!/_3$$

Therefore, to create a hedged portfolio, we sell 1 call option for each $2/3$ shares of stock we buy. Alternatively, we sell 3 calls for each 2 shares we buy. Actually, we would buy 3 call option contracts for every 200 shares of stock purchased.

The hedge ratio is a very useful concept in option trading. It represents the number of calls to sell for each stock to buy in order to have a risk-free portfolio. Indeed, in Exhibit 24A-1b, with a hedge ratio of $2/3$, we create a portfolio whose future cash flow is constant ($63.33 in this specific example).

The hedge ratio can also be used to determine how many stocks to buy in conjunction with zero-coupon bonds in order to synthetically create an option contract. That is, with a call option and stocks, we can create a risk-free bond. Hence, with stocks and a risk-free bond, we can create the payoffs of an option contract.

PRACTICE BOX

We have seen that with $h_c^* = {}^2\!/_3$, a riskless portfolio is created. This Practice Box demonstrates that when $h = {}^1\!/_2$ (that is, a value different from $2/3$), a risky portfolio is obtained.

Problem

Demonstrate that with $h = {}^1\!/_2$, a risky portfolio is obtained.

Solution

A hedge ratio of $1/2$ implies that for every call that is written, $1/2$ share of stock needs to be purchased. We can construct the following table of outcomes:

Cash Flows

Trading Strategy	Today (0)	At Expiration $S_t = S_u = \$110$	$S_t = S_d = \$95$
Write one call option	$+c_0$	$-\$10$	$\$0$
Buy $1/2$ share of stock	$-(1/2)S_0$	$+(1/2)\$110 = \$55$	$+(1/2)\$95 = \$47.50$
Net cash flow	$+c_0 - (1/2)S_0 = ?$	$\$45$	$\$47.50$

We see that with this portfolio, the future outcomes are uncertain (either $45 or $47.50); hence, this portfolio is risky. Only the hedge ratio of $h_c^* = {}^2\!/_3$ creates a certain future cash flow.

STEP 5: SOLVE FOR THE CALL PRICE USING NPV

We now have a standard net present value (NPV) problem. If we select h_c^* as the number of shares of stock to buy, then the future cash flows are certain. With the future cash flows known with certainty, the appropriate discount rate is the risk-free interest rate (r).

The standard one-period NPV problem is written as follows:

$$NPV = \left[\frac{CF_1}{1+r}\right] - I \qquad (24A.2)$$

where CF_1 is the cash flow at time period 1, r is the discount rate, and I is the required investment. In equilibrium, the NPV must be zero. If NPV > 0, all investors will buy such a portfolio, driving its price up. If NPV < 0, all investors will sell such a portfolio short, driving its price down. In reality, prices rarely deviate dramatically from NPV $= 0$.

In our example (see Exhibit 24A-1), the cash flow at the expiration date is

$$-c_u + (h_c^* \cdot S_u) = -c_d + (h_c^* \cdot S_d) = -\$0 + (\tfrac{2}{3})\$95 = \$63.33$$

and

$$I = c_0 - (h_c^* \cdot S_0) = c_0 - (\tfrac{2}{3})\$100 = c_0 - \$66.67$$

Substituting these results into Equation 24A.2 yields the following:

$$\$63.33/(1 + 0.05) = c_0 - \$66.67$$

Solving for c_0, we have

$$c_0 = \$66.67 - (\$63.33/1.05) \cong \$6.36$$

The general expression for the binomial option pricing model for call options is

$$c_0 = h_c^* S_0 + \frac{c_d - h_c^* S_d}{1+r} \qquad (24A.3)$$

In equilibrium, the call option is worth $6.36. If the call price is any other value, an opportunity to generate infinite profit at no risk will exist. (Demonstrate how you could generate unlimited profits if the call is worth $6 or $7.) Hence, in the simplified world depicted in this example, the equilibrium call price will be $6.36.

It is important to point out that we made no reference to the probabilities associated with the stock price moving up or down. Hence, we can correctly infer that for a given stock price today (S_0), option prices are independent of the future expected stock price. This puzzling result can be explained as follows: although the probabilities do not directly affect c_0, they do affect it indirectly. For example, if we increase the probability of S_u, we increase S_0, and an increase in S_0 will increase the value of c_0.

STEP 6. EXTEND THE RESULTS TO MORE THAN ONE PERIOD

If you break the period from 0 to t into an almost infinite number of subperiods and allow the stock price to move up or down by a small amount within each subperiod, then the resultant option pricing model is the famous Black–Scholes option pricing model covered in Chapter 24.[18]

Exhibit 24A-2 demonstrates how we can create a portfolio of put options and the underlying stocks whose cash flow in the future is certain. We first determine that the hedge ratio is $\frac{1}{3}$ (by equating the future cash flow) and then solve for p_0. Hence, exactly as with Exhibit 24A-1, we can determine the put option value.

The hedge ratio is

$$h_p^* = \frac{p_d - p_u}{S_u - S_d}$$

EXHIBIT 24A-2   Hedged Portfolio for a One-Period Binomial Model to Price a Put Option

Part a: A Cash Flow Table

	Cash Flows		
		At Expiration	
Trading Strategy	**Today (0)**	$S_t = S_u = \$110$	$S_t = S_d = \$95$
Buy one put option	$-p_0$	$+p_u$	$+p_d$
Buy h_p share of stock	$-h_p \cdot S_0$	$+h_p \cdot S_u$	$+h_p \cdot S_d$
Net cash flow	$-p_0 - h_p \cdot S_0 = ?$	$+p_u + h_p \cdot S_u$	$+p_d + h_p \cdot S_d$

Part b: An Example Where $S_0 = \$100$, $X = \$100$, $u = 1.10$, $d = 0.95$, $r = 5\%$, and $h_p = \frac{1}{3}$

	Cash Flows		
		At Expiration	
Trading Strategy	**Today (0)**	$S_t = S_u = \$110$	$S_t = S_d = \$95$
Buy one put option	$+p_0$	$-\$0$	$+\$5$
Buy h_p share of stock	$-(\frac{1}{3})\$100$	$+(\frac{1}{3})\$110$	$+(\frac{1}{3})\$95$
Net cash flow	$+p_0 - (\frac{1}{3})\$100 = +p_0 - \$33.33$	$+\$0 + (\frac{1}{3})\$110 = \$36.67$	$+\$5 + (\frac{1}{3})\$95 = \$36.67$

p_0 = the current put price, S_0 = the current stock price, S_t = the stock price at expiration, S_u = the stock price at expiration when it goes up, S_d = the stock price at expiration when it goes down, X = the strike price, and r = the risk-free interest rate.

18. For more details on the binomial option pricing model, see John C. Cox and Mark Rubinstein, *Options Markets* (Englewood Cliffs, N.J.: Prentice-Hall, 1985), Chap. 5.

In our example,

$$h_p^* = \frac{5 - 0}{110 - 95} = \frac{1}{3}$$

In summary, a six-step process is used to determine option prices. First, the stock prices are assumed to move to only one of two future values. Second, the option prices at maturity are determined from the future stock prices. Third, a portfolio of the stock and the option is constructed. Fourth, a specific number of stocks are traded, called the *hedge ratio,* such that the future payoff is certain. Fifth, the option price is determined using a standard NPV approach. Finally, the model is extended to multiple future stock prices. Note that no assumption was made in relation to the stock's expected return or regarding the probabilities that the stock price will get one of the two future values. Thus, for a given stock price, the expected return on the stock does not directly influence the option price. The effect is only through the observed current stock price (S_0).

PRACTICE

24A.1 Suppose there are only two possible states: in State 1, the stock price rises by 50%; in State 2, the stock price drops by 25%. The current stock price is $S_0 = \$50$, the exercise price is $X = \$55$, and the risk-free interest rate for the period is $r = 5\%$.
a. Calculate the put and call hedge ratios.
b. Use the binomial option pricing model to value the put and call options.

24A.2 Using the data in Question 24A.1, how would your answers change if the following information were added?
a. The probability of an upward move is 75%.
b. The probability of an upward move is 100%.

24A.3 A stock price can go up by 20% with a probability of 60% or go down by 10% with a probabil-

ity of 40%. The call price is $\dot{c}_0 = \$10$. If we reversed these probabilities, the option price would not change. Do you agree?

24A.4 Using the information in Question 24A.3, how would your answer change if you were given the information that the stock price will not change with the change in probabilities?

24A.5 Suppose the stock price is $S_0 = \$100$ and the strike price is $X = \$80$. The stock price can go up by 20% or down by 10%. What is the hedge ratio (h_c^*) for a call option? What is the hedge ratio (h_p^*) for a put option?

Appendix 24B An Example Using the Black-Scholes Option Pricing Model

Using a table of normal distributions (rather than computer software) to calculate the call option value, let us use the same parameters employed in the chapter (Section 24.2.1): $S = \$100$, $X = \$100$, $\sigma = 30\%$, $r_c = 7\%$, and $t = 182$ days, which is about $\frac{1}{2}$ year.

We calculate the call price following these three steps:

STEP 1: CALCULATE d_1 AND d_2

Given the parameters just listed and Equation 24.10, we have

$$d_1 = \frac{\ln\left(\frac{100.0}{100.0}\right) + \left[0.07 + \left(\frac{0.3^2}{2}\right)\right]\left(\frac{1}{2}\right)}{(0.3)\sqrt{\frac{1}{2}}}$$

$$= \frac{0.0 + 0.0575}{0.3 \cdot 0.70711}$$

$$= 0.2711$$

Also, from Equation 24.11 we have

$$d_2 = 0.2711 - \left(0.3 \cdot \sqrt{\tfrac{1}{2}}\right)$$

$$= 0.2711 - (0.3 \cdot 0.70711)$$

$$= 0.0590$$

Now that we have d_1 and d_2, we are ready to compute $N(d_1)$ and $N(d_2)$.

STEP 2: INTERPOLATE FOR $N(d_1)$ AND $N(d_2)$

Unfortunately, option prices are very sensitive to estimates of $N(d_1)$ and $N(d_2)$. Therefore, it is important to achieve a high level of accuracy. Exhibit 24B-1 presents values of $N(d)$ for given values of d accurate to four decimals. Our values for d_1 and d_2 are not precisely given in this exhibit. Hence, we need to interpolate between the two nearest values for $N(d)$ in the exhibit:

$d_{1H} = 0.275$　　　$N(d_{1H}) = 0.6083$　　　　$d_{2H} = 0.06$　　　$N(d_{2H}) = 0.5239$
　　From Exhibit 24B-1　　　　　　　　　　　From Exhibit 24B-1

$d_1 = 0.2711$　　　$N(d_{1H}) = ?$　　　　　$d_2 = 0.0590$　　　$N(d_2) = ?$
　　Our estimate　　　　　　　　　　　　　　Our estimate

$d_{1L} = 0.27$　　　$N(d_{1L}) = 0.6064$　　　　$d_{2L} = 0.055$　　　$N(d_{2L}) = 0.5219$
　　From Exhibit 24B-1　　　　　　　　　　　From Exhibit 24B-1

d_{1H}, d_{1L}, d_{2H}, and d_{2L} are the values from Exhibit 24B-1 immediately above and below d_1 and d_2. H represents the value on the high side, and L represents the value on the low side.

The interpolation formula is

$$N(d) = N(d_L) + (d - d_L)\left[\frac{N(d_H) - N(d_L)}{d_H - d_L}\right]$$

Note that we simply add to the lower value $N(d_L)$ some portion of $N(d_H) - N(d_L)$ that becomes larger as $d - d_L$ increases. For example, if $d = d_H$, we get exactly

EXHIBIT 24B-1   Values for N(d) Given d

Second Decimal of d

d	0.0000	0.0050	0.0100	0.0150	0.0200	0.0250	0.0300	0.0350	0.0400	0.0450	0.0500	0.0550	0.0600	0.0650	0.0700	0.0750	0.0800	0.0850	0.0900	0.0950
-2.9000	0.0019	0.0019	0.0018	0.0018	0.0018	0.0017	0.0017	0.0017	0.0016	0.0016	0.0016	0.0016	0.0015	0.0015	0.0015	0.0015	0.0014	0.0014	0.0014	0.0014
-2.8000	0.0026	0.0025	0.0025	0.0024	0.0024	0.0024	0.0023	0.0023	0.0023	0.0022	0.0022	0.0022	0.0021	0.0021	0.0021	0.0020	0.0020	0.0020	0.0019	0.0019
-2.7000	0.0035	0.0034	0.0034	0.0033	0.0033	0.0032	0.0032	0.0031	0.0031	0.0030	0.0030	0.0029	0.0029	0.0028	0.0028	0.0028	0.0027	0.0027	0.0026	0.0026
-2.6000	0.0047	0.0046	0.0045	0.0045	0.0044	0.0043	0.0043	0.0042	0.0041	0.0041	0.0040	0.0040	0.0039	0.0038	0.0038	0.0037	0.0037	0.0036	0.0036	0.0035
-2.5000	0.0062	0.0061	0.0060	0.0060	0.0059	0.0058	0.0057	0.0056	0.0055	0.0055	0.0054	0.0053	0.0052	0.0052	0.0051	0.0050	0.0049	0.0049	0.0048	0.0047
-2.4000	0.0082	0.0081	0.0080	0.0079	0.0078	0.0077	0.0075	0.0074	0.0073	0.0072	0.0071	0.0070	0.0069	0.0069	0.0068	0.0067	0.0066	0.0065	0.0064	0.0063
-2.3000	0.0107	0.0106	0.0104	0.0103	0.0102	0.0100	0.0099	0.0098	0.0096	0.0095	0.0094	0.0093	0.0091	0.0090	0.0089	0.0088	0.0087	0.0085	0.0084	0.0083
-2.2000	0.0139	0.0137	0.0136	0.0134	0.0132	0.0130	0.0129	0.0127	0.0125	0.0124	0.0122	0.0121	0.0119	0.0118	0.0116	0.0115	0.0113	0.0112	0.0110	0.0109
-2.1000	0.0179	0.0176	0.0174	0.0172	0.0170	0.0168	0.0166	0.0164	0.0162	0.0160	0.0158	0.0156	0.0154	0.0152	0.0150	0.0148	0.0146	0.0144	0.0143	0.0141
-2.0000	0.0228	0.0225	0.0222	0.0220	0.0217	0.0214	0.0212	0.0209	0.0207	0.0204	0.0202	0.0199	0.0197	0.0195	0.0192	0.0190	0.0188	0.0185	0.0183	0.0181
-1.9000	0.0287	0.0284	0.0281	0.0277	0.0274	0.0271	0.0268	0.0265	0.0262	0.0259	0.0256	0.0253	0.0250	0.0247	0.0244	0.0241	0.0239	0.0236	0.0233	0.0230
-1.8000	0.0359	0.0355	0.0351	0.0348	0.0344	0.0340	0.0336	0.0333	0.0329	0.0325	0.0322	0.0318	0.0314	0.0311	0.0307	0.0304	0.0301	0.0297	0.0294	0.0290
-1.7000	0.0446	0.0441	0.0436	0.0432	0.0427	0.0423	0.0418	0.0414	0.0409	0.0405	0.0401	0.0396	0.0392	0.0388	0.0384	0.0379	0.0375	0.0371	0.0367	0.0363
-1.6000	0.0548	0.0542	0.0537	0.0532	0.0526	0.0521	0.0516	0.0510	0.0505	0.0500	0.0495	0.0490	0.0485	0.0480	0.0475	0.0470	0.0465	0.0460	0.0455	0.0450
-1.5000	0.0668	0.0662	0.0655	0.0649	0.0643	0.0636	0.0630	0.0624	0.0618	0.0612	0.0606	0.0600	0.0594	0.0588	0.0582	0.0576	0.0571	0.0565	0.0559	0.0554
-1.4000	0.0808	0.0800	0.0793	0.0785	0.0778	0.0771	0.0764	0.0756	0.0749	0.0742	0.0735	0.0728	0.0721	0.0715	0.0708	0.0701	0.0694	0.0688	0.0681	0.0675
-1.3000	0.0968	0.0959	0.0951	0.0943	0.0934	0.0926	0.0918	0.0909	0.0901	0.0893	0.0885	0.0877	0.0869	0.0861	0.0853	0.0846	0.0838	0.0830	0.0823	0.0815
-1.2000	0.1151	0.1141	0.1131	0.1122	0.1112	0.1103	0.1093	0.1084	0.1075	0.1066	0.1056	0.1047	0.1038	0.1029	0.1020	0.1012	0.1003	0.0994	0.0985	0.0977
-1.1000	0.1357	0.1346	0.1335	0.1324	0.1314	0.1303	0.1292	0.1282	0.1271	0.1261	0.1251	0.1240	0.1230	0.1220	0.1210	0.1200	0.1190	0.1180	0.1170	0.1160
-1.0000	0.1587	0.1574	0.1562	0.1551	0.1539	0.1527	0.1515	0.1503	0.1492	0.1480	0.1469	0.1457	0.1446	0.1434	0.1423	0.1412	0.1401	0.1390	0.1379	0.1368
-0.9000	0.1841	0.1827	0.1814	0.1801	0.1788	0.1775	0.1762	0.1749	0.1736	0.1723	0.1711	0.1698	0.1685	0.1673	0.1660	0.1648	0.1635	0.1623	0.1611	0.1599
-0.8000	0.2119	0.2104	0.2090	0.2075	0.2061	0.2047	0.2033	0.2019	0.2005	0.1991	0.1977	0.1963	0.1949	0.1935	0.1921	0.1908	0.1894	0.1881	0.1867	0.1854
-0.7000	0.2420	0.2404	0.2389	0.2373	0.2358	0.2342	0.2327	0.2312	0.2296	0.2281	0.2266	0.2251	0.2236	0.2221	0.2206	0.2192	0.2177	0.2162	0.2148	0.2133
-0.6000	0.2743	0.2726	0.2709	0.2693	0.2676	0.2660	0.2643	0.2627	0.2611	0.2595	0.2578	0.2562	0.2546	0.2530	0.2514	0.2498	0.2483	0.2467	0.2451	0.2435
-0.5000	0.3085	0.3068	0.3050	0.3033	0.3015	0.2998	0.2981	0.2963	0.2946	0.2929	0.2912	0.2894	0.2877	0.2860	0.2843	0.2826	0.2810	0.2793	0.2776	0.2759
-0.4000	0.3446	0.3427	0.3409	0.3391	0.3372	0.3354	0.3336	0.3318	0.3300	0.3282	0.3264	0.3246	0.3228	0.3210	0.3192	0.3174	0.3156	0.3138	0.3121	0.3103
-0.3000	0.3821	0.3802	0.3783	0.3764	0.3745	0.3726	0.3707	0.3688	0.3669	0.3650	0.3632	0.3613	0.3594	0.3576	0.3557	0.3538	0.3520	0.3501	0.3483	0.3464
-0.2000	0.4207	0.4188	0.4168	0.4149	0.4129	0.4110	0.4090	0.4071	0.4052	0.4032	0.4013	0.3994	0.3974	0.3955	0.3936	0.3917	0.3897	0.3878	0.3859	0.3840
-0.1000	0.4602	0.4582	0.4562	0.4542	0.4522	0.4503	0.4483	0.4463	0.4443	0.4424	0.4404	0.4384	0.4364	0.4345	0.4325	0.4305	0.4286	0.4266	0.4247	0.4227

(continued)

EXHIBIT 24B-1   *(continued)*

0.0000	0.5000	0.5020	0.5040	0.5060	0.5080	0.5100	0.5120	0.5140	0.5160	0.5179	0.5199	0.5219	0.5239	0.5259	0.5279	0.5299	0.5319	0.5339	0.5359	0.5378
0.1000	0.5398	0.5418	0.5438	0.5458	0.5478	0.5497	0.5517	0.5537	0.5557	0.5576	0.5596	0.5616	0.5636	0.5655	0.5675	0.5695	0.5714	0.5734	0.5753	0.5773
0.2000	0.5793	0.5812	0.5832	0.5851	0.5871	0.5890	0.5910	0.5929	0.5948	0.5968	0.5987	0.6006	0.6026	0.6045	0.6064	0.6083	0.6103	0.6122	0.6141	0.6160
0.3000	0.6179	0.6198	0.6217	0.6236	0.6255	0.6274	0.6293	0.6312	0.6331	0.6350	0.6368	0.6387	0.6406	0.6424	0.6443	0.6462	0.6480	0.6499	0.6517	0.6536
0.4000	0.6554	0.6573	0.6591	0.6609	0.6628	0.6646	0.6664	0.6682	0.6700	0.6718	0.6736	0.6754	0.6772	0.6790	0.6808	0.6826	0.6844	0.6862	0.6879	0.6897
0.5000	0.6915	0.6932	0.6950	0.6967	0.6985	0.7002	0.7019	0.7037	0.7054	0.7071	0.7088	0.7106	0.7123	0.7140	0.7157	0.7174	0.7190	0.7207	0.7224	0.7241
0.6000	0.7257	0.7274	0.7291	0.7307	0.7324	0.7340	0.7357	0.7373	0.7389	0.7405	0.7422	0.7438	0.7454	0.7470	0.7486	0.7502	0.7517	0.7533	0.7549	0.7565
0.7000	0.7580	0.7596	0.7611	0.7627	0.7642	0.7658	0.7673	0.7688	0.7703	0.7719	0.7734	0.7749	0.7764	0.7779	0.7793	0.7808	0.7823	0.7838	0.7852	0.7867
0.8000	0.7881	0.7896	0.7910	0.7925	0.7939	0.7953	0.7967	0.7981	0.7995	0.8009	0.8023	0.8037	0.8051	0.8065	0.8078	0.8092	0.8106	0.8119	0.8133	0.8146
0.9000	0.8159	0.8173	0.8186	0.8199	0.8212	0.8225	0.8238	0.8251	0.8264	0.8277	0.8289	0.8302	0.8315	0.8327	0.8340	0.8352	0.8365	0.8377	0.8389	0.8401
1.0000	0.8413	0.8426	0.8438	0.8449	0.8461	0.8473	0.8485	0.8497	0.8508	0.8520	0.8531	0.8543	0.8554	0.8566	0.8577	0.8588	0.8599	0.8610	0.8621	0.8632
1.1000	0.8643	0.8654	0.8665	0.8676	0.8686	0.8697	0.8708	0.8718	0.8729	0.8739	0.8749	0.8760	0.8770	0.8780	0.8790	0.8800	0.8810	0.8820	0.8830	0.8840
1.2000	0.8849	0.8859	0.8869	0.8878	0.8888	0.8897	0.8907	0.8916	0.8925	0.8934	0.8944	0.8953	0.8962	0.8971	0.8980	0.8988	0.8997	0.9006	0.9015	0.9023
1.3000	0.9032	0.9041	0.9049	0.9057	0.9066	0.9074	0.9082	0.9091	0.9099	0.9107	0.9115	0.9123	0.9131	0.9139	0.9147	0.9154	0.9162	0.9170	0.9177	0.9185
1.4000	0.9192	0.9200	0.9207	0.9215	0.9222	0.9229	0.9236	0.9244	0.9251	0.9258	0.9265	0.9272	0.9279	0.9285	0.9292	0.9299	0.9306	0.9312	0.9319	0.9325
1.5000	0.9332	0.9338	0.9345	0.9351	0.9357	0.9364	0.9370	0.9376	0.9382	0.9388	0.9394	0.9400	0.9406	0.9412	0.9418	0.9424	0.9429	0.9435	0.9441	0.9446
1.6000	0.9452	0.9458	0.9463	0.9468	0.9474	0.9479	0.9484	0.9490	0.9495	0.9500	0.9505	0.9510	0.9515	0.9520	0.9525	0.9530	0.9535	0.9540	0.9545	0.9550
1.7000	0.9554	0.9559	0.9564	0.9568	0.9573	0.9577	0.9582	0.9586	0.9591	0.9595	0.9599	0.9604	0.9608	0.9612	0.9616	0.9621	0.9625	0.9629	0.9633	0.9637
1.8000	0.9641	0.9645	0.9649	0.9652	0.9656	0.9660	0.9664	0.9667	0.9671	0.9675	0.9678	0.9682	0.9686	0.9689	0.9693	0.9696	0.9699	0.9703	0.9706	0.9710
1.9000	0.9713	0.9716	0.9719	0.9723	0.9726	0.9729	0.9732	0.9735	0.9738	0.9741	0.9744	0.9747	0.9750	0.9753	0.9756	0.9759	0.9761	0.9764	0.9767	0.9770
2.0000	0.9772	0.9775	0.9778	0.9780	0.9783	0.9786	0.9788	0.9791	0.9793	0.9796	0.9798	0.9801	0.9803	0.9805	0.9808	0.9810	0.9812	0.9815	0.9817	0.9819
2.1000	0.9821	0.9824	0.9826	0.9828	0.9830	0.9832	0.9834	0.9836	0.9838	0.9840	0.9842	0.9844	0.9846	0.9848	0.9850	0.9852	0.9854	0.9856	0.9857	0.9859
2.2000	0.9861	0.9863	0.9864	0.9866	0.9868	0.9870	0.9871	0.9873	0.9875	0.9876	0.9878	0.9879	0.9881	0.9882	0.9884	0.9885	0.9887	0.9888	0.9890	0.9891
2.3000	0.9893	0.9894	0.9896	0.9897	0.9898	0.9900	0.9901	0.9902	0.9904	0.9905	0.9906	0.9907	0.9909	0.9910	0.9911	0.9912	0.9913	0.9915	0.9916	0.9917
2.4000	0.9918	0.9919	0.9920	0.9921	0.9922	0.9923	0.9925	0.9926	0.9927	0.9928	0.9929	0.9930	0.9931	0.9931	0.9932	0.9933	0.9934	0.9935	0.9936	0.9937
2.5000	0.9938	0.9939	0.9940	0.9940	0.9941	0.9942	0.9943	0.9944	0.9945	0.9945	0.9946	0.9947	0.9948	0.9948	0.9949	0.9950	0.9951	0.9951	0.9952	0.9953
2.6000	0.9953	0.9955	0.9955	0.9955	0.9956	0.9957	0.9957	0.9958	0.9959	0.9959	0.9960	0.9960	0.9961	0.9962	0.9962	0.9963	0.9963	0.9964	0.9964	0.9965
2.7000	0.9965	0.9966	0.9966	0.9967	0.9967	0.9968	0.9968	0.9969	0.9969	0.9970	0.9970	0.9971	0.9971	0.9972	0.9972	0.9972	0.9973	0.9973	0.9974	0.9974
2.8000	0.9974	0.9975	0.9975	0.9976	0.9976	0.9977	0.9977	0.9977	0.9978	0.9978	0.9978	0.9979	0.9979	0.9979	0.9980	0.9980	0.9980	0.9980	0.9981	0.9981
2.9000	0.9981	0.9982	0.9982	0.9982	0.9983	0.9983	0.9983	0.9984	0.9984	0.9984	0.9984	0.9985	0.9985	0.9985	0.9985	0.9985	0.9986	0.9986	0.9986	0.9986

Source: Financial Risk Management, Inc.

$N(d) = N(d_H)$. If $d = d_L$, we get exactly $N(d) = N(d_L)$, as we would anticipate. Thus, for $N(d_1)$, we have

$$N(d_1) = 0.6064 + (0.2711 - 0.27)\left(\frac{0.6083 - 0.6064}{0.275 - 0.27}\right)$$

$$= 0.6064 + (0.00110)(0.38)$$

$$= 0.6068$$

Similarly, for $N(d_2)$,

$$N(d_2) = 0.5219 + (0.0590 - 0.055)\left(\frac{0.5239 - 0.5219}{0.06 - 0.055}\right)$$

$$= 0.5219 + (0.004)(0.40)$$

$$= 0.5235$$

Now that we know $N(d_1)$ and $N(d_2)$, we are ready to calculate the option price.

STEP 3: COMPUTE THE CALL PRICE

We now substitute the values of $N(d_1)$ and $N(d_2)$ into Equation 24.9:

$$c = (\$100.0 \cdot 0.6068) - (\$100.0 \cdot e^{-0.07/2} \cdot 0.5235)$$

$$= \$60.68 - \$50.55 = \$10.13$$

Note that in using 182 days to expiration, the precise calculation done by a computer program is $c = \$10.06$. Hence, the equilibrium call price is $10.13. Under the five assumptions in this example, we know that the call price has to be $10.13, or else there is arbitrage.

Appendix 24C Continuously Compounded Interest Rates

This appendix compares annually compounded interest rates with continuously compounded interest rates. The Black-Scholes option pricing model (BSOPM) uses continuously compounded interest rates. *Annual compounding* implicitly assumes that interest is paid annually. *Continuous compounding* assumes that interest is paid continuously—that is, more frequently than every second. If we let PV denote present value and FV denote future value, then Equations 24C.1 and 24C.2 express the relationship between PV and FV via annual compounding (r) and continuous compounding (r_c), respectively:

$$FV = PV(1 + r)^t \qquad \text{(Annual)} \qquad \text{(24C.1)}$$

$$FV = PVe^{r_c t} \qquad \text{(Continuous)} \qquad \text{(24C.2)}$$

where e stands for the exponential.[19] Solving for the compound rate, r and r_c, we have

$$r = \left(\frac{FV}{PV}\right)^{1/t} - 1 \qquad (24C.3)$$

$$r_c = \frac{\ln\left(\frac{FV}{PV}\right)}{t} \qquad (24C.4)$$

where ln[ ] is the natural logarithm.

For example, suppose that $t = \frac{1}{2}$ year (hence, $1/t = 2$), $FV = \$105$, and $PV = \$100$. What is the relationship between r_c and r?

$$r = \left(\frac{105.0}{100.0}\right)^2 - 1$$

$$= 0.1025, \text{ or } 10.25\%$$

$$r_c = \frac{\ln\left(\frac{105.0}{100.0}\right)}{\frac{1}{2}}$$

$$= \ln(1.05)/(0.5) = 0.04879/0.5$$

$$\cong 0.09758, \text{ or } 9.758\%$$

Hence, continuous compounding is another method of accounting for the time value of money. Continuous compounding is used in calculating option prices, because it most closely relates to the underlying assumptions of the BSOPM, which assumes a continuous change in the hedge ratio (as illustrated in the binomial option pricing model).

Appendix 24D Calculating Continuously Compounded Standard Deviations

Recall from Chapter 6 that the standard deviation of stock rates of return is calculated by the following equation:

19. Mathematically,

$$\left(1 + \frac{R}{m}\right)^m$$

where R is the quoted rate. This equation will tend to e^R as m goes to infinity. Hence, we say e^R represents continuous compounding.

$$\sigma = \sqrt{\frac{1}{n}\sum_{t=1}^{n}(R_{i,t} - \overline{R}_i)^2} \qquad (24D.1)$$

where $R_{i,t}$ is the rate of return on stock i during period t, R_i is the average rate of return on stock i, and n is the number of historical observations. Chapter 5 presented the interim rate of return (modified for stocks) as follows:

$$R_{i,t} = \frac{P_{i,t} - P_{i,t-1} + D_{i,t}}{P_{i,t-1}} \qquad (24D.2)$$

where $P_{i,t}$ is the price of stock i at t, $P_{i,t-1}$ is the price of stock i at $t-1$, and $D_{i,t}$ is the dividend of stock i, if any, paid at t. The only difference in calculating the standard deviation with continuous compounding is the equation to calculate $R_{i,t}$. With continuous compounding, the proper equation for calculating rates of return is

$$R_{i,t} = \ln\left(\frac{P_{i,t} + D_{i,t}}{P_{i,t-1}}\right) \qquad (24D.3)$$

where ln[ ] is the natural logarithm.

It can be shown that for sufficiently short time periods (or small changes in the stock price), the rates of return given by Equations 24D.2 and 24D.3 are about the same. However, for long holding periods (greater than one week), the differences are more substantial.

To illustrate the magnitude of the differences in the two methods of estimating the standard deviation, let us consider the annual price information of a stock index. The second column in Exhibit 24D-1 gives the index values for a recent decade. The third column gives the continuously compounded rates of return, and the fourth column gives the annually compounded rates of return. As the exhibit shows, the differences between the standard deviations can be sizable. This case was based on data from Hong Kong stocks, which are very volatile. The holding period was assumed to be 1 year, which is fairly long. The less volatile the assets in question and the shorter the holding period, the smaller the differences will be between these methods.

EXHIBIT 24D-1
Illustration of Continuously Compounded Rates of Return Compared with Annually Compounded Rates of Return

Year	Index	Continuously Compounded Rates of Return[a]	Annually Compounded Rates of Return[b]
1	100.0		
2	138.8	0.328	0.388
3	216.6	0.445	0.561
4	556.9	0.944	1.571
5	332.7	−0.515	−0.403
6	136.0	−0.895	−0.591
7	274.1	0.701	1.015
8	373.0	−0.308	0.361
9	317.6	−0.161	−0.149
10	360.9	0.128	0.136
11	634.4	0.564	0.758
	Mean	0.185	0.365
	Standard deviation	0.536	0.624

a. Based on $R_{i,t} = \ln\left(\dfrac{P_{i,t} + D_{i,t}}{P_{i,t-1}}\right)$

b. Based on $R_{i,t} = \dfrac{P_{i,t} - P_{i,t-1} + D_{i,t}}{P_{i,t-1}}$

Note that this index is without dividends included, so $D_{i,t}$ is always zero.

CHAPTER 25

FINANCIAL ENGINEERING

LEARNING OBJECTIVES

After studying this chapter you should be able to:

1. Define financial engineering.

2. Explain how firms benefit from financial engineering.

3. Describe interest rate, currency, and commodity swaps.

4. Describe how swaps are used to mitigate financial risk.

5. Describe recent innovations in instruments used in financial engineering.

INVESTMENTS IN THE NEWS

DERIVATIVES ARE A SENSIBLE WAY TO MANAGE RISK

Bets can go bad. Sears bet that interest rates would go up. They didn't.

The terms of Sears' derivative were a little more complex than the average Super Bowl bet. Here's how the derivative, called an interest-rate swap, worked. Swaps that Sears had entered into over the years required it to pay a fixed, average interest rate of 8.02% on $996 million in 1996. In return it would receive an interest rate pegged to the market rate of interest on the same $996 million.

As interest rates have generally fallen since the time the derivatives were initiated, that floating rate turned out to be 5.44%. Since it was obligated to pay 8.02% and only got 5.44%, it would appear that Sears lost money on the hedge.

Of course, at the same time, the falling interest rates meant Sears was saving money on its regular debt. What the hedge did for Sears was to protect it if interest rates had risen, rather than dropped.

But what remains a mystery is how much—if any—of Sears' derivatives losses have already been recognized as interest expense, or when the remaining losses will be recognized.

Source: Scott Woolley, "Derivatives Are a Sensible Way to Manage Risk," *Forbes*, August 11, 1997, p. 43. Reprinted by Permission of *Forbes* magazine © Forbes Inc., 1997.

Sears is involved with interest rate swaps, by which Sears is obligated to pay a fixed interest rate of 8.02% on its debt; in return it receives a market floating rate, which dropped to 5.44%. This situation induced a $382 million loss to Sears. What are swaps? Why do firms swap assets? The swap is only one financial tool among other sophisticated financial tools that investors employ. Swaps and other tools are discussed in this chapter.

The chapter focuses on the way organizations—individual corporations, individual states, and institutional investors—can use financial securities to manage risk. Specifically, it focuses on equity risk, commodity risk, foreign exchange risk, and interest rate risk, which can have potentially adverse effects on an organization's financial performance. To reduce these financial risks, many organizations rely on complex financial securities. The derivatives discussed in Chapters 22 to 24 are often part of risk management strategies, as are other types of derivatives.

The first part of this chapter covers financial engineering, the technique used to manage financial risk. After discussing what financial engineering is and how firms can use it in their financial strategies, the discussion turns to swaps, a specific financial engineering tool.

25.1 WHAT IS FINANCIAL ENGINEERING?

Although **financial engineering** has several definitions, in this text it is used to mean "the design, the development, and the implementation of innovative financial instruments and processes, and the formulation of creative solutions to problems in finance."[1] Financial engineering typically employs derivative securities such as options, futures, or swaps to manage an organization's existing financial risk exposure. This section elaborates on financial engineering and provides a general decision-making framework for managing financial risks.

The financial engineering process involves three activities. First is the use of innovative financial instruments. For example, S&P 500 index futures contracts can be used to hedge a U.S. equity portfolio. Wheat futures options can be used to hedge a wheat farmer's wheat price risk.

The second activity is the creation of innovative financial processes. An innovative financial process is an alternative way of accomplishing an objective currently achieved by a standard investment technique. These innovations may reduce the costs of financial transactions and expand the set of trading opportunities available to investors. An example of an innovative financial process is the shelf registration rule, which allows firms to issue securities over a period of time rather than all at one time (see Chapter 3).

The final activity in the financial engineering process is the formulation of creative solutions to complex financial problems. As financial securities become more

---

1. John D. Finnerty, "Financial Engineering in Corporate Finance: An Overview," in Clifford W. Smith, Jr., and Charles W. Smithson (ed.), *The Handbook of Financial Engineering: New Financial Product Innovations, Applications, and Analyses* (New York: HarperBusiness, 1990), p. 69.

sophisticated and the marketplace remains volatile, the need for innovative risk management has increased. Thus, financial engineering also addresses complex financial problems that sometimes require custom-designed financial securities.

Some of these financial innovations make everyone happy except the tax collector. Recently, firms have issued preferred stocks, called monthly income preferred securities (MIPS). These vehicles give investors a higher yield relative to the yield of other existing preferred stocks, and the firms can deduct the dividends for tax purposes. Hence, both investors and firms enjoy the new financial innovation, and the IRS loses. Of course, the transaction is not a simple one:

The tax break is made possible because the MIPS are issued by a special-purpose partnership, which then lends the proceeds to its corporate parent. The parent, be it Texaco or GTE, is obligated to pay interest to the partnership, which then passes the money on to investors in the form of dividends.[2]

25.1.1 Financial Engineering at Magma Copper Company

Magma Copper Company is a copper mining company whose profits are sensitive to changes in copper prices. To reduce its exposure to copper price risk, Magma issued $200,000 in "copper interest-indexed bonds." Instead of paying a fixed interest rate on an ordinary bond, on this bond issue Magma must make interest payments that are tied to copper prices. By issuing these bonds, Magma effectively reduces its copper price risk. If copper prices rise, then Magma makes more money from mining copper and, hence, is required to pay a higher interest rate. If copper prices fall, then Magma does not earn as much money from mining copper and gets to pay a lower interest rate. Notice that these bonds have qualities of equity, because both the coupon payment and Magma's equity value vary with the price of copper.

By looking closely at the way Magma reduced its copper price risk, we can see how a firm can employ financial engineering. The process of financial engineering starts with a clear understanding of the financial risk involved. What exactly is the financial risk of changes in such things as exchange rates, interest rates, oil prices, and so forth? The management of a firm must be able to draw the relationship between (1) firm value and the risk variable or (2) firm income and the risk variable. Thus, the first step in financial engineering is to establish the relationship between the firm's value (or income) and risk. For the risk variable we use rv, and for the value of the underlying item we use V. V can represent the income from an investment, the value of a portfolio, or the value of the firm. In our analysis of Magma we use V to represent the income from an investment. Exhibit 25-1a illustrates the relationship between Δv and Δrv, where Δ denotes "change" in the two variables.

Exhibit 25-1 illustrates how the copper price risk of Magma Copper Company can be mapped. This graph, called a **risk profile,** shows the relationship between changes in the firm value (or changes in profitability) and changes in the risk variable. Magma owns copper mines, so its profitability is directly tied to copper prices.

2. *Barron's*, February 27, 1995.

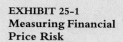

EXHIBIT 25-1
Measuring Financial
Price Risk

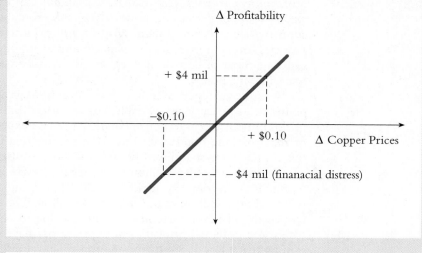

Part a: Risk Profile of
Magma Copper Company
in Relation to Changes in
Copper Prices

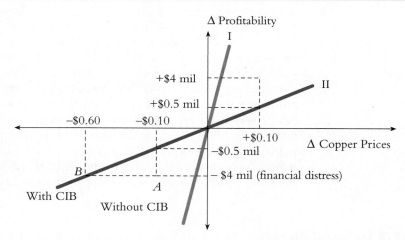

Part b: Risk Profile of
Magma Copper Company
in Relation to Changes in
Copper Prices with the
Issue of Copper Interest-
Indexed Bonds

Note: "With CIB" denotes the risk profile of Magma Copper Company with copper interest-indexed bonds.
"Without CIB" denotes the risk profile of Magma Copper Company with fixed-rate bonds. A-Magma Copper
Company is under financial distress if prices fall by $0.10 per pound. B-Magma Copper Company is under finan-
cial distress if prices fall by $0.60 per pound.

Suppose Magma expects to earn an additional $4 million if copper prices rise to
$1.10 per pound from the current price of $1 per pound. Recall that the risk profile
looks at changes from current levels. If copper prices fall to $0.90 (that is, a price
change of −$0.10), Magma expects profits to fall by $4 million, at which time it
would experience financial distress (it would be unable to pay bondholders).

Exhibit 25-1a shows that as copper prices rise above expected prices, Magma's profitability also rises. Unfortunately, Magma's exposure to copper prices goes both ways. If copper prices fall, so does Magma's profitability. As the graph illustrates, if copper prices fall far enough, Magma will experience financial distress. This link provides strong motivation for management to attempt to minimize the firm's exposure to copper price risk; it illustrates the situation Magma would face if it issued fixed-income bonds.

By issuing copper interest-indexed bonds, Magma links some of its interest expenses to its primary risk variable, copper prices. Exhibit 25-1b illustrates the effect of this bond issue on Magma's copper price risk exposure. Line I represents the case of fixed-income bonds, and Line II represents that of linked bonds. For example, the copper interest-indexed bonds could be constructed so that the interest payments increase by $3.5 million if copper prices rise by $0.10 per pound and fall by $3.5 million if copper prices fall by $0.10 per pound. Hence, the change in profit will be ±$0.5 million rather than ±$4 million. The copper interest-indexed bonds reduce the likelihood of financial distress due to copper price changes. Unfortunately, the potential gains if copper prices rise have also been greatly reduced. Assuming that a loss of $4 million induces financial distress (as before), notice also that with the copper interest-indexed bonds, Magma will not experience financial distress until copper prices fall by $0.60, which is very unlikely.

In this case, bondholders rather than shareholders are exposed to the risk of fluctuating copper prices. When these bonds were issued, the firm's stockholders shifted their copper price risk to bondholders. The stockholders had a less risky security, because bondholders and stockholders share the copper price risk. However, who would want to buy such a bond? Many pension funds hold enormous quantities of bonds, whose returns vary as the general level of interest rates fluctuates. A pension fund can use these indexed bonds to diversify its bond portfolio, as well as perhaps raise the expected yield on the portfolio, because copper prices are not highly correlated with interest rates. Thus, bonds with such unique characteristics give bond portfolio managers the ability to reduce the overall volatility of their portfolios.

25.1.2 Indexed Bonds

Pension funds and other institutional investors that buy bonds have an exposure to inflation risk. If they buy a bond for, say, 10 years, and inflation escalates, then the interest rate will go up to adjust itself to the inflation, and the bond's price may fall sharply. Recently, the U.S. Treasury issued index-linked bonds in which the principle and the interest are linked to the cost of living index. These bonds eliminate inflation risk for both sides—the government and investors. The government knows exactly how much it pays as interest in real terms (which it does not know with unlinked bonds), and investors are released from inflation risk. Thus, linked bonds are an example of how both sides can benefit from the development of a financial product.

25.1.3 Symmetric and Asymmetric Hedging Strategies

The strategy used by Magma is one of several hedging strategies possible with financially engineered investment instruments. Magma's hedging strategy is called a **symmetric hedging strategy,** because the risk of loss was eliminated at the cost of potential gains. Symmetric hedging strategies are identifiable by the straight line representing the hedging strategy ("with CIB" in Exhibit 25-1b).

An alternative strategy is an **asymmetric hedging strategy,** which insures the risk but allows for potential gains if prices move favorably. Protective put buying is an example of an asymmetric hedging strategy. Recall from Chapter 23 that protective put buying is buying stock and put options. The main characteristic of this strategy is that it sets a floor on losses. In the same manner, Magma could buy exchange-traded put options on copper futures contracts to set a floor on its potential losses.

The asymmetric approach to managing financial risk is further illustrated in the case of the state of Texas hedging its oil tax revenues from declining oil prices (see Connecting Theory to Practice 25.1). What exactly is the state of Texas trying to accomplish by this option trading? Exhibit 25-2a illustrates the revenue risk related to oil prices. As oil prices rise, so do the tax receipts from the oil levies. Rather than symmetrically hedging this risk with a crude oil futures contract, the state of Texas opted for an asymmetric hedge. Exhibit 25-2b illustrates the effect of this hedge, assuming that the entire revenue risk is hedged. A floor has been placed on tax receipts, yet the gains from tax levies when oil prices rise have not been entirely eliminated. The gain with increases in oil prices is decreased only by the cost of the put options. This strategy is asymmetric: the chance of a dramatic loss has been eliminated, but the chance of a dramatic gain has not been eliminated.

CONNECTING THEORY TO PRACTICE 25.1

STATES HITTING OPTIONS PITS TO HEDGE RISK

When oil prices sank to $11 a barrel in 1986, the fortunes of Texas plunged, too. Suddenly, the state that had grown rich with the boom in oil found itself short billions of dollars in expected energy tax revenues.

Today, the Lone Star state is trying to avert the havoc that volatile oil prices can wreak on state budgets. With a pilot program unveiled earlier this year, Texas became one of the few but growing number of states to hedge the risks of wildly swinging commodity prices in the commodity markets themselves. What's more, Texas is doing it without the help of Wall Street's financial wizards.

Spearheaded by state Sen. Teel Bivins, Texas started buying options last April to avoid suffering a sharp drop in tax revenue if oil prices tumbled.

(continued)

**EXHIBIT 25-2
Illustration of
an Asymmetric
Hedging Strategy**

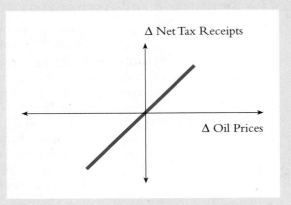

Part a: The State of Texas's Exposure to Oil Price Risk
with No Hedging

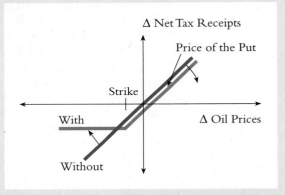

Part b: The State of Texas's Exposure to Oil Price Risk
with Put Options (an asymmetric hedging strategy)

Note: "With" denotes the risk profile of Texas's net tax receipts with futures put options (*net* refers to the total after the cost and benefits of the options are considered). "Without" denotes the risk profile of Texas's net tax receipts with no hedging.

Texas levies a 4.6% tax on every barrel of oil produced in the state, and the revenue it derives from the tax varies according to the price of oil. To avoid a repeat of 1986, Texas has decided to use unclaimed oil royalty monies to buy "put" options that give it the right to sell oil futures at a preset "strike" price any day before the option expires. Thus, if oil prices plunge below the strike price, the state can exercise the option, which effectively allows it to sell oil futures at above-market prices—and to profit from any further declines. Or, instead of selling futures, Texas could simply unload its put option in the market—also at a profit because the option increases in value as the price of oil declines.

(continued)

The profit Texas makes with these methods merely offsets the decline in the tax revenue it collects. "It's not a money-making goal," Texas State Treasurer Kay Bailey Hutchison is quick to note, "it's an insurance policy goal."

Should oil prices remain where they are or rise, the state loses the small outlay it made to buy the put.

Source: Anita Raghavan, "States Hitting Options Pits to Hedge Risk," *Wall Street Journal,* September 8, 1992, p. C1. Reprinted by permission of *The Wall Street Journal,* © 1992 Dow Jones & Co., Inc. All Rights Reserved Worldwide.

MAKING THE CONNECTION

The state of Texas is seeking to ease the pain of tax revenue loss when oil prices decline. Declining oil prices adversely affect Texas in two ways. First, owners of oil wells may simply turn off the wells. With a decline in the number of barrels of oil extracted comes a direct reduction in taxes received by the state. Second, the state tax is 4.6% of the sales price of the oil. When crude oil is selling for $30 a barrel, the state receives $1.38, or $0.046 \cdot \$30$, from each barrel sold. However, if crude oil falls to $15 a barrel, the state receives only $0.69, or $0.046 \cdot \$15$, from each barrel sold. By buying put options on oil, the state of Texas profits if prices fall, thereby reducing the risk of such price changes.

It is not always clear whether symmetric or asymmetric hedging is a better method for risk protection. Exhibit 25-3 illustrates a decision-making framework that can be used to reach an appropriate solution. Each strategy is evaluated on its cost. For example, if intolerable losses would be incurred then a hedging strategy should be pursued. If a particular risk is insignificant, then the most efficient strategy is to ignore the risk and allow it to remain. If a particular risk is significant, then most firms would prefer to hedge it with an asymmetric strategy. However, if the cost of this insurance is high, then the firm must look at symmetric hedging strategies. If the costs of symmetric strategies are high, then the firm may decide to bear the risk (and implicitly receive any benefits that otherwise would have been paid out in the hedge). If a particular risk is intolerable, then the firm *must* hedge against it. If the cost of asymmetric hedging is affordable, then that approach is taken. Symmetric hedging is used if asymmetric hedging is too expensive. Symmetric hedging reduces the risk by eliminating both the downside cost and the upside benefit.

Parts 2 and 3 of this book explained that a diversified portfolio of assets eliminates a large portion of the financial risk in that portfolio. Why, then, should a firm be concerned with managing exposures to financial risk? Won't these risks be diversified away across firms? If so, there is no need for the firm to hedge them. Clearly, the state of Texas is not held in a portfolio, so the concepts related to diversification do not apply. Do the concepts of diversification apply to corporations? We examine this question next.

EXHIBIT 25-3   **Managing Financial Price Risk: a Decision–Making Framework**

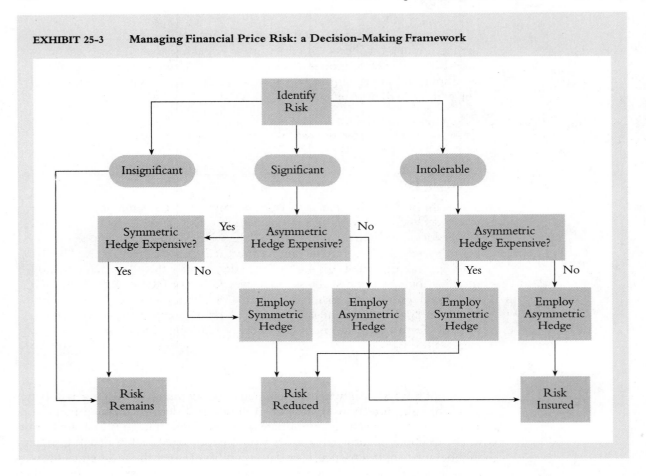

PRACTICE BOX

Problem	Show graphically the effect of the state of Texas pursuing a symmetric hedging strategy (as Magma Copper Company did), such as selling futures contracts, rather than an asymmetric hedging strategy.
Solution	The symmetric hedge would have a symmetric impact on both the gains and the losses in tax receipts. Specifically, the influence of the symmetric strategy could be graphically expressed as follows:

(continued)

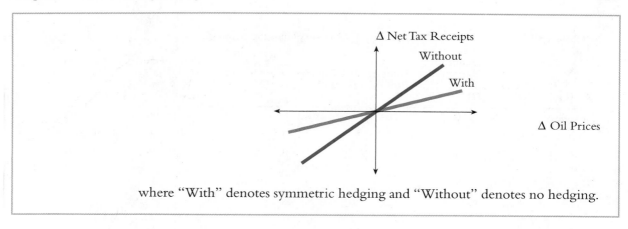

where "With" denotes symmetric hedging and "Without" denotes no hedging.

25.2 WHY PURSUE FINANCIAL ENGINEERING STRATEGIES?

Organizations use financial engineering to manage financial risk for several reasons. These reasons fall into three broad categories: unique situations, situations in which markets are perceived to be inefficient, and situations in which markets are perceived to be efficient.

25.2.1. Unique Situations

Organizations can benefit from financial engineering in two types of unique situations. First, some investors are underdiversified and cannot easily obtain an appropriate level of diversification. For example, the state of Texas is not a security that can be easily diversified. The managers of state revenues and expenses must focus on total risk, not just systematic risk (see Chapter 10). In some firms, such as family-owned companies, major shareholders may not want to lose control by selling shares, but the shareholders may wish to mitigate the effects of adverse movements in the share price.

A second unique situation occurs when the quantity of assets to be hedged is highly correlated with the value of the firm or with the firm's profitability, and the firm (for example, a farmer) invests a high proportion of its wealth in the enterprise. For example, during the planting season a wheat farmer is never sure of the actual quantity that will be harvested. A significant amount of quantity risk makes asymmetric strategies more attractive. Exhibit 25-4 illustrates the possible outcomes for a wheat farmer who either does not hedge, hedges symmetrically with a futures contract ($F_0 = \$3.50$ per bushel), or hedges asymmetrically with put options ($p_0 = \$0.1$ per bushel; strike = $\$3.50$ per bushel). These results are based on the assumptions that it takes $\$250,000$ to run the farm regardless of the weather conditions and that

EXHIBIT 25-4   **The Wheat Farmer P/L for Various Hedging Strategies**

Weather	Wheat Prices (1)	Quantity Harvested (bushels) (2)	Unhedged Profits (3)	Futures P/L (4)	Options P/L (5)	Symmetric Hedge P/L (6) = (3) + (4)	Asymmetric Hedge P/L (7) = (3) + (5)
Drought	$4.5	60,000	$ 20,000	−$100,000	−$10,000	−$ 80,000	$ 10,000
Normal	3.5	100,000	100,000	0	−10,000	100,000	90,000
Rain	2.5	110,000	25,000	100,000	90,000	125,000	115,000

P/L denotes profits and losses.

(1) Price

(2) Quantity

(3) Unhedged Profits = Wheat Price · Quantity Harvested − $250,000.

(4) Futures P/L = ($3.50 − Wheat Price)100,000 Bushels.

(5) Options P/L = max(0, $3.5 − Wheat Price)100,000 Bushels − $10,000 (cost of the put option).

(6) Symmetric Hedge P/L = Unhedged Profits + Futures P/L.

(7) Asymmetric Hedge P/L = Unhedged Profits + Options P/L.

all hedging is done based on the expected harvest of 100,000 bushels of wheat. Also, the weather will either be drought (wheat prices will rise to $4.50), normal (wheat prices will be $3.50), or abundant rainfall (wheat prices fall to $2.50).

Exhibit 25-4 shows that in a drought, wheat prices rise to $4.50, and the quantity harvested falls to 60,000 bushels. The symmetric hedge is disastrous, resulting in a loss of $80,000. The farmer initially used the futures contracts to hedge against falling wheat prices but finds that the hedge results in further losses in a drought. The rise in wheat prices (which is normal during droughts) causes the futures contracts to incur losses at a time when the farmer has lower profits. This result does not occur with asymmetric strategies, such as put options. The farmer can examine these alternative hedging strategies and choose the preferred policy.

These examples show that firms can benefit from financial engineering when they face unique financial risks. When it is difficult to diversify, or when the quantity to be hedged is unpredictable, further analysis is required.

25.2.2 When Markets Are Perceived to Be Inefficient

As discussed in Chapter 12, there is growing evidence that financial markets are not completely efficient. In an inefficient market, investors can successfully engineer a transaction that saves money with certainty. Also, if investors can predict the future direction of an asset's price with some degree of accuracy, then they can benefit from financial engineering. An investor could engage in a strategy known as **selective hedging,** where the investor would hedge only during periods of high risk and not hedge when the risk is minimal. For example, a bank facing interest rate risk may decide not to insure against the downside risk during an election year but to insure against the risk during other time periods.[3] Although this hedging strategy is initially less costly when compared with the full hedging strategy (whether it is an election year or not), it is a dangerous strategy if the bank is wrong about its expectations. It could lose when hedged (an opportunity loss), and when it is not hedged, the result could be very costly. Alternatively, if the bank has the ability to predict changes in interest rates, then it will not lose when hedged, and it will win when not hedged (a highly desirable result).

Continuing this line of thought further, a firm could engage in pure speculation. For example, a copper mining firm may have superior information regarding the future price of copper. With this information, the firm could speculate with derivative securities, hoping to gain from its correct predictions regarding copper prices. This is a very risky strategy, however, because if the firm is wrong, it typically will lose both in its regular business and in the derivative securities.

25.2.3 When Markets Are Perceived to Be Efficient[4]

If markets are efficient, in the sense that future stock prices cannot be predicted, there are still valid reasons to assess and actively manage financial price risk.[5] To set the framework for this discussion, consider the following proposition:

If there are no taxes, no transaction costs, and the firm has a fixed investment policy, then the financial policies (such as financial engineering) will be irrelevant.[6]

In reality, at least one of these three initial assumptions—no taxes, no transaction costs, and fixed investment policy—clearly does not hold. This situation creates an incentive to employ financial engineering tools, even if the market cannot be predicted. The following sections evaluate each assumption to determine its validity.

NO TAXES

Taxes are an unpleasant fact of life. The existence of taxes provides a reason for using financial engineering. Financial engineering strategies can minimize a firm's expected tax burden. Section 25.1 introduced the MIPS, a special type of preferred security that reduces the tax burden. This section demonstrates how progressive taxation may create a benefit if financial innovations are employed. If investors are indifferent to the total risk (as opposed to the systematic risk) of a firm's stock, then they will not mind (and will actually appreciate) a firm's lowering its risk level with derivative securities if derivatives reduce the expected tax burden.

---

3. The bankers may believe that short-term interest rates will stay low because of political pressure and will increase after the election is over.

4. The basic idea for this section can be found in Clifford W. Smith, Jr., Charles W. Smithson, and D. Sykes Wilford, *Managing Financial Risk* (New York: Harper & Row, 1990), chap. 17.

5. Efficiency here is defined in terms of investors' ability to earn excess profits from predicting the future.

6. This is a revised version of Modigliani and Miller's famous Proposition 1. See Franco Modigliani and Merton Miller, "The Cost of Capital, Corporation Finance and the Theory of Investment," *American Economic Review* 48 (June 1958): 261–297.

Let us illustrate one of several possible tax reduction strategies. In the United States, the tax schedule is progressive for firms with earnings less than $81,333,333. The more money a firm earns, the higher its marginal tax rate. As profits increase, not only does the amount paid increase but also the amount paid as a percentage of profits increases. Exhibit 25-5 gives the corporate tax rate schedule for 1997. Exhibit 25-6 illustrates the information in the tax rate schedule. Notice that for low pretax profits, the graphical relationship bends upward. How can a firm use this information and financial engineering to its own advantage?

Consider the following simple example. A small U.S. manufacturing firm sells its specialized products in France. Suppose it is anticipating earning in pretax profits next year either $200,000 or $0, depending on the movement in foreign exchange rates. Also suppose either outcome is equally probable. If the uncertainty could be resolved costlessly, the firm would earn pretax profits of $100,000 (the expected figure) for sure [or after-tax profits of $77,750 ($100,000 − $22,250)]. The following table, based on the data in Exhibit 25-5, outlines the profit in the realistic case where certainty prevails:

	Adverse Move in Rates	Favorable Move in Rates	Hedged Position
Pretax profits	$0	$200,000	$100,000
Taxes[a]	0	61,250[b]	22,250[c]
Net profit	0	138,750	77,750

a. See Exhibit 25-5.

b. $61,250 = $22,250 + 0.39($200,000 − $100,000).

c. $22,250 = $22,250 + 0.39($100,000 − $100,000).

EXHIBIT 25-5 U.S. Corporate Tax Rate Schedule as of October 1997	For Earnings Over	But Not Over	Tax Is	Of the Amount Over
	$ 0	$ 50,000	15%	$ 0
	50,001	75,000	$7,500 + 25%	50,000
	75,001	100,000	$13,750 + 34%	75,000
	100,001	335,000	$22,250 + 39%	100,000
	335,001	10,000,000	$113,900 + 34%	335,000
	10,000,001	15,000,000	$3,400,000 + 35%	10,000,000
	15,000,001	18,333,333	$5,515,000 + 38%	15,000,000
	18,333,334	—	Flat 35%	0

Source: http://www.taxaccountpros.com/taxtable.htm.

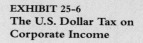

EXHIBIT 25-6
The U.S. Dollar Tax on
Corporate Income

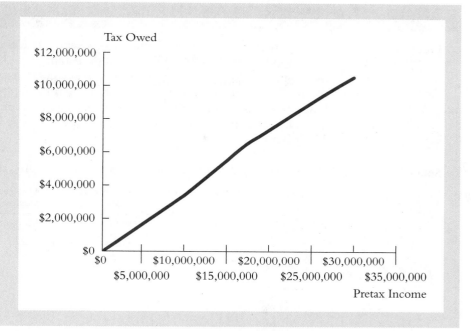

We can use the preceding table to calculate the expected net profit without any hedging:

$$\text{Expected Net Profit} = (\tfrac{1}{2})\$0 + (\tfrac{1}{2})\$138{,}750 = \$69{,}375$$

which is $8,375, or $77,750 − $69,375, *less* than the net profit when the uncertainty has been resolved. Recall that risk-averse investors are typically willing to pay a premium for the reduction in risk. In this case, they are faced with a lower expected income and a higher rate relative to the certainty case. Thus, the reduction in risk results in a higher profit because of the curvature within the tax schedule.

If you could hedge your risk for $7,000, would you do it? You would if you were risk averse. The manufacturing firm could sell French franc futures contracts and hedge its risk. This strategy would definitely be attractive if the hedge cost less than $8,375 (the tax savings). This hedging might even be attractive if it cost more than $8,375 because of the reduction in risk.

The tax benefit from financial engineering will increase if the tax schedule becomes more convex or the variability of pretax profits increases. Financial engineering can also be used to shift income from one year to another, as well as from one country to another, to get additional tax benefits. Thus, financial engineering provides added flexibility to a firm's management.

PRACTICE BOX

Problem

a. Using the tax schedule in Exhibit 25-5, assume that pretax profits are expected to be $50,000 or $150,000 with equal probability based on adverse or favorable moves in exchange rates. Compute the expected after-tax profits, and compare this result with the example in the text. If the uncertainty could be hedged costlessly, how much gain would there be in expected value?

b. Explain how the results in this problem would change if the tax rate were a flat 33% percent.

Solution

a. Based on the data in Exhibit 25-5, we can determine the following:

	Adverse Move in Rates	Favorable Move in Rates	Hedged Position
Pretax profits	$50,000	$150,000	$100,000
Taxes[a]	7,500[b]	41,750[c]	22,250[d]
Net profit	42,500	108,250	77,750

a. See Exhibit 25-5.

b. $7,500; see Exhibit 25-5, Row 2.

c. $41,750 = $22,250 + 0.39($150,000 − $100,000); see Exhibit 25-5, row 4.

d. $22,250; see Exhibit 25-5, Row 4.

From this table we can calculate the expected net profit without any hedging as follows:

$$\text{Expected Net Profit} = (\tfrac{1}{2})\$42,500 + (\tfrac{1}{2})\$108,250 = \$75,375$$

which is only $2,375, or $77,750 − $75,375, *less* than the net profit when the uncertainty has been resolved. Recall that for the more volatile case of either $0 or $200,000, the increase in expected net profits when hedging was $8,375. Hence, we see that as the volatility of pretax profits declines, so does the benefit of hedging. Thus, there is a direct relationship between the volatility of pretax profits and the benefits of hedging.

b. Based on a flat 33% tax rate, we find the following:

	Adverse Move in Rates	Favorable Move in Rates	Hedged Position
Pretax profits	$50,000	$150,000	$100,000
Taxes[a]	16,500[a]	49,500	33,000
Net profit	33,500	100,500	67,000

a. $16,500 = $50,000(0.33).

(continued)

From this table we can calculate the expected net profit without any hedging as follows:

$$\text{Expected Net Profit} = (\tfrac{1}{2})\$33,500 + (\tfrac{1}{2})\$100,500 = \$67,000$$

which is exactly the same as the net profit when the uncertainty has been resolved. Hence, there are no tax benefits to hedging with a flat tax rate.

NO TRANSACTION COSTS

Financial engineering can reduce a firm's expected transaction costs. Transaction costs here include any expenses related to acquiring and maintaining a firm's financial structure. For example, a firm that has a significant amount of debt may benefit from reducing the variability of its profits, which in turn reduces the transaction costs involved if financial distress occurs. Consider the preceding example, where the firm may earn either $200,000 or $0, depending on foreign exchange rate movements. If the firm had an additional $50,000 in interest expense, then the outcomes would be $150,000 or −$50,000. If an adverse move in foreign exchange rates occurred, the firm would experience financial distress.

When a firm experiences financial distress, it may lose valuable employees, suppliers will be reluctant to extend credit, and customers will be skeptical about the firm's ability to support its products over the long run. In addition, the firm may incur many kinds of additional costs, such as legal fees and other professional fees. Hence, managing the financial risk with derivative securities can greatly reduce the likelihood of financial distress and hence avoid these transaction costs.

Recall the example of Magma Copper Company given in Exhibit 25-1. The use of copper interest-indexed bonds reduced the probability of incurring transaction costs related to financial distress. Symmetric strategies using forwards, futures, and swaps, as well as asymmetric strategies using options, can be used to protect the earnings of a corporation. For example, Federal Express Corporation may use fuel options to hedge against rising petroleum prices. This strategy will reduce the likelihood that Federal Express will default on its financial obligations.

FIXED INVESTMENT POLICY

In many cases, financial engineering can be used to expand the set of investment opportunities available to a firm. For example, if a firm is exposed to considerable financial risk, such as commodity price risk, lenders will typically place restrictions on the amount of risk to which the firm can be exposed. If the firm hedges the commodity price risk, lenders will allow the firm to engage in more business, which in turn will enhance the firm's profitability. Thus, by using financial engineering tools, the firm increases its future investment opportunities.

Many firms are able to greatly expand their international trade with financial engineering strategies. For example, a small aluminum wire manufacturer in the

United States could expand its sales if it were able to make forward delivery commitments that were priced in a foreign currency. The ability to manage foreign exchange risk opens many new markets to a firm that is not able to tolerate large amounts of such risk and, thus, must have rigid currency risk management policies.

25.3 SWAPS

Swaps are a recent innovation in financial risk management. A **swap** is a contract between two **counterparties** (the two sides of a swap) who agree to exchange payments based on the value of one asset in exchange for a payment based on the value of another asset. A simplified example would be two bondholders—one holding a floating-rate bond and the other holding a fixed-rate bond—who agree to exchange coupon payments over the life of the bonds.

The three major types of swaps are interest rate swaps, currency swaps, and commodity swaps. Most swaps are cash settled. For interest rate swaps, the exchange of cash payments is based on the level of interest rates. For currency swaps, the exchange of cash payments is based on the level of foreign exchange rates. For commodity swaps, the exchange of cash payments is based on the level of commodity prices.

25.3.1 Interest Rate Swaps

To explain how swaps work, we examine an interest rate swap in detail and then examine how to use interest rate swaps to manage interest rate risk. In an **interest rate swap,** the counterparties exchange interest payments based on specified interest rates. For example, in an interest rate swap, one counterparty typically exchanges fixed-rate interest payments for floating-rate interest payments. This particular swap is called a **fixed for floating swap** (or a **plain vanilla swap**). The two parties in a fixed for floating swap are the **receive fixed counterparty** and the **receive floating counterparty.** The receive fixed counterparty receives payments based on the fixed rate and makes payments based on the floating rate (pay floating). The receive floating counterparty receives payments based on the floating rate and makes payments based on the fixed rate (pay fixed).

For the receive fixed counterparty, the cash exchanged is computed as follows:[7]

$$
\begin{array}{lcl}
\text{Payment} & = & \text{Payment Based on} \quad - \quad \text{Payment Based on} \\
\text{(Receipt)} & & \text{the Floating Rate} \qquad\quad \text{the Fixed Rate} \\
& = & r_{fl}(NP)(t/360) \quad\; - \quad r_{fx}(NP)(t/360)
\end{array}
$$

where r_{fl} denotes the floating rate (which typically is the London Interbank Offer Rate, or LIBOR), r_{fx} denotes the fixed rate, t is the number of days during which

---

7. LIBOR is based on a 360-day year and an actual day count, which we assume here is 180 days. For credit risk reasons, only the net cash flows are exchanged rather than the receive fixed counterparty's paying at 8% and the receive floating counterparty's paying at 7%.

interest accrues (for example, for a semiannual paying swap, $t = 180$), and NP is the **notional principal** (the amount on which the dollar interest calculation is made). For example, if you had a $1,000 loan at 5%, your annual interest payment would be $50, or $0.05 \cdot \$1,000$. With swap payments, the notional principal is equivalent to the loan amount. We can rearrange the above expression as

$$\text{Payment (Receipt)} = (r_{fl} - r_{fx})(NP)(t/360)$$

Hence, when the floating rate exceeds the fixed rate, the receive fixed counterparty has to pay. When the fixed rate exceeds the floating rate, the receive fixed counterparty receives a payment.

For example, a 3-year LIBOR-based swap will have six future payments (one at the end of each semiannual period). If the fixed rate is 7% and the notional principal is $1,000,000, then the future cash flows will depend on the difference between 7% and the current LIBOR rate. For example, if after six months the LIBOR rate is 8%, then the receive fixed counterparty must pay the receive floating counterparty $5,000 [$5,000 = (0.08 − 0.07)$1,000,000(180/360)]. Connecting Theory to Practice 25.2 discusses the motivation for using swaps, along with some of the issues surrounding them. For example, interest rate swaps can be used to realign risks so that all participants are better off or are unaffected. After the rate swap, the hamburger franchisee has, in essence, the fixed-rate loan he desired; the Chicago commercial bank is unaffected; Exim Japan has, in essence, the floating-rate loan it desired; and the insurance company is unaffected.

CONNECTING THEORY TO PRACTICE 25.2

LET'S SWAP

A hamburger franchisee gets his capital from a commercial bank in Chicago, where he can borrow only at a floating rate (say, prime plus 1%) because the bank simply can't risk loading up its balance sheet with any assets of longer duration than 90 days. Why? Because the bank's liabilities—checking accounts, for example—are of very short duration. A checking customer does not want to be told that he has to wait five years for his paycheck to clear.

The restaurateur, meanwhile, would much prefer the safety of a fixed rate over the next five years, even though the longer-term loan will cost him plenty. Indeed, the yield curve is so steep these days that seven-year Treasury notes yield percentage points more than six-month T-bills. That steepness translates immediately into a similar yield curve for the restaurant owner: He's going to pay a certain spread over the relevant Treasury in any event. He's willing to pay the extra points of interest to avoid the risk that the prime will spike up to 15% and bankrupt him.

Now add two more players to the drama: a bond issuer and an insurance company.

(continued)

The bond issuer might be Export-Import Bank of Japan. Its size and prime credit quality give it access to a credit market the restaurant owner doesn't have, namely, publicly traded seven-year notes. The notes are fixed-rate because that's what Exim Japan lenders—pension funds and insurance companies, for the most part—want. Exim Japan's treasurer, however, is willing to take a chance on floating rates. After all, this company is not going to be bankrupted by a sudden jump in the prime, and the yield curve is so abnormally steep that borrowing at the short end is irresistible for borrowers who can stomach the risk.

Solution: rate swaps, mediated by banks or securities firms. In a rate swap, no principal changes hands, just exposures to the yield curve. The hamburger outlet, in effect, picks up Exim Japan's obligation to pay a fixed rate over seven years, while Exim Japan assumes the hamburger outlet's floating-rate exposure. No risk of principal is involved since the players are swapping only streams of interest.

Source: Robert Lenzner and William Heuslein, "The Age of Digital Capitalism," *Forbes,* March 19, 1993, pp. 62–72. Reprinted by permission of *Forbes* magazine © Forbes Inc., 1993.

MAKING THE CONNECTION

The excerpt describes two borrowers: the hamburger franchisee (HF) and the Export-Import Bank of Japan (EI). HF is borrowing at a floating rate and would rather have a fixed rate, whereas EI is borrowing at a fixed rate and would rather have a floating rate. The following diagram illustrates the interest payments of these two firms, where CB denotes the Chicago bank and IC denotes the insurance company:

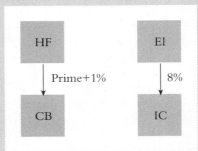

1. HF borrows from CB at a floating rate but wants to borrow at a fixed rate.
2. EI borrows from IC at a fixed rate but wants to borrow at a floating rate.

Now suppose an investment bank (IB) offers a receive floating and pay fixed swap to HF and a receive fixed and pay floating swap to EI. Of course,

(continued)

the investment bank would want to be compensated for its efforts. The resulting cash flows could look something like the following diagram, where IB denotes the investment bank:

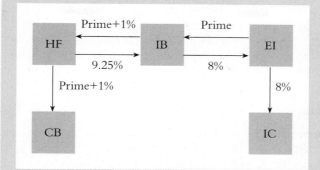

HF and EI swap with the investment bank.

Cash flows to CB and IC are unaffected.

After the swap, HF is essentially paying the fixed rate, because the prime + 1% paid to the CB is received from IB. EI is essentially paying the floating rate, because the 8% paid to IC is received from IB. Finally, IB is making 25 basis points (0.25%), because it gains 1.25% (9.25% − 8%) on the fixed side and loses 1% on the floating side.

In this case, the Chicago commercial bank may be losing out on an opportunity. Its client, the hamburger franchisee, desires, and thus is willing to pay a premium for, a fixed-rate loan. Thus, the bank could generate more profits by making a fixed-rate loan to the franchisee and using interest rate swaps to convert these assets to floating-rate assets.

Swaps, like futures contracts, are a derivative security, but there are three major differences. First, futures contracts involve only one future transaction, whereas swaps typically have several future transactions. Second, futures contracts are typically short term, whereas swaps tend to extend over several years. Hence, futures are used to hedge a single risk exposure over a short time period, whereas swaps are used to hedge multiple exposures over a longer time period. Finally, unlike futures, swaps are typically not mark to market. This lack of marking to market results in swaps' having more credit risk than futures contracts.

25.3.2 Currency Swaps

A **currency swap** requires the exchange of different currencies. The first currency swap occurred in August 1981, between IBM and the World Bank. The details of a currency swap are similar to those of an interest rate swap, except the future exchanges are different currencies.

For example, suppose British Petroleum (BP) expects to receive $900,000 from U.S. sales each quarter for the next 2 years. BP would like to hedge this foreign exchange exposure, but exchange-traded futures contracts do not extend 2 years into the future. BP might find a company such as PepsiCo (PC) that has United Kingdom sales and is headquartered in the United States. PepsiCo would like to convert its U.K. pounds into U.S. dollars. A currency swap could hedge the foreign exchange risk for both parties. Specifically, based on current foreign exchange market conditions, a currency swap could be developed in which BP agrees to swap with PC $900,000 for £600,000 each quarter for the next 2 years. Thus, both British Petroleum and PepsiCo have locked in an exchange rate of $1.5/£ ($900,000/£600,000).

25.3.3 Commodity Swaps

A **commodity swap** requires the exchange of cash based on the value of a specific commodity at specified points in the future. For example, a 3-year crude oil swap with quarterly payments would have twelve (4 quarters · 3 years) cash exchanges. If the contract price in the swap for crude oil was $20 per barrel, then the cash exchange would be the difference between the current price of crude oil and $20. If crude oil was selling for $25 per barrel at a quarterly payment, then one counterparty would receive $5 ($25 − $20) per barrel from the other counterparty.

Another example is the jet fuel price risk that airlines face. When jet fuel prices rise, there is a lag in the airline's ability to pass this higher cost on to passengers in the form of higher ticket prices. Hence, airlines need a security that will be useful in managing future jet fuel purchases. Commodity swaps fulfill this need. Airlines may use jet fuel swaps to lock in their future purchase price of fuel, thus providing stability to their costs. Jet fuel suppliers like commodity swaps because these swaps allow them to lock in a fixed sales price.

Connecting Theory to Practice 25.3 further illustrates a commodity swap. The producer benefits because the sales price uncertainty is eliminated. The refiner benefits because the purchase price uncertainty is eliminated. Thus, the commodity swap helps both producers and refiners better manage their commodity price risk.

CONNECTING THEORY TO PRACTICE 25.3

BIG-STAKES HEDGE STARTS BRANCHING OUT

Commodity swaps, a little-known form of commodity trading for big-stakes players in oil and metals, are burgeoning following the Commodity Futures Trading Commission's [CFTC's] decision not to regulate these off-exchange transactions.

The swaps, which involve the exchange of money and not actual shipments of oil or metal, are designed to neutralize the uncertainties of volatile prices for businesses that produce or use commodities. Swaps are now being written on a widening range of commodities including oil and oil products, as well as gold and base metals such as copper, zinc and aluminum.

(continued)

Jack Cogen, vice president of risk management at Chase Manhattan Bank, says the total value of commodity swaps outstanding now is probably no more than $3 billion, but he predicts the market will grow tenfold over the next few years.

Mr. Yeres [former counsel to the chairman of the CFTC and a partner at Baer Marks & Upham in New York] thinks the commodity-swap market is taking off fast in part because of trading sophistication that has built up in the past five years in the much bigger swap markets for interest rates and currencies. According to industry statistics, about $1 trillion in interest-rate swaps and $317 billion in currency swaps were outstanding at the end of 1988. About 60,000 separate swaps were involved.

Source: Stanley W. Angrist, "Big-Stakes Hedge Starts Branching Out," *Wall Street Journal*, September 26, 1989, p. C1. Reprinted by permission of *The Wall Street Journal*, © 1989 Dow Jones & Co., Inc. All Rights Reserved Worldwide.

MAKING THE CONNECTION

Corporations more frequently are using complex derivative securities to manage their exposure to changes in commodity prices. Although the commodity swap market is small compared with the interest rate swap market and the currency swap market, many believe that it will grow in the future. Commodity swaps are useful tools in managing the risks that corporations face. According to the ISDA (International Swap and Derivatives Association) report for the first half of 1996, the total volume of swaps outstanding in June 1996 was $15.58 trillion in interest swaps and $1.29 trillion in currency swaps.

25.4 RECENT FINANCIAL ENGINEERING INNOVATIONS

Innovations in managing financial risk have been introduced at a rapid pace. In the past, financial risk management depended on available financial opportunities. Today, financial institutions stand ready to offer almost any conceivable opportunity a client may find desirable. Thus, in the assessment of financial strategies to manage risk, the availability of specific financial vehicles is no longer a consideration. In the future, innovative strategies will determine available financial opportunities. This section briefly reviews some of the recent innovations.

Many recently introduced innovative products are related to swaps. In **amortizing swaps,** the notional principal is amortized (reduced) over the life of the swap. Many loans are amortized. Alternatively, in **step-up swaps,** the notional principal is increased over the swap. This unusual variation is applicable to banks with interest rate risk that increases with longer maturities. There are many other variations on swap structures. The demand for exotic swap contracts produces the supply of exotic securities.

Other innovations included caps, floors, and collars. A **cap** is an option-based instrument that sets a ceiling on the impact of a risk variable. For example, an interest rate cap will set a ceiling on the losses incurred if a firm issues a floating-rate loan. Specifically, the cap buyer receives money when rates are up (offsetting losses on a floating-rate loan).

A **floor** is an option-based instrument that sets a minimum on the impact of a risk variable. For example, an interest rate floor will set a floor on the interest paid for an investor who holds a floating-rate bond. Specifically, the floor buyer receives money when rates are down (offsetting losses from holding a floating-rate bond).

A **collar** is a combination of a cap and a floor. For example, a firm that issues a floating-rate loan could enter a collar and receive the benefit of having set a ceiling on rates at the cost of setting a floor on rates. One benefit of collars is that they can be designed to require no initial outlay. Caps and floors both require the payment of an initial premium in a similar way to option contracts.

As the innovation process continues, an increased array of financial vehicles will no doubt be offered. Therefore, it is essential for people involved in investments to have a solid understanding of these financial vehicles.

25.5 THE VALUE AT RISK (VAR)

The Basel Committee on Banking Supervision established rules for risk management that would serve as the foundation for market risk regulation. After long discussions, on January 1, 1998, proposals for setting the capital requirements of banks finally were passed. A host of other nations have since adopted the Basel Committee's recommendations. Basically, the Basel rules aim to tell banks how much equity they should hold in order to face potential losses. This new type of risk management for banks (which can be applied to any other firm) is called value at risk, now well known as *VaR*. Banks still have the option of using their own internal market risk models (that is, value at risk models or a standard model that typically requires higher capital). The VaR defines the regulatory minimum capital that should be held against trading losses. These new regulatory requirements may induce banks to employ derivatives and other new financial tools to help them comply.

The VaR is a value in dollars at which there is a probability of, say, 1% that the bank's trading loss will be greater than or equal to this value. This possible loss corresponds to ten business days. Thus, the VaR is a function of the predetermined probability.

Exhibit 25-7 illustrates the VaR value at a confidence level of 1%. Suppose that the bank's ten business days' trading profit/loss in millions of dollars is estimated to be between −$10 million and +$100 million, as illustrated in the exhibit. Suppose also that there is 1% probability that the trading loss for ten business days will be $5 million or more (see Exhibit 25.7). Then the 1% VaR is $5 million. We can say with 99% confidence level that the bank will not lose more than $5 million. According to the Basel decision, a bank should hold equity of at least 3 times the ten days'

**EXHIBIT 25-7
The VaR Value
at a Confidence
Level of 1%**

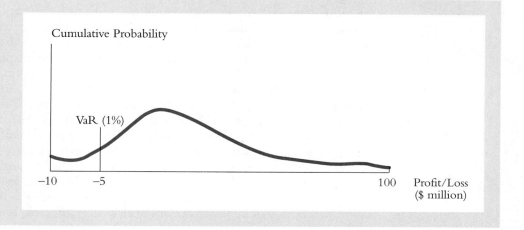

VaR—in this example, at least \$15 (= 5 · 3) million. This is known as the Basel "multiplication factor."[8]

If the distribution of daily trading losses and profits is known, the VaR can be determined easily. However, in practice it is very difficult to estimate this distribution. There are two popular approaches to the estimate: the variance-covariance approach and the historical simulation approach.

The variance-covariance approach relies on the assumption that the returns on financial assets and liabilities follow a multivariate normal distribution. The main drawback of this approach is that distributions of returns are not normal, because in general, they have fatter tails than the tails of the normal distribution. (Furthermore, a normal distribution rate of return is defined from minus infinity to plus infinity, but actual rates of return cannot be smaller than −100%, a case where the asset price drops to zero.) Also, derivatives cannot be analyzed with normal distribution, because the rate of return on derivatives is certainly not normal. Another problem has to do with the difficulty in estimating the variances and covariances of the trading losses and profits induced by the various actions the bank takes.

The historical simulation approach is based on the actual daily distribution of losses and profits from trading. Hence, this approach does not need to assume a normal distribution of returns. The Basel Committee decided that at least 1 year of daily returns should be included in the simulation. Using this historical distribution and, say, 1% left tail probability, the VaR can be calculated simply as the value at which 1% of the observations (returns) are smaller than this value. The drawbacks of the historical simulation approach is that it strongly depends on the time window selected. For example, when the October 1987, October 1997, and August 1998 crashes are included in this historical data, results may be different than when these three events are not included. In other words, historical data may not properly reflect

---

8. Actually, the capital held against the risk is the maximum of the last VaR and the average VaR in the last six months multiplied by the multiplication factor.

the future returns. Because both the variance-covariance method and the historical simulation method contain possible measurement errors, to be conservative, the Basel Committee decided that the multiplication factor would be at least three.

The Basel requirements may have a direct effect on the investor who invests in a bank's stock. To see this, suppose that a given bank has an optimal equity level and an optimal bundle of activities. By the new regulation and, in particular, by the multiplication factor (which may be too high), the bank has to either change its equity level or change its bundle of activities—actions that lead firms to shift from their optimal positions. These shifts will affect the mean rate of return and beta of the bank's stock, and hence possibly the equilibrium stock price. For example, suppose that the bank decides to hold put options on various assets in order to reduce the left tail of the distribution (which, in turn, will imply that less equity needs to be held). Thus, the bank can use derivatives to comply with the Basel requirements. However, recall that holding options will change the risk-return profile of the bank's stock and hence will affect its mean rate of return and the stock's beta.

SUMMARY

Define financial engineering.   Financial engineering is the design, development, and implementation of innovative financial instruments. In the past, exchange-traded derivative securities determined the potential solutions to risk exposure problems. Today, solutions to risk exposure problems determine the derivative securities created.

Explain how firms benefit from financial engineering. Financial engineering can be potentially beneficial in unique situations, as well as in both efficient and inefficient markets. In inefficient markets, selective hedging (hedging only when it is believed to be profitable) or speculative trading may be profitable. In efficient markets, hedging is useful in specific cases based on taxes, transaction costs, and flexible investment policies.

Describe interest rate, currency, and commodity swaps. Swaps are a recent innovation in financial risk management. The three main types of swaps are interest rate swaps, currency swaps, and commodity swaps. An interest rate swap is a contract between two counterparties who agree to exchange payments at specified points in time, and the payments are based on interest rates. Currency swaps are similar, except payments are based on foreign exchange rates. Commodity swaps also are similar, except payments are based on commodity prices. Swaps are beneficial because they typically have multiple future cash flows over several years. Hence, with one swap contract, organizations can achieve their desired hedge.

Describe how swaps are used to mitigate financial risk. Swap contracts are used to offset an organization's financial risk. For example, a bank that will be adversely affected if interest rates rise over the next 2 years may consider entering receive floating and pay fixed interest rate swaps. That way, the loss to the bank when interest rates rise will be offset by gains on the swap.

Describe recent innovations in instruments used in financial engineering. Swaps are now offered based on variable notional principal, such as amortizing and step-up swaps. Caps, floors, and collars are option-based securities designed to place a ceiling on interest costs (caps), a floor on interest receipts (floors), or both (collars). One of the latest innovations is the VaR, a method used by banks and insurance companies to evaluate the various risks they face and to hold a sufficient capital versus this risk.

CHAPTER AT A GLANCE

1. *Hedging strategies can be classified as symmetric or asymmetric:*

Symmetric Hedging

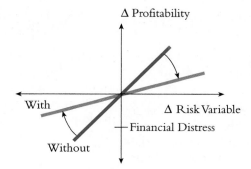

where "With" denotes with symmetric hedging, and "Without" denotes without any hedging.

Asymmetric Hedging

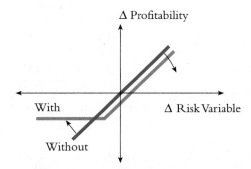

where "With" denotes with asymmetric hedging, and "Without" denotes without any hedging.

2. *Financial engineering is beneficial for the following:*
    a. Unique situations such as underdiversified investors and situations in which there is quantity risk.
    b. Inefficient markets—selective hedging and pure speculation.
    c. Efficient markets—taxes, transaction costs, and flexible investment policies.

KEY TERMS

Amortizing swaps   951

Asymmetric hedging
  strategy   935

Cap   952

Collar   952

Commodity swap   950

Counterparty   946

Currency swap   949

Financial engineering   931

Fixed for floating swap   946   Receive fixed   Selective hedging   940
Floor   952   counterparty   946   Step-up swap   951
Interest rate swap   946   Receive floating   Swap   946
Notional principal   947   counterparty   946   Symmetric hedging
Plain vanilla swap   946   Risk profile   932   strategy   935

REVIEW

25.1 "Because markets are efficient, financial engineering activities are worthless." Evaluate this statement.

25.2 Suppose a new administration decides to alter the corporate tax schedule to make it more "progressive." That is, the higher the pretax income, the higher the percentage tax. In general, how will this influence the benefits of hedging?

25.3 Categorize the following strategies as asymmetric or symmetric hedging strategies. Illustrate your results graphically. (Assume that each strategy is being used as a hedge.)
a. Covered call writing.
b. Protective put buying.
c. Selling futures contracts.
d. Entering a commodity swap.

25.4 Identify and discuss three reasons why a firm may wish to hedge even if the markets are perceived to be efficient.

25.5 Suppose United Parcel Service (UPS) requires its fuel suppliers to guarantee a fuel price for three months in advance. UPS officers realize that the suppliers are charging a large fee (in the form of a markup in price) for this price guarantee. Discuss the various alternatives UPS could pursue to hedge fuel prices.

25.6 How would the risk profile of Magma Copper Company change if it issued 50% debt as fixed-income bonds and 50% debt as bonds linked to copper prices?

25.7 Suppose you own 1,000 shares of AMR, Inc., and are concerned that the current $57 stock price may fall over the next six months. Suppose the six-month $55 strike puts are trading at $4. Show your current risk profile of AMR stock, as well as an asymmetric hedge of the downside risk.

PRACTICE

25.1 When managing financial price risk, investors often ignore "quantity risk." Suppose a financial institution hedges a fixed-rate mortgage portfolio with a receive floating (pay fixed) interest rate swap. The mortgages can be paid off early (which is called *prepayment*). Discuss the risks involved with this type of hedging strategy. What alternative hedging strategies could be pursued?

25.2 Suppose Eastman Kodak (EK) purchases large quantities of silver (used in the production of film). Because the company does not believe the silver market is efficient, it buys excess quantities of silver when prices are low and allows inventories to dramatically decline when silver prices are high. EK also hedges with silver options. Specifically, EK buys out-of-the-money calls when prices are rising to insure a fixed price of silver if prices continue to rise, and it buys out-of-the-money puts when prices are falling to set a floor on the value of the inventory if prices continue to slide. Discuss how the strategic changes in inventory will influence the quantity of options employed.

25.3 The credit risk related to swaps raises many concerns. Discuss, in general, the credit risk of interest rate swaps as compared with a fixed-rate bond (assume you receive fixed and pay floating). Will a distressed counterparty always default on the swap? If not, why not?

25.4 Identify the different securities available to manage interest rate risk. Be sure to categorize the securities as either symmetric or asymmetric.

25.5 Suppose the state of Texas levies a 4.6% tax on every barrel of oil produced in the state. Based on historical data, the Treasury Department in Texas makes the following forecasts:

Likelihood of Outcome	Possible Outcome	Sales Price (per barrel)	Barrels Produced in Texas (in millions)
1/8	Oil crisis	$40	35
5/8	Normal	$20	28
1/4	Overproduction	$15	21

a. Estimate the tax receipts for each possible outcome, as well as the expected tax receipts and the standard deviation of tax receipts.
b. How would your results change if the barrels produced remained the same (at $28 million) for each outcome? Discuss how this quantity risk influences tax receipts.

25.6 Suppose AMR, Inc. (the parent company of American Airlines), is a highly leveraged company that needs to raise $100,000,000 in 15-year bonds. AMR also has an enormous exposure to jet fuel price risk because of American Airlines's consumption of jet fuel. Bond market participants have expressed concern over the default risk engendered by this new bond issue. Design a financially engineered solution to this predicament.

25.7 Suppose a large U.S. stock portfolio manager decides to selectively hedge the entire portfolio over the next year. Specifically, the manager will either hedge the first six months or hedge the last six months. Discuss the possible outcomes of either symmetrically hedging (with index futures con-

tracts) or asymmetrically hedging (with index put options). (Discuss only the cases in which the market is either way up or way down in each six-month period.)

25.8 A major South African gold mine consortium decided to sell gold futures contracts before announcing its decision to sell large quantities of gold in the international markets (which was expected to depress gold prices).
a. Were there any ethical or regulatory violations?
b. Was this a hedge or a speculation? Defend your answer carefully.
c. Suppose the futures price of gold was $350 per ounce, and the consortium hedged 1 million ounces. Discuss the consortium's profits (or losses) if gold fell as expected to $300 or rose to $400 (an unanticipated international crisis).
d. What alternative strategies could the consortium have pursued?

25.9 A U.S. firm that exports its products to the United Kingdom has the following revenues:

If the exchange rate is $1.6/pound, then revenues are zero.
If the exchange rate is $1.8/pound, then revenues are $100,000.

Assume that each event is equally probable. The firm can hedge at the rate of $1.7/pound, ending up with a profit of $50,000 with certainty.
a. If there are no taxes and the firm is risk neutral, would it hedge?
b. If there are no taxes and the firm is risk averse, would it hedge?
c. Suppose the firm is risk neutral and taxes are as follows: for profits up to $50,000, the firm pays 25%, and for profits from $50,000 to $100,000, it pays 40%. Would the firm now hedge? Why or why not? Show the after-tax cash flow with and without hedging. Assume that the revenue is the firm's taxable income.

25.10 Suppose a wheat farmer faced the following outcomes based on weather (as given in Exhibit 25-4):

Wheat Prices	Quantity Harvested (bushels)	Unhedged Profits	Futures P/L	Options P/L	Symmetric Hedge P/L	Asymmetric Hedge P/L
$4.50	60,000	$ 20,000	−$100,000	−$10,000	−$ 80,000	$ 10,000
$3.50	100,000	100,000	0	−10,000	100,000	90,000
$2.50	110,000	25,000	100,000	90,000	125,000	115,000

P/L denotes profits and losses.

Unhedged Profits = Wheat Price · Quantity Harvested − $250,000.

Futures P/L = ($3.50 − Wheat Price)100,000 Bushels.

Options P/L = max(0, $3.50 − Wheat Price)100,000 Bushels − $10,000 (cost of the put option).

Symmetric Hedge P/L = Unhedged Profits + Futures P/L.

Asymmetric Hedge P/L = Unhedged Profits + Options P/L.

The futures and options are for 100,000 bushels. The futures price is $3.50 per bushel, and the strike price of the option is also $3.50. The options cost $10,000.

Suppose there is a probability of ⅓ for each possible wheat price. Which hedging strategy—no hedge, symmetric hedge, or asymmetric hedge—is best according to the mean-variance criterion?

25.11 Assume the state of Texas has the equivalent in revenues of 1 million barrels of oil per year. Also assume that oil will average either $20, $22, or $26 per barrel over the next year with equal probability.
a. The price of a put is $1 per barrel for 1 year with a strike price of $22. Compute the revenues to the state both with and without put options.
b. How will your results in Part a change if Texas decides to hedge only half of its oil price risk?

25.12 Suppose a firm considers a project whose net cash flow is −$50,000 or +$400,000 with equal probability. The fluctuations are caused by possible foreign exchange fluctuations. To finance this project, the firm needs to borrow from a bank. The bank, however, does not approve the loan because of the default risk inherent in the −$50,000 outcome. The bank is willing to approve a loan to finance a project with outcomes of either +$20,000 or +100,000 with equal probability. If both projects require $50,000 to implement, discuss alternatives available to the firm if derivative securities exist to hedge the foreign exchange risk.

25.13 Spiders are shares in the trust that holds all the S&P 500 issues. They trade as regular stocks do on the American Stock Exchange. The following excerpt explains a new financial instrument suggested recently by Morgan Stanley Dean Witter:

This is the sort of customized service that investment banks lavish on big institutional investors: Say you'd like to place a seven-year wager on the Standard & Poor's 500 Index, complete with a warrant that protects your original investment, all packaged in a single security. . . .

Just such an item has emerged from the equity-derivatives workshop of Morgan Stanley Dean Witter, and while nothing fancy to the average rocket-science wizard on any Wall Street desk, the product offers a look at the nifty market plays afforded the big boys but unreplicable by even sophisticated individuals.

Filed with the Securities and Exchange Commission in the form of a debt security to be issued by Morgan Stanley, the product is snappily called Separable Units Mandatorily Exchangeable for Standard & Poor's Depositary Receipts, or Spiders. Spiders are shares in a trust that holds all S&P 500 issues and trades like a regular stock on the American Stock Exchange. The new units consist of a contract to buy a number of Spiders in 2005, coupled with a put warrant guaranteeing the purchase price back in case the S&P is lower at that time than at the issue date.

The client for whom the deal was drawn up is saying, in effect: "Deliver the U.S. stock market to me in seven years' time, complete with any upside, and throw in a

(continued)

money-back guarantee on top of it." Such a flexible investment would be nice to own for anyone who thinks the current market smells a bit like 1973. Early that year, the Dow touched 1000 before a vicious bear market hit; in April 1980 the index was staggering along at 759. . . .

Of course, anyone can hedge or speculate on the index itself by way of CBOE-listed options on the S&P, known as the SPX. But there is no delivery of shares at expiration, only an exchange of cash. And the options can be expensive: The widely traded SPX options are valued at $100 times the index, meaning at current index levels one contract is worth more than $96,000. It takes a pretty big stock portfolio to make that a handy hedge.[9]

a. Suppose that a share of a spider is traded for $96 (that is, 10% of the S&P 500 index, which is 960). You decide to buy 1,000 spiders and 1,000 put options (spiders coupled with put options are the new

asset, as suggested in the excerpt). Use the BSOPM to figure out the price of the put options. Assume that $t = 7$ years, the annual σ of the S&P 500 is 25%, the annual riskless interest rate is 6%, and the spider price is $96.

b. You decide to examine another investment. This time, you buy 1,000 put options and 1,000 call options. Use the put-call parity (see Chapter 24) to determine the call price.

c. Determine your rate of return on these two investments after 7 years if the S&P 500 index will be the following:

(1) 800.

(2) 1100.

For Internet questions visit the Levy Investment Web site at http://levy-invst.swcollege.com.

In a new twist on the growing market for derivative investments, Salomon Inc. sold $60 million of three-year notes whose returns are linked to the stock price of a computer company that had nothing to do with the deal.

The securities, known as Equity-Linked Securities, or ELKs, pay interest of 6.75% annually, but their principal repayment is tied to the stock price of Digital Equipment Corp. The securities, which are listed on the American Stock Exchange, are designed to appeal to yield-oriented investors who are "moderately bullish on Digital," said Larry Bernstein, a Salomon vice president.

The notes allow certain institutional investors, such as income-oriented mutual funds, to sidestep rules that would ordinarily prevent them from buying Digital stock, derivatives experts said. These funds' stated objectives require them to stick with only income-producing invest-

ments, and Digital "pays no dividend," said Emmett Harty, president of the Parallax Group, a Stamford, Conn., derivatives research group.

If Digital's stock price falls, investors will suffer the same damage to principal as if they had owned the stock, but their losses will be somewhat offset by the 6.75% annual interest they receive on the ELKs. If Digital's stock rises, the price appreciation of the securities is capped at 35%—no matter how high the stock goes. Including interest income, that works out to a maximum possible return of about 16% a year over the three years.

A spokesman for Digital took pains to note that the Maynard, Mass., computer maker "has no position" in the offering. "They are free to do what they please," he said of Salomon, adding that although Salomon didn't ask the company's

(continued)

---

9. Michael Santoli, "Playing with Spiders," *Barron's,* January 19, 1998, p. MW15. Reprinted by permission of *Barron's,* © 1998 Dow Jones & Co., Inc. All Rights Reserved Worldwide.

permission to issue the Digital-linked notes, it did make "a courtesy call" to notify them about it in recent months.

While derivatives instruments linked to an unrelated company's stock have occasionally traded privately among big institutional investors, the Salomon ELKs are the first to be publicly traded.

Yesterday, the Salomon ELKs closed at $37.50 on the Amex, unchanged from their initial listing price. Digital's stock rose 37.5 cents a share to $37.875 in New York Stock Exchange composite trading.

Source: "Salomon Debt Links Returns to Stock of Computer Firm," *Wall Street Journal*, July 28, 1993, p. C20. Reprinted by permission of *The Wall Street Journal*, © 1993 Dow Jones & Co., Inc. All Rights Reserved Worldwide.

Questions

1. The bond is sold at $37.50, which is the current price of Digital's stock. Calculate the coupon and the yield to maturity on the assumption that the stock price will be $37.50 at maturity.

2. Calculate the yield to maturity on the assumption that Digital's stock will be $50 at maturity.

3. Investors who invest $10,000 in the bond would like to get back *at least* $8,000 (not including interest) at maturity. What is the minimum stock price to insure this?

4. Explain how the 16% maximum annual rate of return on the ELKs mentioned in the article is obtained. Give a detailed calculation.

5. Salomon can issue a straight bond with a yield to maturity of 7% or the suggested ELKs. Assume that the 7% is obtained with certainty. Suppose the stock price at maturity is estimated to be $87.50 with a probability of ½, $30 with a probability of ¼, or $45 with a probability of ¼. Which bond yield has a better risk-return profile according to the mean-variance rule?

6. Suppose that a few days before maturity the stock price is $50. There is a 100% probability that at maturity the stock price will fall to the range of $45 to $55. What is the maximum price of the ELKs a few days before maturity? What is the minimum price of the ELKs? Explain.

7. Why might the ELKs be attractive to some financial institutions that are bullish on Digital's stock?

8. Suppose you buy the ELKs and add to it a put option (for 3 years) on Digital stock. The strike price is $37.50, and the put costs $5. What is the minimum terminal wealth at maturity on such an investment strategy? What is the minimum rate of return on such a strategy? What is the maximum terminal wealth at maturity? What is the maximum rate of return on such a strategy? What kind of investors might engineer such an investment strategy, and how is it related to the concept of portfolio insurance? Explain your answers to the last two questions. (Hint: Consider pension funds that have a financial commitment to pay a certain sum of money 3 years hence.)

SELECTED REFERENCES

Finnerty, J. D. "Financial Engineering in Corporate Finance: An Overview." *Financial Management* 17(Winter 1988): 14–33.

This article provides an introduction to the potential uses of financial engineering concepts in corporate finance.

Kolman, Joe (ed.). *A Guide to the Derivatives Market.* New York: Derivatives Strategy & Tactics, 1994.

This book presents a series of short articles taken from Derivatives Strategy *that describe several insightful uses of financial engineering.*

SUPPLEMENTAL REFERENCES

Campbell, Tim S., and William A. Kracaw. *Financial Risk Management Fixed Income and Foreign Exchange.* New York: HarperCollins, 1993.

Geanuracos, John, and Bill Millar. *The Power of Financial Innovation.* New York: HarperBusiness, 1991.

Jorion, Phillipe. *Value at Risk: The New Benchmark for Controlling Derivatives Risk.* New York: McGraw-Hill, Inc., 1997.

Kiiskinen, Arto. "Cash for Questions." *Risk* 10, no. 9 (September 1997).

Marshall, John F., and Kenneth R. Kapner. *Understanding Swap Finance.* Dallas, Tex.: South-Western Publishing, 1990.

Singer, Richard. "To VaR, a Sister." *Risk* 10, no. 8 (August 1997).

Smith, Clifford W., Jr., and Charles W. Smithson. *The Handbook of Financial Engineering: New Financial Product Innovations, Applications, and Analyses.* New York: HarperBusiness, 1990.

Smith, Clifford W., Jr., Charles W. Smithson, and D. Sykes Wilford. *Managing Financial Risk.* New York: Harper & Row, 1990.

A

INFORMATION SOURCES

This appendix reviews the major sources of investment information, with addresses and telephone numbers given where relevant. The breadth and depth of available information is astounding.

Major World Markets

Many exchanges provide to new investors information related to the securities they trade. (See Exhibit 1). Public libraries have books that provide additional information on most exchanges. For example, the *NYSE Fact Book* provides information about the New York Stock Exchange.

Governmental Agencies

Governments gather and publish a large quantity of information. For example, the Securities and Exchange Commission (SEC) collects information that companies report to it on a quarterly basis. The SEC is experimenting with electronic access to the firms that file with it. Soon there will be an electronic gateway to a wide range of federal databases of electronically stored public information.

EXHIBIT 1	Major World Exchanges		
Name	**Address**	**Phone**	**Products**
American SE	86 Trinity Pl. New York, NY 10006	(212) 306–1000	Stocks, bonds, option, exotics
Chicago Board OE	400 S. LaSalle St. Chicago, IL 60605	(312) 786–5600	Options
Chicago BOT	141 W. Jackson Blvd Chicago, IL 60604	(312) 435–3500	Futures
Chicago ME	30 S Wacker Dr. Chicago, IL 60606	(312) 930–1000	Futures and options
Commodity Exchange, Inc. (COM EX)	4 World Trade Center New York, NY 10048	(212) 938–2900	Futures and options
National Association of Security Dealers	1735 K Street N.W. Washington, D.C. 20006	(202) 728–8955	Stocks
New York FE	20 Broad St. New York, NY 10005	(212) 656–4949	Futures
New York ME	4 World Trade Center 8th Floor New York, NY 10048	(212) 938–2222	Futures
New York SE	11 Wall Street New York, NY 10005	(212) 656–3000	Stocks

SE = Stock Exchange, BOT = Board of Trade, OE = Options Exchange, ME = Mercantile Exchange, and FE = Futures Exchange.

The Commodities Futures Trading Commission (CFTC) regulates the futures markets and thus is a source of information on the current state of regulation of futures contracts.

The U.S. Council of Economic Advisors publishes the *Economic Report of the President*. The first part of the report contains an analysis of the current status of the United States. The second part provides statistical tables relating to income, employment, and production, which are useful in security analysis. The council also publishes the *Economic Indicators* on a monthly basis for the Joint Economic Committee. This publication contains data and graphs on national output, income, spending, gross national product (GNP), gross domestic product (GDP), costs, profits, unemployment figures, production, and business activity. It also contains new construction data, private housing and vacancy rates, business inventories data, consumer price data, many financial statistics, and some international data.

The Federal Reserve is another source of economic information. It publishes the *Federal Reserve Bulletin, U.S. Financial Data, National Economic Trends,* and other publications that contain useful investment-related information.

The *Federal Reserve Bulletin* is a monthly publication produced by the board of governors of the Federal Reserve System. It contains recent monetary-related statements to the Congress and monetary legal developments and announcements, as well as a host of monetary statistics.

U.S. Financial Data is published weekly by the Research and Public Information Division of the Federal Reserve Bank of St. Louis. It gives weekly highlights concerning such things as unemployment, retail sales, the consumer price index (CPI), and the producer price index (PPI). It also provides data and graphs on loan rates, borrowing figures, savings and money market funds, interest rates, and yields on selected securities.

National Economic Trends is published monthly by the Research and Public Information Division. It provides information on the CPI, the PPI, civilian employment and unemployment rates, payroll employment, industrial production, personal income, retail sales, inventories, GDP, imports and exports, and the federal debt.

The Federal Trade Commission (FTC), in conjunction with the SEC, publishes the *Quarterly Financial Report for Manufacturing Corporations,* which is a good synopsis of the current state of manufacturing in the United States. The Department of Commerce publishes the *Survey of Current Business* and *Business Conditions Digest.* The *Survey of Current Business* is a monthly publication that contains very detailed information on every segment of national income and the GDP. It includes an almost exhaustive review of the business cycle indicators and current business statistics.

Business Conditions Digest is a monthly publication of the U.S. Department of Commerce, Bureau of Economic Analysis. It contains composite indexes, cyclical indicators, national incomes and product data, prices, wages and productivity data, and employment data. It also includes some international comparisons.

The Political Risk Yearbook provides data on international relations, social conditions, sources of power, climate for business, political actors, and banking conditions for every country of the world. It also includes an eighteen-month forecast of regime stability under the most likely regimes, forecasts of turmoil, investment restrictions, trade restrictions, and domestic economic problems.

Associations

Several professional associations provide information as a benefit to their constituents. For example, the Association for Investment Management and Research (AIMR) and the Institute of Chartered Financial Analysts (ICFA) publish the *CFA Digest,* which contains summaries of many recent research articles to help keep executives abreast of innovation.

The American Association of Individual Investors provides a variety of documents useful to individual investors, including a monthly magazine titled *AAII* and an annual publication, *The Individual Investor's Guide to No-Load Mutual Funds.* AAII addresses important topics for the novice investor, as well as some topics of interest to the experienced investor. *The Individual Investor's Guide to No-Load Mutual Funds* provides recent performance information on no-load mutual funds, along with other pertinent information related to mutual funds.

Exhibit 2 provides the names, addresses, telephone numbers, and brief descriptions of the major investment-related associations. Many of these organizations have introductory pamphlets that you may find useful.

Investment Data Sources[1]

Exhibit 3 provides an overview of investment-related data sources. In addition, many magazines cover investment-related issues. For example, *Business Week* has an annual issue on mutual fund performance. *Forbes* covers mutual funds once a year with summary statistics. Other related magazines include *Money, Financial Analysts Journal, Journal of Portfolio Management, Institutional Investor,* and *Fortune.*

Brokerage firms also generate an enormous amount of information related to investments. Access to this information related to investments. Access to this information requires an account with the firm. Many investors have found it beneficial to have multiple accounts to gain access to the reports of different brokerage firms.

---

1. This information is based primarily on *The Individual Investor's Guide to Investment Information,* published by the American Association of Individual Invsteors, 1990, pp. 22–31.

EXHIBIT 2   **Investment–Related Associations**

Name	Address	Phone	Products
The American College	270 Bryn Mawr Ave. Bryn Mawr, PA 19010	(215) 526-1000	Chartered financial consultant
Association for Investment Management and Research	1633 Broadway Suite 1602 New York, NY 10019	(212) 957-2860	Wide array of information for the analyst
College for Financial Planning	4695 S. Monaco St. Denver, CO 80237	(303) 755-7101	Certified financial planner
Futures Industry Association	2001 Pennsylvania Suite 600 Washington, D.C. 20006	(202) 466-5460	Futures
Institute of Chartered Financial Analysts	P. O. Box 3668 Charlottesville, VA 22903	(804) 977-6600	Ethics, information for the analyst
International Association for Financial Planning	2 Concourse Pkwy. Suite 800 Atlanta, GA 30328	(404) 395-1605	Adherence to a code of ethics
Investor Responsibility Research Center	1755 Massachusetts Ave. N.W. Suite 600 Washington, D.C. 20036	(202) 234-7500	Reports on corporate ethical and social behavior or conduct
Licensed Independent Network of CPA Financial Planners	404 James Robertson Pkwy. Suite 1200, Nashville, TN 37219	(615) 242-7351	Fee-only planners
National Association of Personal Financial Advisors	1130 Lake Cook Rd. Suite 105 Buffalo Grove, IL 60089	(800) 366-2732	Fee-only financial planners
National Association of REITs	1129 20th St. N.W. Suite 705 Washington, D.C. 20036	(202) 785-8717	Information on real estate investment trusts
National Futures Association	200 W. Madison St. Suite 1600 Chicago, IL 60606	(312) 781-1300	Futures
National Insurance Consumer Organization	121 N. Payne St. Alexandria, VA 22314	(703) 549-8050	Information on the insurance industry
North American Securities Administrators Association	555 New Jersey Ave. NW Suite 750 Washington, D.C. 20001	(202) 737-0900	Enforcement of "blue sky" laws pertaining to the sale of securities
Securities Industry Association	120 Broadway New York, NY 10271	(212) 608-1500	Information on the securities industry

EXHIBIT 3   **Investment Data Sources**

Name	Frequency	Investment Data Provided
Barron's	Weekly	"Market Laboratory" statistics on indexes, technical analysis, economic indicators; price, volume, and other security data
Business Conditions Digest	Monthly	Economic and business cycle indicators
Corporate Reports	Quarterly, annually	Individual public firm accounting data that can be obtained directly from firms
Directory of Obsolete Securities	Annually	Help in determining the status of a corporation
Federal Reserve Chart Book	Quarterly	Charts on financial and business statistics
Investor's Daily	Daily	Financial news, detailed security data for technical analysis, information from recent corporate reports
Moody's Bond Record	Monthly	Statistics on corporate and municipal bonds regarding quality, yield, and recent price range
Moody's Dividend Record	Annually, twice-weekly updates	Dividend payment information
Moody's Handbook of Common Stocks	Quarterly	10-year firm statistics, including ratios
Moody's Manuals	Annually, twice-weekly updates	Detailed information about companies and their securities
National Economic Trends	Monthly	Data on macroeconomics, with charts
S&P Bond Guide [a]	Monthly	Quality ratings, yields, and recent prices
S&P Stock Guide	Monthly	Firm statistics, including ratios
S&P Stock Reports	Quarterly	Company descriptions, with accounting data
S&P Corporation Records	Bimonthly	Detailed information about companies and their securities
S&P Industry Surveys	Quarterly	Industry analyses, with some firm-specific information
Stocks, Bonds, Bills & Inflation Yearbook	Annually	Return and inflation statistics on a monthly and annual basis
Value Line Investment Survey: Ratings and Reports and Selection and Opinion	Two volumes, weekly updates	Value Line rating and company information, including beta and future estimates
Wall Street Journal	Daily	Daily news, price information, and summary statistics, including quarterly industry analyses and earnings surprises

a. S&P is Standard & Poor's.

B

AIMR CODE OF ETHICS AND STANDARDS OF PROFESSIONAL CONDUCT

THE CODE OF ETHICS

Members of the Association for Investment Management and Research shall:
- Act with integrity, competence, dignity, and in an ethical manner when dealing with the public, clients, prospects, employers, employees, and fellow members.
- Practice and encourage others to practice in a professional and ethical manner that will reflect credit on members and their profession.
- Strive to maintain and improve their competence and the competence of others in the profession.
- Use reasonable care and exercise independent professional judgment.

STANDARDS OF PROFESSIONAL CONDUCT

Standard I: Fundamental Responsibilities

Members shall:

A. Maintain knowledge of and comply with all applicable laws, rules, and regulations (including AIMR's Code of Ethics and Standards of Professional Conduct) of any government, governmental agency, regulatory organization, licensing agency, or professional association governing the members' professional activities.

B. Not knowingly participate or assist in any violation of such laws, rules, or regulations.

Standard II: Relationships with and Responsibilities to the Profession

A. Use of Professional Designation.

1. Membership in AIMR, the Financial Analyst Federation (FAF), or the Institute of Chartered Financial Analysts (ICFA) may be referenced by members of these organizations only in a dignified and judicious manner. The use of the reference may be accompanied by an accurate explanation of the requirements that have been met to obtain membership in these organizations.

2. Holders of the Chartered Financial Analyst designation may use the professional designation "Chartered Financial Analyst," or the mark "CFA," and are encouraged to do so, but only in a dignified and judicious manner. The use of the designation may be accompanied by an accurate explanation of the requirements that have been met to obtain the designation.

Source: Excerpted with permission from *Standards of Practice Handbook, Seventh Edition*. Copyright 1996, Association for Investment Management and Research, Charlottesville, Va. All Rights Reserved.

3. Candidates may reference their participation in the CFA Program, but the reference must clearly state that an individual is a candidate for the CFA designation and may not imply that the candidate has achieved any type of partial designation.

B. Professional Misconduct. Members shall not engage in any professional conduct involving dishonesty, fraud, deceit, or misrepresentation or commit any act that reflects adversely on their honesty, trustworthiness, or professional competence.

C. Prohibition against Plagiarism. Members shall not copy or use, in substantially the same form as the original, material prepared by another without acknowledging and identifying the name of the author, publisher, or source of such material. Members may use without acknowledgment factual information published by recognized financial and statistical reporting services or similar sources.

Standard III: Relationships with and Responsibilities to the Employer

A. Obligation to Inform Employer of Code and Standards. Members shall:

1. Inform their employer, through their direct supervisor, that they are obligated to comply with the Code and Standards and are subject to disciplinary sanctions for violations thereof.

2. Deliver a copy of the Code and Standards to their employer if the employer does not have a copy.

B. Duty to Employer. Members shall not undertake any independent practice that could result in compensation or other benefit in competition with their employer unless they obtain written consent from both their employer and the persons or entities for whom they undertake independent practice.

C. Disclosure of Conflicts to Employer. Members shall:

1. Disclose to their employer all matters, including beneficial ownership of securities or other investments, that reasonably could be expected to interfere with their duty to their employer or ability to make unbiased and objective recommendations.

2. Comply with any prohibitions on activities imposed by their employer if a conflict of interest exists.

D. Disclosure of Additional Compensation Arrangements. Members shall disclose to their employer in writing all monetary compensation or other benefits that they receive for their services that are in addition to compensation or benefits conferred by a member's employer.

E. Responsibilities of Supervisors. Members with supervisory responsibility, authority, or the ability to influence the conduct of others shall exercise reasonable supervision over those subject to their supervision or authority to prevent any violation of applicable statutes, regulations, or provisions of the Code and Standards. In so doing, members are entitled to rely on reasonable procedures designed to detect and prevent such violations.

Standard IV: Relationships with and Responsibilities to Clients and Prospects

A. Investment Process.

A.1 Reasonable Basis and Representations. Members shall:

a. Exercise diligence and thoroughness in making investment recommendations or in taking investment actions.

    b. Have a reasonable and adequate basis, supported by appropriate research and investigation, for such recommendations or actions.

    c. Make reasonable and diligent efforts to avoid any material misrepresentation in any research report or investment recommendation.

    d. Maintain appropriate records to support the reasonableness of such recommendations or actions.

A.2 Research Reports. Members shall:

    a. Use reasonable judgment regarding the inclusion or exclusion of relevant factors in research reports.

    b. Distinguish between facts and opinions in research reports.

    c. Indicate the basic characteristics of the investment involved when preparing for public distribution a research report that is not directly related to a specific portfolio or client.

A.3 Independence and Objectivity. Members shall use reasonable care and judgment to achieve and maintain independence and objectivity in making investment recommendations or taking investment action.

B. Interactions with Clients and Prospects.

B.1 Fiduciary Duties. In relationships with clients, members shall use particular care in determining applicable fiduciary duty and shall comply with such duty as to those persons and interests to whom the duty is owed. Members must act for the benefit of their clients and place their clients' interests before their own.

B.2 Portfolio Investment Recommendations and Actions. Members shall:

    a. Make a reasonable inquiry into a client's financial situation, investment experience, and investment objectives prior to making any investment recommendations and shall update this information as necessary, but no less frequently than annually, to allow the members to adjust their investment recommendations to reflect changed circumstances.

    b. Consider the appropriateness and suitability of investment recommendations or actions for each portfolio or client. In determining appropriateness and suitability, members shall consider applicable relevant factors, including the needs and circumstances of the portfolio or client, the basic characteristics of the investment involved, and the basic characteristics of the total portfolio. Members shall not make a recommendation unless they reasonably determine that the recommendation is suitable to the client's financial situation, investment experience, and investment objectives.

    c. Distinguish between facts and opinions in the presentation of investment recommendations.

    d. Disclose to clients and prospects the basic format and general principles of the investment process by which securities are selected and portfolios are constructed and shall promptly disclose to clients and prospects any changes that might significantly affect those processes.

B.3 Fair Dealing. Members shall deal fairly and objectively with all clients and prospects when disseminating investment recommendations, disseminating material changes in prior investment recommendations, and taking investment action.

B.4 Priority of Transactions. Transactions for clients and employers shall have priority over transactions in securities or other investments of which a member is the beneficial owner so that such personal transactions do not operate adversely to their clients' or employer's interests. If members make a recommendation regarding the purchase or sale of a security or other investment, they shall give their clients and employer adequate opportunity to act on the recommendation before acting on their own behalf. For purposes of the Code and Standards, a member is a "beneficial owner" if the member has

   a. a direct or indirect pecuniary interest in the securities;

   b. the power to vote or direct the voting of the shares of the securities or investments;

   c. the power to dispose or direct the disposition of the security or investment.

B.5 Preservation of Confidentiality. Members shall preserve the confidentiality of information communicated by clients, prospects, or employers concerning matters within the scope of the client-member, prospect-member, or employer-member relationship unless the member receives information concerning illegal activities on the part of the client, prospect, or employer.

B.6 Prohibition against Misrepresentation. Members shall not make any statements, orally or in writing, that misrepresent

   a. the services that they or their firms are capable of performing;

   b. their qualifications or the qualifications of their firm;

   c. the member's academic or professional credentials.

Members shall not make or imply, orally or in writing, any assurances or guarantees regarding any investment except to communicate accurate information regarding the terms of the investment instrument and the issuer's obligations under the instrument.

B.7 Disclosure of Conflicts to Clients and Prospects. Members shall disclose to their clients and prospects all matters, including beneficial ownership of securities or other investments, that reasonably could be expected to impair the member's ability to make unbiased and objective recommendations.

B.8 Disclosure of Referral Fees. Members shall disclose to clients and prospects any consideration or benefit received by the member or delivered to others for the recommendation of any services to the client or prospect.

Standard V: Relationships with and Responsibilities to the Investing Public

A. Prohibition against Use of Material Nonpublic Information. Members who possess material nonpublic information related to the value of a security shall not trade or cause others to trade in that security if such trading would breach a duty or if the information was misappropriated or relates to a tender offer. If members receive material nonpublic information in confidence, they shall not breach that confidence by trading or causing others to trade in securities to which such information relates. Members shall make reasonable efforts to achieve public dissemination of material nonpublic information disclosed in breach of a duty.

B. Performance Presentation.

1. Members shall not make any statements, orally or in writing, that misrepresent the investment performance that they or their firms have accomplished or can reasonably be expected to achieve.

2. If members communicate individual or firm performance information directly or indirectly to clients or prospective clients, or in a manner intended to be received by clients or prospective clients, members shall make every reasonable effort to assure that such performance information is a fair, accurate, and complete presentation of such performance.

GLOSSARY

A

Abnormal rate of return Returns that are above what we would expect to earn, given the level of risk taken.

Accelerated earnings When the growth rate of earnings is increasing.

Accounting anomalies Trading strategies that generate abnormal returns based on observed accounting numbers.

Active investment strategy An investment strategy in which the portfolio manager actively manages investments by altering the proportions of assets in the portfolio.

Actual margin Initial investment as a percentage of the current market value.

Adjusted rate of return The simple rate of return adjusted for the effects of dividends.

Advance–decline line A measure that compares the number of stocks that rose with the number of stocks that fell.

Advanced estimates The first estimate of GDP released about one month after the measurement period.

Agency risk The risk that managers do not act in the owner's best interest.

Aggressive stock A stock with a beta greater than 1.

Alpha The intercept of a regression line.

American depository receipts (ADRs) Receipts for foreign shares held in a U.S. bank.

American-style option An option that can be exercised early.

Amortizing swaps An interest rate swap where the notional principal declines based on an amortization schedule.

Anomalies Unanticipated events that can offer investors the opportunity of earning abnormal returns.

APT performance index a Performance index based on the APT.

Arbitrage A zero investment portfolio that yields positive future returns.

Arbitrage pricing theory (APT) A linear relationship between expected return and risk derived by assuming that there is no arbitrage profit in the market.

Arithmetic average Figure obtained by adding up the returns of *n* observations and dividing this sum by *n*.

Arithmetic method Adds the rates of return and divides by the number of observations.

Asked price Price at which investors can buy securities.

Asked rate The discount rate at which Treasury bills can be purchased.

Asset Something owned by a business, institution, partnership, or individual that has monetary value.

Asset allocation The proportioning of an investment portfolio among asset classes.

Asymmetric hedging strategy A strategy that insures the risk of loss but does not limit the possibility of gain.

At-the-money An option that would generate no cashflow if exercised now and liquidated.

B

Back test A technique to test for abnormal profits by observing how historical prices behaved in response to some event.

Balance sheet An accounting statement showing the assets, liabilities, and equity of a firm on a specific date.

Bank discount rate The interest rate charged to banks when they borrow directly from the Federal Reserve.

Bank reserves The percentage of deposits that banks must hold in noninterest bearing assets.

Bankers' acceptance Money market security that facilitates international trade.

Bar chart A graph showing price movements over time with high, low, and closing prices.

Basis The difference between the current spot price and the futures price.

Benchmark revisions Revisions to GDP made in July for estimates covering the past three years.

Beta The risk index of an individual's assets and portfolios alike; it is a measure of systematic risk.

Bid price Price at which investors can sell securities.

Bid-asked spread Asked price minus the bid price.

Bid rate The discount rate at which Treasury bills can be sold.

Blue chip stock Stock of a large, financially sound corporation.

Bond A financial contract that typically has a stated maturity and periodic interest payments.

Bond indenture A document detailing the terms of a bond issue.

Breadth Volume of orders above and below current price.

Breadth indicators Measures of overall market strength or weakness.

Broker A person who acts as an intermediary between a buyer or seller and the market.

Broker loan rate *See* Call loan rate.

Budget deficit When a government spends more in a given period than its tax revenues.

Bull spread An option strategy designed to allow investors to profit if prices rise, but limit their losses if prices fall.

Business cycle A period expansion and contraction of aggregate economic activity as measured by real GDP.

Business risk The risk that the firm cannot operate profitably.

C

Callable bonds Bonds that can be repurchased by the issuing corporation at a stated price.

Call loan rate Interest rate charged on margin traders.

Call market Trading only occurs at specified times.

Call option A contract giving the right to buy a specified amount of an underlying asset during some period in the future at a predetermined price; gives an investor the right to buy a specified stock at a specified price on or before a specified date.

Candlestick chart A bar chart that includes the opening price as well as the high, low, and closing prices.

Candlestick line A graphical representation of the open, high, low, and closing prices.

Cap An option-based instrument that sets a ceiling on the impact of a risk variable.

Capital asset pricing model (CAPM) A model describing the relationship between beta and expected return.

Capital gains Profits earned when assets are sold at a higher price than purchased.

Capital market A market for bonds with maturities greater than one year and stocks.

Capital market line (CML) The highest sloped line achievable on the expected return and standard deviation graph.

Capital market security Long-term bonds and stocks.

Cash basis Calculated bond rates of return that ignore the accrued interest.

Cash dividend Payments to common stockholders from the firm that issued the stock.

Cash matching strategy An income immunization strategy that assures future cash needs are supplied.

Cash settled The option buyer receives the intrinsic value of the option at expiration automatically.

Cash settlement The exchange of cash rather than the physical asset in a futures contract.

Certainty When the value of an asset is known with probability 1.

Channel A pattern formed when two parallel lines are drawn on a bar chart, showing the up and down prices.

Characteristic line The linear relationship between an asset and the market portfolio.

Churning Excessive trading for the purpose of generating commissions.

Civilian unemployment rate The number of unemployed persons as a percentage of civilians working or actively seeking work.

Closed-end funds A mutual fund that cannot issue more shares.

Closing transaction A transaction that offsets an asset already held.

Coincident indicators Economic statistics that are supposed to move with the business cycle.

Collar An option-based instrument that sets both a ceiling and a floor on the impact of a risk variable.

Commercial paper Unsecured Notes of corporations, usually issued at a discount.

Commission broker A broker who is paid a fee for each trade that is conducted.

Commodity swap A contract to exchange payments based on a specific commodity price.

Common factor A factor that affects all asset prices, not necessarily at the same magnitude, e.g., interest rate, inflation rate, unemployment rate, and rate of return on the market portfolio.

Common-factor news News that affects all stocks.

Common stock A security representing part ownership of a firm.

Concentration ratio A measure of how much of the industry is dominated by the largest firms.

Conduit Firms that sell pooled mortgages.

Conduit theory Capital gains and ordinary income should not be double taxed with investment companies.

Contingent claim *See* Derivative security.

Contingent immunization An investment strategy designed to accommodate both the desire of bond managers to actively trade and the desire of investors to minimize interest rate risk.

Constant dividend growth model The stock valuation model that assumes that dividends grow at a constant rate.

Continuous market Trading can occur any time the exchange is open.

Contraction The phase of the business cycle after a peak and before a trough.

Conversion premium The value of the option to convert in a bond.

Conversion price Par value divided by the conversion ratio.

Conversion ratio The number of stocks per bond issued when the bond is converted.

Conversion value Intrinsic value of a bond if immediately converted.

Convertible bond Contains an option to convert it into some stock.

Convexity A measure of the curvature of the bond's price-yield relationship, used in price immunization strategies.

Corporate bond Debt securities issued by corporations to finance investment in new plant and equipment.

Corporate governance Method of controlling the corporation.

Correlation A unitless measure of the degree of dependency between two assets.

Cost of carry model A futures pricing model based on the implied cost of owning the underlying asset.

Counterparties The two entities participating in a swap.

Coupon-bearing bond Bonds that pay period interest payments.

Coupon payment The fixed periodic interest payment on bonds.

Coupon yield The promised annual coupon rate.

Covariance A measure of the degree of dependency between two assets.

Covered call writing An option strategy composed of buying a stock and writing a call option. The profit/loss from this strategy corresponds to that in put writing..

Covered position Using options when the underlying asset is already owned.

Credit quality A measure of the likelihood of default; letters are assigned such as AAA, AA, and so forth.

Credit risk The risk that the bond issue's interest or principal will not be paid.

Crossborder bonds Bonds that firms issue in the international market.

Cumulative abnormal rate of return (CAR) The amount of abnormal return accumulated over time.

Cumulative preferred stock Dividends accumulate if they are not paid.

Currency swaps A contract to exchange different currencies on specified dates.

Current yield The stated annual coupon payment divided by the current bond price.

Cyclical stock Stock moves with the business cycle.

D

Date of record The date ownership is assessed for dividends.

Day order Order that expires at the end of the day.

Debentures Unsecured bonds.

Declaration date Date dividend is announced.

Defensive stock A stock with a beta less than 1; moves opposite the business cycle.

Depth When traders are willing to trade at prices above and below the current price.

Derivative security An asset that derives its value from another asset.

Direct method A method of reporting the statement of cash flow that gives the cash receipts and payments.

Discount A closed-end fund trading below NAV, as a percent of NAV.

Discount rate The method of quoting Treasury bill interest rates; the required rate of return, given the riskiness of the stock.

Display rule Requires that limit orders placed by customers and priced better than a specialist's or market maker's quote must be displayed.

Dividend discount model (DDM) Valuation Model based on the present value of cash dividends.

Divisible Assets that you are able to buy small portions of.

Divisor A number used in price-weighted indexes that is adjusted for security changes such as stock splits.

Dollar-weighted average rate of return A method of calculating an average rate of return that takes into account the amount invested in each time period.

Dow theory A technical theory that is based on primary, intermediate, and short-term trends.

Dual listing Security listed on more than one exchange.

Duration The holding period that balances the price effect against the reinvestment effect.

Duration drift The change in duration due to the passage of time.

Duration matching strategy An income immunization strategy that matches asset duration with the duration of the liabilities.

E

Efficient frontier The set of all investment strategies with the highest mean for a given variance.

Efficient market A market in which prices reflect all relevant information about the stock.

Efficient portfolio A portfolio that is not dominated by the m-v rule by any other portfolio.

EMT The theory that all assets are correctly priced and that there are no "bargains" in the market.

EPCoR Equal percentage contribution rule.

Equal percentage contribution rule (EPCoR) By this rule, in the CAPM equilibrium each asset contributes the same percent to the portfolio rate premium as well as to its risk.

Ethics The principles on which the correctness of specific actions are determined.

Eurodollars A deposit denominated in U.S. dollars held in a bank outside of the United States.

European-style option An option that cannot be exercised early.

Event anomalies Trading strategies that generate abnormal returns based on specific events.

Ex-ante value Forecasted rate of return used in estimating statistics.

Excess return or abnormal return Deviation from the return predicted by the CAPM.

Ex-dividend date First day when stockholders no longer receive dividends if stock is purchased.

Execution costs The cost of setting prices.

Exercise Make use of a right available in a contract (e.g., in a put option or a call option).

Exercise price See Strike price.

Exercising Buying or selling assets through an option contract.

Expansion The phase of the business cycle after a trough and before a peak.

Expected return A measure of the average return anticipated on an asset.

Expiration date The date on which the option contract expires.

Ex-post average The historical average rate of return on an asset.

Ex-post rate of return Historical rate of return used in estimating statistics.

F

Face value *See* Par value.

Fallen angels Investment grade bonds that have subsequently been downgraded to a speculative grade.

Family of funds Several different mutual funds offered by the same investment company.

Federal agency bond Government agency bond, such as FNMA.

Federal funds Money market securities facilitating interbank borrowing.

Federal funds rate The interest rate charged to banks when they borrow other banks' excess reserves.

Fiduciary Must act for the benefit of another party.

Financial assets Intangible assets, such as stocks and bonds.

Financial engineering The design, development, and implementation of innovative financial instruments and processes, and the formulation of creative solutions in finance.

Financial risk The risk related to debt.

Financial statement A report that contains basic accounting data which help investors understand the firm's financial history.

Financial statement analysis Analysis of a firm's financial statements to assess the worth of its securities as well as its ability to meet its financial obligations.

Firm anomalies Trading strategies that generate abnormal returns based on firm-specific characteristics.

Firm-specific news News that only affects a specific firm.

First market Exchange-traded securities traded on the exchange.

Fiscal policy Taxation and spending policies by a government designed to achieve GDP growth, relatively full employment, and stable prices.

Fixed for floating swap An interest rate swap where the payments are based on a fixed rate and a floating rate.

Floor An option-based instrument that sets a floor on the impact of a risk variable.

Floor broker A person who handles buying and selling futures contracts for others; brokers who are willing to work for other member firms to assist in the trading process.

Foreign exchange expectations The relationship between the current forward foreign exchange rate and the expected future spot exchange rate.

Forward contract A contract to do something in the future, for example, borrow or lend money.

Forward foreign exchange contract Obligates an investor to deliver a specified quantity of one currency in return for a specified amount of another currency.

Forward foreign exchange rate The exchange rate available today to exchange currency at some specified date in the future.

Forward rate The yield covering a period of time starting in the future.

Fourth market Exchange-traded issues traded directly between buyer and seller.

Frictionless market A market where trading is costless to conduct.

Fundamental analysis Assesses the intrinsic value of a firm; trading strategies are based on the asset's publicly available information.

Futures Commission Merchants (FCMs) People qualified to trade futures contracts.

Futures contract An agreement to make or take delivery of an asset at a later date at a given price; the trading price of a futures contract.

G

GCAPM General capital asset pricing model–a model that allows investors to hold a small number of assets in the portfolio.

General obligation bond Backed only by the municipality.

Geometric average Figure obtained by the product of n observations and years (1 + rates of return), taking the $1/n$ root, and subtracting 1.

Geometric compounding Used when assuming any cash payments are reinvested.

Geometric method Compound rate of return that mimics an investor's actual performance.

Good-till-canceled order (GTC) An order to trade that is effective until canceled.

Gross Domestic Product (GDP) The total of goods and services produced in an economy.

Gross spread Difference between the firm commitment price and the issue price.

Growth stock Stocks from smaller firms having sales and earnings growth in excess of the industry average.

H

Hedge The use of a technique used to limit loss potential.

Hedge ratio The number of stocks to buy or sell with options such that the future portfolio value is risk-free.

High grade Bonds with credit quality of AAA or AA.

Holding period rate The rate of return earned on a bond by holding it for the next period.

Horizon matching strategy An income immunization strategy that cash matches over the next few years and duration matches the rest.

I

Immunization strategies Strategies that seek to neutralize the adverse effects of changes in yield to maturity.

Income immunization strategies Those strategies that insure adequate future cash flow.

Income statement An accounting statement showing the flow of sales, expenses, and earnings during a specified period.

Income stock High-dividend paying stock.

Index funds Passively managed funds that try to mimic a specified index.

Index method Method for calculating rates of return that is based on initial and terminal values.

Indifference curve A curve representing points of indifference for assets having different expected returns and standard deviations.

Indirect method A method of reporting the statement of cash flow that takes net income and through a series of adjustments reconciles it to cash from operations.

Industry allocation The decision as to what proportion to invest in each industry.

Inefficient frontier The set of all investment strategies with the lowest variance (below the minimum variance portfolio).

Inefficient portfolio A portfolio that is dominated by the m-v rule by at least one other portfolio.

Inflation risk The risk related to the purchasing power of an investment.

Information asymmetry Differences in information available to different participants.

Initial margin Initial investment in a margin trade, in percent; money the option writer sends to the OCC to sell the specific options.

Initial public offerings (IPOs) Securities traded in the primary market for the first time.

Interest–rate parity The relationship between the forward foreign exchange rate and nominal interest rates.

Interest rate risk The risk faced by bond investors when market interest rates change.

Interest rate swap A contract to exchange payments based on interest rates.

Interim rate of return The rate of return earned between cash flows.

Intermarket spread swap Speculating on bonds in different markets.

Intermediate trend A trend lasting from 3 weeks to 6 months in price data.

International Fisher relationship The relationship between nominal interest rates and inflation rates in different countries.

In-the-money An option that would generate positive cash flow if exercised now and liquidated.

Intrinsic value The value of the option if immediately exercised or zero, whichever is greater.

Investment Financial capital used in an effort to create more money.

Investment bankers Help firms issue IPOs.

Investment company An organization that pools investors' money and invests it in securities.

Investment grade Bonds rated BBB (or Baa) or above.

Investment policy A written document detailing the objectives and constraints for the investment.

Investment trust A closed-end fund.

J

Jensen's' performance index A performance measure based on the SML.

Junk bonds Very risky, higher coupon bonds; *see also* speculative grade.

L

Lagging indicators Economic statistics that are supposed to move behind the business cycle.

Leading indicators Economic statistics that are supposed to move ahead of the business cycle.

Levered portfolio A portfolio partially financed by borrowing.

Life cycle A discernible pattern over the life of an industry.

Limit order Trade only at a specified price.

Linking method Method for calculating rates of return that multiplies one plus the interim rate of return.

Liquidity preference hypothesis (LPH) A hypothesis stating that longer-term bonds should have a higher yield due to investors' preferences for liquidity.

Liquidity premium The difference between the yield based on the unbiased expectations hypothesis and the actual yield.

Load The fee paid as a sales commission to vendors of mutual funds.

Local A person who trades for his own account in a futures pit.

Local expectations hypothesis (LEH) A hypothesis stating that all similar bonds, except maturity, will have the same holding period rate of return.

Long position An agreement to *take* delivery in the futures market.

Long position in an option Refers to buying options.

M

Maintenance margin The dollar amount that must be kept at the OCC throughout the life of the contract; percentage of the dollar amount of securities that must always be set aside as margin.

Margin call A broker calls for more collateral to be posted.

Margin trading Buying securities, in part, with borrowed money.

Mark to market Taking profits and losses daily on futures contracts.

Market A means by which products are bought and sold.

Market capitalization Market value of all shares outstanding.

Market maker Traders who post the bid and asked prices.

Market microstructure The functional setup of a market.

Market order Trade at the best existing price.

Market portfolio The optimum portfolio with riskless borrowing and lending.

Market segmentations hypothesis (MSH) A hypothesis stating that different maturity bonds trade in separate segmented markets.

Marketable security Securities that are easily bought and sold.

Maturity date *See* Expiration date.

Maximum expected return criterion (MERC) Choosing the asset with the highest expected return.

Maximum return criterion (MRC) Choosing the asset with the highest return.

Mean *See* Expected return.

Mean-variance criterion (MVC) Prefer a higher mean and/or a lower variance.

Mean-variance frontier The set of investment strategies with the lowest variance for all possible means.

Mean-variance set *See* Mean-variance frontier.

Mid-market The price around which the market maker derives the bid and asked prices.

Minimum variance portfolio (MVP) The portfolio with the smallest variance from the mean variance set.

Monetary policy Actions by a central bank to control the supply of money and interest rates that directly influence the financial markets.

Money market A market for bonds with maturities of less than one year.

Money market security Short-term bonds, usually less than 1 year.

Mortgage Collateralized bonds, usually real estate.

Mortgage-backed securities Securities whose value depends on a set of mortgages.

Moving average A method of averaging the most recent past price data.

Multiplier A term used when referring to the P/E ratio as a payback measure.

Municipal bond State and local government securities.

Mutual fund A managed pool of money invested in securities.

N

Naked position Using options without holding to any underlying security.

Negotiable certificates of deposit Large denomination certificates of deposit that can be traded.

Net asset value (NAV) Current market value of securities in fund, less liabilities on a per share basis; intrinsic value of a mutual fund.

Neutral stock A stock with a beta of 1.

No-load fund Mutual fund that does not have any sales commissions.

Nominal yield *See* Coupon yield.

Nonmarketable security Securities that cannot be easily bought and sold.

Normal growth firms Firms whose earnings grow at a constant rate.

Not-held orders (NH) Broker is not held liable if he or she is unable to trade.

Notional principal The basis on which swap interest payments are based, similar to the par value of bonds.

O

Objective probability The true unobservable underlying probability.

Odd lot Orders not in size of 100s.

Open-end fund A mutual fund that can issue more shares.

Open interest The number of futures contracts outstanding at a point in time.

Open market operations U.S. Treasury transactions by the Federal Reserve used to influence bank reserves.

Opening transaction The transaction when the initial position is taken.

Opportunity line Represents portfolios that are achieved by combining different levels of borrowing and lending with a single risky portfolio.

Option A legal contract that gives its holder the right to buy or sell a specified amount of an underlying asset at a fixed price.

Option buyer The owner of the option contract.

Option premium The initial purchase or sales price of an option.

Option writer The person from whom the option buyer purchases the option contract.

Out-of-the-money An option that would generate negative cash flow if exercised now and liquidated.

Over-the-counter market A telephone- and computer-linked network for trading securities.

P

Participating preferred stock Dividends are tied to earnings.

Par value Lump sum paid at maturity.

Passive investment strategy An investment strategy in which the portfolio manager does *not* actively manage investments.

Payoff diagram A graph illustrating the value line or the profit and loss line.

Payment date Date dividend check is mailed.

Peak The top of the business cycle.

Percentage financial statements The balance sheet and income statements converted to percentages.

Performance attribution A means to assess the sources of portfolio performance.

Performance index A risk-adjusted measure of how well a portfolio has performed.

Physical asset (also called **real** or **tangible** assets) Tangible assets, such as precious metals or real estate.

Pit A place where all buying and selling of futures contracts takes place.

Plain vanilla swap *See* Fixed for floating swap.

Point-and-figure chart A graph with x's and o's, used to plot price reversals without consideration of time.

Political risk The possibility that a country will take over a firm.

Portfolio A group of securities that are held together in an effort to achieve some future consumption desire.

Portfolio expected return A weighted average of the individual asset's expected return.

Portfolio insurance A strategy in which the maximum risk of loss is set in advance.

Portfolio variance A complex weighted average of the individual assets' variances and covariances (or correlations).

Preference share Preferred shares that have first claim to preferred dividends.

Preferred habitat hypothesis A hypothesis that suppliers and demanders of funds have a preferred region of the yield curve, but can be induced to move.

Preliminary estimates The second estimate of GDP released about two months after the measurement period.

Premium A closed-end fund trading above NAV, as a percent of NAV.

Price continuity Minimal price changes due to transactions.

Price effect The impact on bond prices when interest rates change.

Price immunization Immunization strategies that focus on the current market value of assets and liabilities.

Price risk The risk that bond prices will fall when interest rates rise.

Primary market Where securities are first sold to the public.

Primary offering *See* Seasoned new issue.

Primary trend Long-term trends lasting 4 to 4½ years in price data.

Principal *See* Par value.

Private placement An issue of securities that is not sold to the public.

Private placement memorandum Necessary information on a private placement.

Program trading Trading at least 15 securities at one time.

Prospectus A legal document containing a business plan and other information for investors regarding IPOs.

Protective put buying A strategy of holding a stock and buying out of the money option on this stock.

Purchasing power parity The relationship between two countries' inflation rates and their foreign exchange rates.

Pure yield pick-up swap Moving to bonds with a higher yield.

Put-call parity (PCP) Establishes the pricing relationship between the underlying security, the risk-free interest rate, call options, and put options.

Put/call ratio A measure based on the volume of put and call option trading.

Put option A contract giving the right to sell a specified amount of an underlying asset during some period in the future at a predetermined price.

Put ratio backspread A complex spread strategy used when one believes the stock price will decline but fears the stock price might rise.

Q

Quantity risk The risk taken when the quantity of an asset to be hedged is uncertain.

Quote rule Rule requiring market makers to publish quotations for any listed security when a quote represents more than 1% of the aggregate trading volume for that security.

R

Rally An overall rise in the stock market or in an individual security.

Random walk A statistical concept where future price changes are unpredictable, not based on prior outcomes.

Rate anticipation swap Positioning a bond portfolio based on the perceived direction of future interest rate moves.

Rate of return Dollar profit divided by investment.

Rating agency A firm that assesses the credit risk of a bond.

Ratio analysis A method used to compare financial trends both between firms and for a given firm over time.

Real asset *See* Physical asset.

Real body On a candlestick line, it is the broad part consisting of the difference between opening and closing prices.

Real rate of return An inflation-adjusted rate of return.

Real GDP The inflation-adjusted measure of GDP.

Realized rate of return Rate of return that has already been earned.

Realized yield The holding period return actually generated from an investment in a bond.

Receive fixed counterparty The counterparty of an interest rate swap receiving payments based on the fixed rate and making payments based on the floating rate.

Receive floating counterparty The counterparty of an interest rate swap receiving payments based on the floating rate and making payments based on the fixed rate.

Recession Typically defined as two consecutive quarters of negative real GDP growth.

Registered competitive traders Members of an exchange who trade for their own account.

Registered equity market maker The title of the AMEX market maker.

Regulated investment company An investment company that satisfies Regulation M of the IRS and avoids taxes on security transactions.

Regulations Rules established by governments for the purpose of identifying unacceptable behavior.

Regulatory risk The risk that governments will change the way a firm may operate.

Reinvestment effect The impact on the reinvestment rate when interest rates change.

Reinvestment rate risk The risk of not being able to reinvest coupon payments at as high an interest rate when rates fall.

Reinvestment risk The risk that future cash flows will be invested at a lower rate.

Relative strength A measure of the price performance of one index against another.

Repurchase agreement Sale of a money market security with an agreement to buy it back at a higher price at a specified time.

Resiliency Speed of new orders when prices change.

Resistance An upper bound on prices due to the quantity of willing sellers at that price level.

Revenue bond Backed by a specific project's income.

Reverse repos The opposite side of a repurchase agreement, where one buys securities with an agreement to sell them at a later day at a specified price.

Revised estimates The third estimate of GDP released about three months after the measurement period.

Risk *See* Uncertainty.

Risk averter Someone who dislikes risk, everything else the same.

Risk neutral Someone who is indifferent about risk.

Risk premium The higher return required to take higher risk.

Risk profile A mapping of the change in value or profits and losses to which an organization has exposure.

Risk seeker Someone who likes to take risk and is even willing to pay for it.

Round lots A stock trade that is a multiple of 100.

S

Scalping Investment bankers buying up the good IPOs.

Seasonal anomalies Trading strategies that generate abnormal returns based solely on the time of year.

Seasoned new issue A new stock offering by a company that has sold stock previously.

Second market OTC trades on the OTC market.

Secondary market Where securities trade after they are issued.

Sector allocation The decision as to what proportion to invest in each sector.

Secured bonds Bonds with collateral backing them.

Securities Exchange Act of 1934 An act that regulates the secondary market, established the SEC, gives the federal government authority to establish a margin, and forbids insider trading.

Security An instrument that signifies an ownership position in a stock or a bond, or rights to ownership by an option.

Security market line (SML) The linear relationship between expected return and beta.

Security selection The decision as to what proportion to invest in each security; the process of determining the securities within each asset class that are most suitable.

Selective hedging Hedging during some time periods and not hedging during other time periods.

Semi-strong form of the EMT Prices reflect all relevant publicly available information.

Sentiment indicator An indicator of traders' opinions about the market.

Separation property *See* Separation theorem.

Separation theorem The decision of the optimal portfolio of risky assets (denoted m) is separate from the actual portfolio of the riskless asset and m.

Settle price An average of the trading prices that occur during the last few minutes of the day.

Shadows The thin lines above and below the real body on a candlestick line.

Sharpe's performance index A performance measure based on the CML.

Short position An agreement to *make delivery* in the futures market.

Short selling Selling borrowed securities.

Short-term trend Trends that last less than 3 weeks that are very erratic.

Simple interest The principal times the rate times the time.

Simple rate of return *See* Holding a period rate.

Single Index Model (SIM) A model by which all rates of return are generated by one factor, e.g., GNP, inflation rate, or unemployment rate. This model dramatically reduces the computation load needed to derive the m-v frontier.

Sinking fund Money set aside to repay a bond principal in the future.

Specialist Appointed market maker on the NYSE.

Speculative Securities that involve a high level of risk.

Speculative grade bond Bonds with credit quality below BBB (or Baa).

Speculative stock Very risky stock.

Spot market A market where trades are made for immediate delivery (or within a few days).

Spot rate The yield to maturity of a zero-coupon bond with some stated maturity.

Spread An option strategy in which the investor holds long and short positions on the same type of option, but the contracts have different expiration dates and exercise prices.

Standard deviation A measure of risk, the square root of the variance.

Standard normal distribution A normal distribution with mean 0 and standard deviation 1.

Statement of cash flow An accounting statement showing the flow of cash through the firm.

Step-up swap An interest rate swap where the notional principal increases based on a predetermined schedule.

Stock split When a company issues more new shares in return for existing shares.

Stop order Order to trade if adverse price movement occurs.

Straddle An option strategy in which the investor buys or sells both puts and calls on the same underlying item with the same exercise price and expiration date.

Strike price The predetermined price to buy or sell within the option contract.

Strong form of the EMT Prices reflect all relevant publicly and privately available information.

Subjective probability One's beliefs regarding the actual underlying probabilities.

Subordinated bonds Bonds that stand behind other bonds in the credit line.

Substitution swap Selling overpriced bonds and buying underpriced bonds.

Supergrowth firms Firms whose earnings grow at a high rate for a period of time.

Support A lower bound on prices due to the quantity of willing buyers at that price level.

Swap A contract to exchange payments of some sort at a future date.

Symmetric hedging strategy A strategy where the risk of loss is eliminated but so is the possibility of gain.

Syndicate A group of investment bankers who participate in an IPO, taking some of the risk.

Systematic risk The part of an asset's variance attributable to the overall market fluctuation; the risk related to overall movements in the market.

T

Tangible asset *See* Physical asset.

Technical analysis The process of identifying trends in historical price data and extending them to the future.

Tender offer An attempt to buy large portions of a publicly held firm.

Term repos Repurchase agreements that have a longer holding period.

Term structure of interest rates *See* Yield curve.

Third market Exchange-listed issues traded off the exchange.

Time value Any option value in excess of intrinsic value.

Time-weighted rate of return Calculating returns that measure how invested wealth would grow.

Top-down approach A security selection approach that starts with asset allocation and works systematically through sector and industry allocation to individual security selection.

Trendline A line drawn on a bar chart to identify current trends.

Treynor's performance index A performance measure based on the CAPM.

Trough The bottom of the business cycle.

Turnover Value of securities purchased (or sold, whichever is less) divided by average NAV, a measure of transaction cost.

U

Unbiased expectations hypothesis (UEH) A hypothesis stating that the current implied forward rate is an unbiased predictor of future spot rates.

Uncertainty When more than one possible outcome could occur.

Underwriters Act as intermediaries between the firm and investors.

Underwriter's discount *See* Gross spread.

Unsystematic risk The part of an asset's variance attributable to the individual firm.

Upstairs market Trades arranged by a network of trading desks, usually large blocks.

Uptick Last price is above previous price.

U.S. Treasury bills Short-term government securities issued at a discount.

U.S. Treasury bonds Over 10 years when initially issued, government securities.

U.S. Treasury notes 2 to 10 years when initially issued, government securities.

Utility A measure of an investor's level of "satisfaction" or preference.

V

Variance A measure of risk or the dispersion around the mean.

W

Weak form of the EMT Prices reflect information revealed by historical market-based data.

Wealth effect Investors reacting to interest rates' impact on bond portfolio value.

Writer *See* Option writer.

Y

Yield curve The relationship between yield to maturity and maturity for similar bonds.

Yield to call The internal rate of return on a bond when it is assumed to be called on the first call date.

Yield to maturity The internal rate of return on a bond when held to maturity.

Z

Zero beta An asset with zero beta has a zero correlation with the market portfolio. The expected return on such an asset in equilibrium equals the risk-free interest rate.

Zero-coupon bond Pays no interest and trades at a discount.

Zero-plus tick Last price is same as previous trading price, which was an uptick.

NAME INDEX

A

Abel, Andrew B., 740, 763
Acuff, Marshall, 29
Addison, Andrew L., 322, 450
Alger, Kevin, 94
Allen, Gregory C., 553
Allen, Paul, 445
Altman, Edward I., 582, 586, 587, 601, 602
Amihud, Y., 327
Anderson, Seth C., 489, 493, 494, 519, 520
Angrist, Stanley W., 827, 953
Ankrim, Ernest M., 553
Applegate, Jeffrey, 679
Ariel, Robert A., 448
Arrow, K. J., 214
Arshadi, Nasser, 136
Asikoglu, Yaman, 711
Asquith, Paul, 602

Atanasov, Maria, 145, 213
Attinger, Bill, 654
Ayling, David E., 23, 104

B

Bachelier, Louis, 423, 448, 842
Bae, Sung C., 118
Bailey, Jeffery V., 540
Baker, David, 94
Baker, H. Kent, 144, 763
Ball, R., 427, 448
Ballmer, Steve, 445
Balog, James, 763
Bansal, Ravi, 368
Barber, Joel R., 654
Barnard, Doug, 210
Barron, Robert A., 140
Bary, Andrew, 44, 551, 792
Baumol, William, 66

Bavishi, Vinod B., 406, 804
Beard, T. Randolph, 489
Becker, Skip, 872
Beebower, Gilbert, 445
Benjamin, Jeff, 499
Benos, Alexandros, 117
Berenbeim, Ronald E., 131, 144
Bernanke, Ben S., 740, 763
Bernard, Victor L., 428, 448
Berner, Richard, 734, 735
Bernstein, Larry, 961
Bernstein, Leopold A., 767, 773, 803
Bernstein, Richard, 730
Berry, Michael A., 362, 368
Berton, Lee, 770
Best, Peter, 602
Bhardwaj, R. K., 448
Bierwag, Gerald O., 653, 654
Bivins, Senator Teel, 935

Black, Fischer, 405, 763, 873, 885, 895, 902, 903
Blake, Christopher R., 537, 554
Block, Frank E., 601, 784, 806
Blume, Marshall E., 423, 602
Bogle, John C., 538, 553
Bookstaber, Richard M., 874
Booth, Richard A., 137
Born, Jeffery A., 489, 493, 494, 519, 520
Bower, Richard S., 692
Bradford, C. Steven, 124
Bradley, Edward S., 144
Brauer, Greggory A., 520
Brealey, Richard A., 533, 554
Breyer, Justice Stephen G., 416
Brinson, Gary, 445
Brooks, L. D., 448

Brooks, Robert, 541, 569, 602, 654
Broske, Mary Stearns, 580
Brown, David P., 431, 481
Bruchey, Stuart, 84
Buffett, Warren, 408, 751, 799
Burke, James, 130
Burmeister, Edwin, 362, 368
Burton, Peter, 87
Byrne, Alistair, 602
Byrum, Mike, 288

C

Caires, Bryan de, 23
Campbell, Tim S., 961
Canelo, Peter, 464–465
Cannon, Heather, 695
Cappiello, Frank, 519
Carlson, John, 117
Carnes, W. Stansbury, 737, 739, 744, 763
Casey, John L., 144
Cavanagh, Gerald F., 120,144
Chan, K. C., 448
Chance, Don M., 507, 520, 873, 895
Chang, Eric C., 520
Chen, Nai–fu, 448
Cherry, Michael A., 602
Chiras, D., 902
Chrabaszewski, Rick, 119
Chriss, N., 874
Christensen, B. J., 327
Christensen, Peter Ove, 654
Chugh, Lal C., 706, 707, 708
Ciccarone, Richard, 580
Clark, Don, 445
Clark, Stephen E., 337
Clarke, Roger G., 481
Clash, James M., 521, 713, 728
Clasing, Henry K. Jr, 336
Clements, Jonathan, 370
Clough, Charles, 555
Cochrane, John H., 448
Cogen, Jack, 951
Coggin, T. Daniel, 283
Cohen, A., 214
Cohen, Abby, 750
Cohen, Laurie P., 125
Connolly, Robert A., 448
Cook, Timothy Q., 66
Copper, Mark L., 654

Cornell, Bradfors, 602
Corrigan, E. Gerald, 127
Cottle, Sidney, 601, 784, 803
Cowles, A., 431, 448
Cox, John C., 874
Crawford, Peggy J., 493, 520
Crouhy, Michael, 118
Culp, Michael, 656, 657
Cumby, Robert E., 536, 554

D

Danielson, Morris G., 693
Dattatreya, Ravi E., 874
de Caires, Bryan, 108
Deng Xiao–ping, 491
Dennis, Michael C., 803
Dennis, Robert, 580
Dent, W. Douglas, 519
diBartolomeo, Dan, 520
Dodd, David, 427, 730, 799
Doherty, Jaqueline, 598
Donnelly, Barbara, 704
Donnelly, Terence, 620
Dorfman, John R., 119, 407, 443
Dow, Charles, 463, 464
Downes, John, 24, 485
Duen Li Kao, 601
Dybrig, Philip H., 654

E

Eatwell, John, 24, 117, 448
Edwards, Gary, 129
Edwards, Robert D., 452, 481
Ehrbar, Al, 688
Eichholtz, Piet, 405
Einhorn, Steven, 686–687
Eiteman, David K., 189, 405
Elton, Edwin J., 537, 554
Erb, Claude, 24
Ercan, Metin R., 711
Estep, T., 711
Eun, Cheol S., 536–537, 554
Evans, Frank C., 803
Evans, Richard, 465
Eyssell, Thomas H., 136

F

Fabozzi, D., 66
Fabozzi, Frank J., 66, 80, 117, 602, 653, 874

Fabozzi, T. Dessa, 653
Fama, Eugene F., 326–327, 408, 421–422, 423, 427, 428, 434, 435, 448, 453, 481, 569, 602, 706, 747, 763, 788
Farrell, James L., Jr., 731
Ferris, Stephen P., 507, 520
Figleweski, Stephen, 874
Finnerty, John D., 931, 960
Fisher, I., 159, 189
Fisher, Irving, 392, 405, 427
Fons, Jerome, 580, 602
Fooladi, Iraj, 654
Fouse, William L., 692, 731
Fredman, Albert J., 519
French, F., 326–327, 423, 428, 434
French, Kenneth R., 408, 435, 453, 481, 706, 747, 764, 788
Fridson, Martin S., 118, 602
Friend, Irwin, 431
Front, Marshall, 642
Fullman, Scott H., 915

G

Gao Yan, 117
Garman, C., 602
Gates, Bill, 445
Geanuracos, John, 602, 961
Gehr, Adam K., Jr., 692
Gerstner, Louis V., 769
Gibson, Charles, 786
Gibson, Rajna, 874
Gillard, Barbara, 249–250
Ginsburg, Justice Ruth Bader, 416
Glassman, James K., 751
Glen, Jack D., 536, 554
Glosten, Lawrence R., 118
Goldfield, Steven, 66
Good, Walker R., 214, 692
Goodman, Jordan Elliot, 24, 485
Gordon, Lilli, 66
Gordon, M. J., 665, 693
Gough, David, 769
Graham, Benjamin, 730, 799–801
Granger, D., 423, 448
Granito, Barbara Donnelly, 612
Grasso, Richard A., 372–373

Grazer, Brian, 134
Green, J., 839
Greenspan, Alan, 1, 2, 3, 210, 555
Grinblatt, Mark, 554
Gross, William, 620
Grover, Mary Beth, 518, 713
Gruber, Martin J., 537, 554
Grundy, Kevin, 336
Gultekin, N. Bulent, 423, 902

H

Halpern, Philip, 554
Hammer, Richard M., 144
Hanson, N., 711
Harper, Charles P., 493, 520
Harty, Emmett, 961
Harvey, Campbell R., 24
Hasbrouck, Joel, 89, 117
Hassett, Kevin A., 751
Haugen, Robert A., 448
Hawkins, David, 120, 144, 785
Hendricks, Darryll, 520
Henrikson, 431
Hensel, Chris R., 553
Hensel, Katherine, 22–23
Herman, Tom, 431, 563, 642
Herzfield, Thomas J., 489
Higgins, Huong N., 732
Hirsch, James S., 509
Hirsch, Ray, 115
Hirshleifer, J. H., 214
Hobun, James P., Jr., 803
Hodgos, Charles W., 554
Hoffman, Stuart, 29
Homaifar, Ghassem, 654
Homer, Sidney, 644, 653
Hood, L. Randoph, 445
Horvath, Philip A., 693
Howard, Ron, 134
Hsieh, David S., 368
Hu, Henry T. C., 126, 144
Huang, Roger D., 24
Huberman, Gur, 449
Hull, John C., 873
Hunter, John E., 283

I

Ilmanen, Antli, 602
Ingene, Charles A., 764
Ippolito, 431

J

Jaffe, 423, 427, 431
Jaffee, Thomas, 65
Jasen, Georgette, 444
Jegadeesh, Narasimhan, 449, 452–453, 481
Jennings, Robert H., 481
Jennings, Ross, 803
Jensen, C. Michael, 327, 427, 431, 531, 536, 554
Jensen, Gerald R., 449, 803
Johnson, Hugh, 464
Johnson, Robert R., 449, 803
Jones, Charles P., 427, 428, 429, 448
Jones, H. E., 448
Jorion, Philippe, 449, 961
Josephson, Michael, 130

K

Kahn, Ronald N., 533, 554, 654
Kahn, Sharon, 693, 732
Kahn, Virginia Munger, 492
Kandel, Shmuel, 449
Kao, Duen Li, 582
Kao, G. Wenchi, 175, 189
Kapner, Kenneth R., 961
Karnosky, Denis S., 553
Karpus, George, 482
Keim, Donald B., 423, 602
Kelly, Jonathan, 118
Kendall, M., 449
Kennedy, Justice Anthony M., 416
Keynes, John Maynard, 658
Khorana, Ajay, 554
Kihn, John, 117
Kiiskinen, Arto, 961
Kim, James, 754
Kim, Joseph A., 602
Kimball, Andrew E., 602
King, Benjamin F., 735, 764
Klarman, Seth A., 803
Klein, Harry, 22
Knutson, Peter H., 777, 803
Koehn, Michael, 66
Kogelman, Stanley, 692
Kolman, Joe, 960
Kolodny, Richard, 536–537, 554
Konishi, Atsuo, 874

Kracaw, William A., 961
Kritzman, Mark, 654
Kriz, John J., 127
Kroll, Stanley, 481

L

Labich, Kenneth, 130
Lakonishok, Josef, 449, 539–540, 765
Lane, Brian, 432
Latane, Henry A., 427, 428, 429, 448
Lay, Mark, 555
LeBaron, Dean, 439
Leclery, Marc J., 803
Lederman, Jess, 66, 117, 602
Lee, Ahyee, 448
Lee, Charles C., 489, 520
Lee, Peter, 105
Leeson, Nicholas, 822, 840, 850
Lehmann, Bruce N., 423, 452, 481, 537, 554
Leibowitz, Martin L., 644, 692
Lenzner, Robert, 600
Lerman, Zvi, 379, 380, 381, 406
Levin, Arthur, 132–134
Levingston, Steven E., 465, 471
Levitt, Arthur, 133, 134
Levy, Haim, 118, 189, 214, 327, 328, 379, 380, 381, 406, 541, 569, 602
Liebowitz, Martin L., 653
Lintner, John, 319, 336
Lipin, Steven, 127
Lipper, Kenneth, 599–600
Lipson, Elliot, 260–261
Litterman, Robert, 405
Liu, Pu, 431, 449
Livingston, Miles, 117, 602
Lloyd George, Robert, 492
Lo, Andrew W., 453, 481
Lofthouse, Stephen, 405
Lonergan, Joyce, 754
Long, D., 902
Longstaff, Francis A., 654
Lowenstein, Louis, 144
Lucchetti, Aaron, 805, 822
Ludwig, Robert, 369, 370
Lynch, Peter, 439, 803

M

Ma, Christopher K., 602
Maberly, Edwin, 449
Macaulay, Frederick R., 653
McBain, Robert, 850
Macbeth, J., 902
McElroy, Marjorie B., 362, 368
McFall, Lamm Jr., 764
McGee, Susan, 29
McGeen, Suzanne, 679
McGough, Robert, 136
MacKinlay, A. Craig, 453, 481
McLean, Bethany, 403
McLean, Stuart K., 874
McNamara, Brian M., 140
McQueen, 423
McVey, Edward, 215
Madlem, Peter W., 519
Maffei, Gregory, 445
Magee, John, 452, 481
Maginn, John L., 24, 336, 533, 553
Malkiel, Burton, 24, 336, 407, 411, 439, 448
Manaster, S., 902
Mann, Steven V., 117
Markese, John, 250
Markowitz, Harry M., 196, 214, 328
Marshall, John F., 961
Marshall, William, 654
Martin, Luis, 117
Masih, 423
Matsumoto, Keishiro, 803
Meador, Joseph W., 706, 707, 708
Meehan, John, 307
Mehran, Jamshid, 654
Mendelson, H., 327
Mercer, Jeffrey, 448, 803
Merrill, Charles, 85
Merton, Robert C., 328, 368, 423, 449, 806, 874, 885
Merville, L., 902
Messner, Grace, 730
Metcalf, Gilbert E., 407
Metz, Michael, 791–792, 884
Meulbroek, Lisa K., 144
Meyers, Thomas A., 455, 456, 458, 459, 467, 481

Michael, Tom, 288
Micheletti, Arthur, 260
Milgate, Murray, 24, 117, 448
Milken, Michael, 125
Millar, Bill, 602, 961
Miller, Barry, 803
Miller, M., 327
Miller, Merton, 941
Miller, Michael W., 770
Millman, Gregory J., 806
Mitchell, Constance, 620
Modest, David M., 537, 554
Modigliani, Franco, 80, 117, 941
Moffett, Michael H., 189, 405
Mollner, Laurence, 805
Moore, A. C., 471
Morgenstern, O., 423, 448
Morris, Chip, 115–116
Morris, Gregory I., 481
Moses, Jonathan M., 125
Moy, Ronald L., 448
Mullins, David W., Jr., 602
Munger, Charles, 408
Munoz, Mark, 850
Murphy, Bernadette, 471
Murphy, Michael R., 129, 144
Murray, Roger F., 601, 784, 803

N

Nagorniak, John J., 721
Natale, Robert, 433
Navellier, Louis, 322–323
Neiderhoffer, Victor, 431
Nelling, Edward, 554
Newman, Peter, 24, 117, 448
Nison, Steve, 462, 481
Norwitz, Steven, 215

O

O'Connor, Justice Sandra Day, 416
Officer, D., 902
Ogden, J. P., 449
O'glove, Thornton, 769
O'Hagan, James, 415
O'Neal, Edward, 336, 520
Osborne, 423, 431

P

Palmer, Jay, 699
Pare, Terence P., 408
Park, Keith K. H., 66, 117
Patel, Jayendu, 520
Paulenoff, Michael J., 481
Peavy, John M., 489, 520
Peavy, John W. III, 406
Peers, Alexandra, 580
Penman, Stephen H., 803
Peterson, 428
Peterson, Richard L., 602
Petrie, Thomas A., 764
Pollack, Irving M., 66
Porter, Michael E., 764
Power, William, 127
Prestbo, John A., 322
Price, T. Rowe, 375
Pring, Martin J., 452, 463, 481
Prochniak, Andrea L., 288
Pulliam, Susan, 433
Puri, Shaifali, 851

R

Rabbitt, Paul, 598
Radcliffe, Robert, 541
Raghavan, Anita, 750
Ranny, Richard, 510–511
Rao, Ramesh, 602
Rea, James, 799
Rehnquist, Chief Justice
    William H., 416
Reichel, Frank, 728
Reifman, Shlomo Z., 734
Reilly, Frank K., 175, 189
Reinganum, Marc, 434, 704,
    705
Rendleman, Richard J., Jr.,
    427, 428, 429, 448
Resnick, Bruce G., 536–537,
    554
Roberts, 411, 423
Roberts, Gordon S., 654
Robertson, Malcolm J., 109,
    110, 117, 177, 876
Rogalski, J., 902
Rohweder, Harold C., 732
Roll, Richard, 327, 337,
    368, 427, 449, 453, 481,
    533, 541, 554
Rosen, Kyle, 884
Ross, Stephen A., 327, 337,
    345, 368, 533, 541, 874

Roth, Harrison, 873
Rowe, Timothy D., 66
Rozeff, Michael S., 732
Ruane, William, 408
Rubinstein, Mark, 874
Rudd, Andrew, 336
Ryan, Patrick J., 602

S

Sage, Russell, 842
Salomon, R. S., Jr., 444,
    762
Samuelson, Paul, 842
Santoli, Michael, 961
Sappenfield, Ross, 406
Sarnat, Marshall, 189, 380,
    406
Saunderson, E., 839
Scalia, Justice Antonio, 416
Scarlata, Jodi G., 117
Scherveik, Susan, 711
Schloss, Walter, 408
Scholes, Myron, 327, 427,
    431, 806, 874, 885, 895,
    902
Schulman, David, 749
Schultz, Ellen E., 104
Schwartz, Eduardo, 654
Schwartz, Robert A., 74,
    117, 144
Scott, George Cole, 519
Seijas, Robert W., 117
Serletis, 423
Sesit, Michael R., 160
Seyhun, H. Nejat, 136, 428,
    431, 449
Sharpe, William F., 214, 319,
    328, 336, 368, 525, 533,
    536, 554
Shefrin, Hersh, 144
Sheridan, Titman, 554
Shieh, 428
Shivaswamy, Melkote, 803
Shleifer, Andrei, 368, 489,
    520, 539–540, 765
Siegel, Jeremy J., 189, 206,
    597
Siegel, Lawrence, 104, 107
Silber, William L., 874
Simmonds, David, 23, 108
Simonetti, Gilbert Jr., 144
Singer, Brian D., 553
Singer, Richard, 961
Singh, Ravi, 94

Slifer, Stephen D., 737, 739,
    744, 763
Smith, Clifford W., 82, 118,
    941, 961
Smith, Clifford W., Jr., 874
Smith, D., 431, 449
Smith, Laurence, 369
Smithson, Charles W., 874,
    941, 961
Solnik, Bruno, 66, 378, 396,
    405, 406, 423
Solomon, Jack, 471
Sommerfeld, Ray, 70
Sondergard, 423
Sorensen, Bjarne G., 654
Sorenson, Eric H., 720, 721,
    732
Souter, Justice David H., 416
Speidell, Lawrence S., 406,
    804
Stack, William, 492
Statman, Meir, 144, 481
Steiner, Robert, 85
Steinkuehler, Franz, 143
Stevens, Justice John Paul,
    416
Stigum, Marcia, 66
Stoll, Hans R., 24
Stonehill, Arthur I., 189, 405
Stovall, Robert, 444
Stuckey, John M., Jr., 563
Sturm, Paul, 801
Subrahmanyam, Marti G.,
    874
Sullivan, Michael P., 602
Syed, Azmat A., 431, 449

T

Taylor, Walton R. L., 554
Teitelbaum, Richard, 688
Tewles, Richard J., 144
Thaler, Richard H., 489, 520
Thales, 841
Thomas, Jacob K., 448
Thomas, Justice Clarence,
    416
Thomas, Lee, 654
Thomson, Robert B., II.,
    803
Thorley, 423
Tinic, Seha M., 902
Topkis, Maggie, 445
Treynor, Jack, 528, 554, 764
Trzcinka, Charles, 507, 520

Tsiveriotis, K., 874
Tucker, Alan L., 48, 117
Tuttle, David L., 533, 692
Tuttle, Donald L., 24, 336,
    553
Tyson-Quah, K., 839

V

Veit, E. Theodore, 129
Velasco, S., 403
Vickers, 431
Viet, E. Theodore, 144
Vishny, Robert, 368, 539–
    540, 765
Viskanta, Tadas, 24
Viswanathan, S., 368

W

Ward, Sandra, 438, 884
Wartzman, Rick, 210
Watts, 427
Waxler, Caroline, 555
Weinstein, Stan, 450
Weiss, Kathleen, 489, 520
Weiss, Stephen W., 602
Westerfield, 423
Whitford, David, 191
Wien, Byron, 22
Witkowski, Erik, 520
Wilford, D. Sykes, 941, 961
Williams, Gerald J., 144
Williamson, David A., 720,
    721, 732
Willner, Ram, 654
Winkler, Matthew, 563
Woelfel, Charles J., 804
Wolff, Eric D., 602
Woolley, Scott, 840, 841, 930
Wright, David J., 175, 189

Y

Yoder, James A., 554
Yu, 423
Yuhas, Alan, 337

Z

Zeckhauser, Richard, 520
Zuk, Michael, 65
Zweig, Robert, 507, 520

SUBJECT INDEX

A

Abnormal rates of return
    capital asset pricing model and, 324
    cumulative, 424–425
    efficient market theory and, 410, 412, 422
Accelerating earnings, 706
Accounting anomalies, 434, 438
Accounting concepts, 767–770
Accounting method, for estimating dividend growth rate, 718
Accrual basis, for calculating bond returns, 154–156
Accrued interest, bond prices and, 605–608
Active bond management strategies, 643–645

Active investment strategies, 419
Actual margin, 99
Addison Report, The, 322
Adjusted rate of return, 165–167
Adjusted stock price, 791
ADRs. *See* American Depository Receipts
Advance-decline line, 469–470, 479
Advanced estimate of GDP, 737
Agency risk, 710–711
Aggressive stocks, 304
AIMR. *See* Association for Investment Management and Research
All-or-none order, 97
Alpha stocks, 323, 324, 325, 326

American Bar Association, and pay-to-play practices, 132–133
American Depository Receipts (ADRs), 54, 56
American Stock Exchange (AMEX), 83
    listing requirements, 86
American-style options, 846
    call option boundaries, 889
    put option boundaries, 892–893
Americus Trust, 126
Amortizing swaps, 951
Annuities, 25
Anomalies, efficient market theory and, 422, 433–438
Appraisal costs of initial public offerings, 82
APT. *See* Arbitrage pricing theory

APT performance index, 533
Arbitrage, 93, 192–194, 346
    definitions of, 885
    futures contracts and, 826, 828, 829, 830
    interest rate parity and, 394, 395
    options, 885, 888, 890
Arbitrage pricing theory (APT), 338, 345–346
    assumptions and risk-return relationship, 350–351, 353–354
    capital asset pricing model and, 360–361
    examples of, 346–350
    linear relationship, 354–360
    multifactor model, 361–363
    program trading and, 349–350

Arithmetic average, 162
Arithmetic method
    for calculating equally
        weighted indexes, 173
    of determining average
        rate of return, 163–165
Asked price, 90
Asked rate on Treasury bills,
    33
Asset(s). *See also* Portfolio(s);
        specific assets
    allocation of, 15–16, 420–
        421, 542
    correlation coefficient of,
        227–231
    dependency of, 217–219
    factors affecting price, 4–5
    financial versus physical, 7–
        11
    number of, and risk reduc-
        tion, 261–264
    risk and return on, 49
    risk-free, 292
    underlying, 806, 849–851
Association for Investment
        Management and Re-
        search (AIMR)
    code of ethics, 131–132,
        135, 966
    rate-of-return calculations
        for bonds, standards for,
        154–155
    rate of return standards,
        148, 166
    Standards of Professional
        Conduct, 134–135,
        966–970
Associations, 961–965
Asymmetric hedging strategy,
    935–939
At-the-money options, 849
Autocorrelations, 425
Automated trading, 92–93
Average cost method, 773,
    774, 775, 776
Average rate of return, 162–
    165

B

Back testing, 433
Balance sheet, 767, 770–773
    equity on, 777
    example of, 797

intangibles on, 776–777
inventory evaluation meth-
    ods, 773–776
liabilities on, 777
plant and equipment on,
    776
Bank discount rate, 744
Bankers' acceptances, 35
Bank reserves, 743
Bar charts, in technical analy-
    sis, 453–457
Basel Committee recom-
    mendations, 952–954
Basel multiplication factor,
    953
Basis, pricing futures and,
    827–828
Basket trade, 97
Bear market
    closed-end funds in, 518
    Dow Theory of, 464
Beginning market value
    (BMV), 148
Benchmark revisions of
    GDP, 737
Beta
    characteristic lines, 303–
        306
    common stock portfolio
        management and, 709
    definition of, 22, 301
    fund volatility and, 307,
        308
    in practice, 325, 326
    as risk measure, 301–303,
        523, 540
    SIM, 338–339
    surprise factor and, 351
    uses of, 308–309
    of U.S. market, 314–315
    zero, 354–355
Bid-asked spread, 92
Bid price, 90
Bid rate on Treasury bills, 33
Binomial option pricing
        model, 915–922
Black-Scholes option pricing
        model (BSOPM), 895–
        903
    call options and, 895–897
    convertible securities and,
        905
    empirical evidence regard-
        ing, 899, 902–903

estimating inputs to, 897–
    899
example, 922–926
futures contracts and, 906–
    909
portfolio insurance valua-
    tion using, 904–905
put options and, 897
sensitivity analysis of, 899,
    900–901
warrant valuation using,
    906
Blind bids, 93–95
Blue chip stocks, 43
BMV. *See* Beginning market
    value
Bond(s), 30–31. *See also*
        Bond duration; Bond
        management strategies;
        Bond prices; Bond
        valuation; Bond yield;
        Spreads over Treasuries;
        Yield curve
    callable, 38, 51, 579, 590–
        592, 907
    cash flow characteristics of,
        573, 574
    century, 31
    characteristics of, 31, 32
    convertible, 46–47, 599–
        600, 905
    corporate, 39–40, 106
    coupon-bearing, 39, 156
    crossover, 106
    debentures, 579
    Eurobonds, 588
    federal agency, 38
    general obligation, 39
    high-grade, 577
    indexed, 934
    inflation-indexed, 587–588
    interest rates and, 556
    international, 588–590
    international, rates of re-
        turn on, 382, 404–405
    investment-grade, 577
    junk, 39, 498, 578, 586–
        587
    municipal, 38–39
    rates of return, on accrual
        basis, 154–156
    ratings of, 577–586
    revenue, 39
    risks of, 48–53, 559–562

Samurai, 588
secured, 578–579
speculative grade, 578
subordinated, 578
taxes and, 67, 69–70
Treasury, 33, 105
types of, 32–41
world market, 105–107
yankee, 588
zero-coupon, 39
Bond duration, 624–632
    computational equation
        for, 654–655
    convexity and, 637–639
    definition of, 629
    impact on bond volatility,
        627
    interest rates and, 612
    as measure of holding pe-
        riod, 629–631
    principles of, 632, 635–
        637
    yield to maturity and, 631–
        632, 635, 636
Bond funds. *See* Closed-end
    funds; Open-end funds
Bond indenture, 578
Bond indexes, 174–175,
    642
Bond laddering, 642–643
Bond management strategies
    immunization strategies,
        639–641, 643
    interest rates and, 565–567
    passive versus active, 642–
        645
Bond markets
    economy, relationship to,
        744, 745–746
    international, 588–590
Bond prices
    coupon rate and, 620–624
    length of maturity and,
        615–618
    length to maturity and,
        618–620
    time and, 613–614
    yield to maturity and, 614–
        615
Bond valuation. *See also*
        Bond yield; Spreads over
        Treasuries; Term struc-
        ture of interest rates;
        Yield curve

accrued interest and partial periods, 605–608
compounding interest rates and, 609–611
embedded options and, 592–593
equations for, 603–605
interest rate changes and, 556–558
in practice, 573–576
Bond yield. *See also* Term structure of interest rates
to call, 572
coupon (nominal), 571
current, 571
inflation rates and, 556
realized, 572
yield curve and, 558–562
Book value, of stock, 746–748
BOPM. *See* Binomial option pricing model
Breadth indicators, in technical analysis, 469–472, 479
Breadth of transactions, 74
Broker(s)
commission, 91
commission schedule, 102, 103
dealers, 91
discount, 102
floor, 91
full-service, 101–102
services offered by, 102
Brokerage services, 102
Broker loan rate, 97–98
BSOPM. *See* Black-Scholes option pricing model
Budget deficits, 743
Bull market
bond yields and, 555
Dow Theory of, 463–464
popularity of investment companies and, 485
Bull spread, 866–868
Business cycles, 740–741, 742
Business risk, 52, 710
Butterfly strategies, 882, 883
Buttonwood Tree Agreement, 85, 86, 842
Buyers, of options, 843–844

C

Callable bonds, 38, 51, 579, 590–592, 905
Call feature, 579, 590–592
Call loan rate, 97–98
Call market, 87–88, 108
Call options, 46, 841, 848
Black-Scholes option pricing model and, 895–897
boundaries for, 887–889
covered call writing, 865–866
payoff diagram for, 858
put-call parity, 842
value of, at expiration, 860–861
Call price, 856, 896, 920
Call ratio backspread, 882, 883
Call ratio spread, 882, 883
Candlestick charts, in techical analysis, 459–462
Candlestick line, 460
Cap, 952
Capital asset pricing model (CAPM), 311, 312
arbitrage pricing theory and, 360–361
estimating investor's required rates of return and, 720, 722
proof of, 319–322
shortcomings of, 325, 327–328
using to select stocks, 323–324
Capital gains, 42
rates of return calculations and, 149
taxes on, 66, 69, 157
Capital market, 6
Capital market line (CML), 289–290, 297–299
Jensen's performance index and, 531
Sharpe's performance index and, 525, 526
Capital market securities, 7, 31, 32, 36–41
CAPM. *See* Capital asset pricing model
Cash dividends, 41–42, 674–675

Cash flow (CF), 695–696
rates of return calculations and, 149
statement, 767, 780–783
uneven, 26
Cash levels, as technical indicator, 479–480
Cash matching strategy, 639
Cash settlement, 815, 876
CBOE. *See* Chicago Board Options Exchange
CBOT. *See* Chicago Board of Trade
CDs. *See* Certificates of deposit
Center for Research in Securities Prices (CRSP), 173
Century bonds, 31
Certainty and risk, 192–194, 195
Certificates of deposit (CDs), 35
Channels, 454, 456, 457
Characteristic lines, 303–306
Chartered financial analysts (CFAs), 785
Charting. *See* Technical analysis
Cheat sheets, 432–433
Checking accounts, and mutual funds, 505
Chicago Board Options Exchange (CBOE), 842–843
Chicago Board of Trade (CBOT), 842
Chief executive officers, compensation of, and performance, 138
Churning, 137
Civilian unemployment rate, 743
Clearinghouse, futures trading and, 82–90
Closed-end funds, 56–60, 483–484
in bear market, 518
benefits of, 486
categories of, 486
history of, 485
initial public offerings of, 489
net asset value of, 487–489

premiums and discounts, 488, 493, 494–495
risks of, 489, 490, 491–492
term funds, 482
turnover and, 494
in *Wall Street Journal*, 486–488
Closing transactions, 846
CML. *See* Capital market line
Coincident indicators, 741, 742
Collar, 850, 952
Commercial paper, 33–35
Commission brokers, 91
churning and, 137
initial public offerings and, 137
Commission rates, 102, 103
Commission schedule, 102
Committee for Performance Presentation Standards (CPPS), 148
Commodities contracts. *See* Futures contracts
Commodities Futures Trading Commission (CFTC), 962
Commodity futures, pricing, 833
Commodity swaps, 950–951
Common-factor rate of return, 338–342
Common factor risk. *See* Systematic risk
Common size statements, 788–790
Common stocks. *See also* Common stock valuation; Stock(s)
blue chip, 43
characteristics of, 41–42
classifications of, 42–43
cyclical, 43
defensive, 43
growth, 42, 657
income, 42–43
options, 46
speculative, 43
Common stock selection, 704–723
characteristics of winners, 705–706
dividend discount model inputs and, 716–723

Common stock selection
  (continued)
  duration of stock and,
    714–715
  economic value-added
    model, 701–703
  Graham's guidelines, 800
  market signals and, 712–
    714
  portfolio management and,
    707–715
  risk and, 710–712
Common stock valuation,
    656–682
  analysts' view of, 706–707,
    708
  for assessing investment
    opportunities, 658
  constant dividend growth
    model and, 664–665,
    674–675
  cost of equity capital and,
    675–676
  discounted cash flow prin-
    ciple and, 659–664
  for estimating appropriate
    discount rates, 658–659
  free cash flow model and,
    693–700
  normal-growth firms and,
    667–670
  opportunities for extraor-
    dinary profits and, 666–
    667
  price/earnings ratios and,
    656, 676–682
  reinvestment of earnings
    and, 666
  supergrowth firms and,
    670–674
  for understanding financial
    media, 659
  for valuing common stock
    issue, 658
Composite indexes, 740–741
Compounding interest rates,
    609–611, 926–927
Concentration ratio, 753,
    756
Conduit, 41
Conduit theory, 485
Conservatism, 768, 773
Constant dividend growth
    model, 664–665

cash dividends and, 674–
    675
  cost of equity capital and,
    675–676
Constituency relations and
    ethics, 131
Consumer price index (CPI),
    158
Contingent claims. See De-
    rivatives; Derivative se-
    curity
Contingent immunization,
    643
Continuous market, 88, 108
Contraction phase, of busi-
    ness cycle, 740
Conversion feature, 592–593
Conversion premium, 47
Conversion price, 47
Conversion ratio, 47
Conversion value, 47, 592
Convertible bonds, 46–47,
    599–600, 905
Convexity, 637–639, 641
Corporate bonds, 39–40
  call feature, 590–592
  performance of, versus
    government bonds, 552–
    553
  risk of default, 576–577
  world market, 106
Corporate governance, 128
Correlation, 15
  mean-variance frontier
    and, 269–270
  portfolio risk reduction
    and, 251–266
Correlation coefficient, 227–
    231
Cost of carry model, 832
Counterparties, 946
Coupon-bearing bonds, 39
Coupon payments, 31
Coupon yield, 571
Covariance, 222–227, 228–
    229, 367–368
Covered call writing, 865–
    866
Covered position, 850
CPI. See Consumer price
    index
CPPS. See Committee for
    Performance Presenta-
    tion Standards

Credit quality, 577
Credit risk, 577
CreditWatch, 581–582
Crossover bonds, 106
CRSP. See Center for Re-
    search in Securities
    Prices
Cumulative abnormal rates of
    return (CAR), 424, 429
Cumulative preferred stocks,
    44
Currency futures, pricing,
    830–833
Currency risk, 380–385, 386
Currency swaps, 949–950
Current ratio, 784
Current yield, 571
Cyclical stocks, 43, 740

D

Date of record, 42
Day orders, 96
DCF. See Discounted cash
    flow principle
DDMs. See Dividend dis-
    count models
Dealers, 91
Debentures, 578
Debt ratios, 784, 786
Declaration date, 42
Deep-in-the-money options,
    850
Default risk, 48, 576–577,
    587. See also Margin re-
    quirements; Spreads over
    Treasuries
Defensive stocks, 43, 304
Deflator, 738
Delivery month, 810
Demand and supply analysis,
    753–756
Dependency of assets, 217–
    219
Depth of transactions, 74
Derivative exchanges, 109–
    110
Derivatives. See also Forward
    contracts; Futures con-
    tracts; Option(s); Swaps
  convertible bonds, 46–47
  definition of, 806, 840
  futures, 47
  hazards of, 884

hedging strategies and,
    805–806
  need for regulation of, 127
  risk-return tradeoff, 14
  stock options, 46
  swaps, 47–48
  types of securities, 7
  world market, 108–110
Derivative security, 841
Derivatives Safety and
    Soundness Act (H.R.
    4503), 128
Diamonds, 60
Direct method
  for reporting cash flow, 780
  of determining portfolio
    variance, 232
Discount brokers, 102
Discounted cash flow (DCF)
    principle, 659–664
Discount on closed-end
    funds, 488, 493, 494–
    495
Discount rate
  bank, 744
  on common stocks, 657,
    721
  estimating, 658–659
  on Treasury bills, 33
Display Rule (Rule 11Ac1–
    4), 123, 124
Diversifiable risk. See Unsys-
    tematic risk
Diversification. See also Port-
    folio diversification
  as benefit of mutual funds,
    503, 504–505
  efficient market theory
    and, 418
  indexing and, 543–545
  international, 310, 369–
    370, 374–380, 404–405
  mutual funds and, 215,
    237–238
  super diversification, 335
  in unrelated firms in prac-
    tice, 272–274
Dividend(s)
  growth rate, estimating,
    716–719, 732–733
  as stock market valuation
    tool, 748
Dividend discount models
    (DDMs), 661

assumptions of, 721–722
estimating dividend
growth rate, 716–719,
732–733
estimating investors' registered rate of return,
719–720
implementing, 720–723
inputs for, 722
interpreting results of,
722–723
Dividends per share (DPS)
constant dividend growth
model and, 665–666
financial statement analysis
and, 766
Divisibility, of financial assets, 8, 10
Divisor, 169
Dollar-weighted average rate
of return, 189–190
Double summation formula
for portfolio variance,
235–236
Dow Jones Global Indexes,
179–180
Dow Jones Industrial Average
(DJIA)
biggest one-day declines
in, 305
Dow Theory and, 463–464
formula for, 169
stocks included in, 167–
168
Dow Jones industry groups,
752
Dow Theory, 463–465
DPS. See Dividends per share
Dual listing, 84
Duration. See also Bond
duration
of bonds, 624–632
of common stock, 714–
715
Duration drift, 632, 635
Duration matching strategy,
639–640

E

Earnings. See also Earnings
per share; Price/earnings
ratio
accelerated, 706

as cash dividends, 674–675
reinvestment of, 666
Earnings multiplier, 788
Earnings per share (EPS)
constant dividend growth
model and, 665
dividend growth rate and,
718–719
financial statement analysis
and, 766, 783–784
Earnings/price (E/P) ratio,
677, 679, 720
Economic indicators, 740–
741
*Economic Report of the
President*, 962
Economic value-added
(EVA) model, 701–703
Efficient frontier
calculating, 283–287
common stock portfolio
management and, 709
international diversification and, 379–380, 381
investor's point of view
and, 386–387
with many assets, 270–272
in two-asset case, 267–269
Efficient markets, 14–15, 409
financial engineering in,
941–946
Efficient market theory
(EMT)
analyst's view of, 415
debate about, 407, 439
definition of, 409–410
empirical evidence related
to, 421–433
information set for, 410–
411
investment strategy in inefficient market and, 421
overview of, 408
passive versus active portfolio management and,
419–420
portfolio selection and,
417–419
resource allocation and,
417
semistrong form of, 412,
414, 417–419, 427–430
strong form of, 414–415,
421, 431–433

weak form of, 411–412,
421, 422–426
Efficient portfolios, 267–269
ELKs. See Equity-linked se-
curities
Embedded options
call feature, 590–592
conversion feature, 592–
593
Employee Retirement In-
come Security Act of
1974 (ERISA), 122,
124, 485
EMT. See Efficient market
theory
Ending market value (EMV),
148
Enigmas, 422
Enterprise capitalists, 120
EPS. See Earnings per share
Equally weighted indexes,
172–174
Equal percentage contribution rule (EPCoR),
320–322
Equity, 777
Equity-linked securities
(ELKs), 959–960
ERISA. See Employee Re-
tirement Income Secu-
rity Act of 1974
Ethics
AIMR Code, 131–132,
134–135, 968–972
CEOs' compensation and,
138
churning, 137
conduct of investment
managers and, 138
crisis in, 129–130
definition of, 120
fraud and, 128–131
independent judgment of
financial analysts and,
135
insider trading and, 135–
136
initial public offerings and,
137
product sales commissions
and, 137–138
unethical versus fraudulent
behavior, 131–135
Eurobonds, 588

Eurodollars, 36
European-style options, 846
call option boundaries,
887–889
put option boundaries,
890–893
EVA. See conomic value-
added (EVA) model
Event anomalies, 434, 438
Event studies, 422, 424
Ex-ante rates of return, 147
Ex-ante values, 163
Excess return, 324, 410
Exchange rate(s)
expectations, 393–394
inflation and, 390–391
movements, compared
with interest rate and inflation rate differentials,
397–398
rates of return and, 160–
162
spot, 395–396
Exchange rate risk, 52, 380,
809, 830
Ex-dividend date, 42
Execution costs, 74
Exercise price, 844
Exercising option contracts,
843–844
Expansion phase, of business
cycle, 740
Expectations hypothesis
local (LEH), 568–569
unbiased (UEH), 569
Expected return, 197, 208,
344–345
Expiration date, of option
contract, 845
Ex-post averages, 163
Ex-post rates of return, 147,
709
Extraordinary profit, 410

F

Face value, 31
Fallen angels, 586. *See also*
Junk bonds
Family of funds, 498, 500
FDIC. *See* Federal Deposit
Insurance Corporation
Feasible set, 292
Federal agency bonds, 38

Federal Deposit Insurance Corporation (FDIC), 121
Federal funds market, 36
Federal funds rate, 744
Federal Reserve Board
   function of, 743–744
   margin requirements for options and, 876
   as source of information, 962
Federal Trade Commission (FTC) and Securities Act of 1933, 121
Fiduciary, and ERISA, 122
Financial analyst, independent judgment of, 135
Financial Analysts Federation, 706, 707, 708
Financial assets, contrasted with physical assets, 7–11
Financial engineering, 930–960. See also Swaps
   definition of, 931–932
   in efficient markets, 941–946
   indexed bonds, 934
   in inefficient markets, 940–941
   recent innovations, 932, 951–952
   unique situations from which firms can benefit, 939–940
Financial engineers, 126
Financial planners, 102–104
   ethics of, 137–138
Financial risk, 710
Financial statement analysis, 765–797
   accounting concepts, 767–770
   balance sheets, 770–777
   cash flow statements, 780–783
   earnings per share and, 783–784
   income statements, 778–780
   ratio analysis and, 784–797
   uses of, 766
Financial statements, definition of, 766–767

Firm anomalies, 433–434
Firm-specific news, 340, 352–353
Firm-specific rates of return, 338–342
First-in, first-out (FIFO) method, 773, 774, 775, 776
First market transactions, 83
Fiscal policy, 741, 743
Fixed for floating swap, 946
Floor, 952
Floor, of stock exchange, 83
Floor brokers, 91, 817
Forbes index, 734, 735
Foreign Corrupt Practices Act of 1977, 122–123, 124
Foreign exchange rates
   exchange rate risk and, 52
   expectations, 393–394
   rates of return and, 160–162
Forward contracts, 565, 807–809
Forward foreign exchange rate, 393–394
Forward rate, 565, 807
Fourth market transactions, 84
Fraud, versus unethical behavior, 131–135
Free cash flow model (FCFM), 693–700
Frictionless market, 895
FTC. See Federal Trade Commission
Full-service brokers, 101–102
Fundamental analysis, 42, 414, 418, 421, 427
Futures commission merchants (FCMs), 816–817
Futures contracts, 47, 805. See also Futures pricing
   arbitrage, 826
   characteristics of, 809–812
   clearinghouse and, 818
   definition of, 809
   hedging, 824–825
   investment strategies with, 822–827
   margin requirements and, 818–822

options on, 906–909
   portfolio diversification and, 826–827
   reading financial data on, 812–815
   speculating, 825
   swaps versus, 949
   trading, 816–817
   types of, 812
Futures price, 47, 828, 838
Futures pricing, 827–833
   basis and, 827–828
   of commodity futures, 833
   of currency futures, 830–833
   of stock index futures, 828–830
Future value, 24–25, 163

G

GDP. See Gross domestic product
General capital asset pricing model (GCAPM), 328
General obligation bonds, 39
Geometric average, 162
Geometric compounding, 166–167
Geometric method of determining average rate of return, 164
Geometric Series Theorem, 603
Glass-Steagall Banking Act of 1933, 121, 123
GLOBEX trading system, 93
GNP. See Gross national product
Good-till-canceled (GTC) order, 96
Graham's guidelines, 800
Gross domestic product (GDP), 736–739
Gross national product (GNP), 736–737
Gross spread (GS), 76
Growth stocks, 42

H

Hammer, in candlestick charts, 462

Hanging man, in candlestick charts, 462
Hedging, 7. See also Swaps
   binomial option pricing model and, 917, 921
   derivatives and, 805–806
   futures contracts and, 824–825
   international investment and, 369
   option-stock, 872–873
   selective, 940–941
   symmetric and asymmetric strategies, 935–939, 940
High-grade bonds, 577
Highs and lows, as technical indicator, 472, 480
Holding period, for physical and financial assets, 8, 9, 10
   common stock duration and, 714–715
   common stock valuation and, 661
   price and reinvestment effects and, 625–626, 628–629
Holding period rate, 568
Holding period return (HPR), 148
Horizon matching strategy, 640

I

Immunization strategies
   contingent, 643
   income, 639–641
   price, 641
Inaccurate price discovery, 74
Income effect, 557
Income immunization strategies, 639–641
   cash matching, 639
   duration matching, 639–640
   horizon matching, 640
Income statement, 767, 778–780
Income stocks, 42–43
Independent auditor's report, 784

Index(es), 167–177. *See also*
  Performance indexes
  bond, 174–175
  composite, 740–741
  Dow Jones Industrial Average (DJIA), 167–168
  equally weighted, 172–174
  Forbes, 734, 735
  importance of, 168
  price-weighted, 169–171
  purpose of, 168–169
  stock, 176–177
  value-weighted, 171–172
Indexed bonds, 934
Index funds
  in family of funds, 498
  function of and returns on, 499–500, 503
  negative beta and, 288
  passive portfolio management and, 419–420
Index method, for calculating time-weighted rate of return, 150, 151–153, 156
Index models. *See* Single index model
Index options, 874, 876
Index-related trade, 97
Indifference curves, 290–291, 300
Indirect method, for reporting cash flow, 780
Indirect method, of determining portfolio variance, 233–234
Industrial life cycles, 753
Industry allocation, 543
Industry analysis, 3, 751–756
Inefficient frontier, 267–269, 270–272
Inefficient markets
  financial engineering in, 940–941
  investment strategy in, 421
Inefficient portfolios, 267–269
Inflation
  bond yield and, 556
  exchange rates and, 390–391
Inflation-indexed bonds, 587–588
Inflation rate differentials, 397–398

Inflation rate risk, 50, 711–712
Information
  asymmetry of, 82
  availability of, 10–11, 73
  sources, 961–965
Initial margin (IM), 99, 876, 877
Initial public offerings (IPOs), 76
  announcement of, 79
  cheat sheets on, 432–433
  of closed-end funds, 489
  commission brokers as underwriters of, 137
  lemons, 115–116
  private placement versus, 80–81
  risks of, 78
  Securities Act of 1933 and, 121
  underpricing of, and price discovery, 81–82
  valuation of, 658
Insider trading, 135–136, 143
  Securities Exchange Act of 1934 and, 121, 123
  Supreme Court ruling on, 415–416
Insider Trading and Securities Fraud Enforcement Act of 1988, 123, 124, 135–136
Insider Trading Sanctions Act of 1984, 123, 124, 135
Intangibles, 776–777
Interest rate(s). *See also* Bond valuation
  bond duration and, 612
  bond price and, 624–626
  changes in, 556–558
  compounding, methods of, 609–611, 926–927
  forward, 565
  holding period, 568
  spot, 565–567
Interest rate differentials, 397–398
Interest-rate parity, 394–396
Interest-rate risk, 48–49, 49–50, 712
  contingent immunization and, 643

convexity, 637–639
  duration, 632, 635–637
  immunization strategies, 639–641
Interest-rate swaps, 930, 946–949
Intermarket spread swaps, 644
Intermediate trend, in Dow Theory, 463
Internal rate of return (IRR), 27
International equity index, 536–537
International Fisher relationship, 392–393
International investment
  benefits of, 370–371
  bond markets, 588–590
  currency risk, 380–385
  diversification, 369–370, 374–380, 404–405
  foreign exchange expectations, 393–394
  growth of international market, 371–373
  interest rate parity and, 394–396
  international Fisher relationship, 392–393
  points of view on, 385–389
  purchasing power parity and, 389–392
International markets
  growth of, 371–373
  industry analysis and, 756
International securities, 54, 56
International equity index, 536
Internet, on-line stock trading, 71, 72
In-the-money options, 849–850, 902
Intrinsic value, of option, 852
Inventory evaluation, 773–776
Investment(s)
  asset allocation and, 420–421
  corporate finance contrasted with, 6–7

in an inefficient market, 421
  job opportunities in, 12
  reasons for studying, 11–12
  speculative, 6–7
Investment Act of 1934, 842
Investment Advisors Act of 1940, 122, 123
Investment bankers, 76–80
Investment companies, 483. *See also* Closed-end funds; Open-end funds
  popularity of, 484–485
  regulated, 485
Investment Company Act of 1940, 122, 123, 495
Investment criteria
  maximum expected return criterion (MERC), 197–199
  maximum return criterion (MRC), 196–197
  mean-variance, 202–205
Investment data resources, 963–965
Investment-grade bonds, 577
Investment managers, ethical conduct of, 138
Investment policy, 12–13
  fixed, financial engineering and, 945–946
Investment process, 12–17. *See also* Investment strategies
  investor characteristics, 12–13
  risk-return tradeoff, 14
  separation property, 299–301
Investment strategies. *See also* Bond management strategies; Common stock selection; Immunization strategies; Income immunization strategies; Portfolio strategies
  development of, 14–15
  efficient and inefficient, 266–272
  in efficient market, 417–420
  futures contracts and, 822–827

Investment strategies
  (continued)
  implementation of, 17
  in inefficient market, 421
  linked to EMT, 414
  monitoring, 17
  options and, 862–868,
    872–873, 879–883
  passive versus active, 419–
    420
Investment trusts. *See*
  Closed-end funds
Investment weights, correlation of assets in portfolio, 255–261
Investors
  characteristics of, 12–13
  definition of, 3
  as performance informa-
    tion users, 522
  risk averters, 199
  risk-neutral, 205
  risk seekers, 205–206
  risk tolerance and asset al-
    location, 16
IPOs. *See* Initial public offerings

J

January effect, 435–438
Jensen's performance index,
  531–532, 536
Joint hypothesis, 410
Joint tests, 409
Junk bonds, 39, 498, 578,
  586–587

L

Lagging indicators, 741, 742
Last-in, first-out (LIFO)
  method, 773, 774, 775,
  776
Last-sale-price orders, 97
Leading indicators, 741, 742
Levered portfolios, 296
Liabilities, 777
LIBOR. *See* London Inter-
  bank Offer Rate
Limit orders, 95
Linking method, for calculat-
  ing time-weighted rate
  of return, 150–151, 156

Liquidity
  initial public offering un-
    derpricing and, 82
  marketability and, 10
  ratios, 784, 786
  of security market, 74–75
Liquidity preference hypoth-
  esis (LPH), 569–570
Liquidity premium, 570
Liquidity risk, 51
Load, 495, 503, 506–507
Local expectations hypothe-
  sis, 568–569
Locals, 817
London Interbank Offer
  Rate (LIBOR), 946–947
Long position
  in forward contracts, 807
  in option, 844
Long straddle strategy, 882,
  883

M

Macroeconomic market ana-
  lysis, 736–744, 761–762
Maintenance margin, 99,
  876, 877
Maloney Act of 1938, 121,
  123
Management fees, 507
Managers
  market timing and, 537–
    539
  as performance informa-
    tion users, 522
  Standard and Poor index
    and, 534–536
Margin
  actual, 99
  futures versus stock, 820
  initial, 99, 876, 877
  maintenance, 99, 876, 877
  Securities Exchange Act of
    1934 and, 121
Margin call, 99
Margin requirements
  futures trading and, 818–
    822
  options and, 875–878
Margin trading, 97–100
Market(s). *See also* specific
  markets, e.g., Options
  markets

call, 87–88, 108
  continuous, 88, 108
  definition of, 73
  mixed, 88
Marketability, of financial assets, 10
Marketable securities, 10
Market analysis, 736–751
  bond market and, 745–746
  business cycle and eco-
    nomic indicators and,
    740–741
  fiscal and monetary policy
    and, 741–744
  gross domestic product
    and, 736–739
  macroeconomic factors
    and, 3
  purpose of, 735
  stock market and, 746–751
Market anomalies, efficient
  market theory and, 433–
  438
Market capitalization, 171
Market impact effects, 74
Market makers, 90, 91
Market microstructures,
  87
Market opening/closing or-
  der, 97
Market orders, 95
Market portfolios, 289, 298,
  309–310
Market Reform Act, 124
Market risk, 52
Market segmentation hy-
  pothesis (MSH), 570–
  571
Market timing, 537–539
Market-to-book-value
  (M/B) ratios, 414, 434–
  435, 788
Mark to market cash settle-
  ment, 810–812, 874
Maturity date, of option
  contract, 845
Maximum expected return
  criterion (MERC), 197–
  199
Maximum return criterion
  (MRC), 196–197
Mean return, 197
Mean-variance criterion
  (MVC), 202–205

Mean-variance frontier
  (MVF)
  correlation and, 269–270
  definition of, 267
  in dollars and marks, 388
Mid-market order, 97
Minimum-fill order, 97
Minimum variance portfolio
  (MVP), 268
MIPS. *See* Monthly Income
  Preferred Securities
Monetary policy, 741, 743–
  744
Monetizing, 851
Money machine, 346,
  888
Money market securities, 7,
  31, 32, 33–36
  mutual funds, 498
  world, 105
Monthly Income Preferred
  Securities (MIPSs), 932,
  941
Mortgage(s), 40–41
Mortgage-backed securities,
  41
Moving averages, technical
  analysis and, 465–467
Multiples. *See* Price/earning
  ratios
Multiplicative method, for
  calculating equally
  weighted indexes, 173–
  174
Municipal bonds, 38–39
Mutual funds, 56–60. *See also*
  Closed-end funds;
  Open-end funds
  benefits of, 503–506
  beta risk measurement,
    308
  costs of, 506–511
  diversification benefits of,
    215, 237–238
  empirical evidence of per-
    formance, 536–537
  family of funds, 498, 500
  global stock funds, 501–
    502
  growth of, 1940–1996,
    484
  international, 536–537
  monkey market funds, 498
  no-load and load, 495

prospectus, 495–497
size of, 509
stocks versus, 510–511
types of, 483–503
U.S. stock funds as, 145

N

Naked position, 850
National Association of Securities Dealers (NASD), 121
  automated quotations system, 83, 87
  listing requirements, 86
National Market System (NMS), 87
NAV. *See* Net asset value
Neglected firm effect, 434
Net asset value (NAV), 56, 487–489
Net present value (NPV), 27, 920
Neutral stocks, 304
Newsletters, for investors, 322–323, 472, 537, 538
New York Stock Exchange (NYSE), 83
  Composite Index, 176
  floor brokers, 91
  history of, 84, 85, 842
  listing requirements, 86
  specialists, 91–92
No-load mutual funds, 495
Nominal yield, 571
Nonmarketable securities, 10
Nonparametric tests, 425–426
Normal-growth firms, 666, 667–670
  free cash flow model and, 693–700
Not held (NH) order, 96
Notional principal, 48, 947

O

Objective probabilities, 195
Odd lots, 96
Odd-lot trading, 472
Open-end funds, 56, 483. *See also* Index funds
  empirical evidence of performance, 536–537
  no-load and load, 495

performance averages, 498
prospectus, 495–497
in *The Wall Street Journal*, 499
Opening transactions, 846
Open interest, 812, 815
Open market operations, 743–744
Opportunity line, 289, 294–296
Option(s), 840–883. *See also* Call options; Option contracts; Option prices; Options markets; Put options
  American-style, 846, 892–893
  arbitrage, 885, 888, 890
  at-the-money, 849
  bond valuation and, 592–593
  buyers of, 843–844
  definition of, 841
  development of trading in, 841–843
  European-style, 846, 887–889
  index, 874, 876
  in-the-money, 849–850, 902
  investment strategies using, 862–868, 872–873, 879–883
  margin requirements, 875–878
  out-of-the-money, 849–850, 902
  sellers of, 848
  stocks versus, 848–849
  taxes and, 848, 874–875
  underlying asset and, 849–851
Option boundaries, 886–894
  for call options, 887–889
  put-call parity, 842, 893–894
  for put options, 890–893
Option contracts, 842, 844–848
Option premium, 846
Option prices, 852–862
  intrinsic and time value components, 852–854
  payoff diagrams, 854–862

Options markets, 851–852
  Options Clearing Corporation (OCC) and, 851–852
Option valuation, 884–929. *See also* Black-Scholes option pricing model; Option boundaries
  binomial option pricing model for, 915–922
Option writers, 844
Orders, 95–97
Out-of-the-money options, 849–850, 902
Over-the-counter (OTC) market, 83–84, 86–87
Overtrading, 119

P

Parity relationships, 389–394
Partial periods, bond prices and, 605–608
Participating preferred stocks, 44
Par value, 31, 48
Passive bond management strategies, 642–643
Passive investment strategies, 419
Payment date, 42
Payoff diagrams
  for bull spread, 867
  for covered call writing, 865
  for futures contracts, 823, 824
  for options, 854–862
  for protective put buying, 864
  for put ratio backspread, 880
  for short selling, 857
  for straddle, 882
Pay-to-play practices, 132–133
Peaks, 740
Pension funds
  index-linked bonds and, 934
  performance of, versus S&P index, 537, 538
Percentage financial statements, 788–790
Percent risk, 378–379

Performance attribution, 541–543
Performance indexes
  APT performance index, 533
  caution regarding, 539–541
  comparison of, 533–534
  definition of, 523
  international equity index, 536–537
  Jensen's performance index, 531–532, 536
  Sharpe's performance index, 525–528, 536
  Treynor's performance index, 528–531
Performance measurement
  empirical evidence of mutual fund performance and, 536–537
  international diversification and, 543–545
  performance attribution and, 541–543
  risk measurement and, 523–525
  timing of market and, 537–539
Periodic payment amount, 26
Perpetuity bonds, 575, 559
Personal trading. *See* Insider trading
Physical assets, contrasted with financial assets, 7–11
Pit, 817
Plain vanilla swaps, 946
Point-and-figure charts, in technical analysis, 457, 459
Political risk, 51–52, 370
Portfolio(s), 5, 7
  asset's risk when held with other assets in, 216–219
  definition of, 216
  diversification in, 15–16
  efficient and inefficient, 267–269
  expected rate of return on, 220–222
  levered, 296
  market, 289, 298, 309–310

Portfolio(s) *(continued)*
  minimum variance (MVP),
    268
  opportunity line, 289
  size of, single index model
    and, 343–344
  top-down approach and,
    541–543
  U.S. market, 309–310
  world market, 309–310
  zero, 354–355
Portfolio diversification, 15–
    16
  correlation and risk reduc-
    tion and, 251–266
  correlation coefficient,
    227–231
  efficiency of investment
    strategies, 266–272
  futures contracts and, 826–
    827
  international, 374–380,
    404–405, 543–545
  investment weights guaran-
    teeing perfect return on
    portfolio, 255–261
  number of assets and risk
    reduction, 261–266
  in practice, 272–274
Portfolio insurance, 904–905
Portfolio strategies
  common stock, 707–715
  efficient market theory
    and, 417–419
  hedging, 917, 921
  indexing and, 543–545
  market timing, 537–539
  passive versus active, 419–
    420
Portfolio variance
  correlation and, 252–254
  direct method for calculat-
    ing, 232
  double summation for-
    mula, 235–236
  indirect method for calcu-
    lating, 233–234
  international composition,
    389
  of portfolio composed of
    n assets, 238, 244–248
Predictability, tests for, 422
Preference shares, 44

Preferred habit hypothesis,
    571
Preferred stocks, 43–44
Preliminary estimated of
    GDP, 737
Premium(s)
  on closed-end funds, 488,
    493, 494–495
  convertible, 47
Present value, 4, 25–26
Price(s). *See also* Price/earn-
    ing (P/E) ratio
  asked, 90
  bid, 90
  conversion, 47
  futures, 47, 828, 838
  of initial public offerings,
    76
  market, establishing, 92
  of options, 852–862
Price continuity, 74
Price discovery, 81–82
Price/dividends ratio, 748
Price-earning (P/E) anomaly,
    438
Price/earning (P/E) ratios,
    414, 438, 676–682, 695
  common stock selection
    and, 704, 706, 730
  common stock valuation
    and, 656, 657
  financial statement analysis
    and, 787, 788
  as market signal, 712
  as measure of stock mar-
    ket, 748–749, 750–
    751
Price effect, 625–626
Price immunization, 641
Price received when issued
    (PI), 76–77
Price risk, 49, 561
Price-to-book ratio, 706,
    712, 747
Price-weighted indexes,
    169–171
Pricing. *See* Arbitrage pricing
    theory; Binomial option
    pricing model; Black-
    Scholes option pricing
    model; Capital asset
    pricing model
Primary offering, 76

Primary security market, 75–
    82
Primary trend, in Dow
    Theory, 463
Prime shares, 126
Principal, 31
Private placement, 80–81
Private placement memoran-
    dum, 80
Privileges. *See* Option con-
    tracts
Probabilities, 195
Profitability ratios, 784, 786,
    787
Profit and loss (P&L) state-
    ment, 778
Profit or loss (P/L) line, 854,
    856, 859
Program trading, 93, 349–
    350
Property, plant, and equip-
    ment (PPE), 776
Prospectus, 76, 495–497
Protective put buying, 863–
    864, 885
Public Utility Holding
    Company Act of 1935
    (PUHCA), 121, 123
Purchasing power parity,
    389–392
Purchasing power risk,
    50
Pure yield pickup swaps,
    644
Put-call parity (PCP), 842,
    893–894, 897
Put/call ratio, 472–473
Put options, 46, 841, 848,
    849
  Black-Scholes option pric-
    ing model and, 893
  boundaries for, 890–893
  payoff diagram for, 861,
    862
  protective put buying,
    863–864
  put-call parity, 842
  value of, at expiration,
    861–862
Put price, 856
Put ratio backspread, 879,
    880, 883
Put ratio spread, 882, 883

Q

Quick ratio, 784, 786
Quiet period, 432
Quote Rule (Rule 11Ac1–1),
    123, 124

R

Rally, 4
Random walk, 411–412
Rate anticipation swaps, 644
Rates of return. *See also*
    Index(es)
  abnormal, 412, 422, 424–
    425
  adjusted, 165–167
  after-tax, 156–158
  AIMR standards, 148
  average, 162–165
  on bonds, accrual basis,
    154–156
  on closed-end funds, 487,
    488
  common-factor and firm-
    specific, 338–342
  continuously com-
    pounded, 929
  currency risk and, 380–
    385, 386
  definitions of, 188–189
  dollar-weighted, 189–190
  estimating, 719
  ex-ante, 147
  ex-post, 147, 709
  foreign exchange and,
    160–162
  index method for calculat-
    ing, 150, 151–153, 156
  inflation-adjusted, 158–
    159
  linking method for calcu-
    lating, 150–151, 156
  on portfolio, 220–222
  real, 159
  realized, 147, 353
  risk and, 206
  simple, 148–154
  time-weighted, 150–153,
    165–167
  tracking, 177–180
  uses of, 146–148
Rating agencies, 577

Ratio analysis, financial statement analysis and, 784–794

Real assets, contrasted with financial assets, 7–11

Real body, 460–461

Real GDP, 736, 739, 745–746, 746, 747

Realized rates of return, 147, 353

Realized yield, 572

Real rates of return, 159

Receive fixed counterparty, 946

Receive floating counterparty, 946

Recessions, 743

Registered competitive traders, 91

Registered equity market makers, 91

Regression method, for estimating dividend growth rate, 732–733

Regulated investment companies, 485

Regulation
corporate governance and, 128
definition of, 120
of derivatives, 127
financial innovation and, 126
history of, 120–125

Regulation T, 876

Regulatory risk, 51–52, 711

Reinvestment effect, 625–626

Reinvestment rate risk, 49, 560

Relative strength, technical analysis and, 467–468

Repurchase agreements (repos), 35–36

Resiliency of transactions, 74

Resistance, 457, 458

Resource allocation, and efficient market theory, 417

Return. See also Rates of return; Risk-return tradeoff
abnormal, 324, 410, 412, 422, 424–425

arbitrage pricing theory and, 350–351, 353–354
excess, 324, 410
expected, 197, 208, 344–345
on portfolio, 218
risk-free, 255
tests for predictability, 422
zero, 354–355

Revenue bonds, 39

Reverse repos, 36

Risk. See also Beta; Capital asset pricing model; Diversification; Financial engineering; Spreads over Treasuries
agency, 710–711
arbitrage pricing theory and, 350–351, 353–354
asset allocation and, 15–16
asset dependency and, 219
attitudes toward, 205–206
beta as a measure of, 301–303
business, 52, 710
of call, 51
capital market line and, 297–299
certainty and, 192–194
for common stock, sources of, 710–712
credit, 577
currency, 380–385, 386
default, 48, 576–577
exchange rate, 52
financial, 710
indifference curves and, 290–291
inflation, 711–712
inflation rate, 50
interest rate, 48–49, 49–50, 712
investment criteria and, 196–199
of initial public offerings, 78
liquidity, 51
market, 52
measuring, 523–525
nature of, 194–196
percent, 378–379
political and regulatory, 51–52, 370
price, 49, 561

purchasing power, 50
regulatory, 711
reinvestment, 49, 560
security market line and, 310–315
with single index model, 344–345
sources of, 48–53
systematic, 317–319, 343–344, 710
total, 523
underwriters', 77
unsystematic, 317–319, 343–344
value at risk (VaR), 952–954
variance and, 201–205
zero, 355

Risk aversion, 199–201

Risk-free assets, 292–297

Risk-free return, 255

Riskless interest rate, 194

Risk neutrality, 205

Risk premium, 199, 200–201, 219, 315–317

Risk profile, 191, 932–933

Risk-return tradeoff, 14, 177

Risk seekers, 205–206

Round lots, 44, 96

Rule 12b–1 fees, 507

Rule 144A, 124

S

Samurai bonds, 588

Scalping, 82

Score shares, 126

Seasonal anomalies, 434, 435–438

Seasoned new issue, 76

SEC. See Securities and Exchange Commission

Secondary security market, 75, 83–87

Second market transactions, 83–84

Sector allocation, 543

Secured bonds, 578

Securities. See also Derivatives; Regulation; Securities markets; Securities trading mechanics; specific securities

international, 54–56
laws, summary of, 123–124
marketable and nonmarketable, 10
mortgage-backed, 41
selection of, 15
types of by market classification, 7

Securities Act of 1933, 121, 123, 432

Securities Acts Amendments of 1975, 122

Securities and Exchange Commission (SEC)
creation of, 121, 844
as information source, 961
insider trading acts, 123, 135–136, 415
Rule 12b–1, 507

Securities Exchange Act of 1934, 121, 123

Securities Investor Protection Act of 1970, 122, 124

Securities Investor Protection Corporation (SIPC), 102, 122

Securities Law Enforcement Remedies Act, 124

Securities trading mechanics
automated trading, 92–93
blind bids, 93–95
brokers, 101–103
establishing market prices, 92
financial planners, 103–104
goals of system, 89–90
margin trading, 97–100
participants, 90–92
placing an order, 96–97
short selling, 101
systems, 87–89
types of orders, 95, 95–96

Security analysis, 4

Security custody, 506

Security market(s), 73–110. See also Securities trading mechanics
primary, 75–82
role of, 73–75
secondary, 83–87
world, 104–110

Security market line (SML), 310–315
  Treynor's performance index and, 528, 529
Security selections, 543
Selective hedging, 940–941
Semistrong form of the EMT, 412, 414, 417–419
  evidence related to, 427–430
Sentiment indicators, in technical analysis, 469, 472–473
Separation property, 299–301
Separation theorem, 300
Serial correlations, 425
Settlement date, 97
Settle price, 812
Shadows, 461
Shareholders Communications Improvement Act, 124
Sharpe's performance index, 525–528, 536
Shelf registration, 80, 123, 124
Short position
  in forward contracts, 807
  in options, 844
Short selling, 101, 283–287, 473, 859
Short-term trend, in Dow Theory, 463
Simple interest, 609
Simple rate of return, 148, 148–154
Single index model (SIM)
  calculating asset covariance by, 367–368
  common-factor and firm-specific rates of return, 338–342
  reduction of computations using, 342–343
  risk and expected return with, 344–345
  systematic and unsystematic risk, and portfolio size, 343–344
Sinking funds, 578
Specialists, 91–92
Speculative-grade bonds, 578

Speculation
  on futures, 825
  on stocks, 43
Spiders, 60
Spot exchange rates, 395–396
Spot/future trade, 97, 828
Spot rate, 565–567, 807
Spreads, bull, 866–868
Spreads over Treasuries, 576–590
  bond ratings and, 582–586
  inflation-indexed bonds and, 587–588
  international bond markets and, 588–590
  junk bonds and, 586–587
Spread strategies, 863
Standard deviations, 202
  continuously compounded, calculating, 927–929
  efficient portfolios and, 290
  equation, 202, 208
  as risk measure, 191, 523
  Sharpe's performance index and, 525, 527
Standard normal distribution, 896
Step-up swaps, 951
Stock(s). See also Common stocks
  adjusted price, 791
  aggressive, 304
  alpha, 323
  blue chip, 43
  characteristics of, 41–42
  cyclical, 43, 740
  defensive, 43, 304
  growth, 42
  income, 42–43
  mutual funds versus, 510–511
  neutral, 304
  options, 46
  options versus, 848–849
  preferred, 43–44
  risks of, 48–53
  selecting, using CAPM, 323–324
  speculative, 43
  taxes and, 70

Stock exchanges, 83–84
  characteristics of, 89
  history of, 85
  listing requirements, 86
  national versus regional, 86
  world, 108
Stock indexes, 176–177
Stock index futures, pricing, 828–830
Stock market(s)
  economy, relationship to, 746
  reading financial pages, 44–46
  valuing, 746–751
  world, 107–108
Stock splits, 44
Stop order, 96
Straddle strategies, 863, 881–882
Strike (exercise) price, 844, 856, 891, 897
Strong form of the EMT, 414–415, 421
  evidence related to, 431–433
Subjective probabilities, 195
Subordinated bonds, 578
Substitution effect, 557
Substitution swaps, 644
Super Bowl indicator, 658
Supergrowth firms, 666, 670–671
  economic value-added model and, 702–703
  limited time, 671–674
Support, in technical analysis 457, 458
Surprise factor, 351, 352–353
Swaps, 47–48, 109
  amortizing, 951
  commodity, 950–951
  currency, 949–950
  fixed for floating, 946
  interest-rate, 930, 946–949
  intermarket spread, 644
  plain vanilla, 946
  pure yield pickup, 644
  rate anticipation, 644
  step-up, 951
  substitution, 644
Symmetric hedging strategy, 935–939
Syndicates, 78

Systematic risk, 317–319, 710
  single index model and, 343–344

T

Tangible assets, contrasted with financial assets, 7–11
Taxes, 66–70
  bonds and, 67, 69–70
  capital gains, 66, 69
  financial engineering and, 941–945
  investment companies and, 485
  Monthly Income Preferred Securities and, 932, 941
  mutual funds and, 508
  on options, 848, 874–875
  rates of return, effect on, 156–158
  stocks and, 70
  turnover rates and, 119
Technical analysis, 412, 418
  bar charts and, 453–457
  breadth indicators and, 469–472
  candlestick charts and, 459–462
  definitions of, 451–452
  Dow Theory and, 463–465
  empirical evidence to support, 452–453
  fundamental analysis versus, 451
  moving averages and, 465–467
  point-and-figure charts and, 457–459
  relative strength and, 467–468
  sentiment indicators and, 469, 472–473
Tender offers, 122
Term funds, 482, 484
Term repos, 36
Term structure of interest rates, 562–564
  expectations hypothesis and, 568–569

forward contracts and, 565
forward rates and, 565–567
holding period rate and, 568
liquidity preference hypothesis and, 569–570
market segmentations hypothesis and, 570–571
spot rate and, 565–567
Thin market, 74
Third market transactions, 84
Time value, of option, 852–853
Time value concepts, 24–27
Time-weighted rate of return, 150–153, 165–167
Tokyo Stock Exchange (TSE), 83, 108
TOPIX Index, 176
Tombstone, 78
Top-down approach, to portfolio management, 542–543
Total risk, 523
Traders, 90–92
Trading
costs, 504–505
insider, 121, 123, 135–136, 143, 415–416
volume, 470–472, 480
Trading posts, 83
Transaction costs
commission schedule and, 102
financial engineering and, 945

of mutual funds, 507–508
price setting and, 74
Treasury bills (T-bills), 33, 194
Treasury bonds, 36–38, 105
yield curves for, 559, 560, 561
Trendlines, 453–454, 455
Treynor's performance index, 528–531
Trough, 740
Trust Indenture Act of 1939, 121–122, 123
Truth-issuance act, 121
Turnover
closed-end funds and, 494
tax consequences of, 119
12b–1, 507

U

Unbiased expectations hypothesis, 569
Uncertainty. See Risk
Underwriters, 76–80
Undiversifiable risk. See Systematic risk
Unemployment rate, 743
Unit trusts, 59–60
Unsystematic risk, 317–319
single index model and, 343–344
Upstairs market, 84
Uptick, 101
U.S. Council of Economic Advisors, 962

U.S. Treasury securities. See Treasury bills
Utility, 291

V

Value at risk (VaR), 952–954
Value investing, 800
Value line, 854
Value-weighted indexes, 171–172
Variance. See also Portfolio variance
calculating, 201–202, 208, 229
mean-variance criterion, 202–205
portfolio, 231–236, 238, 244–248
value at risk (VaR) and, 953

W

Warrants, 906
Weak form of the EMT, 411–412, 421
evidence related to, 422–426
Wealth effect, 557
Williams Act of 1968, 122, 124
World market portfolio, 309–310
World security markets, 104–110, 961. See also International investment

Y

Yankee bonds, 588
Yield curve, 558–562. See also Term structure of interest rates
bond returns and, 650–651
shape of, 562–564
Yield to call, 572
Yield to maturity, 556, 558, 571–572, 575, 576
bond pricing and, 614–618
convexity and, 638
duration and, 631–632, 635
estimating investor's required rates of return and, 720
for junk bonds, 587

Z

Zero beta, 354–355
Zero-cost collar, 850
Zero-coupon bonds, 39, 555
put-call parity and, 893
yield to maturity equation for, 559
Zero investment portfolios, 354–355
Zero-plus tick, 101
Zero return, 354–355
Zero-risk portfolios, 828